CIS 500: INFORMATION SYSTEMS *for* DECISION MAKING

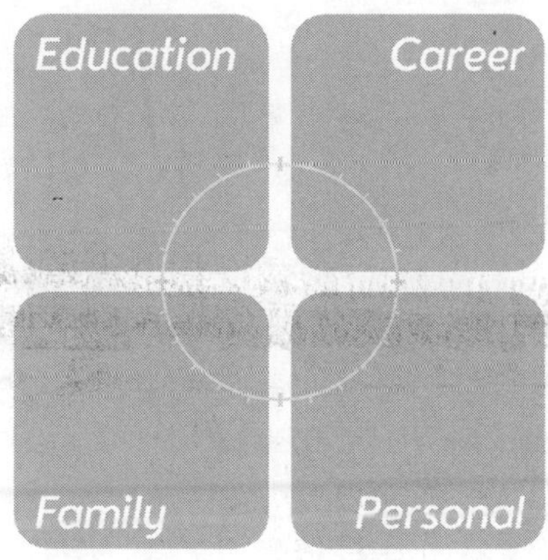

THIRD CUSTOM EDITION

Taken from:

Information Systems Management in Practice, Seventh Edition
by Barbara C. McNurlin & Ralph H. Sprague, Jr.

Managing Information Technology, Fifth Edition
by E. Wainwright Martin, Carol V. Brown, Daniel W. DeHayes, Jeffrey A. Hoffer and William C. Perkins

Excerpts taken from:

Information Systems Management in Practice, Seventh Edition
by Barbara C. McNurlin and Ralph H. Sprague, Jr.

Published by Prentice-Hall, Inc.
A Pearson Education Company
Upper Saddle River, New Jersey 07458

Managing Information Technology, Fifth Edition
by E. Wainwright Martin, Carol V. Brown, Daniel W. DeHayes, Jeffrey A. Hoffer, and William C. Perkins

Published by Prentice-Hall, Inc.

Printed in the United States of America

10 9 8 7 6 5 4 3 2 1

ISBN 0-536-27627-7

2006200215

SB

Please visit our web site at *www.pearsoncustom.com*

PEARSON CUSTOM PUBLISHING
75 Arlington Street, Suite 300, Boston, MA 02116
A Pearson Education Company

BRIEF CONTENTS

CONTENTS

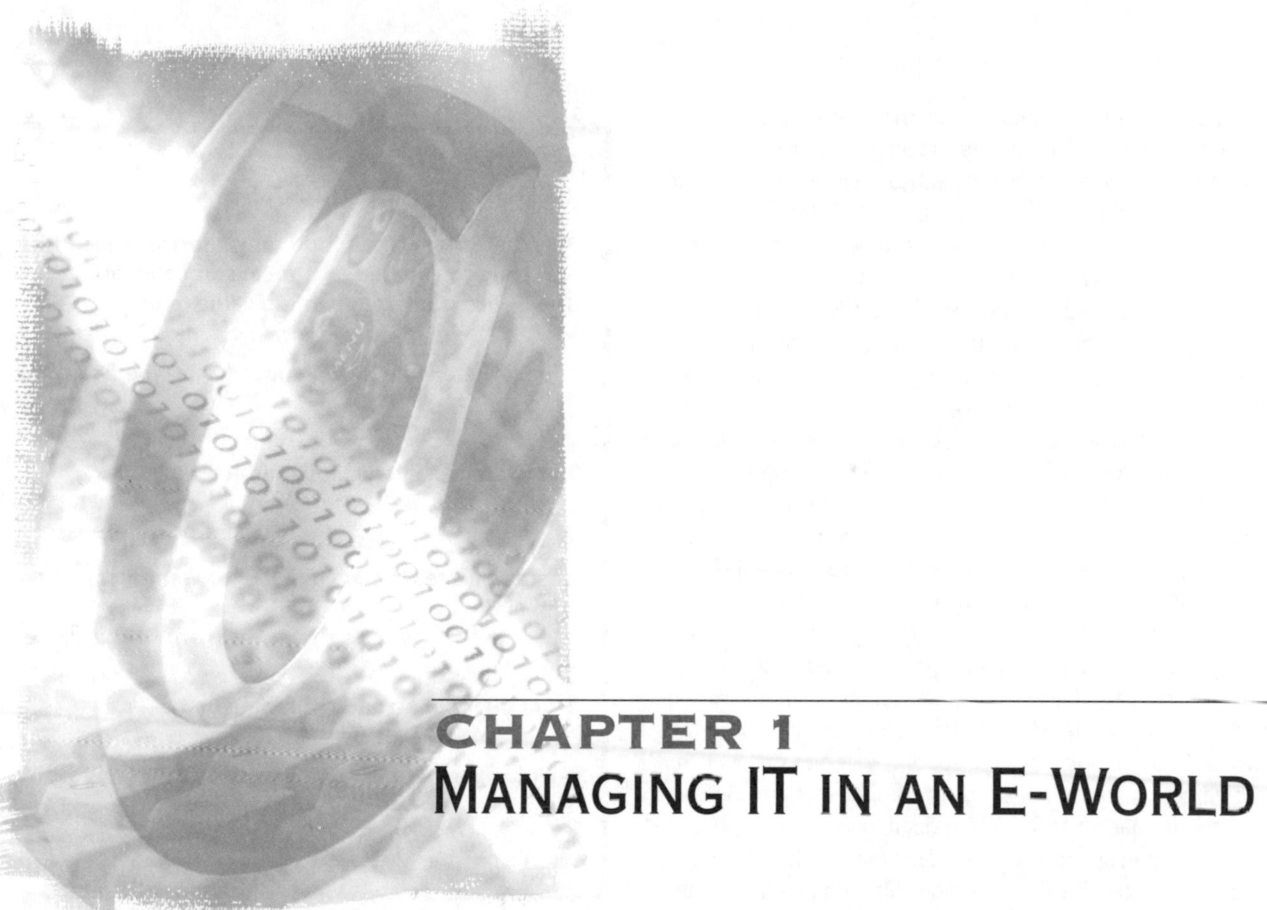

CHAPTER 1
MANAGING IT IN AN E-WORLD

THE INFORMATION REVOLUTION HAS CLEARLY ARRIVED. INVESTMENT IN information technology during the 1990s has been a major contributing factor to unprecedented gains in productivity within the United States during the early 2000s. Traditional firms have integrated the Internet into their everyday business activities. Web-based applications and Internet e-mail have become an additional channel of communication with a firm's traditional customers, its suppliers, and its shareholders.

Today we take for granted that we are part of an electronic world, or *e-world.* Many of us expect to find connections to the Internet not only in our schools and our workplace, but also in our homes. As 60 percent of U.S. homes have also invested in Internet connections for their home computers, government agencies have begun to use Web applications to provide information as well as to collect taxes and receive electronic business documents online. When we travel, we can use wireless networks at airport terminals, high-speed data connections in our hotel rooms, and Internet cafes on the streets of a city or resort town.

Businesses also recognize that they are competing in an e-world in which the technologies that they invested in yesterday could lack the business capabilities that they want today. The rules for business survival can quickly change, and an event in one part of the world can affect financial markets in countries halfway across the globe.

Being a user of **information technology** (IT) in an e-world is also clearly different from being a computer user before we had an easy-to-use browser to navigate across Web sites. Today's elementary school students learn to do research using Web-based resources, and many teens choose to use their discretionary time surfing online rather than watching television. Today's typical undergraduate student is an experienced user of e-mail and Web resources. New graduates are likely to have used the Internet to distribute a resume and to seek out or communicate online with potential employers, perhaps via a Web-based job site.

Managing IT in a business today is also very different from managing IT in a prebrowser world. Business managers expect to have access not only to data about the firm's internal operations

> We define **information technology (IT)** as computer technology (hardware and software) for processing and storing information, as well as communications technology for transmitting information.

from their desktops, but also to external market data and personal organizers with automated meeting reminders. Sales and customer support personnel expect to have access to up-to-date information about customers, as well as documents from sales force members who can be scattered across many locations. When a new business is acquired, employees expect their information systems (IS) to quickly reflect this change as well. Today's workers also typically have little patience for a computer network that is not available or an application that is not easy to use.

The primary objective of this textbook is to help prepare you to be an effective manager in an e-world. Employees with a college degree are expected to be knowledgeable about computer applications and to be ready to help plan and participate in systems implementations. Some of our readers will choose to become IT professionals working in an information systems department or to take a *business technologist* position working side-by-side with business managers and system users.

To set the stage for the remainder of the textbook, we first briefly describe some of the IT trends that are part of today's e-world. Then we present some specific examples of how IT has enabled new ways for a business to compete, for employees to work, and for people to live in a modern society. We then introduce the IS management role in today's organizations, which is a role that has evolved as IT innovations have emerged. This introductory chapter then ends with some learning objectives for each of the four parts of this textbook.

MISPREDICTIONS BY IT INDUSTRY LEADERS

This "telephone" has too many shortcomings to be seriously considered as a means of communication. The device is inherently of no value to us.

—*Western Union internal memo, 1876*

I think there is a world market for maybe five computers.

—*Thomas Watson, chairman of IBM, 1943*

But what [is a microchip] good for?

—*Engineer at the Advanced Computing Systems Division of IBM, 1968*

There is no reason anyone would want a computer in their home.

—*Ken Olson, president, chairman, and founder of Digital Equipment Corp., 1977*

640K ought to be enough for anybody.

—*Attributed to Bill Gates, chairman of Microsoft, 1981*

Dell has a great business model, but that dog won't scale.

—*John Shoemaker, head of Sun's server division, 2000*

[Sources: Kappelman, 2001; Jones, 2003]

RECENT INFORMATION TECHNOLOGY TRENDS

As a user of computers and communication devices, you are well aware that improvements in computer hardware, software, and communication networks have been dramatic and frequent over the past decade in particular. Some of you might, in fact, think that the IT industry's predictions of a "new economy" and "Internet time" led to excessive investments in IT during the late 1990s, especially in the United States. Although these criticisms could be valid, the fast rate of innovations in the IT industry has made it difficult to accurately predict the IT products and services that will be "winners" tomorrow. In fact, IT leaders in the past have publicly made some significant *mis*-predictions about technologies (see the sidebar "Mispredictions by IT Industry Leaders").

Although many of today's tools are technologically complex, they have also become easier to use—more **user-friendly**. Within a relatively short time, IT has not only become commonplace in the workplace, but also commonplace in many homes and public areas. This increased usability and availability have led to the beginnings of what has been called **ubiquitous IT**, in which computers and communications devices will touch almost every aspect of our lives.

For example, personal information devices have become so commonplace that instructions for airplane travelers include warnings about when the use of computers and cellular phones is forbidden. New airplanes are also increasingly being equipped with new technologies that include Internet access from the passenger seat of an airplane in flight. The pervasiveness of IT has also led to new battlefield tactics, in which military commanders have used their cell phones to call opposing commanders and urge them to surrender their units (Samuelson, 2003).

In Part I of this textbook, we will discuss the underlying technology concepts and their historical predecessors in much more detail. For now, let us briefly consider some of the technology developments that have led to this ubiquity of IT and to what has been called a postindustrial, digital economy.

Computer Hardware: Faster, Smaller, Cheaper

Computer-on-a-chip (microcomputer) technology was available as early as the 1970s, but the introduction of the first IBM Personal Computer (PC) in 1981 began to fuel the

Information Revolution. By the mid-1990s, desktop and portable PCs for the business and the home had become "commodity products" available from manufacturers around the world. Today's typical PC has the processing power of an organization's entire computing center of the 1960s. More important, today's PC comes with an easy-to-use operating system with graphical icons, a Web browser, point-and-click devices for screen navigation, and the capability to play music and videos—all at a cheaper price than what the same features would have cost 12 months earlier. Lightweight notebook-sized computers have also become so affordable that they have replaced many of the larger machines on the desktops of business employees and are carried into meetings and taken on business trips.

Today, even smaller, handheld computer devices have become the indispensable business tools to stay in touch with e-mail and other office documents when away from the office. As miniaturized computer devices and cellular phones have also become pervasive in all types of locations, including shopping malls and restaurants, companies have also begun to think about new applications to provide services to mobile users via these handheld devices.

Computer Software: Standardized and Integrated

By the year 2000, some version of Microsoft Corporation's Windows software had become the standard operating system for the vast majority of microcomputers being used as desktop and portable computer "clients." Microsoft's Office Suite (word processing, spreadsheet, database, presentation, and e-mail software sold in a single bundle) and the same company's Web browser are also the *de facto* software standard throughout corporate America today, despite a U.S. government lawsuit charging Microsoft with monopolistic practices. In fact, this standard in U.S. organizations and multinational companies has been a major contributor to the ubiquity of computing and the swift emergence of today's e-world.

The 1990s also brought a tremendous growth in the availability of software packages with integrated modules that could pass common business transactions across functional groups, business divisions, and national boundaries in "real time." Today, these **enterprise system** packages have been widely adopted not only by large manufacturing and service firms based in the United States and around the globe but also by midsized and smaller firms. Some enterprise software packages have versions that have been programmed for specific industries (such as the petrochemicals industry or even higher education). With these standard enterprise system modules to build on, applications that integrate data across traditional and Web-based channels for customers and suppliers are now also available from the same early enterprise system vendors, as well as other vendors that specialize in applications for customer relationship management or supply chain management integration.

One of the early enablers of today's phenomenal progress toward software integration was the giveaway strategy of Netscape Communications, the creator of the first commercial Web browser. The Netscape browser rapidly became a standard tool for accessing the Web (see sidebar "Internet Time").

INTERNET TIME

In the summer of 1994, Tom Pacquin—one of the early employees at Netscape—was asking other employees how long they had been at the company. Their replies were that a 4-month tenure seemed like a year, maybe 2. "Ah," said Mr. Pacquin, "Internet time." This became an inside joke and then was picked up by marketers at Netscape who used the term as a "window" into the company and into a new world in which none of the old rules apply.

[Based on Gomes, 2002]

Computer Networks: High Bandwidth, Global, and Wireless

The standard browser application, along with an Internet communications standard (TCP/IP), led to an unprecedented level of IT investments in the 1990s to obtain a more global reach for employees and organizations. By the year 2000, company networks that linked employees to the Internet had become commonplace. Not only large businesses, but also small businesses and home users, could also take advantage of investments by telecommunications firms in fiber-optic lines during the late 1990s. These high-bandwidth lines sped up Web page retrieval and made possible higher-speed video access. By 2003 many home users could also buy access to high-bandwidth lines using cable modems to connect with cable lines or digital subscriber lines (DSLs) to connect via telephone lines ("land lines").

Today, companies are also investing in wireless technologies to increase the mobile access of their employees and business partners. New subscription services are available for devices that have both microcomputer and cellular capabilities, and companies have invested in developing Web pages for access by these handheld, mobile devices. Satellite and cellular technologies also can link motorists with a central support center for emergency help as well as travel services (such as GM's OnStar), accessible via a computer installed near the car driver's seat.

By the new millennium, more than half of capital expenditures by U.S.-based businesses were for IT purchases. The hardware, software, and network technologies briefly discussed above, as well as other technologies described in detail in the subsequent chapters of this textbook, have ushered in an Internet age that has already had major impacts on the way businesses compete, the way we as employees get our jobs done, and the ways we can choose to live as citizens on this planet. IT can be used today to not just enable, but also to help *shape* business strategies.

Traditional Ways to Compete

The way that businesses compete can be described in three ways (Porter, 1980):

- *Cost*—competing with other businesses by being a low-cost producer of a good or a service
- *Differentiation*—competing with other businesses by offering products or services that customers prefer due to a superiority in characteristics such as product innovativeness or image, product quality, or customer service
- *Focus*—competing on cost or differentiation within a specific market niche

Computers have been used to *lower costs* by automating transaction processing, shortening order cycle times, and providing operational data for decision making since the 1960s, when large firms invested in their first computers. In the 1980s a flood of technology innovations led to increases in IT investments that brought additional efficiency gains—such as shortening the time to develop new products with computer-aided design tools; optimizing a plant floor process with software that has captured a human expert's decision rules; and speedily changing a production line with planning systems that integrate research and development (R&D), production, and sales information.

IT has also played a significant role in enabling businesses to *differentiate* their products or services. By the 1980s firms began to gain a measurable *competitive advantage* from custom IT applications that provided

- sales personnel with information to help them better service a specific customer
- just-in-time supplies for business customers
- new information-based products such as cash management accounts or drug interaction information for healthcare providers

By the 1990s, IT applications had advanced to the extent that many firms were able to compete on *both cost and differentiation*. Some firms also used IT to transform the ways that companies in their industry had previously competed. One of the best known examples of developing IT for competitive advantage was American Airlines' SABRE reservation system, which evolved from an inventory system for American Airlines employees alone to an interorganizational system for large and small travel agencies to process airline flight reservations for American Airlines *and* its competitors.

New Ways to Compete

Although using the Internet to conduct business is still a recent innovation, we can already see some of the major ways that traditional businesses will change the way they compete in order to leverage the Internet's capabilities. For example, by the late 1990s the SABRE reservation system described above was being accessed as a Web-based reservation system for travelers and businesses via an independent intermediary (*www.travelocity.com*) as well as via the Web site for American Airlines (*www.aa.com*). However, because of the open access to the Internet, Web sites for other individual airlines, as well as other new dot-com travel sites (such as *www.expedia.com* and *www.orbitz.com*), became new online competitors, and what was once a major competitive business advantage for American Airlines' parent company was in jeopardy.

The travel industry is therefore one example of how competition in an industry has been restructured by the Internet. Consumers now have direct access to online travel businesses and electronic ticketing, which don't require an in-person visit to a local travel agency with SABRE or some other reservation system. Airline companies also need to fiercely compete on price because ticket prices are now more visible to the purchaser.

Wal-Mart, Dell, and Lands' End are three examples of preexisting companies that have been leveraging the Internet's capabilities to compete in new ways to (1) achieve additional cost efficiencies, (2) acquire the ability to mass customize their products, and (3) reach even more customers.

Wal-Mart. As a large discount retailer, Wal-Mart has used Internet technology standards to increase efficiencies in its transactions with its myriad suppliers. Today it is also emerging a leader in the implementation of radio frequency identification (RFID) technologies to gain even further automation capabilities and eventually even greater cost savings.

Dell Corporation. As a firm that originally sold low-cost microcomputers via phone or catalog, Dell developed software for customer service representatives to electronically capture a customer request, translate the order data into a PC system design with these components, and then electronically "summon the right resources" to fulfill the order. IT therefore enabled Dell to implement not only a low-cost business strategy, but also a "mass customization" strategy (Pine, Victor, and Boynton, 1993). In other words, Dell used IT to create a customized product using an assembly-line process. The company then leveraged the Internet's capabilities to become the first PC manufacturer to have a Web site that allowed the customer to directly place a customized order—a "self-service" application that resulted in Dell needing fewer customer service representations to take custom orders by phone.

Lands' End. Another example of an original catalog company that has leveraged the Internet for mass customization is Lands' End, a clothing retailer. In this case the firm uses the Web's multimedia capabilities to facilitate custom-made purchases of clothing via its Web site. This capability was quickly implemented due to a strategic alliance with a vendor that had developed algorithms to translate customer responses into a computer-generated pattern that was shipped to an offshore manufacturer. The company also developed software to track the status of each order. Within one year of offering the first custom clothing, custom products were among its top 20 products and it had attracted new customers.

The Internet has also drastically reduced the costs for computer linkages with potential customers and suppliers in different geographic locations. For some firms the new e-world has also meant their first opportunity to sell to customers living on different continents. Small businesses can afford to conduct business electronically because of the inexpensive technologies involved. Web sites can be programmed to display screens using a different language, different currencies, and even perhaps local pricing, depending on the user's browser location or selected preference.

WORKING IN AN E-WORLD

The IT innovations in hardware, software, and networks described above have also escalated the level of IT investments to support today's **knowledge workers**, as they have become increasingly dependent on IT to do their jobs. A microcomputer on every desktop has become standard equipment in most organizations, and many workers have access to the Internet.

> Coined in the 1980s, the term **telecommuter** refers to one who works from a location outside the firm's regular offices and "commutes" via telecommunications lines in order to do his or her work.

Another major change has been the development of an IT infrastructure to support workers anytime and anywhere. Sales personnel and other traveling managers are equipped with portable computers and other mobile equipment that give them access to company data anytime (24 hours a day, 7 days a week), while working essentially anywhere (from an off-site office, home office, hotel room, airport, or on the road). Remote access to corporate records is still not always provided due to security concerns, although today the majority of Fortune 500 companies have equipped their sales forces with portable microcomputers in order to be **telecommuters**. Global access is more problematic, but anytime/anywhere access within national borders is now an expected IT service within large firms.

By 1995 measurable gains in workforce productivity due to organizational investments in IT and worker training had been reported, and the United States was able to exploit this temporary productivity advantage over other industrialized nations. When a typical graduate of a business curriculum entered the workforce for the first time, he or she could be expected to have a proficiency in personal productivity tools such as that provided by the standard productivity software suite (Microsoft Office). By 2003 the dependence of knowledge workers on IT was so pervasive that computer virus attacks could result in major productivity losses.

More Productive Teams

Today's knowledge worker also typically uses e-mail to communicate with team members when not in face-to-face settings and to share electronic work documents. Commercial software packages that support collaborative teamwork have been improved over the past decade and now typically have Web-based front ends for ease of use from internal and external networks. Videoconferencing technologies have also recently been adopted as cost-cutting measures as these technologies have improved in functionality and companies have sought to reduce travel expenditures.

Team members who telecommute are also increasingly common. For teams that have members in different time zones, some meetings might require individuals to participate in electronic conversations or videoconferencing sessions from a remote computer outside of regular office hours. In some cities environmental laws have also led to work schedules that include telecommuting for some knowledge workers, such as 4 days in the office and 1 day working outside it.

Virtual Organizations and Free Agents

Today we are also seeing the beginnings of temporary alliances between organizations and individuals in what are called **virtual organizations**. The ubiquity of IT and lowered communication costs via the Internet are making it easier for organizations to contract with other organizations or individuals in order to have access to scarce expertise, perhaps at cheaper labor costs. Some small businesses might have no real office or headquarters at all; the company might be made up of individuals scattered across different locations and might make use of talent wherever it can be found around the globe (see sidebar "Fluid Companies").

A new type of telecommuter who can do knowledge work without being at a specific work location has also emerged: the **free agent**. This means that individuals with specialized skills and IT linkages can work independently as contractors without belonging to any organization. They can post their resumes and sell their skills globally. People choose to be free agents because they have control over their schedules and what projects they work on. Organizations might want free agents because they can quickly expand and contract their human workforce without long-term obligations for salaries and benefits.

ENVISIONING THE FUTURE

User interfaces will finally get out of their desktop metaphor… and use more natural and efficient interaction mechanisms and styles that take better advantage of our human capabilities.

—Andries van Dam

User-aware software will be capable of learning about an individual and adapting itself accordingly.

—Cherri Pancake

Ours may be the last generation that sees and readily knows the difference between real and virtual things.

—Norman I. Badler

We will create superior robots that eventually decide they have no need for us.

—Peter J. Denning

Excerpts from "The Next 1000 Years," *Communications of the ACM* [44:3 (March 2001).]

LIVING IN AN E-WORLD

Although it is too early to predict the long-term impacts of recent IT innovations on the ways we live, we do know from major technological innovations of the past, such as the automobile and the telephone, that the impacts can be far-ranging and unexpected. We also can already see impacts on our daily lives. Cell phones enable us to stay connected with family members without having to find access to a land-line service; the Internet provides access to vast amounts of "free" information that in the past required a phone call to a government agency, a reference librarian, or a company's customer service agent; and Web-based applications, such as online banking, can save us time.

As business managers and citizens of the world, we all need to be vigilant about the implications of new IT developments and help shape their usage, as well as help our society avoid some of the potentially harmful impacts.

FLUID COMPANIES

Companies will be much more molecular and fluid. They will be autonomous business units connected not necessarily by a big building but across geographies all based on networks. The boundaries of the first will be not only fluid or blurred but in some cases hard to define.

[Don Tapscott, coauthor of Digital Capital (Byrne, 2000)]

THE IS MANAGEMENT ROLE IN ORGANIZATIONS

In most organizations an **information systems (IS)** department is given the responsibility for managing the firm's IT assets: its hardware, software, networks, and IS professionals. The specific responsibilities of an IS department have continued to evolve as the range and reach of information technologies have grown.

One way to view this historical evolution of the IS management role is in the form of eras, as shown in Figure 1.1. The characteristics of the first four eras were initially envisioned by Jack Rockart of the Massachusetts Institute of Technology (Rockart 1988), as summarized below.

Accounting Era Back-office computer automation began with accounting	IS professionals were primary decision makers but reported into an accounting function (the first corporate computer user)	Transaction processing was automated with the use of computers for single functions (transactions were aggregated and then processed in a single run or "batch" due to magnetic tape storage)
Operational Era Computer automation expanded to other functions	Business managers became more involved in systems decision making (as applications supported more business functions)	Online systems were introduced for transaction processing (made possible by direct access storage devices using magnetic disks)
Information Era IT investments to support the knowledge worker	End users became direct users of computer applications using user-friendly mainframe and microcomputer tools	Decision support systems that could "interact" with users were introduced (made possible by software tools developed for direct end-user computing)
Network Era IT investments in interenterprise systems	Business managers began to take more of an "ownership" role in IT investments	Computer networking enabled applications with business partners (custom-developed inter-organizational applications)
Internet Era IT investments to support new kinds of e-business	Top management has taken a leadership role in IT decision making to ensure that IT investments are strategically aligned with the business	The Internet and Web-based applications provide a global reach to customers and business partners (enabled by a standard communications protocol and standard Web browser)

Figure 1.1 Five IS Management Eras

> We use the term **information systems (IS) organization** to refer to the organizational department or unit that has the primary responsibility for managing IT.

In the first era (1950s to mid-1960s), the Accounting Era, IS professionals typically reported to an accounting manager, because back-office computer automation began with accounting applications, such as accounts payable. At this time computer applications were batch systems: Transactions were aggregated and then processed in a single run or "batch" due to the reliance on magnetic tape as a storage medium. Because the accounting was the first function to be automated, accountants were also the first business managers to become knowledgeable about IS. Nevertheless, the IS specialists were typically solely in charge of the development and implementation of these applications. According to Rockart, "The information systems staff swept into the department, interviewed the clerks, and designed the systems—most of which were barely understandable to anyone outside the computer hierarchy."

In the Operational Era (beginning mid-1960s), computer automation expanded to other business functions. During this era, online transaction processing also became possible due to the availability of direct access storage devices (that use magnetic disks). These technological advances made possible the development of real-time computerized systems for critical operational transactions, such as those needed for airline ticketing and manufacturing scheduling. IT specialists still dominated the development and implementation of these applications, but business (line) managers became more involved in choosing which systems to implement and participated in the development of systems requirements and system implementation.

The new application focus in the third era (late 1970s to mid-1980s), the Information Era, was the use of IT not just for transaction processing, but also for interactive decision making. End users had access to user-friendly mainframe and, later, microcomputer tools to develop decision support systems. End users were trained to develop database queries and to develop financial models for decision making. During this era the IS organization took on a new and growing role: the support of end users who could develop their own computer applications. These end-user support tasks also evolved from purchasing and installing stand-alone microcomputers, to installing local area networks (LANs), multiuse software, and shared equipment such as printers.

In Rockart's fourth era, the Network Era (beginning in the mid-1980s), firms began to actively pursue the development of custom systems that would give them a competitive advantage and business managers began to take more of an "ownership" role in IT investments. Many of these strategic applications required improved telecommunications capabilities to link across geographically distributed units of the company, as well as electronic linkages with customers, suppliers, and other business partners. With the breakup of the AT&T monopoly in 1984, the IS department also took on what became a much more complex responsibility: the operations and support of telecommunications networks.

In the first half of the 1990s, new enterprise system packages that integrated transaction data across functional "silos" became available for purchase. Large firms were among the earliest to purchase these complex systems. Multinational firms were able to implement the same enterprise system modules in non-U.S. locations by using the language and currency translation capabilities of these packages. These IT investments had very important business implications: Functions that had previously been decentralized could be consolidated (centralized) and business processes could be reengineered, for example, to provide a single point-of-contact for servicing national accounts or global customers, as well as local customers.

The fifth era in Figure 1.1, the **Internet Era**, is usually said to have begun with the widespread dissemination of the commercial Web browser. Beginning in the mid-1990s, U.S.-based businesses began to make major IT investments to develop an e-business capability. Top managers in traditional firms began to take more of a leadership role in IT decision making, because initial e-business investments required some hard decisions about how to respond to potential threats from new online (dot-com) companies and experimental applications with unknown returns. We have now begun the second decade of this Internet Era. The IS management role has evolved to include support for not only a new type of internal network (intranets) but also for remote access by customers and suppliers, including public Web sites for conducting business around-the-clock (24/7).

From these era descriptions in Figure 1.1 we can see that the IS management role has changed not only as new information technologies have expanded the firm's dependence on IT, but also as the firm's business managers have learned how to use IT in new ways.

Managing the IT Assets

Given the increased dependence on IT by businesses in all types of industries, effective management of the firm's IT assets has become a business imperative. Ross, Beath, and Goodhue (1996) argue that IT managers need to focus on managing three types of IT assets: technology, relationship, and human assets (as summarized in Figure 1.2). Some characteristics of these three assets in today's e-world are described below.

Technology Asset. Managing this asset requires effective planning, building, and operating of a computer and communications infrastructure—an information "utility"—so that all employees have the right information available as needed, anytime, anywhere. Just like land-line telephone users expect to receive a dial tone as they initiate a call, computer users expect a network to be up so that they can access data quickly in an easy-to-use form. Today's organizations have become so dependent on IT that when information systems are unavailable, entire departments can't get their work done, customers can't be fully supported, and suppliers can't receive orders for needed materials.

One view of an enterprise-level technology architecture, based on Weill and Broadbent (1998), is shown in Figure 1.3. The IT components layer includes the hardware, systems software, and networks that capture, process, and store transaction data. The IT services layer

IT Asset	Goal
Technology	A well-defined IT architecture with sharable IT platforms and easy-to-use applications
Relationship	A working climate in which IT and business managers share the responsibility and risks, along with selected outside IT partners
Human	An appropriately skilled and supportive internal IT staff and well-managed human resources from strategic IT vendor partners.

Figure 1.2 Three IT Assets

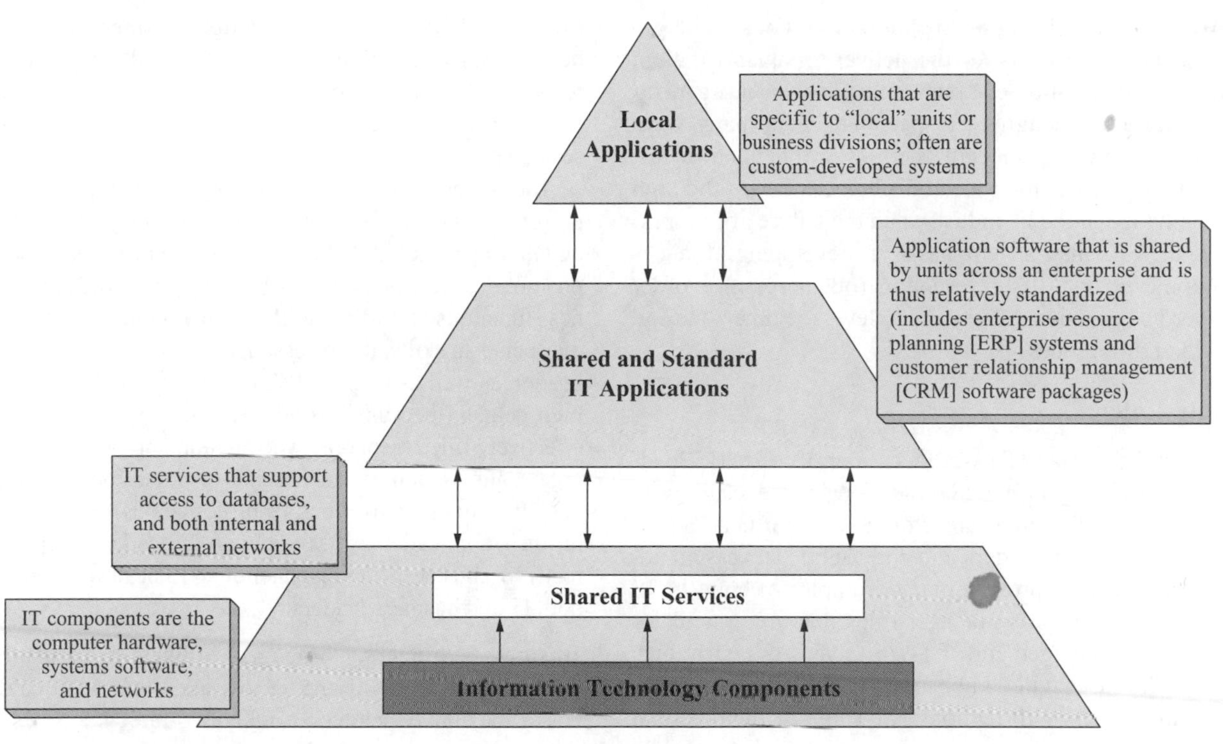

Figure 1.3 Enterprise IT Architecture (Based on Weil and Broadbent, 1998).

can be viewed from an internal user's viewpoint: It includes support for access to e-mail services, shared databases, and both internal and external networks. (In Part I we discuss these information technologies in detail.) The IT manager is held accountable for not only ensuring reliable computer and network operations and support, but also for ensuring business continuity in the event of a virus attack or other unanticipated external event. For those organizations with Web-based retailing applications, customers cannot make a purchase if Web servers are unavailable, so the importance of IT security has escalated.

The top two layers in Figure 1.3 are application software layers. The top layer is applications that are specific to "local" units, business divisions, or specific functions; these are typically applications that have been customized to meet a specific unit's needs. The second layer from the top has grown to be much larger over the past decade. For example, enterprise system packages that support back-office transaction processing belong to this layer. (In Part II we discuss these application categories in detail.)

In a widely distributed, but poorly titled, article published in the May 2003 *Harvard Business Review* (called "IT Doesn't Matter"), Nicholas Carr argues that the primary IS management role today is to manage the costs and vulnerabilities of the computing "utility." The author also argues that because of recent investments in standard application packages, obtaining a competitive advantage from IT is an elusive goal. However, as the large number of letters to the editor published in the subsequent issue of this journal pointed out, competitive advantage doesn't come from the IT investment alone: It comes from the way that the business applies IT to meet strategic goals. Competitive advantage therefore can be achieved not only with customized applications, but also with large, complex enterprise system packages.

Relationship Asset. The relationship asset has become recognized as critically important as we have evolved from the Accounting Era to the Internet Era of IS management. As seen in Figure 1.1, business managers have taken on greater decision-making roles about IT investments and are championing the development and implementation of new IT applications in order to achieve the intended business benefits.

Achieving business value from IT investments therefore requires strong working partnerships between business managers and IT managers (Brown, McLean, and Straub, 2000). According to David Pottruck (Co-CEO of Charles Schwab), IT is so integral to business today that business leaders who do not learn how to partner with their IT leaders will not be successful (see the sidebar "Blending Technology and the Business").

Human Asset. Managing the human asset of an IS organization is also critical for the delivery, implementation, and ongoing operation of systems that enable an organization's strategy. Managing IT specialists is in many ways similar to managing specialists in other functional areas, but there also are some special differences due to the high rate of change in the IT industry and the nature of IT work. Today there is also an emphasis on developing alliances with domestic and offshore vendors (outsourcing) in order to lower IT operational costs and to leverage time zone and peak load differences.

People Roles

Although the human IT asset focuses on IS roles (IS leaders, other IS managers, and IS professionals), the relationship asset points out the importance of IS roles for non-IS specialists (business managers and end users). The case studies in this textbook provide many examples of both the IS specialist and business manager roles that are critical for the effective management of IT in today's organizations. Some of the cases will demonstrate how to play these roles well, while others will demonstrate some of the potential pitfalls that occur when these roles are either not formally assigned or not performed well.

IS Leaders. The **chief information officer** (CIO) began to emerge in the 1980s as large organizations needed high-level general managers, with both technology and business leadership experience, to manage their IT assets. If IT is to play a strategic role in the organization, IS leaders must have a close relationship with the firm's top management team—and one way to achieve that is to have in place a CIO-level position.

Other IS Managers. Today's IS leadership team typically includes IS managers accountable for **data centers**, network operations, and new application solutions; many organizations also have their own IT human resource specialists to ensure that the IT human asset is well-trained and change-ready. IS managers responsible for planning, delivering, and implementing new strategic IT solutions for specific business units or functions are often physically located alongside the business managers they support. In some firms a central unit provides data center and telecommunications operations and support, while IS units responsible for application solutions report directly to a business manager.

IS Professionals. Programmers, software engineers, systems analysts, database developers, Web developers, LAN administrators, and technical support providers all belong to this category. At the end of the 1990s, a shortage of IS professionals to fill such positions was estimated by the Information Technology Association of America (ITAA) to be as large as 1.2 million workers. This led many manufacturing and service firms to seek out alternative resources for technical skills, such as outsourcing firms and other service providers.

Today there is a high demand not just for skilled technical personnel, but also for individuals with a mixture of technology *and* business skills that can fill "business technologist" positions. This role requires knowledge of different business functions and softer skills, such as communication and interpersonal skills. IS professionals who have a business education as well as technical skills are expected to remain in high demand because business technology roles cannot be effectively filled by people who are not employees within the organization (such as outsourcing or other contract personnel). In some organizations IS professionals responsible for business applications work under an IS head who reports directly to a business unit manager or an IS head who reports to both IS and business leaders.

Business Managers. Managers of business units are the internal customers of the IS organization. In today's e-world, the high dependence on IT for strategic business initiatives requires not just IT-literate, but IT-savvy business managers. Many strategic IT projects are therefore jointly led by business and IS managers. This is because the business managers in an organization are the most knowledgeable about what changes in business processes might be required to achieve the greatest business benefits from a new IT solution. Typical examples of key roles played by business managers include

- serving on an advisory or oversight committee that prioritizes and approves requests for large IT investments
- being the business sponsor or "owner" of an IT project
- serving as a business process or functional expert on a project team to develop requirements for a custom application or to select a software package
- participating in the planning and execution of the rollout of a new IT application

End Users. Although IS professionals are also end users of IT, in this textbook we use the term end user to refer to non-IS specialists within an organization. Not every IT project team might have end users as formal team members, but business employees frequently are relied on to give the project team information about their current work tasks and business processes, to participate in the redesign of these processes, and to evaluate designs for online application screens and reports from an end-user perspective. End users who have direct contacts with an organization's customers also play critical roles in IT projects when new systems will affect interactions with customers. In addition, many end users play critical roles in new system training, as well as ongoing "local support" for other end users who are learning new applications and computer tools. Some end users also develop applications using tools such as Excel, Access, and Visual Basic, and the monitoring of these applications is a business manager's responsibility.

THE IMPORTANCE OF INFORMATION SYSTEMS MANAGEMENT

Information technology (IT)—computers and telecommunications—is having the kind of revolutionary, restructuring impact that has been expected and touted for years. The rapid advances in the speed and capacity of computing devices, coupled with the pervasiveness of the Internet, digital storage, wireless and portable devices, and multimedia content, are causing major changes in the way we live and work.

Although IT affects nearly all aspects of human endeavor, this book emphasizes its use in managing and operating organizations, including business enterprises, government organizations, and social and charitable organizations. Any time people work together to jointly pursue objectives, IT is changing the way they work.

Managing and operating IT for these purposes has been a field of practice for some 50 years. First known as *business data processing* and later as *management information systems* (MIS), the field is now called *information technology* (IT). In this book, we distinguish between *IT* (the technology) and the organization that manages the technology, which we call the IS (information systems) organization. IS combines the technologies, people, processes, and organizational mechanisms for fostering the use of IT to improve organizational performance.

New Business Environment

Due to the growth and pervasiveness of IT, organizations are operating in a different environment from just a few years ago. This environment includes:

- **Globalization.** Have you noticed? The world seems to be getting smaller. Events in a faraway land can impact others in another part of the globe. As a result, a major theme in today's world is globalization, whereby companies seek to offer their goods and services around the world. However, the worldwide spread of brands and the emergence of global institutions are encountering major backlashes from groups, and even nations, that want to maintain their local identity. Companies feel this backlash in their use of IT: locales and regions want systems that suit their culture, preferences, or ways of working. In addition, they want jobs to stay put, not move to a far-off country. In response, IS executives are seeking to achieve a balance between implementing a single enterprisewide IT infrastructure and tailoring systems to fit local needs—and locating work where it is best performer.
- **E-enablement.** Doing business electronically has been a fundamental use of computers since the 1950s, but now the Internet has become a hub for conducting business. The before-Internet economy is transforming into an electronic economy where clicks and bricks exist side by side. The dot-com crash might have seemed a hiccup in the increasing use of the Internet for business and commerce. However, it has not deterred companies from e-enabling their businesses, that is, integrating the Internet into how they work. In general, the term *e-business* has the broad connotation of doing business electronically. E-business has much to do with building e-enabled relationships with consumers and other enterprises, not just performing transactions electronically. *E-commerce,* on the other hand, is being used in the more limited sense of buying and selling electronically, as in handling commerce transactions.

  The vision is full interconnectivity among everyone on earth, with the ability to communicate electronically, transfer multimedia files, and access information from around the world at the touch of a button on a wireless device in the blink of an eye.
- **Knowledge Sharing and Knowledge Management.** One aspect of this is the transfer of knowledge between people (sharing), because the most important asset in enterprises is the people and the knowledge they possess. The other aspect is the transfer of knowledge from people's heads into lasting things, such as processes, products, practices, databases, directories, software, and such. People walk out the door each night (or leave the company); these other artifacts do not, but they do grow stale and outdated. This second area is called *knowledge management.* Both aspects have to do with managing people and the knowledge they possess. IT can be used for both.

Emphasis on knowledge work is shifting from procedure based to goal based. At the same time, a major shift is taking place from information access to content management, which includes searching, filtering, synthesizing, assimilating, and sharing knowledge resources. The importance of content management is reinforced by the fact that intellectual assets are considered by many to be the only source of sustainable competitive advantage for organizations.

Management of IS

Although IT is used in space exploration, weapons systems, medicine, entertainment, and many other aspects of human activity, the majority of information technologies are used to manage organizations.

The process of managing IT in organizations is becoming increasingly complex as it becomes more important. To illustrate why, here are just three major trends that impact IT management:

- Governance of IT, that is, deciding who makes which IT decisions, is shifting from being handled exclusively by IS executives to being a collaborative effort between IS and the business.
- The role of IS is shifting from application delivery to system integration and infrastructure development.
- Outsourcing is becoming a way of life for many IS organizations, to the extent that a major responsibility of IS is developing and managing relationships with external service providers (ESPs).

A LITTLE HISTORY

Most people are surprised to learn that the United States passed from the industrial era to the information era in 1957. In that year, the number of U.S. employees whose jobs were primarily to handle information (information workers) surpassed the number of industrial workers. Figure 1.4 shows Marc Porat's well-known division of the economy.

In the late 1950s and early 1960s, though, information technology to support information work hardly existed. Only the telephone was widespread, and even it did not reach every desk. Computers were just beginning to be used in data processing applications, replacing electric accounting machines. Even where computers were in use, their impact was modest.

Most other information work in general offices was done without much support from technology. Xerographic office copiers were introduced in 1959. Electric typewriters were commonplace, but the first word processor would not arrive until 1964. Facsimile machines were used only in specialized applications and would not be in general office use until the 1970s. However, the future of technology support for information workers was extremely bright. Many of the foundations of IT had been invented, and costs were starting their steady long-term fall.

Another milestone was reached in about 1980, when the number of U.S. information workers surpassed the number of U.S. workers in all other sectors combined. In other words, information workers exceeded 50 percent of the U.S. work force. However, the technology to support these infor-

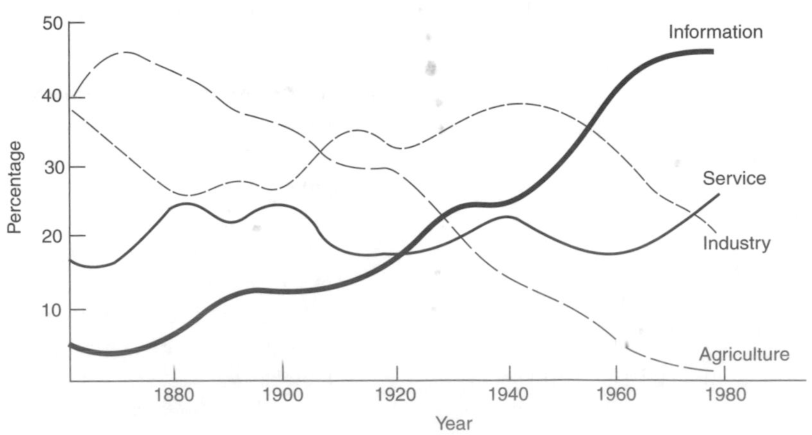

Figure 1.4 Percentage Aggregation of the U.S. Work Force *Source:* Marc U. Porat, *The Information Economy* (Washington, D.C.: Office of Telecommunications Policy, U.S. Department of Commerce, 1977).

mation workers remained slow, expensive, and segmented into special-purpose categories.

IT was initially used to perform manual information work more quickly and more efficiently. Then it was used to manage work better. Now we are well into the third stage of technology assimilation in which IT makes pervasive changes in the structure and the operation of work, business practices, organizations, industries, and the global economy.

The next two sections explore the changes in the work environment and the technical environment.

THE ORGANIZATIONAL ENVIRONMENT

How IT is used depends on the environment surrounding the organization that uses it. This environment includes economic conditions, characteristics of principal resources (especially labor), management philosophies, societal mores, and other factors. This environment changes constantly. Simultaneously, technological advances affect the way IT is used. An ongoing debate centers around whether technology drives change in organizations or merely supports it. This "chicken or egg" debate is giving way to the realization that IT and its use and management coevolve, each influencing the other.

This section explores two aspects of the organizational environment: the external forces that are causing executives to reexamine how their firms compete and the internal structural forces that affect how organizations operate or are managed. It then considers how these environmental trends have led to a new set of goals for the new work environment.

The External Business Environment

Today, the turbulent business world includes shorter and shorter product cycles, a U.S. telecommunications industry in turmoil, investor doubts about corporate truthfulness, and terrorism. IT contributes to this turbulence because it allows information to move faster, increasing the pace at which individuals and organizations can respond to events. One result is higher peaks and lower valleys, caused by an IT-charged herd instinct. The following are the main changes taking place in our global marketplace.

The Internet Economy. This economy began with business-to-consumer (B2C) retailing, selling over the World Wide Web (Web). The pioneer of the Web-only business model was Amazon.com. The action then moved to business-to-business (B2B), with buyers and sellers using Internet exchanges (or e-marketplaces) to find and consummate business deals. eBay is the most well-known exchange, but there are other industry-specific exchanges. The main point is that today's economy is encompassing both old and new ways of operating, and IT is a major underpinning of the way these two worlds interface with each other.

Global Marketplace. The entire world has become the marketplace. To succeed, large companies believe they need to be global, meaning huge and everywhere. Merger mania is occurring across industries as companies aim for this goal. Mergers even cross national boundaries. It is not unusual for a British food company to own U.S., French, and other food and beverage companies, or for a Swiss pharmaceutical company to buy out its American and Japanese counterparts.

In addition, the Internet enables companies to work globally—with three main operating arenas, Asia/Pacific, the Americas, Europe and the Middle East and Africa (EMEA)—and work around the clock by passing work from one region to the next, following the sun.

The global marketplace has become a two-way street. Firmly entrenched companies find unexpected competitors from halfway around the world bidding on work via the Internet. Parts and subassemblies are being manufactured in many countries to cut overall labor costs and then shipped to other countries for final assembly.

The Internet also allows small firms to have a global reach. Norwegians can order extra-hot chili sauce from Texas. Europeans can order books over the Internet from U.S. companies before those books become available in their own country's bookstores. And so on. The business environment is now global, but local tastes still matter. As noted earlier, local backlashes against globalization are a factor global enterprises need to include in their planning.

Business Ecosystems. A new term is creeping into the business lexicon: *ecosystem*. An ecosystem is a web of relationships surrounding one or a few companies. For example, Microsoft and Intel are the center of the Wintel ecosystem that has dominated the PC world. Yet, although they dominate the PC ecosystem, they are far less dominant in other ecosystems, such as the Internet ecosystem and the wireless communications ecosystem. The point about ecosystems is that they appear to follow biological rules rather than industrial-age, machine-like rules. They require flexibility because relationships change more frequently; they are more organic. Relationships and coevolution require a different corporate mindset from the command-and-control mindset of the past.

Decapitalization. Tangible items, such as capital, equipment, and buildings, were the tenets of power in the industrial age. Today, intangible items, such as ideas, intellectual capital, and knowledge, have become the scarce, desirable items. You could say that the business world is moving from tangible to intangible; it is decapitalizing. For this reason, managing talent has become as important as managing finances. Without talent, ideas dwindle, the new-product pipeline shrivels up, and the company becomes less competitive. More and more talk focuses on managing intellectual capital (the knowledge in people's heads).

Faster Business Cycles. The tempo of business has accelerated appreciably; companies do not have as much time to develop new products or services and move them into the marketplace. Once on the market, their useful lives tend to be shorter as well, so speed has become of the essence. Efforts to accelerate time to market or to reduce cycle time often depend on innovative uses of IT.

Accountability and Transparency. The rise and fall of dot-coms probably should have been expected; some of their business plans truly could not make money. However, the ensuing debacle in the overbuilt telecommunications industry and the corporate financial shenanigans in several industries around the world have shaken investor confidence and led to calls for greater transparency of corporate operations and greater accountability of corporate officers. These events are likely to increase the pressure for corporate ethics. IT will surely play a role in implementing the ensuing regulations and fostering transparency. Discussions of IT ethics might also increase.

Rising Societal Risks of IT. Since the last edition of this book, IT has negatively affected millions of people—through network shutdowns, computer viruses, identity thefts, e-mail scams, movement of white-collar jobs to lower-cost countries, and such—which has led to increasing calls for government regulation and for vendors and corporations to take action. This edition includes more discussion of the societal risks that accompany the societal benefits of IT.

Now, more than in the past, CIOs need to address the dark side of IT, which includes protecting the privacy of individuals whose information they store and securing their networks, databases, and computers from cybercrime, computer viruses, and such. They also need to consider the societal effects of outsourcing, and ease, as much as possible, the human misery that comes from employees losing their job or having to oversee work performed in distant places.

The Internal Organizational Environment

The work environment is also changing, and the art of managing people is undergoing significant shifts. These changes are profound enough to change organizational structures. Frances Cairncross, management editor at the *Economist,* writes in her book *The Company of the Future* that the relationship between IT and enterprise structure is growing more widespread and deeper. She believes that the company of the future will look much like the Japanese *keiretsu* (the associations of independent and interdependent businesses working in concert). Here are some of the changes we see affecting how people work and how organizations operate. Some support Cairncross's belief.

From Supply-Push to Demand-Pull. In the industrial age, companies did their best to figure out what customers wanted. Firms were organized to build a supply of products or services and then "push" them out to end customers on store shelves, in catalogs, and such. The Internet, which allows much closer and one-to-one contact between customer and seller, is moving the business model to demand-pull. In this model, companies offer customers the components of a service or product, and the customers create their own personalized versions, creating the demand that pulls the specific product or service they want through the supply chain, or rather, the demand chain.

To move to this consumer-pull mass customization business model, companies need to essentially reverse their business processes to be customer facing. In fact, this model can lead to suppliers and customers cocreating products and services. For example, book buyers who put their critiques of books on Amazon.com's Web site are, in a sense, cocreating part of Amazon's service to other book buyers.

Here's another bookseller example. Borders is the second-largest book retailer in the United States. Its president has decided to replace the industry's supply-push approach with a new demand-pull approach. Traditionally, and still today, booksellers push those books that publishers pay them to promote in their bookstore windows, on near-the-door tables, and in other high-traffic areas.

Borders' president thinks these short-term incentives might actually hurt overall sales in categories, so he is shifting Borders to "category management," which means publishers will help comanage 250 book categories, reports Trachtenberg. In return for being part of the decision-making process by recommending titles to Borders, the publishers will help pay for the market research Borders will do to find out what book buyers want. For instance, Borders wants to find out which books are bought on impulse, which ones sell better when the cover is showing, which types should be grouped together, where sections should be located, and even how to price books.

Borders' competitors are watching this demand-pull experiment with great interest. Some doubt that it will work, reports Trachtenberg, arguing that selling books is not like selling screwdrivers or prescription drugs. One thing Borders has already learned through its market research, though, is that one-fourth of its cookbooks are bought as gifts.

Customer-centricity is another term for this trend. It means replacing product-centric thinking with customer-centric thinking. The result: Organizational structures shift from product groups to customer groups. One way to view this shift is to see it as turning traditional thinking inside out. When companies focus on products, they are thinking inside-out. When they think about customers and customer groups, they think outside-in.

Although you might think this shift means keeping customers happy, it can actually have the opposite effect for some customers. When companies create customer clusters using data warehousing and data mining techniques, they find out which clusters are profitable and which are not. They may then institute policies that cater to the profitable customers and charge or let go the unprofitable ones.

Self-Service. Bank automated teller machines (ATMs) were an early example of customer self-service. The 1990s saw an increase in systems that let consumers access corporate computer systems to purchase products, inquire about the state of an order, and, in general, do business with the firm online on their own. FedEx was one of the first companies to leverage the Web by allowing customers to directly access its package-tracking system via its homepage. Today, companies that ship products via FedEx have links to the same homepage, providing that service to their customers. When customers serve themselves, employees can do other kinds of work.

Real-Time Working. A term that has been around for at least 15 years but has only recently gained traction (and use in vendor marketing materials) is the *real-time enterprise.* The genesis of this notion, we believe, was the military, whose personnel fly planes and drive tanks using instrument panels. These panels show the pilots and soldiers the surrounding terrain as it exists at the moment, so that they can respond to changes and threats in real time. The term has been adopted in business and means operating a business in as close to real time as possible, using computer systems to indicate the state of the "business terrain" as it exists at the moment.

For example, members of a sales team about to talk to a potential global customer can have up-to-the-minute information about that customer—late-breaking news about the company, recent management changes, latest orders to the company (if any), sales tips from other employees—all gathered for them from many sources.

Other examples of real-time working are knowing inventories as of right now (not 1 week or 1 month ago), knowing cash on hand right now (not at the end of last month), and being able to reach someone when you need them, perhaps via instant messaging. With accurate, current information on company operations, customer orders, inventory stocks, and on-demand access to others, people have better information to make decisions. Thus, businesses are making a major push to have real-time information in hand and real-time access to people, which are not easy feats, especially for enterprises with global operations.

Team-Based Working. The trend is toward people working together on projects. Rather than depending on chains of command and the authority of the boss, many organizations emphasize teams to accomplish major tasks and projects. Peter Drucker's classic article in the *Harvard Business Review* uses the analogy of a symphony, where each member of the team has a unique contribution to make to the overall result. Task-oriented teams form and work together long enough to accomplish the task, then disband. This project-based working, where people sometimes work simultaneously on several projects with different teams across different organizations, is generating major interest in information systems called *groupware.* Groupware provides IT support for meetings, collaborative work, and communications among far-flung team members. Cairncross believes the increased ability to collaborate in new ways using IT is one of the forces driving the changes in organizational structures and that enterprises that use the technology to work in new collaborative ways will be the winners.

Anytime, Anyplace Information Work. Information workers are increasingly mobile, so computers are needed not just for accessing information, but also for communicating with others. One of the hallmarks of IT today is that the communication capabilities of computers are seen as more important than their computing capabilities. Communication technology has developed to the point where information work can be done anywhere with a laptop computer, cell phone, or PDA. Electronic mail, voice mail and instant messaging (IM) cross time zones to allow work to be conducted anytime, anywhere. People sporadically work from home, rather than commute every day, and they work in their preferred geographical location, even if it is remote from the main office. The advances in wireless technology enable people to work in an airport, at a customer site, while walking, and so on.

Outsourcing and Strategic Alliances. To become more competitive, organizations are examining which work they should perform internally and which they should give to others. *Outsourcing,* having a third party perform information work for you, may be a simple contract for services or a long-term strategic alliance. Between these two extremes are a variety of relationships that are redefining the way organizations work together. The thinking is: We should focus on what we do best and outsource the other functions to people who specialize in them to make us more world-class in all our functions. The result is becoming known as the *extended enterprise.* IT is providing the information and communication means to manage complex sets of relationships.

Demise of Hierarchy. In the traditional hierarchy, people performing the same type of work are grouped together and overseen by a supervisor. The supervisor allocates the work, handles problems, enforces discipline, issues rewards, provides training, and so on. Management principles such as division of labor and chain of command define this traditional work environment.

This structure is no longer best in many instances. Self-managed groups, whether working on an assembly line or in an insurance company, provide much of their own management. They have lower absenteeism, yield higher productivity, produce higher quality work, and are more motivated than workers in traditional settings.

A major reason for the demise of hierarchy is that the more turbulent business environment—represented by the changes just noted—challenges the premises of a hierarchical structure because it cannot cope with rapid change. Hierarchies require a vertical chain of command where lines of responsibility do not cross and approval to proceed on major initiatives is granted from above. This communication up and down the chain of command can take too much time in today's environment. IT enables team-based organizational structures by facilitating rapid and far-flung communication.

Goals of the New Work Environment

As a result of these changes in the internal and external organizational environment, enterprises around the world are redefining their work environment—a tumultuous proposition, at best—without any true guidance. We see the following overarching goals for thriving in the new work environment:

- Leverage knowledge globally
- Organize for complexity
- Work electronically
- Handle continuous and discontinuous change

Leverage Knowledge Globally. Knowledge is now being called *intellectual capital* to signify its importance. This is not the knowledge in an expert system or a Lotus Notes database, but rather the knowledge in people's heads. Knowledge that people know but cannot really explain to others is called *tacit knowledge,* as opposed to explicit explainable knowledge. Companies that are able to leverage tacit knowledge globally will be successful—provided, of course, its use is directed by a sound strategy.

Brook Manville and Nathaniel Foote of McKinsey & Company point out that knowledge-based strategies begin with strategy, not knowledge. Intellectual capital is meaningless unless companies have the corporate fundamentals in place, such as knowing what kind of value they want to provide and to whom.

They also point out that executing a knowledge-based strategy is not about managing knowledge but about nurturing people who have the knowledge, tapping into the knowledge that is locked in their experience. Although companies have numerous systems in place to share explicit knowledge, the key to unlocking tacit knowledge is a work environment in which people want to share. A manufacturer that tried to foster greater knowledge transfer while downsizing discovered that the combination was impossible. Why would employees share what they know when the bosses were looking for ways to consolidate expertise?

The means to tap tacit knowledge is to foster sharing and to support the sharing with technology. E-mail and groupware can provide the interconnection, but the driving force is the culture. When people want to share, they form *worknets*—informal groups whose collective knowledge is used to accomplish a specific task. The sharing and leveraging of knowledge happens through organizational "pull"—people needing help from others to solve a problem—rather than organizational "push," which overloads people with information. Therefore, leveraging knowledge is all about raising the aspirations of each individual, say Manville and Foote.

Organize for Complexity. A second overarching goal of companies, whether they recognize it or not, is to be able to handle complexity. Why? One reason is that the world has become so interconnected that simple solutions no longer solve a problem. Another reason is that issues are systemic. Corporate decisions can have an environmental impact, a human resources impact, an economic impact, and even an ethical impact. Furthermore, capturing marketshare oftentimes requires allying with others who have complementary expertise. Alliances increase complexity; so does specialization. Have you bought shampoo, crackers, or tires lately? These used to be fairly straightforward decisions. Today, the choices are so numerous that consumers can spend an inordinate amount of time making a selection. To thrive in such an age, companies need to be organized to be able to handle complexity.

Work Electronically. Just as the marketplace is moving to the market*space,* the workplace is moving to the work*space.* Taking advantage of the Internet, and networks in general, is a third major goal of enterprises these days. But just as the move from horse and buggy to train to automobile to jet plane each was not simply a change in speed, but a change in kind, so, too, is the move to working in a space rather than a place a change in kind. It requires different organizing principles, management tenets, compensation schemes, organizational structures, and such. It also changes how organizations interact with others, such as their customers.

George Gilder, columnist and author, noted that business eras are defined by the plummeting price of the key factor of production. During the industrial era, this key factor was horsepower, as defined in kilowatt hours. It dropped from many dollars to 7.5 cents. For the past 40 years, the driving force of economic growth has been transistors, translated into millions of instructions per second (MIPS) and bits of semiconductor memory. The latter has fallen 68 percent a year, from $7 per bit to a millionth of a cent. Gilder thinks that we are now at yet another "historic cliff of cost" in a new factor of production, bandwidth. "If you thought the price of computing dropped rapidly in the last decade, just wait until you see what happens with communications bandwidth," said Gilder, referencing a remark by Andy Grove, CEO of Intel.

MIPS and bits have been used to compensate for the limited availability of bandwidth. The microchip moved power *within* companies, allowing people to vastly increase their ability to master bodies of specialized learning. Microchips both flattened corporations and launched new corporations. Bandwidth, on the other hand, moves power all the way to consumers. That is the big revolution of the Internet, Gilder contends, and the reason behind the move to relationship marketing with consumers.

In an era of bandwidth abunda
changes. For example, TV is based on
chical model with a few broadcast stat
and millions of passive broadcast receivers (televisions). The result is "lowest-common-denominator" entertainment from Hollywood. The Internet, on the other hand, is a "first-choice" culture, much like a bookstore. You walk in and get your first-choice book. First-choice culture is vastly different from lowest-common-denominator culture, says Gilder. As the Internet spreads, the culture will move from what we have in common to one in which our aspirations, hobbies, and interests are manifested.

Handle Continuous and Discontinuous Change. Finally, to keep up, companies will need to innovate continually—something most have generally not been organized to do. Continual innovation, however, does not mean continuously steady innovation. Innovation occurs in fits and starts. Change takes two forms: continuous change (the kind espoused by total quality management techniques) or discontinuous change (the kind espoused by reengineering). When a product or process is just fine, but needs some tuning, continuous change improves its efficiency. However, when it is not fine, discontinuous change is needed to move to an entirely new way of working. The two often form a cycle. Companies need to be able to handle both for their products and processes.

These four major goals underlie the new work environment. This organizational environment sets the backdrop for exploring the emerging technology environment.

THE TECHNOLOGY ENVIRONMENT

The technology environment enables advances in organizational performance. The two have a symbiotic relationship; IT and organizational improvements coevolve. IT evolution can be described using the four traditional areas of hardware, software, data, and communication.

Hardware Trends

In the 1950s and 1960s, the main hardware concerns of data processing managers were machine efficiency and tracking new technological developments. Batch processing was predominant; online systems emerged later. At that time, hardware was centralized, often in large showcase data centers behind glass walls.

In the mid-1970s, processing power began to move out of the central site, but only at the insistence of users who bought their own departmental minicomputers and word processors. In the 1980s, mainly due to the advent of personal computers (PCs), this trend accelerated far beyond the expectations of most people, especially IS managers.

Now this trend is well established. Client-server computing forms the underlying structure. A *client* machine on the desktop, a laptop, or a handheld provides the user interface, and a *server* on the network holds the data and applications. This same client-server model is used for interacting with the Web.

The major development in hardware toward mobile and handheld devices is led by two factions: telecommunications companies (and the cell phone manufacturers that serve them) and handheld computer manufacturers, such as Palm and Microsoft. Functionality is expanding with devices handling both voice and data. Use of wireless hardware has become the norm for the anytime-anyplace workforce.

These hardware trends are further distributing processing beyond organizational boundaries to suppliers and customers. The result is the movement of enterprisewide hardware and processing power out of the control—although perhaps still under the guidance—of the IS organization.

Software Trends

The dominant issue in software and programming in the 1960s was how to improve the productivity of in-house programmers—those who created mainly transaction processing systems. Occasionally, IS management discussed using outside services, such as time-sharing services, application packages, and contract programming from independent software houses. The software industry was still underdeveloped, though, so application development remained the purview of IS managers.

Later, programming issues centered first around modular and structured programming techniques. Then the topic expanded to life cycle development methodologies and software engineering, with the goals of introducing more rigorous project management techniques and getting users more involved in early stages of development. Eventually, prototyping (quick development of a mock-up) became popular.

Then two other software trends appeared. One, purchased software became a viable alternative to in-house development for many traditional, well-defined systems. Two, IS managers began to pay attention to applications other than transaction processing. Software to support decision support systems (DSS), report generation, and database inquiry shifted some programming from professional programmers to end users.

During the 1990s, the push for open systems was driven primarily by software purchasers who were tired of being locked in to proprietary software (or hardware). The open systems movement continues to demand that different products work together, that is, *interoperate*. Vendors initially accommodated this demand with hardware and software black boxes that performed the necessary interface conversions, but the cost of this approach is lower efficiency.

Another major trend in the 1990s was toward enterprise resource planning (ERP) systems, which tightly integrate various functions of an enterprise so that management can see cross-enterprise financial figures and order and manufacturing volumes. Some firms implemented ERP to replace legacy systems that were not Y2K compliant (i.e., the systems would think that an "02" would mean 1902 rather than 2002). Implementing ERP involves integrating components, which is called systems integration, rather than application development. Implementation has been expensive and troublesome, especially for companies wanting to modify the ERP software to fit their unique processes. However, for many large corporations, their ERP system has become their foundation information system, in essence, defining their IT architecture.

Like hardware, software is becoming more network-centric. Rather than replace legacy systems, many companies are adding Web front ends to broaden access to the systems to employees, customers, and suppliers. Companies are establishing corporate portals where employees log into their company intranet to use software housed at that site. This approach moves the software from being decentralized (on PCs) to being centralized (on a server somewhere).

Another change in software is the move to Web Services. Web Services are packages of code that each perform a specific function and have a URL (Uniform Resource Locator; an address on the Internet) so that they can be located via the Internet to fulfill a request. For example, if you have accessed FedEx's Web site to track a package, you have used a Web Service. MacAfee's virus protection also is delivered to PCs using a Web Services approach. The software industry is morphing into a Web Services industry.

The significance of Web Services is that it moves software and programming to being truly network-centric; the network becomes the heart of the system, linking all Web Services. Packages of code can be concatenated to produce highly tailored and quickly changed processes. In the past, once software was programmed to handle a process in a specific way, it essentially cast that process in electronic concrete because the process could not change until the software was modified. The tenet of Web Services is that a process is defined at the time it is executed, because each Web Service decides at that time which of its many options to use to answer the current request. The world of Web Services entails its own jargon, standards, and products. Importantly, it builds on the past—functions in legacy systems can be packaged to become Web Services.

Data Trends

The evolution of the third core information technology area—data—has been particularly interesting. At first, discussions centered around file management and techniques for organizing files to serve individual applications. Then generalized file management systems emerged for managing corporate data files. This more generalized approach led to the concept of corporate databases to serve several applications, followed a few years later by the concept of establishing a data administration function to manage these databases.

In the 1970s, the interest in data turned to technical solutions for managing data—database management systems. As work progressed, it became evident that a key element of these products was their data dictionary. Dictionaries now store far more than data definitions; they store information about relationships between systems, sources and uses of data, time cycle requirements, and so on.

For the first 20 years of information processing, discussions about data concerned techniques to manage data in a centralized environment. It was not until the advent of fourth-generation languages and PCs that interest in letting employees directly access corporate data began. Then users demanded it.

In addition to distributing data, the major trend in the early 1990s was expanding the focus from data resources to information resources, both internal and external to the firm. Data management organizes internal facts into data record format. Information management, on the other hand, focuses on concepts (such as ideas found in documents, especially digital documents such as Web pages) from both internal and external sources. Thus, *information resources* encompass digitized media, including voice, video, graphics, animation, and photographs.

Managing this expanded array of information resources requires new technologies. Data warehousing has arisen to store huge amounts of historical data from such systems as retailers' point-of-sale systems. Data mining uses advanced statistical techniques to explore data warehouses to look for previously unknown relationships in the data, such as which clusters of customers are most profitable. Similarly, massive amounts of document-based information are organized into document repositories and analyzed with document mining techniques. In addition, as noted earlier, businesses now emphasize intellectual capital management. Some believe knowledge can reside in machines; others believe it only resides in people's heads. Either way, knowledge management is of major importance in the new economy because intangibles hold competitive value.

The Web has, of course, broadened the term *data* to mean "content," which encompasses text, graphics, animation, maps, photos, film clips, and such. Initially, Web content was managed by the content creators, such as marketing departments. However, with the huge proliferation of sites, enterprises realized they needed to rein in all the exuberance in order to standardize formats, promote their brands in a common manner, establish refresh cycles for their content, and create approval and archival processes. Content management has become very important, and as one manager observed, it is a lot like running a newspaper.

Two major data issues now facing CIOs are security (protecting data from those who should not see it) and privacy (safeguarding the personal data of employees and customers). Furthermore, regulations (such as the Sarbanes-Oxley Act in the United States) now require company officers to verify their financial data. Because the processes that handle financial data are undoubtedly automated, CIOs need to document and ensure the accuracy of these processes. Thus, numerous aspects of data safeguarding have become important.

Communications Trends

The final core information technology is telecommunications. This area has experienced enormous change and has now taken center stage. Early use of data communications dealt with online and time-sharing systems. Then interest in both public and private (intracompany) data networks blossomed.

Telecommunications opened up new uses of information systems, and thus it became an integral component of IS management. Communications-based information systems were used to link organizations with their suppliers and customers. In the early 1980s, a groundswell of interest surrounded interorganizational systems, because some provided strategic advantage. Also during the 1980s, the use of local area networks (LANs) to interconnect PCs began. PCs started out as stand-alone devices, but that only took advantage of their computing capabilities. It soon became clear that they had communication capabilities as well, so companies jammed even more wires in their wiring ducts to connect desktops to each other and then to the corporate data center.

Until the Internet appeared, enterprises leased lines from telecommunications carriers to create wide area networks (WANs) that linked their offices and factories. The only publicly available telecommunication system was the voice telephone system. Transmitting data from PCs in small offices that did not have leased lines generally entailed using a modem to dial-up a computer at another site.

The Internet changed all that. Internet Service Providers (ISPs) appeared seemingly overnight to provide PC users with a local number for dialing into the Internet to search the Web, converse in a chat room, play text-based games, send e-mail, and transfer files. The Internet provided for data the equivalent of the worldwide voice network. Today, the Internet's protocol has become the worldwide standard for LANs and WANs. In fact, it will soon be the standard for voice as well.

The latest development in telecommunications technology is wireless—wireless long distance, wireless local loops (the last-mile connection of a home or office), wireless LANs (increasingly handled by Wi-Fi technology), and even wireless personal area networks (PANs). Wireless does not just enable mobility; it changes why people communicate, how they live, and how they work. It is a paradigm shift, and we are in the early days of wireless.

THE MISSION OF IS ORGANIZATIONS

With the organizational and IT environments as backdrops, we now turn to the mission of the IS organization. In the early days, transaction processing systems acted as "paperwork factories" to pay employees, bill customers, ship products, and so on. During that era, the performance of the IS organization was defined by efficiency (or productivity) measures such as the percentage of uptime for the computer, throughput (number of transactions processed per day), and the number of lines of program code written per week.

Later, during the MIS era, the focus of IS departments shifted to producing reports for "management by exception" or summary reports for all levels of management. This era gave us the classic IS objective to "get the right information to the right person at the right time." In this era, IS was judged on effectiveness measures (in addition to the efficiency measures of the previous era).

For today's environment, the mission of IS organizations has broadened to the following:

To improve the performance of people in organizations through the use of IT.

The objective is improvement of the enterprise, not IS, so, ideally, IS performance is based on business outcomes and business results. IT is but one contributor to improving enterprise performance. This book focuses on the resources used by IS organizations.

A SIMPLE MODEL

We propose a simple model to describe the IS function in organizations. Figure 1.5 represents the process of applying IT to accomplish useful work. On the left is the technology, and on the right are the users who put it to work. The arrow represents the process of translating users' needs into systems that fill that need. In the early days of IT, this translation was performed almost entirely by systems analysts.

Figure 1.6 is a simple representation of what has happened over the past 50 years. Technology has become increasingly complex and powerful; uses have become increasingly sophisticated. Information systems are now viewed as system products and users have become customers. The increased distance between the two boxes represents the increasingly complex process of specifying, developing, and delivering these system products. It is no longer feasible for one system analyst to understand the fine points of all the technologies needed in an application as well as the nuances of the application. More specialization is required of systems professionals to bridge this wider gap.

Systems professionals are not the only ones who can help bridge this gap between the technology and its users. Technology has become sophisticated enough to be used by many employees and consumers. At the same time, they are becoming increasingly computer literate; many employees even develop their own applications. Figure 1.7 depicts this trend. Today, some of the technology is truly user-friendly, and some applications, such as Web page development, database mining, and spreadsheet manipula-

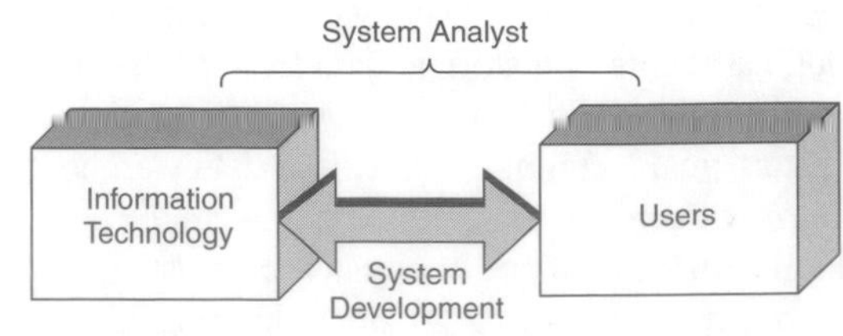

Figure 1.5 A Simple Model of Technology Use

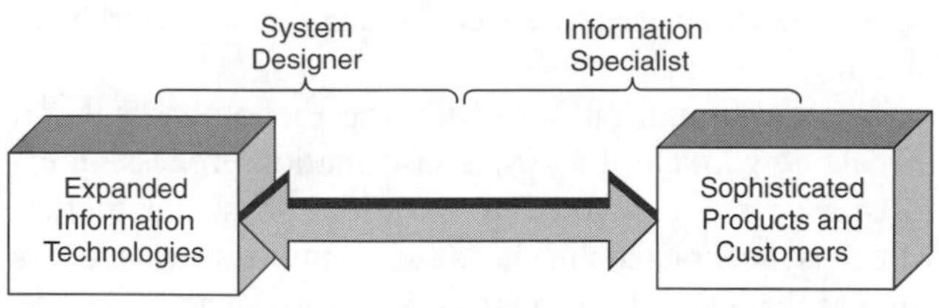

Figure 1.6 Systems Professionals Bridging the Technology Gap

tion, are handled by non-IT staff. Transaction systems, however, are still developed by professional developers, either inside or outside the firm.

The main point of this discussion is that technology is getting more complex, applications are becoming more sophisticated, and users are participating more heavily in the development of applications. The net result is that management of the process is becoming more complex and difficult as its importance increases.

A BETTER MODEL

Expanding the simple model gives us more guidance into managerial principles and tasks. We suggest a model with four principal elements:

1. A set of technologies that represent the IT infrastructure installed and managed by the IS department
2. A set of users who need to use IT to improve their job performance
3. A delivery mechanism for developing, delivering, and installing applications
4. Executive leadership to manage the entire process of applying the technology to achieve organizational objectives and goals

Let us look more carefully at each of these elements.

The Technologies

Several forces contribute to the increased importance and complexity of IT. One, of course, is the inexorable growth in computing and communications capacity accompanied by significant reductions in cost and size of computers and telecommunications components. Another is the merging of the previously separate technologies of computers, telephones/telecom/cable TV, office equipment, and consumer electronics. Still a third contributor is the ability to store and handle multiple forms of data—including voice, image, and graphics—and integrate them, resulting in multimedia. Here is a brief list of some rapidly growing technology areas:

- Handheld wireless devices and multifunction cell phones
- Web Services
- Wireless networks
- Convergence of voice, data, and video
- Integration of consumer electronics and IT

These technologies form products that are useful to employees, customers, suppliers, and consumers. No longer relegated primarily to automating transactions, information systems now fill major roles in management reporting, problem solving and analysis, distributed office support, customer service, and communications. In fact, most activities of information workers are supported in some way by IT; the same is becoming true of suppliers, customers, business trading partners, and consumers.

The Users

As IT becomes pervasive, user categories expand. The users of electronic data processing and MIS once were relatively easy to identify; they were inside the company. These systems performed clear-cut processes in specific ways. Now, though, many people want open-ended systems

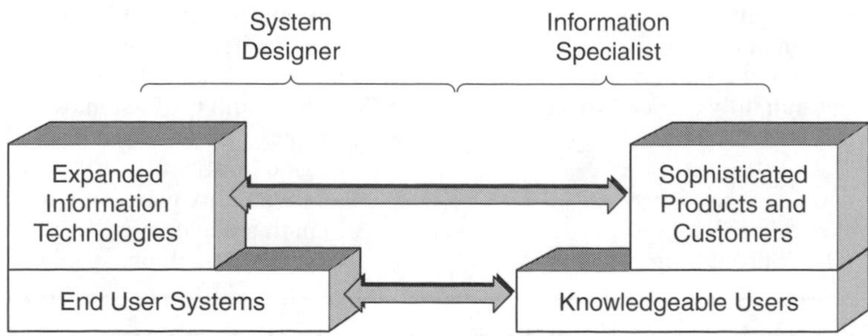

Figure 1.7 Users Bridging the Technology Gap

that allow them to create their own processes on the fly. They want systems that act as a tool, not dictate how to perform a task.

If we concentrate only on business use of IT, one helpful dichotomy divides the activities of information workers into two: procedure-based activities and knowledge-based (or goal-based) activities. The value of this model is that it focuses on the important characteristics of information workers—their job procedures and knowledge—rather than on the type of data (e.g., numbers versus text) or the business function (production versus sales), or even job title (managerial versus professional).

Procedure-based activities are large-volume transactions, where each transaction has a relatively low cost or value. The activities are well defined; therefore, the principal performance measure is efficiency (units processed per unit of resource spent). For a procedure-based task, the information worker is told what to accomplish and the steps to follow. Procedure-based activities mainly handle data.

Knowledge-based activities, on the other hand, handle fewer transactions, and each one has higher value. These activities, which can be accomplished in various ways, must therefore be measured by results, that is, attainment of objectives or goals. Therefore, the information worker must understand the goals because part of the job is figuring out how to attain them. Knowledge-based activities are based on handling concepts, not data. Figure 1.8 summarizes these two kinds of information-based work, giving several examples from banking.

Some authors use the words *clerical* and *managerial* to refer to these two types of activities. Looking at the attributes, however, it is clear that managers often do procedure-based work, and many former procedure-based jobs now have knowledge-based components. Furthermore, the distinction between manager and worker is blurring.

The most important benefit of this dichotomy is that it reveals how much of a firm's information processing efforts have been devoted to procedure-based activities, which is understandable because computers are process engines that naturally support process-driven activities. As important as they are, though, it is clear that procedure-based activities are the wave of the past. The wave of the future is applying IT to knowledge-based activities. For the task "pay employees" or "bill customers," the system analyst can identify the best sequence of steps. On the other hand, the task "improve sales in the Asian market" has no best process. People handling the latter work need a variety of support systems to leverage their knowledge, contacts, plans, and efforts.

System Development and Delivery

In our model, system development and delivery bridge the gap between technology and users, but systems for procedure-based activities differ from systems for knowledge-based information work.

The left side of Figure 1.9 shows the set of technologies that form the IT infrastructure. Organizations build systems on these technology resources to support both procedure-based and knowledge-based activities. The three main categories, called *essential technologies,* are computer hardware and software, communication networks, and information resources. We call the management of them *infrastructure management,* which includes operations, that is, keeping the systems that use these technologies up and running.

The right side of Figure 1.9 shows the two kinds of information work: procedure based and knowledge based.

Procedure Based

- High volume of transactions
- Low cost (value) per transaction
- Well-structured procedures
- Output measures defined
- Focus on process
- Focus on efficiency
- Handling of data
- Predominantly clerical workers
- Examples
  - Back office
  - Mortgage servicing
  - Payroll processing
  - Check processing

Knowledge Based

- Low volume of transactions
- High value (cost) per transaction
- Ill-structured procedures
- Output measures less defined
- Focus on problems and goals
- Focus on effectiveness
- Handling of concepts
- Managers and professionals
- Examples
  - Loan department
  - Asset/liability management
  - Planning department
  - Corporate banking

Figure 1.8 A Dichotomy of Information Work

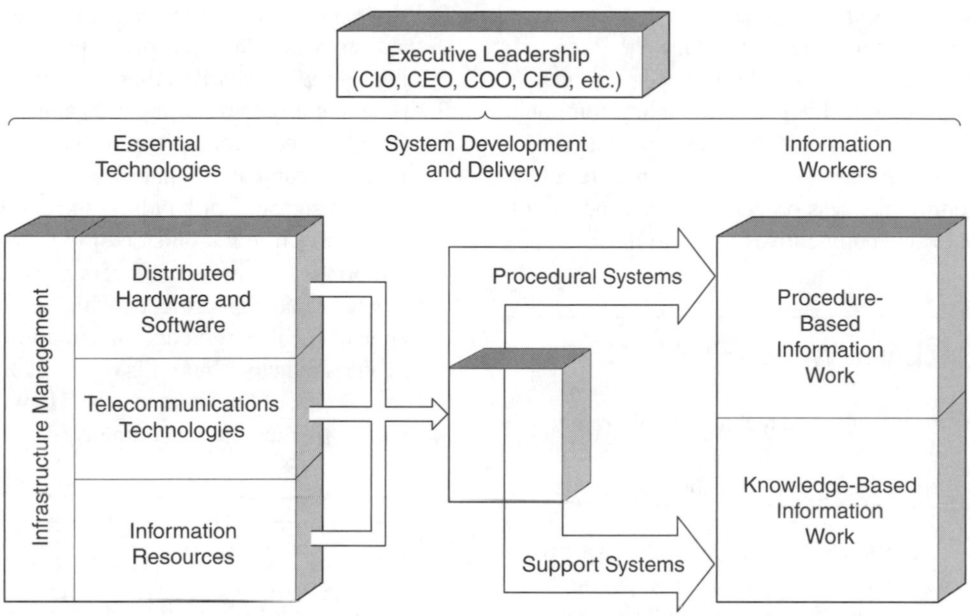

Figure 1.9 A Framework for IS Management

These two categories arc not distinct or separate, of course, but it is helpful to keep their major differences in mind because they lead to different approaches, and frequently different teams, in the bridging of systems development and delivery.

In between the technologies and the information workers is the work of developing and delivering both procedure-based systems and support systems.

IS Management

The fourth component of this book's model is executive leadership. IT leadership comes from a chief information officer (CIO) who must be high enough in the enterprise to influence organizational goals and have enough credibility to lead the harnessing of the technology to pursue those goals. However, the CIO, as the top technology executive, does not perform the leadership role alone, because IT has become too important to enterprise success to be left to one individual. Thus, CIOs work with their business peers, C-level executives—CEO, COO, CFO—and the heads of major functional areas and business units. The technology is becoming so fundamental and enabling that this executive team must work together to govern and leverage it well.

To summarize, this model of the IS function has four major components:

1. The technology, which provides the electronic and information infrastructure for the enterprise
2. Information workers in organizations, who use IT to accomplish their work goals
3. The system development and delivery function, which brings the technology and users together
4. The management of the IS function, with the overall responsibility of harnessing IT to improve the performance of the people and the organization

SUMMARY

In this chapter, you learned the basics of managing IT in an e-world—not just from the perspective of the manager but from the consumer and worker's viewpoints as well. Traditional methods of competition for business were compared to the new methods that have evolved in the e-world and revolutionized the work industry and the work force in the past decade.

Not only has the business structure changed in order to support the new technology, but the electronic age has also forced businesses to redefine their work environments and develop new goals. Any business that plans on staying competitive must have goals that capitalize on a global economy, electronic speed, and continuous change. Companies must develop new, more secure methods for handling and processing valuable data.

Computers and the Internet have also changed how companies vie for new consumers, as well as serving those same customers. In some cases, the customers have become a part of the process, often customizing the products they buy.

The IS management model has expanded, and now it must deliver the essential technologies, including computer hardware and software, communication networks, and information resources. Organizations have been forced to adapt and retool their entire business process in a short period of time if they want to stay competitive and up-to-date.

CHAPTER REVIEW QUESTIONS

1. Define the term information technology. Who manages IT?
2. What types of productivity in a business are associated with IT investments?
3. What are some of the IT innovations of the past two decades that have led to "ubiquitous" computing?
4. How do portable technologies help employees work more effectively?
5. What are three major trends that have impacted IT management and actually changed it?
6. What is customer-centric thinking, as opposed to product-centric thinking?
7. How has the role of the business manager changed since computers were first used in business organizations?
8. How has the IT revolution changed the way workers are asked to do their jobs? How have the jobs themselves changed?
9. What are the new goals of the workplace environment?
10. How have the definitions of data and the handling of it changed over the past 10 years?
11. What is the mission of the IS department?
12. List some of the technology areas that the IS person is now responsible for.
13. What are some of today's challenges for managing the human aspect?
14. How has the role of the business manager changed since computers were first used in business organizations?
15. What is an example of a potential "unintended" consequence of IT that needs to be monitored?

CHAPTER DISCUSSION QUESTIONS

1. The process of managing IT has become increasingly complex over the past few years. Is it better or worse to have more people involved in the process? Discuss pros and cons.
2. More and more companies are outsourcing products and services. What new problems arise for the IT manager with regard to these decisions?
3. The main problem for any company is handling the growth of the communications and computing capacity in any company. What ideas do you have for managing this growth or handling the communications aspect? Try to think outside of the box.
4. Tomorrow's business managers need to understand how to manage IT projects, which includes learning some of the IT jargon and information. How can a business manager build his or her IT knowledge and stay abreast of the latest trends? How can the IT manager help others in the company?

CASE STUDY: BLENDING TECHNOLOGY AND THE BUSINESS

Blending technology and the more traditional business disciplines has always been a challenge, one that I recognized in my early days at another company. I volunteered to do a job in what was then "data processing," generating projects and managing them, primarily to run the internal systems of the business. I was not embraced as part of the business but rather operated in my own little domain. I had a hard time getting their attention.

This experience began to teach me some important lessons. The business managers who refused to help got the worst outcomes: Their projects were delayed, inadequate, and more expensive than we had planned. I concluded that it wasn't intentional: They couldn't appreciate the potential of their involvement. Many of them didn't see technology as integral to their business; instead, they saw IT merely as a tool. Information technology is now so integral to business that a business leader must be smart about the key elements and trade-offs.

[Adapted from Pottruck and Pearce, 2000]

Case Study Discussion Questions

Question One

This piece was written several years ago. Based on your experience, is the problem of business managers *not* accepting IT a thing of the past, or does it still exist?

Question Two

Query some people in the business industry and ask them how well IT is integrated into their business model.

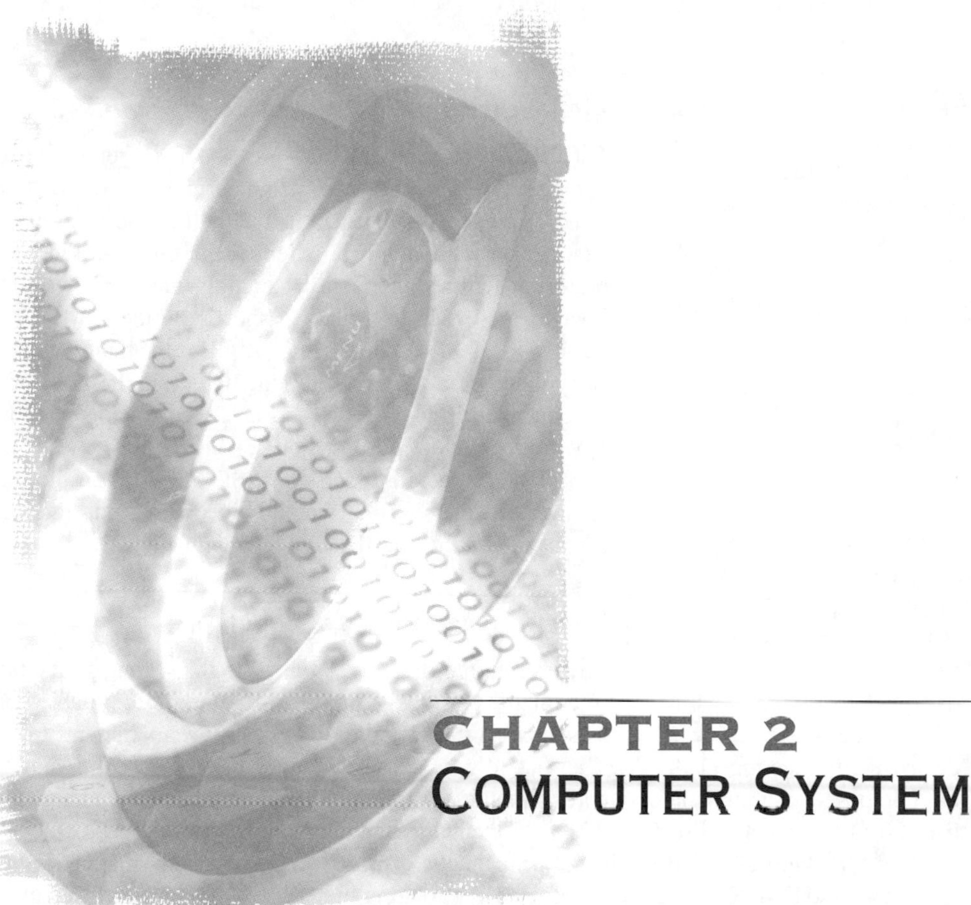

CHAPTER 2
COMPUTER SYSTEMS

CHAPTER 1 HAS SET THE STAGE FOR THE DETAILED STUDY OF INFORMATION technology (IT) and your role in harnessing that technology. We can now take a closer look at the building blocks of information technology and the development and maintenance of IT systems.

Our definition of IT is a broad one, encompassing all forms of technology involved in capturing, manipulating, communicating, presenting, and using data (and data transformed into information). Thus, IT includes computers (both the hardware and the software), peripheral devices attached to computers, communications devices and networks—clearly incorporating the Internet—photocopiers, facsimile machines, cellular telephones and related wireless devices, computer-controlled factory machines, robots, video recorders and players, and even the microchips embedded in products such as cars, airplanes, elevators, and home appliances. All these manifestations of IT are important, and you need to be aware of their existence and their present and potential uses in an organizational environment. However, two broad categories of IT are critical for the manager in a modern organization: computer technology and communications technology. Both of these technologies have had, and continue to have, a gigantic impact on the structure of the modern organization, the way it does its business, its scope, and the jobs and the careers of the managers in it.

Perhaps the first important point to be made in this chapter is that the division between computer and communications technology is arbitrary and somewhat misleading. Historically, computer and communications technologies were independent, but they have grown together over the years—especially in the 1980s and 1990s. Distributed systems exist in every industry, and these systems require the linking of computers by telecommunication lines. World Wide Web-based systems, delivered either via an intranet within the organization or via the Web itself, are becoming increasingly prevalent. Almost every manager at every level has a microcomputer on his or her desk. The computer is connected by telecommunication lines to a corporate computer and usually to the Internet. Today, the information systems organization often has responsibility for both computing and communications. The switches used in telephone networks are computers, as are the devices used to set up computer networks such as routers and gateways. It is still convenient for us to discuss computing technology as distinct from communications technology, but the distinctions are becoming even more blurred as time passes. In reality, computer/communications technology is being developed and marketed by the computer/communications industry.

This chapter concentrates on computer **hardware**, as distinct from computer **software**. Computer hardware refers to the physical pieces of a computer system–such as a CPU, a printer, and a disk drive–that can be touched. Software, by contrast, is the set of programs that controls the operations of the computer system.

EVOLUTION OF COMPUTER SYSTEMS

At present, early in the twenty-first century, the computer/communications industry is easily the largest industry in the world in terms of dollar volume of sales. This is a remarkable statement, given that the first large-scale electronic computer was completed in 1946. The ENIAC (Electronic Numerical Integrator And Computer), which was built by Dr. John W. Mauchly and J. Presper Eckert, Jr., at the Moore School of Electrical Engineering at the University of Pennsylvania, was composed of more than 18,000 vacuum tubes, occupied 15,000 square feet of floor space, and weighed more than 30 tons (see Figure 2.1). Its performance was impressive for its day—the ENIAC could perform 5,000 additions or 500 multiplications per minute.

First Generation of Computers

The ENIAC ushered in the so-called first generation of computers, extending from 1946 through 1959. Vacuum tubes were the distinguishing technology utilized in the first generation machines. After several one-of-a-kind laboratory machines, the first production-line machines—the Sperry Rand Univac, followed shortly by the IBM 701—became available in the early 1950s. But the major success story among first generation machines was the IBM 650, introduced in 1954. The 650 was designed as a logical move upward from existing punched-card machines, and it was a hit. IBM expected to sell 50 of the 650s but, in fact, installed more than 1,000, which helped IBM gain its position of prominence in the computer industry.

Second Generation of Computers

The invention of the transistor led to the second generation of computers. Transistors were smaller, more reliable, and less expensive and gave off less heat than vacuum tubes. The second generation machines generally used magnetic cores (minute magnetizable washers strung on a lattice of wires) as their primary memory, compared to the vacuum tubes or magnetic drums, where spots were magnetized on the surface of a rotating metal cylinder, that were used in the first generation. Memory sizes were increased considerably,

Figure 2.1 The ENIAC (Courtesy of Bettmann/CORBIS).

perhaps by a factor of 20, and execution speeds increased as well, again perhaps by a factor of 20. IBM again dominated this era, largely on the strength of the popular 7000-series large machines and the record-breaking sales of the 1400-series small machines.

Third Generation of Computers

The beginning of the third generation has a specific date—April 7, 1964—when IBM announced the System/360 line of computers. The System/360, as well as third generation machines from other vendors, was based on the use of integrated circuits rather than individual transistors. Early in the third generation, magnetic cores were still used as primary memory; later, semiconductor memories replaced cores. Memory sizes and execution speeds continued to climb dramatically. With the third generation, the notion of upward compatibility was introduced. When customers outgrew (ran out of capacity with) one model in a product line, they could trade up to the next model without any reworking of implemented applications. Perhaps the most drastic change was that the third generation machines relied on revolutionary, sophisticated operating systems (complex programs), such as IBM's OS, to actually control the computer's actions. As one might expect, the System/360 and the System/370 that followed were the dominant computers of the late 1960s and 1970s (see Figure 2.2).

Fourth Generation of Computers

Unfortunately, there is no neat dividing line between the third and fourth generations of computers. Most experts and vendors would agree that we are now in the fourth generation, but they don't agree on when this generation started or how soon we should expect the fifth generation (if ever). Changes since the introduction of the System/360 have tended to be evolutionary, rather than revolutionary. New models or new lines based on new technologies were announced by all major vendors on a regular basis in the 1970s, 1980s, 1990s, and early 2000s (although many of the players have changed). Memory sizes have continued to climb, and speeds have continued to increase. An innovation later in the fourth generation was to incorporate multiple processors into a single machine. The integrated circuits of the third generation became LSI (large-scale integration) circuits and then VLSI (very-large-scale integration) circuits. Through VLSI the entire circuitry for a computer can be put onto a single silicon chip smaller than a fingernail. Communication between terminals and computers, and between computers themselves, first began during the third generation, but the use of this

Figure 2.2 A Configuration of the IBM System/360 (Courtesy of IBM Archives. Unauthorized use not permitted.).

technology came of age during the fourth. With the spread of distributed systems and various local and long-distance network arrangements, some commentators refer to communication as the distinguishing feature of the fourth generation.

The Development of Minicomputers

Parallel with the third and fourth generations, an important splintering occurred within the computer industry. As IBM and the other major vendors, such as Sperry Rand, Burroughs, NCR, Honeywell, and Control Data, competed for industry leadership with more powerful, larger machines, a number of smaller, newer firms recognized a market niche for small machines aimed at smaller businesses and scientific applications. Successful firms in this minicomputer market included Digital Equipment Corporation (DEC), Data General, and Hewlett-Packard. These minicomputers were just like the larger machines (which came to be called mainframes), except that they were less powerful and less expensive. The minicomputer vendors also worked very hard at developing easy-to-use applications software. As the minicomputer market evolved, many of the mainframe vendors, such as IBM, moved into this area.

The Development of Microcomputers

Another splintering within the industry took place in the late 1970s and 1980s with the introduction and success of the microcomputer, which is based on the computer on a chip (see Figure 2.3), or microprocessor. Apple and other companies pioneered the microcomputer business, finding a market niche below the minicomputers for home use, in very small businesses, and in the public school system. Then, in late 1981, IBM entered the market with its Personal Computer, which quickly became the microcomputer standard for the workplace. In fact, the Personal Computer, or PC, became so much of a standard that most people use the terms *microcomputer*, *Personal Computer*, and *PC* interchangeably (and we will do so in this book, as well). Subsequent developments included greatly increased speed and capabilities of microcomputers, as well as the introduction of a variety of IBM "clones" in the marketplace by other vendors. The widespread acceptance of microcomputers in the business world placed significant computing power at the fingertips of virtually every manager. The connection of all these microcomputers (as well as the connection of the larger machines) through company intranets and the worldwide Internet changed the entire face of computing in the mid- and late 1990s.

BASIC COMPONENTS OF COMPUTER SYSTEMS

For historical completeness, we should note that there are really two distinct types of computers—digital and analog. Digital computers operate directly on numbers, or digits,

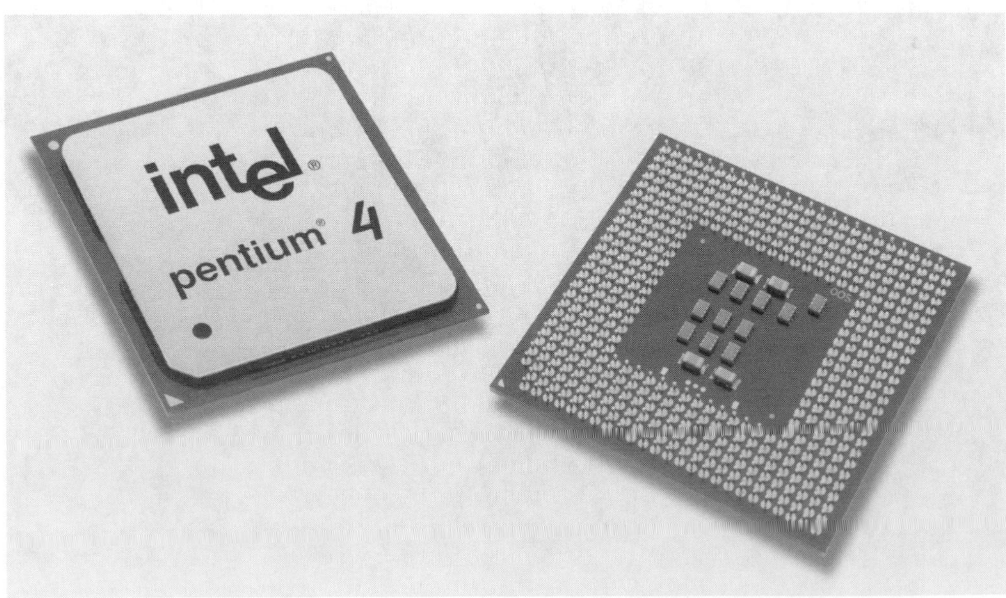

Figure 2.3 Intel® Pentium® 4 Processor Built on 90 nm (nanometer) Technology (Courtesy of Intel Corporation).

THE MICROPROCESSOR CHIP NEARS 35

In late 1971, Intel Corporation announced the first microprocessor in a trade-magazine ad that heralded "a new era in integrated electronics." But even Intel didn't anticipate the scope of the revolution it was unleashing on business and society. Today the world's chip population has swollen to nearly one trillion, including 25 billion microprocessors. Ever since Intel's first microprocessor, the 4004, these chips have grown increasingly powerful in periodic leaps and bounds (see Table 2.1). In 1996, Intel Chairman Andrew S. Grove predicted that this inexorable march would continue for at least 15 more years, perhaps 30. By 2011, he envisioned microprocessors with a billion transistors that would chew through 100,000 MIPS (millions of instructions, or operations, per second). Grove's estimates are holding true–in fact, he might well have been low in his predictions! In late 2003 the fastest Pentium 4 chips boasted 55 million transistors and speeds of 3,200 MIPS. Therefore, that 2011 chip will be crammed with the power of over 30 Pentium 4s.

Table 2.1 The Evolution of the Intel Microprocessor

Chip	Public Debut	Initial Cost	Number of Transistors	Initial MIPS
4004	11/71	$200	2,300	0.06
8008	4/72	$300	3,500	0.06
8080	4/74	$300	6,000	0.6
8086	6/78	$360	29,000	0.3
8088	6/79	$360	29,000	0.3
i286	2/82	$360	134,000	0.9
i386	10/85	$299	275,000	5
i486	4/89	$950	1.2 million	20
Pentium	3/93	$878	3.1 million	100
Pentium Pro	3/95	$974	5.5 million	300
Pentium II	5/97	$775	7.5 million	266[a]
Pentium III	2/99	$696	9.5 million	500[a]
Pentium 4	11/2000	$819	42 million[b]	1,500[a]
Pentium 4 with Hyper-Threading Technology	11/2002	$637	55 million[b]	3,060[a]
1286 (?)	2011	n/a	1 billion	100,000

[a]The numbers reported for the Pentium II, Pentium III, Pentium 4, and Pentium 4 with Hyper-Threading Technology are actually megaHertz (millions of cycles per second), not MIPS. This measure would be the same as MIPS if one instruction were executed each cycle.

[b]Intel did not make public the number of transistors on the Pentium 4 and Pentium 4 with Hyper-Threading Technology chips. The numbers in the table came from Rendleman, 2002, and might not be comparable to the other transistor figures.

Source: Business Week (December 9, 1996): 150, with updates from the Intel Web site, 1997, 1999, 2000, and 2002, and from Rendleman, 2002.

Of course, Silicon Valley-based Intel Corporation is not the only chipmaker, but it is the largest and the most important. Intel supplies over 80 percent of the all-important microprocessor chips used to power IBM and IBM-compatible microcomputers. Advanced Micro Devices (AMD), which produces Intel-compatible chips, is the only other major player in this market, with about a 15 percent market-share. Other manufacturers of processor chips (largely for more powerful machines) include IBM, Hewlett-Packard, and Sun Microsystems. IBM also produces the processor chips used in Apple microcomputers.

However, the worldwide semiconductor industry consists of much more than processor chips. Although U.S. firms dominate the processor market (all the firms mentioned above are from the United States), four of the five leading producers of the random access memory chips used in PCs are from outside the United States–Samsung Electronics (Korea), Hynix Semiconductor (Korea), Infineon Technologies (Germany), and Elpida Memory (Japan). The fifth major player is Micron Technology of the United States. Intel is at the top of the heap in terms of **flash memory** production, as used in digital cameras and music players, followed by Samsung, Toshiba (Japan), and AMD. Another rapidly growing segment of the semiconductor industry consists of **digital signal processor** (**DSP**) chips. DSP chips convert analog images or sounds in real time (meaning with essentially no delay) to a stream of digital signals. DSP chips are used at the heart of digital cellular telephones, digital audio receivers, cable modems, and handheld computers, and they are also used in traditional products such as kitchen appliances and electric motors and in new products such as hearing aids and digital-video editing systems. Texas Instruments (which, like Intel, also introduced a microprocessor chip in 1971) is the leader in sales of DSP chips, but Agere Systems (United States), Analog Devices, Inc. (United States), Infineon, Motorola, NEC Electronics (Japan), and Renesas Technology (Japan) are also major players. In another market segment, IBM is the leading producer of custom-made chips, called application-specific integrated circuits, or ASICs, followed by rivals such as Texas Instruments and NEC Electronics. Several of the chip manufacturers already mentioned, including IBM, do **foundry** work, which involves the production of chips for other companies that have been designed by those companies. The leaders in the foundry business, however, are a trio of Asian chipmakers–Taiwan Semiconductor Manufacturing Company, United Microelectronics Corporation (Taiwan), and Chartered Semiconductor Manufacturing Ltd. (Singapore). The semiconductor industry is gigantic and rapidly expanding, with worldwide revenues forecast to reach $200 billion annually by 2005.

[Adapted from Port, 1996; Rendleman, 2002; Park and Kunii, 2002; Ante, Port, Einhorn, and Park, 2003; and Edwards, Ihlwan, and Engardio, 2003]

just as humans do. Analog computers manipulate some analogous physical quantity, such as voltage or shaft rotation speed, which represents (to some degree of accuracy) the numbers involved in the computation. Analog computers have been most useful in engineering and process-control environments, but digital machines have largely replaced them even in these situations. Thus, all of our preceding discussion relates to digital computers, as does that which follows.

Underlying Structure

Today's computers vary greatly in size, speed, and details of their operation—from handheld microcomputers costing around $100 to supercomputers with price tags of more than $30 million. Fortunately for our understanding, all these machines have essentially the same basic logical structure (as represented in Figure 2.4). All computers, whether they are microcomputers from Dell or mainframes from IBM, are made up of the same set of six building blocks: input, output, memory, arithmetic/logical unit, control unit, and files. Our discussion of how computers work will focus on these six blocks and their interrelationships.

In addition to the blocks themselves, Figure 2.4 also includes two types of arrows. The broad arrows represent the flows of data through the computer system, and the thin arrows indicate that each of the other components is controlled by the control unit. A dashed line encircles the control unit and the arithmetic/logical unit. These two blocks together are often referred to as the **central processing unit**, or **CPU**, or as the **processor**. (Historically, the memory was also considered part of the CPU because it was located in the same physical cabinet, but with changes in memory technologies, memory is now regarded as a separate entity from the CPU.)

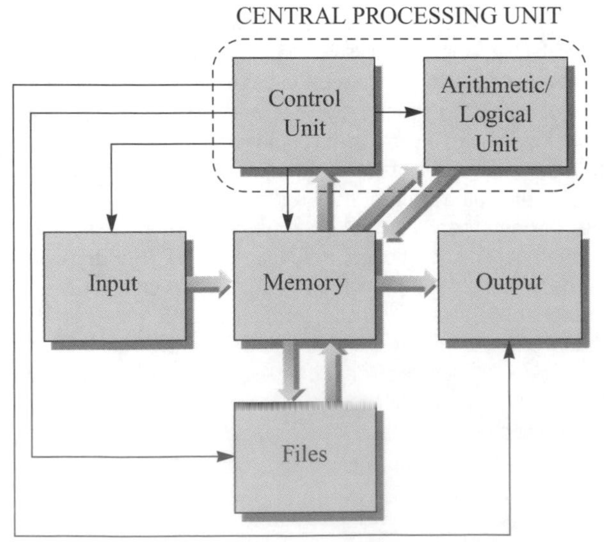

Figure 2.4 The Logical Structure of Digital Computers

Input/Output

To use a computer, we must have some means of entering data into the computer for it to use in its computations. There are a wide variety of input devices, and we will mention only the most commonly used types. The input device that you as a manager are most likely to use is a keyboard on a microcomputer or a terminal. We will talk more about microcomputers (PCs) later, but they include all the building blocks shown in Figure 2.4. A **terminal** is a simpler device than a PC; it is designed strictly for input/output and does not incorporate a processor (CPU), or at least not a general-purpose processor. Most terminals consist of a keyboard for data entry and a video display unit (a television screen) to show the user what has been entered and to display the output from the computer. The terminal is connected to a computer via some type of telecommunication line. In addition to their use by managers, terminals are widely used by clerical personnel involved in online transaction processing. Today microcomputers are replacing many terminals.

Special types of terminals are also in widespread use as computer input devices. Point-of-sale terminals have largely replaced conventional cash registers in major department stores, and automatic teller machines (ATMs) are commonplace in the banking industry. These devices are simply terminals modified to serve a specific purpose. Like the standard terminals described above, these special-purpose devices serve as both input and output devices, often incorporating a small built-in printer to provide a hard-copy record of the transaction.

Terminals allow users to key data directly into the computer. By contrast, some input methods require that data be recorded on a special input medium before they can be entered into the computer. Until the 1980s, the most common form of computer input involved punched cards and a punched-card reader. Users keyed in data at a punched-card keypunch machine, which translated the keystrokes into holes in a punched card (employing a coding scheme known as Hollerith code). The punched cards were then carried to a punched-card reader directly attached to the computer; the reader read the cards one at a time, interpreting the holes in the cards and transmitting the data to the memory. Until the early 1980s, U.S. government checks, many credit-card charge slips, and class enrollment cards at most universities were punched cards. Computers often had a card punch attached as an output device to produce checks, enrollment cards, and other punched-card output. However, punched cards were a nuisance to handle and store, and they have disappeared because of the communications developments of the past two decades.

Other input methods employing special input media have not disappeared, although their importance has shrunk. With a key-to-tape system or a key-to-disk system, data entry personnel key in data at a microcomputer or a terminal attached to a midrange computer. The computer records the data as a series of magnetized spots (using some type of coding scheme) on the surface of a magnetic tape (similar to the tape used in a home videocassette recorder) or a magnetic disk (similar in appearance to an old-style phonograph record). After a significant quantity of data has been recorded, an output magnetic tape is created and hand-carried to the primary computer system, where it is mounted in a magnetic tape unit. This unit then reads the tape, interpreting the magnetized spots on the surface of the tape and transmitting the data to the memory.

Some input methods read an original document (such as a typed report or a check or deposit slip) directly into the computer's memory. Check processing is handled this way in the United States through the **magnetic ink character recognition** (**MICR**) input method. Most checks have the account number and bank number preprinted at the bottom using strange-looking numbers and a special magnetizable ink. After a check is cashed, the bank that cashed it records the amount of the check in magnetizable ink at the bottom of the check. A computer input device called a magnetic ink character reader magnetizes the ink, recognizes the numbers, and transmits the data to the memory of the bank's computer. **Optical character recognition** (**OCR**) is an input method that directly scans typed, printed, or hand-printed material. A device called an optical character reader scans and recognizes the characters and then transmits the data to the memory or records them on magnetic tape.

Imaging goes even further than OCR. With imaging, any type of paper document, including business forms, reports, charts, graphs, and photographs, can be read by a scanner and translated into digital form so that the document can be stored in the computer system. Then this process can be reversed so that the digitized image stored in the computer system can be displayed on a video display unit, printed on paper, or transmitted to another computer. However, the characters in the image cannot be easily processed as individual numbers or letters. Imaging is often accomplished through a specialized image-management system, which is a microcomputer-based system.

An increasingly important way of entering data into a computer is by scanning a **bar code label** on a package, a product, a routing sheet, a container, or a vehicle. Bar code systems capture data much faster and more accurately than systems in which data are keyed. Thus the use of bar codes is very popular for high-volume supermarket checkout, department store sales, inventory tracking, time and attendance records, and health care records. Bar codes are also valuable for automated applications such as automotive assembly control and warehouse restocking. There is actually a wide variety of bar code languages, called *symbologies*. Perhaps the most widely known symbology is the Universal Product Code, or UPC, used by the grocery industry.

Just as we must have a way of entering data into the computer, the computer must have a way of producing results in a usable form. We have already mentioned displaying results on a video display unit, printing a document on a small printer built into a special-purpose terminal, and punching cards. Output can also be written on a magnetic tape or a magnetic disk (such as a 3.5-inch floppy disk), which could be useful if the data will be read back later into either the same or another computer.

The dominant form of output, however, is the printed report. Computer printers come in a variety of sizes, speeds, and prices. At the lower end are serial printers, which are usually employed with microcomputers. They usually employ a nonimpact process (such as an ink-jet or laser-jet process), and they typically operate in a speed range of 3 to 15 pages per minute. Printers used with larger computers may be line printers or page printers. Line printers operate at high speeds (up to 2,200 lines per minute) and print one line at a time, usually employing an impact printing mechanism in which individual hammers force the paper and ribbon against the appropriate print characters (which are embossed on a rotating band or chain). Page printers, which produce up to 800 pages per minute, print one entire page at a time, often employing an electrophotographic printing process (like a copying machine) to print an image formed by a laser beam.

In part to counteract the flood of paper that is threatening to engulf many organizations, microfilm has become an important computer output medium. The output device is a **computer output microfilm** (**COM**) recorder that accepts the data from the memory and prepares the microfilm output at very high speeds, either as a roll of microfilm or as a sheet of film called a microfiche that contains many pages on each sheet. **Voice response units** are gaining increasing acceptance as providers of limited, tightly programmed computer output. Cable television shopping services and stock price quotation services often use voice output in conjunction with touch-tone telephone input.

A relatively new buzzword used to describe computer input and output is **multimedia**. A multimedia system uses a microcomputer to coordinate many types of communications media—text, graphics, sound, still images, animations, and video. The purpose of a multimedia system is to enhance the quality of, and interest in, a presentation, whether it is a corporate briefing, a college lecture, an elementary school lesson, or self-paced instruction. The sound and video usually come from a compact disk (CD) or digital video disk (DVD) played on a CD or DVD player built into the microcomputer. Graphics or photographs used as part of the presentation might have been scanned via an imaging system, and artwork created with a graphics program on the computer; these images are then stored in the computer's files. The key is that the microcomputer controls the entire multimedia presentation.

To summarize, the particular input and output devices attached to a given computer will vary based on the uses of the computer. Every computer system will have at least one input device and at least one output device. On the computers you will be using as a manager, keyboards, video display units, printers, CD and DVD players, and disk drives will be the most common input/output devices.

Computer Memory

At the heart of the diagram of Figure 2.4 is the **memory**, also referred to as main memory or primary memory. All data flows are to and from memory. Data from input devices always goes into memory; output devices always receive

VOICE INPUT TO COMPUTERS

Voice input to computers is becoming a reality, although we cannot converse with today's machines as easily as Starfleet officers can talk with the computer system on the *USS Enterprise*. But we are certainly moving in that direction! Economical software packages are now available to run on microcomputers operating under Windows 2000 or XP that permit users to "dictate" to the computer and have the computer produce a word-processed document. Until recently, however, the accuracy of **speech recognition software** was suspect, with the best packages achieving recognition accuracy only a little above 90 percent—nearly one error in every ten words. In late 2002 and mid-2003, *PC Magazine* tested the latest upgrades from the two leading speech recognition software packages for PCs and found that both packages achieved 95 to 98 percent accuracy after an hour of dictation, correction, and retraining. With these numbers, speech recognition software is getting close to becoming a productivity-enhancing tool—at least for users with limited typing skills, disabilities, repetitive stress injuries from overusing a computer keyboard, or no time to do anything except dictate (such as medical doctors). For most of us, speech recognition software might provide an interesting supplement to the keyboard and mouse, but it is not going to replace these traditional means of input in the short run.

PC Magazine's Greg Alwang was most impressed with the Dragon NaturallySpeaking Preferred 7 package (from ScanSoft; street price $200). After the required five minutes of training of the software, he was able to attain initial accuracy of 90 to 95 percent on dictation, depending on the document. The accuracy figure went up to 96 to 98 percent after an hour or so of use. Furthermore, NaturallySpeaking Preferred 7 contains automatic punctuation to save the user from dictating commas and periods, and it is supported on handheld Pocket PCs (more on these small computers later) so that users can dictate while on the road. IBM's ViaVoice for Windows Release 10 Pro edition (list price $100) was nearly as good on dictation accuracy, but it did not perform as well in terms of attaining hands-free operation of a PC. With NaturallySpeaking Preferred 7, Alwang was easily able to navigate around the document and correct his dictation errors by voice alone, with only minimal command errors. ViaVoice, however, required a combination of voice, keyboard, and mouse commands to navigate and make corrections.

At least in the short run, dictation to the computer is probably not the most important application of speech recognition—that honor falls to interactive voice response systems that provide up-to-date information and services through a call center, with the user providing voice input via a telephone. In this case the software runs on a server (a larger computer) at the call center. The leading suppliers of these call-center speech recognition/voice response systems are ScanSoft, Inc., and Nuance Communications. Such systems are now widely used for such activities as providing access to flight arrival and departure information, permitting phone-based Web browsing, tracking packages, and checking online brokerage accounts. At Yahoo!, subscribers pay $4.95 a month to interact with a virtual responder named Jenni, who can help them check the weather and find sports scores. Amtrak has a perky virtual attendant named Julie who provides schedule, fare, and train-status information. Users prefer these speech recognition/voice response applications to the alternative of multiple touch-tone responses, but they are expensive to develop. Amtrak has spent $4 million over 3 years on speech-related hardware, software, and integration, but the Amtrak executives think it is well worth the cost. Payback will be less than a year, based on reduced labor costs in call centers—voice systems cost about 25 cents per call, compared to about $5 for a human responder. Estimates of the size of the call-center speech recognition/voice response system market vary widely, with Giga Information Group conservatively predicting a cumulative $4 billion in sales by 2006. PC-based speech recognition software is getting close to being a mainstream application, and call-center speech recognition/voice response systems are already in the mainstream.

[Adapted from Alwang, 2002, 2003; and Keenan, 2002]

their data from memory; two-way data flows exist between files and memory and also between the arithmetic/logical unit and memory; and a special type of data flows from memory to the control unit to tell the control unit what to do next. (This latter flow is the focus of the section of this chapter entitled "The Stored-Program Concept.")

In some respects the computer memory is like human memory. Both computers and humans store data in memory in order to remember it or use it later. However, the way in which data are stored and recalled differs radically between computer memory and human memory. Computer memory is divided into cells, and a fixed amount of data can be stored in each cell. Further, each memory cell has an identifying number, called an *address*, that never changes. A very early microcomputer, for example, might have 65,536 memory cells, each capable of storing one character of data at a time. These cells have unchanging addresses varying from 0 for the first cell up to 65535 for the last cell.

A useful analogy is to compare computer memory to a wall of post office boxes (see Figure 2.5). Each box has its own sequential identifying number printed on the box's door, and these numbers correspond to the addresses associated with memory cells. In Figure 2.5 the address or identifying number of each memory register is shown in the upper-left corner of each box. The mail stored in each box changes as mail is distributed or picked up. In computer memory, each memory cell holds some amount of data until it is changed. For example, memory cell 0 holds the characters MAY, memory cell 1 holds the characters 2005, memory cell 2 holds the characters 700.00, and so on. The characters shown in Figure 2.5 represent the contents of memory at a particular point in time; a fraction of a second later the contents could be entirely different as the computer goes about its work. The contents of the memory cells will change as the computer works, while the addresses of the cells are fixed.

Computer memory is different from the post office boxes in several ways, of course. For one thing, computer memory operates on the principle of "destructive read-in, nondestructive read-out." This means that as a particular piece of data is placed into a particular memory cell, either by being read from an input device or as the result of a computation in the arithmetic/logical unit, the computer destroys (or erases) whatever data item was previously in the cell. By contrast, when a data item is retrieved from a cell, either to print out the item or to use it in a computation, the contents of the cell are unchanged.

Another major difference between post office boxes and memory cells is in their capacity. A post office box has a variable capacity depending upon the size of the pieces of mail and how much effort postal employees spend in stuffing the mail in the box. A memory cell has a fixed capacity, with the capacity varying from one computer model to another. A memory cell that can store only one character of data is called a **byte**, and a memory cell that can store two or more characters of data is called a **word**. For comparability, it has become customary to describe the size of memory (and the size of direct access files) in terms of the equivalent number of bytes, even if the cells are really words.

Leaving our post office analogy, we can note that there are several important differences between the memory of one computer model and that of another. First, the capacity

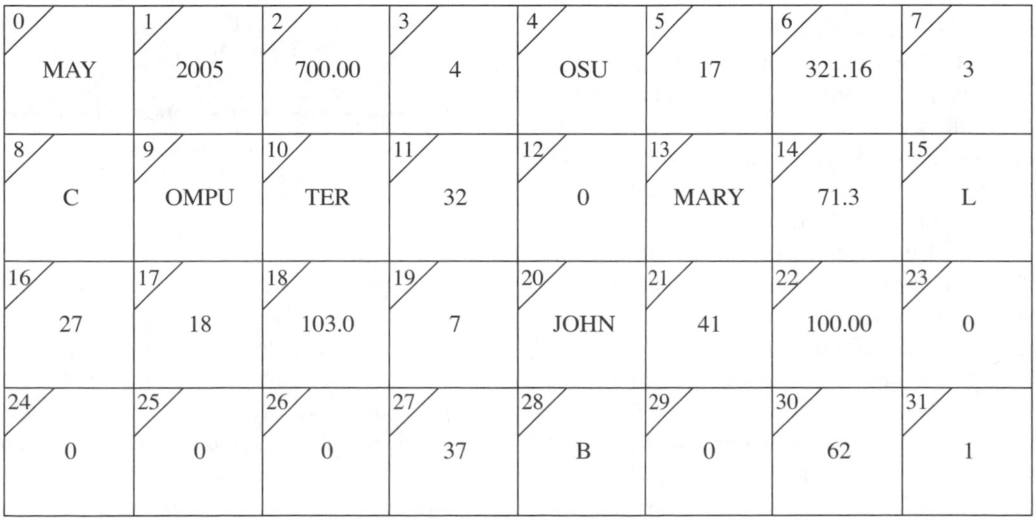

0 MAY	1 2005	2 700.00	3 4	4 OSU	5 17	6 321.16	7 3
8 C	9 OMPU	10 TER	11 32	12 0	13 MARY	14 71.3	15 L
16 27	17 18	18 103.0	19 7	20 JOHN	21 41	22 100.00	23 0
24 0	25 0	26 0	27 37	28 B	29 0	30 62	31 1

Figure 2.5 Diagram of Computer Memory

of each cell might differ. In a microcomputer each cell may hold only 1 digit of a number, whereas a single cell in a mainframe may hold 14 digits. Second, the number of cells making up memory may vary from several million to many billion. Third, the time involved to transfer data from memory to another component may differ by an order of magnitude from one machine to another. The technologies employed in constructing the memories may also differ, although all memory today is based on some variation of VLSI circuits on silicon chips.

Bits and Coding Schemes. Each memory cell consists of a particular set of circuits (a small subset of the VLSI circuits on a memory chip), and each circuit can be set to either "on" or "off." Because each circuit has just two states (on and off), they have been equated to 1 and 0, the two possible values of a binary number. Thus, each circuit corresponds to a *bi*nary digi*t*, or a **bit**. In order to represent the decimal digits (and the alphabetic letters and special characters) for processing by the computer, several of these bits (or circuits) must be combined to represent a single character. In most computers eight bits (or circuits) represent a single character, and a memory cell containing a single character, we know, is called a byte. Thus, eight bits equals one byte in most machines.

Consider a particular example. Assume that we have a computer where each memory cell is a byte. (A byte can contain one character.) Then memory cell number 327, for instance, will consist of eight circuits or bits. If these circuits are set to on-on-on-on-off-off-on (or, alternatively, 1111 1001), this combination may be defined by the coding scheme to represent the decimal digit 9. If these bits are set to 1111 0001, this may be defined as the decimal digit 1. If these bits are set to 1100 0010, this may be defined as the letter B. We can continue on like this, with each character we wish to represent having a corresponding pattern of eight bits.

Character	EBCDIC Binary	Character	ASCII-8 Binary
A	1100 0001	A	1010 0001
B	1100 0010	B	1010 0010
C	1100 0011	C	1010 0011
D	1100 0100	D	1010 0100
E	1100 0101	E	1010 0101
F	1100 0110	F	1010 0110
G	1100 0111	G	1010 0111
H	1100 1000	H	1010 1000
I	1100 1001	I	1010 1001
J	1101 0001	J	1010 1010
K	1101 0010	K	1010 1011
L	1101 0011	L	1010 1100
M	1101 0100	M	1010 1101
N	1101 0101	N	1010 1110
O	1101 0110	O	1010 1111
P	1101 0111	P	1011 0000
Q	1101 1000	Q	1011 0001
R	1101 1001	R	1011 0010
S	1110 0010	S	1011 0011
T	1110 0011	T	1011 0100
U	1110 0100	U	1011 0101
V	1110 0101	V	1011 0110
W	1110 0110	W	1011 0111
X	1110 0111	X	1011 1000
Y	1110 1000	Y	1011 1001
Z	1110 1001	Z	1011 1010
0	1111 0000	0	0101 0000
1	1111 0001	1	0101 0001
2	1111 0010	2	0101 0010
3	1111 0011	3	0101 0011
4	1111 0100	4	0101 0100
5	1111 0101	5	0101 0101
6	1111 0110	6	0101 0110
7	1111 0111	7	0101 0111
8	1111 1000	8	0101 1000
9	1111 1001	9	0101 1001

Figure 2.6 EBCDIC and ASCII Computer Coding Schemes

Two common coding schemes are in use today. The examples given above are taken from the Extended Binary Coded Decimal Interchange Code (commonly known as EBCDIC, pronounced eb'-si-dic). IBM originally developed EBCDIC in the 1950s, and IBM and other vendors still use it. The other common code in use is the American Standard Code for Information Interchange (ASCII), which is employed in data transmission and in microcomputers. Figure 2.6 lets you compare the ASCII and EBCDIC codes for the alphabet and decimal digits, but you do not need to know these codes—only that they exist!

The bottom line is that a coding scheme of some sort is used to represent data in memory and in the other components of the computer. In memory, circuits in a particular cell are turned on and off, following the coding scheme, to enable us to store the data until later. It turns out that circuits are also used to represent data in the control and arithmetic/logical units. In the input, output, and files, the coding scheme is often expressed through magnetized spots (on and off) on some media, such as tape or disk. In data transmission, the coding scheme is often expressed through a series of electrical pulses or light pulses. In summary, the coding scheme is vital to permit the storage, transmission, and manipulation of data.

Arithmetic/Logical Unit

The **arithmetic/logical unit**, like memory, usually consists of VLSI circuits on a silicon chip. In fact, the chip pictured in Figure 2.3 is the Intel Pentium 4 processor chip used in today's top-of-the-line microcomputers. In many respects, the arithmetic/logical unit is very simple. It has been built to carry out addition, subtraction, multiplication, and division, as well as to perform certain logical operations such as comparing two numbers for equality or finding out which number is bigger.

The broad arrows in Figure 2.4 represent the way in which the arithmetic/logical unit works. As indicated by the broad arrow from memory to the arithmetic/logical unit, the numbers to be manipulated (added, subtracted, etc.) are brought from the appropriate memory cells to the arithmetic/logical unit. Next, the operation is performed, with the time required to carry out the operation varying, depending on the computer model. The speeds involved vary from several million operations per second up to billions of operations per second. Then, as indicated by the broad arrow from the arithmetic/logical unit to memory in Figure 2.4, the result of the operation is stored in the designated memory cell or cells.

Computer Files

As applications are being processed on a computer, the data required for the current computations must be stored in the computer memory. The capacity of memory is limited (although it can go over 250 billion bytes on some large machines), and there is not enough space to keep all the data for all the concurrently running programs (e.g., Microsoft Excel, Microsoft Word, Netscape Navigator, Lotus Notes) in memory at the same time. Adding additional memory might be possible, but memory is relatively expensive. In addition, memory is volatile; if the computer's power goes off, everything stored in memory is lost. To keep vast quantities of data accessible within the computer system in a nonvolatile medium but at more reasonable costs than main memory, file devices—sometimes called secondary memory or secondary storage devices—have been added to all but the tiniest computer systems. File devices include magnetic tape drives, hard (or fixed) disk drives, floppy (or removable) disk drives, and CD (or optical) drives. All but the optical drives record data by magnetizing spots on the surface of the media, using a binary coding scheme.

The broad arrows in each direction in Figure 2.4 illustrate that data can be moved from particular cells in memory to the file and that data can be retrieved from the file to particular memory cells. The disadvantage of files is that the process of storing data in the file from memory or retrieving data from the file to memory is quite slow relative to the computer's computation speed. Depending upon the type of file, the store/retrieve time could vary from a very small fraction of a second to several minutes. Nevertheless, we are willing to live with this disadvantage to be able to store enormous quantities of data at a reasonable cost per byte.

Sequential Access Files. There are two basic ways to organize computer files: sequential access and direct access. With **sequential access files**, all the records that make up the files are stored in sequence according to the file's control key. For instance, a payroll file will contain one record for each employee. These individual employee records are stored in sequence according to the employee identification number. There are no addresses within the file; to find a particular record, the file device must start at the beginning of the sequential file and read each record until it finds the desired one. It is apparent that this method of finding a single record might take a long time, particularly if the sequential file is long and the desired record is near the end. Thus, we would rarely try to find a single record with a sequential access file. Instead, we would accumulate a batch of transactions and process the entire batch at the same time.

Sequential access files are usually stored on magnetic tape. A **magnetic tape unit** or magnetic tape drive is the file device that stores (writes) data on tape and that retrieves (reads) data from tape back into memory. Even with batch processing, retrieval from magnetic tape tends to be much slower than retrieval from direct access files. Thus, if speed is of the essence, sequential access files might not be suitable. On the other hand, magnetic tapes can store vast quantities of data economically. For example, a tape cartridge that can store up to 800 million bytes of data can be purchased for under $10, or a high-performance tape cartridge with a capacity of 40 billion bytes can be purchased for under $40.

Until the mid-1980s, the magnetic tape used with computers was all of the reel-to-reel variety, like old-style home tape recorders. Then 1/2-inch tape cartridges were introduced, and in 1988 the sales of magnetic tape cartridge drives overtook the sales of reel-to-reel drives for the first time. The tape cartridges are rectangular and thus easier to store than round reels, and, more importantly, the cartridges can be automatically loaded and ejected from the tape drives. With reel-to-reel, an operator must mount each individual tape; with cartridges, an operator can place an entire stack of cartridges into a hopper at one time and let the drive load and eject the individual cartridges. Thus, fewer operators are needed to handle a cartridge-based tape system.

Direct Access Files. A **direct access file**, stored on a **direct access storage device** (**DASD**), is a file from which it is possible for the computer to obtain a record immediately, without regard to where the record is located in the file. A typical DASD for a computer consists of a continuously rotating stack of disks (or perhaps only one disk), where each disk resembles an old-style phonograph record (see Figure 2.7). A comb-shaped access mechanism moves in and out among the disks to record on and read from hundreds of concentric tracks on each disk surface. The hard drives found on almost all microcomputers are an example of direct access files. Typical internal hard drives for PCs store from 20 to 160 billion bytes (gigabytes) and cost from \$50 to \$200. The speed at which data may be read from or written on a hard drive is quite fast, with transfer rates up to 100 million bytes (megabytes) per second possible.

EMC Corporation, based in Hopkinton, Massachusetts, has become the market leader in storage systems for large computers by devising a way to link together a large number of inexpensive, small hard drives (such as those used in PCs) as a substitute for the giant disk drives that were previously used. EMC has developed a specialized computer and sophisticated software to control this **redundant array of independent disks** (**RAID**) approach so that data can be supplied to the mainframe or other large computer rapidly, reliably, and less expensively per byte than the giant disk drive approach (Judge, 1999). As an example, EMC's Symmetrix DMX 3000 model can be configured with from 192 to 576 hard drives, each with a storage capacity of either 73 or 146 gigabytes, giving a total storage capacity from 14 terabytes (trillion bytes) up to a maximum of over 84 terabytes (EMC Web site, 2003).

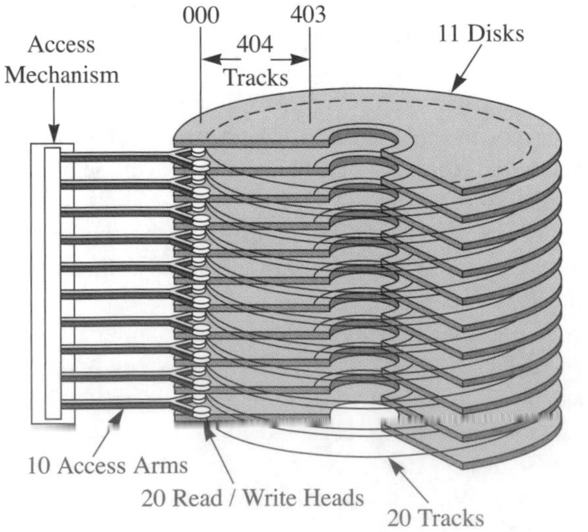

Figure 2.7 A Schematic Diagram of a Magnetic Disk Drive

In contrast to these fixed-disk, large-capacity, fairly expensive file devices, direct access devices can also be portable or employ a removable disk, be relatively small, and be quite inexpensive. For instance, a removable 3.5-inch high-density disk for a microcomputer can store up to 1.44 million bytes (1.44 megabytes) of data and costs less than 50 cents. The disk drive itself costs under \$100. These 3.5-inch disks are protected by a permanent hard plastic case, but they are sometimes called floppy disks. "Floppy disk" is a misnomer for today's disks, but the name originated with their 5.25-inch predecessor disks for microcomputers, which were made of flexible plastic without sturdy cases and were in fact "floppy." The transfer rate to read to or write from a floppy disk varies, but a common transfer rate is 0.06 million bytes (megabytes) per second—a very slow rate compared to other DASDs.

A newer, higher-capacity DASD, with a removable disk, is Iomega Corporation's Zip drive. A Zip drive may be installed internally in a PC or attached externally. A Zip disk is slightly larger than a conventional floppy disk, and about twice as thick; its capacity is either 100, 250, or 750 megabytes on a single removable disk, depending upon the Zip drive. A 750-megabyte Zip drive costs about \$180, and each disk for this drive is about \$13; this Zip drive reads or writes at speeds up to 7.5 megabytes per second. The smaller-capacity 250-megabyte Zip drive costs about \$125, and each disk for this drive is about \$11; the transfer rate for reading or writing is up to 2.4 megabytes per second (Iomega Web site, 2003). These transfer rates are not particularly fast, but the low cost and durability of the Zip drive have made it quite popular for backing up and transporting large data files.

Iomega Corporation also offers an attractive line of portable hard drives to back up very large data files and move these large data files from one computer system to another. Iomega's HDD Portable Hard Drives come with capacities varying from 20 gigabytes to 60 gigabytes. The 60-gigabyte drive costs about \$360 and has a maximum sustained transfer rate of 30 megabytes per second (Iomega Web site, 2003).

The newest and smallest portable DASD for PCs utilizes flash memory—as used in digital cameras and portable music players—rather than a magnetizable disk. This device goes by various names, depending upon the manufacturer or the commentator, including a Jump Drive (Lexar), DiskOnKey (M-Systems), Mini USB Drive (Iomega), flash drive, or simply keychain drive. **Keychain**

drive is perhaps the most descriptive, because the device is not much larger than the average car key (see Figure 2.8). As an example, Iomega's Mini USB Drive is available in 64, 128, and 256 megabyte sizes, with prices of about $40, $60, and $90. These keychain drives are designed to plug into a standard universal serial bus (USB) port on a PC. With a USB 2.0 port, the computer can read data from Iomega's 256-megabyte keychain drive at a rate of 5 megabytes per second and write data to the keychain drive at a rate of 3.5 megabytes per second. To use a keychain drive, take off the top of the drive, exposing the USB connector. Plug the connector into the USB port on a PC, and the computer will recognize it automatically—then just use the keychain drive as you do any other drive! The keychain drive is an economical and extremely convenient way to transport significant amounts of data. The 3.5-inch floppy disk was on its way out even before the keychain drive came on the scene, but the keychain drive should certainly hasten the floppy disk into oblivion (Armstrong, 2002, and Iomega Web site, 2003).

The key to the operation of direct access files is that the physical file is divided into cells, each of which has an address. The cells are similar to memory cells, except that they are much larger, usually large enough to store several records in one cell. Because of the existence of this address,

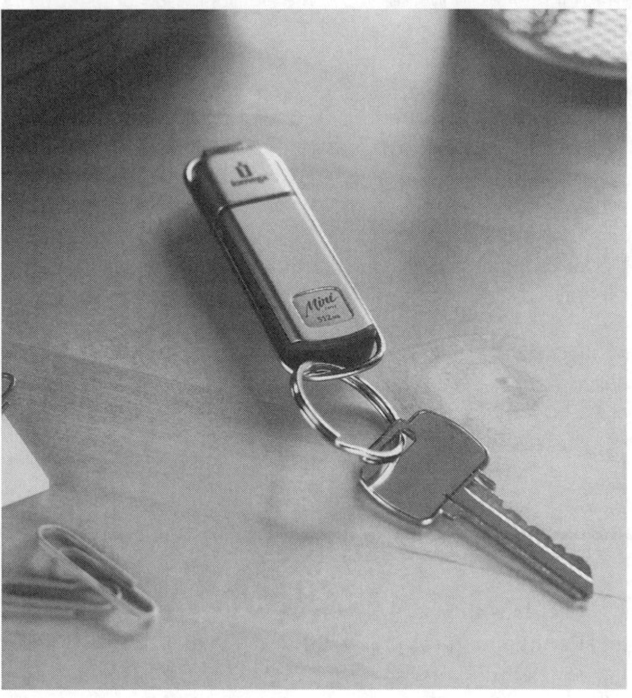

Figure 2.8 Keychain Drive: Iomega's Mini USB Drive (Photo courtesy of Iomega Corporation).

it is possible for the computer to store a record in a particular file address and then to retrieve that record by remembering the address. Thus, the computer can go directly to the file address of the desired record, rather than reading through sequentially stored records until it encounters the desired one.

How does the computer know the correct file address for a desired record? For instance, assume that an inventory control application running on the computer needs to update the record for item number 79032. That record, which is stored somewhere in DASD, must be brought into memory for processing. But where is it? At what file address? This problem of translating from the identification number of a desired record (79032) to the corresponding file address is the biggest challenge in using direct access files. Very sophisticated software is required to handle this translation.

Online processing requires direct access files, and so does Web browsing. Airline reservation agents, salespeople in a department store, managers in their offices, and Web surfers from their home or office machines will not wait (and in many cases cannot afford to wait) the several minutes that might be required to mount and read the appropriate magnetic tape. On the other hand, batch processing can be done with either sequential access files or direct access files. Sequential access files are not going to go away, but all the trends are pushing organizations towards increased use of direct access files. First, online processing and Web browsing absolutely require direct access files. Second, advancements in magnetic technology and manufacturing processes keep pushing down the costs per byte of direct access files. Third, the newer optical disk technology (see the box "Optical Disk Storage") provides drastically lower costs per byte of direct access files for applications where somewhat slower data retrieval speeds are acceptable. Fourth, and most important, today's competitive environment is forcing organizations to focus on speed in information processing, and that means an increasing emphasis on direct access files.

Many major computer installations today have so many DASD units that they are collectively referred to as a disk farm. It is not unusual for a large installation to have many trillions of bytes (terabytes) of disk storage online.

Control Unit

We have considered five of the six building blocks represented in Figure 2.4. If we stopped our discussion at this point, we wouldn't have much. Thus far we have no way of controlling these various components and no way of taking advantage of the tremendous speed and capacity we have

OPTICAL DISK STORAGE

A newer type of direct access file storage for computer systems, the **optical disk**, is becoming more and more important. Some writers have argued that the optical disk might spell the end of the floppy disk: After all, rewritable versions of the optical disk are now available that have hundreds of times the capacity of a standard floppy disk, a transfer rate much faster than a floppy, and a price that is quite economical (e.g., see Wildstrom, 2000). An optical disk is made of plastic coated with a thin reflective alloy material. Data are recorded on the disk by using a laser beam to burn microscopic pits in the reflective surface (or in some cases alter the magnetic characteristics of the surface), employing a binary coding scheme.

Two primary types of optical disks are in common use with computers today: a **compact disk** (**CD**) and a **digital video disk**, or **digital versatile disk** (**DVD**). Then each of these optical disk types has three primary variations: a read-only disk (**CD-ROM** or **DVD-ROM**, where ROM stands for Read Only Memory); a recordable disk (**CD-R** or **DVD-R**, where R stands for Recordable); and a rewritable disk (**CD-RW** or **DVD-RW**, where RW stands for ReWritable). A CD has much less capacity than a DVD: Standard capacity for a CD is 700 megabytes of data or 80 minutes of audio recording, while standard capacity for a two-sided DVD is 4.7 gigabytes, more than enough for a full-length movie. Some experts believe that DVDs will eventually replace CDs and VHS videocassettes, but that won't happen overnight. A significant advantage of DVD drives is that they are backward compatible with CDs, so that a DVD drive can play all types of CDs as well as DVDs. The media are quite inexpensive, with blank CD-Rs costing under a $1, blank CD-RWs under $1.50, blank DVD-Rs under $5, and blank DVD-RWs under $7 each.

The readable CD or DVD is familiar as a way of distributing music, computer software, and even movies. It can only be read and cannot be erased; a master disk is originally created, and then duplicates can be mass produced for distribution. Thus, a readable optical disk is particularly useful for distributing large amounts of relatively stable data (such as music, computer software, a book, a movie, or multimedia material) to many locations.

A recordable optical disk was once called a **WORM** (Write Once-Read Many) disk. A recordable CD or DVD can be written on by the computer—but only once! Then it can be read many times. Recordable optical disks are quite appropriate for archiving documents, engineering drawings, and records of all types.

A rewritable CD or DVD is the most versatile form of optical disk because the data can be recorded and erased repeatedly. Writing on a rewritable optical disk is a three-step process: (1) Use laser heat to erase the recording surface; (2) use a combination of laser and magnetic technology to write on the recording surface; and (3) read, via a laser, what has been written to verify the accuracy of the recording process. This type of optical disk is a strong candidate to replace the venerable floppy disk, particularly now that software products let the user "drag" files to an optical disk (using a mouse) just like to any other drive.

One more complication arises with regard to recordable and rewritable DVDs—vendors have created multiple formats that are not always compatible. Thus, a rewritable DVD is only rewritable with the appropriate DVD writer drive. There are two different recordable formats, labeled DVD-R and DVD+R, and three different rewritable formats, labeled DVD-RW, DVD+RW, and DVD-RAM. Happily, DVD drives are beginning to appear that will read and write all major CD and DVD formats. One such drive is Iomega's Super DVD Writer/All-Format Internal Drive, priced at about $250. This drive is rated 4x2x8x when using the DVD-RW format. The numbers mean that the speed of writing on this drive is 4x (which translates to 5.5 megabytes per second), the speed of rewriting is 2x (2.75 megabytes per second), and the speed of reading is 8x (11.0 megabytes per second). When using a CD with the CD-RW format, the drive is rated 24x16x32x, which translates to writing at 3.6 megabytes per second, rewriting at 2.4 megabytes per second, and reading at 4.8 megabytes per second (Iomega Web site, 2003). (Note that the baseline 1x differs from DVD to CD: With DVD, 1x equals 1.375 megabytes per second; with CD, 1x equals 0.15 megabytes per second.)

As an example of optical storage used with large computer systems, the IBM Enhanced 3995 Optical Library C-Series uses *either* rewritable or WORM 5.25-inch removable disk cartridges, with a cartridge holding up to 5.2 gigabytes of data. The 3995 Model C38 incorporates 258 cartridges, giving a total online capacity of 1.341 terabytes (1.341 trillion bytes) for the optical library system. You can double the capacity to 2.682 terabytes by attaching a Model C18 expansion unit to the Model C38. This optical library system is capable of a sustained data transfer rate of 2.3 to 4.6 megabytes per second, with a burst data transfer rate of 6 megabytes per second.

[Portions adapted from Wildstrom, 2000; Iomega Web site, 2003; and IBM Web site, September 2003a]

described. The **control unit** is the key. It provides the control that enables the computer to take advantage of the speed and capacity of its other components. The thin arrows in Figure 2.4 point out that the control unit controls each of the other five components.

How does the control unit know what to do? Someone must tell the control unit what to do by devising a precise list of operations to be performed. This list of operations, which is called a program, is stored in the memory of the computer just like data. One item at a time from this list is moved from memory to the control unit (note the broad arrow in Figure 2.4), interpreted by the control unit, and carried out. The control unit works through the entire list of operations at electronic speed, rather than waiting for the user to tell it what to do next. What we have just described is the **stored-program concept**, which is the most important idea in all of computing.

THE STORED-PROGRAM CONCEPT

Some person must prepare a precise listing of exactly what the computer is to do. This listing must be in a form that the control unit of the computer has been built to understand. The complete listing of what is to be done for an application is called a **program**, and each individual step or operation in the program is called an **instruction**. The control unit carries out the program, one step or instruction at a time, at electronic speed.

When a particular computer model is designed, the engineers build into it (more precisely, build into its circuitry) the capability to carry out a certain set of operations. For example, a computer might be able to read an item of data keyed from a keyboard, print a line of output, add two numbers, subtract one number from another, multiply two numbers, divide one number by another, compare two numbers for equality, and perform several other operations. The computer's control unit is built to associate each of these operations with a particular instruction type. Then the control unit is told which operations are to be done by means of a program consisting of these instructions. The form of the instructions is peculiar to a particular model of computer. Thus, each instruction in a program must be expressed in the precise form that the computer has been built to understand. This form of the program that the computer understands is called the **machine language** for the particular model of computer.

Not only will the form of the instructions vary from one computer model to another, so will the number of different types of instructions. For example, a small computer might have only one add instruction, while a large one might have a different add instruction for each of several classes of numbers (such as integer, floating point or decimal, and double precision). Thus, the instruction set on some machines could contain as few as 20 types of instructions, while other machines could have more than 200 instruction types.

In general, each machine language instruction consists of two parts: an operation code and one or more addresses. The operation code is a symbol (e.g., A for add) that tells the control unit what operation is to be performed. The addresses refer to the specific cells in memory whose contents will be involved in the operation. As an example, for a hypothetical computer the instruction

Operation Code	Addresses	
A	470	500

means the computer should add the number found in memory cell 470 to the number found in memory cell 500, storing the result back in memory cell 500. Therefore, if the value 32.10 is originally stored in cell 470 and the value 63.00 is originally stored in cell 500, the sum, 95.10, will be stored in cell 500 after the instruction is executed. Continuing our example, assume that the next instruction in the sequence is

M	500	200

This instruction means move (M) the contents of memory cell 500 to memory cell 200. Thus, 95.10 will be placed in cell 200, erasing whatever was there before. (Because of nondestructive read-out, 95.10 will still be stored in cell 500.) The third instruction in our sequence is

P	200

which means print (P) the contents of memory cell 200 on the printer, and 95.10 will be printed.

Our very short example contains only three instructions and obviously represents only a small portion of a program, but these few instructions should provide the flavor of machine language programming. A complete program would consist of hundreds or thousands of instructions, all expressed in the machine language of the particular computer being used. The person preparing the program (called a programmer) has to know each operation code and has to remember what data he or she has stored in every memory cell. Obviously, machine language programming is very difficult and time-consuming.

Once the entire machine language program has been prepared, it must be entered into the computer, using one of the input methods already described, and stored in the computer's memory. This step of entering the program in memory is called loading the program. The control unit then is told (somehow) where to find the first instruction in the program. The control unit fetches this first instruction and places it in special storage cells called registers within the control unit. Using built-in circuitry, the control unit interprets the instruction (recognizes what is to be done) and causes it to be executed (carried out) by the appropriate components of the computer. For example, the control unit would interpret the add instruction above, cause the contents of memory cells 470 and 500 to be sent to the arithmetic/logical unit, cause the arithmetic/logical unit to add these two numbers, and then cause the answer to be sent back to memory cell 500.

After the first instruction has been completed, the control unit fetches the second instruction from memory. The control unit then interprets this second instruction and executes it. The control unit then fetches and executes the third instruction. The control unit proceeds with this fetch-execute cycle until the program has been completed. Usually the instruction that is fetched is the next sequential one, but machine languages incorporate one or more branching instructions that, when executed, cause the control unit to jump to a nonsequential instruction for the next fetch. The important point is that the control unit is fetching and executing at electronic speed; it is doing exactly what the programmer told it to do, but at its own rate of speed.

One of the primary measures of the power of any computer model is the number of instructions that it can execute in a given period of time. Of course, some instructions take longer to execute than others, so any speed rating represents an average of some sort. These averages might not be representative of the speeds that the computer could sustain on the mix of jobs carried out by your organization or any other organization. Furthermore, some machines operate on four bytes at a time (microcomputers), while others operate on eight bytes at a time (many larger machines). Thus, the speed rating for a microcomputer is not comparable to the speed rating for a larger machine. In the 1980s the most commonly used speed rating was **MIPS**, or millions of instructions per second executed by the control unit. This measure has largely gone out of favor because of the "apples and oranges" nature of the comparisons of MIPS ratings across classes of computers.

Another speed rating used is **MegaFLOPS** or **MFLOPS**—millions of floating point operations per second. These ratings are derived by running a particular set of programs in a particular language on the machines being investigated. The ratings are therefore more meaningful than a simple MIPS rating, but they still reflect only a single problem area. In the LINPACK ratings, the problem area considered is the solution of dense systems of linear equations using the LINPACK software in a FORTRAN environment (Dongarra, 2003). MFLOPS ratings when solving a system of 100 linear equations include .00169 for a Palm Pilot III; 51 for an AMD K6-II (500 MHz); 62 for a Gateway G6-200 Pentium Pro; 558 for a Compaq Server D520e (667 MHz); 1,486 for an IBM eServer pSeries 655 (1.7 GHz); and 1,635 for an HP Integrity Server rx2600 (1.5 GHz). These are all single processor machines. MFLOPS ratings when solving a system of 1,000 linear equations vary from 49 for a Hewlett-Packard 9000/730 (one processor); 5,187 for a Sun UltraSPARC II (30 processors); 7,699 for an IBM RS/6000 SP Power3 (16 processors); 29,360 for a Cray T932 (32 processors); and 45,030 for a NEC SX-5/16 (16 processors) (Dongarra, 2003). Of course, these LINPACK ratings are not very meaningful for applications where input/output operations are dominant, such as most business processing.

These published speed ratings can be useful as a very rough guide, but the only way to get a handle on how various machines would handle your organization's workload is **benchmarking**. Benchmarking is quite difficult to do, but the idea is to collect a representative set of real jobs that you regularly run on your computer, and then for comparison actually run this set of jobs on various machines. The vendors involved will usually cooperate because they want to sell you a machine, but there can be severe problems in getting existing jobs to run on the target machines and in comparing the results once you get them.

Computer publications often do their own benchmarking, as illustrated in Table 2.2 in which *PC World* identifies the top seven computers in a class it calls "desktop PCs—power system." *PC World* has created a representative mix of common business applications it calls PC WorldBench 4, which it ran on all machines in this class. The performance score is a measure of how fast a PC can run this mix as compared with *PC World*'s baseline machine, a Gateway Select 1200 with a 1.2-gigaHertz (GHz) Athlon processor, 128 megabytes of memory, and a 20-gigabyte hard drive. For example, the ABS Ultimate M5 in Table 2.2 is 1.4 times as fast as the baseline system.

PC World goes on to combine this PC WorldBench 4 performance score (valued at 25 percent of the overall rating) with other factors such as price (10 percent), base configuration (10 percent), extra features (10 percent), graphics quality (15 percent), setup and ease of use (5 percent), and vendor's reliability and service (25 percent) to arrive at an overall rating for each machine, as shown in the far right column of Table 2.2.

Again, processing speeds vary across machines, but all computers use the stored-program concept. On all computers a machine language program is loaded in memory and executed by the control unit. There is a great deal more to the story of how we get the machine language program, but suffice it to say at this point that we let the computer do most of the work in creating the machine language program. Neither you nor programmers working for your organization will write in machine language; any programs will be written in a language much easier and more natural for humans to understand.

Table 2.2 Benchmarking: Top Seven Desktop PCs—Power System

System	Processor	Street Price	PC WorldBench 4 Performance Score[a]	Overall Rating
ABS Ultimate M5	2.2-GHz Athlon XP 3200+	$2739	140 (outstanding)	92
Dell Dimension 8300	3.2-GHz Pentium 4	$3807	127 (good)	86
Dell Dimension XPS	3.06-GHz Pentium 4	$3807	127 (good)	86
Micro Express MicroFlex 30A	2.167-GHz Athlon XP 3000+	$1999	131 (good)	86
Sys Technology Performance 3200+	2.2-GHz Athlon XP 3200+	$2690	136 (outstanding)	84
@Xi Computer MTower 3000+	2.167-GHz Athlon XP 3000+	$1993	133 (very good)	82
Acer Veriton 7600G	3-GHz Pentium 4	$1937	122 (fair)	80

[a]The descriptive labels are those assigned by *PC World*.
Source: PC World (October 2003): 144–146.

EXTENSIONS TO THE BASIC MODEL

In the previous section we considered the underlying logical structure of all digital computers, and we found that all computers are made up of the set of six building blocks shown in Figure 2.4. Now let us note that Figure 2.4 is an accurate but incomplete picture of many of today's computers. To be complete, the figure should be extended in two ways. First, today's computers (both microcomputers and larger machines) often have multiple components for each of the six blocks rather than a single component. Machines may have multiple input devices, or multiple file devices, or multiple CPUs. Second, the architecture of today's machines often includes several additional components to interconnect the basic six components. For example, magnetic disk file devices usually have a disk controller that interfaces with a data channel connected to the CPU. In this section we want to extend our basic model to incorporate these additional ideas and thus present a more complete picture of today's (and tomorrow's) computer systems.

Communications within the Computer System

Controller. As a starting point for the extended model, let us note that appropriate **controllers** are needed to link input/output devices such as terminals, DASDs, and sequential access devices to the CPU and memory of large computer systems. The exact nature of the controller will vary with the vendor and the devices being linked, but the controller is usually a highly specialized microprocessor attached to the CPU (through another new component called a data channel) and to the terminals or DASDs or other devices (see Figure 2.9). The controller manages the operation of the attached devices to free up the CPU (and the data channel) from these tasks.

For example, a DASD controller receives requests for DASD read or write activity from the data channel, translates these requests into the proper sets of operations for the disk device, sees that the operations are executed, performs any necessary error recovery, and reports any problems back to the data channel (and thus to the CPU). A communications controller has the job of managing near-simultaneous input/output from an attached set of terminals, ensuring that the messages from each terminal are properly collected and forwarded to the data channel, and that responses from the data channel are properly sent to the right terminal.

Data Channel. The **data channel** is just as critical as the controller. A data channel is a specialized input/output processor (yet another computer) that takes over the function of device communication from the CPU. The data channel's role is to correct for the significant mismatch in speeds between the very slow peripheral devices and the fast and critical CPU. When the CPU encounters an input/output request (including requests for disk or tape reads and writes) during the execution of a program, it relays that request to the data channel connected to the device in question (the number of data channels varies with the machine). The CPU then turns to some other job while the data channel oversees input/output.

The data channel often includes some amount of buffer storage (a special type of memory), so that it may move large blocks of data into and out of main memory at one time. In this way, the data channel has to interrupt the CPU only when it is ready to move a large data block; during most of the time the CPU can continue to process another job. The

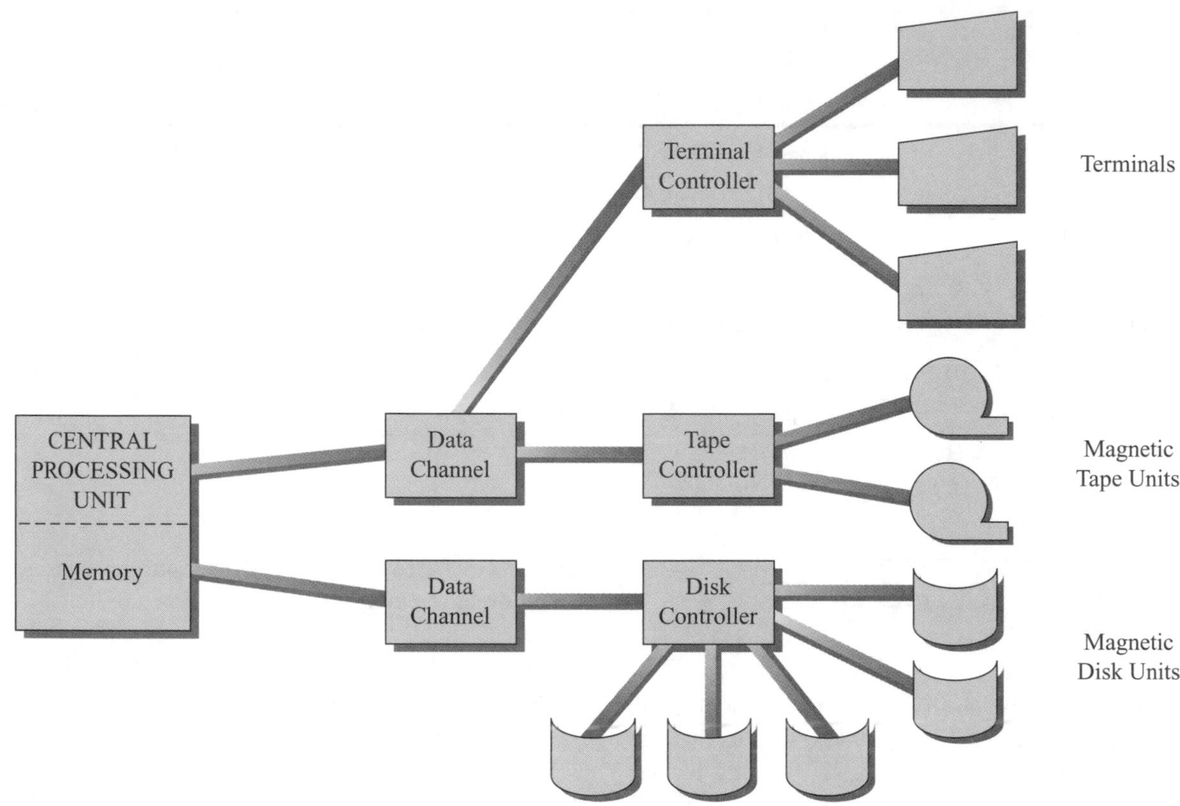

Figure 2.9 Data Channels and Controllers

data channel, on the other hand, must wait on data transmitted from the controller as it gathers an input block, or it must wait for the controller to accept a block of output data.

Another way in which the data channel sometimes operates is by cycle stealing. In this variation, the data channel has only a small amount of buffer storage in which it receives data. For example, when this small buffer fills up during a disk read, the channel steals a cycle from the CPU and places the contents of the buffer in main memory. This operation has minimal impact on the CPU (it loses only one cycle out of thousands) and allows the data channel to employ an area of main memory as its buffer.

Cache Memory

Thus far we have considered two (or perhaps three) levels of storage devices: main or primary memory, which is very fast and quite expensive; and secondary memory, which we can subdivide into not-so-fast and not-so-expensive DASDs and slow and inexpensive sequential access storage devices (magnetic tapes). Now add **cache memory**, which was originally employed as a very high-speed, high-cost storage unit used as an intermediary between the control unit and the main memory (Grossman, 1985). The term *cache* (pronounced cash) is French for a hidden storage place. The cache is intended to compensate for one of the speed mismatches built into computer systems—in this case, that between fetching data from main memory (and moving data to the arithmetic/logical unit or other internal registers) and executing an instruction. The CPU can execute an instruction much faster than it can fetch data (which requires electronically moving the data from memory to the arithmetic/logical unit). Thus, in a conventional architecture, the critical CPU often waited for the completion of a data fetch.

With cache memory, an entire block of data is moved at one time into the cache, and then most data fetches take place from the higher-speed cache to the arithmetic/logical unit. The success of cache memory depends upon two characteristics of the data to be used by the CPU—locality of reference and data reuse. Locality of reference means that if a given piece of data is used, there is a high probability that a nearby piece of data will be used shortly thereafter. Data reuse means that a block of data will be kept in the cache until it has not been recently referenced; then it will be replaced by a block of data that has been requested. The use of cache memory should optimize the use of the critical CPU.

After its successful use as an intermediary between the CPU and main memory, cache memory was incorporated into DASD controllers. The basic idea is similar, except the speed mismatch is greater between the relatively slow DASD and the much faster data channel. Again, the keys to success of the cache are locality of reference and data reuse. A large block of data is moved from DASD to the cache, and then (hopefully) most data fetches take place from the cache rather than DASD itself. A microprocessor in the DASD controller manages the cache memory, keeping track of the frequency of reference to the data in the cache and moving blocks of data into and out of the cache in an attempt to optimize the use of the data channel (and, indirectly, the CPU). Figure 2.10 illustrates the use of cache memory both in the CPU and in a DASD controller. Cache memory (in the CPU and in the DASD controller) represents an important way in which the conventional storage hierarchy has been extended. Cache memory is becoming a part of many components of the hardware, including high-speed communication modules and special-purpose CPUs such as array processors. Even more layers may be added to the storage hierarchy as system designers seek to balance cost, capacity, and performance.

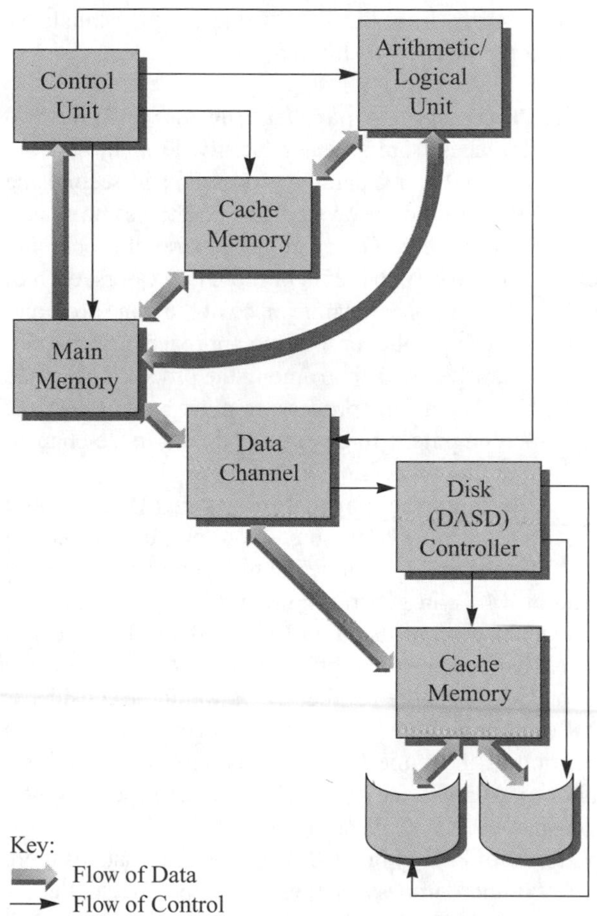

Figure 2.10 Partial Logical Structure of Computer Incorporating Cache Memory

Multiple Processor Configurations

One of the most intriguing extensions to the basic model is the use of multiple CPUs or processors as part of a single computer system. A **multiprocessor** is a computer configuration in which multiple processors (CPUs) are installed as part of the same computer system. Without using the multiprocessor terminology, we actually considered such a system when we discussed the use of data channels (which are themselves processors) with a single primary CPU. Sometimes the term *front-end processor* is used instead of data channel, but in either case the additional processor (or processors) is used to offload handling of input/output from the primary CPU.

Symmetric Multiprocessors. An increasing number of larger computers now make use of multiple processors as a way of increasing their power (usually measured by throughput). In these cases, two, three, or more CPUs are installed as part of the same computer system. The term **symmetric multiprocessor (SMP)** refers to multiprocessor machines in which all the processors or CPUs are identical, with each processor operating independently of the others. The multiple CPUs equally share functional and timing access to and control over all other system components, including main memory and the various peripheral devices, with each CPU working in its own allotted portion of memory. One CPU might handle online transaction processing, while a second deals with engineering calculations, a third works on a batch payroll system, and a fourth operates as a Web server.

Vector Facilities. An example of an asymmetric multiprocessor is a **vector facility**, a specialized multiple processor configuration designed to handle calculations involving vectors. For these calculations, the same operation is to be performed on each element of the vector. By installing a number of parallel, relatively inexpensive microprocessors (operating under control of a primary control unit and thus a single program), all these operations can be performed simultaneously. The keys to whether a vector facility is worthwhile are the percentage of the total calculations that involve vectors and the lengths of the vectors themselves. The higher the percentage and the longer the vectors, the more valuable the vector facility. For research and development activities, vector facilities are often worthwhile, but their value for most business information processing is limited.

Parallel Processors. A **parallel processor (PP)** has two major differences from a vector facility. First, there is no single primary CPU in a parallel processor, and, second, the various CPUs are not always performing the same operation at the same time. For example, a parallel processing machine may have 16, 64, 256, or more processors, each of which would work on a separate piece of the same program. In order to use a parallel processing approach, the program must somehow be divided up among the processors and the activities of the various processors must be coordinated. Many supercomputers, to be discussed later in the chapter, employ a parallel processing architecture.

The term **massively parallel processor (MPP)** is used to describe machines with some large number of parallel CPUs. There is no firm guideline to distinguish between a PP and an MPP; in general, however, 32 or more parallel CPUs would be considered an MPP if the different CPUs are capable of performing different instructions at the same time, or 1,000 or more parallel CPUs would be considered an MPP if the different CPUs must all carry out the same instruction at the same time. An example of a massively parallel machine is the IBM RS/6000 SP supercomputer (code name ASCI White) purchased by the U.S. Department of Energy in 2000. This machine contains more than 8,100 microprocessors operating in parallel and is capable of 12.3 *trillion* calculations per second, which made it the world's fastest supercomputer for about 2 years.

We are just beginning to learn how to take advantage of the incredible power of parallel processing machines. At present, the user must specifically tailor his or her programs to utilize the parallel CPUs effectively. For the short term, parallel processors will be most useful in universities and research laboratories and in a few specialized applications that demand extensive computations such as extremely high-volume transaction processing.

TYPES OF COMPUTER SYSTEMS

In our earlier discussion of the various generations of computers, we introduced some terminology—microcomputers, minicomputers, and mainframes—that has been applied to different types of computer systems. Now we want to expand our taxonomy of computer types to include the full range of computer systems available today. In our discussion we will indicate the primary uses of each type of system as well as the major vendors. Our discussion must begin with a significant caveat. Although there is some agreement on the terms we will be using, there is no such agreement on the parameters defining each category or on the computer models that belong in each type. Even if there were such agreement today, there would not be tomorrow as new technologies are employed and new computer models are introduced.

Generally speaking, the boundaries between the categories are defined by a combination of cost, computing power, and purpose for which a machine is built—but the *purpose* is the dominant criterion. Listed in order of generally increasing cost and power, the categories we will use are microcomputers, workstations/midrange systems, mainframes, and supercomputers (see Table 2.3). You will note that the ranges of cost and power in Table 2.3 are often overlapping, which reflects the differences in purpose for which the machines have been designed. Remember also that MFLOPS (millions of floating point operations per second) is only a very rough comparative measure of power.

Please note that the category boundaries in Table 2.3 are extremely fuzzy. The boundary between microcomputers and workstations/midrange systems has been arbitrarily set at $3,000, but the technology employed is quite similar on both sides of this boundary (at least in terms of PCs and workstations). On the other hand, the type of work done on these classes of machines is quite different, as indicated in the table, so we have chosen to separate them. Historically, workstations and midrange systems have been considered as distinct categories, but they now overlap so much in cost, power, and applications that we have chosen to combine them in a single category that stretches all the way from microcomputers to the much larger mainframes and supercomputers. Moreover, some workstations use technology similar to supercomputers—the primary difference might be the number of parallel processors. Low-end mainframes have significantly less power than high-end workstations/midrange systems, but have been designed for the widest possible range of applications. Some sources use the term *servers* instead of workstations/midrange systems, but we disagree with this label because a wide variety of machines including microcomputers, workstations/midrange systems, mainframes, and supercomputers can and do perform in a server capacity.

Microcomputers

Microcomputers, often called micros or **personal computers** or just PCs, cost from $300 to $3,000. They generally have less power than workstations/midrange systems, but

Table 2.3 Types of Computer Systems

Category	Cost	MFLOPS	Primary Uses
Microcomputers	$200–$3,000	20–400	Personal computing Client in client/server[a] applications Web client Small business processing
Workstations/midrange systems	$3,000–$1,000,000	40–4,000	Departmental computing Specific applications (office automation, CAD[b], other graphics) Midsized business general processing Server in client/server applications Web server, file server, local area network server
Mainframes	$1,000,000–$20,000,000	200–8,000	Large business general processing Server in client/server applications Large Web server Widest range of applications
Supercomputers	$1,000,000–$100,000,000	4,000–100,000,000	Numerically intensive scientific calculations Very large Web server

[a]Client/server applications involve dividing the processing between a larger computer operating as a server and a smaller machine operating as a client.

[b]CAD is an abbreviation for computer-aided design.

the dividing line between these categories is faint. In general, microcomputers can be carried or moved by one person, and they usually have only a single keyboard and video display unit (which is why they are called personal computers). **Desktop PCs** are the most familiar, but PCs also come in **laptop** or **notebook** models in small briefcase-like packages weighing under 10 pounds and in newer, smaller **handheld** or **palmtop** models weighing in at a pound or (usually) less. An intriguing new variation of the notebook computer is the tablet PC, where the user writes on an electronic tablet (the video screen folded flat on top of the PC) with a digital pen (see the sidebar entitled "Is a Tablet PC Right for You?").

By the second half of the 1980s, the most popular microcomputer for business use was the IBM Personal Computer, designed around microprocessor chips built by Intel and the PC-DOS operating system (a software package) created by Microsoft. In the first decade of the twenty-first century, IBM-compatible machines still dominate the business marketplace, but the overwhelming majority of these machines are being sold by vendors other than IBM. In fact, in 2002 IBM chose to outsource the production of IBM desktop computers to Sanmina-SCI Corporation to reduce costs (Ante and Henry, 2002). (IBM continues to produce its own popular ThinkPad laptop computers.) The sales leader in the PC marketplace is Dell, which developed as a direct-sales vendor, originally by mail and telephone and now predominantly via the World Wide Web. After its 2002 acquisition of Compaq Computer, Hewlett-Packard is challenging Dell for market leadership. Other major players include a trio of Japanese firms—Fujitsu, Toshiba (both of which sell only laptop and tablet microcomputers in the United States), and NEC—as well as Gateway (which has also used the direct-sales approach, although not as successfully as Dell), and, of course, IBM. In response to competitive pressures, all the PC vendors, including Dell, Hewlett-Packard, and IBM, have lowered their prices and introduced multiple microcomputer lines.

IBM-compatible machines in the early years of the twenty-first century employ mostly Intel Pentium 4 chips, with older Pentium chips and AMD Athlon chips also in use. Most of these machines use some version of the Microsoft Windows operating system (either Windows 2000 or Windows XP).

In addition to IBM-compatible machines, the only other contender in the business environment is the Apple Macintosh. Initially, the Macintosh found tough going in the business world against the entrenched IBM microcomputers, but its easy-to-use graphical interface won it many converts in the late 1980s and early 1990s. Then Macintosh sales seemed to hit a plateau, and Apple struggled until it introduced the iMac in 1998. The colorful iMac added a spark to the Apple product line and made Apple profitable again, although Apple's market share is still very small—about 3 percent of the U.S. microcomputer market in 2003. However, Apple appears to have built a safe niche for itself through innovative products such as the very successful iPod MP3 music player; its AirPort wireless networking gear; and a new software product, iLife, which is a suite of video, music, and photography software that allows users to develop professional-looking home movies (Burrows, 2003). Between Apple and the myriad of PC-compatible vendors, the microcomputer market is extremely competitive and should remain so for the foreseeable future.

Microcomputers have been put to a myriad of uses. In the home, they have been used for record-keeping, word processing, and games; in the public schools, for computerized exercises, educational games, and limited programming; in colleges, for word processing, spreadsheet exercises, presentations, and programming. In the corporate environment they are used for word processing, spreadsheets, presentations, small database applications, and programming; as terminals into larger computers; and as clients in client/server applications. Stand-alone microcomputers in a large organizational setting are a thing of the past: For managers to do their jobs, they need microcomputers linked into the corporate computer network so that they can access data and applications wherever they exist. Microcomputers have also become important for small businesses, where they do operate as stand-alone machines or on small local area networks (LANs). The growing supply of software developed for a particular type of small business (e.g., a general contractor, hardware store, or farmer), coupled with the relatively low price of microcomputers, has opened up the small business market. In the last half of the 1990s, microcomputers also became the point of entry for all types of users into the Internet and the World Wide Web—microcomputers are the universal Web client for all of us!

Workstations/Midrange Systems

Historically, workstations and midrange systems have been considered as distinct categories of computers, but they now overlap so much in cost, power, and applications that we have chosen to combine them in a single category that stretches all the way from microcomputers to the much larger mainframes and supercomputers. Somewhat arbitrarily we have defined this type of computer system as costing from \$3,000 (the top of the microcomputers category) to \$1,000,000 (near the bottom of the mainframes category), with power ranging from 40 to 4,000 MFLOPS.

It is enlightening to trace the roots of the two aspects of this middle-of-the-road category of computers. *Workstation* is one example of the confusing terminology that abounds in the computing field. In one use of this term, workstation means any type of computer-related device at which an individual may work. Thus, a personal computer is a workstation, and so is a terminal. However, the term workstation is also used to describe a more powerful machine that is still run by a microprocessor but might or might not be used by a single individual. This more powerful type of workstation is one of the two bases for our second category of computers. **Workstations** are, in fact, grown-up, more powerful microcomputers. Workstations at the lower end of the range tend to have only one "station"—a keyboard and a high-quality video monitor at which to "work," although that is not usually true for the upper-end machines. Workstations are based on the microprocessor chip, but the chips are more powerful than those used in microcomputers. Workstations were originally deployed for specific applications demanding a great deal of computing power, high resolution graphics, or both, but

PALMTOP WARS

The smallest microcomputers—**palmtop** machines, also called handheld computers or **personal digital assistants** (**PDAs**), which weigh under a pound and cost from $200 to $800—are beginning to catch on as business tools in a big way. Early in the twenty-first century, two palmtop operating systems (and the various devices running these operating systems) dominate the marketplace: the Palm operating system and Microsoft's Windows Mobile for Pocket PC operating system. Palm (recently renamed palmOne) has the largest market share—around 50 percent—but Microsoft is closing the gap.

Palm had first-mover advantage, with the first successful pen-based computer. With a large and growing installed base (now over 30 million Palm-powered devices sold), built on superb contact and calendar management functionality on clean-looking, user-friendly devices, Palm attracted scores of software developers who turned out thousands of varied applications to run on the Palm. Meanwhile, Microsoft had several false starts as it tried to break into the palmtop market. Microsoft's first real success occurred in 2000 with the introduction of the **Pocket PC** version of its pint-sized Windows CE operating system. Hewlett-Packard, Casio Computer, and Compaq Computer offered early Pocket PC devices, and although they offered some advantages in functionality over the Palm handhelds, they were more complex to use and more difficult to interface with the desktop PC. Numerous improvements in the Pocket PC operating system and the associated handheld devices have occurred over the past few years, as they have in the Palm operating system and Palm devices. In part because of the dominance of Microsoft in the desktop market, the Pocket PC has steadily gained market share, although it still trails Palm.

Current products using the Palm operating system include the Palm Tungsten and Zire models, the Sony Clié, and the Handspring Visor and Treo. Pocket PCs on the market include the Hewlett-Packard iPaq line (the name was inherited from Compaq Computer), the Dell Axim, and products from Toshiba, Audiovox, and ViewSonic. It is easy to synchronize both Palms and Pocket PCs with the user's desktop computer via a small "cradle" and easy-to-use software; it is also easy to synchronize the newer devices with the desktop via Bluetooth short-range wireless communication. In addition, built-in Wi-Fi wireless networking in the newer models permits both Palms and Pocket PCs to bypass the desktop PC to receive and send e-mail and to surf the World Wide Web.

Many observers believed that the palmtop market would be a replay of the desktop market, with Palm in the role of Apple, and that it was only a matter of time before the Pocket PC became the standard for the business community. Others, including Carl Zetie of Giga Information Group, believe that the market dynamics of the palmtop market are much more complex than those of the desktop, and that "there's still everything to play for—and, in fact, no guarantee that any single 'winner' must emerge" (Zetie, 2002). It is unclear whether the Microsoft advantages of built-in support for Microsoft Office documents, easy integration with Microsoft Exchange, and the Microsoft name will overcome Palm's huge advantage in installed base and available applications software. It certainly looks like the palmtop wars will continue.

[Adapted from Green, 2000; Zetie, 2002; Ewalt, 2003; and Wildstrom, July 14, 2003]

they more recently have been used as Web servers, in network management, and as servers in client/server applications. Furthermore, because of their very strong price-performance characteristics compared to other types of computers (see Table 2.3), workstations have made inroads into the domains of traditional midrange systems (such as departmental computing and midsized business general processing) and mainframes (large business general processing). These inroads made by workstations into the midrange systems domain have been so significant that we have chosen to combine these categories for our discussion. Today it is almost impossible to decide which machines in this broader category should still be considered "workstations" and which should be considered "midrange systems."

The development of the **reduced instruction set computing** (**RISC**) chip is largely responsible for the success of this class of machines, at least at its upper end. You will recall from our earlier discussion that some computers have a large instruction set (mainframes) while others have a considerably smaller instruction set (microcomputers). The designers of the RISC chips based their work on a reduced instruction set, not on the complete instruction set used on mainframe chips. By working with a reduced instruction set, they were able to create a smaller, faster chip than had been possible previously. Variations of these RISC chips power most of the machines at the upper end of the workstations/midrange systems category today.

Turning to the second aspect of our workstations/midrange systems category, we begin by noting that

IS A TABLET PC RIGHT FOR YOU?

The newest variation of the microcomputer is the **tablet computer**, powered by the Microsoft Windows XP Tablet PC Edition operating system and manufactured by several vendors, including Acer, Fujitsu, Hewlett-Packard, Gateway, and Toshiba. All these systems provide a flat, tablet-like surface on which the user can "write" with a digital pen. Then the Windows software stores the handwriting digitally or, if you wish, converts the handwriting into type. (According to users, the conversion of handwriting into type is good, but not perfect.) For a professional person who takes lots of notes, a tablet PC seems like a great idea!

There are at least three different approaches to building a tablet computer: One of these, used by Toshiba and Acer, is a modification of the clamshell approach as used in all notebook computers. When the screen is up, the tablet PC looks like any other notebook computer (see Figure 2.11). The difference is that the screen pivots 180 degrees and folds flat over the keyboard to form a tablet (shown on the left in Figure 2.11). The second approach, used by Fujitsu, does not have a mechanical keyboard at all, so it is flat all the time—much like an electronic clipboard. The user enters data by writing with the special pen or by tapping the appropriate keys on a virtual keyboard displayed on the screen. The final approach, used by Hewlett-Packard, employs a detachable keyboard that can serve as a base somewhat like a standard notebook, or can fold behind the screen, or can be removed entirely. The H-P tablet slides into a docking station with or without the keyboard attached.

The software is the key to the successful use of a tablet PC, and the consensus seems to be that the software is getting better but is not all the way there yet (Foley, 2003, and Wildstrom, August 4, 2003). *Information Week*'s John Foley tested two tablet PC applications from Microsoft, both of which use the pen device to write on the screen in digital ink. Windows Journal was the more stable and easy-to-use of the two, having shipped as part of the Windows XP Tablet PC Edition as part of its initial release in 2002. With Windows Journal, the user takes notes and makes sketches on what appears to be endless pages of a legal pad. OneNote is an add-on to Windows released in 2003, and—although trickier to master than Journal—has a lot more capabilities: It is a note-taking application that lets the user combine handwritten or typed notes with drawings, graphics, digital photographs, audio clips, and Web pages—a true multimedia application (Foley, 2003).

The promise of the tablet PC is apparent, and—eventually—many professional workers will be using a tablet PC or one of its successors for note-taking. How soon is eventually? Is a tablet PC right for you?

[Adapted from Greene and Park, 2002; Wildstrom, 2002; Foley, 2003; and Wildstrom, August 4, 2003]

Figure 2.11 Views of the Hewlett-Packard Compaq Tablet PC TC 1000 (Courtesy of Hewlett-Packard).

traditional **midrange systems** have always had an identity crisis—no one knew for sure what to call them or what machines belonged in this category. Until the 1990s, commentators used the label of **minicomputers** for this category (see the section entitled "Evolution of Computer Systems" earlier in this chapter). Originally, these machines were just like the larger mainframe machines, except that they were less powerful and less expensive. For a while the larger minicomputers were even called **superminicomputers**, which is a strange name, using both *super* and *mini* as prefixes. These traditional midrange systems were very important, serving as departmental computers, handling specific tasks such as office automation, and acting as the server in a client/server architecture. Many midsized businesses used one or more midrange systems to handle their corporate data processing. Some analysts suggested that the traditional midrange systems category would disappear, squeezed between increasingly powerful microcomputers and workstations from the bottom and entrenched mainframe systems from above, but that did not happen. Instead, both workstations and midrange systems have "morphed" into the complex, intertwined category that we have chosen to call **workstations/midrange systems**. These systems are primarily employed as servers for client/server applications, Web serving, file and database serving, and network management. They vary from relatively small systems that serve one user or a single department up to enterprise-wide systems that have assumed many of the roles of mainframe computers.

It can be useful to divide this category into several smaller categories. At the low end come machines that are essentially high-powered PCs, typically built around Intel microprocessors (such as the Xeon, Celeron, or Pentium 4 processor) and often using Windows NT Server, Windows 2000 Server, or Windows 2003 Server as the server operating system. It is also possible to run the UNIX or Linux operating system on these Intel-based servers, but this is not as common.

At the high end are machines that are powered either by RISC processors developed by the vendor (such as Hewlett-Packard, Sun Microsystems, or IBM) or top-of-the-line Intel microprocessors such as the Itanium 2 or Pentium 4. For the most part these high-end machines run either the Linux operating system or some variation of the UNIX operating system. In this market subsegment the leaders are IBM, Hewlett-Packard, and Sun Microsystems. Other vendors include Silicon Graphics, Inc. (United States), Fujitsu, and Dell. As an example, IBM's entry in this UNIX/Linux market subsegment is its eServer pSeries workstation (formerly RS/6000), employing IBM-developed RISC chips with copper (not aluminum) wiring. Among the many models in the eServer pSeries are the pSeries 630 with up to four processors and the pSeries 690 with up to 32 processors. The newer models in the pSeries line are powered by IBM's POWER4+ 64-bit microprocessor, described by IBM as a "server on a chip." The POWER4+ chip contains two processors, a high-bandwidth switch (for fast internal communications), a large memory cache, and an input/output interface—over 180 million transistors in total on a single chip! (IBM Web site, May 6, 2003) The pSeries and its predecessor RS/6000 series have been a tremendous success for IBM, with well over 1 million systems shipped to commercial and technical customers throughout the world. (See also the sidebar entitled "World's Fastest Supercomputer Revisited" later in this chapter.)

A third subcategory is made up of machines that are most identifiable with the "midrange systems" side of the mix. These machines have survived and prospered because they offer much better input/output capabilities than those from the workstations side of the mix and because an extensive array of easy-to-use commercial applications software has been developed for them. In addition, thousands of organizations have developed extensive specialized software to run on midrange systems, and these "legacy" systems cannot easily be converted to run on other types of hardware. On the other hand, these remaining midrange systems have incorporated RISC chips, have embraced UNIX and Linux, and are largely used as servers today. Thus, they are quite different from traditional midrange systems.

The primary example of such a midrange system is IBM's eServer iSeries (formerly the AS/400) family of computers. In the 1980s, IBM's System/34, System/36, and System/38 became the most popular business computers (not including microcomputers) of all time. Most of these machines were replaced by IBM's AS/400 (which was first introduced in 1988 and has been a major success for IBM), and many additional AS/400s were sold. The name was changed in 2000 to the eServer iSeries, and the beat goes on. Today's eServer iSeries models employ 64-bit copper-based RISC technology. iSeries models vary from relatively small machines, such as the single-processor iSeries 800 with a sample configuration price tag under $25,000, to the model iSeries 890, which can incorporate as many as 32 processors and might cost hundreds of thousands of dollars. All the iSeries machines use IBM's proprietary OS/400 operating system, but even this operating system now incorporates support for the UNIX and Linux operating systems (IBM Web site, September 2003).

Mainframe Computers

The **mainframes** are the "bread-and-butter" machines of information processing and the heart of the computing systems of most major corporations and government agencies. Our earlier discussion of the evolution of computing dealt primarily with the various generations of mainframe computers. The range of mainframe power and cost is wide, with MFLOPS varying from 200 to 8,000 and cost from $1,000,000 to $20,000,000. A mainframe can handle thousands of terminals (or microcomputers acting as terminals), and the machine requires a good-sized computer room and a sizable professional staff of operators and programmer/ analysts. The strength of mainframes is the versatility of the applications they can handle: online and batch processing, standard business applications, engineering and scientific applications, network control, systems development, Web serving, and more. Mainframes also operate as very large servers in a client/server environment. Because of the continuing importance of mainframes in corporate computing, a wide variety of peripheral equipment has been developed for use with these machines, as has an even wider variety of applications and systems software. This development, by the way, has been carried out by computer vendors, other equipment manufacturers, and companies that specialize in producing software, known as software houses.

Historically, competition has been fierce in the mainframe arena because of its central role in computing. The dominant vendor has been IBM since the late 1950s. The current generation of IBM mainframes is the eServer zSeries (formerly the System/390 series). The newest machines in the zSeries, code-named T-Rex but officially labeled the zSeries 990, were introduced in 2003, and they vary from a single-processor model to a 32-processor model. All these machines are built around the IBM multichip module (MCM), a grouping of 16 chips employing leading-edge copper wiring and silicon-on-insulator technology and containing over 3.2 billion transistors. The 32-processor model can have up to 256 gigabytes of main memory. Development of the zSeries 990 required 1,200 IBM developers and an investment of $1 billion over a 4-year period. A 32-processor zSeries 990 mainframe is able to process 9 billion instructions per second, a threefold improvement over IBM's previous most powerful mainframe. Furthermore, multiple systems can be combined in a Parallel Sysplex, a multisystem environment that acts like a single system. Through a combination of hardware and software, especially the z/OS operating system, a zSeries Parallel Sysplex can incorporate up to 32 individual machines, each of which can have up to 32 processors (IBM Web site, May 13, 2003).

IBM's choice of the code name for its new mainframe as it was being developed, T-Rex, is an interesting one. Some commentators have described the mainframe computer as a dinosaur nearing extinction, and IBM seems to be responding to those criticisms with the T-Rex—the most feared of the dinosaurs and, now, the most feared of the large computer systems. IBM calls the zSeries 990 "the world's most sophisticated server." IBM has maintained its preeminent position in the mainframe arena through solid technical products, excellent and extensive software, extremely reliable machines, and unmatched service.

Competition in the mainframe arena is a little less fierce than it used to be. Two vendors, Amdahl (United States) and Hitachi (Japan), dropped out of the mainframe market in 2000. Fujitsu (Japan) purchased Amdahl, and Hitachi bowed out of the mainframe market to concentrate on other market segments. Amdahl and Hitachi are particularly interesting cases because they succeeded for many years by building machines that were virtually identical to IBM's, often with slightly newer technology, and then by selling them for a lower price. Now Fujitsu is the only remaining vendor offering IBM "plug compatible" mainframes. The only other major players in the mainframe market are Unisys (United States) and Groupe Bull (France). Unisys was formed years ago as the merger of Burroughs and

Figure 2.12 IBM eServer zSeries 990 (Courtesy of IBM Archives. Unauthorized use not permitted.).

Sperry (remember that Sperry built the very first production-line computer), so Unisys has been in the mainframe business a long time.

All the major mainframe vendors, including IBM, fell on hard times in the early 1990s. Because of stronger price/performance ratios from other classes of machines, especially microcomputers and workstations, the primary focus of new systems development in the first half of the 1990s was on client/server applications designed to run on these more cost-effective platforms. The last half of the 1990s saw a marked movement back to mainframes, although demand slackened before and after January 1, 2000, largely because companies were wrapped up in solving the year 2000 (Y2K) problem and then in attending to other IS problems they had let slip while working on Y2K. IBM and other vendors have introduced new technology (such as copper wiring on chips and silicon-on-insulator technology), added UNIX and Linux options to proprietary operating systems, and slashed prices drastically. The addition of Linux capability has been particularly important in the twenty-first century resurgence of the mainframe, with many companies finding out that it is more economical to run multiple Linux virtual servers on a single mainframe than to run (say) 40 Intel-based servers (Greenemeier, 2002). The role of the mainframe will continue to evolve as we move further into the twenty-first century, with more emphasis on its roles as keeper of the corporate data warehouse, server in sophisticated client/server applications, powerful Web server, and controller of worldwide corporate networks.

Supercomputers

The high-end supercomputers are specifically designed to handle numerically intensive problems, most of which are generated by research scientists, such as chemists, physicists, and astronomers. Thus, most of the high-end supercomputers are located in government research laboratories or on major university campuses (even in the latter case, most of the machines are largely supported by grants from the National Science Foundation or other government agencies). Midrange supercomputers, however, have found a variety of uses in large business firms, most frequently for research and development efforts, Web serving on a massive scale, data mining, and consolidating a number of smaller servers.

Until the mid-1990s, the acknowledged leader in the high-end supercomputer arena was U.S.-based Cray Inc. However, IBM mounted a concerted effort in supercomputers in the 1990s, and IBM now clearly holds the top spot (see sidebar entitled "World's Fastest Supercomputer Revisited"). In the June 23, 2003, online listing of the world's top 500 supercomputers, the top 100 machines were distributed as follows: IBM 49, Hewlett-Packard 12, Dell and Hitachi 5 each, Cray Inc. and NEC 4 each, and 8 other vendors with 3 machines or fewer, plus 8 self-made machines (i.e., built by the using organization) (Top 500, 2003). These large computers use one or more of three high-performance computer architectures: parallel vector processing, massively parallel processing, and symmetric multiprocessing. All three of these multiprocessor arrangements were described earlier in this chapter in the section entitled "Extensions to the Basic Model." As an example, the Cray T3E can incorporate up to 2,176 MPPs and operate at speeds up to 3 teraflops (3 trillion floating point operations per second). The Cray SV1ex is based on a symmetric multiprocessing model (SMP), with up to 32 SMP nodes, each of which can consist of up to 32 processors, permitting speeds over 1 teraflop. The newest and most powerful Cray machine is the X1, which is a vector massively parallel processing machine with symmetric multiprocessing nodes. The Cray X1 is based on ultrafast individual processors capable of 12.8 gigaflops each; 64 of these processors can be installed in a single cabinet, giving up to 819 gigaflops of peak computing power. The maximum configuration for the X1 then consists of 64 cabinets containing 64 processors each, providing up to 52.4 teraflops of computing power (Cray Inc., 2002).

In addition to the vendors mentioned above, two other important vendors of midrange supercomputers are Silicon Graphics, Inc., and Sun Microsystems, both powerhouses in high-performance workstations. An interesting development in the supercomputer arena occurred in 1996 when Silicon Graphics, Inc., acquired Cray Research, thus becoming (for a time) the world's leading high-performance computing company. Cray Research continued to operate as a separate unit, focusing on large-scale supercomputers. Then in 2000, Tera Computer Company purchased Cray Research from Silicon Graphics, Inc., with the combined company renamed Cray Inc. In the supercomputer arena as in other areas, sometimes it is hard to keep up with the players!

SUMMARY

Obviously, there is a lot more to IT than the digital computer, but the computer was definitely the key technological development of the twentieth century. The computer has had an outstanding impact on organizations and on our lives, and it has captured our imaginations like no other recent development.

However, the current definition of IT encompasses all forms of technology involved in capturing, manipulating, communicating, presenting, and using data. Thus, IT includes computers, peripheral devices attached to computers, communications devices and networks, photocopiers, facsimile machines, cellular telephones and wireless devices, robots, video recorders and players, etc. But for the IT person in a business or company, the key areas of responsibility are computer technology and communications technology.

To summarize, all computer systems are made up of some combination of six basic building blocks: input, output, memory, arithmetic/logical unit, files, and control unit. All these components are controlled by a stored program that resides in memory and is brought into the control unit one instruction at a time, interpreted, and executed. The basic model has been extended in several directions over the years, primarily by adding controllers and data channels to interface the slower peripheral devices (input, output, disks, and tapes) with the much faster CPU. Many machines include a multilevel storage system, including high-speed cache memory. To gain more power, multiple processors have been employed in a single computer system in a variety of configurations. Whatever the machine configuration, the computer system is still controlled by stored programs or software.

While the numbers and specific details covered in this chapter and in this book will quickly become outdated, the basic principles presented should be valid for the foreseeable future.

CHAPTER REVIEW QUESTIONS

1. What are the distinguishing characteristics of the current (or fourth) generation computers?
2. Distinguish between microcomputers, workstations/midrange systems, mainframes, and supercomputers. Give approximate speeds and costs.
3. List the six building blocks that make up digital computers and describe the flows of data that occur among these blocks.
4. Distinguish between the contents of a memory cell and the address of a memory cell. What is the difference between a byte and a word or a bit and a byte?
5. What are the advantages and disadvantages of using direct access files versus using sequential access files? Why do organizations bother to use sequential access files today?
6. Explain the importance of the stored-program concept. Include the role of the control unit in your explanation.
7. What are the full names for the following acronyms: OCR, CPU, MFLOPS, CD-RW, MIPS, MPP, DASD, SMP, UPC, CD-ROM, PP, DVD?
8. Describe what is meant by benchmarking. When and how would you carry out benchmarking?
9. What is cache memory? Where would it be used and why?
10. Distinguish between a symmetric multiprocessor computer and a parallel processor computer. Which is the most important at this time for business information processing and why?

CHAPTER DISCUSSION QUESTIONS

1. This chapter discusses advantages and limitations of handheld computers (PDAs, etc.), but technology is constantly changing and improving. Given your personal knowledge of what is available in today's marketplace (phones, PDAs, iPods, etc.), how has technology changed since this chapter was written?
2. Do an Internet search for current processing speeds of computers and Intel chips/microprocessor chips. Compare the current speeds to the speeds five years ago.
3. IBM has been a dominant force in the computer industry since the late 1950s. Why was this the case? Why were so many large corporations committed to "Big Blue" (as IBM is affectionately known), at least until the early 1990s? Is there any one company dominant in today's marketplace?
4. Apple Computer has had a varied career and impact on technology. What device has Apple introduced in the past decade that has "saved" the company? What new product is it producing that might change the way the company is viewed in the future (think chips)?
5. Are mainframe computers a thing of the past? Will smaller computers take over the marketplace?

CASE STUDY: WORLD'S FASTEST SUPERCOMPUTER REVISITED

In August 2001, the U.S. Department of Energy installed a powerful IBM RS/6000 SP supercomputer (code name ASCI White) that is dedicated to simulating nuclear explosions. The Department of Energy (DOE) computer contains more than 8,100 microprocessors and is capable of processing 12.3 *trillion* calculations per second, making it the fastest supercomputer ever built (at the time).

The DOE machine contains 512 nodes, each of which contains 16 copper-based Power3-II microprocessors, all managed by a central point-of-control running advanced management software to make the most of the hardware. (Most other microprocessors use aluminum wiring, which does not conduct electricity as well as copper and thus is slower.) The RS/6000 SP contains a switch to move data between nodes at speeds up to 800 megabytes per second. The price tag on this supercomputer was around $110 million.

A few years later, it is time for the next round of the "world's fastest supercomputer." The DOE has awarded IBM a contract valued at $216 to $267 million to build the *two* fastest supercomputers in the world, with a combined peak speed of 467 trillion calculations per second (teraflops). The first system, code named ASCI Purple, will be capable of up to 100 teraflops and will be employed to simulate the aging and operation of U.S. nuclear weapons, ensuring the safety and reliability of the stockpile without underground testing. ASCI Purple will be powered by 12,544 POWER5 microprocessors, IBM's next generation microprocessor; 64 of these microprocessors will be placed in each of 196 nodes. Then the nodes will be able to communicate with one another at the incredible rate of 12,500 billion bytes (gigabytes) per second.

The second system, code named Blue Gene/L, will take longer to develop and will be more powerful still. When completed, Blue Gene/L will employ 130,000 microprocessors and will be capable of up to 367 teraflops. Blue Gene/L will be a research machine to develop and run simulations of very complex physical phenomena of national interest, such as turbulence, prediction of material properties, and the behavior of high explosives.

The price tags for these massive supercomputers would be too steep for commercial users, but IBM uses essentially the same technology as in ASCI White, although on a much smaller scale (and thus at a more reasonable price), in the eServer pSeries 690. For example, Merck & Co., one of the world's largest pharmaceutical companies, is purchasing five pSeries 690 systems, each with 32 processors, as an addition to 2 IBM RS/6000 SP supercomputers already in use. Merck will use these supercomputers in the basic research aspects of the drug development process, including database searching and chemical property computation. IBM estimates that more than 70 percent of all IBM supercomputers sold are used for commercial applications, including tasks like Web serving on a massive scale, business intelligence and data mining (more on this in Chapter 7), handling large parallel databases, and simply consolidating large numbers of smaller servers.

[Adapted from IBM Web site, 2000; April 2002; October 2002]

Case Study Discussion Questions

Question One

Do some research on the Internet to see when Blue Gene/L came into existence. What is this technology capable of? What areas (scientific, medical, etc.) will benefit from its supertechnology?

Question Two

How do you see computer technology evolving? Will there be a next supercomputer or is that an outdated term?

Question Three

What does the future hold in terms of possibilities for new devices to help mankind? Think outside the box or as a science fiction writer might think. What could possibly be a usage of computer technology that we need or might want, but don't think is possible in today's world?

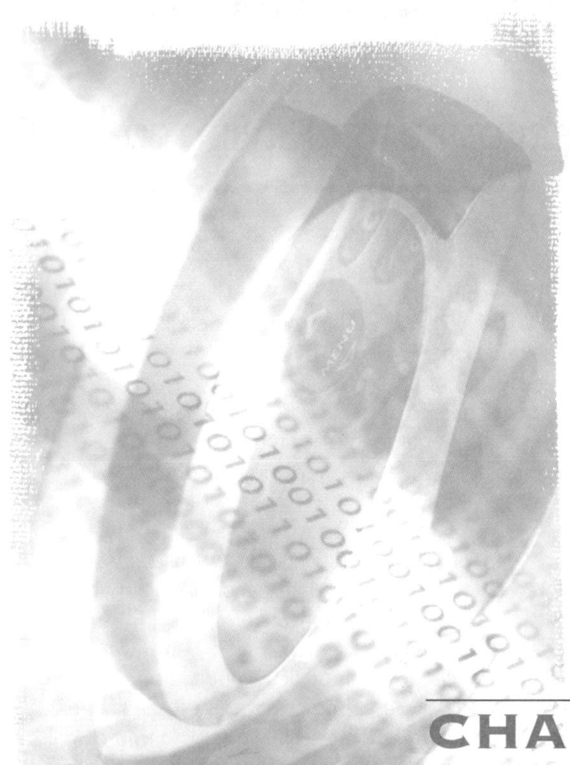

CHAPTER 3
COMPUTER SOFTWARE

IN MANY RESPECTS THIS CHAPTER IS MERELY A CONTINUATION OF CHAPTER 2, which concentrated on computer hardware, or the physical pieces of a computer system. We learned that all the hardware is controlled by a stored program, which is a complete listing (in a form that the computer has been built to understand) of what the computer is to do. Such a stored program is an example of computer software, the topic of this chapter. Software is the set of programs (made up of instructions) that control the operations of the computer system. Computer hardware without software is of little value (and vice versa). Both are required for a computer system to be a useful tool for you and your organization. Thus, this chapter will explain more fully the symbiotic relationship between computer hardware and software.

As important as understanding computer hardware is, it is even more important for you as a manager to understand software. First, appropriate software is required before hardware can do anything at all. Second, most organizations spend several times as much money on software as they do on hardware. This ratio of software to hardware costs is rapidly increasing over time. In the first decade of the twenty-first century, a software company, Microsoft Corporation, is arguably the most successful and most influential company in the entire computer arena.

Third, and most personally relevant, you will be dealing directly with a number of important software packages, such as spreadsheets, word processors, and Web browsers, whereas the only hardware you are likely to interact with is a workstation (most likely a microcomputer, not one of the higher-powered workstations discussed in the previous chapter). Whatever your job in an organization, you are also likely to be involved in software development or acquisition efforts as a member of a project team or as an end user. If your field is marketing, you might well be involved with the creation of a new sales reporting system; if your field is finance, you might develop a computer model to evaluate the impact of a possible merger; if you are an operations manager, you might participate in the development of a new inventory reporting system. For a variety of reasons, therefore, it is important that you understand the various types of computer software and the ways software is used within an organization.

EVOLUTION OF COMPUTER PROGRAMMING

First and Second Generation Languages

Computer software has, of course, been around as long as computer hardware. Initially, all software was written in machine language, as described in "The Stored-Program Concept" section of Chapter 2. Each instruction in a machine language program must be expressed in the precise form that the particular computer has been built to understand. If, for instance, we want to subtract the number found in memory cell 720 from the number found in memory cell 600, storing the result in cell 600, then the machine language instruction (for a hypothetical computer) would be

Operation Code	Addresses	
S	720	600

A complete program to carry out a particular application (e.g., compute the payroll or prepare a management report) would consist of hundreds or thousands of similar instructions expressed in the machine language of the particular computer. The programmer would have to look up (or memorize) each operation code and remember what data have been stored in every memory cell. Machine language programming was (and is) an exacting, tedious, time-consuming process, but it was the only option available on the earliest computers.

Computer software developers soon created **assembly languages** that used the computer itself to perform many of the most tedious aspects of programming. For example, easily remembered mnemonic operation codes are substituted for the machine language operation codes (e.g., SUB for S or SUB for something as unintelligible as 67 on some machines). Symbolic addresses are substituted for a memory cell address (e.g., GPAY for 600). Thus, if our single instruction above is part of a payroll program where we want to subtract deductions (DED) from gross pay (GPAY), we can write

SUB	DED	GPAY

Writing instructions such as this is much easier (and less error-prone) than writing machine language instructions, particularly when we consider that there are likely to be 50 different operation codes and hundreds of memory cell addresses to remember in even a moderate-sized program.

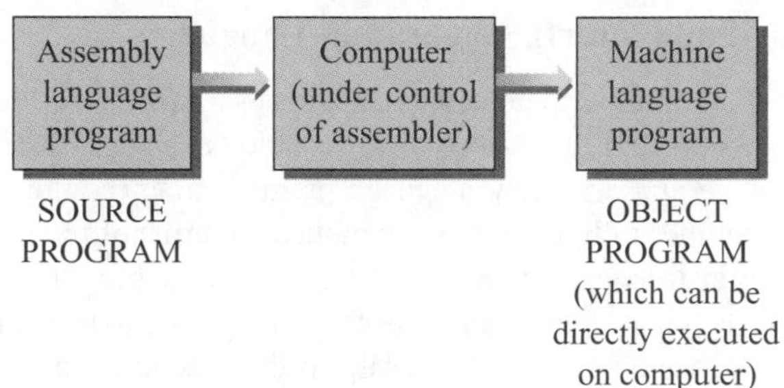

Figure 3.1 Assembler Translation Process

The entire assembly language program is written using instructions similar to the one above. Then the computer, under the control of a special stored program called an **assembler**, converts these mnemonic operation codes and symbolic addresses to the machine language operation codes and memory cell addresses. The assembler program simply keeps a table of conversions for operation codes and addresses and makes the substitutions as necessary. Figure 3.1 illustrates this translation process from the assembly language program (the program containing mnemonic codes and symbolic addresses) to the machine language program. The assembly language program is also called the **source program**, and the resulting machine language program is the **object program**. Once the translation process has been completed, the outcome machine language program is loaded into memory and carried out by the control unit (as described in Chapter 2). The machine language for a particular computer is referred to as the first generation language, or 1 GL, and the assembly language that came along later is called the second generation language, or 2 GL.

Assembly language programming was popular for business applications for many years (until about 1970), and a few major firms and some computer professionals still use assembly language. Popular assembly languages have included SOAP (Symbolic Optimization Assembly Program), Autocoder, and BAL (Basic Assembly Language). Assembly language programming is much easier than machine language programming, but it still requires the programmer to employ the same small steps that the computer has been built to understand; it still requires one assembly language instruction for each machine language instruction. Thus, even after the advent of assembly languages, efforts continued to make it easier to tell the computer what the user wanted done. The results are today's third and fourth generation languages (3 GLs and 4 GLs).

Third and Fourth Generation Languages

The third and fourth generation languages represent a radical departure from the first two generations. Both machine language and assembly language programming require the programmer to think like the computer in terms of the individual instructions. With 3 GLs and 4 GLs, the programmer uses a language that is relatively easy for humans to learn and use but has no direct relationship to the machine language into which it must eventually be translated. Thus, the 3 GLs and 4 GLs are designed for humans, not computers! Typically, each 3 GL or 4 GL instruction will be translated into many machine language instructions (perhaps 10 machine language instructions per 3 GL instruction, or 100 machine language instructions per 4 GL instruction). Furthermore, although each type of computer has its unique 2 GL, the 3 GLs and 4 GLs are largely machine independent. Thus, a program written in a 3 GL or 4 GL can be run on many different types of computers, which is often a significant advantage.

Third generation languages are also called **procedural languages**, because they express a step-by-step procedure devised by the programmer to accomplish the desired task. The earliest procedural language was FORTRAN (an abbreviation for FORmula TRANslator), which was developed by IBM in the mid-1950s. Other popular procedural languages include COBOL (COmmon Business Oriented Language), PL/1, BASIC, PASCAL, ADA, and C. These third generation languages (particularly FORTRAN, BASIC, C, and COBOL) are still very important today, and a later section of this chapter will expand on these introductory remarks. Estimates vary, but it is likely that at least two-thirds of the programs in use today were written in 3 GLs.

A source program in any one of these languages must be translated into the machine language object program before the computer can carry it out. For 3 GLs (and for 4 GLs), the language translator is called a **compiler** if the entire program is translated into machine language before any of the program is executed, or an **interpreter** if each source program statement is executed as soon as that single statement is translated. Historically, the BASIC language was usually interpreted, while most other 3 GLs have been compiled. However, BASIC compilers now exist, and interpreted COBOL is sometimes used during program development.

Figure 3.2 depicts the process of compiling and running a compiled procedural language program, such as C, FORTRAN, or COBOL. This process is quite similar to that used for assembly language programming (see Figure 3.1), with the labels changed as appropriate. The key is that the entire program is translated into an object program, and then the object program is loaded and executed. Dealing with the entire program in this manner has the advantage that an efficient machine language program (one that executes rapidly) can be produced because the interrelationships among the program statements can be considered during the compilation process; dealing with the entire program has the disadvantage that the programmer does not learn about errors until the entire program has been translated.

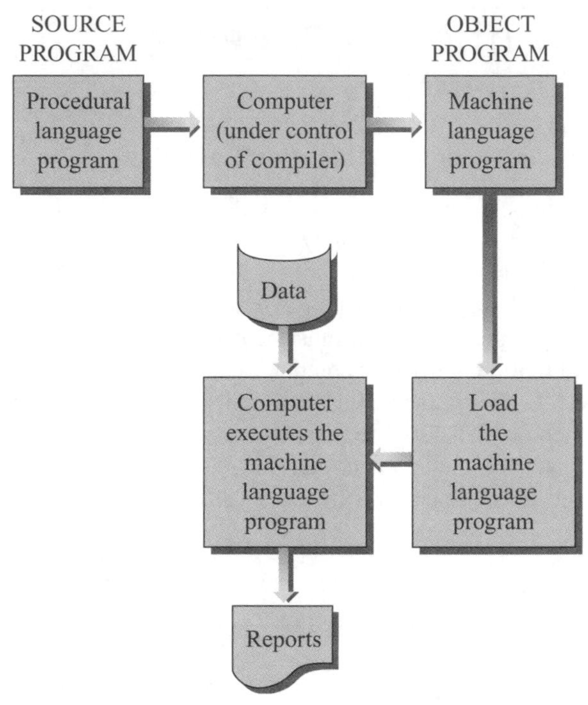

Figure 3.2 Compiling and Running a Procedural Language Program

Figure 3.3 shows the process of interpreting and running an interpretive language program, such as BASIC. With an interpreter, only one statement from the source program is considered at a time. This single statement is translated into machine language, and if no errors are encountered, it is immediately executed. The process is re-

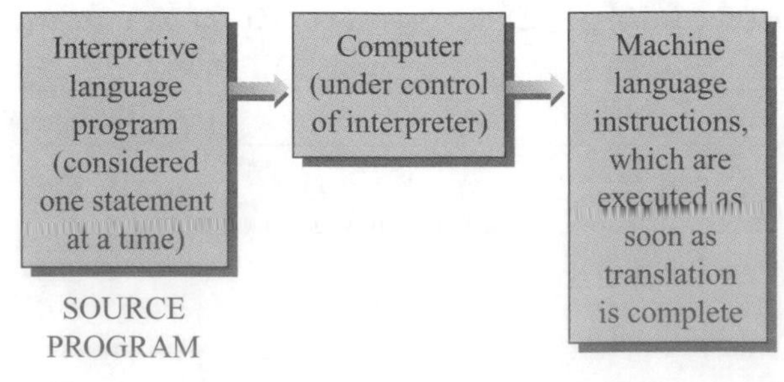

Figure 3.3 Interpreting and Running an Interpretive Language Program

peated, statement after statement. This interpretive process lends itself to interactive programming in which the programmer composes the program at a workstation, keys in one statement at a time, and is almost immediately provided feedback if an error is made. If there are no errors, output is produced immediately after the last statement is entered. The machine language program resulting from the interpretive process is usually much less efficient than one resulting from compilation because only one source program statement is being considered at a time. On the other hand, program development might be sped up because of the immediate feedback to programmers when they make an error. With an interpreter, there is often no true object program, because the machine language instructions are discarded as soon as they are executed. Furthermore, if the program is executed repeatedly, each source statement is translated again each time it is executed, which is quite inefficient compared with the compilation process.

Fourth generation languages—also called **productivity languages** and **nonprocedural languages**—are even easier to use than the third generation languages. To employ a 3 GL, the programmer must devise a step-by-step procedure to accomplish the desired result and express this procedure in the form of 3 GL statements. With a 4 GL, the computer user merely gives a precise statement of what he or she wishes to accomplish, not an explanation of how to do it. Thus, the order in which statements are given in a 4 GL is usually inconsequential. Furthermore, each 4 GL statement is usually translated into significantly more machine language instructions than a single 3 GL statement, sometimes by a factor of 100. Thus, 4 GL programs are easier to write, shorter, and less error-prone than 3 GL programs, which in turn have the same advantages over their 2 GL predecessors. Fourth generation languages, for the most part, use an interpreter to translate the source program into machine language. Please note that the 3 GLs and 4 GLs are essentially the same from one computer model to the next, but the translation programs (compilers and interpreters) must be specific to the particular computer model.

With these advantages, why aren't all programs written in 4 GLs today? First, some of the 4 GLs, like IFPS and SAS, are not general-purpose languages and cannot be used easily for many types of programs. On the other hand, FOCUS and CA-Ramis are indeed general-purpose 4 GLs. More important, many programs are not written in 4 GLs because of concern for efficient use of the computer resources of the organization. For the most part, 4 GL programs translate into longer machine language programs that take much longer to execute than the equivalent programs written in a 3 GL. (Similarly, 3 GL programs often translate into longer machine language programs that take more time to execute than the equivalent 2 GL programs.) The upshot of these arguments is that many one-time programs or infrequently used programs (such as a decision support system or a specialized management report) are written in 4 GLs, while most production programs (those that will be run every day or every week) are written in 3 GLs. In the case of infrequently used programs, human efficiency in writing the program is more important than computer efficiency in running it; for production programs, the opposite is often the case.

In the late 1990s and early 2000s, new programming languages have gained popularity that are still predominantly 3GLs but also have some 4 GL characteristics. These languages are usually described as **object-oriented programming** or **visual programming** languages. Object-oriented programming (OOP) languages such as Smalltalk and C++ came first; these languages are built on the idea of embedding procedures (called methods) in **objects,** and then putting these objects together to create an application. A newer object-oriented programming language, Java, and a visual programming language, Visual Basic, provide a graphical programming environment and a paint metaphor for developing user interfaces. These newer entries in the programming arena as well as 3 GL and 4 GL languages will be described more fully later in the chapter. Overall, the programming environment in most large organizations is now more diverse than ever, with most organizations using some combination of conventional 3 GLs, 4 GLs, object-oriented programming, and visual programming. The trend is towards more object-oriented and visual programming, but significant 4 GL programming and even more 3 GL programming is still being carried out.

KEY TYPES OF SOFTWARE

In the previous section we considered the evolution of computer programming. These programming languages—from assembly language to COBOL to FOCUS to C++ to Java—have been used over the past several decades to create an incredible array of software products, including the language translators themselves. We now want to categorize the various types of computer software that have been created and gain an understanding of how they work together.

To begin our look at the key elements of computer software, let us step back from the details and view the big picture. It is useful to divide software into two major categories:

1. Applications software
2. Support software

Applications software includes all programs written to accomplish particular tasks for computer users. In addition to our payroll computation example, applications programs would include an inventory record-keeping program, a word-processing package, a spreadsheet package, a program to allocate advertising expenditures, and a program producing a summarized report for top management. Each of these programs produces output that users need to do their jobs.

By contrast, **support software** (also called **systems software**) does not directly produce output that users need. Instead, support software provides a computing environment in which it is relatively easy and efficient for humans to work; it enables applications programs written in a variety of languages to be carried out; and it ensures that the computer hardware and software resources are used efficiently. Support software is usually obtained from computer vendors and from specialized software development companies called software houses.

The relationship between applications software and support software might be more readily understood by considering the software iceberg depicted in Figure 3.4. The iceberg's above-water portion is analogous to applications software; both are highly visible. Applications software directly produces results that you as a manager require to perform your job. However, just as the iceberg's underwater portion keeps the top of the iceberg above water, the support software is absolutely essential for the applications software to produce the desired results. (Please note that the iceberg analogy is not an accurate representation of the numbers of applications and support programs; there are usually many more applications programs than support programs.) Your concern as a manager will be primarily with the applications software—the programs that are directly relevant to your job—but you need to understand the functions of the primary types of support software to appreciate how the complete hardware/software system works.

APPLICATIONS SOFTWARE

Applications software includes all programs written to accomplish particular tasks for computer users. Portfolio management programs, general ledger accounting programs, sales forecasting programs, material requirements planning (MRP) programs, electronic mail programs, and desktop publishing packages are all examples of applica-

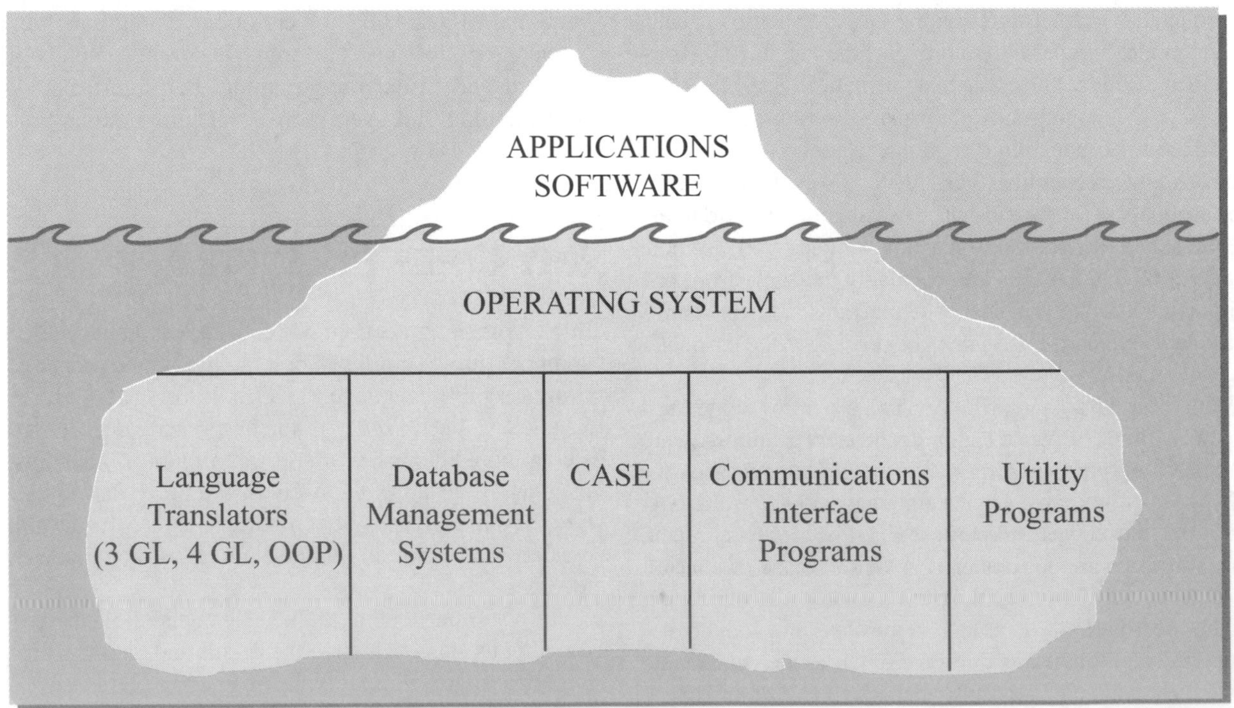

Figure 3.4 The Software Iceberg

tions software. Each of you will be using applications software as part of your job, and many of you will be involved in developing or obtaining applications software to meet your organization's needs.

Because applications software is so diverse, it is difficult to divide these programs into a few neat categories as we will do with support software later in the chapter. Instead, we will begin with a brief look at the sources of applications software, and then we will give two examples of accounting packages to illustrate the types of commercial packages that are available for purchase. Finally, we will look at personal productivity packages for handling many common applications (e.g., word processing, spreadsheets).

Where do we obtain software? Support software is almost always purchased from a hardware vendor or a software house. Only the very largest information systems organizations would even consider writing utility programs or modifying operating systems or compilers. Applications software, however, is sometimes developed within the organization and sometimes purchased from an outside source. Standard applications packages, such as word processing, database management systems, electronic mail, and spreadsheets, are almost always purchased. Applications that are unique to the organization—a one-of-a-kind production control system, a proprietary foreign exchange trading program, a decision support system for adoption or rejection of a new product—are almost always developed within the organization (or by a consulting firm or software company under contract to the organization). The vast middle ground of applications that are quite similar from one organization to the next, but which might have some features peculiar to the particular organization, might be either purchased or developed.

These middle-ground applications include accounts payable, accounts receivable, general ledger, inventory control, MRP, sales analysis, and personnel reporting. Here, the organization must decide whether its requirements are truly unique. Does the organization have the capability of developing this application in-house? What are the costs and benefits of developing in-house versus purchasing a package? This make-or-buy decision for applications software is an important one for almost every organization. Let us note at this point that the rising costs of software development tend to be pushing the balance towards more purchased software and less in-house development.

Until the mid-1980s virtually all software development done within an organization was done by the formally constituted information systems organization. The exceptions were engineers, scientists, and a few computer jocks in other user departments. A revolution called end-user computing has occurred in the past two decades, and now end users such as you do much of the internal software development. There are at least three reasons for the end-user computing revolution. First, the information systems organization was unable to keep up with the demand for new applications software, and significant backlogs of jobs developed. Second, a more knowledgeable, more computer-oriented group of users was created through the hiring of college graduates and the use of various internal and external training programs. Third, and perhaps most significant, powerful desktop computer systems became affordable, and software vendors developed relatively easy-to-use tools that made it possible for interested, but not expert, users to carry out significant software development. These tools include the fourth generation languages and the query languages associated with database management systems. This trend toward end-user computing will continue, in our view, with many of you becoming involved in software development early in your careers.

Of course, not all internal software development is now done—or should be done—by users. For the most part, information systems organizations have not shrunk because of end-user computing; they simply have not grown as rapidly as they might have otherwise. The information systems organizations (or consulting companies or software vendors) continue to develop and maintain the large, complex applications. The IS organizations also tend to develop applications that apply to multiple areas within the organization and those applications for which efficiency is paramount, such as sales transaction processing. The IS organizations employ the same tools used by end users, but they also do a substantial portion of their work using COBOL and other 3 GLs, OOP, and, in some instances, CASE (computer-aided software engineering) tools.

Examples of Applications Packages

Often applications software will be purchased from an outside source. To continue our look at applications software, we will consider one category of commercially available software—accounting packages—as a representative of the many categories that exist. Many commercial accounting packages are available, but we will focus on only two such packages: one inexpensive package designed for small businesses and one somewhat more expensive package designed for midsized and larger businesses.

The package designed for smaller businesses is Peachtree Complete Accounting, with a retail price of $300 for a single-user version. This package has all the features that a small to midsized business would need, including general ledger, accounts receivable, accounts payable, inventory, payroll, time and billing, job costing, fixed asset accounting, and analysis and reporting tools. The Peachtree Today "My Business" pages, illustrated in Figure 3.5, provide a concise, graphical way for the business to review key financial information with a quick glance at a set of Web pages. The "My Business" pages display up-to-date graphical or tabular information on sales and receipts (see Figure 3.5), purchases and payables, and general ledger accounting. Other features built into Peachtree Complete Accounting include the ability to generate customer quotes, create and track sales orders and back orders, maintain an audit trail, track inventory items by detailed attributes, and customize forms, reports, and screens. *PC Magazine* gives Peachtree Compete Accounting a high rating—four out of five possible dots—and it costs $200 less than *PC Magazine*'s top-rated product. "This whale of a product is one you should consider if your inventory tracking needs are great," says *PC Magazine*'s Kathy Yakai. "Despite its large feature set, Peachtree Complete is a relatively easy program to use. Peachtree Complete's reporting capabilities have always been strong" (Yakai, 2003, p. 35).

The second package, or rather an extensive set of modules that can be purchased independently, is the ACCPAC Advantage Series Corporate Edition, produced by ACCPAC International, Inc., a subsidiary of software giant Computer Associates International, Inc. ACCPAC Advantage Series Corporate Edition (there is also an enterprise edition for medium to large businesses, a small business edition, and a discovery edition) is a Web-based, modular financial management system for midsized businesses that supports as many as 10 concurrent users. The ACCPAC software resides on a Web server, with only a Web browser needed on workstations to access the application. The central module of ACCPAC Advantage Series is the System Manager, which controls access to all ACCPAC accounting applications and information. The System Manager module manages security, ensures data integrity, handles bank reconciliation and tax processing, and permits creation of customized reports. Other available modules include General Ledger, Accounts Payable, Accounts Receivable, Inventory Control, Order Entry, Purchase Orders, U.S. Payroll, Canadian Payroll,

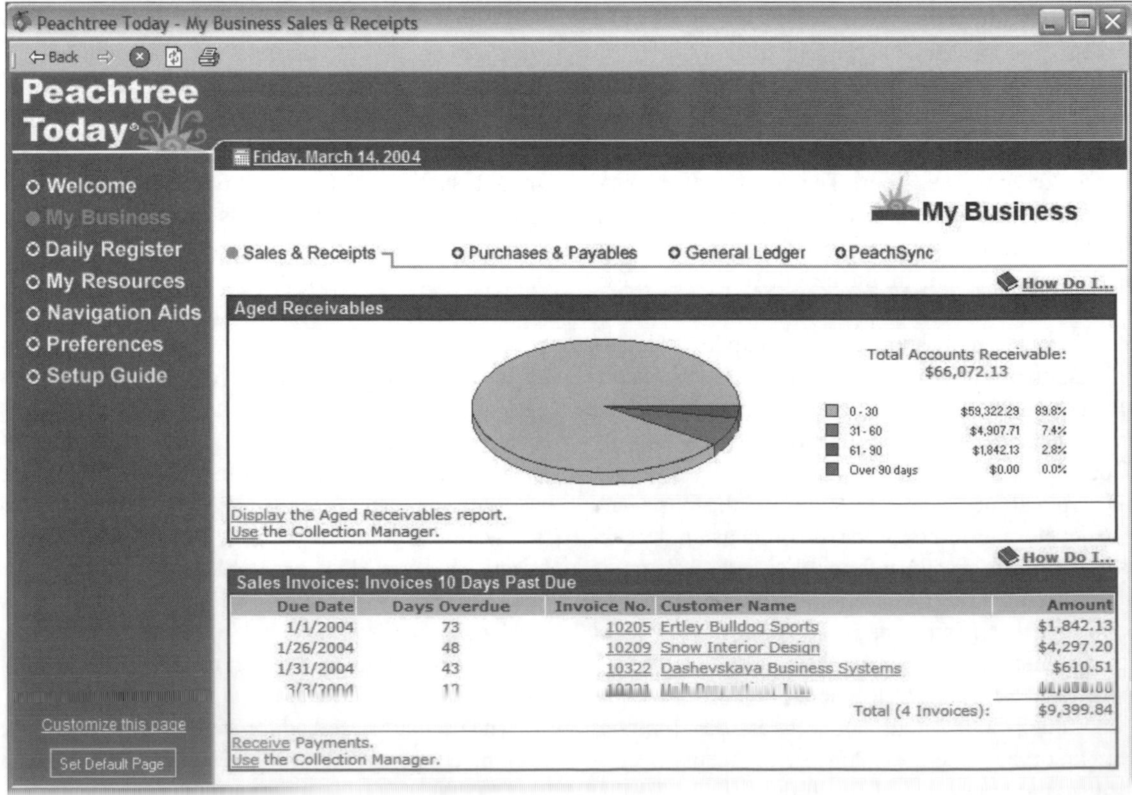

Figure 3.5 Peachtree Today "My Business" Page from Peachtree Complete Accounting (Reproduced with permission of Best Software SB, Inc. The peach device, Peachtree Complete, and Peachtree Today are registered trademarks of Best Software SB, Inc.).

General Ledger Consolidations, Project and Job Costing, Multicurrency, and Intercompany Transactions. The idea, of course, is for each organization to select and employ the modules needed to run its business. These modules are priced at $1,000 each. In addition, there is a fee of $900 to $1,300 per user (up to 10), depending on the database management system used with ACCPAC Advantage Series. ACCPAC options are also available, including a financial diagnostic and strategic analysis tool (CFO), an easy-to-use report generator (Query), an electronic funds transfer direct payroll option, a sales analysis tool, and a sales optimizer tool. These options cost from $500 to $1,000 each. Thus, the total cost of an ACCPAC Advantage Series installation will be much higher than that for Peachtree Complete Accounting, but ACCPAC Advantage Series will be able to handle a much larger business.

Personal Productivity Software

From your personal standpoint as a manager, the category of applications software that we have chosen to call **personal productivity software** is probably the most important of all. These are the packages that you and your fellow managers will use on a regular basis: word processing, spreadsheets, presentation graphics, electronic mail, desktop publishing, microcomputer-based database management systems, Web browsers, statistical packages, and other similar easy-to-use and extremely useful packages. These packages are microcomputer-based, and they have been developed with a friendly, comfortable graphical user interface (GUI).

Exciting things continue to happen in the personal productivity software area. The true beginning of this area came in 1979 with the introduction of VisiCalc, the first electronic spreadsheet. With VisiCalc, microcomputers became a valuable business tool, not just a toy or a hobby. The financial success of VisiCalc convinced many enterprising developers that there was money to be made in developing software packages that individuals and companies would buy and use. Within a few years a deluge of products appeared—a mixture of good and bad—that has not stopped flowing. The results have been truly marvelous for the businessperson with a willingness to experiment and a desire to become more productive. Most of the microcomputer products are quite reasonably priced (often a few hundred dollars), because the successful products can expect to reap large rewards on their volume of sales. Furthermore, a number of excellent publications have developed (such as *PC Magazine*, *PC World*, and *Smart Computing*), which carefully review the new products to assist us in choosing the right packages. Hardly a month goes by without the announcement of an exciting new package that might become the new VisiCalc, Lotus 1-2-3, WordPerfect, or Microsoft Excel.

Word Processing. Word processing might be the most ubiquitous of the personal productivity software packages. In many organizations the first users of microcomputers were the secretaries using early word-processing packages (often WordStar). As secretaries learned the advantages of word processing, particularly the ability to make corrections in a draft without retyping the entire document, managers began to think that it might be more convenient for them, too, to have a microcomputer on their desk so that they could draft letters and reports directly at the keyboard rather than writing them out longhand. There is an art to composing at the keyboard, but once a person has the hang of it, his or her productivity (in terms of written output) can easily be doubled or tripled, as compared to writing longhand. Thus, word processing has made major inroads into the corporate world at the managerial level.

The newest versions of the popular word-processing packages make it easy to get addicted to them. For example, Microsoft Word underlines words that might be misspelled

DO YOUR ACCOUNTING ON THE WEB!

Accounting for small businesses can now be done on the World Wide Web! Several companies, including Peachtree Software, make accounting software accessible via the Web so that the bookkeeper, small business owner, or other designated employee can enter accounting data, check inventory levels or financial information, and create reports from anywhere at anytime. Peachtree Software calls its online accounting service ePeachtree, and the fees are quite reasonable. The ePeachtree basic accounting service–which includes general ledger, sales and receivables, purchasing and payables, inventory, job and project tracking, and sales tax tracking–is $150 per year for a single user (plus a single outside public accountant at no additional fee), with an add-on fee of $102 per year for each additional user. ePeachtree also has available a payroll service add-on for an additional $96 per year. On its ePeachtree Web page, Peachtree stresses its security measures, including the use of Secure Sockets Layer (SSL) encryption technology and a secure "firewall" server (more on these security measures in Chapter 8). From a small business standpoint, a big plus for using ePeachtree or a similar service is that the firm never again has to spend the money or take the time to upgrade its accounting software–the vendor automatically handles all upgrades. The only software the business needs is a Web browser!

[Adapted from Peachtree Software Web site, 2003]

so that you can correct them as you type; lets the user change fonts, margins, and columns easily; rewrites sentences to make them grammatically correct with the click of a mouse; links any text directly to an Internet file; and converts Web files directly to Word format so they are ready to use. Another popular capability is mail merge—the ability to automatically print the same letter (with the address and salutation changed, of course) to everyone on a mailing list. Other popular word-processing packages include Corel WordPerfect, Lotus Word Pro, and Sun's StarOffice Writer. All these packages try to achieve "what you see is what you get," or WYSIWYG, and all succeed to a great extent. The idea is that the text you see on the computer screen should be as close as possible to the resulting printed text. In choosing a word processor, most of us tend to prefer whichever word processor we worked with first. Increasingly, though, organizations have settled on a standard office suite (more on this later), and thus we use the word processor included in that standard suite, usually Microsoft Word. The important thing is not which word processor you use, it is forcing yourself to choose and use any one of the better word processors in order to improve your productivity in writing.

Spreadsheets. Second only to word processing in popularity are electronic spreadsheet packages, the most widely used of which is Microsoft Excel. Other popular spreadsheet packages are Lotus 1-2-3 and Corel Quattro Pro. After the early success of VisiCalc, Lotus 1-2-3 became the spreadsheet standard in the early 1980s and held that leadership position for over a decade. With the growth of software office suites and the dominance of Microsoft in the operating system arena, 1-2-3 has fallen behind Excel as the spreadsheet of choice, but Lotus is still an excellent product with a strong following.

The idea of the electronic spreadsheet is based on the accountant's spreadsheet, which is a large sheet of paper divided into many columns and rows on which the accountant can organize and present financial data. The spreadsheet approach can be used for any application that can fit into the rows and columns framework, including budget summaries for several time periods, profit and loss statements for various divisions of a company, sales forecasts for the next 12 months, an instructor's gradebook, and computation of various statistics for a basketball team.

The intersection of a row and a column is called a cell. Each row in the spreadsheet is given a label (1, 2, 3, etc., from the top down), as is each column (A, B, C, etc., from left to right), and a cell is identified by combining the designations of the intersecting row and column (see Figure 3.6). In a budget summary spreadsheet, for example, cell C4 might contain $32,150, the budgeted sales income for the second quarter. Similarly, cell C2 might contain the heading information "Second Quarter." To enter data into a cell, the cursor is positioned on that cell and the user merely keys in the appropriate data.

But the power of a spreadsheet program does not come from keying numeric data into particular cells, although that is certainly done. The power comes in part from the use of formulas to combine the contents of other cells, letting the program make the calculations rather than doing them by hand. For example, let us assume that cell C9 in our budget summary example is to contain the total income for the second quarter, which is the sum of cells C4, C5, C6, and C7. Rather than adding C4 through C7 by hand, the user enters a formula in cell C9 that tells the program to total the contents of those four cells. One way to express that formula in Microsoft Excel is = +C4+C5+C6+C7. The program then computes the sum and places it in cell C9. More importantly, if a change has to be made in one of the numerical entries, say in cell C5, the sum in cell C9 is automatically corrected to reflect the new number. This feature makes it very easy to modify assumptions and conduct "what if" analyses using a spreadsheet package.

Among the "big three" spreadsheet packages mentioned earlier, there is little difference in the basic approach, although the details do vary. The normal display when using Excel, for example, is a portion of the spreadsheet (a window) with a menu, icons, and a control area at the top of the screen. Using the arrow keys, the user navigates around the spreadsheet to the cell where the entry is to be made. Note that the window automatically changes to keep the cursor cell visible. As numerical or heading information is keyed in, it appears both in the control area at the top of the screen and in the desired cell. If a formula is keyed in, however, the formula appears in the control area while the resulting numerical value is placed in the cell. The user accesses the various commands in Excel through the menu and icons at the top of the screen. If a particular string of commands is likely to be used repeatedly, it is possible to create a "macro" (a program). The user then employs a few keystrokes to call the macro rather than entering the entire string of commands.

Projecting profit for a hypothetical company will serve as a specific spreadsheet application. The Second Company wishes to project its profit for the years 2005 through 2009, given a set of assumptions about its quantity sold, selling price, fixed expenses, and variable expenses. For example, quantity sold of the only product is assumed to be 2,000 units in 2005, increasing 5 percent per year for each year thereafter. Price is assumed to be $50 per unit in 2005, increasing at 8 percent per year. Rent is $1,000 in 2005, growing

	A	B	C	D	E	F	G
1			SECOND COMPANY PROJECTED PROFIT				
2							
3			2005	2006	2007	2008	2009
4							
5	Quantity sold		2000	2100	2205	2315	2431
6	Price		$ 50.00	$ 54.00	$ 58.32	$ 62.99	$ 68.02
7							
8	Total income		$ 100,000	$ 113,400	$ 128,596	$ 145,827	$ 165,368
9							
10							
11	Fixed costs:						
12	Rent		$ 1,000	$ 1,100	$ 1,200	$ 1,300	$ 1,400
13	Salaries		$ 20,000	$ 22,000	$ 24,200	$ 26,620	$ 29,282
14	Equipment leases		$ 4,000	$ 4,200	$ 4,410	$ 4,631	$ 4,862
15	Utilities		$ 5,000	$ 6,000	$ 7,200	$ 8,640	$ 10,368
16	Office supplies		$ 500	$ 475	$ 451	$ 429	$ 407
17							
18	Total fixed costs		$ 30,500	$ 33,775	$ 37,461	$ 41,619	$ 46,319
19							
20	Variable costs:						
21	Unit material cost		$ 8.00	$ 10.00	$ 12.00	$ 14.00	$ 16.00
22	Unit labor cost		$ 4.00	$ 4.16	$ 4.33	$ 5.11	$ 5.62
23	Unit supplies cost		$ 1.00	$ 1.00	$ 1.00	$ 1.00	$ 1.00
24							
25	Total material cost		$ 16,000	$ 21,000	$ 26,460	$ 32,414	$ 38,896
26	Total labor cost		$ 8,000	$ 8,736	$ 9,540	$ 11,820	$ 13,652
27	Total supplies cost		$ 2,000	$ 2,100	$ 2,205	$ 2,315	$ 2,431
28							
29	Total variable costs		$ 26,000	$ 31,836	$ 38,205	$ 46,548	$ 54,979
30							
31	Total costs		$ 56,500	$ 65,611	$ 75,666	$ 88,168	$ 101,298
32							
33							
34	Profit before taxes		$ 43,500	$ 47,789	$ 52,930	$ 57,660	$ 64,070

Figure 3.6 Microsoft Excel Spreadsheet

at $100 per year. Similar assumptions are made for each of the other categories of fixed and variable costs. The resulting spreadsheet is shown in Figure 3.6, which indicates that the Second Company is projected to make $43,500 in profit before taxes in 2005 and $64,070 in 2009.

How were these numbers in the spreadsheet determined? Many of the numbers in the 2005 column were keyed directly in as initial assumptions. However, eight of the numbers in the 2005 column and all of the numbers in the remaining columns were determined by formulas, letting the program perform the actual calculations. For instance, 2000 was actually keyed into cell C5 and 50.00 into cell C6. Cell C8, however, contains a formula to multiply quantity sold times price, =+C5*C6. Figure 3.7 shows the formulas behind the numbers in Figure 3.6. If the cursor is positioned on cell C8 in the spreadsheet, the number 100,000 will appear in the spreadsheet but the formula =+C5*C6 will appear in the control area at the top. Similarly, cell C18 contains a formula to add the contents of cells C12, C13, C14, C15, and C16; one way of expressing this formula is =SUM(C12:C16). Cell D5, the quantity sold in 2006, also contains a formula. In this case the quantity sold in 2006 is to be 5 percent greater than the quantity sold in 2005, so the formula is =+C5*1.05. Not surprisingly, the formula in cell E5 is =+D5*1.05. Thus, any changed assumption about the quantity sold in 2005 will automatically affect both total income and profit in 2005 and quantity sold, total income, and profit in all future years. Because of this cascading effect, the impact of alternative assumptions can be easily analyzed after the original spreadsheet has been developed. This is the power of a spreadsheet package.

Database Management Systems. After word processing and spreadsheets, the next most popular category of personal productivity software is microcomputer-based database management systems (DBMSs). The most widely used package is Microsoft Access; other popular packages include FileMaker Pro, Corel Paradox, Alpha Five, and Lotus Approach. dBase was the desktop DBMS leader in the 1980s but has now largely disappeared. All these packages are based on the relational data model. The basic ideas behind these packages are the same as those to be discussed for large machine DBMSs, but the desktop DBMSs are generally easier to use. With the aid of macros and other programming tools (such as Visual Basic for Applications in the case of Access), rather sophisticated applications can be built based on these DBMS packages.

Presentation Graphics. Presentation graphics is yet another important category of personal productivity software. Most spreadsheet packages incorporate significant graphics capabilities, but the specialized presentation graphics (sometimes called business graphics) packages have even greater capabilities. Used for creating largely

	A	B	C	D	E	F	G
1			SECOND COMPANY PROJE	CTED PROFIT			
2							
3			2005	2006	2007	2008	2009
4							
5	Quantity sold		2000	=+C5*1.05	=+D5*1.05	=+E5*1.05	=+F5*1.05
6	Price		50	=+C6*1.08	=+D6*1.08	=+E6*1.08	=+F6*1.08
7							
8	Total income		=+C5*C6	=+D5*D6	=+E5*E6	=+F5*F6	=+G5*G6
9							
10							
11	Fixed costs:						
12	Rent		1000	=+C12+100	=+D12+100	=+E12+100	=+F12+100
13	Salaries		20000	=+C13*1.1	=+D13*1.1	=+E13*1.1	=+F13*1.1
14	Equipment leases		4000	=+C14*1.05	=+D14*1.05	=+E14*1.05	=+F14*1.05
15	Utilities		5000	=+C15*1.2	=+D15*1.2	=+E15*1.2	=+F15*1.2
16	Office supplies		500	=+C16*0.95	=+D16*0.95	=+E16*0.95	=+F16*0.95
17							
18	Total fixed costs		=SUM(C12:C16)	=SUM(D12:D16)	=SUM(E12:E16)	=SUM(F12:F16)	=SUM(G12:G16)
19							
20	Variable costs:						
21	Unit material cost		8	=+C21+2	=+D21+2	=+E21+2	=+F21+2
22	Unit labor cost		4	=+C22*1.04	=+D22*1.04	=+E22*1.18	=+F22*1.1
23	Unit supplies cost		1	1	1	1	1
24							
25	Total material cost		=+C5*C21	=+D5*D21	=+E5*E21	=+F5*F21	=+G5*G21
26	Total labor cost		=+C5*C22	=+D5*D22	=+E5*E22	=+F5*F22	=+G5*G22
27	Total supplies cost		=+C5*C23	=+D5*D23	=+E5*E23	=+F5*F23	=+G5*G23
28							
29	Total variable costs		=+C25+C26+C27	=+D25+D26+D27	=+E25+E26+E27	=+F25+F26+F27	=+G25+G26+G27
30							
31	Total costs		=+C18+C29	=+D18+D29	=+E18+E29	=+F18+F29	=+G18+G29
32							
33							
34	Profit before taxes		=+C8-C31	=+D8-D31	=+E8-E31	=+F8-F31	=+G8-G31

Figure 3.7 Cell Formulas for Microsoft Excel Spreadsheet

textual presentations, but with embedded clip art, photographs, graphs, and other media, the leaders in this field are Microsoft PowerPoint, Corel Presentations, and Lotus Freelance Graphics. For design of more complex business graphics, the leading packages are Microsoft Visio, Adobe Illustrator, CorelDraw, and Macromedia FreeHand.

World Wide Web Browsers. A very important type of personal productivity software is the **Web browser** used by an individual to access information on the World Wide Web. The Web browser is the software that runs on the user's microcomputer, enabling the user to look around, or "browse," the Internet. Of course, the user's machine must be linked to the Internet via a modem connection to an Internet service provider (ISP) or a connection to a local area network (LAN), which is in turn connected to the Internet. The Web browser uses a hypertext-based approach to navigate the Internet. **Hypertext** is a creative way of linking objects (such as text, pictures, sound clips, and video clips) to each other. For example, when you are reading a document describing the Grand Canyon, you might click on the link The View from Yavapai Point to display a full-screen photograph of that view or click on the link The Grand Canyon Suite to hear a few bars from that musical composition.

Two primary Web browsers are in use in the first decade of the twenty-first century: Netscape and Microsoft's Internet Explorer. Netscape had first-mover advantage but has now been eclipsed by Internet Explorer in terms of number of users. From the user's standpoint, the great thing about this browser battle is that both products are free—the price is unbeatable! Both Microsoft and Netscape (now a subsidiary of America Online, or AOL) make money by functioning as an ISP and by developing software and applications for use on the World Wide Web.

In recent versions of Internet Explorer, Microsoft has introduced the idea of the **Active Desktop**, which Microsoft describes as a customizable "dashboard" for your Windows-based PC. The Active Desktop lets the user place both Windows icons (such as shortcuts to programs that you use frequently) and Hypertext Markup Language (HTML) elements (such as links to Web sites that you visit frequently) on the Windows home screen. The HTML elements can be dynamic, too. Users can, for example, place a Web page containing a weather report or a news feed on the desktop and have it updated at regular intervals so that the content is always fresh.

Web browsers are based on the idea of **pull technology**. The browser must request a Web page before it is sent to the desktop. **Push technology** is also important. In push technology, data are sent to the client (usually a PC) without the client requesting it. E-mail is the oldest and most widely used push technology—and certainly e-mail spam is the most obnoxious form of push technology. In the 1990s the most familiar Web example of push technology was PointCast (a free download package), which delivered customized news ticker-tape style to the user's desktop. However, this provider-to-end-user use of push technology has essentially gone out of existence (and so has PointCast) because of a flawed economic model. Other uses of push technology have been more successful. For example, it is commonplace for technology vendors (such as Microsoft) and corporations to distribute software patches and new versions of software via push technology, often on an overnight basis. Similarly, many organizations have pushed sales updates and product news to their sales representatives and field service technicians around the world. But what if the users are only occasionally online, with much of their work done offline?

BackWeb Technologies Limited—which describes itself as the "offline Web company"—has the answer with offline portal access and proactive delivery of information using its Polite technology. A **portal** is simply a standardized entry point to key information on the corporate network. When an employee is online, he or she goes through the portal to find the needed information. With the BackWeb system, a copy of the corporate portal is set up on the user's PC. When the PC is online, BackWeb's Polite technology takes advantage of otherwise unused bandwidth to update the portal's contents, such that network performance is never affected by the portal replication. Thus, the user can do most of his or her work offline using the offline portal. The newest version of BackWeb's Proactive Portal Server introduces two-way replication, which lets users work in a portal offline and then automatically replicates changes and additions once they reconnect to the network. In an important move, software giant SAP plans to package Proactive Portal Server with its mySAP software. Offline portals, serviced by push technology, can increase the productivity of today's mobile employees when they are on the road and disconnected from the network (BackWeb Web site, 2003; and Kontzer, 2003).

Electronic Mail and Groupware. Electronic mail has become the preferred way of communicating for managers in most businesses today. It is asynchronous (no telephone tag) and unobtrusive, easy to use and precise. Groupware incorporates not only electronic mail, but also much more. Groupware has the goal of helping a group become more productive and includes innovative ways of data sharing, such as Lotus Notes' threaded discussion groups.

Other Personal Productivity Packages. Desktop publishing gives the user the ability to design and print an in-house newspaper or magazine, a sales brochure, an annual report, and many other things. The more advanced word-processing packages, such as Microsoft Word and Corel WordPerfect, provide the capability to arrange the document in appropriate columns, import figures and tables, and use appropriate type fonts and styles. The popular specialized desktop publishing packages, such as Adobe PageMaker, Adobe InDesign, Adobe FrameMaker, Quark XPress, and Microsoft Publisher, are even more powerful.

There are a number of other categories of personal productivity packages. Two important security packages are Norton Internet Security (from Symantec), which combines the best antivirus product with the best software firewall solution, and McAfee Internet Security (from Network Associates). Personal information managers provide an easy-to-use electronic calendar plus storage of telephone numbers, addresses, and other personal information. For an individual not working as part of a group, Lotus Organizer is often the top choice; for those working in a group, groupware products such as Lotus Notes and Microsoft Outlook provide these capabilities. Goldmine Business Contact Manager (from FrontRange), ACT! (from Interact Commerce), and NOW Up to Date & Contact Manager (from Power On Software) are examples of contact management programs that let the user track past and potential customers.

A widely used and valuable package for creating, distributing, and commenting on electronic documents is Adobe Acrobat. Project scheduling software includes Microsoft Project, FastTrack Schedule (from AEC Software), and SureTrak Project Manager (from Primavera). Among the popular packages for image editing are Adobe Photoshop, Adobe Photoshop Elements (a reduced-version package designed for hobbyists), Jasc Paint Shop Pro, and Roxio PhotoSuite. For video editing, three strong software packages are Pinnacle Studio, Adobe Premiere Pro, and Avid Xpress. Valuable reference packages include Rand McNally StreetFinder & TripMaker (from Global Marketing Partners), Microsoft Streets & Trips, and Microsoft Encarta (a true multimedia encyclopedia).

The list of personal productivity software presented here could certainly be extended, but today's most important categories have been mentioned. New packages and new categories will certainly be introduced in the next few years.

Office Suites. New versions of the popular personal productivity software packages have been introduced every year or so in the late 1990s and early 2000s, but two other developments have been even more important in redefining the personal productivity software area. First, the key players have evolved over time, with some firms being purchased by others and some products being sold to a different vendor. IBM's purchase of Lotus Development Corporation in 1995 was perhaps the most significant shift among the players. The popular WordPerfect word-processing package has been batted around like a ping-pong ball; first Novell purchased the WordPerfect Corporation, and then Novell sold the WordPerfect package to Corel. The popular packages of 2 or 3 years ago likely still exist, but they might not have the same corporate home.

Second, an even more important development is the combining of certain of these personal productivity software packages into integrated suites of applications for use in the office. With the strong popularity of the Microsoft Windows operating system, the major software players scrambled to introduce **office suites**, also known as **application suites**, that are compatible with Windows. Of course, Microsoft, as the developer of Windows, had the inside track in terms of producing Windows software packages and a Windows office suite. In the first decade of the twenty-first century, the Microsoft Office suite is overwhelmingly the dominant entry in the marketplace. Three other office suites are worth mentioning: Corel WordPerfect Office, Lotus SmartSuite, and Sun StarOffice.

Microsoft Office (version 95, then 97, 2000, XP, and now 2003) was the first suite and has captured a dominant market share, but the other three suites have strong features, popular products, and a distinct price advantage. The Microsoft Office 2003 suite includes Word (word processing), Excel (spreadsheet), PowerPoint (presentations), and Outlook (e-mail, contacts, and scheduling) in the standard edition. The small business edition adds Publisher (desktop publishing) and a version of Outlook with Business Contact Manager, and the professional edition adds Access (database management system) to the small business package. The suggested retail price is $399 for the standard edition, $449 for the small business edition, and $499 for the professional edition. The other players in the office suite arena have had difficulty keeping up with Microsoft. Microsoft was the first mover, controls the operating system, has good individual products (although not always the best individual products), and has done a better job of integrating the individual products than Corel and Lotus.

Lotus SmartSuite Millennium Edition 9.8 includes seven primary products: Word Pro (word processing), 1-2-3 (spreadsheet), Freelance Graphics (presentations), Approach (database management system), Organizer (time management), FastSite (Web publishing), and SmartCenter (information manager). The retail price is under $300, but the street price is often under $40. Corel WordPerfect Office 11 includes three primary products in its standard edition: WordPerfect (word processing), Quattro Pro (spreadsheet), and Presentations (presentations). The professional edition adds Paradox (database management system). The retail price is about $300 for the standard edition and $400 for the professional edition, but the street price is under $40 for the standard edition and under $120 for the professional edition. The Sun StarOffice 7 office suite, which retails for $79, includes five products: Writer (word processing), Calc (spreadsheet), Impress (presentations), Draw (graphics), and Base (database management system). For all these suites, the price to upgrade from an earlier edition is considerably less than the retail price. All these suites provide excellent value for the investment. It seems clear that the future of certain personal productivity software products (word processing, spreadsheet, presentations, and database management system) lies in office suites because of the ability to move data among the various products as needed.

SUPPORT SOFTWARE

Support software has been designed to support applications software behind the scenes rather than to directly produce output of value to the user. There are several types of support software, such as the language translators we encountered earlier in this chapter. In our discussion of the evolution of computer programming, we noted that programs written in second, third, and fourth generation languages must be translated to machine language before they can be run on a computer. This translation is accomplished by support software called assemblers, compilers, and interpreters. We now want to take a systematic look at the various types of support software.

The Operating System

The most important type of support software is the operating system, which originated in the mid-1960s and is now an integral part of every computer system. The **operating system** is a very complex program that controls the operation of the computer hardware and coordinates all the other software, so as to get as much work done as possible with the available resources. Users interact with the operating system, not the hardware, and the operating system in turn controls all hardware and software resources of the computer system.

Before operating systems (and this was also before PCs), computer operators had to physically load programs and start them running by pushing buttons on the computer console. Only one program could be run at a time, and the computer was often idle while waiting for an action by the operator. Now the operator's job is much easier and the computer is used more efficiently, with the operating system controlling the starting and stopping of individual programs and permitting multiple programs to be run at the same time. The operating system on a PC also helps the user by providing an easy-to-use graphical user interface (GUI).

There are two overriding purposes for an operating system: to maximize the work done by the computer system (the throughput) and to ease the workload of computer users. In effect, the operation of the computer system has been automated through the use of this sophisticated program. Figure 3.8 illustrates some of the ways in which these purposes are advanced by the operating system. This somewhat complex diagram presents the roles of the operating system in a large computer system. To make these roles more understandable, we will concentrate on the diagram's individual elements.

First, note that the human operator at the top of the diagram interfaces only with the operating system, the local input job stream, and the local output job stream. The interface with the operating system is usually done by entering simple commands at an operator console (a specialized terminal). The interface with the local input job stream

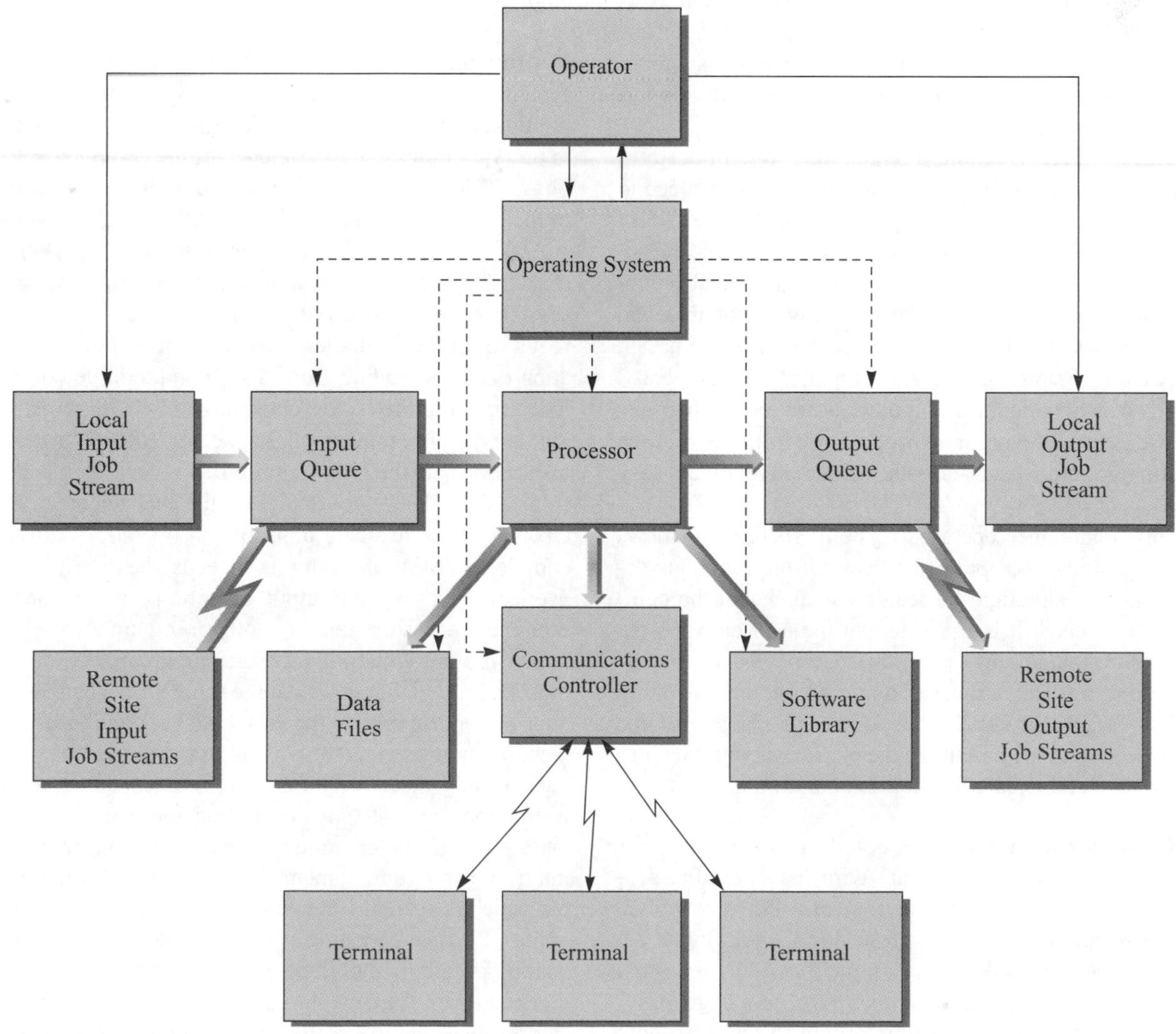

Figure 3.8 The Role of the Operating System

usually involves mounting tapes or changing removable disk packs, and the interface with the local output job stream means separating and distributing printed output.

The operating system, either directly or indirectly through other support software, controls everything else that takes place in Figure 3.8. It controls the inflow and outflow of communications with the various terminals and microcomputers (often through a specialized communications interface program). Using priority rules specified by the computer center manager, the operating system decides when to initiate a particular job from among those waiting in the input queue; similarly, the operating system decides when to terminate a job (either because it has been completed, an error has occurred, or it has run too long). The operating system decides which job to print next, again based on priority rules. It stores and retrieves data files, keeping track of where everything is stored (a function sometimes shared with a database management system). The operating system also manages the software library, keeping track of both support and applications programs.

The advantage of letting the operating system perform all the above tasks is that it can react at electronic speed to select the next job, handle multiple terminal sessions, select the appropriate software from the library, and retrieve the appropriate data file. Thus, the expensive and powerful central processing unit (CPU) can be kept as busy as possible, and the throughput from the system can be maximized. Further, the operating system can create a computing environment—in terms of what operators and other users see on their terminal screens and what they need to key in to instruct the operating system what to do—in which it is relatively easy to work.

A microcomputer operating system, such as Windows 2000 or Windows XP, performs many of the functions described above, although the scale is smaller and the complexity is reduced. It is still true that the user employs the operating system to start a program, to retrieve data, to copy files, and so on. The purpose of a microcomputer operating system is exactly the same as the purpose of a large machine operating system: to maximize the work done by the computer system and to ease the workload of human users.

Job Control Language. As noted, it is necessary for computer users to communicate with the operating system, often by keying in instructions at a PC or terminal. These instructions must be expressed in the particular **job control language**, or **JCL**, that is understood by the operating system being used. This job control language varies significantly from one operating system to the next, both in terms of the types of instructions and the detailed syntax. For example, with the PC-DOS or MS-DOS operating system (used on IBM and IBM-compatible PCs before Windows became popular), to change directories, one types CD\ followed by the name of the new directory; to list the current directory, one types DIR; to copy a file named MEMO from the A drive to the C drive, one types COPY A:MEMO C:. These are examples of the job control language. The JCL is even simpler for a Macintosh or a PC operating under Windows 2000 or XP. In this case, the user may click or double-click on an icon to start an application or retrieve a file. The JCL is much more complex for a larger machine, but the ideas are the same. To run a payroll program, for example, JCL is used to tell the operating system the name of the program to be run, the names of the data files that are needed, instructions for output of data, and the account number to be charged, among other things.

Multiprogramming or Multitasking. Operating systems often incorporate two important concepts—multiprogramming (or multitasking) and virtual memory—in order to increase the efficiency of the computer's operations. These concepts are concerned with the management of the memory and the CPU time of the computer system.

On larger machines, **multiprogramming** is often employed to overlap input and output operations with processing time. This is very important because the time required for the computer to perform an input/output operation (such as reading from disk) is quite large compared to the time required to execute an arithmetic instruction. In fact, a typical computer might execute 100,000 arithmetic instructions in the time required to read a single record from a disk. Thus, it would be quite inefficient to let the CPU remain idle while input/output operations are being completed. Multiprogramming keeps the CPU busy by overlapping the input/output operations of one program with the processing time of another program.

For multiprogramming, several programs (say 5 to 10) must be located in memory at the same time. Then the operating system supervises the switching back and forth among these programs so that the CPU is almost always busy. When the currently executing program encounters an input/output instruction, an interrupt occurs and the operating system takes control. The operating system stores the status of the interrupted program in memory so that this information will be available when the interrupted program gets another shot at the CPU. The operating system then decides which of the waiting programs should be executed next, and it resets the computer with the new program's status. Then the operating system gives control to the new program, which executes until it encounters an input/output instruction. Thus, the operating system controls the switching back and forth among programs that is involved in multiprogramming.

The switching among programs in multiprogramming may be triggered by time as well as by an event (the occurrence of an input/output instruction). Time-driven multiprogramming (sometimes called **time-sharing**) is the usual mode of operation when large numbers of users are simultaneously using a computer (midrange or larger) from terminals or microcomputers serving as terminals. In this environment, each user is allocated a small slice of CPU time (e.g., a few milliseconds). When a particular user's turn arises, her program runs for those few milliseconds, carrying out thousands of instructions. Then a time interrupt occurs, and the operating system transfers control to the next user for his slice of time. Unless the number of concurrent users becomes excessively high, these bursts of available time occur so rapidly that it appears to the user that he or she is the only person using the computer.

On smaller computers, including microcomputers, the term **multitasking** is used to describe essentially the same function as multiprogramming on larger machines. In both cases the operating system controls the switching back and forth among programs stored in memory. There are two basic types of multitasking: *preemptive* and *cooperative*. In preemptive multitasking, the operating system allocates slices of CPU time to each program (the same as time-driven multiprogramming above). In cooperative multitasking, each program can control the CPU for as long as the program needs. In practice, multitasking means that a user can print a report at essentially the same time as he or she recalculates a spreadsheet, all the while monitoring for new electronic mail.

Virtual Memory. Whereas multiprogramming or multitasking is primarily concerned with the management of CPU time, **virtual memory** is concerned with the management of main memory. At present, virtual memory is used only on larger computer systems. Virtual memory makes it appear to the user that an unlimited amount of main memory is available, meaning that individual programs can be much larger than the actual number of memory cells. More importantly, virtual memory permits multiprogramming to operate more efficiently. How does this work?

The trick is the creative use of direct access storage devices (DASDs), with the operating system switching portions of programs (called pages) between main memory and DASDs. Unless all the programs are small, it is difficult to get enough programs stored in memory for multiprogramming to operate efficiently. For example, three large programs might occupy all of the memory, and it might be common for all three programs to be processing input/output instructions at the same time. This leaves the CPU idle, which is undesirable. The cost of adding enough real memory to store 10 programs at a time—to permit efficient multiprogramming—might be prohibitive. The virtual memory concept recognizes that only one segment of a large program is being executed at a time, while the bulk of the program is inactive. Therefore, with virtual memory, only a few pages of the program (perhaps only one) are kept in main memory, with the rest relegated to a DASD. Because only a small portion of each program is located in memory, portions of a sufficient number of programs can be stored in memory to permit efficient multiprogramming.

Of course, it is often necessary for the operating system to bring new portions of a program (new pages) into memory so they can be executed. This swapping of pages between a DASD and main memory is called, appropriately enough, paging. The size of pages varies, but each is often a few thousand bytes. When we combine the concepts of multiprogramming (switching among pages of programs already in memory) with virtual memory (requiring frequent page switches from DASDs to memory), then we begin to realize the incredible complexity of tasks carried out by the operating system.

Multiprocessing. Despite the similarity between the terms, multiprocessing is quite different from multiprogramming. **Multiprocessing** refers to the processing, or work, that takes place when two or more CPUs are installed as part of the same computer system. Each CPU works on its own job or set of jobs (often using multiprogramming), with all the CPUs under control of a single operating system that keeps track of what the various CPUs are doing. This is complexity piled on complexity! It is easy to see that today's computer systems would be much less efficient and of very limited use to us without the powerful operating systems that exist and are continually being upgraded.

Sources of Operating Systems. For the most part, operating systems are obtained from the manufacturer of the hardware, although some other company might have written the operating system. For example, when you buy a new microcomputer from Gateway or Dell it likely comes equipped with Windows XP, an operating system from Microsoft. Most of the popular operating systems are **proprietary systems** that were written expressly for a particular computer system. Examples are PC-DOS and MS-DOS, which are the same operating system written by Microsoft for IBM microcomputers and IBM compatibles, respectively; Windows 2000 and Windows XP, which are newer systems written for IBM-compatible microcomputers; MVS and

VM, which are two alternative large machine operating systems offered by IBM; and OS/400, which is the operating system for IBM's iSeries (formerly AS/400) line of midrange systems.

In contrast to these proprietary systems, the popular UNIX operating system and the newer Linux operating system are **open systems**. UNIX and Linux are not tied to a particular computer system or hardware manufacturer. Bell Laboratories originally developed UNIX, with subsequent versions created by the University of California at Berkeley, AT&T, and a variety of hardware manufacturers. For example, Sun Microsystems and IBM have developed their own versions of UNIX—Solaris for Sun and AIX for IBM. UNIX is powerful and flexible, and it is portable in that it will run on virtually any computer with a C language compiler (UNIX was written in C; more on C later).

Linux is a cut-down version of UNIX originally written by a young Finnish programmer, Linus Torvalds, in 1991. Torvalds made his new operating system compact and flexible, and he decided to share Linux freely. The only stipulation to the free use of Linux is that if a programmer makes modifications or extensions to Linux, he or she agrees to share them with the rest of the worldwide Linux community. Torvalds then has the final say on everything that goes into Linux. Although a knowledgeable computer programmer can download Linux for free and get it operating on his or her machine, most users (including corporations) need a bit more help and buy a Linux "distribution" from a vendor such as Red Hat, Corel, and SuSE. This distribution includes the free Linux system plus additional software, documentation, and a way of installing the software. Linux received a significant boost when many of the major players in the information technology field, including IBM, Hewlett-Packard, Intel, and Dell, agreed to push its use. IBM, in fact, has made Linux the centerpiece of its information technology strategy and now offers Linux on all of its varied computer platforms, from PCs and workstations to mainframes and supercomputers. Consequently, Linux has taken market share away from UNIX and is holding down the growth of Microsoft Windows on servers.

Many of the newer computers, such as high-powered workstations and supercomputers, run only UNIX or Linux. Many computer professionals would like to see UNIX or Linux become the standard operating system for all computer systems. That appears unlikely in the foreseeable future, but the use of Linux in particular will continue to spread, at least for Web servers, network servers, and other larger machines. Some organizations have even adopted a strategy of carrying out all new applications software development in a UNIX or Linux environment and gradually moving existing applications to UNIX or Linux. In particular, many client/server applications have been designed to run on a UNIX- or Linux-based server. Linux continues to move into the large computer arena, where it is likely to coexist with vendor operating systems like VM or OS/400 in major corporate and government data processing centers.

A **server operating system**, also called a **network operating system (NOS)**, is software running on a server that manages network resources and controls the operation of a network. To state this in another way, a server OS is an operating system that has been enhanced by adding networking features. For example, a server OS allows computers on a network to share resources such as disk drives and printers; it also handles the server-side of client/server applications. Major players in the server OS market include several variations of UNIX, Microsoft Windows NT Server, Microsoft Windows 2000 Server, Microsoft Windows 2003 Server, Novell NetWare, and Linux. According to the Framingham, Massachusetts-based firm IDC, Microsoft is dominant in this market, with 55 percent of the new server OSs shipped in 2002. Linux comes in second, with 23 percent of the market, followed by the various flavors of UNIX at 11 percent and Novell NetWare at 10 percent. IDC also sees continued growth for both Microsoft and Linux in the server OS arena through at least the year 2007 (Hines, 2003).

At the microcomputer level, Microsoft Windows is even more dominant, with about 94 percent of the market. The remainder is almost evenly split between Linux (for IBM-compatible machines) and Mac OS (for Apple's Macintosh machines) (Hines, 2003). Linux is growing in this market sector, but it is no real threat to Microsoft. Because most new IBM-compatible machines come preloaded with Windows XP, it is the *de facto* standard for microcomputers as of this writing.

In summary, all of the widely used operating systems in use today will continue to evolve over the next several years, with each becoming more complex and more powerful. Paradoxically, microcomputer operating systems will at the same time become much easier to use. It appears likely that the movement towards Linux for larger machines will continue, and that Windows will continue to dominate the microcomputer market—although Linux might make some inroads here. The server operating system market is where a major Windows-Linux battle appears to be developing.

One of the important notions in the information technology area is that of an **IT platform**, which is defined as the set of hardware, software, communications, and standards an organization uses to build its information systems. Now we are in the position to point out that the

IS LINUX THE FUTURE?

Linux, an open source operating system with a penguin as its mascot, has become the hot software for running Web sites, with estimates indicating that well over 50 percent of the Web servers (computers that serve up Web or intranet pages) are now running the Linux operating system. Linux is also being used to run database servers, electronic mail servers, and application development servers. The result is that Linux now controls about 25 percent of the server operating system market, and that percentage appears likely to increase. Information technology managers like Linux because it is cheap and reliable and it performs well. They also feel that they need an alternative to Microsoft Windows, and they appreciate the availability of development tools through the Internet. On the negative side, the biggest concern is the limited availability of business software written for Linux. Other weaknesses cited include the existence of multiple versions of Linux and the limited availability of training and education.

Linux is also being used on computers other than midrange and low-end servers. At the high end, IBM reports that several of its customers are replacing numerous servers with new IBM zSeries mainframes running Linux. The Securities Industry Automation Corporation (SIAC), a wholly-owned subsidiary of the New York and American Stock Exchanges, replaced a number of UNIX-based servers with a single zSeries mainframe running Linux virtual servers under IBM's z/VM operating system (z/VM is the current version of IBM's VM operating system). This mainframe examines, processes, and issues e-mail activity reports on 15 to 20 million e-mail transactions a day. SIAC indicates that the use of Linux on a mainframe has resulted in reduced server and maintenance costs, greatly improved scalability, and 100 percent availability. Deutsche Telekom AG replaced 25 UNIX servers with a single IBM zSeries mainframe running two dozen virtual Linux partitions. The workload includes e-mail, internal Web sites, and network support. The benefits include higher security and reliability as well as reduced administration and operating costs. Sonera Entrum, a subsidiary of Finland's largest telecommunications company, consolidated all of its services for its digital subscriber line (DSL) customers on a single zSeries mainframe running IBM's z/VM operating system with about 500 virtual Linux servers. The benefits include increased reliability, better customer service, and, most important, lower cost of operation because of reduced administration and maintenance costs.

At the low end, Linux has found its way into about 3 percent of new desktop PCs. As perhaps a sign of the times, Wal-Mart is selling $200 Linux-based PCs. In Spain, the region of Extremadura is giving away over 10,000 Linux-based PCs to residents. A new group, the Linux Desktop Consortium, has been formed to promote the use of Linux on corporate and home desktops. The movement of Linux to the desktop is slow, but Linus Torvalds, who created Linux in 1991, calls desktop Linux "inevitable." Torvalds indicated that "We already have all of the tools, in open-source software, necessary for 80 percent of the office workers in the world: an office suite including spreadsheet, word processor, and presentation program; a Web browser; graphical desktop with file manager; and tools for communication, scheduling, and personal information management" (Weiss, 2003). In addition to its use in conventional computers of all sizes, Linux is finding its way into a variety of consumer-electronics devices, including TiVo TV program recorders and Sony PlayStation video game consoles.

Linux with 25 percent of the server market? Linux on microcomputers being sold at Wal-Mart? Linux in TiVo and PlayStation? Multiple copies of Linux running on a mainframe? Perhaps Linux *is* the future.

[Adapted from Ricadela, 2002; Greene, 2003; Greenemeier, 2003; IBM Web site, 2003; Ketstetter, Hamm, Ante, and Greene, 2003; and Weiss, 2003]

operating system is usually the single most critical component of the platform. Thus, it is common to discuss an MVS (mainframe) platform, a UNIX platform, a Windows XP platform, or a Linux platform.

Third Generation Languages

As illustrated in Figure 3.4, the underwater portion of the software iceberg includes support software in addition to the critical operating system. It is useful to divide this support software into five major categories: language translators, database management systems, CASE tools, communications interface software, and utility programs. Let us consider languages and language translators first.

The third generation languages, which are more commonly called procedural or procedure-oriented languages, are the workhorses of the information processing field. As mentioned earlier, support software in the form of compilers and interpreters is used to translate 3 GL programs (as well as 4 GL and OOP programs) into machine language programs that can be run on a computer. The procedural languages do not enjoy the near-total dominance of a decade ago, but they are still the languages of choice for many computer professionals, scientists, and engineers. During the 1990s and the early part of the 2000s, 4 GLs, DBMSs, application generators, object-oriented languages, and visual languages have gained ground on the 3 GLs (in part because of the growth of end-user computing), but they will not replace the 3 GLs in the next few years. There are several reasons why the procedural languages will remain popular. First, most computer professionals are familiar with one or more procedural languages and will be reluctant to change to something new. Second, the procedural languages tend to produce more efficient machine language programs (and thus shorter execution times) than the 4 GLs and other newer alternatives. Third, new versions of the procedural languages continue to be developed, each generally more powerful and easier to use than the previous version. For example, object-oriented versions of C, COBOL, and PASCAL are now available.

Using a procedural language requires logical thinking, because the programmer must devise a detailed step-by-step procedure to accomplish the desired task. Of course, these steps in the procedure must be expressed in the particular statement types available in the given procedural language. Writing a procedural program is generally viewed as just one stage in the entire program development process. Table 3.1 provides one possible listing of the various stages in the program development process. Note that writing the program does not occur until stage four. Stage eight is debugging, which literally means to get the bugs or errors out of the program. The most difficult stages in this program development process tend to be one and two—the proper identification of the problem and the development of an algorithm, which is a step-by-step description (in English) of the actions necessary to perform the task. In stage three, the algorithm is converted into a structure chart, which is a pictorial representation of the algorithm, or pseudocode, which is an English-language-like version of the program. Throughout the entire process, logical thinking and a logical progression of steps are required to effectively use a procedural language.

Perhaps the most significant change in the procedural languages from their beginnings is that they are more amenable to **structured programming**. A structured program is one that is divided into modules or blocks, where each block has only one entry point and only one exit point. When a program is written in this form, the program logic is easy to follow and understand, and thus the maintenance and correction of such a program should be easier than for a nonstructured program. The consequence of structured programming is that few if any transfer statements (often implemented as a GO TO statement) are required to transfer control to some other portion of the program. Therefore, structured programming is often referred to as GO TO-less programming, although the modular approach is really the central feature of a structured program. The newer versions of all the procedural languages encourage highly structured programs.

BASIC. BASIC is a good place to begin a brief look at three popular procedural languages because it is the simplest of them. BASIC, which is an acronym for **B**eginner's **A**ll-purpose **S**ymbolic **I**nstruction **C**ode, was developed in the early 1960s by John Kemeny and Thomas Kurtz at Dartmouth College. Their purpose was to create an easy-to-learn, interactive language for college students that would let the students concentrate on the thought processes involved in programming rather than the syntax.

The early versions of BASIC were interpreted rather than compiled, but BASIC compilers have popped up in the past decade or two. Unfortunately, there are many versions of BASIC

Table 3.1 Stages in the Program Development Process

Stage 1	Problem identification
Stage 2	Algorithm development
Stage 3	Conversion of algorithm to computer-understandable logic, usually in form of structure chart or pseudocode
Stage 4	Program preparation
Stage 5	Keying program into computer
Stage 6	Program compilation
Stage 7	Execution of program with test data
Stage 8	Debugging process using test data
Stage 9	Use of program with actual data

developed by various computer manufacturers and software houses, and they are often incompatible. Attempts at standardization came too late, which is one reason why businesses have been loath to adopt it. Also, BASIC has historically lacked the mathematical capabilities, data management capabilities, and control structures necessary to carry out business and scientific processing efficiently. Newer versions of BASIC have addressed these shortcomings, however, as well as added the capability of developing graphical user interfaces (more on this later). These developments promise a greater role for BASIC in the future.

To illustrate BASIC, consider the following sample problem: Write a BASIC program that will find the average of a set of numbers input by the user. Use a negative number to indicate the end of the data. A BASIC program to solve this problem is shown in Figure 3.9, together with the screen dialog that occurred when the program was run on a microcomputer using a simple data set. Although the details of programming are not important, you will note that most of the instructions are quite intuitive—even the uninitiated would correctly guess the meaning of most instructions.

BASIC PROGRAM

```
10    REM  THIS PROGRAM FINDS THE AVERAGE OF A SET OF NUMBERS
20    REM      INPUT BY THE USER. A NEGATIVE NUMBER IS USED
30    REM      TO INDICATE THE END OF THE DATA.
40    PRINT "ENTER AS MANY POSITIVE NUMBERS AS YOU WISH,"
50    PRINT "WITH ONE NUMBER ENTERED PER LINE."
60    PRINT "WHEN YOU HAVE ENTERED YOUR ENTIRE SET OF NUMBERS,"
70    PRINT "ENTER A NEGATIVE NUMBER TO SIGNAL THE END OF DATA."
80    LET COUNT = 0
90    LET TOTAL = 0
100   INPUT NUMBER
110   IF NUMBER < 0 GO TO 150
120   LET TOTAL = TOTAL + NUMBER
130   LET COUNT = COUNT + 1
140   GO TO 100
150   LET AVG = TOTAL / COUNT
160   PRINT "THE AVERAGE OF YOUR NUMBERS IS"; AVG
170   PRINT "YOU ENTERED"; COUNT; "NUMBERS TOTALING"; TOTAL
180   END
```

SCREEN DIALOG WITH ABOVE BASIC PROGRAM

(Responses keyed in by user are underlined; computer responses are not underlined.)

```
OK
RUN
ENTER AS MANY POSITIVE NUMBERS AS YOU WISH,
WITH ONE NUMBER ENTERED PER LINE.
WHEN YOU HAVE ENTERED YOUR ENTIRE SET OF NUMBERS,
ENTER A NEGATIVE NUMBER TO SIGNAL THE END OF DATA.
?23
?45
?1
?78.6
?–9
THE AVERAGE OF YOUR NUMBERS IS 36.9
YOU ENTERED 4 NUMBERS TOTALING 147.6
OK
```

Figure 3.9 BASIC Program and Accompanying Screen Dialog

C. For scientific and engineering programming, the most important language is C, which was written by Dennis Ritchie and Brian Kernighan in the 1970s. C is a very powerful language, but hard to use because it is less English-like and closer to assembly language than the other procedural languages. The C programming language features flexibility of use, economy of expression, versatile data structures, modern control flow, and a rich set of operators. Because of these strengths, C is widely used in the development of microcomputer packages such as word processing, spreadsheets, and database management systems, and it is gaining on FORTRAN (more on this language later) for scientific applications. Further, C has better data management capabilities than FORTRAN and other scientific languages, so it is also being used in traditional business data processing tasks such as payroll, accounting, and sales reporting.

C was originally developed for and implemented on the UNIX operating system, and its use grew as UNIX spread. In fact, the UNIX operating system was written in C. C programs have a high level of portability: A C program can usually be transported from one computer system to another—even from a mainframe to a microcomputer—with only minor changes. C has been adopted as the standard language by many college computer science departments, and it is widely used on microcomputers. On large research computers, it is not unusual for C and FORTRAN to be the only languages ever used.

C's strengths are its control structures and its mathematical features. To illustrate, suppose that the result of one trial of a simulation experiment is an estimated profit for the firm for the next year. Twenty such trials have been made, each producing an estimated profit for the next year. As an example, write a C program to compute the mean and variance of the estimated profit figures, entering in the data from the keyboard, one estimated profit figure per line.

A C program to solve this problem is given in Figure 3.10. The statements beginning and ending with /* and */ are comments. The *for* statement near the top of the program is a C statement to control repeated execution of a set of instructions. Some of the mathematical statements are obvious, and some are not, but the program gets the job done.

```
#include<stdio.h>
/* C program to compute means and variances
of simulated profit figures */

main()
{
/* Variable declaration and initialization */
  int index;
  float sum=0.0,sumsq=0.0,trial,mean,var;
/*Control repeated execution using for statement */
  for (index = 1; index <=20; ++index)
  {
      printf("Enter a profit figure:\n");
      scanf("%f",&trial);
      sum += trial;
      sumsq += trial*trial;
}/*End control for */
  mean = sum/20.0;
  var = (sumsq/19.0) - (sum*sum)/(19.0*20.0);
  printf("Mean Value is = %f\n",mean);
  printf("Variance is = %f\n",var);
}/*End of program */
```

Figure 3.10 C Program

COBOL. COBOL, which is an acronym for **CO**mmon **B**usiness-**O**riented **L**anguage, is a language specifically devised for traditional business data processing tasks. It was developed by a computer industry committee (originally the short-range committee of the Conference on Data Systems Languages, or CODASYL; later the COBOL Committee of CODASYL) in order to provide an industry-wide common language, closely resembling ordinary English, in which business data processing procedures could be expressed. Since its inception in 1960, COBOL has gained widespread acceptance because it is standardized, has strong data management capabilities (relative to the other 3 GLs), and is relatively easy to learn and use. COBOL is by far the most popular language for programming mainframe computers for business applications.

COBOL programs are divided into four distinct divisions. The first two divisions are usually fairly short. The IDENTIFICATION DIVISION gives the program a name and provides other identifying information, and the ENVIRONMENT DIVISION describes the computer environment in which the program will be run. The ENVIRONMENT DIVISION is also the portion of the program that has to be changed to transport the program from one computer model to another. The DATA DIVISION, which is often quite long, defines the entire file structure employed in the program. The PROCEDURE DIVISION corresponds most closely to a BASIC or C program; it consists of a series of operations specified in a logical order to accomplish the desired task. The combination of all these divisions, especially the DATA DIVISION, makes COBOL programs quite long compared with other procedural languages. COBOL has been correctly described as a verbose language.

Our sample COBOL program is designed to compute and print monthly sales commissions for the salespersons of a large corporation. Each salesperson earns a 1 percent commission on the first \$50,000 in sales during a month and a 2 percent commission on all sales in excess of \$50,000.

The data have already been keyed in and are stored as a data file on a magnetic disk. One record has been prepared for each salesperson, containing the person's name and sales for the month. The output is to be a line for each salesperson, showing the name, monthly sales, and sales commission. In addition, the program is to accumulate the total commissions for all salespersons and to print this amount after all the salespersons' records have been processed.

Figure 3.11 provides a COBOL program to accomplish this processing. Again, the details are not important, but note the four divisions of the program and the sheer length of this relatively simple program.

```
1      8   12
       IDENTIFICATION DIVISION.
       PROGRAM-ID. COMMISSIONS-COMPUTE.
       AUTHOR. JOE PROGRAMMER.
       ENVIRONMENT DIVISION.
       CONFIGURATION SECTION.
       SOURCE-COMPUTER. IBM-4381.
       OBJECT-COMPUTER. IBM-4381.
       INPUT-OUTPUT SECTION.
       FILE-CONTROL.
           SELECT SALES-FILE ASSIGN DA-3380-S-IPT.
           SELECT COMMISSIONS-FILE ASSIGN DA-3380-S-RPT.
       DATA DIVISION.
       FILE SECTION.
       FD SALES-FILE
           LABEL RECORD OMITTED
           RECORD CONTAINS 80 CHARACTERS
           DATA RECORD IS IN-RECORD.
       01  IN-RECORD                        PICTURE X(80).
       FD  COMMISSIONS-FILE
           LABEL RECORD OMITTED
            RECORD CONTAINS 132 CHARACTERS
           DATA RECORD IS PRINT-RECORD.
       01  PRINT-RECORD                PICTURE X(132).
        WORKING-STORAGE SECTION.
       01  SALES-RECORD.
           05  NAME                    PICTURE A(30).
           05  FILLER                  PICTURE X(10).
           05  SALES                   PICTURE 9(8)V99.
           05  FILLER                  PICTURE X(30).
       01 COMMISSION-RECORD.
           05  FILLER                  PICTURE X(10).
           05  NAME-OUT                PICTURE A(30).
           05  FILLER                  PICTURE X(10).
           05  SALES-OUT               PICTURE $$$,$$$,$$$.99.
           05  FILLER                  PICTURE X(10).
           05  COMMISSION              PICTURE $$$$,$$$.99.
           05  FILLER                  PICTURE X(47).
       77  TEMP-COMMISSION             PICTURE 9(6)V99.
       77  TOTAL-COMMISSIONS           PICTURE 9(10)V99  VALUE 0.
       77  TOTAL-COMM-EDITED           PICTURE $$,$$$,$$$,$$$.99.
       01  MORE-DATA                   PICTURE X          VALUE 'Y'.
           88   THERE-IS-MORE-DATA                       VALUE 'Y'.
           88   THERE-IS-NO-MORE-DATA                     VALUE 'N'.
```

Figure 3.11 COBOL Program

```
1      8   12
       PROCEDURE DIVISION.
       MAIN-CONTROL.
           PERFORM INITIALIZATION.
           PERFORM READ-PROCESS-PRINT UNTIL THERE-IS-NO-MORE-DATA.
           PERFORM COMPLETE.
           STOP RUN.
       INITIALIZATION.
           OPEN INPUT SALES-FILE, OUTPUT COMMISSIONS-FILE.
           MOVE SPACES TO COMMISSION-RECORD.
       READ-PROCESS-PRINT.
           READ SALES-FILE INTO SALES-RECORD
               AT END MOVE 'N' TO MORE-DATA.
           IF THERE-IS-MORE-DATA
               MOVE NAME TO NAME-OUT
               MOVE SALES TO SALES-OUT
               IF SALES GREATER 50000
                  COMPUTE TEMP-COMMISSION = .01*50000+.02* (SALES-50000)
               ELSE
                  COMPUTE TEMP-COMMISSION = .01*SALES
               MOVE TEMP-COMMISSION TO COMMISSION
               WRITE PRINT-RECORD FROM COMMISSION-RECORD
                  AFTER ADVANCING 1 LINES
               ADD TEMP-COMMISSION TO TOTAL-COMMISSIONS.
       COMPLETE.
           MOVE TOTAL-COMMISSIONS TO TOTAL-COMM-EDITED.
           DISPLAY 'TOTAL-COMMISSIONS ARE' TOTAL-COMM-EDITED.
           CLOSE SALES-FILE, COMMISSIONS-FILE.
```

Figure 3.11 COBOL Program *(continued)*

Other Procedural Languages. There are many other procedural languages in addition to BASIC, C, and COBOL. The granddaddy of the procedural languages is FORTRAN. Originally introduced by IBM in the mid-1950s, it quickly became the standard for scientific and engineering programming. FORTRAN is still widely used today, in good part because of the significant investment made in the development of FORTRAN scientific software.

PL/1 (Programming Language One) was developed by IBM in the mid-1960s as a language to do both mathematical and business-oriented processing. IBM hoped that PL/1 would replace both FORTRAN and COBOL, but it obviously did not. Some companies switched from COBOL to PL/1 and have remained staunch PL/1 users, but their numbers are limited.

In the 1980s, PASCAL was often the favorite language of college computer science departments, and it was widely used on microcomputers. PASCAL has greater mathematical capabilities than BASIC, and it handles data files better than FORTRAN. However, PASCAL never caught on outside of universities except as a microcomputer language, and its popularity has now waned in favor of C.

ADA is a language developed under the direction of the U.S. Department of Defense as a potential replacement for COBOL and FORTRAN. It was first introduced in 1980 and does have strong scientific capabilities. However, it was not widely adopted outside the federal government. ADA has not disappeared, but its use has diminished even within the Department of Defense.

Special-purpose procedural languages have also been developed. For instance, SIMSCRIPT, GPSS, and SLAM are all special-purpose languages designed to help simulate the behavior of a system, such as a production line in a factory. Perl is a special-purpose language used primarily for writing Common Gateway Interface (CGI) scripts for World Wide Web applications. Our listing of procedural languages is incomplete, but it is sufficient for our purposes. The bottom line is that these workhorse languages are still important, because they are the primary languages used by the majority of computer professionals.

Fourth Generation Languages

There is no generally accepted definition of a fourth generation language, but there are certain characteristics that most 4 GLs share. They generally employ an English-like syntax, and they are predominantly nonprocedural in nature. With a 4 GL, the user merely gives a precise statement of what is to be accomplished, not how to do it (as would be done for a procedural language). For the most part, then, the order in which instructions are given in a 4 GL is unimportant. In addition, 4 GLs do not require the user to manage memory locations in the program like 3 GLs, resulting in less complex programs.

The 4 GLs employ very high-level instructions not present in 3 GLs, and thus 4 GL programs tend to require significantly fewer instructions than their 3 GL counterparts. This in turn means that 4 GL programs are shorter, easier to write, easier to modify, easier to read and understand, and less error-prone than 3 GL programs. Fourth generation languages are sometimes called very-high-level languages in contrast to the high-level third generation languages.

The roots of fourth generation languages date back to 1967, with the introduction of RAMIS (originally developed by Mathematica, Inc., and now sold by Computer Associates as CA-Ramis). Another early entry that is still is use today is FOCUS (from Information Builders, Inc.). Initially, these products were primarily available on commercial time-sharing networks (like Telenet and Tymnet), but direct sales of the products to customers took off around 1980. By the mid-1980s, FOCUS was estimated to command about 20 percent of the market, with RAMIS following with 16 percent (Jenkins and Bordoloi, 1986).

In the late 1980s and early 1990s, the 4 GL market became even more splintered as new versions of the early 4 GLs were rolled out and a wide variety of new products entered the marketplace. The emphasis of the products appearing in the 1990s was on *portability*—the ability of the 4 GL to work with different hardware platforms and operating systems, the ability to work over different types of networks, and the ability to work with different database management systems (Lindholm, 1992). In the late 1990s and early 2000s, the 4 GLs changed again. First, most 4 GLs added a Web interface so that they could be used from a PC without requiring any special software on the PC. Second, and even more important, the focus of these products shifted to **business intelligence** and the 4 GL label essentially disappeared. Today's business intelligence software tools are designed to answer queries relating to the business by analyzing data (often massive quantities of data), thereby providing "intelligence" to the business that will help it become more competitive. Of course, this focus on business intelligence is not that different from the focus of 4 GLs in the past; it really is an evolution, not a drastic change.

Some of the 4 GL products are full-function, general-purpose languages like CA-Ramis and FOCUS and have the complete functionality necessary to handle any application program. Thus, they are direct competitors with the 3 GLs. Other 4 GLs were created to handle a particular class of applications, such as statistics, decision support, or financial modeling. For example, SAS (from SAS Institute) began as a limited-purpose 4 GL focusing on decision support and modeling. SAS Business Intelligence has now expanded to an integrated suite of software for business intelligence in an enterprise, with extensive capabilities in data access, data management, data analysis, and data presentation. Among the more popular business intelligence packages today are WebFOCUS (a Web-based, business-intelligence-oriented version of FOCUS), Cognos Business Intelligence Series 7, Brio Intelligence, MicroStrategy 7i, and Microsoft Data Analyzer (MacVittie, 2002). To gain a better perspective on the nature of a 4 GL, we will take a brief look at one of the most popular and enduring 4 GLs, FOCUS.

FOCUS. FOCUS is an extremely versatile general-purpose 4 GL. Versions of FOCUS are available to operate under the control of all the major operating systems mentioned earlier in this chapter. Information Builders, Inc. describes FOCUS as a "host-based reporting" system and as "the corporate standard for enterprise business information systems," while WebFOCUS is described as "the standard for enterprise business intelligence" (Information Builders Web site, 2003). FOCUS consists of a large number of integrated tools and facilities, including a FOCUS database management system, a data dictionary/directory, a query language and report generator, an interactive text editor and screen painter, and a statistical analysis package. Of particular importance, FOCUS has the ability to process data managed both by its own DBMS (FOCUS files) and by an external DBMS or external file system (non-FOCUS files). We will concentrate on perhaps the most widely used of the FOCUS capabilities, the query language and report generator.

Consider the following problem situation. A telephone company wishes to prepare a report for its internal management and its regulatory body showing the difference between customer bills under two different bill computation approaches. One of these bill computation methods is the traditional flat rate based on the size of the local calling area; the other is so-called measured service, in which the customer pays a very small flat rate for a minimum number of calls and then pays so much per call (21 cents in the example) for calls above this minimum. Massive FOCUS data files already exist containing all the necessary raw data for an extended test period, with each record including customer number, area, type of service, number of calls during the time period, and the length of the time period (in months). The telephone company wants a report for present flat rate customers in area two only, showing the difference between the two billing approaches for each customer and the total difference over all flat rate customers in area two.

Figure 3.12 shows a FOCUS program (more commonly called a FOCEXEC) that can produce the desired report. As with our 3 GL examples, the individual instructions are not important, but let us consider the major pieces of the program. After some initial comments, the program begins with the TABLE command, which calls the query/report generator function of FOCUS. The data file is called TEST. Up to the first END, the instructions sum the variables TOT_CALLS and MONTHS for each customer in each area

FOCUS PROGRAM

(FOCEXEC)

```
-*
-*      THIS FOCEXEC GIVES THE BILL DIFFERENCES FOR ALL
-*      CUSTOMERS WITH FLAT RATE SERVICE IN AREA TWO, AS WELL
-*      AS THE TOTAL OF THESE BILL DIFFERENCES.
-*
TABLE FILE TEST
SUM TOT_CALLS MONTHS AND COMPUTE
AVG_CALLS/D12.2=TOT_CALLS/MONTHS;
BY CUST BY AREA IF SERV CONTAINS FL
ON TABLE HOLD AS BDATA
END
DEFINE FILE BDATA
FRATE/D4.2=IF AREA CONTAINS 'ON' THEN 12.10
             ELSE IF AREA CONTAINS 'TW' THEN 13.40
             ELSE 14.51;
MRATE/D4.2=7.35;
K/I1=IF AVG_CALLS GT 30 THEN 1 ELSE 0;
MESSRU/D12.2=(AVG_CALLS–30)*.21*K;
BILL_DIFF/D12.2=FRATE–(MRATE+MESSRU);
END
TABLE FILE BDATA
HEADING CENTER
"2004—TWO"
"SERV = FL"
SUM BILL_DIFF NOPRINT MONTHS NOPRINT AND COMPUTE
      AVG_BILL_DIFF/D12.2=BILL_DIFF/MONTHS;
IF AREA EQ TWO ON TABLE COLUMN–TOTAL BY AREA BY CUST
END
```

FOCUS OUTPUT

```
                    2004—TWO
                    SERV = FL
   AREA   CUST   AVG_BILL_DIFF
   TWO    4122        4.87
          4125        8.28
          4211       -5.33
            *           *
            *           *
            *           *
   TOTAL            2,113.88
```

Figure 3.12 FOCUS Program and Output

if the type of service is FL, and then divide one sum by the other to get an average number of calls per month (AVG_CALLS). The DEFINE FILE BDATA computes the rates by the two approaches as well as the difference between the two rates, storing these computed values in the temporary file BDATA. Finally, the TABLE FILE BDATA computes the average bill difference, AV_BILL_DIFF, and prints the report shown at the bottom of Figure 3.12.

Note that the FOCUS program is not particularly intuitive, but it is quite short for a reasonably complex problem. It is also largely nonprocedural in that the order of most statements does not make any difference. Of course, the conditional IFs and BYs must be appropriately placed.

Future Developments. The fourth generation languages are evolving even more rapidly than those in the third generation, particularly with the addition of easy-to-use business intelligence options and easy-to-interpret graphical output and colorful displays. Furthermore, with the increasing capabilities of today's computers, the lack of efficiency of execution of 4 GL programs vis-à-vis 3 GL programs is of little concern. For these reasons and others mentioned earlier (increasing computer sophistication of managers, continuing backlogs in the information systems department), the use of 4 GLs will continue to grow. The strongest element of growth will come from end-user computing, but information systems departments will also shift towards 4 GLs, especially for infrequently used applications.

Fifth generation languages will also emerge in the twenty-first century, although it is too soon to be specific about their form and functionality. One possibility is that the fifth generation languages will be **natural languages**, in which users write their programs in ordinary English (or something very close to it). Users will need little or no training to program using a natural language; they simply write (or perhaps verbalize) what they want done without regard for syntax or form (other than that incorporated in ordinary English). At present there are no true natural languages, but some restricted natural language products have been developed that can be used with a variety of database management systems and 4 GLs. Commercial developments in the natural language area have, however, been slower than expected.

Markup Languages

Before turning to object-oriented programming languages, we should mention the markup languages, which are neither 3 GLs, 4 GLs, nor OOP languages. Currently the best known of the markup languages is **HTML**, or **Hypertext Markup Language**. HTML is used to create World Wide Web pages, and it consists of special codes inserted in the text to indicate headings, bold-faced text, italics, where images or photographs are to be placed, and links to other Web pages, among other things. VRML, or virtual reality modeling language, provides the specifications for displaying three-dimensional objects on the Web; it is the 3-D equivalent of HTML. HTML and the other markup languages are not really programming languages in the sense that we have been using this term; they are simply codes to describe the way the completed product (the Web page, the 3-D object, and so on) is to appear.

XML, or **eXtensible Markup Language**, is destined to become even more important than HTML. XML is used to facilitate data interchange among applications on the Web; it is really a metalanguage standard for specifying a document markup language based on plain-text tags. Let's see what this means. XML was developed by the W3C, the World Wide Web Consortium, whose goal is to develop open standards for the Web. Other W3C standards are **HTTP** (**Hypertext Transfer Protocol**) and HTML.

XML is a pared-down version of SGML (standard generalized markup language), which was itself developed by the International Standards Organization (ISO) in 1986. HTML is another subset of SGML with which we are more familiar. Both HTML and XML employ plain-text tags (i.e., made up of ordinary letters, numbers, and special characters) as a way to "mark up" a document. However, the similarities between HTML and XML end there. HTML tags tell a Web browser how to display various elements on a Web page, while XML tags identify the nature of the associated data. For example, one XML tag might identify a customer name as a customer name, another might identify a customer's address as an address, another might identify a number as a product number, and yet another might identify the quantity sold as the quantity sold. Entire sets of XML tags are being defined for particular industries and situations.

The key is that XML is a metalanguage: For each industry or unique situation, a set of XML tags can be created to identify the data elements employed in that situation. XML makes it relatively easy to identify and share data in order to achieve data integration across organizational boundaries. XML is "extensible" in that new tags can be defined as needed, and XML allows the separation of the presentation of the data from the data themselves. Through the use of text tags, for example, a company can identify specific pieces of data on a Web page (such as a customer order) and can extract the desired data for use in another application. It seems likely that the use of XML tags in Internet documents might eventually replace electronic data interchange, or EDI. EDI depends upon carefully designed, rather cumbersome formatting of the data to be exchanged; XML replaces that formatting with customized tags. Thus, XML provides an easy and effective way to identify and share data.

An XML specification (like HTML) consists of tags (enclosed in angle brackets: < >). However, XML tags are intended to convey the meaning of data, not the presentation format. For example, an HTML tag such as <H1>This data to be displayed in Heading 1 format</H1> tells the browser to display data using the Heading 1 format. By contrast, the XML tags given below are an attempt to represent the meaning of the data related to games.

```
<Game type="College Football" date="10/11/2003">
    Indiana vs. Northwestern. This was an overtime game.
    <Score team="Indiana">31</Score>
    <Score team="Northwestern">37</Score>
</Game>
```

The top-level tag <Game> specifies that what follows are details about a game. The attributes for Game (type and date) provide specific details about the information that follows. The end of details about the game is indicated by the</Game> tag. One of the key features of XML is its ability to have nested tags, i.e., tags within tags. The "Score" tags provide an example of how one can use this feature to add meaning to the information contained within the <Game></Game> tags.

XML tags (unlike HTML tags) are not fixed. Programmers can use any tags that suit an application's needs. However, all applications that are going to process a given set of data need to understand and agree upon the tag names they intend to use. It is important to realize that data specified using XML do not provide any indication as to how to display the data. The data display for a set of XML documents is controlled by the use of XSL (extensible style language) specifications. These specifications indicate how to display XML data in different formats, such as HTML.

Object-Oriented Programming

In the early years of the twenty-first century, the hottest programming languages (at least in terms of interest and experimentation) are not 4 GLs or natural languages, but **object-oriented programming** (**OOP**) languages. OOP is not new (it dates back to the 1970s), but it has received renewed attention because of the increased power of workstations and the excellent GUIs that have been developed for these workstations. OOP requires more computing power than traditional languages, and a graphical interface provides a natural way to work with the OOP objects. OOP is neither a 3 GL nor a 4 GL, but an entirely new paradigm for programming with roots in both the procedural 3 GLs and the nonprocedural 4 GLs. Creating the objects in OOP is somewhat akin to 3 GL programming in that the procedures (called methods) are embedded in the objects, while putting the objects together to create an application is much closer to the use of a 4 GL.

The fundamental ideas of OOP are to create and program various objects only once and then store them for reuse later in the current application or in other applications. These objects might be items used to create the user interface, like a text box or a check box, or they might represent an entity in the organization, such as Employee or Factory.

One of the first OOP languages was Smalltalk, a language developed by researchers at Xerox to create a way that children could learn how to program. Smalltalk never really took off as a children's programming tool, but it was used marginally in the business world. Managers thought programming would become more efficient if programmers only had to create objects once, and then were able to reuse them in later programs. This would create a "toolbox" from which programmers could just grab the tool they needed, insert it into the program, fine-tune it to meet the specific needs of the program, and be done.

The most prominent OOP languages today are C++, an object-oriented version of the original C language, and Java, a platform-independent language developed by Sun Microsystems. C++ is a superset of the C language, in that any C program can also be a C++ program, but C++ introduces the power of reusable objects, or classes. Java is a general-purpose programming language well-suited for use on the World Wide Web, and it has quickly gained widespread acceptance by most vendors and by programmers everywhere.

Java programs come in three flavors: stand-alone applications, applets, and servlets (see the section of this chapter entitled "Languages for Developing Web Applications"). Stand-alone applications are run on your desktop, whereas **applets** are programs that are downloaded from a Web server and run on your Web browser. Servlets are programs that reside in and are run on a Web server. Java programs are designed to run on a **Java virtual machine**, a self-contained operating environment (including a Java interpreter) that behaves as if it is a separate computer. Such an operating environment exists for most operating systems, including UNIX, Linux, Macintosh OS, and Windows, and this virtual machine concept implements the "write once, run anywhere" portability that is Java's goal. The Java virtual machine has no access to the host operating system (whatever it is), which has two advantages:

- *System independence.* A Java application will run exactly the same regardless of the hardware and software involved.

- *Security.* Because the Java virtual machine has no contact with the host operating system, there is almost no possibility of a Java application damaging other files or applications.

Other object-oriented languages that are gaining prominence are those that are part of the .NET framework from Microsoft. Introduced in early 2002, the .NET framework allows programmers to write programs in a variety of OOP languages, including Visual Basic .NET (abbreviated as VB.NET), C# (pronounced "C sharp"), and J# (pronounced "J sharp") (see the sidebar entitled "J2EE vs. .NET").

As an example of an OOP program, consider Figure 3.13(A), written in Visual Basic 6.0. It is important to note that Visual Basic 6.0 is actually considered to be a pseudo-OOP language, because it supports most, but not all, features of an OOP language (see below for these features). Visual Basic 6.0 is a very popular language for developing applications. Figure 3.13(A) is a simple Visual Basic program designed to compute the average, highest, and lowest grades of a college student. Figure 3.13(B) shows the screen layout (GUI interface) designed for this application, using Visual Basic's click, drag, and drop tools. The user enters his or her grades in Chemistry, Calculus, English, and History, and the program computes the average, highest, and lowest grades. Note that the program itself looks very much like a 3 GL program, while the screen design becomes a much simpler task in Visual Basic (or any OOP language) than in a 3 GL.

To work with an OOP language, one must think in terms of objects. The programmer must start by defining those entities that are referred to as classes. A class is the blueprint or specifications for creating an object. To work with the class, we must create an instance of the class, which is then referred to as the object. An object has attributes, or properties, that can be set by the programmer, or even by the user when the program is running, if the programmer desires. An object also has methods—predefined actions taken by the object. Objects can also respond to events, or actions taken upon the object. Objects, properties, methods, and events can all be a bit difficult to comprehend at first, so let's use an example that might be more familiar to you—the family dog.

We can think of a dog and identify various attributes, which programmers call properties, to differentiate one dog from another dog. Each dog has height, weight, color, coat thickness, eye color, snout shape, and many other features that might differ from other dogs (see Figure 3.14 left). Each of these properties thus has a value. Each dog, independent of its property values, also does several actions; programmers call these methods. Eat, sleep, run, and fetch are examples of these methods. Dogs also respond to several actions done to them; these are called events. Hearing their name called, being petted, or even being

J2EE VS. .NET

Java 2 Enterprise Edition (**J2EE**) and **.NET** are two competing frameworks proposed by an alliance of companies led by Sun Microsystems and Microsoft, respectively, as platforms for application development on the Web using the object-oriented programming paradigm.

J2EE, as the name suggests, is based on the Java language. In fact, J2EE is not the name of a product. Instead, it is a collection of 13 different Java-based technologies put together in a particular fashion. Thus, theoretically it is possible to buy each of these technologies from different vendors and mix-and-match them as needed. In practice, however, it is typical for a company to buy a product that implements the J2EE specification from a single vendor. Popular choices in this regard include Websphere from IBM, Weblogic from BEA, and SunOne from Sun. One of the key advantages of J2EE is that because everything is Java-based, the products can be run on a variety of platforms, e.g., Windows, UNIX, and Linux.

By contrast, applications written for Microsoft's .NET framework are designed to run only on the Windows platform. However, unlike J2EE, where one is limited to using Java as the programming language, in .NET a programmer can choose among a variety of languages such as VB.NET, C#, J# (a variant of Java), and even C++. In fact, within a single application a programmer can, for example, choose to write portions of the program in VB.NET and others in C#.

There has been a lot of debate as to which framework is better. The answer depends on several tangible and intangible factors. In the end, we think that the decision regarding which technology to adopt will be based largely on the following factors:

- *Available programmer expertise*
- *Complexity of the Web application* For large applications that have significant scalability and security requirements, the J2EE framework provides the flexibility needed to achieve the desired architectural and performance goals.
- *Degree of Web services support needed* Both J2EE and .NET are quite comparable in terms of their support for Web services standards including XML. The difference lies in the fact that support for XML is an integral part of the .NET framework, whereas at this time XML support has to be "bolted on" in J2EE.

kicked are examples of events to which the dog responds (see Figure 3.14). The code in Figure 3.15 shows an example of a class called Dog, written in Java.

We said that to work with a class, we must create an instance of the class called an object—this process is called instantiation. From our class definition of a dog (Figure 3.15), we know that it has various properties, methods, and events. For a family without a pet, however, all that family has is a class definition. When the family goes to the animal shelter to rescue a furry friend, they now have an instance of the class, or an actual dog.

The code in Figure 3.16 shows how a Dog can be instantiated from the class definition in Figure 3.15. We instantiate a new Dog and then call the display method in the newly created dog object.

Objects also have two important features that make them even more useful. One of them is encapsulation. Encapsulation allows the object's creator to hide some (or even all) of the object's inner workings from other programmers or users. This keeps the object's integrity very high, exposing only parts of the object that will not cause the object to crash. Let's apply this to our dog example. For a dog to sur-

```
Private Sub btnCalculate_Click()
' Declare variables
Dim sClasses(3) As Single
Dim sMean, sHigh, sLow As Single, x As Integer
' Initialize variables
sClasses(0) = CSng (txtCalculus.Text)
sClasses(1) = CSng (txtChemistry.Text)
sClasses(2) = CSng (txtHistory.Text)
sClasses(3) = CSng (txtEnglish.Text)
sMean = 0
sHigh = 0
sLow = 100
' Do calculations
For x = 0 To 3
        sMean = sMean + sClasses (x) / 4
        If sClasses (x) > sHigh Then
                sHigh = sClasses (x)
        End If

        If sClasses (x) < sLow Then
                sLow = sClasses (x)
        End If
Next x
' Write out results
txtStatistics.Text = "Your average grade is" & sMean & vbCrLf
txtStatistics.Text = txtStatistics.Text & "Your highest grade is" & sHigh & vbCrLf
txtStatistics.Text = txtStatistics.Text & "Your lowest grade is" & sLow
End Sub
----------------------------
Private Sub btnClear_Click()
' Clears the contents of the text boxes
txtChemistry.Text = " "
txtCalculus.Text = " "
txtEnglish.Text = " "
txtHistory.Text = " "
txtStatistics.Text = " "
End Sub
----------------------------
Private Sub Exit_Click()
' Quits the program
End
End Sub
```

Figure 3.13(A) Visual Basic Program

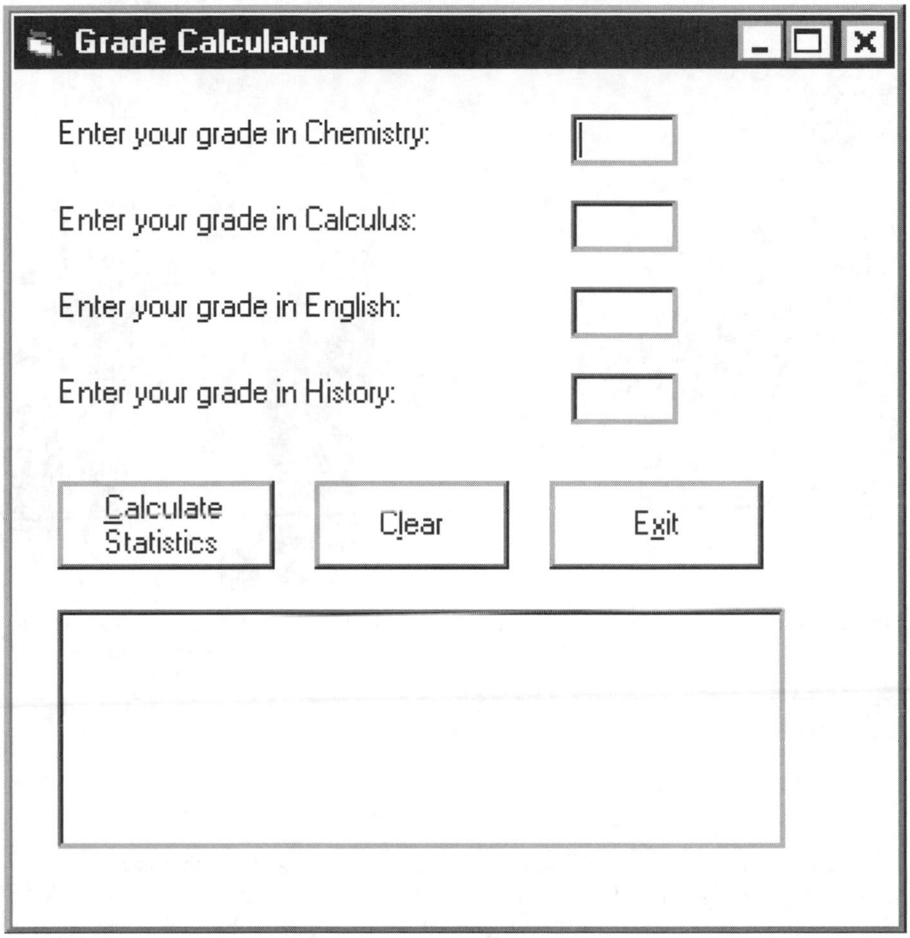

Figure 3.13(B) Visual Basic Screen Layout

vive, it needs vitamins, nutrients, proteins, and carbohydrates. These items must get into the dog's bloodstream and be carried to the muscles and organs that need them. However, we as dog owners do not try to inject the items directly into the bloodstream or the organs; we merely buy dog food at the store and set it out for our pet. The dog eats the food and digests it, and the nutrients are carried to their proper places. You could thus say that the digestive system of the dog has been encapsulated. We do not need to know how it works, nor in most cases do we even care. It has been created to work the way it is, although if it were to start behaving incorrectly, we might take the dog to see a programmer—the veterinarian!

The second feature is called inheritance. Inheritance means that we can create subclasses and superclasses from classes, and they then automatically have properties, methods, and events of their related class. For example, if I have a class called animal, I know that dog should be a subclass of animal. A dog is a type of animal (not the other way around) and should take on the properties, methods, and events of the class animal. Visual Basic does not support inheritance, which is the primary reason that it is not a true OOP language.

Object-oriented programming is one of the most sought-after skills in the job market of the early twenty-first century. Despite OOP's supposed natural way of thinking about the world, it is difficult to find good object-oriented programmers. Older programmers who learned programming in structured languages like C and COBOL often do not want to be retrained, and some younger programmers do not like OOP languages because they can be very difficult to learn. It can also take longer to develop an object-oriented program than a structured program, and objects must be reused several times before any overall cost and time savings are realized.

Languages for Developing Web Applications

The emergence of the Internet has led to the increasing need for developing Web-based applications. Although

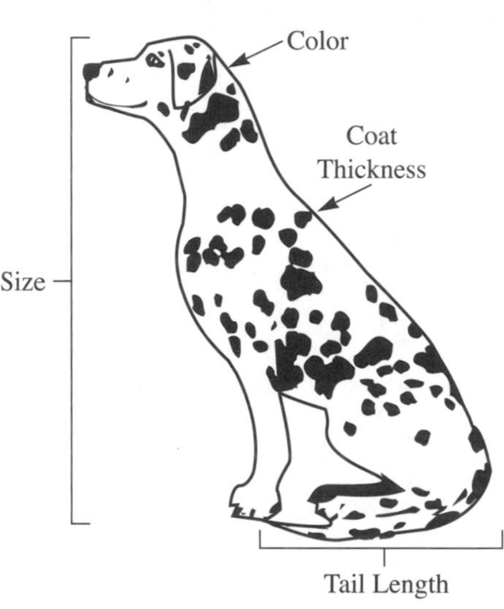

All are examples of properties

The dog wags its tail in response to an *event*, being petted

Figure 3.14 A Dog as an Object

these applications range in complexity from very simple applications that allow user registration to applications that enable business-to-business transactions, they all have the following things in common:

- All Web applications are based on an n-tier architecture (where n >= 2). The typical system consists of three tiers: a user interface (client), a Web or application server, and a database server.
- The user interacts with the system (on his or her machine) through Web-based forms. Data entered into the forms are sent to the server, where a server application program processes them. This program might write parts of this information to a database (residing on a different machine).

The most common user interface encountered by users is an HTML form. This form might either be static or dynamic (i.e., produced by a program). An example of a dynamic HTML form that can be used to order grocery items is shown at the top of Figure 3.17. The ASP.NET code needed to generate this page is shown below the HTML form. Please note that the user simply enters the heading, the labels, the items in the list, and the possible values of these items, and the code is automatically generated by Active Server Pages (ASP). The code is a mixture of general HTML tags and some tags that are specific to ASP.NET, e.g., asp:DropDownList. The *runat* portion of the form specifies that a program on the server that generated this page should be called when the user clicks on the button of type Submit (labeled Calculate Cost) on the form. The data from each of the user interface elements are passed on to the program on the server.

The program that processes the data is shown in Figure 3.18. This program retrieves the data from the form and stores the data items in session variables named item, state, and qty, respectively. After this, the program redirects control to the next page that needs to be displayed—that is, confirm.aspx. However, before this page is loaded, the load function shown in Figure 3.19 is called. Here, we retrieve the values stored in the session and assign them to various elements of our page to be displayed. The result is the new page shown in Figure 3.19.

The example shown in Figures 3.17 through 3.19 is written using ASP.NET. All Web application development technologies or server-side programming environments operate using a similar model in that they all provide mechanisms for generating dynamic Web pages, encoding complex business logic on the server side as well as reading and writing to a variety of database management systems. Common examples of server-side programming

```
public class Dog{
    double height;
    double weight;
    String color;

        public Dog (double someheight, double someweight, String somecolor)
    {
        height = sometype;
        weight = someweight;
        color = somecolor;
    }

        //methods
        public void sleep() {
        //code to make a dog sleep will go here
        }
        public void run() {
        //code to make a dog run will go here
        }

        public Object fetch() {
        //code to make a dog fetch will go here
        //this method will return the item fetched
        }
    public void display()
    {
    System.out.println("The Height of Animal is: " + height);
    System.out.println("The Weight of Animal is: " + weight);
    System.out.println("The Color of the Animal is: " + color);
    }
}
```

Figure 3.15 Java Class Called Dog

environments are CGI using Perl, Java Servlets and Java Server Pages (JSP), Microsoft's Active Server Pages (ASP, ASP.NET), and Allaire's ColdFusion. Currently, Java Servlets/JSP (for all platforms, especially UNIX and Linux) and ASP/ASP.NET (primarily for Windows) are the preferred technologies for developing e-business solutions.

```
public class AnimalTest
{
    public static void main(String args[])
    {
        Animal myanimal;

        myanimal = new Dog("10.5", 30,"Black");
        myanimal.display();
    }
}
```

Figure 3.16 Java Instantiation of a New Dog

Database Management Systems

A **database management system (DBMS)** is support software that is used to create, manage, and protect organizational data. A database management system works with the operating system to store and modify data and to make data accessible in a variety of meaningful and authorized ways.

A DBMS adds significant data management capabilities to those provided by the operating system. The goal is to allow a computer programmer to select data from disk files by referring to the content of records, not their physical location. This makes programming easier, more productive, and less error-prone. Also, this allows systems professionals

WHY IS OBJECT TECHNOLOGY VALUABLE?

One reason that the term "object oriented," or "OO," is often confusing is that it is applied so widely. We hear about object-oriented user interfaces, object-oriented programming languages, object-oriented design methodologies, object-oriented databases, even object-oriented business modeling. A reasonable question might be: Is this term used because OO has become a synonym for "modern and good," or is there really some substantial common thread across all these object-oriented things?

I believe that there is such a common thread, and that it makes the object paradigm useful in all these diverse areas. Essentially it is a focus on the "thing" first and the action second. It has been described as a noun-verb way of looking at things, rather than verb-noun. At the user interface, first the object is selected, then the action to be performed on the object. At the programming language level, an object is asked to perform some action, rather than a procedure called to "do its thing" on a set of parameters. At the design level, the "things" in the application are defined, then the behavior (actions) of these things is described.

Object technology provides significant potential value in three areas, all closely related: productivity, maintainability, and paradigm consistency. We must change application development from a people-intensive discipline to an asset-intensive discipline. That is, we must encourage and make feasible the widespread reuse of software components. It is exactly in this "reusable component" arena that object technology can contribute significantly. The aspects of object technology that help in reuse are encapsulation (which allows the developer to see a component as a "black box" with specified behavior) and inheritance (which encourages the reuse of code to implement identical behavior among different kinds of objects).

[Radin, 1996]

responsible for database design to reorganize the physical organization of data without affecting the logic of programs, which significantly reduces maintenance requirements. These objectives are given the umbrella term *data independence*. For example, a DBMS would allow a programmer to specify retrieval of a customer record based only on knowledge of the customer's name or number. Furthermore, once the customer record is retrieved, a DBMS would allow direct reference to any of the customer's related order or shipment records (even if these records are relocated or changed).

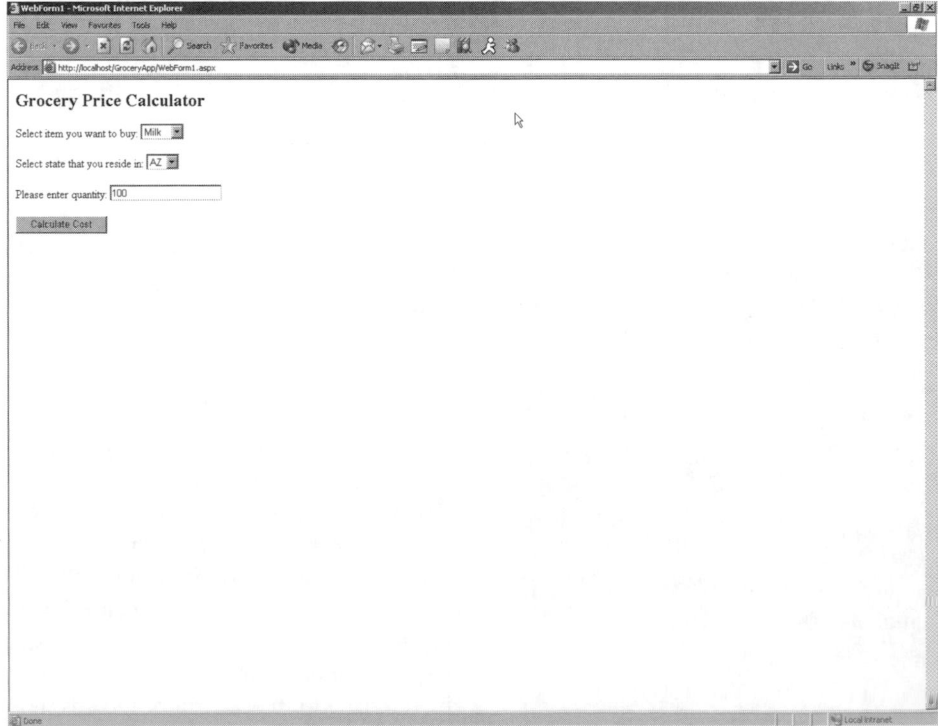

Figure 3.17 Grocery Store HTML Form and Accompanying Code

```
<%@ Page Language="vb" AutoEventWireup="false" Codebehind="WebForm1.aspx.vb"
Inherits="GroceryApp.WebForm1"%>
<!DOCTYPE HTML PUBLIC "-//W3C//DTD HTML 4.0 Transitional//EN">
<HTML>
        <HEAD>
                <title>WebForm1</title>
                <meta name="GENERATOR" content="Microsoft Visual Studio.NET 7.0">
                <meta name="CODE_LANGUAGE" content="Visual Basic 7.0">
                <meta name="vs_defaultClientScript" content="JavaScript">
                <meta name="vs_targetSchema" content="http://schemas.microsoft.com/intellisense/ie5">
        </HEAD>
        <body>
                <form id="Form1" method="post" runat="server">
                        <P>
                                <asp:Label id="Label1" runat="server" Width="340px" Height="40px" Font-
                                Bold="True" Font-Size="Large">Grocery Price Calculator</asp:Label></P>
                        <P> </P>
                        <P>
                                <asp:Label id="label3" runat="server" Width="242px">Select item you want
                                to buy:</asp:Label>
                                <asp:DropDownList id="item" runat="server">
                                        <asp:ListItem Value="Eggs">Eggs</asp:ListIte m>
                                        <asp:ListItem Value="Milk">Milk</asp:ListItem>
                                        <asp:ListItem Value="OJ">OJ</asp:ListItem>
                                </asp:DropDownList></P>
                        <P> </P>
                        <P>
                                <asp:Label id="label2" runat="server" Width="242px">Select state that you reside
                                in:</asp:Label>
                                <asp:DropDownList id="state" runat="server">
                                        <asp:ListItem Value="IN">IN</asp:ListItem>
                                        <asp:ListItem Value="AZ">AZ</asp:ListItem>
                                        <asp:ListItem Value="IL">IL</asp:ListItem>
                                </asp:DropDownList></P>
                        <P> </P>
                        <P>
                                <asp:Label id="Label4" runat="server" Width="164px">Please enter
                                quantity:</asp:Label>
                                <asp:TextBox id="Qty" runat="server"></asp:TextBox></P>
                        <P> </P>
                        <P>
                                <asp:Button id="Submit" runat="server" Width="183px" Text="Calculate
                                Cost"></asp:Button></P>
                </form>
        </body>
</HTML>
```

Figure 3.17 Grocery Store HTML Form and Accompanying Code *(continued)*

Thus, a DBMS allows access to data based on content (e.g., customer number) as well as by association (e.g., orders for a given customer).

A **database** is a shared collection of logically related data that is organized to meet the needs of an organization. A related term is a *data warehouse*, a very large database or collection of databases, to be considered in Chapter 6. A DBMS is the software that manages a database. A DBMS is a very complex and often costly software package, ranging in price from under $500 for a personal computer product to $200,000 or more for a DBMS on a large mainframe computer.

Note that the **relational DBMS** is the most common type of DBMS. With the relational model, the data are arranged into simple tables, and records are related by storing common data in each of the associated tables. Many DBMS products use the relational model, including Microsoft Access and SQL Server from Microsoft

```
Public Sub submit_Click(s As Object, e As EventArgs)

Session.add("item", item.SelectedItem.Text)
Session.add("state", state.SelectedItem.Text)
Session.add("qty", Qty.Text)
Response.sendRedirect("confirm.aspx")

End Sub
```

Figure 3.18 Program to Process Data from Grocery Store HTML Form

Corporation, Paradox by Corel, DB2 by IBM, and Ingres by Computer Associates.

File Organization. The computer files are stored on the disk using the file organization provided by the operating system and special structures added by the DBMS. Although their exact details can be treated as a "black box" in most cases, it is useful to know some of the terminology and choices. Three general kinds of file organizations exist: sequential, direct, and indexed (see Figure 3.20).

A **sequential file organization** arranges the records so that they are physically adjacent and in order by some sort key (usually the unique key that distinguishes each record from another). Thus, a sequential customer file would have

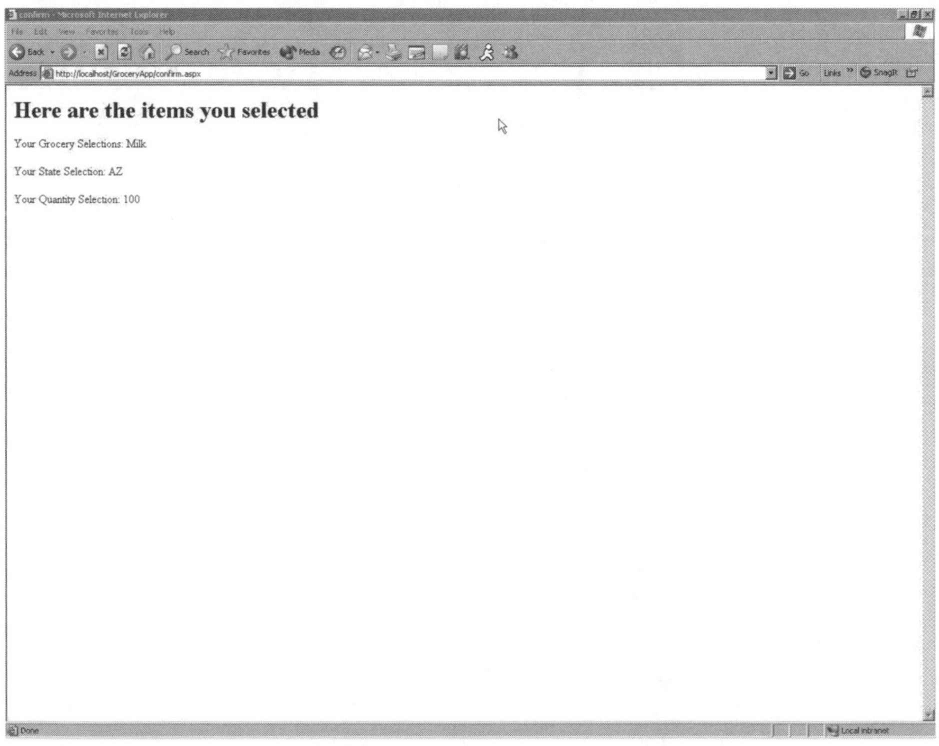


```
Private Sub Page_Load(ByVal sender As System.Object, ByVal e As System.EventArgs)
Handles MyBase.Load
    'Put user code to initialize the page here
    item.Text = Session.Item("item")
    state.Text = Session.Item("state")
    Quantity.Text = Session.Item("qty")
  End Sub

End Class
```

Figure 3.19 Grocery Store Confirmation Web Page and Code That Generates It

the records arranged in order by customer name or identifier. Sequential files use very little space and are fast to use when the records are to be retrieved in order, but they are inefficient when searching for a particular record because they must be scanned front to back. Also, when records are added or deleted, the whole file must be rearranged to accommodate the modifications, which can be time-consuming.

A **direct file organization** also uses a key for each record, but records are placed and retrieved so that an individual record can be rapidly accessed. The records are located wherever they can most quickly be retrieved, and the space from deleted records can be reused without having to rearrange the file. The most typical method employed is a hashing function. In this case, the record key, such as the customer number, is mathematically manipulated (by some algorithm) to determine the location of the record with that key. It is possible that several keys can "collide" to the same location, but such synonyms are easily resolved. Direct files are extremely fast for accessing a single record, but because the keys that exist at any point in time are usually arbitrary, sequential processing of direct files requires a long and tedious scan and usually sorting of the records.

Indexed file organizations provide a compromise between the sequential and direct access capabilities. The record keys only are arranged in sequence in a separate table, along with the location of the rest of the data associated with that key (this location field in the table is called a pointer). This "lookup" table or index is similar to a card catalog in a library, in which the author name, book title, and topics are different types of keys and the book catalog number is a pointer to its location in the library. To access the records sequentially, the table is completely scanned one entry at a time, and as each entry is encountered, its associated data record is retrieved. To access the records individually, the table is scanned until a match with the desired key is found and only the desired record is retrieved; if no match is found, an error is indicated. Because the table is quite small (just enough space for the key and location of every record, compared to possible hundreds or thousands of characters needed for the whole record—remember the analogy of the card catalog in a library), this scan can be very fast (certainly considerably faster than scanning the actual data). For a very large table, another table can be created to access the first table (which is, of course, nothing more than a specialized file itself). Popular names for such methods of indexes on top of indexes are indexed sequential access method (ISAM) and virtual storage access method (VSAM).

Finally, because in a database we want to be able to access records based upon content (e.g., by customer number) as well as by relationship (e.g., orders for a given customer), a DBMS along with the operating system must also provide a means for access via these relationships. Record keys and location pointers are these means. For example, we could store pointers in a customer record and its associated order records to link all these related records together (see Figure 3.21). Such a scheme is called *chaining* or a *list structure*. Alternately, we could store the customer number in each of its associated order records and use tables or hashing functions to locate the related record or records in other files. Relational DBMSs use this scheme.

Sequential File Organization

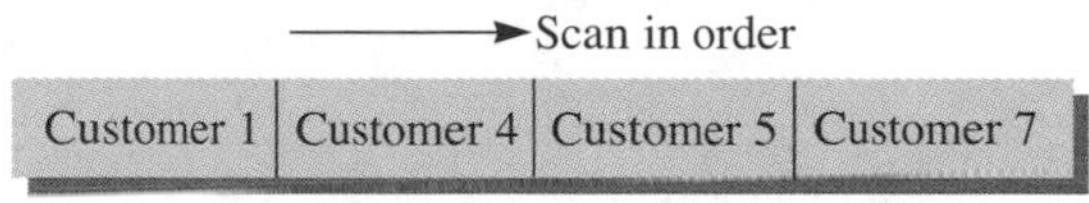

Direct File Organization

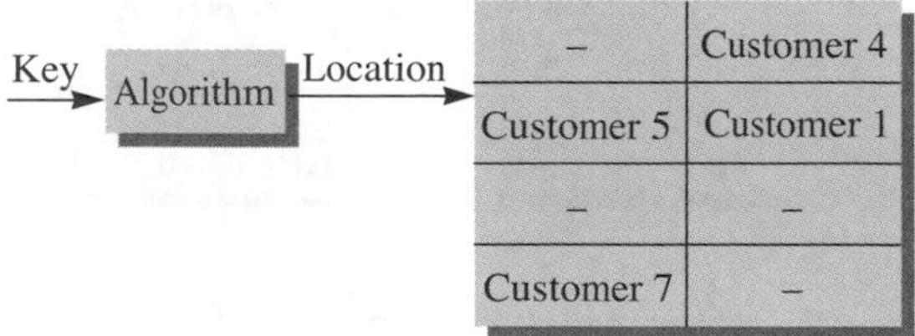

Indexed File Organization

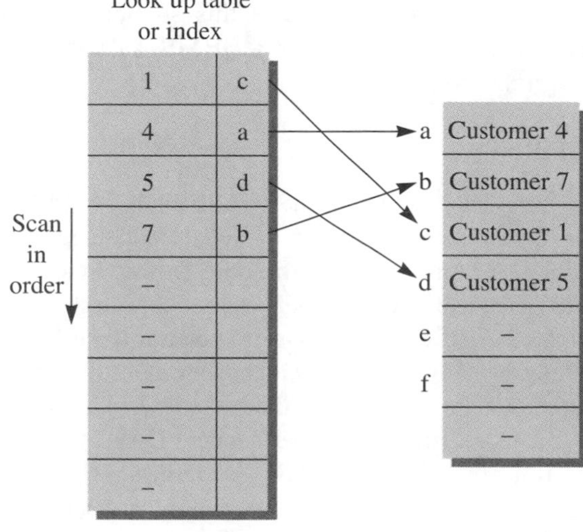

Figure 3.20 File Organizations

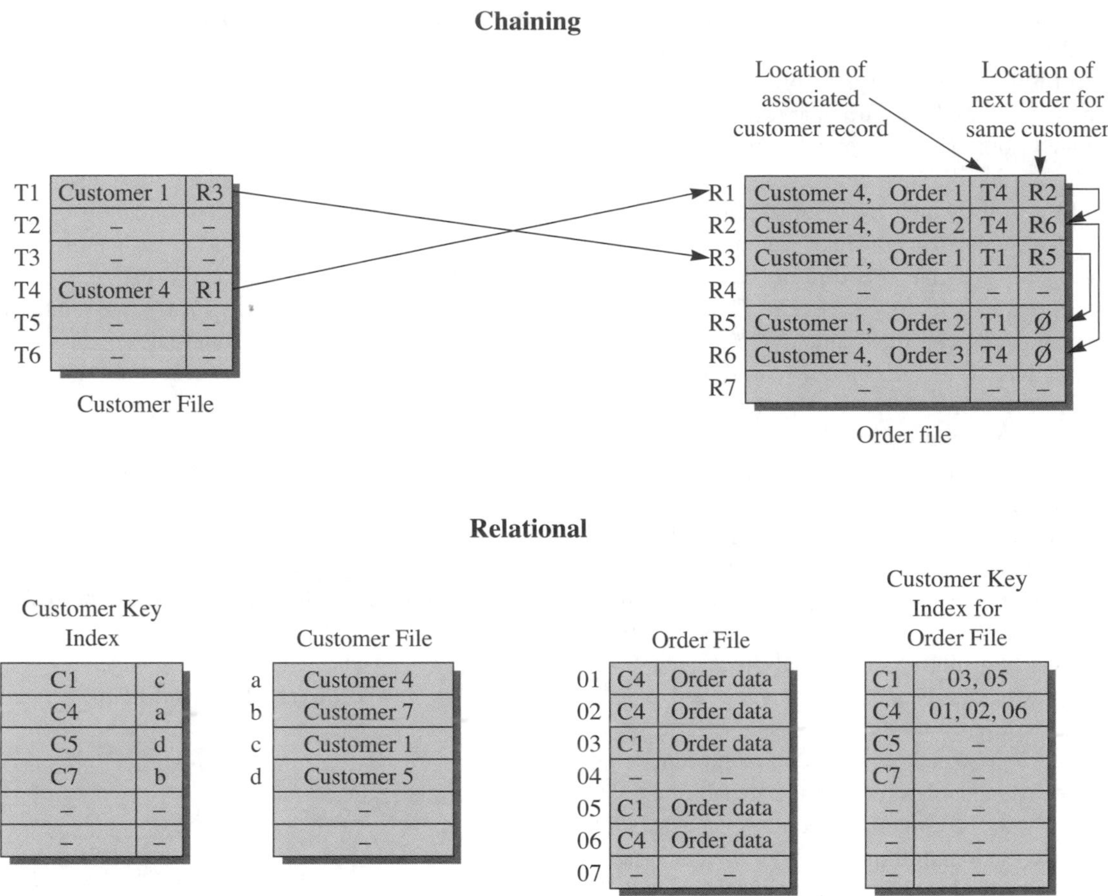

Figure 3.21 Schemes for Relationships Between Files

Database management systems are a very important type of support software, and this section has introduced some basic ideas about a DBMS, a database, and file organization.

CASE Tools

It was originally predicted that CASE tools would have a major impact on computer professionals, and that has been true for some professionals in some firms. However, the growth of the use of CASE tools has been much slower than anticipated. **CASE**, an acronym for **computer-aided software engineering**, is actually a collection of software tools to help automate all phases of the software development life cycle. In those firms that have adopted CASE tools—and there are many of them—CASE has radically changed the jobs of systems analysts and programmers. In particular, the job of the analyst or programmer involves more up-front work in clearly defining the problem and expressing it in the particular specifications required by the CASE tool. Then the tool assists in the back-end work of translating the specifications to the required output, such as a data flow diagram or a COBOL program.

There has been a recent surge in the use of CASE tools for object-oriented development based on the **Unified Modeling Language**, or **UML**. UML is a general-purpose notational language for specifying and visualizing complex software, especially large, object-oriented projects. Examples of such UML-based CASE tools are IBM's Rational Rose and Borland's Together. Note that CASE is only beginning to make an impact. CASE has the potential of providing a productivity boost to an area of the company (the information systems organization) that needs such a boost.

Communications Interface Software

Communications interface software has become increasingly important with the explosion in the number of local area networks (LANs) and wide area networks (WANs) and with the growing importance of the Internet and the World Wide Web. We have already discussed perhaps the most important type of communications interface software, the Web browser, which is software that runs on the user's computer enabling the user to look around, or "browse," the Internet.

Communications packages on large computers with many attached workstations have the awesome task of controlling the communications of these workstations, or terminals, with the central computer. This software collects the messages from the terminals, processes them as necessary, and returns the responses to the proper terminals. These packages are often designed to work closely with a particular operating system. For example, IBM's CICS (Customer Information Control System) and TSO (Time Sharing Option) are communications packages designed to work with IBM's MVS operating system (now called the z/OS operating system). Similarly, IBM's CMS (Conversational Monitor System) is designed to work with the VM operating system (now z/VM). IBM has also created versions of CICS that work with AIX, IBM's UNIX operating system; Solaris, Sun's UNIX operating system; and HP-UX, Hewlett-Packard's UNIX operating system. These UNIX/CICS combinations made it much easier for IBM's customers to move their applications to UNIX and provide evidence of the importance of UNIX. More recently, IBM has also created a version of CICS to work with Windows NT Server. Microcomputer communications packages (in workstations attached to large computers) have the much simpler task of making the microcomputer act as if it were a particular type of terminal that can be handled by the large computer communications package.

In addition to the Web browser, two additional items of communication interface software became important in the last decade. **Telnet** is a communications interface package designed to permit a user to log into a remote computer from whatever computer he or she is currently using. The key is that the computer currently being used must be attached to the same network as the remote computer. In some cases this "same network" might be a LAN on a corporate or educational campus, while in other cases this network might be the worldwide Internet. The user invokes the Telnet program and identifies the remote computer he or she wishes to log into. The connection is made, and then the user simply logs into the remote computer as if he or she were on-site. One of this textbook's authors taught in Europe for several summers, and he has a computer account at the European university. He regularly logs into that European computer via Telnet to carry out business there. Another valuable communications interface package is **FTP**, which is short for **File Transfer Protocol**. This package is designed to transfer files from one computer system to another. In effect, the user logs into the two computer systems at the same time, and then copies files from one system to the other. The files being transferred might be programs, textual data, images, and so on.

Utility Programs

This is obviously a catch-all category, but an important one nevertheless. On large computers, utility software includes programs that load applications programs into an area of memory, link related programs and subprograms, merge two files of data, sort a file of data into a desired sequence (e.g., alphabetical order on a particular data item), and copy files from one place to another (e.g., from a DASD to magnetic tape). Utility programs also give the user access to the software library. In most cases the user communicates with these utility programs by means of commands in the job control language. On a microcomputer, utility programs are used to zip (compact) and unzip large files for easier transport, to reorganize the hard drive to gain disk space, to check for computer viruses, and for many other tasks.

THE CHANGING NATURE OF SOFTWARE

In the process of investigating the various categories of computer software, we have noted many of the important trends in the software arena. Building upon our earlier discussions, we can explicitly identify the significant developing patterns in the software field, emphasizing those that have the most direct relevance to you as a manager. The following are seven key trends that we have identified:

1. More complexity of hardware/software arrangements.
2. Less concern with machine efficiency.
3. More purchased applications, and more portability of these applications from one computer platform to another. Conversely, more use of open source (free or inexpensive) support software, such as Linux.
4. More programming using object-oriented and visual languages, especially Java and Visual Basic .NET.
5. More emphasis on applications that run on intranets and the Internet, especially using the World Wide Web.
6. More user development.
7. More use of personal productivity software on microcomputers.

More Complexity of Hardware/Software Arrangements

To a much greater extent, varying configurations of hardware will be tied together by sophisticated software packages. We discussed multiprocessing and parallel processing, which involve multiple CPUs in one machine controlled by the operating system. Another way of configuring machines is to cluster several computers together, sharing common disk devices, all under control of their separate operating systems. Applications software is being split among machines as organizations move to multi-tier client/server or Web-based arrangements. With Web-based systems, the only software stored on the workstation is the browser, but there often are both an applications server and a database server involved in running the application. These more complex hardware/software arrangements have little direct impact on you as a manager; they are ways in which computer systems will be made more powerful to assist in the efficient and effective running of a business.

Less Concern with Machine Efficiency

The cost per instruction on computers will continue to drop dramatically, as it has for the past four decades. That is, machine cycles will continue to get cheaper. On the other hand, personnel costs, both for computer professionals and managers, will continue to climb. Thus, as time passes, we will be more concerned with human efficiency and less concerned with machine efficiency. This reduced concern for machine efficiency has both direct and indirect impacts on you as a manager. It means that software tools that improve human efficiency, such as visual and object-oriented languages, query languages, and CASE tools, will become more popular for computer professionals and, where appropriate, for managers. It also will lead to the development of executive workstations with voice and natural language interfaces, which are terribly inefficient from the machine standpoint.

More Purchased Applications

The higher personnel costs for computer professionals mean higher costs for in-house development of new applications software. In addition, the present backlogs for internal development of new applications are not going to disappear in the short run. The demand for new applications is also not going to slacken, particularly with the infusion of an increasing number of computer-literate managers into organizations. Add to this mix a vigorous software industry marketing an incredible variety of software packages, and it is easy to predict a continuing growth in purchased applications software. Furthermore, more of the purchased applications will be portable from one computing platform to another or will work with a variety of support software (especially database management systems). This gives companies more flexibility in their choice of computing platforms.

Another major reason for purchasing software is to correct internal business processes that are not working as well as they should. Most software packages designed to handle standard business tasks such as payroll, accounts payable, general ledger, and material requirements planning incorporate excellent procedures in the package, and by implementing the package the organization is required to adopt these improved procedures. Thus, the organization is forcing the "reengineering" of its processes by implementing the software package. This is particularly true for so-called enterprise resource planning packages. The advantage to you of the trend towards more purchased applications is that you will be able to get new applications you need implemented more quickly; the disadvantage is that the purchased software might not be able to do precisely what you want done in the way in which you want it done.

Although organizations are likely to purchase *more* of their applications in the future, it might be that they purchase *less* of their support software. The rising popularity of open source support software, such as the Linux operating system, means that more applications software is being developed to run on these open source platforms. As time goes on, organizations might be able to spend more of their information technology budget on applications and less on support software.

More Programming Using Object-Oriented and Visual Languages

In part because of the emphasis on GUIs, Visual Basic .NET, Java, and similar object-oriented and visual programming languages will gain even more widespread acceptance. These languages lend themselves to developing GUI interfaces such as those used on the World Wide Web, and many believe that they are easier to learn and use than the traditional 3 GLs. The increased use of these languages is also consistent with the lessened concern over machine efficiency noted above, because they tend to produce quite inefficient code. From the manager's perspective, the use of these languages will tend to give you the applications you need more quickly, and the GUI will make the screens more attractive and easier for you and your employees to use.

More Emphasis on Applications That Run on Intranets and the Internet

This is a very important and powerful trend, but we are somewhat premature in introducing it at this point in the book. We will explore the idea of intranets and the Internet in the next chapter. After that discussion this trend will be more meaningful. For now, note that intranets are networks operating within an organization that use the same technology as the worldwide Internet, and that the Internet is a network of networks spanning the globe. More and more organizations are creating or buying applications that run on their internal intranet or the Internet because it is both easy and economical to make these applications available to everyone who needs them.

More User Development

This trend hits close to home because you and your fellow managers will carry out more software development efforts yourselves. For the most part, you will work with personal productivity software, 4 GLs, and query languages that are easy to learn and use. Why will this increase in user development occur? Because it is easier and quicker for you to develop the software than to go to the information systems organization and work with them on the development (often after an extensive wait). This will be the case for many situations where you need a one-time or infrequently used report, or a decision support system to help you with a particular decision. Managers will continue to rely on the information systems organization (or on purchased software) for major ongoing systems, such as production control, general ledger accounting, and human resource information systems.

More Use of Personal Productivity Software

This final trend is the most important one for most of you. The use of personal productivity software, especially Web browsers, spreadsheet packages, and database management systems, will grow for managers and other professionals. Packages with a well-designed GUI will increasingly be the software of choice, because a GUI makes the software easier to learn and use. Your workstation, linked to a LAN and the worldwide Internet, will become as indispensable as your telephone (and eventually will *become* your telephone). You will use it almost every hour of every working day for electronic mail, Web browsing, word processing, spreadsheets, database management, presentation graphics, and other applications. In fact, most of you will find the microcomputer so essential that you will carry a notebook version or an even smaller palmtop computer with you when you are out of your office.

THE SOFTWARE COMPONENT OF THE INFORMATION SYSTEMS INDUSTRY

Many software products have been mentioned in this chapter, as well as many software vendors, but we lack a frame of reference from which to view the software subindustry. There are two primary groups of players in the software arena: hardware manufacturers and software houses. Many of the major hardware vendors—companies such as IBM, Sun Microsystems, Hewlett-Packard, Fujitsu, and Unisys—have a major presence in the mainframe/midrange/server computing market. In this big/midrange machine market, customers usually buy their operating systems and much of their support software from their hardware vendors—and sometimes a large proportion of their applications software as well. Thus, many of the major players in the hardware market are also major players in the software market. For example, IBM, the largest hardware vendor, is the second largest software vendor in the world in terms of revenue, trailing only Microsoft.

The software houses form an interesting and competitive group, although they are increasingly dominated by a single firm. Microsoft is the largest and most influential software house, and its dominance is growing. Microsoft is based in Redmond, Washington, and until 2000 was headed by Bill Gates, reportedly the richest person in the world. Gates is still the Chairman of the Board and Chief Software Architect of Microsoft. Other major software vendors include Computer Associates, based in Islandia, New York, which produces a variety of mainframe and PC-based software packages, with particular strength in mainframe database, job scheduling, security, and systems management software; Oracle (Redwood Shores, California), which began by specializing in mainframe DBMSs but has now branched out into other areas, notably enterprise resource planning systems (integrated software to run a business); SAP (Germany), which is the market leader in the enterprise resource planning area with its R/3 package; PeopleSoft (Pleasanton, California), which moved into the number two position in enterprise resource planning systems with its 2003 purchase of J. D. Edwards for $1.7 billion in stock; and Novell Inc. (Provo, Utah), a major provider of network management and network security software, as well as Web services packages. Until 1995, Lotus Development Corporation would have been listed as a major player in this group, but IBM bought it that year. The hottest Lotus product, and certainly one of the big reasons for IBM's interest, is Lotus Notes, a groupware product designed to aid in information transfer and efficient communication among large groups of people. IBM continues to buy promising software houses, including its 2003 purchase of Rational Software for $2.1 billion in cash. Rational, which now operates as a division of IBM Software, produces software to assist in the development of major applications, especially when using an object-oriented approach. In addition to these big software houses, there is a multitude of medium-sized to small-sized software firms. Many of the smaller firms tend to rise and fall rapidly based on the success or failure of a single product, and many small firms have gone bankrupt when they tried and failed to develop additional products.

A third group of players in the software subindustry, not as important as the first two, is the consulting firms. The key players are changing so rapidly that it is difficult to keep up, as the major public accounting firms spin off or sell off their consulting practices, sometimes to hardware vendors (IBM purchased PricewaterhouseCoopers Consulting). For the most part, the software developed and sold by these firms has been an outgrowth of their consulting practices and thus tends to be applications software geared to particular industries in which they have consulted extensively. There are also many smaller firms in the information systems arena that are difficult to categorize either as a software house or a consulting firm because they truly operate as both. Their consulting jobs often involve writing or modifying software for a particular firm and then moving to another firm within the same industry to do a similar job.

To complete the software story, we should mention that some excellent software can be obtained from noninformation systems companies that have developed software for their own use and then later decided to market the product. The software business is dominated, however, by the software houses and the hardware manufacturers.

SUMMARY

Both computer hardware and software are required for a computer system to perform useful work. The hardware actually does the work—adding two numbers, reading a record from disk, printing a line—but the software controls all of the hardware's actions. Thus, understanding software is critical to comprehending how computer systems work. From a financial perspective, most organizations spend several times as much money on software as they spend on hardware. Also, managers deal directly with a variety of software packages, but rarely deal with hardware other than their own workstation. For all these reasons, software is a vital topic for aspiring managers to understand.

Software comes in a variety of shapes and sizes, figuratively speaking. Applications software consists of all programs written to accomplish particular tasks for computer users. Support software establishes a relatively easy-to-use computing environment, translates programs into machine language, and ensures that the hardware and software resources are used efficiently. The most important piece of software is the operating system that controls the operation of the hardware and coordinates all of the other software. Other support software includes language translators, communications interface software, database management systems, and utility programs.

Applications software is often developed within the organization using third generation procedural languages, such as COBOL or C, fourth generation nonprocedural languages like FOCUS or SAS, or newer languages, such as C++ or Java. Historically, nearly all the internal software development has been carried out by computer professionals in the information systems organizations. In the past decade, however, more of the development has been done by end users, using 4 Gls and DBMS query languages. The trend that affects managers even more is the growing availability and use of personal productivity software, such as spreadsheets and database systems. It's anticipated that the trend toward more user development of personal productivity packages will continue and will grow.

Almost all of an organization's support software and an increasing proportion of its applications software is purchased from outside the firm. The hardware manufacturers appear to supply the bulk of the support software and some of the applications programs for larger computers. Independent software houses (not associated with hardware manufacturers) are particularly important sources of mainframe applications software and microcomputer software of all types. Consulting firms are also a valuable sources of applications software. When purchasing software, the organization must consider the quality and fit of the software package and the services and stability provided by the vendor.

CHAPTER REVIEW QUESTIONS

1. Describe the four generations of computer programming languages and how they differ among the various generations. How do object-oriented programming, HTML, and XML fit into these generations?
2. List at least five categories of personal productivity software packages. Which product is your personal favorite and why? What are the strengths and weaknesses of the product you are describing?
3. What are the purposes of an operating system? What are the primary tasks carried out by a mainframe operating system?

4. What is the difference between multiprogramming and multiprocessing?
5. What is virtual memory and why is it important?
6. List the six major categories of support software.
7. Explain the concept of structured programming? Why is it important?
8. What are the primary advantages and disadvantages of a fourth generation language over a third generation language? What might be a characteristic of a fifth generation language?
9. What are the primary characteristics of an object-oriented language? How does it differ from a third or fourth generation language?
10. What is the difference between push and pull technology? Give examples of each.
11. Describe the three different types of file organizations and how they work.
12. What does CASE stand for? What is the purpose or CASE tools and who is most likely to use them?
12. Provide the full names for the following acronyms: JCL, 4 GL, DBMS, COBOL, XML, HTML, OOP, DASD, CASE, BASIC.

CHAPTER DISCUSSION QUESTIONS

1. What do you think is the most important advancement in computer software over the past five years? Why?
2. As a student, what is the most useful personal productivity software for you? Why? What do you anticipate will be your favorite software package when you enter the business world?
3. Based on your experience with computers, which one category of personal productivity software needs the most work to make it useful to managers? What type of development is needed? How would you go about doing that task?
4. What are the pros and cons of having managers involved in the end-user computer process? Do managers bring strengths or weaknesses to that process? Should they be involved at all?

CASE STUDY: THE SEMANTIC WEB

Just as it seems that people and businesses are getting the knack of using the World Wide Web somewhat effectively, a bigger and better network—the Semantic Web—is coming along. Led by Timothy Berners-Lee, the father of the present Web, a collaborative effort is underway under the auspices of the World Wide Web Consortium (W3C) to have key aspects of the new Semantic Web in place by 2005. The Semantic Web will be a smart network that will appear to understand human language and will make computers almost as easy to work with as other humans. The basic idea is to annotate any type of data, any content on the Web, with specialized tags that will identify the data's meaning and the context in which the data exist. Then computers will be able to process semantic relationships between items to respond to human language queries as if they truly understand the words being used.

Building the Semantic Web will require three key items of software. The first item is XML, or eXtensible Markup Language, as described in the "Markup Languages" section of this chapter. The XML tag is a label to identify an item as a part number, or a price, or a photograph of a product—but these tags do not explain the specific meaning of the part number, price, or photograph. Instead, the tags will point to a combination dictionary and thesaurus for XML tags, called the RDF, or Resource Description Framework, which is the second required item of software. The RDF, for instance, will permit the computer to understand that two different tags—say <purchase> and <buy>—actually mean the same thing. The third required piece of software is the ontology, an online encyclopedia that lays out the detailed relationships among XML terms and RDF concepts.

To illustrate the use of the future Semantic Web, consider the hypothetical case of an automobile manufacturer that needs to find the perfect part for a new car that is under development. The manufacturer could instruct a semantic search tool to find a bolt that is lightweight, resistant to heat, and a specific size, that costs less than one cent, and that can be delivered to the plant at a particular time each week. By accessing the semantic tags in online product catalogs from a variety of suppliers, the search tool could compare and evaluate the options and present the manufacturer with a list of bolts that best meet the stated criteria. It is the semantic tags, and the ability of the computer to process those tags and understand the semantic relationships among them, that permit the computer to accomplish this task.

Just as the World Wide Web was the most important software innovation in the 1990s, the Semantic Web is quite likely to be the most important software innovation in the first decade of the twenty-first century. "We expect the Semantic Web to be as big a revolution as the original Web itself," says Richard Hayes-Roth, Hewlett-Packard Co.'s chief technology officer for software (Port, 2002, p. 97).

[Adapted from Port, 2002; and Ewalt, 2002]

Case Study Discussion Questions

Question One

This article was written in 2002, so much has occurred with the Semantic Web since then. Go online and research this network. Where does it stand now?

Question Two

What are the reasons for building a Semantic Web? What capabilities will it have? What is the biggest challenge for bringing the Semantic Web into being?

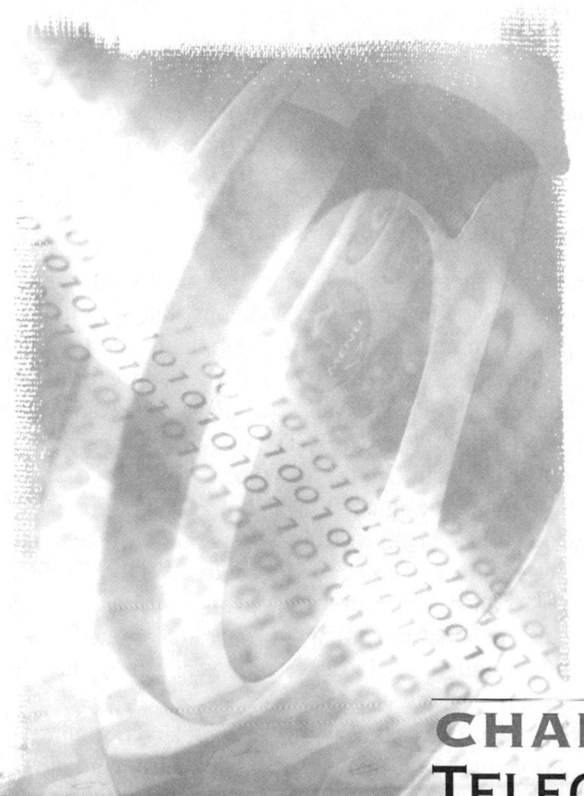

CHAPTER 4
TELECOMMUNICATIONS AND NETWORKING

THIS CHAPTER IS THE THIRD OF A QUARTET OF CHAPTERS DEVOTED TO the building blocks of information technology. So far we have considered hardware and software, but there are two more critical building blocks to go. The hardware and software must have *data* to be processed to produce useful results. If every computer were a stand-alone unit with no connection to other computers or computer-related equipment, then hardware and software and data would be the end of the story as far as computers are concerned. In fact, until about 30 years ago, that *was* the end of the story. Today, however, virtually all computers of all sizes communicate directly with other computers by means of an incredible variety of networks. For computers in organizations, these networks include intraorganizational local area networks (LANs), backbone networks, and wide area networks (WANs) as well as the worldwide Internet. For home computers, the most important network is the Internet. In addition to computer (or data) communications, today's organizations also depend heavily on voice (telephone) and image (video and facsimile) communication. This chapter explores the increasingly important topic of telecommunications and networking.

This chapter's goal is to cover only the telecommunications and networking technology that you as a business manager need to know. You need to understand the roles and general capabilities of various types of transmission media and networks, but you do not need to know all the technical details. You certainly need to know the important terminology and concepts relating to telecommunications and networking. Most important, you need to understand the interrelationships among hardware, software, and telecommunications and networking so that you can use the full gamut of information technology to increase your productivity and your organization's effectiveness.

Change is everywhere in the information technology domain, but nowhere is change more evident and more dramatic than in the realm of telecommunications and networking. A communications revolution is taking place that directly or indirectly affects the job of every manager, and the primary catalyst is the Internet and the World Wide Web (an application that runs on the Internet).

The breakup of American Telephone & Telegraph (AT&T) in 1984 created an environment in which a large number of firms competed to develop and market telecommunications equipment and services. Partially because of this increased competition, innovation in the telecommunications and networking arena has been at an all-time high. Digital networks, fiber-optic cabling, cellular telephones, the ability to send both voice and data over the same wires at the same time, and wireless networks have contributed to the revolution.

At the same time, most large U.S. businesses have restructured internally to reduce layers of middle management and create a leaner organization (as introduced in Chapter 1). They have also decentralized operations in order to respond more quickly to market opportunities and competitors' actions and have created cross-functional teams to improve business processes and carry out projects. The net result of these internal changes is that communication has become more important than ever for the remaining, often geographically dispersed, managers. They need rapid, reliable voice and data communication with other parts of the company and with suppliers and customers. Small businesses are also more dependent upon communication than ever before, and developments such as local area networks (LANs), cellular telephones, and increased functionality of the public wired telephone network have helped fill this need. Internal needs and external competition and innovation combined to create a latter-twentieth-century communications revolution that is continuing into the new millennium. The aim of this chapter is to help you become a knowledgeable participant in the communications revolution.

THE NEED FOR NETWORKING

Let us be more precise in justifying the need for networking among computers and computer-related devices such as printers. Why do managers or other professionals working at microcomputers need to be connected to a network? Why are small computers often connected to larger machines? Why are laser printers often attached to a LAN? Why is it critical for many businesses to be connected to the Internet? In our judgment, there are five primary reasons for networking.

Sharing of Technology Resources

Networking permits the sharing of critical (and often expensive) technology resources among the various users (machines) on the network. For example, by putting all the microcomputers in an office on a LAN, the users can share a variety of resources, such as a high-speed color printer that is a part of the network. The users can also share software that is electronically stored on a file server (another microcomputer designated for that particular purpose). All these devices are connected by wiring and are able to communicate with one another under control of a LAN software package called a server (or network) operating system. When a particular user wants to print a color brochure or a color transparency, it is sent electronically from the user's machine to the network printer.

Sharing resources is also important for larger computers. It is quite common for mainframes or midrange computers to share magnetic disk devices and very high-speed printers. Further, wide area networks (WANs) permit the sharing of very expensive resources such as supercomputers. The National Science Foundation has funded five national supercomputer centers across the United States, and researchers from other universities and research laboratories are able to share these giant machines by going through their local computer network into a national high-speed backbone network such as Abilene (more on this network later in the chapter).

Sharing of Data

Even more important than the sharing of technology resources is the sharing of data. Either a LAN or a WAN permits users on the network to get data (if they are authorized to do so) from other points, called nodes, on the network. It is very important, for example, for managers to be able to retrieve overall corporate sales forecasts from corporate databases to use in developing spreadsheets to project future activity in their departments. In order to satisfy customers, automobile dealers need to be able to locate particular vehicle models and colors with specific equipment installed. Managers at various points in a supply chain need to have accurate, up-to-date data on inventory levels and locations. Accountants at corporate headquarters need to be able to retrieve summary data on sales and expenses from each of the company's divisional computer centers. The chief executive officer, using an executive information system (see Chapter 6), needs to be able to access up-to-the-minute data on business trends from the corporate network.

NETWORKS WILL CHANGE EVERYTHING

In the early 1990s, Paul Saffo, a fellow at the Institute for the Future, developed a fascinating set of forecasts about the effect of information technologies on the way we would work, play, and conduct business in the years to come. So far, his projections have been right on. "The short answer is that networks will change everything," said Saffo. "In the next 5 years, networks will be supporting a shift to business teams from individuals as the basic unit of corporate productivity. In the 10-year time frame, we'll see changing organizational structures. In 20 to 30 years, we'll see a shift so fundamental, it will mean the end of the corporation as we know it." According to Saffo, organizations have started down the path to a pervasive interconnectivity of workstations that will result in an entirely new "virtual" corporate structure.

[Adapted from Wylie, 1993]

In some instances data might be retrieved from a commercial, public database external to the firm, such as LexisNexis or Dow Jones Newswires.

Of course, the ultimate sharing of data is now occurring via the **World Wide Web** on the Internet. By conservative estimates, there are now at least 600 million users of the Web at sites around the world, and this number continues to grow rapidly. Each of these users has easy (and often free) access to an incredible array of information on any topic. The user begins by using a search engine such as Google or a favorite reference site, and then follows hypertext-based links to seek out the desired data. In short, the Web has created a new and exciting way of sharing data.

Distributed Data Processing and Client/Server Systems

With **distributed data processing**, the processing power is distributed to multiple computers at multiple sites, which are then tied together via telecommunications lines. **Client/server systems** are a variant of distributed systems in which the processing power is distributed between a central server system, such as a mainframe, midrange computer, or powerful workstation, and a number of client computers, which are usually desktop microcomputers. Distributed and client/server systems tend to reduce computing costs because of their reliance on more cost-effective microcomputers and workstations.

There are many examples of distributed systems. One is the use of laptop computers by a company's sales force, where orders and sales data are transmitted over the telephone network to the corporate computer center. A second example is the use of a client/server application for general ledger accounting, with desktop microcomputers as the clients and a high-powered workstation as the server. In most cases such a package is implemented over a LAN in a single building or a cluster of buildings (a campus). A third example, also a client/server system, involves the creation of a commercial real estate database on a server located at the real estate firm's main office. The client machines are microcomputers located in the firm's branch offices or customer offices, with the clients and server linked via the public telephone network. In any case, it is the existence of a telecommunications network that makes distributed data processing a feasible and often attractive arrangement.

Enhanced Communications

Networks enhance the communications process within an organization (and between organizations) in many important ways. The telephone network has long been a primary means of communication within and between organizations. Electronic mail over the corporate computer network has become a mainstay of communication in many major organizations in the past decade or so, and the development of the Internet has extended the reach of these electronic mail systems around the world. Electronic bulletin boards (including internal, regional, and national bulletin boards) and mass electronic mailing lists for people with common interests permit multiparty asynchronous communication on an incredible array of topics. Instant messaging permits synchronous text communication over the Internet. And video communication, especially videoconferencing, provides a richer medium to permit more effective communication.

Direct data communication links between a company and its suppliers or customers, or both, have been successfully used to give the company a strategic advantage (this topic is more fully explored in Chapter 7). The SABRE airline reservation system is a classic example of a strategic information system that depends upon communication provided through a network. Recent developments to be discussed later in this chapter—such as Integrated Services Digital Network (ISDN) and digital subscriber line (DSL)—permit both voice and data communications to occur over the same telecommunications line at the same time. Starting with "plain old telephone service" (POTS) networks and continuing with today's LANs, WANs, and the Internet, networks have enhanced the communication process for individuals and organizations.

Marketing Outreach

In the last decade the Internet has become an important new marketing channel for a wide variety of businesses. Marketing is communication, of course, but it is a very specialized type of communication. Most midsized and larger business firms have a major presence on the World Wide Web, with extensive Web sites providing information on the firms' products and services and, in many cases, an online ordering capability. Many smaller firms are also using the Web for marketing outreach, perhaps by creating a Yahoo! store. Chapter 7 will consider the wide variety of marketing activities undertaken on the World Wide Web.

AN OVERVIEW OF TELECOMMUNICATIONS AND NETWORKING

Networking—the electronic linking of geographically dispersed devices—is critical for modern organizations. To participate effectively in the ongoing communications revolution, managers need to have a rudimentary understanding of the various telecommunications and networking options available to their organizations.

The prefix *tele-* simply means operating at a distance. Therefore **telecommunications** is communications at a distance. There are a number of other terms or abbreviations that are used almost interchangeably with telecommunications: data communications, datacom, teleprocessing, telecom, and networking. We prefer telecommunications because it is the broadest of these similar terms. It includes both voice (telephone) and data communications (including text and image). Teleprocessing means that the computer processing is taking place at a distance from where the data originates, which obviously requires telecommunications. Networking is the electronic linking required to accomplish telecommunications.

One might think that only a wire, or some other conduit, is needed for telecommunications, but it is much more complex than that! To begin a detailed consideration of telecommunications, first consider the primary functions performed by a telecommunications network, as listed in Table 4.1. The most obvious of these functions is the *transmission* of voice or data, or both, using the network and the underlying media. The *processing* involves making sure that an error-free message or data packet gets to the right destination. Subfunctions of processing include editorial, conversion, and routing. *Editorial* involves checking for errors and putting the communication into a standardized format, and *conversion* includes any necessary changes in the coding system or the transmission speed when moving from one device on the network to another. In networks where alternative paths are possible between the source and the destination of a communication (particularly WANs and the Internet), *routing*—choosing the most efficient path—is an important task. Closely related to the processing function is *network control*, which includes keeping track of the status of various elements of the system (e.g., which elements are busy or out of service) and, for some types of networks, checking each user periodically to see if the user has a communication to send. A not-so-obvious but critical function is the provision of an *interface* between the network and the user; hopefully this interface will make it easy and efficient for a manager or any other network user to send a communication. The next major section explores the variety of ways in which the functions listed in Table 4.1 can be delivered.

Table 4.1 Functions of a Telecommunications Network

Function	Brief Description
Transmission	Movement of voice and/or data using network and underlying media
Processing	Ensuring that error-free communication gets to right destination
Editorial	Checking for errors and putting communication into standardized format
Conversion	Changing coding system or speed when moving from one device to another
Routing	Choosing most efficient path when multiple paths are available
Network control	Keeping track of status of network elements and checking to see if communications are ready to be sent
Interface	Handling interactions between users and the network

KEY ELEMENTS OF TELECOMMUNICATIONS AND NETWORKING

We believe that you as a business manager need to understand certain key elements about telecommunications and networking to participate effectively in the communications revolution—to know what the options are for the business systems you need. These key elements include certain underlying basic ideas, such as analog versus digital signals and switched versus private lines; the variety of transmission media available; the topology (or possible arrangements) of networks; the various types of networks, including LANs and WANs; and the network protocols employed on these networks. This section will be rather technical and will involve a number of difficult concepts, so it might require some effort on your part to keep sight of the big picture of telecommunications.

Analog and Digital Signals

Perhaps the most basic idea about telecommunications is that the electronic signals sent on a network may be either analog or digital, depending on the type of network. Historically, the telephone network has been an **analog network**, with voice messages sent over the network by having some physical quantity (e.g., voltage) continuously vary as a function of time. This analog signal worked fine for voice transmission because it required the significant variations provided by an analog signal (corresponding to variations in human speech characteristics) and was insensitive to minor degradations in signal quality. On the other hand,

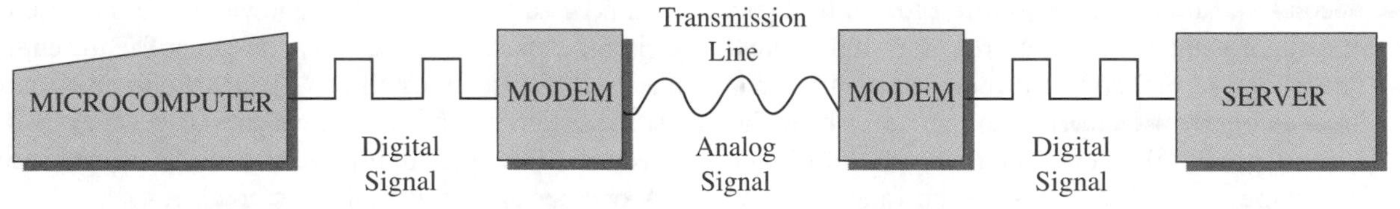

Figure 4.1 The Use of Modems in an Analog Network

computer data consist of a string of binary digits, or bits—a string of zeros and ones—to represent the desired characters. The form of this computer data does not mesh well with analog transmission. First, only two distinct signals—representing zeros and ones—need to be sent, and second, the data are extremely sensitive to degradations in signal quality. Noise in a telephone line could easily cause a zero to be interpreted as a one or vice versa, and the entire message might become garbled. Because of this problem with noise, data cannot be sent directly over the analog telephone network.

Two solutions are possible to the problem of transmitting computer data. The original solution, and one that is still widely used, is to convert the data from digital form to analog form before sending it over the analog telephone network. This conversion is accomplished by a device called a **modem**, an abbreviation for a *mo*dulator/*dem*odulator (see Figure 4.1). Of course, the data must be reconverted from analog form back to digital form at the other end of the transmission line, which requires a second modem. The conversion (or modulation) carried out by the modem may be of different types. Figure 4.2 illustrates the use of amplitude modulation (two different voltage levels to represent zero and one), frequency modulation (two different frequencies of oscillations to represent zero and one), and phase modulation (the use of a phase shift to represent the change from a zero to a one or vice versa). The use of modems and the analog telephone network is an acceptable way to transmit data for many applications, but it is severely limited in terms of transmission speeds and error rates.

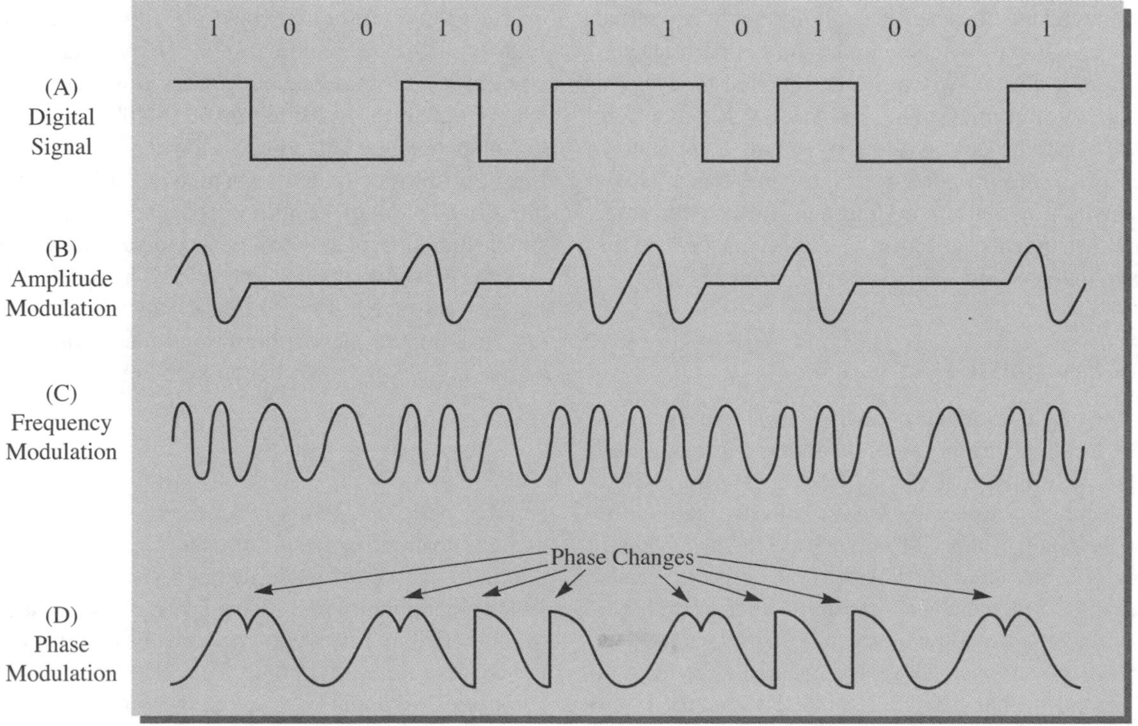

Figure 4.2 Digital and Analog Signals. (Adapted from Andrew S. Tanenbaum, Computer Networks. 4th ed. © 2003. Reprinted by permission of Prentice Hall, Inc., Upper Saddle River, New Jersey.).

The second and longer-term solution to the problem of transmitting computer data is to develop **digital networks** specifically designed to directly transmit zeros and ones, as in Figure 4.1 (A). Digital networks have the advantages of potentially lower error rates and higher transmission speeds, and modems are no longer necessary. Because of these advantages, the networks that have been specifically created for the purpose of linking computers and computer-related devices are digital. Furthermore, the telephone network is gradually being shifted from an analog to a digital network. Digital services such as ISDN and DSL (to be explored later in this chapter) are now available in many parts of the United States for users seeking higher-speed access to the Internet over the public telephone network.

This shift of the telephone network from analog to digital is due in part to the increasing volume of data being transmitted over the network, but there is also a significant advantage to transmitting voice signals over a digital network. Digital voice transmission can provide higher quality transmission—less noise on the line—just as digital recording provides higher fidelity CDs. Most of our telephone instruments are still analog devices, so the signal sent from the instrument to the nearest switching center (which may be operated either by the telephone company or your own organization) is still an analog signal. These telephone switches, however, are rapidly being converted from analog to digital switches. When the analog voice signal arrives at a digital switch, it is converted to a digital voice signal for transmission to a digital switch somewhere else, which may be across town or across the country. Thus, an increasing proportion of the voice transmission between switching centers is digitized. In the future our telephone instruments will also be digital devices, so the entire telephone network will eventually become digital.

Speed of Transmission

Whether the signal is digital or analog, another basic question is the speed of transmission. Please note that by speed we *do not* mean how fast the signal travels in terms like miles per hour, but rather the volume of data that can be transmitted per unit of time. Terms such as *bandwidth*, *baud*, and *Hertz* (*Hz*) are used to describe transmission speeds, whereas a measure such as bits transmitted per second (bits per second, or bps) would be more understandable. Happily, the three terms mentioned above are essentially the same as bits per second in many circumstances. **Bandwidth** is the difference between the highest and the lowest frequencies (cycles per second) that can be transmitted on a single medium, and it is a measure of the medium's capacity. (Sometimes it is necessary to divide the bandwidth into multiple channels, all carried on a single medium, to utilize the entire capacity. Thus, the transmission speeds we discuss are really data rates for the one or more channels carried on the single medium.) **Hertz** is simply cycles per second, and **baud** is the number of signals sent per second. If each cycle sends one signal that transmits exactly one bit of data, which is often the case, then all these terms are identical. To minimize any possible confusion, we will talk about bits per second, or bps, in this chapter. In information technology publications, *baud* was formerly used for relatively slow speeds such as 2,400 baud (2,400 bits per second) or 14,400 baud (14,400 bps), while *Hertz* (with an appropriate prefix) was used for higher speeds such as 500 megaHertz (500 million bps) or 2 gigaHertz (2 billion bps). More recently, the term *baud* has fallen into disfavor, but *Hertz* is still widely used in PC advertisements. For clarity, we will stick with *bps* in this chapter.

The notion of bandwidth, or capacity, is important for telecommunications. For example, approximately 50,000 bits (0s and 1s) are required to represent one page of data. To transmit this page using a 14,400 bps modem over an ordinary analog telephone line would take 3.5 seconds. If one were transmitting a large data file (such as customer accounts), that bandwidth or capacity would be unacceptably slow. On the other hand, to transmit this same page over a 128,000 bps (128 kbps) DSL line would take only four-tenths of a second. Graphics require approximately one million bits for one page. This would require a little over a minute for transmission at 14,400 bps over an analog telephone line, or about 8 seconds over a 128 kbps DSL line. Full-motion video transmission requires the enormous bandwidth of 12 million bps, and thus data compression techniques must be employed to be able to send video over the existing telephone network. The bandwidth determines what types of communication—voice, data, graphics, stop-frame video, full-motion video—can reasonably be transmitted over a particular medium.

Types of Transmission Lines

Another basic distinction is between private (or dedicated) communication lines and switched lines. The public telephone network, for example, is a switched-line system. When a communication of some sort (voice or data) is sent over the telephone network, the sender has no idea what route the communication will take. The telephone company's (or companies') computers make connections between switching centers to send the communication over the lines they deem appropriate, based on such factors as the length of the path, the amount of traffic on the various routes, and the capacity of the various routes. This switched-line system usually works fine for voice communications. Data communications, however, are more sensitive to the differences in line quality over different routes and to other local phenomena, such as electrical storms. Thus, a data communication sent from Minneapolis to Atlanta over the telephone network might be transmitted perfectly at 11 A.M., but another communication sent from Minneapolis to Atlanta 15 minutes later (a different connection) might be badly garbled because the communications were sent via different routes.

One way to reduce the error rate is through private lines. Most private lines are dedicated physical lines leased from a common-carrier company such as MCI, Sprint, or AT&T. A company might choose to lease a line between Minneapolis and Atlanta to ensure the quality of its data transmissions. Private lines also exist within a building or a campus. These are lines owned by the organization for the purpose of transmitting its own voice and data communications. Within-building or within-campus lines for computer telecommunications, for example, are usually private lines.

The last basic idea we wish to introduce is the difference among simplex, half-duplex, and full-duplex transmissions. With **simplex transmission**, data can travel only in one direction. This one-way communication is rarely useful, but it might be employed from a monitoring device at a remote site (monitoring power consumption, for example) back to a computer. With **half-duplex transmission**, data can travel in both directions but not simultaneously. **Full-duplex transmission** permits data to travel in both directions at once, and, therefore, provides greater capacity, but it costs more than half-duplex lines. Ordinary telephone service is full-duplex transmission, allowing both parties to talk at once, while a Citizen's Band (CB) radio provides half-duplex transmission, allowing only one party to transmit at a time. Modems sometimes have a switch that lets the user choose between full-duplex and half-duplex operation, depending upon the type of transmission desired.

Transmission Media

A telecommunications network is made up of some physical medium (or media) over which communications are sent. Five primary media are in use today: twisted pair of wires, coaxial cable, wireless, satellite (which is a special form of wireless), and fiber-optic cable.

Twisted Pair. When all uses are considered, the most common transmission medium is a **twisted pair** of wires. Most telephones are connected to the local telephone company office or the local private branch exchange (PBX) via a twisted pair. Similarly, many LANs have been implemented by using twisted pair wiring to connect the various microcomputers and related devices. A twisted pair consists of two insulated copper wires, typically about 1 millimeter thick, twisted together in a long helix. The purpose for the twisting is to reduce electrical interference from similar twisted pairs nearby. If many twisted pairs will run parallel for a significant distance—such as from a neighborhood to a telephone company office—it is common to bundle them together and enclose them in a protective sheath.

The transmission speeds attainable with twisted pairs vary considerably, depending upon such factors as the thickness of the wire and the distance traveled. On the analog voice telephone network, speeds from 14,400 to 56,000 bps are commonplace. When a digital service such as ISDN or DSL is used on the telephone network, speeds of 128,000 bps are typical, while inbound DSL speeds might be even higher, up to 1.544 million bps. Much higher speeds—16 million bps and more—can be obtained when twisted pairs are used in LANs. Multiple twisted pairs in a single cable can support speeds up to 100 million bps when used in a Fiber Distributed Data Interface (FDDI) or Fast Ethernet LAN, or even up to 1 billion bps (1 gbps) with Gigabit Ethernet (more on these LAN types later). The speeds of twisted pair and other media are summarized in Table 4.2.

Coaxial Cable. **Coaxial cable**, or **coax** for short, is another common transmission medium. A coaxial cable consists of a heavy copper wire at the center, surrounded by insulating material. Around the insulating material is a cylindrical conductor, which is often a woven braided mesh. Then the cylindrical conductor is covered by an

Table 4.2 Telecommunications Transmission Speeds

Transmission Medium	Typical Speeds
Twisted pair—voice telephone	14.4 kbps–56 kbps
Twisted pair—digital telephone	128 kbps–1.544 mbps
Twisted pair—LAN	10 mbps–100 mbps
Coaxial cable	10 mbps–1 gbps
Wireless LAN	6 mbps–54 mbps
Microwave	50 kbps–100 mbps
Satellite (per transponder)	50 kbps–100 mbps
Fiber-optic cable	100 mbps–100 gbps

KEY: bps = bits per second
kbps = thousand bits per second, or kilo bps
mbps = million bits per second, or mega bps
gbps = billion bits per second, or giga bps

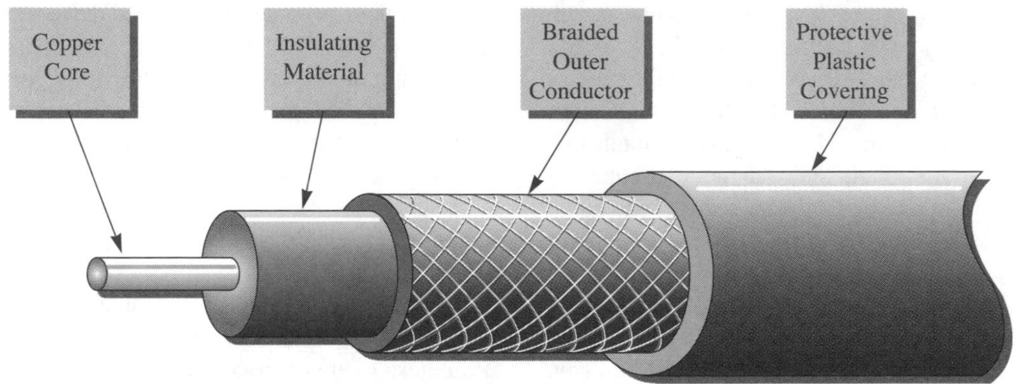

Figure 4.3 Construction of a Coaxial Cable

outer protective plastic covering. Figure 4.3 illustrates the construction of a coaxial cable.

Because of its construction, coaxial cable provides a good combination of relatively high transmission speeds and low noise or interference. Two kinds of coaxial cable are in widespread use—**baseband coax**, which is used for digital transmission, and **broadband coax**, which was originally used for analog transmission but which is now used for digital transmission as well.

Baseband coax is simple to use and inexpensive to install, and the required interfaces to microcomputers or other devices are relatively inexpensive. Baseband offers a single digital transmission channel with data transmission rates ranging from 10 million bits per second (10 mbps) up to perhaps 1 billion bps (1 gbps), depending primarily on the distances involved (longer cables mean lower data rates). Baseband coax was widely used for LANs and for long-distance transmission within the telephone network, although much of this coax has now been replaced by fiber-optic cabling.

Broadband coax, which uses standard cable television cabling, was originally installed for analog transmission of television signals, but it increasingly employs digital transmission. A single broadband coax can be divided into multiple channels, so that a single cable can support simultaneous transmission of data, voice, and television. Broadband data transmission rates are similar to those for baseband coax, and high transmission speeds are possible over much longer distances than are feasible for baseband coax. Because of its multiple channels and additional capacity, broadband coax has been more enduring than baseband. Broadband coax is still widely used for cable television and LANs that span a significant area, often called metropolitan area networks.

Wireless. Strictly speaking, wireless is not a transmission medium. **Wireless** is broadcast technology in which radio signals are sent out into the air. Wireless communication is used in a variety of circumstances, including cordless telephones, cellular telephones, wireless LANs, and microwave transmission of voice and data.

A **cordless telephone** is a portable device that may be used up to about 1,000 feet from its wired telephone base unit. This permits the user to carry the telephone to various rooms in a house or take it outdoors on the patio. By contrast, a **cellular telephone** (carried in a pocket, purse, or briefcase) may be used anywhere as long as it is within range—about 8 to 10 miles—of a cellular switching station. At present, these cellular switching stations are available in all metropolitan areas of the United States and most rural areas. The switching stations are low-powered transmitter/receivers that are connected to a cellular telephone switching office by means of conventional telephone lines or microwave technology. The switching office, which is computer-controlled, coordinates the calls for its service area and links the cellular system into the local and long-distance telephone network.

Wireless LANs are growing in popularity. They have the obvious advantage of being reasonably easy to plan and install. A wireless system provides networking where cable or wire installation would be extremely expensive or impractical, such as in an old building. A wireless LAN also permits users of mobile devices such as handheld or laptop computers to connect to the LAN (and thus the Internet) whenever they are within range of a wireless access point, such as in a coffee shop or an airport terminal. A wireless LAN is less secure than a wired LAN and more susceptible to interference, which might increase the error rate and force the wireless LAN to operate at a slower data rate. Most wireless LANs operate in the range of 6 to 11 million bps, with a few newer wireless LANs operating at speeds up to 54 mbps.

Microwave has been in widespread use for long-distance wireless communication for several decades. Microwave is line-of-sight transmission—there must be an unobstructed

WAL-MART PUSHES RFID

Wal-Mart has decided that it is time to get serious about the introduction of **radio frequency identification**, or **RFID**, as a successor to the now-familiar bar codes. Wal-Mart's Chief Information Officer Linda Dillman recently announced that the company will require its 100 top suppliers to begin using RFID for selected applications by January 2005. Wal-Mart's action will likely force other retailers to adopt RFID to remain competitive, and its wider use will bring down the costs, which is critical for RFID to be successful.

RFID tags, which are about the size of a postage stamp, combine tiny chips with an antenna. When a tag is placed on an item, it automatically radios its location to RFID readers on store shelves, checkout counters, loading bay doors, and possibly shopping carts. With RFID tags, inventory is taken automatically and continuously. RFID tags can cut costs by requiring fewer workers for scanning items; they also can provide more current and more accurate information to the entire supply chain. According to analyst Emme P. Kozloff, Wal-Mart could save $8.4 *billion* a year by 2007 by installing RFID in many of its operations.

For widespread RFID use to become a reality, however, costs must come down and other potential problems must be resolved. At present, tags run about 10 cents apiece, and RFID won't be feasible until this cost is under a penny. Wal-Mart and other retailers also have to worry about possible radio interference, and they have the difficult job of convincing consumers that the tags are not a threat to personal privacy. However, with Wal-Mart pushing it, RFID seems destined to play a significant role on the retail scene.

[Adapted from Khermouch and Green, 2003]

straight line between the microwave transmitter and the receiver. Because of the curvature of the Earth, microwave towers have to be built, typically about 25 to 50 miles apart, to relay signals over long distances from the originating transmitter to the final receiver. These requirements for towers, transmitters, and receivers suggest that microwave transmission is expensive, and it is, but long-distance microwave is less expensive than burying fiber-optic cable in a very long trench, particularly if the right of way for that trench has to be obtained. Microwave is widely used for long-distance telephone communication and, to a lesser extent, for corporate voice and data networks; transmission speeds up to 100 mbps are possible.

Other line-of-sight transmission methods exist in addition to microwave. For short distances (such as from one building to another), laser or infrared transmitters and receivers, mounted on the rooftops, are often an economical and easy way to transmit data.

Satellite. A special variation of wireless transmission employs **satellite communication** to relay signals over very long distances. A communications satellite is simply a big microwave repeater in the sky; it contains one or more transponders that listen to a particular portion of the electromagnetic spectrum, amplify the incoming signals, and retransmit back to Earth. A modern satellite may have around 40 transponders, each of which can handle an 80 mbps data transmission, 1,250 digital voice channels of 64 kbps each, or other combinations of data channels and voice channels. Transmission via satellite is still line-of-sight transmission, so a communication would have to be relayed through several satellites to go halfway around the world (see Figure 4.4).

One interesting, but annoying, aspect of satellite transmission is the substantial delay in receiving the signal because of the large distances involved in transmitting up to the satellite

DR. PEPPER GOES WIRELESS

Dr. Pepper/Seven Up Inc., of Plano, Texas, is trying something new: monitoring the operation of its vending machines via wireless technology. Isochron Data Corp. is conducting the pilot test for Dr. Pepper. For the pilot, Isochron has installed a specialized microcomputer (hardware and software from VendCast) and a two-way paging device (from Motorola) in a dozen vending machines. The VendCast software collects inventory, sales, and "machine-health" data at each vending machine, and then, on a daily basis, the VendCast server at Isochron's network operations center polls each machine. A dome antenna atop the vending machine allows broadcast and reception via a narrowband personal communications services wireless network run by SkyTel Communications. The data are aggregated and stored at Isochron, and then—with the VendCast client software installed on their PCs—managers and sales personnel at Dr. Pepper can access the data via a secured Web site. Rick Harris, manager of channel research at Dr. Pepper, is excited about the business value of the data being collected, both for daily operations and in the potential for data mining (see Chapter 6). "Information like this is a great asset to have to consider new placements of vending machines, or locations where multivendor machines might be warranted, such as in front of a Wal-Mart or high-traffic supermarket." Harris indicates that a Dr. Pepper salesperson can use the data "to plan loading of trucks and truck routes. Ideally, he'd like to spend his time filling an 80 percent empty machine rather than one that's maybe only 30 percent depleted."

[Adapted from Lais, 2000]

BLUETOOTH IS HERE!

Harald Bluetooth was a tenth-century Viking king in Denmark. Now a new wireless technology named in his honor allows communication among a wide variety of devices, such as mobile telephones, desktop and notebook computers, palmtop computers, DVD players, and printers, eliminating cables and permitting communication where it used to be impossible. **Bluetooth** is short-range radio technology that has been built into a microchip, enabling data to be transmitted wirelessly at speeds of 1 million bits per second. The price for Bluetooth cards (including the microchip) is a bit steep—$100 for a 3Com Bluetooth PC Card and $129 for a Palm Bluetooth Card in late 2003—but the price is expected to drop as demand grows. The Bluetooth Special Interest Group's founding members were two leading mobile phone manufacturers, Ericsson and Nokia; two leading notebook computer vendors, IBM and Toshiba; and Intel, the leading producer of microprocessor chips. They have been joined by many other companies, including Agere, Microsoft, and Motorola as promoter members. The Bluetooth Special Interest Group has developed Bluetooth technology standards that are available free of royalties to any company that wishes to use them. Products using Bluetooth technology have to pass interoperability testing prior to release. Thus far, more than 1,000 Bluetooth products of all kinds are available for purchase, and Bluetooth support is embedded in leading operating systems such as Microsoft Windows XP, Apple Computer's Mac OS X, and Palm OS.

The possibilities are endless for the use of Bluetooth. By adding Bluetooth cards (containing the microchip) to a notebook computer and a palmtop, a business traveler is able to synchronize the data in a notebook computer and palmtop simply by placing both devices in the same room. Bluetooth can eliminate the need to use cables to connect the mouse, keyboard, and printer to a desktop computer. An array of Bluetooth-equipped appliances, such as a television set, a stove, a thermostat, and a home computer, can be controlled from a cellular phone—all from a remote location, if desired. The Bluetooth Special Interest Group has designed the microchips to include software controls and identity coding to ensure that only those units preset by their owners can communicate. As a specific example, Federal Express (FedEx) is using Bluetooth technology in the handheld computers—called the PowerPad—that all FedEx couriers will carry with them during pickup and delivery cycles each day to collect package tracking information, provide dispatch messages to couriers, communicate with dispatch centers, and exchange information with other devices such as printers and signature capture devices. Interest in Bluetooth is strong, and a new Frost & Sullivan research report indicates that shipments of Bluetooth devices will double in 2003, to 70 million units shipped. Watch out for the Viking king! Bluetooth is here!

[Adapted from Bluetooth Web site, 2003, and Clark, 2003]

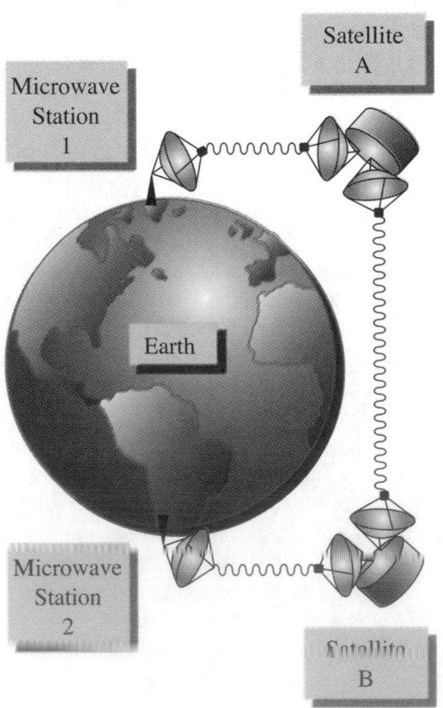

Figure 4.4 Satellite Communications

and then back down to Earth. This is particularly true for the geostationary earth orbit (GEO) satellites, which are positioned 22,000 miles above the equator such that they appear stationary relative to the Earth's surface. The minimum delay for GEO satellites is just under one-third of a second, which is an order of magnitude larger than on fiber-optic connections or Earth-bound microwave covering the same ground distance.

Interest in the use of satellites by corporations was heightened in the 1990s by the development of Ku-band satellite technology and the new very small aperture terminals (VSATs). VSATs are small satellite dishes with a 3-foot or smaller antenna, which are much less costly than their bigger cousins. Ku-band broadcasts at a higher frequency than the older C-band, and thus a smaller antenna can receive the signals. A typical VSAT data transmission rate up to a satellite is 19.2 kbps, with rates from the satellite to the VSAT of 512 kbps or more.

Another recent development is the interest in low earth orbit (LEO) satellites, which orbit at a distance of only 400 to 1,000 miles above the Earth, compared to 22,000 miles above the earth for GEO satellites. Because of their rapid motion, it takes a large number of LEO satellites for a complete system; on the other hand, because the satellites are close to the Earth, the ground stations need less power for communication and the round-trip delay is greatly reduced. Several years ago (1997) it appeared as though nearly 1,700 LEO satellites would be launched by 2006—more than 10 times the 150 commercial satellites in orbit at that time (Schine, et al., 1997)—but that is not happening. Let's see why.

The first major LEO project was Iridium, which launched 66 satellites to offer mobile telephony, paging, and data communication services. Investors in the $5 billion Iridium project included Motorola, Lockheed Martin, and Sprint; Motorola managed the project. The satellites were all flying and the Iridium system went live in 1998, with two-page advertisements splashed in major magazines such as *Business Week.* The Iridium customer would have an individual telephone number that would go with him or her anywhere on Earth, enabling the customer to make and receive calls from even the most remote places on the globe. Unfortunately, the prices to use the Iridium service were too high and it never caught on. Iridium filed for bankruptcy in 1999, and for a time it appeared likely that the satellites would be allowed to fall out of orbit. But Iridium got a second chance! A group of investors paid $25 million for the satellites and other assets of the original Iridium (quite a bargain!), and started satellite telephone service again in March 2001 (Ewalt, 2001). The old Iridium needed 1 million customers to break even; the new Iridium needed only tens of thousands. Many of these customers came from the U.S. military, which signed a deal for unlimited use for up to 20,000 soldiers. The British military is another customer, as are many news media representatives (Maney, 2003). The cost is still substantial for the reborn Iridium, but not nearly as high as before: The telephone, which weighs a little under a pound, costs about $1,500, and calls cost $1.50 per minute. In addition, there is a $60 activation fee and a $20 monthly subscription fee.

A competing LEO satellite system, Globalstar, has also had a troubled history. With its 48 LEO satellites, Globalstar does not provide complete coverage of the planet, but it does offer service in over 100 countries. The cost of Globalstar's Skyline 120 plan (in the United States and the Caribbean) is $50 per month for 120 included minutes (42 cents per minute), plus 75 cents per minute for additional minutes.

The plug was pulled on a third proposed LEO satellite system, named Teledesic, in October 2002. The original plan for Teledesic, which was sponsored by Craig McCaw (who built McCaw Cellular before selling it to AT&T), Bill Gates (Microsoft), and Boeing, was to create a 288-satellite network to provide low-cost, high-speed Internet access, corporate networking, and desktop videoconferencing. The number of satellites was later reduced to 30, each with a larger "footprint" on the Earth, but even that plan was cancelled in 2002 before any Teledesic satellites were launched. All these LEO satellite systems seemed like good ideas at the time they were planned, but the expenses involved were massive. Furthermore, the LEO systems took so long from concept to deployment that competing, less expensive technologies—such as cell phones, DSL, and cable—had made massive inroads into the potential market before the satellites were launched.

Fiber Optics. The last and newest transmission medium—**fiber-optic** cabling—is a true medium, not a broadcast technology. Advances in optical technology have made it possible to transmit data by pulses of light through a thin fiber of glass or fused silica. A light pulse can signal a 1 bit, while the absence of a pulse signals a 0 bit. An optical transmission system requires three components: the light source, either an LED—a light-emitting diode—or a laser diode; the fiber-optic cable itself; and a detector (a photodiode). The light source emits light pulses when an electrical current is applied, and the detector generates an electrical current when it is hit by light.

Fiber optics are much faster than other media and require much less space because the fiber-optic cable is very small in diameter. Fiber-optic cables are more secure because the cables do not emit radiation and, thus, are very difficult to tap. They are also highly reliable because they are not affected by power-line surges, electromagnetic interference, or corrosive chemicals in the air. These benefits are leading telephone companies to use fiber optics in all their new long-distance telephone lines, lines connecting central office sites, and most of their new local lines from central office sites to terminuses located in subdivisions. (The advantages of speed and security are obvious; the size is important because many of the cable ducts already installed lack room for more coax, but can hold the thinner fiber-optic cabling.) The high cost of the required equipment and the difficulty of dealing with the tiny fibers make this an unattractive medium for most LANs, except when it is used as a backbone to connect multiple LANs and where very high speeds or high security needs exist.

Transmission speeds for fiber range up to 1 billion bits per second (1 giga bps or 1 gbps) for large diameter fiber (50 to 100 micron core, which does not include any protective covering) to as high as 100 gbps for small diameter fiber (10 microns or less). The fact that the smaller diameter fiber has much larger capacity might be surprising, but light reflections are greatly reduced with a smaller fiber—the light ray bounces around less—permitting higher transmission speeds. The large diameter fiber is multimode, meaning that several light rays are traversing the fiber simultaneously, bouncing off the fiber walls, while the small diameter fiber is single mode, with a single light ray at a time propagated essentially in a straight line without bouncing. Single-mode fiber, unfortunately, requires higher-cost laser light sources and detectors than multimode fiber. In a recent development, the light ray sent through a single-mode fiber can be split into 80 or more different colors, each carrying its own stream of data. In this process, called dense wave division multiplexing, prisms are used to send these multiple colors down a single fiber. Today, much of the fiber being installed by telephone companies is 8-micron single-mode fiber with a transmission speed, using wave division multiplexing, of 10 gbps. The outside diameter (including protective covering) of this single-mode fiber is only 125 microns, which is about one-fiftieth the outside diameter of a typical coaxial cable. Thus, both the speed and size advantages of fiber optics are significant.

Topology of Networks

The starting point for understanding networks is to recognize that all telecommunications networks employ one or more of the transmission media discussed previously. But what do the networks look like in terms of their configuration or arrangement of devices and media? The technical term for this configuration is the topology of the network. There are five basic network topologies—bus, ring, star, hierarchical or tree, and mesh (see Figure 4.5)—plus an unlimited number of variations and combinations of these five basic forms.

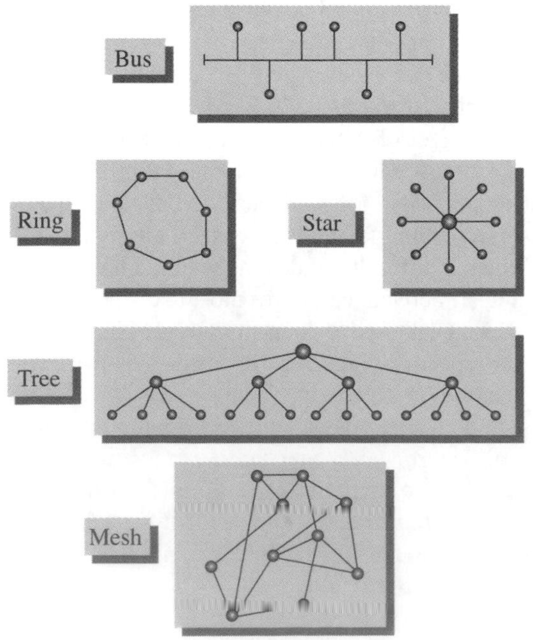

Figure 4.5 Network Topologies

Bus. The simplest topology is the linear or **bus topology**. With the bus, all network devices share a single length of cable (coax, fiber, or twisted pair). One of the network devices is usually a file server with a large data storage capacity. An obvious advantage of the bus is the wiring simplicity. A disadvantage is its single-point failure characteristic. If the bus fails, nodes on either side of the failure point cannot communicate with one another.

Ring. The **ring topology** is similar to the bus except that the two ends of the cable are connected. In this case, a single cable runs through every network device, including (usually) a file server. The wiring for the ring is slightly more complicated than for the bus, but the ring is not as susceptible to failure. In particular, a single failure in the ring still permits each network device to communicate with every other device.

Star. The **star topology** has a mainframe or midrange computer, a file server (usually a microcomputer), or a networking device at its center, with cables (or media of some type) radiating from the central device to all the other network devices. This design is representative of many small-to-medium computer configurations, with all workstations and peripherals attached to the single midrange computer. It is also encountered in LANs. Advantages of the star include ease of identifying cable failure, because each device has its own cable; ease of installation for each device, which must only be connected to the central device; and low cost for small networks where all the devices are close together. The star's primary disadvantage is that if the central device fails, the whole network fails. A cost disadvantage might also be encountered if the network grows, for a separate cable must be run to each individual device, even if several devices are close together but far from the central device.

Tree. The fourth basic topology is the **tree**, or hierarchical. This topology is sometimes called a hierarchical star, because with some rearrangement (spreading the branches out around the central device), it looks like an extension of the star. The configuration of most large and very large computer networks is a tree, with the mainframe at the top of the tree connected (through data channels) to terminal controllers such as a multiplexer and perhaps to other smaller computers. Then these terminal controllers, or smaller computers, are, in turn, connected to other devices such as terminals, microcomputers, and printers. Thus, the tree gets "bushy" as one traverses it from top to bottom.

The tree has the same primary disadvantage as the star. If the central device fails, the entire network goes down. On the other hand, the tree arrangement possesses a great deal of flexibility. The cost disadvantage of the star might not appear when devices are added to the network, for the use of intermediate devices (multiplexers, small computers) removes the necessity of connecting every device directly to the center.

Mesh. In a **mesh topology** most devices are connected to two, three, or more other devices in a seemingly irregular pattern that resembles a woven net, or a mesh. A complete mesh would have every device connected to every other device, but this is seldom done because of the cost. The public telephone network is an example of a mesh topology; another example is the system of networks that makes up the Internet.

The ramifications of a failure in the mesh depend upon the alternative paths or routes available in the vicinity of the failure. In a complex mesh, like the telephone network, a failure is likely to have little impact, except on the devices directly involved.

More Complex Networks. Now the fun begins, because the previous five network topologies can be combined and modified in a bewildering assortment of networks. For example, it is quite common to attach multiple bus or ring LANs to the tree mainframe computer network. Two ring LANs may be attached via a fiber-optic cable, which is in effect a very simple bus network.

National and international networks are much more complex than those we have considered thus far, because the designers have intentionally built in a significant amount of redundancy. In this way, if one transmission line goes out, there are alternative routes to almost every node or device on the network. As an example, the **vBNS+** network (originally the very high-performance Backbone Network Service, or vBNS) operated by MCI is shown in Figure 4.6. vBNS+, which was developed through a cooperative agreement between MCI and the National Science Foundation (NSF), links NSF-supported supercomputer centers (labeled on Figure 4.6) and provides points of presence (PoPs) where other users (including both researchers and commercial users) may link into vBNS+ from the Internet. vBNS+ employs a dual backbone topology based upon rings connecting the east and west coasts, with the addition of a link from Chicago to Memphis, a loop up to Seattle, extra links in the northeastern United States, and spurs going off the ring to other sites. As another example, the long-distance telephone network is a mesh topology, with numerous paths possible to connect most metropolitan areas.

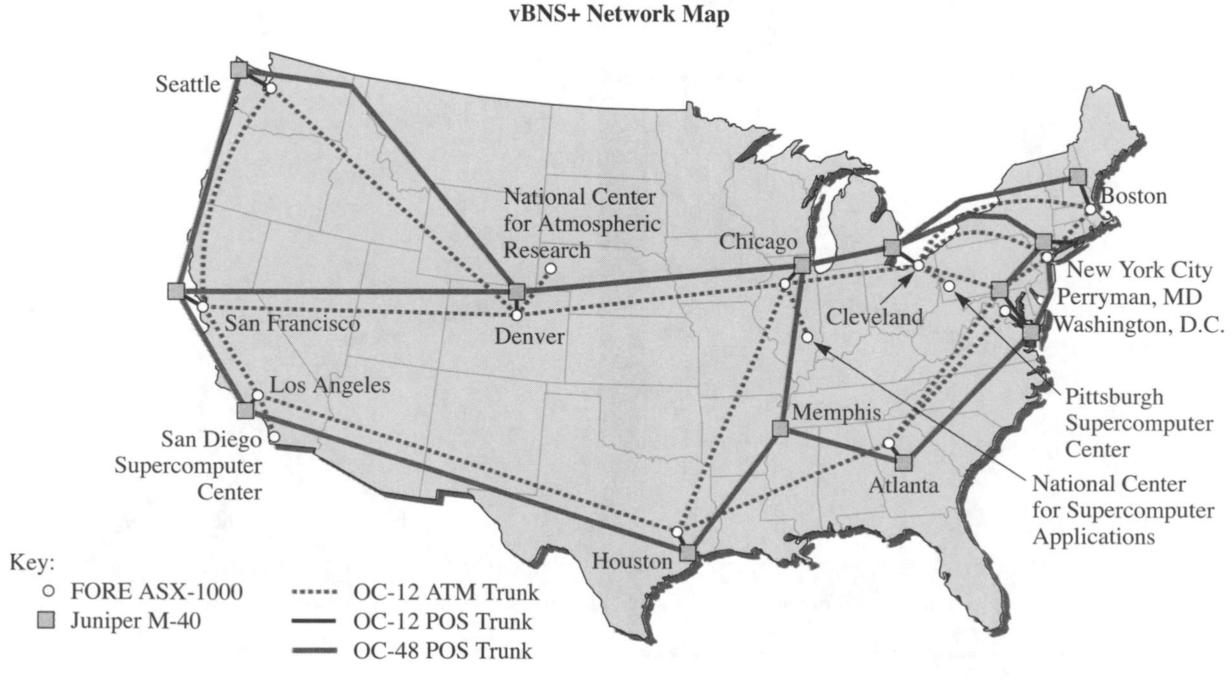

Figure 4.6 vBNS+ Network Map

Types of Networks

Thus far we have considered two key elements of telecommunications networks: the transmission media used to send the communications and the arrangement or topology of the networks. Now we turn to the categorization of networks into basic types. Please note that the categories employed here are somewhat arbitrary—but we believe extremely useful—and might differ from those used in other references. The types of networks to be described include computer telecommunications networks, private branch exchange (PBX) networks, local area networks (LANs), backbone networks, wide area networks (WANs), the Internet, and Internet2.

Computer Telecommunications Networks. It is almost easier to describe this initial type of network by what it is not. It is not a PBX network, a LAN, or a WAN. What we are calling a **computer telecommunications network** is the network emanating from a single medium, large, or very large computer, or a group of closely linked computers. This type of network usually is arranged as a tree (see Figure 4.5) with coaxial cable and twisted pair as the media. Until the early 1980s, this was usually the only type of network (except for the telephone network) operated by an organization that did business in one building or a group of adjacent buildings (a campus). In many organizations even today the predominant communication with the central computer is through the computer telecommunications network. This type of network is controlled by the central computer, with all other devices (e.g., terminals, microcomputers, and printers) operating as subordinates or "slaves" on the network. IBM's mainframe architecture was originally based on this type of network, although LANs and other network types may now be linked to a mainframe or large computer.

This is not a bad arrangement, but it puts a tremendous communications control burden on the central computer. For this reason it is quite common to add a front-end processor or communications controller to the network—between the central computer and the rest of the network—to offload the communications work from the central computer (see Figure 4.7). A front-end processor or communications controller is another computer with specially designed hardware and software to handle all aspects of telecommunications, including error control, editing, controlling, routing, and speed and signal conversion.

PBX Networks. **Private branch exchanges**, or **PBXs**, have been around for many years, but today's digital

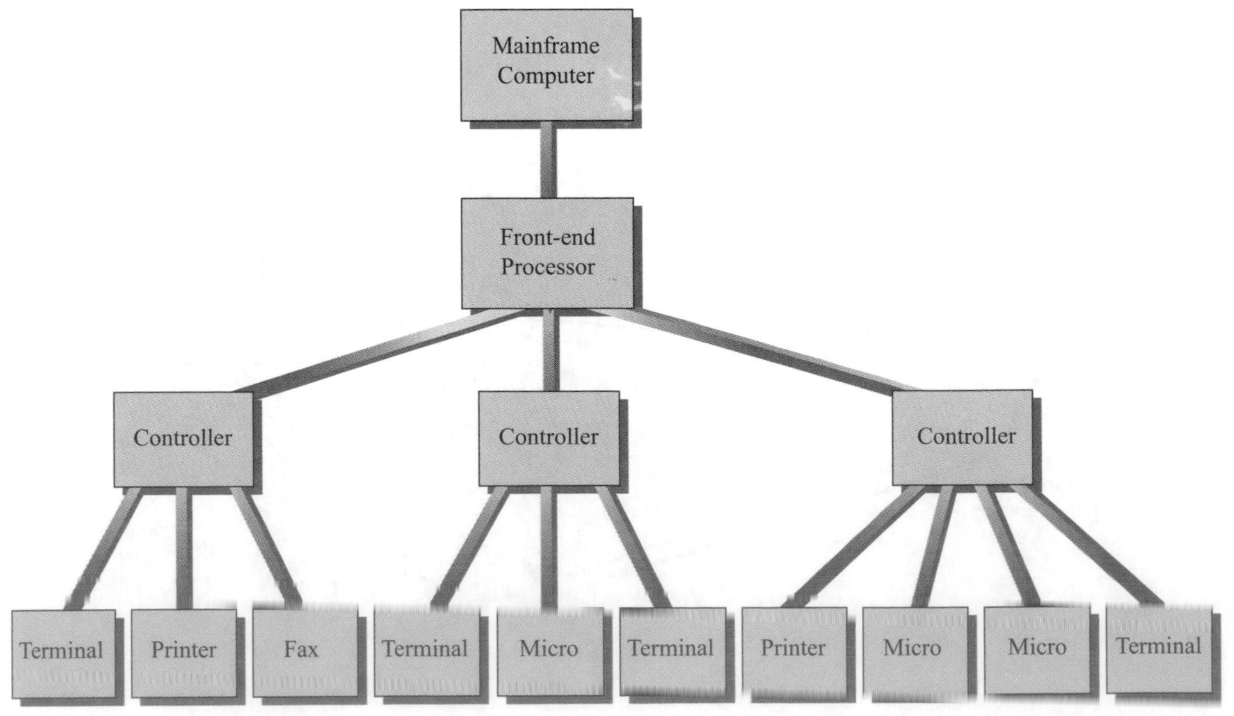

Figure 4.7 Computer Telecommunications Network

PBXs have extensive capabilities not possessed by their predecessors. The initial PBXs were switchboards run by human operators to operate an internal telephone system within an organization. Later PBXs worked in the same way except that electromechanical relays performed the switching rather than human operators. Today's digital PBX consists of a digital switch operated by a built-in computer, and the PBX has the capability of simultaneously handling communications with internal analog telephones, digital microcomputers and terminals, mainframe computers, and the external telephone network. The newest PBXs are IP-enabled (Internet Protocol-enabled), meaning that they can handle the new IP digital telephones running over wiring that was formerly reserved for data communications. IP telephony is sometimes referred to as voice-over-IP telephony. Figure 4.8 provides a schematic representation of a PBX.

It is obvious from Figure 4.8 that a PBX can serve as the central device in a star or a tree network. The media used are typically some combination of coax, twisted pair, and fiber (if high speeds are essential). If a mainframe computer is attached to the PBX, the PBX can function as the front-end processor for the mainframe. In terms of the telephone network, the PBX translates analog telephone signals to digital form before sending them over the digital network. Except for telephone instruments, all the devices shown in Figure 4.8 are digital, including the ISDN devices to be discussed later.

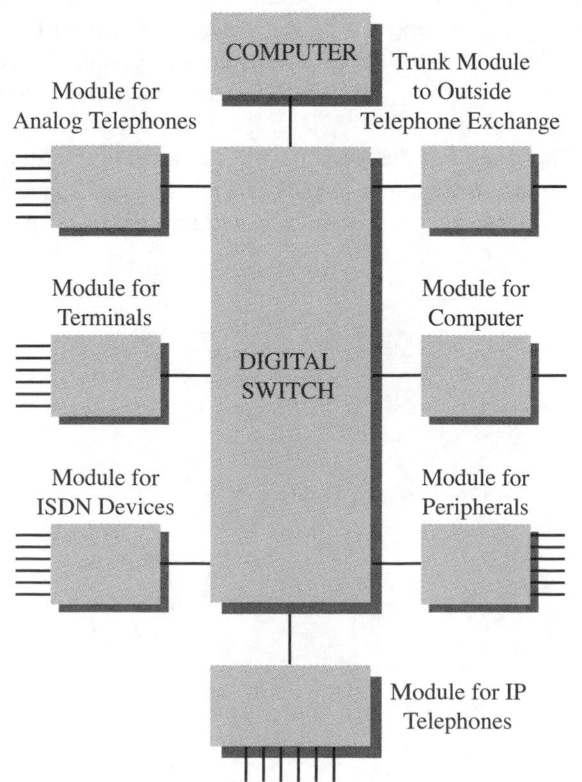

Figure 4.8 Schematic Representation of a PBX

A PBX has several advantages. It can connect all, not just some, of the telecommunications devices in a building or campus; it can use existing telephone wiring, which is a major advantage; it can carry voice and data over the same network; it can connect in a transparent way to the external telephone network; and it has a very high potential throughput rate. On the negative side, the maximum speed for a single channel (as distinct from overall throughput) is fast enough for telephone and most terminal traffic but painfully slow for shipping a large computer file from the mainframe to a remote server. PBXs are also complex and expensive pieces of equipment.

Local Area Networks. A **local area network (LAN)** is first and foremost a *local* network—it is completely owned by a single organization and generally operates within an area no more than 2 or 3 miles in diameter. LANs are data networks that generally have a high data rate of several million bps or more.

A LAN differs from a computer telecommunications network in that a LAN contains a number of intelligent devices (usually microcomputers) capable of data processing rather than being built around a central computer that controls all processing. In other words, a LAN is based on a peer-to-peer relationship, rather than a master-subordinate relationship. A LAN differs from a PBX network in that a LAN handles only data, is not part of the telephone system, and requires new wiring. But a LAN does have a great deal in common with a PBX network in that both are aimed at establishing communication between a variety of devices in order to share data and resources and to facilitate office or factory automation. Thus, PBXs and LANs are often seen as competing technologies.

LANs exist in a variety of topologies, but four of these—for which standards have been developed by the Institute for Electrical and Electronic Engineers (IEEE) and subsequently adopted by both national and international standards organizations—are clearly dominant today. These four LAN standards are officially designated as IEEE 802.3 (contention bus design), IEEE 802.4 (token bus design), IEEE 802.5 (token ring design), and IEEE 802.11, including 802.11a, 802.11b, and 802.11g (wireless design).

Wired Local Area Networks. The **contention bus** design was originally developed by Xerox and subsequently adopted by Digital Equipment Corporation (now part of Hewlett-Packard) and Novell, among others. This design is usually referred to as **Ethernet**, named after the original Xerox version of the design. The contention bus is obviously a bus topology (see Figure 4.5), usually implemented using coaxial cable or twisted pair wiring. Communication on an Ethernet LAN is usually half-duplex—that is, communication in both directions is possible, but not simultaneously. The interesting feature of this design is its contention aspect—all devices must contend for the use of the cable.

With Ethernet, devices listen to the cable to pick off communications intended for the particular device and determine if the cable is busy. If the cable is idle, any device may transmit a message. Most of the time this works fine, but what happens if two devices start to transmit at the same time? A collision occurs and the messages become garbled. The devices must recognize that this collision has occurred, stop transmitting, wait a random period of time, and try again. This method of operation is called a **CSMA/CD protocol**, an abbreviation for carrier sense multiple access with collision detection. In theory, collisions might continue to occur and thus there is no upper bound on the time a device might wait to send a message. In practice, a contention bus design is simple to implement and works very well as long as traffic on the network is light or moderate (and thus there are few collisions).

The original Ethernet design, now called **shared Ethernet**, employs a contention *bus* as its logical topology, but it is usually implemented as a physical *star* arrangement (see Figure 4.9). The usual way of creating a shared Ethernet LAN is to plug the cables from all the devices on the LAN into a **hub**, which is a junction box containing up to 24 ports into which cables can be plugged. Embedded inside the hub is a linear bus connecting all the ports. Thus, shared Ethernet operates as a logical bus but a physical star.

Switched Ethernet is a newer variation of Ethernet providing better performance at a higher price. The design is similar to shared Ethernet, but a switch is substituted for the hub and the LAN operates as a logical star as well as a physical star. The switch is smarter than a hub—rather than passing all communications through to all devices on the LAN, which is what a hub does, the switch establishes separate point-to-point circuits to each device and then forwards communications only to the appropriate device. This switched approach dramatically improves LAN performance because each device has its own dedicated circuit, rather than sharing a single circuit with all devices on the network. Of course, a switch is considerably more expensive than a simple hub.

The **token bus** design employs a bus topology with coaxial cable or twisted pair wiring, but it does not rely on contention. Instead, a single token (a special communication or message) is passed around the bus to all devices in a specified order, and a device can only transmit when it has the token. Therefore, a microcomputer must wait until it receives the token before transmitting a message; when the message is sent, the device sends the token on to the next device. After some deterministic period of time based on messages sent by other devices, the device will receive the token again.

The token bus design is central to the **Manufacturing Automation Protocol (MAP)**, which was developed by General Motors and adopted by many manufacturers.

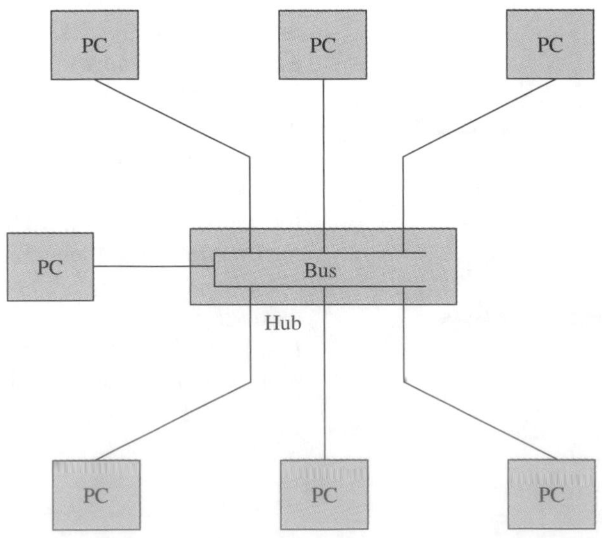

Figure 4.9 Shared Ethernet Topology: Logical Bus, Physical Star

MAP is a factory automation protocol (or set of standards) designed to connect robots and other machines on the assembly line by a LAN. In designing MAP, General Motors did not believe it could rely on a contention-based LAN with a probabilistic delay time before a message could be sent. An automobile assembly line moves at a fixed rate, and it cannot be held up because a robot has not received the appropriate message from the LAN. Therefore, General Motors and many other manufacturers have opted for the deterministic token bus LAN design.

The third LAN standard is the **token ring**, originally developed by IBM, which combines a ring topology (see Figure 4.5) with the use of a token as described for the token bus. A device attached to the ring must seize the token and remove it from the ring before transmitting a message; when the device has completed transmitting, it releases the token back into the ring. Thus, collisions can never occur, and the maximum delay time before any station can transmit is deterministic. The usual implementation of a token ring involves the use of a wire center into which cables from individual devices are plugged, creating a physical star but a logical ring.

All three types of wired LAN designs are widely used today. Token bus dominates the manufacturing scene, and Ethernet leads token ring by a wide and growing margin in office applications. But the hottest type of LAN in the early twenty-first century is the wireless LAN, to which we will now turn.

Wireless Local Area Networks. **Wireless LANs**, commonly known as **Wi-Fi** (short for wireless fidelity), represent only a small proportion of LANs in operation today, but a rapidly growing proportion. Wi-Fi technology has obvious advantages for people on the move who need access to the Internet in airports, restaurants, and hotels. Wi-Fi is also gaining acceptance as a home or neighborhood network (see the sidebar entitled "Making Wi-Fi Work"), permitting an assortment of laptop and desktop computers to share a single broadband access point to the Internet. Wireless LANs are also moving into the corporate and commercial world, especially in older buildings and confined spaces where it would be difficult or impossible to establish a wired LAN or where mobility is paramount. Even in newer buildings, wireless LANs are often being employed as *overlay networks.* In such cases Wi-Fi is installed in addition to wired LANs so that employees can easily move their laptops from office to office and can connect to the network in places such as lunchrooms, hallways, and patios (Dennis, 2002, p. 266).

Today's wireless LANs use one of four standards incorporated in the IEEE 802.11 family of specifications. All four standards use the shared Ethernet design (logical bus, physical star; see Figure 4.10) and the **CSMA/CA protocol**, which is an abbreviation for carrier sense multiple access with collision avoidance. CSMA/CA is quite similar to CSMA/CD used in traditional Ethernet, but it makes greater efforts to avoid collisions. In one approach to collision avoidance, any computer wishing to transmit a message

MAKING WI-FI WORK

Millions of people are setting up wireless networks. Here's how it's done, using a network with a PC and one or more laptops.

1. Get a high-speed net connection. You can subscribe to a cable-modem or DSL phone service for about $40 a month. The modem is usually free, and you can do the installation yourself in a few minutes.
2. Buy a Wi-Fi access point. The size of a clock radio, this box includes an Internet router and a two-way Wi-Fi radio. It costs $100 to $250.
3. Connect access point to modem and desktop. Plug cables into the back of the modem and PC. Install the software on the PC and follow the directions.
4. Buy a wireless antenna for each laptop. These credit-card devices run $30 to $50.
5. Install antenna and antenna software on laptop. Install the antenna before you install the software, or it won't work properly.
6. Congratulations! Your network is up and running. Test the signal strength by wandering around with the laptop.
7. Whoops! The signal is weak. Most people find reception in their homes is hampered by walls and other obstructions. Signal strength will remain stronger if you move upstairs or downstairs just above or below the access point.
8. Don't panic! You have options. You can buy a signal booster, which attaches to the router and costs about $100. You can sometimes boost the strength of the router's signal online, with help from the manufacturer's service department.
9. Telecommuting? O.K., panic! If you work at home with a laptop that has been configured for the office, you may need to reconfigure it with help of your employer.
10. Expand! Now that you have connected the desktop and laptop to your network, you can buy another antenna to include your TiVo, digital home theater, or gaming console in the network.

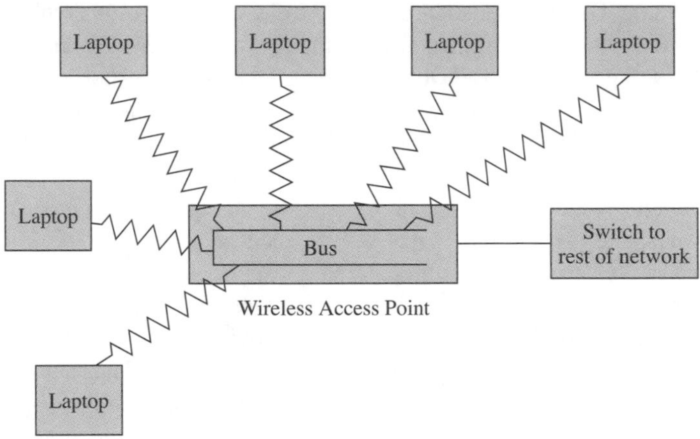

Figure 4.10 Wireless Local Area Network Topology

first sends a "request to transmit" to the wireless access point. If no other computer is transmitting, the wireless access point responds by sending a "clear to transmit" signal to all computers on the wireless LAN, specifying the amount of time for which the network is reserved for the requesting computer.

In order to establish a wireless LAN, a wireless **network interface card (NIC)** must be installed in each computer. The wireless NIC was referred to as an antenna in the "Making Wi-Fi Work" sidebar, but it is really more than that—the NIC is a short-range radio transceiver that can send and receive radio signals. At the heart of a wireless LAN is the **wireless access point**, or **WAP**, which is a radio transceiver that plays the same role as a hub in a wired Ethernet LAN. The WAP receives the signals of all computers within its range and repeats them to ensure that all other computers within the range can hear them; it also forwards all messages for recipients not on this wireless LAN via the wired network.

The most popular wireless LAN standard in the early twenty-first century is 802.11b, which operates in the 2.4 GHz (gigaHertz) band at data rates of 5.5 to 11 mbps. The range of 802.11b LANs is typically 300 to 500 feet, which is greater than that of 802.11a, the next most widely used wireless LAN standard. The 802.11a standard operates in the 5.8 GHz band at data rates up to 54 mbps. The problem with 802.11a is that the range is only about 150 feet; in fact, the 54 mbps data rate can be sustained reliably only within about 50 feet of the WAP. The newest standard is 802.11g, which uses a different form of multiplexing in the 2.4 GHz band to achieve the same range as 802.11b (300 to 500 feet) with data rates up to the 54 mbps of 802.11a. Currently 802.11g products are more expensive than those

WIRELESS MOOCHERS

Wireless Internet access—known by the term Wi-Fi, for wireless fidelity—is quickly gaining popularity among people seeking high-speed Internet connections when they are away from their home or office. The signal from a typical wireless access point (WAP) only extends for about 300 feet in any direction, so the user must find a "hot spot" to be able to access the Internet while on the road. Sometimes hot spots are available for free or for a small fee. For instance, some Schlotzsky's delicatessens, Omni Hotels, and Hampton Inns offer hot spots for free; some McDonald's restaurants, Starbucks coffee shops, and Borders bookstores offer hot spots for a fee. By the end of 2003, Gartner Group estimates that there will be 29,000 Wi-Fi hot spots in North America, ranging from retail establishments to entire city neighborhoods.

The hot spots work; they do attract customers—and moochers! The manager of a Hampton Inn in Michigan reports seeing local salespeople, who were not staying in the hotel, lurking in the lobby or sitting in cars as they checked their e-mail or surfed the Web using the hotel's wireless network. A homeowner in Oregon confirms that a digital moocher was parked at the end of his driveway using a hot spot that the homeowner had set up to share with his neighbors. One executive could not get a room at a Wyndham Hotel offering wireless access, so he checked into another hotel without Wi-Fi and ended up driving back to the Wyndham several times to check his e-mail in the lobby. Another executive sat outside a closed Starbucks after midnight, in frigid temperatures, to check his e-mail. Wi-Fi is growing in popularity, and enthusiasts will go to great lengths to find hot spots!

[Adapted from Wingfield, 2003]

for 802.11b, but 802.11g's higher data rate should make it an attractive alternative for new wireless LANs.

Higher-Speed Wired Local Area Networks. LAN technology continues to advance in the first decade of the twenty-first century. The top speed of a traditional Ethernet LAN is 10 mbps, but **Fast Ethernet,** operating at 100 mbps, is being used in many newer LANs (and backbone networks, to be discussed in the next section) where greater capacity is needed. Fast Ethernet uses the same CSMA/CD architecture and the same wiring as traditional Ethernet. The most popular implementations of Fast Ethernet are *100 Base-T*, which runs at 100 mbps over category 5 twisted-pair cabling (four pairs of wires in each cable), and *100 Base-F*, which runs at 100 mbps over multimode fiber-optic cable (usually two strands of fiber joined in one cable). Although the wiring for Fast Ethernet could handle full-duplex communication, in most cases only half-duplex is used.

Even newer and faster than Fast Ethernet is **Gigabit Ethernet**, with speeds of 1 billion bits per second and higher. The fastest Ethernet in general use is 1-gbps Ethernet, commonly called *1 GbE*. 1 GbE running over twisted-pair cables is called *1000 Base-T*; amazingly, 1000 Base-T still runs over one category 5 cable (four pairs of wires) by using an ingenious procedure to send streams of bits in parallel. There are two versions of 1 GbE when running over fiber-optic cabling: *1000 Base-SX* uses multimode fiber, and *1000 Base-LX* uses either multimode fiber or single-mode fiber depending on the distances involved (up to 1,800 feet with multimode fiber or over 16,000 feet with single-mode fiber). 1 GbE is often used in backbone networks, to be discussed in the next section. 10-gbps Ethernet is currently under development, and several researchers have proposed 40-gbps Ethernet. 10-gbps Ethernet, called *10 GbE*, will run over multimode fiber for short distances and single-mode fiber for longer distances, using full-duplex communication between only two computers at a time. Ethernet speeds keep going up, suggesting that Ethernet will continue to be the preferred networking approach for high-speed LANs and backbone networks for the foreseeable future.

Just as Fast Ethernet is sort of a traditional Ethernet grown up, so is **Fiber Distributed Data Interface (FDDI)** related to a traditional token ring LAN. A traditional token ring LAN operates at a maximum speed of 16 mbps. By contrast, FDDI employs a token ring architecture to deliver 100 mbps. FDDI was originally developed to operate with fiber-optic cable (hence the name) but now operates on either copper media (usually category 5 twisted-pair cable) or fiber-optic cabling. FDDI is actually a dual-ring technology, with each ring running in the opposite direction to improve fault recovery. With FDDI, the primary ring is active until a fault is detected, at which time the secondary ring is activated. Although still in use today, the future of FDDI seems limited because of advances in Ethernet technology.

Backbone Networks. **Backbone networks** are the in-between networks—the middle distance networks that interconnect LANs in a single organization with each other and with the organization's WAN and the Internet. For example, the corporate headquarters of a large firm might have multiple buildings spread out over several city blocks. Each floor of a large building might have its own LAN, or a LAN might cover an entire smaller building. All these LANs must be interconnected to gain the benefits of networking—enhanced communications, the sharing of resources and data, and distributed data processing. In addition, the LANs must also be connected to the company's WAN and, in most cases, to the Internet. A backbone network is the key to internetworking (see Figure 4.11).

The technology involved in backbone networks is essentially the same as that described for LANs, but at the high end. The medium employed is usually either fiber-optic cabling or twisted-pair cabling, providing a high data transmission rate, often 100 mbps or more. The topology may be a ring (FDDI) or a bus (Fast Ethernet or Gigabit Ethernet) or some combination. The only new terminology we need to introduce relates to the hardware devices that connect network pieces together or connect other networks to the backbone network.

We have already introduced the hub, the switch, and the wireless access point. A hub, we know, is a simple device into which cables from computers are plugged; it may also be used to connect one section of a LAN to another. Hubs forward every message they receive to all devices or sections of the LAN attached to it, whether or not they need to go there. A **wireless access point** is the central device in a wireless LAN that connects the LAN to other networks. A **bridge** connects two LANs, or LAN segments, when the LANs use the same protocols, or set of rules (more on this later); a bridge is smart enough to forward only messages that need to go to the other LAN. A **router**, or a **gateway** (a sophisticated router), connects two or more LANs and forwards only messages that need to be forwarded but may connect LANs that use different protocols. For example, a gateway is used to connect an organization's backbone network to the Internet. A **switch** connects more than two LANs, or LAN segments, that use the same protocols. Switches are very useful to connect several low speed LANs (e.g., a dozen Ethernet LANs running at 10 mbps) into a

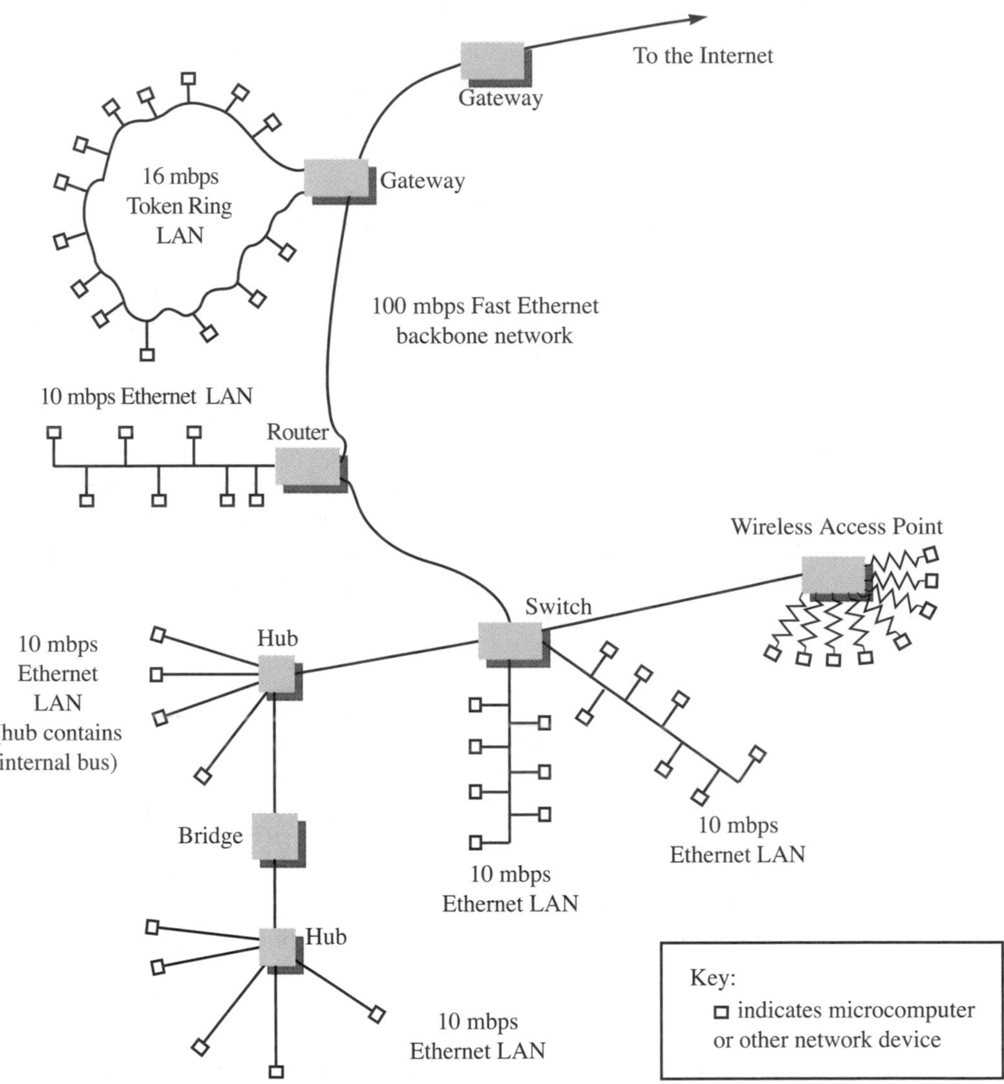

Figure 4.11 Sample Backbone Network

single 100 mbps backbone network (running Fast Ethernet). In this case the switch operates very much like a multiplexer. The top vendors of these hardware devices include Cisco, 3Com, and Lucent Technologies.

Wide Area Networks. Today's more complex, more widely dispersed organizations need **wide area networks (WANs)**, also called long-haul networks, to communicate both voice and data across their far-flung operations. A WAN differs from a LAN in that a WAN spans much greater distances (often entire countries or even the globe), has slower data rates (usually below 622 mbps), and is usually owned by several organizations (including both common carriers and the user organization). In addition, a WAN employs point-to-point transmission (except for satellites), whereas a LAN uses a multiaccess channel (such as the bus and ring). We will note some exceptions, but for the most part WANs rely on the public telephone network.

DDD and WATS. The easiest way to set up a WAN is to rely on ordinary public telephone service. **Direct Distance Dialing (DDD)** is available through the local telephone company and a long-distance carrier—AT&T, MCI, Sprint, or others—and can be used for voice and data communications between any two spots served by the telephone network. Of course, the speed for data transmission is quite limited (up to 56 kbps, depending upon the modem), data error rates are relatively high, and the cost per hour is very expensive. **Wide Area Telephone Service (WATS)** is also available, in which the organization pays a monthly fee for (typically) unlimited long-distance telephone service using the ordinary voice circuits. WATS has the same advantages and disadvantages as DDD. However, the cost per hour of WATS is somewhat less than DDD, but the customer pays for it whether it is used or not, while DDD is only paid for when it is used. DDD is appropriate for intermittent, limited-volume data transmission at relatively slow speeds, while WATS is used for more nearly continuous, somewhat larger volumes of data to be transmitted at relatively slow speeds.

Leased Lines. Another, sometimes attractive, alternative is to lease dedicated communications lines from AT&T or another carrier. If a manufacturing company has three plants geographically separated from corporate headquarters (where the mainframe computer or large servers are located), it might make sense to lease lines to connect each of the three plants to headquarters. These leased lines are generally coaxial cables, microwave, or fiber-optic cables of very high capacity, and they are less prone to data errors than ordinary voice lines. The leased lines are expensive, ranging from hundreds of dollars per month for distances of a few miles up to tens of thousands of dollars per month for cross-country lines.

The most common leased lines operate at a data transmission rate of 1.544 mbps and are referred to as **T-1 lines**. In order to effectively use this high data transmission rate, organizations must employ multiplexers at each end of a T-1 line to combine (or separate) a number of data streams that are, individually, much less than 1.544 mbps.

Leased lines with capacities higher than T-1 are also available. Four T-1 lines are combined to create a T-2 trunk, with a capacity of 6.312 mbps, but T-2 trunks have largely been bypassed in favor of T-3 trunks (consisting of seven T-2s), with a data transmission capacity of nearly 45 mbps. T-3 links are available between major cities, although the costs are much higher than for T-1 lines. T-4 trunks also exist (made up of six T-3s), with a huge capacity of 274 mbps.

The newest and highest capacity leased lines (and also the most expensive) are fiber-optic transmission lines, or SONET lines. **SONET**, which is an abbreviation for **Synchronous Optical Network**, is an American National Standards Institute (ANSI) approved standard for connecting fiber-optic transmission systems. Data transmission rates for SONET lines are shown in Table 4.3. Note that the slowest SONET transmission rate (OC-1) of nearly 52 mbps is faster than the T-3 rate of 45 mbps. All the links in the vBNS+ network shown in Figure 4.6 are SONET lines, with the faster of the two dual backbones operating at OC-48 (2.488 gbps) and the slower dual backbone and all other links operating at OC-12 (622 mbps). vBNS+ is truly a high-performance, high-bandwidth network.

Table 4.3 SONET Circuits

SONET Level	Data Transmission Rate
OC-1	51.84 mbps
OC-3	155.52 mbps
OC-9	466.56 mbps
OC-12	622.08 mbps
OC-18	933.12 mbps
OC-24	1.244 gbps
OC-36	1.866 gbps
OC-48	2.488 gbps
OC-192	9.953 gbps
OC-768	39.812 gbps

Key: mbps = million bits per second
gbps = billion bits per second

Satellite. Satellite microwave communication is being used by an increasing number of organizations that are setting up a WAN. The satellite or satellites involved are owned by companies such as Loral Space and Communications, Hughes Electronics Corporation, and Intelsat, and the user organization leases a portion of the satellite's capacity. The user organization either provides its own ground stations or leases time on a carrier's ground stations, as well as communication lines to and from those ground stations. The use of Ku-band transmission with relatively inexpensive VSAT ground stations is making satellite transmission very popular for organizations with many remote locations. Both Kmart and Wal-Mart, for example, use VSAT networks to link their thousands of stores with their corporate headquarters. V-Crest Systems, a member of the Volkswagen Group, runs a VSAT network for all the Porsche, Audi, and Volkswagen dealerships throughout the United States. Through the VSAT network, V-Crest provides information services for order placement, warranty processing, parts and vehicle location, customer tracking, financing, insurance, accounting, inventory control, and service management.

ISDN. Another way of implementing a WAN is an **Integrated Services Digital Network (ISDN)**. ISDN is a set of international standards by which the public telephone network is offering extensive new telecommunications capabilities (including simultaneous transmission of voice and data over the same line) to telephone users worldwide.

So-called narrowband ISDN is now available in many areas of the world. ISDN is digital communication, using the same twisted pairs already used in the present telephone network.

ISDN capabilities are made possible by hardware and software at the local telephone company office and on the organization's premises (such as a digital PBX) that divide a single telephone line (twisted pair) into two types of communication channels. The B, or bearer, channel transmits voice or data at rates of 64 kbps, faster than is possible using a modem. The D, or data, channel is used to send signal information to control the B channels and to carry packet-switched digital data.

So far, two narrowband ISDN services have been offered. The basic rate offers two B channels and one 16 kbps D channel (a total data rate of 144 kbps) over a single twisted pair. Each basic rate line is capable of supporting two voice devices and six data devices, any two of which can be operating simultaneously. The primary rate provides 23 B channels and one 64 kbps D channel (for a total data rate of 1.544 mbps) over two twisted pairs. Although not yet widely available, broadband ISDN—using fiber-optic cabling—offers data transmission rates of over 150 mbps. Therefore, ISDN provides a significant increase in capacity while still using the public telephone network.

Further, the D channel brings new capabilities to the network. For instance, the D channel can be used for telemetry, enabling remote control of machinery, heating, or air conditioning at the same time the B channels are being used for voice or data transmission. The D channel can also be used for single-button access to a variety of telephony features, such as call-waiting and display of the calling party's number.

A number of innovative uses of ISDN have been implemented. In a customer service application, an incoming call from a customer comes in over one of the B channels. The D channel is used to automatically signal the file server to send the customer's record to the service representative's workstation over the second B channel. In a marketing application, a salesperson sends alternative specifications or designs to a potential buyer's video screen over one B channel while simultaneously talking to the buyer over the second B channel.

The developments in ISDN are a part of the digitization of the public telephone network. However, ISDN has never caught on in a big way, and it now seems destined to be bypassed by other digital developments such as DSL (to be covered in a later section) and IP (Internet Protocol) telephony. At present, ISDN service is available on most telephone lines in the United States. But ISDN service is still relatively expensive. As an example, to obtain a basic rate ISDN line from SBC (a regional Bell operating company), the installation fee is $113 and the monthly line charge is about $40 for voice and data services. In addition, an ISDN modem is required. What advantages does this ISDN line provide? ISDN permits the user to be a more effective telecommuter (working from home), to share a computer screen display with another user at a distant location, to conduct desktop videoconferencing, to transfer large data files with ease, and to access the Internet at 128 kbps (combining the two B channels), over twice as fast as an ordinary modem.

Packet-Switched Networks. **Packet-switched networks** are quite different from the switched-circuit (DDD and WATS, ISDN) and dedicated-circuit (leased lines, satellite) networks previously described. In switched- and dedicated-circuit networks, a circuit is established between the two computers that are communicating, and no other devices can use that circuit for the duration of the connection. In contrast, a packet-switched network permits multiple connections to exist simultaneously over the same physical circuit. **Packet switching** is a store-and-forward data transmission technique. Communications are sent over the common carrier network, divided into packets of some fixed length, perhaps 300 characters (see Figure 4.12). Control information is attached to the front and rear of this packet, and it is sent over a communications line in a single bundle. Packet switching is quite different from usual voice and data communications, where the entire end-to-end circuit is tied up for the duration of the session. With packet switching, the network is used more efficiently because packets from various users can be interspersed with one another. The computers controlling the network will route each individual packet along the appropriate path.

A **packet assembly/disassembly device (PAD)** is used to connect the user organization's internal networks (at each of its locations) to the common carrier network. The organization must, of course, pay a fee to make use of the common carrier network. In some cases the user organization provides the PADs and pays a fixed fee for a connection into the common carrier network plus a charge for the number of packets transmitted. In other cases the user organization might contract with a firm that manages and operates the entire WAN for the user organization, including the PADs needed at each location. This contracting-out practice used to be called a **value added network**, or **VAN**, but that terminology has largely disappeared. Today such a packet-switched WAN is usually called a managed network. In the United States, managed network services are available from AT&T, Sprint, MCI, and Infonet Services Corporation. Packet-switched networks are quite common,

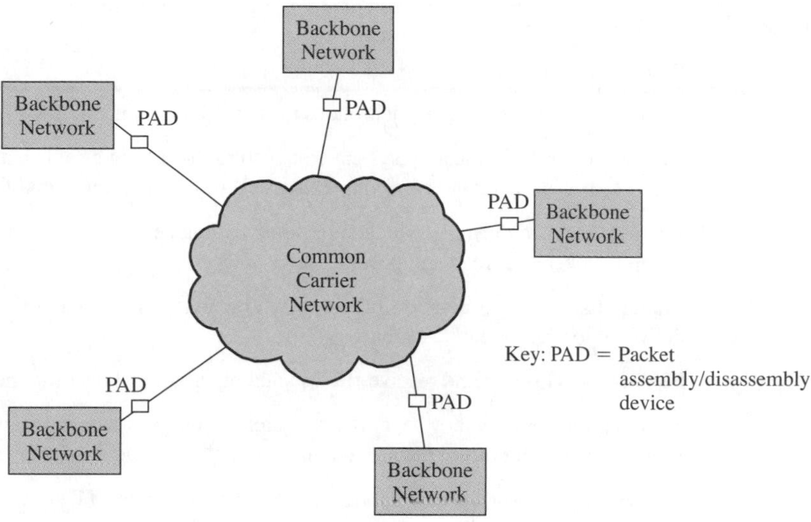

Figure 4.12 Packet-Switched Network Connecting Five Organizational Locations

including some networks like vBNS+ that serve a limited audience and others like the Internet that are available to anyone or any organization that wishes to buy the networking service.

ATM. One of the newer entries on the WAN as well as the backbone network scene is **ATM**, or **Asynchronous Transfer Mode**. ATM is based on the idea of packet switching as described earlier. For ATM, each packet is rather small—a total of 53 bytes, including 48 bytes of data and 5 bytes of control information attached to the front of the packet. ATM was originally created for use in WANs to carry both data and voice traffic, which helps explain the small packet size—the small packet is an appropriate size for voice traffic, but it is very small for data traffic. ATM is a telecommunications standard for broadband ISDN.

ATM does not really describe a line transmission technology, such as contention bus or token ring; it is a switching technology with usual speeds from 155 mbps in each direction up to 622 mbps. ATM operates as a full-duplex circuit, so the total throughput varies from 310 mbps (155 mbps times 2) up to 1.24 gbps (622 mbps times 2). An ATM network uses switches arranged in a mesh topology (see Figure 4.5), usually running on fiber-optic cables or category 5 twisted-pair cables. In brief, ATM is fast packet switching with short, fixed-length packets.

Because of the fast data transmission rates, ATM networks gained a foothold in the WAN arena and in backbone networks; they were also used in some LANs. However, ATM uses protocols that differ from the Internet's Transmission Control Protocol/Internet Protocol (TCP/IP), so it is necessary to convert ATM addresses into TCP/IP addresses (and back) to access the Internet from an ATM network. Thus, with the ascendancy of the Internet, ATM fell into disfavor. ATM has had some successes, and it is now widely used deep within the public telephone network (Tanenbaum, 2003, p. 62). It is not, however, a common choice for WANs or backbone networks.

Virtual Private Networks. A **virtual private network (VPN)** provides the equivalent of a private packet-switched network (as discussed earlier) using the public Internet. A VPN provides a moderate data rate (up to 2 mbps) at a very reasonable cost, but the network's reliability is low. To establish a VPN, the user organization places a VPN device (a special router or switch) on each Internet access circuit to provide access from the organization's networks to the VPN. Of course, the user organization must pay for the access circuits and the Internet service provider (ISP). The VPN devices enable the creation of VPN *tunnels* through the Internet. Through the use of encapsulation and encryption, these tunnels ensure that only authorized users can access the VPN. The primary advantages of VPNs are low cost and flexibility, while the disadvantages include low reliability, unpredictable transmission speeds, and security concerns. An organization can create a VPN itself, or it can contract with a vendor such as AT&T or MCI to manage and operate the VPN.

Internet. Almost last, but certainly not least, of the network types we will consider is the ubiquitous Internet. The Internet could be considered a gigantic WAN, but it is really

Table 4.4 Internet Applications

Name of Application	Purpose of Application
Electronic mail, or e-mail	Easy-to-use, inexpensive, asynchronous means of communication with other Internet users
Instant messaging	Synchronous communication system that enables the user to establish a private “chat room” with another individual to carry out text-based communication in real time over the Internet
Usenet newsgroups	Internet discussion groups, which are essentially huge electronic bulletin boards on which group members can read and post messages
Listserv	Mailing list such that members of a group can send a single e-mail message and have it delivered to everyone in the group
File Transfer Protocol, or FTP	Permits users to send and receive files, including programs, over the Internet
Gopher	Menu-based tool that allows the user to search for publicly available data posted on the Internet by digging through a series of menus until the sought-after data are located
Archie	Allows the user to search the publicly available anonymous FTP sites to find the desired files
Veronica	Allows the user to search the publicly available Gopher sites using key words until the sought-after data are located
World Wide Web, or the Web	Hypertext-based tool that allows the user to traverse, or surf, the Internet by clicking on a link contained in one document to move to another document, and so on; these documents might also include video clips, recordings, photographs, and other images

much more than that. The **Internet** is a network of networks that use the TCP/IP protocol (to be discussed later in the chapter), with gateways (connections) to even more networks that do not use the TCP/IP protocol. By January 2003 there were approximately 172 million hosts (number of IP addresses that have been assigned a name) on the Internet (Internet Software Consortium, 2003). An “educated guess” of the number of Internet users in September 2002 was 605 million, with over 182 million users in Canada and the United States (Nua.com, 2003). An incredible array of resources—both data and services—is available on the Internet, and these resources are drawing more users, which are drawing more resources, in a seemingly never-ending cycle.

The Internet has an interesting history, dating back to 1969 when the U.S. Department of Defense created ARPANET to link a number of leading research universities. Ethernet LANs incorporating TCP/IP networking arrived in the early 1980s, and NSFNET was created in 1986 to link five supercomputer centers in the United States. NSFNET served as the backbone (the underlying foundation of the network, to which other elements are attached) of the emerging Internet as scores of other networks connected to it. Originally, commercial traffic was not permitted on the Internet, but this barrier was broken in the late 1980s and the floodgates opened in the early 1990s. In 1995 the National Science Foundation withdrew all financial support for the Internet, and began funding vBNS+ (see Figure 4.6)—which is sometimes considered as part of Internet2 (discussed next).

The Internet has no direct connection to the U.S. government or any other government. Authority rests with the Internet Society, a voluntary membership organization. The governing body of the society is the Internet Architecture Board, which is entirely made up of volunteers. Similarly, the Internet receives no government support now that NSF funding has ended. Users pay for their own piece of the Internet. For an individual, this usually means paying an Internet service provider (ISP) a monthly fee to be able to dial a local number and log into the Internet. The smaller ISPs, in turn, pay a fee to hook into the Internet backbone, which is a network of high-bandwidth networks owned by major ISPs such as AT&T, UUNet/MCI, Sprint, and Aleron.

The Internet provides the four basic functions: electronic mail, remote login, discussion groups, and the sharing of data resources. Electronic mail was really the first “killer app” of the Internet—the first application that grabbed the attention of potential users and turned them into Internet converts. Electronic mail provides an easy-to-use, inexpensive, asynchronous means of communication with other Internet users anywhere in the world. A newer variant of electronic mail, **instant messaging (IM)** is a synchronous communication system that enables the user to establish a private "chat room" with another individual to carry out text-based communication in real time over the Internet. Typically, the IM system signals the user when someone on his or her private list is online, and then the user can initiate a chat session with that individual. Major players in the IM market are America Online, Yahoo!, Microsoft, and IBM Lotus.

Remote login permits a user in, say, Phoenix, to log into another machine on which she has an account in, say, Vienna, using a software program such as Telnet. Then she can work on the Vienna machine exactly as if she were there. Discussion groups are just that—Internet users who have gathered together to discuss some topic. **Usenet newsgroups** are the most organized of the discussion groups; they are essentially a set of huge electronic bulletin boards on which group members can read and post messages. A **listserv** is a mailing list such that members of the group can send a single e-mail message and have it delivered to everyone in the group. This usually works fine as long as users remember whether they are sending a message to an individual in the group or to the entire group. Do not use the reply function in response to a listserv message unless you intend your reply to go to the entire group!

The sharing of data resources is a gigantic use of the Internet. **File Transfer Protocol**, or **FTP**, is a program that permits users to send and receive files, including other programs, over the Internet. For ordinary FTP use, the user needs to know the account name and password of the remote computer in order to log into it. Anonymous FTP sites have also been set up, however, which permit any Internet user to log in using "anonymous" as the account name. As a matter of courtesy (and to track accesses), most anonymous FTP sites ask that the user enter his e-mail address as the password. Once logged in, the user may transfer any files located at that anonymous FTP site. **Gopher** is a menu-based tool that allows you to search for publicly available information posted on the Internet by digging (like a gopher) through a series of menus until you find what you want. **Archie** is a tool that allows you to search the publicly available anonymous FTP sites worldwide to find files. And **Veronica** performs a similar function with Gopher sites, searching the publicly available Gopher sites using key words to identify the data you are after.

Early in the twenty-first century, FTP is still popular, but Gopher, Archie, and Veronica have largely disappeared, subsumed by the tremendous capabilities of the **World Wide Web**, or **WWW**, or just the **Web**. The Web is a hypertext-based way of traversing, or "surfing," the Internet. With hypertext, any document can contain links to other documents. By clicking on the link with the computer mouse, the referenced document will be retrieved—whether it is stored on your own computer, one down the hall, or one on the other side of the world. More than this, the Web provides a graphical user interface (GUI) so that images, photographs, sound bites, and full motion video can be displayed on your screen as part of the document (provided your computer is appropriately equipped). All this material is delivered to your computer via the Internet. The World Wide Web is the second "killer app" of the Internet, and it has accelerated the already rapid telecommunications revolution.

To use the World Wide Web, the user's machine must have a Web browser program installed. This software package permits the machine to access a Web server, using either a dial-up telephone connection (with a modem) or a direct connection through a LAN. The most popular browser is Microsoft's Internet Explorer. When a user first logs into the Web, she is connected to a "home" server at her ISP or her own organization. She can then surf the Web by clicking on hypertext links, or she can search for a

IM ABUSE IS RAMPANT IN WORKPLACE

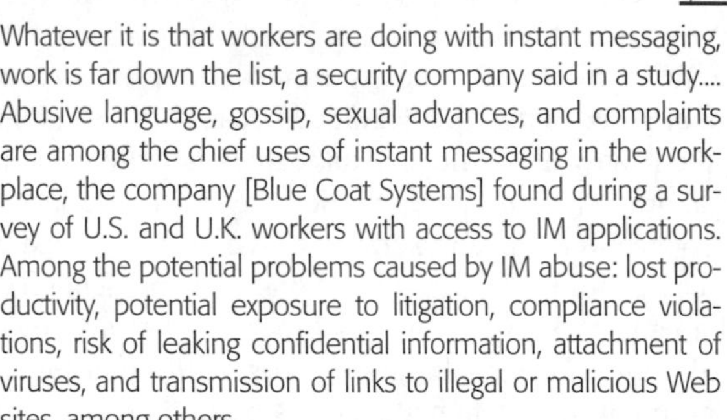

Whatever it is that workers are doing with instant messaging, work is far down the list, a security company said in a study.... Abusive language, gossip, sexual advances, and complaints are among the chief uses of instant messaging in the workplace, the company [Blue Coat Systems] found during a survey of U.S. and U.K. workers with access to IM applications. Among the potential problems caused by IM abuse: lost productivity, potential exposure to litigation, compliance violations, risk of leaking confidential information, attachment of viruses, and transmission of links to illegal or malicious Web sites, among others.

"There are currently 40 million business users of IM, and there are genuine business benefits to the immediacy of IM," said Steve Mullaney, Blue Coat's marketing VP. "The technology is not going to go away. But left unchecked, instant messaging could ultimately cause more business problems than it solves."

The solution, from [Blue Coat's] point of view, is to make IM a full member of the enterprise IT club, subject to the same level of restriction, monitoring, and enforcement as e-mail, Internet use, and other better-established applications. Blue Coat also recommended development of company policies regarding appropriate use of instant messaging, basing those policies on a "log it, manage it, control it" triad.

[Ferrell, 2003]

particular topic using a Web crawler, or "search engine" program. Or, if she knows the address of the site she wishes to visit—this address is called the **Uniform Resource Locator** (**URL**)—she can enter the address directly into her browser. For Web site addresses, or URLs, she expects to visit frequently, she can save the address as a "bookmark" in her browser so that all she must do is click on the appropriate bookmark to return to the Web site.

In the early days of the Web (say, 1992 to 1995), a great deal of factual information was on the Web, but very little of commercial interest. Today, however, all major organizations, and many lesser ones, have a significant presence on the Web. The Web gives businesses a new way to provide information about their products and services, a new way to advertise, and a new way to communicate with customers and suppliers and potential customers and suppliers. With increasing frequency, the Web is being used to complete sales, particularly of products, such as software, that can be delivered via the Internet and of products such as books, CDs, and clothes, that can be delivered via regular mail. (We will talk more about electronic commerce via the Web in Chapter 7.) Designing appealing Web pages has become an art—firms want to make sure that their pages convey the right image. Figures 4.13 and 4.14 show the home pages of two leaders in the information technology field, Microsoft and Hewlett-Packard.

DSL, Cable Modem, and Satellite. How does an individual user access the Internet? In the workplace, most users are connected to a LAN, which in turn is connected to the organizational backbone network, and then to the Internet. From home or a small office, connections are most often made from a dial-in modem, operating at speeds up to 56 kbps. ISDN service is also available in most parts of the United States with data transfer rates up to 128 kbps. Early in the twenty-first century, three newer, higher-speed alternatives burst on the scene: **digital subscriber line** (**DSL**), **cable modem** connection, and **satellite** connection. Taken together, these are referred to as **broadband** connections.

DSL is a service offered by telephone companies using the copper wires already installed in homes and offices; it uses a sophisticated modulation scheme to move data over the wires without interfering with voice traffic—that is, both a voice conversation and an Internet hookup can be active at the same time over a single DSL line. DSL is sometimes called a "last mile" technology in that it is used only for connections from a telephone switching station to a home or office, not for connections between switching stations. Data transfer rates on DSL are very fast, varying from 384 kpbs to 1.544 mbps downstream from the Internet to the home or office machine and usually 128 kbps upstream from the home or office machine to the Internet. This differential in upstream and downstream speed is not usually a problem, because users typically do not send as much data *to* the Web as they receive *from* the Web. Furthermore, the DSL line is dedicated to the single user, so these speeds are guaranteed. As an example of the costs, self-installation of the SBC Yahoo! DSL basic package in Indianapolis is almost free—as part of a special offer, the $99 modem is offset by a $99 instant credit if the user signs a 1-year agreement. A network interface card is included if needed. Activation is free, and the user needs to pay only taxes and a $14.95 shipping and handling fee. The monthly fee for the first year is $26.95, which does not include regular voice telephone service but does include basic Yahoo! ISP service. There is a $200 charge for a technician to install DSL.

A cable modem connection is very competitive to DSL in both price and speed. In this case the service is obtained from the cable television company and the data are transmitted over the coaxial cables already used by television. These cables have much greater bandwidth than twisted pair copper wires, but traditionally they transmitted data only in one direction—from the cable television company to the home. Reengineering of the cable television system was necessary to permit the two-way data flow required for Internet connections. Current download speeds with a cable modem range up to 3 mbps, with upload speeds considerably slower (256 kbps is common). However, cable modem speeds might be degraded because users are sharing the bandwidth of the coaxial cable; as more users in a neighborhood log into the Internet, the slower the speed of the connections. As an example of the costs, the installation charge for Cox Communications cable modem service in Phoenix is $100, or the customer can use a free self-installation kit. A cable modem costs $90, and the customer might be able to get it free as part of a special offer. Then the monthly service charges are $39.95 for cable television customers. No additional ISP is needed; Cox Communications provides the connection to the Internet.

The third alternative, a satellite connection, tends to be the most expensive option, but for customers in rural areas it might be the only choice. The uplink operates from 50 to 128 kbps, with the downlink from 400 to 700 kbps with bursts up to 1.5 mbps. Satellite broadband connections can be one-way service or two-way service. For one-way service, the customer must contract with a wired ISP (dial-up, DSL, or cable modem) for the uplink, while the satellite supports the downlink. The downlink is just like the usual terrestrial link, except that the satellite transmits data to the computer via a satellite dish at the customer's home or office. The two-way satellite service transmits and receives

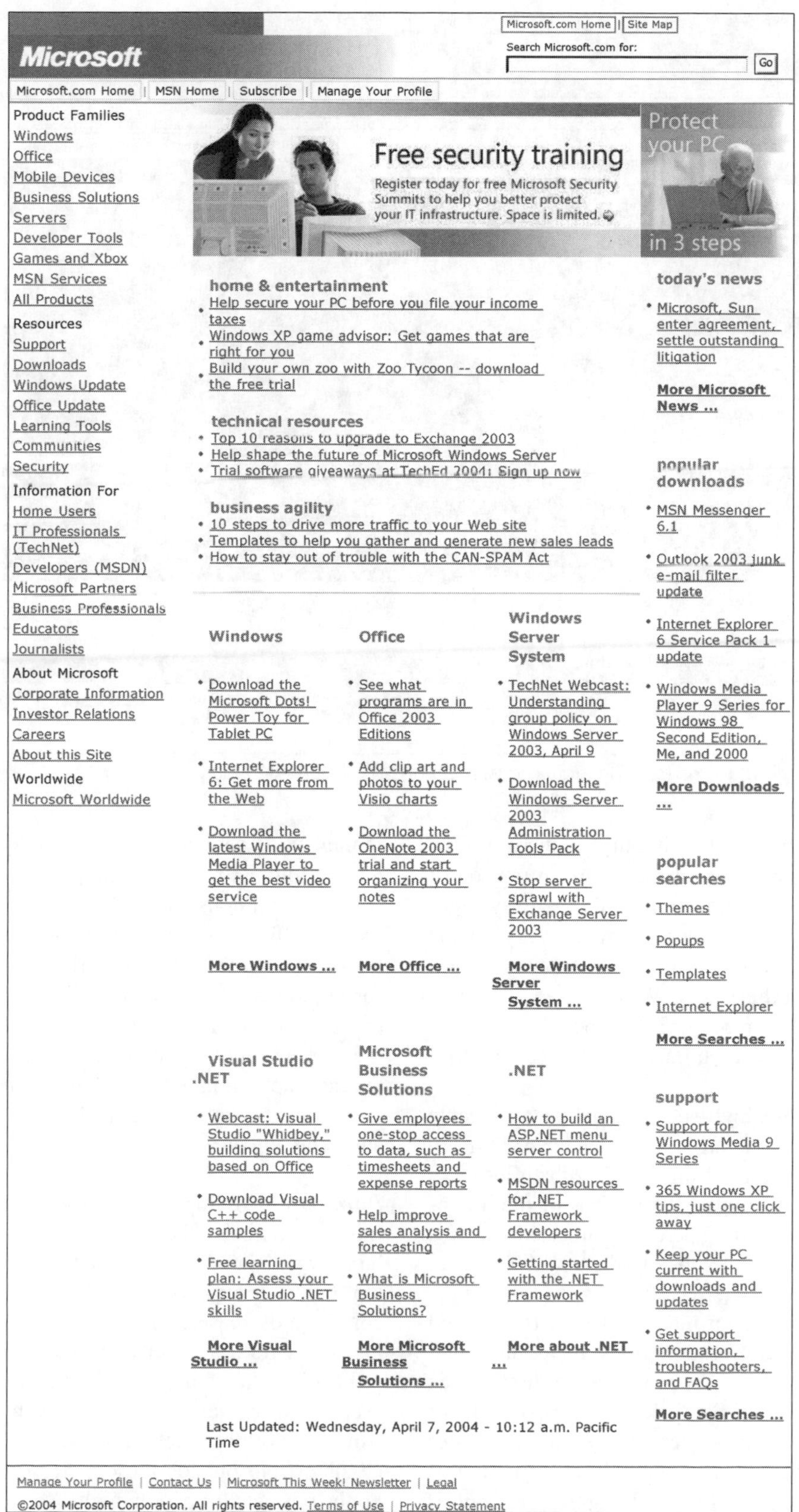

Figure 4.13 Microsoft Home Page (Reproduced with permission from Microsoft Corporation).

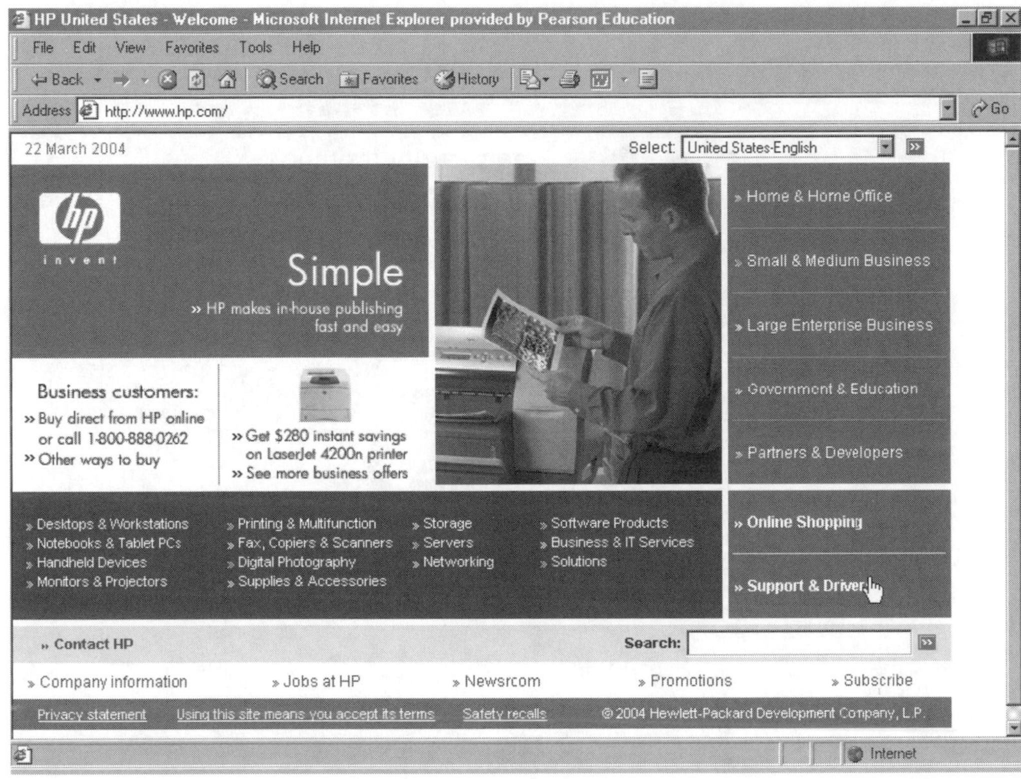

Figure 4.14 Hewlett-Packard Home Page (Reproduced with permission of Hewlett-Packard Company).

signals directly via the satellite without needing a ground line to support the connection for the upstream portion of the broadband service. As an example of a two-way satellite service, DirecWay (from Hughes Network Systems) is available from any location in the United States with a clear view of the southern sky. With a 1-year service agreement, the installation fee is $600 (including a satellite dish, a modem, and installation) and the monthly charge is $59.99.

In the battle to provide high-speed Internet access, cable modem connections have a strong early lead over DSL. In mid-2003 there were about 22 million broadband users in the United States, with roughly two-thirds of them connected by cable modem and 30 percent connected via DSL (Crockett, Ihlwan, and Yang, 2003; Jesdanun, 2003). Both cable modem and DSL users have been growing rapidly, and that growth should continue. However, the United States is far behind several other nations, including South Korea, Japan, and Canada, in the proportion of households with broadband service. In South Korea, three-fourths of all households have broadband service, and the data rates are roughly triple U.S. rates at a monthly cost that is just over half the average U.S. cost. In Japan, 27 percent of households have broadband service, compared to 10 percent in the U.S. Broadband in Japan averages 10 mbps for only $23 a month. Broadband adoption in Canada is up to 36 percent of all households. If the U.S. is to catch up, it will require efforts on the part of the government to remove regulatory roadblocks and perhaps provide tax incentives for broadband investments, efforts on the part of service providers to reduce prices and increase speeds, efforts on the part of venture capitalists to promote broadband content startup companies, and efforts on the part of content developers to promote legal file-sharing (Crockett, Ihlwan, and Yang, 2003).

Intranets. An important spin-off from the success of the Internet has been the creation of **intranets** within many large organizations. An intranet is simply a network operating within an organization that employs the TCP/IP protocol. In most cases, an intranet consists of a backbone network with a number of connected LANs. Because the protocol is the same, the organization may use the same Web browser, Web crawler, and Web server software as it would use on the Internet; however, the intranet is not accessible from outside the organization. It might or might not be possible for people within the organization to access the Internet.

DENIAL-OF-SERVICE ATTACKS, WORMS, VIRUSES PLAGUE THE INTERNET

It seems as though every month we read about—or experience first-hand—reliability and security problems on the Internet, such as denial-of-service attacks, worms, and viruses. In July 2003, Microsoft's Web site was inaccessible for almost 2 hours when a denial-of-service attack overwhelmed the site with traffic. Another denial-of-service attack hit the Web site of Knight Ridder's 31 daily newspapers (including the Miami Herald, the Philadelphia Inquirer, and the San Jose Mercury News) for several hours in September 2003. These denial-of-service attacks most likely came from one or more small programs, readily available for downloading from the Web, that were planted in the computers of unsuspecting users all over the world. Then, at some signal from the mastermind, the programs in these multiple computers started requesting access to the Microsoft or Knight Ridder site, over and over and over again. With these repeated requests from multiple computers, all in a matter of seconds, the sites simply could not handle the traffic and were essentially shut down. This congestion is like repeatedly dialing a telephone number so that everyone else dialing the same number will always get a busy signal. Thus, the perpetrators "denied service" to the legitimate users of the Web sites.

Viruses and worms are quite similar; both can play havoc with the operation of an infected computer. A virus is a program or piece of code that is loaded onto your computer without your knowledge and against your wishes; it can attach itself to other programs and can replicate itself. A worm is a special type of virus that can replicate itself and use memory but that cannot attach itself to other programs. Among the many virus and worm attacks in 2003 were the Slammer attack in January, which infected vulnerable computers by exploiting a known flaw in Microsoft's SQL Server 2000 database program; the Blaster attack in early August, which affected newer versions of Microsoft Windows through a vulnerability in its Remote Procedure Call interface; and the Sobig attack in late August, which worked to identify hiding spots for the worm and more e-mail addresses to propagate itself. Among the many repercussions of these attacks, the Slammer attack disrupted operations for police and fire dispatchers outside Seattle, who had to resort to pencil and paper for hours, and the Blaster attack brought portions of CSX Transportation's 23,000-mile rail network to a halt and delayed Amtrak's Washington, D.C. commuter trains by 2 hours. On a more personal note, the Blaster worm infected the home computer of one of this book's authors, forcing him to restart his computer multiple times until he was able to remove the worm. The Internet is important to all of us, and it is becoming even more important, but it has a long way to go to achieve reliability and security.

[Adapted from Bridis, 2003; Foley, 2003; Kreiser and Hulme, 2003; Babcock, 2003; and Associated Press, 2003]

Some commentators have referred to the Internet as the "information superhighway." That is wrong, as Bill Gates, the chairman of Microsoft, has pointed out in his book, *The Road Ahead* (1995). The Internet is merely the predecessor of the information superhighway; we are not there yet. Before we have a true information superhighway, we need gigantic increases in bandwidth, more reliability and security (see the sidebar entitled "Denial-of-Service Attacks, Worms, Viruses Plague the Internet"), more accessibility by the entire population, and more applications. We are only beginning to scratch the surface of possibilities for the Internet and the information superhighway beyond.

Internet2. In reality, **Internet2** is not a network type, although it does run a leading-edge, very high-bandwidth network; it is a not-for-profit consortium of over 200 universities, working in partnership with over 60 leading technology companies and the U.S. government, to develop and deploy advanced network applications and technologies. Internet2 hopes to accelerate the creation of tomorrow's Internet, a true "information superhighway." The three primary goals of Internet2 are to

- create a leading-edge network capability for the national research community
- enable revolutionary Internet applications based on a much higher-performance Internet than we have today
- ensure the rapid transfer of new network services and applications to the broader Internet community

Internet2's "leading-edge network for the national research community" is named Abilene, and its operation center is in Indianapolis (see Figure 4.15). This is a very high-performance network, with all but one of the links in Figure 4.15 operating at 9.953 gbps (OC-192). You can go online at *loadrunner.uits.iu.edu/weathermaps/Abilene* and see how busy the network currently is. Abilene is a backbone network used by the Internet2 universities; it provides an effective interconnection among regional networking aggregation points, called gigaPoPs, that have been formed by the Internet2 universities. Created by the Internet2 community, Abilene is a partnership of Internet2, Qwest Communications, Cisco Systems, Nortel Networks, and Indiana University. Please note that Abilene is engaged in a healthy, even cooperative sort of competition with vBNS+, another very high-performance network operated by MCI (see Figure 4.6). There is a significant overlap of vBNS+ customers and Internet2 members, and MCI engineers

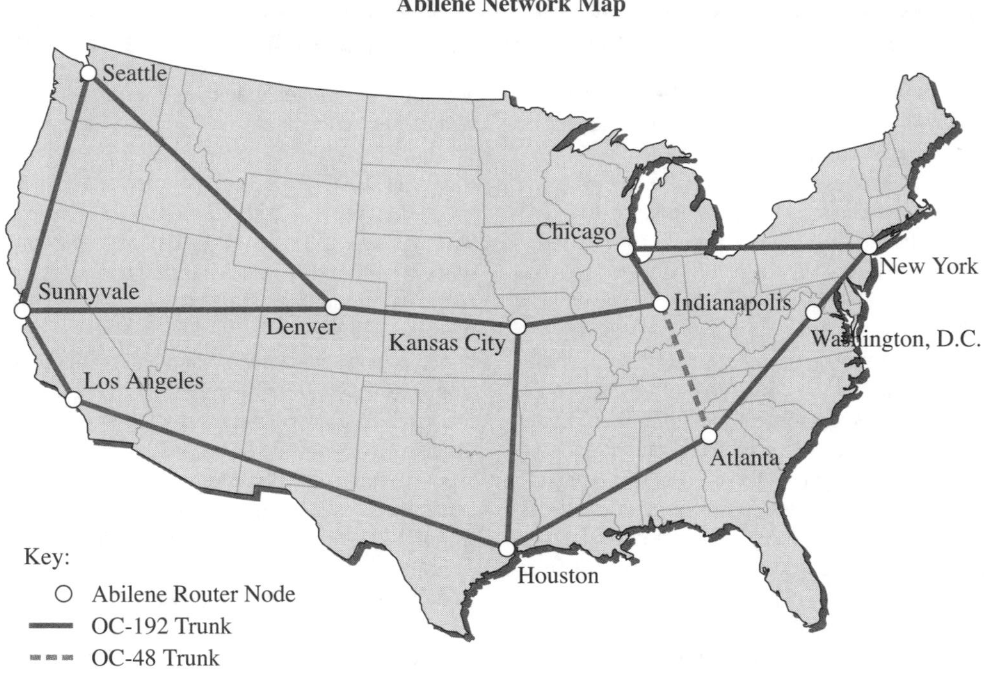

Figure 4.15 Abilene Network Map

have participated in several Internet2 projects. In fact, the vBNS+ and Abilene networks have a connection through the network access point in Chicago. vBNS+, Abilene, and the other Internet2 projects are the precursors of tomorrow's Internet.

Network Protocols

There is only one more major piece to our network puzzle. How do the various elements of these networks actually communicate with one another? The answer is by means of a **network protocol**, an agreed-upon set of rules or conventions governing communication among elements of a network, or, to be more precise, among layers or levels of a network. In order for two network elements to communicate with each other, they must both use the same protocol. Therefore, the protocol truly enables elements of the network to communicate with one another.

Without actually using the protocol label, we have already encountered several protocols. LANs, for example, have four widely accepted protocols: contention bus, token bus, token ring, and wireless. Historically the biggest problem with protocols is that there have been too many of them (or, to look at the problem in another way, not enough acceptance of a few of them). For example, IBM and each of the other major hardware vendors created their own sets of protocols. IBM's set of protocols is collectively termed Systems Network Architecture or SNA. IBM equipment and equipment from another vendor, say, Hewlett-Packard, cannot communicate with each other unless *both* employ the same protocols—IBM's, or H-P's, or perhaps another set of "open systems" protocols. The big challenge involved in integrating computers and other related equipment from many vendors into a network is *standardization* so that all use the same protocols!

In the past two decades considerable progress has been made in standardization and acceptance of a set of protocols—although we are not ending up where most commentators would have predicted in the late 1980s. At that time, it appeared that the **OSI** or **Open Systems Interconnection Reference Model**, developed by the International Organization for Standardization (ISO), would become the standard set of protocols. The OSI model defines seven layers (see Figure 4.16), each of which will have its own protocol (or protocols). The OSI model is only a skeleton, with standard protocols in existence for some layers (the four LAN protocols are part of the data link layer), but with only rough ideas in other layers. All major computer and telecommunications vendors—including IBM—announced their support for the OSI model, and it appeared that OSI was on its way.

For better or worse, the movement toward the OSI model was essentially stopped in the 1990s by the explosion of the role of the Internet and the creation of numerous intranets within major organizations. Both the Internet and intranets employ TCP/IP, or Transmission Control Protocol/Internet Protocol, as their protocol. TCP/IP is not

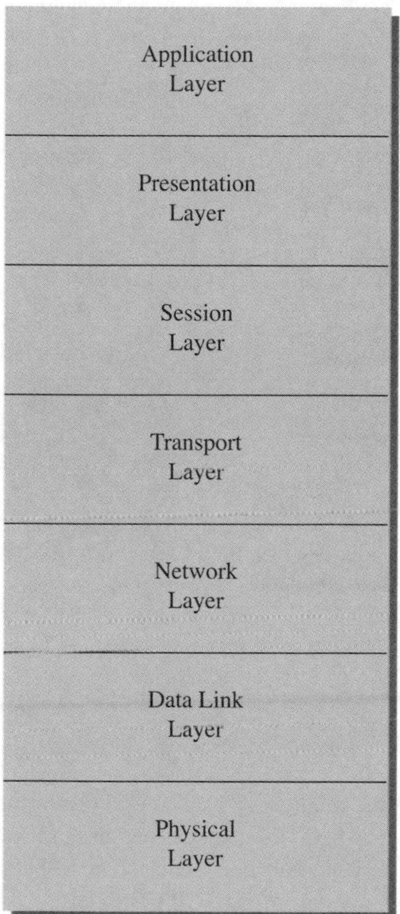

Figure 4.16 Seven Layers of the OSI Reference Model

part of the OSI reference model, and it is a less comprehensive set of protocols than OSI, correspondingly roughly to two of the seven OSI layers. Both the OSI model and TCP/IP are important, for different reasons, so we will explore both sets of protocols. The OSI model provides an extremely useful framework for considering computer networks, so it is a good place to begin. The TCP/IP model, augmented with some other ideas, is the *de facto* standard set of protocols for networking in the early twenty-first century, so we will turn to TCP/IP after considering the OSI model.

OSI Reference Model. Because of the importance of the OSI model, and because it will give us a conceptual framework to understand how communication takes place in networks, we will briefly discuss each of the layers in the OSI model and an example of how data can be transmitted using the model (see Figure 4.17). This is a very complex model because it must support many types of networks (e.g., LANs and WANs) and many types of communication (e.g., electronic mail, electronic data interchange, and executive information systems).

Physical Layer. The physical layer is concerned with transmitting bits (a string of zeros and ones) over a physical communication channel. Electrical engineers work at this level, with typical design issues involving such questions as how many volts should be used to represent a 1 and how many for a 0.

Data Link Layer. For the data link layer to work, data must be submitted to it (by the network layer) in the form of data frames of a few hundred bytes. Then the data link adds special header and trailer data at the beginning and end of each frame, respectively, so that it can recognize the frame boundaries. The data link transmits the frames in sequence to the physical layer for actual transmittal and also processes acknowledgment frames sent back by the data link layer of the receiver and makes sure that there are no transmission errors.

Network Layer. The network layer receives a packet of data from the transport layer and adds special header data to it to identify the route that the packet is to take to its destination. This augmented packet becomes the frame passed on to the data link layer. The primary concern of the network layer is the routing of the packets. The network layer often contains an accounting function as well in order to produce billing information.

Transport Layer. Although not illustrated by Figure 4.17, the transport layer is the first end-to-end layer encountered. In the lower layers of the OSI model, the protocols are between a sending device and its immediate neighbor, then between the neighbor and its immediate neighbor, and so on, until the receiving device is reached. Starting with the transport layer and continuing through the three upper layers, the conversation is directly between the layer for the sending device and the corresponding layer for the receiving device. Thus, the upper four layers are end-to-end protocols.

The transport layer receives the communication (of whatever length) from the session layer, splits it into smaller blocks if necessary, adds special header data defining the network connection(s) to be used, passes the packet(s) to the network layer, and checks to make sure that all the packets arrive correctly at the receiving end. If the network connection requires multiplexing for its efficient use, the transport layer also handles this (and in a manner transparent to the higher layers).

Session Layer. Through the session layer, users on different machines may establish sessions between them. For most applications the session layer is not used, but it would allow a user to log into a remote computer or to transfer a

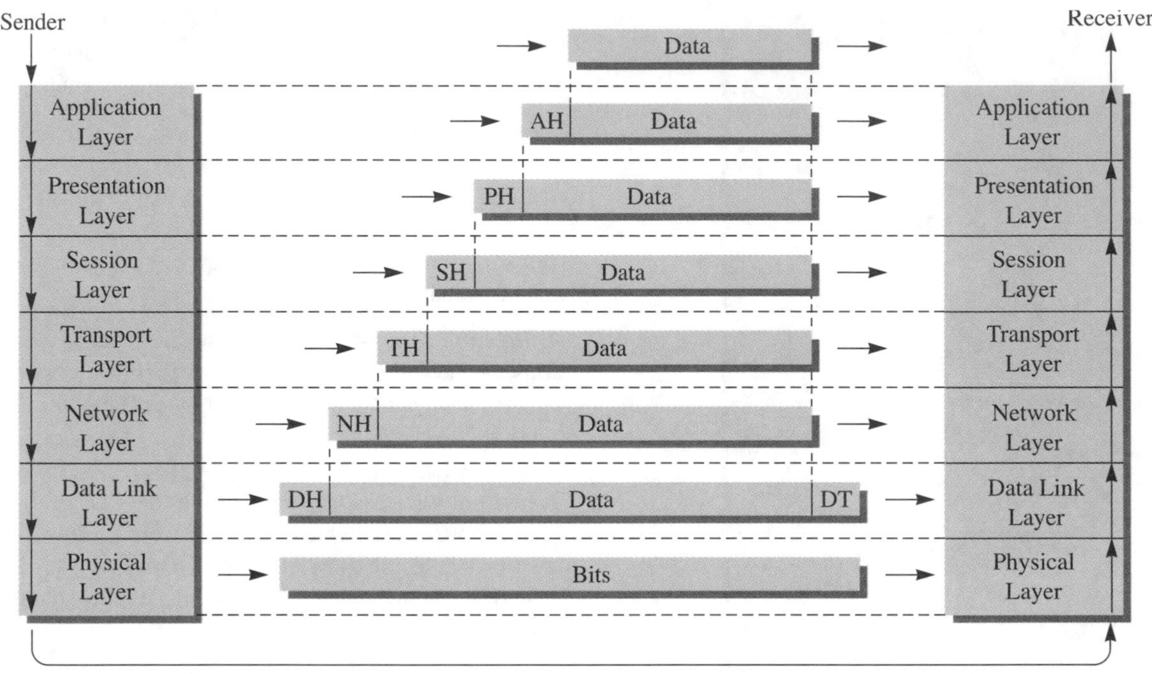

Figure 4.17 Data Transmission Based on OSI Model

file between two computers. The session layer may provide several services to the users, including dialog control (if traffic can only move in one direction at a time) and synchronization (so that a portion of a communication received need not be retransmitted even if the network fails).

Presentation Layer. The presentation layer, unlike the lower layers, is concerned with the information to be transmitted, rather than viewing it as a string of bits. The presentation layer accepts as input the communication as internally coded by the sending device and translates it into the standard representation used by the network. (The presentation layer on the receiving device reverses this process.) In addition, the data may be cryptographically encoded if it is especially sensitive. Like the layers below and above, the presentation layer adds a header to the data before sending it to the layer below.

Application Layer. The uppermost layer deals with the wide variety of communications-oriented applications that are directly visible to the user, such as electronic data interchange, file transfer, electronic mail, and factory floor control. There will always be differences across different terminals or systems, and a protocol is required for each application (usually implemented in software) to make each of these devices appear the same to the network. For a group of users to communicate using electronic mail, for example, the devices they employ must all use the same application layer/electronic mail protocol. The OSI electronic mail protocol, known as MOTIS, gained acceptance in some parts of the world but has largely been replaced by SMTP, which is at least unofficially part of the TCP/IP model.

Data Transmission Using the OSI Model. Figure 4.17 provides an illustration of data transmission based on the OSI model. The sender has some data to be transmitted to the receiver. The sender, for example, might be a manager at a workstation who wishes to transmit a query to the corporate executive information system located on a large server in another state. The manager types in a query, which is temporarily stored in the workstation in electronic form. When the manager hits the Enter key, the query (data) is given to the application layer, which adds the application header (AH) and gives the resulting augmented data item to the presentation layer. The presentation layer converts the item into the appropriate network code, adds a presentation header (PH), and passes it on to the session layer. The session layer might not do anything, but if it does, it will end by attaching a session header (SH) and passing the augmented item to the transport layer. The transport layer does its work, adds a transport header (TH), and sends the resulting packet to the network layer. The network layer, in turn, does its work, adds a network header (NH), and sends the resulting frame to the data link layer. The data link layer accepts the frame, adds both a header (DH) and a trailer (DT), and sends the final bit stream to the physical layer for actual transmission to the receiver.

When the bit stream reaches the receiver, the various headers (and trailer) are stripped off one at a time as the communication moves up through the seven layers until only the original query arrives at the receiver, which, in our example, is a large server. Perhaps the easiest way to understand this entire process is that the original data go through a multilevel translation process (which is really much more than translation), with each layer acting as if it were directly communicating with the corresponding receiving layer. Most important, the entire process should take place in a device/system independent way that is totally transparent to the user.

TCP/IP. **TCP/IP**, or **Transmission Control Protocol/Internet Protocol**, is not part of the OSI reference model, although it roughly corresponds to the network and transport layers. TCP/IP is used in many non-Internet networks, including vBNS+ and Abilene, as well as in the UNIX and Linux operating systems and in Microsoft Windows. Most important, TCP/IP is the protocol used on the worldwide Internet and on numerous intranets operating within organizations. Thus TCP/IP, not OSI, has become the *de facto* standard protocol for networking around the world. Nevertheless, TCP/IP is only a partial set of protocols, not a fully developed model. Thus computer scientists and commentators have, in effect, developed an augmented TCP/IP model. First we will consider the TCP/IP protocols themselves, and then we will turn to the extended TCP/IP model.

The IP portion of the TCP/IP protocol corresponds roughly to the network layer of the seven-layer model, while the TCP portion corresponds approximately to the transport layer. TCP/IP accepts messages of any length, breaks them into pieces smaller than 64,000 bytes, sends the pieces to the designated receiver, and makes sure that the pieces are correctly delivered and placed in the right order (because they might arrive out of sequence). TCP/IP does not know the path the pieces will take and assumes that communication will be unreliable. Thus, substantial error-checking capabilities are built into TCP/IP itself to ensure reliability.

The original Internet developers envisioned the complete networking protocol as having four layers—the networking and transport layers as the middle layers, with a hardware layer below these two layers and an application layer above them (Dennis, 2002, p. 14). From a practical standpoint, this four-layer view of the world is not too different from the OSI model, because the presentation and session layers are often not used. The four-layer model's hardware layer then corresponds to both the data link and physical layers of the OSI model. In this extended TCP/IP model, the application layer includes protocols such as SMTP (for e-mail), HTTP (for Web pages), and FTP (for file transfer). The transport layer is TCP, of course, and the network layer is IP. Then the hardware layer would include the various LAN standards, ATM, FDDI, ISDN, SONET, and DSL, among others. This extended TCP/IP model represents reality in terms of the standard set of networking protocols in the early twenty-first century.

SNA. The extended TCP/IP model, perhaps with some ideas borrowed from the OSI model, clearly represents the future in terms of network protocols. Nevertheless, IBM's **Systems Network Architecture** (**SNA**) remains an important standard. SNA, like OSI, is really a suite or grouping of protocols. IBM created SNA to allow its customers to construct their own private networks. In the original 1974 version of SNA, only a simple tree topology emanating from a single mainframe was permitted. By 1985, however, arbitrary topologies of mainframes, minicomputers, and LANs were supported.

SNA is a very complicated suite of protocols because it was designed to support the incredible variety of IBM communication products, teleprocessing access methods, and data link protocols that existed before SNA. We do not need to explore the details of the SNA suite, but it might be useful to note that the newer OSI model was patterned after SNA in several ways: Both employ the concept of layering, use seven layers, and incorporate essentially the same functions. The contents of the two sets of layers, however, are quite different, especially in the middle three layers (called the network, transport, and session layers in OSI). Although IBM still supports SNA, it also supports both TCP/IP and elements of the OSI model under the umbrella of its late-1980s **Systems Application Architecture** (**SAA**), which is really a philosophy rather than a set of protocols.

We now have all the pieces of the network puzzle. Network protocols provide the means by which various elements of telecommunications networks can communicate with one another. Thus, networks consist of physical media, arranged according to some topology, in a particular type of network, with communication throughout the network permitted through the use of particular protocols.

THE EXPLODING ROLE OF TELECOMMUNICATIONS AND NETWORKING

We have already stressed the critical role of telecommunications and networking several times, but to make the point even stronger, we will discuss how the role of telecommunications and networking is exploding in organizations today. In fact, many authorities suggest that the network (not the computer) is the most critical and most important information technology of the future. To illustrate this explosion, we will consider four areas of operation in which telecommunications networks are of critical and growing importance.

Online Operations

The dominant activities of many organizations have now been placed online to the computer via a network. For banks and other financial institutions, teller stations (as well as automated teller machines) are all online. Tellers directly update your account when you cash a check or make a deposit. The bank does not care what branch in what city you use, because your account is always up-to-date. Not quite as obviously, insurance companies have most of their home office and branch office activities online. When an insurance claim is made or paid, when a premium is paid, or when a change is made to a policy, those activities are entered online to the insurance company network. These and other financial institutions (such as brokerage firms and international banks) simply could not operate as they do without telecommunications networks.

The computerized reservations systems of the major airlines are another example of an indispensable use of online systems. Virtually all travel agencies in the United States are now online. Computerized reservation systems constitute the core marketing strategy of the major airlines. The major airlines introduce new versions of their reservation systems every few years, with significant new features built into each revision. For example, Delta, United, and American Airlines provide LANs to link travel agency microcomputers, permitting the agencies to integrate a wide variety of travel agency management applications with reservations processing. All this activity makes sense when one considers that the airlines make more money on their reservation systems, per dollar spent, than they make flying passengers. Historically, the airlines make 8 to 10 percent profit overall in a good quarter, while the reservation systems, through user fees and increased sales, make as much as 20 percent profit.

In the late 1990s the airlines and private vendors moved one step further by giving users the ability to make their own reservations online, effectively bypassing travel agents entirely. Each of the major airlines has its own Web site where users can buy tickets and select seats on future flights. Even more capability is available on the Web sites of three major online travel companies: Travelocity (part of Sabre Holdings, a spin-off from American Airlines), Expedia (developed by Microsoft, and now part of USA Interactive, formerly USA Networks), and Orbitz (created by five airlines—American, Continental, Delta, Northwest, and United). These sites provide information, process ticket sales for flights from all airlines, and offer other travel services such as hotel and rental car reservations. To access Travelocity, go to *www.travelocity.com* ; for Expedia, the Web site is *www.expedia.com*; and for Orbitz, go to *www.orbitz.com*.

Connectivity

Connectivity is a very popular buzzword among major U.S. and international corporations. Most large (and many smaller) organizations now provide every managerial and professional employee a personal workstation, and these workstations are connected to a network structure (often an intranet) so that each employee has access to every person, and every system, with which he or she might conceivably need to interact.

Connectivity to persons and organizations outside the firm is also important. American Hospital Supply Corporation created a strategic advantage by providing connectivity with the hospitals it served. DaimlerChrysler Corporation has installed a system to tie its dealers to the corporation so that deviations from expected sales are spotted quickly. All the automobile manufacturers are stressing connectivity with their suppliers so that they can adjust orders efficiently. Thus, connectivity throughout the customer-manufacturer-supplier chain is a critical element.

Electronic Data Interchange and Electronic Commerce

Electronic data interchange, or **EDI**, will be covered more completely in Chapter 7, but it is certainly part of the exploding role of networking. EDI is a set of standards and hardware and software technology that permits business documents (such as purchase orders, invoices, and price lists) to be transferred electronically between computers in separate organizations. For the most part, the transmission of EDI documents takes place over public networks, including the Internet. The automobile industry is perhaps the most advanced in the use of EDI, but many other firms and industries have also adopted this technology.

Electronic commerce (also called e-business) is a broad term that incorporates any use of telecommunications and networking to conduct commercial activities. EDI is part of electronic commerce, but the most explosive electronic commerce area involves commerce over the World Wide Web. Electronic commerce includes online catalogs, online ordering, online payment for goods and services, and sometimes online delivery of products. A number of virtual stores and shopping malls have been set up on the Web, and an incredible array of products is offered. One interesting and colorful electronic commerce venture is described in the sidebar "Virtual Florist." Electronic commerce over the Web is burgeoning, and there is no end in sight. The authors of this book, for example, have purchased software and electronic books on the Web and immediately downloaded them; registered online for conferences; made hotel and airline reservations; and purchased books, CDs, and a variety of gifts on the Web for offline delivery. Shopping on the Web is becoming important for most consumers. As you will learn in Chapter 7, electronic commerce is even more important for businesses than for consumers.

Marketing

In addition to electronic commerce, telecommunications is being used for many exciting projects in the marketing area. Two examples are the use of laptop microcomputers by salespersons and the use of telecommunications for telemarketing and customer support. All business organizations sell products and services, although the distribution channels vary widely. The sales function is often performed either by sales representatives employed by the firm or by independent agents aligned with the firm (e.g., an insurance agent). In either case, telecommunications is being widely used to provide support for the sales personnel. In the last few years, instant messaging (IM) has become an important tool for customer support, especially for firms such as online retailer Lands' End and most of the major Wall Street stock and bond traders.

This sales support is not always as direct as the two examples above. Such support often takes the form of online information describing product or service characteristics and availability. This up-to-the-minute information makes the sales representative or agent more competitive and increases the organization's profitability (as well as increasing the chances of retaining productive sales personnel). The importance of this instantaneous information is apparent for a St. Louis-based Merrill Lynch stockbroker talking to a client who is considering the purchase of a stock on the New York Stock Exchange, but it is almost as critical for a parts clerk at a Honda dealership in Oregon dealing with a disgruntled customer. The parts clerk can use his networked computer to check the availability of a needed part in Honda regional warehouses in the United States and can immediately place the order from the nearest warehouse that has the part.

VIRTUAL FLORIST

The Virtual Florist is an Internet Web site operated by the Internet Florist, St. Paul, Minnesota, with a URL of *www.virtualflorist.com.* The home page includes the Virtual Florist logo of a bouquet of yellow tulips appearing to come out of a computer screen, as well as a seasonal animated message, e.g., "Send a boo-tiful arrangement" (at Halloween) or "Bring the colors of the season inside" (in November). The home page has two primary segments, Have FRESH FLOWERS Delivered Today and Send a FREE Virtual Flower Card, as well as a tab to enable a recipient to pick up a virtual flower card. You may send anyone a virtual bouquet or virtual card (as long as he or she has an e-mail address), and it really is free! The user picks out the appropriate virtual bouquet or card from among a large number of screen displays of beautiful flowers and interesting cards. After the user personalizes the bouquet or card with a message, an e-mail message is sent to the lucky person who is to receive the bouquet. Then the recipient "picks up" the bouquet from the Virtual Florist Web site and it is displayed on his or her screen. After several days, the virtual bouquet and all records are destroyed. Of course, what the Virtual Florist wants the user to do is return to this site to order a real bouquet. Clicking on "Have FRESH FLOWERS Delivered Today" links the user to the Internet Florist home page, and to the wide selection of roses, blooming plants, fresh arrangements, stuffed animals, balloons, and flower arrangements for special occasions such as a birthday, anniversary, or birth of a baby. The user may order online via the Web or call a toll-free telephone number. In most cases same day delivery is available anywhere in the United States or Canada if the order is submitted by 2 P.M. in the time zone of the delivery.

[Adapted from Virtual Florist Web site, 2003]

THE TELECOMMUNICATIONS INDUSTRY

There are three major segments of the telecommunications industry: (a) carriers, who own or lease the physical plant (cabling, satellites, cellular towers, and so forth) and sell the service of transmitting communications from one location to another; (b) equipment vendors, who manufacture and sell a wide range of telecommunications-related equipment, including LAN software and hardware, routers, hubs, wireless access points, digital switches, multiplexers, cellular telephones, and modems; and (c) service providers, who operate networks and deliver services through the network, or provide access to or services via the Internet. This third

THE TELECOM REVOLUTION CONTINUES . . .

. . . IN FIBER OPTICS TO THE HOME

Telecom revolutions have a way of sneaking up on you. The latest upheaval may be upon us—and it's the result of rare industry cooperation. In late May, Verizon Communications, SBC Communications, and BellSouth announced that they would jointly develop standards that will allow them to roll out ultrafast fiber-optic lines right to customers' doorsteps. All three have begun to lay fiber in select neighborhoods, including a Verizon project in suburban Virginia. Fiber to the home would boost connectivity speeds by a factor of 20, making current DSL and cable broadband services run like mules next to a Kentucky Derby champion. Faster lines could unleash an explosion of new services, ranging from video-on-demand to more realistic games. "A few years from now," says Danny Briere, CEO of researcher TeleChoice Inc., "we'll look back at this [pact] as a milestone."

[Crockett, Haddad, and Rosenbush, 2003, p. 68]

. . . IN SENSOR NETWORKS

Already, companies from British supermarket Tesco PLC to Shell Oil Co. have deployed first generation [sensor] systems to monitor inventories and check the status of pumps at gas stations. That's just the beginning. Within 5 years, these sensor computers could be shrunk to the size of a grain of sand and deployed over much of the globe, resulting in thousands of new networks. Look for them to be scattered across farms and battlefields to monitor minute chemical and temperature changes and slapped onto trucks and shipping boxes to trace inventory automatically.

Sensor networks promise a mammoth extension of the Internet. To date, the Web has been a showcase for the human brain. It specializes in the words, numbers, music, and images that mankind produces. With sensors, the network stretches to the far vaster field of global activity. This means such networks can cover every single thing that moves, grows, makes noise, or heats up. Potentially, much of the world will be bugged. Moreover, these bugs will be doing most of the work. "Most of the data traffic won't be between human beings this time around but between these silicon cockroaches," says Bob Metcalfe, the networking pioneer who has invested in Ember Corp., a sensor-network startup in Boston.

[Green, 2003, p. 100]

. . . IN NETWORK-ENABLED UTILITY COMPUTING

The concept is one of the most compelling in the history of computing: make information technology as easy to use as plugging into an electrical outlet. This idea is commonly called utility computing, and many experts believe it's going to sweep the infotech world like a digital tidal wave. IBM, for one, is spending $800 million this year on marketing its vision of utility computing, which it calls e-business on demand.

"We think this is the third major computing revolution—after mainframes and the Internet," says analyst Frank Gillett of Forrester Research. The idea is that the power plant-like computing systems of the future will operate both at remote data centers and within a company's offices—under a variety of novel payment schemes. Whatever setup, the systems can be managed by the company's own tech staff or by outsiders. And rather than requiring customers to buy computer servers outright for use inside their own walls, hardware makers, including IBM, Sun Microsystems, and Hewlett-Packard, each offer computing-as-used payment options.

[Hamm and Burrows, 2003, p. 96]

segment includes America Online, Microsoft Network, Yahoo!, and a wide variety of ISPs.

As an important historical footnote, the entire complexion of the telecommunications industry changed in 1984 with the breakup of AT&T into the long-distance telephone and equipment-centered AT&T and the regional Bell operating companies (RBOCs). Although the various pieces that resulted from the divestiture were still large, there was no longer a single monolithic entity in control of most telecommunications in the United States. Just before the AT&T breakup, technological developments in long-haul communications (microwave, satellites, and fiber optics) made the development of long-distance networks to compete with those of AT&T economically feasible. Thus came the rise of MCI, Sprint, and other long-distance carriers. Furthermore, court decisions and management policies served to effectively split AT&T (and each of the regional operating companies) into two businesses—regulated and nonregulated. The original carrier portion of the business was still regulated, but the nonregulated portion could now compete actively in the computer/communications equipment market. AT&T, and to a lesser extent the operating companies, became major players as equipment vendors.

The 1984 AT&T divestiture also had significant managerial implications for the telecommunications function in a user organization. Prior to 1984 the telecommunications manager had a relatively easy job, dealing with AT&T for almost all of his or her telecommunications needs and receiving high-quality, reliable service for a regulated price. After divestiture, the job got much tougher. Now the manager has to deal with a variety of carriers and equipment vendors (often including AT&T), and also has to make sure that all the various pieces fit together.

The twenty-first century will bring even further change, not all of it predictable, to the telecommunications industry. In much of the world the government-owned telephone carriers have shifted to private ownership. In the United States, the Telecommunications Reform Act of 1996 resulted in increased competition for telephone service (both voice and data). To a great extent, everything is now up for grabs: Within limits specified by the act, the local telephone companies may enter the long-distance market and perhaps the cable television market; the cable television operators may enter the local and long-distance telephone markets; and the long-distance telephone companies may enter the local service market and perhaps the cable television market.

The growth of mobile telephony has changed the landscape, and it appears likely that telephony over the Internet will result in further change. In late 2003 there were 147 million cell phones in the United States, compared to 187 million traditional phone lines. At the present rate of growth, mobile phones will overtake the regular telephone business in 2005 (Rosenbush, et al., 2003, p. 110). The players in the telephone industry are changing as well, with the RBOCs recombining to form megacompanies such as SBC, Verizon, and BellSouth. Perhaps the more things change, the more they stay the same: The Bell companies are numbers one (Verizon), two (Cingular, formed by BellSouth and SBC), and three (AT&T Wireless, spun off from parent AT&T) in the wireless telephone market. The telecommunications equipment manufacturers, including such firms as Lucent Technologies, Nortel Networks, and Alcatel, had disastrous financial results in the years surrounding the turn of the twenty-first century but seem to be recovering as we near the midpoint of the new century's first decade. These are exciting—and nerve-racking—times for companies in the broadly defined telecommunications industry.

MANAGING TELECOMMUNICATIONS

In this view, the telecommunications system is an electronic highway system. Generally, IS departments have been responsible for designing, building, and maintaining that information highway in the same way that governments are responsible for building and maintaining streets, roads, and freeways.

Once built, the network, with its nodes and links, provides the infrastructure for the flow of data, information, and messages. This flow is managed not by IS professionals, but by users, just as users manage the flow of vehicles on physical highways. Government agencies provide standards and laws for the flow of highway traffic that are enforced by the police and highway patrol. In the same way, IS departments select and enforce telecommunications standards for information traffic while governments divvy up the spectrum for different wireless uses. This analogy could be pursued in more detail, but the point is clear: Telecommunications is the basis for the way people and companies work today. It provides the infrastructure for moving information, just as a transportation system, such as shipping lanes, railroad right of ways, and the airspace, provides the infrastructure for the movement of people and goods.

This analogy presents telecommunications as a linking mechanism, which it is. However, the Internet has also opened up a different view of telecommunications, that of providing a *cyberspace,* a place where people can "exist" in a virtual world, where organizations can conduct business, and in fact, a place where organizational processes exist. It is an online world, a sort of cybercity. This view, too, is providing the foundation for the online economy.

However, even more is happening. Just about everything about telecommunications is shifting, from the industry itself to the protocols (the languages networks use to communicate with each other).

THE EVOLVING TELECOMMUNICATIONS SCENE

Telecommunications is exciting, perhaps too exciting for many people given the plethora of bankruptcies and plummeting prices of telecommunications stocks. The early 2000s can be viewed as a respite from and a correction of the excesses of the late 1990s when telecommunications expectations separated from reality. Even with the downturn, though, changes occurred, and the rate of change is accelerating. To give an inkling of what is happening, here are some of the major changes that are taking place.

A New Telecommunications Infrastructure Is Being Built

The oldest part of the telecommunications infrastructure is the telephone network, commonly called the public switched telephone network (PSTN), or affectionately called POTS (plain old telephone service). This global network was built on twisted-pair copper wires and was intended for voice communications. It uses analog technology (signals sent as sine waves) and circuit switching, which means a virtual (temporary) circuit is created between caller and receiver and that circuit is theirs alone to use; no other parties can share it during the duration of their telephone call. Although appropriate for delivering high-quality voice, circuit switching is inefficient because of all the unused space in the circuits when no sound is being transmitted.

The overhead of establishing a circuit was tolerable for voice calls because they lasted several minutes, notes an in-depth telecommunications study by PricewaterhouseCoopers (PwC), before it became part of IBM Global Services. However, data traffic is sent in bursts that last less than a second. Opening and closing circuits at this rate is not economical, so the basic traffic-handling mechanism for data had to change.

PSTNs were also built on the premise of dumb voice telephones; therefore, they needed intelligent switches in the network to perform all the functions. Telephone company central offices house the intelligent switches that implement all the services, including call waiting, caller ID, call forwarding, conference calling, and so on.

The new telecommunications infrastructure being built around the world is aimed at transmitting data. The wired portion consists of fiber-optic links (glass fiber rather than copper wire) sending digital signals (ones and zeros instead of sine waves). The wireless portion consists of radio signals. Both use packet switching; messages are divided into packets, each with an address header, and each packet is sent separately. No circuit is created; each packet may take a different path through the network. Packets from any number of senders and of any type, whether e-mails, music downloads, voice conversations, or video clips, can be intermixed on a network segment. These networks are able to handle much more and a greater variety of traffic. Packet nets also can handle voice. The analog voice signals are translated into ones and zeros, compressed, and packetized.

Unlike voice-centric networks, data-centric networks assume intelligent user devices that provide the addressing information; therefore, the network only needs store-and-forward routers to route the packets. This architecture allows new kinds of services to be deployed much more rapidly, notes the PwC study, because the basic functions of the network need not be changed. Thus, for example, it was easy to add the World Wide Web as a new kind of layer on the Internet infrastructure. Other such layers are multiplayer gaming, e-mail, and file transfer. This infrastructure would not have been possible with PSTN. Witness the promise of videophone, which was announced at the 1939 World's Fair in New York. It still has not arrived, except over the Internet.

The Internet can handle new kinds of intelligent user devices, including Voice-over-IP (VoIP) phones, personal digital assistants (PDAs), gaming consoles, and all manner of wireless devices. It can allow these devices to handle different kinds of services, such as voice, e-mail, graphics, gaming, and so forth. Thus, the global telecommunications infrastructure is changing from a focus on voice to a focus on data.

THE TELECOMMUNICATIONS INDUSTRY IS BEING TRANSFORMED

The telecommunications infrastructure of old was originally provided by monopolies such as AT&T in the United States and government-owned postal, telephone, and telegraph agencies (PTTs) in other countries, such as Nippon Telephone and Telegraph (NTT) in Japan, Telefónica de España in Spain, and so on. Gradually, the telecommunications industry has been deregulated, country by country, although in many countries the PTT has simply become the private monopoly. Even so, competition in the industry has increased.

The telecommunications industry is becoming like the computing industry, says Rich Karlgaard, publisher of *Forbes* magazine, in that each year brings predictable improvements. In fact, he believes the industry is now more competitive than the computer industry. Computer processing power has followed Moore's Law of doubling every 18 months since 1959; and it appears likely to continue at that rate for 10 more years, yielding processors with speeds of a trillion bits per second. Bandwidth on fiber, on the other hand, is now doubling capacity every 4 months.

The telecommunications industry basically has two kinds of carriers: long-distance carriers, known as interexchange carriers (IXCs), and local exchange carriers (LECs). In the United States, the deregulation of AT&T in 1984 left AT&T in the IXC business and spun off seven LECs called Regional Bell Operating Companies (RBOCs): USWest, Bell South, Ameritech, Bell Atlantic, Northwest Bell, Southwestern Bell (now SBC), and Pacific Bell. Today, only four remain; they have bought up the others.

These RBOCs provided local access to the long-distance carriers and had a monopoly on this local loop. In short, they handled *the last mile:* the connection between a subscriber and the telephone company's central office (neighborhood switch) where the network switching equipment resides. This last mile has proven to be the bottleneck in telecommunications.

Visualize the world's networks as huge fire hoses, transmitting at the whopping speed of a terabit (10^{12} bits per second) over fiber-optic cable. Then visualize the twisted-pair phone line coming into your home or business as a straw, only operating at speeds of 56 kbps (104 bits for second) for a modem or 1.2 mpbs (10^6 bits per second) for a digital subscriber line (DSL). DSL runs over the same copper wire but has improved electronics that boost the speed, allows simultaneous voice and data, and is always on, eliminating the need to dial in. The *last mile problem* is the bridging of this fire-hose-to-straw gap. See Figure 4.18.

In the 1990s, the RBOCs began encountering competition for this last mile. So the jargon expanded. RBOCs

Bits Per Second	*Notation*	*Abbreviation*	*Amount*	*Term*	*Technologies*
1,000,000,000,000	10^{12}	1 tbps	Trillion	Terabits	Optical fiber potential (and higher)
100,000,000,000	10^{11}	100 gbps			
10,000,000,000	10^{10}	10 gbps			Optical wireless local loop (20G), OC-768 (40G), WMAN (100G)
1,000,000,000	10^9	1 gbps	Billion	Gigabits	Microwave LANs (1.5G–2.0G), OC-48 (2.5G), ATM (2.5G), Gigabit Ethernet (1G), WMAN (24G)
100,000,000	10^8	100 mbps			OC-12 (622M), ATM (155M to 622M), T4 (274.176M), OC-3 (155.52M), Faster Ethernet (100M), infrared (100M), WMB (100–400M)
10,000,000	10^7	10 mbps			T3 (44.736M), E3 (34.318M), frame relay (10M), Ethernet (10M), WLANs (10M), cable modem (10M), Wi-Fi (11–54M)
1,000,000	10^6	1 mbps	Million	Megabits	T2 (6.132M), infrared LAN (4M), stationary 3G wireless (2M), E1 (2.048M), DSL (1.544M to 7M), T1 (1.544M), Wi Max (1.5–10M)
100,000	10^5	100 kbps			Wireless local loop (428K), mobile 3G wireless (384K), ISDN (128K), 2G wireless (128K)
10,000	10^4	10 kbps			Modems (56K), 2.5G wireless (57K)
1,000	10^3	1 kbps	Thousand	Kilobits	2G wireless (9.6K to 14.4), infrared LAN (9.6K)
100	10^2	100 bps			
10	10^1	10 bps			

FIGURE 4.18 Telecommunication Technologies and Their Speeds

became known as incumbent local exchange carriers (ILECs) and the new competitors became competitive LECs (CLECs). The importance of CLECs is the new kinds of connection options they have brought to businesses and homes, such as cable modems, optical fiber, wireless, satellite, and faster wire lines. In response, ILECs have bundled local phone access with Internet access, and ISPs use their brand name recognition to expand into the local carrier market, becoming CLECs. You really need a scorecard to see who's who.

To illustrate these twists and turns in the telecommunications industry in the United States over the past 20 years, consider the following case of ICG, whose history has mirrored these changes.

CASE EXAMPLE

ICG COMMUNICATIONS

ICG Communications is a facilities-based CLEC providing voice and data services in 25 metropolitan areas in the United States. ICG serves approximately 6,000 customers, including ISPs, IXCs, and corporate customers with medium to large businesses.

It all began in the mid-1980s in Denver, Colorado. Teleport Denver, Ltd. (TDL), built a satellite teleport with eight earth stations so it could transmit voice around the world. It could reach five continents in a single satellite hop.

In 1984, when AT&T was forced to divest itself of its local telephone companies, TDL management looked into the possibilities of offering local telephone service to Denver. They originally planned to lease circuits from the local RBOC, but the costs were too high, so they decided to install their own private fiber-optic links to connect to the international exchange carriers that carried long-distance voice calls.

Then, in the late 1980s, when a new breed of telecommunications provider arose—the CLECs—TDL management again extended their view, this time to providing long-distance as well as private-line services to businesses.

Once the Denver network was in place in the early 1990s, its new parent, IntelCom Group, expanded its geographic presence by buying other companies that provided fiber telecommunications services. In the mid-1990s, management signed fiber lease agreements with electric utilities—an innovative strategy at the time—that allowed them to more quickly and cost-effectively expand ICG's services.

Then ICG expanded its offerings beyond fiber-based transport to offering switched services by installing switches in its key markets. In 1995, ICG also formed a strategic alliance with Southern New England Telephone through which it could offer an SS7-switched network across the United States.

The Telecom Act of 1996 allowed ICG to enter the local telephone market, so it began aggressively building staff and regional networks in California, Colorado, the Southeast United States, and the Ohio Valley. It also signed a 7-year agreement with Lucent Technologies to purchase switching systems and technical services. It entered the local telephone market in 1997, offering local, long-distance, and calling-card services to small- and medium-sized businesses. By the end of the year, ICG was serving 141,000 lines in several markets.

In 1998 and 1999, ICG moved into the Internet services arena. It merged with Netcom On-Line Communications Services, a major ISP. Hence, it could also offer data services.

In 1999, it sold the Netcom U.S. consumer customer base to MindSpring, another major ISP, to focus on Netcom's backbone network, which has 227 points of presence serving some 700 U.S. cities. ICG also entered into an agreement with MindSpring whereby MindSpring would use ICG's data network and network management capabilities. This agreement moved ICG into becoming an "Internet enabler" for ISPs.

During the first half of 1999, ICG signed a number of multiyear agreements with ISPs to provide them with access, transport, and network management services. In late 1999, it sold off its fiber-optic division and its satellite division because management decided to focus on providing (1) access and transport to ISPs, (2) telecommunications services to businesses across the United States, and (3) direct connectivity to IXCs.

When the dot-com bubble burst, ICG was not immune. The company filed for Chapter 11 bankruptcy to gain protection from its creditors, and the Bankruptcy Court of Delaware accepted its plan for reorganization. After gaining financing to reemerge, ICG moved out of bankruptcy in late 2002.

Its focus is providing broadband, dial-up Internet access, dedicated Internet access, voice and Internet Protocol (IP) solutions, and fiber-optic transport services. Its latest offerings are voice and Web conferencing and a bundled offering of voice, data, long distance and telecom—thereby combining analog and digital communications.

As this case shows, ICG has moved from providing traditional voice telephone service via satellite to becoming an Internet infrastructure provider to seeking shelter in bankruptcy and reemerging as an Internet provider. It is an interesting story that mirrors the fate of the strongest CLECs and shows that all roads are indeed leading to the Internet and its IP protocol.

The Internet Is the Network of Choice

Although it may feel like old news now, the biggest telecommunications story of the past 10 years has been the Internet, the global packet-switching network that is the epitome of next-generation networks. What has surprised most people was the Internet's surprisingly fast uptake for business uses and then the fast plummet of the dot-com and telecommunications industries. However, in both arenas, the crashes were needed reactions to the excesses of the late 1990s. In the mid-1990s, the Internet caught most IS departments by surprise, not to mention the hardware and software vendors that serve the corporate IS community. Many executives are relieved that the Internet pace of the late 1990s has now slowed down so that they can plan their online business strategies rather than feel the need to react quickly to dot-com invasions in their industry.

The Internet actually began in the 1960s; it was funded by the U.S. Department of Defense's Advanced Research Projects Agency and was called ARPANET. The network was intended for electronic shipment of large scientific and research files. It was built as a distributed network, without a controlling node, so that it could continue to function if some of its nodes got knocked out in a nuclear war. Much to the surprise of its creators, it was mainly used for electronic mail among government contractors, academics, researchers, and scientists.

In 1993, the Internet was still mainly a worldwide network for researchers, scientists, academics, and individuals who participated in news groups. It was all text, no graphics. It had e-mail for sending messages, maintaining e-mail lists, and interacting with news groups. It had file transfer protocol (FTP) for sending files, Telnet for logging onto another computer, and Gopher for searching and downloading files from databases.

That all changed in 1994 when the World Wide Web was invented by Tim Berners-Lee at CERN in Geneva. This graphical layer of the Internet made it much more user-friendly. Web sites had addresses specified by their URL. Its multimedia Web pages were formatted using HTML. The Web sites could be accessed via an easy-to-use browser on a PC. Hyperlinks hidden behind highlighted words on a Web page, when clicked, would jump to the linked page. Following the links became known as "Web surfing." This graphical electronic world was first populated by homepages of computer geeks and young people. The Web's use by businesses began skyrocketing a few years later, in the late 1990s.

The Internet has done for telecommunications what the IBM PC did for computing: It brought it to the masses. In 1981, when the IBM PC was introduced, its architecture was open; all the design specifications were published. This openness led to thousands of peripheral manufacturers, component makers, and clone makers producing compatible products. An entire industry developed around this open architecture. The same has happened with the Internet because it provides the same kind of openness, this time in the telecommunications arena. Vendors have a standard set of protocols to work with so that products can work with each other. Businesses do not need to commit to a proprietary architecture. Like the PC, this openness yields the most innovative solutions and the most competitive prices.

The Internet has three attributes that make it important to corporations: ubiquity, reliability, and scalability. It is global, thus it is ubiquitous. Enterprises, both large and small, potentially have global reach with a browser and global presence with a Web site. As noted earlier, the Internet was designed to survive computer crashes by allowing alternate routing. This capability makes it highly reliable. People might not be able to access a crashed server, but they can still access all other nodes that are operating. The Internet has also been able to sustain incredible growth since its beginning. Specific Web sites can handle tremendous amounts of traffic, in the tens of millions of hits a day, if they have been properly designed. That is scalability!

Today, the protocols underlying the Internet have become the protocols of choice in corporate networks for internal communications as well as communications with the outside world. The norm is now end-to-end IP networks.

To illustrate how a company might build a corporate network from scratch utilizing the Internet, here is the fictitious example of XYZ Company.

CASE EXAMPLE

XYZ COMPANY

XYZ Company, which makes and sells widgets, is in the process of installing a corporate network. The CTO has a myriad of decisions to make. Of course he wants employees to be able to access each other, corporate data, and the Internet, so he will create an IP network using the Internet's standard protocol, TCP/IP, which packages data into packets, each with a header that tells where it is to be delivered.

The Internet will be the heart of XYZ's corporate operation. Hence the CTO will create an intranet for use by employees, an extranet for use by suppliers and some large customers, and of course, the Internet as the all-important central public network.

The CTO has a basic way of thinking about all the computer-based devices in his company: He sees them as either clients or servers. Computers, handhelds, cell phones, and wired phones used by the employees are clients; they make requests of other computers. Computers that respond to these requests are servers. They can act as storage devices for shared files for teams or departments or even customers. They may house shared applications or shared peripherals or they can connect the client devices to a network, including the Internet. Now that IP phones offer good voice quality, he may opt for them as well.

Serving Remote Users

Every PC will be outfitted with a Network Interface Card (NIC) that lets it talk to the network. XYZ has four choices of communication wiring: twisted pair (the standard telephone line), coaxial cable (like cable TV), fiber-optic (glass fiber that carries signals via light pulses), and wireless. Fiber carries tremendous amounts of traffic and is expensive; therefore, it is mainly used in backbone networks. Each NIC will support the medium the company will be using.

Each computer also needs a network operating system. These days, it is part of the computer's operating system. Furthermore, some of the machines need a modem to convert (modulate) the digital signal from the computer to an analog signal for the telephone or cable system, and vice versa.

For employees working from computers in their homes, who need to transmit larger and larger files such as PowerPoint presentations, the CTO could choose DSL modems, which communicate at 1.2 mbps (10^6). Or he could choose cable modems, which communicate at a whopping 10 mbps. Like DSL, cable modems are not available everywhere. Also, like DSL, they are always on; no dial-up is needed. However, this convenience can present security problems because the session code does not change as it does with dial-up sessions.

The CTO needs to decide how to connect these remote users to the corporate network and provide the speed and security they need. The salespeople, for instance, no longer have company-supplied offices; their offices are in their homes. They have company-supplied laptops and PDAs; they dial in from hotels, client sites, or their homes or use an always-on personal communication service (PCS) for e-mail.

Serving Local Users

In the office, all the computers and telephones will be connected directly to an always-on LAN.

The various LANs in XYZ's offices will use three types of computers to route traffic.

- *Hubs* are repeaters; they forward packets of data from one machine to another. When a number of computers share a hub, data sent from one goes to all the others. This configuration can get congested with many computers, so hubs will only be used within a work group.
- *Switches* are smarter; they only forward packets to the port of the intended computer using the addressing information in each packet's header. Switches will be used to connect work groups.
- *Routers* are smarter still; they use a routing table to pass along a packet to the next appropriate router on a network. Thus, they can direct packets via the most efficient route or relay packets around a failed network component. Routers also link network segments that use different protocols, such as linking an Apple-Talk network with an Ethernet network. Routers also can connect to WANs. XYZ will use routers to connect its LANs to a WAN.

The CTO will likely choose the Fast Ethernet Protocol for his IP-based LANs. It has a speed of 100 mpbs (10^8) to accommodate employees' multimedia and video needs. Using Ethernet, when a computer has a message to send, it broadcasts the stream of packets and then listens for an acknowledgment of receipt. If it does not receive a reply within a specified time, it rebroadcasts, presuming the packets collided with packets from other computers and did not reach their destination.

The LAN will give in-office employees an always-on connection to the company's intranet, its employee-only Web site that is protected from the outside world by a firewall. The firewall is a server that lets in e-mail but does not permit access to applications or executable code. The intranet will essentially be "the office" for XYZ, because it will house all the firm's forms, processes, and documents. It will also be accessible by remote employees.

Communicating Between Offices

XYZ employees need to communicate between sites, so they need some sort of WAN. As expected, the CTO has choices here as well. Asynchronous transfer mode (ATM) is high speed—up to 622 mpbs (10^8). ATM is used by telephone companies for their network backbones; they then offer ATM services to companies like XYZ for their WANs. However, due to the high cost of ATM long-distance bandwidth, the CTO might not be able to afford it.

A fairly new option to link several offices in a city or to link floors within a building is Gigabit Ethernet, which operates at speeds of 1 gbps (10^9 bits per second). One hundred gigabit Ethernet (10^{11}) is on the horizon. Gigabit Ethernet has been outselling ATM because it is less costly. It is definitely the option the CTO would prefer.

These issues are some of the major considerations for the CTO. He is definitely going to base all his decisions on being IP-centric.

Extranets. Not long after creating intranets for employees, businesses realized they could extend the concept into extranets—a special part of the intranet for use by trading partners, customers, and suppliers for online commerce. The following case of National Semiconductor illustrates the use of an extranet and shows how the company tackled the challenge of conducting business online globally.

CASE EXAMPLE

NATIONAL SEMICONDUCTOR

National Semiconductor, with headquarters in Santa Clara, California, designs and manufactures semiconductor products used in personal computers, consumer electronics products (cars, cameras, cell phones, and so on), and telecommunications systems. National is focusing on its key competency—advanced analog and mixed analog/digital signal technologies—for use in the newest breed of electronic devices, information appliances, which are low-cost, easy-to-use, wireless devices that interact with the Internet without the use of a PC. National has sales of $2 billion and employs some 11,000 people around the globe.

To gain market share and move into new markets in Europe, South America, and Asia, National looked to the Web. It created an intranet that the sales force could access to keep up-to-date on products and place orders. It created the "National Advisor" using Internet-based push technology to electronically send news, sales reports, and customer information to the sales force and its management.

National also created an extranet for distributors and channel partners and a Web site for design engineers who use its components in electronic and telecommunications products. This Web site contains descriptions of more than 30,000 products in the form of PDF databooks. Design engineers can view these databooks and order samples either via the Web or through distributors.

To give far-flung engineers decent download times of these 10k-to-200k-size files, National initially installed mirrored servers in Germany and Hong Kong and planned for eight more sites. However, management discovered that the logistics of maintaining 10 such sites would be a nightmare as well as cost prohibitive at approximately $4 million a year.

They thus turned to outsourcing to a company with data centers around the globe that offers hosting and other Internet infrastructure services. It replicates Web sites on edge servers, which are servers close to users (on the edge of the Internet), so that download speed is fast. Some servers even perform language

(Case continued)

(Case continued)

translation so that when a request is made, the closest edge server detects the type of user device, type of network, and country (and its regulations) and adapts the content to those conditions.

The cost would be $400,000 a year, or one-tenth the in-house cost. More importantly, performance was so much better that National could reach markets in Asia, Eastern Europe, Indonesia, and Latin America, where Internet service was generally slow. In addition, the company could distribute daily customer data and market information within 24 hours, which would speed product development and responses to design engineers' queries.

National's Web site now supports 1 million design engineers around the globe who download more than 10,000 databooks a day, in about 2 seconds each. The company only needs to replicate its site once; the hosting company takes care of the global coverage. Finally, National receives reports on which pages are being accessed in each part of the world, which is important information to the sales and marketing staff.

Digital Convergence Has Become a Reality

Digital convergence is the intertwining of various forms of media—voice, data, and video. Convergence is now occurring because, as just noted, IP has become the networking protocol of choice. When all forms of media can be digitized, put into packets, and sent over an IP network, they can be managed and manipulated digitally and integrated in highly imaginative ways. IP telephony and video telephony have been the last frontiers of convergence—and now they are a reality.

IP Telephony. Recently, enterprises have been investigating the use of the Internet to transmit voice to replace their telephone systems. This new Internet use is called Voice-over-IP (VoIP), Internet telephony, or IP telephony. According to James Cope, it works in the following manner: A special IP phone with an Ethernet jack in the back instead of the standard telephone jack is attached to a company LAN, perhaps through a PC. Rather than the analog signals sent by traditional phones, the IP phone generates a digital signal. That signal is routed over the LAN just like any other data in packets either (1) to another IP phone on the LAN, (2) through the company's WAN to a distant IP phone on another of the company's LANs, or (3) through an IP voice gateway to the PSTN to a standard telephone.

Few companies have yet given up their telephone networks for a VoIP network, but as the cost differential continues, more will switch. Like other devices on a network, IP phones have an IP address, so they can be easily moved to another location and still be located.

IP telephony became the hot telecommunications technology in 2004. Until that time, voice quality over the Internet was poor, so people were not interested in switching to digital IP phones. But by 2003, voice quality was sufficient for early adopters, and surprisingly Cisco became the largest IP telephone company, shipping over 3 million IP phones by mid-2004 and purportedly shipping over 2 million in the third quarter of 2004 alone. (As the primary supplier of Internet routers, Cisco also expects to sell lots of its routers to telecommunications companies as they switch their networks from analog to digital networks.)

Voice has become another digital media that can be managed electronically, from one's PC, for example. One new possibility this digitization presents is ad hoc conferencing (or just-in-time collaboration, as it is also called). For instance, with the appropriate VoIP infrastructure, two people instant messaging with each other via their computers could seamlessly switch to a voice conversation, talking rather than typing. Furthermore, because each person's telephone, instant messaging, and e-mail share one address book, they can instant message, phone, or e-mail others to join their call just by clicking on their names. Anyone in the conference can pull up a PowerPoint slide or a spreadsheet to discuss a point on it—or even scribble on it—or view a new video clip. They can even archive the call and send it to other people.

Video Telephony. The same is happening with video telephony, which is not video conferencing via a PBX, but rather video over IP. With the appropriate IP infrastructure, video telephony can be, say, launched from an instant-messaging conversation. IP phones with cameras also facilitate it, phone to phone.

Oodles of new converged products are flooding the marketplace now that high-quality voice has become IP based. In fact, when VoIP is mentioned these days, it is done so in the context of collaboration. The point is not so much that VoIP offers essentially free voice calling worldwide over IP networks. The point is that VoIP now permits cost-effective, full-media collaboration worldwide. That is a new paradigm, which can change how businesses work. One early effect has been the boom in offshore outsourcing.

In addition, some new converged offerings add *presence,* by indicating how someone can be reached at a particular moment, often through a green indicator beside the appropriate contact option in the converged address book. Such a system then automatically dials that option. Presence will likely become a major feature of converged IP systems.

The Toronto Pearson International Airport illustrates the reality of digital convergence via IP.

Digital convergence is setting up a collision among three massive industries, state Stephen Baker and Heather Green. The first is the $1.1 trillion computer industry, led by the United States. The second is the $225 billion consumer electronics industry, which has Asian roots and new aggressive Chinese companies. The third is the $2.2 trillion telecommunications industry, with leading wireless players in Europe and Asia and data networking leaders in Silicon Valley. These industries need each other to offer converged services. Innovative offerings and services are now being released by large and small companies alike. It is not yet clear which business models or offerings will emerge as the big winners. It is only clear that this is a disruptive time for all three industries, note Baker and Green, as it likely is for a host of other industries as well, such as the music, television, gaming, and movie industries, to name just four.

The Rate of Change Is Accelerating

Although no one seems to know for sure, many people speculate that data traffic surpassed voice traffic either in 1999 or 2000. Changes are still moving at a fast clip, even with the retrenching in the telecommunications industry. Author George Gilder explains why he believes the pace of IT change is picking up, and even more importantly, why it will increase faster still.

Gilder notes that the technologies of sand (silicon chips), glass (fiber optics), and air (wireless telecommunications) are governed by exponential rules. *Mead's Law,* named after Carver Mead of California Institute of Technology, says that N transistors on a sliver of silicon yield N^2 performance and value. It is the rule of semiconductors, which is why this technology has been so powerful. This law of semiconductors now is joined *by the law of the telecosm*—networking N computers yields N^2

CASE EXAMPLE

TORONTO PEARSON INTERNATIONAL AIRPORT

Toronto Pearson International Airport is Canada's busiest airport, with 3 terminals serving 65 airlines and 24.5 million passengers in 2003. In April 2004, a new terminal opened that Cisco touts as a next-generation showcase because its infrastructure is a single, common-use IP network.

The network is *common use* because its infrastructure is shared by all the airport tenants. Its backbone is two independent high-speed rings for reliability and growth, with over 100 network switches, 1,000 IP phones, and 1,000 wireless access points. There is no separate telephone network, just one IP network that combines 14 communications systems and that supports integrated voice, data, and video.

Each tenant has a private LAN for its own voice, data, and video applications. The LAN is accessed via virtual private networking (VPN) technology so that it is private and secure. Yet each network can be accessed from anywhere in the terminal with the appropriate authorization by just plugging in, either via a wired or a wireless access point. The wireless network is highly restricted and tightly controlled so that the data traveling over it is also private and secure.

In essence, the airport authority acts as a service provider to the airlines, tenants, and passengers. The network is used for all applications. For passenger check-in, for instance, the gates have IP phones as well as data connections. Each gate can be used by any airline; the gate crew just plugs in to access the airline's voice and data services. Passengers can also check in at any kiosk for any flight for any airline, which has reduced congestion.

Baggage tracking is integrated with passenger reconciliation via the network, improving security. The network also supports security systems, emergency responses, video surveillance, and network security.

The network and the interlinked applications it permits have reduced network operations costs, consolidated network support (because there is only one network), increased operational efficiency in the terminal (in baggage handling and check-in), enhanced security and made it consistent, and increased capacity (handling 15 percent more passengers soon after the terminal opened).

performance and value. Combining the two laws leads to the compounding force of exponentials that have been sweeping through the world economy.

To get a sense of the power of exponents and why it is inexorable, consider the story of the emperor of China and the inventor of chess, says Gilder. The emperor was so exultant with the invention of chess that he told the inventor he could have anything he wanted in his kingdom. The inventor thought for a moment and then said, "Just one grain of rice, your majesty, on the first square, two on the second, four grains of rice on the third, and so on through the 64 squares of the chess board."

Of the two possible outcomes to this story, one is that the emperor goes bankrupt, because at 10 grains per square inch, 2^{64} grains of rice would cover the entire surface of the earth with rice fields two times over, oceans included. The other possibility, which is even more alarming, is that the inventor loses his head. Confronted with exponential technologies, emperors often decapitate. One rule of this story is "Keep an eye on the emperor," says Gilder, because they can suppress the spread of technology quite effectively. The governments of many countries have done just that in stifling IT through their PTTs.

It is also worth noticing, says Gilder, that at the halfway point (the 32nd square), the emperor only needs to give 2^{32} grains of rice (4 billion), which he could easily do from his rice fields. Therefore, nothing much happens during the first 32 squares. But after that, look out.

To relate this story to the present day, Gilder presents the following astounding facts: In 1995, exactly 32 doublings of computer power had occurred since the invention of the digital computer after World War II. Therefore, since 1995, we have been on "the second half of the chess board," and a stream of profound developments has taken place. E-mail outnumbered postal mail for the first time in 1995—95 billion external e-mails to 85 billion postal mails. The number of PC sales overtook the number of TV sales in late 1995. And on and on. Such changes will only accelerate, he predicts. For this reason, everyone in business must become comfortable with technology to cope with a world of ever-increasing technological change.

The Optical Era Will Provide Bandwidth Abundance

Gilder also predicts an abundance of bandwidth around the world. He notes that an economic era is defined by the plummeting price of the key factor of production. During the industrial era, that key factor was horsepower, as defined in kilowatt hours, which dropped from many dollars to 7.3 cents. Since the 1960s, the driving force of economic growth has been the plummeting price of transistors, translated into MIPS and bits of semiconductor memory. The latter has fallen 68 percent a year, from $7 some 35 years ago to a millionth of a cent today.

We are now at another historic cliff of cost in a new factor of production: bandwidth. "If you thought the price of computing dropped rapidly in the last decade, just wait until you see what happens with communication bandwidth," says Gilder, referencing a remark by Andy Grove, CEO of Intel. Up to this point, we have used MIPS and bits to compensate for the limited availability of bandwidth, says Gilder, but now we are moving into an era of bandwidth abundance.

Fiber-optic technology is just as important as microchip technology. Currently, 40 million miles of fiber-optic cable have been laid around the world. However, half of it is dark; that is, it is not used. The other half is used to just one-millionth of its potential, because every 25 miles it must be converted to electronic pulses to amplify and regenerate the signal. The bandwidth of the optical fiber has been limited by the switching speed of transistors, 2.5 to 10 billion cycles per second.

The intrinsic capacity of each thread is much greater. There is 10 times more capacity in the frequencies used in the air for communication, from AM radio to KU-band satellite. The capacity of each thread is 1,000 times the switching speed of transistors—25 terahertz. As a result, using all-optical amplifiers (recently invented), we could send all the telephone calls in the United States on the peak moment of Mother's Day on one fiber thread. Putting thousands of fiber threads in a sheath creates an era of bandwidth abundance that will dwarf the era of MIPS and bits. Or to give a more personal example from *Business Week,* downloading a digital movie, such as *The Matrix,* takes more than 7 hours using a cable modem and 1 hour over Ethernet; it would take 4 seconds on an optical connection.

Over the next decade, bandwidth will expand 10 times as fast as computer power and completely transform the economy, predicts Gilder.

The Wireless Century Begins

The goal of wireless is to do everything we can do on wired networks, but without the wire, says Craig Mathias of Farpoint Group, an expert on wireless telecommunications. A better term than *wireless* would be *radio*, because most wireless is over-the-air radio signals—for nationwide networks as well as LANS.

Einstein defined a wired telegraph as being a very long cat with its head in Los Angeles and its tail in New York. When you pull its tail, it meows in Los Angeles. Wireless is the same, but there is no cat, says Mathias. Wireless actually goes back to Benjamin Franklin, who believed energy could move through the air. Then Guglielmo Marconi created the first radio in an 1895 broadcast.

The problem with wireless is that radio waves are nondeterministic; that is, you cannot tell if a transmission will reach its intended antenna. Furthermore, as people move around, the relationship between the transmitter and the receiver changes. That's how calls get dropped. Wireless networks also experience interference, echoes, fading, and power limitations.

Wireless communications have been with us for some time in the form of cell phones, very small aperture terminals (VSATs), pagers, building-to-building microwave links, infrared networks, and wireless LANs in warehouses. Tomorrow's uses span a vast spectrum. We are on the cusp of an uptick in wireless use, says Mathias.

Frank Dzubeck, a long-time telecommunications consultant, agrees, stating that whereas the twentieth century was the Wireline Century, the twenty-first century will be the Wireless Century. The motivation for laying copper wire, cable, and fiber throughout the twentieth century was voice communications. The motivation for wireless is data. Dzubeck sees wireless equivalents arriving that rival today's wireline technologies. But before delving into these alternatives, it's important to understand the distinction between licensed and unlicensed radio frequencies.

Licensed versus Unlicensed Frequencies. Some frequencies of the radio spectrum are licensed by governments for specific purposes; others are not. The distinction has become very important in the wireless arena because it has led to the rapid innovation, and resulting tumult, the telecommunications industry is currently experiencing.

Anyone can create a wireless device to operate in unlicensed frequencies without first getting a license from the government, notes Heather Green. Wi-Fi and other technologies mentioned here use unlicensed frequencies. This has led to greater competition, more innovation, and faster changes in unlicensed technologies than in those using licensed frequencies. The licensed portions of the spectrum are owned by large companies that can afford government licenses that give them a monopolistic hold on specific frequencies. In the absence of competition, these companies have tended to be more plodding in introducing new innovations. But now they face more fleet unlicensed competitors.

The devices that tap unlicensed frequencies are cheaper than their licensed counterparts because they do not need to absorb the huge billion-dollar licensing fees. This discrepancy has caused major pricing disparities, which is good for consumers, but not for licensees.

The downside of the unlicensed frequencies, though, is the possibility of collisions between signals in these parts of the radio spectrum. That is why, notes Green, there is so much lobbying in the United States for the U.S. Federal Communications Commission to take away frequencies from the major TV broadcasters and open it up for unlicensed uses.

This section discusses wireless technologies for networks that cover different distances, from a few feet to thousands of miles, as shown in Figure 4.19:

- *Wireless Personal Area Networks (WPANs).* Networks that provide high-speed connections between devices that are up to 30 feet apart.
- *Wireless Local Area Networks (WLANs).* Networks that provide access to corporate computers in office buildings, retail stores, and hospitals, or access to Internet "hot spots" where people congregate.
- *Wireless Metropolitan Area Networks (WMANs).* Networks that provide connections in cities and campuses at distances up to 30 miles.
- *Wireless Wide Area Networks (WWANs).* Networks that provide broadband wireless connections over thousands of miles

WPANs. For distances of a few feet, the high-bandwidth wireline technology is USB—the ubiquitous port on PCs for fast connections to printers, monitors, DVD drives, and the like. The equivalent wireless technology, notes Dzubeck, is IEEE 802.15, which is also known as ultrawideband (UWB) and 802.15.3 (WiMedia). It can transmit from 100 to 400 Mbps (or higher), and it uses unlicensed bandwidth. Green foresees UWB being used to transmit huge files from a laptop sitting in the trunk of a salesperson's car to the PDA being held in the front seat. However, standards are not yet in place.

WLANs. For distances greater than several hundred feet, the high-speed wireline technology has been Ethernet, transmitting at 4 to 10 Mbps. Its wireless counterpart is IEEE 802.11, also known as Wi-Fi. Some people call Wi-Fi the wireless technology for the last 100 feet. Using a wireless modem card, which is essentially a radio transmitter, a laptop or PDA can transmit at 11 Mbps. Newer 802.11 standards are increasing speed and distance.

Wi-Fi is replacing wired LANs in offices and creating wireless LANs where none previously existed—hot spots. A hot spot is an area around a Wi-Fi relay antenna that transmits the wireless signal from a laptop or PDA to a nearby computer or to an ISP to link to the Internet. Some hot spots are public; some are private; some are free; others

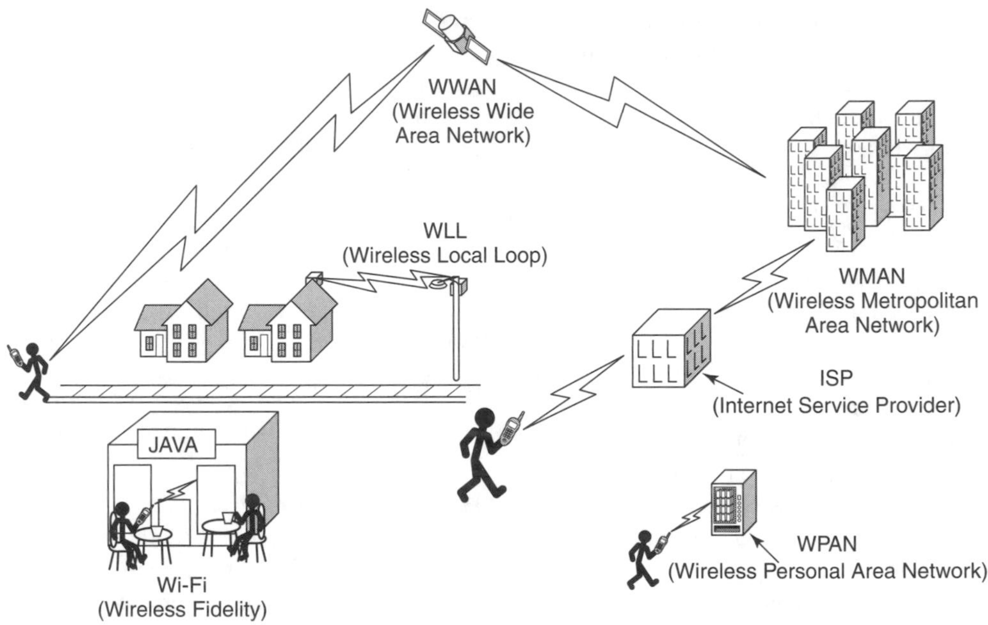

FIGURE 4.19 The Span of Wireless

charge by use or subscription. They are now found wherever people congregate—in restaurants, airports, hotel lobbies, parks, convention centers, and so on.

One private use of Wi-Fi is in cash registers, notes Green, so that salespeople can check inventory and prices at the register rather than having to check the racks. Such uses will grow, she believes, especially for people who must be on the move in an area, such as a hospital, a construction site, a warehouse, an airport terminal, and such.

The following example is a fairly typical use of a WLAN in manufacturing. The importance of this example is that the LAN is used to provide visibility into manufacturing operations, which is a crucial first step that companies need to make internally to take advantage of online commerce.

WMANs. For distances of 10 to 30 miles, three wireline technologies have been used for local-loop connections and access to cable networks: T-1, cable modem, and DSL.

The wireless equivalent to these wireline technologies is 802.16, which can deliver speeds of 5 to 10 Mbps over these distances. The stationary version is called WiMax (Worldwide Interoperability for Microwave Access). Like Wi-Fi, WiMax creates a hot spot around its radio antenna. It is perfect for aggregating 802.11 hot spots, notes Dzubeck, giving them access to a long-distance carrier network. Proprietary broadband microwave transmission capabilities have been around for years, notes Green, connecting buildings on a campus, for example. What is new with WiMax is that it is attempting to standardize the technology. Once it no longer uses proprietary technology, equipment costs will plummet.

The mobile version of 802.16 (also called WiMax) could replace cellular technologies, such as GSM, which is used in cell phones, notes Dzubeck. As yet, though, there are no standards for mobile WiMax. It also has a competitor in the licensed spectrum, notes Green, called Mobile-Fi. It, too, lacks standards. Green envisions both technologies eventually providing high-speed (1.5 Mbps) connections to devices being used in moving vehicles and trains.

Cellular companies offer a third option called 3G (third generation), which also uses licensed spectra. The new 3G networks are slower (.3 to .5 Mbps), notes Green, but they are reliable and widely available, unlike Mobile-Fi or WiMax. Some cities already have wireless broadband Internet access via a 3G mobile phone network.

Wireless local loop. Within the WMAN category is the local loop, or "the last mile," where individual homes and offices are connected to a telephone company's central office a few miles away. Eventually, high-speed wireless will be available for the last mile, notes Dzubeck. Newly released spectra (71 to 76 GHz, 81 to 86 GHz, and 92 to 95 GHz) will enable high-speed connections of 2.48 Gbps and 100 Gbps (in its next generation) for up to 1 mile. This speed is carrier-grade quality, so it will be used to replace fiber in the last mile.

CASE EXAMPLE

BMW

BMW builds more than 1 million vehicles a year in Germany and the United States. It opened a facility in South Carolina, and more than 30 suppliers have built facilities nearby to work with BMW. When this plant was slated to take on the manufacture of the company's sport utility vehicle, BMW wanted to implement the new assembly line quickly, which meant helping its suppliers scale up quickly as well.

Real-time delivery of data to the suppliers was one key to moving quickly. Suppliers needed accurate inventory data on the components they were supplying to BMW so that they knew when to make just-in-time deliveries to the plant. BMW uses SAP's ERP system to track parts inventory. To gather the inventory data that needed to be fed into the ERP, BMW decided to place bar codes on each part. The bar codes could then be scanned as the parts moved through the assembly process so that BMW's planners, operations personnel, and suppliers would know the current status of all parts.

Originally, BMW used Intermec bar code scanners attached to hard-wired data terminals at different locations on the plant floor. But more recently, it upgraded to Intermec's wireless scanning system. The scanner terminals transmit the data from the bar code readers to the SAP ERP via a wireless network that covers the entire 2-million-square-foot plant. The system uses radio frequency (RF) technology. The move to wireless allows BMW to more quickly reconfigure or expand the data collection system. Stations are simply moved; they do not need to be rewired.

A number of BMW's suppliers have followed suit and have implemented wireless data collection networks in their operations. As a result, the supply chain—from supplier to supplier warehouse to BMW's production line to shipment to a dealer—is supported by a flow of data that travels over interconnected wireless and wired networks.

WWANs. Whether the subject is wireless WANs or LANs, the only two wireless technologies are infrared light and radio airwaves (sine waves at specific frequencies) up into the microwave range. Figure 4.20 shows the electromagnetic spectrum and the broadcast frequencies where the different technologies lie.

The most familiar wide area mobile wireless technology is cell phones, where cell refers to a geographic area with a radio transmitter and receiver. The range of a cell explains why a cell phone used in a moving car fades in and out: As the call is passed from one cell to another it fades out of one range and into another. In essence, a cell phone is like a miniature radio station, says Roth, broadcasting on a certain bandwidth. With the cellular structure, a phone only needs to compete for bandwidth with other phones in the cell. Cell phones operate in the upper radio waves in the microwave frequency band of 2.4 to 5 GHz.

1G cellular. First-generation (1G) cell phones used analog technology and circuit switching. Callers were charged for the amount of time they used the circuit, not for the amount of information transmitted. And, like a telephone or modem, users dialed in.

In the early 1980s, Europe had nine cell phone standards. But seeing the need for one standard to allow continent-wide communication, the European countries developed a digital standard called Global System for Mobile Communications (GSM). GSM operates at a slow 9.6 kbps, but it has encryption to prevent eavesdropping. GSM has become the mobile telephony standard, even in the United States. Unlike the computing industry, a number of the leading global telecom manufacturers are outside the United States. NTT is in Japan, Ericsson is in Sweden and Nokia is in Finland.

2G cellular. Second-generation (2G) cellular, which predominates today, uses digital technology, but is still circuit switched. Although not developed to provide data transmission, 2G phones can carry data. Anyone who has used a laptop computer with a wireless modem to communicate is familiar with 2G data transmission. The Louisville Metro Sewer District provides an example.

2G also can carry messages using short messaging service (SMS). SMS is packet based and is used for paging and short messages, often from one cell phone to another. SMS is a large driver of wireless data services. It

Frequency	*Frequency Name*	*Technologies*	*Spectrum Uses*
3,000 EHz 300 EHz 30 EHz		Gamma rays	
3 EHz 300 PHz 30 PHz		X-rays	
3 PHz		Ultraviolet radiation	
		Visible light	
300 THz 30 THz 3 THz 300 GHz		Infrared radiation	
30 GHz	Extra high frequency	Microwave	Wireless Local Loop (71–95 GHz) Terrestrial microwave
3 GHz	Super high frequency		Satellites (0.5–51.4GHz)
	Ultra high frequency	Radio waves	Wireless LANs (2.4–5.0 GHz) 3G wireless (1,800–2,200 Mhz) 1G cellular (800–900 MHz) UHF TV (500–800 Mhz)
300 MHz	Very high frequency		VHF TV (175–216 MHz) FM radio (88–108 MHz)
30 MHz	High frequency		
3 MHz	Medium frequency		Wireless local loop (1.25 MHz) AM radio (540–1800 KHz)
300 KHz	Low frequency		GSM 2G wireless (200 KHz)
30 KHz 3 KHz 300 HZ 30 HZ	Very low frequency		
7.5 HZ	Earth		

FIGURE 4.20 The Electromagnetic Spectrum and Broadcast Frequencies

has been hugely popular with Scandinavian teens who use it for instant messaging. And in Japan, NTT DoCoMo introduced i-mode phones for Internet services and e-mail in 1999. Within a year, NTT had 6 million subscribers and some 12,000 i-mode sites. Many were for consumer uses, such as banking, ticketing, weather reports, paying bills, and so on.

3G cellular. The goals of third-generation (3G) technologies are to provide WANs for PCs and multimedia devices to access the Internet or to tap other wireless services at data rates of 384 kbps for mobile and 2 mbps fixed. These speeds are orders of magnitude greater than 2G wireless services. They could support multimedia and video. Some believe that low-bandwidth wireless services, such as the BlackBerry e-mail pager and SMS, are still the true killer applications.

It is too early to tell what the killer apps of wireless will be, because the promise of 3G networks is alluring. As Peter Howe notes, "Coming soon to your cell phone: Everything!" Cell phones have gone from just being telephones to being cameras, camcorders, televisions, mes-

CASE EXAMPLE

LOUISVILLE METRO SEWER DISTRICT

In 1997, Jefferson County, Kentucky, received 13 inches of rainfall in 4 hours. Sewers and drains overflowed, causing 40,000 homes to be flooded. The damage was $200 million, notes Owen Thomas. At the time, the repair workers had cell phones and walkie-talkies, but they had to return to headquarters to get assignment details and look up customer records—a process that slowed their response to the flooding.

In July 2001, the county again experienced heavy rains. Three storms in one weekend left 12 inches of rain. The pressure in the drainage system was so high that manhole covers blew off. But this time, the repair crews had laptops that could connect to district databases by wireless modems, so they could view maps of neighborhoods, locate broken water mains and pipes, and check out the most likely areas of damage—the downtown brick sewers built before the Civil War in the 1850s.

As customers called in for emergency repairs, the operators at the sewer district's headquarters entered the orders into a database, which the work crews could immediately access from the field. Thus, they were able to quickly install auxiliary pumps, for example, which prevented neighborhoods from flooding. In fact, Jefferson County cleaned up its storm damage in a few days, whereas the rest of the state took weeks, notes Thomas.

The wireless network uses off-the-shelf network software and a CRM database. The system has not only saved the sewer district millions of dollars by preventing damage, but the district also can operate with fewer people. Each field technician can now do the work of two, and the IT staff has been cut, even though the call center has been expanded to 24-hour service. The field technicians cannot imagine doing their job without their laptops, states Thomas.

saging and gaming devices, Etch-A-Sketch art screens, flash cards, small computers, and digital wallets. They may become whatever consumers want in the future, he notes. The uses truly are exploding. South Korea's SK Telecom even claims to have ring tones that are silent mosquito repellents. Another claims to be a smoke detector. Phones that can send signals to devices remotely, such as starting the home air conditioner so the house is cool when the owner arrives, are being called smart phones.

Of course, one mitigating factor with cell phones is battery life. Companies are investing lots of resources to resolve this issue. Another mitigating factor is input, due to the tiny keyboards found on most cell phones. Speech recognition has long been hailed as the solution to the input problem. Time will tell whether that's what consumers will want, notes Howe. It's part of the digital convergence noted earlier.

Cell phones are also becoming multimodal, supporting 802.11 as well as cellular technology. With this development, notes Mathias, the cell phone can become the relay point between the Internet (via Wi-Fi) and other devices, such as a notebook computer, PDA, camera, or some other device. In fact, Mathias believes cell phones with Wi-Fi will act as a type of router, because it is a far cheaper solution than installing a WAN radio in every device, each with its own WAN service (and monthly fee).

Wireless mesh networks. Mathias goes so far as to say that wireless mesh networks will become very important. A *mesh network* is a type of network in which many nodes are both end points and relay points. That is, each node can generate traffic, receive traffic, or pass traffic along to a nearby node.

What's important about a wireless mesh network, notes Mathias, is that it is far more flexible than a wired mesh network because its links are radio signals, not wires. Paths through a wireless mesh can change, depending on traffic loads, transmission conditions, and such. He believes they are the most flexible network structure ever created. Furthermore, the more users, the more capacity. The downside, though, is that it uses a lot of battery power (a precious commodity these days).

Even so, he believes they will influence the future of wireless.

VSAT (Very Small Aperture Terminal). Stationary *wireless* broadband is best provided today by VSAT, which is why this technology has taken off, notes Mathias. Just look on the roofs of gas stations and chain stores. They all have small VSAT dishes. The speed is 0.5 mbps. Hughes, for instance, provides two-way satellite at hundreds of bits per second—better than dial-up. Numerous wideband VSAT-based services will come online in the next couple of years, he predicts.

Obviously, companies use the Internet to sell their products and services. One company that was an early Internet user has also become an early wireless user, extending its Internet presence to cell phones. That company is American Greetings. Here is the history of its use of the Web.

Is Wireless Secure? Security is a major issue today, notes Mathias. When both wireline and wireless use the IP proto-col, both will rely on the same kinds of security. Until that happens, though, different approaches are needed. Wireless security is not really a major additional concern, notes Mathias, because signals fade fast when they travel through the air. Eavesdroppers need special equipment to pick up radio signals from far away. Radio scrambling and spread-spectrum technologies add security, encryption protects data, and eventually, 802.11i will provide a framework for security.

However, the network is often not the main problem, notes Mathias. Security leaks happen at the end, in the notebook computers; therefore, the data need to be encrypted on the equipment. Security issues are gradually being addressed; the area requires eternal vigilance

Is Wireless Safe? Although a lot of attention is focused on wireless services, a troubling question has not yet been answered: Are these transmissions safe for humans? The higher-frequency services are in the microwave range. They use almost the same frequency as microwave ovens. Microwave frequencies are more dangerous than lower-frequency radio waves because they cause molecules to vibrate faster, causing heat as the molecules rub against each other. This is how microwave ovens cook food. The power limits on cell phones, wireless modems, and WLANs (3 watts) aim to protect people from this short-term microwave heating phenomenon, says Roth. Microwaves operate at 500 watts. Long-term effects from low-level vibrations that do not raise body temperature are still possible, though. Some studies on rats showed damage to DNA, which can cause diseases such as cancer.

Although such health concerns have been dismissed by many scientists and scientific studies, their confidence has not settled the issue. Many have long believed that electromagnetic radiation from power lines, electrical appliances, and computers can interfere with the body's bioelectromagnetic field, causing an imbalance. These imbalances leave people feeling drained, fatigued, and stressed out. Although it is likely that our bodies can rebalance disruptions caused by occasional exposure to electromagnetic radiation (EMR), frequent bombardment likely has an effect. It is probably difficult to directly link exposure to disease; it is more likely that exposure will gradually lower a body's immunity.

The amount of radiation emitted by cell phones is limited by governments, but these limits are averages. Spikes are possible, and these are known to kill cells; therefore, holding a cell phone next to one's head for prolonged periods of time is not wise. Voice use of cell phones by young people is especially disturbing. Thus, it is quite possible that there could soon be a backlash against wireless devices similar to the protests against genetically modified organisms. Objective research is needed and protection could become a hot topic. Anyone care for metal-lined hats?

In conclusion, the success of wireless is guaranteed, Mathias says, because people will not give up being mobile. There is no substitute technology, but we advise prudent use.

Messaging Is a Killer App

What has proven true with data communication technologies over and over again is that the killer application is messaging. As noted earlier, the original inventors of the Internet expected it to be used by researchers to send files back and forth. Instead, researchers used it mainly for e-mail. And e-mail has remained a major use. In the wireless arena, the BlackBerry messaging service is indispensable to many people, and the driving force for wireless data services using 2G phones in Scandinavia and Japan has been SMS.

Likewise, instant messaging (IM) has become an important mode of communication. Importantly, it appears to be the current preferred mode of communication among young people. In his 2004 keynote address at Networld + Interop, Andy Mattes, president and CEO of Siemens Information and Communications Networks, USA, included two brief video clips of five children, ages 8 to 11, talking about how they communicate with their friends. Behind several of them was a computer screen, often showing a couple of rows of open IM chat boxes, lined up side by side. As the children explained, they use IM to chat with all of their friends at the same time. One boy only uses the phone once a day, to call his Mom (who works in the computer industry). Another girl says that she does not use the phone because then she can only talk to one friend at a time. And

CASE EXAMPLE

AMERICAN GREETINGS

American Greetings, a $2.2-billion greeting card company, was a pioneer in utilizing the Web. It launched its Web site in 1996, featuring paper greeting cards, electronic greeting cards, flowers, and gifts.

At Business OnLine97, a conference sponsored by Giga Information Group, the director of electronic marketing for American Greetings described how his firm decided to take advantage of the Web to sell its greeting cards.

The First Web Site

The director noted that his team began its thinking by asking, "Who is our biggest competitor?" The answer was not the other paper-and-ink greeting card competitors. The answer was "forgetfulness." People forget to buy greeting cards. The people who forget the most are those who are on the Internet—men. Although the team could not address forgetfulness at the retail store level, they could address it via the Web—to a potentially huge market—on a self-serve basis.

The company created a Web-based reminder service whereby a consumer can sit down for one-half hour and enter 6 months' worth of upcoming events that require greeting cards, such as birthdays and anniversaries. Once American Greetings has this list, it will send the consumer an e-mail reminder to buy a card shortly before each event. Or, the consumer can select a card on the Web site, and American Greetings will address and mail it and send a follow-up e-mail to the consumer stating when the card was mailed.

The electronic marketing group then realized that being able to talk directly to consumers could be used as a value-added service. As a promotion, they sent 50,000 e-mail messages to people who had asked to be reminded of Mother's Day. But rather than simply send the reminder, they offered free postage for any Mother's Day card bought online. The response was overwhelming. In fact, it was far more successful than the group expected. An even more recent Mother's Day promotion swamped the site.

To build brand loyalty, the electronic marketing group went further by taking advantage of a unique attribute of the Web—personalized marketing. American Greetings has some 35 licenses with well-known brands. One, for instance, is with the National Football League. The electronic marketing group has leveraged these 35 licenses using the profile each consumer fills out for the reminder service. For instance, if a consumer notes in his profile that he is a football fan, he may receive a special promotion to buy a specific NFL card when he visits AmericanGreetings.com.

The manager's goal for all of these services—reminder service, electronic cards, and personalized online marketing has been to build brand loyalty and establish switching costs so that customers will purchase all of their greeting cards from his company.

Not only is he targeting the consumer market, but he is also aiming at the enterprise market, especially salespeople and bosses. These people are likely to see greeting cards as a nice gesture, which will help them maintain and improve relationships with customers or subordinates.

Forming an Online Alliance

The demographics of card buying have changed over the past 20 years. Twenty years ago, 65 percent of greeting cards were bought in specialty card shops. Today, 66 percent are bought in mass retail chains, where the buyers are younger. American Greetings is the leader in this mass retailing channel. To continue as a leader, the company had to find new ways to offer greeting cards. The Internet is one possible channel.

To tap that channel, the electronic marketing group extended American Greetings' alliance with Wal-Mart to the Web. When consumers visit Wal-Mart's online greeting card section, they are actually sent to American Greetings' Web site through a special side-door Wal-Mart entrance. American Greetings then gives Wal-Mart a percentage of sales from these consumers' online purchases.

By using the side-door approach to link the two sites, American Greetings can track the origin of the purchaser and thereby pay Wal-Mart the agreed-on percentage. In addition, American Greetings can make its site appear to be part of Wal-Mart, strengthening Wal-Mart's brand. In reinforcing Wal-Mart's Web-based distribution channel, American Greetings also becomes a value-added partner, which is important if Wal-Mart decides to consolidate greeting-card suppliers.

(Case continued)

(Case continued)

In addition, to spur purchasing on the Web as well as at Wal-Mart's stores, American Greetings has given online purchasers of greeting cards a money-off coupon that they can print out on their printer and take to a Wal-Mart store. Thus, each partner hopes to increase the traffic of the other. In so doing, they tighten their alliance, both in the marketplace and the Web marketspace.

Consolidating Its Online Presence

AmericanGreetings.com is the online greeting and personal expression subsidiary of American Greetings. Its network of sites in early 2002 was one of the world's top 15 Web sites, with more than 16 million unique monthly visitors. The company says it offers the largest selection of online greetings. To achieve that status, the company has acquired BlueMountain.com, Egreetings.com, BeatGreets.com (featuring musical greetings from over 200 artists), and Gibson Greetings.

American Greetings sees its mission as helping "people everywhere express their innermost thoughts and feelings, enhance meaningful relationships, and celebrate life's milestones and special occasions."

Moving to Wireless

Today, members of American Greetings' online card club, who pay $14 a year for membership, receive a choice of thousands of greeting cards, and they can create and print paper cards, invitations, package decorations, business cards, newsletters, stickers, and more on their color printers. Their personalized site contains their profile, favorites list, address book, list of cards sent and to whom, and a reminder list.

To extend the usefulness of membership, American Greetings teamed up with Nokia in 2002 to create a wireless Web presence. Using the WAP browser built into a Nokia phone, members can access American Greetings' WAP-based Web site to send an electronic greeting, either to another phone or to a computer. The company reasons that when people have idle time, besides checking e-mail or playing a game using their cell phone, they also might want to send a funny animated card to someone.

she does not use e-mail because it is like regular mail—slow. In short, they prefer to chat with many friends at once. IM gives them this capability.

Many see IM as the killer app of wireless as well, not just for teenagers, but for businesses. Steven Cherry points out that the U.S. Navy's Office of the Chief of Naval Operations turned to IM to communicate with its displaced employees who could not use the secure telecommunications system following the September 11, 2001, terrorist attacks. Top naval officers now use this specially designed and secured IM system routinely to communicate with each other and with their staffs. In addition, the U.S. Navy has connected 300 ships at sea with IM. Whereas teenagers use IM to chat, corporations and other enterprises are using it to quickly ask a question of someone, to share documents, and to exchange notes, says Cherry.

Newer technologies will allow messaging to become even more personal. This is one reason why camera phones have become so popular: a picture is often more personal than a voice description. Photo messaging will add to voice and text messaging. Video messaging is more personal still. Video phones will allow others to be there—a sick grandparent will be able to attend a graduation, a traveling mom will be at a grade school play, and a far-off relative can help celebrate a birthday party.

The key attribute of IM is that it provides *presence,* which means that a person on your buddy list can see when you are using a computer or device (if it has the appropriate IM software and service) and therefore knows that you are present and available to receive an instant message. Presence is being built into collaboration software, Webcasts, and online games as well. The downside of presence, of course, is that people with large buddy lists can be deluged with instant messages whenever they have their phone or computer on.

Always on is the communication mode of the future because it allows instant notification. For example, a sales team may ask to receive news releases and intranet entries about their specific clients or their main competitors, so they are always up-to-date. If the team's devices support a team calendar, team members might be able to schedule a quick telephone conference call if they receive important news, such as a competitor trying to snag an important customer or information about a market test. Or, they might just collaborate asynchronously via SMS. On-the-go multiparty collaboration is an important use of low-bandwidth wireless devices, and it could become the same with high-bandwidth devices. Or, a collector might ask for instant notification when specific items within specific price ranges come up for auction. The service might give the collector one-click transaction capabilities so the collector can bid on an item once he or she receives notification.

Mei Chuah, a researcher at Accenture Labs, foresees cell phones, their IM capabilities, and online commerce commingling physical and virtual worlds. She believes the cell phone will become a person's portal to other people, physical things, and virtual entities as well. All will be part of a person's social network. Personal devices (including our cars) will be "socialized" by having communication capabilities and will potentially communicate wirelessly with each other. Phones will have sensing and even control capabilities. For example, a software robot in the phone will "sense" what friends are doing, and connect those who are, say, watching the same TV program or downloading the same song. Once companies realize they can sell more products and services to consumers by creating social activities (including virtual ones) around their products or services, even more types of things will be given communication capabilities, Chuah believes.

Furthermore, she sees the physical and virtual worlds interconnecting, with social networks in one moving to the other. People in virtual worlds already hold parties over the Internet. Such socializing in one world will flow to socializing in the other. Furthermore, items in one world will move to the other. Chuah cites the example of the virtual sword won by an advanced player in the online game Everquest being sold on eBay. Wireless communications will eventually link both worlds, she believes, and the nexus will be the cell phone.

A current-day example of using IM to sell products is Keebler's RecipeBuddie.

Coming: An Internet of Things

Wireless communications are not just for people, of course. A machine-to-machine Internet is coming, note Andy Reinhardt and Heather Green. Machines will likely use Wi-Fi as one wireless communication protocol. Another protocol is ZigBee, a radio-based communication standard used by tiny sensors. Such sensors might monitor the main systems in a vehicle; the inventory of ice cream in vending machines; a building's HVAC system; or the soil moisture, nutrients, and temperature in a field as well as a myriad of other uses.

The sensors are designed to send specific bits of information, be long lasting, require little energy, and communicate efficiently. With ZigBee, the sensors pass their information on to the next sensor in a sort of bucket-brigade fashion, with the last one passing the data to a computer for analysis or communication, notes Green.

Yet another protocol that involves communication among things is radio-frequency identification (RFID). Like the bar code, it is a technology that involves small tags affixed to objects that provide information about the object. For example, an RFID tag on a package could tell a scanner where it is going, where it has been, the temperature range it has experienced (if that is important to the contents), and so on.

The problem CIOs face is tying such new sensor-based systems into their corporate databases. It is likely that the communication systems will use a mix of wired and wireless technologies, as appropriate. That is just one challenge.

THE ROLE OF THE IS DEPARTMENT

This long discussion of telecommunications gives just a glimpse into its complexity as well as its increasing importance. Given this central role of telecommunications networks, what is the IS department's role? We believe IS has three roles: create the telecommunications architecture for the enterprise, run it, and stay close to the forefront of the field.

A network architecture needs to contain a set of company policies and rules that, when followed, lead to the desired network environment. The key challenge in network design is connectivity. *Connectivity* means allowing users to communicate up, down, across, and out of an organization. The goal is not a single coherent network, but rather finding the means to interface many dissimilar networks. One guiding principle is to build systems that are coherent at the interfaces so that users think they are only dealing with one network.

The second key concept in architecture design is *interoperability,* which means the capability for different computers, using different operating systems and on different networks, to work together on tasks—exchanging information in standard ways without any changes in functionality and without physical intervention. A truly interoperable network would allow PCs, laptops, handhelds, devices, and objects to interoperate, even while running different operating systems and communicating over IP networks. This interoperability is the goal of architecture and is the main job of the IS department.

The second job of the IS department is to operate the network. Suffice it to say here that many companies are outsourcing this work to companies that specialize in network management because the area is so complex, there are too few network specialists to go around, and network infrastructures are costly investments.

The third job of IS is to stay current with the technology. In this day and age, if an IS department is not already experimenting with how handheld devices can interact with its

Web site, they are behind competitors who are. Keeping abreast of telecommunications requires continually peering into the future and testing out new ideas. It is a crucial job of IS departments, even when budgets are tight.

SUMMARY

The telecommunications and networking area has existed for considerably longer than computer hardware and software, but the developments in all three areas have merged in the past two decades to put more emphasis on telecommunications than ever before. The late 1990s and early 2000s saw the era of networking come into its own. Networks provide enhanced communication to organizations and individuals and permit the sharing of resources and data. They are also essential for implementing distributed data processing and client/server systems. The exploding role of telecommunications and networking is evident in many organizational activities, including online operations, EDI, and electronic commerce, forever changing the way people do business. In addition, businesses have an intense desire to improve organizational communication through universal connectivity. Truly, a communications revolution is underway, with networking and the Internet at the heart of it.

The technology of telecommunications and networking is extremely complex, perhaps even more so than computer hardware and software. By concentrating on a number of key elements, we have developed a managerial-level understanding of networks. Communication signals may be either analog or digital. It is easier to transmit data digitally, and there is a concerted movement toward digital transmissions today. Networks employ a variety of transmissions media (such as coaxial and fiber-optic cable) and are configured in various topologies (such as rings and trees). Major network types include computer telecommunications networks, emanating from a mainframe or midrange computer; digital PBX networks for both voice and data; LANs for high-speed communication within a restricted area; backbone networks to connect LANs together, and possibly to connect to WANs and the Internet; WANs for communication over a long haul; and the Internet.

The Internet, and especially the World Wide Web, has been front-page news over the past several years as the world becomes wired. WANs and the Internet are highly dependent upon facilities owned and operated by the telephone companies and other carriers. To enable the devices attached to any type of network to communicate with one another, protocols (or rules of operation) have to be agreed upon. The success of the Internet has led to the acceptance of TCP/IP as today's *de facto* networking protocol.

The first generation of the Internet economy was wired. The second generation will be unwired. This untethering has already changed how we live our lives and do our work. Today, telecommunications is all about connecting. The number of possible connections is exploding worldwide.

CHAPTER REVIEW QUESTIONS

1. What are the five primary reasons for networking? Describe each one of them and how each particular area of networking affects and enhances businesses.
2. Define telecommunications. What are the primary functions performed by a telecommunications network?
3. Explain the differences between analog and digital communication. How does the modem factor into these two forms of communication?
4. How has the telecommunications industry changed over the past decade?
5. A telecommunications network is made up of some type of physical medium over which communications are sent. What are the five primary media in use today? Describe them and how they work. Describe the types of situations where each would be used.
6. What is Bluetooth technology?
7. How does fiber-optic technology work?
8. Discuss the advantages and disadvantages of the four primary types of local area networks, which are contention bus, token bus, token ring, and wireless.
9. Explain the differences between accessing the Internet via a modem, ISDN, DSL, a cable modem, and a satellite. Which of these access mechanisms is likely to become more important in the future?
10. What is a LAN? A WAN? When would you use one as opposed to the other?
11. What are some of the disadvantages of wireless communication?
12. What is a wireless moocher?
13. Identify these acronyms or initials: LAN, WAN, RFID, DSL, LEO, FTP, FDDI, vBNS, PBX, ISDN, SONET, EDI.
14. Why is the idea of a standard network protocol, such as the OSI reference model, important?
15. Explain the difference between the Internet and an intranet. What is Internet2?
16. Three important protocols discussed in this chapter were OSI, TCP/IP, and SNA. In one or two sentences per protocol, tell what these names stand for and describe the basic purposes of the three protocols.
17. What are some definitive examples of how telecommunications has changed the business world in marketing, operations, and connectivity?

18. Name the three segments of the telecommunications industry. Describe them.

CHAPTER DISCUSSION QUESTIONS

1. What are some possible applications for Bluetooth technology in business in the future that might not even have been thought of yet?
2. What are the implications of fiber-optic technology for the future?
3. Has the popularity of the Internet and the related adoption of TCP/IP by many organizations and networks helped or hindered the movement towards a single standard protocol such as OSI? Why?
4. Although having a wireless device is handy, it can also be an intrusion. People need some privacy. They should not always be reachable, and there are situations where cell phones are disruptive. Wireless devices have also been found to be dangerous by virtue of their distractive capability when used in a car. Should the use of wireless devices be regulated in any fashion? What about the security issues of wireless communication? Discuss.

CASE STUDY: KEEBLER

In September 2002, Keebler, the cookie and cracker company, launched RecipeBuddie on its Web site, notes Gordon Bass. "She" is an instant-messenger bot that converses with people who IM her. But she only talks about recipes, using her database of 700 recipes to, say, help someone figure out what to cook for dinner. Keebler's goal, of course, is for her to get people to buy more Keebler products. She has been given the personality of a humor-filled suburban housewife, which seems to best fit the demographics of Keebler's audience: suburban women ages 25 to 54.

Her origin is ActiveBuddy, a company founded by Timothy Kay that builds interactive agents (bots) to run on IM networks, private networks, and wireless networks. RecipeBuddie, for example, sits on someone's AOL IM buddy list and can answer natural-language questions about recipes. She can be accessed at www.keebler.com.

Emedia, the developer of Keebler's Web site, built RecipeBuddie using the scripting language BuddyScript (from ActiveBuddy). Development entailed writing scripts to reply to user questions. For RecipeBuddie, each natural-language response acknowledges the other party, repeats the request, and makes a suggestion, which is often one or more recipes. Scripting entailed making the link between what people might ask about (cooking dinner for the kids, a picnic lunch, no onions, feeling sad, etc.) and recipes in the database. Emedia initially wrote 2,000 pieces of dialog for RecipeBuddie, notes Bass.

Once developed, Emedia had to get permission to launch RecipeBuddie on the three major IM networks: AOL, MSN, and Yahoo! ActiveBuddy receives a fee every time RecipeBuddie is accessed. Keebler tracks the number of people who put RecipeBuddie on their buddy list, the number of messages exchanged with RecipeBuddie, and the number of recipes viewed and printed.

RecipeBuddie has been very successful, exceeding Keebler's expectations. The main developer, Anna Murray of Emedia, notes three lessons she learned from building the bot. One, users really like to converse with bots, so a lot more can be done with them. Two, scripting is like writing a novel, so it needs to be done by just a couple of people, and they need to work together very closely. And three, others, besides the original scripters, should be able to add their own content, such as answers to frequently asked questions.

Case Study Discussion Questions

Question One

How is the use of bots affecting our perception of reality as a society? For example, do you think that Keebler customers are really aware that they are conversing with a bot rather than an ordinary person?

Question Two

In the past, companies employed telephone operators who answered personal questions and directed the customer to the right individual. Now everything on the phone services is automated (press this button and then that button, etc.), and it's virtually impossible to have your questions answered by a real person when you contact a company. Is this an advancement/improvement or the downfall of society and interpersonal relationships? How do you feel when you can't get your questions answered by a real person? Is there an in-between answer for companies to pursue that will satisfy everyone's needs? Should Keebler continue the use of bots or go back to real people?

Question Three

What are some other ways that bots could be used to improve a business? Try to think outside the box and into the future.

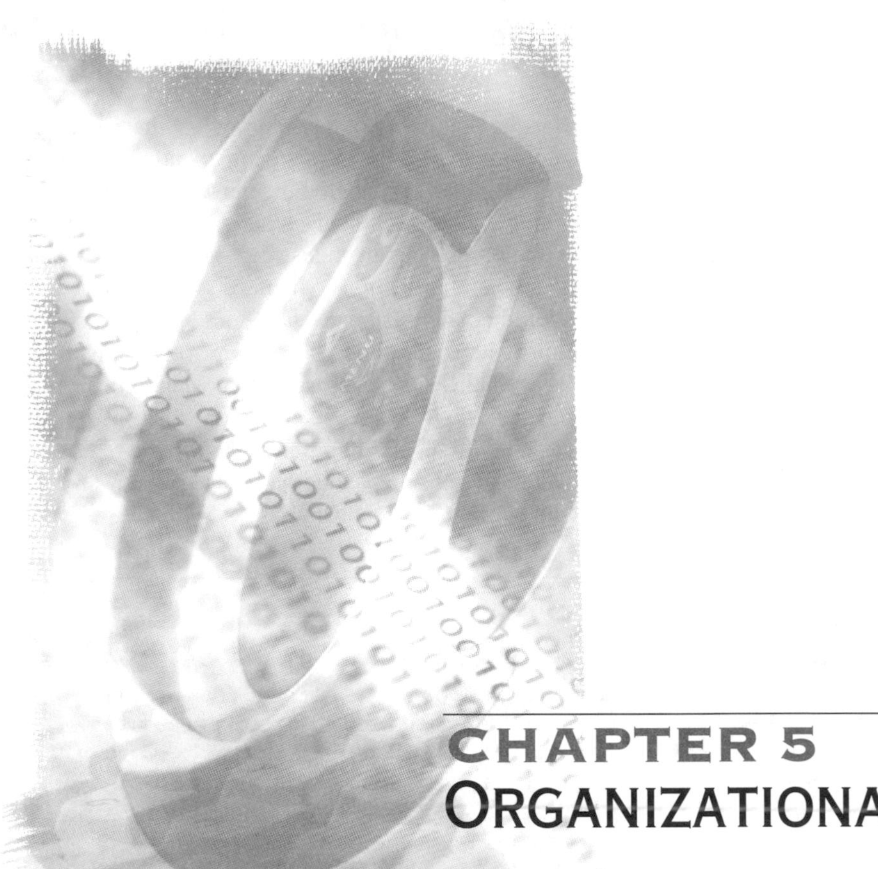

CHAPTER 5
ORGANIZATIONAL SYSTEMS

INFORMATION TECHNOLOGY (IT) IS A KEY ENABLER FOR ORGANIZATIONS of all sizes, both public and private. Businesses and other organizations are not the same as they were a decade ago. They are more complex but have fewer layers of management; they tend to offer more customized products and services; they are increasingly international in scope; and they are heavily dependent on the accurate and timely flow of information. And this change in organizations is accelerating, not decelerating.

As a current or future manager, you must be aware of IT and its potential impact on your job, your career, and your organization. You cannot afford to leave consideration of IT solely to the information systems (IS) specialists. As a business manager, you must perform many critical roles if you and your organization are to be successful: conceptualize ways in which IT can be used to improve performance; serve as a consultant to the IS specialists who are developing or implementing applications for your organization; manage the organizational change that accompanies new IT applications; use the technology applications and help enhance them; and facilitate the successful implementation of new IT applications.

Where do we start getting you ready for your new roles? We start with an *awareness* of how IT is being used in a variety of organizations. The first five chapters of this book have already begun the process of building awareness of IT applications. This chapter and the following two chapters will provide a systematic introduction to a wide variety of IT applications. We think you will be impressed with the breadth of areas in which IT is being employed to make organizations more efficient and effective. We hope these three chapters will stimulate your thinking about potential applications in your present or future organization. Most of the obvious applications are already in place. Nearly every organization uses a computer to handle its payroll, keep inventory records, and process accounts receivable and payable; almost every organization uses a telephone system and facsimile machines. But many applications remain to be discovered, most likely by managers like you.

APPLICATION AREAS

To consider a topic as broad as IT applications, some type of framework is needed. We have divided applications into those that are *interorganizational* systems and those that are *intraorganizational* systems. Electronic commerce or e-business applications, including electronic data interchange

CRITICAL ISSUES OF IS MANAGEMENT

For 14 years—from 1988 through 2001—Computer Sciences Corporation conducted an annual survey of senior IS executives at leading manufacturing and service companies worldwide to identify the top issues they were facing. In the most recent survey, the top two issues were "optimizing enterprise-wide IS services" and "optimizing organizational effectiveness." Enterprise resource planning (ERP) systems, together with applications such as groupware and data warehousing (all covered in this chapter), are aimed at providing high-quality, consistent IS services throughout the organization. IT applications such as customer relationship management, groupware, data mining, decision support systems, expert systems, and executive information systems provide managers with the information and the tools they need for effective decision making. These applications are considered in this chapter and the next.

The third-place concern in the survey was "organizing and utilizing data." A variety of IT applications, including data warehousing, data mining, groupware, decision support systems, executive information systems, knowledge management systems, and ERP systems (topics covered in this chapter and the next chapter), help organize and utilize data to improve the organization's performance. Number four on the list of critical issues was "connecting to customers, suppliers, and/or partners electronically." Numerous IT applications, including electronic mail, groupware, ERP systems, electronic data interchange, and especially e-business applications (topics covered in this chapter and Chapter 7), help build the electronic connection between an organization and its trading partners.

In the aftermath of 9/11, it is no surprise that the fifth-place concern in the survey was "protecting and securing information systems." None of the application areas discussed in Chapters 6 through 8 focuses primarily on this issue, although security considerations are paramount in the implementation or upgrading of any application. We will return to the topic of protecting and securing information systems in the final two chapters of this book. Number six on the list of critical issues was "updating obsolete systems," which is exactly what organizations try to do when they implement ERP systems and other enterprise-wide applications, as discussed in this chapter.

[Survey results from Computer Sciences Corporation, 2001]

(EDI) systems, represent obvious examples of interorganizational systems, or systems that span organizational boundaries. The importance of applications that link businesses with their end consumers (B2C) or link businesses with other business customers or business suppliers (B2B) has been fueled by the growth of the Internet. Knowledge about e-business applications is so important today that we devote all of Chapter 7 to this topic.

To provide some structure to the broad range of intraorganizational systems, we have divided these applications into two major categories: enterprise systems, designed to support the entire enterprise (organization) or large portions of it, and managerial support systems, designed to provide support to a specific manager or a small group of managers. This chapter covers enterprise systems, such as transaction processing systems and groupware, as well as the critical concept of client/server architecture. Chapter 6 deals with systems specifically designed to support managers, such as decision support systems and expert systems.

Figure 5.1 lists these two major categories of applications, along with representative application areas that fall within each category. This figure provides the primary framework for our discussion of intraorganizational IT applications in this chapter and the following chapter. Please note that the application areas are neither unique nor exhaustive. For example, some specific applications fall in two or more application areas (such as enterprise resource planning systems also being transaction processing systems). Further, it is easy to argue that an application area such as groupware is both an enterprise system and a management support system. Somewhat arbitrarily, we have chosen to discuss group support systems, which is an important subset of groupware concerned with supporting the activities of a small group in

Enterprise Systems
- Transaction Processing Systems
- Enterprise Resource Planning Systems
- Data Warehousing
- Customer Relationship Management
- Office Automation
- Groupware
- Intranets
- Factory Automation

Managerial Support Systems
- Decision Support Systems
- Data Mining
- Group Support Systems
- Geographic Information Systems
- Executive Information Systems
- Business Intelligence Systems
- Knowledge Management Systems
- Expert Systems
- Neural Networks
- Virtual Reality

Figure 5.1 Types of Application Systems

a specific task or a specific meeting, as a management support system while discussing the broader category of groupware as an enterprise system. Despite these caveats, however, the application areas given in Figure 5.1 encompass the overwhelming majority of specific applications, and the terminology reflects standard usage.

CRITICAL CONCEPTS

Before we turn to specific examples of the various application areas, we must consider a number of important concepts that are intertwined throughout all the applications. An understanding of these concepts is a prerequisite to an understanding of the applications.

Batch Processing versus Online Processing

One of the fundamental distinctions for computer applications is **batch processing** versus **online processing**. In the early days of computers, all processing was batched. The organization accumulated a batch of transactions and then processed the entire batch at one time. For example, all inventory transactions (in and out) were recorded on paper during the day. After the close of business for the day, the transactions were keyed into a type of computer-readable medium, such as magnetic tape. The medium was then physically carried to the computer center, and the entire inventory was updated by processing that day's batch against the master inventory file on the computer. By the beginning of the next business day, the master inventory file was completely up-to-date and appropriate inventory reports were printed. Figure 5.2 represents this batch processing approach in a simplified form.

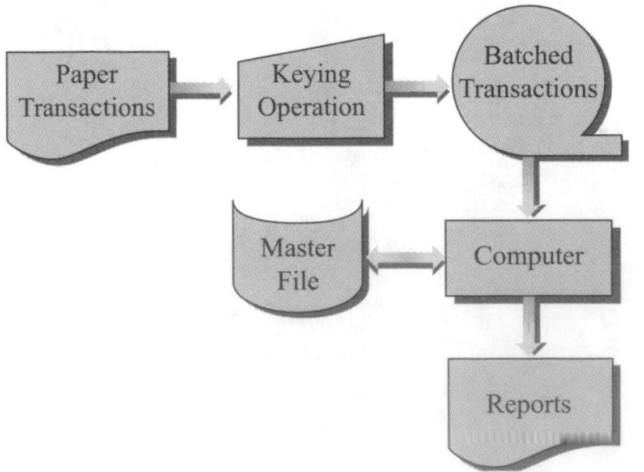

Figure 5.2 Batch Processing (Simplified)

The major problem with batch processing is the time delay involved before the master file is updated. Only at the beginning of the business day, for example, will the master inventory file be up-to-date. At all other times the company does not really know how many units of each product it has in stock.

As the technology improved, online processing was developed to avoid the time delay in batch processing. With a fully implemented online system, each transaction is entered directly into the computer when it occurs. For example, in an online inventory system a shipping clerk or sales clerk enters the receipt or sale of a product into a workstation (a sophisticated cash register) connected by a telecommunications line to the server computer, which holds the inventory master file. As soon as the entry is completed, the computer updates the master file within a fraction of a second. Thus, the company always knows how many units of each product it has in stock. Figure 5.3 depicts such an **online system**.

A fully implemented online system is also called an **interactive system**, because the user is directly interacting with the computer. The computer will provide a response to the user very quickly, usually within a second. Not all online systems, however, are interactive. Some systems, often called **in-line systems**, provide for online data entry, but the actual processing of the transaction is deferred until a batch of transactions has been accumulated.

A fully online system has the distinct advantage of timeliness. Why then aren't all present-day systems online? There are two reasons—cost and the existence of so-called natural batch applications. In most cases batch systems are much less expensive to operate than their online counterparts. There are usually significant economies associated with batching, both in the data-entry function and the transaction processing. But if the data-entry function can be accomplished when the original data are captured (such as with a sophisticated cash register), an online data entry/batch processing system might be less expensive than a straight batch system. The decision of batch versus online becomes a trade-off between cost and timeliness. In general, online

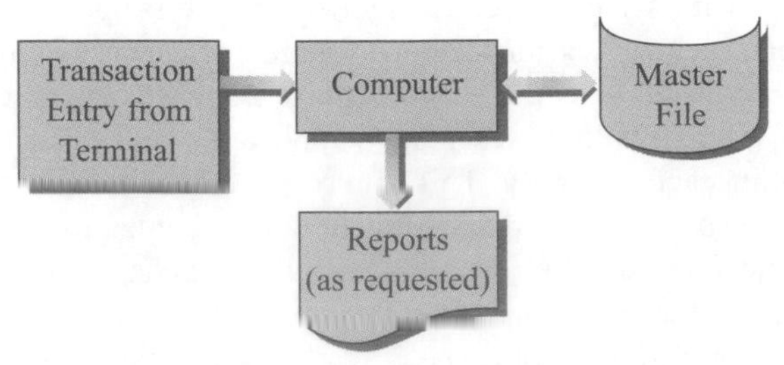

Figure 5.3 Online Processing

costs per transaction have been decreasing and the importance of timeliness has been increasing. The result is that most applications today use online data entry and an increasing proportion also use online processing.

The exception to this movement to online processing has been the natural batch applications. An organization's payroll, for example, might be run once a week or once every two weeks. There is no particular advantage to the timeliness of online processing; the organization knows when the payroll must be run. Even in this instance, there might be advantages to online data entry, to permit convenient changes in employees, exemptions, deductions, and wage rates. Thus, hybrid online data entry/batch processing systems will continue to exist.

Functional Information Systems

Instead of considering the two major categories and associated application areas of Figure 5.1, it is possible to create a framework based strictly on the organization's primary business functions—a **functional information systems** framework. For example, consider an organization in which the primary business functions are production, marketing, accounting, personnel, and engineering. Applications may then be categorized as part of the production information system, part of the marketing information system, or part of the accounting information system, and so on. This functional approach is simply an alternative way of classifying applications.

In this alternative view, the overall IS is composed of multiple subsystems, each providing information for various tasks within the function. In turn, each functional subsystem consists of a possibly interrelated series of subsubsystems. For example, the production information system is likely to include interrelated subsystems for sales forecasting, production planning, production scheduling, material requirements planning, capacity requirements planning, personnel requirements planning, materials purchasing, and inventory. The marketing information system may include subsystems for promotion and advertising, new product development, sales forecasting (hopefully tied into the production sales forecasting subsystem), product planning, product pricing, market research, and sales information. The accounting information system, which is generally the oldest and most fully developed functional system, is likely to include computerized versions of the entire journal and ledger system, plus a cost or responsibility accounting system and a financial reporting system for preparing reports for stockholders and other external groups.

One of the most important trends in the latter 1990s and the early 2000s is the movement toward integration of these functional information systems. Often these integration efforts have begun by focusing on a **business process**—the chain of activities required to achieve an outcome such as order fulfillment or materials acquisition—rather than on functions. Such a focus on process makes it easier to recognize where formerly distinct information systems are related and thus where they should be integrated (e.g., use common data and perform an activity only once). Sometimes the internal information systems department has developed these integrated systems, but more often software packages called enterprise resource planning (ERP) systems have been purchased from outside vendors. We will return to these ERP systems later in the chapter.

Vertical Integration of Systems

Another important characteristic of some systems is that they operate across levels of the organization or, in some instances, across independent firms occupying different levels in an industry hierarchy, such as an automobile manufacturer and the associated independent dealers. (More on these interorganizational systems will be covered in Chapter 7.) A system that serves more than one vertical level in an organization or an industry is called a **vertically integrated information system**. For example, in a single firm, a vertically integrated sales information system may capture the initial sales data and produce invoices (acting as a transaction processing system), summarize these data on a weekly basis for use by middle managers in tracking slow- and fast-selling items as well as productive and unproductive salespeople (acting as a decision support system), and further analyze these data for long-term trends for use by top managers in determining strategic directions (acting as an executive information system).

In a somewhat similar way, a national fast-food chain might develop a sales information system with modules both for operating units (company stores and franchises) and for the national organization. Thus, data collected at the store level using the operating unit module are already in the appropriate form to be processed by the national organization module. These basic data are transmitted via telecommunication lines to the national organization on a periodic basis, perhaps each night. The extent of vertical integration is an important characteristic of applications.

Distributed Systems and Client/Server Systems

Distributed systems, sometimes called **distributed data processing**, refers to a mode of delivery rather than a traditional class of applications like transaction processing or decision support systems. With distributed systems, the processing power is distributed to multiple sites, which are then tied together via telecommunications lines. Local area networks (LANs) and wide area networks (WANs) are both used to support distributed systems. We should note that there are a variety of operational functions that can be distributed, including data collection and entry, data editing and error correction, file location, and processing. In our view, only the last function—processing—represents distributed systems. Whether or not the processing power is distributed, it is often appropriate to distribute data collection and entry as well as data editing and error correction to the sites at which the transactions occur (e.g., the sales floor in a department store and the dock in a warehouse). File location, however, would never be distributed unless at least some processing power is also distributed.

Thus, we are defining distributed systems as systems in which computers of some size (microcomputers, midrange computers, mainframes, and so forth) are located at various physical sites at which the organization does business (headquarters, factories, stores, warehouses, office buildings) and in which the computers are linked by telecommunication lines of some sort in order to support some business process. The economics of distributed systems are not perfectly clear, but have tended to favor distribution. For the most part, communication and support costs go up with distributed systems while computer costs go down. Placing smaller microcomputers and workstations at noncentral sites is generally less expensive than expanding the capacity of a large system at the central site. Distributed systems do have disadvantages, such as greater security risk because of easy accessibility, dependence on high-quality telecommunications lines, and greater required coordination across sites. In most instances, however, the disadvantages are outweighed by the economic advantages. The distributed mode of computing has become the norm for business firms around the world.

In the 1990s a particular type of distributed system known as a **client/server system** moved to center stage, and this type of system continues to enjoy the spotlight in the twenty-first century. With this type of system, the processing power is distributed between a central server computer, such as a midrange computer or a powerful workstation, and a number of client computers, which are usually desktop microcomputers. The split in responsibilities between the server and the client varies considerably from application to application, but the client usually provides the graphical user interface (GUI), accepts the data entry, and displays the immediate output, while the server maintains the database against which the new data are processed. The actual processing of the transaction may occur on either the client or a server. For example, in a retail client/server application, the client might be the sophisticated cash register on the sales floor while the server is a workstation in the back office. When a credit sale is made, the data are entered at the register and transmitted to the server, the server retrieves the customer's record and updates it based on the sale, the server returns a credit authorization signal to the register, and the sales document is printed at the register. At the close of the billing cycle, the server prepares the bills for all the customers, prints them, and produces summary reports for store management.

Now that we have a general idea about the nature of a client/server system, let us explore the three building blocks of such a system. First, the client building block, usually running on a PC, handles the user interface and has the ability to access distributed services through a network. Sometimes the client also does the processing. Second, the server building block, usually running on a bigger machine (a high-end PC, workstation, midrange computer, or even a mainframe), handles the storage of data associated with the application. This associated data might be databases, groupware files (to be discussed later), Web pages, or even objects for object-oriented programs. Sometimes the server (or even another server) does the processing. The third building block is **middleware**, a rather vague term that covers all the software needed to support interactions between clients and servers. The *Client/Server Survival Guide* refers to middleware as "... the slash (/) component of client/server. In this first approximation, middleware is the glue that lets a client obtain a service from a server."

Middleware can be divided into three categories of software: server operating systems, transport stack software, and service-specific software. The server operating system, also called a network operating system, has the task of creating a *single-system image* for all services on the network, so that the system is transparent to users and even application programmers. The user does not know what functions are performed where on the network—it looks like a single system. The primary server operating systems are Microsoft Windows NT Server, Microsoft Windows 2000 Server, Microsoft Windows 2003 Server, Novell NetWare, several variations of UNIX, and Linux. Transport stack software allows communications employing certain protocols, such as Transmission Control Protocol/Internet Protocol (TCP/IP), to be sent across the network. The server operating system often encompasses some elements of the needed transport stack software, but other middleware products might also be required. The service-specific software is used to carry out a particular service such as electronic mail or the World Wide Web's Hypertext Transfer Protocol (HTTP).

Consider the split in responsibilities between the client and the server. The question is where the actual processing of the application is done. Originally, all client/server systems had only **two tiers**—a client tier and a server tier. If most of the processing is done on the client, this is called a *fat client* or *thin server* model. If most of the processing is done on the server, then it is a *thin client* or *fat server* model. For example, Web servers and groupware servers are usually fat servers (i.e., the processing is largely done on the server for Web and groupware applications), while database servers are usually thin servers (i.e., the processing is largely done on the client). In the mid-1990s **three-tier client/ server systems** became popular. In the most popular three-tier configuration, an application server that is separate from the database server is employed. The user interface is housed on the client, usually a PC (tier 1), the processing is performed on a midrange system or workstation operating as the application server (tier 2), and the data are stored on a large machine (often a mainframe or midrange computer) that operates as the database server (tier 3).

Let us consider some examples of client/server systems. A regional Bell operating company created a three-tier expense reporting system for use by its thousands of employees, and a natural gas company developed a three-tier facilities management application to improve decision making on the maintenance of its natural gas wells. An east-coast electric utility company used a three-tier approach to revamp its customer service system. The new system enables the utility's 450 service representatives to gain access to the multiple databases the company maintains on its 1.5 million customers. The service representatives use PCs as clients (tier 1) working through four servers that process the customer inquiries (tier 2) by accessing data from the company mainframe (tier 3). For a more complete description of a three-tier client/server application, see the sidebar entitled "Processing Prescription Drug Claims at Liberty Health."

In the early twenty-first century, there is a renewed emphasis on the thin client model to service remote areas, small locations, and traveling employees, where it is difficult to update the client software regularly. As an example, Maritz Travel Company, a $1.8 billion travel management company, used a thin client approach based on Microsoft Corp.'s Windows NT Terminal Server Edition and MetaFrame software, from Citrix Systems, Inc. With the Citrix approach, applications execute on a server and are merely displayed on the client, with the client acting as a "dumb" terminal. Maritz initially licensed 15,000 Citrix users and plans to extend the applications to nearly 50 of its remote offices. Richard Spradling, the chief information officer of Maritz, identifies many advantages to the thin client approach. According to Spradling, it is much easier to update only the servers; users automatically access the most current version of an application; performance of the applications has improved; and, over time, Maritz will spend less money on hardware by purchasing thin client devices rather than standard PCs or other fat clients (Wilde, 1999).

PROCESSING PRESCRIPTION DRUG CLAIMS AT LIBERTY HEALTH

Liberty Health is a supplemental health insurer based in Markham, Ontario. After a slow start in its efforts to migrate to client/server technology, Liberty Health concentrated on getting its most mission-critical system—processing claims for prescription drugs sold at more than 3,500 pharmacies across Canada—into a three-tier environment. The clients were PCs, running Windows, located in the pharmacies (tier 1); the application servers were Sun workstations and Hewlett-Packard midrange systems (tier 2); and the database server was a Unisys mainframe computer (tier 3). Programmers initially used the C and C++ programming languages to develop the tier 1 and tier 3 components of the system. They used a specialized development tool, BEA Systems' Tuxedo, to develop the transaction processing component (tier 2). Later development work was done using Information Advantage's DecisionSuite. Transaction volumes have grown substantially over the period since the point-of-sale prescription claims system became operational, and the system has handled the increased volume without difficulty, according to Bob Jackson, Liberty Health's IT development support officer.

[Adapted from Ruber, 1997]

TRANSACTION PROCESSING SYSTEMS

Let us begin our survey of applications with the "granddaddy" applications, the ones that started it all—**transaction processing systems**. These systems process the thousands of transactions that occur every day in most organizations, including sales; payments made and received; inventory shipped and received; hiring, firing, and paying employees; and paying dividends. In addition to producing the documents and updated records that result from the transaction processing (such as invoices, checks, and orders), these systems produce a variety of summarized reports that are useful to upper-level management.

Transaction processing systems are life-or-death systems for "paperwork" organizations, such as banks and insurance companies, and critical systems for the overwhelming majority of medium and large organizations. These systems were the first computerized systems, and they still use the majority of large-machine computing time in most organizations. For the most part, these transaction processing systems can be justified by traditional cost-benefit analysis. These systems are able to process transactions more rapidly and more economically (and certainly more accurately) than a manual (human) system. Transaction processing systems might be mainframe-based or midrange-based, or they might be two-tier or three-tier client/server systems. Most of the latest systems being implemented are client/server systems, but there are many, many mainframe- or midrange-based transaction processing systems still in use.

As a manager, you do not need to know the details of these systems. You only need to have an understanding of a transaction processing system's general nature, importance, and complexity. Therefore, we will limit our discussion to two representative transaction processing systems for single business functions—payroll and a sales order entry system.

Payroll System

At first glance, a payroll system seems fairly simple. Operators input the number of hours worked for each employee (usually employing online data entry), and the system batch processes these transactions to produce payroll checks. While this one-sentence description is correct, it represents only the tip of the iceberg, because it involves only about 10 percent of the system. The payroll processing subsystem also must keep year-to-date totals of gross income, social security income, individual deductions, various categories of taxes, and net income. It also must incorporate the ability to compute federal, state, and local taxes, as well as social security contributions, and it must handle both mandatory and voluntary deductions.

What other subsystems are necessary? Figure 5.4 lists the primary subsystems in most payroll systems and the tasks the subsystems must accomplish. Thus, the payroll system is both commonplace and complex. The payroll system is usually easy to justify on a cost-benefit basis because it would take an incredible number of payroll clerks to complete a modern payroll and maintain all the associated records.

Subsystems to accomplish:

- Payroll processing, including updating year-to-date master file
- Capture hours-worked data
- Add/delete employees
- Change deduction information for employees
- Change wage rates and salaries
- Creation of initial year-to-date master file
- Calculate and print payroll totals for pay period, quarter, and year
- Calculate and print tax reports for pay period, quarter, and year
- Calculate and print deduction reports for pay period, quarter, and year
- Calculate and print W-2 forms at end of year
- Interface with human resources information system
- Interface with budget information system

Figure 5.4 Components of a Payroll System

Order Entry System

We will illustrate a mainframe- or midrange-based order entry system, but an order entry system could certainly employ client/server technology. The basic idea behind an online order entry system is simple. As orders are received (whether in person, by mail, or by telephone), the sales representative enters the information into the system. The data entry might be via a microcomputer on the sales representative's desk or possibly through a point-of-sale transaction recording system (a sophisticated cash register that doubles as a terminal). The computer then updates the appropriate files and prints an invoice, either at the point-of-sale terminal, the sales representative's desk, or in the computer center.

Once again, this basic explanation tells only a small part of the story. Figure 5.5 provides a more complete description and shows how each transaction (sale) interacts with as many as six files on the computer system. In addition to the invoice, more than a dozen types of computer output might be generated. For example, the computer can check the credit status of the customer and reject the sale if the customer's credit limit will be exceeded. If the item ordered is in stock, a multipart shipping document is printed; if the item is not in stock, a message is sent (via the PC) to the customer to ask if he or she wants to backorder the item. Periodically or on demand, the order entry system will print out sales reports organized by item or by customer, customer statements, inventory reports, backorder status reports, and

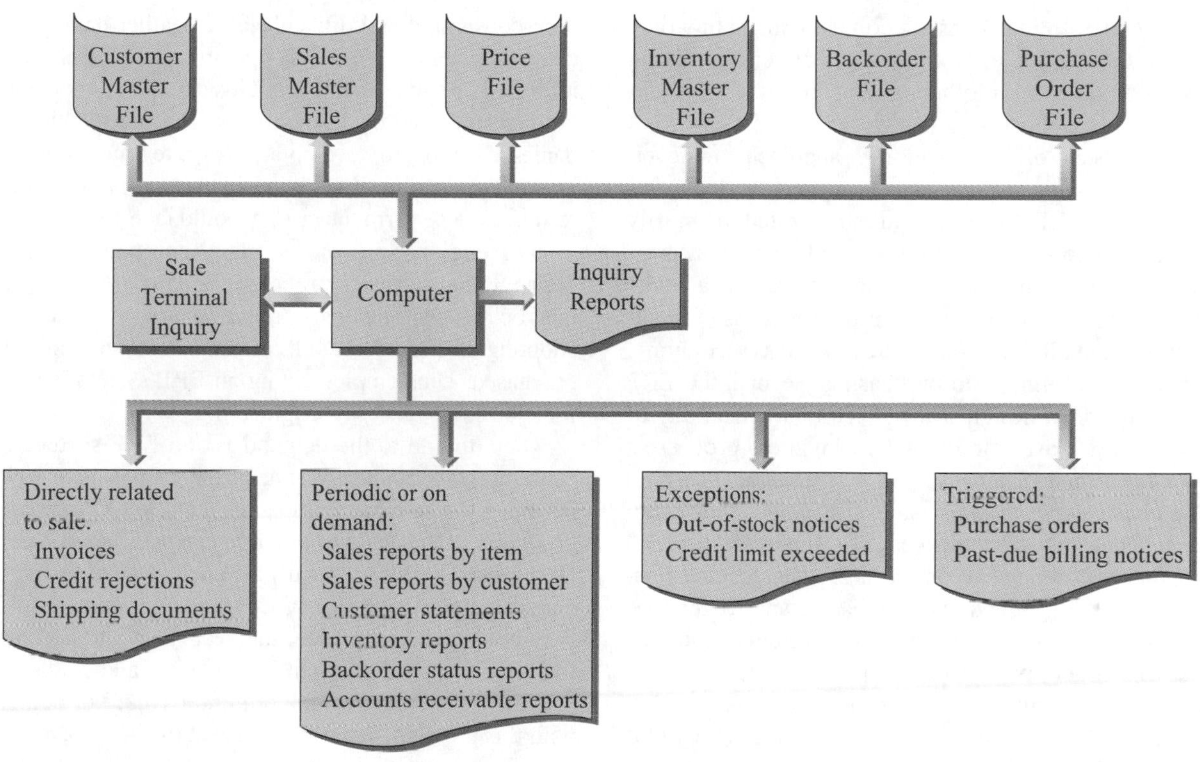

Figure 5.5 Online Order Entry System

accounts receivable reports. The system will also generate reports when exception conditions occur, such as when an item is out of stock or when a customer attempts to exceed the established credit limit. In these cases management action might be necessary. The order entry system can automatically print out purchase orders when an item is out of stock; it can also print out past-due billing notices for customers. A primary advantage of such an online system is that inquiries can be answered in a few seconds.

An important order entry system variant is an interorganizational system in which the orders are placed directly by the customer or the customer's computer (more on e-business applications in Chapter 7). An early, pre-Internet example was the American Hospital Supply Corporation's ASAP system in which order entry terminals, linked to AHSC's computer, were placed on the customers' (hospitals') premises, and hospital personnel placed orders themselves by keying them in. This made placing orders much more convenient for the customers and at the same time greatly reduced the delays and costs associated with printing and mailing order forms. More recently, orders have been placed by the customer's computer to the seller's computer using electronic data interchange (EDI)—which will be discussed in Chapter 7. By the late 1990s, the World Wide Web had taken the order entry process one step further by making it easy for both consumers and businesses to do their own order entry via a Web browser and an Internet connection. For example, many businesses use the Web to order networking equipment from Cisco Systems, and both businesses and consumers use the Web to order PCs from Dell Inc. In fact, several of the authors of this book have used the Web to order PCs from Dell.

ENTERPRISE RESOURCE PLANNING SYSTEMS

Enterprise resource planning (ERP) systems are also transaction processing systems, but they go well beyond traditional transaction processing system functionality—and thus deserve treatment as a separate application area. An ERP system is a set of integrated business applications, or modules, that carry out common business functions such as general ledger accounting, accounts payable, accounts receivable, material requirements planning, order management, inventory control, and human resources management. Usually these modules are purchased from a software vendor. In many cases a company might buy only a subset of these modules from a particular vendor, mixing them with modules from other vendors and with the company's existing applications.

An ERP system differs from earlier approaches to developing or purchasing business applications in at least two ways. First, the ERP modules are integrated, primarily through a common set of definitions and a common database. As a transaction is processed in one area, such as the receipt of an order, the impact of this transaction is immediately reflected in all other related areas, such as accounting, production scheduling, and purchasing. Second, the ERP modules have been designed to reflect a particular way of doing business—a particular set of business processes. Unlike a functional IS approach, ERP systems are based on a value-chain view of the business in which functional departments coordinate their work. To implement an ERP system, then, a company is committing to changing its business processes. If a company is purchasing an ERP system, the company might need to change its processes to conform to those embedded in the software package. The company adapts to the ERP software package, not vice versa.

Why has ERP become such a hot topic in the late 1990s and early 2000s, with most large and medium-sized firms either installing ERP systems or seriously thinking about it? The benefits from ERP will be specific to a given firm, but some common benefits have emerged. In many cases the companies are not happy with the old way of doing business—by separate functional departments—and they do not have the *integration* of applications (and therefore the data) to support their decision-making and planning needs. The current applications often do not "talk" to each other, making it a time-consuming and difficult job to gather data, present a coherent picture of what is happening in the firm, and make informed decisions and plans. This situation is not new, but, until recently, packaged solutions were not available to companies. The cost to develop a set of integrated applications internally is prohibitive; even if the company had the IS resources to perform the task, it would take years. From previous reengineering efforts, many companies know that their internal business processes need to be changed, and they believe that the best and easiest way to fix them is by adopting the processes built into an ERP system that can be purchased. Thus, implementing an ERP system is a way to force business process reengineering.

Then, to add to the demand for an ERP system, along came the year 2000 problem. In the mid- to late 1990s, it became clear to many companies that their key application programs would cease to function correctly when dates past December 31, 1999, were used. When these programs were coded—often using COBOL—the programmers allowed only two digits to represent the year. They did not imagine that their programs, written in the 1970s and 1980s, would still be used when the millennium arrived. For companies with this problem, the effort and cost to change every reference from a two-digit year to a four-digit year in their programs would be substantial. Adopting an ERP system, which was developed in the 1990s and correctly provided for dates beyond the year 2000, seemed to be an easy, albeit expensive, solution to the **Year 2000 problem**. Rarely was the year 2000 problem the sole reason to implement an ERP system, but if the company was not happy with its existing, nonintegrated set of applications, then the year 2000 problem might well have tipped the balance.

WHY PURCHASE AN ERP PACKAGE?

In a recent research study, three researchers–including one of the authors of this book–identified seven benefits gained by purchasing an ERP package. Three of these factors were overall business benefits, two were IT-related benefits, one benefit included both business and IT benefits, and the final factor was the avoidance of year 2000 maintenance costs. The three overall business benefits were data integration (improving access to data across business units, functions, processes, and the enterprise), new ways of doing business (implementing redesigned business processes, moving to a process orientation, and reducing costs of doing business), and global capabilities (supporting globalization with common processes and country-specific capabilities). The flexibility/agility benefit provided both business benefits (supporting competitive agility and business growth) and client/server architecture benefits. The two IT-related benefits were IT purchasing benefits (achieving time, cost, and reliability advantages from purchasing as opposed to building the system) and IT architecture cost reduction (reducing costs associated with systems operations and maintenance).

In considering the relative importance of these seven benefits, the authors distinguished between the purchase of an ERP by a company for its *value-chain* activities of materials management, production and operations, and sales and distribution, and the purchase of an ERP for *support* activities such as financial accounting and human resources. Data integration was the most highly sought-after benefit for both value-chain and support purchasers, and it was significantly more influential for value-chain purchasers than for support purchasers. Global capabilities were rated significantly higher by value-chain purchasers than support purchasers. Both IT purchasing benefits and year 2000 compliance were rated higher by support purchasers.

[Adapted from Brown, Vessey, and Powell, 2001]

It should be emphasized that implementation of an ERP system is extremely difficult because the company must change the way it does business. Further, ERP systems are very expensive. A typical large-scale ERP implementation costs tens of millions of dollars and takes a year or more. These implementation costs include not only the software licenses but also hardware and network investments and often consulting costs.

Further, choosing the right ERP software is a difficult task. The leading vendors are SAP, PeopleSoft, Inc. (which purchased ERP vendor J. D. Edwards in 2003), Oracle, and Baan; several smaller companies also offer ERP software. For ERP purchases, there are strong arguments for picking a single vendor, such as the tight integration of applications that is possible and the standardization of common processes. On the other hand, choosing a single vendor could also reduce flexibility for the adopting company. A "best of breed" or mix-and-match approach with multiple vendors might enable the company to meet more of its unique needs and reduce reliance on a single vendor; conversely, such an approach typically makes implementation more time-consuming and complicates system maintenance. With either approach, it is usually essential to employ the vendor or another consulting firm, or both, to assist in the implementation process. For large, multidivisional firms, implementing an ERP system is a very complex, challenging task that needs the best minds and careful attention of internal IS specialists, internal business managers, and external consultants. Most ERP implementations show positive results, but not always right away (see the sidebar entitled "Enterprise Systems Show Results, But Not Always Right Away"). The potential payoff of an ERP system, in terms of better information for strategic and operational decision making and planning, and greater efficiency, profitability, and growth, makes the efforts and the costs worthwhile.

ENTERPRISE SYSTEMS SHOW RESULTS, BUT NOT ALWAYS RIGHT AWAY

The infamous reputation of enterprise systems (ERP, CRM) is lots of money for little value. Yet more than three-quarters of companies implementing enterprise systems say they've achieved at least half of the value they initially expected from the technology, according to a study by Accenture. The companies that extracted value had two things going for them: time and follow-through. Within a year of implementation, most companies failed to realize many hoped-for benefits, such as reduced headcount and more accurate business planning. But after two years, the majority saw payback of every type of benefit except increased revenue.

[Ware, November 1, 2003]

The complexity of installing enterprise-wide systems has led to some spectacular failures in recent years. High-flying shoemaker Nike, Inc., stumbled last quarter [i.e., the first quarter of 2001], when problems related to a complex installation of supply chain software from i2 Technologies, Inc., forced it to write off $100 million in inventory and miss its sales goals. In the last two years, both Phoenix, Arizona-based PETsMART, Inc., and Hershey, Pennsylvania-based candy maker Hershey Foods Corp. saw revenues suffer as a result of problems implementing ERP systems from SAP. "The lesson learned from failures like Nike is that having to customize complex environments can kill you," says Joshua Greenbaum, principle of Enterprise Applications Group, in Daly City, California.

[Orzech, 2001]

An Example ERP System: SAP R/3

The most popular of the ERP systems is SAP R/3, developed by a German firm, SAP AG, headquartered in Walldorf, Germany. On the strength of the R/3 system and its newer Web-based variant mySAP, SAP is one of the top software firms in the world. According to an SAP brochure, 19,000 organizations worldwide run SAP software solutions. These organizations use SAP software at more than 60,000 locations in 120 countries.

SAP R/2 was a mainframe-based ERP; R/3 is a client/server system employing a common, integrated database with shared application modules. SAP R/3 handles both TCP/IP and Systems Network Architecture (SNA) communication protocols. SAP developed R/3 using its own fourth generation language (4 GL), named ABAP/4, which is the key piece of SAP's ABAP/4 Development Workbench. Customers may use ABAP/4, if they wish, to modify or enhance the standard R/3 modules. However, ABAP/4 will be of primary interest to companies that wish to employ an integrated 4 GL toolkit to develop applications, including managerial support systems, in addition to SAP standard modules. In 1999, SAP launched mySAP, which is both an umbrella concept for SAP's strategy of allowing its users to work through the World Wide Web *and* a brand name for the new Web-enabled versions of its R/3 software. Included under the mySAP label are a wide variety of enterprise software modules, including a robust ERP module (see Figure 5.6 and Figure 5.7).

The family of SAP R/3 software products fits the general description of an ERP system given above. It is a tightly integrated system consisting of numerous modules. A company may choose to implement some or all of these

Analytics
- Strategic enterprise management
- Business analytics

Financials
- Financial accounting
- Managerial accounting
- Financial supply chain management
- Manager self-service

Human Resources
- Employee transaction management
- Employee lifecycle management
- E-recruiting
- Employee relationship management
- Employee self-service
- HR analytics

Operations
- Purchase order management
- Inventory management
- Production management
- Maintenance and quality
- Delivery management
- Sales order management

Corporate services
- Real estate management
- Incentive and commission management
- Travel management

Figure 5.6 Key Functional Areas of mySAP ERP

modules. Most important, implementation of R/3 requires that the company change its business processes to conform to the processes built into the software.

Let us take a closer look at SAP R/3 and mySAP. At the very heart of an SAP implementation is the SAP R/3 Enterprise Core. Extensions can be added to the R/3 Enterprise Core, as desired, in various application areas—financials, supply chain management, product lifecycle management, human resources, and travel management. SAP R/3 Enterprise consists of the Core, the Extensions, and the SAP Web Application Server.

At the next level up in terms of comprehensiveness, mySAP ERP is a bundled ERP solution that incorporates SAP R/3 Enterprise as its core and adds mySAP Human Resources, mySAP Financials, and SAP NetWeaver. NetWeaver is SAP's integration and application platform to ensure seamless interaction with virtually any other SAP or non-SAP software. Figure 5.6 lists the key functional areas of mySAP ERP. Note that mySAP ERP is a relatively comprehensive package, with strength in the operations area as has historically been the case for SAP.

In addition to the modules bundled in mySAP ERP, other available modules in the mySAP Business Suite

Business Intelligence
- Data warehousing
- Business intelligence platform and tools

Customer Relationship Management
- Marketing, sales, and service
- Analytics
- E-commerce

Enterprise Portal
- Knowledge management
- Collaboration

ERP
- *See Figure 6.6*

Financials
- Strategic enterprise management
- Financial supply chain management
- Corporate services such as real estate management

Human Resources
- Employee lifecycle management
- Employee relationship management
- Employee transaction management

Marketplace
- Business partner management
- Self-service procurement
- Supplier enablement

Mobile Business
- Mobile business applications, including
  - Mobile asset management
  - Mobile time and travel
  - Mobile supply chain management

Product Lifecycle Management
- Lifecycle data management
- Program and project management
- Quality management

Supplier Relationship Management
- Contract management
- Plan-driven or self-service procurement
- Supplier connectivity

Supply Chain Management
- Supply chain planning
- Collaborative planning, forecasting, and replenishment
- Vendor-managed inventory

Figure 5.7 mySAP Business Suite Modules (in bold), with a Sample of Key Capabilities for Each Module

include business intelligence, customer relationship management, enterprise portal, marketplace, mobile business, product lifecycle management, supplier relationship management, and supply chain management (see Figure 5.7 for a sample of the key capabilities for each module). In the human resources module, the employee self-service area is an interesting one—it gives employees more active participation in the organization's human resources programs by permitting them to review and update their own address data, submit travel expenses or leave applications, view and print summary pay information, and check their own benefits selections and vacation balances. The names and sample capabilities of the modules should provide a reasonable understanding of what most of the modules do, but let us expand on three relatively new modules. Business intelligence provides a data warehousing capability within R/3 (more on data warehousing shortly), as well as tools to extract key information from the warehouse. Enterprise portal provides a secure, unified entry point into the organization's knowledge base as well as a comprehensive collaboration environment. Marketplace provides support for e-business on a robust, secure platform; marketplace provides self-service procurement, forward and reverse auction capabilities (more on this in Chapter 7), and, for suppliers, automated order management, up-to-date content delivery, and efficient customer billing.

All the above mySAP modules are generic software packages that would work in most businesses. In addition, the early years of the twenty-first century have seen the development of *industry solutions* by SAP and other ERP vendors that are tailored to the special needs of particular industries. SAP, for example, currently offers 23 specific industry solutions, including automotive, banking, chemicals, health care, insurance, pharmaceuticals, and retail. The trend is for more specialization of ERP packages, with variations for smaller businesses being introduced and more industry solutions under development.

Companies may choose to implement some or all of the SAP modules. Motorola's Semiconductor Products Sector, for example, chose to use the human resources modules, including payroll. Motorola, Inc., purchased the payroll module as a solution to the year 2000 problem. Motorola has implemented SAP payroll and employee record-keeping for all 25,000 U.S.-based employees, which, at the time it was installed, made it the largest North American R/3 payroll implementation. ERP implementation is such a challenging task that most companies employ a consulting firm to assist them; in Motorola's case, Price Waterhouse served as the consultant (SAP, 1997). DIRECTV, a unit of Hughes Electronics Corp. headquartered in El Segundo, California, chose to implement SAP R/3 modules for financials, materials procurement, and project tracking and costing to support its extremely rapid growth, which was largely through acquisition. DIRECTV, using Deloitte & Touche as its consulting partner, installed the R/3 modules as well as an Oracle database on a Hewlett-Packard HP 9000 server. According to DIRECTV Chief Information Officer Bob Pacek, the implementation went smoothly: "We went from a handshake to going live in only 11 months." He attributes that accomplishment to DIRECTV's decision to avoid customization insofar as possible (Wreden, 1999). MassMutual Financial Group is implementing several modules of mySAP, including employee self-service, payroll, and benefits administration from the human resources area; general ledger, budget, treasury, fixed assets, and travel and expenses from the financials area; and business-to-business procurement (buying) (SAP, 2000).

In contrast to these partial applications, Hyundai Motor Company is deploying mySAP modules, including the SAP automotive industry solution, to consolidate and automate its supply chain, financial, human resources, and procurement processes in its first North American assembly plant, now under construction in Montgomery, Alabama (Bacheldor, February 3, 2003). As part of an outsourcing agreement with EDS, Dial Corporation is scrapping enterprise software packages from Oracle, Siebel Systems, and Manugistics and moving to a single suite from SAP. The SAP implementation will include manufacturing, supply chain, finance, accounting, performance management, and customer relationship management software and is expected to cost $35 million, including licenses, implementation services, and maintenance. According to Dial Chief Information Officer Evon Jones, Dial went with SAP because "SAP and the processes with SAP's software are regarded as best in class and will drive operational efficiencies, particularly when you start to get greater visibility within your supply chain" (Bacheldor, July 25, 2003).

For more detailed descriptions of SAP implementations at several firms, see the section entitled "What is the Experience with ERP?" in Vollmann, Berry, Whybark, and Jacobs (2004, pp. 123–130). Also see the sidebar entitled "Toyota Motorsport Accelerates Formula One Operations with SAP." Today, Web-enabled ERP software systems are still a hot commodity.

DATA WAREHOUSING

In order to create a data warehouse, a firm pulls data from its operational systems—the transaction processing systems we have just discussed—and puts the data in a separate "data warehouse" so that users may access and analyze the data without endangering the operational systems. Thus, **data warehousing** is the establishment and maintenance of a large data storage facility containing data on all (or at least many) aspects of the enterprise. If the data warehouse is to be useful, the data must be accurate, current, and stored in a useable form; in addition, easy-to-use data access and analysis tools for managers and other users must be provided to encourage full use of the data.

TOYOTA MOTORSPORT ACCELERATES FORMULA ONE OPERATIONS WITH SAP

SAP announced that Toyota Motorsport GmbH, Toyota's German-based motorsport subsidiary, is implementing software from SAP's automotive industry solution to streamline ERP processes across its Formula One racing operations. Toyota Motorsport is replacing its existing, nonintegrated systems with SAP for Automotive, including mySAP Product Lifecycle Management, mySAP Supply Chain Management, mySAP Human Resources, and mySAP Financials.

Having won seven world championship titles with its World Rally Championship program, Toyota decided to enter Formula One racing in 1999. The entire car, including the engine and chassis, is completely designed and constructed at Toyota Motorsport's headquarters in Cologne, Germany. In order to operate a Formula One racing program, 20,000 to 30,000 made-to-order parts are required, and these parts must be quickly available. Further, the parts must be analyzed on an ongoing basis. Toyota Motorsport felt that SAP software was the best choice to efficiently manage the enormous amount of data required for the racing program's success, as well as to control its supply chain, production, and financial processes cost effectively.

"Applying knowledge effectively translates into competitive edge," said Thomas Schiller, IT general manager for Toyota Motorsport. "After comprehensive evaluation of several vendors, we found that SAP could best enable the solid data foundation that is critical to our business. SAP gives us a strategic advantage, ensuring high availability of reliable information across our operations to make faster and more informed decisions. With its integrated solutions and powerful scope of functionality, SAP enables us to effectively execute these decisions and accelerate our production and supply chain processes."

[Adapted from SAP, 2003]

Establishing a data warehouse is time-consuming and expensive. Three types of software tools are needed: warehouse construction software, warehouse operation software, and warehouse access and analysis software. Warehouse construction software is required to extract relevant data from the operational databases, make sure the data are clean (free from error), transform the data into a useable form, and load the data into the data warehouse (see Figure 5.8). Software tools to construct the warehouse include products such as Advantage Data Transformer (from Computer Associates), IBM DB2 Warehouse Manager, Informatica Powercenter, Oracle Warehouse Builder, and SAS/Warehouse Administrator.

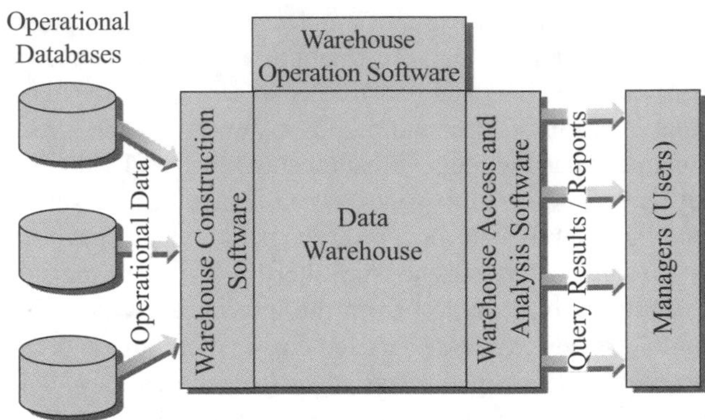

Figure 5.8 Key Elements of Data Warehousing

Operation software is required to store the data and manage the data warehouse. Data warehouse storage is typically accomplished by database management systems such as Advantage Ingres (from Computer Associates), IBM DB2, Microsoft SQL Server, NCR Teradata, Oracle, and Sybase; specialized warehouse management software is offered by Computer Associates, IBM, Information Builders, SAS Institute, and others.

The widest variety of software tools is available in the warehouse access and analysis area. Information catalog tools, such as Computer Associates' PLATINUM Repository, tell the user what is in the warehouse. Analysis and reporting tools enable a user to produce customized reports from the data warehouse, perhaps on a regular basis. Among these tools are Information Builders' WebFOCUS, MicroStrategy's 7i, Oracle's Darwin, and SAS Institute's Enterprise Miner. Visualizing the data might be important, using tools such as Computer Associates' CleverPath Forest & Trees and SAS Institute's SAS/INSIGHT. Some software packages, such as IBM's DB2 Universal Database Data Warehouse Edition, include tools to accomplish warehouse construction, operation, and access and analysis. This IBM product incorporates Intelligent Miner Modeling, Visualization, and Scoring modules to accomplish warehouse access and analysis. We will defer further consideration of these analysis tools until the next chapter, when we consider decision support systems, data mining, and executive information systems in more detail. In our judgment, creation and maintenance of the data warehouse is an enterprise system, while these end-user reporting and analysis tools are designed for management support—the topic of Chapter 6.

Companies of all shapes and sizes are successfully using data warehousing. Let us consider some examples. Gart Sports, a retailer with annual revenues of $681 million, acquired Sportmart in 1997 to become the largest sporting goods chain west of the Mississippi River. Among Gart's most essential tasks after the Sportmart purchase was the consolidation of the inventory information from the two firms' separate databases. Gart chose to create the combined database on IBM AS/400 servers using IBM's DB2 database management system. Gart also employed JDA Software Group's Merchandising Management System as its warehouse management software, combined with JDA's Retail Ideas software used to carry out queries and produce reports to satisfy Gart's unique requirements. The data warehouse occupies 400 gigabytes of disk storage, with more than 50 Gart employees accessing the warehouse. In addition to using the warehouse to manage inventory, Gart also produces performance-related reports for budget management and analysis of store operations as well as to assess the effectiveness of its advertising strategies by product and geography (Singer, 2000).

Harrah's Entertainment, with 18 casinos in 8 states, has annual revenues of $2 billion. Harrah's has created a data warehouse to track and analyze customer spending in all its casinos through its Total Gold system. All major guest transactions are captured, including those at slot machines and gaming tables, through the use of a magnetic membership card. To encourage use of the card, members receive vouchers or coupons each time it is used. John Boushy, senior vice president of information technology and marketing services, believes that "The information and analytical capabilities resulting from our new warehouse enable us to understand our customers better, to determine what adds value to each individual, and to market to them in a highly customized fashion." Boushy adds, "The system can predict a customer's profitability, even with very little transaction information. This enables us to react quickly to changes in behavior that may indicate possible attrition." Harrah's has implemented its data warehouse on an NCR massively parallel processor server, using NCR's Teradata database and warehousing software. The setup cost of the new data warehouse, which is capable of handling more than 100 terabytes of data, was about $2 million for hardware, software, and conversion expenses. Boushy expects payback of this cost within two years. According to Boushy, "Our warehouse has enabled us to develop world-class relationship marketing capabilities, which are leading to greater profits" (Singer, 1999).

Continental Airlines, Inc., won the 2003 Data Warehouse Institute Award for the best enterprise data warehouse. The original objective of the warehouse was to accurately forecast passenger bookings, but it is now used for a much wider variety of applications, including revenue management, customer relationship management, fraud detection, and management of crew payrolls. Continental's data warehouse, which is based on hardware and software from NCR's Teradata division, incorporates data from 41 sources, including flight schedules, seat inventory, revenue and ticketing data, profiles of OnePass frequent flyers, employee records, and crew payrolls. Thirteen hundred employees in 35 departments have access to the data, with most using Brio Software's query and reporting software. According to Continental, the data warehouse has been a big success, with millions of dollars in savings as well as revenue increases of several million dollars.

As user demands on the warehouse increased over time, Continental's data warehousing team reworked the data warehouse to operate on a near-real-time basis. The mainframe and COBOL tools that originally handled the transformation and loading of the data have been replaced by custom-built C++ software running on a network of Windows-based servers. Now users analyze flight operations and reservations data that is only seconds old. The data warehouse's near-real-time architecture and automated data transformation capabilities are two of the best practices that earned Continental the best enterprise data warehouse award (Whiting, July 28, 2003). Data warehousing has the potential to let companies understand and utilize the data that they are already collecting as they run their businesses.

CUSTOMER RELATIONSHIP MANAGEMENT

A type of application that often pulls much of its data from the organization's data warehouse is **customer relationship management**, or **CRM**. A CRM system attempts to provide an integrated approach to all aspects of interaction a company has with its customers, including marketing, sales, and support. The goal of a CRM system is to use technology to forge a strong relationship between a business and its customers. To look at CRM in another way, the business is seeking to better manage its own enterprise around customer behaviors.

A variety of software packages have been created to manage customer relationships, but most depend upon capturing, updating, and utilizing extensive profiles of individual customers. These profiles are often stored in a data warehouse, and data mining (discussed in Chapter 6) is used to extract relevant information about the firm's customers. Furthermore, customer profiles are made available online to all those in the company who might interact with a customer. In addition, Web-based front-ends have been

BANKING ON A WAREHOUSE AT FIRST UNION

After more than 80 acquisitions, First Union Corporation, of Charlotte, North Carolina, is now the nation's sixth largest bank and eighth largest brokerage, with assets of $230 billion and operating earnings of $3.7 billion. First Union needed a large, integrated data warehouse to incorporate the data from the legacy systems and customer databases of its acquisitions as well as its own legacy systems and databases. First Union made the decision to build the new warehouse, with a capacity of 27 terabytes, on an IBM RS/6000S platform running an Informix relational database management system. Analysts at First Union employ SAS Institute software products to carry out high-end data modeling and data mining on the data warehouse, and the analyses are proving valuable to the bank.

The story does not end with the data warehouse. First Union took the data warehousing approach one step further by creating a targeted, easily used **data mart**, which is simply a smaller, more focused version of a data warehouse created for "drop-in shopping," much like a neighborhood convenience mart. First Union designed its data mart, known as Sigma, to analyze customer profitability and to deliver customized marketing more efficiently. Sigma, which runs on the same RS/6000S with the same Informix relational database as the data warehouse, extracts all its information from the warehouse. Sigma is considerably smaller than the data warehouse—only five terabytes. Executives and sales managers access the data mart using MicroStrategy's DSS Web software (a browser-based, easy-to-use data analysis tool) on the First Union intranet. In total, about 250 analysts, managers, and executives access the warehouse and the data mart.

By evaluating the performance of products, branches, and regions, and using cross-selling analyses, First Union has increased revenues, customer satisfaction, and employee productivity. First Union also hopes to expand its commercial business with small-business customers by determining which delivery channels are the most popular and then enhancing service in those areas. Bob DeAngelis, manager of First Union's Enterprise Knowledge Group, believes that studying the interactions with customers is critical. "This enables us to better match our offerings and service levels with the customers' needs, including the assignment of relationship managers to those customers with complex relationships."

[Adapted from Singer, 1999]

created so that a customer can interact with the company online to obtain information about products and services offered by the company, to place an order, to check on the status of an existing order, to seek answers from a knowledge base, or to request service. CRM software packages enable organizations to market to, sell to, and service customers across multiple channels, including the Web, call centers, field representatives, business partners, and retail and dealer networks.

The CRM market is quite fragmented, with many of the newer options focused on a specific industry or market—so-called vertical CRM applications. One useful way of viewing the CRM market divides it into the following five segments (Schwartz, 2003):

- *Traditional out-of-the-box CRM.* This segment includes all the enterprise vendors, including CRM industry leader Siebel Systems, Inc., Oracle, PeopleSoft, and SAP. These applications have a great deal of horizontal functionality, such as call center support, sales-force automation, and marketing support. It is often necessary for the company's IT department, perhaps with the assistance of a consulting firm, to customize the software by adding some elements and removing others to fit the specific business or industry needs.
- *Traditional CRM with templates for specific vertical industries.* All the major enterprise vendors except Oracle offer this option, each with CRM solutions available in 20 or more vertical categories. The company's IT department selects the functionality needed for the specific business; it is often necessary for the IT department or a consultant to customize the template to meet the firm's specific needs.
- *Traditional out-of-the-box CRM with application development hooks.* This segment sounds similar to the previous "templates" approach, but in reality is quite different. In this category, vendors provide a series of reusable software objects that can be combined as needed to build an application best suited to the company's needs. Vendors in this segment include E.piphany, Chordiant Software, Kana Software, Inc., and Oracle. The reusable objects incorporate the basic CRM functionality needs for every business as well as the most common needs within a variety of industries.
- *Industry-specific vertical CRM packages.* This category has seen the most growth in the early twenty-first century, with packages available in most major vertical industries. For example, in the retail industry, key vendors are Blue Martini Software, JDA

Software Group, Inc., and Retek, Inc. In the consumer goods industry, vendors include CAS and MEI Group; in financial services, leading vendors are Chordiant Software, Metavante Corporation, Pegasystems Inc., and Pivotal Corporation. Firepond, Inc., Kana Software, Inc., and Pegasystems are three key vendors in the health care industry. Other leading vendors include Reynolds and Reynolds Company in the automotive industry, Interface Software, Inc., in the legal arena, and Dendrite International in the pharmaceutical industry.

- *Custom solutions from vertical systems integrators.* Vendors in this category include Accenture, Computer Associates, IBM Global Services, and Unisys. A custom solution tends to be very expensive but might be necessary for companies with unique or very specific business or industry needs. In most cases the **systems integrator** will start with a vertical template and add functionality as necessary.

Without calling them CRM applications, we have already described two examples of CRM projects using a data warehouse: Harrah's Entertainment and First Union Corporation. Other examples abound: Online brokerage Quick & Reilly Inc. is using Siebel's sales-force automation tools to offer its customers investment options based on what it already knows about them. Quick & Reilly began investing $10 million in call-center and sales-force automation software in 1998. Within 6 months of initial implementation, the CRM system boosted the rate at which brokers convert sales prospects into customers by up to 20 percent. "That's a real return on investment," said Edward M. Garry, Quick & Reilly's vice president for customer relationship management (Kerstetter, Hamm, and Greene, 2002).

Pharmaceutical manufacturer Eli Lilly & Company has implemented sales-force automation, call-center, and other CRM applications from Siebel to support its efforts in branding its drugs (Lilly manufactures antidepressant Prozac as well as many other drugs). "Branding is more important to drug companies nowadays," said Roy Dunbar, chief information officer at Lilly. "Patients used to call their doctors; now, a patient on one of our drugs can pick up the phone and call us." Based on its CRM systems, Lilly has initiated the Lilly Answer Center, which uses the Web and call-center technology to stay in close contact with customers (Greenemeier, September 22, 2003).

A CRM implementation in a pharmaceutical company also helps drive sales and improve the bottom line. With CRM, a drugmaker can identify which physicians are most receptive to their salespeople, calculate potential revenue from physician relationships, and customize interactions with high-priority physicians. Kos Pharmaceuticals Inc., a manufacturer of drugs to treat chronic cardiovascular and respiratory diseases, implemented CRM in 2003 for its 500 sales representatives. "Our sales staff is growing, and we needed to make sure they communicate with each other, especially if they're calling on the same doctors," said Lisa Barry, senior manager of sales systems at Kos. "The sales force seems happier [with the CRM in place], and the physicians like that different sales reps can tell a continuous story" (Greenemeier, October 29, 2003).

In perhaps the largest implementation of CRM software ever, Hewlett-Packard is scrapping a number of different CRM applications across its business channels and installing the eBusiness Applications package from Siebel Systems, Inc., as a unified platform. The CRM project will consolidate Hewlett-Packard's direct and indirect sales channels, including thousands of direct-sales representatives, marketing professionals, contact-center representatives, and partner resellers. Eventually, the project could involve over 50,000 users. "From a customer-experience perspective, it was absolutely imperative to move rapidly," said Mike Overly, vice president of customer operations for HP Global Operations. Hewlett-Packard expects to gain a unified view of customers across all channels and drive operating efficiencies, saving the company tens of millions of dollars (Dunn, 2003). In the early 2000s many companies have publicly stated that they were becoming more customer-focused—and some companies are carrying through on such statements in a very significant way by installing a CRM system.

OFFICE AUTOMATION

Office automation refers to a set of office-related applications that might or might not be integrated into a single system. The most common applications are electronic mail, word processing, voice mail, copying, desktop publishing, electronic calendaring, and document imaging, along with document preparation, storage, and sharing.

Office technology has taken major strides since World War II. Document preparation has evolved from manual typewriters, to electric typewriters with a moving carriage, to the IBM Selectric typewriters with the "golf ball" typing element, to memory typewriters, to expensive terminals connected to a minicomputer, to stand-alone microcomputers, and now to microcomputers linked via a LAN. Copying has moved from mimeograph machines to fast photocopiers and facsimile machines. The telephone has moved from a simple instrument with no dial or keys to a

CRM: DESPERATELY SEEKING SUCCESS

Not all CRM projects are successes, but that does not seem to be deterring corporate investment in CRM applications. An AMR Research study shows that only 16 percent of CRM initiatives have returned value to the company. The remaining projects include some that have failed but more that are unclear whether they have succeeded or failed because the companies have not defined successes or goals for their CRM projects. "Companies must define their CRM strategy up front, and that strategy will define what success looks like and which metrics are important," according to Kevin Scott, a senior research analyst with AMR Research.

Despite these mixed results, 35 percent of executives surveyed in a recent *CIO Magazine* Tech Poll indicated that their organizations will launch CRM projects in the next year. Similarly, a recent IDC forecast calls for a 6.7 percent annual growth rate for CRM expenditures from 2002 to 2007, resulting in $12.1 billion in CRM software annual revenue by 2007.

Given this continued growth in CRM projects with only limited success thus far, what must companies do to give their CRM initiatives the best chance of succeeding? *CIO Magazine* suggests three best practices:

- Be prepared for organizational change—collaboration across the enterprise will be required.
- Keep it simple—make sure your application has an easy-to-use interface and that your vendor will work with you to provide user training.
- Align your vendor's definition of success with your own—make sure your vendor understands your company's definition of success.

[Adapted from Ware, August 1, 2003]

dial telephone, and then from a simple touch-tone telephone to a versatile touch-tone instrument with features such as automatic redial, call forwarding, call waiting, multiparty calling, and caller identification. To a great extent, however, these devices still do not talk to each other today—but IT will change that! In the office of the future, these devices and others will be connected via an integrated voice/data/image network, as shown in Figure 5.9. In our discussion of the components of this figure, we will mention those connections that exist today.

Word Processing and Application Suites

A number of excellent word-processing packages have been developed for microcomputers, the most common workstations in today's offices. Microsoft Word is clearly the market leader, but there is also support for Corel WordPerfect and Lotus Word Pro. These software packages are typically sold as part of an application suite that includes spreadsheet, presentation, database, and possibly other applications. The advantage of a suite is that it is possible to copy and paste from one application to another in the same suite; for instance, a Microsoft Office user can copy a portion of an Excel spreadsheet to the clipboard and paste the portion directly into a Word document she is preparing. In a small office or high-print-volume situation, a high-quality printer can be connected directly to a PC. It is more common, however, for office PCs to be on a LAN so documents can be sent electronically from the preparing workstation to a high-quality printer, as depicted in Figure 5.9.

Electronic Mail

Electronic mail (e-mail) systems permit rapid, asynchronous communication between workstations on a network, eliminating telephone tag. Most systems incorporate such features as sending a note to a distribution list, forwarding a note to someone else with an appended message, replying to a note without reentering the address, and filing notes in electronic file folders for later recall. All the authors of this book use electronic mail on a regular basis, and we feel we could not do without it.

Of course, there are potential drawbacks to e-mail communication. Because it is so easy to use, the volume of e-mail can become overwhelming, particularly standard messages sent to a distribution list. Spam—unsolicited e-mail that most of us regard as junk—is the bane of e-mail users in the decade of the 2000s. E-mail is also less personal because it is dependent on text signals alone (but see the sidebar "E-mail Smileys for All Occasions"). Some people use offensive words and phrases that they would never use in face-to-face conversation, called "flaming." Privacy issues arise because of the opportunity for electronic monitoring by supervisors. For most organizations and most users, however, these drawbacks are totally overshadowed by the advantages of rapid, asynchronous communication.

Variants of e-mail include electronic bulletin boards, listservs, computer conferencing, chat rooms, and, most recently, instant messaging (IM). An electronic bulletin board is a repository (a disk on a computer) on which anyone with access to the bulletin board and the computer account number can post messages and read other messages. Bulletin boards can be operated within an organization (employing

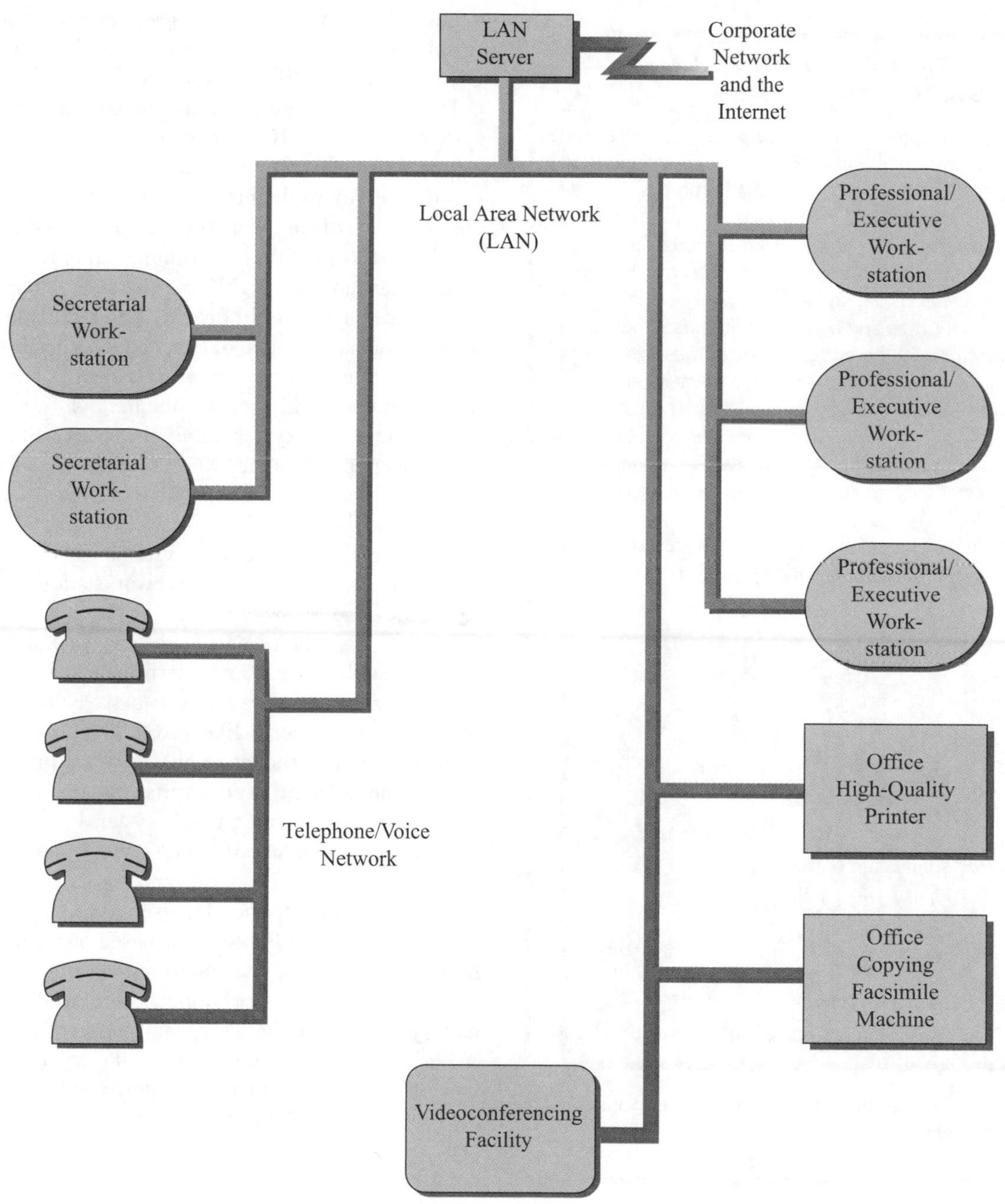

Figure 5.9 Office of the Future Network

the usual communication links), or over the Internet. A listserv is a computerized mailing list that accepts a message sent to the listserv address and forwards it to everyone on the particular mailing list.

Computer conferencing is similar to a bulletin board, but it is set up around a particular topic. For example, a professional society can set up a computer conference to consider changes in its annual meeting program. The announcement of the topic and the Web address (or account number) at which the conference will be held are published in the society's newsletter, which can be distributed electronically via a listserv. Users participate in the conference by logging into the conference, entering an opinion, and reading other participants' opinions. Chat rooms are real-time versions

E-MAIL SMILEYS FOR ALL OCCASIONS

As e-mail has spread through corporate America and around the world, new conventions for communication have been created. Perhaps the most humorous of these conventions is the digital smiley face and the numerous variations which have evolved from the original smiley. When you tilt your head to the left and use your imagination, the original digital smiley :-) looks like a little face with a colon for eyes and a hyphen for a nose. The use of this digital smiley at the end of an e-mail message means something like "just kidding," as in the following message copied from an electronic bulletin board. The subject is uncontrollable scalp flaking, and one writer is proposing a new remedy: "I find that rinsing my scalp with vinegar will cut down on it for a while, if you don't mind smelling like a salad :-)"

But the variants of the digital smiley are even more fun. Here are some variants along with their interpretations:

:-(	I'm unhappy
:-D	I'm laughing
B-)	I'm cool
:*)	I'm drunk
{(:-)	I have a toupee
}(:-(	I have a toupee and it's windy
:-8	I'm talking out of both sides of my mouth
[:-)	I'm wearing a Walkman
d:-)	I'm a baseball player
:-?	I'm smoking a pipe
<<<<(:-)	I'm a hat salesman
':-)	I accidentally shaved off one eyebrow

Try creating your own smileys and spice up your own e-mail messages!

[Adapted from Miller, 1992]

of computer conferencing (synchronous communication) conducted on the Internet, with an incredibly wide array of topics. IM is a synchronous communication system that enables the user to establish a private chat room with another individual to carry out text-based communication in real time over the Internet.

The first popular e-mail systems were mainframe or minicomputer-based, which makes sense because e-mail predated client/server systems. They were also designed to run under proprietary operating systems (e.g., not UNIX). Examples are Digital Equipment's VaxMail and ALL-IN-ONE and IBM's OfficeVision and PROFS (Professional Office System). The more advanced mainframe-based systems, such as PROFS, packaged e-mail together with electronic calendaring and other related features. In this mainframe environment, the e-mail system runs on the mainframe, with the workstation being used as a terminal. With PROFS, the main menu included a calendar with the current date highlighted, a clock, a message area where other users could directly communicate with this workstation, and a menu of other choices, such as process schedules (electronic calendaring), open the mail, search for documents, and prepare documents. Some of these mainframe e-mail systems are still in use, although they are not as popular as they once were because they do not have a GUI interface or the functionality of the newer groupware systems.

The second wave of e-mail systems was designed to run on UNIX servers (high-powered workstations running the UNIX operating system). Popular systems include Pine and Elm. This type of e-mail system runs on the server, with the PC being used as a terminal; again, there is no GUI interface. These systems do not have the functionality of mainframe systems like PROFS, but they are much more economical to operate on a per-user or per-message basis. It should come as no surprise that many colleges and universities still use these UNIX systems.

The development of POP-servers and POP-mail demonstrates how PC-based front-ends can be used to provide a friendlier interface for users. POP stands for post office protocol, and POP-mail is based on an analogy with post office boxes. To use POP-mail, a POP-client such as Eudora or Pegasus must be loaded on the PC. Various e-mail systems, including Pine, can be used as a POP-server. All incoming mail is kept on the POP-server until the user logs on and asks for mail to be downloaded to his or her own machine; this is analogous to traditional mail being kept in a post office box until the patron opens the box and empties it. The user processes the mail on his or her own machine, using the GUI provided by Eudora or Pegasus. The user can read mail, throw some of it away, store some in electronic file folders, and prepare responses to some of it. After processing the mail on the PC, the user reopens a connection to the POP-server on the host computer and uploads any outgoing messages.

The third wave of e-mail systems were LAN-based client/server software systems that incorporated well-designed GUI interfaces, complete with small inboxes, outboxes, wastebaskets, attractive fonts, color, and other GUI features. Some examples are cc:Mail by Lotus and

Microsoft Mail. If an organization wants e-mail only, these packages are sufficient. LAN-based e-mail systems were very popular in the 1990s, but have largely been replaced in the 2000s by the more robust groupware systems such as Lotus Notes/Domino and Microsoft Outlook/Exchange. A variation of this third wave of client/server e-mail systems is Internet mail, which has become very popular for small business and home use. For Internet mail, the client software is the user's Web browser, and the server software is located on a high-powered Web server operated by an Internet service or software provider. The user must, of course, have access to the Internet via an Internet service provider (ISP) or an organizational link to the Internet. Examples of these Internet mail systems, which are usually free, are Microsoft Hotmail, Netscape Mail, and Juno E-mail on the Web.

Progressive organizations, however, are ready to move beyond simple e-mail. They want the greater functionality of the older mainframe systems plus the GUI interface of the POP-mail and LAN-based systems. They want electronic calendaring and document sharing. The answer is groupware. We will discuss groupware as a separate category of applications below, after we have completed our discussion of the office of the future. Groupware is, in fact, a significant step toward the hypothetical office of the future.

Future Developments

Today, the telephone/voice network in most companies is totally independent of the computer/data network. In the office of the not-so-distant future, these networks will be combined into one integrated office network. Newer workstations include a voice receiver and a voice speaker and can function as a telephone. Some users are already using their workstations to make telephone calls over the Internet. When the technology has matured and the appropriate connections to the office and external networks have been made, the functions of today's telephones are likely to be totally subsumed by the workstation itself.

Today, almost all offices have facsimile machines to receive electronically transmitted documents and produce a hard copy version. Faxes can also be sent and received via a PC. However, conventional copying machines are still stand-alone devices. In the future, the copying machine will be integrated into the office network and will absorb the function of the stand-alone facsimile device. Single or multiple copies of a document may be printed either at the copying machine, from a workstation in the same office, or from a remote site. The all-in-one machines (printer, copier, scanner, and facsimile), such as the Hewlett-Packard OfficeJet d155xi, are early examples of these integrated devices.

Document storage is another evolving area of office automation. It is not unusual for today's organizations to store their business documents online, often using magnetic or optical disk technology. More and more of these documents will be stored digitally in the future, particularly with the growing use of imaging technology. With imaging, any type of paper document—including reports, graphs, and photographs—can be read by a digital scanner and translated into digital form so that it can be stored in the computer system. Later this process can be reversed, so that the digitized image stored in the computer system can be printed on paper, displayed on a video display unit, or transmitted to another workstation.

A facility possessed by a limited but growing number of organizations—a videoconferencing facility—is shown at the bottom of Figure 5.9. Such facilities permit face-to-face, or, more properly, image-to-image meetings and conferences without the need for costly and time-consuming travel. By tying the videoconferencing facility into the integrated office network, computer-generated reports and graphics can also be shared during the conferences.

Whereas separate videoconferencing facilities work well for larger group meetings, desktop videoconferencing is now a reality, and as quality improves it will become quite popular for one-on-one and small group conferences. The screen on a desktop PC is so small, however, that we do not think desktop videoconferencing will prove satisfactory for large group conferences. Splitting an already small screen into multiple smaller images will reduce the sense of being there, reducing the effectiveness of the conference. Thus, we believe that the office of the future will include a separate videoconferencing facility (usually a conference room) where a large group of people can participate in a conference with a large group at another location.

As an example of both group and desktop videoconferencing, let us consider the newest offerings from Polycom, Inc., headquartered in Pleasanton, California. With its 2001 acquisition of PictureTel Corporation, Polycom solidified its position as the worldwide market leader in voice- and videoconferencing. Polycom iPower 9000 Series group videoconferencing units have list prices from $15,500 to $26,500 per unit for the iPower 9400 and from $18,000 to $29,000 per unit for the top-of-the-line iPower 9800. In each case the lower figure is the price of the base system with no monitors and support for only IP network connection; the higher figure includes a dual monitor package and the ability to connect to an additional type of network. Polycom iPower 9000 Series units operate at 30 frames per second (comparable to television quality) when operating at 256 kbps and above. This network speed can be obtained via a LAN connection, digital subscriber line (DSL), cable modem, or combined Integrated Services Digital Network (ISDN) lines. Included in the iPower 9800 is a feature, called Limelight, that causes the camera to focus on the current speaker. Limelight works by triangulating from the sounds received at four tiny, built-in microphones in order to focus on the speaker or, if several people are speaking almost at once, to zoom out and show all the people who are speaking. Another capability included in the iPower 9800 is ImageShare, a unique tabletop interface that lets users access a laptop computer and share its screen display with other videoconferencing participants. At the desktop level, Polycom's ViaVideo II, with a list price of $599 and a street price of $529 or less, is a compact, portable system that plugs into the universal serial bus (USB) port on a standard PC. The ViaVideo II is designed to operate at 15 frames per second (fps) at network speeds from 32 kbps up to 320 kbps (motions will appear jerky at 15 fps), or at 30 fps at network speeds above 320 kbps. This desktop system does not provide large-system picture quality, but it does provide full-screen, full-motion video with full duplex audio when used with an appropriate network connection.

In summary, the ideal office network shown in Figure 5.9 does not exist. Offices have secretarial and professional/executive workstations in ever-increasing numbers, and these devices are usually linked via a LAN. Today telephony is not typically accomplished on the same network, and the facsimile machine is not on the LAN. The use of videoconferencing is increasing, but still not commonplace.

As organizations move toward office automation, they have learned some important lessons. First, the process of office automation must be coordinated—each office unit cannot go its own way. The various islands of automation must be made compatible. In most organizations the IS organization has been given the responsibility for corporate-wide office automation. Second, the emphasis must be on the information requirements—the problems being solved—in office automation as in other IT applications. Third, training and education of all parties involved is a necessary prerequisite for a successful system. Fourth, office automation should be an evolutionary process, moving toward the mythical office of the future, but not expecting to get there overnight. Fifth, the redefinition of the functions of the office and the restructuring of individual roles are required to achieve the maximum benefits of office automation.

GROUPWARE

Earlier in this chapter, we argued that ERP systems deserved treatment as a separate application area because of their currency and importance, despite the fact that ERP systems are, indeed, transaction processing systems. Now we wish to make the same argument for including groupware as an application area vis-à-vis office automation. Clearly, groupware is part of office automation, but it is a very critical part that deserves special attention.

Groupware is an industry term that refers to soft*ware* designed to support *groups* by facilitating collaboration, communication, and coordination. Nowadays, the term **collaboration** or the phrase **collaborative environment** is often used as a synonym for groupware. In choosing a groupware product, the decision maker must decide what functions are required and seek a product (or a combination of products) that provides these features. Some groupware features are electronic mail, electronic bulletin boards, computer conferencing, electronic calendaring, group scheduling, sharing documents, electronic whiteboards, meeting support systems, workflow routing, electronic forms, desktop videoconferencing, learning management systems, and IM. None of the leading groupware packages provide all the functions that a company might want, but in many cases add-on packages can be purchased to fill the gaps.

One might guess that the heart of a successful general-purpose groupware product is electronic mail, and that might be right—but the key feature that put industry leader Lotus Notes in the top position is its outstanding ability to share documents of all types. Electronic calendaring and group scheduling are also important, and these have been strengths of Novell GroupWise. The third major player, Microsoft Exchange, is a relative newcomer in this market, but Exchange has easily passed GroupWise to move into the number two position (Emigh, 2003). Other players in the groupware marketplace include Oracle with its Collaboration Suite, Thruport Technologies with its HotOffice product, Groove Networks with its Groove Workspace product, and Web Crossing. All the groupware players are moving to support real-time collaboration based on presence awareness, or the ability to detect others' online availability (which is the key technology underlying IM). An interesting specialized groupware area deals with electronic meeting support systems, and we will talk more about this area in the next chapter.

Groupware, like ERP systems, is a growth area in the software industry as well as an evolving area (see the sidebar entitled "Real-Time Collaboration"). To gain a greater understanding of this area, let us take a closer look at a leading groupware product, Lotus Notes.

An Example Groupware System: Lotus Notes

Lotus Development Corporation's first important product was 1-2-3, and it became the dominant spreadsheet package in the 1980s and early 1990s. The second important product was Notes, a groupware system originally featuring strong document-sharing features and a reasonable e-mail package that has grown into a more full-featured product. Notes—and Lotus's expertise in developing PC and client/server software—were important to IBM, which paid $3.5 billion to purchase Lotus in 1995. IBM was already a software powerhouse, as we have noted earlier in this book, but its strength was in large machine software. IBM believed it needed to bolster its PC software prowess to compete with Microsoft in that market, and it also wanted the Notes groupware product. IBM has allowed Lotus to operate as a separate business unit, and so far the buyout seems to have benefited both IBM and Lotus. Notes continues to be the leader in the groupware marketplace (in terms of number of "seats"), followed by second-place contender Microsoft Exchange.

Users can configure the welcome page of Lotus Notes to their liking; Figure 5.10 shows the slightly customized welcome page used by one of the authors of this book. At the top left of the screen is the menu bar containing the menus of commands used to perform tasks within Notes. Just below the menu bar is a row of icons that permit the user to perform tasks quickly by clicking the mouse on an icon. Below the row of icons is an address box. To go to a Web address you have not visited before, enter the Uniform Resource Locator (URL) in the address box; to go to a page you have previously visited, click the down arrow at the right end of the address field and select the appropriate URL from the drop-down list. To the right of the menu bar is the navigation bar that allows you to navigate in Notes just as you would in a Web browser (Notes is, in fact, a Web browser). Down the left side of the screen are the bookmark buttons, which represent a powerful way to navigate to Web pages as well as to Notes databases, views, and documents. In the big area of the screen, the upper left quadrant shows the most recent entries in the user's Notes inbox, the upper right quadrant shows the "to do" list and calendar entries for the current day, and the lower half contains "hot spot" links to the user's mail, calendar, contacts (address book), "to do" list, and personal journal.

Some established Notes users prefer to work from the workspace page, shown in Figure 5.11, which served the function of the welcome page in earlier versions of Notes. The workspace page also contains the menu bar, the row of icons, the navigation bar, and the bookmark bar. Now, however, most of the screen is occupied by the workspace,

REAL-TIME COLLABORATION

Many business-technology managers see a lot of value in using the Internet to keep people in constant and instantaneous communication with one another, yet they're not certain when that vision will become reality. It's happening, but only in bits and pieces, as with telecommuters who communicate with co-workers using IM and employees who attend project-team meetings via Web conferencing. This concept, known as real-time collaboration, focuses on the person-to-person aspect of a company's broader collaboration strategy. On occasion, technologies such as IM and Web conferencing are being used to collaborate in real time with customers, partners, and suppliers.

But are the technologies and concept advanced enough to build a strategic organizational plan around real-time collaboration? That's a question business-technology managers are asking, and there are numerous challenges to achieving that goal in the near future. Many of the technologies available don't follow standards and don't link to each other easily, and the performance of multimedia delivery over the Internet hasn't reached a high degree of consistency. Then there are the cultural issues involved in getting people to embrace a completely different way of working. "Real-time collaboration apps aren't ready for prime time," says Forrester Research analyst Erica Rugullies.

On a positive note, analysts think it will be only a few years before big visions for real-time collaboration are realized. Big-name vendors such as IBM Lotus Software, Microsoft, Oracle, Siemens, and Sun Microsystems are promising—and in some cases already offering—collaboration tools that embrace standards-based technologies such as XML, Web services, Java 2 Enterprise Edition, and voice over IP. The resulting flexibility will let collaborative components be sewn together to create an always-on architecture. The plan from the IT community is to let collaborative features be embedded in various enterprise applications, launched from numerous communication tools, and consumed by just about any device. "There's a larger vision here than a group of disconnected services," says Rob Koplowitz, senior director of product marketing for Oracle. "Customers are beginning to see this as an infrastructure play."

[Kontzer, November 17, 2003]

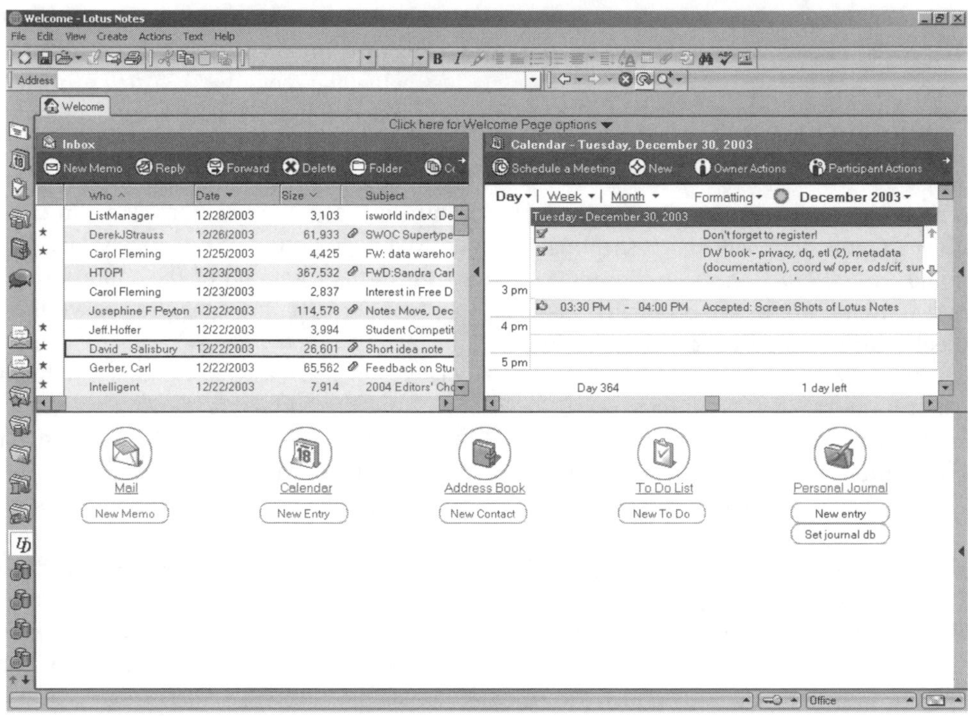

Figure 5.10 Lotus Notes® Welcome Page (Copyright © 2004 IBM Lotus Software. Lotus Notes is a registered trademark of IBM Lotus Software. Used with permission of IBM Lotus Software.).

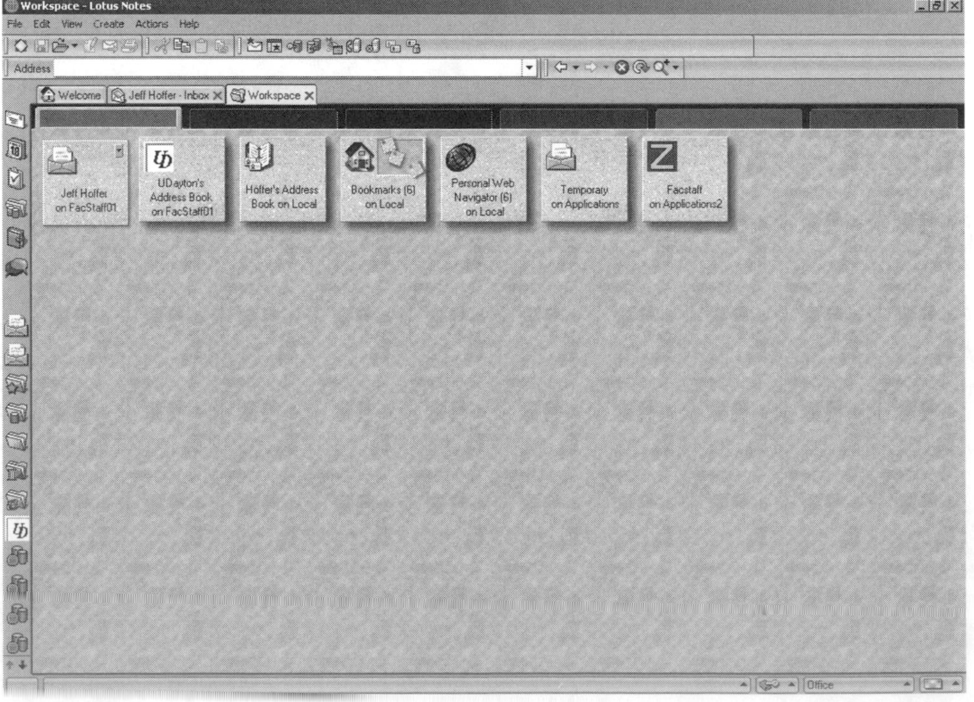

Figure 5.11 Lotus Notes® Workspace Page (Copyright © 2004 IBM Lotus Software. Lotus Notes is a registered trademark of IBM Lotus Software. Used with permission of IBM Lotus Software.)

which in turn contains icons representing databases. These databases are the heart of Notes; each contains a collection of documents relating to the same topic. The database on the left is the mailbox, which is an entry point into the e-mail features of Notes. The other databases refer to a university address book, a personal address book, personal bookmarks, a personal Web navigator, and two databases related to applications. The user opens a database by double-clicking on the relevant icon.

When the user opens the mailbox—either by clicking the mail bookmark button on the left side of any page (the top icon, which looks like a piece or mail) or the mail hot spot in the bottom area of the welcome page—the inbox view of the mailbox is displayed, as shown in Figure 5.12. In addition to the bars and icons appearing on the welcome or workspace page, a view action bar appears above the listing of e-mail messages in the larger window to the right. The actions listed relate to the current view. For the inbox view, the entries are new memo, reply, forward, delete, folder (i.e., move to folder), copy into, and tools; all these, except tools, are common actions used in processing e-mail. Most of the screen is divided into a navigation pane on the left and an active view pane on the right. In the inbox view, the active view pane lists the user's mail messages, tells who sent the message, the date it was sent, the size of the message, and the subject assigned by the sender. To open a message a user double-clicks on it. A star immediately to the left of the sender's name indicates unread messages. The navigation pane on the left lists a number of views and folders that can be used to manage the mail. For instance, the folder "drafts" contains messages you are working on but have not yet sent; the "to do" folders contain task lists that have been created by the user; and the set of file folders with names such as Academic Dishonesty, Accounting, ACM, and Administrative Committee constitute the electronic filing system for this user. Notes also has a valuable electronic calendaring feature that you access by clicking on the calendar bookmark button on the left side of the page (the second icon, which looks like a page of a desk calendar) or by clicking on the calendar hot spot on the welcome page. Several different calendar views are available, including a one-day view, a one-week view, and a one-month view.

As mentioned above, the real strength of Notes is its document-sharing abilities. This is done through various shared databases. Some of the databases might be set up so that the user can only read documents, not modify them or add new ones; in other databases, such as discussion

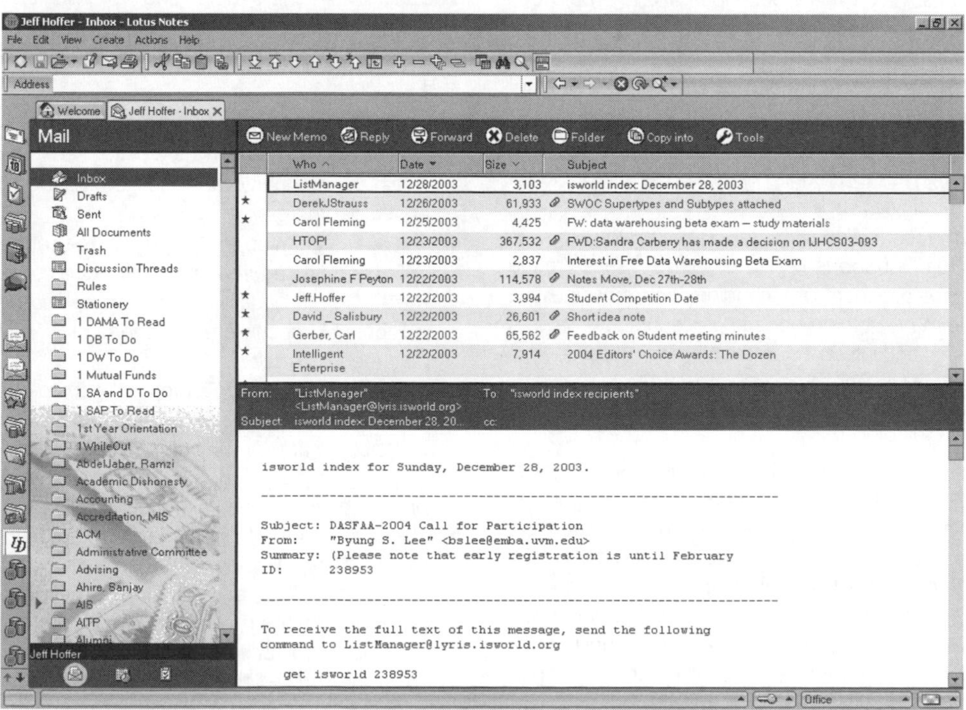

Figure 5.12 Lotus Notes® Inbox (Copyright © 2004 IBM Lotus Software. Lotus Notes is a registered trademark of IBM Lotus Software. Used with permission of IBM Lotus Software.).

groups, all participants are encouraged to enter into the discussion. We already said that to open a database from the workspace page, the user double-clicks on its icon. To open a database from any other page, first click on the database bookmark button on the left side of the page (this button appears to be a cylinder, or a hard drive, in front of a file folder). This opens the database bookmark page, showing all the databases that the user has bookmarked. (These bookmarked databases are likely to be the same as those represented by database icons on the workspace page.) The user opens a database by double-clicking on the relevant database listing. What if the user has not bookmarked the desired database? The database bookmark page also contains "Find a Database" and "Browse for a Database" selections. The opening screen of any database looks similar to Figure 5.12, with appropriate tool buttons, a navigation pane to the left, and a list of topics or documents in the view pane to the right. The user double-clicks on a document to display it.

How does all this work? Lotus Notes is a client/server system, with the large files (databases) stored on the server, which Lotus calls a "Domino server powered by Notes." The user can opt to store databases on the PC hard drive, but master copies of the large corporate or departmental databases of documents are stored on the server. Corporate files are replicated from one Notes server to another on a regular basis, so that everyone in the organization has access to the same version of a document. The Lotus Notes client, operating on a PC, is used to access the server with appropriate password protection. This access might either be directly across a LAN or via a dial-up modem. Any Web browser on the Internet can also access Notes. Of course, the Notes client is itself a Web browser. A major advantage of using Notes as the browser is that Notes gives you the ability to store copies of Web pages as documents in a Notes database.

Finally, another strength of Lotus Notes is its ability to serve as a development platform, allowing companies to create their own Notes applications customized for their needs. In fact, a growing number of these specialized applications are available commercially through third-party vendors, including project management, human resources, help desk, document management, health care, sales and marketing, and imaging applications.

AT HERTZ, LOTUS NOTES/DOMINO IS #1

Hertz rents cars from approximately 7,000 locations in more than 150 countries. Given this global span, Hertz employees must communicate and collaborate on an ongoing basis with people all over the world. Forms must be completed and routed to people in other offices or countries. Changes in policies and regulations must be quickly distributed to a widely dispersed workforce. To streamline these and other global tasks, Hertz depends increasingly on IBM Lotus Notes and Domino and on related Lotus technologies such as IBM Lotus Instant Messaging, Web Conferencing, Team Workplace, and Domino.Doc.

"For us, Lotus Domino is key to efficiency," says Claude Burgess, senior vice president of technology and e-business at Hertz. "It takes so many of the mundane procedures we have as a global organization and lets us automate them to cut costs, eliminate travel, speed processes, and add security. The processes won't go away, and so making them more efficient is extremely important."

One Domino application that touches the lives of most of Hertz's 15,000 Lotus Notes users is its home-grown eForms system. With eForms, Hertz employees can electronically complete and process any of about 500 types of forms that used to exist only on paper. "With eForms I can submit the forms in seconds," says Burgess. "Our Domino-based workflow application routes it to the appropriate people automatically, and any questions or annotations stay with the form, creating a history for the next person who gets it and eliminating questions that slow things down." Burgess indicates that eForms has reduced the amount of paper Hertz prints by 70 percent and has greatly speeded up forms processing. "Form contents are more secure, and we don't lose data. Everything is routed and processed correctly not just by luck, but because the software makes it happen."

Other Lotus communication and collaboration applications at Hertz include:

- The use of IBM Lotus Team Workplace to create Web-based workrooms where project teams formed to digitize processes within the company can manage the associated documents and track progress.
- The use of Domino.Doc to publish the company's employee policy and procedure manual, as well as other internal documents. Domino.Doc is a Domino-based solution that enables collaborative document management throughout the entire document life cycle.
- The use of Lotus Web Conferencing to hold regular meetings between multidisciplinary teams in dispersed locations. "For instance," Burgess indicates, "we can all be looking at a graphical display of information while making changes to it on the shared screen as the team interaction dictates."
- The use of Lotus Domino Everyplace to send critical information to profit center managers' phones, personal digital assistants (PDAs), or other mobile devices. "These people are always on the move, and aren't often in their office or at their desks to receive messages," says Burgess. "But the faster we can get them crucial information, such as a last-minute change in fleet availability, the better they're able to do their jobs."

[Adapted from IBM, 2003]

INTRANETS

The notion of an intranet was introduced in Chapter 4: An **intranet** is a network operating within an organization that employs the TCP/IP protocol, the same protocol used on the Internet. In most cases an intranet consists of a backbone network with a number of connected LANs. Because the protocol is the same, the organization may use the same Web browser, Web crawler, and Web server software that it would use on the Internet. The intranet, however, is not accessible from outside the organization. The organization decides whether or not people within the organization have access to the Internet.

An intranet presents some incredible advantages to the organization. If an organization already has an internal network of interconnected LANs plus an operating Web server and Web browsers on most workstations, as most organizations do, then implementing an intranet is a relatively easy task involving some programming on the Web server. With minimal effort the full functionality of a localized World Wide Web, including e-mail and document sharing, is available within the organization. The Web browser is a "universal client" that works with heterogeneous platforms. Furthermore, virtually no training is needed to implement an intranet because users already know how to use a browser. Deploying a new intranet application is simple—just send an e-mail message containing the URL (address) of the new application to users.

Even if the organization does not have a Web server and Web browsers, the costs are not overwhelming. Web browsers are inexpensive or free, and a minimal Web server complete with software can be obtained for well under $10,000. Intranets are easy enough to set up that in some organizations the first intranet was set up by end users (such as engineers), not by the IS organization, to enable sharing of particular documents.

Intranets serve a variety of important uses within organizations. None is more important than those of the CareWeb intranet at the Boston-based CareGroup HealthCare System. The CareGroup includes six hospitals, 2,500 health care professionals, and 800,000 patients in the northeastern United States. The CareWeb intranet, introduced in 1998, consolidates medical records from geographically dispersed patients, clinics, and laboratories into a single clinical database and makes these records accessible to health care professionals via a Web browser.

In April 2000 the Secure Patient/Physician Communication application, a clinical database, was implemented on the CareWeb intranet. "With our clinical systems on the Web, if I am an E. R. doctor and a 53-year-old patient rolls in with chest pain, I am able to compare that day's events with what happened [to him] a year ago," say Dr. John Halamka, chief information officer of CareGroup. Furthermore, CareGroup officials firmly believe that CareWeb has enabled them to increase the quality of patient care while reducing expenses by about $1 million per year.

With patients' medical histories available on the intranet, health care professionals can easily determine information such as past surgeries, medications used, and allergies. Patients can also access their own medical records over the intranet—as long as they have a browser and the requisite password—to check prescriptions and request referrals to specialists. Another intranet application gives insurance providers access to CareWeb so that insurance transactions can be conducted over the Web. Insurance providers can transmit information on benefits and eligibility of patients to CareGroup, and CareGroup has made referral and authorization applications available on the intranet. Soon it will be possible to submit claims over CareWeb. Nearly 300 applications are currently available on CareWeb. They run the gamut from those discussed above to a signature authorization program to financial analysis to medical analysis, such as an application used for calculating kidney functions (Henry, 2000).

At Seagate Technology, Inc., the world's largest manufacturer of disk drives, an intranet and an associated secure extranet permit Seagate's sales force, distributor representatives, and representatives of original equipment manufacturers (OEMs) that use Seagate components to access timely and accurate information on Seagate product availability and pricing. The notion of an **extranet** will be explored more fully in Chapter 7, but it refers to an Internet-based application that permits key trading partners (in this case distributors and OEMs) to access another organization's intranet. Seagate has implemented 15 client/server applications on its intranet to support its forecasting, quoting, and order management activities; there are up to 1,000 users of these critical applications.

The fact that the Seagate intranet is available to key trading partners has made development of applications more challenging. Seagate has chosen to use a Java-based approach to building applications and employs Marimba's Castanet software to deliver and manage the client/server applications. When a new or updated application is completed, an IS professional loads it on a centralized server that also hosts a Castanet Transmitter. When users log on, the Castanet Tuner on their desktop or laptop automatically downloads the latest version of the Java-based application. The use of Java and Castanet permits the client software to be kept up-to-date easily on the wide variety of PCs used by distributors, OEMs, and Seagate's sales force. With its intranet applications, Seagate has significantly improved its sales processes by providing current, easily accessible information on product availability, pricing, and sales volumes to its sales staff and its key trading partners (Earthweb.com, 2000).

When originally introduced, intranets were seen as competing with full-service groupware products such as Lotus Notes and Microsoft Exchange (Varney, 1996). Both fostered communication within the organization. Intranets did not provide the full range of groupware services, but they were much less expensive. Over time, intranets and groupware have grown closer together. Groupware has fully embraced the Internet, and groupware clients such as Lotus Notes are now Web browsers. Today many intranets employ the groupware client as the Web browser. At the same time, intranets became so complex and cumbersome to use that it was necessary to provide some structure, some organization so that users could find what they needed on the intranet. The answer was a **portal**—software that provided a structure and thus easier access to internal information via a Web browser. (If the organization desires, those external to the organization can also use portals, but that is a topic for Chapter 7.) This added software meant that intranets became more expensive. Portal software is available from a large variety of software firms, both large and small, including groupware vendors IBM, Microsoft, and Oracle. Among other portal vendors are BEA Systems, Corechange, Plumtree, Sun Microsystems, Sybase, and Vignette Corp.

IBM, for example, has built a gigantic intranet using its own groupware tools. According to IBM officials, the company's intranet is now a staple provider of information to employees. A recent internal survey found that 54 percent of IBM employees rank the intranet as among their three preferred sources of company information. Almost two-thirds of IBM employees rate the intranet as a tool that is critical to their performance, with the same proportion indicating that it is a time-saver.

IBM has been using the intranet for employee-to-employee collaboration, including a gigantic World Jam, when all employees worldwide were invited to log into a marathon chat session over a 72-hour period. More than 50,000 employees logged into World Jam to participate in 10 moderated discussion forums considering themes relevant to day-to-day life at the world's largest IT company. IBM also uses the intranet to provide information on all facets of work life, including health care benefits, unit performance updates, expense accounting, procurement, and stock purchasing. The intranet is working—more than 80 percent of IBM's U.S. employees who enrolled for health benefits last year did so via the intranet, and more than 140,000 received their health benefits information entirely online. The bottom line for IBM was about $1 million in savings (Mcdougall, 2001).

FACTORY AUTOMATION

The roots of **factory automation** lie in (1) numerically controlled machines, which use a computer program, or a tape with holes punched in it, to control the movement of tools on sophisticated machines, and in (2) **material requirements planning (MRP)** systems, which rely on extensive data input to produce a production schedule for the factory and a schedule of needed raw materials. The newer **computer-integrated manufacturing (CIM)** combines these basic ideas not only to let the computer set up the schedules (as with MRP) but also to carry them out through control of the various machines involved (as with numerically controlled machines).

POWERFUL PORTALS

The clunky intranet has given way to sophisticated corporate portals, and analysts predict these portals may soon become the new metaphor for desktop computing in business. Portals were once viewed merely as a way to provide easy access to internal information via a Web browser. But a new wave of software has helped the concept of in-house portals evolve into much more. This new generation of portals is so easy to use and effective in providing access to crucial data, reports, applications, and processes that many companies are using portals as their new desktop, replacing the Windows start button and a variety of commonly used applications.

A wide range of large companies and organizations are rolling out portals that are expected to cut costs, free up time for busy executives and managers, and add to the bottom line. That has prompted some to describe company portals as the next "killer application."

In simple terms, a company portal is an internal World Wide Web. The portal's home page, or start page, is displayed in a Web browser and generally includes search engines, as well as essential tools such as an appointment calendar and e-mail interface. Portal products are software suites that contain scores of applications that perform a variety of functions. Portal software vendors also offer special utilities—Plumtree Software calls them "gadgets"—that let users add other features such as stock tickers, clocks, and hotel, restaurant, and weather information. More sophisticated portals provide strategic, company-specific data.

Corporate information and technology managers say the portals they're rolling out this year are already contributing millions of dollars to the bottom line. Others say their return on investment will be measured in minutes and hours of employee time that is better and more profitably used.

[Konicki, 2000]

Computer-integrated manufacturing is one of the primary ways by which manufacturers are facing the challenges of global competition. Through the various components of CIM, manufacturers are increasing productivity and quality while simultaneously reducing the lead time from the idea stage to the marketplace for most products. A list of strong proponents of CIM reads like a who's who of manufacturing—General Motors, John Deere, Ford Motor Co., Weyerhaeuser, FMC, and Kodak, among others.

CIM systems fall into three major categories: engineering systems, manufacturing administration, and factory operations. Table 5.1 lists the acronyms used in this section on factory automation. The engineering systems are aimed at increasing the productivity of engineers and include such systems as computer-aided design and group technology. Manufacturing administration includes systems that develop production schedules and monitor production against these schedules; these systems are usually termed manufacturing resources planning systems. Factory operations include those systems that actually control the operation of machines on the factory floor. Computer-aided manufacturing and shop floor control are examples of such systems.

Engineering Systems

Computer-aided design (CAD) is perhaps the most familiar of the engineering systems. CAD involves the use of computer graphics—both two-dimensional and three-dimensional—to create and modify engineering designs. **Computer-aided engineering (CAE)** is a system designed to analyze the functional characteristics of a design and simulate the product performance under various conditions in order to reduce the need to build prototypes. CAD and CAE permit engineers to conduct a more thorough engineering analysis and to investigate a wider range of design alternatives. Advanced CAD/CAE systems store the information they generate in a database that is shared with the other components of CIM, such as CAM.

Group technology (GT) systems logically group parts according to physical characteristics, machine routings through the factory, and similar machine operations. On the basis of these logical groupings, GT is able to identify existing parts that engineers can use or modify rather than design new parts, simplifying the design and manufacturing processes. **Computer-aided process planning (CAPP)** systems plan the sequence of processes that produce or assemble a part. During the design process, the engineer retrieves the closest standard plan from a database (using the GT classification of the new part) and modifies that plan rather than starting from scratch. The resulting plans are more accurate and more consistent, thereby reducing process planning and manufacturing costs.

Table 5.1 Abbreviations Used in Factory Automation

Acronym	Full Name
CIM	computer-integrated manufacturing
CAD	computer-aided design
CAE	computer-aided engineering
GT	group technology
CAPP	computer-aided process planning
MRP	material requirements planning
MRP II	manufacturing resources planning
SCM	supply chain management
CAM	computer-aided manufacturing
AGV	automated guided vehicle
MAP	Manufacturing Automation Protocol
SFC	shop floor control

Manufacturing Administration

Manufacturing resources planning (MRP II) systems usually have three major components: the master production schedule, material requirements planning, and shop floor control. The master production schedule component sets the overall production goals based on forecasts of demand. The MRP component then develops a detailed production schedule to accomplish the master schedule, using parts explosion, production capacity, inventory, and lead-time data. The shop floor control component releases orders to the shop floor based on the detailed production schedule and the actual production accomplished thus far. To use a recent buzzword, MRP II systems attempt to implement just-in-time (JIT) production. Note that MRP II does not directly control machines on the shop floor; it is an information system that tries to minimize inventory and employ the machines effectively and efficiently.

In our discussion of ERP systems earlier in this chapter, we noted that MRP is often one of the key modules of an ERP system. Thus, such an ERP system ties together the manufacturing production schedule with the other important aspects of running an enterprise, including sales and distribution, human resources, and financial reporting. The latest type of manufacturing administration system, however, goes beyond ERP and outside the boundaries of the firm itself: **Supply chain management (SCM)** systems are designed to deal with distribution and transportation of raw materials and finished products throughout the supply chain and to incorporate constraints caused by the supply chain into the production scheduling process. These supply chain management systems are often interorganizational in nature (a customer and its suppliers) and are commonly implemented by an SCM module from an ERP vendor or an SCM package from a vendor such as i2 or Manugistics.

Factory Operations

Factory operations systems go a significant step further than MRP II—they control the machines. By definition, **computer-aided manufacturing (CAM)** is the use of computers to control manufacturing processes. CAM is built around a series of computer programs that control automated equipment on the shop floor. In addition to computer-controlled machines such as automated drill presses and milling machines, CAM systems employ automated guided vehicles (AGVs) to move raw materials, in-process materials, and finished products from one workstation to another. AGVs are loaded using robot-like arms and then follow a computer-generated electronic signal (often a track under the floor that has been activated) to their next destination. Workers are used only to maintain the equipment and handle problems. Because job setups (preparing a machine to work on a new part) are automated and accomplished in minimum time, CAM permits extremely high machine utilization. With the low setup time, very small batches (even as small as one) can be produced efficiently, shortening production lead times and reducing inventory levels.

SCM HELPS DELIVER THANKSGIVING TURKEYS

Perdue Farms produces more than 48 million pounds of chicken products and almost 4 million pounds of turkey products each week. For Thanksgiving, Perdue will ship roughly 1 million whole turkeys—and all these turkeys will arrive at the supermarkets within 24 hours of processing. This logistics task is much easier for Perdue because the company invested $20 million in Manugistics supply chain management software, including forecasting and supply chain planning tools. With the aid of the SCM system, Perdue has gotten much better at delivering the right number of turkeys to the right customers at the right time, according to Chief Information Officer Don Taylor. "As we get to November, we have live information at our fingertips," he says.

Perdue also uses technology to make sure its products arrive fresh. Each of its delivery trucks is equipped with a global positioning system, so dispatchers always know where the trucks are and can send out replacement trucks if necessary. Some supermarkets have vendor-management inventory control systems, which allow Perdue to track sales of its products in real time. "We're always looking at new technologies as they come along to see what makes sense for us," Taylor says. And SCM certainly makes sense for Thanksgiving turkeys.

[Adapted from Luttrell, 2003]

As this brief description has implied, a CAM system is very sophisticated and requires a great deal of input data from other systems. Product design data would come from CAD, process design data from CAPP, and the master production schedule and material requirements from MRP II. The CAM system must also be able to communicate electronically with the machines on the shop floor.

The manufacturing communications network is likely to employ the **Manufacturing Automation Protocol (MAP)**, pioneered by General Motors and now accepted by nearly all major manufacturers and vendors. MAP is a communications protocol (a set of rules) to ensure an open manufacturing system. With conformance to MAP by all vendors, seamless communication between all equipment on the factory floor—regardless of the vendor—is possible. MAP is a user-driven effort, and the details of the concept are evolving. Nevertheless, MAP is a reality in factory automation upon which future systems will be based.

Within factory operations applications, **shop floor control (SFC)** systems are less ambitious than CAM but are still important. These systems provide online, real-time control and monitoring of machines on the shop floor. For example, the SFC system might recognize that a tool on a particular milling machine is getting dull (by measuring the metal that the machine is cutting per second) and signal this fact to the human operator on duty. The operator can then take corrective measures, such as instructing the SFC to change the tool or changing it himself or herself, depending on the system.

Robotics

Outside the broad area of CIM, robotics is one other aspect of factory automation that deserves mention. Robotics is, in fact, one branch of the artificial intelligence tree. (Artificial intelligence is discussed in the next chapter.) With robotics, scientists and engineers are building machines to accomplish coordinated physical tasks in the manner of humans. For over two decades, robots have been important in manufacturing to accomplish simple but important tasks, such as painting and welding. Robots perform repetitive tasks tirelessly, produce more consistent high-quality output than humans, and are not subject to such dangers as paint inhalation or retinal damage. Newer robots incorporate a certain amount of visual perception and thus are able to perform assembly tasks of increasing complexity. Industrial robots are expensive, but they are becoming economically viable for a wider range of tasks as their capabilities are extended. Robots and CIM are producing a vastly different "factory of the future" based on IT.

System Integration

Integration is by far the biggest software problem CIOs face.That is why offerings that integrate systems generate so much interest. The increasing complexity of IT, with systems from various eras and technologies that must coexist and even work together, makes the integration challenge even more difficult to solve. That is why large integrated enterprise-wide systems have been adopted: to replace the myriad "silo" systems with one interconnected one.

CIOs have long strived to integrate the information systems in their organizations so that they work together. However, integration is complex and expensive, and it can cause systems to crash. But competitive pressures have raised the importance of integrating business processes and, thus, the underlying information systems. The trend away from in-house software development toward the use of off-the-shelf software has furthered the need for integration. Online business requires integrating systems across organizations.Technology vendors have responded with a number of products to facilitate the integration of systems.

Three main approaches to integration are:

- DBMSs
- ERP systems
- Middleware

The DBMS approach takes a data-oriented view to integration. DBMSs allow applications to share data stored in a single or distributed database.The applications can come from a number of sources, but they employ a common DBMS.

The ERP approach takes an application view of integration. All applications come from a single vendor and are specifically designed to communicate with each other.

The middleware approach takes a third-party approach; applications communicate with each other through third-party translation software.

Each of the three approaches has advantages and disadvantages, depending on the conditions in the enterprise. Typically, organizations use a combination of the three. Indeed, a quick look at vendor strategies reveals a mixture of the approaches. Oracle, firmly in the DBMS market, has moved toward offering enterprise applications. SAP, a major ERP vendor and long a competitor of Oracle, has modified its products to use standard DBMSs, including that of Oracle. The three approaches are not mutually exclusive.

ERP Systems

An ERP system aims to integrate corporate systems by providing a single set of applications from a single vendor operating with a single database.The goal is to provide the means to integrate business departments and functions across an organization. ERP vendors offer a complete set of business applications, including order processing, HR management, manufacturing, finance and accounting, and CRM. By automating many of the tasks involved in business processes and standardizing the processes themselves, the ERP system can provide substantial payback to a company if the system is installed properly.

The history of ERP contains both successes and failures, though the failures have been especially notable. Scott Buckhout and his colleagues reported on a study of ERP implementations in companies with more than $500 million in revenues. The average cost overrun was 179 percent, and the average schedule overrun was 230 percent. Despite these overruns, the desired functionally was 59 percent below expectations, on average. Only 10 percent of the implementation projects actually finished on time and within budget; another 35 percent of the projects were canceled. Even IT companies have had problems. Dell canceled its ERP project after 2 years and expenditures of more than $200 million.

Some of the failures can be attributed to factors common to other IS projects, such as the system's large size and complexity. However, ERP systems differ in a significant way from other systems, which is not always recognized. Because they are designed to integrate and streamline numerous business functions, they have significant implications for the way the firm is organized and operates. Many failures result from too much attention being given to the technical aspects of the system and too little attention being given to its organizational impacts.

An ERP system contains a model of the business that reflects assumptions about the way the business operates. The vendor makes these assumptions and designs the system to reflect the vendor's understanding of business processes in general. As a result, the business model embedded in the ERP system may be different from the way the business actually operates. Even though the ERP system can be customized to some degree, configuring the system entails compromises.The company must balance the way it wants to operate with the way the system wants the company to operate.

To realize the benefits of ERP–integrated systems and integrated business processes–a company must therefore change its organizational structure and culture. From his extensive studies of ERP, Thomas Davenport stresses that companies that have derived the greatest benefits have viewed ERP (he prefers the term *enterprise system, ES*) primarily in strategic and organizational terms, not in technical terms; they "stressed the enterprise not the system."The managers have asked: "How might an ES strengthen our competitive advantages? How might it erode them? What will be the system's effect on our organization and culture?

CASE EXAMPLE

COLGATE-PALMOLIVE

Colgate-Palmolive Company is a 190-year-old consumer products leader. In the mid-1990s, it faced a competitive crisis. Sales of personal care products dropped 12 percent and operating profits dropped 26 percent in North America. Colgate-Palmolive had a decentralized structure, with national or regional control in more than 200 countries. This structure produced independent operations that were expensive to coordinate, slow to respond to market changes, and constrained company growth. Management needed to develop new products, reduce product delivery cycles, and reduce the cost of operations.

Management's vision was to abandon the decentralized structure and become a truly global company with an integrated business environment and standardized business processes. Their first step toward this vision was to integrate their supply chain in 80 countries and distribution to 200 countries.The goal was to reduce the annual cost of the supply chain by $150 million and to standardize business processes. A key element to achieving this integration was a global ERP system.

After setting up a prototype environment in the United States, Colgate was convinced that the SAP R/3 modules for sales and distribution, materials management, finance, and HR would provide the functionality and flexibility it needed worldwide. Management also decided on Oracle's relational DBMS and a Sun hardware platform running the Solaris operating system. The current network has 270 servers, 11 terabits of data storage, and can support 3,000 concurrent users accessing the network from PCs around the world. The global ERP implementation took 5 years and cost $430 million.

The company quickly met its goals, realizing savings of $50 million the first year and $100 million the second. These savings were invested into creating and marketing new products, including the successful Target toothpaste, which allowed Colgate to regain the number one market position for toothpaste in the United States that they had lost 34 years earlier. The company also reduced the product delivery cycle by more than 60 percent. Integration allowed regional cooperation on purchasing, resulting in larger contracts with fewer suppliers, which saved $150 million the first 2 years.

Colgate also accrued substantial savings in IT operations. The old, highly complex, decentralized IT infrastructure, which had many data centers and local applications, was streamlined. Data centers around the world were consolidated from 75 to 2. The complexity of the global data networks was also simplified. SAP's R/3 provides a standard for applications, although the core support for the applications remains with each division.

The success of Colgate's ERP project stems from senior management convincing all employees that the company faced a crisis that only a dramatic change in strategy and organization could solve. The need for global restructuring of strategies and operations drove the need for a global, integrated IT infrastructure. The initial focus on the supply chain led to immediate positive results, validating management's strategy and providing support for the organizational changes. Colgate was also under pressure to integrate its operations from its larger customers, who had already begun to integrate their own operations. The ERP project was actually part of a larger project to rethink and realign Colgate's business strategies, structures, processes, and systems.

Do we need to extend the system across all our functions, or should we implement only certain modules? What other alternatives, if any, for information management might suit us better than an ES?"

As an example of a successful implementation of ERP, consider Colgate-Palmolive.

Middleware

Most organizations have a wide range of applications, new and old, from a variety of vendors, running on numerous platforms. Replacing or rewriting these applications is not feasible. One option is to employ a class of development products known as *middleware*. As its name implies, middleware is software that works between and connects applications, allowing them to share data.Without middleware, applications would have to be modified to communicate with each other, usually by adding code to each application, perhaps causing unintended negative effects. Middleware acts as a translator between the applications so that they do not need to be changed.

As Woolfe points out, middleware simplifies development by acting as the glue that binds the components, allowing them to work together. A plethora of middleware is avail-

INTERAPPLICATION COMMUNICATIONS FACILITIES:LINK COMPONENTS

- Application programming interfaces (APIs): provide a standard way of interfacing
- Remote procedure calls (RPCs): enable a dialogue between two geographically dispersed applications
- Object request brokers (ORBs): allow applications or utilities to inter-work in standard ways
- Message-oriented middleware (MOM): uses asynchronous message passing for inter-application communications

TRANSACTION MANAGERS: HANDLE TRANSACTIONS ACROSS MULTIPLE PLATFORMS

- Standard query languages (SQLs): standardize the way in which databases are accessed
- TP monitors (CICS,for example): monitor online transaction processing with a database
- Two-phase commit: a protective mechanism for transactions that fail to complete successfully

UTILITIES: PROVIDE GENERAL SERVICES

- Directory services: resource allocation
- Time services: timing
- Security services: encryption,and so on
- Software distribution:including configuration control

Figure 5.13 Types of Middleware Used in Client-Server Applications. *Source:* Roger Woolfe, "Managing the Move to Client-Server," Wentworth Research Program (now part of Gartner EXP, Stamford, CT), 1995.

able, as Figure 5.13 illustrates. Some are for communicating among applications, others are for managing transactions across platforms, and still others provide general services, such as security, synchronization, or software distribution.

One type of middleware that has gained popularity is Enterprise Application Integration (EAI) products. EAI tools typically use a message broker to transfer data between applications. They allow users to define business processes and make data integration subject to rules that govern those processes.As an example, a rule might state that data moves automatically from the purchasing application to the accounts receivable application only after the appropriate person has signed off on the purchase. Companies acquire a central module plus the interfaces needed to connect the applications.To handle unique integration needs, EAI vendors provide custom programming to modify the EAI modules to fit the company's requirements. Here is an example of a use of such middleware.

CASE EXAMPLE

A TELECOMMUNICATIONS FIRM

In the highly competitive telecommunications industry, a company must offer a wide range of products and services and be able to rapidly modify them to respond to market changes and new technologies.As a result, processing customer requests for new and updated services is a major source of company cost and customer dissatisfaction. It has been estimated that 65 percent of new and change orders in the telephone industry have errors that must be corrected after the fact. This situation leads to tens of millions of dollars in unnecessary direct costs and a 20 percent annual customer churn. The result: significantly reduced profits.

To improve the process and retain customers, one telecommunications company implemented a CRM system. However, processing requests for new phone lines still was tedious because each request required interacting with three back-office applications before the CRM system could respond to the customer. Most of the connectivity was manual, not automated, so response to customer requests was still unacceptable. To address the problem, the company looked to EAI so that no new ordering process would be needed; the existing process would simply be automated.

(Case continued)

(Case continued)

With the new EAI system, processing a customer request begins with the customer calling the call center, which creates a CRM-based order. The customer's name and address are passed to the ERP system, which retrieves the necessary information for the provisioning application to validate the request and ensure that the new service is compatible with the customer's existing services. The telephone service is specified and, if appropriate, a new phone number is allocated. Pricing is retrieved from the packaged accounting system before all the information is returned to the call center for presentation to the customer through the CRM system.

The process is now entirely automated. What used to take days or weeks is now handled in minutes while the customer is on the line, tremendously improving customer responsiveness. Processing costs have been reduced, errors eliminated, and customer churn lowered. No new applications were required and the existing applications remained untouched.

INTERNET-BASED SYSTEMS

HKEx's system is actually a good introduction to Internet-based systems. AMS/3 is not Internet based, but it allows Internet access for online trading as well as other actions. The Internet has opened up the options HKEx can offer. Internet users have become so sophisticated that Internet-based systems must now be scalable, reliable, and integrated both internally and externally with the systems of customers and business partners. In developing such systems, companies have learned they must negotiate programming language differences. For example, a system may have to port old COBOL applications to Java, reconcile interface discrepancies, and interface with back-end legacy applications, often without documentation or past experience with those systems.

Internet-based systems are where the system development action is occurring. This section discusses three aspects of Internet-based systems: a framework, a language, and an environment.We examine these aspects for the following reasons:

- *Application Servers* because they appear to provide the preferred framework for developing Internet-based systems
- *Java* because customers are demanding open systems; they do not want to be tied to a single vendor's proprietary technology. Java is a fairly open language that has evolved from client-side programming to being a server-side application development standard
- *Web Services* because they are touted as the development environment of the future

Application Servers

Originally conceived as a piece of middleware to link a Web server to applications on other company systems, the application server has grown into a framework for developing Internet-based applications. Figure 5.14 illustrates the basic application server architecture. A set of application servers is connected to create a single virtual application server. This virtual server takes requests from clients and Web servers (on the left), runs the necessary business logic, and provides connectivity to the entire range of back-end systems (on the right).

In addition to providing middleware and integration functions, application servers have become application development platforms, with a wide range of development and automatic code generation tools. They can provide common functions, such as security and database connectivity, notes Radding, they can store business logic components (forming the building blocks for applications), and they provide development capabilities inherited from CASE [now called integrated development environments (IDEs)]. In short, they aim to increase programmer productivity by automating and managing many of the technical tasks in developing and running Internet-based applications. They also provide scalability. As demands on applications grow, a company can increase the power of its virtual application server by either installing more servers or replacing smaller servers with larger ones. The application server also provides automatic load balancing among the multiple servers.

Java

If companies are to develop Internet-based systems quickly, as the e-business environment demands, they need component-based development tools. If, in addition, the

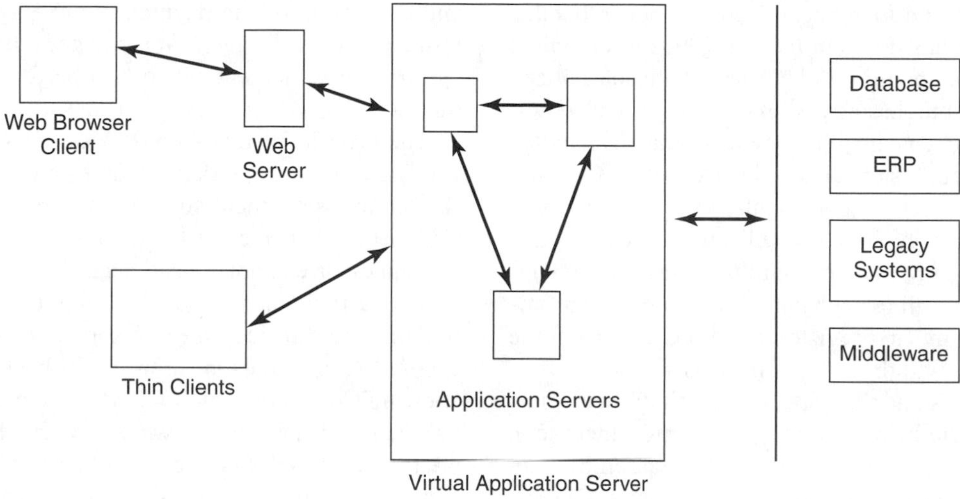

Figure 5.14 Application Server Architecture

systems being developed are to be portable and scalable, then the companies need to employ an open system architecture. For both component-based tools and open systems, industry standards are necessary. Currently, some of the most widely used standards for Internet-based systems development have evolved from Java.

Java was originally developed to provide applets that run on Web clients. However, it quickly evolved into a full programming language with the goal of providing platform independence; that is, Java applications could run on any system through a *Java virtual machine*. This promised application portability was dubbed "write-once, run-anywhere." That promise has not been met, though. Java performed poorly relative to other languages, such as C++.Therefore, companies have not converted their client applications to Java. However, Java has evolved into a standard platform for developing server-side applications.

The two major components in the Java server-side platform are Enterprise JavaBeans (EJBs) and the Java 2 Enterprise Edition (J2EE) software specification. EJBs emerged on the developer scene in 1998 when Sun Microsystems unveiled a specification for creating server-based applications using software components. EJBs are preconfigured pieces of code that IS staff no longer have to build from scratch. They can be as simple as an order entry form or as complicated as a virtual shopping cart that even protects shopper privacy. Use of EJBs can greatly enhance programmer productivity. Microsoft competes with its own version of components called COM (Component Object Model) components. (Note the term *object*. OO programming has become increasingly important in system development.)

J2EE defines a standard for developing Internet-based enterprise applications. It simplifies enterprise application development by basing it on a collection of standard server-side application programming interfaces (APIs), providing a set of services to modular components, and handling many of the core functions for the applications. Components include an API for database access, security modules that protect data in the Internet environment, and modules supporting interactions with existing enterprise applications. J2EE also supports XML.

Together, J2EE and EJBs provide an alternative to building online business systems from scratch or buying packaged online business systems because of their multi-vendor platform capability and pre-built, reusable components.

Web Services

The vision of Web Services is that modules of code can be assembled into services, which, in turn, can be linked to create a business process at the moment it is needed and run across enterprises, computing platforms, and data models. There are a couple of ways to build a Web Service. One is to wrap an XML wrapper around an existing piece of code that performs a specific function, thus exposing it. Then give that Web Service an Internet address and let others use it, for a fee.

John Hagel III and John Seely Brown point out that this is what Citibank has done. In the late 1990s when online exchanges were popping up like weeds, Citibank noticed that although the purchasing process was handled electronically, the actual exchange of money was generally handled manually or through special banking networks. Citibank had expertise in electronic payments, so it created a payment processing Web Service called CitiConnect.

When a company plans to purchase, say, office supplies through an online exchange, the company can utilize CitiConnect by first registering with CitiConnect the bank accounts to withdraw funds from as well as the purchasing employees and their spending limits. When a purchase is made, the buyer clicks on the CitiConnect icon on the screen. That click automatically assembles an XML-wrapped message that contains the buyer's ID, the amount of the purchase, the supplier's ID, the withdrawal bank account number, the deposit bank account number, and the timing of the payment, note Hagel and Brown. Using predefined rules, that message is then routed to the appropriate settlement network to perform that financial transaction.

The benefits of this Web Service are substantial, note Hagel and Brown. Settlement times are 20 to 40 percent shorter, and settlement costs are half or less. In addition, Citibank has extended its brand into a new market, and the exchanges have happier customers.

This arrangement also illustrates the second way to build a Web Service: use one someone else has already exposed. Commerce One drew on Citibank's Web Service, allowing Commerce One to focus on the other aspects of its business. Hagel and Brown believe companies will couple their own Web Services with those of others to create complex, yet flexible, best-in-class systems. To illustrate the basics of building a Web Service, consider the following simplified example.

CASE EXAMPLE

BUILDING A WEB SERVICE

A graphical example of building a Web Service from an existing in-house application is shown in Figure 5.15. Following is a much simplified description of that process.

Step 1: Expose the Code. A currency conversion Web Service is created by *exposing* the currency conversion code of a credit card processor by encapsulating it in an XML wrapper.

Step 2: Write a Service Description. A description of the currency conversion service is written using WSDL (Web Services Definition Language). Housed in an XML document, this description describes the service, how to make a request to it, the data it needs to perform its work, the results it will deliver, and perhaps the cost to use it.

Step 3: Publish the Service. The currency conversion service is then published by registering it in a UDDI (Universal Discovery, Description, and Integration) registry. Publishing means that its service description, along with its URL (its address), is housed in the registry for others to find. The registry is essentially a Web Services yellow pages.

Step 4: Find a Currency Conversion Web Service. The currency conversion service can now be found by, say, a pricing Web Service. The pricing Web Service sends a request in the form of an XML document in a SOAP (Simple Object Access Protocol) envelope to one or more registries. This special envelope is also based on XML. This particular request of the UDDI registry asks for a listing of currency conversion Web Services. The reply is sent in an XML document in a SOAP envelope back to the requestor.

Step 5: Invoke a Web Service. The pricing service can now bind to and invoke the selected currency conversion service by sending it an XML message in a SOAP envelope asking it to, say, convert US $1,250.25 into Australian dollars. The currency conversion service performs the task and returns the answer in an XML document in a SOAP envelope and quite likely invokes a payment Web Service to be paid for performing that conversion service.

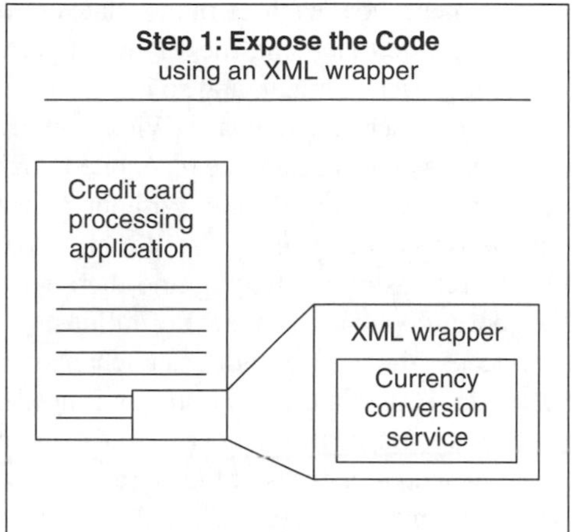

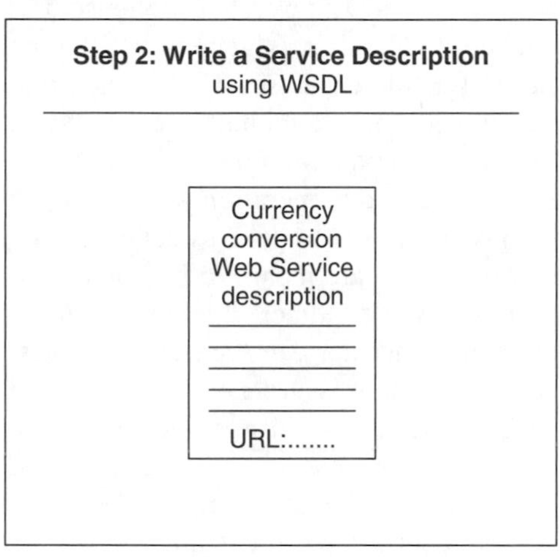

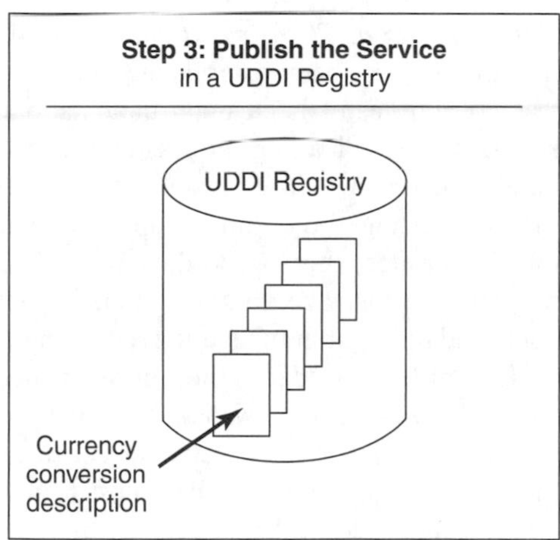

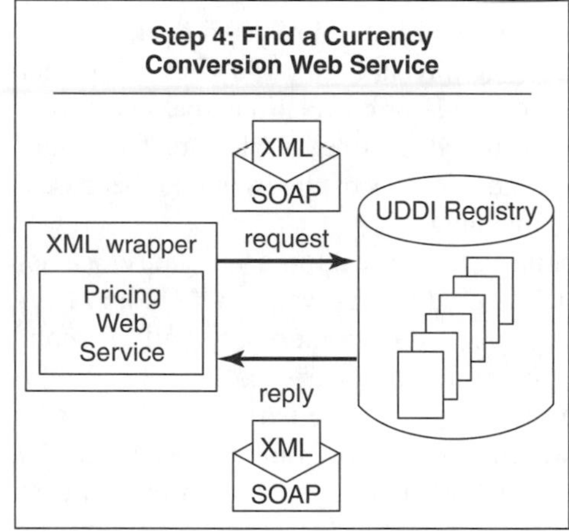

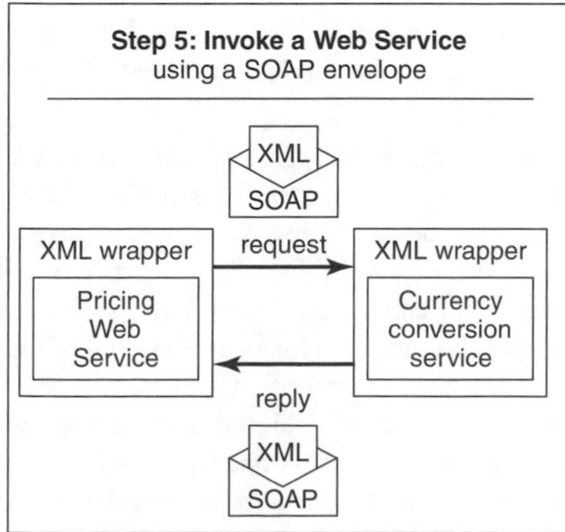

Figure 5.15 Building a Web Service

Data Warehouses

Data warehouses appeared in the early 1990s, a bit before ERP systems. Like ERP systems, they, too, spurred getting record-based data into shape. Data warehouses house data used to make decisions. The data is generally obtained periodically from transaction databases–five times a day, once a week, or maybe just once a month. The warehouse thus presents a snapshot at a point in time.

Data warehouses differ from operational databases in that they do not house data used to process daily transactions. Operational databases are meant to be updated to hold the latest data on, say, a customer's flight reservation, the amount of product in inventory, or the status of a customer's order. Data warehouses are not. They are not updated as events occur, only at specific points in time. In addition, unlike transaction databases, data warehouses are used with tools for exploring the data. The simplest tools generate preformatted reports or permit ad hoc queries. Yet warehouses are reaching beyond reporting on internal data. They are being combined with purchased data, such as demographic data, late-breaking news, and even weather reports, to uncover trends or correlations that can give a company a competitive edge. For example, a retailer might put the umbrellas and raincoats by the front door because a surprise storm is moving in.

The most common type of data in a warehouse is customer data, which is used to discover how to more effectively market to current customers as well as noncustomers with the same characteristics. As a result, the marketing department has, in large part, been the driving force behind warehouses. They want to use customer data–from billing and invoicing systems, for example–to identify customer clusters and see the effect different marketing programs have on these clusters.

Data warehouses are seen as strategic assets that can yield new insights into customer behavior, internal operations, product mixes, and the like. However, to gain the benefits, companies must take the often-delayed step of reconciling data from numerous legacy systems. When the perceived benefits appear to outweigh the costs, companies tackle the tremendous task.

Due to the strategic nature of such uses of data, warehousing projects need sponsorship from top management, not only to provide funding and guide the project in truly strategic uses, but also to ensure that departments cooperate and yield up their data for cross-correlations.

Key Concepts in Data Warehousing. As with all other areas of IT, data warehousing has its own set of terms and concepts. Here are a few of them.

Metadata: Defining the data. One of the most important elements in a data warehouse is its metadata; that is, the part of the warehouse that defines the data. Metadata means "data about data." Metadata explains the meaning of each data element, how each element relates to other elements, who owns each element, the source of each element, who can access each element, and so on.

Metadata sets the standard. Without it, data from different legacy systems cannot be reconciled, so the data will not be clean; that is, comparable. Without comparable data, the warehouse is not of much use. So an important aspect of data warehousing is creating and then enforcing common data definitions via metadata definitions.

Because the world continues to change, so, too, does the metadata. Thus, a metadata librarian is needed to keep it up-to-date, to enforce the standards, and even to educate users about metadata features of the warehouse. Metadata can be used not only to understand the data in the warehouse, but also to navigate through the warehouse.

Quality data: The biggest challenge. Once metadata definitions have been established, the largest job of data warehousing teams is cleaning the data to adhere to those standards. This cleaning process is onerous, lament warehousing teams, because legacy data often has definitions that have changed over time, gaps, missing fields, and so on. Sometimes, the source data was not even validated properly, for instance, to ensure that the postal code field contained the right number and type of characters.

The older the data, the more suspect its quality. However, because users want to track items over time, even with poor quality, data warehousing teams cannot discard the old, poor-quality data. They must find ways to align it with the more recent data, generally by estimating the data that should be in the missing fields, realigning figures based on the newer formulas, and so forth. This grueling manual task is one of the largest the warehousing team must perform.

Data marts: Subsets of data warehouses. When data warehousing was first espoused, the ideal was to build one huge, all-encompassing warehouse. However, that goal has not always proved feasible or practical. For one thing, search times can be excruciatingly long in huge warehouses. For another, the cost may be too high.

Thus, the concept of data marts became popular. A *data mart* is a subset of data pulled off the warehouse for a specific group of users. A data mart is less expensive to build and easier to search. For these reasons, some companies have started their data warehouse work by first building data marts. Then they populate the data warehouse by drawing from these marts. This approach is the reverse of what was espoused just a few years ago when purists believed that data should go from a data warehouse to data marts.

The main challenge in following this mart-to-warehouse approach is that the company must have unifying metadata, so that the data in all the marts uses the same definitions. Otherwise, the data cannot be meaningfully correlated in the warehouse.

Steps in a Data Warehousing Project. A typical data warehousing project has five main steps.

1. ***Define the business uses of the data.*** Warehousing projects that are run solely by IS departments without a sponsoring user department are generally unsuccessful. The data needs a business use to demonstrate payback.
2. ***Create the data model for the warehouse.*** This means defining the relationships among the data elements. This process can be quite a challenge, especially when commingling data from a number of systems.
3. ***Cleanse the data.*** This notorious step requires moving the data out of the operational systems and then transforming it into the desired standardized format. Specific tools can help cleanse standard kinds of data, such as names and addresses, but defining the transformations is often manual, as is filling in gaps.
4. ***Select the user tools.*** Consider the users' point of view and then select the tools they will use and train them to use them.
5. ***Monitor usage and system performance.*** Warehouse teams need to be particularly alert to changes in use. In many cases, usage begins slowly. But when it catches on, performance can degrade seriously as the system and the team are swamped with requests. If, however, the team monitors use and creates standard queries that serve groups of users rather than individuals, the team can reduce its workload and speed up system response time as well.

The following lengthy case example illustrates numerous ways one company is using its data for competitive advantage. The case illustrates use of ERP, data warehousing, and the Web, not only for internal use of data, but as the basis for new revenue-generating services to customers and suppliers. It shows how innovative companies can use advanced information management technologies. This case is based on a paper that won one of the awards in the Society for Information Management's annual paper competition. This competition attracts some of the best in-depth descriptions of IS management in practice. The company is Owens & Minor.

CASE EXAMPLE

OWENS & MINOR

Owens & Minor (OM), headquartered in Richmond, Virginia, distributes name-brand medical and surgical supplies from 14,000 suppliers to over 4,000 hospitals, integrated health-care systems, and group purchasing organizations throughout the United States. OM employs 2,700 people and had sales of $3.8 billion in 2001.

As Don Stoller, Director of Information Management, and his co-authors point out, OM is in the middle of its value chain. The supply side begins with raw material suppliers who sell to manufacturers (such as Johnson & Johnson), who sell to OM (the distributor), who then sells to health-care providers (such as hospitals), who sell to patients. In this field, distributors compete for contracts between manufacturers and health-care providers.

In the mid-1990s, OM bought a competitor, doubling OM's size to $3 billion. However, merging the two cultures proved so difficult that OM recorded its first loss. This loss spurred management to implement a new three-part strategy:

1. Achieve operational excellence
2. Follow and support patient care
3. Turn information into knowledge and then into profit

This strategy depended on building a leading-edge IT infrastructure and an IT R&D culture, which it did. In 1999, it won an award for its industry-leading ebusiness infrastructure. Here is what OM did.

(Case continued)

(Case continued)

Achieving Operational Excellence

OM augmented its ERP system to automate order forecasting, which improved inventory turns, reduced ordering rates from five times a week to once a week, and improved customer service. OM also installed an activity-based costing system to separate the cost of its products from the cost of delivery. Thus, customers, such as hospitals or purchasing groups, could pay just for the delivery service they wanted. Some wanted delivery to a loading dock; others wanted delivery to an emergency room. Some customers saved large amounts of money with this new option, and OM increased its sales. A new warehouse management system that uses handheld devices also increased OM's operational efficiency.

Following and Supporting Patient Care

OM implemented an Internet-based inventory management system, called OM-Direct, so that customers could order over the Internet, even using handheld devices. For example, when a hospital signs up for this service, it can ask OM to place bar codes on the products and establish replenishment levels. Then, when a hospital employee scans the bar code with, say, a Palm device, enters the on-hand inventory of that product, and uploads the data to OM's system, the system automatically reorders the product, if needed. Some 1,100 customers signed up for OM-Direct during its first 2 years.

To serve smaller customers and suppliers, such as physicians' offices, small hospitals, and small specialist suppliers, OM teamed up with trading exchanges to provide online marketplaces for these members to buy and sell products and even use OM-Direct. The exchanges have encouraged these customers to start using the Internet for ordering, even though they only offer 1,700 of OM's 150,000 products.

Turning Information into Knowledge and Profit

Most interestingly, OM initiated a data warehousing and decision-support initiative, building one subject area at a time (sales, inventory, accounts receivable, and so on), and permitting queries across the subject areas. During the first year, much of the work was handled by a system integrator familiar with building data warehouses. After that, it became the responsibility of a 12-person OM team that included a director, a manager, three developers who add new subject areas and load data, one data administrator, and six business analysts, who work with the users.

Initially, the warehouse was for internal use only. Within the first 30 months, some 500 OM employees in sales, marketing, supply chain management, finance, and other departments had learned to use the BusinessObjects tool to make queries or create reports from the warehouse, report Stoller et al.

For several reasons, the warehouse team then investigated offering decision support over the Web. Customers were asking sales reps for more information; some requesting up to 30 reports a month. Why not let the customers serve themselves? Also, the Web would allow casual users, such as customers or executives who do not want to learn Business-Objects, to access the data in the data warehouse. Furthermore, OM realized that customers and suppliers were asking for information to run their own businesses because they did not have the systems or technology in-house. Delivering this information over the Web could give OM a competitive advantage by strengthening its relationships with trading partners, giving it a market-leading feature to entice new customers, and even turning the data warehouse into a new service; in fact, a new source of revenue.

To assist its trading partners, OM created an extranet and asked a pilot set of customers and suppliers to list the kinds of information they needed to, say, reduce their costs or better manage their inventories. From these lists, the OM warehousing team created queries and let these partners pilot test the system for 4 months. During that time, OM debated whether to offer this service for free or for a fee. It decided to charge money, reasoning that the information would appear more valuable if it had a price. Furthermore, the fees would be reasonable, especially compared with the up-front data warehousing costs partners would be able to avoid.

When the service, called Wisdom, was rolled out, it became the first "e-business intelligence application" in the medical and surgical supply distribution industry, state Stoller et al.

All users have a profile of the information they can access. Every access is checked by the security system. Every query contains the user's account number so that the system knows which information can be used to answer the query. The browser interface is easy to use; people point and click on over 50 predefined queries, or, more recently, make ad hoc queries.

OM has continued to improve the service. Suppliers and customers can now add external data, such as data from other manufacturers, into OM's data warehouse so they can study more relationships and perform more "what if" investigations.

For example, a typical-size hospital spends $30 million a year buying all its medical and surgical supplies. Hospital groups can have a difficult time analyzing purchases across all their hospitals, because each has a disparate system. Rather than invest in consolidating the systems themselves, hospital groups would rather purchase data about their own transactions from, say, a distributor who is well placed in the value chain to have that information.

OM has thus become an important "infomediary," note Stoller et al., because hospital purchasing staffs may have a much easier time getting the purchasing information they need from OM than from their own hospital. They can then discover, for instance, which purchases were "on contract" with OM, and thus had the lower contract price, and which were not. Oftentimes, up to 40 percent of hospital purchases are off-contract, which costs these hospitals money they need not spend. Furthermore, purchasing managers can see how many suppliers they use for the same product and negotiate higher-volume discounts from just one or two. They can also see ordering frequency and optimize it by increasing order volumes, perhaps. In addition, they can more easily spot delivery problems.

OM's Wisdom service turns out to be equally valuable to suppliers, such as Johnson & Johnson. Wisdom has over 30 queries and 100 reports for suppliers to watch their products move out to consumers. They can analyze their marketshare in specific regions, analyze product shelf life, coordinate shipping from several locations, see on-contract purchasing (and help customers increase the levels), analyze drop shipments (which are more expensive than OM distribution), and so forth.

Wisdom has become a valuable service to both OM suppliers and customers, and it becomes more valuable the more sales or purchases go through OM rather than through other distributors. In fact, Wisdom led to over $60 million in new business in 1 year because it is providing visibility throughout OM's value chain. Because partners pay for its use, there is constant pressure to keep it market leading, note Stoller et al.

The next step is to turn the data warehouse into an industry-wide warehouse by asking suppliers and customers to place all their data there. If this occurs, conceivably, other distributors might become paying customers of Wisdom as well. Or, as OM and three competitors have agreed, they will establish an independent, neutral health care information exchange.

Document Management

Now we turn to managing document-based information. Management of *internal* document-based information has traditionally rested with the vice president of administration, who has traditionally overseen records management (document records, not data records). Technologies used to manage documents have included micrographics (microfilm and fiche) and computer output microfilm (COM), generally in stand-alone systems. That is, until the Internet arrived. Now corporate intranets house many former paper-based internal documents.

External document-based information, on the other hand, has generally been the responsibility of corporate librarians. Yet, as the amount of such external information grows and as more of it has become computerized, it is increasingly being included in IS executives' jurisdiction. Again, it has been the Web that has brought these external documents to the attention of CIOs, yet many of them consider documents to be the least manageable form of information.

Even in today's Internet-rich world, paper still plays a major role in most enterprises. And while paper is around, there is a need to move seamlessly between digital and printed versions of documents. Hence, the importance of document management. The field of electronic document management (EDM) uses new technologies to manage information resources that do not fit easily into traditional databases. EDM addresses organizing and managing conceptual, descriptive, and ambiguous multimedia content.

Using IT to manage documents is a challenge for enterprises because most of their valuable information is in documents, such as business forms, reports, letters, memos, policy statements, contracts, agreements, and so on. Moreover, most of their important business processes are based on or driven by document flows. While computer systems have mostly handled facts organized into data records, far more valuable and important are the concepts and ideas contained in documents. Reports drawn from computerized databases fill important roles in status assessment and control. Oftentimes they must be accompanied by a memo or textual report that explains and interprets the report. Meetings, phone conversations, news items, written memos, and non-computerized reports are usually rated more important by managers. Technology applied to handling documents promises to improve these forms of communication.

A document can be described as a unit of "recorded information structured for human consumption." It is recorded and stored; therefore, a speech or conversation for which no transcript is prepared is not a document. This definition accommodates "documents" dating back to cuneiform inscriptions on clay tablets. What has changed are the ways information is represented and the ways documents are processed. Information previously represented

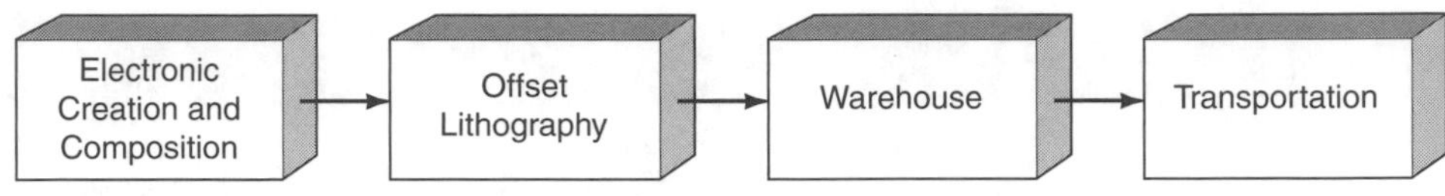

Figure 5.16 Traditional Publishing Process

primarily by text is now also represented by graphical symbols, images, photographs, audio, video, and animation. Documents previously created and stored on paper are now digitally created, stored, transported, and displayed.

Applying technology to process traditional documents changes what documents can accomplish in organizations. A definition more oriented to technology comes from *Byte* magazine.

> *A document is a snapshot of some set of information that can*
>
> - *incorporate many complex information types;*
> - *exist in multiple places across a network;*
> - *depend on other documents for information;*
> - *change on the fly (as subordinate documents are updated);*
> - *have an intricate structure or complex data types such as full-motion video and voice annotations; and*
> - *be accessed and modified by many people simultaneously (if they have permission to do so).*

It is hard to think of anything more pervasive and fundamental to an organization than documents. The impact of applying emerging technologies to document management is potentially significant. EDM promises to advance the management of conceptual information, thereby improving the levels of support and productivity for manager and professional. With documents as the primary vehicle for business processes, EDM contributes to business process redesign and quality improvement. Numerous EDM applications generate value. In this section, we will examine three:

1. To improve the publishing process
2. To support organizational processes
3. To support communications among people and groups

The concept of just-in-time (printing, publishing, and forms processing) pervades the design philosophy in all three areas.

Improving the Publishing Process. Technology enables a major restructuring of the process of publishing and distributing paper documents. For those organizations that produce documents as a product or as support for a product, this change is reengineering their document production processes. The stages of the traditional process, designed primarily for high-volume and high-quality documents, is shown in Figure 5.16. The document is created, generally with the use of electronic tools, and a photographic plate is made for an offset printing press. The offset press requires long print runs to amortize the extensive setup costs. Thus, a large quantity of documents is produced and stored in a warehouse and then documents are shipped to their destination when they are required. R. R. Donnelley & Sons Company, the country's largest publisher, estimates that 60 percent of the total cost of delivering these documents is in storage and transportation.

Figure 5.17 shows the steps in the revised publishing/distribution process using newer technologies. Documents are stored electronically, shipped over a network, and printed when and where they are needed. The major benefits result from reducing obsolescence (revisions are made frequently to the electronically stored version), eliminating warehouse costs, and reducing or eliminating delivery time.

Here is an example of how a traditional printing process has been changed by emerging technologies.

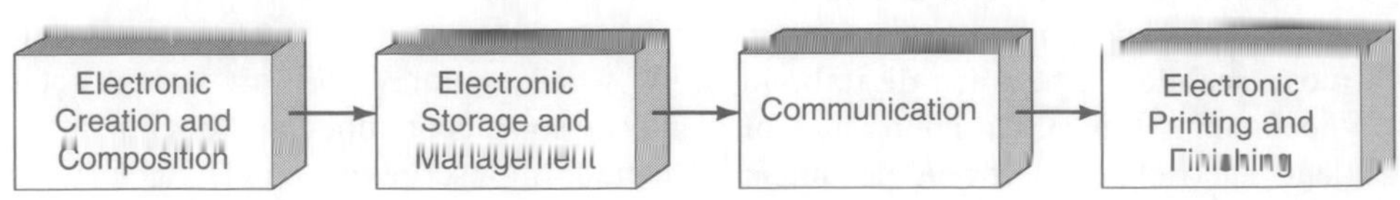

Figure 5.17 Reengineered Publishing Process

CASE EXAMPLE

HICSS PERSONAL PROCEEDINGS

The Hawaii International Conference on System Sciences has been held each January since 1967. It brings together academics and professionals to discuss research papers from a wide variety of computer-related subjects.

The conference proceedings have made an important contribution to the literature for many years. But with more than 450 papers averaging 10 pages each in length, the proceedings have grown to 4,500 pages in 9 volumes weighing 25 pounds. As a result, conference management decided to produce a paper book of abstracts with a CD-ROM of the full papers tucked in a sleeve inside the back cover. This publishing approach reduced the paper problem, but many participants wanted to see the full papers during the presentations and discussions. They had been using the paper versions to take notes and to understand additional details of the presentation.

Conference management then introduced personal proceedings. A month before the conference, participants can use a Web site to choose 20 papers they would like to have in their personal paper proceedings. The papers they choose are printed on a Xerox Docutech machine with their name on the cover and delivered to them at the conference. Additional papers can be printed individually at the conference using the conference print-on-demand service for a nominal fee. This new use of print-ondemand technology has helped the conference meet the participants' needs while cutting costs and reducing paper.

Supporting Communications among People and Groups. The value of documents is that they transfer information across time and space. Of course, the Internet can handle such communication, but when all members of a group do not have Internet access, or do not use it frequently, companies may need to continue to rely on paper documents. EDM can be used to facilitate such communications among people and groups. In the broadest sense, all EDM applications support this function. The following case illustrates using various technologies to communicate with customers via paper and ensure that each customer gets the right pieces of paper.

CASE EXAMPLE

TAPIOLA INSURANCE GROUP

Tapiola is a group of three insurance companies with headquarters in Espoo, Finland, a suburb of Helsinki. By Finnish law, an insurance company can sell only one type of insurance; therefore, each of Tapiola's three companies sells either life, non-life, or pension insurance. Tapiola calls itself "an insurance department store."

Some 90 percent of insurance in Finland is sold by five insurance groups; Tapiola is the fourth-largest group. It has 14 percent of the market with 1.5 million customers and 3 million policies. Each year its mailroom sends out 4 million letters, so printing is an important and expensive part of its operation.

Formerly, the Tapiola group offered 150 kinds of insurance policies and had 300 different insurance policy forms. Half of the forms were in Swedish and half were in Finnish because both are official languages in Finland. The policy forms were preprinted by an outside print shop, generally on sprocket-fed

(Case continued)

(Case continued)

computer paper. Then the forms were filled in by printers connected to their IBM mainframes.

This mode of operation presented several problems. If a change was made to a form, the inventory of old forms had to be discarded. Reprinting new forms often took weeks. That time represented possible lost revenue. Also, the computer printers could print on only one side of each sheet of paper. Finally, for more complex policies, Tapiola had to use large-size computer paper that was often unwieldy to handle and mail.

Document-Processing Goals

The production manager and the insurance applications development manager looked around for an alternate way to print policies and statements. They had several goals. One was, of course, to reduce costs. A second goal was to stop using preprinted forms. Their third goal was to give Tapiola marketing people new ways to advertise insurance products by making computer-generated letters to customers more flexible. The fourth and most important goal was to make Tapiola "the most personal insurance company in Finland." These two systems managers wanted their computer-generated correspondence to prospective and current policyholders to appear more "human," as if a Tapiola employee had used a typewriter to write a personal reply to an inquiry or request for information.

Centralized Solution

To overcome the computer-generated appearance of their output, they switched to plain paper printers from Rank Xerox, the European subsidiary of Xerox Corporation. Xerox is best known for its photocopiers, but it is increasingly creating products for electronic document processing where a document can include text, data, images, and graphics. Conversion of the output equipment at Tapiola took 15 months, during which time it reduced its 300 preprinted forms to 4.

Four New Forms

The four new forms are actually four types of standard European A4-cut paper. (In the United States, the equivalent would be the 8 1/2 x 11 sheet of paper.) The first form is a plain white A4 sheet of paper. It is used for internal communications within Tapiola.

The second form is the same blank white paper with four holes punched along the left-hand side to fit in the standard European four-ring binder. (In the United States, the standard is a three-ring binder.) This form is also mainly for internal use.

The third form has the Tapiola logo preprinted in green in the upper left-hand corner, and both sides of the paper have the word "Tapiola" printed in tiny, faint green letters over most of the page. This form is the standard company stationery, and it has become one of Tapiola's standard computer printout forms for communicating with the outside world.

The fourth form is the same as the third except that it has a 4 x 6-inch (10 x 15cm) perforated area in the lower right-hand corner. This form is used for all their insurance policy bills. The tear-off portion can be paid at any bank; the money and information about the payment go directly from the bank to Tapiola.

Programming and Conversion

Reprogramming the IBM applications was extremely easy, because only the output routines needed to be changed. That programming took 2 work years of application programmer time. In addition, one systems programmer spent 6 months working with Xerox on the IBM-to-Xerox system software interfaces. One forms designer spent 15 months redesigning all 300 preprinted forms into 240 printing formats for the application programmers. About 60 forms disappeared altogether because they were found to be unnecessary; the remaining 240 forms are not all different because one-half of them are in Swedish and the other half are in Finnish.

The conversion was done in two stages. First, customer policy statements were printed in a form-like manner on two sides of the new-size paper. These looked somewhat like the old forms so that policyholders could understand the changeover. Then, the terse, table-like data was replaced with text to make the statements look more like personal letters.

Envelope Stuffing

Interestingly, these redesigns of customer documents were the easy part of the conversion. The more difficult and sensitive part was making sure that each envelope contained the correct pieces of paper. Because Tapiola was now using smaller sheets of paper, each envelope often needed to include several sheets, and, of course, Tapiola did not want to put a cover letter for one policyholder into the same envelope as a statement for another policyholder.

To solve this problem, the company found an envelope insertion machine made by PMB Vector in Stockholm, Sweden. This machine contains a microprocessor that can read an eight-dot code printed at the top of each sheet of paper. Thus, the Xerox printer not only prints the correspondence but, at the same time, it prints a code at the top of each sheet of paper–one code for all pages to go in one envelope. The Vector insertion machine makes sure that each envelope only contains pages with the same code.

Decentralized Expansion

This document-processing conversion was just one part of the effort to improve and humanize customer correspondence. In the midst of the document redesign, Tapiola also decided to move some printing of customer correspondence to its 62 branch offices.

To illustrate how a remote printer is used, consider the case of a female policyholder who has received medical care. She can mail the medical bills to Tapiola or visit her local office in person. If she visits them and presents her bills to a Tapiola employee, that employee uses a desktop machine to access the policyholder's data from the central database. If she has brought all the proper documents needed for reimbursement, the employee can initiate a direct electronic payment from a Tapiola bank account to her personal bank account, no matter which bank they both use.

Once a day, Tapiola transmits all such electronic transactions to its bank, and those transactions are cleared that same day. (The five major Finnish banks have collaborated and created a sophisticated and fast banking system.) The employee then gives the policyholder a letter verifying the transaction. That letter is generated by the central IBM computer but is printed on the local Xerox printer. If the policyholder is missing some information, the employee can create a personalized letter explaining what is missing by assembling phrases stored in the central database and then printing the letter on-site.

The people at Tapiola Data recommend that other IS organizations become involved in electronic document management by first looking at the output their computers are generating. It was not difficult to mix traditional host computing with document processing technology.

A poll of Finnish citizens showed that Tapiola is seen as a dynamic company, and it has the best reputation among young people of all the insurance groups. The people at Tapiola Data believe their use of document-processing technology is helping to build and reinforce this image.

Supporting Organizational Processes. Documents are still the vehicle for accomplishing many processes in organizations. Typical examples include processing a claim in an insurance company, hiring a new employee, or making a large expenditure. The documents are primarily forms that flow through the organization carrying information, accumulating input and approval from a sequence of people. Many such workflow systems still rely heavily on the physical circulation of paper forms.

Using IT to support these processes generates significant value in reducing physical space for handling forms, faster routing of forms (especially over geographical distances), and managing and tracking forms flow and workload. Two trends in organizations have increased the importance of workflow systems: total quality management and business process reengineering.

In addition to improving transaction-oriented business processes with EDM, many organizations are improving the management processes of reporting, control, decision making, and problem solving as well. Several EISs now supply documents to supplement the more traditional data-based reports. Organizations with a custom-developed EIS also add so-called soft information in the form of documents.

To give an example of how one organization improved a work process via a new document management system, consider the Tennessee Valley Authority.

CASE EXAMPLE

TENNESSEE VALLEY AUTHORITY

The Tennessee Valley Authority (TVA) is the largest supplier of power in the United States, serving some 8 million customers in the eastern United States by generating energy using fossil, hydroelectric, and nuclear fuels. Not long ago, the nuclear division, which has three facilities, revamped its maintenance management system—a system that relies on documents, such as manuals from vendors, drawings, and work instructions, that are regulated by government.

(Case continued)

(Case continued)

TVA spends more than $48 million a year creating maintenance work orders and then planning and performing the work. One plant alone processes 14,000 work orders a year. Government regulations that oversee the documentation of this work contribute significantly to TVA's high maintenance costs.

The improvement project was handled by a team from various parts of the nuclear operation. They analyzed and charted the existing work processes, determined which improvements were most needed, and investigated how those improvements could be achieved. They spent 350 hours interviewing people and looked at 15 other utilities.

One thing they discovered was that the work orders were inextricably linked to document workflow and the ways procedures were managed. Previously, the three areas–work order management, document workflow, and procedure management–had been viewed as separate, and thus managed separately. Upon investigation, the team realized that every work order included accompanying diagrams, documentation, and procedure instructions. However, the three were not always in sync. For example, a work order might be planned several months in advance, but in the meantime, procedures might be changed, yet those changes were not noted when the work order was about to be performed.

The new process designed by TVA electronically combines maintenance orders in one system with procedural document management in another system and eliminates a number of existing systems that did not talk to one another. Maintenance workers can now access documentation on equipment, parts, and records as well as work instructions from desktop machines. Work orders are generated electronically and then routed for approval with the most current drawings and procedures electronically attached. In addition, the documents are indexed by, say, piece of equipment, and the three plants now use the same systems. Thus, maintenance people can review past activity and better plan for the future.

The system has been successful, but the team underestimated the change management effort needed. They did not realize they had to bring many employees up-to-speed on using computers; some had not used keyboards. In addition, the team realized they should have set expectations differently. Rather than emphasize the benefits of the new systems to each employee (because sometimes the new systems required more work of some employees), the team should have emphasized the benefits of the system to TVA, which were significant.

The average amount of human time spent processing a work order has decreased by almost half, from 39 hours to 23 hours; labor savings are large. More importantly, maintenance workers now have captured data for improving processes.

Content Management

We now turn to the other form of document-based information: Web content. Many corporate intranets now house documents that used to be paper based. In some cases, these documents appear in PDF form on the intranet, which is like taking a photograph of the pages so that the pages cannot be changed.

The question for CIOs has become: How should we manage all the internal and external content on our Web sites? The field that addresses this question is called *content management.* It deals with managing Web-based content of all types, writes Chuck Tucker in the Gartner EXP report entitled *Dealing in Web Currency.* A major reason content has become important to CIOs, he notes, is because it is a core management discipline underlying online business. Without production-level Web content management processes and technologies, large-scale online-business is not possible. The content on Web sites attracts customers, answers questions, and handles transactions. If the content is not refreshed frequently, perhaps as news occurs, or if it is full of errors, or if it cannot handle transaction volumes, a company's Web channel will stave off rather than attract customers.

Content is no longer static; it is active. It can cause actions to happen. An underlying reason is the adoption of XML. XML is used to put tags on data that give that data meaning. Computers use the meanings to manipulate the data and perform work. In essence, use of XML moves Web content from being in a human-only readable format to being in a computer-readable format. Thus, the content can be passed to back-end transaction processing systems and cause an action to take place, such as ordering a book or configuring a recently ordered computer. XML is an intrinsic part of managing Web content because it is the language for manipulating the content to work with transaction applications, which is the basis for e-commerce.

In the beginning, when Web sites were new, Web content was managed as follows: Someone in a department, usually HR or marketing, decided to use this new communication channel. They designed a format, decided on the sections on the site, and wrote the content or gathered it from written documents. The department then gave all this content to the Webmaster to publish. When new material needed to be added, they gave it to the Webmaster, who turned it into HTML and published it to the Web site. Before long, the Webmaster became the publishing bottleneck; time to publish got longer and longer. This homegrown method was not only inefficient, but it also did not present a good image to Web site visitors.

To create a content management strategy, states Tucker, companies need to understand the three phases of the content management life cycle and the goals for each one. As shown in Figure 5.18, the three phases, which can be viewed as input—process—output, are:

1. Content creation and acquisition
2. Content administration and safeguarding
3. Content deployment and presentation

Managing Content Creation and Acquisition. Each phase needs a different emphasis to be effective, notes Tucker. Content creation and acquisition, for instance, needs to focus on *creating content quality*. That is why it might be wise to buy some content from specialists, which is called syndicated content, rather than create it in-house. For example, why create a stock ticker or a weather report or a news feed? Draw on the ones that already exist.

High-quality in-house content comes from subject matter experts and local employees. Thus, the best organizational structure is to distribute content creation and maintenance to employees in HR, marketing, sales, and field offices. They should be responsible not only for creating their content, but also for keeping it updated and fresh.

To avoid anarchy, though, these dispersed experts should be directed centrally and use centrally created formats and an automated workflow system that moves their work along. The system might even send them reminder e-mails of publishing deadlines. Finally, to improve content quality, it is wise to create a feedback loop so that comments from Web site visitors reach these content creators. Then these creators know what types of content attract visitors and customers.

Content Administration and Safeguarding. The emphasis in this phase, like any operational phase, is *efficiency*, states Tucker. The goal is to achieve the most with the least effort. Content management software tools can help. These tools are used to identify types of content and the business rules that apply to each type. For example, publication of press releases on a Web site should follow business rules that state that each release will first be approved by the manager of corporate communications, each press release will use the standard press release format, and each release will move to the archive file 1 month after being published. Business rules form the heart of content administration. They present the parameters for the automated workflow for each type of content, thus relieving the Webmaster bottleneck.

So, whereas content creation should be distributed, content administration should be centralized. This structure permits overall central guidance of distributed creative efforts. However, it does present some vexing challenges. One involves the approval process of foreign-language content. Companies that create an approval process believing that all content will be in, say, English, create translation bottlenecks for themselves if they expect all drafts to be translated into English for approval and then translated back into the original language once the document is approved. Companies need to consider multilanguage issues when creating their workflows, selecting their content management software, and designing their Web sites.

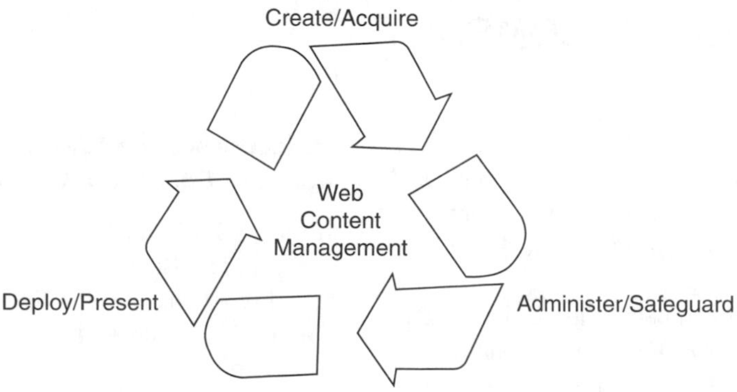

Figure 5.18 The Web Content Management Life Cycle. *Source:* Tueber, Chuck, *Dealing in Web Currency,* Gartner EXP, 56 Top Gallant, Stamford, Ct, June 2001.

Content Deployment and Presentation. The third phase of the content management life cycle is the output phase, distributing content to Web site visitors. The emphasis in this phase should be on *effectiveness*, that is, presenting the content so that it attracts visitors, allows them to navigate the site easily, and leads them to the desired actions, notes Tucker.

Because this phase can determine the success of a firm's e-commerce efforts, it is best to design a Web site beginning with this phase, then move on to ensuring content quality and processing efficiency. The Eastman Chemical Company example that follows illustrates this outside-in viewpoint; most companies take an inside-out view. Eastman redesigned its site to take its customers' point of view rather than its internal organizational point of view. The change had a major positive impact.

Today, most Web sites need certain features to attract and keep visitors. Two such features are personalization and localization. Personalization means allowing Web site visitors to customize how they view the page. For instance, some visitors to consumer sites may want lots of sports news but little international news. On the other hand, business visitors to corporate sites might want the site to open to the products they buy or recent news pertinent to their industry. Web content software gives site builders the ability to offer site visitors viewing options. Once selected, the choices are stored in the users' profile and referenced every time they visit the site. Companies can also use personalization to offer complementary products, such as corkscrews to wine buyers, notes Tucker, or take into account a customer's past buying record.

Localization, on the other hand, means tailoring a site to a culture, market, or locale. For instance, a site may be designed to present its content in the language of the country or region of the visitor. Likewise, localization may mean making appropriate currency conversions automatically. Localization is crucial for companies involved in global e-commerce.

Finally, a growing issue in deployment is multichannel distribution; that is, being able to display the site in the manner appropriate to each type of device, from PC to cell phone. Ideally, the information comes from a common repository, rather than existing in several places, and is put in the appropriate form when requested, notes Tucker. Otherwise, if the same content is stored in several places, it can get out of sync. Central storage is important to maintain content quality.

In summary, the way to manage content is to understand the goal of each phase of the content life cycle–quality, efficiency, or effectiveness–and design the phase with that goal in mind. In addition, there should be a feedback loop, so that Web site visitors can tell Web site content creators which content is most useful to them. Such a loop can then drive continual improvement in the Web site.

To illustrate how one company is managing its Web content, consider Eastman Chemical, whose story appeared in Tucker's report entitled *Dealing in Web Currency*.

CASE EXAMPLE

EASTMAN CHEMICAL COMPANY

Eastman Chemical Company, which is located in Kingsport, Tennessee, is a global manufacturer of chemicals, fibers, and plastics. Founded in 1920 to make chemicals for Eastman Kodak, it was spun off in 1994. Annual sales were $5.4 billion in 2001.

Management considers the company a leader in using IT. Eastman.com was operational in 1994, several years before most companies had Web sites. Originally the site was used for HR and recruiting. Over time, as more content was added, the site became a hodge-podge of different sections targeted at different audiences, structured like Eastman's organization chart.

Redesigning the Web Site to Take the Customer Viewpoint

In mid-1999, Eastman initiated a companywide effort to become more customer focused and launched a major ecommerce program. This was the catalyst for rethinking the Web site design. The redesign was championed by the vice presidents of e-commerce and corporate communications because their departments jointly managed content.

The e-commerce group provides the tools and processes for employees to create and update Web content. The corporate communications department enforces corporate content policy and approves all Web content for correct use of trademarks, brands, terminology, and so on.

In line with the corporate refocus, the two groups decided to change the Web site structure from presenting an inside-out view based on Eastman's corporate structure to presenting an outside-in view with sections devoted to the markets the company serves.

A packaging customer who bought plastics from two Eastman operations formerly had to search the site to find who supplied plastics. Once found, each section had a different navigational system. In the redesign, a single section on food packaging was created for all Eastman operations dealing with packaging.

Eastman worked with a Web design company on the new site architecture, site map, and layout.

Upgrading the Content Management Software

At the same time, Eastman searched for content management software to replace home-grown software in use since 1994. The flat HTML files created a maintenance bottleneck because each page had to be updated separately and required a programmer to translate the content into HTML.

Eastman selected a content management product to create pre-approved templates for employees to use, then forward the pages to corporate communications for approval. This approach eliminated the programmer bottleneck. The software manages employees' rights to update, add, and publish content. Each user ID has a security level and permissible functions associated with it.

Pulling all the business content together for the new site turned out to be a massive effort. Once the content had been compiled, cataloged, and approved, moving from the old system and server to the new system and new content proved to be a second major undertaking.

Benefits of the Site Redesign

The benefits of the redesign were far greater than expected. Within 6 months, overall traffic doubled, and hits to the new market sections, where Eastman sells its products, increased from 30 percent to 60 percent of total hits. Today, traffic has tripled, and 70 percent of the hits are in the market sectors. Adding new content significantly helped increase traffic, but so, too, did the customer focus.

Eastman underestimated the value of the technical product data sheets published on the site, especially to people outside the United States who previously were unable to get this information easily or quickly. More than 50 percent of the site traffic is from outside the United States. Customers report that the technical data has also significantly accelerated their internal decision-making processes.

To manage the technical data, Eastman uses an internally developed product catalog. Formerly, a data sheet could exist in multiple locations, which led to quality problems, because each had to be updated separately. With the product catalog, the data is stored once and is pulled into a data sheet when needed. Thus, Eastman can ensure that everyone sees the same data on a chemical, even in two different markets.

The site has a public part that anyone can access and a protected part for customers only. Once customers are registered and have a user name and password, they can place orders, look at their order history and status, and browse the product catalog in this protected part. They can also personalize their view of the site to some extent and create their own catalog of the products they normally order.

Since the redesign, Eastman has continued to expand the site. It recently improved search capabilities and added a synonym directory, which has proven important because site visitors often use different names for the same product.

Moving Forward: Globalization and Localization

Globalization and localization are major issues. Eastman has a presence in more than 30 countries and sells in all major regions of the world. A significant portion of sales comes from overseas, so the company wants to allow a site visitor to choose one of, say, eight languages and see the relevant content in that language. If it had treated English as a foreign language during the 1999 redesign, it could add other languages easily. Thinking globally in all content management decisions is a necessity.

Another major challenge is finding a workable global approval process. Checking for adherence to content policies by corporate communications is quick today because all content is in English. However, translation into multiple languages and adaptation to local cultures can significantly complicate and lengthen this approval process. Retranslation into English for corporate approval is too expensive to be feasible. The e-commerce and corporate communications departments are currently working on creating a workable translation and approval process for content originating in other languages.

Eastman has learned that it is best to push content management to the source as much as possible so as not to create bottlenecks at central control points. It also learned the value of consistent organization throughout the Web site. This helps present a cohesive image of the company to site visitors. Having the content management system pull information from the product catalog also ensures data consistency.

Managing Blogs. The term *blog* is short for *"Web log"* or "weblog." A blog is a Web site where an individual makes intermittent Web postings. It is akin to a personal online journal. People write and post on blogs as a form of self-expression. What do they write about? They write about whatever comes to mind. They may write about their private life or their work life. Most blogs also invite comments from others, which appear on the blog as well. Blogs are a different form of Web content, but they still need to be managed. Enterprises need to establish guidelines for employees who choose to blog.

Blogs are powerful tools for democratizing online expression, notes Dan Farber. According to Farber, "Combine blogs with social networks and presence services (such as instant messaging and global positioning), and you have a new person-to-person, information-sharing connection fabric." In short, individuals can compete with major media via blogs, and they can have major impacts such as influencing politics or company policies. Some forward-thinking companies have recognized the power of this immediate form of publishing and communication. One corporate use of blogs is for crisis management. A blog can be more appropriate than e-mail in managing a crisis (such as a fire or a security breach). All the postings can be on one site, in journaling style, rather than passed as disconnected e-mails, notes Farber.

What readers seem to trust about blogs, that they do not trust about conventional media, is their opinionated and personal nature. These characteristics present both opportunities and challenges to organizations. For example, Farber notes that Microsoft employee Robert Scoble's popular blog about the company's forthcoming version of Windows, Longhorn, is not vetted by Microsoft. It's Scoble's opinions. But he does admit that he talks to the company's public relations department to be sure he does not divulge company-confidential information, notes Farber. Scoble's blog can be found at http://radio.weblogs.com.0001011

Employees who are not careful about the information they blog can find themselves in trouble. A hypothetical case study of a blogger who works for a disposable-glove manufacturer is presented in the September 2003 issue of the *Harvard Business Review.* Known as "Glove Girl," her highly popular blog has increased sales of a company glove, but she has also talked about competitors' products, potential deals, and industry statistics–all from her own point of view, not the company's. This case poses the question, "What should company management do about Glove Girl?" to four experts. It's a question all top management teams should be asking themselves.

One of the experts is Ray Ozzie, Chairman and CEO of Groove Networks, a company that provides software for group collaboration. He notes in his comments that he believes employee blogs are "more often than not" good for companies. But companies need policies to guide employees in expressing themselves via Weblogs or Web sites, while both protecting the company and reflecting positively on it. He notes that in 2002 his company developed such a policy, shown in the following case example, to address four concerns:

1. That readers would see blogs as official company communications rather than personal opinions
2. That confidential information would be disclosed, intentionally or not
3. That a party–the company, an employee, a customer, or other–could be disparaged on a blog
4. That a blog might violate the quiet period imposed by securities regulations, during which time a company cannot discuss an upcoming securities-related event

Ozzie's advice in the case, and to executives in general, is to create a policy for their firm and to become more familiar with blogging–even perhaps write their own blog, as he does at www.ozzie.net, to "communicate convincingly with employees, markets and shareholders."

Getting Closer to Customers

The first wave of using the Internet in the working-outward arena involved the use of Web sites to sell products and services and manage customer relations. Many types of products can now be purchased online, from books, CDs, and flowers to automobiles, legal services, and wine. The advantages of selling online are numerous and seem obvious. Figure 5.19 lists some of these advantages. Indeed, it is not difficult to find success stories, such as Dell, E*TRADE, and Cheap Tickets. However, the potential problems are also numerous and have become more obvious since the dot-com bust. Figure 5.20 lists some of the potential problems faced in creating a B2C system.

Use of the Internet has now become much more sophisticated. CRM systems are used to learn more about customers (and perhaps noncustomers). Whether you visit a firm's Web site, call it from your home, office, or cell phone, or buy something from it, the firm is keeping track and combining that information to create a profile of you. CRM systems for managing these profiles are the next wave of enterprise systems, following on the heels of ERP. ERP focused on internal data. CRM focuses on customer data.

CASE EXAMPLE

GROOVE NETWORKS

Employee Guidelines for Personal Web Sites and Weblogs

In general, the company views personal Web sites and Weblogs positively, and it respects the right of employees to use them as a medium of self-expression.

If you choose to identify yourself as a company employee or to discuss matters related to the company's technology or business on your Web site or weblog, please bear in mind that, although you and we view your Web site or weblog as a personal project and a medium of personal expression, some readers may nonetheless view you as a de facto spokesperson for the company. In light of this possibility, we ask that you observe the following guidelines:

- Please make it clear to your readers that the views you express are yours alone and that they do not necessarily reflect the views of the company. To help reduce the potential for confusion, we would appreciate it if you put the following notice–or something similar–in a reasonably prominent place on your site (e.g., at the bottom of your "about me" page):

  The views expressed on this Web site/weblog are mine alone and do not necessarily reflect the views of my employer.

If you do put a notice on your site, you needn't put it on every page, but please use reasonable efforts to draw attention to it–if at all possible, from the home page of your site.

- Take care not to disclose any information that is confidential or proprietary to the company or to any third party that has disclosed information to us. Consult the company's confidentiality policy for guidance about what constitutes confidential information.
- Please remember that your employment documents give the company certain rights with respect to concepts and developments you produce that are related to the company's business. Please consult your manager if you have questions about the appropriateness of publishing such concepts or developments on your site.
- Since your site is a public space, we hope you will be as respectful to the company, our employees, our customers, our partners and affiliates, and others (including our competitors) as the company itself endeavors to be.
- You may provide a link from your site to the company's Web site, if you wish. The Web design group has created a graphic for links to the company's site, which you may use for this purpose during the term of your employment (subject to discontinuation in the company's discretion). Contact a member of the Web design group for details. Please do not use other company trademarks on your site or reproduce company material without first obtaining permission.

Finally, the company may request that you temporarily confine your Web site or Weblog commentary to topics unrelated to the company (or, in rare cases, that you temporarily suspend your Web site or weblog activity altogether) if it believes this is necessary or advisable to ensure compliance with securities regulations or other laws.

Examples of CRM are scattered throughout this text. CRM systems are both a boon and a bane, depending on how intrusive you think they are. You may be pleased when companies e-mail you offers that you want to take advantage of, such as a reduced-fare flight to a city you want to visit on the weekend. Or, you may see them as invading your privacy. In response to privacy concerns, some countries have passed privacy-protection laws to require companies to inform customers of whether and under what circumstances customer information is shared with others.

On the other side of the coin, IT and the Internet have changed what customers value. They now expect service to be fast; the key term is on-demand. Online business enables firms to respond quickly by drastically reducing the time needed to respond to customer requests for company, product, and price information, to process an order, and to get products to customers.

Global accessibility: The Internet eliminates geographic boundaries.

Reduced order processing: Automated order processing improves efficiency.

Greater availability: The company is available online 24 hours a day, 7 days a week.

Closer customer relationships: With a direct link to customers,the company can quickly address concerns and customize responses.

Increased customer loyalty: With improved customer service and personalized attention comes greater customer loyalty.

New products and services: With direct links to customers, the company can provide information-based products and services.

Direct marketing: Manufacturers can bypass retailers and distributors, selling directly to customers.

Figure 5.19 Advantages of B2C E-Business

WORKING INWARD: BUSINESS-TO-EMPLOYEE

The essence of using IT strategically inside the enterprise has been, and continues to be, focused on improving business processes. Use of the Internet internally is no exception. It has revolved around building intranets.

Building an Intranet

An intranet is a private company network that uses Internet technologies and protocols, and possibly the Internet itself. The network is intended for employees only, and departments have used them to disseminate information and policies, provide needed forms, and even permit online transactions of former paper-based processes (such as filling out an expense requisition or changing a benefit). Applications use the Web interface and are accessed through browsers; communications use several protocols, including Hypertext Transfer Protocol (HTTP) for addressing Web sites, Hypertext Markup Language (HTML) for Web content structuring, and Transmission Control Protocol/Internet Protocol (TCP/IP) for network routing. The result is open systems using nonproprietary technologies.

The benefits of intranets have been significant: wider access to company information, more efficient and less expensive system development, and decreased training costs. By using an intranet's open-system architecture, companies can significantly decrease the cost of providing companywide information and connectivity. One of the most important attributes of intranets is that they support any make or brand of user device–from high-end worksta-

Technical: The information systems are not always reliable or may be poorly designed.

Logistics: Getting products to customers around the world in a timely manner brings physical barriers to the virtual business.

Personnel: Few people have expertise in dealing with the new environment,both in technical and business arenas.

Legal: Doing business across geographic boundaries means dealing with multiple legal systems.

Competitive response: The ease of creating a Web presence brings low barriers to entry for competitors.

Transparent prices: Customers can easily compare prices across Web sites,reducing profit margins.

Greater competition: The elimination of geographic boundaries means a firm must compete with competitors from around the world.

Figure 5.20 Potential B2C Problems

tion to PC, to laptop, to handheld device–as well as existing databases and software applications. Such interconnectivity has been the promise of open systems for many years. The Internet provides the connecting protocols to make the open-system promise a reality.

Furthermore, investments in a companywide electronic infrastructure are significantly less than building a proprietary network. Companies only need the servers, browsers, and a TCP/IP network to build an intranet. If, in addition, the company wishes to use the infrastructure of the Internet to geographically extend its intranet, the only additional components needed are firewalls, which keep the public from accessing the intranet, and local access to the Internet. Figure 5.21 shows the basic architecture of an intranet. The link to the Internet allows the company to expand its intranet worldwide easily and inexpensively–a significant benefit that was unthinkable before the Internet.

Finally, because an intranet uses the browser interface, users do not need extensive training on different products. In addition, due to the HTML standard and the availability of easy-to-use Web page authoring tools, employees can easily create their own Web pages for whatever purpose they need. As a result, all employees are potential site creators, reducing the IS department's programming bottleneck, while adhering to companywide standards. An additional benefit is that companies only need to record information in one place, where it can be kept up-to-date for access by all employees no matter where in the world they are located.

Due to the ease with which Web sites can be created, many employees have built their own, leading to a proliferation of sites with company information. To control the situation, IS departments have created corporate portals that act as gateways to firms' internal resources, information, and Internet services. This solution brings access to company data and applications together in a single site. Employees simply need a browser. At the same time, the portal provides IS management with a way to monitor and control the growth of internal Web sites, and the portal provides a link to Internet resources external to the company,

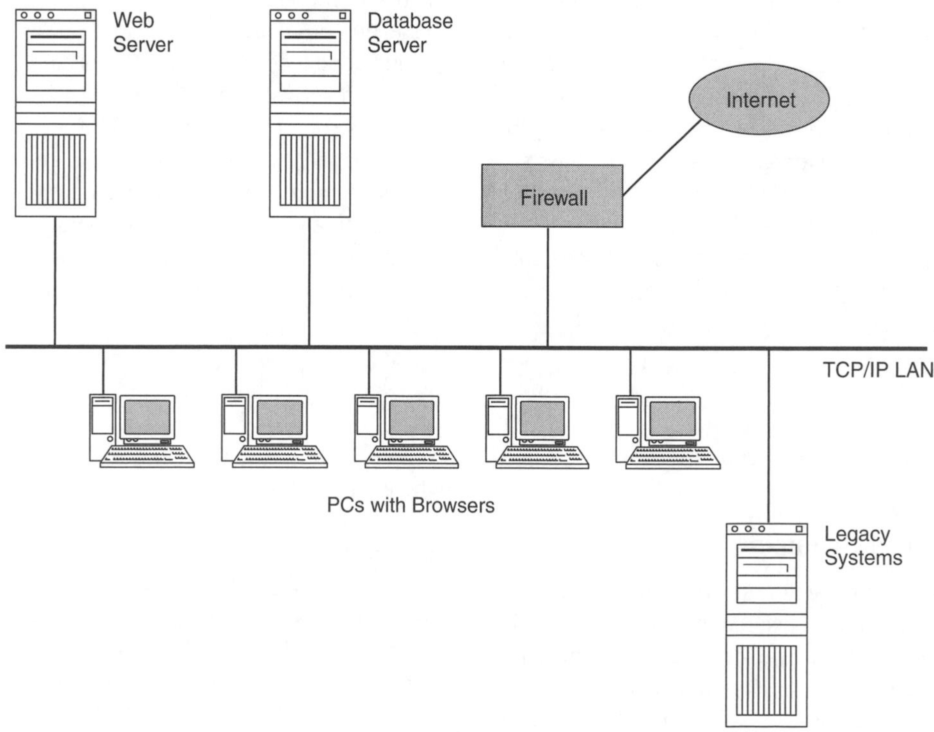

Figure 5.21 Intranet Architecture

CASE EXAMPLE

GE POWER SYSTEMS

Being a marketing man, when Jeff Immelt became chairman of General Electric (GE) in September 2001, he surveyed the sales force. He found that they were spending more time in the office searching for information they needed to sell GE products than out with their customers. He challenged all the business units to reverse the ratio, notes Anthes.

One business unit, GE Power Systems, sells multimillion-dollar turbines and turbine parts and services to energy companies. It answered the challenge by building a Web-based sales portal for its salespeople. In essence, the portal is meant to be their main source of information by linking them to numerous information sources–some inside GE, some outside–without requiring changes to the underlying systems.

The main data feeds into the portal are from the existing Oracle and Siebel databases on sales, parts, pricing, inventory, customers, and such. The portal also has a news feed from the outside. The coordination of all the information is handled by portal software from Vignette. The software assembles dynamic *portlets* that present salespeople with personalized, up-to-date data views. The portlet might show, for instance, the status of the salesperson's customers' orders, recent news stories that mention the salesperson's customers, price changes, sales performance for the month, and so on.

Vignette's system manages the content and its presentation to the salespeople; a special Oracle data mart for the portal pulls the appropriate data from the other systems at the appropriate intervals. Some data, such as customer master file updates, is pulled in real time (when the update takes place), whereas other data, such as turbine installations, is updated weekly, notes Anthes.

The Web server aspects of the system are handled by BEA System's WebLogic Server, and SiteMinder from Netegrity handles security and user sign-ons. When a salesperson wants to access an application through the portal, SiteMinder uses an authorization table that has access permissions to determine whether to grant the user access to the system. Formerly, salespeople had to enter a different password for each application. Now, they only enter one password to get into the portal.

Power Systems' IT organization was able to build this portal in just 6 months' time by following GE's rigorous project management methodology and by using rapid prototyping ("launch and learn," they call it), building incomplete versions of the portal for salespeople to test out and critique at the annual sales conference and elsewhere.

The portal's architecture is flexible enough to be extended to include more types of information and to permit access to more applications. In short, the portal has greatly enhanced the usefulness of GE Power Systems' existing systems to its salespeople by giving them a single port of entry to them all.

such as sites for industry news, customers, and business partners. GE Power Systems is a case in point.

Fostering a Sense of Belonging

Intranets are evolving into very important enterprise structures. In fact, in some enterprises, the intranet is seen as the enterprise. It houses videos of executives explaining the enterprise's vision and mission. It includes all the internal forms, rules, and processes. Need to file an expense report? Go to the intranet. Need to make travel reservations? Use the intranet. In short, the intranet embodies the company's processes and culture and can be accessed anywhere an employee has a connection to the Web.

Although this convenience can ease the life of employees, it can also feel colder and more impersonal than the traditional office setting. Frances Cairncross, author of *The Company of the Future*, believes the challenge for corporate management of widely dispersed enterprises today is maintaining cohesion, which takes a lot more effort than when employees are colocated. With so many employees working out of their home, car, hotel room, airport, or customer site, she believes it is important to create a sense of belonging.

CASE EXAMPLE

WIRE NOVA SCOTIA

Industry Canada has a Community Access Program (CAP) that provides a one-time grant to 10,000 Canadian communities to set up a CAP site, which is a public Internet access site for use by a rural community to stimulate its economic development, note Professors Bruce Dienes and Michael Gurstein. The CAP grant also pays for a summer field worker (age 16 to 30) to set up the site and encourage local businesses, government, and community groups to use the CAP site and the Internet.

Cape Breton, a region in Canada's Nova Scotia province, has become quite impoverished. Its main livelihoods–fishing, coal, and steel–have dried up, and many residents have moved away. University College of Cape Breton opened a center to research and incubate ways to use IT to stimulate Nova Scotia's economy, especially Cape Breton's. The center is not funded, thus its operation depends on funding from the projects it gains.

The Challenge

The center was most interested in the CAP opportunity, but Drs. Gurstein and Dienes knew that success required the CAP sites to be coordinated and work together. Acting alone, these rural sites would fail. The center could serve as a coordinating site, providing access to government and industry services, such as job listings, health information, and online banking. It could also help with marketing locally created products and services.

The goal of a CAP initiative for Nova Scotia would be to help site staff strategize with rural groups–school boards, corporate sponsors, libraries, regional development agencies, and others–to form collaborative networks to increase economic activity via "rural informatics," enabling rural enterprises to offer their goods and services globally.

The challenge was how to remotely coordinate and manage CAP sites spread across the province's wide geographic area given the limited finances.

The Solution

The initiative to address this challenge was called Wire Nova Scotia (WiNS). It would coordinate the youth workers at 67 CAP and other community access sites scattered throughout Nova Scotia. Six regional coordinators would have notebook computers and cell phones to supervise the youth workers. The Cape Breton center would house the main server. The heart of this community would be a password-protected intranet for use by the youth field workers, supervisors, and central staff.

One face-to-face orientation and training session was held for the youth workers and their supervisors so that they knew each other before going off to establish their Internet access site in a small community. Supervisors also held a few training sessions in the field. It turns out that those who attended these sessions had an easier time integrating into the WiNS community. Those who did not attend a session had a much harder time gaining the sense of belonging.

Building an Online Community

From then on, WiNS was managed almost totally online. The intranet supported email, e-mail lists, real-time chat, and online conferences. E-mail gave the dispersed field workers an outlet for peer interaction, which greatly increased morale. Being remote, many of them worked alone most of the time. E-mail gave them peers to talk with and a community to belong to.

The heart of the system was the WebBoard that provided a means for online group discussions. The formal organizational structure occurred online, using various online conferences.

General Conferences. All WiNS staff used the WebBoard to hold general conferences for

- WiNS-wide announcements
- Business development: Staff generated and shared ideas on ways to help local businesses increase their income stream
- Technical support: Participants helped each other on the technical aspects of running their Internet access site. Conferences fostered field workers' dependence on one another rather than just on the central technical staff.

Personal Conferences. Each field worker had a personal conference area where he or she filed weekly reports and site

(Case continued)

(Case continued)

usage statistics. Only the worker and his or her regional coordinator could access this site. Coordinators could review the logs and sometimes head-off problems before they grew too large.

Regional Conferences. Each region also held regional conferences via the intranet to plan joint ventures among nearby sites or to coordinate regional promotions. Regions also held real-time online chat meetings to foster informal socializing amongst their field workers. These sessions not only helped build a sense of community, but they often spread innovations among the sites quickly.

Coordinator Conferences. Finally, the WiNS coordinator held a weekly online staff conference with his six regional coordinators, which helped them learn from and support one another. Each coordinator supervised 10 to 25 sites across Nova Scotia, and each had different expertise. The weekly conferences gave them a way to meet and tap each other's expertise.

In all, Dienes and Gurstein believe the only way the 67 sites in WiNS could have operated successfully that summer was via an intranet. It permitted remote management and created a sense of belonging among far-flung remote sites that could not otherwise have been attained at a cost the initiative could afford.

An intranet can provide the foundation for creating a sense of belonging by giving a means of communicating and creating communities. Whether enterprises use intranets to help employees feel part of the culture is up to them. Whether they are successful is yet another issue. Cairncross believes this goal should be a major use of intranets because the care of employees is one of the most important things enterprises do. Here is an example of one intranet used for that purpose.

WORKING OUTWARD: BUSINESS-TO-CUSTOMER

In most industries, companies need sophisticated computer systems to compete. For airlines, hotels, and rental car companies, a computer reservation system–either their own or someone else's–is a must. In the drug and hospital wholesaling industries, those that had automated order entry and distribution systems gobbled up those that did not have such systems. In financial markets, computerized trading and settlement systems are replacing open-outcry systems. And the list goes on.

As industry leaders increase the sophistication of their systems to concurrently address the four hallmarks of competitiveness—quality, service, innovation, and speed—their competitors must do the same or find themselves at a disadvantage. Using IT (or any technology) as the basis for a product or a service can, in some cases, be viewed as moving up a series of experience curves.

Jumping to a New Experience Curve

The traditional view of an experience curve is that the cost of using a new technology decreases as the firm gains more experience with it. However, in *Strategic Choices* Kenneth Primozic, Edward Primozic, and Joe Leben present the view that more experience leads to a set of connected curves, rather than one continuous learning curve, as shown in Figure 5.22.

Each curve represents a different technology or a new combination of technologies in a product or service as well as in the product's manufacturing or the service's support. Moving to a new curve requires substantial investment in a new technology, and the company often must choose from among competing technologies, none of which is yet the clear winner. A firm that correctly identifies a new market and the technologies to exploit it can shift to the new experience curve and successfully open up a new industry segment. However, management sometimes has such an emotional attachment to the current experience curve that it fails to see the next one and thus loses its market share to swifter competitors. This has repeatedly happened in the computer field. Mainframe manufacturers ignored minicomputer firms. Then minicomputer firms ignored PC manufacturers (considering PCs to be toys). Then PC manufacturers ignored operating system firms, that is, Microsoft. And they, in turn, initially ignored the Internet.

To demonstrate this principle of experience curves and the need to keep up or lose out, consider the authors' example on page 209.

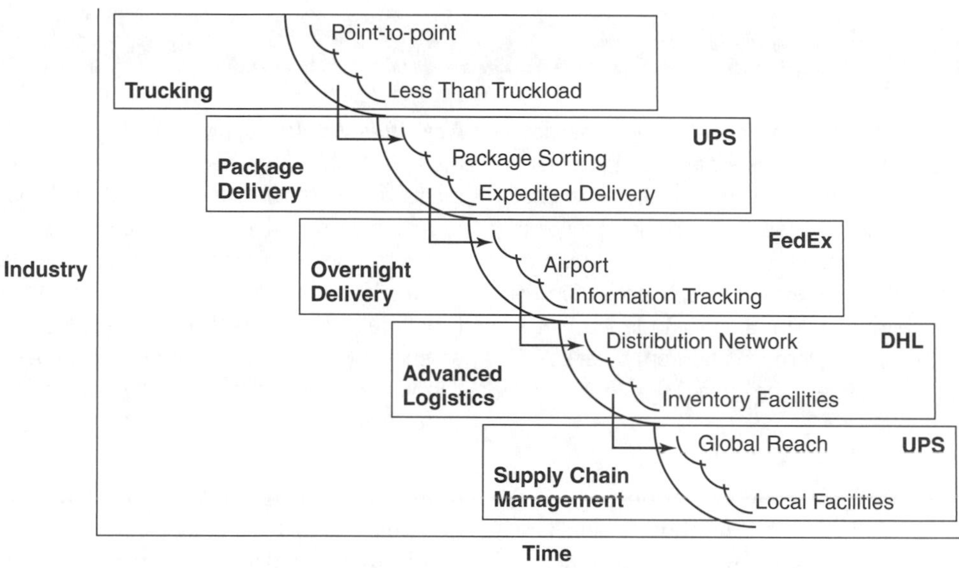

Figure 5.22 The Shipping Industry. *Source:* Based on Kenneth Primozic, and Joe Leben, *Strategic Choices: Supremacy, Survival, or Sayonara* (New York: McGraw-Hill, 1991).

CASE EXAMPLE

THE SHIPPING INDUSTRY

Primozic et al. present an intriguing discussion of the shipping industry (which we have extended) to illustrate their concept of experience curves.

The Original Industry: Trucking

The trucking industry initially shipped two types of truckloads of goods: full point-to-point truckloads and less than truckloads (LTLs), as shown in the upper left of Figure 5.22.

New Industry 1: Package Delivery. Once United Parcel Service (UPS) based its entire business on LTL shipping, a new industry segment was born: package delivery. As a result of this new experience curve, the shipping industry changed, and UPS actually became much larger than the trucking companies because it served a market with far more customers. The new technology that was key to UPS' success–and thus represented this particular experience curve–was the efficient sorting of packages at distribution centers in order to maximize use of its trucks.

New Industry 2: Overnight Delivery. UPS, however, did not guarantee a delivery time nor did it track packages. FedEx capitalized on these two missing functions, jumped to a new experience curve, and started yet another new industry segment: overnight delivery. FedEx became larger than UPS because it tapped an even larger market. And for UPS and other package carriers to compete, they, too, had to invest in the technologies to guarantee delivery and track packages.

Needless to say, IT played a crucial role in this experience curve. In fact, the Internet began playing a role when UPS allowed customers to order package pickup online and when FedEx created a Web page that enabled customers to query the whereabouts of a package directly from its package-tracking database. That Web site, which went live in November 1994, had 12,000 customers a day doing their own package tracking, saving FedEx $2 million just that first year.

New Industry 3: Advanced Logistics. In the late 1990s, a third industry emerged: advanced logistics. Due to their distribution

(Case continued)

(Case continued)

networks and inventory facilities, overnight delivery services could handle inventory for large corporate clients and guarantee overnight delivery of these inventoried items. On this experience curve, client companies outsource not only their inventory, but also distribution to FedEx, Airborne Express, UPS, and other carriers. Clients include computer manufacturers, auto parts suppliers (to handle after-sales service), health-care diagnostic labs, retailers, even movie studios (to ship film to and from theaters). IT continues to play an integral role in the offered services.

New Industry 4: Supply Chain Management. Most recently, the industry has morphed again. Major players are becoming clients' supply chain partners, providing all the services needed to get a client's product from the loading dock to the customer's premises. These companies have extended beyond advanced logistics by having the global reach and local presence (in far-flung locations) that their clients need to move their goods. In essence, these players become their client's distribution function, which requires all of the parties involved to work even more closely with each other.

The case example of Cisco and UPS on page 212 illustrates this latest industry. Notice how Cisco taps UPS's global reach and experience with European carriers to complete its supply chain. Also notice how closely linked the companies are becoming, with UPS employees responsible for some of Cisco's inventory and for some of the data in Cisco's ERP system, thereby giving Cisco more visibility into its downstream supply chain.

The Emergence of Electronic Tenders

An important development is occurring in the working-outward arena. Initially, IT was embedded in products and services because of its computational capabilities. For example, cars and elevators have computers that make them operate more efficiently. Toys have computers to make them more fun. Now, due to the Internet and wireless networks, the communication capabilities of computers are being extended and emphasized, often in these same products and services. These additions are literally transforming these goods. In essence, we would characterize these additions as adding *electronic tenders.*

An electronic tender is an electronic communication capability in a product or service that allows that product or service to be tended; that is, cared for, attended to, or kept track of by another computer. Electronic tenders open a seemingly unlimited set of possibilities for using IT in the working-outward arena. For example, consider a vehicle and its computers. Those computers can be programmed to perform diagnostics while the vehicle is running. Those diagnostics could be monitored by the car dealer (or an intermediary service provider), in real time, as a service to the owner. If something seems out of kilter, the owner could be notified, perhaps in real time. Likewise, packages and luggage with bar codes or other forms of identification can be tracked and found (if lost). The list of the uses of electronic tenders is endless.

Electronic tenders are occurring with services as well. A growing number of enterprises keep track of their customer interactions, culling them to understand clusters of customers and their buying patterns. Again, the options are endless. The goal is to get closer to the customer. You will learn more about electronic tenders and B2C in Chapter 7.

SUMMARY

Early in the twenty-first century, virtually all large and midsized businesses and an increasing number of small businesses depend on enterprise IT systems. These systems support almost every function of the business, from procuring raw materials to planning the production schedule to distributing the product, from recording and summarizing sales figures to keeping track of inventory, from paying employees and suppliers to handling receivables, from maintaining the organization's financial records to enabling employees to communicate more effectively. Modern organizations simply cannot do business without enterprise IT systems.

Transaction processing systems are central to the operations of almost every business. These workhorse systems, which were the very first IT applications installed in most businesses, process the thousands of transactions that occur every day, including sales, payments, inventory, and payroll. In recent years many larger businesses have turned to enterprise resource planning (ERP) systems as a way to achieve an integrated set of transaction processing applications. ERP systems typically consist of a number of modules to handle the sales and distribution, manufacturing, financial reporting, and human resources areas, and the organization can buy a subset of these modules to satisfy its needs.

Transaction processing systems handle the volume of transactions generated as a firm does business, and they also produce summary reports on these transactions. They do not, however, provide this transactional data in a form that enables managers to use the data in decision-making activities—data warehousing does this. With data warehousing, organizational data are made accessible from a storage area that is distinct from that used for operational transaction processing. When combined with easy-to-use analysis tools—which are discussed in the next chapter—the data warehouse becomes a critical information resource for managers to enable strategic and operational decision making.

Office automation systems affect every knowledge worker in a firm. Word processing, electronic calendaring, electronic mail, and many other applications are most commonly delivered via an employee's PC attached to the organization's network. Groupware is an increasingly popular way of providing office automation functionality in an integrated package. Lotus Notes, the most popular groupware package today, provides an excellent document-sharing capability as well as calendaring, e-mail, and other features. Intranets—networks within an organization that employ Internet standards—offer employees easy access to an organization's internal information via a Web browser. Factory automation, especially computer-integrated manufacturing, applies IT to the task of increasing efficiency and effectiveness in the manufacturing process.

As important as these various enterprise systems are, they are certainly not the whole story in terms of IT applications. Chapter 6 focuses on managerial support systems designed to provide support to a manager or managers, and Chapter 7 explores the topic of e-business applications.

CHAPTER REVIEW QUESTIONS

1. Consider the enterprise systems application areas listed in Figure 5.1. Which application areas are most important today? How do some of the areas cross over from enterprise systems to managerial systems?
2. What are the fundamental differences between batch processing and online processing? What is in-line processing?
3. Why aren't all present-day systems online?
4. What is a vertically integrated information system? Give an example.
5. Describe how a client/server system works and when an organization would choose to implement one.
6. Define middleware and list three categories.
7. What are the primary categories of modules that are likely to be offered by a major ERP vendor?
8. What are the primary reasons for implementing an ERP system?
9. What are the major difficulties in the implementation of such a system and what have been some notable ERP failures?
10. What aspects of the automated office do you encounter in the workplace today?
11. Define groupware and the features included in a groupware product.
12. What is an intranet and how is it used in business? List advantages and disadvantages.
13. What are the steps that must take place in a data warehousing project?
14. Explain the three phases of content management.
15. Define these acronyms: CIM, CAD, MRP, MAP, GT, MRP II.

CHAPTER DISCUSSION QUESTIONS

1. Differentiate between a two-tier client/server system and a three-tier client/server system. Differentiate between a fat client and a thin client. Why would a firm choose one of these approaches over the others when implementing a client/server system?
2. Consider an office environment with which you are somewhat familiar. What changes have occurred in the preparation of documents over the past decade? Why do you think these changes have occurred? Have they been technology-driven or people-driven, or both?
3. Based on your reading and knowledge from other sources, in what ways has the phenomenon of the Internet influenced office automation?
4. Many large firms have adopted groupware, and others are still using older mainframe-based UNIX server-based, or LAN-based e-mail systems. What explains this difference? Why have some firms moved quickly to groupware, while others are moving more slowly?
5. All of us come in contact with distributed systems almost every day, even if it is only while shopping. Describe a distributed system with which you have come in contact. In your view, what are the advantages and disadvantages of this system? Is the system you described a client/server system?

6. Consider a Weblog for a company. What are some of the advantages and disadvantages for the company of having such a site? Should the business have a policy for controlling information on the Weblog, or does this fly in the face of what a Weblog is all about?

CASE STUDY: CISCO SYSTEMS AND UPS SUPPLY CHAIN SOLUTIONS

In the late 1990s, Cisco committed itself to manufacturing products within 2 weeks of receiving an order, but it could not guarantee delivery. Customers were responsible for getting their products shipped from Cisco, located in San Jose, California, to their own premises. Shipping to Europe was especially taxing on customers.

To improve the situation, Cisco turned over its European supply chain to UPS Supply Chain Solutions (UPS SCS), a division of UPS, for reengineering and management.

Some 90 percent of Cisco's products are configured and ordered over the Web. Within 24 hours of receiving an order, Cisco sends the customer an email that states that the order has been accepted and that indicates when it will be produced.

When the product for a European customer is ready, Cisco notifies UPS SCS. Within 24 hours, UPS SCS picks up the order and books cargo space to move it to its European distribution center in the Netherlands, where it arrives 2 to 3 days later. In this shipping process, SCS handles customs clearance, documentation, billing, and carrier selection.

Once at the European distribution center, the order is shipped to the customer in one of two ways. If it is a complete order or if the customer chooses to receive the order in several shipments, UPS SCS ships the product directly using its cross-docking facility. If the product is only part of an order, it is held until the rest of the order is received, then shipped. In some cases, fast-moving products are inventoried at the Netherlands site. UPS SCS personnel manage the site's inventory levels (meeting Cisco's specifications) and handle the last bill-of-material update in Cisco's ERP system once a product has been ordered for dispatch.

UPS SCS uses its own system to find the best shipper to move the package from the Netherlands center to the customer site. In essence, the system issues an electronic request for quote to all approved shippers in the system. The system uses the information they supply to calculate the price, transit time, and service level for the shipment and then places a shipping order. The UPS SCS system also updates Cisco's system so that customers can find out their order status via Cisco's Web site. Until an order is filled, customers can even make changes, such as changing the delivery address.

The systems of the two companies have become increasingly linked. Each movement of a product is recorded in both systems.

UPS now handles over 1 million boxes a year for Cisco through its Netherlands distribution center. Because UPS can ensure reliable transit times, Cisco is able to now promise delivery times for its European customers. In addition, these customers have only one point of contact for their shipments: the UPS SCS distribution center. And Cisco has online visibility into its downstream supply chain–to customer delivery in Europe–which it did not have before.

Case Study Discussion Questions

Question One

Cisco and UPS have merged many of their activities to create one seamless operation between two companies. The advantages of such a situation are obvious and noted in the case study. Can you think of any disadvantages?

Question Two

Aside from order fulfillment and transportation, what are some other areas of a company that might benefit from streamlining their business through technological improvements or the Internet?

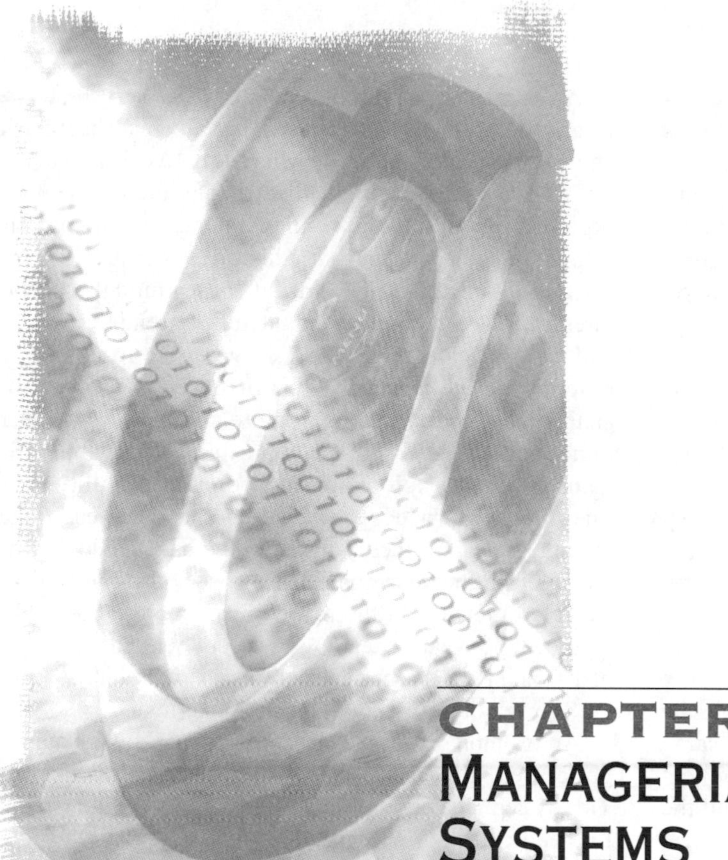

CHAPTER 6
MANAGERIAL SUPPORT SYSTEMS

MANAGERIAL SUPPORT SYSTEMS ARE THE TOPIC OF THIS SECOND OF THREE chapters devoted to our survey of information technology (IT) application areas. Managerial support systems are designed to provide support to a specific manager or a small group of managers, and they include applications to support managerial decision making such as group support systems, executive information systems, and expert systems. In contrast, the previous chapter dealt with enterprise systems designed to support the entire organization or large portions of it, such as transaction processing systems, data warehousing, groupware, and intranets. Together these two chapters provide a relatively comprehensive picture of the applications of IT within a single organization (*intraorganizational* systems). To complete the survey of IT applications, Chapter 7 will focus on *e-business applications* that span organizational boundaries, including B2C and B2B applications using the Internet. Taken as a set, these three chapters encompass the great majority of IT applications in use today.

The enterprise systems discussed in the previous chapter are critical for running a business or any other type of organization, and you will be dealing with many such enterprise systems, especially transaction processing systems and groupware. Nevertheless, these enterprise systems have been designed to support the organization as a whole, not you in particular or even a group of managers. Managerial support systems, in contrast, are intended to directly support you and other managers as you make strategic and tactical decisions for your organizations. For example, interactive decision support systems (DSSs) are designed to help managers and other professionals analyze internal and external data. By capturing the expertise of human experts, expert systems advise nonexperts in a particular decision area. Group support systems are designed to make group work, especially meetings, more productive. Executive information systems (EISs) provide easy-to-navigate summary data for the managers of an organization. This chapter will explore these and other managerial support systems that are increasingly important in running modern organizations.

DECISION SUPPORT SYSTEMS

A **decision support system (DSS)** is a computer-based system, almost always interactive, designed to assist a manager (or another decision maker) in making decisions.

A DSS incorporates both data and models to help a decision maker solve a problem, especially a problem that is not well structured. The data are often extracted from a transaction processing system or a data warehouse, but that is not always the case. The model might be simple, such as a profit-and-loss model to calculate profit given certain assumptions, or complex, such as an optimization model to suggest loadings for each machine in a job shop. DSSs and many of the systems discussed in the following sections are not always justified by a traditional cost-benefit approach; for these systems many of the benefits are intangible, such as faster decision making and better understanding of the data.

Figure 6.1 shows that a DSS requires three primary components: model management to apply the appropriate model, data management to select and handle the appropriate data, and dialog management to facilitate the user interface to the DSS. The user interacts with the DSS through the dialog management component, identifying the particular model and data set to be used, and then the DSS presents the results to the user through this same dialog management component. The model management and data management components largely act behind the scenes, and they vary from relatively simple for a typical spreadsheet model to quite complex for a mathematical programming-based scheduling model.

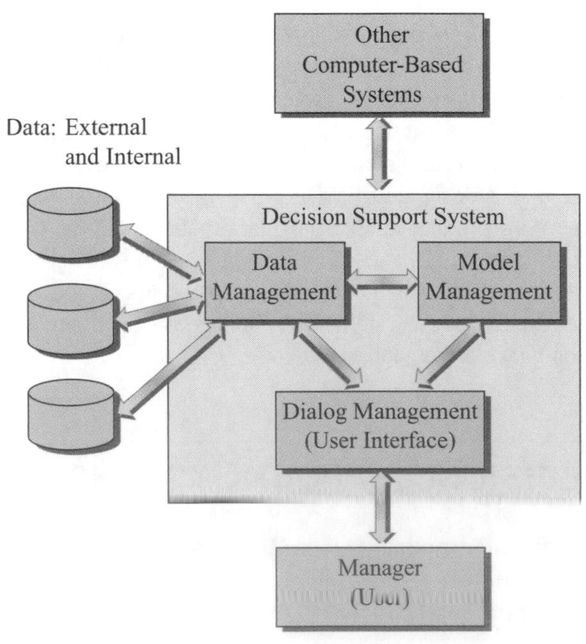

Figure 6.1 Decision Support Systems Components

An extremely popular type of DSS is a pro forma financial statement generator. Using a spreadsheet package such as Lotus 1-2-3 or Microsoft Excel, a manager builds a model to project the various elements of the organization or division financial statement into the future. The data employed are historical financial figures for the organization. The initial (base) model incorporates various assumptions about future trends in income and expense categories. After viewing the results of the base model, the manager performs a series of "what-if" analyses by modifying one or more assumptions to determine their impact on the bottom line. For example, the manager might explore the impact on profitability if the sales of a new product grew by 10 percent per year, rather than the 5 percent incorporated in the base model. Or the manager might investigate the impact of a higher-than-expected increase in the price of raw materials, such as 7 percent per year instead of 4 percent per year. This type of financial statement generator is a simple but powerful DSS for guiding financial decision making.

An example of a DSS driven by transactions data is a police-beat allocation system used by a California city. This system enables a police officer to display a map outline and call up data by geographic zone, which shows police calls for service, types of service, and service times. The system's interactive graphics capability lets the officer manipulate the maps, zones, and data to consider a variety of police-beat alternatives quickly and easily and takes maximum advantage of the officer's judgment.

Other DSS examples include an interactive system for capacity planning and production scheduling in a large paper company. This system employs detailed historical data and forecasting and scheduling models to simulate overall performance of the company under differing planning assumptions. A major oil company developed a DSS to support capital investment decision making. This system incorporates various financial routines and models for generating future plans; these plans can be displayed in either tabular or graphic form to aid in decision making. A major airline uses a DSS to help aircraft controllers deal with aircraft shortage problems that might arise at an airport because of delayed or canceled incoming flights or mechanical problems for aircraft on the ground. The DSS, which uses a network optimization modeling technique, helps controllers use spare aircraft more effectively as well as evaluate possible delay-and-swap options. Over an 18-month period, this DSS saved the airline more than $500,000 in delay costs.

All the DSS examples cited are more properly called **specific DSSs**. These are the actual applications that assist in the decision-making process. In contrast, a

A POTPOURRI OF DSS EXAMPLES

Virtually every issue of *Interfaces* contains a discussion of one or more new DSSs. To illustrate, we briefly describe three quite different decision support systems presented in the July–August 2002 and January–February 2003 issues of *Interfaces*.

"STEP-UP: A decision support system for transforming the dislocated U.S. defense workforce" (Vitolo and Vance, 2002) describes a DSS developed to assist in the retraining and placement of workers who lose their jobs when a defense facility (in this case, the Philadelphia Naval Shipyard and Base) is closed. STEP-UP was developed by a Penn State research team based at the Center for Applied Behavioral Studies and was funded by a grant from the U.S. Department of Labor. STEP-UP requires three data components: an extensive profile for each dislocated worker, a listing of available job positions in growth industries in the general area of the closed base, and a compendium of training programs available in the area. STEP-UP provides flexible matching capabilities to help dislocated workers identify potential job matches or evaluate training programs that will prepare the worker for available jobs. Working with a counselor, the dislocated worker can use STEP-UP to probe the job market based on his or her competencies, "knowledge, skills, and abilities," or achievements such as a certification or a license. Where skills gaps with available positions exist, STEP-UP suggests appropriate training. Employers can also use STEP-UP to identify suitable candidates for job openings. STEP-UP is currently installed at two locations of the Private Industry Council of Philadelphia and is regularly used by 15 to 20 managers, counselors, and job-placement specialists. Since its inception, STEP-UP has supported processing of over 15,000 clients and has recorded job openings for almost 2,000 employers. STEP-UP is fundamentally a counseling support system, and it seems to be a very useful tool.

In the same issue of *Interfaces*, Gupta, Peters, Miller, and Blyden (2002) describe a DSS to help the distribution network of Pfizer/Warner-Lambert (with annual sales of over $30 billion) plan its operations. The DSS actually consists of five models—three are simulation models that work together to support long-run planning of warehouse capacities in the network, a fourth is a mathematical programming model that produces plans for distribution of Pfizer/Warner-Lambert products over the planning horizon, and the fifth is an inventory investment model employing multiple approaches suggested in the inventory management literature (such as the traditional item-level statistical safety-stock model and high-level square-root-of-N models). Based on these principal components, variations of the DSS have been used for a variety of strategic and tactical decision making, including determining whether the company should expand the number of regional distribution centers, deciding on the best long-term U.S. distribution network for the consolidation of the premerger Warner-Lambert and Pfizer networks, and setting up a new pharmaceutical delivery network. At the operational level, a DSS has been developed that contains a toolkit of diagnostic models, analyses, and standardized reports designed to monitor distribution and transportation operations, identify opportunities for improving short-run operations, and provide information to support immediate decisions. The quantified benefits of Pfizer/Warner-Lambert's DSS include annual savings of over a half million dollars in freight costs, the elimination of customer deductions of several hundred thousand dollars annually, and the creation of a strategic manufacturing technology plan that could save $5.9 million annually.

A quite different type of DSS has been developed for Continental Airlines to minimize the costs of schedule disruptions caused by unexpected events such as inclement weather, aircraft mechanical problems, and crew unavailability (Yu, Argüello, Song, McCowan, and White, 2003). Because of such disruptions, crews might not be properly positioned to service their remaining scheduled flights. CALEB Technologies has developed the CrewSolver DSS to generate optimal or near optimal crew-recovery solutions to cover open flights and return crews to their original schedules in a cost-effective manner while honoring government regulations, contractual rules, and quality-of-life requirements. CrewSolver is a real-time, always available DSS operated by a crew coordinator from a graphical user interface. CrewSolver employs live operational data from the system operation control database as well as a complete crew file. When a disruptive event occurs, the crew coordinator requests a recovery solution, and CrewSolver employs a mathematical programming model (solved by a heuristic-based search algorithm) to generate up to three solutions, from which the crew coordinator chooses one. Solutions consist of reassigning crews from one flight to another, deadheading crews to cover a flight or return back to base, holding crews at their current location, assigning crews additional duty periods, moving a crew's layover to a different city, and using reserve crews to cover flights left uncovered by active crews. The results from the use of CrewSolver have been impressive: Continental Airlines estimates that it saved $40 million during 2001 from the use of CrewSolver to recover from four major disruptions: snowstorms that hit Newark, New Jersey just before New Year's Eve and again in March, heavy rains that closed the Houston airport for a day in June, and the terrorist attacks on September 11, 2001.

decision support system generator is a software package that provides a set of capabilities to build a specific DSS quickly and easily (Sprague and Carlson, 1982). In the previous pro forma financial statement example, Microsoft Excel or Lotus 1-2-3 can be viewed as a DSS generator, whereas a specific Excel or 1-2-3 model to project financial statements for a particular division of a company is a specific DSS.

DATA MINING

In Chapter 5 we introduced data warehousing—the idea of a company pulling data from its operational systems and putting the data in a separate data warehouse so that users may access and analyze the data without interfering with the operational systems. In that discussion we touched on the variety of software tools available for analysis of data in the warehouse, but deferred a more complete discussion until this chapter. Our argument was that the creation and maintenance of the data warehouse is an enterprise system, in that the data warehouse supports the entire organization by making the data available to everyone, whereas the analysis of the data is performed by and/or for a single manager or a small group of managers and is, therefore, a managerial support system. Without explicitly mentioning it, we have already begun the more detailed discussion of these tools for analyzing data in the warehouse, for the DSSs described in the previous section often pull the data they need directly from the organizations' data warehouses.

Data mining employs a variety of technologies (such as decision trees and neural networks) to search for, or "mine," "nuggets" of information from the vast quantities of data stored in an organization's data warehouse. Data mining, which is sometimes considered a subset of decision support systems, is especially useful when the organization has large volumes of transaction data in its warehouse. The concept of data mining is not new, although the term became popular only in the late 1990s. For at least two decades, many large organizations have used internal or external analysts, often called management scientists, to try to identify trends, or patterns, in massive amounts of data by using statistical, mathematical, and artificial intelligence techniques. With the development of large-scale data warehouses and the availability of inexpensive processing power, a renewed interest in what came to be called data mining arose in recent years.

Along with this renewed interest came a variety of high-powered and relatively easy-to-use commercial data mining software packages. Among these packages are Oracle 9i Data Mining and Oracle Data Mining Suite (formerly Darwin), SAS Enterprise Miner, IBM Intelligent Miner for Data (as well as related products IBM Intelligent Miner Modeling, Visualization, and Scoring), and KnowledgeSEEKER, KnowledgeSTUDIO, and KnowledgeExcelerator from Angoss Software Corp. *Datamation*'s Data Mining and Business Intelligence Product of the Year for 2003 is SAS Text Miner, which has the ability to handle textual information, pulling data out of letters, memos, medical records, and documents of all kinds and finding themes and patterns in these documents (Gaudin, 2003). These packages vary widely in cost, ranging from under a thousand dollars for some desktop packages to over $100,000 for some enterprise packages that run on large servers. Consultants are often required to fully utilize the capabilities of the more comprehensive packages.

What are the decision techniques or approaches used in data mining? One key technique, decision trees, is embedded in many of the packages. A decision tree is a tree-shaped structure that is derived from the data to represent sets of decisions that result in various outcomes—the tree's various end points. When a new set of decisions is presented, such as information on a particular shopper, the decision tree then predicts the outcome. Neural networks, a branch of artificial intelligence to be discussed later in this chapter, are incorporated in most of the high-end products. Other popular techniques include linear and logistic regression; association rules for finding patterns of co-occurring events; clustering for market segmentation; rule induction, the extraction of if-then rules based on statistical significance; nearest neighbor, the classification of a record based on those most similar to it in the database; and genetic algorithms, optimization techniques based on the concepts of genetic combination, mutation, and natural selection.

For completeness, let us introduce a term related to data mining, but with a difference—**online analytical processing**, or **OLAP**. OLAP has been described as human-driven analysis, whereas data mining might be viewed as technique-driven. OLAP is essentially querying against a database, employing OLAP software that makes it easy to pose complex queries along multiple dimensions, such as time, organizational unit, and geography. The chief component of OLAP is the OLAP server, which sits between a client machine and a database server. The OLAP server understands how data are organized in the database and has special functions for analyzing the data. In contrast, data mining incorporates such techniques as decision trees, neural networks, and genetic algorithms. An OLAP program extracts data from the database and structures it by individual dimensions, such as region or dealer. Data mining software searches the database for patterns and relationships, employing techniques such as neural networks.

Of course, what you can do with data mining is more important to you as a manager than the decision techniques employed. Typical applications of data mining are outlined in Table 6.1. Whatever the nature of your business, the chances are good that several of these applications could mean increased profits. Most of these applications focus on unearthing valuable information about your customers.

Many examples of successful data mining operations have been reported in IT magazines. Farmers Insurance Group, a Los Angeles-based provider of automobile and homeowners insurance, uses data mining to develop

Table 6.1 Uses of Data Mining

Application	Description
Cross-selling	Identify products and services that will most appeal to existing customer segments and develop cross-sell and up-sell offers tailored to each segment
Customer churn	Predict which customers are likely to leave your company and go to a competitor and target those customers at highest risk
Customer retention	Identify customer characteristics associated with highest lifetime value and develop strategies to retain these customers over the long term
Direct marketing	Identify which prospects should be included in a mailing list to obtain the highest response rate
Fraud detection	Identify which transactions are most likely to be fraudulent based on purchase patterns and trends
Interactive marketing	Predict what each individual accessing a Web site is most likely interested in seeing
Market basket analysis	Understand what products or services are commonly purchased together (e.g., beer and diapers) and develop appropriate marketing strategies
Market segmentation	Segment existing customers and prospects into appropriate groups for promotional and evaluation purposes and determine how to approach each segment for maximum results
Payment or default analysis	Identify specific patterns to predict when and why customers default on payments
Trend analysis	Investigate the difference between an average purchase this month versus last month and prior months

competitive rates on its insurance products. For example, Farmers used IBM's DecisionEdge software to mine data on owners of sports cars. Typically, these drivers are categorized as high-risk and thus pay high insurance premiums. However, Farmers discovered that a sizeable group of sports-car owners are married, 30 to 50 years old, own two cars, and do *not* have a high risk of accidents. Farmers adjusted the premiums for this group downward and believes that the company gained a competitive advantage in this market segment (Davis, 1999).

Vermont Country Store (VCS), a Weston, Vermont-based catalog retailer of traditional clothing, personal items, and housewares, uses SAS Institute's Enterprise Mining data mining software to segment its customers to create appropriate direct marketing mailing lists. "We concentrate on profitability, which we have learned can be increased by identifying the top echelon of customers and mailing them the larger catalog," according to Erin McCarthy, manager of statistical services and research at VCS. VCS also uses data mining to determine the mailing lists to be used for special campaigns. For example, VCS uses Enterprise Miner to research Christmas buying patterns and create a special Christmas campaign list, selecting just customers who order during the holidays. These customers can be even further segmented by their level of purchases and the types of products they buy, with focused catalogs sent to each separate group. "Our ultimate goal," says McCarthy, "is to be able to limit, or stabilize, the number of contacts we have with customers and still grow our market. For instance, if we're going to mail a catalog to a certain group of people five times a year, we want to know the best five offers to make them. Data mining is helping us do that" (Dickey, 1999).

Florida Hospital, an 11-campus, Orlando-based healthcare organization, has implemented IBM's Intelligent Miner in an effort to identify relationships in its patient data. Florida Hospital's initial data mining project was to predict which patients suffering from congestive heart failure were most likely, after being treated and released, to be readmitted or, even worse, to die. Data mining identified unsuspected clusters of data involving patient care that the hospital used as a starting point for making changes in its clinical procedures. In another study, the hospital used Intelligent Miner to investigate patterns associated with the care being given by individual physicians and the total charges they generate. That study is helping the hospital's chief medical officers establish standard care guidelines and clinical best practices. Early in 2000, Florida Hospital created a new standard care plan for patients with pneumonia and acute pneumonia. "We're using Intelligent Miner to validate whether patients on the standard care plan at one campus do better than those who are not on the plan at other campuses," reports Alexander Veletsos, information systems director at the hospital (Gwynne, 2000).

Data mining *requires* a well-designed and well-constructed data warehouse with well-maintained data in it. Before any organization thinks about data mining, it must ensure that it is capturing essential data and that the data are complete and accurate. For example, Merck-Medco, the prescription mail-order unit of pharmaceutical giant Merck & Co., Inc., based in Montvale, New Jersey, had to spend four years working on its unwieldy database of patient and treatment records before it had a warehouse ready for data mining. At Merck-Medco, this became a major data reengineering effort to clean up the data (ensure that they are

DATA MINING WORKS AT MERCK-MEDCO

Evan Marks, vice president for marketing at Merck-Medco, believes that the company's data mining system, named ExpeR$_x$t, "helps you ask the right questions and deliver your information even if you're not sure what patterns you're looking for." One pattern the system has uncovered is already saving Merck-Medco customers millions of dollars.

Using ExpeR$_x$t, Merck-Medco analyzed the effectiveness of certain treatments for gastric-intestinal ailments. Cost data led Merck-Medco to seek alternative treatments to the most frequently prescribed drug. The result was identification of an alternative and less costly drug that could prove effective for many patients and could even work more quickly. "Data mining didn't tell us about the new treatment," says Marks, "but it did indicate that many of our customers had high costs in this area, and that led us to look for alternatives in the medical literature."

The new drug saved one Merck-Medco client with two million employees about $10 million in prescription drug costs. Merck-Medco has since applied the program to many other customers, helping to cut their costs by an average of 10 to 15 percent with just this one change.

Overall, ExpeR$_x$t is now used by 400 analysts throughout Merck-Medco, and Marks expects to find similar cost-saving alternative treatments through the use of data mining.

[Adapted from McCarthy, 1997]

internally consistent) and align the data into a meaningful framework within which data mining could be conducted. However, the effort appears to be worth it at Merck-Medco, as reported in the sidebar "Data Mining Works at Merck-Medco" (McCarthy, 1997). Data mining offers exciting possibilities for learning about customers, particularly for companies that have well-established data warehouses.

GROUP SUPPORT SYSTEMS

Group support systems (GSSs) are an important variant of DSSs in which the system is designed to support a group rather than an individual. GSSs, sometimes called group DSSs or electronic meeting systems, strive to take advantage of the power of a group to make better decisions than individuals acting alone. GSSs are a specialized type of groupware (see Chapter 5) that is specifically aimed at supporting meetings. Managers spend a lot of their time in group activity (meetings, committees, conferences); in fact, some researchers have estimated that middle managers spend 35 percent of their work week in meetings and that top managers spend 50 to 80 percent of their time in meetings. GSSs represent an attempt to make these group sessions more productive.

GroupSystems, developed at the University of Arizona (and now marketed by GroupSystems.com, formerly Ventana Corporation), is an excellent example of GSS software (Nunamaker, et al., 1991, GroupSystems.com Web site, 2003). GroupSystems customers include major corporations such as Agilent Technologies, Boeing, Ernst & Young, Lucent, and PricewaterhouseCoopers, and government organizations such as the Federal Aviation Administration, Federal Reserve Bank, U.S. Department of Education, and the U.S. Army, Navy, and Air Force. In a typical implementation (see Figure 6.2), a computer-supported meeting room is set up containing a PC for each participant, all linked by a local area network (LAN). A large public screen facilitates common viewing of information when this is desired. GroupSystems, which is installed on each machine in the network, provides computerized support for idea generation, organizing ideas, prioritizing (such as voting), and policy development (such as stakeholder identification).

Each participant in a group session (for example, a brainstorming session) has the opportunity to provide input anonymously and simultaneously via the PC keyboard. This can encourage creative thinking because no one can be ridiculed for a "stupid idea." Each idea or comment is evaluated on its merits rather than by who offered it. Similarly, in a voting session the participants will not be swayed by how someone else votes. Thus, a GSS such as GroupSystems should generate more high-quality ideas as well as decisions that truly represent the group.

Recent work in the GSS area has moved beyond support of the traditional group session. The new focus is to

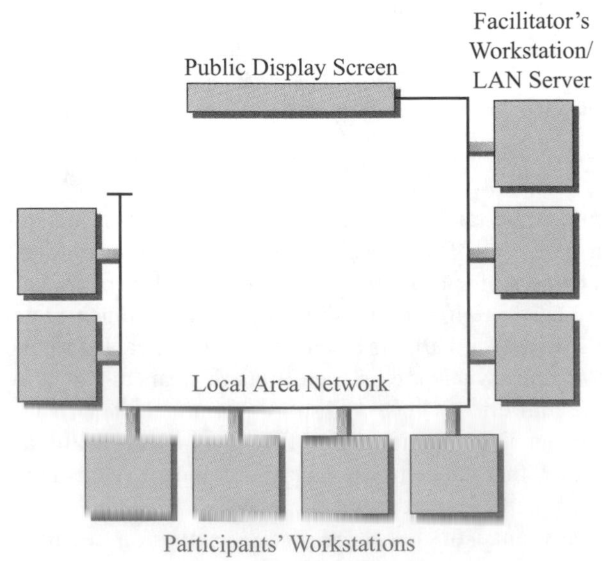

Figure 6.2 Group Support System Layout

GSS WORKS FOR EASTMAN CHEMICAL, NOKIA TELECOMMUNICATIONS

Eastman Chemical wanted to have creative problem-solving sessions to generate ideas in order to better meet customer needs, but the company found that traditional meetings were unproductive and time-consuming. Eastman installed GroupSystems, and it has paid off in a major way. In a recent GroupSystems session, 400 ideas were generated during a 2-hour session with nine people. During the same GSS session, similar ideas were combined and weighted voting was employed to pick out the top ideas for implementation. Dr. Henry Gonzales, manager of polymer technology at Eastman, stated, "We found that with GroupSystems, we had more unusual ideas, a richer pool to choose from, and we got to the point a lot faster. I did a study and calculated that the software saved 50 percent of people's time, and projected a cost savings of over $500,000 for the 12 people [who used the GSS] during a year's time. So we bought another license, and are upgrading to another facility so more people can use the technology."

Finland-based Nokia, the world's second largest cellular telephone manufacturer, had developed an environmental policy with the objective of sustainable development in accordance with the International Chamber of Commerce charter. To implement this policy, the switching platforms research and development department decided that it was necessary to integrate environmental issues into the design process. To make this happen, idea-generating workshops using GroupSystems were held for the product design experts. As an example, the initial GroupSystems workshop generated 90 pages of ideas, voting results, and survey results, providing valuable feedback on both environmental and other aspects of product design.

The environmental ideas produced by the GSS sessions were carefully examined and rewritten as check lists, which in turn became the heart of Nokia's new "Design for Environment" system. The result was the integration of "Design for Environment" into the product design at key "influencing points" in the product life cycle process, such as writing requirements and specifications.

[Adapted from GroupSystems.com Web site, 2003]

NEGOTIATION SUPPORT SYSTEMS

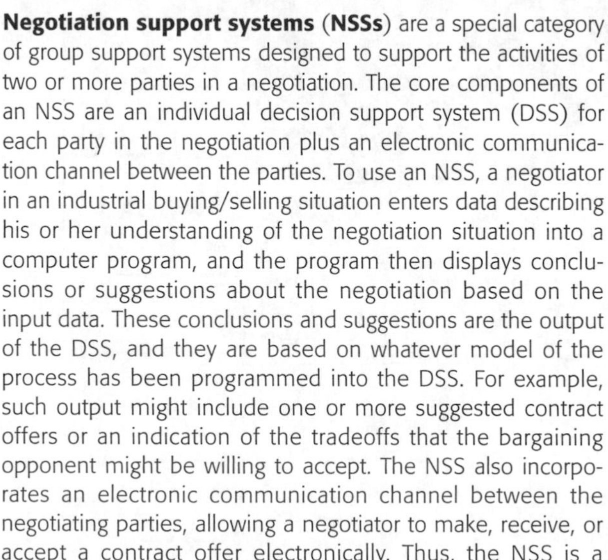

Negotiation support systems (**NSSs**) are a special category of group support systems designed to support the activities of two or more parties in a negotiation. The core components of an NSS are an individual decision support system (DSS) for each party in the negotiation plus an electronic communication channel between the parties. To use an NSS, a negotiator in an industrial buying/selling situation enters data describing his or her understanding of the negotiation situation into a computer program, and the program then displays conclusions or suggestions about the negotiation based on the input data. These conclusions and suggestions are the output of the DSS, and they are based on whatever model of the process has been programmed into the DSS. For example, such output might include one or more suggested contract offers or an indication of the tradeoffs that the bargaining opponent might be willing to accept. The NSS also incorporates an electronic communication channel between the negotiating parties, allowing a negotiator to make, receive, or accept a contract offer electronically. Thus, the NSS is a

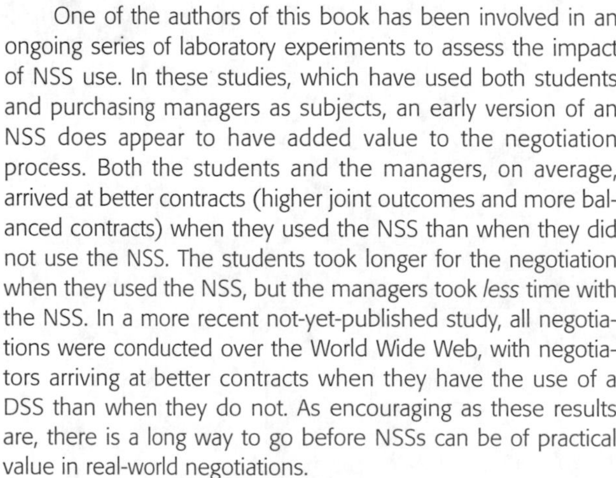

bargaining aid available to the negotiator if and when he or she chooses to use it.

One of the authors of this book has been involved in an ongoing series of laboratory experiments to assess the impact of NSS use. In these studies, which have used both students and purchasing managers as subjects, an early version of an NSS does appear to have added value to the negotiation process. Both the students and the managers, on average, arrived at better contracts (higher joint outcomes and more balanced contracts) when they used the NSS than when they did not use the NSS. The students took longer for the negotiation when they used the NSS, but the managers took *less* time with the NSS. In a more recent not-yet-published study, all negotiations were conducted over the World Wide Web, with negotiators arriving at better contracts when they have the use of a DSS than when they do not. As encouraging as these results are, there is a long way to go before NSSs can be of practical value in real-world negotiations.

[Adapted from Perkins, Hershauer, Foroughi, and Delaney, 1996]

support the work team in all its endeavors, whether the team is operating in a "same time, same place" traditional meeting or in a "different time, different place" mode—that is, as a **virtual team**. The client/server version of GroupSystems, called GroupSystems MeetingRoom, provides rich support for a "same time, same place" traditional meeting, while GroupSystems OnLine allows group members to use GroupSystems over the World Wide Web or an intranet, or both, via a standard Web browser, permitting group members to participate in the group session no matter where they are or when they are able to contribute.

GEOGRAPHIC INFORMATION SYSTEMS

Geographic information systems (GISs), spatial decision support systems (SDSSs), location-based services, geodemographics, computer mapping, and automated routing are names for a family of applications based on manipulation of relationships in space. Geographic technologies such as GISs capture, store, manipulate, display, and analyze data spatially referenced to the earth. As Figure 6.3 shows, GISs—a generic term for systems that specialize in geographic data—feature a rich user display and an interactive environment that is highly engaging to human decision makers.

Fields as diverse as natural resource management, public administration, NASA, the military, and urban planning have been using GISs for four decades. Scientists, planners, oil and gas explorers, foresters, soldiers, and mapmakers have matured this technology, developing sophisticated capabilities for creating, displaying, and manipulating geographic information. In the 1990s geographic technologies came to the attention of business users as the power of desktop computing merged with widespread access to geographic data. In the new century geographic technologies are moving into key business functions enabled by technologies such as radio frequency identification (RFID) tags, global positioning system (GPS) satellite transmitters and receivers, and spatial capabilities now included in production quality database management systems (DBMSs). More important, many firms are learning that most business data have inherent spatial meaning.

Business Adopts Geographic Technologies

Geographic technologies in business were a well-kept secret for many years; the earliest business adopters of GISs seldom talked about it because of its competitive value. Firms such as Arby's and McDonald's—whose ability to succeed depends on being in a better location than competitors—used GISs for site location to become among the first to

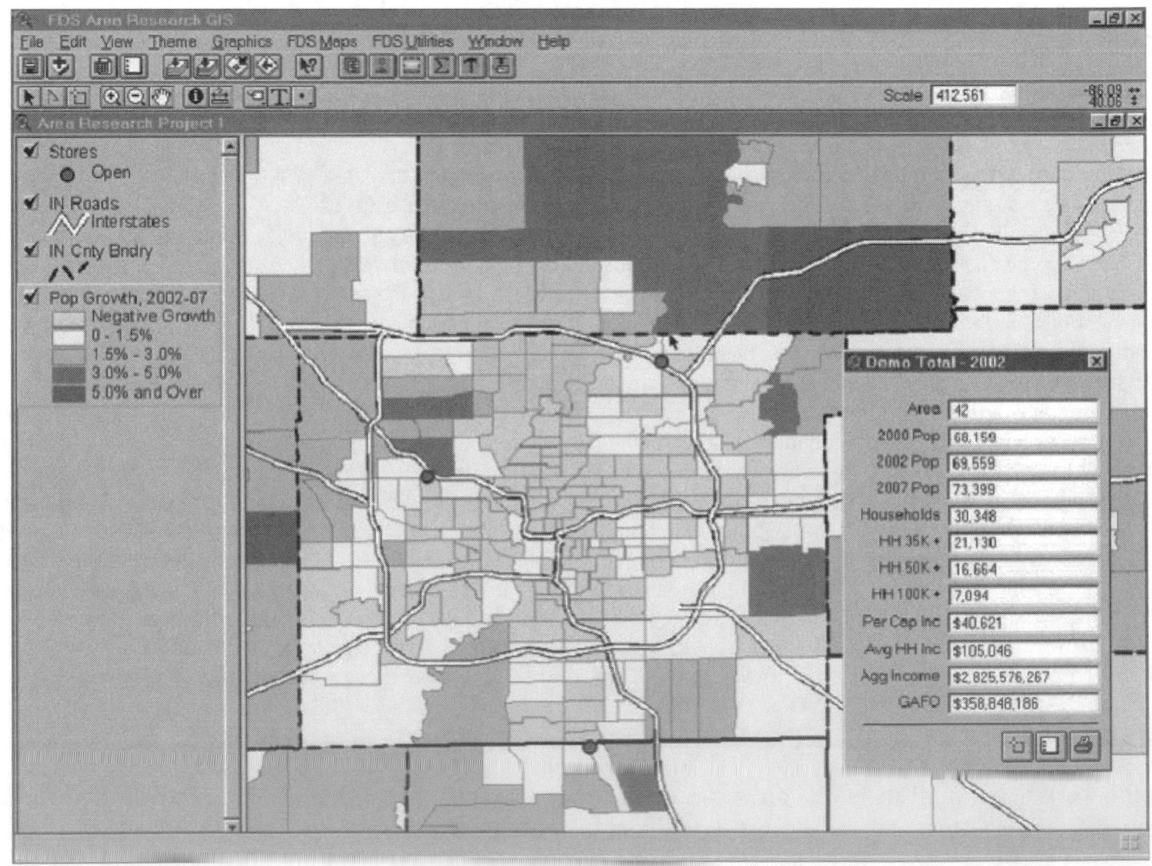

Figure 6.3 Department Store Analysis (Reprinted courtesy of Environmental Systems Research Institute, Inc. Copyright © 2003 Environmental Systems Research Institute, Inc. All rights reserved.)

recognize the business benefits of geographic technologies. Other applications include market analysis and planning, logistics and routing, environmental engineering, and the geographic pattern analysis bankers use to show that they do not "redline" areas—that is, unfairly deny loans by location. Today, many sources provide high quality geographically encoded data; few companies need to digitize maps or photographs.

As these examples illustrate, many functional areas in business are using geographic technologies such as GISs to recognize and manage their geographic dependencies. The research arm of Federated Department Stores, Inc. (which operates over 450 Macy's, Bloomingdale's, The Bon Marché, Burdines, Goldsmith's, Lazarus, and Rich's-Macy's stores in 34 states, Guam, and Puerto Rico) is an example: Beginning in the late 1990s, Federated used a GIS for simple map production and analysis. Dozens of proprietary, industry, and public data sources including internal sales information were underutilized because of the difficulty of linking them. Because many of their most experienced retail analysts had little interest in computing, the capabilities languished until a team of five analysts identified a GIS as a key integration capability (*ArcNews Online*, 2003). The resulting system came together just in time to support a major business initiative to find sites for a new type of small store in existing markets. The GIS allowed comparison between potential and actual performance in hundreds of existing markets; mapping the data clearly showed untapped potential and supported market development (see Figure 6.3).

Furthermore, location-dominated businesses such as retailing are learning how to use spatial analysis to support more than site location (see the sidebar later in this chapter entitled "Beyond Location, Location, Location"). Sears is a notable example of building from a site-location competence to bring spatial capabilities to logistics and, along the way, improve customer service for Sears, Homelife, and Brand Central stores. Home delivery "hit rate" (delivery within the window) improved from 78 percent to over 90 percent while reducing the delivery window from 4 to 2 hours, something customers truly valued. Other benefits included lower mileage per stop, increased deliveries per truck, and eventually a reduction in the number of warehouses operated (*ArcNews*, 1996).

It is hard to find an industry or government agency that does not have spatial analysis needs. Health care, transportation, telecommunication, homeland security, law enforcement, natural resources, utilities, real estate, banking, and media all need to locate people or assets, or both, in space and to predict their behavior. For example, the National Center for Health Statistics at the Centers for Disease Control and Prevention uses a GIS to improve policy making by mapping health concerns ranging from diseases to homicides (NCHS, 2004).

What's Behind Geographic Technologies

Two approaches to representing spatial data are widely used: the raster approach and the vector approach. Both types of data have been commonly managed in a data model that stores related data in layers known as coverages or themes. Recently, a new model, the geodatabase model, has emerged based on object-oriented data concepts.

Raster-based GISs rely on dividing space into small, equal-sized cells arranged in a grid. In a GIS these cells (rasters) can take on a range of values and are aware of their location relative to other cells. Like pixels on a computer screen, the size of the cells relative to the features in the landscape determines the resolution of the data. Satellite imagery and other remote sensing applications exploit the ability of the raster approach to identify patterns across large areas. Although this approach offers continuous data, objects of interest must be inferred or extracted from the rasters, making the precision of the original data collection crucial.

Raster approaches have dominated business applications in natural resources. Analysis of raster data using statistical techniques and mathematical models allows meteorologists to distinguish rain from snow and foresters to identify diseased areas within a forest. Precision farming is a recent application that uses raster-based GISs with GPS satellite receivers to plan and deliver the specific treatment (herbicide, pesticide, fertilizer) only to the part of the field that needs it. In addition to achieving cost savings by avoiding unneeded chemical use, precision farming can reduce environmental problems and improve overall soil quality and retention (*GPS World*, 1995).

Vector-based GISs have seen widespread use in public administration and utilities and are the most common approach used in business. Vector systems associate features in the landscape with either a point, a line, or a polygon. Points are often used to represent small features such as ATMs, customer addresses, power poles, or items in motion, like trucks. Lines are for linear features such as roads and rivers and can be connected in networks. Polygons represent areas and surfaces, including lakes, land parcels, and regions—such as sales territories, counties, and zip codes. The relationships between the vector elements are called their topology; topology determines whether features overlap or intersect. Vector systems can distinguish, for example, an island in a lake, two roads crossing, and customers within a 2-mile radius of a retail site. However, vector data are not continuous; the resulting overlaps and gaps between features affect presentation and analysis, and thus must be explicitly dealt with by specialized personnel.

The most common data model for both vector and raster data is the **coverage model** in which different layers or themes represent similar types of geographic features in the same area and are stacked on top of one another (see Figure 6.4). Like working with transparent map overlays, layers allow different geographic data to be seen together, and they facilitate geographic manipulation and analysis.

Questions that geographic analysis can answer include the following:

- What is adjacent to this feature?
- Which site is the nearest one?
- What is contained within this area?
- Which features does this element cross?
- How many features are within a certain distance of a site?

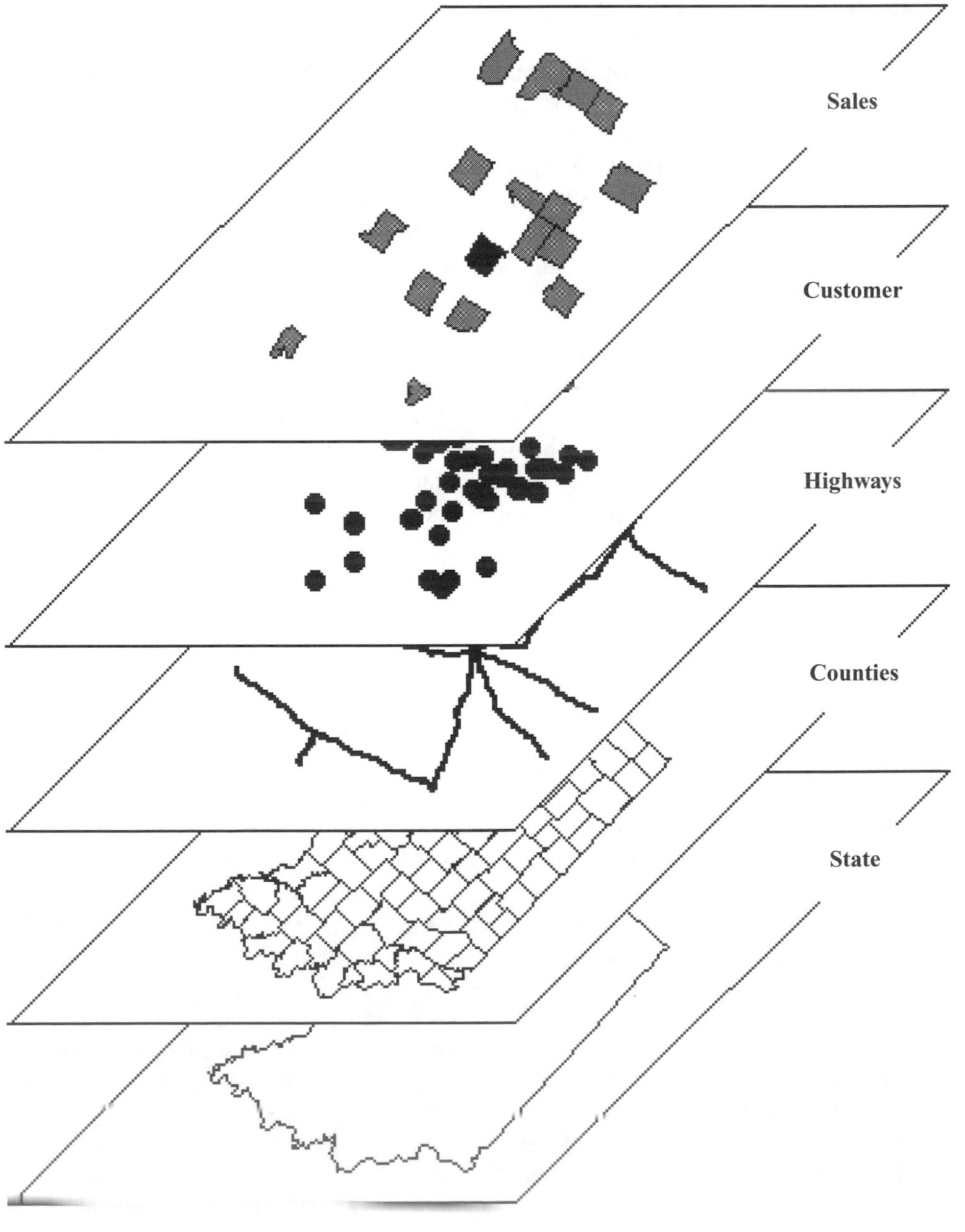

Figure 6.4 Map Layers in a GIS

Infinite zoom, panning and centering, finding the distance between two points, querying and labeling features, and changing symbols and colors on demand are basic capabilities for any GIS. Desktop GISs also provide for spatial manipulation such as intersection and union, the assignment of geographic references to addresses through geocoding, and standard query language support for interacting with attribute data. Once limited to high-end workstations, advanced GIS applications are now moving to the desktop and even the palmtop to automate sophisticated decision support tasks such as finding the shortest/fastest/safest route from A to B or grouping sales or service territories to minimize internal travel distance, equalize potential, or omit the fewest prospects.

Although the coverage data model facilitates incorporation of data from different sources into a single map for analysis and presentation, it is limited in its ability to relate objects to each other or to link objects in the system by their behavior in the world. A new model, called the **geodatabase model**, draws on object-oriented database concepts, which do not require the spatial data to be stored in separate indexes from their attributes (as vector data require) or that all items in the database be the same size (as raster data require) (Zeiler, 1999). In the geodatabase model, a feature such as a land parcel is defined not just by spatial references but by business rules which might specify its relationship to other objects such as adjacent parcels (e.g., "has at least one contiguous boundary"), owners ("has only one"), or administrative units ("is in only one fire district"). Further, this approach results in fewer problems with data accuracy while accommodating raster, vector, surface, address, coordinate, and other spatial data in one database.

Issues for Information Systems

Business applications of GISs are often initially introduced into a company to support a single user such as a market researcher. However, the power of GISs cannot be contained, and soon it spreads within and across groups, as we see with the Sears story above. Few IS organizations are in a position to develop a geographic application from scratch, but thanks to the maturity of GIS tools, this is seldom necessary. Desktop geographic systems contain scripting languages and support application program interfaces with popular desktop software packages as well as map object libraries (such as MapObjects from ESRI and MapX from MapInfo Corp.) and Internet-based interactive mapping application packages (such as Microsoft Corp.'s MapPoint Web Service).

Data sources for GISs include internal sources such as customer databases and warehouse locations and external ones such as street networks and advertising media market maps purchased from data vendors. Both new users and IS personnel are often unfamiliar with cost and quality issues for geographic data. For example, although geographic files for zip codes are often included at no additional cost in packaged desktop GIS software, the U.S. Postal Service updates zip codes on an ongoing basis, resulting in a decay in the accuracy of existing data sources. Additional issues emerge when geographic data are needed for an area outside the United States; if the data are available, they might be less accurate, more difficult to obtain, and more expensive.

Vendors for geographic technologies are seldom household words in IS; major players include Environmental Systems Research Institute (ESRI), MapInfo, AutoCAD, Microsoft, Tactician, and Intergraph Corp. GISs are increasingly integrated and integratable—map-enabled Web sites, which were an advanced technology a few years ago, are now available as an add-in using eXtensible Markup Language (XML) and .NET. Ongoing developments in geographic technologies include

- more advanced graphics, particularly three-dimensional and dynamic modeling to simulate movement through time and space, such as the path of a hurricane
- geography in your hand—the continued proliferation of spatial technologies into handheld devices for consumer use in location-based services
- linking spatial capability with wireless capability—not just access to data whenever you need it, but deployment and redeployment of the right assets—both human and nonhuman—to the right place
- radio frequency identification (RFID) technologies, which are dropping in cost and spurring new applications of spatial location to inexpensive objects, even individual garments and consumer products
- use of spatial technologies to tame out-of-control data warehouses and point-of-sale (POS) data (see the sidebar entitled "Beyond Location, Location, Location")

EXECUTIVE INFORMATION SYSTEMS/BUSINESS INTELLIGENCE SYSTEMS

The key concept behind an **executive information system (EIS)** is that such a system delivers online current information about business conditions in an aggregate form easily accessible to senior executives and other managers. An EIS is designed to be used directly by these managers without the assistance of intermediaries.

BEYOND LOCATION, LOCATION, LOCATION— GISs AND RETAILER LOYALTY CARD PROGRAMS

Not surprisingly, retailing has been one of the first business sectors to embrace GISs (e.g., Baker and Baker, 1993). Recently, retailers have come to see how geographically-enabled tools can help build traffic at existing stores (not just locate new ones) while taming the large volumes of data collected via point-of-sale (POS) systems. Researchers at the University of Alabama found distinct spatial patterns in the adoption of a customer loyalty card program for a major national retailer (disguised at the request of the firm). GIS made quick work out of address matching to analyze the first year's shopping behavior for nearly 18,000 loyalty program customers in a large Midwestern U.S. city, seamlessly incorporated census data on 300,000 people in the market area, and even determined the influence of billboard locations. Key insights that could come only from GIS-enabled spatial analysis include:

- Close proximity (living within 0.6 mile) to an innovator—someone adopting in the first 2 days—increased by 13.2 percent the chances you would join the program during the first year.
- Of course, distance from home to the store matters, but GIS shows that the distance effect was much stronger than expected. For each mile away from the store you live, you are 13.4 percent less likely to join the loyalty card program.
- Billboard locations were crucial. Nonadopters were, on average, 5.1 miles away from a billboard (compared to 2.5 miles for first-week adopters); even within a 3-mile ring of the store, nonadopters live farther from the nearest billboard than adopters.

People are always someplace in space, whether at home, working, shopping, or traveling. Retailers who understand the importance of location are exploiting the power of spatial analysis to make more effective decisions not just about store location, but about the spatial effect of different marketing innovations and strategies.

[Adapted from Allaway, Murphy, and Berkowitz, 2004]

An EIS uses state-of-the-art graphics, communications, and data storage methods to provide the executive easy online access to current information about the status of the organization.

Dating only to the late 1980s in most cases, EISs represent the first real attempt to deliver relevant summary information to management in online form. Originally, EISs were developed for just the two or three top executive levels in the firm, but that caused many problems of data disparity between the layers of management. The most important internal data—dealing with suppliers, production, and customers—are generated under the control of lower-level managers, and they need to know what is being reported higher up in the organization. As a result, today the user base in most companies has been broadened to encompass all levels of management in the firm—and sometimes even managers in customer and supplier organizations.

EISs employ transaction data that have been filtered and summarized into a form useful for the executives in the organization. In addition, many successful EISs incorporate qualitative data such as competitive information, assessments, and insights. This emphasis on competitive information has become so important in the last few years that many organizations now call their EISs **business intelligence systems** or **competitive intelligence systems** (see the sidebar entitled "Global Competitive Intelligence at Dow AgroSciences"). In summary, an EIS is a hands-on tool that focuses, filters, and organizes an executive's information so he or she can make more effective use of it.

Let us take Geac Performance Management (formerly Comshare MPC) as an example of a software platform for developing an EIS/business intelligence system. Geac Performance Management has its roots in an earlier product named Commander EIS, but it has now moved beyond a relatively simple EIS that summarizes data for top managers to a full-blown management planning and control system. Geac Performance Management is a client/server and intranet-based software tool consisting of a number of modules to monitor, measure, and manage business performance. Available modules include strategy management, planning, budgeting, financial consolidation, forecasting, and management reporting and analysis. If additional EIS/business intelligence features are desired, a companion product from Geac named Comshare Decision can be used to develop customized business intelligence, decision support, and OLAP applications as part of a comprehensive EIS. The client for Geac Performance Management is simply a Web browser.

Geac Performance Management permits customization of a large number of easy-to-use and easy-to-interpret displays to present key information to managers; the software package allows business users to view information in whatever way makes sense to them, including charts, graphs, maps, spreadsheets, ad hoc queries and calculations, and even proactive personal alerts when a specified condition occurs. In addition, it provides exception monitoring, an intelligent "drill-down" capability to identify relevant detailed information, multiple business perspectives (such

GLOBAL COMPETITIVE INTELLIGENCE AT DOW AGROSCIENCES

"Have you heard the latest about Monsanto? Can you believe the recent program Bayer launched? Rumors, news, and updates on competitors are everywhere. Yet how do we make sense of it all and stay focused on the information that really matters? Thanks to the newly launched Global Competitive Intelligence (GCI) Web site, all Dow AgroSciences employees can now efficiently learn competitive information while sharing what they hear in the marketplace." These lines begin an internal newsletter article that announced GCI to Dow AgroSciences employees in 1999.

In 1997, Dow AgroSciences management set an objective of establishing competitive intelligence as part of its company's culture. Eighteen months prior to this decision, two independent "skunk works" projects had yielded positive business results. The skunk works approaches were simple. One involved establishing Hypertext Markup Language (HTML) pages posted to a Web site on the company's intranet, where competitive information was posted and accessible by password. The other approach involved assigning an individual within each business unit as a competitive intelligence "focal point." Competitive information was fed to these focal points, who then distributed the information to all other focal points by e-mail, who in turn distributed information to sales and marketing personnel where appropriate.

Based on the business benefits realized from these early approaches, competitive intelligence was established as a global center of expertise within Dow AgroSciences. The result was the Global Competitive Intelligence (GCI) system. GCI is an intranet-based system that utilizes an Oracle database and is supported by a network of human resources (focal points) covering global operations. The intranet interface is simple to use yet is driven by a powerful database. The system is accessible to any Dow AgroSciences employee throughout the globe via the company's intranet. Currently, four levels of access have been built into the database. Level 1, which includes public information about the industry and competitors, is accessible to all employees who have access to the intranet. Competitive intelligence focal points and selected managers have access to additional information at Level 2, including public articles provided by a news service as well as reported competitive activities (rumors). Level 2 also includes detailed competitive profiles, updated annually. Level 3 is reserved for top management use, and Level 4 is for database administration.

The GCI system provides competitive observations and published news to permit employees to gain a clearer understanding of a competitor's strategy. Key competitive companies are profiled annually with the results of the analyses posted to dynamic pages within GCI. Information used in profiling companies includes corporate and divisional strategy assumptions, a history of business agreements, plant locations and research and development sites, product sales, financial assumptions, key personnel, and a SWOT analysis. Dow AgroSciences has integrated information from the GCI system into its business planning cycle and utilizes the analyses for licensing and acquisition activities. Through the use of the GCI system, the company has a designated network of people responsible for collecting, analyzing, and sharing competitive information with the entire organization on a global basis.

[Adapted from Fowler, 2000]

as region or product), multiple scenarios for planning (best, worst, most likely), and charting of cause/effect linkages among plan elements. Examples of Geac Performance Management displays are shown in Figure 6.5. Other leading commercial EIS products include SAS/EIS from SAS Institute, PilotWorks from Pilot Software, and Executive Dashboard from Qualitech Solutions. Commercial business intelligence platforms, which perform many of the same functions but are more narrowly focused than the EIS products, include Business Objects Enterprise 6.1, Cognos Enterprise Business Intelligence, Hyperion Performance Suite, and MicroStrategy 7i Business Intelligence Platform.

Perhaps the earliest EIS described in print is the management information and decision support (MIDS) system at the Lockheed-Georgia Company (Houdeshel and Watson, 1987). The sponsor for MIDS was the Lockheed-Georgia president, and a special staff reporting to the vice president of finance developed the system. An evolutionary approach was used in developing MIDS, with only a limited number of displays developed initially for a limited number of executives. For example, a display might show prospective customers for a particular type of aircraft or might graphically depict both forecast and actual sales over the past year.

Over time, more displays were developed and more executives were added to the system. The initial version of MIDS in 1979 had only 31 displays developed for fewer than a dozen senior executives. By 1985, 710 displays had been developed, 30 senior executives and 40 operating managers were using the system, and the mean number of displays viewed per user per day was up to 5.5. Many factors had to come together for MIDS to be successful, but perhaps the most important was that the system delivered the information (based on quantitative and qualitative data) that senior executives needed for them and their company to be successful.

More recently, EISs have been created and used successfully in many other large companies such as Phillips Petroleum, Dun & Bradstreet Software, Coca-Cola Company,

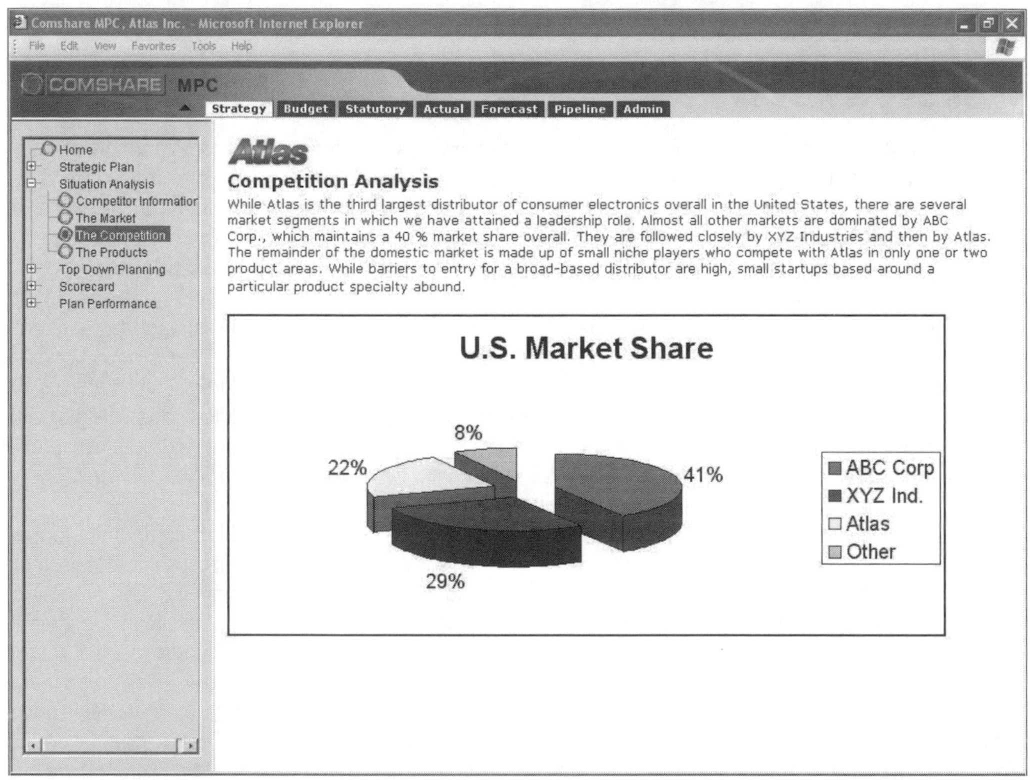

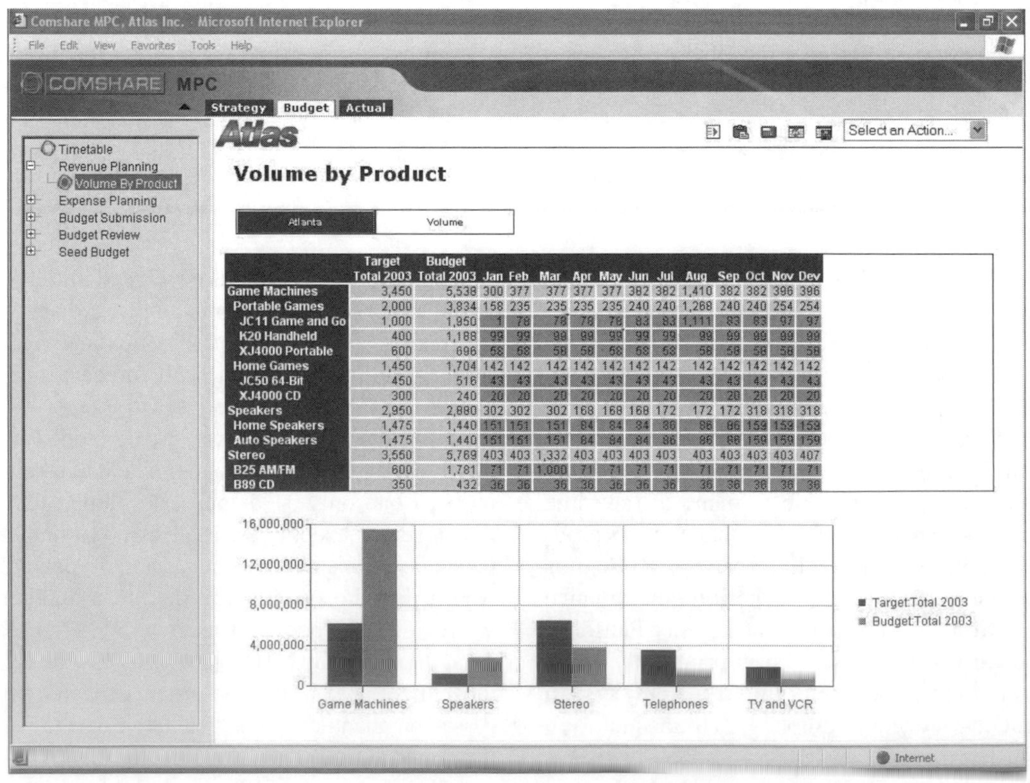

	Target Total 2003	Budget Total 2003	Jan	Feb	Mar	Apr	May	Jun	Jul	Aug	Sep	Oct	Nov	Dev
Game Machines	3,450	5,538	300	377	377	377	377	382	382	1,410	382	382	396	396
Portable Games	2,000	3,834	158	235	235	235	235	240	240	1,268	240	240	254	254
JC11 Game and Go	1,000	1,950	1	78	78	78	78	83	83	1,111	83	83	97	97
K20 Handheld	400	1,188	99	99	99	99	99	99	99	99	99	99	99	99
XJ4000 Portable	600	696	58	58	58	58	58	58	58	58	58	58	58	58
Home Games	1,450	1,704	142	142	142	142	142	142	142	142	142	142	142	142
JC50 64-Bit	450	516	43	43	43	43	43	43	43	43	43	43	43	43
XJ4000 CD	300	240	20	20	20	20	20	20	20	20	20	20	20	20
Speakers	2,950	2,880	302	302	302	168	168	168	172	172	172	318	318	318
Home Speakers	1,475	1,440	151	151	151	84	84	84	86	86	86	159	159	159
Auto Speakers	1,475	1,440	151	151	151	84	84	84	86	86	86	159	159	159
Stereo	3,550	5,769	403	403	1,332	403	403	403	403	403	403	403	403	407
B25 AM/FM	600	1,781	71	71	1,000	71	71	71	71	71	71	71	71	71
B89 CD	350	432	36	36	36	36	36	36	36	36	36	36	36	36

Figure 6.5 Example Geac Performance Management Displays (Courtesy of Geac Computer Corporation Limited. Copyright © 2003 Geac Computer Corporation Limited.).

Fisher-Price, Conoco, Inc., and CIGNA Corporation. The following paragraphs focus on four other companies that have recently installed EISs.

Based in Calgary, Alberta, Petro-Canada is a leader in the Canadian petroleum industry. Petro-Canada's oil and gas division has recently used Comshare Decision to create an integrated information system with easier, more consistent, and timely access to information for business decision-making processes—an EIS. Petro-Canada calls the new system "The Dashboard Project," which means having the key performance measures and analytical data available for view on a dashboard so that managers can look forward through the "windshield of opportunity." By using Comshare Decision's integrated solution for analysis and performance measurement, all levels of decision makers have access to the same numbers and views and have confidence that the data are current, correct, and verifiable. The new system provides a single user interface for all required information in an intuitive, flexible manner, including executive views, graphs, charts, drill-down capabilities, alarms, and alerts. Furthermore, the data visualization capabilities let decision makers have the data presented in the way that makes most sense for them (*DM Review*, 2000).

Domino's Pizza, Inc., with retail sales exceeding $3 billion per year, has also gone with the Comshare Decision approach to developing an EIS. "The rich functionality of the Web interface will allow us to provide consistent delivery whether the user is at our headquarters, in one of our regional offices, in our international offices, or on the road," states George Azrak, vice president of information systems development at Domino's Pizza. "Comshare gives us a lot of flexibility to tailor the system for an executive, middle manager, heavy-duty analyst, and even a user who is just looking for some packaged information—we can serve all our users. And the data visualization techniques for detecting hidden problems in operational data are a big hit with our users" (Geac Web site, 2003).

Dean Health System, a Madison, Wisconsin-based health care organization, originally used Comshare Decision to develop an EIS to provide its geographically diverse, multispecialty clinics with the ability to carry out detailed analysis and reporting at the local level. In 2003, Dean Health System took a further step by using the Geac Performance Management budgeting module to integrate and improve its budgeting process enterprise-wide. According to Ron Thomas, decision support administrator at Dean Health System, the enhanced EIS "will empower our departmental directors with immediate access to information they need to be accountable for the success of their operations." Krispy Kreme Doughnut Corporation, which produces more than 2.7 billion doughnuts a year, implemented all modules of Geac Performance Management to create its comprehensive EIS. "Formerly, we used a combination of financial reporting and consolidation software and spreadsheets," said Frank Hood, CIO of Krispy Kreme. "Those systems and processes left little time for analysis of the information, were not tightly integrated to many of our data stores, and were just too cumbersome and fragmented for us to ever realize the benefits of a true performance management system. We believe the increase in integration combined with gains in analytical reporting efficiency [through the use of Geac Performance Management] will translate into improvements in operational and management effectiveness" (Geac Web site, 2003).

KNOWLEDGE MANAGEMENT SYSTEMS

Knowledge management systems (KMSs) are systems that enable individuals and organizations to enhance learning, improve performance, and, hopefully, produce long-term sustainable competitive advantage. Simply stated, a KMS is a system for managing organizational knowledge. A KMS may be designed to support "communities of practice" focusing on different key knowledge areas; in this case the KMS enables connections from people to people (e.g., expert directories), people to knowledge (e.g., knowledge repositories), and people to tools (e.g., community calendars, discussion forums). On the other hand, a KMS may consist of elaborate structuring of knowledge content (e.g., taxonomies), carefully packaged and disseminated to people. In the former case, a KMS is all about technology, while in the latter case the technology is necessary but not central. We will return to these different types of KMSs later in this section.

KMSs use various hardware and software applications to facilitate and support **knowledge management (KM)** activities. What then is KM? KM is a set of management practices that is practical and action-oriented. In other words, KM involves the strategies and processes of identifying, creating, capturing, organizing, transferring, and leveraging knowledge to help individuals and firms compete (O'Dell and Grayson, 1998). KM is concerned with behavior changes to reflect new knowledge and insights. KM is not about relying on technology to improve processes; rather, KM relies on recognizing the knowledge held by individuals and the firm. Therefore, a KMS is the technology or vehicle that facilitates the sharing and transferring of knowledge for the purpose of disseminating and reusing valuable knowledge that, once applied, enhances learning and improves performance.

Why has KMS received so much attention recently, and why are so many projects labeled KMS projects? There are two explanations. First, one trigger leading to the development of KM and KMS is related to firm valuation. For example, Microsoft's net value was estimated by examining its market value based on stock prices minus net assets. The enormous difference was attributed to the knowledge held by individuals and the organization (e.g., routines, best practices). In a similar time frame, "knowledge assets" began to appear on a few firms' balance sheets in their annual reports. Hence, there is a growing awareness and consensus that "knowledge" will enable firms to differentiate themselves from others and to compete effectively in the marketplace.

Second, tangible benefits accrue from implementing KM and KMS initiatives. Although the benefits are specific to a given firm, there are both *operational improvements* and *market improvements*. Operational improvements focus on internal activities and include cost savings (e.g., faster and better dissemination of knowledge), efficient processes (e.g., best practices), change management processes (e.g., behavior changes), and knowledge reuse (e.g., high quality standards). In contrast, market improvements focus on external activities such as performance (e.g., increased sales), cost savings (e.g., lower costs of products and services), and customer satisfaction.

The goal of a KMS is to tap into the knowledge of the individual and the organization and disseminate it throughout the firm to derive operational and market improvements. Furthermore, a KMS is different from other systems because it considers the content contained within the system—that is, the system is only as good as what is in it! Based on a study of more than two dozen successful KMSs recently implemented in various firms, there are three KMS characteristics that need to be considered in describing a KMS: First, the extent to which there is formal management and control of the KMS; second, the focus of the KM processes, such as knowledge creation, capture, organization and packaging, access, search and dissemination, and application; and third, the extent to which reusability of knowledge is considered (e.g., the 80-20 rule, or 20 percent of the knowledge content that potentially could be contained in a KMS is likely to be of most value to 80 percent of the users) (Dennis and Vessey, 2003).

A KMS might have very little formal management and control, as in the case of "communities of practice" (COPs). Designed for individuals with similar interests, a COP KMS provides a vehicle to allow members of such a community to exchange ideas, tips, and other knowledge that might be valuable to the members of the community. There is no formal management or control of such a KMS; rather, the members are responsible for validating and structuring their knowledge for use within the KMS. Each member of the COP is responsible for the knowledge content, with a great likelihood that such knowledge will be applicable to only a few members. In other words, there is very little, if any, organizing and packaging of knowledge, making the search and applicability even more difficult. Hopefully, there will be occasions where a single item of knowledge content will be important to many members of the COP, although these occasions might be few in number.

In contrast, a KMS might have extensive formal management and control. There might be a KM team to oversee the process of validating the knowledge prior to dissemination. Such a team provides structure, organization, and packaging for how knowledge is to be presented to the users. These dedicated resources ensure that knowledge content entered into the KMS has been thoroughly examined and that it will meet the 80-20 rule.

This discussion does not imply that a KMS must be characterized as binary—that is, having either little or extensive formal management and control, knowledge processing, or knowledge reusability. Rather, there is a spectrum of KMSs that are designed to meet the specific needs of a given firm. In the case of a COP KMS, it is not clear whether the focus is either operational or market improvements. On the other hand, the KM team approach attempts to accomplish both operational and market improvements. Although KMSs are still growing with much room for advancement, many firms observe their KMS evolving from one form to another as they learn from their experience and as their strategic needs and resources change. Such evolution suggests that firms are enjoying the benefits accrued from tapping into their employees' and organizational knowledge. Moreover, they find a strategic need to continue their efforts to unveil the hidden treasures within and outside their organizational boundaries.

Two Recent KMS Initiatives within a Pharmaceutical Firm

Corporate KMS. A KM team was formed to develop an organization-wide KMS serving multiple communities of practice. The operation of a community of practice involves a combination of software and processes. Each community has a designated coordinator whose job is to ensure that the community thrives (some communities have two or three coordinators). The coordinators are volunteers and receive no extra compensation; however, they do tend to become highly visible members of their communities. The coordinator performs many specific functions such as welcoming new members, developing and maintaining standards of conduct and standards for knowledge within the community, maintaining the community calendar, monitoring the discussion forums, ensuring the knowledge in the community is appropriate, serving as the primary point of contact and external ambassador for the community, and many other items.

The portal software used to support the communities of practice provides approximately 150 tools of which only a handful are regularly used. The three most commonly used tools are the discussion forum, tips, and calendar. As the name suggests, the discussion forum is a tool that enables question-and-answer discussions among members of the community. Any member of the community can pose a question or a request in the discussion forum, which is available to all members. Likewise, all members can respond to the items posted in the discussion. Each discussion item in the forum is typically started as its own thread and there are often two or three active discussion threads, depending on the community's size. The community's coordinator typically reviews the items in the discussion forum and archives older discussions. Sometimes the coordinator will decide that a particular item is useful and relevant over the long term and should be moved to the tips area. In that case the coordinator or the contributors to the discussion will prepare a more formal version to be stored in the tips area.

The tips tool enables any member of the community to write a short entry that documents some sort of best practice advice that the contributor believes might be of interest to the community as a whole. The full text of all tips is searchable, so the members of the community can find tips of interest.

The coordinator maintains the community calendar. Members of the community typically e-mail the coordinator with suggested calendar items, which the coordinator posts. Typical calendar items include face-to-face meetings held by part or all of the community, seminars and workshops offered by members of the community, and more formal presentations likely to be of interest to the community.

Field Sales KMS. A different KM team was formed to lead the development of the field sales KMS. Unlike the corporate KMS, this KM team's mission was to design and build *both* the content and the structure of the KMS. Therefore, a knowledge taxonomy was developed so that knowledge about each of the drugs sold by the firm was organized separately. Sales representatives would have access to knowledge only about the drugs they sold.

Sales operations and brand management would develop initial drafts of the knowledge content, which they would provide to the KM team. The KM team would format the documents and put them in the proper locations in the KMS according to the taxonomy. Although the system was intended to be the primary knowledge repository used by the field sales representatives and the sales managers, all knowledge communication with the field sales representatives was expected to be conducted through the field sales KMS. Instead of mailing paper marketing materials and advisories, for example, managers would now create them in Word and PowerPoint and post them into the field sales KMS.

The KM team also realized that it was important to enable the field sales representatives themselves to contribute sales tips and practical advice for use by other sales representatives. However, because of strict government regulatory control over communication with the physicians, all such tips needed first to be approved by the firm's legal department. A formal four-step process was therefore developed for validating all content sent in from the field sales representatives. Tips were first vetted by the KM team itself to make sure the content was coherent and complete. Next, the tip was submitted to the legal group to ensure that the content was consistent with all rules, regulations, and good promotional practice guidelines. Then the tip was sent to the brand management team to ensure that it was consistent with the marketing strategy for the drug. Next, the tip was sent to the sales operations group for peer review by a panel of five sales representatives to ensure the contribution had real value. Finally, once the tip had been approved, it was entered into the field sales KMS. Although this sounds like a lengthy process, most tips were processed within 2 weeks of receipt. Field sales representatives were rewarded by receiving sales points for each tip that was ultimately accepted (these points were part of the usual commission structure received by all sales representatives; the points received for each tip were equivalent to approximately $60).

Although there were several iterations of user interfaces to best align with changing taxonomies, the knowledge structure for the current system was designed in what the team called a "T-structure," which had two distinct parts. Across the top of the "T" (and presented horizontally near the top of the Lotus Notes screen) was the general sales knowledge designed to be pertinent to all sales divisions. This contained knowledge on topics such as rules and guidelines for sales promotions, templates for sales processes, forms for sales functions, and directories with phone numbers of key experts within the U.S. business unit. Down the middle of the "T" (and presented vertically near the left edge of the Lotus Notes screen) was the division-specific knowledge, which typically pertained to drugs sold by that division. This contained information such as fundamental sales information on the drugs sold by the sales representatives, competitive analyses, results in recent drug trials, and letters from expert physicians. Tips and best practices submitted by the field sales representatives would either fit across the top or down the side of the screen depending on whether they focused on general sales knowledge or on product-specific knowledge.

ARTIFICIAL INTELLIGENCE

The idea of **artificial intelligence (AI)**, the study of how to make computers do things that are currently done better by people, is about 50 years old, but only in the last two decades have computers become powerful enough to make AI applications commercially attractive. AI research has evolved into six separate but related areas; these are natural languages, robotics, perceptive systems (vision and hearing), genetic programming (also called evolutionary design), expert systems, and neural networks.

The work in **natural languages**, primarily in computer science departments in universities and in vendor laboratories, is aimed at producing systems that translate ordinary human instructions into a language that computers can understand and execute. Robotics was considered in the previous chapter. **Perceptive systems** research involves creating machines possessing a visual and/or aural perceptual ability that affects their physical behavior. In other words, this research is aimed at creating robots that can "see" or "hear" and react to what they see or hear. With **genetic programming** or **evolutionary design**, the problem is divided into multiple segments, and solutions to these segments are linked together in different ways to breed new "child" solutions. After many generations of breeding, genetic programming might produce results superior to anything devised by a human. Genetic programming has been most useful in the design of innovative products such as a satellite support arm with a novel shape that prevents vibrations from being transmitted along the truss, and General Electric Co.'s energy-efficient halogen light bulb, which is 48 percent brighter than a standard halogen bulb (Port, 2000).

The final two branches of AI are the ones most relevant for managerial support. The **expert systems** branch is concerned with building systems that incorporate the decision-making logic of a human expert. A newer branch of AI is **neural networks**, which is named after the study of how the human nervous system works, but which in fact uses statistical analysis to recognize patterns from vast amounts of information by a process of adaptive learning. Both these branches of AI are described in more detail in the following sections.

EXPERT SYSTEMS

How does one capture the logic of an expert in a computer system? To design an expert system, a specialist known as a knowledge engineer (a specially trained systems analyst) works very closely with one or more experts in the area under study. Knowledge engineers try to learn everything they can about the way in which the expert makes decisions. If one is trying to build an expert system for estate planning, for example, the knowledge engineer works with experienced estate planners to see how they do their job. What the knowledge engineer has learned is then loaded into the computer system, in a specialized format, in a module called the knowledge base (see Figure 6.6). This knowledge base contains both the inference rules that are followed in decision making and the parameters, or facts, relevant to the decision.

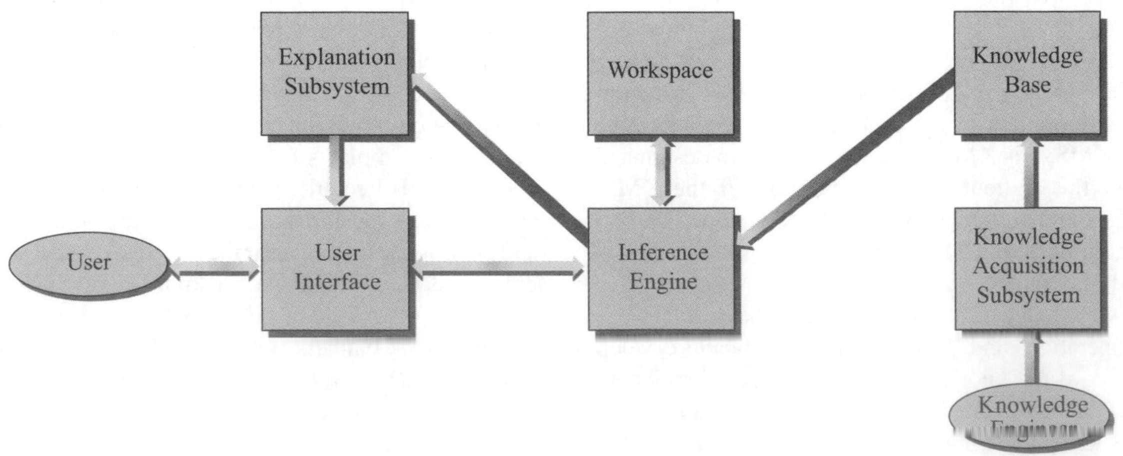

Figure 6.6 Architecture of an Expert System

The other major pieces of an expert system are the inference engine and the user interface. The inference engine is a logical framework that automatically executes a line of reasoning when supplied with the inference rules and parameters involved in the decision; thus, the same inference engine can be used for many different expert systems, each with a different knowledge base. The user interface is the module used by the end user—for example, an inexperienced estate planner. Ideally, the interface is very user-friendly. The other modules include an explanation subsystem to explain the reasoning that the system followed in arriving at a decision, a knowledge acquisition subsystem to assist the knowledge engineer in recording inference rules and parameters in the knowledge base, and a workspace for the computer to use as the decision is being made.

Obtaining an Expert System

Is it necessary to build all these pieces each time your organization wants to develop and use an expert system? Absolutely not. There are three general approaches to obtaining an expert system, and only one of them requires construction of all these pieces. First, an organization can buy a fully developed system that has been created for a specific application. For example, in the late 1980s, Syntelligence, Inc., developed an expert system called Lending Advisor to assist in making commercial lending decisions for banks and other financial institutions. Lending Advisor incorporated the many factors involved in approving or rejecting a commercial loan, and it was installed in several banks. In general, however, the circumstances leading to the desire for an expert system are unique to the organization, and in most cases this "off-the-shelf" expert system option is not viable.

Second, an organization can develop an expert system itself using an **artificial intelligence shell** (also called an **expert systems shell**). The shell, which can be purchased from a software company, provides the basic framework illustrated in Figure 6.6 and a limited but user-friendly special language with which to develop the expert system. With the basic expert system functions already in place in the shell, the system builder can concentrate on the details of the business decision being modeled and the development of the knowledge base. Third, an organization can have internal or external knowledge engineers custom-build the expert system. In this case the system is usually programmed in a special-purpose language such as Prolog or Lisp. This final approach is clearly the most expensive, and it can be justified only if the potential payoff from the expert system is quite high and no other way is possible.

Examples of Expert Systems

Perhaps the classic example of an expert system is MYCIN, which was developed at Stanford University in the mid-1970s to diagnose and prescribe treatment for meningitis and blood diseases. General Electric Co. created an expert system called CATS-1 to diagnose mechanical problems in diesel locomotives, and AT&T developed ACE to locate faults in telephone cables. Schlumberger, Ltd., an international oil company, developed an expert system named Dipmeter to give advice when a drill bit gets stuck while drilling a well. These examples and others are concerned with diagnosing problem situations and prescribing appropriate actions, because experts are not always present when a problem occurs.

Diagnosis of a different sort is made by an expert system at the American Stock Exchange that has been built to help detect insider trading on the exchange. This expert system, named Market Surveillance, is designed to support analysts in making recommendations on whether to open

EXPERT SYSTEM HELPS CAMPBELL KEEP THE SOUP STIRRING

Campbell Soup Company makes its soup in hydrostatic canned food product sterilizers, or cookers, that are over 70 feet tall and incorporate a variety of equipment. Cooker malfunctions can mean significant lost production time, which Campbell obviously tries to minimize. When Aldo Cimino, an expert at diagnosing cooker problems, announced his pending retirement, Campbell decided to "clone" the expertise of this 44-year veteran diagnostician by building an expert system. "Decades of expertise that had benefited Campbell were on the verge of walking out the door forever," said Alan Carr, Campbell's director of business systems. "Several goals were quickly determined [for the new expert system]. The expert system would have to be able to replace Aldo Cimino, and it should be useful as a training tool for production and maintenance engineers."

Campbell hired a team from Texas Instruments (TI) to create the expert system, named COOKER, using TI's Personal Consultant as the expert systems shell. The team watched Cimino perform his job and conducted extensive interviews with him over a period of several weeks; then the information provided by Cimino was captured in a series of rules placed in the knowledge base. The expert system was implemented on a PC deployed on the factory floor so that it could be quickly used by workers when problems arose. Early returns suggest that COOKER is working quite well, and that Aldo Cimino is enjoying his retirement.

[Adapted from *I/S Analyzer*, 1995]

an investigation of suspected insider trading. The relevant database of stock price activity is entered into the expert system, and the analyst responds to a series of questions from the system. The output consists of two scores—the first is the probability that an investigation should be opened and the second is the probability that an investigation should not be opened (Exsys Inc., 2003).

Earlier we mentioned that expert systems were used to assist in making commercial lending decisions as early as the 1980s. Today, over one-third of the top 100 commercial banks in the United States and Canada use FAST (Financial Analysis Support Techniques) software for credit analysis. This expert-systems-based software gives a credit analyst access to the expertise of more experienced analysts, speeding up the training process and increasing productivity. FAST also provides a complete range of traditional analytical reports on both a historical and a pro forma basis (Exsys Inc., 2003).

Expert systems often serve in an advisory role to decision makers of all kinds. For example, the IDP (individual development plan) Goal Advisor is an expert system that assists a supervisor and an employee in setting short-range and long-range employee career goals and the developmental objectives to reach these goals. Nestle Foods has developed an expert system to provide information to employees on their pension fund status. Using the expert system, an employee can conduct a private "interview" with a pension fund expert and ask what-if questions about benefits. The expert system enables the employee to make more knowledgeable personal financial planning decisions without requiring extensive personnel department consultation. EXNUT is an expert system developed by the National Peanut Research Laboratory and the U.S. Department of Agriculture to help peanut farmers manage irrigated peanut production. Based on extensive data collected from individual peanut fields throughout the growing season, EXNUT makes recommendations for irrigation, fungicide treatment, and pest management. The results are quite positive: The fields managed by EXNUT have consistently produced higher yields and high-quality peanuts using less water and less fungicide than those managed without the expert system (Exsys Inc., 2003).

Scheduling is another important area for expert systems. Expert systems currently in use include a truck routing and scheduling system that determines the sequence of stops on a route to provide the best service and a factory design system that organizes machines and operators to provide an efficient flow of materials through the factory and use the resources efficiently. As another example, General Motors created the Expert Scheduling System, or ESS, to generate viable manufacturing schedules. GM used both IntelliCorp's Knowledge Engineering Environment expert system shell and the Lisp programming language to build the system. ESS incorporates heuristics that had been developed by an experienced factory scheduler into the system, and it also links directly into GM's computer-integrated manufacturing (CIM) environment so that real-time plant information is used to generate the plant floor schedules (*I/S Analyzer*, 1995).

Some expert systems specialize in sifting through massive sets of rules or other data, sometimes called case-based reasoning. The United Nations employs an expert system called the Entitlements System to interpret the

EXPERT SYSTEMS PAYING OFF FOR SOME FIRMS

Once touted as potentially revolutionizing business operations, you don't hear much about expert systems these days, although proponents claim more enterprises than you might expect have adopted them. But can expert systems help your enterprise run leaner and smarter?

In the early days of expert systems, "there was too much technobabble that wasn't backed up by actual business cases," admitted Mike Will, director of research and development for Picodoc Corp., which develops tools for creating relatively small expert systems. Systems created with Picodoc's product, PicoXpert, have no more than 500 rules and run on the Palm handheld platform.

At a higher level are automated network-based expert systems. Sometimes these systems are built into other products, such as the network protocol analysis and monitoring developed by Network Instruments. According to Douglas Smith, president of Network Instruments, the expert component starts working after the software identifies a specific event such as a delay in data transmission. "The system examines all the streams of data," Smith explained. "It can determine, say, whether the delay is network-based or just that somebody left to go to the bathroom. It saves IT shops a lot of time."

At the high end are mainframe-based expert systems deployed by organizations such as airlines and huge shippers used for efficiently deploying equipment and crews. Will claimed that it would be exorbitantly expensive for those organizations to hire enough people to perform such ongoing analyses. Yet, deploying aircraft and crews inefficiently would result in untold losses for those companies, he claimed.

The bottom line, Will acknowledged, is that, while expert systems can make many companies operate more efficiently, they had better be ready to invest a lot of time and, in many cases, money, developing and tweaking them.

[Haskin, 2003]

complex salary regulations for all employees of the U.N. Secretariat worldwide. The pay for U.N. employees is determined by a base salary plus entitlements, and the entitlements include benefits based on location of work plus other contractual agreements. The rules and regulations for the entitlements fill three volumes of several hundred pages each. Using PowerModel software from IntelliCorp, the U.N. has built an expert system that determines and applies entitlements automatically, employing an online knowledge base containing the entitlements rules. The expert system also reassesses the entitlements whenever an employee's status changes (Baum, 1996).

NEURAL NETWORKS

Whereas expert systems try to capture the expertise of humans in a computer program, neural networks attempt to tease out meaningful patterns from vast amounts of data. Neural networks can recognize patterns too obscure for humans to detect, and they adapt as new information is received.

The key characteristic of neural networks is that they *learn*. The neural network program is originally given a set of data consisting of many variables associated with a large number of cases, or events, in which the outcomes are known. The program analyzes the data, works out all the correlations, and then selects a set of variables that are strongly correlated with particular known outcomes as the initial pattern. This initial pattern is used to try to predict the outcomes of the various cases, and these predicted results are compared to the known results. Based on this comparison, the program changes the pattern by adjusting the weights given to the variables or by changing the variables. The neural network program then repeats this process over and over, continuously adjusting the pattern in an attempt to improve its predictive ability. When no further improvement is possible from this iterative approach, the program is ready to make predictions for future cases.

This is not the end of the story. As more cases become available, these data are also fed into the neural network and the pattern is once again adjusted. The neural network learns more about cause-and-effect patterns from this additional data, and its predictive ability usually improves accordingly.

Commercial neural network programs (actually, these are shells) are available for a reasonable price, but the difficult part of building a neural network application is data collection and data maintenance. Still, a growing number of applications are being deployed. Neural networks are typically used either to predict or categorize, but to do so in an inductive manner rather than deductively. Table 6.2 lists examples of current uses of neural networks.

Here are some examples of neural networks. BankAmerica uses a neural network to evaluate commercial loan applications. American Express uses a neural system to read handwriting on credit card slips. The state of Wyoming uses a neural system to read hand-printed numbers on tax forms. Oil giants Arco and ChevronTexaco are using neural networks to help pinpoint oil and gas deposits below the Earth's surface. Mellon Bank installed a neural network credit card fraud detection system. When a credit card is swiped through the card reader in a store, the transaction is sent to Mellon's neural system. By analyzing the type of transaction, the amount spent, the time of day, and other data, the neural network makes a fraud prediction in 45 seconds or less and either denies the transaction or feeds the predictive score to a human analyst who makes the final decision. Spiegel Catalog, Inc., which depends on catalogs to generate sales for its mail-order business, uses a neural network as a way of pruning its mailing list to eliminate those who are unlikely to order from Spiegel again.

Neural networks are also being used to manage portfolios. Deere & Company's pension fund has been using neural networks to manage its portfolio of over $100 million since 1993. The fund monitors a pool of 1,000 U.S. stocks on a weekly basis. For each stock a neural network models the future performance of the stock as a function of the stock's exposure to 40 fundamental and technical factors and provides an estimate of its weekly price change. The company then selects a portfolio of the top 100 stocks and allocates the fund proportionately based on predicted

Table 6.2 Uses of Neural Networks

Categorization	Prediction/Forecasting
Credit rating and risk assessment	Share price forecast
Insurance risk evaluation	Commodity price forecast
Fraud detection	Economic indicator predictions
Insider trading detection	Process control
Direct mail profiling	Weather prediction
Machinery defect diagnosis	Future drug performance
Character recognition	Production requirements
Medical diagnosis	
Bacteria identification	

LOAN STAR

Household Financial Corporation is a $10 billion consumer finance business with headquarters in Prospect Heights, Illinois, and 1,400 branch offices in 46 states. In the late 1990s, Household developed an object-oriented software system named Vision to integrate all phases of the consumer lending process; Vision also connects to an intelligent underwriting system that returns lending decisions in minutes rather than hours or days. Built into the Vision system are neural network components that help Household make smarter decisions about its customers.

For instance, say a credit card holder calls, irate about a late fee. He's not a profitable customer for the company; he carries a single card with little or no balance and has spurned Household offers for credit insurance products and equity loans. Why should the Household service rep cancel the late fee? Vision knows why. The system "takes into consideration the potential lifetime value of the customer," says Ken Harvey, now Household's chief information officer.

Turns out this customer took out a school loan six years ago and a small auto finance deal for a used car three years ago from another company. His modest income has gone up significantly two years running. Considering these variables, Vision can recognize this late fee as a first offense by a recent college graduate who handles his finances well and may be in the market for significant new loans in the next year. Vision authorizes the service rep to waive the fee. Then the system can prompt the rep with suggestive selling for this now-happy customer—does he know that Household can pay off that old car loan and offer attractive terms on a loan for a newer vehicle?

Taken in sum, the system ties the company more closely to existing and prospective customers. Loan approvals are faster, sales proposals more targeted, and customer service more responsive. Cutting out the waiting game and creating more desirable products helps Household forge a customer intimacy that ultimately translates to profits, which in today's stock-market-driven environment is the ultimate in enterprise value.

[Slater, 2000]

returns. The annual pension fund return has been well in excess of industry benchmarks (NeuroDimension, 2000).

Another use of neural networks is in targeted marketing, where marketing campaigns are targeted to potential customers who have the same attributes that resulted in sales for previous campaigns. A security system has been developed that uses neural technology to recognize a person's face to grant that person access to a secured area. Washington, D.C.-based start-up Psynapse has based its network intrusion protection system named Checkmate on a neural network; Checkmate conducts a real-time assessment of each visitor to a network, and if it notes behavior that indicates an attempted security breach, it automatically terminates the intruder's access (Orzech, 2002).

Neural networks have also been used to forecast the number of admissions to a hospital on a given day and to discover relationships among the admissions data that are not otherwise visible. In this study neural networks produced forecasts of the same overall quality as traditional methods, but in less than half the time. Furthermore, neural networks were able to prove the value of a specific medical treatment through analysis of the admissions data; this treatment had long been claimed to be beneficial but proving the benefit had been difficult until neural networks came along (Z Solutions, 2003).

In the late 1980s and 1990s, expert system and neural network applications received a great deal of hype in the popular press. The AI applications were supposedly going to solve many of the decision problems faced by managers. Today, industry has adopted a more realistic view of AI applications: AI is not a panacea, but there are a significant number of potentially valuable applications for AI techniques. Each potential application must be carefully evaluated. The result of these careful evaluations has been a steady growth, but not an explosion, in the development and use of expert systems and neural networks to help businesses cope with problem situations and make better and more consistent decisions.

VIRTUAL REALITY

Virtual reality is a fascinating application area with rapidly growing importance. **Virtual reality**, or **VR**, refers to the use of computer-based systems to create an environment that seems real to one or more senses (usually including sight) of the human user or users. The ultimate example of VR is the holodeck aboard the U.S.S. Enterprise on *Star Trek: The Next Generation*, where Data can be Sherlock Holmes in a realistic setting with realistic characters and where Jean-Luc Picard can play the role of a hard-boiled private eye in the early twentieth century.

VR exists today, but with nowhere near the reality of the Enterprise's holodeck. You might have played a video game where you don a head-mounted computer display and a glove to get directly into the action. The use of VR in a non-entertainment setting falls primarily into three categories—training, design, and marketing. Training examples will be presented first, followed by examples of the use of VR in design and in marketing.

The U.S. Army uses VR to train tank crews. Through multiple large video screens and sound, the soldiers are seemingly placed inside a tank rolling across the Iraqi desert, and they have to react as if they were in a real tank battle. In the field of medicine, medical students are learning through collaboration and trial-and-error on virtual cadavers, which is much less expensive than using actual bodies. As an example, researchers have created 3-D animations of hematomas—bleeding between the skull and brain—of virtual patients who have suffered head damage in an automobile accident. Using a virtual-reality head-mounted display and virtual-reality gloves, students work together to diagnose and treat the patient (Hulme, 2002).

Amoco has developed a PC-based VR system, called "truck driVR," for use in training its drivers. Amoco believed that the VR system was a cost-effective way of testing how well its 12,000 drivers performed under a variety of hazardous driving conditions. This immersive VR system, which cost approximately $50,000 to develop, employs a helmet that holds the visual and auditory displays and completely immerses the user in the virtual world. To make truck driVR realistic, multiple views are provided to the user, including views of both left and right rear-view mirrors that are displayed only when the user moves his or her head to the left or right (*I/S Analyzer*, 1997).

Duracell also employs VR for training. Duracell was installing new equipment to manufacture a new line of rechargeable batteries, and the company needed to train its factory personnel on the new equipment in a safe and cost-effective manner. The Duracell system, which is nonimmersive (no helmet or special glasses), also runs on a PC and incorporates a parts familiarization module, an operations module, and a troubleshooting module. With this system the user is able to completely explore the new piece of equipment within the desktop virtual world. "With the use of that special mouse [a Magellan space mouse], the user can walk around it [the equipment], they can get underneath it, they can get on top of it," says Neil Silverstein, a training manager at Duracell. "They can fly into the smallest crevices of the machine, something that you can never do in the real world because you might lose a finger." Duracell is quite pleased with the results. The training is standardized and completely safe, and there is no need for on-the-job training (*I/S Analyzer*, 1997).

VR use in training might become even more prominent as the result of a project called Virtual Environments for Training, which is a collaboration among the Center for Advanced Research in Technology for Education, the Lockheed Martin Space Systems Advanced Technology Center, and the University of Southern California Behavioral Technology Laboratories. The purpose of this project is to develop training systems that integrate VR with a tutoring system that uses natural dialogue and "learns." For example, an intelligent martial arts tutor would learn the student's fighting style and thus become increasingly difficult for the student to beat. The intelligent tutor would also know what the student has already learned and adjust the training accordingly. The training would take place within an immersive virtual environment, using head-mounted displays and input devices such as 3-D mice and data gloves (Wohl, 2000).

Superscape Inc. specializes in the creation of innovative, high-quality, interactive 3-D applications. Superscape created interactive training materials that visualize a Ford Motor Company factory floor, including forklift trucks, to make plant workers more aware of the potential hazards on the factory floor. The company teamed with Discovery.com to build an application named "Inside the space station," which permits online PC users to control the 3-D space station environment, including docking the space shuttle, rotating solar panels, and manipulating mechanical arms. Superscape has also been heavily involved in the development of 3-D games, including the Harry Potter game for LEGO. The company's Swerve technology has been developed to create games for wireless devices, including the newer mobile phones. Among the games developed using Superscape Swerve technology are MotoGP, Jet Fighter, Astrosmash 3D, Chesscapade, and Speedboat Race (Superscape, 2003).

On the design side, several automobile manufacturers have used VR to assist in the design of automobiles. With this system, an automotive engineer—usually wearing special glasses and a special glove to be able to interact with the system—is able to sit in the driver's seat of a future automobile. The engineer turns the steering wheel and uses buttons and knobs as though he or she were in a real car. By letting the engineer get the feel of this future car, the manufacturer hopes that problems in the dashboard and controls design can be corrected before actual—and expensive—prototypes are even built.

An air conditioning/furnace manufacturer is using VR to permit engineers to walk through an existing or proposed product. By walking through a furnace, for example, the engineer gets a perspective of the design from a completely different vantage point. The engineer starts thinking of all the ways in which the design could be improved that were not obvious before. VR also allows the mock-up of products long before physical prototypes are created. This enables designers to get the real look and feel of the product and even get feedback from focus groups. Imagine sitting in the cab of a large farm combine before it is ever built and getting an understanding of the line of sight that the operator will have. Is the steering wheel blocking important gauges? Where should the mirrors be placed?

VR is increasingly being used for marketing on the Web. Interactive 3-D images of a company's products and services are beginning to appear on company Web sites; these images provide a more comprehensive view of the product as well as differentiate the Web site from those of competitors. Internet Pictures Corp., or iPIX, headquartered in Oak Ridge, Tennessee, is the leader in a field that the company calls "immersive imaging"—the capture, processing, hosting, and distribution of rich media to Internet sites and Internet-enabled devices. Of particular interest are the "virtual tours" created by iPIX for the real estate industry, the travel and hospitality industry, and educational institutions. On these virtual tours, the user logs on the appropriate Web site and can experience a 360-degree view from a particular camera location. If you are house-hunting, you can get a 360-degree view of the living room and the kitchen in a home for sale; if planning a vacation, you can get a 360-degree view of the grounds and the lobby of a resort hotel; if selecting a college, you can get a 360-degree look at key buildings on campus. Figure 6.7 shows a virtual-tour view of the living room of a home for sale in Las Vegas. By using the buttons at the bottom of the picture, the user can turn a full 360 degrees in either direction, stop the movement, or zoom in and out. An even newer use of immersive imaging is to capture up-to-date information about assets in order to be prepared for an emergency. Immersive imaging can provide visual documentation of the layout of facilities and the location of critical elements, such as exits and fire extinguishers, for use by emergency workers; it can also verify compliance with regulatory guidelines (Internet Pictures Corporation, 2003; Ortiz, 2003).

The development of VR is in its infancy, and it will be a long time before anything remotely approaching the Enterprise's holodeck is possible. Nevertheless, many vendors are developing VR hardware and software, and numerous valuable VR applications are beginning to appear.

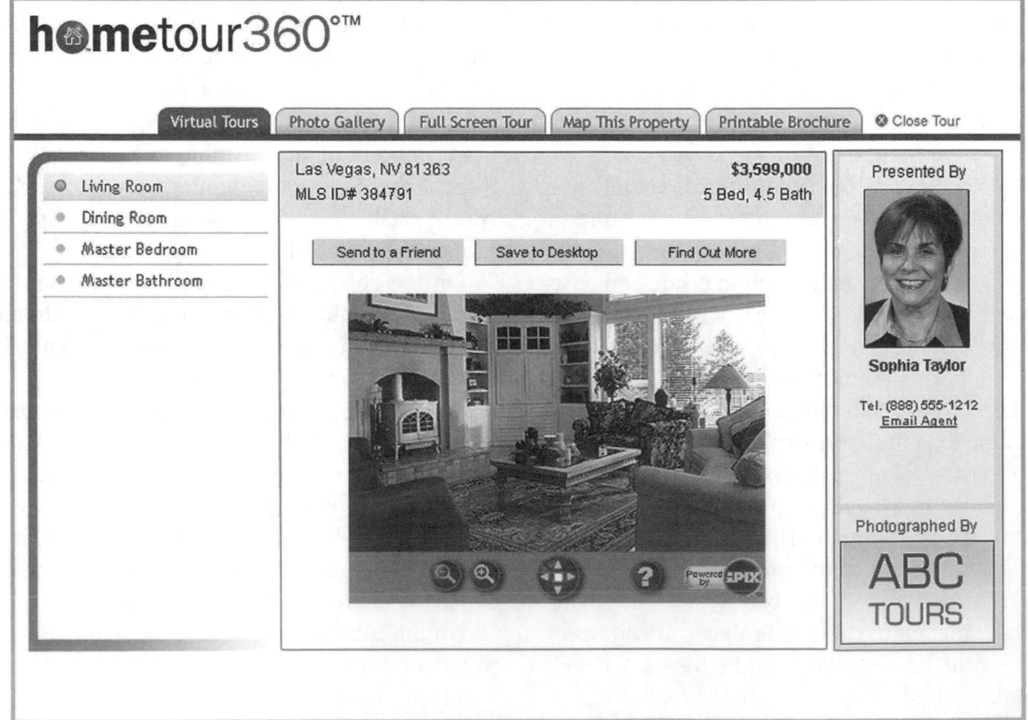

Figure 6.7 Hometour 360° Virtual Tour of Living Room (Courtesy of Homestore, Inc. Copyright © 2004 Homestore, Inc.).

HOW TO DESIGN CARS AND SCARE CHILDREN

Robert DeBrabant decided to use GM's cutting-edge 3-D virtual-reality technology to entertain 370 children visiting the automaker on its most recent "Take Your Child to Work" day. He had designers create a pterodactyl cartoon character that pokes its beak directly into the faces of the kids sitting in the room and wearing specially designed headsets. The image proved to be a bit too true-to-life: One little girl screamed and started crying.

DeBrabant runs GM's Envisioning Center, a three-screened, theaterlike room where engineers view three-dimensional images of model-car designs. They can view the images from any angle, and at such exact scale that they can walk up to the screen and use rulers to measure the width and height of any detail. Designers can change a car's color at the click of a mouse. They can even reconfigure the way lighting and background affects a model.

The center allows for meticulous inspection of design detail. For example, a designer can manipulate the image of the car until it almost seems that he or she can reach into the interior and manipulate the steering wheel. "Designers can study how much headroom a driver has, how ergonomic the dashboard controls are, and make absolutely sure that every aspect of the vehicle is perfect," DeBrabant says. Engineering teams on different continents frequently interact in virtual reality using the center's collaboration capability and can manipulate the 3-D models as easily as their U.S. counterparts.

[Konicki, 2002]

SUPPORTING DECISION MAKING

If you think about it, most computer systems support decision making because all software programs involve automating decision steps that people would take. In the mainframe era, the earliest commercial uses of computers aimed to automate such decisions as analyzing sales, updating accounts payable, calculating payroll payments, and recording credit card charges and payments. Since those early days of the 1950s and 1960s, use of computers to support decision making has become increasingly sophisticated, either completely taking over complex decisions or supporting people who make complex decisions. A whole host of technologies has been aimed at this use of computers, including:

1. Decision support systems (DSSs)
2. Data mining
3. Executive information systems (EISs)
4. Expert systems (ESs)
5. Agent-based modeling

Decision making is a process that involves a variety of activities, most of which deal with handling information. To illustrate such a process, here is a scenario (see page 238) about a vice president with an ill-structured problem and how he confronts it using a variety of decision-making technologies.

This scenario illustrates the wide variety of activities involved in problem solving. Where does the decision making start and stop? Which are the crucial decisions? It really does not matter because all the activities are part of the overall process of solving the problem. The scenario also illustrates the wide variety of technologies that can be used to assist decision makers and problem solvers. They all aim to improve the effectiveness or efficiency of the decision-making or problem-solving process.

TECHNOLOGIES THAT SUPPORT DECISION MAKING

Whereas the purpose of tractors, jackhammers, and steam engines has been to enhance humans' physical capabilities, the purpose of computers has been to enhance our mental capabilities. Hence, a major use of IT is to relieve humans of some decision-making tasks or help us make more informed decisions. At first, IT relieved us of procedure-based decisions—those that involved easily discernible procedures. Software now has progressed to the point where computers can make goal-based decisions. The following are five technologies that support decision making: DSSs, data mining, EISs, ESs, and agent-based modeling.

Decision Support Systems

During the 1970s and 1980s, the concept of decision support systems (DSSs) grew and evolved out of two previous types of computer support for decision making. One was management information systems (MISs), which provided (1) scheduled reports for well-defined information needs, (2) demand reports for ad hoc information requests, and (3) the ability to query a database for specific data. The second contributing discipline was operations research/management science (OR/MS), which used mathematical models to analyze and understand specific problems.

CASE EXAMPLE

A PROBLEM-SOLVING SCENARIO

Using an EIS to compare the budget with actual sales, a vice president of marketing discovers a sales shortfall in one region. Drilling down into the components of the summarized data, he searches for the apparent causes of the shortfall, but can find no answer. He must look further, so he sends an e-mail message to the district sales manager requesting an explanation. The sales manager's response and a follow-up phone call also reveal no obvious single cause, so he must look deeper.

The vice president investigates several possible causes:

- *Economic conditions.* Through the EIS and the Web, he accesses wire services, bank economic news letters, current business and economic publications, and the company's internal economic report on the region in question. These sources, too, reveal no serious downturn in the economic conditions of the region.
- *Competitive analysis.* Using the same sources, he investigates whether competitors have introduced a new product or launched an effective ad campaign or whether new competitors have entered the market.
- *Written sales reports.* He then browses the reports of sales representatives to detect possible problems. A concept-based text retrieval system allows him to quickly search on topics, such as poor quality, inadequate product functionality, or obsolescence.
- *A data mining analysis.* He asks for an analysis of the sales data to reveal any previously unknown relationships buried in the customer database and relevant demographic data.

The vice president then accesses the marketing DSS, which includes a set of models to analyze sales patterns by product, sales representative, and major customer. Again, no clear problems are revealed.

He thus decides to hold a meeting with the regional sales managers and several of the key salespeople. They meet in an electronic meeting room supported by group DSS (GDSS) software such as GroupSystems by Ventana Corporation. During this meeting they examine the results of all the previous analyses using the information access and presentation technologies in the room, brainstorm to identify possible solutions, and then develop an action plan.

No discernible singular cause has led to the shortfall in sales, so the group decides that the best solution is to launch a new multimedia sales campaign that sales representatives can show on their laptop computer when they visit customers.

The vice president then enters a revised estimate of sales volume into the financial planning model, taking into account the new sales promotion plan, and distributes it to the sales force in the region.

He holds a sales meeting in the GDSS room and by video conference launches the new campaign and trains sales personnel in the use of the multimedia presentation.

The definition of DSSs that prevails today was described in *Building Effective Decision Support Systems,* by Ralph Sprague and Eric Carlson. They define DSSs as:

- Computer-based systems
- That help decision makers
- Confront ill structured problems
- Through direct interaction
- With data and analysis models.

The last two items have become the basis of the architecture for DSSs, which Sprague and Carlson call the DDM paradigm: the dialog (D) between the user and the system, the data (D) that supports the system, and the models (M) that provide the analysis capabilities. Sprague and Carlson make the point that a good DSS should have balance among the three capabilities. It should be easy to use to support the interaction with non-technical users; it should have access to a wide variety of data; and it should provide analysis and modeling in numerous ways.

The Architecture for DSSs The model in Figure 6.8 shows the relationships among the three components of the DDM model. The software system in the middle of the figure consists of the database management system (DBMS), the model base management system (MBMS), and the dialog generation and management system (DGMS).

The dialog component. The dialog component links the user to the system. It can take any number of styles. One dialog style uses a mouse to access pull-down menus and move icons on a color screen to get a graphical presentation of analysis results. The Apple Macintosh introduced this style in the 1980s. The current standard is the browser interface.

The data component. Data is either accessed directly by the user or is an input to the model component. Typically, summarized data, rather than transaction data, is used and put into extract files. Extract files are used for security, ease of access, and data integrity reasons. They keep the all-important transaction systems away from end users. Most recently, the data component has taken the form of data warehousing and data mining.

The model component. Models perform the analysis in a DSS, generally using a mathematical representation of the problem. There are many kinds of models: strategic, tactical, and operational, as well as model-building blocks and subroutines. Together, they can be thought of as the model base. Models need to fit with the data, they need to be kept up-to-date, users need to understand and trust them, and if several models are used, they need to work together.

Basically, there are two kinds of DSSs: institutional and "quick hit." Institutional DSSs are generally built by professionals, often decision support groups. They are intended for organizational support on a continuing basis, and they are generally written using a decision support language. The following case example illustrates an institutional DSS.

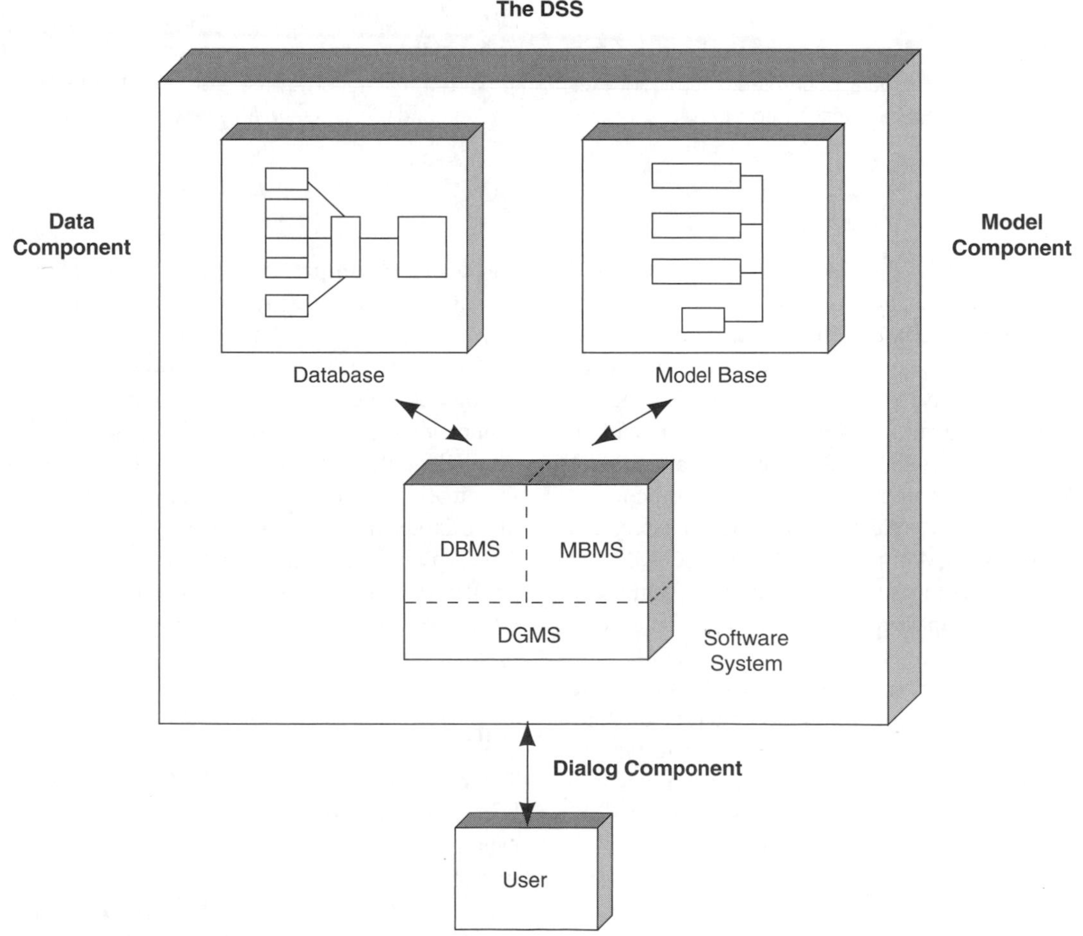

Figure 6.8 Components of a Decision Support System (DSS)

CASE EXAMPLE

ORE-IDA FOODS

Ore-Ida Foods, Inc., is the frozen food division of H. J. Heinz and has a major share of the retail frozen potato market. Its marketing DSS must support three main tasks in the decision-making process.

- *Data retrieval,* which helps managers find answers to the question, "What has happened?"
- *Market analysis,* which addresses the question, "Why did it happen?"
- *Modeling,* which helps managers get answers to, "What will happen if . . . ?"

For *data retrieval,* a large amount of internal and external market data is used. External data, such as economic indexes and forecasts, is purchased. However, the company makes limited use of simple data retrieval. Only about 15 to 30 pages of predefined reports are prepared each sales period.

Market analysis is the bulk (some 70 percent) of Ore-Ida's use of DSS and is used to analyze, "Why did such and such happen?" Data from several sources is combined, and relationships are sought. The analysis addresses a question such as, "What was the relationship between our prices and our share of the market for this brand in these markets?"

Modeling for projection purposes offers the greatest potential value to marketing management. The company has found that, for successful use, line managers must take over the ownership of the models and be responsible for keeping them up-to-date. The models must also be frequently updated, as market conditions change and new relationships are perceived.

As the example above illustrates, an institutional DSS tends to be fairly well defined, it is based on predefined data sources (heavily internal, perhaps with some external data), and it uses well-established models in a prescheduled way. Variations and flexible testing of alternative what-if situations are available, but such tests are seldom done during interaction with the ultimate decision maker.

A "quick-hit" DSS, on the other hand, is developed quickly to help a manager make either a one-time decision or a recurring decision. A quick-hit DSS can be every bit as useful for a small company as for a large one. One type of quick-hit DSS is a reporting DSS, which can be used to select, summarize, and list data from existing data files to meet a manager's specific information needs, such as to monitor inventory in a region, compare actual to planned progress on a project, or follow a trend. A second type of quick-hit DSS is a short analysis program, which can analyze data and print or display the data. These programs can be written by a manager, they generally use only a small amount of data, and they can be surprisingly powerful. Finally, a third type of quick-hit DSS can be created using a DSS generator, which builds a DSS based on the input data. As an example of a powerful short analysis that shows quick-hit DSS in practice, consider the DSS used by the vice chairman of a services company with offices throughout the United States and Europe.

The example on page 241 shows that simple programs of 100 lines of code are indeed practical and can be used to support real-life decisions. In this case, a 40-line program was adequate for the initial evaluation of the ESOP. Eventually, of course, the programs for this system became much larger, but the 40-line program started everything. This example also illustrates the concept of iterative development (a form of prototyping), which is a key concept in DSS development. Other examples of DSSs are given by Sprague and Watson in *Decision Support for Management.*

Data Mining

The data component of the DSS architecture has always been a crucial part of the success of DSSs. Recently, however, many of the advances in DSSs have been in the area of data warehousing and data mining. In fact, Hugh Watson of the University of Georgia and Paul Gray of Claremont Graduate School have devoted a book to the subject, *Decision Support in the Data Warehouse.*

CASE EXAMPLE

A MAJOR SERVICES COMPANY

The vice chairman of the board at a major services firm was considering a new employee benefit program: an employee stock ownership plan (ESOP). He wanted a study made to determine the possible impact of the ESOP on the company and to answer such questions as: How many shares of company stock will be needed in 10, 20, and 30 years to support the ESOP? What level of growth will be needed to meet these stock requirements?

He described what he wanted—the assumptions that should be used and the rules that should be followed for issuing ESOP stock—to the manager of the information services department. The information services manager herself wrote a program of about 40 lines to perform the calculations the vice chairman wanted and then printed out the results. These results showed the impact of the ESOP over a period of 30 years, and the results contained some surprises.

The vice chairman presented the results to the executive committee and, partially based on this information, the ESOP was adopted. Some of the other executives became excited about the results of this analysis and asked if the computer program could be used to project their individual employee stock holdings for 10, 20, and 30 years. The results of these calculations aroused even more attention. At this point, it was decided to implement the system in a more formal fashion. The company treasurer became so interested that he took ownership of the system and gradually expanded it to cover the planning, monitoring, and control of the various employee benefit programs.

Data warehouses hold gigantic amounts of data for the purpose of analyzing that data to make decisions. The most typical use of data warehouses has been users entering queries to obtain specific answers. However, an even more promising use is to let the computer uncover unknown correlations by searching for interesting patterns, anomalies, or clusters of data that people are unaware exist. Called data mining, its purpose is to give people new insights into data. For example, data mining might uncover unknown similarities within one customer group that differentiates it from other groups. Data mining is an advanced use of data warehouses, and it requires huge amounts of detailed data. The most frequent type of data mined these days is customer data because companies want to know how to serve their customers better. Such an example, Harrah's Entertainment, appears on pages 242–243.

Executive Information Systems

As the name implies, executive information systems (EISs) are systems for use by executives. Originally, some people argued that CEOs would not use computers directly and quoted CEOs who agreed with them. But that has not been the case. EISs are used by executives to:

- *Gauge company performance:* sales, production, earnings, budgets, and forecasts
- *Scan the environment:* for news on government regulations, competition, financial and economics developments, and scientific subjects

Using the DDM model described earlier, an EIS can be viewed as a DSS that (1) provides access to (mostly) summary performance data, (2) uses graphics to display the data in an easy-to-use fashion, and (3) has a minimum of analysis for modeling beyond the capability to drill down in summary data to examine components. For example, if sales in a region are denoted as "red" (meaning, below planned targets), the executive can perhaps drill down by country, sales office, and maybe even salesperson to better understand where the shortfall is occurring (on page 244). The experience at Xerox is an example of the successful development and use of an EIS. In many companies, the EIS is called a *dashboard* and may look like a dashboard of a car.

CASE EXAMPLE

HARRAH'S ENTERTAINMENT

Harrah's Entertainment of Memphis, Tennessee, is owner of 26 casinos around the United States, including the Rio in Las Vegas, Harrah's at Lake Tahoe, and Harrah's North Kansas City on a riverboat on the Missouri River.

To better know its customers, Harrah's encourages them to sign up for its frequent-gambler card, Total Rewards. In return for inserting the card in a gaming machine when they play it, gamblers can receive free hotel rooms, free shows, free meals, and other giveaways.

Some 25 million Harrah's customers have a Total Rewards card, reports Joe Nickell, just by filling out their name, age, address, and driver's license number. When they insert the card in a machine, it tracks what they do. Thus, on Nickell's 4-hour-and-40-minute visit to the Rio in Las Vegas, Harrah's learned that he placed 637 wagers on nine slot machines, his average bet was 35 cents, and he lost $350.

Until its Total Rewards program began in 1998, Harrah's only knew how much money each of its 40,000 machines made, notes Nickell, not which customers were playing them. Furthermore, each casino operated independently. Customers might receive VIP treatment at one casino, but not at another.

When competition among casino owners increased in the late 1990s due to legalization of gambling on Indian reservations and riverboats, Harrah's realized it needed to reward its best customers to keep them coming back. But first it had to find out who they were, which was the rationale behind its Total Rewards program.

Harrah's estimated it was getting 36 percent of its customers' gambling money in 1998. It further calculated that a 1-percent increase would equal $125 million in more revenue, states Nickell. Thus, Harrah's goal has been to increase the gambling "wallet share" of each of its customers. During 2001, Harrah's calculated its share had increased to 42 percent.

Using Data Mining to Understand Its Customers

Harrah's mined its Total Rewards database to uncover patterns and clusters of customers. It has created 90 demographic clusters, each of which is sent different direct mail offers—a free steak dinner, a free hotel room, and such—to induce them to pay another visit to any Harrah's casino.

Harrah's has gotten to know its customers well. From just a person's gender, age, distance from any casino, gaming machines played, and amounts of bets, it can fairly accurately estimate the long-term value of that customer. The company creates a gaming profile of each customer and a personalized marketing campaign, offering giveaways appropriate to that customer's cluster, all with the goal of encouraging customers to spend their gambling time at Harrah's rather than at competitors' casinos.

Over time, Harrah's compiles a profit-and-loss for each customer to calculate how much "return" it is likely to receive for every "investment" it makes in that customer. It also tracks how each customer responds to its direct mail offers, ratcheting up or down its giveaways based on changes in that customer's expected long-term value.

Harrah's goes to this much trouble to know its customers, says Nickell, because it learned from mining its Total Rewards database that much of its $3.7 billion in revenues (and 80 percent of its profit) comes from its slot-machine and electronic-gaming-machine players. It is not the high rollers who are the most profitable. In fact, Harrah's discovered that only 30 percent of those who spend between $100 and $500 on each visit bring in 80 percent of Harrah's revenue and close to all its profits. These slots and gaming players are the locals who gamble often.

Using Data Mining to Improve Its Business

"Harrah's Entertainment has the most devoted clientele in the casino business," writes Gary Loveman, CEO. That loyalty is reflected in its bottom line: Its 26 casinos increased their same-store revenues 16 quarters in a row. Data mining has shown Harrah's the link between revenue and customer satisfaction. Customers who report being "very happy with their experience at Harrah's" have increased their spending by 24 percent, whereas those who report being "disappointed" decreased their spending by 10 percent.

Harrah's strategy is to increase loyalty by treating its best customers well. In so doing, Loveman and his predecessor have followed a decidedly different strategy to the casino business than competitors. Others have built lavish facilities and amenities—dazzling attractions in their buildings, high-end shopping malls, spas, and such—to attract new kinds of customers, not just gamblers.

Harrah's has focused on its most lucrative customers—its local slots players—using what Loveman calls a "data-driven marketing" strategy. Rather than devise a marketing strategy first, Harrah's has let the data suggest the marketing ideas based on its mining of customer satisfaction surveys and reward-card data. The data suggested that Harrah's could increase loyalty by focusing on same-store revenue growth by encouraging locals to visit their nearby Harrah's casino often using *appropriate* incentives. Data mining also showed that most locals prefer $60 in casino chips over a free hotel stay with two free dinners and $30 in chips.

To hone customer service even more, Harrah's has divided its Total Rewards program into three tiers—Gold, Platinum, and Diamond—with Diamond customers receiving the highest level of customer service, because they have the highest value. Through mining its customer satisfaction surveys, Harrah's discovered that these gamblers value fast service and friendliness. So Harrah's does its best to make sure they do not wait in line to park their car, check in at the hotel, or eat in the restaurant. And to encourage non-Diamond card gamblers to aspire to receive these same perks, Harrah's makes the differences in service obvious. Marketing to customer aspiration is working "wonderfully," notes Loveman.

Furthermore, because Harrah's sees customer satisfaction as being so important to increasing revenue, it now links employee rewards to customer-satisfaction scores on the two important metrics: speed and friendliness. When a casino's rating increases 3 percent on customer satisfaction surveys, every employee in that casino receives a bonus. In 2002, during the recession, when gambling revenues only increased by 1 percent in one city, the Harrah's casino increased its customer satisfaction rating by 14 percent.

In addition, the company is using data mining to understand its individual slot machines, such as why customers prefer some machines over others. From what it has learned, Harrah's has reconfigured its casino floor.

In all ways possible—from the parking valets to the telemarketers to the individual slots themselves—Harrah's is using insights from its data-driven strategy to treat its best customers the way they say they want to be treated and thereby gain their loyalty and more of their gambling wallet share.

Within the first 2 years of operation of Total Rewards, revenue from customers who visited more than one Harrah's casino increased by $100 million. Due mainly to this program, Harrah's has become the second largest casino operator in the United States, and has the highest 3-year ROI in its industry, notes Nickell.

Stories like the Xerox case appear frequently in the public and trade press. The implication is that computers are finally being used by executives to help them perform their job better. The underlying message is that executive use is just a matter of installing popular software packages, and the only reason more executives are not using computers is their timidity. However, the situation is not that simple. Successful IT support of executive work is fraught with subtle pitfalls and problems. Consider the following description of a failure.

Doing It Wrong. Hugh Watson, a professor at the University of Georgia, has worked with many corporations in the development of EISs. Watson describes a (hypothetical) company and its well-intentioned effort to develop and install an EIS. The IS director at Genericorp had heard of successful EIS experiences. He thought that such a system would be valuable to his company, so he arranged for a presentation by a DSS vendor, which was well received by the executive team. After some discussion, they decided to purchase the product from the vendor and develop an EIS. The allocated budget was $250,000.

They assembled a qualified team of IS professionals who interviewed executives concerning their information needs (whenever the executives could find the time) and developed an initial version of the system consisting of 50 screens to be used by five executives. The response from these executives was quite good, and in some cases enthusiastic. Several of them seemed proud to finally be able to use a computer, says Watson.

With the system delivered, the development team turned it over to a maintenance team and moved on to new projects. The maintenance team was to add new screens and new users—in short, to evolve the system. Nine months later, little had happened, apparently because other systems maintenance projects had become more urgent. About this time, a downturn in revenue generated cost-cutting pressures on nonessential systems; the EIS was discontinued.

CASE EXAMPLE

XEROX CORPORATION

Paul Allaire became the executive sponsor of Xerox's EIS project while he was corporate chief of staff. Although he felt that an EIS would be valuable to the executive team, he insisted that it earn its usefulness, not that it be "crammed down their throats." In fact, the system began small and evolved to the point where even skeptical users became avid supporters.

Improved planning was a clear objective from the start. For example, Allaire describes the problem of getting briefing information to executives before regular executive meetings. Due to the time req-uired to prepare the materials and mailing delays to international offices, many executives ended up reading 100 pages or more the night before a meeting without access to related information or time for discussions with staff. When the materials were put on the EIS, the executives had enough information or preparation time to make the necessary decisions.

The EIS helped make strategic planning more efficient and resulted in better plans, especially across divisions. Instead of each division preparing plans that were simply combined, the EIS allowed the executives to explore interrelationships between plans and activities at several divisions. The EIS played an important role at Xerox during Allaire's tenure.

What went wrong? Watson identifies five problems that serve as a guide to the "hidden pitfalls" in developing a successful EIS.

1. ***Lack of executive support.*** Although it has been listed as a potential problem in system development for years, executive support is crucial for EIS for several reasons. Executives must provide the funding, but they are also the principal users so they need to supply the necessary continuity.
2. ***Undefined system objectives.*** The technology, the convenience, and the power of EISs are impressive, maybe even seductive. However, the underlying objectives and business values of an EIS must be carefully thought through.
3. ***Poorly defined information requirements.*** Once the objectives of the system are defined, the required information can be identified. This process is complicated because EISs typically require nontraditional information sources, such as judgments, opinions, and external text-based documents, in addition to traditional financial and operating data.
4. ***Inadequate support staff.*** The support staff must have technical competence of course, but perhaps more important is that they have an understanding of the business and the ability to relate to the varied responsibilities and work patterns of executives. A permanent team must manage the evolution of the system.
5. ***Poorly planned evolution.*** Highly competent systems professionals using the wrong development process will fail with EISs. An EIS is not developed, delivered, and then maintained. It needs to evolve over time under the leadership of a team that includes the executive sponsor, the operating sponsor, executive users, the EIS support staff manager, and IS technical staff.

Although EIS development is difficult, many organizations report that it is worth the effort. Avoiding the pitfalls identified by Watson improves the probability of a successful EIS. Many questions must be answered when considering an EIS. Some of the answers are specific to the organization—who it will serve, where and when it will be developed—so it would serve no purpose to discuss them here. However, the other questions—why, what, and how—have more general answers.

Why Install an EIS? There are a range of reasons for wanting an EIS. The following motivations are listed in the sequence of strongest to weakest, as far as probable project success is concerned.

- *Attack a critical business need.* An EIS can be viewed as an aid to deal with important needs that involve the future health of the organization. In this situation, almost everyone in the organization can clearly see the reason for developing an EIS.

- *A strong personal desire by the executive.* The executive sponsoring the project may want to get information faster or have quicker access to a broader range of information. Or the executive might want the ability to select and display only desired information and then probe for supporting detail. Or the executive might want to see information presented in graphical form. Within divisions, once corporate management begins using an EIS, division management feels at a disadvantage without one.
- *"The thing to do."* An EIS, in this instance, is seen as something that today's management must have to be current in management practices. The rationale given is that the EIS will increase executive performance and reduce time wasted looking for information.

A strong motivation, such as meeting a critical business need, is more likely to assure top management interest in, and support of, the project. At the other extreme, a weak motivation can lead to poor executive sponsorship of the project, which can result in trouble. Thus, motivation for the EIS is fundamental to its success because it helps determine the degree of commitment by the senior executives.

What Should the EIS Do? This question is second only to motivation as a critical success factor. It determines the extent to which executives will make hands-on use of the system. It is important that all the people associated with the project have the same understanding of just what the new system is expected to do and how it will provide executive support.

In general, EIS and dashboards are used to assess status. At their heart, both should filter, extract, and compress a broad range of up-to-date internal and external information. They should call attention to variances from plans and also monitor and highlight the critical success factors of the individual executive user. Both are a structured reporting system for executive management, providing them with the data and information of their choice in the desired form. Both are for monitoring what is going on in the company and in the outside world. With this information at hand, executives can work to resolve any problems they uncover.

An EIS or a dashboard can start small and quickly with this data-and-information approach and still accomplish something useful. For example, EIS developers asked the company president of one large insurance company the 10 things he would look at first after returning from vacation. He gave them this list. Two weeks later, they gave him an EIS "system" with those 10 items listed on the main menu as the first iteration of the EIS. The president was delighted and was soon asking for more!

This data-and-information approach uses information the executives already get or would like to get. But the EIS provides it faster, in more convenient form, pulling information together that previously had to be viewed separately and using graphics to aid comprehension. See page 246 for another example of an EIS in the form of a dashboard.

Expert Systems

Expert systems (ESs) are a real-world use of artificial intelligence (AI). AI is a group of technologies that attempts to mimic our senses and emulate certain aspects of human behavior, such as reasoning and communicating, says Harvey Newquist a well-known consultant and columnist in the field. AI technologies include ESs, neural networks, fuzzy logic, machine translation, speech recognition, and natural language.

AI has been a promising technology for at least 40 years. In the early 1990s, that promise finally began to unfold, quietly. In particular, ESs, also called knowledge-based systems, became one of several system development methodologies. They have become a prolific application of AI. The auto industry uses them to troubleshoot robots and check cars for noise and vibration. Telecommunications firms use them to diagnose switching circuits. Financial services firms use them to choose financial planning and tax planning alternatives. And the list goes on.

ESs are not new. The first was the Logic Theorist developed in 1956 by Allen Newell and Herbert Simon of Carnegie-Mellon University together with J. C. Shaw of the Rand Corporation. The field changed in the 1970s with the introduction of two AI languages, LISP and Prolog, which made the systems easier to develop. They brought ESs out of the lab and into businesses. The field changed again with the introduction of PC-based tools, called shells, that used conventional languages, such as C.

Definition. An ES is an automated analysis or problem-solving model that deals with a problem the way an expert does. The process involves consulting a base of knowledge or expertise to reason out an answer based on the characteristics of the problem. Clyde Holsapple and Andrew Whinston define an ES as a computer-based system composed of:

- A user interface
- An inference engine

CASE EXAMPLE

GENERAL ELECTRIC

In Spring 2001, the CIO of General Electric (GE) received the first executive dashboard. Now, most senior GE executives have a real-time view of their portion of GE. Each dashboard compares expected goals (sales, response times, etc.) with actual, alerting the executive when gaps of a certain magnitude appear. The CIO's dashboard, for instance, shows critical GE applications. Green means the system is up and running OK, yellow means there is a problem, and red means the system is down. When systems remain red or yellow for a given time, the CIO can have the dashboard system send an e-mail to the developers in charge. The CIO can also pull up historical data to see whether the event appears to be one-time or recurring.

GE's goal is to gain better visibility into all its operations in real time and give employees a way to monitor corporate operations quickly and easily. The system is based on complex enterprise software that interlinks existing systems. GE estimates that it saves $1.6 billion a year from the system.

GE's actions are also moving its partners and business ecosystem closer to real-time operation. For example, GE has installed online kiosks at some Home Depot stores. Customers can order an appliance, choose a delivery date and time, and learn, at that moment, whether that delivery can be made.

Likewise, GE has installed sensors on a number of its products—turbines, aircraft engines, and locomotives, to name a few. These sensors record what is happening on its attached object and transmit that data via satellite to a GE remote monitoring center. If, for instance, there is something wrong with a jet engine, GE learns of that event in real time from the sensor, uses its systems and people to determine a probable cause, and notifies the airline. Likewise, GE can tell its customers how efficiently a GE turbine is running, in real time, and work with the customer on improving that efficiency.

- Stored expertise (in the form of a knowledge base)

The *user interface* is the interface between the ES and the outside world. That outside world could be another computer application or a person. If a person is using the system directly, the user interface contains the means for the user to state the problem and interact with the system. Some systems use multiple-choice graphics, voice, and even animation in the interface. When the system is interacting with another application, though, the interface is the program that presents the facts to the expert system.

The *inference engine* is that portion of the software that contains the reasoning methods used to search the knowledge base and solve the problem. The expert system generally asks questions of the user to get the information it needs. Then, the inference engine, using the knowledge base, searches for the appropriate knowledge and returns a decision or recommendation to the user. Unlike conventional systems, ESs can deal with uncertainty. Users can answer, "Yes (0.7)," meaning, "The answer is probably yes, but I'm only 70 percent certain." In these cases, the system may produce several possible answers, ranking the most likely one first.

The *knowledge* base contains facts and data relevant to the specific application.

Knowledge Representation. Knowledge can be represented in a number of ways. Following are three ways: cases, nodes in a network, and rules.

Case-based reasoning (CBR). One way to represent knowledge is as a case. ESs using this approach draw inferences by comparing a current problem (or case) to hundreds or thousands of similar past cases. CBR is best used when the situation involves too many nuances and variations to be generalized into rules.

Evan Schwartz and James Treece provide an excellent example of a CBR system: the Apache III system used by the intensive care unit at St. Joseph Mercy Hospital in Ypsilanti, Michigan. When 33-year-old Sharon entered the hospital with a potentially fatal respiratory disease, the physicians and nurses in intensive care entered her vital statistics and medical history into a workstation running Apache III. The system drew on records of 17,448 previous intensive care patients to predict whether Sharon would live or die. Its first prediction was that she had a 15 percent chance of dying.

As the statistics were entered daily, the system compared her progress to the base of previous cases. Two weeks later, the prediction of death soared to 90 percent, alerting the physicians and nurses to take immediate corrective action. Then, literally overnight, her chance of dying dropped to 60 percent, and 12 days later to 40 percent. She did recover. The intensive care unit's director credits the system with catching the increased likelihood of death days before his staff would have seen it. The Apache III system is helping the unit respond faster and control costs better.

Neural networks. A second way to store knowledge is in a neural network. Although they are not seen as expert systems, neural networks are a type of decision-making system. They are organized like the human brain. The brain is a network of neurons—nerve cells—that fire a signal when they are stimulated by smell, sound, sight, and so forth. As Brian O'Reilly explains, scientists believe that our brains learn by strengthening or weakening these signals, gradually creating patterns. A neural network contains links (called synapses) and nodes that also fire signals between each other. Neural networks are more intelligent than the other forms of knowledge representation discussed here because they can learn.

O'Reilly presents a good description of how a neural network learns by describing how a simple one might evaluate credit applications. As shown in Figure 6.9, the first layer of this neural net has six "neurons" that represent the criteria for distinguishing good credit risks from bad credit risks. The six criteria are high salary, medium salary, owns a home, less than 3 years on the current job, prior bankruptcy, and has a dog. (The dog probably does not have an effect, but who knows?) Each of the six is connected to the two neurons in the second layer: profitable customer and deadbeat.

To train the system to distinguish between the two, the network is fed the example of an applicant with a high salary who owns a house and has a dog. Each of these three neurons sends a signal of equal strength to both the profitable customer and deadbeat neurons because it has not been trained.

The network is trained by telling the two second-level neurons the outcome of this previous loan: It was paid back. The profitable neuron sends a signal back to the three saying, in effect, "You are right, send a stronger signal next time." The deadbeat neuron, on the other hand, replies with, "You are wrong, send a weaker signal next time." The network is then given many more examples so that it learns the predictors of profitable customers and deadbeats, readjusting its signal strengths with each new case.

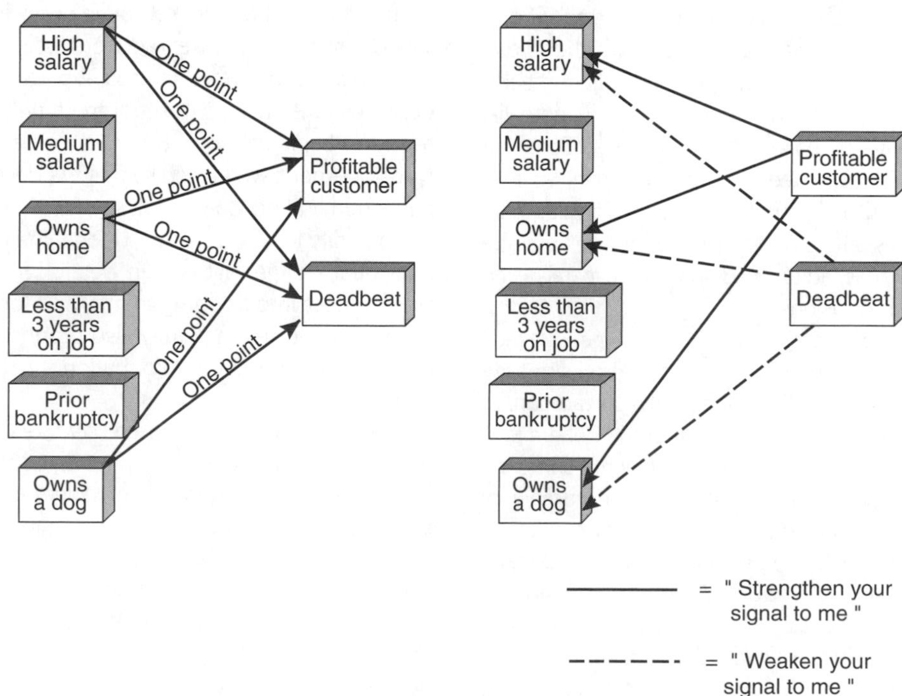

Figure 6.9 Training a Neural Network. *Source:* Brian O'Reilly, "Computers That Think Like People," *Fortune,* February 27, 1989, pp. 90–93.

CASE EXAMPLE

AMERICAN EXPRESS

In 1988, American Express (AmEx) implemented the Authorizer's Assistant, an ES that approves credit at the point of sale. It started as an R&D project, took 2 years to develop, and was put into production with 800 rules. Today, it has over 2,600 rules and supports all AmEx card products around the world. Its purpose is to minimize credit losses and catch fraud. It saves the company millions of dollars a year and has been a phenomenal success.

Whenever an AmEx card is run through a point-of-sale device, the transaction goes into AmEx's credit authorization system (CAS), which is a very important system for AmEx because, in essence, it gives away money. CAS is implemented worldwide and operates 24 × 7. It is such a significant system that the company president is notified if it is down for 45 minutes or more.

Coprocessor systems, such as the Authorizer's Assistant, have been added to CAS. The Authorizer's Assistant authorizes credit by looking at whether cardholders are creditworthy, whether they have been paying their bills, and whether a particular purchase is within their normal spending patterns. It also assesses whether the request for credit could be a potential fraud. Before deploying Authorizer's Assistant, transactions that were not automatically approved by CAS were referred to a person for analysis and a decision. The most difficult credit-authorization decisions are still referred to people, but the Authorizer's Assistant has automated judgment to raise the quality of authorization decisions.

Authorization decisions are driven by the type of credit charge—store, restaurant, and so on. They are also influenced by whether cardholders are in their home city, on vacation, or traveling. A hotel bill or charges in a city other than where they reside would point to the latter. To detect fraud while someone is on vacation, the credit authorizer looks at the number of charges per day. An appropriate question for the system to ask would be, "Is the cardholder's spending velocity 'in pattern' (following his or her typical spending pattern)?" Customer servicing issues and credit policies are also taken into account in the authorization decision. For example, a restaurant charge needs to be handled differently from a camera store charge, because the restaurant charge happens after the service has been rendered and the purchase, unlike a camera, cannot be resold. AmEx also does not want to embarrass a cardholder in the social setting of a restaurant.

Development of the System

The Authorizer's Assistant is a rules-based expert system, and in creating the rules, AmEx had to refine its company policies. One example was the commonly used phrase "sound credit judgment." Before the system was built, this phrase was often used but never defined. Developing the system forced the company to define the phrase in quantifiable rules.

A rule might be framed in terms of the question, "Does this person shop at this store or often buy this kind of merchandise?" If the answer is "yes," the charge would be "in pattern." If the amount is high, another rule might ask, "Does the cardholder pay his or her bill on time and is his or her 12-month credit history good?"

The rules were generated by interviewing authorizers with various levels of expertise. Five were assigned to work with the developers. Some were the top experts (who made correct decisions at least 90 percent of the time); others had a track record of being right only 80 to 89 percent of the time. Both types of experts were used so that the developers could compare good and not-so-good decisions.

To codify the experts' knowledge, the developers studied individual charge histories in detail, broke down the decision process into its components, and focused on each one to refine it. Sometimes they also proposed cases to the experts and recorded the information they asked for to make a decision.

Two kinds of knowledge are captured in the Authorizer's Assistant: policy knowledge and judgment knowledge. Policy knowledge is like textbook knowledge. Judgment knowledge is applied to bend the rules set down in the policy to benefit the cardholder (and keep his or her business). This type of knowledge is very important because it enhances customer service in the eyes of cardholders. Thus, the rules in the system protect the company against loss and the cardholder from embarrassment.

The seven developers also spent several weeks working in the credit authorization environment so that they could understand what the experts were talking about. The system was designed to mimic how people made credit authorization decisions. The knowledge engineers (developers) thus had to develop expertise in credit and fraud as well as in the analysis of cardholder charge patterns. In essence, they acted as credit authorizers for a short time, talking to real cardholders and making authorization decisions on the telephone on the fly. This experience helped them realize how time-sensitive authorization decisions can be. The cardholder may be waiting at an airline counter to get the charge approved; a delay could cause the cardholder to miss the flight. The system had to be designed to deal with this type of customer-sensitive situation; AmEx does not want to embarrass a cardholder by bringing him or her to a telephone unnecessarily.

The vice president of risk management states that the system can be adapted quickly to meet changing business requirements. For example, if a large manufacturing company falls on hard times, AmEx can change the rules that apply to the cities where that company is a major employer so that it can respond compassionately and quickly to credit issues that inevitably will arise. In all, management reaction to the Authorizer's Assistant has been very positive.

Once the network is trained, the high-salary neuron might send a signal worth 10 points to the profitable neuron, whereas the homeowner neuron might send only 2 points. And the less-than-3-years-on-the-job neuron may send 2 points to the deadbeat neuron and a minus 2 points to the profitable one. Because owning a dog is irrelevant, it will send zero points to both. New applications will be evaluated based on these learned patterns.

Neural networks have been used by an automaker to detect defective motors, by oil drillers to describe the progress of underground rock cracking based on sensor data, by a manufacturer to track manufacturing variations to determine the optimum manufacturing conditions, and by computer manufacturers to recognize hand printing.

Rules-based systems. A third way to store knowledge in an ES knowledge base is through rules. In fact, this is the most common form of knowledge representation. The rules are obtained from experts who draw on their own expertise, experience, common sense, ways of doing business, regulations, and laws to state the rules. Rules generally present this knowledge in the form of if-then statements. The number of rules determines the complexity of the system, from 50 to many thousand. Rules are appropriate when knowledge can be generalized into specific statements.

One of the first commercially successful ESs was built by American Express. It is still in use today and is actually a fundamental part of the company's everyday credit card operation. It is a rules-based ES. That story appears on pages 248–249.

Degree of Expertise. The degree of expertise in an ES can be characterized by the kind of assistance it might provide to a person. It might function as an assistant, a colleague, or a true expert.

As an *assistant*, the lowest level of expertise, the ES can help a person perform routine analyses and point out those portions of the work where the expertise of the human is required. The Dipmeter Advisor developed by Schlumberger Ltd. falls into this category. It reads charts produced by instruments that have been lowered into an oil well that is being drilled. Reading such charts, looking for a small amount of significant data, is a tedious job for humans. The ES reads the charts and indicates those portions where human experts should concentrate their attention.

As a *colleague*, the second level of expertise, the system and the human can "talk over" the problem until a "joint decision" has been reached. In this use, the human may employ the "why" and "how" features of the ES to understand the system's train of logic. ESs move beyond the capabilities of DSSs because they are not only able to solve a problem but also explain to some extent how they solved the problem and provide a reliable means of solving similar problems. When a colleague system seems to be going down the wrong track, the human can put in more information to get it back on track to reach a joint decision.

As an *expert*, the highest level of expertise, the system gives answers that the user accepts, perhaps without question. This means that the system performs as well as the top 10 to 20 percent of the experts in the field.

Agent-Based Modeling

Agent-based modeling is a simulation technology for studying emergent behavior; that is, behavior (such as a traffic jam) that emerges from the decisions of a large number of distinct individuals (drivers), notes Eric Bonabeau, president of Icosystem, which builds such modeling systems.

The simulation contains computer-generated agents, each making decisions typical of the decisions an individual would make in the real world. Thus, if modeling a day theme park, the agent representing a family of four would make different decisions than the agent representing teenagers on a date. Bonabeau believes modeling the confluence of a huge number of individual behaviors under-lies understanding the mysteries of why businesses, markets, consumers, and other complex systems behave as they do. In modeling the behavior of highly complex systems via individual agents, agent-based systems often arrive at counterintuitive results. He states that this decision-making technology can be used to predict the unpredictable, and he gives numerous examples of how it has been used. Here are just a few.

- Nasdaq was going to switch its tick size from eighths to decimals, believing that the change would allow stock buyers and sellers to negotiate more precisely and decrease the buy–ask price spread. Using agent-based modeling, with agents representing all the players in its stock market, each making decisions based on real-world strategies, Nasdaq found that the smaller tick size would actually increase the buy–ask price spread because it reduced the market's ability to do price discovery.
- A European retailer wanted to redesign its incentive plan for its country managers. At the time, incentives were based on having the fewest stock-outs (a product running out of stock on the shelves). However, this incentive encouraged hoarding, spoilage, and high-cost rush orders. Agent-based modeling recommended basing incentives both on low stock-outs and on storage costs, because it would connect managers' local behavior with the organization's global performance.
- Southwest Airlines wanted to revamp its cargo operations. The dispatchers loaded cargo onto the flight that would reach the destination soonest. But the result was piles of packages at the end of the day, high security costs, and endless loading and unloading of packages. Agent-based modeling found that costs would be lower and packages would arrive just as quickly by putting them on a plane that would eventually land in the destination city.
- A company planned to change its recruiting practices from hiring college graduates who fit its company culture to hiring experienced people. Agent-based modeling demonstrated that this change would lead to higher staff turnover (which the company had expected) and a decrease in the company's knowledge base (which the company had not expected). Thus, if it was to change [illegible] recruiting practices, it would need to find ways to capture the knowledge of experienced employees before [illegible] left.

These five seemingly competing technologies that support decision making often overlap and combine. For example, some DSS products incorporate tools and techniques from AI. In the form of agents, DSSs are providing the delivery vehicle for ESs, knowledge representation, natural language query, and voice and pattern recognition. The result is intelligent DSSs that can suggest, learn, and understand managerial tasks and problems. Likewise, data mining is often part of a DSS or EIS. In fact, the next section demonstrates how these decision support technologies and other technologies are being mixed and matched to form the foundation for the real-time enterprise.

TOWARD THE REAL-TIME ENTERPRISE

The essence of the phrase *real-time enterprise* is that organizations can know how they are doing at the moment rather than waiting days, weeks, or months for needed information, as has been the case. It is often equated to an airline pilot trying to fly the plane using time-delayed sensors or trying to drive a car without split-second information about what is happening on the highway.

Through IT, organizations have been able to see the status of operations closer and closer to real time. The Internet is giving companies a way to disseminate closer-to-real-time information about events, such as a large customer order or cancellation, a supply chain disruption, weather or governmental disruption, important news, and so forth.

The notion has gotten to the hype point. It is prominent in vendor advertising. That means the notion has some validity, but it is not as easy to achieve as vendors might lead you to believe. This real-time reporting is occurring on a whole host of fronts. Following are just five of those fronts: enterprise nervous systems (to coordinate company operations), straight-through processing (to reduce distortion in supply chains), real-time CRM (to automate decision making relating to customers), communicating objects (to gain real-time data about the physical world), and vigilant information systems (to move to a sense-and-respond culture).

Enterprise Nervous Systems

One approach to the real-time enterprise is to build an enterprise nervous system. In an interesting white paper from Tibco and Gartner, the two companies state that an enterprise nervous system (the technical means to a real-time enterprise) is a kind of network that connects people, applications, and devices. This system differs from many past systems in four ways:

1. It is *message based,* which means that applications, devices, and people communicate with each other via messages. As the Internet has shown, sending messages is a very efficient and effective way of dispersing information among huge numbers of parties.
2. It is *event driven,* which means that when an event occurs—a car arrives at a dealer's lot, a passenger boards a plane, a factory ships a truckload of parts—that event is recorded and made available.
3. It uses a *publish-and-subscribe* approach, which means that the information about the event is "published" to an electronic address and any system, person, or device authorized to see that information can "subscribe" to that address's information feed, which is automatically updated whenever a new event occurs. Portal technology has a similar self-service characteristic. A company posts information on its portal, and if you are authorized to see that information, you can access it when you want, or subscribe to receive it automatically in real time. This approach is one way to inform hundreds, thousands, or millions of people or systems of an event in real time in a format customized to their system or device.
4. It uses *common data formats,* which means the data formats used in disparate systems are reduced to common denominators that can be understood by other systems and shared.

Below is an example of one such nervous system.

CASE EXAMPLE

DELTA AIRLINES

Delta Air Lines has implemented an enterprise nervous system that is, over time, incorporating the disparate systems the airline had in the late 1990s. At that time, Delta had 60 million lines of code, 70 databases, and 30 technology platforms, most of which did not communicate with each other nor share their data, notes Tom Stewart.

Now, Delta has a nervous system that has gotten rid of over 30 of the databases and one-fourth of the code, and the consolidation is continuing. This system manages the airline's gate operations. Delta has 2,200 flights a day, one every 39.3 seconds, says Stewart. Each is managed by the system, in real time. When a flight has a gate change, for example, everyone who needs to know about that change–gate attendants, baggage handlers, caterers, passengers–gets the data in the appropriate way. Passengers, for instance, receive the information on screens above each gate.

The system was installed by the Feld Group, notes Stewart, led by Charlie Feld, the former CIO of Frito-Lay who installed a real-time system at Frito-Lay and has gone on to do the same at a number of other companies. At Frito-Lay, all the sales force had laptops to record every sale in real time; all the executives had PCs to see the sales. As a result, Frito-Lay took back $40 million less in stale product each year, sales force paperwork dropped by 40,000 hours a year, and Frito-Lay's revenue increased from $3 billion to $4.2 billion in just 3 years.

At Delta, Feld drew on software from Tibco, which provides the foundation for the enterprise nervous system. Feld believes the best way to get a real-time enterprise is to use a publish-and-subscribe approach using EAI products. Using the Tibco products, which include a type of messaging middleware, disparate applications can talk to each other. The software puts the data in these systems into common forms so it can be understood by the numerous applications.

Generally, to start down this EAI path, a company needs a system that is large enough to affect customers, impress the CEO, and intrigue the IT organization, states Stewart. At Delta, this first system was a new gate-and-boarding system. The system is big, it is used by 60,000 Delta employees and 100 million customers, and it affects everything from maintenance crews to reservation clerks to Delta's frequent flyer program. Formerly, the various functions had their own systems and databases. The new system replaced them all with one set of data. Now, when an event occurs, it ripples to everyone. Delta is now expanding those ripples out to its partners who also serve its passengers: caterers, security companies, and such.

CASE EXAMPLE

A REAL TIME INTERACTION ON A WEB SITE

As an illustration of a real-time interaction via a Web site, consider an example from E.piphany, a company that sells real-time CRM software as a component of its suite of CRM products. Following is the sequence of events (1 to 11), as noted in Figure 6.10:

1. A potential hotel guest visits the Web site of a hotel chain that uses E.piphany's software.
2. The site visitor clicks on a hotel in the Orlando area. Information on that real-time event flows to the real-time server powered by E.piphany software.
3. The server initiates a number of requests to create a profile of that customer.
4. It may request past history of interactions with that customer from the E.piphany data mart. Those interactions would include not only Web site interactions but also call center interactions, hotel stays, and so on.
5. The server may request past billing information from the chain's ERP system.
6. It may want past purchase history from the hotel's e-commerce system.
7. Using all those pieces of information, the server then uses its analytics to make some real-time offers to the Web site visitor.
8. If it is off-season in Orlando, hotel management may have created a business rule that says, "For any repeat customer considering booking at least a 2-night stay at this hotel in off-season, offer a 20 percent discount." If, indeed, this customer has stayed at the chain before, the server can make that offer on the spot, probably in a very noticeable pop-up box on the Web site.
9. Or the server might use the E.piphany *real-time mining tool* to make an offer based on the customer's past stays at the hotel, having mined that information from the compiled profile. For instance, it might ask if the customer still wants a king-size bed in a nonsmoking quiet room, as in the past.
10. Or, using the E.piphany *collaborative filtering* technology, based on preferences of other hotel guests with a similar profile, the system might offer three special choices: a laptop computer in the room, a bottle of wine, or a half hour massage at the hotel's spa. Generally, the real-time mining and collaborative filtering tools are used together.
11. The Web site visitor's responses to all the offers are recorded and taken into account by the E.piphany software and used when making offers to other Web site or call center visitors.

In a call center, the call center representatives would have the same kinds of technology support for making decisions and verbally making these offers (and recording responses) over the phone.

Besides the real-time nature of this interaction, another feature is that the system learns from each interaction. Thus, it includes the latest responses in its real-time decision making and offers, keeping up with trends and honing its knowledge of clusters of customers and non-customers.

Straight-Through Processing

The notion of a real-time enterprise has generated two buzzwords worth knowing. One is *zero latency,* which, according to Gartner EXP, was coined in 1998 and means reacting quickly to new information (with no wait time). The premise is that faster action leads to a competitive edge.

The second term is *straight-through processing,* which means that transaction data is entered just once in a process or a supply chain. The Delta example shows straight-through processing within an enterprise. The notion applies even more in supply chains. In fact, reducing lags and latency in supply chains is a major goal these days.

As the *Economist* points out, supply chains experience a bullwhip effect when they do not have straight-through processing. A customer order can trigger a company to generate an order to its supplier, who, in turn, generates its own orders to its suppliers. But generally, these orders are larger because the supplier wants to compensate for unforeseen events. Those upstream suppliers, in turn, order from their suppliers, and their orders are often larger as well. Moving upstream through the supply chain there is

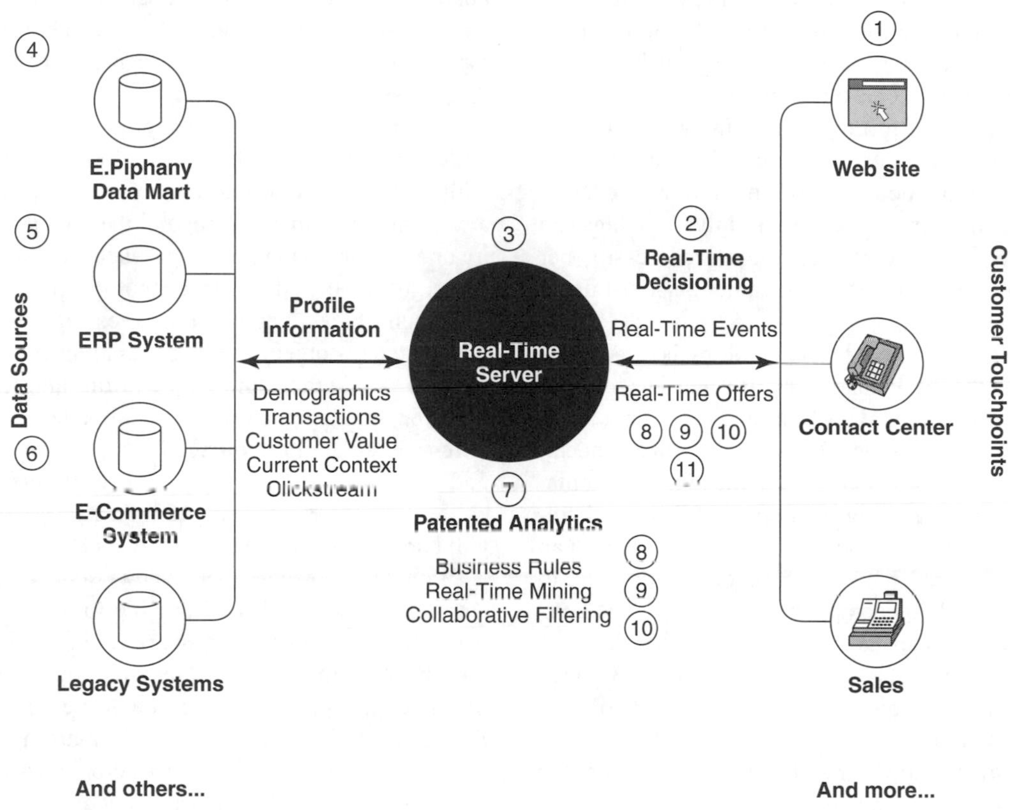

Figure 6.10 A Real-Time Interaction on a Web Site. *Source:* Reprinted with permission of E.piphany, Inc., www.epiphany.com.

increasingly greater variance from the original order. If the customer then cancels the order, that cancellation ripples through the supply chain with the upstream firms experiencing the *bullwhip effect* (a small change by a customer results in a huge change upstream).

Real-time information through the supply chain would likely reduce that ever-growing discrepancy from reality and thus reduce the bullwhip effect. In short, if this supply chain had straight-through processing, the original customer order would be entered only once and all suppliers at all levels in the chain would see the original order and respond accordingly. This is a tall task, but the approach being used is similar to the enterprise nervous system with events, messaging, and publish-and-subscribe features.

Real-Time CRM

Another view of a real-time response might occur between a company and a potential customer, perhaps via a customer call center or a Web site. An example of real-time automated decision making using some of the technologies discussed in this chapter is on pages 252–253.

Communicating Objects

The notion of the real-time enterprise is intriguing for yet another reason. The *Economist* articles on the subject mention sensors and tags that provide information about the physical world via real-time data. We take the editorial freedom of calling them *communicating objects*.

A communicating object can tell you what it is attached to, where it is located, where it belongs, and a lot more information about itself. Technically speaking, such an object is a radio frequency identification device (RFID). It is a small chip that contains information about the object it is attached to, such as a jet engine, a hotel uniform, or a package—anything someone wants to keep track of.

As Glover Ferguson of Accenture explains, communicating objects are also called *smart tags*. They can be as small as a match head, and they are implanted on a wafer surrounded by a coil of wire that serves as the tag's antenna. The antenna allows the tag to be polled by a reader that passes within a few feet. The tag can be passive (read only) or active (send out signals). Those that are larger can be read from further away. Any number of tags can be read by a reader at once, so multiple items on a pallet can be read simultaneously, not one at a time, even in harsh weather conditions. Most importantly, these tags can carry far more information than their predecessor, bar codes. They can carry the history of an item, not just its ID code and price.

In 2003, RFID became a hot technology because Wal-Mart announced that by January 2005 it wanted its top suppliers to place RFID tags on all pallets, cases, and high-ticket items. (Wal-Mart's schedule has since been extended.) The U.S. Department of Defense announced its own initiative the same year. Foreseeing the impact of RFID technology in 1997, the Uniform Product Council (UPC) began an initiative called "Sunrise 2005" to encourage retailers to make their systems RFID compliant by that time. The UPC recognized that bar codes have 11 digits, but that the electronic product codes (EPCs) used by RFID have 13 digits. Retrofitting legacy systems to accommodate the two additional digits is akin to the Y2K challenge CIOs faced in the late 1990s. Efforts to retrofit the old bar code system to the new EPCs required for RFID will be mammoth.

RFID presents a number of potentially other large costs to CIOs. The tags can accumulate histories of products. How much more storage and bandwidth will a company need to capture and communicate all this data? Where should the data be stored and for how long? What sorts of new programs will be needed to analyze the data? In short, CIOs need to understand how well their existing architectures and infrastructures can accommodate RFID and the changes that will be needed, notes Levinson. Advocates of consumer privacy are concerned about RFID tags placed on individual products.

Ferguson believes smart tags are going to transform industries because one day they will talk to one another, which will change how work is handled. For example, Seagate, the disk drive manufacturer, has a smart tag on each individual disk it manufactures. Each type of disk must go through a specific sequence of processes, depending on its type. The checklist on the tag directs it through the correct sequence and ensures that each step is completed before the next one begins. The tags have allowed Seagate to uncover more sources of production errors than in the past, notes Ferguson. A key is the object's ability to capture new information.

Communicating objects are also major theft-prevention devices because they are cheap enough to affix to often-stolen items, such as cartons of liquor and PC motherboards. In the case of motherboards, when one is illegally taken offsite, it can automatically be disabled by the owner, thereby preventing its use. Tags can even be more effective than a set of keys in safeguarding a location, notes Ferguson. People entering an area may be required to wear an RFID wristband. Likewise, these tags can keep people with Alzheimer's disease in appropriate areas, sending out a warning when they are beyond the bounds of their facility or are near a dangerous area, such as a staircase.

Ferguson notes that this technology gets really interesting when objects begin communicating with each other, which he calls object-to-object communication. Theft prevention is a stand-alone application, and new forms of inventory management (say, by a business partner) are a "four walls" application. At first, PCs were stand-alone and used within companies. But the Internet unleashed entirely new uses of PCs and their successors. The same will happen with smart tags, predicts Ferguson.

With these objects, a whole new "silent commerce" will emerge. "Fresh" fish will be able to tell you if they are really fresh, because their smart tag can tell you whether they have been frozen at any time since being caught. Variable pricing could become more of the norm. In Singapore, for instance, cars carry smart tags, and drivers are charged variable prices for where they drive in the city and when. The prices are set to encourage or discourage driving at different places at different times. It is an example of real-time traffic control.

Vigilant Information Systems

The premise of the real-time enterprise is not only that it can capture data in real time, but also that it has the means to act on that data quickly. One theory for how to act fast was espoused in the 1950s by Colonel John Boyd, a U.S. Air Force fighter pilot. He believed he could win any dogfight in 40 seconds (or less). In fact, he put money on his ability. He challenged any fighter pilot, stating that starting from any position of disadvantage he would have his jet on the challenger's tail within 40 seconds or he would pay the other pilot $40. He is said to have never lost a bet, even to pilots in superior aircraft.

He called his theory the OODA (Observe, Orient, Decide, Act) loop because it consisted of the following four actions:

- *Observe* where the challenger's plane is,
- *Orient* himself and size up his own vulnerabilities and opportunities,

- *Decide* which maneuver to take, and
- *Act* to perform it before the challenger could go through the same four steps.

Boyd's goal was to operate *inside* his challenger's loop, that is, to take the four steps faster. By outthinking other pilots, he could outmaneuver them, which often led to confusing them. An OODA loop is shown in Figure 6.11.

Western Digital has used this type of thinking to move itself closer to operating in real time with a sense-and-respond culture that aims to operate faster than its competitors. See the Case Example on pages 256–258.

The Dark Side of Real Time

Given the advantages of more real-time activities, what are the disadvantages? Glover Ferguson believes that object-to-object communication could compromise privacy. He asks, "At what point does an object's ability to track, record, and communicate with other objects invade an individual's rights?" There is no cut-and-dried answer; it depends on the circumstances. It is a political issue, not a technical one, and many CEOs are going to face this question in the future, Ferguson believes. Does knowing the exact location of a company truck every minute of the day and night invade a driver's privacy? Can citizens disable their smart cars to drive where they please without being tracked? The answers, notes Ferguson, lie in CEOs understanding the context of the use of smart tags and the sensitivities that can arise in those contexts.

Omar El Sawy of the University of Southern California points out that in the era of speed, a situation can become very bad, very fast—much faster than in a slower economy. He believes that speed must be balanced with caution. People in a high-speed environment need deep visibility into the workings of their environment and must watch constantly for signals that something bad is likely to happen.

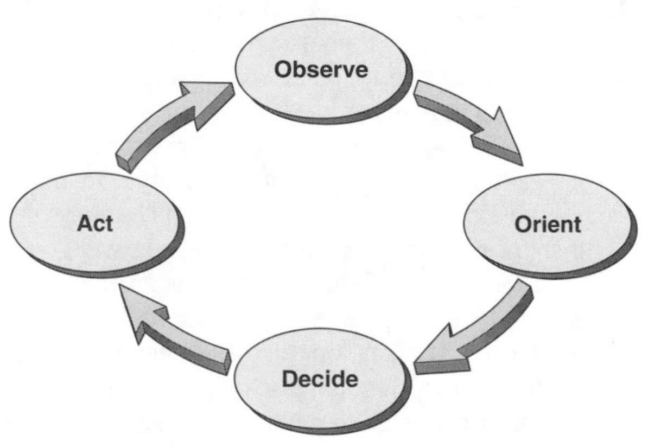

Figure 6.11 An OODA Loop

It is worth noting that when the New York Stock Exchange allowed programmed trading (stock trading by computers rather than people), the exchange learned after a bad experience that it also had to introduce "circuit breakers" to stop deep dives in the market caused by the systems reacting so quickly to actions by other systems. Enterprises may need to introduce similar kinds of circuit breakers when they depend heavily on systems to make decisions and perform actions for them.

SUPPORTING COLLABORATION

In her book, *The Company of the Future*, France Cairncross states that the company of the future will be a collection of online communities, some internal, some that reach outside the organization's boundaries into its business ecosystem, some that are designed and formed outright, and some that just grow on their own. She believes that a main job of executives and managers is to foster these communities and the collaboration they engender. A major job of CIOs is therefore to provide the technology to support online communities and online collaboration. Cairncross is not alone in her thinking.

Teams: The Basis of Organizations

In the *Harvard Business Review,* Peter Drucker's article, "The Coming of the New Organization," became the most reprinted article in the article's first year. Apparently it struck a responsive chord. In that article, Drucker states that organizations are becoming information based, and that they will be organized not like a manufacturing organization, but more like a symphony orchestra, a hospital, or a university. That is, each organization will be composed mainly of specialists who direct their own performance through feedback from others—colleagues, customers, and headquarters.

This move is being driven by three factors, says Drucker. One, knowledge workers are becoming the dominant portion of labor, and they resist the command-and-control form of organization. Two, all companies, even the largest ones, need to find ways to be more innovative and entrepreneurial. Three, IT is forcing a shift. Once companies use IT to handle information rather than data, their decision processes, management structure, and work patterns change.

For example, spreadsheets allow people to perform capital investment analyses in a few hours. Before this

CASE EXAMPLE

WESTERN DIGITAL

Western Digital, with headquarters in Lake Forest, California, manufactures hard drives for PCs, storage systems, and home entertainment systems. It has nearly 17,000 employees, revenues of $3 billion a year, manufacturing plants in Malaysia and Thailand, and customers around the globe.

The industry has short product cycles and experiences intense competition, which keeps product quality high and prices low. Western Digital's main challenge has been to keep up with customers' relentless demands for more storage and faster access while keeping its costs down.

Companies that have not kept up have not survived. Western Digital has survived, even excelled, notes Robert Houghton, Western Digital's CIO, and his coauthors. IT and OODA-loop thinking have been part of this success, providing management with integrated data to manage enterprise-wide and the ability to respond to changes more rapidly.

The Underlying Vigilant Information System

Houghton's IS organization built what they call a *vigilant information system* (VIS), which Houghton et al. define as a system that is "alertly watchful." It is complex, and it builds on the firm's legacy systems. It essentially has four layers, as shown in Figure 6.12:

- *Raw data layer.* The first (bottom) layer consists of raw data from customer orders, customer payments, costs of drives, test data on drives, and so on.
- *Functional application layer.* The second layer, the *observe* layer, consists of the transaction systems (ERP, point of sale, logistics, etc.) that Western Digital uses to run its business. Each application performs its specific functions using the raw data form the first layer.
- *Business intelligence layer.* The third layer, the orient layer, consists of analysis and reporting systems that use data from the data warehouse (drawn from the second layer systems) to analyze Western Digital's performance—financial, factory, and quality performance.
- *Dashboard layer.* The top layer, the decide and act layer, consists of two types of dashboards, one for use in factories (to optimize operations) and one for use by corporate (to plan and forecast). The dashboards display key performance indicators and metrics, they permit drill down, and they issue alerts when data is not within preset boundaries. Western Digital employees use this layer to decide what to do and, in some cases, initiate actions via the dashboard.

The dashboards give factory and corporate management real-time visibility into operations. Houghton et al. define real-time as being "sufficiently vigilant for the process being monitored." Thus, for the factory dashboards, real time means "as close as possible to real time." For the corporate dashboards, real time means "after the data has been validated and synchronized among the data feeds so that all the noise has been filtered out." It is the links between these four layers that have turned Western Digital's formerly disparate systems into a coordinated vigilant information system that funnels the appropriate real-time data to the dashboards.

The Changed Business Processes

As important as the underlying VIS is, it had to be complemented by appropriate business processes to give Western Digital a way to operate *inside* its competitors' OODA loops. Management knew that new dashboards on their own would not change the company's decision-making culture. Therefore, three new company policies were drafted to leverage the VIS:

1. The company's strategic enterprise goals must be translated into time-based objectives and aligned across the company so that management has one set of metrics to manage.
2. Key performance indicators (KPIs) must be captured in real time, and be cmparable, so that teams can compare operations across groups and business units, thereby improving performance companywide.
3. Decision making should be collaborative, to coordinate actions company-wide. To achieve this new style of working, the dashboards have become the focal point in many regularly scheduled meetings, and teams have worked to ensure that people with different expertise are involved in the meetings, from afar, if

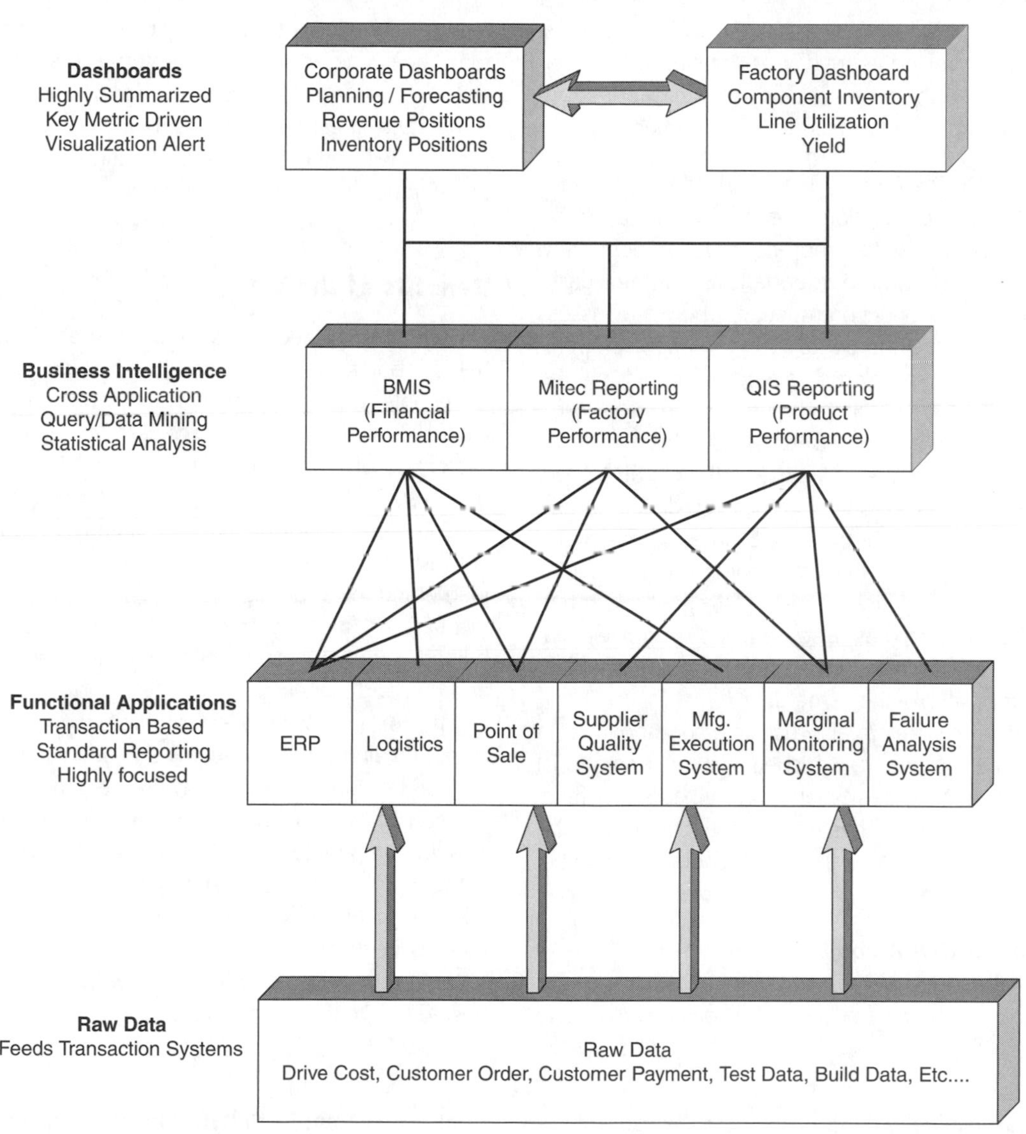

Figure 6.12 Architecture of Western Digital's Vigilant Informaton System. *Source:* R. Houghton, O. El Sawy, P. Gray, C. Donegan, A. Joshi, "Vigilant Information Systems for Managing Enterprises in Dynamic Supply Chains: Real-Time Dashboards at Western Digital," *MIS Quarterly Executive,* Vol. 3, No. 1, March 2004, pp. 19–35. Used with permission.

necessary. It has taken teams quite a while to figure out what information others need to participate in decision making while being "virtually there" rather than in the room.

Each dashboard contains its appropriate real-time metrics and KPIs, and each metric and KPI has its own target level and a variance setting. When a variance is exceeded, the appropriate executive is alerted.

The Shop-Floor OODA Loop. The shop-floor supervisors in the factories, who manage closest to real time, operate on the tightest OODA loop. They receive a page or a flashing light on their dashboard when one of their variances

(Case continued)

(Case continued)

is violated. The time from alert to action is often minutes, rather than the former hours or days. Sometimes, they can diagnose and resolve the problem using their dashboard because the dashboards can be used to initiate actions.

The Factory OODA Loop. The production managers, who oversee multiple production lines, operate on an OODA loop that is not as tight as the shop-floor OODA loop. They, too, receive alerts, but a more important use of their dashboard is at their daily production meeting, where they assess yesterday's performance and discuss ways to improve operations. The "yesterday problems" already handled by the shop-floor supervisors are filtered out. So the production managers only see the unresolved issues, which reduces their information overload and quickens their OODA loop, note Houghton et al. As a result, their daily production meetings have dropped from 5 hours to 1.5 hours. These meetings involve 15 people, so the dashboard system provides production managers significant time savings in these meetings alone. The system has also reduced micromanagement; there is no longer haggling about who has the right data because they all see the same data.

The production managers also use their dashboard in a learning mode, performing "health checks" of the operational aspects of the factory to see what is and what is not functioning well. Western Digital has learned that the shorter the OODA loop, the more frequent the health checks need to be, state Houghton et al.

The Corporate OODA Loop. Corporate executives receive alerts on their dashboards, and they find they can uncover root causes faster because of the dashboards, note Houghton et al. But they mainly use their dashboards to perform health checks for the enterprise as a whole. Their OODA loop is not as tight as the factory loop, but their decisions often affect the factories. Many decisions require consultation with others, so people routinely send screen shots or references to screens to others so that they all see the same data when discussing an issue.

Benefits of the VIS

The VIS has, indeed, quickened all three OODA loops and helped to link decisions across them. Management's goal is to be able to initiate a change in the factories in the same work shift as the company receives a change request from a customer. When it reaches this speed of responsiveness, it believes it will gain market share, note Houghton et al.

Corporate performance has already improved measurably. Margins have doubled since the dashboards were implemented over 3 years ago. Management attributes the increase, in part, to the dashboards because they have helped improve data visibility, supply chain management, and demand planning.

The VIS is moving Western Digital toward a sense-and-respond culture where it learns and adapts quickly in a coordinated fashion. The sensing (observe and orient) is handled by the VIS, whereas the responding (decide and act) is handled by the people. In this environment, timing is important. There is no point in accelerating sensing if no action can be taken, and there is no point in accelerating responding if there is no fresh information. The two need to be in sync, note Houghton et al., which is how Western Digital's three nested OODA loops now work.

technology was available, these investment analyses generally had to be based on opinion because the calculations are so complex. With computing, the calculations become manageable. More importantly, the assumptions underlying the calculations can be given weights. In so doing, investment analysis changes from being a budgeting question to being a policy question, says Drucker, because the assumptions supporting the business strategy can more easily be discussed.

IT also changes organizational structure when a firm shifts its focus from processing data to producing information, he says. Turning data into information requires knowledge, and knowledge is specialized. The information-based organization needs far more specialists than middle managers who relay information. Thus organizations are becoming flatter, with fewer headquarters staff and more specialists in operating units. Even departments have different functions. They set standards, provide training, and assign specialists. Work is done mainly in task-focused teams, where specialists from various functions work together as a team for the duration of a project.

Team-based organizations work like hospitals or orchestras, says Drucker. Hospitals have specialty units, each with its own knowledge, training, and language. Most are headed by a working specialist, not a full-time manager. That specialist reports to the top of the hospital, reducing the need for middle management. Work in the units is done by ad hoc teams that are assembled to address a patient's condition and diagnosis. Symphony orchestras are similar. They have one conductor, many high-grade specialists, and other support people.

Drucker believes that we are at the beginning of the third evolution in the structure of organizations. The first, which took place around 1900, separated business ownership from management. The second, in the 1920s, created the command-and-control corporation. The third, happening now, is the organization of knowledge specialists.

Why should IS executives be interested in supporting groups? Robert Johansen, of the Institute for the Future and an author of two books on group working, notes that systems that support groups are important because most people spend 60 to 80 percent of their time working with others. Yet, from informal polls he has taken, people seem to feel they are most productive when they are working alone. Thus, they are not happy about how they work with others. This finding reveals a need for systems that support groups.

Groupware—electronic tools that support teams of collaborators—represents a fundamental change in the way people think about using computers, says Johansen. The things people need to work with others are different from the things they need to work alone. Thus, groupware is different from past software.

Groupware that takes full advantage of IT needs to be just another part of corporate information systems, says Johansen. The products need to be built on existing platforms—e-mail systems, LANs, departmental systems, and public network services, such as the telephone or the Internet. Use of these technologies must advance beyond the "horseless carriage" stage and lead to new organizational structures, he believes.

Given these three opinions on the importance of group working and the need for systems to support such collaboration, we turn to exploring the kinds of groups that exist and the kinds of systems that support their collaboration.

UNDERSTANDING GROUPS

Collaboration is all about getting work done in a group, rather than individually. However, groups differ from one another, and their work styles vary depending on a number of factors. Here are some characteristics of groups.

Characteristics of Groups

Not all groups are the same. Different types emerge for different tasks. Some of the characteristics that differentiate groups include membership, interaction, hierarchy, location, and time.

Membership. Groups can be open, where almost anyone can join. Or they can be closed, where membership is restricted. Actually, a gray scale between open and closed indicates the degree of difficulty in gaining membership.

Interaction. The group can be loosely coupled, where the activity of each member is relatively independent of the other members. Salespeople who have their own sales territories often fall into this category. Or the group can be tightly coupled, such as a project team where the work of each member is tied closely to the work of the other members. As in the case of gaining group membership, group couplings range widely from loose to tight.

Hierarchy. A group can be just one part of a chain of command. Large public events, such at the Olympics or the Rose Parade, for instance, are planned and conducted by a hierarchy of committees. At the top is an ongoing committee that sets the general plans years in advance and selects the site and the top people for putting on each event. The top committee then oversees the work of the various detail committees. In addition, each of the detail committees may have subcommittees working on specific portions of their responsibility. This same hierarchy of committees occurs in large IT projects, such as implementing ERP, or in defining IT policies, such as an enterprise's overall IT architecture.

Location. Group members may be collocated or dispersed. In the past, location influenced how they collaborated. When collocated, they could meet face-to-face. When dispersed, they either had to travel or use video conferencing to read each other's body language. But IT is making long-distance personal contact easier. More and more, teams and groups can work together effectively while remaining dispersed. In some cases, groups in Asia perform their work on a project and then pass that work on to a European group when their Asian workday ends. The European group progresses the work, then passes it to a group in the Americas when the European workday ends. In this type of group working, location allows round-the-clock work. This work-style is not yet a common phenomenon, but it does happen.

Time. There are two aspects to the time dimension of group work: duration of the group and time intensity of the work. The work of some groups is short-lived. An ad hoc committee might be formed to uncover the root cause of a recurring problem, for instance, and then disband once that cause has been found. Other groups last for a long time; functions in an organization, such as HR or finance, are examples.

On time intensity, some groups' members work full-time on the group's work. Other groups only require intermittent work by their members. Of course, time intensity usually varies—high intensity at times interspersed with low intensity at other times.

We cite these characteristics to illustrate that providing computer-based support for groups is not uniform because of the many variations. Initially, support was for intra-company groups. However, the Internet has led to the ability to provide worldwide support for global teams that cross organizational lines. The main issues are what types of groups need support and why.

Types of Groups

Here is a list of just a few of the many, many kinds of groups.

- ***Authority groups*** involve formal authority (and often hierarchy), such as boss and subordinates or team leader and team members. Membership is closed and coupling is tight, but location is irrelevant in more and more cases, and generally these groups work full-time. In matrix management, people may have two bosses, one technical and one administrative.
- ***Intra-departmental groups*** can have members all doing essentially the same work, full-time, often under the same boss. Membership is closed, seniority generally exists, and interaction can range from tight (only do one job, on their own) to loose coupling (work with their neighbor). Location is generally close, but, as in the case of globally dispersed departments serving different parts of the world, they can be dispersed. These groups generally rely on LANs, departmental computers, and intranets to collaborate.
- ***Project teams*** generally have members who work full-time to accomplish a goal within a specific schedule. Generally, membership is closed, coupling is tight, and a hierarchy can exist. To obtain the expertise they need, these teams often have dispersed membership. They also have a limited duration: to the end of the project. Some teams bring in experts to fill special needs. For instance, a team creating a document might call on an editor near the end or a graphics person to add diagrams and handle document formatting.
- ***Interdepartmental work groups*** pass work from department to department (purchasing, receiving, accounts payable) in a chain, forming a super group. Membership is closed, coupling is tight, and hierarchy tends not to be present. In support areas, such as finance, HR, and even IT, companies have been creating shared services departments that collocate people doing similar work. Formerly, these people were in remote offices, perhaps performing several jobs. Now they work full-time on one job in a center of expertise. In some cases, the function has been outsourced, which generally moves the entire function to the provider's site.
- ***Committees and task forces*** are formed to deal with a subject area or issue. Generally, neither requires full-time participation. Committees are usually ongoing; task forces just deal with the issue and disband. Membership may not be quite as closed as a project team, and interaction might not be as tightly coupled. Generally, the work is not full-time; although, in the case of a merger, an IT architecture team may need to temporarily work full-time to design the IT architecture of the merged enterprise.
- ***Business relationship groups*** are relationships with customers, groups of customers, suppliers, and so on. Membership often is closed in that a new organization may have to earn acceptance. Interaction is loosely coupled. A hierarchy is not likely, but favored customers and suppliers can have dominating influences. Generally, these are meant to be long-lived, but that may or may not be true, depending on changes in the business ecosystem.
- ***Peer groups*** meet to exchange ideas and opinions. Examples are fraternal organizations, repairmen who call on each other for help, and prospects called together for a sales presentation. Membership can range from relatively open to closed, and the interaction tends to be loosely coupled. Hierarchy usually is not much in evidence. Often the group has dispersed members who meet face-to-face rarely but may keep in close contact electronically.
- ***Networks*** are groups of people who socialize, exchange information, and expand the number of their personal acquaintances.
- ***Electronic groups*** include chat rooms, multi-user domains, user groups, and virtual worlds, all formed on the Internet to socialize, find information, entertain themselves, gain comfort, or just experiment with the online world. Membership is generally wide open, interaction is loosely coupled, there is usually no hierarchy, and the members are widely dispersed and most likely never meet face-to-face.
- ***Communities of practice (CoPs)*** is a term coined by the people at the Institute for Research on Learning

to refer to a group of people who work or socialize together for so long that they have developed an identifiable way of doing things. Such communities arise naturally at school, at work, in volunteer organizations, and in sports clubs. Some CoPs form as a way to share ideas about a technology they all use. Others form as a way to get work done faster and easier; they informally devise shortcuts and practices. Generally, CoPs have open membership. They last as long as their members see them as useful.

- ***Network armies*** is a term coined by Richard Hunter of Gartner EXP in his book *World Without Secrets: Business, Crime, and Privacy in the Age of Ubiquitous Computing* to mean a widely dispersed group of people that forms to further a cause. Hunter sees the open source movement as a network army. So are most grassroots movements, such as groups opposed to globalization, terrorist organizations, and animal rights activists. Leaders emerge and membership is usually open. Network armies increasingly use electronic means to further their agendas.

These final two types of groups—communities of practice and network armies—are probably unfamiliar because they have only recently been identified. They are likely to increase in the future because they take advantage of IT, they have the flexibility to form and act quickly (which is an advantage in our faster-moving world), and they could increasingly wield power. Thus, we delve into each a bit more.

Communities of Practice

The "father" of CoPs is Etienne Wenger, who identified them and has studied them since authoring the definitive book on CoPs, *Communities of Practice: Learning, Meaning, and Identity*. In an article with William Snyder of Social Capital Group, Wenger and Snyder point out that CoPs are all about managing knowledge that is, capturing and spreading know-how, ideas, innovations, and experience. CoPs are an organizational form that complements other means for sharing knowledge. In fact, in some enterprises, CoPs form the foundation of their knowledge management efforts. Wenger and Snyder define them as informal groups that form around a passion for or expertise about something. This "something" can vary from deep-water drilling to check processing, they note. The subject matter really does not matter; the goal in forming a CoP is to share members' experiences, expertise, and problems.

Though informal, some CoPs have had a profound effect on their enterprise by driving strategies, creating new lines of business, spreading best practices, solving seemingly intractable problems, retaining people, and increasing the level of expertise in some areas. To date, few enterprises have formally recognized CoPs or supported them. Without support, CoPs can be difficult to organize and then sustain.

Being informal, CoPs resist being managed. However, some enterprises have seen their value and have learned how to nurture them. Wenger and Snyder believe these enterprises are the forward-thinking ones. They have learned how to provide the infrastructure and climate for these self-organizing entities to form of their own volition, meet and share via numerous channels (face-to-face, e-mail, IM, video conferencing), and even strengthen the organization's formal mechanisms. As an example, consider DaimlerChrysler and its support of CoPs, which began in the Chrysler Corporation in the late 1980s.

Although CoPs cannot be designed, they can be nurtured. Wenger and Snyder believe companies need to perform three nurturing acts to garner benefits from CoPs: identify potential CoPs, provide them with an infrastructure, and measure them appropriately.

Identifying Potential CoPs. To identify potential CoPs, companies can provide the means and experience for developing them by providing CoP consultants. Thereby, an employee interested in forming a CoP can explore the possibility with someone who understands CoPs and can help the employee interview potential members to see what sorts of problems the community should address to provide real value to members. The employee and consultant can then plan an initial activity to not only address the identified problems, but also link them to the company's agenda. But to even get off the ground, say Wenger and Snyder, the members need to personally "connect" to the group's intent; otherwise, people will not participate.

Providing a CoP Infrastructure. To provide a CoP infrastructure, executives need to give CoPs legitimacy because they lack resources and formal standing in the enterprise. Sometimes that means extolling the contributions of CoPs and the people who organize them, instituting compensation systems that reward collaboration, and budgeting money to build IT systems that CoPs need. In some instances, membership is not open; an employee must be recognized as an expert to be invited to join. Thus, there is formal recognition of the esteem of belonging. Having executive sponsors also provides a kind of CoP infrastructure, as does linking them to a corporate university, if one exists, or paying for them to participate in CoP activities. Providing support to organize events is also a form of infrastructure.

CASE EXAMPLE

DAIMLERCHRYSLER

In the late 1980s, when Chrysler Corporation was about to go out of business because of competition from Japanese auto companies, CoPs played a large role in its survival, write Etienne Wenger, Richard McDermott, and William Snyder in their book *Cultivating Communities of Practice*. In the late 1980s, it took Chrysler 5 years to bring a vehicle to market; competitors took as little as 3. To compete, management had to reinvent how the company worked. Its organizational structure at the time was functional, with design units passing vehicle designs to manufacturing units that then passed back the designs after modifying them for manufacturability.

To reduce this iterative process, which added significant time to development, the company reorganized into "car platforms," such as Jeep, minivan, truck, or small car. Engineers and other workers reported to only one platform. This change reduced development time to 2.5 years—a significant improvement. However, it also led to multiple versions of parts, uncoordinated relationships with suppliers, and mistakes repeated among the platform groups, write the authors.

Employees with similar jobs needed to communicate across the platforms, but the new structure did not foster that interchange. So, some began meeting informally. Rather than formalize these cross-platform groups, they became known as Tech Clubs; in essence, CoPs that were supported and sanctioned by top management.

They began to take responsibility for their area of expertise by conducting design reviews. They even revived the old idea of creating "engineering books of knowledge," which are databases that store the information engineers need to do their job, such as compliance standards, lessons learned, and best practices. Such books only succeed when the users "own" them and naturally keep them up-to-date as part of their everyday work.

Once community members within Chrysler saw the value of their book to their work, ownership took hold. They now spend much of their meeting time debating the items that should be in the chapters, and the wording that should be used, to be sure what they state is correct. The books are intended to deal with the real problems they face. Wenger, McDermott, and Snyder point out that the engineers find these debates and discussions to be just as important as the final documents because they learn a lot from interacting with their peers. Thus, while they are building practice standards they are also building a community. The two go hand-in-hand in successful CoPs, the authors note.

The Chrysler division now has over 100 Tech Clubs, and a team is introducing the concept to its parent, DaimlerChrysler. In fact, this team helps Tech Club coordinators in the United States and Germany launch their clubs, produce useful knowledge resources for members, and keep their clubs vibrant and relevant. The Tech Club support team also helps ensure that the clubs are working on common technology platforms so that they can share knowledge across clubs.

Wenger, McDermott, and Snyder point out that these Tech Clubs provide DaimlerChrysler with the crucial matrix structure they need to have engineers focus on their platform yet share their knowledge across platforms without the administrative headaches that formal matrix structures have required.

Measuring CoPs. To measure CoPs appropriately often means measuring their contributions in nontraditional ways because their effects may not be immediate. Their contributions may only show up in the formal organization (on a team or department's work), not in the community's work. It is not always possible to identify a good idea as originating in a CoP. To assess CoPs, note Wenger and Snyder, listen to the stories members tell about their CoP, such as how a comment at a CoP gathering spurred an idea, solved a major problem, or accelerated a project. Such anecdotes generally do not count in formal measurement programs, but collecting stories systematically can paint a picture of the kinds of contributions specific CoPs are making. In some cases, such collections of stories can even lead to estimates of money saved or revenues generated.

CoPs are emerging first in knowledge-based enterprises. But to flourish, executives need to understand their characteristics and how they work. Wenger and Snyder see CoPs as an emerging business form that will be as familiar in the near future as business units and business teams are today.

Network Armies

As noted earlier, Richard Hunter coined the term *network army*, which he defines as a set of individuals and communities aligned by a cause. They have moral and intellectual influencers as opposed to formal leadership. Major differences may exist among members' overall beliefs. As an example, consider the civil liberties community in the United States, which includes members from both the left and right wings of the dominant political parties. Network armies are as permanent as their common agenda; their cohesive force is their value system. Their communications are in open forums that anyone can join. Modern communication technologies, including the photocopy machine, the fax machine, and most recently the Internet, have dramatically increased the reach of network armies.

Network armies have existed for a long time, but they can now appear suddenly with a lot of power because of three developments: (1) high-speed information flows due to a common language (English) and communication system (Internet), (2) the geometrically expanding power of networks (adding one person geometrically increases the number of interconnections), and (3) the international visibility now afforded just about any cause. Network armies go about their business in the open; anyone can join in or listen in to their discussions. As a result, says Hunter, the network army is the social and political structure that suits a world without secrets.

One of the intriguing observations Hunter makes about network armies is that hierarchies (like traditional businesses, governments, and armies) have a tremendously difficult time fighting network armies because they have no single leader; they are like a hydra with many heads. They are so dispersed and part of the fabric of society that they are difficult to find, let alone fight. Hunter believes network armies are on the rise. An example of a network army appears on page 264.

Having explored types and characteristics of groups, we turn our attention to systems to support collaboration.

SYSTEMS TO SUPPORT COLLABORATION

The activities of groups can be divided into two generic categories. One is communication and interaction. Communication means transmitting information from one person to another or to several others; interaction means back-and-forth communication over time. Two, groups are involved in decision making and problem solving. The members reach a decision or form a consensus. Both types of group activities are needed in collaboration. Historically, systems supporting group work have originated from one or the other of these two major functions. Office systems, and in particular e-mail, support people-to-people communication. Researchers in the area of computer-supported cooperative work generally have emphasized technology to aid communication, such as enhanced computer conferencing and systems to assist two or more people to work on the same project. On the other hand, group DSS work has evolved from the DSS community and focuses on reaching a conclusion, decision, or consensus, even though it includes technology to support communication.

A second way to view the work of groups is the way Geraldine DeSantis of Duke University and Brent Gallupe of the University of Minnesota did in one of the early frameworks. Their matrix, shown in Figure 6.13, has proximity of group members on one dimension (together/dispersed) and duration of interaction on the other (limited/ongoing). The figure gives one technology example per cell. Note that this matrix is relevant for both communication and decision making. For example, decision making has been the intent of decision rooms, whereas LANs are usually perceived mainly as supporting communication.

Groups in close proximity and with a limited decision-making duration might use a decision room where every attendee uses a computer to participate in the group's deliberations. An example of such a room is presented shortly. Groups that are dispersed and have a limited decision-making duration might use decision rooms connected via video conferencing. Or, as at one highly advanced lab with two facilities, they might communicate via video walls. Standing by one wall allowed employees to converse in real time with someone standing by the wall at the other site. People would meet at the wall to make decisions or just to converse (as a person would when happening upon a colleague in a hallway).

Close-proximity groups with ongoing decisions could use a local decision network, IM, or perhaps a chat room on an intranet. Dispersed groups with ongoing decisions could also use an intranet, if appropriate, or a secure decision system. An example is presented shortly.

Yet a third way to categorize the work of groups uses a variation of the DeSantis-Gallupe matrix by having time on one dimension (same time/different time) and place on the other (same place/different place). This third view has become dominant, so it is used here. Bob Johansen of the Institute for the Future (IFTF) is a leader in the field of

CASE EXAMPLE

THE OPEN SOURCE MOVEMENT

Richard Hunter of Gartner EXP believes that the open source movement is a prime example of a network army. Open source means that (1) the complete source code must be distributed with any and all distributions, and (2) anyone can modify and redistribute the code to anyone to use. A prime example of open source software is Linux, the operating system whose kernel was written by Linus Torvalds. The opposite of open source is proprietary software, which is sold only in its compiled state (undecipherable by humans) and is not allowed to be changed except by the developer.

Open source is mainly about how software is developed, enhanced, and managed. The open source movement is a community with a shared culture, where people earn their membership by the quality of the code they produce. Members are volunteers; no one is paid. They do it for fun (they love to code), to hang around with other like-minded developers ("fiery brains," says Hunter), and to be part of a worthy cause. Torvalds' goal in developing Linux was to "write software that does not suck." He reasoned that the best way to do that would be to let interested software developers chip in and improve any part that attracted them. Thus, it is a culture of mavericks who want lots of personal autonomy, guided by minimal conformance.

The movement has a massive flat structure with 4 "influencers" (including Torvalds), 6 to 8 distributors who package versions, some 200 project leaders who manage active projects, and some 750,000 volunteer developers (as of late 2001). The number is probably higher now. The developers follow the influencers because they have the same values. This flat structure is possible, says Hunter, because the Internet allows the influencers to communicate directly with the developers, and vice versa. Hence, the influencers know what the volunteers think, which can make it both harder for them to lead as well as to mislead. In addition, all communications are open via bulletin boards, e-mail lists, and other Internet-based channels that anyone can join.

Hunter notes that when he and his Gartner colleagues critiqued the viability of open source software in 1999, they believed it would capture 15 percent of the server operating system market. "We did not realize this was a disruptive technology that could change the software world," he notes. Less than 2 years later, after "getting it," he and his colleagues significantly increased their assessment to predicting that open source would be used in 80 percent of businesses by year-end 2003.

Hunter now believes it is not wise to underestimate the claims of network armies, as Microsoft apparently did. The worst mistake a business can make is to become the nemesis of a network army, and that is what Microsoft did in 1998. Until that time, the open source movement's only goal was to write useful software. However, in August 1998, Microsoft saw the open source movement as a threat and wrote an internal paper that proposed ways to eliminate it. That study, of course, fell into the hands of an open source member, states Hunter, because this is a world without secrets. The open source movement always distrusted Microsoft, and that distrust hardened into rage once the study was published on the Web under the moniker, *The Halloween Papers*.

Microsoft's past tactics for addressing competitors are not appropriate for dealing with a network army, writes Hunter. There are no open source revenues, so Microsoft cannot undercut prices (as it did in bundling its browser into Windows and destroying Netscape). There is no one to negotiate with, so the movement cannot be bought and then taken apart (as many past competitors have been).

All "negotiations" with a network army must be in public, notes Hunter, and consist of actions, not words, which is what Microsoft is now doing. Its executives are arguing against the movement in public forums, hoping to dissuade executives from using open source software. But when it first denied, and then acknowledged, that it was using such software itself to support Hotmail and other services due to the superiority of the open source software, Microsoft lost credibility. Open source members only believe actions. They want people to do the right thing because they see their cause as a moral one.

Hunter believes Microsoft thought it was up against a rival business and tried to use the tactics it used successfully against other businesses. However, a network army is more like a religion than a business, and you do not fight a religious movement by telling its members that they are worshippers of an evil, false god. Better to find some way to work with them on projects of mutual interest as a means of establishing personal trust. However, Microsoft has not wanted to coexist with anyone, so it has taken a different route. It is a dangerous route, Hunter believes. Businesses that face a network army cannot make it go away without addressing the underlying issues. Treating a network army like a business is bound to backfire.

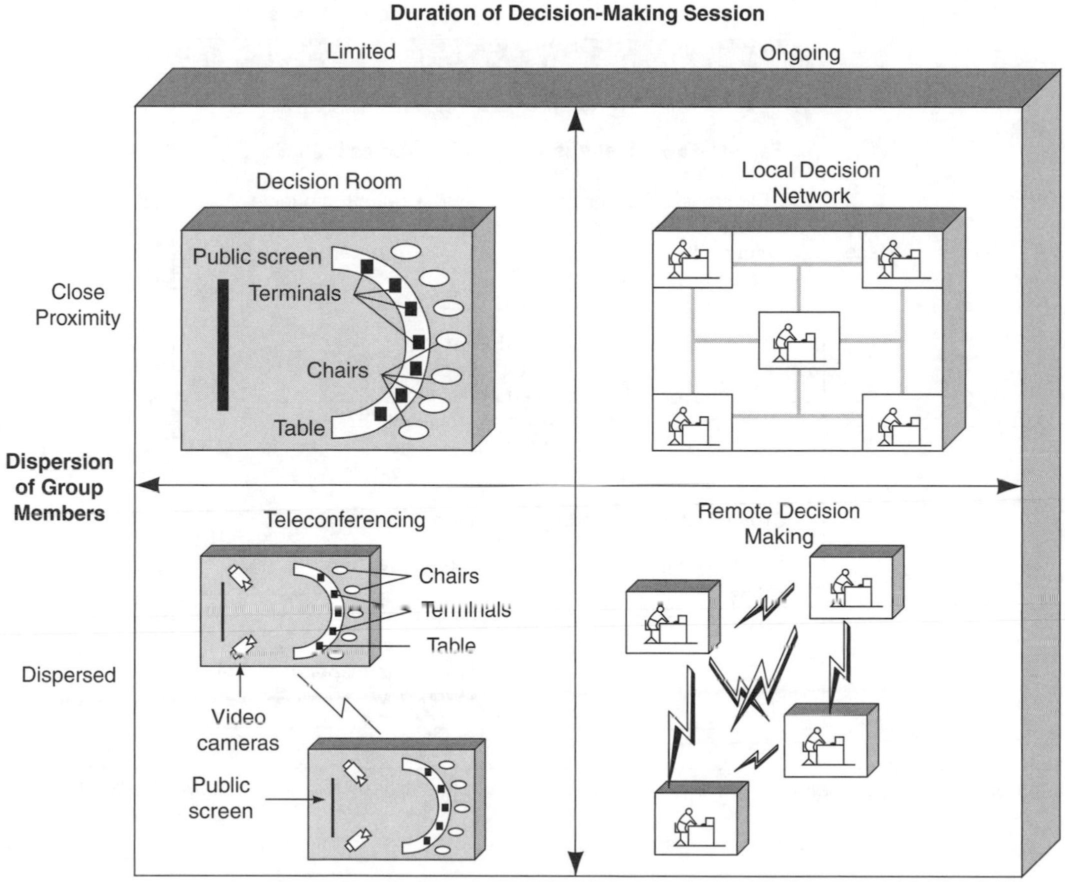

Figure 6.13 Framework for Group Decision Support. *Source:* G. DeSantis and B. Gallupe, "Group Decision Support Systems: A New Frontier," *Data Base,* Winter 1985, pp. 10–15.

groupware. He and his colleagues at IFTF extended the DeSantis-Gallupe matrix to form the time/place framework shown in Figure 6.14.

The two values, either same or different, on each dimension designate whether the group members are communicating and interacting over time and/or distance. The "same time/same place" cell in the upper left, for example, includes electronic meeting support systems. The "different time/different place" cell in the lower right incorporates such communication-oriented systems as e-mail, computer conferencing, and use of Lotus Notes.

Until recently, there has been little integration among the systems in the cells, even though it is clear to researchers and developers that supporting collaboration must aim to permit anytime, anyplace group working. But that is changing. Systems used by individuals are also being used by groups, as demonstrated by Western Digital's use of digital dashboards. In addition, systems used in meetings are also being used to "extend" those meetings over time after the participants have dispersed. For instance, a Lotus Notes database might be used in a meeting as well as outside of it. Instant messaging is used in both settings, as are the dashboards at Western Digital. The Internet has aided in extending the use of systems among the cells.

Supporting "Same Time/Same Place" Collaboration

Supporting "same time/same place" collaboration has generally meant supporting meetings, and a lot of work has focused on this area. One study found that the average executive in a U.S. company spends more than 800 hours a year in meetings. Not only does this figure represent a large portion of total work hours (on the order of 30 percent), but even worse, the executives reported that they

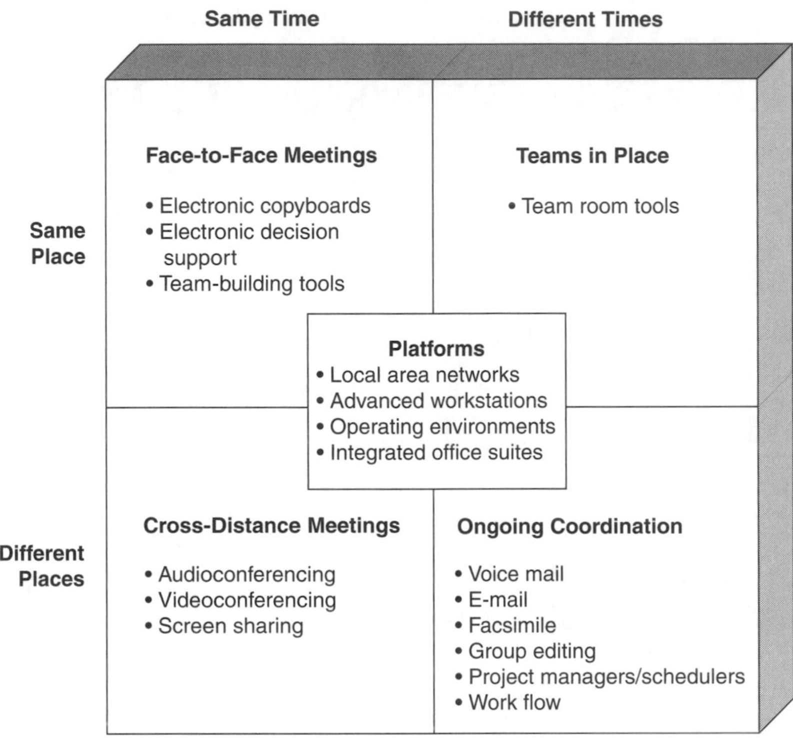

Figure 6.14 Groupware Options. *Source:* Courtesy of Robert Johansen of the Institute for the Future, Menlo Park, CA.

considered about 240 of those hours to have been wasted in useless meetings.

The Problem with Meetings. From the many meetings we have attended, many shortcomings have been evident. Meetings often have no agenda or only a superficial one. No problems are clearly spelled out in advance, and no specific action items are proposed to address the problems. If actions (or motions) are proposed, alternatives are not fully considered. If documentation about the issues has been provided before the meeting, some members choose not to study it; they expect to be briefed at the meeting. The chairperson may do little or no follow-up between meetings to see that the members carry out their assignments.

Some meetings are doomed from the start. Key people arrive late or do not attend at all. Necessary information does not arrive. Some group members have forgotten to fulfill their assignments. Then the meeting chairperson may do a poor job of managing the meeting time. Discussion may be allowed to wander from the subject. Time may be spent on briefing attendees or on routine matters—reviewing and correcting minutes of prior meetings, getting committee progress reports, and so on. Such meetings tend to run over their allotted time, with important items receiving poor consideration. Often, too, a few people dominate the discussion; not infrequently, these people are repetitious, saying the same things over and over. Conversely, some people do not speak up and contribute their ideas.

Finally, many meetings are wasteful from a cost standpoint. A meeting involving even a few managers and professionals costs hundreds of dollars per hour in salaries alone; large meetings can easily cost thousands of dollars per hour. If travel is required, costs are even higher. Add to these considerations the fact that the participants are unavailable for other activities while tied up in the meetings.

IT Can Help. The goals of systems for improving meetings are to (1) eliminate some meetings, (2) encourage better planning and better preparation for those meetings that must be held, and (3) improve the effectiveness of meetings that are held.

Eliminate some meetings. The most likely candidates for elimination are the meetings that do not call for a group decision or group action but are simply for group updating. Progress report meetings are an example, particularly if progress (actual progress versus planned progress) can be reported frequently by e-mail, the company intranet, or an electronic team meeting place. Meetings where key people cannot attend or where needed information is not yet available can be canceled at the last moment. E-mail, voice mail, and IM systems allow the word to be spread rapidly. Intranets allow progress and status reports to be posted in a form that is easily available to everyone. In short, some of the work done in meetings can be shifted from the "same time/same place" cell to the "different time/different place" cell in the time/place matrix.

Better preparation for meetings. Computer conferencing can play a significant role in improving preparation for meetings. A computer conferencing system is actually a form of enhanced e-mail. Participants can log on at their convenience, read all entries made by others since they last logged on, and make their contributions. In the planning stage of a meeting, such a system can be used to obtain reactions to the proposed agenda, and those reactions might spur debate and alternatives. Furthermore, routine matters may be handled before the meeting, such as review and approval of minutes, receiving committee progress reports, voting on routine action items, and so on. Group members can give attention to these matters at their convenience, saving valuable synchronous meeting time for more important business. The chairperson can also use the conferencing system for follow-up activities. Finally, the system can provide a written record of pre- and post-meeting communications.

Improve the effectiveness and efficiency of meetings. One of the major benefits of meeting support systems is improved meeting efficiency and effectiveness. Meetings are more effective when the ideas generated by the group are more creative and everyone in the group is actively involved. Meetings are more effective when group commitment happens quickly. Following is a case in point.

Supporting "Same Time/Same Place" Presentations and Discussions

A second "same time/same place" situation that can benefit from group support tools is traditional presentation-discussion sessions found in classrooms, conference sessions, and business meetings. In an article in the *Communications of the ACM*, Robert Davison and Robert Briggs10 explored the advantages of using a Group Support System (GSS) in a presentation-discussion session held in a workshop setting. The system was similar to the one used by Burr-Brown. Each member of the audience had a workstation, all interconnected by a LAN, with a public screen to show the group's interactions. The presenter had a separate screen for audiovisuals used in the presentation.

To begin their exploration, Davison and Briggs made the following seven hypotheses about the potential advantages and disadvantages of attendees using a GSS at the workshops:

- ***More opportunities for discussion.*** Using a GSS would eliminate the need to divide available airtime among potential speakers because participants could contribute simultaneously. The parallel, non-oral communication channels would multiply the time available to the audience. In addition, because they would be communicating online, the participants could interact with each other during the actual presentation, which further multiplied available airtime.
- ***More equal participation.*** Because the GSS provides many parallel communication channels, loud or strong personalities probably would not dominate the discussion. Unlike oral discussions, the amount contributed by one person was expected to be independent of the amount contributed by others. This expectation was more likely to lead to a more equal distribution of discussion among the attendees.
- ***Permanent record of discussion.*** The GSS would capture a permanent electronic transcript of the online discussion. Thus, both participants and presenters could access the details long after the discussion was over.
- ***Improved feedback to presenters.*** With unrestricted airtime for audience members and a permanent record of their discussion, presenters anticipated more comments as well as more detail in those comments. Furthermore, the anonymity allowed by the GSS would reduce some participants' concerns about negative repercussions if they contributed unpopular, critical, or new ideas. Thus, the presenters could receive more unfiltered critical analysis of their work using the GSS.
- ***Improved learning.*** The GSS was also expected to reduce attention blocking; that is, the loss of attentiveness caused by people trying to remember what they want to say during the presentation. Working in parallel, participants could record ideas when they occurred, then return their attention to the presentation. With more discussion

CASE EXAMPLE

BURR-BROWN CORPORATION

Burr-Brown Corporation, with headquarters in Tucson, Arizona, manufactures and sells electronics parts to other electronic manufacturers. It has about 1,500 employees and $180 million in annual sales.

When the University of Arizona, also in Tucson, created a decision room in its IS department, the CEO of Burr-Brown decided to use it for management's 3-day annual strategic planning meeting. He was so pleased with the results that the firm used it again the following year for the same purpose.

The Decision Room

The room has 24 workstations arranged in a semicircle on two tiers. Up to 48 people can use the room, 2 persons per workstation. In an adjacent control room is the file server, and at the front of the room is a facilitator's control station, as well as a rear projection screen for video, slides, and movies, and a white board. All the participants' workstations and the facilitator's workstation are connected by a LAN.

The university has developed a number of decision room software tools, and more than 100 groups have used their decision room. That software is now marketed under the name GroupSystems by GroupSystems.com.

The Electronic Brainstorming System is the most popular of the tools; it is used by more than 70 percent of the groups. Like most of the tools, it allows participants to simultaneously and anonymously key in ideas on a specific question. After an idea is entered and sent to the file server, the participant can see the ideas entered by others.

After the brainstorming portion of a meeting, many groups use the Issue Analyzer to organize the ideas. A Voting Tool ranks ideas and a Topic Commenter attaches comments to ideas already in the system. Finally, the groups can use the Policy Formation software to study alternatives. Most group "discussions" using these tools are done via keyboards rather than by talking. However, some other tools do encourage face-to-face discussions.

Burr-Brown's Use of the Room

Burr-Brown's annual strategic planning meetings had always been held off-site, with some 9 to 10 executives attending. When they used the decision room, 31 executives attended. The IS department at the university provided a meeting facilitator to help plan the meeting and then facilitate it.

During the meeting, the facilitator explained each tool before it was to be used. The facilitator also kept participants on track and was the neutral leader of the meeting so that Burr-Brown's CEO could attend as a participant. In addition, an assistant facilitator and three other assistants also were present. They helped the participants use the hardware and software, made copies of the documents generated by the system, and so on.

Before the meeting, several planning meetings were held to settle the meeting agenda. Each of the 11 divisions was asked to prepare a document to describe its 1-year action plan and rolling 5-year plan, including objectives and projected budgets. Participants received these plans before the meeting.

The agenda for the 3-day meeting was:

- Day 1: Long-term strategy planning
- Day 2: Short-range action planning
- Day 3: Wrap-up in both areas

The meeting began with the group using the workstations to generate ideas about expected corporate performance in the coming years. They then organized these ideas to create the framework for discussing each division's plans.

For the next day and a half, they entered comments on the 5-year strategic plans and 1-year action plans of each division, one division at a time.

They also spent some time brainstorming ways to accomplish the year's objectives and then ranking the ideas. The group settled on specific actions they would take on the top seven issues.

On the last afternoon, they divided into four groups to discuss important topics face-to-face. The planning meeting ended with the four groups presenting their recommendations.

Executives' Reactions

After the 3-day session, the participants were asked to summarize their reactions to the decision room. They reported the following.

- **It increased involvement.** One senior vice president commented that the decision room allowed them to do in 3 days' time what would have taken months. The CEO noted that the past sessions could not be larger than

10 people to be manageable; and in those sessions, only two or three people really spoke up. With the decision room, 31 people were able to attend without hampering deliberations, and the group's comments were much more open than in the past.

During one 1-hour electronic brainstorming session, 404 comments were made, with the fewest number of comments from any of the 24 workstations, some of which had two users, being 4 and the highest being 27. Seven workstations contributed more than 20. Thus, contributions were relatively evenly distributed across the group.

The group had mixed reactions about the efficiency of the system. In a post-session questionnaire answered by 26 participants, 11 stated that it was more efficient than past meetings, 9 said it was not, and 6 were neutral. However, the majority agreed that the facilitator was important in helping them use the room.

- **The planning process was more effective.** Several executives mentioned two aspects of the session that enhanced its effectiveness. The main one was anonymity. Due to anonymity, more people asked more questions and made more suggestions than they did in the former meeting format where all discussion was verbal, which identified the contributor.

  Second, the planning process itself was extremely educational, said the CEO. "People walked in with narrow perceptions of the company and walked out with a CEO's perception. This is the view that is sought in strategic planning, but is usually not achieved," he commented 3 months after the session. This type of education had not happened at previous planning sessions.

One Year Later

One year later, 25 executives participated in a 2-day session. About 16 had attended the year before. This year, the intent of the meeting was different. It was to critique plans so that their impact on others and the support they needed from others were more explicit.

After the CEO described the firm's objectives and the economic climate, the planning session began with the group critiquing the previous year's results, company-wide. The 2-day session ended with each business unit manager commenting on the ideas received about his or her particular unit and how those ideas might affect the unit's action plan.

From the previous year's session, they learned that brainstorming is effective if the groups are structured properly. A large group can consider a few issues, such as corporate objectives, and present ideas on those topics. But a large group cannot "converse" because of the large number of ideas to consider.

For "dialogs," Burr-Brown found it best to form several small groups, with each group addressing a few issues. One person puts in a statement, another person comments on it, then someone else comments, and so on. In the second year, they conducted small group dialogs and found them effective.

The company also learned that the discussion room is not a substitute for a planning process. It is excellent for generating many ideas in a short time. However, because face-to-face interaction is reduced, people are less likely to make commitments and agree on courses of action than in a face-to-face setting. Therefore, Burr-Brown does not use the room to reach consensus.

The communications manager recommends that others planning to use such a room tell the participants about the room beforehand. Just send them an e-mail that describes the room and includes a photograph, he suggests. Also, explain to paraticipants how their comments will be used because the use probably will affect how they answer questions. In all, Burr-Brown participants were pleased with the candor and objectivity the decision room elicited. They believe its use has enhanced their annual planning meetings.

time, reduced attention blocking, increased participation, improved feedback, and a permanent record, GSS users would retain more knowledge from a presentation than when they used conventional methods.

- *Remote and asynchronous participation.* In addition, people who do not attend a presentation could still benefit by reading and contributing after the event. However, this opportunity does not mean replacing all face-to-face conferences and presentations with distributed online interaction. Many people find casual conversations in hallways and over meals to be as valuable as formal presentations.
- *Potential negative effects.* Despite such benefits, Davison and Briggs were concerned that online discussions during presentations might be a mixed blessing. Human attention is limited, so online discussions might distract participants to the point where they lose the thread of the presentation. Such distractions could outweigh other benefits. Furthermore, the online discussions could digress from the concepts in the presentation or even devolve into flaming. In addition, the

anonymity of online discussion could hinder the evolution of a social community among the participants

To explore these hypotheses, Davison and Briggs conducted some experiments at a conference known for its interactive workshop-like sessions. See the Case Example on pages 271–272.

Supporting "Different-Place" Collaboration

One of the most promising uses of groupware is ongoing coordination by groups who work in different places, and perhaps at different times. With the increasing marketplace emphasis on cycle-time reduction, companies can use the globe and its three main regions (Europe, Asia, and the Americas) to extend their workday to round-the-clock by passing work from groups in one region to the next at the end of each one's workday, as the following personal example attests.

> *I had that experience for the first time a few years ago. On one of my first writing projects, the author of the report, who worked in England, e-mailed me his thoughts and questions on the topic at the end of his workday. During my workday, while he was sleeping, I did some thinking and research on the topic, and e-mailed my thoughts and findings back to him at the end of my day. While I slept, he worked. He and I worked this way, swapped long e-mails, for about 1 week. But we got at least 2 weeks' worth of work done. It was tremendously exhilarating and productive without either of us having to work long hours.*

One of the results of using IT to support collaboration is the formation of virtual teams; they exist in space, but not in one place. Some never meet face-to-face. These teams often form to handle a project, then disband after the project is complete. They tend to operate in three cells of Johansen's matrix.

- *Same time/same place:* Typically, the team meets face-to-face initially to develop the basic plan and objectives.
- *Different time/different place:* They then communicate by e-mail and do data gathering and analysis separately.
- *Same time/different place:* If their technology is strong enough, they may have audio or video conferences to discuss developments and progress toward goals.

A case example of a successful virtual team, as described in the award-winning paper to the Society for Information Management by Carman et al. appears on pages 273–276.

As this discussion of systems to support collaboration has shown, there is a spectrum of group working situations and many types of IT-based support. Furthermore, use of collaboration software can change structure within one enterprise, working relationships between enterprises, and working relationships between people in different parts of the world. To conclude the chapter, we look at research findings about using the lessons from managing one type of dispersed group to managing other types.

MANAGING COLLABORATION IN VIRTUAL ORGANIZATIONS

This chapter on collaboration has presented some intriguing glimpses into the dramatic changes occurring in organizational structures. Frances Cairncross, Peter Drucker, Etienne Wenger, and others believe that the organization of the future will be much more like networks of communities and teams than the hierarchical bureaucracies of the past. The question is: With CoPs, network armies, and global virtual teams becoming more predominant, how are such nontraditional collaborative structures to be managed?

Professor M. Lynne Markus of Bentley College, Brook Manville of Saba Software, and the late Carole Agres of Claremont Graduate School explored this question by looking to the open source movement. Here is their thinking, which appeared in a *Sloan Management Review* article.

They, too, cite Drucker, who stated that the job of executives in managing knowledge workers is not to tell them what to do (manage them), but rather to tell them where the organization is going (lead them). It is akin to leading volunteers who, though unpaid, labor for a cause out of commitment and the expectation of having a voice in the operation. Markus et al. note that CoPs, self-employed freelancers, and industries experiencing the emergence of networked organizational forms all point to a workforce with a more volunteer-like mindset—in spirit if not in fact. The authors researched the open source movement to help the managers of one knowledge-based organization that was having governance troubles. The traditional forms of governance were causing employees to feel distant and leave. The authors' research led them to two conclusions:

1. Executives of increasingly virtual organizations should think about expanding the kinds of motivators they use. The open source movement demonstrates that while money is a motivator for volunteers, gaining a high reputation among peers, taking pride in contributions, and being able to improve and use high-quality software are strong motivators as well.
2. Executives of increasingly virtual organizations should consider adopting a governance structure that

CASE EXAMPLE

HICSS

As part of the Hawaii International Conference on System Sciences (HICSS), 43 participants attended a 3-hour tutorial on business process reengineering. The workshop had 24 laptops placed around two sets of tables, along with two large screens—one to show the PowerPoint slides for the presentation and the other to show the contents of the electronic discussion. To overcome concerns about politeness, the presenter encouraged the participants to use the equipment by saying that he considered typing while he was talking to be both polite and desirable. However, only eight comments were submitted during the 3 hours. Similarly low levels of participation occurred in two later 9-minute paper presentation sessions. Again, informal interviews revealed a widespread fear of rudeness.

Davison and Briggs hypothesized that because the attendees had not used a GSS during a presentation, they might not imagine how non-intrusive it could be. They also hypothesized that participants might not realize how easy the software was to use. Therefore, the following day, they used the GSS for three 90-minute sessions. Each session had three paper presentations.

As each session began, the moderator asked participants to use the GSS to respond to the question, "What are the most pressing research issues facing the technology-supported learning research community?" Everyone contributed an idea and then responded online to an idea contributed by someone else.

The first presenter told the group that the oral discussion following the presentations would draw from the online discussion. Two subsequent speakers asked for online responses to specific questions. All others asked for critical feedback about their presentations. As soon as the first speaker began, members of the audience started typing. Participants contributed 275 comments during the three sessions, ranging from 20 to 54 per presentation. About 94 percent of comments were presentation related, with no instances of flaming. Furthermore, during other sessions with no GSS, oral contributions to the post-presentation discussions came from no more than four people. Observations in the GSS-supported sessions showed that contributions came from all over the audience.

One Year Later

During the following year, Davison and Briggs refined both their GSS methods and their questionnaire. They then conducted a more rigorous follow-up study at the next HICSS conference. The study addressed three primary research questions: What effect would GSS have on participation and perceived learning? Would the GSS be perceived as a detrimental distraction? What effect would GSS use have on the perceived value of the presentations and discussions?

At this conference, 34 laptops in a workshop setting let participants have a clearer view of the large public screen. All GSS-supported sessions began with a brief hands-on activity related to the session topic. A moderator invited online participation at the beginning of each presentation, and most presenters added their encouragement. Participants were urged to raise key issues from the online discussions during the post-presentation discussions. After the sessions, Davison and Briggs administered their survey questionnaire. They received data from 173 participants. Of those, 73 reported having used GSS, whereas 70 reported they had not.

Results of the Survey

From the survey, Davison and Briggs learned that GSS users were significantly more willing to participate in the discussions than non-GSS users, and they reported doing so at significantly higher levels. The participants in both the GSS-supported and standard presentations had equal opportunity to contribute to oral discussion and did so at approximately equal rates. However, the participants who used the GSS also contributed hundreds of comments to the online discussions, so their overall participation was substantially higher. Furthermore, a much higher percentage of the audience got involved in the GSS discussion than in the oral discussion. Thus, it appears that the GSS may have accomplished its primary purpose: to increase participation and learning. But at what cost?

Overall, participants were comfortable with the amount of distraction and digression in the sessions. Only three GSS users and four non-GSS users reported negative reactions—too few for meaningful statistical analysis. Thus, the GSS did not appear to create widespread perceptions of undue distraction or digression.

(Case continued)

(Case continued)

No online flaming occurred, and nearly all the online contributions were relevant to the presentations. Content analysis of the online transcripts suggested that participants grasped the key concepts of the presentations, which is further evidence the GSS did not distract them from the oral delivery of information.

Overall, the respondents also reported receiving positive value from the conference sessions and the GSS. This response suggests that the GSS enabled the groups to increase the quantity of something they valued—the discussions and feedback—without reducing its quality. Many participants chose to take electronic transcripts with them at the end of each session, whereas others downloaded transcripts from the Internet. Thus, the value derived from the discussion was extended beyond the walls of the presentation hall.

fosters self-governance by employees. Although the open source movement appears to have all the trappings of chaos waiting to happen, it is actually very well disciplined because its governance mechanisms foster self-governance.

Here is some of their thinking in these two areas.

Motivating a Virtual Workforce

Markus, Manville, and Agres suggest that managers in virtual organizations put in place motivators that reinforce each other. Open source contributors volunteer for many often-interlocking reasons. They love to build software. That is pure joy for them, states Eric Raymond, who wrote "The Cathedral and the Bazaar," an online paper that has been influential in touting the benefits of open source development of software. They take pride in helping others and giving something back to society. They often believe that software should be given away, as it is in university computer science labs where open source flourishes. In addition, they receive the personal benefit of having better software for their own use. One obligation in this culture is to send software enhancements to the author to be checked. Another is to make the enhancements widely available.

Like academia, open source is a "reputation culture," note Markus et al. Reputation is the measure of success. Gaining a reputation for uncovering bugs and making good fixes spreads because open source contributions are highly visible. Every project includes a credit list of the people who have contributed, note Markus et al. This culture is also a gift type of culture. Reputation is gained by what the contributors give away, rather than what they control (as in the exchange culture found in traditional business). In a gift culture, there is abundance. In open source, there is plenty of computing power, network bandwidth, storage space, and such. A good reputation can lead to a job or venture capital. Although money cannot be earned from the software, it can be earned by selling support or education.

Markus, Manville, and Agres thus recommend that reputation may be the symbol of success in other kinds of knowledge work. Managers should use this "coin of the realm" to motivate employees in their virtual organization.

Governing Virtual Organizations

Managing open source appears to be an impossible task because there are at least 750,000 developers, all of whom signed up on their own volition and can stop volunteering at any time. Yet, note Markus et al., many open source projects work well because they employ three governance principles: managed membership, rules and institutions, and social pressures.

Managed Membership. Open source work has a well-defined leadership, with the originator often maintaining a lead role in development and distribution. Or a lead team might rule, dividing the work, refereeing coordination across teams, and so on. Leaders are rarely elected. Although anyone can be involved in searching for bugs and fixes (in most open source work), project authority only comes from being given it by, say, the project's core team based on the quality of one's work on the project. In some cases, even working on a project may require being voted in. Thus, membership is limited, making it manageable.

Rules and Institutions. One rule is the open source license—how the software can be used. The license may, for instance, permit any form of commercial use or not allow commercial versions at all. Other rules relate to how members and leaders are chosen or how voting and discussions are conducted. All communications are generally done over the Internet and occur in phases for a specific length of time. For instance, there can be a request-for-discussion phase, a call-for-votes phase, and a results

CASE EXAMPLE

BOEING-ROCKETDYNE

Boeing-Rocketdyne is the major U.S. manufacturer of liquid-fueled rocket engines, which are used to launch communication satellites. When the company faced significant competition and price pressures from Eastern European companies, it initiated a project called SLICE (Simple Low-Cost Innovative Engine). SLICE's business objectives were dramatic: Reduce the cost of the rocket engine to one-tenth, get the engine to market 10 times faster than the Space Shuttle's main engine, and increase the useful life of the rocket engine by 300 percent. In short, it was a breakthrough project. So much so that none of the senior technical managers thought the goals were possible, and these managers, as a group, had hundreds of years of experience designing rocket engines. Only one advanced program manager was willing to give the project a try.

The team faced many challenges. The first was work style. To get the best people on the project, they needed to come from different disciplines and different organizations. Management would not allow them to be taken off their regular work, so they could not be collocated. They had to work virtually, using electronic collaboration technology, without holding face-to-face meetings. Furthermore, the members had not worked together as a team, so they had different product experiences and used different design processes. Finally, they had to submit only one design, a design that Rocketdyne's conservative senior management would accept.

Despite these challenges, the project was a tremendous success. It lasted 10 months, during which time the team held 89 online meetings using a collaborative technology called the Internet Notebook. The members created and critiqued 20 designs and submitted more than 650 entries into the notebook. The seven senior technical managers who reviewed the project at its conclusion stated that it had surpassed its objectives. The design was approved for the next phase: testing the assumptions about how the liquid would flow through the components.

The design accomplished the following:

- The engine's thrust changer had only 6 parts, down from more than 450.
- The manufacturing cost was estimated to be $1.5 million, down from $20 million.
- Quality was predicted to be Nine Sigma, up from the industry standard of Six Sigma, which meant one failure in 10 billion.
- Development cost was $47,000, down from $4.5 million.

The team was awarded the Department of Defense's Advanced Research Program for "validating a process for virtual collocation teams."

In addition, none of the team members spent more than 15 percent of his or her time on the project, the team stayed within its budget (even though the project took longer than expected), and the total engineering hours were one-half normal using the collaborative technology.

Lessons Learned

Why was the team so successful? Carman and his colleagues studied the life of this project and suggested the following success factors.

A Prior Formal Agreement on Sharing Intellectual Property Was Crucial. Boeing-Rocketdyne anticipated the need for close cooperation on some significant projects well before the SLICE team was formed. Therefore, they began developing a partnership agreement to govern such teams. It turns out that the legal aspects of intellectual property are complicated, so they need time to be defined. Because this agreement was in place when the SLICE team began its work, the team members could move ahead quickly without being concerned about who was able to know what.

The Technology Had to Fit the Team's Virtual Meetings. The team's collaborative technology—the Internet Notebook—was developed by a third party based on the list of requirements drawn up by several of the team members. The technology allowed the team members to

- Access the notebook from anywhere.
- Create, comment on, reference-link, search, and sort entries that could consist of sketches, snapshots, hotlinks to desktop applications, texts, or templates.
- Use an electronic white board for near-instantaneous access to entries.

(Case continued)

(Case continued)

Thus, from the outset, the team had a technology suited to its needs, at least as the team initially defined them. The team focused its early discussions on creating a coordination protocol for facilitating its collaborative use. Figure 6.15 shows how the team members rated these features.

The team adapted ways of working that required it to change the fundamental way the members were used to collaborating: from face-to-face discussions to complete reliance on technology, from sharing information sparingly (only when someone needed to know the information) to sharing all information with everyone all the time, and from using personal collaborative tools (such as company-specific e-mail systems) to using a single system. Initially, the team believed that all information would be captured and shared among all members all the time. The result would be a much greater emphasis on knowledge management and retrieval, beyond just communication.

Being Creative Required New Rules of Engagement. The team learned that its ability to be creative required meeting three requirements:

1. Jointly understand problems, possible solutions, analysis methods, and language
2. Interact frequently as a team, with all members "present," to share work-in-progress, brainstorm ideas, and test out solutions
3. Be able to create new information quickly based on a particular conversation or problem, and then equally quickly discard information that was no longer needed.

The team members discovered they needed to adapt the traditional work practices of a collocated team to function as a creative body. Figure 6.16 shows how the need to be creative is accommodated in collocated teams, and what the SLICE team members learned they would need to do to adapt these needs to their noncollocated situation.

The Focus of the Team's Effort Changed over Time. As the project evolved, the team learned that it had to shift its thinking among three components, from thinking about strategy (how to fulfill the partnership agreement), to implementing a technology that would support collaboration of the dispersed team structure, to actual work practices that would leverage the technology. It learned that the strategy practices needed to be in place before the work or technology practices so that members did not have to be concerned with both doing the work and negotiating information-sharing arrangements at the same time.

Furthermore, the team discovered it needed the technology in place before it could think about work practices because the work style depended on the support technology. Along the way, members also learned that the technology had to be flexible enough to be adapted to different ways of working because some of their initial work practices did not work as well as hoped. So, over the course of the project, they evolved their practices, and the tool had to support this evolution.

Figure 6.17 shows the allocation of effort over the course of the project among these three components of the project: strategy, technology, and work practices. As can be seen, the

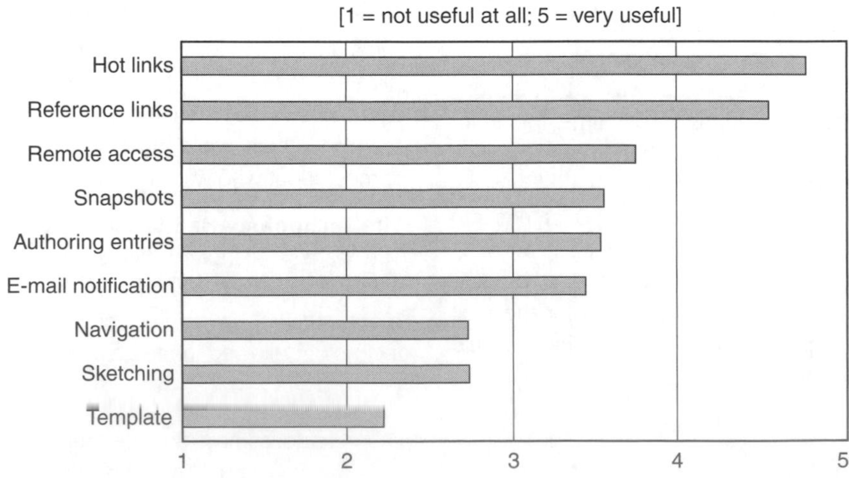

Figure 6.15 Ratings of Notebook Features for Information Retrieval. *Source:* Reprinted with permission of R. Carman et al., "Virtual Cross-Supply Chain Concept Development Collaborative Teams: Spurring Radical Innovations at Boeing-Rocketdyne," first place winner of 2000 paper competition of the Society for Information Management

Core Needs of Creative Teams	*Practices of Colocated Teams*	*Practices Adapted by Virtual Teams*
Development of shared understanding	• Lead engineer is "spoke-in-the-wheel" for coordinating information and consolidating ideas into new design proposals, which constitute the shared understandings of the team.	• From spoke-in-the-wheel coordination (with lead manager/engineer in center) to democratic coordination • Encourage development and use of common-language metaphors
Frequent opportunities for interaction with team members	• Colocation allows for frequent and spontaneous interaction.	• Coupling use of knowledge repository with frequent teleconferences • Allowing one-on-one discussions when need arises but documenting results for everyone
Rapid creation and sharing of context-specific transient information	• Most discussion is verbal and undocumented, and it is hard to capture the context.	• Promote only minimal cataloging of new information, even to the extent of restricting it to "touchstones" and "placeholders" • Timely and frequent discussions of new entries in knowledge repository to enable members to learn the context

Figure 6.16 Structuring Core Processes for Virtual Teams. *Source:* Reprinted with permission of R. Carman et al., "Virtual Cross-Supply Chain Concept Development Collaborative Teams: Spurring Radical Innovations at Boeing-Rocketdyne," first place winner of 2000 paper competition of the Society for Information Management.

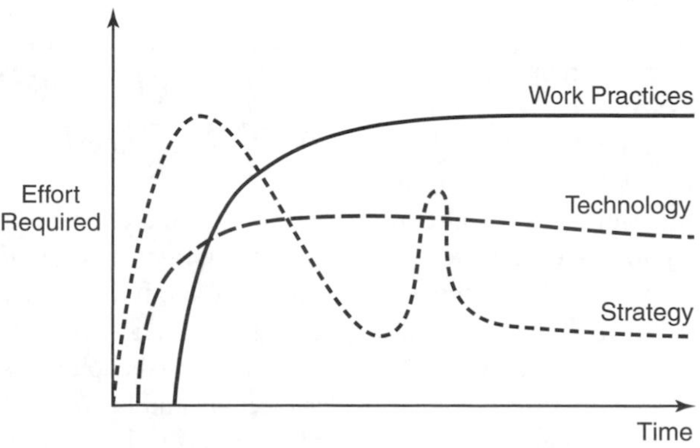

Figure 6.17 Effort Distribution over the Team's Life Cycle. *Source:* Reprinted with permission of R. Carman et al., "Virtual Cross-Supply Chain Concept Development Collaborative Teams: Spurring Radical Innovations at Boeing-Rocketdyne," first place winner of 2000 paper competition of the Society for Information Management.

(Case continued)

(Case continued)

team needed to focus on both the technology and its own work practices over the entire span of the project. For example, a technology facilitator was required to attend all teleconferences so that problems could be fixed immediately. Members never knew when someone would not understand how to perform a particular operation or a server would go down and communications would need to be rerouted. In addition, throughout the project, as the team found work practices not working, members devoted some effort to decide on better ways of working. In the end, this attention paid off.

As noted, the SLICE team at Boeing-Rocketdyne was immensely successful, in large part due to the advanced collaboration technology it used. As usual, though, the technology was necessary but not sufficient. The team also needed a carefully developed partnership agreement in place before work began and work practices to leverage the technology, which needed to evolve as the team members discovered a technology's usefulness.

phase, note Markus et al. Each phase has its own rules. Most voting is democratic, but some is not.

Social Pressures. To have teeth, rules need means to enforce compliance and resolve disputes. To bring continual non-compliers into line, open source groups generally use social pressures. For example, a group may flame someone, which means sending the disobeyer angry e-mail. Or members may spam the person, that is, overwhelm the person with e-mail. Or members may simply shun the person by not responding to that person's e-mail. Generally, after such treatment, the disobeyer learns the rules of the community and falls into line. Such pressures can even be turned on leaders who act inappropriately, note Markus et al.

Conflicts that end badly can cause volunteers to simply leave an open source group because it kills their motivation to contribute. Generally, open source groups use escalated sanctions to resolve conflict and bring non-compliers into line. They also monitor work, which represents another type of social pressure.

These social pressures work because reputation is so important, and because the work is so visible to everyone. Also underlying all the governance mechanisms are the shared values of the culture, which place emphasis on self-control (to maintain one's reputation) and social control (monitoring each other's behavior). Needless to say, IT is a key enabler for all these governing mechanisms, permitting the distributed software development, coordination among the participants, and group-wide enforcement of the rules via the various social controls.

Markus, Manville, and Agres recommend that managers in virtual organizations consider adopting these practices from the open source movement because intrinsic motivation and self-management are as important in virtual organizations as they are in open source. Furthermore, managers should consider rewarding collective results (as happens when an open source product gains commercial success) along with individual benefits. They should also foster development of reputation through the assignment of project lead roles and other mechanisms.

However, adopting the tenets of open source to managing in a virtual organization needs to take into account that a strong shared culture is a precondition for the governance mechanisms to work. A virtual organization without such a culture may not have the same results. Furthermore, Markus et al. question whether the mechanisms for governing programmers performing challenging work can apply equally well to employees performing routine activities. In short, self-governance is at the heart of managing virtual organizations. Without self-governance and strong reinforcing conditions, such social governance mechanisms might not work.

A MODEL FOR MANAGING KNOWLEDGE

Due to the increasing emphasis on knowledge, some now call it *intellectual capital* to distinguish it from the other kinds of capital that firms possess. Giga Information Group, a research firm, has published a model for managing intellectual capital. As shown in Figure 6.18, the model is circular and has four stages, which represent what people generally do with knowledge. First they create it or capture it from a source. Next, they organize it and put it into categories for easy retrieval. Then they distribute it (push) or access it (pull). Finally, they absorb another's knowledge for their own use or to create more new knowledge. Thus, the cycle begins again.

The four stages create three types of capital: human, structural, and customer.

- ***Human capital.*** This form of intellectual capital consists of knowledge, skills, and innovativeness of employees as well as company values, culture, and philosophy. It is created during the knowledge creation–capture and knowledge absorption–reuse stages because these two stages focus on getting people together to share knowledge. They deal with the *people* aspects of knowledge management. Their main question is, "How do we get people to have more knowledge in their heads?"
- ***Structural capital.*** This is the capabilities embedded in hardware, software, databases, organizational structure, patents, and trademarks that support employees as well as relationships with customers. Structural capital is formed in the knowledge organization–categorization and knowledge distribution–access stages because these stages focus on moving knowledge from people's heads to a tangible company asset. These stages deal with the *technology* issues surrounding knowledge management and sharing. Their main question is, "How do we get knowledge out of people's heads and into a computer, a process, a document, or another organizational asset?"
- ***Customer capital.*** This form of intellectual capital is the strength of a company's franchise with its customers and is concerned with its relationships and networks of associates. Furthermore, when customers are familiar with a company's products or services, the company can call that familiarity customer capital. This form of capital may be either human (relationships with the company) or structural (products used from the company).

Based on a series of case studies, Giga discovered that the human capital stages and the structural capital stages require different mindsets. Hence, companies have had to use different approaches to grow each one; and the techniques for one do not work for the other. The companies that focused on human capital used touchy-feely people-centric approaches. In some cases, no technology was used at all. The companies that focused on structural capital took a typical IS approach: using technology to solve a problem. Little talk addressed individuals, communities, and work practices; talk mainly centered on yellow pages of experts, knowledge bases, and such. However, to succeed in leveraging intellectual capital, companies need to do both.

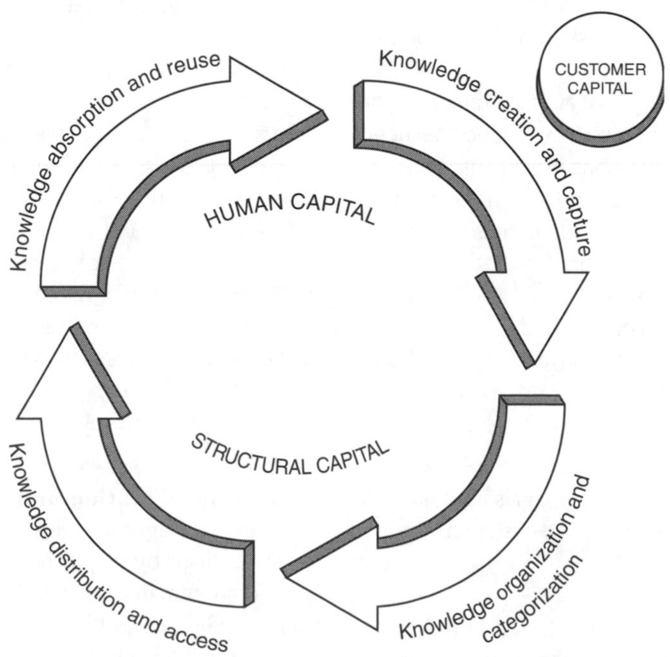

Figure 6.18 A Knowledge Management Framework. *Source:* Reprinted with permission from *Best Practices in Knowledge Management,* Giga Information Group, 1997.

CASE EXAMPLE

BUCKMAN LABORATORIES

Buckman Laboratories, an industrial chemical company based in Memphis, Tennessee, has some 1,200 employees around the world. The concept of sharing knowledge and best practices has been around in Buckman for more than 15 years. In fact, the company's code of ethics reinforces the sharing culture. Buckman believes that successfully transferring knowledge depends 90 percent on having the right culture and 10 percent on technology.

To bring the knowledge of all Buckman's employees to bear on a customer problem anywhere in the world—whether in Europe, South Africa, Australia/New Zealand, or Japan—Buckman established a knowledge transfer system called K'Netix, the Buckman Knowledge Network. The goal of K'Netix was to get people who had not met each other, but belonged to the same business, to communicate with each other and develop trust in each other: trust that one person was interested in the other's success, trust that what one person received from others was valid and sincere, and enough trust in the culture to help someone else.

Ten years ago sharing was accomplished mainly by people traveling all over the world to see each other, with lots of face-to-face conversations and meetings. Today, such meetings still occur, but the technology helps people stay in touch between these meetings, making communications more continuous.

When employees need information or help, they ask via forums, which are Buckman-only online forums over the Internet. In all, seven forums in TechForum are organized by industry and are open to all employees.

One particularly influential conversation, which set the tone for companywide sharing, took place over TechForum and concerned Buckman's global sales awards. A large cash award was split among the top three salespeople worldwide; the top 20 got plaques. It was based on a formula that took many factors into account. The salespeople, however, were unhappy with the formula. When this discussion appeared on the companywide forum, then-CEO Bob Buckman jumped into the fray and decided that the entire company should iron out the problems in front of all employees. Hundreds of messages were recorded, and the entire award structure was restructured online in front of everyone. It was a rare opportunity to allow everyone to share in an important, yet sensitive, company subject. Moreover, top management did not dictate the results. This conversation reinforced the sharing culture.

The conversations are the basis for transferring knowledge around the company. So the important ones are captured. Volunteer experts identify conversations that contain valuable information and, more importantly, valuable streams of reasoning. This information is then edited to remove extraneous material, given key words, and stored in the forum library. In essence, Buckman is capturing the artifacts of its virtual teams in action. In so doing, it is creating a self-building knowledge base, which can be used for what-if analyses and can be mined to create new knowledge.

The prime benefit is timely, high-quality responses to customer needs. For example, a new employee in Brazil was scheduled to visit a customer who had a particular problem. The salesperson posted both the problem and a suggested solution in a forum and sought advice from anyone with more experience. A response came quickly: "I've faced this problem and your pH is too high; it will cause odors and ruin the paper. Bring the pH down by two points. That won't hurt the process, and it will clear up the problem." As a result, this new employee, who had only modest experience, was able to present a proposal with the experience of a 25-year veteran, and make the sale.

Now we turn to specifics of what companies have done to build human capital, structural capital, and customer capital.

Building Human Capital

The emphasis in building human capital, notes Giga, is to answer the question, "How do we get people to have more knowledge in their heads?" Giga sees four ways: create it, capture it, absorb it, and reuse it.

Knowledge Creation and Capture. This phase deals with generating knowledge, either by nurturing employees to create it or by acquiring it from outside. Hence, it deals with both human capital and customer capital. As noted earlier, the Giga cases that emphasized this phase of managing knowledge have used high-touch approaches, such as creating a sharing culture, urging people to meet either in person or electronically, and encouraging innovation.

As another example of what a company can do to promote knowledge sharing globally, consider the approach that Buckman Laboratories has taken. (See page 278) This description is based on Brewer's work.

Knowledge Absorption and Reuse. This phase of building human capital addresses the notion of getting knowledge into people's heads where it can be enhanced and reused. Irrespective of whether people believe that knowledge only exists in minds or can exist in computers, the Giga cases that emphasized this phase of managing knowledge used high-touch approaches. They too focused on nurturing interactions among people, recognizing the knowledge brokers who exist in companies, and supporting communities of practice.

Recognizing knowledge brokers. "The Rudy problem." Simply discovering who has what knowledge is a step in the right direction to fostering knowledge sharing. Yet when possessing knowledge is not rewarded by management, neither is sharing, as the following story illustrates.

At a knowledge management conference, Dr. Patricia Seemann, who headed up a knowledge management project at a pharmaceutical company, told the story of Serge and Rudy (fictitious names but real people). Serge, she said, was a "real" manager. He had a three-window office, a big desk, and a title. If you asked him what he did the past year, he would say, "I registered 600 products in 30 countries." Rudy, on the other hand, is a headache, his manager says, because he does not work. He just stands around and talks all day. Whenever you see him, he is talking to someone. When you ask him what he did the past year, he says, "I sort of helped out."

The company downsized and guess who got laid off? Rudy. And then what happened? His department fell apart because there was no one to help, to provide guidance. When they fired Rudy, they fired their organizational memory, said Seemann. He was a crucial, yet unrecognized asset, because he was willing to share his knowledge.

While at this company, Seemann and her team created a yellow pages guide of company knowledge brokers. Guess who was in the book and who was not? Rudy, of course, was in the book. Serge was not, and neither was top management. How can companies fix what she calls "the Rudy problem"? One way is to create a technical career track and promote knowledge brokers. Giving Rudy a title would have made an enormous difference, Seemann said, because it would have sent a signal that knowledge sharing was recognized in the company. Companies cannot appoint knowledge brokers. They just emerge. And when they do emerge, they need support.

One approach to fostering knowledge sharing: T-shaped managers. If not understanding Rudy's role in the organization is how not to foster knowledge sharing, what is a way to nurture it? Morton Hansen of Harvard Business School and Bolko von Oetinger of Boston Consulting Group propose what they call T-shaped managers. These are executives who have both a vertical role (such as running a business unit) and a horizontal role (such as sharing knowledge with their peers in other business units).

The goal of this structure is to circumvent the limitations of knowledge management systems: They can only house explicit knowledge (not implicit know-how), they cannot foster collaboration by just making documents available, and their directories of experts can get out-of-date quickly. T-shaped management is especially important in organizations with autonomous business units because it helps counterbalance their tendency to compete with each other and hoard expertise.

Whereas the value of T-managers' vertical work is measured by traditional bottom-line financial performance, the value of their horizontal work is measured in five ways, note Hansen and von Oetinger:

1. Increased company efficiency from transferring best practices among business units
2. Better decisions by soliciting peer advice
3. Increased revenue by sharing expertise, again, among peers who are experts in areas in question
4. Development of new business ventures by cross-pollinating ideas
5. Moving strategically through well-coordinated efforts among peers

However, success in these five areas does not just happen. Knowledge sharing requires clear incentives. The company needs to reward sharing. Furthermore, sharing needs to go both ways—give and take. Benchmarking across business units can encourage underperformers to ask for help. Success also requires formalizing cross-unit interactions, state Hansen and von Oetinger. It does not mean creating bureaucracy, but rather creating peer-level collegial support (and confrontation). It also means picking and choosing which cross-unit requests to fulfill based on expected business results and how much someone can really contribute.

BP (see page 280) is exemplary in its use of the T-manager concept, state Hansen and von Oetinger. The insight Hansen and von Oetinger learned from studying BP is that mechanisms must be put in place to both foster and guide managers' knowledge-sharing activities; otherwise, they start to take up too much time and produce few results.

CASE EXAMPLE

BP

BP is in the energy business. It merged with Amoco in 1998, with ARCO in 2000, and Castrol and Veba Aral in Germany in 2002; it now has 100,000 employees in 100 countries. BP's approach to T-shaped management began in the early 1990s in BPX, its oil and gas exploration division. To cut layers and increase accountability, John Browne, then head of BPX and now head of BP, divided the division into 50 autonomous business units. Unfortunately, each business unit head focused only on his or her unit, not on BPX.

To get the business unit heads working together, Browne instituted peer groups in 1993, each with about 12 business unit leaders in similar businesses. No bosses were allowed in these peer groups, so the discussions would be candid and not consist of political posturing. Sharing did increase, but it was not until 1994 when these groups were made responsible for allocating capital within their group and for setting their performance levels that their sharing started to truly impact BPX's performance. The peer group members finally saw the financial value of sharing expertise. When Browne became CEO in 1995, he instituted peer groups BP-wide.

BP has also created cross-unit networks around areas of shared interest. However, BP found, unfortunately, that these several hundred networks cost a lot of time and money (with people flying all over the globe) without resulting in better results. Thus, the number and use have been limited.

BP has also instituted the practice of identifying a limited number of "human portals" who connect people, so that everyone is not trying to network with everyone else. Typically these people are not the top executives, note Hansen and von Oetinger, and typically they have been at BP a long time and in many jobs and locations.

IT plays a role in these various knowledge-sharing activities. An electronic yellow pages identifies experts, and multimedia e-mail and desktop video conferencing permit easier virtual team meetings, report Hansen and von Oetinger.

Since the mergers, BP has reorganized its business units into new peer groups that are more strategically focused. As Hansen and von Oetinger note, the evolution continues.

One T-Shaped Manager's Experiences

One BP T-shaped executive, who heads BP's gas business unit in Egypt, illustrates this new mode of operation. Formerly, whenever his business unit needed help, he would call headquarters. Now, he looks to his peers in other gas units.

His job essentially has two roles, one vertical and one horizontal. He is CEO of the business unit, so he is responsible for its profit-and-loss statement, capital investment decisions, and such. He is also expected to participate in cross-unit activities, which take up some 20 percent of his time. These activities can undermine his vertical role, so he and the seven gas-production peers in the Mediterranean and Atlantic region in his peer group limit their meetings to business purposes. Knowledge sharing is not enough of a reason to meet. Instead, they meet to decide how to allocate capital amongst themselves and how to meet production targets set by their division's executive committee.

In his knowledge-sharing role, in addition to collaborating, he also connects people, acting in some ways like a "human portal," suggesting who might help solve a problem, for example. He also gives advice to peer business units when asked and when he feels he can contribute. He was personally involved in 3 of 20 of his business unit's "peer assists" one year, report Hansen and von Oetinger. In addition, he also requests peer assists, receiving 10 assists one year from BP business units around the world.

Due to all BP's networking, people know where expertise lies, so they go directly to the expertise rather than through headquarters. And because sharing is rewarded, bosses know who is sharing (and requesting assistance) and who is not. In its knowledge-sharing efforts, BP has aimed to change management activities, not corporate structure, to gain the benefits of knowledge sharing while preserving the autonomy of its business units so that they can more quickly and effectively serve their local markets.

Building Structural Capital

The Rudy story also fits with this second subject, building structural capital, because that is what Seemann and her team aimed to do in creating the online yellow pages of knowledge brokers. Her goal was to increase their value. Those yellow pages are a form of structural capital. As noted earlier, companies that emphasize building structural capital generally use high-tech approaches.

Knowledge Organization and Categorization. This phase is often handled by creating best practices knowledge bases or metadata indexes for documents. A few have even tried to measure intellectual capital. Following are two examples, one that focused on improving a knowledge-support process and one that looked into valuing intellectual capital.

CASE EXAMPLE

A PHARMACEUTICAL COMPANY

A project at a major pharmaceutical company was aimed at improving the process of developing new drugs and getting them approved by the U.S. Food and Drug Administration (FDA), a process that takes 5 to 10 years, costs $250 million, and can yield revenues of $1 million a day per drug once it reaches the market.

This project, described at the Knowledge Imperative Conference, revolved around creating a "knowledge infrastructure," one that manages information, enables understanding, and supports learning. The crux of the matter was to understand the customer's needs. In this case, the FDA is the primary customer; however, insurance companies, doctors, and consumers are also customers. The company sells all of them knowledge about disease, treatment, and how a drug will work in particular scenarios. When employees understand the type of knowledge they need to create for these customers and their role in its creation, they will identify better ways to work.

The project began by studying and codifying 60,000 pages of documents filed with the FDA to discern how the teams developing drugs and filing their results were sharing knowledge. These regulatory files explain to the FDA what the company knows about a drug, how it learned those things, and what conclusions it has reached.

The knowledge-infrastructure project team found the files lacking. Each file should have four parts: purpose, content, logic, and context. Only one of the files had a statement of purpose, which stated the problem to be solved. A file without a statement of purpose shows that the author does not know the reason for the document. Many files had contradictions, which told the team that the authors had not talked to each other. For instance, they disagreed on whether the drug should be taken once or twice a day.

To rectify the situation, the study team created a generic knowledge tree of the questions the FDA asks when deciding whether to approve a drug. The top of the tree has their three main questions: Is it safe? Does it work? Does it have sufficient quality? The tree lays out the supporting questions for these three main questions, in layers, which shows the teams which questions they need to answer to the FDA's satisfaction. It also shows people why others need specific information, thus giving them a context (beyond trust) for sharing.

In a pilot project, the knowledge-infrastructure team used a different process with one team: writing as a tool for thinking. They got the team to write up their 10-year drug study before they did it, so that the team members were clear about the data they needed to gather and present to the FDA. Furthermore, they wrote the report template publicly as a team. To create the template, they wrote critical points that had to be in the report on Post-It notes. Next, they prioritized the points on huge sheets of paper on the meeting-room wall. Then they designed studies to prove the points that had to be proven. In creating this virtual prototype of the knowledge to be presented to the FDA, publicly, on the wall, they could physically see what knowledge was needed. They created a common mental model of the results. It was a powerful technique.

They have seen tangible progress in filling in the report sections on content, logic, context, and purpose. In another case, where an existing drug was to be registered for use with a new disease, the team had not made much progress in 2 years' time. After they were shown the knowledge tree over a 2-day period, they were able to submit the file to the FDA in 3 months (they had previously estimated 18 months), and the FDA approved it in 18 months (the team had estimated 3 years).

CASE EXAMPLE

SKANDIA FUTURE CENTERS

The charter for Skandia Future Centers is organizational prototyping. One project, the knowledge exchange, has addressed the question of putting a value on intangibles, such as knowledge.

Today, some 70 percent of investments in the United States are for intangibles; in Sweden it is 90 percent. However, no common mechanism for establishing their value nor trading that value is yet available. A knowledge exchange increases the accessibility of hidden knowledge and will act as a multiplier for wealth creators, both people and organizations.

Skandia's knowledge exchange began as a network for exchanging knowledge using software akin to Lotus Notes. Over time, it has evolved into a Web-based trading arena where people can buy and sell knowledge assets. It is now based on Nonet, a Notes-like product from Metaphor, a Spanish company.

It has two test sites called ICuniverse.com (IC stands for intellectual capital) and Futurizing.com. On ICuniverse.com, for example, before responding to an e-mail message, the recipient and the sender first agree on a price to be paid to the responder, perhaps via an auction. Thus, people are paid for the knowledge they provide. Ideas and writings can be housed on ICuniverse.com and resold, which gives high yield to currently unvalued intellectual assets.

The two sites run on an infrastructure (IQport) owned by NatWest in the United Kingdom and were built over several years' time. IQport includes software and a financial clearing mechanism so that information that is generally thrown away can be wrapped into a package and given a price tag. The sites are linked to two accounts at NatWest; one is in financial currency (traditional money), the other is in digital currency, which can be used to purchase other knowledge. Skandia is testing this concept because it could become a new global currency. It is part of the new digital economy.

The knowledge exchange project has been self-organizing from the start. The center simply provides the arena for "knowledge entrepreneurs" or "knowledge nomads"—people who go from arena to arena working on their latest ideas. Thus, the center supports a nontraditional working model.

To illustrate its migration, the project began with IT people from the United Kingdom who were then joined by IT people from Sweden and the United States. Later, students and the professor from Venezuela who developed Nonet for oil companies were the mainstay. The students collaborated with the professor at the center and with Metaphor, the Spanish company that bought Nonet. Today, the knowledge exchange team has people from Sweden and Denmark.

The question that Skandia Future Centers is now asking itself is: How can we reward knowledge nomads? They do not want a career; they want a journey and freedom. Their lifestyle does not fit into traditional organizational models, yet working with them helps speed up accounting and organizational remodeling because they act like bees, moving among research centers pollinating companies with ideas.

Skandia Future Centers provides an example of delving into the world of valuing knowledge. Few firms have ventured into this realm, but because Skandia deals in knowledge and wants to experiment with the future, this is one area it has explored.

Knowledge Distribution and Access. This phase emphasizes both pushing knowledge out to users (distribution) and accommodating users who pull information to themselves (access). The Giga cases that emphasized this phase also used high-tech approaches. They focused on implementing networks and networking tools to access human and structural capital. Intranets and groupware were important IT-based tools. To illustrate one enterprise's approach, we turn to a U.S. energy company discussed in the Giga report on page 283.

Building Customer Capital

Customer capital is the strength of a company's franchise with its customers, the percentage of customer "mindshare" in its industry. Brand recognition is part of customer capital. Familiarity with one's products is another. One of the most fascinating case studies in the Giga knowl-

CASE EXAMPLE

A U.S. ENERGY COMPANY

In this highly autonomous energy company, the 15 business units each focused on their own performance. To instill sharing in this culture, these units would have to see the benefits themselves. In addition, many of the employees were concerned they would not get credit for their good ideas. To overcome both issues, management decided to focus on promulgating best practices across the business units. A best practice was defined as a practice, know-how, or experience that had proven effective or valuable in one organization and might be applicable to another, notes Giga.

With management encouragement, a number of programs to collect best practices arose. For example, 13 groups in the refining division documented best practices using Lotus Notes. They documented "hard" practices (such as distilling techniques) and "soft" practices (such as training) and recorded metrics, where possible. The division estimated it saved $130 million a year utilizing each other's best practices, notes Giga. Similar programs appeared in other divisions.

Yet, these efforts were disparate, so an enterprising manager within IS gathered all the statistics together and presented them to top management to demonstrate how the company could be nurtured to become a learning company. With top management support, an important booklet was created to align the various divisions. It explained the company's mission, vision, values, total quality management (TQM), and environmental policies. It became the guide for sharing best practices.

In fact, the TQM principles of focusing on processes, measuring processes, and continuously improving them, which the company's employees understood and used, played an important role in espousing knowledge distribution and reuse.

One example was in its capital projects management process. This process is used to manage some $4 billion worth of projects a year. In benchmarking this process, management discovered it had some gaps. Therefore, the process was redesigned, and management of capital projects improved. Seeing the benefits of this process orientation, the corporate office funded other cross-business-unit initiatives that fostered sharing.

However, there was still no central responsibility for knowledge distribution and reuse, and such centralization would not fit the culture well. To solve this problem, certain people were designated "technical knowledge experts" because they knew about best practices across the company. Their job was to disseminate tacit knowledge. To do that, they looked for technical ways to turn tacit knowledge into explicit knowledge. Lotus Notes, as noted earlier, was commonly used to house best practices. It links best practice databases across the 15 operating companies. Employees are encouraged to use Notes to describe best practices, search for a mentor on a subject they need to know about, and find best practices. Notes has also been used to support processes. For example, it is used to coordinate the around-the-clock work of 100 employees in the refining company. In creating this workflow system, the employees reengineered the work so coordination worked more smoothly.

The company has also created online discussion databases, some 50 of them, to encourage sharing and reduce travel. Some of the networks have attracted hundreds of employees, leading to a more networked culture. In turn, some of these networks have led to face-to-face get-togethers, which have further spurred sharing on common topics, such as how to reduce energy costs, improve quality, and hone public relations in different cultures.

In short, this company has spurred best practice sharing wherever it makes sense, mainly guided by the interests of the employees. The results have not only been cost savings, but also a change in employee perception, based on the results of employee satisfaction surveys. Employees responded that there was increased emphasis on processes and more sharing of best practices across the company.

CASE EXAMPLE

A NORTH AMERICAN BANK

After the U.S. savings and loan debacle and the devaluation of real estate in the 1980s, the vice president of organizational learning and leadership development at a North American bank asked, "Why have banks become so exposed to risk in their lending practices?" The answer he arrived at was, "Because they do not understand the new information age and its underpinning collateral." At the time, and still today, banks lent money against hard assets, such as a shopping mall. However, the value of such assets can dissipate almost overnight, making them risky collateral. "Perhaps there is less risk in lending against soft assets, such as a group's knowledge of a programming language or a patented process," he reasoned. Knowledge in a person's head does not disappear overnight. However, the vice president had no way of valuing such intangibles. He continued to work on the problem of knowledge valuation. Over time, his thinking changed the way the bank evaluated new hires and reshaped some of its operations.

To begin his quest on how to value knowledge, or intellectual capital, he drew on the ideas of human capital and structural capital, and then added his own: customer capital.

Human capital was the know-how to meet customer needs; he asked bank managers to measure it by assessing how fast their teams learned. To increase human capital, he shifted emphasis at the bank from training (pushing instruction to people) to learning (getting people to pull the instruction they needed to them), because he believed the crux of increasing human capital was increasing the pace at which an organization learns. He believed people learned when they "owned" their learning and took responsibility for applying it to improve their performance. He developed a list of skills needed to serve customers and gave employees numerous ways to learn these skills, from reading specific books to choosing a mentor.

Structural capital was the organizational capabilities needed by the marketplace. The vice president measured structural capital by uncovering the percentage of bank revenue that came from new services and similar metrics. He believed that although it takes human capital to build structural capital, the better the bank's structural capital, the higher its human capital; one feeds the other. Thus, he generated structural capital from human capital by creating a competitive intelligence "library" about the industry that the bank considers a valuable "intellectual capital repository." Rather than being a library of documents, however, it was a map that showed the kinds of knowledge the bank held and where it existed, whether in an employee's head or a database.

Customer capital was the intellectual assets in the minds of customers related to the bank. The vice president's team measured three aspects: depth of knowledge about the bank in a customer organization, breadth of knowledge by a customer, and loyalty to the bank. To strengthen these aspects, the vice president believed the bank needed to assist its customers' employees in learning. Some of that learning pertained to learning more about the bank, which required making the bank's values and strategies congruent with those of its customers. The vice president therefore helped senior bank officials determine customer needs, establish a common language for communicating with customers, develop a sense of purpose for the relationship, and, most importantly, make learning within the customer organization an important part of the bank's services. The vice president believes that assisting customers will increase his bank's customer capital: depth, breadth, and loyalty. Thus, his knowledge management efforts focused outwardly as well as inwardly.

edge management report, all of which are anonymous, is the one about the vice president who derived the notion of customer capital. Above is that story, based on that report.

To recap, Figure 6.19 shows the key activities in each of the four stages, the form of capital each supports, the skills required of people, and the tools and techniques that are proving valuable for that stage.

The Cultural Side of Knowledge Management

Success in managing knowledge comes as much from changing organizational behavior as it does from implementing new technology, notes Cyril Brooks. His company, Grapevine, offers a product for managing information and knowledge. He notes that besides the platitude of "create a culture that rewards sharing," few people recommend

Phase	*Emphasis*	*Skills/People*	*Tools/Techniques*
Creation and Capture Generate new knowledge Make tacit knowledge explicit Hire people with the right knowledge Create culture of sharing Encourage innovation Incentives for sharing	Human capital Customer capital	Knowledge harvesters Knowledge owners Mentoring/coaching Partner with universities Teamwork Business intelligence Top management	Easy-to-use capture tools E-mail Face-to-face meetings Knowledge tree Write-to-think Feedback
Organization and Categorization Package knowledge Add context to information Create categories of knowledge Create knowledge vocabulary Create metadata tags for documents Measure intellectual capital	Structural capital	Academics Knowledge editors Librarians Knowledge architects Authors Subject matter experts IS	Frameworks Cull knowledge from sources Best practices databases Knowledge bases Knowledge thesaurus Knowledge indexes Measurement tools
Distribution and Access Create links to knowledge Create networks of people Create electronic push and pull distribution mechanisms Knowledge sharing	Structural capital	Publishers Top management IS	HTML Groupware, Lotus Notes Networks, intranets Navigation aids Search tools
Absorption and Reuse Stimulate interaction among people The learning organization Informal networks	Human capital	Group facilitators Organizational developers Matchmakers Knowledge brokers	Team processes Electronic bulletin boards Communities of practice Yellow pages

Figure 6.19 Knowledge Management Stages. *Source:* Reprinted with permission from *Best Practices in Knowledge Management,* Giga Information Group, 1997.

specifics on how to reduce the cultural roadblocks that can hinder knowledge management projects. He describes some cultural barriers, which he calls "red flags."

Watch Out for Cultural Red Flags. Cultural barriers can shut down knowledge management efforts because knowledge management is really about cooperation and sharing. To reach these lofty goals, efforts need to turn the tacit knowledge in people's heads into explicit knowledge in a process, product, or other organizational artifact. Thus, knowledge-management work must tap people's motivations to share and cooperate. Without the motivation, knowledge databases, for example, are not updated or errors are ignored. Or people avoid contributing to a knowledge-sharing network for fear they will give away their best ideas and lose their "competitive advantage" against their peers in the company. Such red flags are not obvious; they are often subtle, yet harmful, says Brooks.

Here are a few of his behavioral red flags that can derail a knowledge-management effort:

- ***Being seen as a whistle-blower or messenger of bad news.*** Few people want to betray their boss, so they avoid presenting early warnings or disagreeing with internal documents. In organizations where "messengers get shot," sharing good news is fine, but sharing bad is not, which defeats the full value of sharing.
- ***Losing one's place as a knowledge gatekeeper.*** Although knowledge brokers are important in organizations, their self-value comes from their controlling the knowledge they house and sharing it only with whom and when they choose. They may see a knowledge management system that encourages the free flow of ideas as decreasing their value, and therefore fight it.
- ***Knowledge sharing really does take time.*** Because sharing takes time, experts may hide so that they are not bothered by requests from others. Others may not participate in, say, presenting their ideas, which may benefit the organization as a whole but have no personal reward, so they think.

These reactions are human; therefore, knowledge-management efforts often need to build "cultural workarounds" so that these kinds of reactions do not block the work. Brooks offers some suggestions. For example, to reduce concerns about being a messenger, the system might allow only limited dissemination of some ideas or give people the ability to rank feedback comments based on their significance. To counter concerns about losing personal advantage, contributions could require authorship or comments might always be linked to the original items. To reduce time consumption, the reward structure could reward contributions based on their value.

In addition to cultural red flags, management red flags are also a concern. Three management red flags are

1. Saying the project is not cost-justifiable because the benefits are intangible
2. Concern that too much participation will reduce employee productivity
3. Concern that creating the taxonomy of knowledge categories will be just too expensive to undertake

Reducing these concerns is an important aspect of knowledge management. Some examples for mitigating these management roadblocks, says Brooks, include illustrating the value of serendipity that has occurred due to sharing, as illustrated in vendor case studies; ensuring that the new system promotes feedback to contributors, which can increase productivity; and drawing on vendor expertise to create knowledge taxonomies rather than start from scratch.

As Brooks points out, organizational culture is an important aspect of knowledge-management efforts and a key determinant of success.

Design the System to Match What the Users Value. Thomas Stewart, a well-known writer in the knowledge-management field, agrees and makes the important point that knowledge needs to be managed within the context where value is created. In short, the system needs to be designed to fit the people who will use it and gain value from it. He notes that many official knowledge-management efforts have come to naught because they did not create the place where people first look for knowledge. On the other hand, a number of grassroots, unofficial efforts have succeeded.

Stewart gives the example of three consultants who created an informal, unofficial Notes-based e-mail list in their company to have a place to collaborate online. Anyone could join the list; to date, it has attracted over 500 company employees. It has actually become the premier knowledge-sharing mechanism in the company even though it is difficult to search and generates a lot of messages, which fill up e-mail boxes. It works, notes Stewart, for four reasons:

1. It is demand driven. Some 80 percent of the traffic is members asking each other, "Does anyone know anything about....?"
2. It roots out tacit knowledge. People contribute what they know, which might not be recorded anywhere in the company.
3. It is right in front of the members in their e-mail boxes every day.
4. It is full of intriguing and strongly held opinions, which the members find most interesting.

The system is like a conversation rather than a library; thus, it is about learning rather than teaching. That is a major difference, notes Stewart. It was designed to manage knowledge in the context where value is created. Given the high number of failed knowledge-management projects, Stewart suggests answering the following three questions before launching off:

1. Which group will use this knowledge space? Once determined, make them responsible for the content.
2. What kind of knowledge does the group need? Once known, that knowledge needs to be managed within that group's content because that is where the value arises. A knowledge-management system or resource should only deal with a single group that creates value in the same way.

3. What is the company culture; is it composed of reusers or originators? The difference matters. A repository of things promotes a reuse culture; an online chat room helps originators, but not vice versa.

Beware of creating a system that supports the wrong culture, warns Stewart. There is really no such thing as a generic knowledge-management system. Each one needs to fit a knowledge-sharing group. Answering these questions will help uncover the structure and content of a knowledge-management resource that will add value and actually be used.

As an example of a knowledge-management project that has worked and has followed many of the tenets espoused by Stewart, consider the work at Partners HealthCare System in Boston. Notice how it takes into account the health-care culture.

SUMMARY

We have now completed our two-chapter survey of intraorganizational IT application areas. Chapter 5 focused on application areas that support the entire organization or large portions of it, including transaction processing systems, data warehousing, and office automation. At the conclusion of Chapter 5, we argued that modern organizations cannot do business without these enterprise IT systems. In this chapter we have concentrated on managerial support systems such as DSSs, EISs, and neural networks. These managerial support systems are just as critical to the individual managers in a business as the enterprise systems are to the firm as a whole. Modern managers simply cannot manage effectively and efficiently without managerial support IT systems.

Several types of managerial support systems are designed to support individual managers in their decision-making endeavors without the aid of artificial intelligence. Decision support systems (DSSs), data mining, geographic information systems (GISs), and executive information systems (EISs) all fall into this broad grouping. A DSS is an interactive system, employing a model of some sort, that assists a manager in making decisions in a situation that is not well structured. The prototypical example of a DSS is carrying out what-if analyses on a financial model. Data mining is concerned with digging out nuggets of information from a data warehouse, again using a model; thus data mining can be considered as a subset of the broader DSS construct. A geographic information system is based on spatial relationships; many, but not all, GISs incorporate a model and are used as a DSS. In contrast, an EIS does not usually involve a model. An EIS provides easy online access to current aggregate information about key business conditions. A business intelligence system is a newer variant of an EIS incorporating special tools to capture and display competitive information. In general, a DSS, data mining, or a GIS provides specific information of value to a manager working on a particular problem, while an EIS provides aggregated information of value to a wide range of managers within the firm.

Group support systems (GSSs) and knowledge management systems (KMSs) provide support to a group of managers, although in quite different ways. A GSS provides support to a group of managers engaged in some sort of group activity, most commonly an in-person meeting, whereas a KMS is a system for managing organizational knowledge and sharing it with the appropriate group. A GSS, which is a specialized type of groupware, consists of software running on a LAN that permits all meeting participants to simultaneously and anonymously make contributions to the group discussion by keying in their ideas and having them displayed on a large public screen, if desired. The software facilitates various group tasks, such as idea generation, organizing ideas, prioritizing, and policy development. With a KMS, knowledge may be shared within a community of practice (a group of managers with similar interests) via knowledge repositories, discussion forums, and community calendars, or within a broader grouping of employees via a carefully structured package of knowledge content.

Artificial intelligence (AI) is used to support the individual manager in our third grouping of managerial support systems. By capturing the decision-making logic of a human expert, an expert system provides nonexperts with expert advice. A neural network teases out obscure patterns from vast amounts of data by a process of adaptive learning. In both cases the user is led to better decisions via AI. Closely related to AI is virtual reality, where computer-based systems create an environment that seems real to one or more human senses. Virtual reality has proved particularly useful for training and design activities, and it is increasingly being used for marketing on the Web.

The enterprise systems, for example, are primarily large-scale systems that would be purchased from an outside vendor or custom developed by the internal IS organization or an external consulting firm. In particular, enterprise resource planning, office automation, groupware, and factory automation are almost always purchased from an outside vendor. These are all massive systems that require similar functionality across a wide variety of firms. Of course, the internal IS department or a consultant may customize them to the organization. Data warehousing and intranets are often implemented with purchased package software, but there might also be internal or consultant development. Historically, the internal IS organization developed most transaction processing systems, but even these systems are likely to be purchased today, as shown by the growth of ERP systems, unless the firm's requirements are unique.

By contrast, the business manager or a consultant (internal or external to the firm) is likely to develop many managerial support systems expressly for the manager. In most cases the business manager or consultant would start with an underlying software tool (such as a DSS generator, expert systems shell, neural network program, or data mining tool) and develop a specific implementation of the tool that satisfies the need. The manager is unlikely, however, to develop a group support system, EIS, or KM system; these multi-user systems are more akin to enterprise systems in terms of their acquisition.

CHAPTER REVIEW QUESTIONS

1. Describe the three primary components that make up any decision support system and how they interact.
2. Explain the difference between a specific decision support system (DSS) and a DSS generator. Give an example of each.
3. Describe two examples of specific DSSs that are being used to assist in decision making. Use either textbook examples or other examples you've heard about.
4. Negotiation support systems (NSSs) and group support systems (GSSs) are both variants of DSSs. Explain how an NSS and a GSS differ from other DSSs.
5. Explain both data warehousing and data mining and how they are related.
6. List at least two techniques (decision technologies) that are used in data mining.
7. List at least three uses of data mining.
8. Give an example of how data mining could be used to change a company's policies or actions.
9. What is the purpose of a group support system (GSS)? What are the potential advantages and disadvantages of using a GSS?
10. Compare the raster-based and vector-based approaches to geographic information systems (GISs). What are the primary uses of each approach?
11. What are the distinguishing characteristics of an executive information system (EIS)? Why have these systems become a part of business intelligence in many companies?
12. What is knowledge management and what is a knowledge management system? How does the concept of a community of practice relate to knowledge management?
13. Briefly describe the areas of artificial intelligence (AI) research. Indicate why business people are most interested in the expert systems and neural networks areas.
14. What are the three approaches to obtaining an expert system? What are the pluses and minuses of each approach?
15. What are the five problems that serve as hidden pitfalls in developing a successful EIS?
16. Describe two examples of expert systems that are being used to assist in decision making (examples don't necessarily have to come from the text).
17. What are two examples of neural networks that are being used to assist in decision making?
18. Describe two examples of the use of virtual reality in an organized setting.

CHAPTER DISCUSSION QUESTIONS

1. Review data mining and data warehousing. In addition to data mining, which of the other application areas may be used in conjunction with data warehousing?
2. What are the primary distinctions between DSSs and expert systems?
3. How do group support systems and groupware relate to one another? Which one is important today? Do you think this will be important in the future?
4. Consider an industry or a company with which you have some familiarity and identify at least one possible application of GISs (geographical information systems) in that industry or company. What are some areas where GISs might be useful in the future?
5. Explain the concept of "drilling-down" as used in executive information systems (EIS). Is drilling-down used in other IT applications? How do these applications relate to EIS?
6. Explain the original role that was to be played by an EIS and then describe how this role has been modified over time. Why has this role change occurred?
7. According to the trade press, the success record of knowledge management systems has been modified over time. Why has this role change occurred?
8. Consider any companies or industries with which you are familiar and identify how they have used at least one possible application of expert systems.
9. Is there an industry or company that you are familiar with that could use a neural network? How and why?
10. Which of the application areas discussed in this chapter is more useful for a small to mid-sized business? Defend your answer.

CASE STUDY: PARTNERS HEALTHCARE SYSTEM

Not too long ago, Tom Davenport of Accenture's Institute for Strategic Change and John Glaser, CIO of Partners HealthCare System in Boston, described how Partners HealthCare System is delivering just-in-time knowledge.

The problem the physicians at Partners HealthCare hospitals and physician groups face is the deluge of new knowledge they need to know but cannot possibly keep up with on their own. The solution has been to present physicians with the new knowledge they need when they need it through the information technology they already use in their work. In essence, this approach makes knowledge management part of their job, not a separate activity, and it can deliver knowledge just when a patient really needs it.

The work at Partners HealthCare began on a small, doable scale: using the doctors' online order entry system to notify doctors of drug interactions when they enter a prescription order. The system checks the patient's medical record, looking for allergic reactions to the drug (or a similar drug) and alerts the physician. The doctor can inquire about the reaction, and, if it was mild, override the computer's recommendation to switch to another medication.

The system can also tell the doctor about a newer, more effective drug or inform him or her of another drug the patient is taking that can lead to a bad interaction. Or, if the doctor is ordering a test, the system can describe a newer, more effective test for the noted symptom. Or the system can warn the doctor that the prescribed medication could worsen a patient disease.

This integrated system is built on knowledge bases (databases of knowledge about the patient, drugs, tests, medical research, and such) and a logic engine (which, as its name implies, performs the logical interconnections between the various kinds of knowledge in the knowledge bases).

The system also has an event-detection mechanism, which alerts a physician when it learns of an event that can endanger the health of a patient. For example, when the patient's health indicators deviate from the norm while the patient is in the hospital, the doctor or a nurse is notified via pager. This capability brings knowledge management into real time, note Davenport and Glaser.

However, this system could not be bought. It had to be built by Partners HealthCare. It was a large investment, but it was made because too many patients at Partners were experiencing drug interactions. Management had to fix that problem. One of the steps it took was to form committees of top clinicians to identify the knowledge that needed to be in the knowledge bases and keep it up-to-date. The drug therapy committee makes the medication recommendations, whereas the radiology committee develops the logic to guide radiology testing. Participation in each committee is seen as prestigious, which is crucial to the success of the system, so that busy physicians give time to the committee work.

Another step Partners took was to only address the most critical processes. Furthermore, the system is simply seen as a recommendation system. It does not make final decisions. Those are left up to the physicians. The combined human–computer system seems to be working. Some 380 orders (out of 13,000 a day) are changed due to a computer suggestion. Some one-third to one-half of orders with drug interactions are cancelled, and some 72 percent of treatments are changed when the event-detection system sounds an alert. Partner's strong measurement culture helps it gather such statistics and see the benefits of the system.

In summary, Davenport and Glaser believe that embedding knowledge in the systems and work processes that professionals use is the way to achieve just-in-time knowledge management and dramatically improve an organization's performance.

Case Study Discussion Questions

Question One

What did it take for this system to be created and become effective? Can you think of a similar application for delivering real-time knowledge in another industry?

Question Two

What are some dangers or risks for patients with this healthcare system? Are there any?

Question Three

Can you think of any situations where ethics might be a factor in how artificial intelligence is handled?

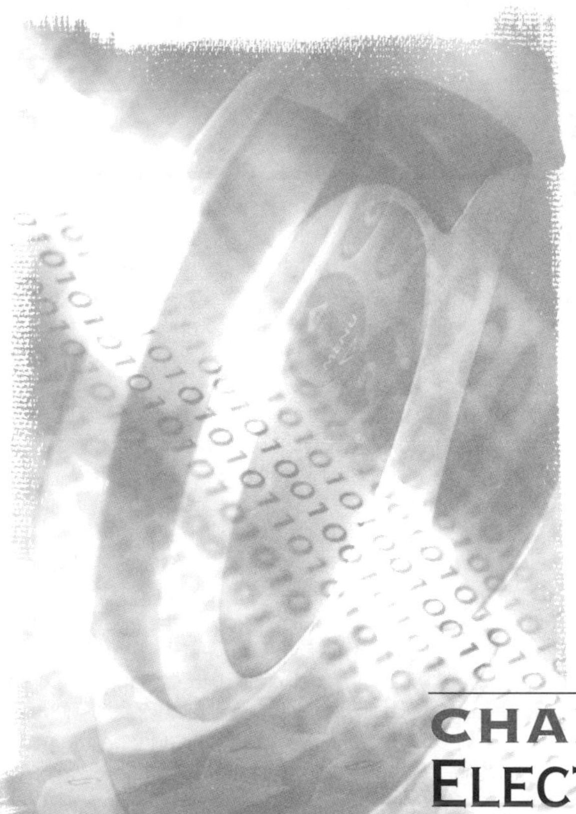

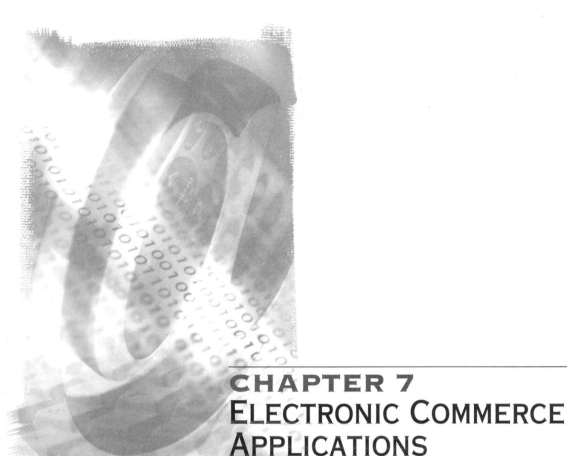

CHAPTER 7
ELECTRONIC COMMERCE APPLICATIONS

As discussed in Chapter 1, today we are in the early years of an e-world: a new digital economy in which a global network of computers links individuals, organizations, and nations in real time. Chapter 5 and Chapter 6 focused on enterprise-wide applications and managerial support systems. This chapter focuses on **electronic commerce** (e-commerce) applications that are designed to extend an organization's reach beyond its own organizational boundaries and to interact with customers, suppliers, and other business partners.

Although e-commerce applications to conduct business transactions beyond organizational boundaries did not originate with the Web, the development of the first commercial Web browser (Netscape Navigator) in the mid-1990s led to an explosive demand for the development of commercial Web sites: hypertext applications stored on Web servers connected to the Internet. By the end of the 1990s, online ways of gathering information and conducting business had become a new way of doing business for many U.S.-based businesses, and new terminology had entered the vernacular to describe them.

> **Electronic commerce** is the electronic transmission of buyer/seller transactions and related information between individuals and businesses or between two or more businesses that are trading partners.

For example, one of the most visible phenomena has been the emergence of new businesses that communicate with their customers online and gain revenues entirely based on traffic to their Web sites, referred to as "pure-plays" or **dot-coms** (an artifact of the suffix ".com" in the Internet domain address for commercial organizations). Between 2000 and 2002, many of these dot-com firms closed, and many investors lost money due to stock holdings or venture capital invested in dot-com and related information technology (IT) companies.

However, at the same time that this dot-com meltdown was occurring, traditional (bricks-and-mortar) businesses that existed before the Web were continuing to learn how to design and implement e-commerce applications to complement, extend, or even transform their ways of doing business—and to regain some of the market share won by the dot-com start-ups in the preceding years. Traditional companies that integrate *offline and online* business strategies are referred to today as "bricks and clicks" or **clicks-and-mortar** firms.

In the following section we give a brief history of the Internet and the major IT innovations that led to its rapid growth. Since legal and regulatory environments also have affected the Internet's growth, we also provide a brief discussion of some important legislative impacts.

We then turn to a discussion of the Internet's potential influence on strategic opportunities and threats at both the industry level and the individual business level. Examples of successful business-to-consumer (**B2C**) and business-to-business (**B2B**) applications for different types of e-business models (including direct-to-customer retailing and online intermediaries) will then be described in detail. The chapter ends with a discussion of what makes a good Web site from a customer perspective.

Continued growth in e-commerce application investments has been forecast for the near future due to the proven advantages of conducting business via the Internet: This open communications network of networks has a relatively cheap entry cost, a transmission speed measured in microseconds or seconds, a multimedia communications capability via the Web, and a global reach to other businesses as well as a growing number of potential customers. A more theoretical explanation for why the Internet is likely to become an even more attractive vehicle for e-commerce in the coming years is provided by **Metcalfe's Law**, which states that

> *the value of a network to each of its members is proportional to the number of other users, expressed as* $(n^2 - n) / 2$.

Stated differently, there are increasing returns to be gained as more and more organizations create Web sites and more individuals gain access to the Internet.

E-COMMERCE TECHNOLOGIES

The *commercial* history of the Internet is actually quite short. The Internet has its roots in **ARPANET,** a network of federal government and research and development firms in the private sector that grew to include educational institutions and other nonprofit organizations outside of the United States. In 1991 the nonprofit organization in the United States responsible for managing the Internet backbone at that time (the National Science Foundation) lifted the original ban on commercial usage of the Internet. In 1994 the first commercial **Web browser** was released as a free product by its developers in an attempt to quickly build demand for its software and services. The rapid diffusion of first the Netscape browser and then Microsoft's browser (Internet Explorer), quickly ushered in the opportunity for businesses connected to the Internet anywhere in the world to reach individual consumers and other businesses.

Today, the Internet is a network of computer networks that use the Transmission Control Protocol/Internet Protocol (TCP/IP) protocol with gateways to even more networks that do not use the TCP/IP protocol. The Web (World Wide Web) is a subset of the Internet, with multimedia capabilities. Web documents are composed in standard markup languages (Hypertext Markup Language [HTML]) and stored on servers around the globe with standard addresses (Uniform Resource Locators [URLs]) that are accessible via a hypermedia protocol (Hypertext Transfer Protocol [HTTP]). Initially, these Web technologies were created for a scientific community to exchange documents.

No single organization owns the Internet; each organization or end user pays for its software and hardware (for clients and servers) and network access. Beginning in 1993, the rights for registering Web site addresses (domain names) were held solely by a U.S. federal contractor, Network Solutions Inc., but site registration is now overseen by ICANN, the Internet Corporation for Assigned Names and Numbers.

Figure 7.1 summarizes some of the major IT developments since the commercial introduction of the browser. Commercial organizations initially created a "Web presence" with hyperlinked text documents for their stakeholders (customers, shareholders) and the public. Web technologies to support interactivity with the user were then developed, along with flashier designs to capture the "eyeballs" of Web site visitors. By 1998 the term Web "portal" emerged to refer to sites that were designed to be a user's initial gateway to other Web sites.

Technologies for B2C Applications

The implementation of secure ways to transmit sensitive transactions and a standard for credit card processing by 1998 were catalysts for the development of Web sites with online sales and service capabilities. By this time the Internet had become a proven channel for supply chain and customer-facing business interactions that held the potential for a competitive advantage. Web developers began to focus on technologies not only to improve the online sales or auction bidding experiences, but also to provide new channels for around-the-clock customer service. The collection of clickstream metrics and personal data from Web site users, as well as the acceptance of Web "**cookies**" stored on the user's hard drive, enabled the customization of Web sites for the individual or organizational user. Web browsers also continually improved in functionality and ease-of-use, and by the new millennium they provided a standard interface to access interactive multimedia (audio, video, animation), with essentially no special end-user training.

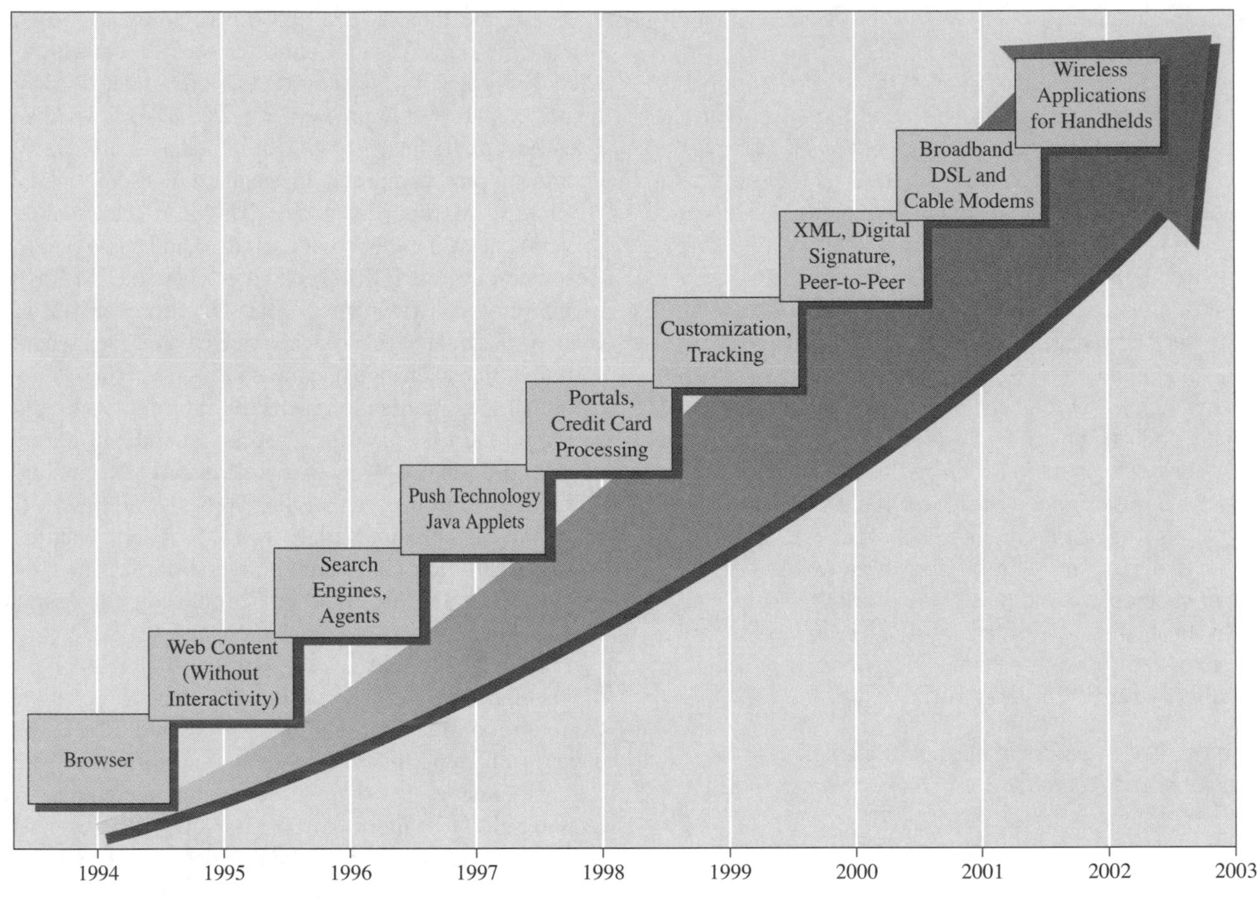

Figure 7.1 Internet Technology Innovations for E-Commerce

Compared to e-mail or the telephone, the Web is therefore a richer communications medium, even with the narrowband connections using "plain old" telephone lines or wireless networks. However, in the United States during the early 2000s, broadband access via cable modems or digital subscriber line (DSL) telephone lines became increasingly available in, or near, U.S. cities or towns with a sizable population: between May and November 2003 alone, at-home broadband connections in the United States increased by 27 percent (Nielsen/Net Ratings, 2003). Increased broadband access to the home users also enabled virtual reality applications in which a consumer can "walk through" a mall, be "measured" for clothing, "try out" a toy, or "view" real estate that is for sale.

By 2004 handheld cellular devices with Internet access that had been more heavily used in other countries (e.g., Finland and Japan), were also fueling IT innovations for mobile e-commerce applications (**m-commerce**). The rate of growth of m-commerce applications in the United States is expected to be dependent on the emergence of standard and secure wireless networks, as well as applications designed to address the constraints of small, handheld devices that might only be used for short periods of time and in physical environments with very different characteristics (e.g., noise, lighting) than the typical portable laptop computer.

The past decade has also seen technology innovations that enable peer-to-peer (**P2P**) applications. The promise of P2P was rapidly recognized due to the fast rise of a music-sharing service (using an MP3 standard) via the Napster.com Web site. However, the initial version of the Web site was short-lived: it was found to be in violation of U.S. copyright laws and shut down by the federal government. Today, other Web sites facilitate P2P file-sharing between client computers using a different business model, and a similar concept, called **grid computing**, that takes advantage of unused computer processing power on desktops to accomplish massive parallel processing computations.

Technologies for B2B Applications

From an economic standpoint, one of the most important technology advances has been the development of standards for a markup language (eXtensible Markup Language, or **XML**) to facilitate the transmission of business documents via B2B applications. XML standards have been endorsed by the cross-industry World Wide Web Consortium (**W3C**), and XML has become a standard language for enabling e-business activities due to its precise "tagging" capabilities. XML also enables a flexible, low-entry form of **electronic data interchange,** or **EDI** applications.

Before the commercialization of the Internet, many companies had developed IT solutions for e-commerce with trading partners based on agreed-upon standards for business document transmission, using proprietary applications that became known as EDI. By the early 1990s over half of the Fortune 1000 had implemented EDI applications using a private telecommunications network of leased lines or a value-added network (VAN) provided by a third party (see the sidebar entitled "How EDI Works").

For large discount retailers like Wal-Mart, EDI applications became an integral part of their business strategies. For large manufacturers, the automated data flows between business partners enabled just-in-time (JIT) manufacturing processes. For example, Chrysler's EDI system in the early 1990s supported 17 million transactions per year with a portion of its 1,600 external suppliers. For these large firms, the costs of developing these customized systems were more than offset by benefits such as

- reduced cycle times for doing business
- cost savings for automated transaction handling and the elimination of paper documents
- improved interfirm coordination and reduced interfirm coordination costs

HOW EDI WORKS

EDI is usually implemented by computer-to-computer communication between organizations. A customer sends a supplier a purchase order or release to a blanket order via a standard electronic document. There is no manual shuffling of paperwork and little, if any, reentering of data. The supplier's computer system checks that the message is in an acceptable format and sends an electronic acknowledgment to the customer. The electronic order then feeds the supplier's production planning and shipping systems to schedule the shipment.

When the order is ready to ship, the supplier sends the customer an electronic notice of the pending shipment. The customer's computer checks that the shipment information corresponds to the order and returns a message authorizing the shipment. The supplier then sends a message that includes the truck number, carrier, approximate arrival time, and bill of lading. The customer's computer alerts the receiving dock of the expected arrival; receiving personnel visually verify the shipment upon arrival for quality, and the shipment is accepted.

A contract signed by EDI business partners determines when an electronic order is legally binding, which could be when it is delivered, after the message is read, or after it has been checked. A contract also determines whether all messages must be acknowledged. Usually, the customer must guarantee that if it issues a correctly formatted and acknowledged order, then it is obliged to accept and pay for the requested goods.

The technical success of EDI depends on standards. Standards for EDI are necessary because computer file formats, forms, data and transaction definitions, and the overall methods of processing data can vary considerably across companies and especially across countries. Standards provide a way to decouple the different EDI participants as much as possible, yet still facilitate data exchange.

An electronic business document is called a transaction set. Header and trailer records contain batch control information, such as the unique identifiers of the sender and receiver, a date, the number of line segments, and so on. Each transaction set also has a unique identification number and a time stamp. An EDI translation program converts an incoming EDI format so that it can be read by an application program, and vice versa.

The specific standard for a transaction set is established between the business partners of an EDI relationship. EDI standards are of three types: proprietary formats designed for one or more organizations and their trading partners, industry-specific formats that are designed to match specific industry needs (e.g., automotive), and generic formats for use by any trading partners. In some industries a major industry player or a consortium of companies have established a standard, whereas in other industries a formal body with large representation may have established a standard.

The American National Standards Institute (ANSI) has coordinated standard-setting activities in the United States. ANSI X.12 formats exist for standard documents in many U.S. industries—including chemicals, automotive, retail merchants, textiles, and electrical equipment. Some of these U.S. standards were developed by an industry group. For example, the Automotive Industry Action Group (AIAG) was created by Ford, General Motors, and Chrysler along with 300 large suppliers. For some industries, the usage of uniform standards for product identification (product codes) is also key to EDI cost savings.

Nevertheless, according to Senn (2000), fewer than 100,000 out of the several million potential business users of EDI applications within the United States had implemented EDI due to constraints such as

- start-up coordination challenges (including EDI standard agreements and legal issues)
- start-up and ongoing IT costs for one or more of the trading partners (including the maintenance of the proprietary systems and the high costs of third-party VANs)

Because of these EDI shortcomings and the development of a secure digital signature capability (see the sidebar entitled "Digital Signatures"), industry watchers projected that B2B applications would grow very rapidly in the first half-decade of the new millennium. Although this projected rate of growth was overly optimistic, and Web-based XML is still considered less efficient than proprietary EDI applications for well-defined, repetitive, and high-volume transactions with business partners, the usage of Web forms with XML "tags" in combination with extranet applications is expected to continue to grow.

DIGITAL SIGNATURES

Digital signatures use cryptography to convert data into a secret code for transmission over a public network. These technologies are often considered the most secure and reliable form of electronic signature because they use public-key infrastructure technologies to ensure that the electronic message has not been altered during transmission.

Say you wanted to draft and complete a contract with a customer using a digital signature. To do so, you'd first have to acquire a digital certificate—the electronic equivalent of an ID card. Several companies, including VeriSign and Entrust Technologies, are licensed to issue such certificates. Once you sign up, the provider transmits the certificate to your computer. You also receive two digital keys—one private and one public.

To sign a document, you enter a password or PIN and affix your electronic signature—the private key—to the document. The person or company receiving your document would then use the public key to unlock your certificate and verify that the signature is valid. Once confirmed, they could sign the document using their own digital tools and return it to you. Throughout the process, the software documents the date and time of each signing, while built-in security measures ensure that the documents haven't been altered anywhere along the process.

[J. Brown, 2000]

Web technologies have also been used to develop e-marketplaces (or exchanges) hosted by buyers, suppliers, third-party service providers, or a consortia of buyers or suppliers. The recent trend has been for companies to create their own B2B applications to support bids from their preferred suppliers or customer orders, using off-the-shelf software from software vendors such as Ariba, Inc., and Commerce One, Inc., that supports alternative EDI transmission methods. However, the economic recession in the United States that began in March 2000 severely "dampened" the rate of investments in Internet-related B2B innovations. After the huge IT expenditures for Y2K and euro compliance had been paid for, an e-business "reality check" set in and the venture capitalists began to demand profits, not just promises, from the Internet-related start-ups. Despite this slow-down in IT innovations, the growth of the commercial usage of the Internet has continued to evolve as traditional companies have learned to leverage earlier IT innovations *as well as business innovations*. The economic slowdown has also led to a better balance between the demand and supply of IT personnel who are skilled in Web technologies.

Technologies for IT Security

One of the biggest potential constraints to the diffusion of Internet-based e-commerce applications for consumers, as well as for businesses, was the initial lack of security for Internet transactions. Two major security issues are how to control access to a computer that is physically networked to the Internet and how to ensure that the security of a given communication, such as a business transaction, is not violated.

The primary way to control access to corporate or individual computers is by means of a **firewall**. Firewalls are devices that sit between the Internet and an organization's internal network (or an individual's computer) in order to block intrusions from unauthorized users and hackers from remote sites. A firewall can be a router, a personal computer, a host, or a collection of hosts. A company's public Web site typically sits outside the firewall, and many firms use outside vendors to host their external Web sites for not only security reasons but also for peak load balancing. Unknown to the Web site user, a company's Web site may therefore be on a vendor's server, and e-mail or other communications may initially be received by a third party, not a computer (or person) internal to the company that owns the domain name.

Encryption is the primary way to ensure the security of a business transaction or other communication. Today's encryption systems are based on two decoding keys and

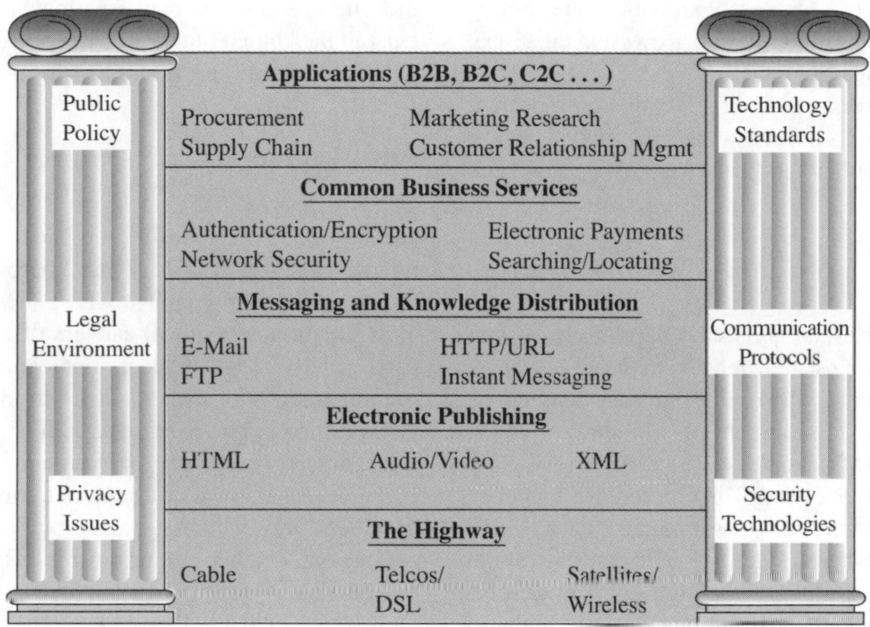

Figure 7.2 E-Commerce Framework (Adapted from Applegate, Holsapple, et al. 1996; Kalakota and Whinston, 1996).

mathematical principles for factoring a product into its two prime numbers. One decoding key is used to encipher (code) a message; a second decoding key is used to decipher it. The enciphering key makes it easy to encode a message, but deciphering requires a key available only to the message's intended recipient. If the enciphering key is the product of two very large prime numbers, the key is expected to have a relatively long life before being vulnerable to a hacker. For example, it took a group of 600 academics and hobbyists using computers of 1993 vintage just under 1 year to identify the two prime numbers for a 129-digit product. A somewhat larger product is estimated to be indecipherable within a person's lifetime (Gates, 1995).

An Internet standard for secure transactions for payment via credit card systems was initiated in 1996 by a consortium that included banks, two major credit card players (MasterCard and Visa), and other major industry players (GTE, IBM Corp., Microsoft Corporation, Netscape). The first version of this new standard, Secure Electronic Transaction (SET), was released in June 1997. Similarly, the implementation of a digital signature capability was viewed as a catalyst for B2B applications.

Companies have also made IT security investments in order to protect the corporation from intentional attacks and viruses that originate with Internet communications. In particular, programs that exploit security flaws in Microsoft's operating systems or application programs have been major targets. In most cases software vendors had already identified the flaws, but companies had not kept up-to-date with security patches made available on the vendor's Web site. Denial-of-service and intentional virus attacks are criminal acts, and the legal systems of national governments need to play strong legislative and oversight roles to help businesses and individuals avoid the high costs of recovering from intentional security breaches.

As shown in Figure 7.2, the IT applications, services, and communications technologies that enable e-commerce depend on two types of pillars: a technology pillar and a legal and regulatory environment pillar. The standards for the Web have evolved under the guidance of consortia such as the W3C, industry consortia, as well as various watchdog groups. These activities are part of the right-hand support pillar in Figure 7.2. The left-hand support pillar includes actions by governments and legal systems, which we will discuss in the following section.

LEGAL AND REGULATORY ENVIRONMENT

Given the Internet's origins and short commercial life, the legal and regulatory environment in the United States has played a major role in shaping the Internet's capabilities for e-commerce as it exists today. However, we expect the role of the U.S. government to be less dominant in the coming years, as the Internet user population grows and the global **digital divide** becomes less severe.

Below we briefly discuss four issues that have been at the forefront of public concern within the United States: tax policies, copyright laws, antitrust (monopoly) laws, and privacy issues.

Tax Policies

Within the United States, taxes on sales of products and services are collected at the state level. Given the lack of physical geography associated with online purchase transactions over the Internet, the development of a uniform sales tax policy requires federal action. During the years of early Internet growth under President Bill Clinton, the executive branch of the federal government supported a "hands-off" policy for taxing Web-based sales as a deliberate attempt to foster the growth of a global superhighway. The government's vision was for a national information superhighway that would link homes, businesses, and government, and IT innovations for e-commerce were expected to fuel the development of the infrastructure to make this a reality.

In October 2001 this federal policy was scheduled to be reconsidered by Congress, and opposition to a hands-off policy had been growing under lobbying efforts by groups such as the National Retail Federation and the International Council of Shopping Centers. However, the September 11, 2001 terrorist attacks on the United States diverted attention from sales tax revenues to security concerns, and the hands-off policy was not replaced. By 2004, however, many state governments had begun taxing Internet purchases, and there was a multi-state government initiative underway to develop an interstate tax program with common collection and audit procedures (referred to as the Streamlined Sales Tax Project).

Copyright Laws

In the United States most major software vendors have been involved in a copyright suit at some time in the recent past. In 2001 the most closely watched copyright suit involved the P2P file-sharing service operated by Napster.com, which was found to be in violation of copyright laws and was closed down. In 2004 the court challenge by The SCO Group against the GPL licensing of the Linux operating system is expected to continue to receive considerable media attention.

Given the galloping rate of IT innovations, software copyrights have been difficult to enforce at a national level. Intellectual copyright laws in general also continue to be difficult to enforce at an international level, as the laws that exist in the United States are not upheld by many countries outside Western Europe and North America.

Antitrust Laws

The two biggest antitrust lawsuits by the Department of Justice against IT industry companies have involved monopoly violations by AT&T and Microsoft.

The 1982 ruling against AT&T ("Ma Bell") led to the 1984 creation of regional carriers ("Baby Bells") as local carriers. The 1996 Telecommunications Act opened up retail markets still further and led to mergers among Baby Bells and other carriers. By 2004 the telecommunications industry was still a hypercompetitive industry that included cable, wireless, regional carriers, long-distance providers, and Internet service providers (ISPs) competing against one another, acquiring spin-offs, and merging with one another.

In early 2000 a federal court judge ruled that Microsoft was in violation of antitust laws due to its tight coupling of its Windows operating systems and its Internet Explorer browser. However, the potential penalty of splitting up Microsoft into two companies—one company for systems software (e.g., Windows) and one company for application software (e.g., Microsoft Office suite)—was not invoked. By the end of 2003, Microsoft products still dominated the desktop operating system, browser, and office productivity suite markets.

Whether the U.S. and European antitrust laws will become an obstacle to global competition for IT industry companies in the near future is an unanswered question. However, one irony is already apparent: a key enabler for the rapid diffusion of the Internet has been the existence of Microsoft products as industry "standards" not only in the United States but also in most multinational firms.

Privacy Issues

The first privacy legislation within the United States dates from the 1970s. However, privacy issues associated with individual consumer data have gained significant attention within the United States with the growth of e-commerce applications and the continued introduction of new technologies to capture consumer data and behaviors, including the usage of cookies. To date, privacy rights advocacy groups have played a major role in ensuring that companies have, and uphold, privacy standards. For example, when a top Internet advertising firm, DoubleClick, revealed its plans for user profiling (by combining anonymous data about Web surfers with personal information stored in other consumer databases), advocacy groups sent out an alert, the Federal Trade Commission (FTC) began to investigate, and DoubleClick aborted its plan.

Watchdog groups and nonprofit organizations have also been a deterrent to individual data misuse by Web site owners. By the end of 2002, more than 90 percent of U.S.-based retailing Web sites provided explicit statements of their own privacy policies—what the firm will or will not do with any individual data collected from usage of their Web site (E-Tailing Group, 2002). Independent organizations also administer programs that validate a firm's responsible behavior toward Web site visitors, and the approved commercial Web site typically displays a visible logo signalling their validated trustworthiness (see the sidebar entitled "TRUSTe Trustmark").

TRUSTe TRUSTMARK

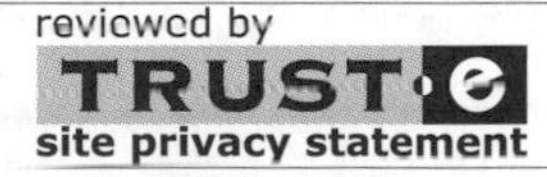

TRUSTe believes that an environment of mutual trust and openness will help make and keep the Internet a free, comfortable, and richly diverse community for everyone. As an Internet user, you have a right to expect online privacy and the responsibility to exercise choice over how your personal information is collected, used, and shared by Web sites. The TRUSTe program was designed expressly to ensure that your privacy is protected through open disclosure and to empower you to make informed choices.

A cornerstone of our program is the TRUSTe "trustmark," an online branded seal displayed by member Web sites. The trustmark is awarded only to sites that adhere to established privacy principles and agree to comply with ongoing TRUSTe oversight and consumer resolution procedures. Privacy principles embody fair information practices approved by the U.S. Department of Commerce, Federal Trade Commission, and prominent industry-represented organizations and associations. The principles include:

- **Adoption and implementation of a privacy policy** that takes into account consumer anxiety over sharing personal information online.
- **Notice and disclosure** of information collection and use practices.
- **Choice and consent**, giving users the opportunity to exercise control over their information.
- **Data security and quality and access** measures to help protect the security and accuracy of personally identifiable information.

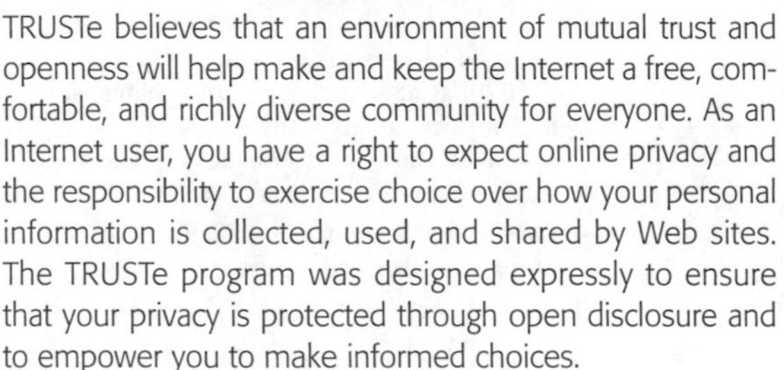

[TRUSTe Web site, accessed January 2004. Logo used with permission of TRUSTe.]

However, it should be kept in mind that until now the U.S. brand of capitalism and the U.S. laws protecting freedom of expression have been the primary shapers of e-commerce because of the historical roots of the Internet and the Silicon Valley innovations of the past decade. As more non-U.S. businesses conduct e-commerce via the Internet, the influence of U.S. approaches will be less dominant, and international agreements are expected to become more important.

STRATEGIC OPPORTUNITIES AND THREATS

Frameworks for thinking about a firm's strategic opportunities and threats have been developed by management strategy guru Michael E. Porter since the early 1980s. In particular, management strategists have used Porter's **competitive forces model** to help businesses anticipate and plan strategic responses to the competitive forces within a firm's industry (Porter, 1985; Porter and Millar, 1985). The five competitive forces are: supplier power, customer power, the threat of new entrants (same products/services), the threat of substitute products/services, and the responses of competitors within the same industry to any of these same forces.

Porter's competitive forces model can also be a useful starting place for thinking about the commercial opportunities and threats introduced by the Internet at the industry level. Figure 7.3 summarizes Porter's general predictions due to the influence of the Internet from the perspective of a traditional company: potential opportunities are shown with a plus (+) sign, potential threats with a minus (–) sign (Porter, 2001).

Looking first at the opportunities due to the Internet that Porter identifies, Porter concludes that (1) the procurement of supplies via the Internet can increase the traditional company's power over its suppliers, (2) the size of a potential market is expanded due to the Internet, and (3) powerful distribution channels between the traditional company and its customers can be eliminated. The first and third opportunities here refer to the potential to bypass companies between the producer or service provider and the customer for that product or service.

However, as can be seen in Figure 7.3, Porter also identifies a large number of threats to the traditional company due to the Internet. Among these threats are:

1. There is a migration to price competition because it's difficult to keep product or service offerings proprietary.
2. The widening of the geographic markets increases the number of potential competitors.

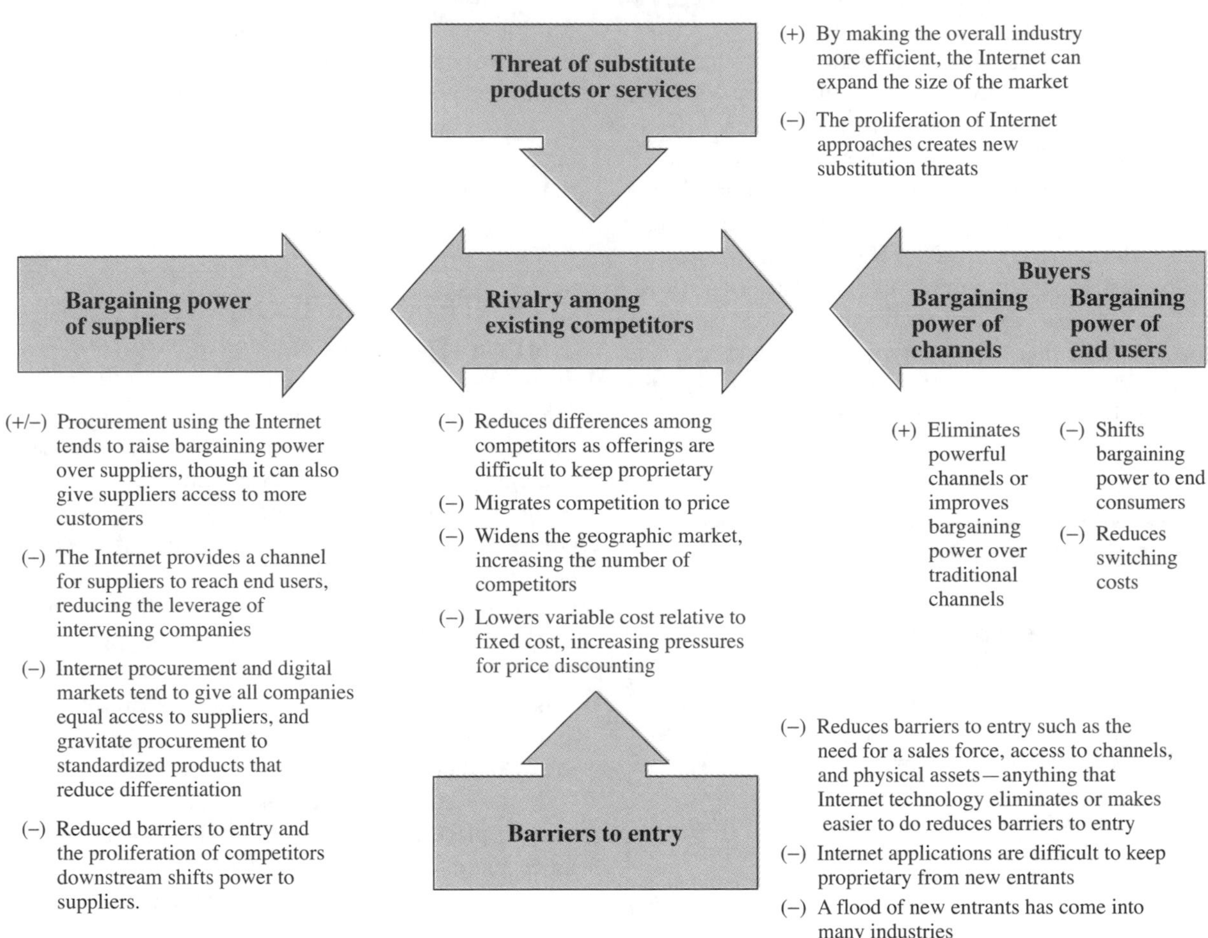

Figure 7.3 How the Internet Influences Industry Structure (Reprinted by permission of *Harvard Business Review*. "How the Internet Influences Industry Structure," by Michael Porter. *Harvard Business Review* March 2001. Copyright © 2004 by the Harvard Business School Publishing Corporation. All rights reserved.).

3. The Internet reduces or eliminates some traditional barriers, such as the need for an in-person sales force and distribution channels.
4. Customers increase their bargaining power as the Internet reduces switching costs for the customer.

The third threat captures the concern that new dot-com competitors might be able to quickly chip away at a traditional firm's profit margins (Ghosh, 1998) due to the ease and speed with which a Web site can be introduced. The first and fourth threats suggest that it will be much more difficult for a company to compete based on differentiation—i.e., the differentiation of the company's products or services based on quality, customer service, or some other unique value perceived by the customer.

Of course, there is a potential danger in using competitive models that were initially based on ways of doing business in earlier decades. For example, Porter's model fosters single-industry thinking, but the Internet provides the potential for cross-industry alliances and marketplaces not possible in the offline world. Porter's 5-force model was conceptually developed two decades ago, when we did not have a global computer network to link commercial businesses with one another and to people across the world. Another potential shortcoming is the masking of the potential for new kinds of dot-com intermediaries to exist between a firm and its customers, as well as between a firm and its suppliers. As will be seen from our examples in subsequent sections of this chapter, the digital nature and global reach of the Internet also makes possible new online aggregators of information and business transactions between multiple buyers and sellers.

When considering the strategic opportunities and threats associated with the Internet, two pre-Internet "lessons" about using IT to provide a competitive advantage should also be considered. The first pre-Internet lesson is that a competitive advantage is likely to be sustainable for an appreciable time if the IT application was designed to leverage a unique competitive capability or strength of the company that owns the application, as this makes the impact of the application more difficult to replicate (Clemons, 1991). For example, IT applications using new handheld computer technologies that were implemented by Frito-Lay, Inc., in the 1980s were able to leverage a preexisting competitive capability of the company: a superior sales and distribution workforce. The handheld computers enabled the direct sales force to be even more effective in pricing promotions for different types of retail outlets that sold its highly perishable food products. IT also eliminated a lot of evening paperwork for the salesperson.

A second pre-Internet lesson was that although sometimes an early-mover advantage is possible, "first movers"—that is, firms that implement an innovative IT application first—do not necessarily gain a sustainable competitive advantage. Marc Andreessen, the cofounder of Netscape, who saw the company lose its first-mover advantage to Microsoft, has warned of the pitfalls of assuming that there will be a long-term first-mover advantage in an Internet era:

> *Most first movers end up lying facedown in the sand, with other people coming along and learning from their mistakes. . . . Being the first mover with the right approach is very important. Being the first mover with the wrong approach means you're dead.*
>
> —MARK ANDREESSEN (as quoted in Anders, 2001)

For example, American Airlines was *not* the first airline to develop an online reservation system for travel agents to connect to but instead was a fast follower with its SABRE rservation system. Initially, the SABRE system saved the travel agent the time and cost of calling an AA salesperson. When the airline industry was deregulated in 1978, the system was expanded to service reservations for all major airline carriers, who paid a transaction fee for each ticket sold. Its parent firm (the AMR Corporation) continued to invest in its online reservation system and expanded its offerings to include other travel industry businesses that relied on travel agents for some of their sales (such as hotels and rental cars). It became the market leader in airline ticket sales and gained control over a primary sales channel for the travel industry; by the end of the 1990s it was one of the largest privately owned computer systems in the world. The SABRE group was also one of the first in the travel industry to form strategic alliances with businesses in other industries, such as an alliance in which Citibank credit card purchases earned frequent flyer credits with American Airlines. These investments were able to provide a sustainable competitive advantage for AMR for almost three decades.

In the e-world of the second half of the 1990s, the SABRE group initially leveraged its earlier online reservation system and alliances with travel businesses to launch a B2C Web site (Travelocity.com) that bypassed its traditional intermediary: the travel agent. However, within a few years it had lost its differentiation advantages and was competing with other online intermediaries primarily on price: as predicted by Porter, the Internet lowered the entry barriers, and the new competition led to lower switching costs for the customer and price visibility that before had only been visible to the travel agent.

E-BUSINESS MODELS

Porter's 5-forces model establishes a starting point for thinking about competitive moves within an industry. Before looking at new business models for e-commerce from the perspective of an individual company, let us first discuss the potential benefits for two dominant types of e-commerce applications: B2C and B2B.

B2C Applications

The growth of business-to-consumer (B2C) e-commerce worldwide depends on the number of consumers that have Internet access. Between 2000 and 2002 the number of U.S. consumers who bought a product online increased 78 percent, the number who made a travel reservation online increased 90 percent, and the number who did banking online increased by 164 percent (Pew, 2002). The demographics of Web users within the United States have also become more mainstream (Greenspan, 2004): The number of men and women is approximately equal and the largest age group of Americans (ages 30 to 49) is also the largest user group (47 percent of total users).

The 1999 Christmas holiday season is usually pointed to as a major event in the e-commerce evolution: Online shopping approached 1 percent of holiday retail sales within the United States for the first time. By 2003 the percentage of online sales had approached 5 percent. In addition, Web sites are beneficial to users not only for online purchasing, but also for other types of prepurchase and postpurchase support. For example, based on one survey of Web users during the 2000 holiday period, 24 percent actually bought gifts online, but another 32 percent used the sites for price comparisons and the remaining 45 percent used the Web to look for gift ideas online (Schwartz, 2001).

The potential seller benefits from B2C applications will, of course, depend on the market in which the seller competes and whether companies in the industry traditionally have sold directly to consumers. However, as summarized in Figure 7.4, the potential benefits include lower sales channel costs, an extended customer reach, an around-the-clock sales and service capability, as well as new ways to do market research. If a product or service can be digitized, it might also be possible to complete not only an online sale, but also an immediate online distribution of the product or service to the customer.

B2B Applications

Although the early B2B applications were proprietary EDI systems using private networks that were not economically feasible for many smaller businesses, by the early 1990s there was a large installed base of these systems. Because these proprietary systems were also highly reliable and efficient, it has taken several years for businesses to be willing to invest in Internet technologies to either complement or replace these early proprietary systems. Similar to the benefits achievable with EDI applications, B2B applications via the Internet can increase the speed and decrease the transaction costs for transactions with business suppliers and business customers.

In addition, however, B2B applications via the Internet can be used to achieve other benefits: (1) linkages with new suppliers and new business customers, including the creation of new marketplace exchanges for buyers and sellers that have no geographic boundaries, and (2) improved relationships with suppliers and customers. Stated differently, B2B e-commerce enables firms to optimize a "web" of transactions and relationships between buyers and sellers (Applegate et al., 1996). Many of these applications use extranets and are a type of supply-chain system (as described in Chapter 5). Although the predictions for the growth of this type of B2B e-commerce were too optimistic at the end of the 1990s, the expectation is that both the United States and Europe will make major B2B technology investments during the first decade of the new millennium (CyberAtlas, 2002).

Just as new dot-com companies emerged for B2C or C2C e-commerce, dot-com companies for B2B e-commerce began to emerge in the mid-1990s. Many of these dot-com companies were a new kind of online intermediary: exchanges that created a marketplace in cyberspace for buyers and sellers. However, just as there was a dot-com meltdown for B2C sites beginning in March 2000, a large number of early dot-com B2B sites also closed down by the end of 2002.

Figure 7.5 provides one explanation for the lack of survival of the B2B dot-coms that were a new type of online intermediary: independent intermediaries will not survive if there are highly consolidated buyer markets or highly consolidated seller markets.

Stated differently, the survival of an independent intermediary depends on the fragmentation of both its buyers and sellers: It needs to compete in a marketplace in which there is a highly fragmented base of sellers as well as a highly fragmented base of buyers. As shown in Figure 7.5, if the number of buyers is small, the buyers will have a lot of "buyer power" and will not likely want to pay an independent intermediary for an online service that they could provide themselves. Similarly, if the number of sellers is small, the sellers will theoretically use their own supplier power rather than pay an intermediary for an online service that they could provide themselves.

Another alternative is for a group of buyers or sellers to band together, as a consortium or other type of alliance, to create their own intermediary. One example of this consortium approach is Covisint (pronounced coh-viz-int), which

Seller Benefits	Buyer Benefits
24/7 access to customer for sales and support	Sales and service anytime, anywhere
Lower costs from online channel	Easy access to product/service information
Multimedia opportunities for marketing	Easy access to product/service pricing
New ways to research potential markets	Agents to help find things, compare costs, and complete a sale
New ways to distribute (if product/service can be digitized)	Immediate delivery of digitized product/service
Global reach to buyers	Global access to sellers

Figure 7.4 Potential Benefits to Sellers and Buyers

- If Buyers and Sellers are Fragmented, **Independent Intermediaries** are likely to be successful.

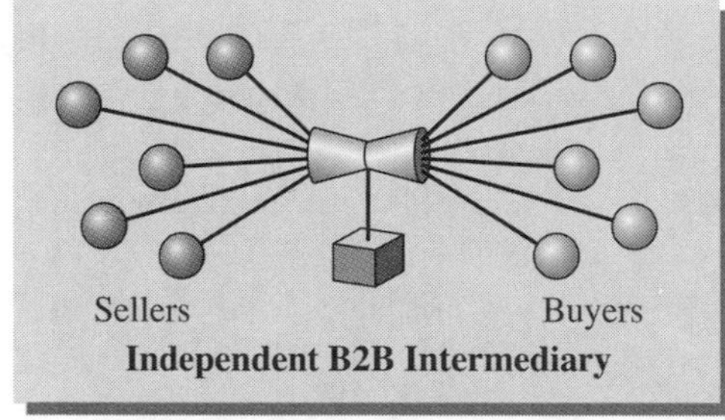

- If **Sellers** are Concentrated, Sellers are likely to dominate.

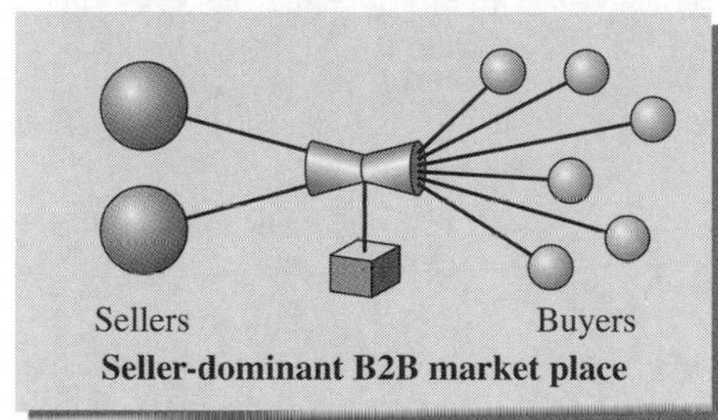

- If **Buyers** are Concentrated, Buyers are likely to dominate.

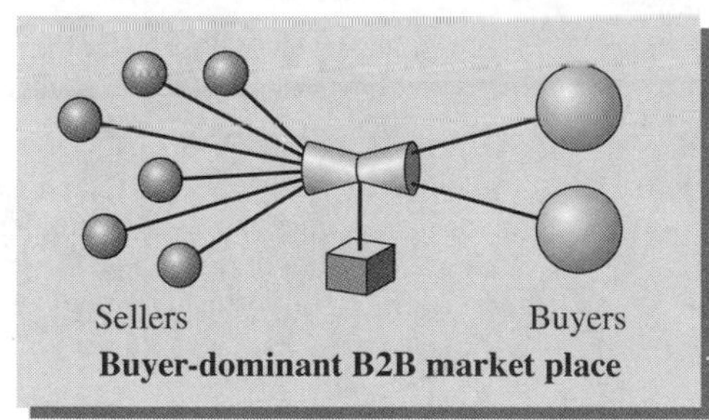

Figure 7.5 Opportunities for B2B Marketplaces

was an intermediary established by the Big 3 automobile manufacturers. However, like Covisint, such a consortium might also face operational and information-sharing constraints due to government regulations about competitor collaboration or resistance among the competing companies for other reasons.

Another explanation for the meltdown of independent online B2B intermediaries is that companies prefer to make their own procurement deals with other businesses rather than purchase through an intermediary. This appears to be true when the products being purchased are production materials that need to meet company-specific and product-specific requirements: The companies would rather have software to run their own exchange or just electronically communicate with their suppliers.

For the procurement of commodity MRO supplies (materials, repair, and operations), however, the usage of some sort of public or private B2B exchange might be more likely as companies seek to achieve cost savings. However, to capture the benefits of an exchange requires investing in new software as well as standardizing procedures (CyberAtlas, 2002). Ariba is an example of a software vendor that assists large business customers in creating their own private exchanges with potential suppliers; these B2B software vendors may also still host an online purchasing exchange for smaller businesses that cannot afford to set up their own private exchange.

Atomic Business Models

Both consultants and academic authors have focused on identifying sustainable models that individual firms can use to leverage the capabilities of the internet for B2C or B2B applications. For example, in their book *Place to Space*, Weill and Vitale (2001) identify eight "atomic" business models that can be used alone or in combinations. Summary descriptions of these eight models (based on Straub, 2004) are provided in Figure 7.6.

Business Model	Description	Customer *Relationship* Owner	Customer *Data* Owner	Customer *Transaction* Owner
1. Content provider	Provides content (e.g., information, digital products, services via intermediaries)	No	No	No
2. Direct-to-customer	Provides goods or services directly to customer, often surpassing traditional channel players	Yes	Yes	Yes
3. Full-service provider	Offers a full range of services in one domain (e.g., financial, health care) directly as well as via complementors attempting to own the primary customer relationship	Yes	Yes	Yes
4. Intermediary	Brings together buyers and sellers by concentrating information (e.g., search engines, auctions)	Yes	Yes	No
5. Shared infrastructure	Brings together multiple competitors to cooperate by sharing common IT infrastructure	No	Yes	Yes
6. Value net integrator	Coordinates value net (or value chain) activities by gathering, synthesizing, and distributing information	No	Yes	No
7. Virtual community	Facilitates and creates loyalty to an online community of people with a common interest, enabling interaction and service provision (Note: virtual communities facilitate cross-selling and up-selling)	Yes	Yes	No
8. Single point of contact	Provides a firm-wide, single point of contact, consolidating all services provided by a large, multibusiness organization (by customer events)	Yes	Yes	Yes

Figure 7.6 Eight Business Models and Their E-Business Assets (Based on Weill and Vitale 2001, Straub 2004).

Weill and Vitale argue that the value propositions for these eight business models differ according to the degree to which three e-business assets are captured *online*:

- *The Customer Transaction.* The ability to capture revenues from the online transaction (revenues from selling a product or providing a service or facilitating such a sale or service; for example, fees might be collected from a business seller for selectively highlighting a seller's products or from a buyer who uses the site to help select a seller).
- *The Customer Data.* The ability to capture online data that yield insights about the customer's purchasing needs (and to use that data to increase revenues via cross-selling to the customer or providing the information to other businesses).
- *The Customer Relationship.* The ability to influence a customer's behaviors (such as being able to provide to a customer an online purchase recommendation that the customer "trusts" because of an established relationship with the Web site).

As shown in Figure 7.6, for example, in a direct-to-customer e-business model, the owner of the Web site captures all three assets online: the transaction, the customer data, and the customer relationship. In an intermediary e-business model, however, the customer transaction takes place between the buyers and sellers that the intermediary brings together. The intermediary can, however, capture data about the customer's purchasing or information needs and also can establish a relationship with the customer as a trusted business intermediary.

Below we provide examples of dot-com and clicks-and-mortar companies that have been successful in developing several of these e-business models.

DIRECT-TO-CUSTOMER EXAMPLES

In a direct-to-customer model, the seller and buyer communicate directly. When a traditional manufacturing firm sets up an e-business site for direct communications with its customers, this often means that it is bypassing a distribution channel traditionally used in the past: Its customer can bypass this traditional sales and customer service channel and can communicate directly with the product's manufacturer. When a traditional direct retailer sets up an e-business site, this means that a customer now has an additional channel that can be used to gather information or communicate directly with the retailer. The customer can still go to a store or telephone a catalog retailer, but now the customer also has the option of using the retailing Web site.

In contrast, for a new dot-com business, customer communications are primarily (if not completely) via the Internet. In addition, the new dot-com business is faced with a significant logistics challenge: the development of efficient offline processes and information systems to complete the order fulfillment process. The inadequate order fulfillment capabilities of dot-coms in general became widely recognized after the publicized delivery failures for online holiday purchases in 1999. This major execution weakness by online retailers also contributed to the wake-up call among venture capitalists and the rapid closing of dot-com Web sites by the end of 2000.

Weill and Vitale also distinguish direct-to-customer models based on whether the products being sold are produced by the company that has the Web site or are products produced by a third party. Firms that sell third-party products online, rather than their own products, face the greatest hurdles at developing a successful online strategy. As can be seen from Porter's 5-forces model (Figure 7.3, p. 298), third-party retailers face the threat of lower barriers to entry for new competitors, as well as the threat of increased competition based on price.

Below we describe three examples of successful implementations of a direct-to-customer e-business model:

- Amazon (*www.amazon.com*), a dot-com pioneer in online retailing of third-party products that had its first profitable fiscal year in 2003
- Dell Corporation (*www.dell.com*), a traditional direct seller of made-to-order microcomputers, which has leveraged a sales channel via the Web to become a market leader
- Lands' End (*www.landsend.com*), a traditional catalog company that developed the capability to give online tools to customers that enable them to make orders for new custom clothing via its Web site

Amazon.com

One of the dot-coms most widely associated with the rise of the Internet is Amazon.com. Its founder, Jeff Bezos, has been recognized as a visionary in e-tailing and as committed to delivering its promises to customers. Amazon was able to use its early-mover position to quickly "brand" itself as a trusted dot-com retailer. This strong dot-com brand also helped Amazon to have the financial backing it needed before it could reach profitability, which did not occur until almost a decade after it was founded (fiscal year 2003).

Amazon.com was named after the Earth's biggest river. Launched as a totally online retailer in 1994, the site initially displayed the slogan "Earth's Biggest Bookstore." However, the company quickly expanded its online offerings to include other products found in physical bookstores, such as music CDs and videos. The Web site had more than 1 million customers after 2 years in operation, and by May 2000 it had 17 million customers.

Initially, Amazon.com was a new entrant that was a major threat only to traditional booksellers, including two bricks-and-mortar chains (Borders Books and Barnes & Noble) that in the mid-1990s were pursuing an aggressive offline growth strategy: the building of superstores. However, by mid-1999 (when venture capital in the United States was still plentiful), Amazon began to expand into other consumer products and created a multistore online mall, and thus became a competitor of Wal-Mart and Sears, Roebuck and Co.

Amazon.com's home page (see Figure 7.7) therefore includes tabs to its Web-based stores that sell a wide range of consumer goods, from electronics to kitchenware to outdoor furniture. Amazon has also expanded its business model to sell used books and has an auction capability (see Intermediary Models discussion below). The Amazon site also prominently displays logos of other retailers, including those essentially "hosted" by Amazon.com. For example, Amazon's year 2000 holiday revenues were significantly helped by its alliance with the traditional retailer Toys R Us. In contrast, in the year 2000 its major online bookseller competitor, Barnesandnoble.com (or bn.com), was pursuing an expansion into digital books for downloading and online course materials for students who registered with Barnes & Noble University. By 2004, Amazon.com listed on its Web site the names of two traditional department stores among its featured retailer partners: the discount retailer Target and the more upscale Marshall Field's.

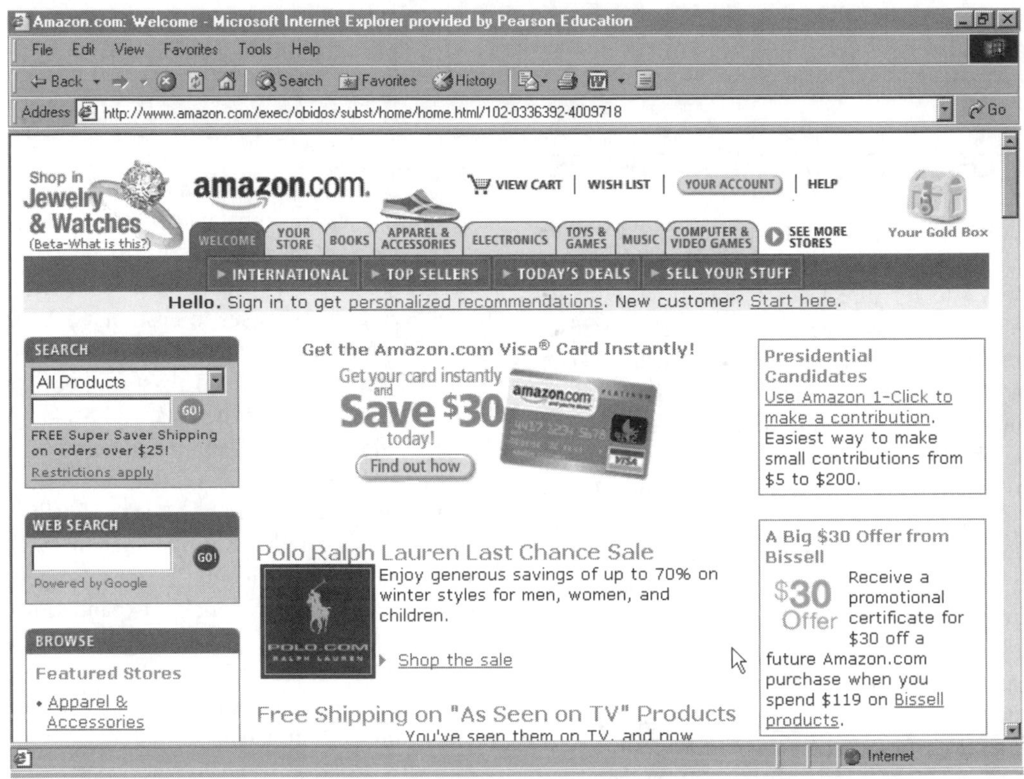

Figure 7.7 Amazon.com Home Page (© 2004 Amazon.com, Inc. All rights reserved.).

Amazon was able to develop these profitable clicks-and-mortar retailing alliances because of its widely recognized capability of providing a superior online shopping experience for its customers. It patented its "one-click" sales capability and also was the first to develop a tailoring capability that provides purchase recommendations based on a return customer's purchases and those by other online customers.

The excerpts from a 2000 review published in the *Wall Street Journal* by the personal computing critic Walter Mossberg in the sidebar "Online Shopping at Amazon.com" describes the customer experience on this site. Mossberg also refers to the virtual "community" that Amazon established by having customers share their candid opinions about purchases they had made (book reviews); in later years the Web site offered opportunities to chat with others with the same interests (a kind of book club) and to set up gift registries. In 2001, Amazon.com received the highest customer satisfaction score for any service company (online or offline) from the American customers who participated in the survey.

As in other dot-coms that sell tangible products, the development of efficient offline processes and information systems to complete the order fulfillment process became a major logistics challenge and a barrier to achieving profitability. Amazon.com's early success with delivery logistics as a dot-com book retailer has been attributed to its access to a major distribution infrastructure first built by another company. For example, when other dot-com companies failed to deliver on holiday sales at the end of 1999, Amazon was able to keep the trust of its customers by fulfilling 99 percent of its orders in time for the Christmas holiday. However, its expansion into

ONLINE SHOPPING AT AMAZON.COM

Amazon has won the loyalty of millions by building an online store that is friendly, easy to use, and inspires a sense of confidence and community among its customers. People trust Amazon, partly because it knows their tastes and does what it promises. Most purchases arrive on time and exactly as ordered. The company sends e-mails to tell when the order was processed and, later, when it was shipped. An order can be cancelled before it ships without going through the usual wrangling. If something goes wrong, Amazon usually forgives the shipping charge or upgrades the type of shipping.

The shopping experience is just terrific. The site is easy to navigate, even though it features 15 different departments. Searching is easy and excellent. The site intelligently personalizes the pages you see to highlight merchandise of a type you've bought before and to suggest similar items.

[Adapted from Mossberg, 2000b]

other products in 1999 also meant that the company had to execute a gigantic expansion of its warehouse and delivery systems, as well as its distribution facilities, to handle products for which it kept an inventory (including electronics).

The business rationale for this aggressive product expansion strategy was that the company had succeeded in becoming a brand name trusted by consumers for a safe online and reliable post-purchasing experience. To be successful at this strategy, however, it not only had to ensure that it still had a superior customer interface for sales and customer support but also had reliable back-office order fulfillment processes. By August 2003, Amazon.com clearly was the "department store" with the most online visitors: 43 percent of the online visits were to Amazon.com, with Wal-Mart and Target each having less than 10 percent (Hitwise, 2003). After considerable investments in its backend processes and systems, Amazon also reported its first profitable fiscal year at the end of 2003.

Dell.com

Companies in the computer hardware and software industries were early online direct-to-customer retailers because they were able to take advantage of the early penetration of Internet access in the homes of people who were likely to be more computer literate and therefore customers who would be likely to buy a computer based on catalog information and savvy about Internet security measures for online purchasing. Dell Corporation (formerly Dell Computer Corporation) was one of the first of the PC retailers to establish a customer-driven PC configuration capability that let customers customize their order (see Figure 7.8).

Dell initially developed software to support this "mass customization" strategy as a direct catalog retailer. The customer representative used the software to electronically capture a customer request, translate the order data into a design with these components, and then electronically "summon the right resources" to fulfill the order. Dell's "make-to-order" business model also meant that Dell didn't need to spend money to purchase, assemble, and store products that no one might buy. It also enabled a just-in-time supply chain to keep down inventory costs. Since Dell is also assembling computers with commodity components, whose prices tend to quickly fall, its make-to-order model also can yield additional cost savings by purchasing components as needed.

Launched in July 1996, Dell's Web site therefore leveraged the original software application used by customer service representatives to create a "self-service" application.

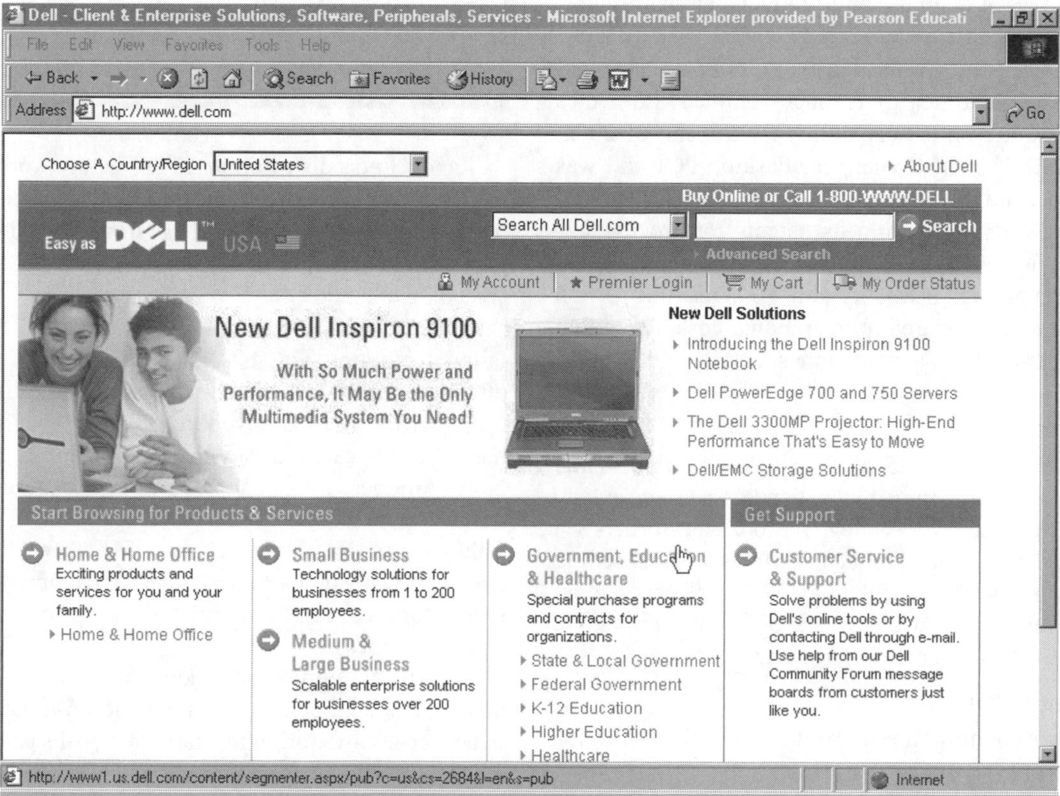

Figure 7.8 Dell.com Home Page (Used with permission of Dell Corporation.).

Businesses and individuals could bypass ordering by phone through Dell employees by ordering directly via Dell's Web site at their own convenience. Customers could also use the Web site to interactively experiment with different computer configurations using a "choiceboard" capability and could determine what the total price would be *before* finalizing their order: Without speaking to another human, a buyer chooses from menus of computer specifications, components, preloaded application software, customer support options, and delivery options, and the computer is delivered at the specified price to the requested location in a few days.

For its B2B online sales, Dell developed Premier Pages that are tailored to the needs of its business customers. For example, Dell assists procurement managers in selecting a small number of configurations to fit their infrastructure standards and employee needs, which can include the business' standard application software. These options are displayed for the business' employees on a secure Web page for this company only, and the employees can order one of the standard configurations at a prenegotiated price. By 2001, more than 50,000 business customers had Premier Pages customized for their employees (including universities that set up standard configurations for student purchases).

Dell's prior catalog model and build-to-order business model were well suited for rapid expansion to a clicks-and-mortar strategy. In contrast, build-to-channel manufacturers such as Compaq Computer and Hewlett-Packard (now merged into one company) had to evolve entirely new business processes in order to compete online with Dell's direct-to-customer online capability. By the end of 2002, Dell was No.1 in market share for desktop PCs and was also the No.1 Internet retailer (see the sidebar entitled "Dell's Way"). By leveraging its patents for process improvements, as well as its ERP and extranet systems, the company's operating costs were only 10 percent of its $35 billion revenues, compared to operational costs twice that percentage at Hewlett-Packard (Jones, 2003).

DELL'S WAY

Year	Event
1984	Michael Dell founds PC's Limited, the forerunner of Dell Computer
1988	Initial public offering of Dell stock: 3.5 million shares at $8.50 each (9 cents, adjusted for splits).
1993	Dell becomes one of the top five computer system makers worldwide. It starts selling its machines in Japan.
1996	Customers begin buying Dell computers over the Internet at *www.dell.com.*
1997	Dell opens a production and sales center in Xiamen, China. In 1999, Dell is ranked number six in China in PC shipments. By September 2002, it eclipses IBM as the top foreign PC seller. (Domestic PC maker Legend still outsells it 6 to 1.)
1999	Dell grabs the top spot in the U.S. PC market.
2000	Dell stock hits an all-time high of $58.13 a share in March.
2001	Dell overtakes Compaq in worldwide PC and U.S. server sales. It loses both leads when Compaq announces plans to merge with Hewlett-Packard.
2002	Dataquest reports that Dell has reclaimed the top spots in both worldwide PC and U.S. server sales from the merged HP-Compaq.

[Jones, 2003]

Landsend.com

Founded in 1963 as a retailer of, first, sailing equipment and then clothes and home furnishings, Lands' End traditionally marketed its products via catalog and took sales orders via telephone and mail orders. In the late 1990s it began selling its products online. Management viewed three characteristics of its traditional business as significant competitive advantages for online direct-to-customer retailing:

- a recognized brand name
- their own manufactured products (not third party products)
- a strong, in-place distribution infrastructure from its traditional offline catalog business

Lands' End's distribution infrastructure worked well for fulfilling sales orders of items in inventory, and the company realized additional profits from the lower order-processing costs from customers using its public Web site (Piccoli et al., 2003).

In October 2001, Lands' End also began to offer custom-tailored clothing via its Web site shown in Figure 7.9 after forming an alliance with Archetype Solutions, Inc. (ASI). ASI's founder (Robert Holloway) had previously had a 17-year career at clothing manufacturer Levi Strauss North America, which had been an early experimenter with online orders of customized clothing but relied on sales via a third-party distribution channel. Another ASI executive had been a consultant at McKinsey & Company and an engineer for a firm in the fabric industry prior to joining the startup business.

Lands' End purchased a noncontrolling interest in ASI and developed a contract that gave it a 6-month lead time in new custom tailoring technologies. ASI's patents included the algorithms that are used to translate a customer's measurements into a pattern for cutting fabric, which is electronically sent to manufacturers of the custom clothing orders. Software to track a customer's order across non-U.S. manufacturing sites and shippers was also put in place to monitor the handoffs between Lands' End, ASI, offshore manufacturing sites, and shippers.

Lands' End began with custom orders for chino pants (men's and women's) and added custom jeans and men's shirts by late 2002. By 2003, its Web site sales of custom chinos and jeans accounted for 40 percent of sales of those items, and repeat purchasers for custom clothing were reported to be high among those individuals making custom orders via the Web. One reason for this high customer satisfaction was that the company retained its usual return policy: even if the clothing was custom-ordered, customers could return it. They were also encouraged to "try again" by providing additional information to Lands' End to help improve the fit. In this way the company also got feedback that ASI could use to improve its software algorithms.

Successful Online Direct-to-Customer Models

These three successful direct-to-customer examples have some common, IT-related strengths. All three companies have developed B2C Web sites that use advanced technologies that support customized interactions with their customers. Amazon's Web site tailors its content to match the customer's expected preferences and Amazon customers can also personalize the Web site display for their own third-party product needs. As sellers of their own products, Dell and Lands' End take the customization a step further and provide online tools that enable a mass customization sales strategy: customers design their own products, which these companies then make to order.

In addition, all three of these companies have implemented back-office order fulfillment systems that enable them to fulfill the order quickly and reliably. As traditional catalog companies, Dell and Lands' End have continued to improve their preexisting capabilities to support their online sales. Dell has leveraged its ERP system to provide extranet links with suppliers, including providers of computer display devices that coordinate their direct shipping to the customer with Dell's shipping of the computer's custom components. Lands' End was able to create a partnership with a new firm founded by a former president of a competitor (Levi Strauss). As a new dot-com, Amazon had to develop a back-office order fulfillment capability; although it initially jump-started this new capability with an alliance, Amazon continued to invest heavily in technology and process improvements for its warehouses in order to compete with discount department stores such as Wal-Mart and Sears.

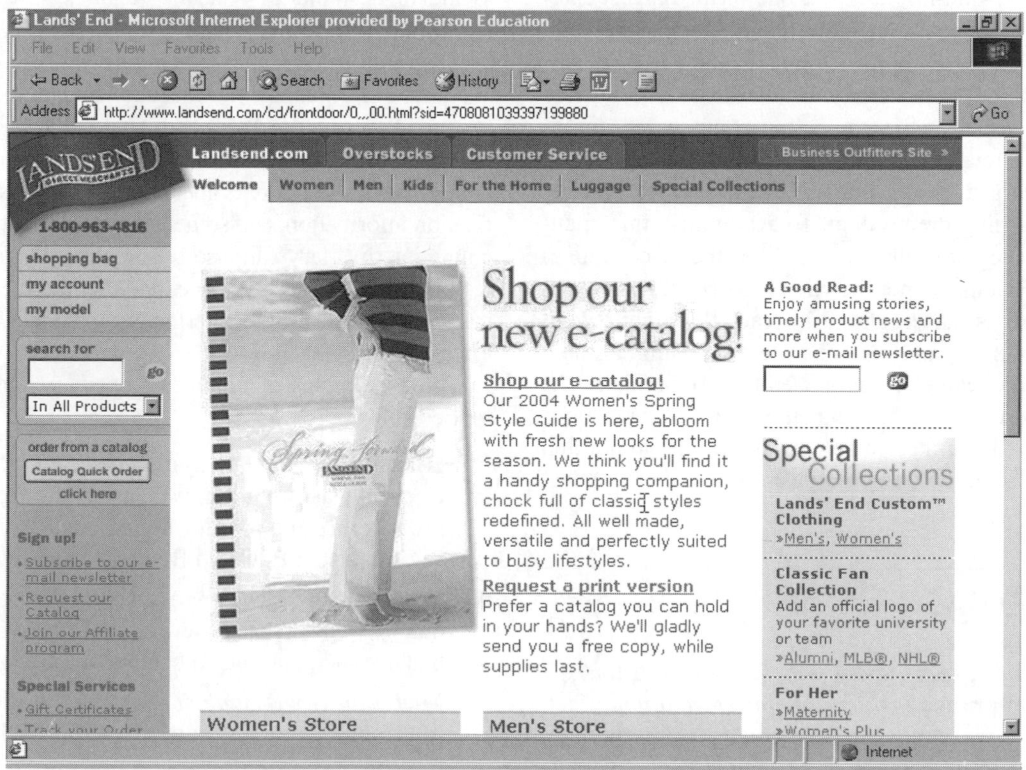

Figure 7.9 Landsend.com Home Page (© 2004 Lands' End, Inc. Used with permission.).

Online Activity (2002)	No. U.S. Internet Users
Buy a product	73 million (62%)
Buy or make a reservation for travel	59 million (50%)
Bank online	37 million (32%)
Participate in an online auction	22 million (20%)
Buy or sell stocks	14 million (12%)

Source: Pew Internet & American Life Project Surveys, 2002

Figure 7.10 Common Online Activities by U.S. Consumers

According to a 2002 survey, the most common online activities of U.S. consumers that result in a business transaction include buying a product, making travel reservations, banking online, participating in an online auction, and buying or selling stocks (see Figure 7.10). According to a recent Ernst and Young study (Straub, 2004), individual products that sell best via the Internet are likely to be (1) specialty items or unusual, (2) information-intensive, (3) nonperishable, and (4) of small enough size and weight to have relatively low shipping costs. Among the best-selling services are those that are information-intensive, such as financial brokerages and travel reservation businesses.

For the clicks-and-mortar firm, one of the biggest challenges is how to *integrate* its online and offline channels and provide a single face to the customer and maintain efficiency. From the customer perspective, the challenge is to provide consistent services, whether the customer purchases a product online, at a retail store, or via an offline catalog service and then uses a different channel for customer service, including returning the product. To accomplish this, managers need to integrate both place (offline) and space (online) business operations; sometimes this is difficult because of incentive systems that might be in place that only reward employees for sales and customer service using a single channel (in-store, call centers, or Web-based). Similarly, the IT groups that support offline and online business operations also need to be integrated in some way in order to develop applications that support a single-face-to-the-customer goal.

INTERMEDIARY EXAMPLES

In the mid-1990s, there was a widespread belief that the Internet would primarily have a *disintermediation* effect; That is, direct-to-customer strategies could circumvent traditional intermediaries. However, the reality is that both online intermediary dot-com businesses have emerged *and* traditional intermediaries have evolved to be successful clicks-and-mortar intermediaries. In addition, as the size of the Internet has increased, a number of "hubs" have emerged that are used as gateways to other sites (Barabasi, 2002).

Weill and Vitale (2001) identify six different subtypes of intermediaries; their salient characteristics are summarized in Figure 7.11. In contrast to the direct-to-customer business model, businesses that pursue the intermediary model typically own the Customer Relationship and Customer Data, but not usually the Transaction Data. Intermediaries in general are successful when they develop a value proposition that increases their linkages to both buyers and sellers. For example, a successful auction intermediary where sales are made to the highest bidder typically requires sufficiently large numbers of buyers and sellers.

The value proposition for an intermediary also is based on the degree to which the intermediary can provide "complete" service. According to Weill and Vitale (2001), for example, the intermediary can lower costs for potential buyers by providing relevant searching capabilities, product/ service specification information, and sometimes fulfillment services. An online intermediary can also create a marketplace in which the buyer determines the price, and the intermediary locates the seller—such as the intermediary model developed by Priceline.com.

Three examples of online intermediary models are described below:

- eBay, Inc. (*www.ebay.com*), a dot-com pioneer in electronic auctions that was one of the first to achieve profitability and is today not only a C2C intermediary, but also a B2C and B2B intermediary
- Yahoo! (*www.yahoo.com*), an early dot-com intermediary that has recently leveraged IT innovations and business acquisitions to become a leading portal
- Manheim (*www.manheim.com*), a traditional B2B intermediary for the sale of used cars that has leveraged the Internet to reduce purchasing and sales costs for its sellers and buyers and to provide remote, real-time bidding during physical auctions.

Intermediary Type	Intermediary Role	Revenue Source(s)
Electronic Auction	Links *high-bid buyer* & seller: sellers list items (specs), buyers bid	Listing fees, % of sale, additional services
Reverse Auctions	Links *low-bid seller* & buyer: buyers list needs (specs), sellers bid	Listing fees, % of sale, additional services
Electronic Markets (Exchanges)	Links (or matches) buyer & seller: sellers list items (specs)—sometimes fixed price, buyers purchase items	Listing fees, % of sale, additional services
Aggregators	Creates market: collects & analyzes comparative information for buyer or seller	Preference listing fees, % of sale, additional services
Electronic Malls	Creates marketspace: creates virtual site for sellers that want to leverage brand proximity	"Rents" from sellers, memberships from buyers, advertising fees, % of sale, additional services
Portals	Information hub: aggregated information, categorized and searchable	Preference listing fees, advertising fees, additional services

Figure 7.11 Key Characteristics of Six Subtypes of Intermediaries (Based on Weill and Vitale, 2001).

eBay

eBay.com, an early dot-com auction, brings together individual buyers and sellers from all over the world who might not otherwise find each other. Launched in 1995, eBay.com captured about 80 percent of the online auction market by the year 2000, with more than $5 billion in merchandise sales from 250 million auctions and global participants. Although profitable from the beginning, its net income is still somewhat modest due to its relatively low charges for its services.

The online auction model, shown in Figure 7.12, is based on revenues captured as a percentage of the auction sale, as a listing fee, and for additional services to facilitate the transaction. Initially, the eBay business model was a consumer-to-consumer (C2C) application; that is, the typical user assumed that he or she was part of a "community" of individual buyers and sellers. However, many eBay sellers today are small businesses: liquidators, wholesalers, small retail shops, or at-home entrepreneurs (Guernsey, 2000). eBay today is therefore also a B2C and B2B intermediary, and to foster relationships with the small business in particular, the company provides extensive online advice and periodically holds workshops in various regions.

eBay has also grown its service capabilities via acquisitions. For example, it created a fixed-price trading capability for direct sales of previously owned goods when it purchased the dot-com start-up Half.com. For auction sales there is also a "Buy It Now" capability in which the buyer agrees to pay a price specified by the seller before the auction period is scheduled to be over. In 2003 it also purchased PayPal, which provided eBay with its own third-party payment capability: an account established by the user that does not depend on having a personal credit card. Since PayPal also provides payment services to other Web sites, it has become an additional revenue source for eBay. eBay also collects fees from sellers for "extras" such as additional digital photos with a listing, the highlighting of a listing, and setting a "reserved price" (such as a minimum price or a "Buy It Now" capability).

As an intermediary that hosts millions of auction sales simultaneously, in real time, eBay's IT operations are of critical importance. In addition to capacity planning for its servers, the company has also had to quickly recover from denial-of-service attacks and other security breaches in recent years. Its primary value to sellers and buyers is low search costs, so the design and execution of its site search capabilities must also be of the highest quality. It owns the relationship with its buyers and sellers and the data on the items being sold, but the transaction itself takes place between the buyer and seller.

Like other online intermediaries dealing with the public at large, eBay also faces considerable sales transaction risks, such as buyers with inadequate funds, sellers who misrepresent their goods, or sellers who do not deliver their goods. Since maintaining the trust of buyers and

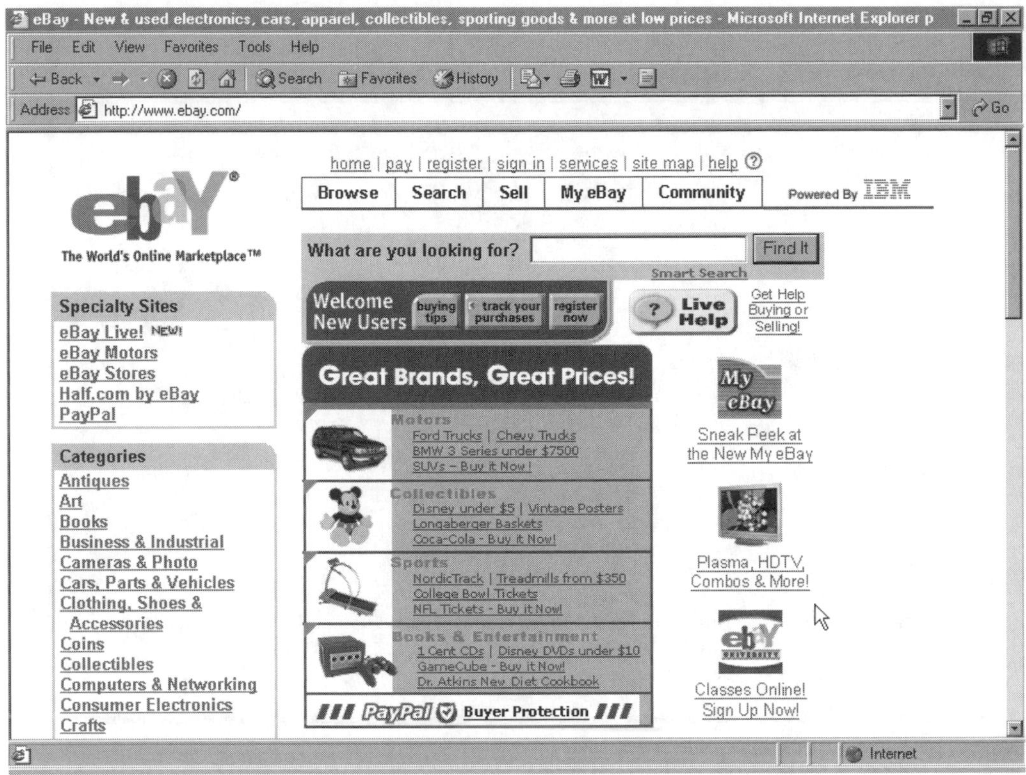

Figure 7.12 eBay.com Home Page (These materials have been reproduced with the permission of eBay, Inc. Copyright © eBay, Inc. All rights reserved.).

sellers is a key to its survival, one of eBay's early tactics for self-policing was to encourage buyers to rate their sellers, and vice versa. Nevertheless, for legal reasons, eBay also states that it is only a venue: "We are not involved in the actual transaction . . . we have no control over the quality, safety or legality of the items advertised" (Weber, 2000). The company also offers insurance coverage for items of certain types and value, plus it facilitates a process to resolve disputes between buyers and sellers.

eBay also has to continually monitor its sites for the sale of inappropriate items or even illegal items. For example, eBay has had to delete listings for items related to recent tragic events in the United States—including the 9/11 terrorist attacks on the World Trade Center and Pentagon and the explosion of the NASA space shuttle Columbia (see the sidebar entitled "eBay Items Yanked").

eBay ITEMS YANKED

eBay deleted several items billed as debris from the space shuttle *Columbia* from the online auction site Saturday, warning that anyone attempting to sell fragments from the doomed shuttle could be prosecuted. It's unclear what kind of debris was listed, but eBay spokesman Kevin Pursglove said that many of the items were pranks. The listings were immediately yanked from the site, and executives may report the sellers to federal authorities. The San Jose–based company has become a barometer of pop culture and current events. But eBay must also deal with morbid postings and attempts to capitalize on human tragedy, and it frequently pulls items.

[The Associated Press, 2003]

Yahoo!

Yahoo! (see Figure 7.13) was launched in April 1994 by a pair of Ph.D. candidates at Stanford University who wanted a way to keep track of Web sites for their own personal interests. It quickly became well known as a site that provided useful links, in an organized way, to help Web users link to other sites. That is, its intermediary business model is to be a Web *portal* that Web users go to first. Some of the ways that portals become hubs for large numbers of users is to offer free services. For example, Yahoo! offers free e-mail and chat rooms and allows users to customize their own home page (MyYahoo!) with specific stock quotes, the relevant horoscope, and so on. By March 2001, Yahoo! had 125 million registered users worldwide.

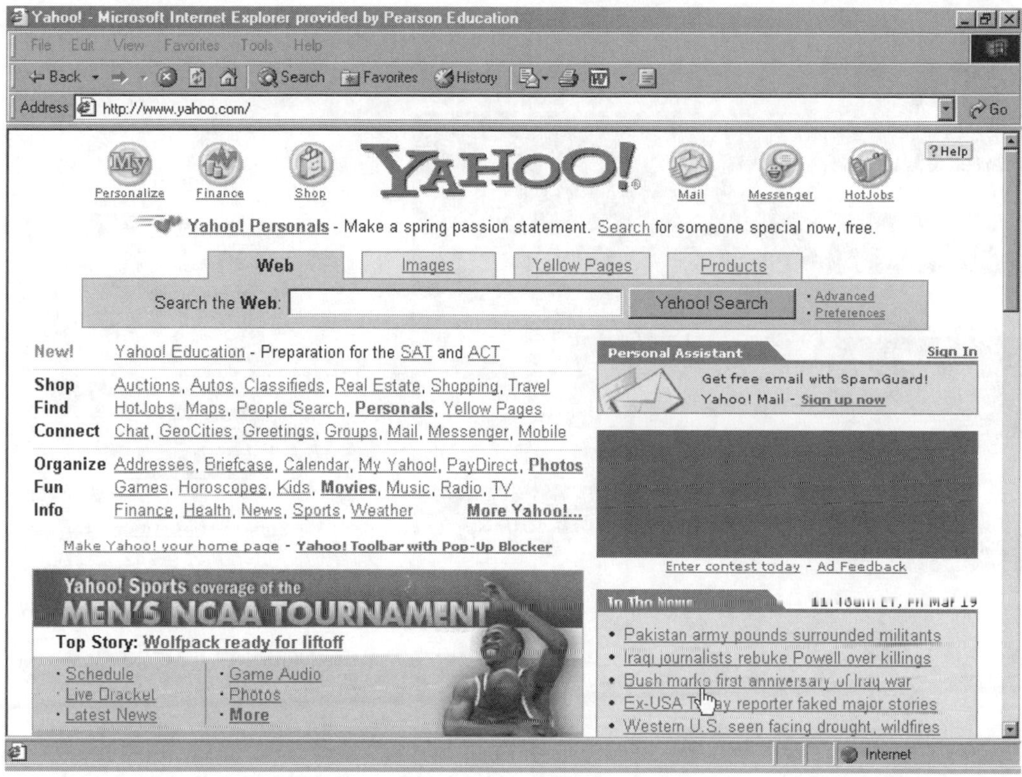

Figure 7.13 Yahoo.com Home Page (Reproduced with permission of Yahoo! Inc. Copyright © 2004 by Yahoo! Inc. YAHOO! and the YAHOO! logo are trademarks of Yahoo! Inc.).

As a portal, the site owns only the customer relationship. Its primary source of revenue has been fees for advertisements on its sites. Initially, these were direct marketing communications using "banner" ads that the user could click on to go to the advertised site. However, like other portals in the late 1990s, Yahoo! began to offer additional services to keep users on its site longer—what came to be referred to as a "walled garden" approach, a term coined by the CEO of one of its competitors (Weill and Vitale, 2001). Yahoo! has also expanded its model to include revenues from sales—including online "shops" (like a shopping mall) and its own auctions site. It also has attempted to be a hub for B2B marketplaces.

Under a new CEO beginning in May 2001, Yahoo! has continued to be one of the most popular Internet hubs as it has changed its business model. In late 2001 it acquired HotJobs.com, a major player in the online job-search market. In mid-2002 it launched a cobranding alliance with SBC Communications, Inc., in order to capitalize on the opportunity to become a new portal for DSL home adopters within the United States, and within the next 12 months it acquired a search technology firm (Inktomi) and an Internet advertising leader (Overture Services) in order to compete with a growing search and advertising competitor (Google). After these acquisitions, its revenue sources included banner ads, paid searches (placing Web site links next to the results of an online search), subscriptions for services (including personal ads), and fees from its SBC broadband partnership. In late 2003 it was the third most frequented site by U.S. users at home or at work (after Microsoft and Time Warner, Inc.) and its instant messenger service was one of the top five Internet applications used (Nielsen/Net Ratings, November 2003; December 2003).

Manheim

Manheim (Figure 7.14) is a used car "remarketer" that in 2003 had 32,000 employees and 116 physical auction sites worldwide, generating more than $2.4 billion in annual revenues. The company provides a marketplace where consignors that own the cars—including rental car companies, car fleet managers in corporations, leasing companies, banks, manufacturers, and licensed auto dealers—can sell their used car inventories to wholesale car retailers.

The typical auction facility has 10 to 15 physical lanes, with cars streaming down the lanes, an auctioneer who

Figure 7.14 Manheim.com Home Page (Used with permission of Manheim.).

settles the bidding, a full-service reconditioning operation, precertification service, and post-sale arbitration of the vehicles. Manheim also services the transfer of car ownership to the buyer, including transport of the used car to the buyer's lot.

In early 2000, Manheim launched a new business unit (Manheim Online) to develop a B2B Web portal for a new online business as well as to provide online support for the physical auctions. For example, vehicles at a physical auction site can be inspected and registered, a sales price is set in consultation with the seller, and a full description (with digital photos) is loaded on the Web site. If a licensed used car dealer agrees to buy the car for the preset price, based on the online description, then there might be appreciable savings in depreciation and holding costs for the seller. The Web site also has a search capability that enables dealers to find used vehicles that meet their requirements. In 2002, Manheim launched Manheim Simulcast, enabling buyers to remotely view and purchase vehicles as they are being offered in the lanes at the physical auction sites.

Most U.S. states have laws that restrict car manufacturers from competing with car sales dealers, so the potential "supplier" threat of car manufacturers reaching directly to customers and bypassing car dealerships is still quite low. In the early days of the Internet, the conventional wisdom was that online car purchasing would be unlikely because consumers would want to test-drive a vehicle. However, online intermediaries that link consumers with used car consignors, either bypassing used car dealers or collecting fees from used car dealers for customer leads, have become a major threat. For example, a dot-com pioneer was Autobytel.com, which refers customers to dealers in the customer's geographical area that have cars with the characteristics that the customer is looking for and then collects fees from dealers (which by the year 2000 numbered more than 5,000 dealers). Other sites that facilitate online purchasing of used (and new) cars, which are owned by groups of dealers, have also emerged (e.g., AutoNation).

Successful Online Intermediary Models

Like the direct-to-customer examples we reviewed earlier, online intermediaries have achieved their current success by continuously innovating with IT. eBay overcame some early server reliability problems and has maintained an outstanding record for systems availability and reliability. Yahoo! grew new technology capabilities via aggressive acquisitions following the dot-com meltdown. Manheim attracted the new IT skillset that it needed by setting up a new business unit (subsidiary) and by using its central-site auction facilities to capture feedback from the used car dealers.

In addition, these three intermediaries have all continued to evolve their business models to not only increase revenues but also to provide value to their buyers and sellers. eBay has expanded into certification services in order to provide auction services for products that yield higher service fees (such as used cars). eBay has also considerably changed its original buyer/seller mix to include many small businesses selling their products online, as well as large companies, including Dell, that sell their inventory remainders. Under a new CEO, Yahoo! evolved its business model to capture new sources of revenue and to compete with a new competitor with a leading search engine technology (Google).

The sustainability of Manheim's B2B clicks-and-mortar model will depend on the continued fragmentation of its buyers and its sellers, as well as its ability to continue to provide unique value-added services to its used car dealers. Although Manheim has evolved its online Web site to facilitate purchases that bypass its own physical auction sites, other online intermediaries, including eBay, have become Manheim's competitors in the development of a capability to bring online buyers who do not need to see a car to sellers who own the car. Since in other intermediary ventures, the online buyers also include consumers, the demand for a B2B intermediary (traditional or online) for the used car industry could also significantly decline in the future.

SPECIAL ISSUE: WHAT MAKES A GOOD WEB SITE?

For e-commerce applications that use a Web site, the company's Web site *is* the company. This means that the design and operation of the Web site is of critical importance for dot-com as well as clicks-and-mortar firms.

A useful framework for thinking about Web site designs from a human-computer interface perspective is the 7Cs framework in Figure 7.15 developed by Rayport and Jaworski (2004). These 7Cs take into account both the functional and the aesthetic characteristics of a good Web site. Using Rayport and Jaworski's framework, we can analyze Web sites known for their superior customer experience and then compare them to the Web sites of other companies that are pursuing similar e-business models.

Other usability frameworks have also been widely disseminated. For example, Microsoft's Usability Guidelines (MUG), include five categories: content, ease-of-use, made-for-the-medium (including customer tailoring), promotion, and emotion (affective reactions to the site). Two acknowledged writers on human factors topics also have regularly published guidelines for Web site design on their Web sites: Walter Mossberg, a long-time columnist for the *Wall Street Journal*, and Jakob Nielsen, a human factors researcher.

Context	Site's layout and design—functionally vs. aesthetically dominant or both (integrated)
Content	Text, pictures, sound, and video that Web site contains, including offering dominant "store types"
Commerce	Site's capabilities to enable commercial transactions—functional tools and pricing
Community	Ways that the site utilizes user-to-user communication to enable feelings of membership and shared common interests
Connection	Extent to which the site is linked to other sites—links out and in
Customization	Site's ability to tailor itself to different users or to allow users to personalize the site
Communication	Ways that the site enables site-to-user, user-to-site, or two-way communications

Figure 7.15 7Cs Framework for Web Site Design (Based on Rayport and Jaworski, 2004).

M-Commerce Web Site Design Issues			
7Cs Framework		**Mobile Setting** to support consumer's limited attention	**Mobile Device Constraints** to complement the insufficient display of mobile devices
Context	*Focal Point*	Linking structure that connects pages seamlessly but efficiently	Section breakdown that organizes information in separate pages
	Interface Implementation	• Menu structured in a shallow rather than a deep hierarchy • Layered sequential process rather than field selection process	Summary and key words that give a whole picture of information separated over pages
Content	*Focal Point*	The adaptive supply of product information and promotional messages to a user's setting	Multimedia mix to utilize both visual and audio channels
	Interface Implementation	Proximate selection method that makes nearby located objects easier to choose (gas stations, bank accounts)	• Conversion of visual information to audio format • Use of non-speech sound
Community	*Focal Point*	Interactive communication by connecting the people with similar needs	To accelerate interactive information exchange despite inferior input/output devices
	Interface Implementation	Connection to shopping companions who share interests in common	SMS, and graphics describing products, transferred through a user's phone book
Customization	*Focal Point*	Tailoring enhanced by information on users' mobile setting	Filtering unnecessary information, so that a small screen contains only information that is highly useful
	Interface Implementation	Proximate selection method that emphasizes the objects of interest, by combining a user's mobile setting (location, time, and resource) with his or her personal interests	Personalized service based on known user profile (content and layout configuration without a need of log-in registration)
Communication	*Focal Point*	Broadcast messages relevant to a consumer's environment	Alternative methods for interactive communication that overcome text typing with awkward input devices
	Interface Implementation	Targeted advertising suitable at the point-of-purchase	Customer feedback in multiple-answer or multimedia formats
Connection	*Focal Point*	Pathways that present Web sites relevant to users' changing environment	To reduce the probability of feeling lost given pathways provided
	Interface Implementation	Adaptive map that shows the information about nearby stores	Icon that gives a link to the starting page with one click of the 'cancel' button
Commerce	*Focal Point*	Secure payment method demanding minimal cognitive attention	Condensed checkout process
	Interface Implementation	Insertion of authentication into mobile phones	One-click checkout process made available by storing a consumer's address, payment method, and preferred delivery options

Source: Lee and Benbasat, 2003

Figure 7.16 Designing an Interface for Mobile Devices

Given the increase in wireless networks and handheld devices that can access the Internet, today's developers must also consider what makes a good Web site display not only on desktop computer screens, but also on much smaller devices. Researchers warn that the applicability of design principles for an application intended for display on desktop computer screens should not be assumed to be the same as for an application to be displayed on a cellular phone.

More specifically, the developer needs to take into account not only the differences in hardware (e.g., screen size, keyboard, etc.), but also differences in typical usage. For example, the typical mobile user might use the device for only a short time, and in very different contexts (while traveling, shopping, walking down a street, etc.).

Lee and Benbasat (2003) have identified some of the design elements that address the consumer's limited attention as well as the deficient displays of today's typical handheld devices for each of the 7Cs shown earlier in Figure 7.15. For Commerce, for example, a secure payment method that demands minimal cognitive attention is needed, as well as a condensed checkout process suitable for a small display (see Figure 7.16).

Other key attributes of a good Web site are related to the characteristics of the operational environment—both the client side and the Web server side, as well as networks being accessed. Common technical problems that need to be anticipated include download delays and search problems, as well as security weaknesses (Straub, 2004).

For example, many users consider more than a few seconds to be an intolerable online delay for a screen to appear. User tolerance for download times will likely be a function of the users' goals, where they are working (at home versus the office), whether they are connected to a highspeed communications line or not, whether the download involves multimedia, and the user's expectations for the download time. The delay in download time can be at the server side, the client side, and/or be a function of the network infrastructure between the client and server.

Getting Closer to Customers

The first wave of using the Internet in the working-outward arena involved the use of Web sites to sell products and services and manage customer relations. Many types of products can now be purchased online, from books, CDs, and flowers to automobiles, legal services, and wine. The advantages of selling online are numerous and seem obvious. Figure 7.17 lists some of these advantages. Indeed, it is not difficult to find success stories, such as Dell, E*TRADE, and Cheap Tickets. However, the potential problems are also numerous and have become more obvious since the dot-com bust. Figure 7.18 lists some of the potential problems faced in creating a B2C system.

Use of the Internet has now become much more sophisticated. CRM systems are used to learn more about customers (and perhaps noncustomers). Whether you visit a firm's Web site, call it from your home, office, or cell phone, or buy something from it, the firm is keeping track and combining that information to create a profile of you. CRM systems for managing these profiles are the next wave of enterprise systems, following on the heels of ERP. ERP focused on internal data. CRM focuses on customer data.

Examples of CRM are scattered throughout this text. CRM systems are both a boon and a bane, depending on how intrusive you think they are. You may be pleased when companies e-mail you offers that you want to take advantage of, such as a reduced-fare flight to a city you want to visit on the weekend. Or, you may see them as invading your privacy. In response to privacy concerns,

Global accessibility: The Internet eliminates geographic boundaries.
Reduced order processing: Automated order processing improves efficiency.
Greater availability: The company is available online 24 hours a day, 7 days a week.
Closer customer relationships: With a direct link to customers, the company can quickly address concerns and customize responses.
Increased customer loyalty: With improved customer service and personalized attention comes greater customer loyalty.
New products and services: With direct links to customers, the company can provide information-based products and services.
Direct marketing: Manufacturers can bypass retailers and distributors, selling directly to customers.

Figure 7.17 Advantages of B2C E-Business

Technical: The information systems are not always reliable or may be poorly designed.

Logistics: Getting products to customers around the world in a timely manner brings physical barriers to the virtual business.

Personnel: Few people have expertise in dealing with the new environment, both in technical and business arenas.

Legal: Doing business across geographic boundaries means dealing with multiple legal systems.

Competitive response: The ease of creating a Web presence brings low barriers to entry for competitors.

Transparent prices: Customers can easily compare prices across Web sites, reducing profit margins.

Greater competition: The elimination of geographic boundaries means a firm must compete with competitors from around the world.

Figure 7.18 Potential B2C Problems

some countries have passed privacy-protection laws to require companies to inform customers of whether and under what circumstances customer information is shared with others.

On the other side of the coin, IT and the Internet have changed what customers value. They now expect service to be fast; the key term is *on-demand*. Online business enables firms to respond quickly by drastically reducing the time needed to respond to customer requests for company, product, and price information, to process an order, and to get products to customers.

Customers also now expect convenience. They want more than one-stop shopping; they want a single point of contact in the company. CRM allows the gathering and managing of customer information so that whoever interacts with the customer has all the relevant customer information at hand.

Customers further expect personalization of service. Online business allows direct, ongoing communication with customers; thus, preferences and buying patterns can be tracked and analyzed to provide individual service. By reducing the time to process orders, online business allows firms to customize products to individual customers. Thus, products from music CDs to PCs to bicycles to automobiles can be made to order online.

Online business forces companies to rethink their pricing of products and services. Customers now have access to a wide range of competitive prices and sellers for products, driving down profit margins and the price of products. Some observers have speculated that online business will drive profit margins to miniscule levels. Although some initial studies have confirmed the lower prices for goods purchased online, the highest volume sellers do not always have the lowest prices. Prices are offset by branding, awareness, and customer trust.

The Internet is not used only to sell to customers online. It is also used to provide services to customers. In fact, sometimes it can be difficult to know which is more valuable, the product or the service. For instance, what is more valuable, a piece of machinery or the ongoing monitoring of that machinery and receiving an alert before it malfunctions?

The current focus is on staying in closer contact with customers, understanding them better, and eventually, becoming customer driven by delivering personalized products and services. As Frances Cairncross notes, the shift taking place is from running a company to keeping customers happy. This shift is having a profound effect on company structure and offerings. On page 317 is an example of a Brazilian company that has taken the implications of the Internet to heart in its organization and offerings, moving from manufacturing, to services, to online services: Semco.

Semco is an unusual company, being employee-driven as it is. However, its forays into using the Internet to expand its business provide lessons for others. This text contains numerous examples of how companies have leveraged the Internet and the electronic tenders IT provides to get closer to customers, sell them complementary goods, or provide them with auxiliary services.

To demonstrate a completely different side of the working-outward arena, we turn to the other side of the coin, from being a seller to being a buyer.

Being an Online Customer

Companies large and small are transacting business via the Internet. Some use it as their main means of business, even after the dot-com crash. Here is an example of one entrepreneur—Terence Channon, CEO of TerenceNet—who is a heavy user of the Internet as both a buyer and seller of services. The story on page 318, comes from Gartner EXP.

CASE EXAMPLE

SEMCO, S. A.

In a *Harvard Business Review* article, Ricardo Semler describes his company's progress into the digital economy. In a recent book, *The Seven-Day Weekend*, he further explains his unusual company. Semco is a Brazilian manufacturer of heavy equipment, such as industrial grade mixers. Semco's transformation is just as unconventional as the company's history would predict. He notes that his company has grown to $160 million in revenue, but he has resisted defining what businesses Semco is in because that would limit his employees' thinking. He prefers for the employees to choose the work they want to do.

Since 1990, the number of employees at Semco has increased from 450 to 3,000. More importantly, it has moved significantly beyond being a manufacturer. First it expanded into services, which have higher profit margins, and more recently into the marketspace of online business services over the Internet.

In 1999, almost 75 percent of Semco's revenues came from services. The shift from manufacturing to services was actually quite natural, states Semler; the employees led the march by listening to what customers wanted, not by following directives from the top of the company. Semler believes that by giving his employees freedom, they simultaneously act in their own best interest and in the best interest of Semco and lead to change naturally. On the other hand, when management defines the limits of the business, change becomes forced and frustrating.

As an example of natural change, Semler notes that they made cooling towers for commercial buildings in the early 1990s. Over time, though, the owners of these high-rises complained to Semco salespeople about the hassles of maintaining these towers. Some of the salespeople proposed starting a service business to maintain these systems. They would charge the customers 20 percent of the savings they generated (thus letting the customers keep 80 percent), and they would give Semco 80 percent of that revenue and keep 20 percent as their pay in the form of commissions. The business proved successful, saving customers money, reducing their hassles, and moving Semco into the service business.

In fact, the property owners were so pleased that they asked Semco to manage other parts of their buildings: the air conditioning compressors, cleaning, security, general maintenance, and so on. As the business grew, Semco teamed up with Cushman & Wakefield, a major property manager, to launch 50-50 ventures in Brazil. The result is a $30-million property management business.

Semler expects 15 percent of revenues to come from Internet-based services, another major shift that is occurring naturally at Semco. Most of the online business initiatives to date have grown out of the firm's expansion into services. For example, in a joint venture with Johnson Controls, Semco manages retail facilities. In making their rounds and talking to store managers, Semco's employees noticed how much money retailers were losing from lost inventories. One employee asked for a 1-year paid sabbatical to study the possibilities of offering online business services to these retailers. His sabbatical was approved, and he later proposed a joint venture with the largest inventory tracking company, RGIS. Within 2 years, Semco had become the largest inventory manager in South America.

In addition, Semco's property management work showed the inefficiency of the construction industry, so it teamed up with Johnson Controls and Cushman & Wakefield to create an online exchange for the commercial construction industry. Now, all the parties in a project, from architects and engineers to banks and project managers, use this exchange to hold multiparty online real-time chats, issue proposals, send bids, share drawings and documents, and even hire people.

Semco has expanded into the e-world even further, teaming with a virtual trade show company to host virtual trade fairs associated with the exchange so that companies too small to exhibit their products in trade shows can exhibit them online. Semco and its partners held eight such shows the first year.

All of this change has occurred by following the employees. When they have a good idea, Semco management is likely to provide the funding to test it out. The company has had more winners than losers taking this self-organizing approach, and it has led Semco naturally into marketspace.

CASE EXAMPLE

A DAY IN THE LIFE OF AN E-LANCER

TerenceNet is an online consulting, development, and research firm that delivers solutions to small- and medium-sized businesses. A fair amount of its work is procured from Elance (www.elance.com), a Web site that puts freelancers in touch with firms seeking bids for projects. Elance charges a commission of 10 percent of the value of jobs set up through the service. The following is a typical day's journal for Channon's use of Elance.

8:15 a.m. My working day starts with e-mail and checking Elance. I signed up with Elance a few years ago to see what kinds of online work were being offered for freelancers. I think I was one of Elance's first customers. The site's first postings were mainly for online work—Web development and the like—just what my firm does. Recently, I have noticed engineers advertising for AutoCAD drawings, so the site seems to be broadening.

There are lots of freelance Web sites and online marketplaces, but I like Elance because it's where I got my first paid job. I won a job through another site—but never got paid. Elance is a very active site, with 30 to 40 new postings a day; others only have three to four.

This morning I bid on 10 projects.

11:05 a.m. I check Elance several times a day or when I get an e-mail notification that I have received a message, like right now. I've logged onto My-Elance—my own personal Elance Web page—that shows all the work I have bid on, which bids are open and which are closed, and all the projects where my bids have been declined or accepted. It also shows all the projects I have offered, the number of bids I have received, and so on.

A company is considering me for a job I bid on, so its new message to me is flagged. This company tells me it has set up a private message board on Elance for us to talk privately about the work.

At first, I used Elance to supplement my company's income. Now I can pretty much count on the site as a revenue source. It may not be steady revenue, but there are enough postings on it, and I win enough of my bids that I can rely on it for work.

I put considerable thought into the bids I make. Some people just cut-and-paste a generic statement of what they do. I don't do that; I respond to a request by setting out exactly what we can do and pointing to examples of similar work. I think this shows commitment and knowledge.

3:00 p.m. When you sign up on Elance, it's like joining a community. Everything is very open. I can see who is bidding on a job, read their experience, look at the work they have done (such as Web sites they have developed), and see how they have responded to a posting. I can also see who has won a bid.

There's a lot of trust involved on both sides because we don't have contracts. I have to trust that the client will pay me. The client has to trust I will do the work. Elance has a feedback board where I can see that I have a top rating from the companies I have worked for and from the people who have worked for me. Everyone can see these ratings.

I have found everyone to be very professional on Elance, cordial in fact. The bidders all feel as if we are in this together; we don't feel or act like competitors. Naturally, we promote ourselves and our work—but we do not talk down others. I've made some wonderful contacts on Elance. Some short jobs have turned into relationships. TerenceNet is now on retainer with one company because it liked our initial work.

Another company liked our development work and wanted more functionality on its Web site. We were busy at the time so I put a posting on Elance. I got 30 bids in 5 days. When I whittled them down to the bid with the best example of the kind of work I wanted, it was from a company in Bulgaria. This company did the work at a fair price and delivered on time, and I have since given it other work. I had to pay via Western Union, but Elance has a payment system where you can transfer funds between bank accounts.

7:30 p.m. One last check on Elance. Usually, there are not many new job postings in the evening, but I want to make sure I have responded to all my messages. There are 10 new postings tonight—one for designing a business card, two for company logos, one for 1 million Web site addresses, one for writing a press release, and one for programming in Dreamweaver. None of them interests me.

I put out a posting for some Palm work a few days ago and gave it a 5-day bid period. I'm surprised I have received nine bids so far. I did not know there were so many wireless developers out there.

There are not many job postings on the weekends, so I'm taking this weekend off to spend with my family.

A major point of the Semco and TerenceNet case examples is that both are very customer-centric. They keep themselves attuned to the market by continually asking what customers need. This customer-centricity is also changing the strategic use of IT in the working-across arena.

WORKING ACROSS: BUSINESS-TO-BUSINESS

Streamlining processes that cross company boundaries is the next big management challenge, notes Michael Hammer, a well-known consultant in the IT field. Companies have spent a lot of time and effort streamlining their internal processes, but their efficiencies generally stop at their corporate walls. The winners will be those that change their processes to mesh with others they deal with so that they have chains of activities performed by different organizations, notes Hammer. This is not a technical challenge, as most have viewed supply chain management (SCM), but a process and management challenge, he believes.

Working across businesses takes numerous forms. Here are three. One involves working with cosuppliers, a second is working with customers in a close mutually dependent relationship, and the third is building a virtual enterprise, in fact, one that might evolve into an e-marketplace.

Coordinating with Cosuppliers

Collaborating with noncompetitors is a type of working across. For example, two food manufacturers might have the same customers (supermarkets and other retailers) but not compete with each other. Hammer calls such companies "cosuppliers." Their form of working across is illustrated in the example below.

What has deterred cosuppliers from working together has been the lack of convenient ways to share information quickly and easily, notes Hammer. The Internet takes away that deterrent. In fact, companies can reduce costs through sharing anywhere they use similar resources, such as warehouse space in the same city or shipping between the same two cities.

Hammer recommends companies begin working with cosuppliers by first making their own processes efficient, then collaborating on new joint processes (which is new territory for many companies). Eliminate duplicate activities, focus on customer needs, and let the work be done by the company in the best position, he suggests.

Deciding what type of relationship two enterprises want with each other in many ways determines many factors regarding their relationship. Do they want a loose, close, or tight relationship?

Establishing Close and Tight Relationships

The action in strategic use of IT and the Internet has moved to the most difficult area, working *across* companies. This

CASE EXAMPLE

GENERAL MILLS AND LAND O' LAKES

The seven largest U.S. food manufacturers have about 40 percent of the supermarket shelf space for dry goods. That volume is high enough to support their own fleet of delivery trucks, notes Michael Hammer. However, they have only 15 percent of the refrigerated goods business, which is not enough volume to fill up their refrigerated trucks for one supermarket. Thus, they use one truck to deliver to several supermarkets, which is less efficient because of traffic delays.

To address this problem, General Mills (maker of Yoplait yogurt) teamed up with Land O' Lakes to combine their deliveries on General Mills trucks. The result is better use of the trucks and higher supermarket satisfaction (due to fewer late shipments). Land O' Lakes ships its butter to General Mills' warehouse, either for delivery on the same truck or for pick up by the customer. In fact, notes Hammer, the coordination has been so beneficial that the two are looking into integrating their order-taking and billing processes, again, because they have duplicate processes where they might be able to only have one. To fill their trucks even further, they are creating joint initiatives for customers to order more from both companies at the same time.

means having relationships with various players in one's business ecosystem—investment banks, advertising agencies, specialist providers, suppliers, distributors, retailers, even competitors. Such relationships often have accompanying linking information systems. As Marcus Blosch and Roger Woolfe point out in the Gartner EXP report *Linking Chains: Emerging Interbusiness Processes,* companies need to determine what level of system integration they want in each case: loose, close, or tight.

- In *loose integration,* one party provides another party with ad hoc access to its internal information. The information may or may not be confidential, and it is accessed when it is needed. An example might be a builder of small power units that lets suppliers and customers check specifications on its Web site, note Blosch and Woolfe. The business processes remain distinct. Such limited integration requires little risk or cost.
- In *close integration,* two parties exchange information in a formal manner. Some of that information is probably confidential, and although the two parties' processes are distinct, they do handle some tasks jointly. For instance, they jointly manage the sharing. An example is airlines sharing pricing data with each other so that they can provide more seamless service to customers using several airlines on one trip. This level of integration leads to greater benefits, so there is greater impetus to make the relationship succeed. However, risks do increase because confidentialities are shared. Costs of integration are also higher than in loose integration.
- In *tight integration,* two parties share at least one business process, as partners, in a business area that is important to them. Generally, high volumes of data are exchanged, the data can be highly confidential, and the data includes key events, such as price changes. An example could be a supplier and retailer sharing a common inventory process. The intent is to synchronize operations to reduce costs and speed response time. Tight integration is the most risky because it is business critical and the most costly to integrate. In some cases, it may be difficult to identify where one organizational boundary ends and the other begins because the two become so intermeshed.

The point to note, state Blosch and Woolfe, is that due to the high costs and risks, companies can only have a few tight relationships. Those would be where the benefits outweigh the costs and risks. That implies that tight relationships are the ones that encompass genuinely critical processes and where working tightly with another party adds significant value. Blosch and Woolfe thus see companies having a pyramid of interbusiness relationships, as shown in Figure 7.19: a few tight ones, some close ones, and many loose ones. The loose ones have basic conformance to integration requirements (such as a negotiated agreement and shared information). Tight ones have advanced conformance as well as significant detail and ongoing maintenance in their agreements.

To illustrate a close relationship that is becoming a tight one, consider the case of The Sara Lee Bakery Group, one of the first food manufacturers to use a specific information technology to establish close relationships with supermarket chains. Based on that experience, it has more recently moved to establish some tight relationships. The case comes from Blosch and Woolfe.

	Numbers of Relationships	Potential Benefit	Cost of Integration	Risk
Tight	Few	•••	•••	•••
Close	Some	••	••	••
Loose	Many	•	•	•

• Basic conformance •• Intermediate conformance with significant detail ••• Advanced conformance with significant detail and ongoing maintenance

Figure 7.19 The Integration Pyramid. *Source:* Marcus Blosch and Roger Woolfe, *Linking Chains: Emerging Interbusiness Processes,* Gartner EXP, August 2001.

CASE EXAMPLE

SARA LEE BAKERY GROUP

Sara Lee Bakery Group (SLBG), formerly Earthgrains, with headquarters in St. Louis, Missouri, is the second-largest bakery in North America. It specializes in fresh-baked branded goods and private-label refrigerated dough and toaster pastries. Worldwide, SLBG has 26,000 employees.

Fresh-baked goods are delivered to retailers by direct store delivery. Delivery people stand in line at the retailer's back door to have their deliveries counted. To reduce labor costs, retailers have reduced the number of hours their back door is open. SLBG requires more trucks to accommodate the reduced hours. The lines become longer and more time is wasted.

Dealing with the Backdoor Bottleneck

SLBG was one of the first food manufacturers to introduce scan-based trading (SBT), selling bread on consignment. On the first day of the new arrangement, SLBG buys back the bread on the retailer's shelf, which moves the inventory value to the bakery group's balance sheet.

At the end of each day, the store sends the scan data from its point-of-sale checkout system for all SLBG products sold that day to its retail headquarters, which then transmits the data to SLBG via EDI or the Internet. The retailer also uses that scan data to post sales to its accounts payable system, and SLBG posts to its accounts receivable system. The retailer pays SLBG electronically based on the scan data.

More recently, SLBG has established a shared database with 100 stores, hosted by a third party, viaLink. This database facilitates price and item synchronization. Once SLBG has created an electronic connection to viaLink, it can easily expand to other trading relationships because viaLink handles translations between trading partners' systems.

Benefits of SBT

SLBG now has 2,143 stores at seven retailers across the United States on SBT. The retailers like SBT because they no longer have money tied up in inventory and they pay for bread after it is sold. SLBG likes the arrangement because it receives the scan data, which it uses to improve its merchandizing. SBT also saves time. Delivery people no longer line up at the back door nor deliver only during the backdoor hours. They stock the shelves themselves.

SLBG uses the saved time to improve the quality of work for its delivery people (less stress in making deliveries), to reduce the number of delivery routes, and to reinvest the time in callbacks in the afternoon to restock the shelves to make the store look better for the before-dinner rush of shoppers.

The shared database eliminates "chasing deductions," which is a huge non-value-added activity in the industry.

Seven Prerequisites for SBT

Over the years, SLBG has learned seven prerequisites for creating SBT relationships.

The first is to deal with the major point of contention—shrinkage—right up front. Shrinkage is the amount of product "lost" at the retail store due to theft, misplacement, or other reasons. SLBG deals with shrinkage by agreeing to split the loss 50-50 up to a maximum amount; thus, accountability is shared with the retailer.

Second, SLBG requires the retailer to have an SBT executive sponsor—an executive from headquarters who makes SBT a priority for the retailer. Individual stores cannot initiate SBT on their own because they do not have the authority or the money to create the necessary systems or interfaces.

Third, SLBG requires the retailer to assign a point person. SBT projects touch many people on both sides. SLBG has a project manager as its point person for the retailer. It only wants to have to contact one person at the retailer as well.

Fourth, to plan the relationship, SLBG asks the retailer to create a cross-functional group—the executive sponsor along with people from purchasing (merchandising), finance, accounting, security, operations, and IS. IS is involved because converting existing systems costs a retailer between \$50,000 and \$100,000. One required change is the creation of a path between scan data and accounts payable, which is not a natural path. If the retailer has not been using EDI, SLBG provides a package for transmitting data securely over the Internet.

Fifth, SLBG asks the retailer to create an as-is process map of how its process currently works and a to-be process map of how it will work in the future. The two processes are vastly different. The data and money move on different paths, and in-store processes need to change. For example, the vice president of operations needs to allow SLBG staff in the retail store after noon.

(Case continued)

(Case continued)

Sixth, SLBG only works with retailers that have invested in achieving almost 100 percent accuracy in their point-of-sale system, because that system determines how much money SLBG is paid. A system that is only 95 percent accurate gives SLBG a 5-percent shrinkage from the outset, which SLBG will not accept.

Seventh, SLBG does not initiate SBT until prices have been synchronized with the retailer.

Managing SBT Relationships

SBT is managed by a 10-person team that is headed by a vice president. The group includes EDI coordinators who handle the technical aspects of receiving SBT data. Project managers integrate customer-driven projects, such as SBT. An analysis group monitors SBT data to ensure that each store is staying within its agreed shrink limits. The analysis group also sends out quarterly invoices to reconcile shrink differences.

Rolling out SBT to a retailer's stores requires lots of coordination. Store employees need to know, "Next Monday everything is going to change." The SBT team works with SLBG's account manager for the retailer to make sure store employees understand the new routine. Store receivers need to understand that SLBG will no longer be standing in line. Store management needs to know delivery people may be tending shelves in the afternoon. SLBG delivery people need to be much more careful about their record keeping—SLBG's income depends on those records.

SLBG's ordering process, in which counting items every day is an integral part, allowed it to move fairly easily to SBT. Manufacturers that do not count individual items, such as soft drink and snack food companies, have a more difficult time making the switch. This is one reason that SBT has not spread more quickly in the industry; it has not yet touched the 85 percent of the grocery items stocked from retailer warehouses.

Becoming a Customer-Centric Value Chain

A company's value chain consists of its upstream *supply chain* (i.e., working with its suppliers of raw materials and parts) and its downstream *demand chain* (i.e., working with its distributors and retailers to sell its products and services to end customers). Traditionally, most companies make-to-stock. They build vehicles or package mutual funds and then push them to customers. This is the supply-push world.

Today, we are seeing the rise of the reverse—a demand-pull world—where a customer's order triggers creation of the customized product or service the customer has defined. The chain of events is reversed from supply-push to demand-pull, from running a company to keeping customers happy. Dell is a prime example of this customer-centric, demand-pull business model. In fact, it has become the model that many companies admire and would like to emulate. The case on page 320 also illustrates the benefits of having a tightly integrated value chain.

Pros and Cons of Demand-Pull. Value chain transparency is a much-talked-about concept. It should, for instance, reduce the number of duplicate orders. During the late 1990s, for instance, when a component was in short supply, manufacturers sometimes duplicated an order for the component with several suppliers just to ensure a steady supply. An order for 10,000 memory chips might appear as 30,000, greatly exaggerating the true demand. In late 2000, when both the dot-com and telecommunications bubbles burst, large amounts of back orders disappeared just about overnight, partly because of this duplicate ordering phenomenon, catching manufacturers unaware. Transparency about orders might prevent such drastic downswings.

Creating private exchanges, such as Dell is doing, changes the level of cooperation among firms as well. Information passes through the chain in a burst and is available to all parties at the same time, rather than sequentially over time. The result, notes Cairncross, is that suppliers and even customers become collaborators in improving efficiency throughout the process. Working closely also introduces technological changes more rapidly. Suppliers would be hard-pressed to keep up without a close working relationship and electronic ties. In fact, some have implemented software that automatically notifies every relevant supplier when a change is made so that they are working from the latest specifications.

One con to demand-pull is the infrastructure. The manufacturer's infrastructure becomes its suppliers' infrastructure as well, binding them more tightly together. If the infrastructure is not robust, crashes can affect the entire ecosystem dependent on the exchange. Another drawback is that such close working requires trust, notes Cairncross. Divulging confidential information to suppliers, such as canceled orders, could hurt the company if it is passed to competitors or Wall Street (perhaps causing the stock price to fall). Furthermore, suppliers that provide parts to competing PC manufacturers must ensure that information from one does not leak to another. This containment of information within a company is often referred to as building "Chinese walls" between the groups that work for competing customers. However, no such containment can be absolute, notes Cairncross. Innovations that employees learn from one customer can naturally seep to another.

Becoming customer-centric is not easy, especially for supply-push companies. Their computer systems, processes, and people follow that model, essentially casting the organization in electronic concrete. That is why the promise of CRM is so alluring. It helps companies shift their attention from managing their operations to satisfying their customers.

Getting Back-End Systems in Shape

To have a hope of working across, internal back-end systems need to be in shape. Most, if not all, B2B systems must integrate with these existing back-end systems, which has proven particularly challenging. Back-end systems cover a wide range of applications, including accounting, finance, sales, marketing, manufacturing, planning, and logistics. Most of these systems have been around for years, operate on a variety of platforms, and were not designed to integrate with other systems. Modifying these systems entails many risks, particularly when the integration must cross organizations. Luckily, most organizations have a head start on interorganizational integration because they have been working for a number of years on internally integrating their systems.

Understanding the need for internal integration, many companies replaced, or are currently replacing, their old back-end systems with newer ones using database management systems (DBMS) and ERP systems. The benefits of DBMS and ERP systems have always stemmed from their ability to provide integration. Recognizing the importance of online business, DBMS and ERP vendors have modified their products to integrate with Internet-based applications. In doing so, the vendors provide platforms for building B2B systems.

Another approach to establishing B2B integration is to create an extranet, as Dell has done. An extranet is a private network that uses Internet protocols and the public telecommunication system to share part of a business' information or operations with suppliers, vendors, partners, customers, or other businesses in a secure manner. An extranet is created by extending the company's intranet to users outside the company. The same benefits that Internet technologies have brought to corporate intranets have accelerated business between businesses.

Whatever the approach, the goal is to extend the company's back-end systems to reengineer business processes external to the company. Example activities include sharing product catalogs, exchanging news with trading partners, collaborating with other companies on joint development efforts, jointly developing and using training programs, and sharing software applications between companies. Initially, the benefits come in the form of greater cost and time efficiencies. Ultimately, the systems will change the structure of industries.

SUMMARY

As this chapter is being written, we have less than one decade of experience with e-commerce applications that use the Web. The technologies have continued to evolve, although the fast rate of change in the second half of the 1990s has slowed down due to the economic slowdown in the United States in the first few years of the new millennium. The legal and regulatory environments of the United States in particular have also shaped the current e-commerce landscape, although there will be a much larger global influence in the coming decades.

Today we do have the advantage of competitive forces models at the industry level and online e-business models based on real-world examples with which to evaluate a given firm's e-business strategy and the potential opportunities and threats for a given industry. Both dot-com survivors and successful clicks-and-mortar companies pursuing direct-to-customer and intermediary e-business models provide examples of potentially viable approaches for the coming years. Less clear is the viability of B2B exchanges that are owned by an independent company or a consortium of companies. We also now have some useful frameworks for what makes a good Web site for desktop and laptop screens, although designs for m-commerce applications are still in an experimental stage.

Over the years, a few innovative companies have achieved strategic advantage using IT. These firms served as models of what could be done, but most companies did not have the resources or skills to follow their example. With the growth of the Internet and the development of online business, IT has become a strategic tool in every industry.

As their employees become dispersed, enterprises are looking for ways to bring cohesion. Intranets and portals are ways to use IT strategically inside the firm. In working outward, enterprises are creating electronic tenders to provide services that make their products more valuable and help them better know their customers and develop more personal relationships with them. This customer-centric view, now so prevalent in the business world, is affecting the strategic use of IT in working across. Value chains are looking to shift from supply-push to demand-pull. As IT continues to evolve, so do its strategic uses.

CHAPTER REVIEW QUESTIONS

1. Define the terms e-commerce, dot-com, clicks-and-mortar, B2C, and B2B
2. What major e-commerce benefit can be provided by extensible Markup Language (XML), but not by Hypertext Markup Language (HTML)?
3. What is meant by a first-mover advantage, and what are some of the reasons that being a first-mover might not actually be a competitive advantage?
4. Describe some U.S. laws that have influenced the nature of e-commerce via the Internet.
5. What are some of the primary benefits of e-commerce via B2C Web sites for buyers and sellers?
6. Choose one of the five competitive forces in Porter's model and describe the opportunities and threats for a specific industry of your choosing.
7. Describe two privacy issues of consumers that are due to e-commerce applications.
8. Describe some of the distinguishing features of a direct-to-customer e-business model.
9. What are some of the distinguishing features of an intermediary e-business model?
10. What do you see as some of the competitive strengths of Amazon.com? Dell.com? Landsend.com?
11. Describe one way that eBay has extended its auction model.
12. Compare the usage of the Internet in the United States with other countries.
13. Describe why expertise in Web page design is of critical importance to any online retailer.
14. What is one of the ways that the dot-com meltdowns in the early 2000s have influenced the recent growth of e-commerce?
15. What is m-commerce and why is it the next e-commerce frontier?

CHAPTER DISCUSSION QUESTIONS

1. Provide evidence to support the following statement: The growth of e-commerce is due to both business and technological innovations.
2. Provide an argument to either support or refute the following statement: In applications for trading partners, the customer holds the greatest power.
3. Briefly describe the potential of the Internet as a new customer service (support) channel.
4. Describe a customer experience that you had on a retailing Web site. Was it satisfactory or not? How could it have been improved, knowing what you know now?
5. Choose three firms within the same industry that have well-established Web sites. Based on these sites, compare and contrast the B2C e-commerce benefits that these companies appear to be achieving.
6. Use the 7Cs framework of Rayport and Jaworski to evaluate the Web sites of two competitors.
7. Describe some of the ways the Internet has or has not impacted the way you live in today's world (some examples might be reading news, making travel plans, buying items, etc.).

CASE STUDY: DELL

Dell, headquartered in Austin, Texas, sells PCs, servers, handhelds, and other equipment directly to customers, either individuals or organizations. It is the largest seller of PCs in the world mainly because of its prices, which are a direct result of its customer-centric business model.

When a customer custom configures a PC online on Dell's Web site, the order information is fed into Dell's production schedule and an e-mail is sent to the customer stating when the computer will be shipped.

However, Dell does not make its computers; its suppliers do. Some 30 of its 200 suppliers get close to 80 percent of Dell's business. That is very few suppliers, notes Cairncross; most PC manufacturers have thousands of suppliers. Dell created an extranet for its suppliers so that they can see order information and Dell's production schedule. In fact, they can grab this information and feed it into their own production systems.

In essence, says Cairncross, Dell's extranet is moving toward becoming a private marketplace, where orders arrive from customers and are distributed to suppliers. In fact, Dell is working toward making the information available to suppliers of its suppliers—two tiers down. Its goal, says Cairncross, is transparency, giving the entire industry a clearer view of supply and demand so that they can see what is selling, and perhaps what buyers are paying, all the while maintaining the privacy of suppliers.

Because suppliers can see through this demand chain and find out which of their components are being ordered and for what kinds of computers closer to real time, they can forecast better. The result is less inventory in the supply chain. Reduced inventory is *very* important in the PC business, notes Cairncross, because some 80 percent of the cost of a PC is in its components. Prices have dropped quickly in the industry; 1 percent every 2 weeks is not uncommon. So the longer they keep inventory, the more money they lose. The fewer days they need to keep inventory, the less money they tie up in it, and the less money they lose.

Dell has a reverse physical value chain from other PC manufacturers. They have supply-push; Dell has demand-pull. Dell also has a demand-pull financial value chain. In the supply-push model, the manufacturer borrows money from a bank to build-to-stock. It then repays the bank, with interest, after the stock has been sold. In Dell's demand-pull financial model, customers pay for their PC when they place their order. Thus, Dell gets paid before it builds the computers. Hence, it borrows less money and pays less interest, lowering its costs and its prices.

Case Study Discussion Questions

Question One

Research another company similar to Dell that has changed its business through a customer-centric business model and a demand-pull chain. How has this impacted its bottom line financially?

Question Two

If a demand-pull marketplace can be good for large businesses, think about the ramifications for small business owners. Discuss how this one area could not only increase the profitability of small business owners, but also encourage individuals to attempt a business of their own.

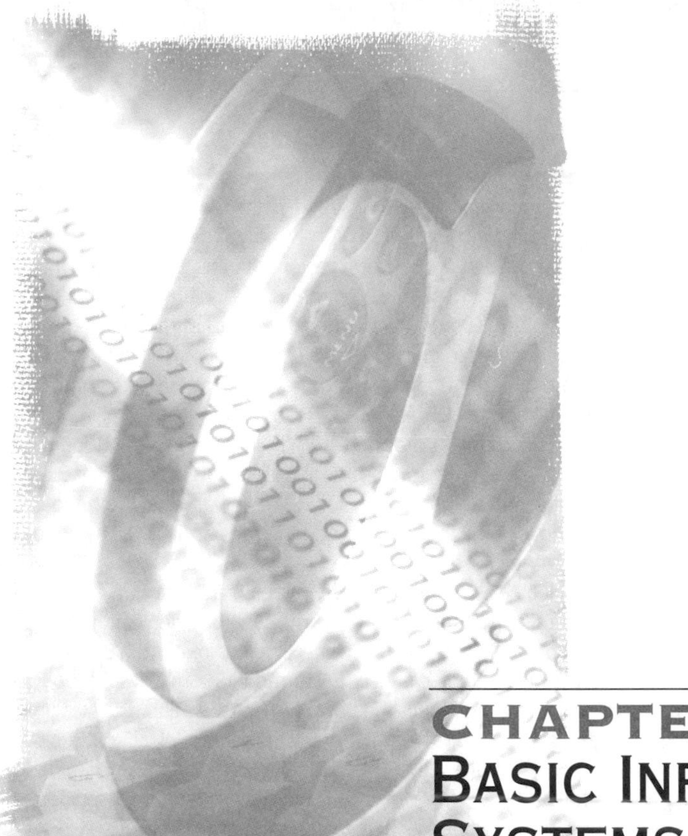

CHAPTER 8
BASIC INFORMATION SYSTEMS CONCEPTS

"It's the SYSTEM's fault!"
"The SYSTEM is down."
"My SYSTEM can't be beat!"
"Don't buck the SYSTEM."

PHRASES SUCH AS THESE REMIND US THAT THE TERM "SYSTEM" CAN BE used to refer to an information system with hardware, software, and telecommunications components or that the term "system" can be used to refer to something much broader than an information system. For example, a systems perspective helps us to understand the complex relationships between different business units and different types of events within an organization so that when we change one aspect of a business we can anticipate the impact on the entire business. The ability to manage organizations as systems with interrelated processes is crucial for success in today's fast-changing business environments.

Today's business managers are being asked to play major roles in systems project teams with internal information systems (IS) specialists and/or outside vendors and consultants, and one of their key roles will be to help provide a high-level systems perspective on the business. Business and information technology (IT) managers must work together to determine the best scope for a systems project to meet the business's needs, as well as the business's requirements for financial returns on its IT investments. With IS personnel, business managers will also help develop and review graphical diagrams of the ways in which the organization currently works, as well as new ways. This chapter will therefore familiarize you with some of the specific methods and techniques that software developers use to describe both current (As-Is) and future (To-Be) systems in the abstract.

Today there is also a heightened sensitivity to system security and reliability. At the end of this chapter we describe a variety of controls that are associated with best practices for system development and implementation in particular.

THE SYSTEMS VIEW

Peter Senge and other management gurus have argued that more holistic systems thinking is needed to enable organizations to more quickly adapt to today's complex, fast-changing environments. According to Senge (1990), systems thinking is

- a discipline for seeing wholes
- a framework for seeing interrelationships rather than things
- an antidote to the sense of helplessness one feels when confronted with complexity

This section provides some templates for analyzing, describing, and redesigning systems. The systems concepts we discuss are general ones, although we will use many information systems examples.

What Is a System?

A **system** is a set of interrelated components that must work together to achieve some common purpose. An example of what happens when system components do not work together appears in Figure 8.1. This house has all the components (rooms, doors, windows, plumbing, electrical wiring) necessary for a functioning home, but the components just do not fit together. For example, the outside steps do not lead to a door. The lesson here is that even when a given component is well-designed, simple, and efficient to operate, the system will malfunction if the components do not work together.

Further, a change in one component could affect other components. For example, if the marketing group (one component part of a business) sells more of some product than expected, the production group (another component) would have to special-order materials or pay overtime to produce more than the planned amount. If the interrelationships between these functions (components) are not well managed, an unanticipated result might be a rise in the costs of goods sold, leading to the company actually losing money from increased sales.

An **information system (IS)** can be defined in a very broad way as the collection of IT, procedures, and people responsible for the capture, movement, management, and

Figure 8.1 An Example of Poor Design

distribution of data and information. As with other systems, it is crucial that the components of an IS work well together. That is, the components must be consistent, minimally redundant, complete, and well connected with one another.

Seven Key System Elements

Systems share the seven general system elements briefly defined as follows:

1. **Boundary.** The delineation of which elements (such as components and storage) are within the system being analyzed and which are outside; it is assumed that elements within the boundary are more easily changed and controlled than those outside.
2. **Environment.** Everything outside the system; the environment provides assumptions, constraints, and inputs to the system.
3. **Inputs.** The resources (data, materials, supplies, energy) from the environment that are consumed and manipulated within the system.
4. **Outputs.** The resources or products (information, reports, documents, screen displays, materials) provided to the environment by the activities within the system.
5. **Components.** The activities or processes within the system that transform inputs into intermediate forms or that generate system outputs; components may also be considered systems themselves, in which case they are called subsystems, or modules.
6. **Interfaces.** The place where two components or the system and its environment meet or interact; systems often need special subcomponents at interfaces to filter, translate, store, and correct whatever flows through the interface.
7. **Storage.** Holding areas used for the temporary and permanent storage of information, energy, materials, and so on; storage provides a buffer between system components to allow them to work at different rates or at different times and to allow different components to share the same data resources. Storage is especially important in IS because data are not consumed with usage; the organization of storage is crucial to handle the potentially large volume of data maintained there.

Figure 8.2 graphically illustrates how these seven elements interrelate in a system.

These elements can also be used to describe specific computer applications. For example, in Figure 8.3 a payroll application and a sales-tracking application are described in terms of five system elements, excluding boundary and environment.

Another important system characteristic is the difference between **formal** versus **informal systems** within organizational contexts. The formal system is the way an organization was designed to work. When there are flaws in the formal system, or when the formal system has not been adapted to changes in business situations, an informal system develops.

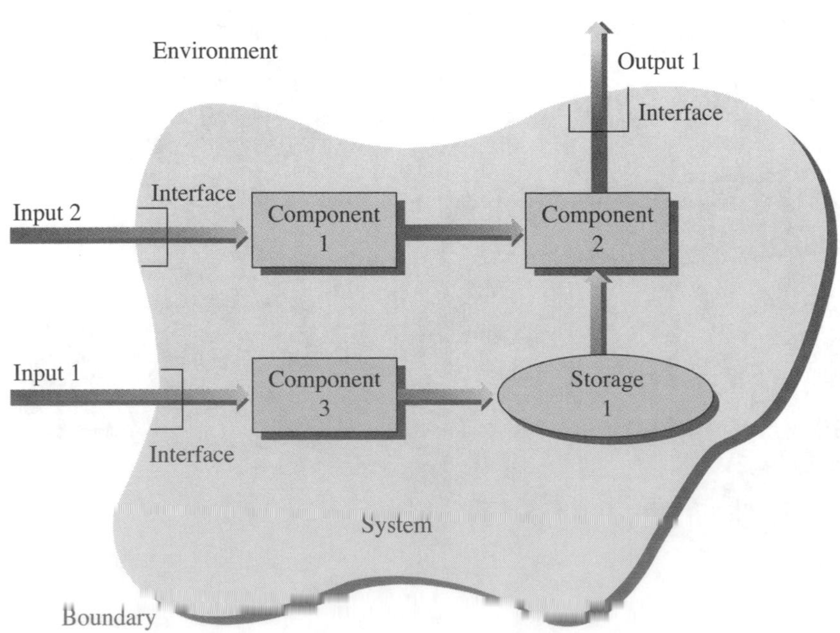

Figure 8.2 General Structure of a System

System:	Payroll	Sales Tracking
Inputs	Time cards Vouchers	Customer orders Customer returns of goods
Outputs	Paychecks W-2 forms	Monthly sales by product Monthly sales by territory
Components	Calculate total pay Subtract deductions	Accumulate sales by product and compare to forecast
Interfaces	Match time cards to employees Sort paychecks by department	Translate customer zip code into territory code
Storage	Employee benefits Pay rates	Product list Sales history Sales forecasts

Figure 8.3 System Component Examples

Recognizing that an organization's formal system is not necessarily equivalent to the real system is crucial when analyzing a business situation or process. For example, if workers continue to reference a bill-of-materials list that contains handwritten changes rather than a computer-printed list for a new shop order, an informal system has replaced the formal information system. In this case, the real system is actually the informal system or some combination of the formal and informal systems.

Three system characteristics that are especially important for analyzing and designing information systems are: determining the system boundary, breaking down a system into modules (decomposition), and designing interfaces between old and new systems.

System Boundary. The system **boundary** delineates what is inside and what is outside a system. A boundary segregates the environment from the system or delineates subsystems from each other. A boundary in the systems world is often arbitrary. That is, we can often choose to include or exclude any component in the system. The choice of where to draw the boundary depends on factors such as these:

1. **What can be controlled.** Elements outside the control of the project team are part of the environment, and the environment often places a constraint on the system scope. For example, if a preexisting billing system is treated as part of the environment of a new product management system, the product management system could be limited to devising products that can be priced and billed in ways already supported.
2. **What scope is manageable within a given time period.** Complex systems often take so long to design and develop that the envisioned systems solution could no longer be the best choice by the time the project is complete.
3. **The impact of a boundary change.** As the business changes or new information about the organization is uncovered, a different system boundary can appear to be beneficial. This decision requires careful analysis of the impact of such a change.

Component Decomposition. A system is a set of interrelated components. A component of a system that is itself viewed as a system (or a set of interrelated components) is called a **subsystem (module)**. The components of a subsystem can be further broken down into more subsystems. The process of breaking down a system into successive levels of subsystems, each of which shows more detail, is called hierarchical (or functional) decomposition. An example is provided in Figure 8.4.

Five important goals of **hierarchical decomposition** of a system are the following:

1. **To cope with the complexity of a system.** Decomposition of a complex system allows us to break the system down into understandable pieces.
2. **To analyze or change only part of the system.** Decomposition results in specific components at just the right level of detail for the job.
3. **To design and build each subsystem at different times.** Decomposition allows us to respond to new business needs as resources permit.
4. **To direct the attention of a target audience.** Decomposition allows us to focus on a subset of components of importance to a subset of the total user population.
5. **To allow system components to operate more independently.** Decomposition allows problem components to be isolated and components to be changed, moved, or replaced with minimal impact on other components.

Interfaces. An **interface** is the point of contact between a system and its environment or between two subsystems. In an information system, the functions of an interface are generally as follows:

Filtering. Disposing of useless data (or noise)
Coding/decoding. Translating data from one format into another (for example, switching between two-part

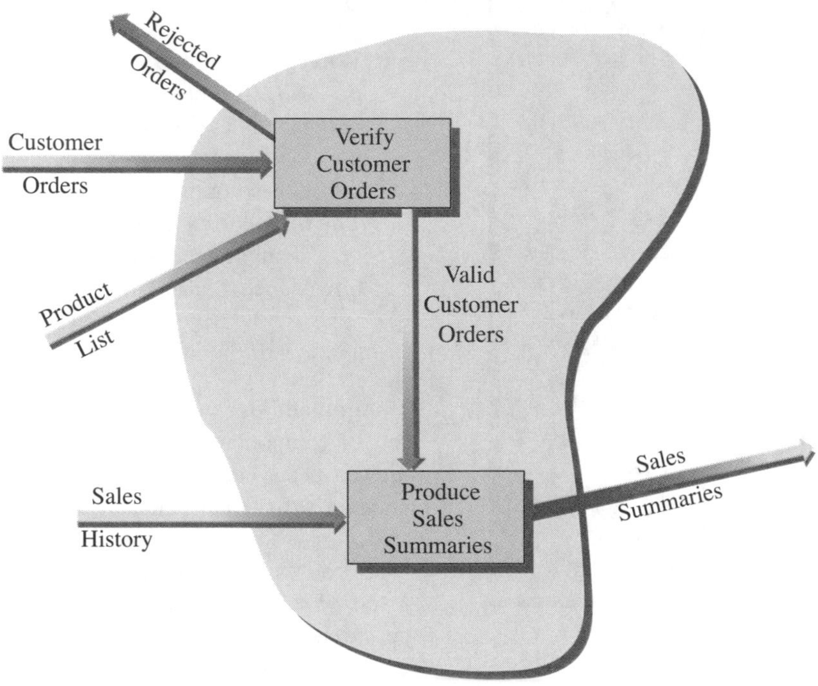

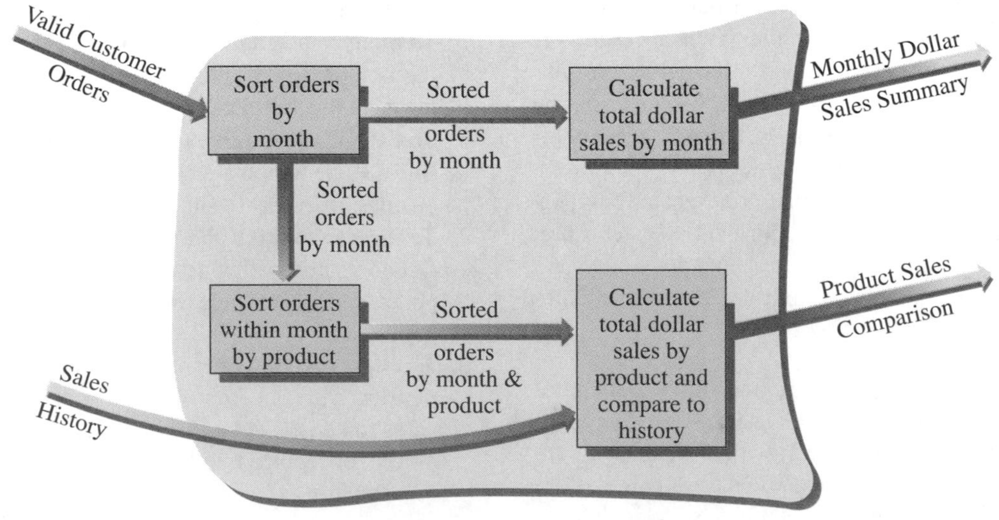

Figure 8.4 Sales Summary Reporting System and Subsystem

numbering schemes, one used by marketing and another used by engineering)

Error detection and correction. Checking for compliance to standards and for consistency; by isolating this task in interfaces, other components can concentrate on their more essential responsibilities

Buffer. Allowing two subsystems to work together without being tightly synchronized, as by having the interface collect data until the next component is ready to accept the data

Security. Rejecting unauthorized requests for data and providing other protection mechanisms

Summarizing. Condensing a large volume of input into aggregate statistics or even mathematical parameters to reduce the amount of work needed by subsequent subsystems

Interfaces also can be built between preexisting independent systems. For example, a company might contract with an outside organization (possibly a bank) to process payroll checks or with a market research firm to capture competitor sales data. In each case an interface is built that allows the external system to communicate with the company's internal systems. Different formats for data, different identifications for customers or employees, and various other differences in definitions and coding need to be translated to support this type of interface. Sometimes these interfaces are called bridges because they connect two "island" systems.

Bridge programs are relatively common. Bridges are expedient ways to accomplish the goal of expanding the capabilities of any one system. Rather than take the time to redesign two systems into one (e.g., to reduce redundant steps, to share common data, and to discontinue duplicate processing and calculations), the two systems are simply interfaced.

Another important objective of an interface is **system decoupling**. Two highly coupled system components require frequent and rapid communication, thus creating a dependence and bottleneck in the system. If one of the components fails, the other cannot function; if one is modified, the other might also have to be modified. Appropriately designed interfaces result in the decoupling of system components. The principal methods of system decoupling are these:

Slack and flexible resources. Providing alternative paths to follow when one component breaks down or slows down, such as having an interface reroute data transmissions to public carriers if the company's private data communications network becomes busy

Buffers. Storing data in a temporary location as a buffer or waiting line that can be depleted as the data are handled by the next component, as in collecting customer orders over the complete day and allowing an order-filling batch program to allocate scarce inventory to highest-need jobs

Sharing resources. Creating shared data stores with only one program (part of the interface component) maintaining the data, thus avoiding the need to synchronize multiple step updating or to operate with inconsistent multiple copies of data

Standards. Enforcing standards that reduce the need for two components to communicate, as in adopting a business policy that requires all interunit transfer of information about customers to be done using the company standard customer identification code

Decoupling allows one subsystem to remain relatively stable while other subsystems change. By clustering components into subsystems and by applying various decoupling techniques, the amount of design and maintenance effort can be significantly reduced. Because business is constantly changing, decoupling can significantly reduce an organization's systems maintenance burdens.

Organizations as Systems

Several useful frameworks exist to conceptualize how information systems fit into organizational systems. The framework in Figure 8.5, based on the Leavitt diamond, graphically depicts four fundamental components in an organization that must work in concert for the whole organization to be effective: people, information technology, business processes, and organization structure.

Figure 8.5 also suggests that if a change in IT is made in an organization—such as the introduction of a new software application—this change is likely to affect the other three components. For example, *people* will have to be retrained, methods of work (*business processes*) will have to be redesigned, and old reporting relationships (*organization structure*) will have to be modified. The important principle here is that:

> *Each time we change characteristics of one or more of these four components, we must consider compensating changes in the others.*

This raises an interesting question: With which of the four components do we start? There is no universal answer to this question, and organizational politics can play a key role in this decision. For example, organization theorists have argued that changes in technology can lead to organizational changes (technological imperative); that organizational factors can drive changes in technology (organizational imperative); and that changes are difficult to predict because

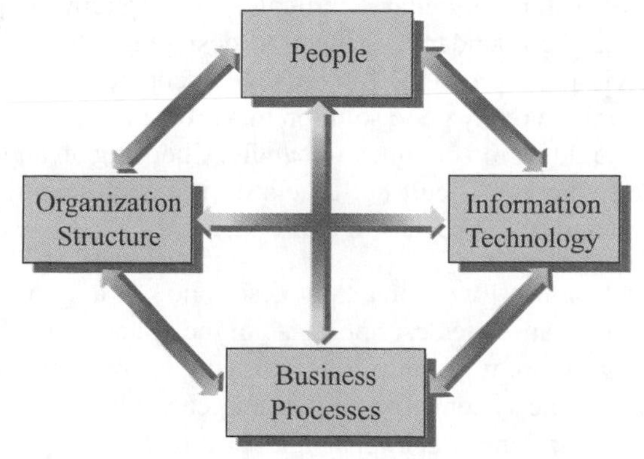

Figure 8.5 Fundamental Components of an Organization

of variations in purpose, processes, and organizational settings (Markus and Robey, 1988). In the 1990s many large U.S. companies chose to make large-scale changes in the way they conducted business by replacing custom information systems with a large software package (such as an enterprise resource planning [ERP] system) in which a vendor embedded the "best practices" for a business function or even an industry.

Systems Analysis and Design

A major process used in developing a new information system is called **systems analysis and design (SA&D)**. SA&D processes are based on a systems approach to problem solving. Here we describe several fundamental principles associated with good SA&D techniques that stem from the key system characteristics described previously.

The first two principles are these:

- *Choose an appropriate scope.* Selecting the boundary for the information system greatly influences the complexity and potential success of an IS project.
- *Logical before physical.* You must know *what* an information system is to do before you can specify *how* a system is to operate.

System Scope. Often the fatal flaw in conceiving and designing a system centers on choosing an inappropriate system scope. Apparently the designer of the house in Figure 8.1 outlined each component separately, keeping the boundaries narrow and manageable, and did not see all the necessary interrelationships among the components. Turning to a business situation, when a salesperson sells a cheaper version of a product to underbid a competitor, that salesperson has focused only on this one sale. However, the costs of handling customer complaints about inadequacy of the product, repeated trips to install upgrades, and other possible problems make this scope inadequate.

The system boundary indicates the system scope. Defining the boundary is crucial to designing any system or solving any problem. Too narrow a scope could cause you to miss a really good solution to a problem. Too wide a scope could be too complex to handle. Choosing an appropriate scope is difficult but crucial in problem-solving in general and in IS projects in particular.

Logical before Physical. Any description of a system is abstract because the description is not the system itself, but different system descriptions can emphasize different aspects of the system. Two important general kinds of system descriptions are logical and physical descriptions. Logical descriptions concentrate on *what* the system does, and physical descriptions concentrate on *how* the system operates. Another way to say this is "function before form."

Returning to our example of a house as a system, as an architect knows, function precedes form with the design of a new house. Before the house is designed, we must determine how many people will live in it, how each room will be used, the lifestyle of the family, and so on. These requirements comprise a functional, or logical, specification for the house. It would be premature to choose the type of materials, color of plumbing fixtures, and other physical characteristics before we determine the purpose of these aspects.

We are often anxious to hurry into designing the physical form before we determine the needed functionality. The penalty for violating the function before form principle is increased costs—the cost and efforts to fix a functional specification error grow exponentially as you progress to the physical. We must get the logical or functional specifications right to understand how to choose among alternate physical implementations.

As an example of the difference between a logical and a physical information system, consider a class registration system. A **logical system** description would show such steps as submitting a request for classes, checking class requests against degree requirements and prerequisites, and generating class registration lists. A **physical system** description would show whether the submission of a request for classes is via a computer terminal or a touch-tone telephone, whether the prerequisite checking is done manually or by electronic comparison of transcript with course descriptions, and so on.

Problem-Solving Steps. The three following principles, or problem-solving steps, have also been associated with good SA&D processes. In fact, they are recommended as good principles for problem-solvers in general.

- A problem (or system) is actually a set of problems; thus, an appropriate strategy is to keep breaking a problem down into smaller and smaller problems, which are more manageable than the whole problem.
- A single solution to a problem is not usually obvious to all interested parties, so alternative solutions representing different perspectives should be generated and compared before a final solution is selected.
- The problem and your understanding of it could change while you are analyzing it, so you should take a staged approach that incorporates reassessments; this allows an incremental commitment to a particular solution, with a "go" or "no-go" decision after each stage.

Later in this chapter we will introduce a generic life cycle process for developing new systems, as well as some specific techniques used by SA&D professionals. First, however, let us develop a shared understanding of the "what" that is driving many IS development and implementation projects today: systems to support cross-functional business processes.

BUSINESS PROCESSES

In the 1990s many organizations began to transform their businesses in an effort to sense and respond more quickly to global threats and demands for cost-cutting. Many of these transformation efforts were directed at moving away from a functional "silo" approach to a more process-oriented approach. Organizing work and work structures around business processes—rather than business functions or business products—requires a new mindset in which basic assumptions are challenged and change is embraced.

A **business process** is a set of work activities and resources.

Identifying Business Processes

According to Peter Keen (1997), the identification of a firm's core processes is a key analytical task. For example, a typical manufacturing firm may have six core processes: sensing the market, developing product, sourcing of materials, manufacturing product, selling product, and fulfilling customer order. A firm's core processes should not be viewed just as its workflows. Rather, these business processes should be viewed as the firm's assets and liabilities. By evaluating the worth of a given process to a firm's competitiveness, managers should be able to identify a small number of processes that need their attention the most.

Figure 8.6 shows one way in which managers can evaluate the importance of a given business process. Folklore processes are those processes that are carried out only because they have been in the past; they are often difficult to identify because they are so embedded in an organization's tasks. When they are identified, they should be abandoned because they create no economic value. Keen also warns that the importance (salience) of a given process is not necessarily the same in different companies in the same industry or even in the same company under different circumstances.

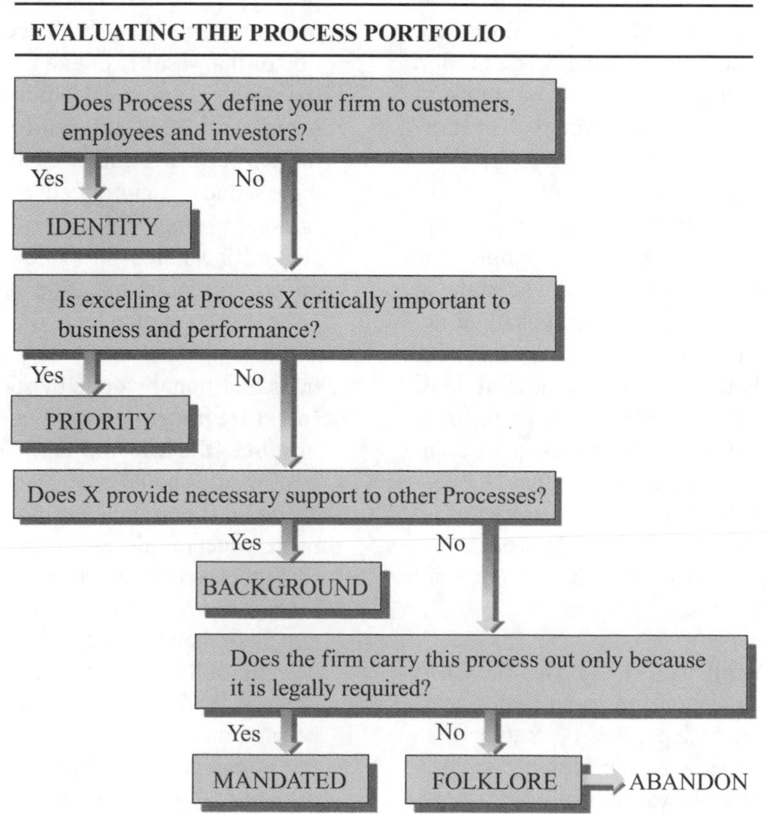

Figure 8.6 Evaluating Business Processes (Keen, 1997)

Business Process Redesign

In a seminal article published in the *Harvard Business Review*, reengineering expert Michael Hammer urged companies to start with a "clean slate" and use IT to radically change the way they did business: "Don't automate; obliterate!" By the early 1990s, consulting firms had developed expertise in what came to be referred to as **business process reengineering (BPR)**: radical business redesign initiatives that attempt to achieve dramatic improvements in business processes by questioning the assumptions, or business rules, that underlie the organization's structures and procedures, some of which could have been in place for decades.

Simple questions like "why," "what if," "who says so," and "what do our customers think," can lead to breakthrough insights that result in totally new business processes. The goal is to achieve an order of magnitude improvement, rather than incremental gains.

Two BPR success stories described by Hammer (1990) have now become classic examples.

Accounts Payable at Ford Motor Company. During an initial redesign of its accounts payable process, Ford concluded that it could reduce head count by 20 percent in this department. The initial solution was to develop a new accounts payable system to help clerks resolve document mismatches. This solution was based on the assumption that problems with coordinating purchase orders, shipment documents, and invoices are inevitable. The proposed new system would help prevent the document mismatches.

Ford's managers were reasonably proud of their plans until the designers discovered that Mazda Motor Corp. accomplished the same function with just five people. The difference was that Ford based its initial system solution on the old business assumptions. In particular, Ford had not questioned its assumption that it could not pay a vendor without an invoice. When Ford questioned its assumptions, a truly reengineered solution was identified, as follows: capture the receipt of goods at the loading dock using computer scanners and use the negotiated price to pay the vendor based on a validated receipt of goods—instead of an invoice. When Ford took a "clean slate" approach, the company achieved a 75 percent improvement gain—not the original projected 20 percent.

Mutual Benefit Life Insurance. Mutual Benefit Life's old insurance application processing was a 30-step process that involved 19 people in 5 departments. Rather than automating the old workflows across multiple people in multiple departments, the process was radically redesigned. Under the reengineered process, an individual case manager is empowered to handle the entire loan application process. This was accomplished by supporting the case manager with an advanced PC-based workstation, expert system software, and access to a range of automated systems. Time to issue a policy dropped from 3 weeks to about 3 hours.

In both of these examples IT played a key role as an enabler of radical business process redesign. Hammer and Champy (1993) encourage managers to go through exercises that help them think about how IT can be used to break old assumptions and rules. Three examples of rule-breaking IT are provided in Figure 8.7.

Hammer (1990) advocated the use of key principles for redesigning business processes. A consolidated list of six principles is presented below.

1. **Organize business processes around outcomes, not tasks.** This principle implies that one person should perform all the steps in a given process, as in the case of Mutual Benefit Life, where one manager handles the whole application approval process. IT is used to bring together all the information and decision-making resources needed by this one person. Often this principle also means organizing processes around customer needs, not the product.
2. **Assign those who use the output to perform the process.** The intent of this principle is to make those most interested in a result accountable for the production of that result. For example, Hammer reports the case of an electronics equipment manufacturer that reengineered its field service function to have customers perform simple repairs themselves. This principle reduces nonproductive overhead jobs, including liaison positions. Principles 1 and 2 yield a compression of linear steps into one step, greatly reducing delays, miscommunication, and wasted coordination efforts. Information technologies, like expert systems and databases, allow every manager to perform functions traditionally done by specialty managers.
3. **Integrate information processing into the work that produces the information.** This principle states that information should be processed at its source. For example, at Ford this means that the receiving department, which produces information on goods received, should also enter this data, rather than sending it to accounts payable for processing. This puts data capture closest to the place where data entry errors can be detected and corrected, thus minimizing extra reconciliation steps. This principle also implies that data should be captured once at the primary source, thus avoiding transmittal and transcription errors. All who need these data work from a common and consistent source. For example, the true power of electronic data interchange (EDI) comes when all information processing related

Old Ways to Work	Information Technology	New Ways to Work
Field personnel (such as sales and customer support staff) need to physically be located in an office to transmit and receive customer and product data	Portable computers with communications software and secure networks that allow remote access to company data	Field personnel access data and respond to messages wherever they are working
Client data is collected in different databases to support different points of contact with the client	Centralized databases that capture transactions from different parts of the business and are accessible via a network	Client data can be accessed simultaneously by employees working in different business units
Only experts can do a complex task *(see Mutual Benefit Life Insurance example)*	Expert systems that have knowledge rules used by company experts when they do this task	Generalists can do a complex task previously only done by an expert

Figure 8.7 How IT Enables New Ways to Work

to an EDI transaction works from a common, integrated database.

4. **Create a virtual enterprise by treating geographically distributed resources as though they were centralized.** This principle implies that the distinction between centralization and decentralization is artificial with IT. Technologies such as teleconferencing, group support systems, e-mail, and others can create an information processing environment in which time and space are compressed. Hammer reports on the experience of Hewlett-Packard, which treats the purchasing departments of 50 manufacturing units as if they were one giant department by using a shared database on vendor and purchase orders. The result is 50 percent to 150 percent improvement in key performance variables for the purchasing function.
5. **Link parallel activities instead of integrating their results.** This principle says that related activities should be constantly coordinated rather than waiting until a final step to ensure consistency. For example, Hammer suggests that different kinds of credit functions in a financial institution could share common databases, use communication networks, and employ teleconferencing to coordinate their operations. This would ensure, for example, that a customer is not extended a full line of credit from each unit.
6. **Have the people who do the work make all the decisions, and let controls built into the system monitor the process.** The result of this principle is the drastic reduction of layers of management, the empowerment of employees, and the shortcutting of bureaucracy. This principle emphasizes the importance of building controls into a system from the start, rather than as an afterthought (see the section entitled "Information Systems Controls to Minimize Business Risks" at the end of this chapter).

However, not all BPR projects of the early 1990s were successes. In fact, Keen (1997) points out that Mutual Benefit Life, whose radical reengineering example was described above, was taken over by regulators due to insolvency about the time Hammer lauded it as a success story. By the mid-1990s many firms began to acknowledge that a combination approach of both radical change and incremental change (such as continuous improvements as part of quality management initiatives) was more successful (El Sawy, 2001).

By the mid-1990s client/server versions of enterprise system packages had also become widely available, making it possible for large companies to implement systems that would support complex processes across multiple functions for the first time: Earlier attempts to become more process-oriented had been aborted because systems to support their reengineered processes were too difficult to custom develop. For example, as described in Chapter 6, enterprise resource planning (ERP) packages offered by vendors such as SAP and PeopleSoft provide integrated software modules that use the same centralized database for manufacturing, purchasing, and accounting transactions. Similarly, packages to support customer relationship management (CRM) by vendors such as Siebel Systems provide modules that can integrate customer data from multiple communication "channels," which are typically managed by different business units (marketing, sales, and customer support).

PROCESSES AND TECHNIQUES TO DELIVER INFORMATION SYSTEMS

We turn now to processes and techniques for developing information systems. Our intent here is to introduce the key concepts that underlie the toolkits of system professionals. We also emphasize topics of use to both IS specialists and business managers who are asked to participate in, or lead, systems projects.

The Information Systems Life Cycle

Figure 8.8 presents the three phases of a generic **systems development life cycle** model: Definition, Construction, and Implementation.

In the *Definition* phase, end users and systems analysts conduct a multistep analysis of the current business operations and the information system or systems in the area of concern. Current operations and systems are described via both process-oriented and data-oriented notations. Process-oriented analysis concentrates on the flow, use, and transformation of data. Data-oriented analysis focuses on the kinds of data needed in a system and the business relationships between these data. Problems with current operations and opportunities for achieving business value through new IT capabilities are identified. A business case is made for the feasibility of new systems, and one solution is chosen. This solution is detailed in a requirements statement agreed to by all parties. If a software vendor has already developed a "packaged" system that meets these requirements, this phase also includes steps to identify and select the best packaged solution. The Definition phase of the life cycle is very much a cooperative effort between business and systems professionals. Doing this phase right can have significant impact on the competitive use of IT.

The *Construction* phase entails the designing, building, and testing of a system that satisfies the requirements developed in the Definition phase. The system first is logically described, and then its physical design is specified. Programs and computer files are designed, and computer technology is chosen. Inputs such as business forms and computer screens are designed, as well as outputs such as reports. After the physical design is accepted as feasible (technically, economically, and operationally), the computer software is programmed and tested. Users play a major role in acceptance testing to verify that the system requirements have been met.

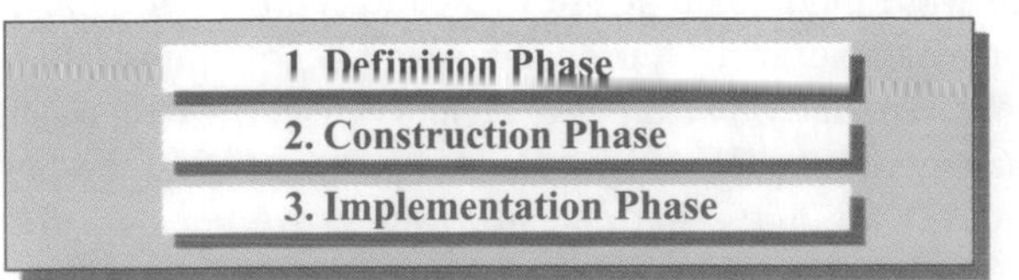

Figure 8.8 Generic Systems Life Cycle

In the *Implementation* phase, business managers and IS professionals work together to install the new system, which often involves converting data and procedures from an old system. The installation of a new system can occur in a variety of ways, such as in parallel with operation of the old system or in a total and clean cutover. The implementation phase also includes the operation and continued maintenance of the system. Maintenance is typically the longest stage of the systems life cycle and incurs the greatest costs. It includes system changes resulting from flaws in the original design, from changing business needs or regulations, and from incorporating new technologies.

In the following chapters we will discuss in more detail some specific methodologies for developing and implementing custom software solutions (Chapter 9) and for purchasing and implementing packaged software solutions (Chapter 10). All these methodologies are based on the generic three-phase life cycle for systems development described above. Although many IS organizations customize these approaches—including expansion or contraction of the specific number of phases or steps, or using different names—there is agreement among IS specialists on the generic activities that are required for developing a quality system that meets the organization's needs.

Structured Techniques for Life Cycle Development

Just as architects use blueprints as abstract representations of a house, IS professionals have developed techniques for representing system requirements and designs. In this section we describe some of these techniques.

Today, IS development projects range in size from a single-user application for a desktop machine to one that will be used by thousands of people in a large organization. The scope of today's large development projects has brought system builders up against both cognitive and practical limitations: The scale and complexity of these projects exceed the capacity of one developer or even a single team of manageable size. Effective large system development requires more systematic approaches that allow partitioning of the problem so that many developers can work on the project simultaneously. Increasing the scale also increases the number of parties involved. Systems projects today can require coordination across multiple project managers and even involve IS professionals in a customer or supplier organization (such as some e-commerce applications discussed in Chapter 7). System builders must be able to communicate with other IS professionals about what system modules do and how they do what they do. IS project managers must be able to coordinate and monitor progress and understand the commitments they are asking business managers and IS project team members to make.

A body of tools has emerged to document system needs and requirements, functional features and dependencies, and design decisions. Called **structured techniques**, these techniques exist for all phases of the systems development process, and many variations have emerged. Additionally, the techniques could be embodied within a larger approach called a **system development methodology**. A methodology is a framework consisting of guidelines, tools, and techniques for managing the application of knowledge and skills to address all or part of a business issue. A systems development methodology, then, consists of processes, tools, and techniques for developing systems. In addition to the types of structured tools discussed in the sections that follow, these methodologies prescribe who should participate and their roles, the development stages and decision points, and specific formats for system documentation.

This section will provide a conceptual introduction to the most common structured techniques in a general life cycle development framework. Two major approaches to systems building have emerged: procedural-oriented and object-oriented. Procedural-oriented systems have historically been the most common, as they appropriately represent a large class of business activities. They include data-oriented as well as sequential, process-oriented activities such as tabulating time cards and printing paychecks, inventory handling, and accounts payable. Object-oriented (O-O) techniques are a newer approach to systems development. Considered by some to be revolutionary and by others to be evolutionary, O-O techniques are better suited to the development of graphical user interfaces (GUIs) and multimedia applications, but they require an entirely new way of thinking for veteran IS professionals.

Procedural-Oriented Techniques

In the past the vast majority of IS development projects have involved automating an existing paper-oriented business process or updating and expanding an existing automated or partially automated business process. This reality is reflected in the fundamental procedural approach to systems development: describe what you have, define what you want, and describe how you will make it so.

As shown in Figure 8.9, this approach involves documenting the existing system (the As-Is model), creating a

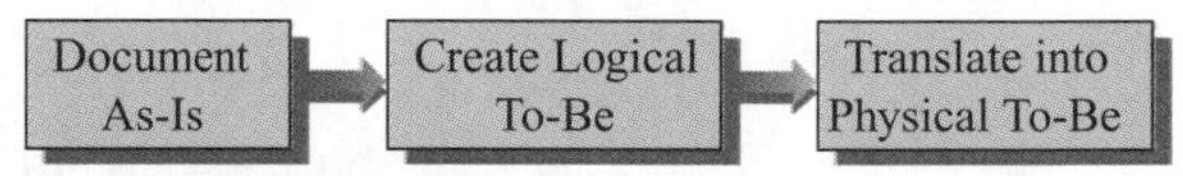

Figure 8.9 Three-Step Modeling Approach

model of the desired future system (the Logical To-Be model), and then interpreting the logical future model as a physical system design (the Physical To-Be model). The motivation for following such a process derives in part from human nature. Most people find it easier to imagine the future by conceiving of how it is different from today. A systematic effort to document the existing system can also yield important insights about its deficiencies and worker ideas about improvements.

This sequential approach is also effective when a new business process is being implemented at the same time that a new system is being implemented; it helps ensure that the new process will work in concert with the new IS, not against it. As described previously, business process redesign became increasingly common during the 1990s.

Describing the three models in Figure 8.10 requires a significant amount of effort prior to building the software. Business managers are often surprised at the demands placed on them to support this definition phase. The objective of this process is to have a thorough description of what the construction phase for the system will entail, so that the project risks can be assessed and planned for with some level of confidence or the decision can be made to abandon the project. In fact, actual software coding during the construction phase typically represents less than one-quarter of the entire systems development effort (Page-Jones, 1988).

The As-Is model provides a baseline for the system: Why build a new one if it will not do more than the old one, do it faster, or avoid existing problems? The As-Is model typically includes both logical and physical models.

Although developing the As-Is model can be user-intensive, the majority of the effort is typically involved with developing the second model: abstracting the As-Is model into the Logical To-Be. Logical To-Be modeling involves a critical appraisal of existing work processes in order to

- identify major subprocesses, entities, and their interactions
- separate processing from the flow of data
- capture relationships between data elements
- determine those entities and processes within the project scope, and those that are not

Creation of the Physical To-Be model is a task dominated by IS specialists, as it requires technology expertise to map

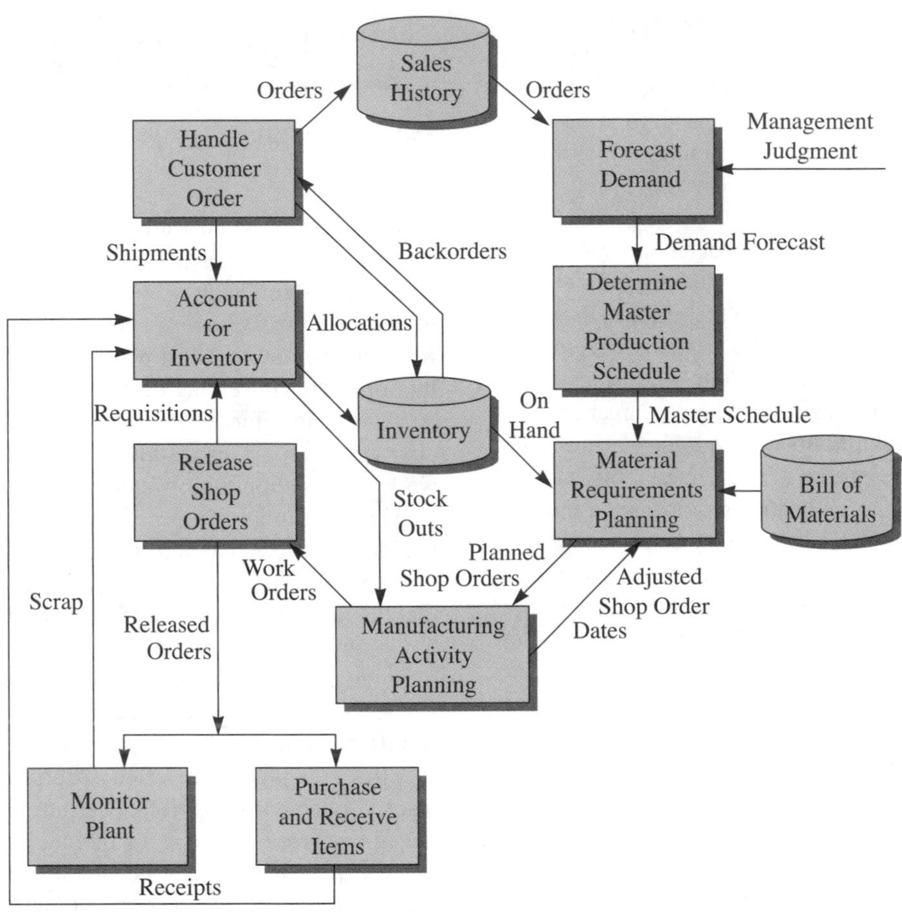

Figure 8.10 Physical Model of a System

the logical requirements to available technology. Although information systems are implemented with specific hardware and software, participants in systems development efforts are cautioned to resist the urge to make decisions related to design and implementation until as late as possible in the project. Premature fixation on a particular technology has often led to unsatisfactory outcomes because it can cause important aspects of the system to go undiscovered or put undue emphasis on *how* to do something before there is certainty about *what* needs to be done. In reality, although no IS project is truly a "clean slate," delaying judgment until the Physical To-Be stage is the recommended strategy.

After a new system has been implemented and is operational, a diagram like that in Figure 8.10 would be used to show a physical model of the key system components and their relationships. It uses the following symbols:

Boxes	for	Major modules
Cylinders	for	Databases
Arrows	for	Flow of data

Note, however, that this diagram makes no references to details such as what type of computer hosts the software or what language it is written in. Instead, the Physical To-Be model is a high-level model. It communicates how the new system will work and helps identify any dependencies that might lead to downstream impacts, such as data integrity problems or inadequate process definitions.

Distinct tools are used at each stage of procedural-oriented development. The output from one stage serves as the input for the next. As firms gain experience with systems development, they often develop a preference for certain tools or adopt variations in the notation. The following section introduces some of the most common tools, concepts, and terminology using widely recognized notation. The tools will be presented with the model (As Is, Logical To-Be, Physical To-Be) with which they are most closely associated, using a common business example throughout: accounts payable. An accounts payable example is useful because accounts payable activities interact with other business activities (such as purchasing and receiving), are familiar to most managers and business students, and are common across industries.

Tools for the As-Is Model

Whether a system is entirely manual or highly automated, the functions and flows of the existing business activity must be captured. Knowledge of a business process is rarely entirely in the possession of a single person, and there could be disagreements on the actual or preferred processes. Procedures, policies, manuals, forms, reports, and other documentation are used along with individual and group interviews to identify existing processes, external participants such as vendors and other functional departments, other databases or applications, and the inputs and outputs of the activities concerned.

A **context diagram** positions the system as a whole with regard to the other entities and activities with which it interacts. This provides a common frame of reference for project participants and helps define the project scope. Figure 8.11 illustrates a context diagram for an accounts payable system. We can see from this diagram that the accounts payable function both receives input from vendors and sends output to them. Other accounting functions receive summary information about payables activities, whereas purchasing provides the input needed to process payables. Vendors, accounting, and purchasing are all considered to be outside the project scope for this development effort.

Another common tool for documenting the As-Is system is a work process flow diagram, as shown in Figure 8.12. This flow chart identifies the existing information sources (purchase order file, receipts file), information sources that are updated (changes to payables), the order in which steps occur (approvals before checks are printed), and some of the dependencies (need to know whether vendor is new or not). The way in which exceptions are handled should also be captured (e.g., what happens to invoices not approved). No two workflow diagrams are identical, because they capture the unique patterns and procedures—formal and informal—of a company.

The work process flow diagram and other As-Is tools serve to point out where the existing system does and does not perform as desired. Common problems include repeated handling of the same document, excessive wait times, processes with no outputs, bottlenecks, and extra review steps. This shows how systems development efforts are closely associated with business process redesign efforts.

Tools for the Logical To-Be Model

In this step systems developers build a high-level model of a nonexistent system: the system that the users and managers would like to replace the one they have now. The Logical To-Be model is an abstraction that identifies the processes and data required for the desired system *without* reference to who does an activity, where it is accomplished, or the type of computer or software used. The model describes the "what," rather than the "how." Stated differently, it separates the information that moves through the business process from the mechanisms that move it (e.g., forms, reports, routing slips). This is important because IT enables information to be in more than one place at the same time; paper does not possess this attribute. By leaving physical barriers behind, the analyst can better determine how to exploit IT. This abstraction step can be difficult for first-time business participants because it appears to ignore issues crucial to their daily work (e.g., specific forms, reports, routing slips). Understanding that the Logical To-Be model encompasses information flows, rather than physical flows (paper, money, products), is the key.

The Logical To-Be model is most closely associated with the **data flow diagram** or **DFD** (see Hoffer et al., 1999, for a thorough discussion of DFDs). The DFD notation itself is technology independent; the symbols have no association with the type of equipment or the humans that might perform the process activities or store

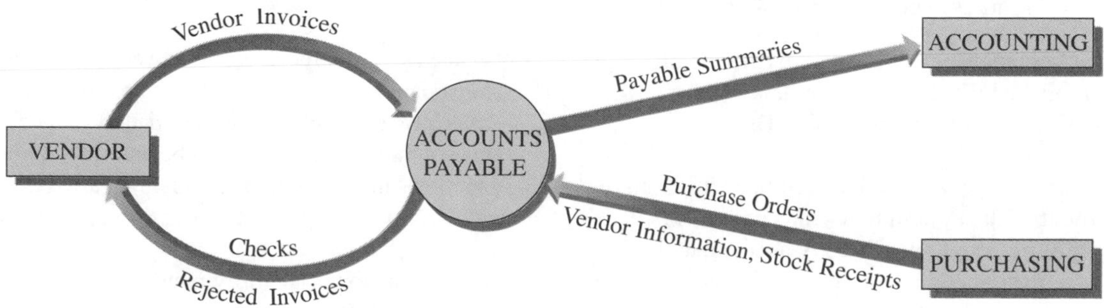

Figure 8.11 Context Diagram for Accounts Payable System

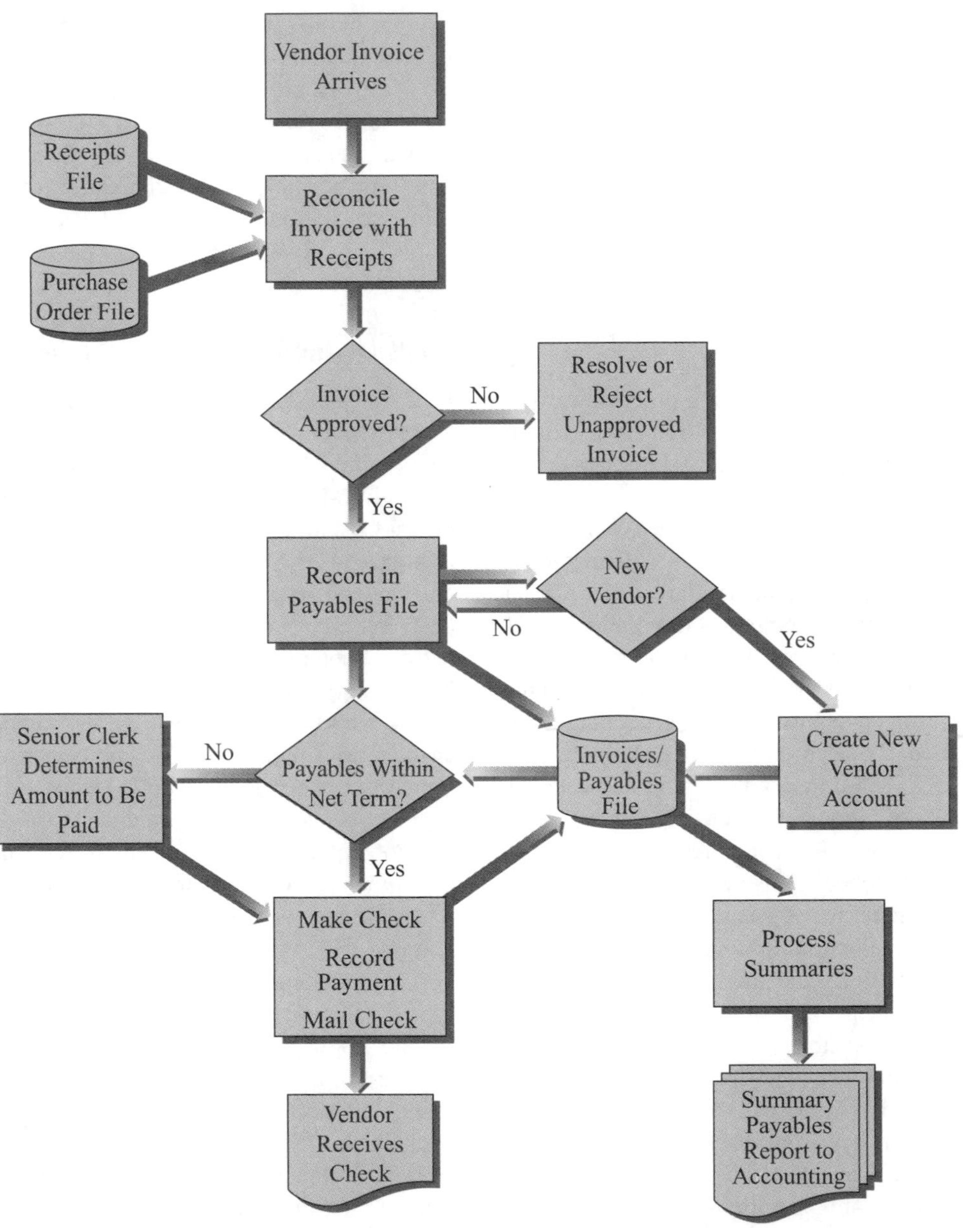

Figure 8.12 Work Process Flow Diagram for Accounts Payable

the data. DFD creation typically involves groups of people and is accomplished through multiple iterations.

Four types of symbols are used in DFDs:

External Entity. A square indicates some element in the environment of the system that sends or receives data. External entities might not directly access data in the system but must get data from processing components of the system. No data flows between external entities are shown. External entities have noun labels.

Data Flow. Arrows indicate data in motion—that is, data moving between external entities and system processes, between system processes, or between processes and data stores. Timing and volume of data are not shown. Data flows have noun labels. Because data flow labels often sound similar, and there could be hundreds of distinct data flows in a project, numbers might also be assigned.

Process. Circles represent processing components of the system. Each process has to have both input and output (whereas an external entity may have either input, output, or both). Processes have verb phrase labels as well as a numerical identifier.

Data Store. Open rectangles depict data at rest—that is, data temporarily or permanently held for repeated reference by one or more processes. Use of a data store implies there is a delay in the flow of data between two or more processes or a need for long-term storage. Each data store contained within the system must have both input and output (i.e., be populated and be used) within the system. Data stores that are outside the system may provide only input or only output. Data stores have noun labels and a unique identifier.

The process of creating data flow diagrams is as follows:

- Identify the entities that supply or use system information.
- Distinguish processes from the data that they use or produce.
- Explicate business rules that affect the transformation of data to information.
- Identify logical relationships.
- Pinpoint duplicate storage and movements of data.

In Figure 8.13(A) a "top-level" DFD for the Accounts Payable system is shown. Consistent with the context diagram of Figure 8.11, the dashed line delineates the system boundary. The system includes four processes (circles). Data stores internal to this system (D2, D3, and D4) serve as buffers between the process components (e.g., to compensate for different processing rates of the components or to permit batch processing of transactions), as well as semi-permanent storage for auditing purposes.

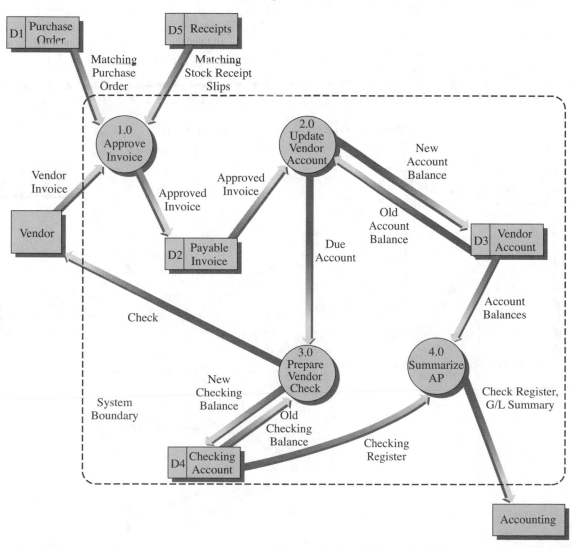

Figure 8.13(A) Top-Level Data Flow Diagram for Accounts Payable System

Because this is a top-level DFD, or macro view, processing details are not depicted. For example, this top-level diagram does not show what happens to exceptions—such as what the process does to deal with invoices that do not match purchase orders or shipment receipt records.

A key to the effectiveness of DFD modeling is the enforcement of strict hierarchical relationships. Each process (circle) on the top-level DFD has a lower-level DFD that documents the subprocesses, data stores, and data flows needed to accomplish the process task. This "explosion" continues for each subprocess until no further subprocesses are needed to describe the function. A process at the lowest level in the model must be definable by a few descriptive sentences. Figure 8.13(B) is the next-lower-level explosion DFD for Process 1.0 (Approve Invoice) in Figure 8.13(A). The process decomposition relationship is shown by the process numbering scheme (1.1, 1.2, etc.).

The lower-level DFDs can result in the identification of additional data stores and data flows as well as subprocesses, but the exploded DFDs must balance with their higher-level counterparts. All data flows identified in a lower-level DFD must be accounted for in the description, source, and destination of data flows at the higher level. During the Logical To-Be defining process, external entities and data flows sometimes will need to be added to higher-level DFDs to assure completeness. It is not uncommon for business systems to have four or five levels of DFDs before exhausting all subprocesses.

When complete, DFDs tell a story about the business process that does not depend upon specific forms or technology. The rigor imposed by the explosion, aggregation, balancing, and documentation of DFDs results in more than simple circle-and-arrow diagrams. For example, from reviewing the accounts payable DFDs, we see:

1. Purchase orders and shipment receipt records are produced by systems outside the accounts payable system (because they are shown as inputs from the environment—that is, outside the system boundary).
2. The payable invoice data store temporarily stores and groups invoices after invoice approval and before subsequent vendor account updating and check writing (data flows into and out of D2).

These statements describe two aspects of the accounts payable organizational data flows as we want them to be

(B) Second-Level DFD for Process 1.0 in Top-Level

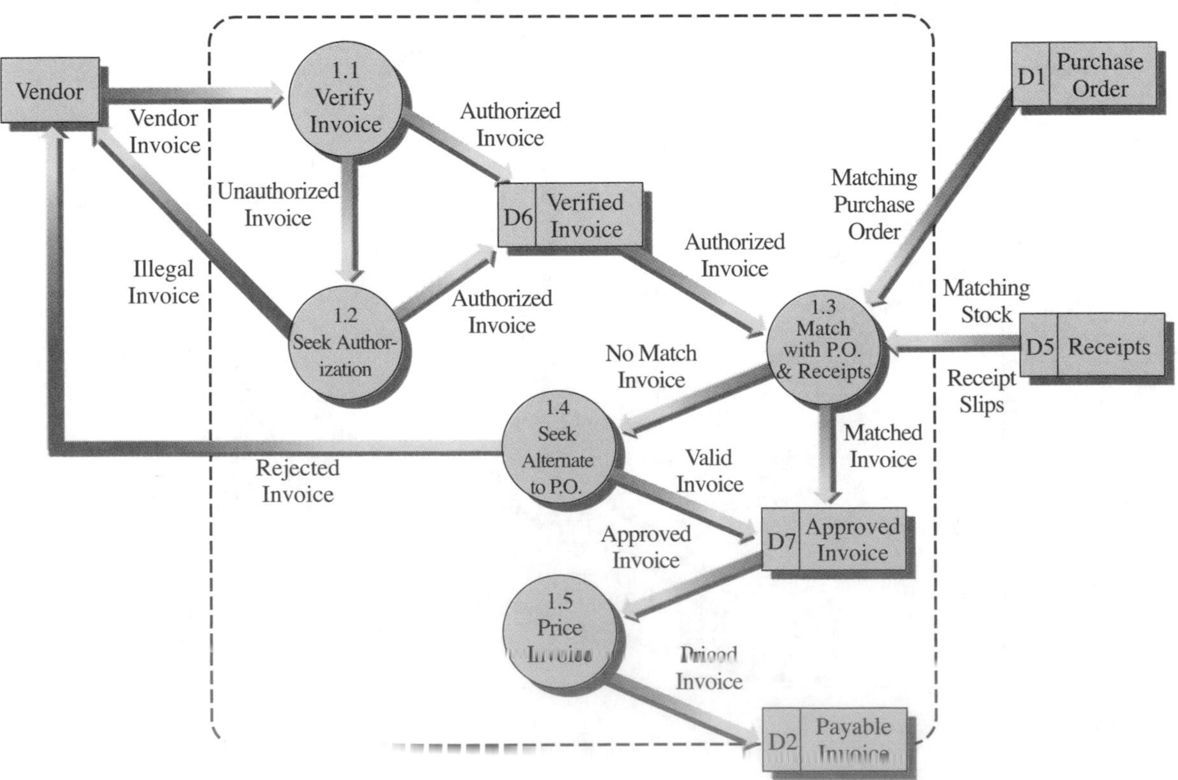

Figure 8.13(B) Second-Level Data Flow Diagram for Accounts Payable System

without implying computerization or any other form of new system implementation.

In addition to diagrams such as in Figure 8.13 (A) and (B), each external entity, process, data flow, and data store is documented as to its content. The documentation also shows how the components are related; for example, the description for the Vendor entity would include both inbound and outbound data flows. Similarly, the data store documentation includes the individual data elements that are input into the store and matches them to output descriptions.

The accuracy and completeness of a DFD model is crucial for the process of converting the Logical To-Be model into the Physical To-Be design. However, prior to commencing this physical design step, additional logical modeling is required to define the system's data elements and relationships.

A **data model** is created by logically defining the necessary and sufficient relationships among system data. The specialized terminology for the four levels of data modeling is provided here.

Data elements are the lowest unit of data. These represent individual types of data such as "purchase order number," "vendor name," or "quantity received."

Entity instances are groupings of related data elements that correspond to a single entity in the world. For example, an entity instance would be all the different data elements needed to represent an invoice.

Entities (or data entities) are groups of entity instances. As such, all the instances have the same structure because they all have the same data elements. This entity then represents a collection of like items, such as all invoices or the transactions that make up a checking account.

Data stores (or databases) are groups of entities that have a relationship. This highest level captures the relationship between entities, such as how invoices can be associated with a purchase order.

The most common approach to defining data elements in a DFD is to create a **data dictionary/directory (DD/D).** The goal of the data dictionary entry is to describe the data element as completely as possible; these entries should err on the side of too much information, rather than too little. This is also the place to capture whether elements are calculated, how many decimal places are required, and how an element may be referred to in external systems that reference it. Figure 8.14 shows a typical data dictionary entry for the data element Purchase Order (PO) Number.

Accounts Payable Project Data Dictionary Entry for PO Number

Label	**PO Number**
Alternate Names	Purchase Order Number. PO Number. PO#
Definition	Unique identifier for an individual purchase order: alpha character designates the division. The five digit number is assigned in sequential order at the time of creation.
Example	C07321
Field Name	PO_Num
Input Format	A##### (single alpha followed by five integers, no spaces or symbols allowed)
Output Format	Same as input format
Edit Rules	No values below 1000 allowed in numeric portion: currently using A-E as division code indicators.
Additional Notes	At conversion to the former system in 1991, numbers below 1000 were discontinued. Each division writes about 700–1,000 purchase orders per year. PO Numbers cannot be re-used.
Storage Type	Alphanumeric, no decimals
Default Value	None
Required	Each purchase order must have one PO Number.

Prepared by: JDAustin	Date: 8/27/97	Version No.: 1

Figure 8.14 Data Dictionary Sample Entry

Figure 8.15 Entity-Relationship Diagram for Invoice and PO

In addition to the detail at the data element level, the relationships between entities must be determined. The **entity-relationship diagram**, also known as the E-R diagram or ERD. Figure 8.15 shows that the data entity "Vendor Invoice" is related to the data entity "Purchase Order" by the relation type "includes." Furthermore, the numerals next to the data entities show that a many-to-one relationship has been defined. This means that one invoice can refer to only one purchase order number but that a purchase order number can have many invoices associated with it.

The E-R diagram in Figure 8.15 thus reflects an existing business rule:

Vendor invoices cannot include items from more than one purchase order.

The motivation for such a business rule could lie in difficulties related to manual paper processing. However, IT can be used to break this rule by eliminating the problems of manually reconciling invoices to multiple purchase orders. If this decision rule is changed, the E-R diagram would be changed to reflect a new many-to-many relationship desired in the Logical To-Be system.

In summary, creating a Logical To-Be model requires the abstraction of existing business processes from the As-Is model into representations that separate data flows from processes and entities, accurately identify business rules, and capture the relationships among data. Though a demanding effort, the creation of a complete To-Be model for complex systems is our best assurance that the new system will improve upon the existing one.

The next step is to develop a physical model based on the Logical To-Be model—including all the decisions necessary to determine how the logical requirements can be met. In preparation for the following Physical To-Be model discussion, Figure 8.16 identifies relational database terminology (as used in a physical model) that corresponds to the various logical E-R model terms. For each pair of terms, a corresponding example from the accounts payable system is also provided.

Tools for Documenting the Physical To-Be System

The end deliverables from the Logical To-Be modeling process are called the **system requirements**. Any proposed system design must address the need for each requirement, provide a substitute, or justify its exclusion. Of course, the objective is to meet as many of the requirements as possible without jeopardizing project scheduling and budget constraints.

Making the Logical To-Be model "physical" requires additional analysis and a host of decisions. Tools for physical design include those that represent how processes and data stores will be partitioned, how program control will be handled, and how the database will be organized.

One of these tools is called a **program structure chart**. Figure 8.17 shows the program structure chart for a subsystem called "Handle Customer Order." Boxes represent subprocess modules, and arrows represent the flow of control during program execution. The diagram is read from top to bottom starting from the left and moving to the right. Flags (arrows with circles) come in two forms: data couples (open circle) and control flags (filled circle). Both flags direct the program modules to take action. Data couples cause action to be taken based on the data passed to the module, whereas control flags cause program execution based on the result of another module's processing. The module at the top controls all these processes and is

Logical Data Modeling Terms	Physical Data Terms	Example
Data Store	Database	Accounts Payable Database
Entity	File or Table	Purchase Order (D1)
Entity Instance	Record or Row	All information on purchase order number C07321
Data Element	Field	PO Number

Figure 8.16 Key Terms for Logical Data Modeling

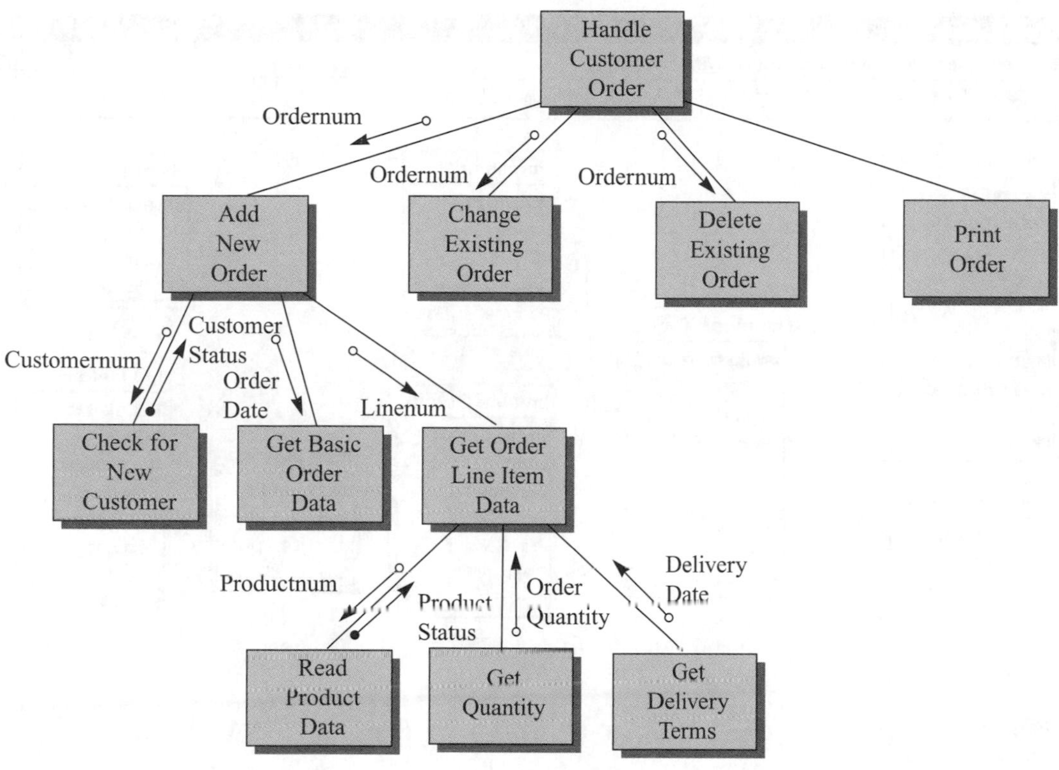

Figure 8.17 Program Structure Chart

the only means by which other program modules can interact with any of the subprocesses.

Program structure charts have rules for determining when they are complete by evaluating design factors such as cohesion and coupling (Page-Jones, 1988). Cohesion requires that each component within the system has a well-defined function and that all components cooperate to achieve an overall system goal. Coupling refers to the degree to which components are dependent on one another. Similar to DFDs, a complex system will have many program structure charts organized in a hierarchy of greater to lesser detail.

Data design issues must also be resolved for a specific database and application architecture. The number, content, and relationship of data tables and their elements must be defined. For example, a closer look at the accounts payable system reveals that purchase orders, receipts, and invoices may contain several similar data elements. An Item Master table is created into which data about all invoice items must be entered. Figure 8.18 shows the Item Master table and its relationship to other tables in the accounts payable database. The creation of this table greatly facilitates the reconciliation of receipts and purchase orders to invoices.

Our final example for the Physical To-Be model is layouts for system interfaces with end users. The most common interfaces are online screen layouts and report layouts. In the Logical To-Be modeling, the need for an interface was identified, as well as its frequency of use and information content. In the Physical To-Be modeling, the specific interface design is addressed.

Figures 8.19 and 8.20 show draft layouts for an input screen and a report for the accounts payable system. Layouts such as these are often developed in close consultation between systems designers and the end users who will be directly working with a computer display. Today's system building tools allow for easy prototyping of such interfaces by end users before the system itself is actually built. Systems today are also frequently built with some flexibility, so that the user can directly control design options for reports and data entry forms in order to adapt to changing needs of the business or the user of the report.

You have now considered some of the tools used to capture system needs, document business rules, and uncover hidden dependencies and relationships as part of the process of developing a new computer system using procedural-oriented techniques.

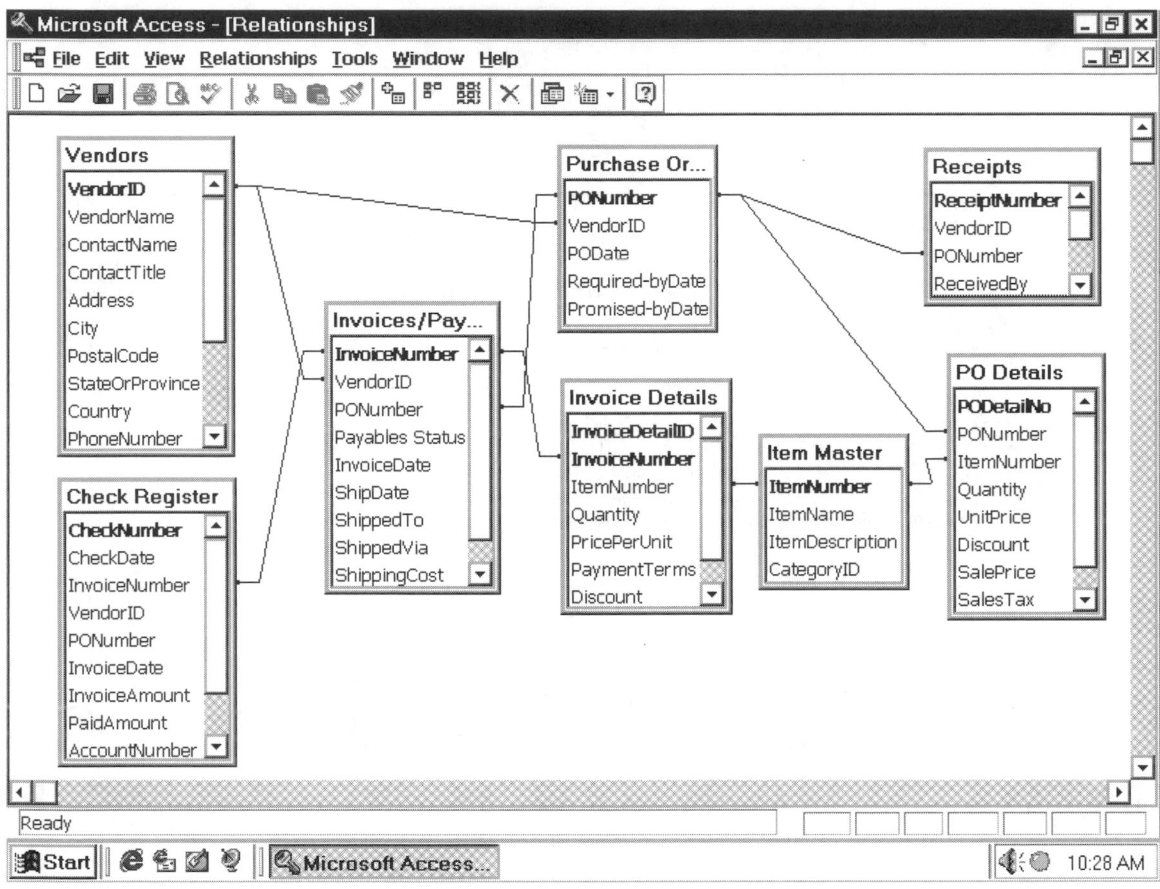

Figure 8.18 Relationships for Data Elements in Accounts Payable Tables (Access Implementation) (Screen shot reprinted with permission from Microsoft Corporation).

Object-Oriented Techniques

An object orientation (O-O) to systems development became common in the 1990s as the demand grew for client/server applications, graphical interfaces, and multimedia data. Objects can be used with any type of data, including voice, pictures, music, and video. An object approach is also well suited for applications in which processes and data are "intimately related" or real-time systems (Vessey and Glass, 1994). As described in Chapter 3, common O-O programming languages include C++, Java, and Visual Basic.

One of the primary advantages of an O-O approach is the ability to reuse objects programmed by others (see Figure 8.21). According to industry observers, successful O-O approaches can produce big payoffs by enabling businesses to quickly mock up prototype applications with user-friendly GUI interfaces. Application maintenance is also simplified.

Software objects are also a key concept behind the sharing of software for an emerging type of network-centric computing: Web services. A Web service enables computer-to-computer sharing of software modules via the Internet on an as-needed basis: A computer program (which could be another Web service) "calls" a Web service to perform a task and send back the result. This type of "dynamic binding" occurs at the time of execution and therefore greatly increases application flexibility as well as reduces the costs of software development. The computer program's owner who uses the service could pay the owner of the Web service on a subscription basis or per use. Existing examples of Web services include currency conversions (e.g., U.S. dollars to euros), credit risk analysis, and location of a product within a distribution channel.

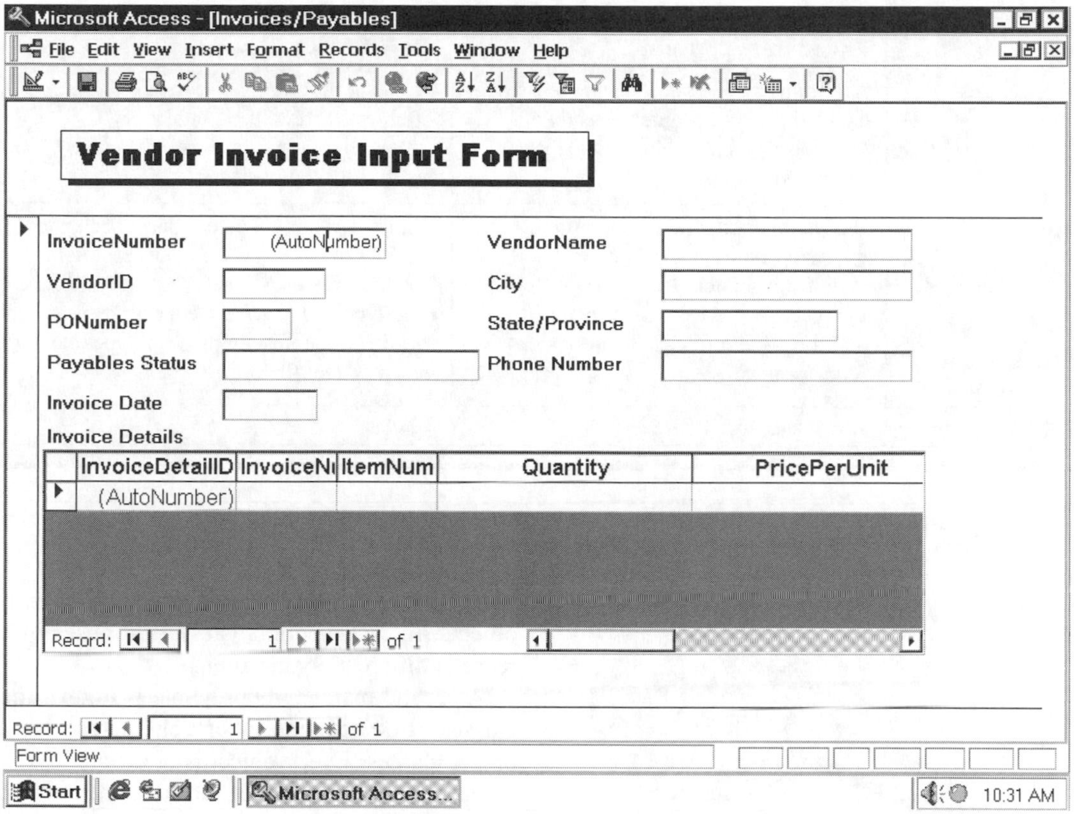

Microsoft Access - [Invoices/Payables]

File Edit View Insert Format Records Tools Window Help

Vendor Invoice Input Form

InvoiceNumber	(AutoNumber)	VendorName	
VendorID		City	
PONumber		State/Province	
Payables Status		Phone Number	
Invoice Date			

Invoice Details

InvoiceDetailID	InvoiceN	ItemNum	Quantity	PricePerUnit
(AutoNumber)				

Record: 1 of 1

Record: 1 of 1

Form View

Start | Microsoft Access... | 10:31 AM

Figure 8.19 Input Form Layout for Vendor Invoice (Screen shot reprinted with permission from Microsoft Corporation).

Check Register

Account Number 2936

	CheckNumber	CheckDate	InvoiceNumber	VendorID	PONumber	InvoiceDate	InvoiceAmount	PaidAmount
	482441	8/3/98	C1523	178	A00702	7/20/98	1,925.50	1,925.50
	482442	8/3/98	1398752	52	C00321	7/24/98	408.92	408.92
	482443	8/3/98	E17982	104	E00052	7/23/98	1,500.00	1,200.00
	482444	8/3/98	175632	89	C00323	7/24/98	10,328.72	10,328.72
TOTAL							14,163.14	13,863.14
	482445	8/4/98	R1689	13	B00824	7/27/98	505.17	505.17
	482446	8/4/98	M568930	97	B00825	7/28/98	12,327.18	11,094.46
	482447	8/4/98	897532	152	A00704	7/28/98	765.15	765.15
	482448	8/4/98	C1527	178	D00376	7/30/98	1,534.83	1,534.83
TOTAL							15,132.33	13,899.61
MONTHLY TOTAL							29,295.47	27,762.75

Figure 8.20 Check Register Report Layout with Sample Data

	Procedural Approach	Object-Oriented Approach
Defining the Task	A team of business managers prepares a detailed design document specifying, as precisely as possible, how the program should do the task.	The O-O programmer searches a library of objects (prewritten chunks of software) looking for those that could be used for the business task.
The Process	Programmers divide up the design and write thousands of lines of code from scratch. If all goes well, the pieces work together as planned and the system fulfills the design requirements.	Within days, a few objects have been put together to create a bare-bones prototype. The business user gets to "test-drive" the prototype and provide feedback; by repeatedly refining and retesting the prototype, the business gets a system that fulfills the task.
Elapsed Time	Months.	Weeks.

Figure 8.21 The Promise of Object-Oriented Approaches (Based on Verity and Schwartz, 1991).

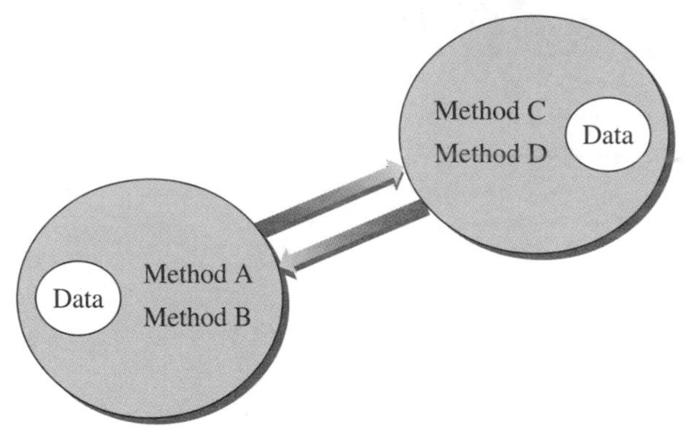

Figure 8.22 Message Passing

Core Concepts

An **object** is a person, place, or thing. However, a key difference between an entity in data modeling and an object is that data attributes as well as the methods (sometimes called operations or behaviors) that can be executed with that data are part of the object structure. The attributes of an object and its methods are *hidden* inside the object. This means that one object does not need to know the details about the attributes and methods of another object. Instead, objects communicate with each other through *messages* that specify what should be done, not how it should be done (see Figure 8.22).

Storing data and related operations together within an object is a key principle of O-O approaches, referred to as **encapsulation**. Encapsulation also means that systems developed using O-O techniques can have loosely coupled modules, which means they can be reused in other O-O applications much more easily. This is why O-O approaches should theoretically result in faster project completion times: New systems can be created from preexisting objects. In fact, vendors can sell libraries of objects for reuse in different organizations.

A second major O-O principle is **inheritance**. That is, classes of objects can inherit characteristics from other object classes. Every object is associated with a *class* of objects that share some of the same attributes and operations. Object classes are also typically arranged in a hierarchy, so that subclasses inherit attributes and operations from a superclass. For example, if a bird is a superclass, the bird object's attributes and operations could be inherited by a specific type of bird, such as a cardinal.

Unified Modeling Language (UML) for O-O Modeling

Techniques and notations for O-O analysis and design modeling have now been standardized under a Unified Modeling Language (UML).

Logical modeling begins with a use-case diagram that captures all the actors and all the actions that they initiate. (The actors are similar to external entities in a data flow diagram.) For example, the actors for a software application to support the renting of videos would include customers who are registered members, noncustomers (browsers) who could choose to become members, a billing clerk, a shipping clerk, and an inventory system. As shown in Figure 8.23, nine different functions initiated by these actors are modeled as Use Cases.

Each Use Case is also described in a text format using a standard template. Common elements in a template are Use Case Name, Actor, Goal, Description, Precondition, and Postcondition, as well as Basic, Alternate, and Exceptional

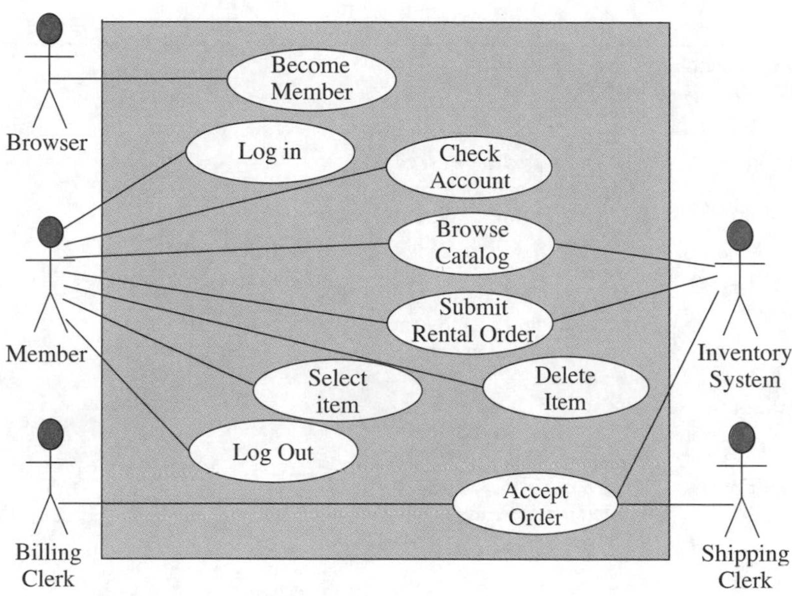

Figure 8.23 Use Case Diagram (Reprinted from Chand, 2003).

Flow events, which describe the actor's actions and the system's response. The events to be documented for one of the use cases (Become Member) in Figure 8.23 are shown in Figure 8.24.

UML also has many other types of diagrams. Three examples for a student registration system are shown in Figure 8.25:

- An extended relationship use-case diagram to logically model event flows beyond initial requirements
- A sequence diagram to capture the messages that pass between object classes
- A class diagram with each object's attributes and methods as well as a model of the relationships between object classes

INFORMATION SYSTEMS CONTROLS TO MINIMIZE BUSINESS RISKS

Suppose you and your partner with whom you have a joint savings account separately go to the bank one day to withdraw the same $500 in savings. Or suppose an inventory clerk enters a wrong part number to record the issue of an item from the storeroom, which results in an out-of-stock status, which automatically generates a purchase order to a supplier, who then begins production, and so on. These situations illustrate just some of the ways in which potential human errors when interacting with information systems can create business risks. However, they are only a small part of the potential risks associated with the use of IT.

Other common system security risks include: (1) risks from criminal acts, (2) risks due to staffing changes and project management deficiencies, and (3) risks from natural disasters. All these risks have the potential for not only dissatisfied customers, but also considerable business expenses for error correction. There is also the risk of potential losses due to lawsuits and negative publicity, which even the world's largest software vendors don't want to receive (see the sidebar entitled "Regaining Customer Trust at Microsoft").

Because of the importance of this subject, elsewhere in this textbook we will also provide discussions of potential IT-related business risks and how to manage them.

Here we discuss some of the management controls to address risks that are specifically associated with the three phases of the software life cycle. Although the security and reliability issues will differ somewhat due to the nature of the software application, this list of control mechanisms provide a starting point for understanding the role of the IS professional (including project managers, analysts, and programmers) in helping to ensure that business risks have been accounted for. However, the identification of potential control risks is to a large extent a business manager's responsibility.

First we describe different types of control mechanisms that need to be considered. Then we describe specific

Use Case Name:	Become Member	
Actors:	Browser	
Goal:	Enroll the browser as a new member	
Description:	The Browser will be asked to complete a membership form. After the Browser submits the application form, the system will validate it and then add the Browser to the membership file and generate a password that is e-mailed to the Browser.	
Pre-condition:	The systems is up and the Browser is logged in as a guest	
Post-condition:	The Member password e-mailed to the Browser/ Member is logged	
Basic Flow		
	Actor action:	System response
	1. This use case begins when the Browser clicks the membership button	
		2. Display the membership form
	3. Browser completes and submits the application	
		4. Check for errors 5. Check the membership database for prior membership 6. Create a password 7. Add new or updated member record to the membership database 8. Send an e-mail to the actor with the password The use case ends
Alternate Flow	Prior membership handling	5.1. Update membership record 5.2. Inform the browser Continue from step 6 of Basic Flow
Exception Flow	Errors in membership application	
		4.1. Identify errors 4.2. Return errors to Browser
	4.3. Browser corrects errors	
		Continue from step 4 of Basic Flow

Figure 8.24 Become Member Use Case (Reprinted from Chand, 2003).

examples of control mechanisms for error detection, prevention, and correction that need to be addressed during the three life cycle phases (Definition, Construction, and Implementation). Although these "proven" mechanisms are recommended responses, both business and IS managers also need to recognize that when new information technologies are introduced they likely will also introduce new control risks.

Types of Control Mechanisms

Control mechanisms include management policies, operating procedures, and the auditing function. Some aspects of control can be built into an information system itself, whereas others are the result of day-to-day business practices and management decisions. Information system controls, for example, are needed to maintain data integrity,

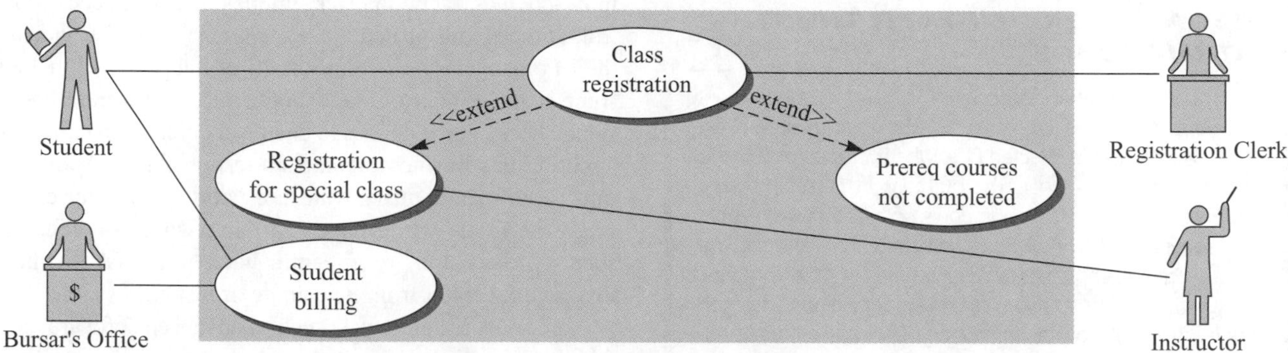

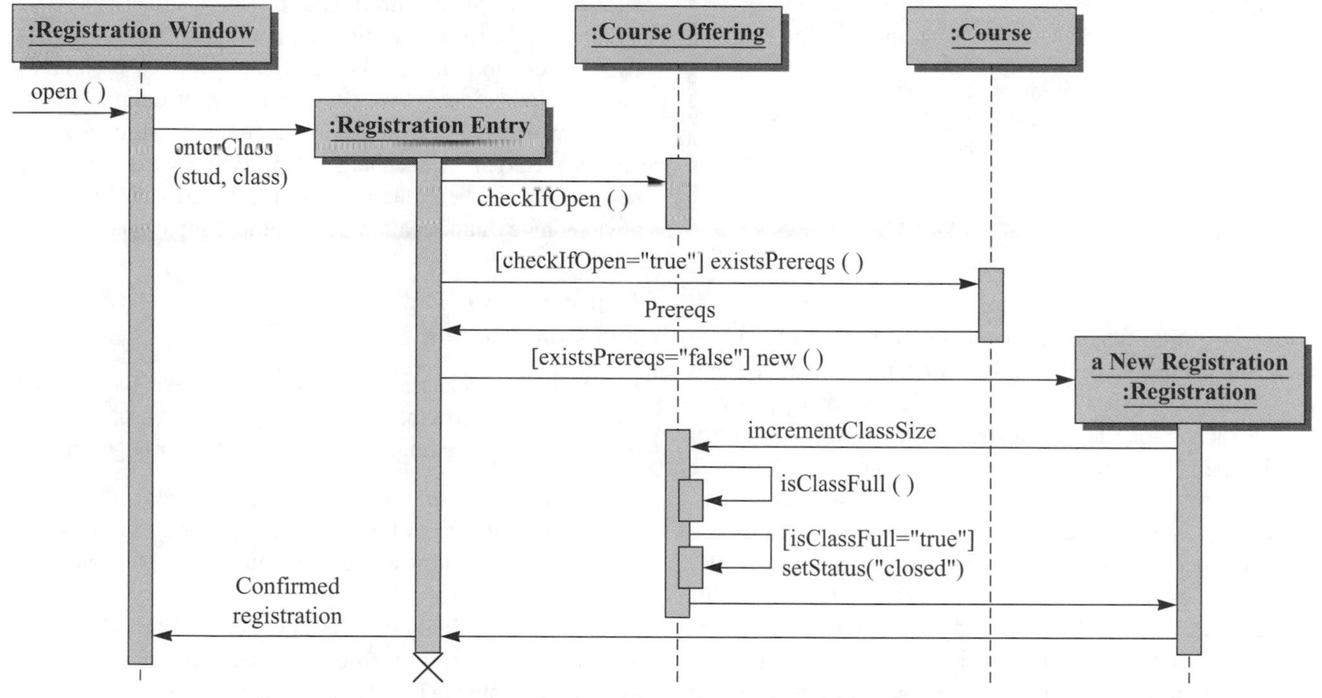

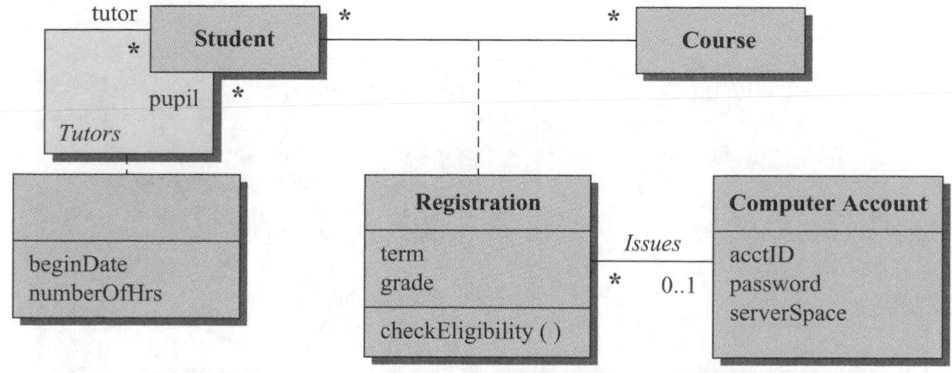

Figure 8.25 UML Diagrams for Student Registration System

REGAINING CUSTOMER TRUST AT MICROSOFT

Computer users worldwide raced to protect themselves from a malicious electronic "worm" designed to allow hackers to gain access to infected PCs. Whatever the origin of the worm, one thing is clear: The outbreak increases pressure on Microsoft to make its Windows software more reliable and secure. In 2002, Bill Gates launched an initiative, called "Trustworthy Computing," to change the way the company designs and builds software. Among other actions, Microsoft added 10 weeks of training for 8,500 of its software engineers. The company also reportedly spent more than $200 million in 2002 to improve the security of its Windows program for corporate servers.

But experts give Microsoft mixed grades for its follow-through, saying the company hasn't changed its methods enough to avoid the kinds of flaws that make attacks by viruses and worms possible in the first place. Ultimately, that could hurt Microsoft where it matters most–in the corporate wallet.

[Adapted from Guth and Bank, 2003]

allow only authorized access, ensure proper system operation, and protect against malfunctions, power outages, and disasters. Throughout the systems development process, the needs for specific controls are identified and control mechanisms are developed to address these needs. Some mechanisms are implemented during the system design, coding, or implementation. Others become part of the routine operation of the system, such as backups and authorization security, and still others involve the use of manual business practices and management policies, such as formal system audits. Figure 8.26 shows some of the control approaches usually employed in the indicated phases of the systems life cycle.

Security controls related to the technology infrastructure—such as backup power supplies, network access control, and firewall protection—are typically the purview of the IS organization. In addition, IS developers will include some standard controls in all applications. However, specifying checks and balances to ensure accurate data entry and handling is a business manager's responsibility. Managers must carefully identify what are valid data, what errors might be made while handling data, what nontechnical security risks are present, and what potential business losses could result from inaccurate or lost data.

Some new technologies, such as advanced software tools for system testing, have improved an organization's control processes, whereas other new technologies (such as Web applications) have introduced new control risks. The increase in distributed computing applications over the past two decades in general has significantly increased a company's reliance on network transmission of data and software—which requires additional technical and managerial controls (Hart and Rosenberg, 1995). Below we discuss only some of the most common control mechanisms that apply to a wide range of application development situations.

Controls in the Definition and Construction Phases

In the initial two phases of the systems life cycle, the accurate and reliable performance of the system can be assured by the use of standards, embedded controls, and thorough testing.

Methodology Standards. The reliable performance of a system depends upon how well it was designed and constructed. No amount of automated checks can override errors in the software itself.

One way to avoid errors is to develop standard, repeatable, and possibly reusable methods and techniques for system developers. The use of standard programming languages and equipment means that systems developers will

Life Cycle Phase	Control Mechanism
Definition and Construction	• Methodology Standards • Validation Rules and Calculations • System Testing
Implementation	• Security • Backup and Recovery • Auditing Roles

Figure 8.26 Pre- and Post-Installation Controls

be more familiar with the tools and will be less likely to make mistakes. A common method is to create a library of frequently used functions (such as calculation of net present value or a sales forecasting model) that different information systems can utilize. Such functions can then be developed and tested with great care and reused as needed, saving development time and reducing the likelihood of design and programming flaws. Most organizations also have standards for designing user interfaces, such as screen and report layout rules and guidelines.

The importance of standards also extends to the documentation of the system during construction and the following period of maintenance and upgrades. If future programmers do not have access to systems documentation that is complete and accurate, they could be unaware of prior changes. Documentation for the system's users also needs to be complete and accurate so that system inputs are not incorrectly captured and system outputs are not incorrectly used.

Validation Rules and Calculations. Each time a data element is updated, the new value can be checked against a legitimate set or range of values permitted for that data. This check can be performed in each application program where these data can be changed (e.g., in a payables adjustment program that modifies previously entered vendor invoices) and in the database where they are stored. Edit rules are also used to ensure that data are not missing, that data are of a valid size and type, and that data match with other stored values.

Providing a screen display with associated data can be a very useful edit check. For example, when a vendor number is entered, the program can display the associated name and address. The person inputting or modifying data can then visually verify the vendor information. Edit rules can also ensure that only numbers are entered for numeric data, that only feasible codes are entered, or that some calculation based on a modified data value is valid. These edit checks are integrity rules that control the data's validity.

Various calculations can be performed to validate processing. Batch totals that calculate the sum of certain data in a batch of transactions can be computed both manually before processing and by the computer during processing; discrepancies suggest the occurrence of data entry errors such as transposition of digits. Though they are not foolproof, such approaches, along with automated edits, go a long way toward assuring valid input.

A **check digit** can be appended to critical identifying numbers such as general ledger account numbers or vendor numbers; the value of this check digit is based on the other digits in the number. This digit can be used to quickly verify that at least a valid, if not correct, code has been entered, and it can catch most common errors.

Business managers and their staffs are responsible for defining the legitimate values for data and where control calculations would be important as a part of the information captured in the data dictionary. Furthermore, business managers must set policy to specify if checks can be overridden and who can authorize overrides. Validation rules should permit business growth and expansion, yet reduce the likelihood of erroneous data.

System Testing. Certainly the most common and effective of all IS controls is complete system testing. Each program must be tested individually and in combination with the other programs in the application. Managers develop test data that have known results. Programs are run with typical and atypical data, correct and erroneous data, and the actual results are compared to what should be produced. Testing occurs not only when systems are initially developed, but also when systems are modified. (See Chapter 9 for a description of additional roles played by users when testing a system.)

Controls in the Implementation Phase

Not all the elements necessary to assure proper systems operation can be built into an application. Avoiding and detecting inappropriate access or use, providing data backups and system recovery capabilities, and formally auditing the system are all ongoing control mechanisms. As mentioned earlier, many application-level controls work in concert with managerial controls. User-managers are responsible for being familiar with any firm-wide control mechanisms and identifying when additional ones are needed for a specific application.

Security. The unauthorized use of data can result in a material loss, such as the embezzlement of funds, or in losses that are harder to measure, such as the disclosure of sensitive data. In any case, the security of data and computers is necessary so that employees, customers, shareholders, and others can be confident that their interactions with the organization are confidential and the business's assets are safe.

Security measures are concerned with both logical and physical access. Logical access controls are concerned with whether users can run an application, whether they can read a file or change it, and whether they can change the access that others have. Managers work with systems personnel to identify and maintain appropriate authorization levels based on work roles and business needs. Two mechanisms for controlling logical access are authentication and authorization (Hart and Rosenberg, 1995):

Authentication involves establishing that the person requesting access is who he or she appears to be. This is typically accomplished by the use of a unique user identifier and a private password.

Authorization involves determining whether or not authenticated users have access to the requested resources. This is typically accomplished by a computer check for permission rights to access a given resource.

Encryption techniques are used to encode data that is transmitted across organizational boundaries. Data may be stored in an encrypted form and then decrypted by the application. Unless a user knows the decryption algorithm, an encrypted file will be unreadable.

The physical security of specific computers and data processing centers must also be established. Badge readers; voice, fingerprint, and retina recognition; or combination locks are common. Formal company statements about computer ethics raise awareness of the sensitivity of data privacy and the need to protect organizational data. When combined with knowledge of the use of transaction or activity logs that record the user ID, network location, time-stamp, and function or data accessed, many security violations could be discouraged.

Because no security system is foolproof, detection methods to identify security breaches are necessary. Administrative practices to help deter computer security abuses have been compiled by Hoffer and Straub (1989). Detection methods include:

- Hiding special instructions in sensitive programs that log identifying data about users
- Analysis of the amount of computer time used by individuals
- Analysis of system activity logs for unusual patterns of use

With the rise of end-user computing and use of the Internet, additional risks due to inappropriate behaviors while using these tools have emerged, as well as issues stemming from work-related use of home PCs. Today, organizations are developing similar controls to manage intranets and access to external Web sites from intranets.

Backup and Recovery. The ultimate protection against many system failures is to have a backup copy. Periodically a file can be copied and saved in a separate location such as a bank vault. Then, when a file becomes contaminated or destroyed, the most recent version can be restored. Of course, any changes since the last copy was made will not appear. Thus, organizations often also keep transaction logs (a chronological history of changes to each file) so these changes can be automatically applied to a backup copy to bring the file up to current status.

A common flaw in backup plans is storing the file backup in the same location as the master file. If stored in the same location, a backup is no more likely to survive a fire, flood, or earthquake than its source file. A secure, offsite location for the backup must be provided, along with a foolproof tracking system.

Some organizations (such as airlines, banks, and telephone networks) can operate only if their online computer systems are working. One approach is to provide redundant systems and operations that "mirror" the production system and data located at a distant facility. This improves the chances of an effective recovery from a widespread power or network outage or a natural disaster. If data recovery processing via another location is immediately available, these locations are known as "hot sites."

Managers and IS professionals together need to determine how frequently backup copies are needed, the business cost of recovering files from backup copies, and how much should be spent on specialized backup resources. As with any security procedure, the ongoing backup and recovery costs need to be in line with the potential organizational benefits and risks.

Auditing Roles. Critical business processes are subject to periodic formal audits to assure that the processes operate within parameters. As more and more organizations have become dependent on information systems in order to operate their business, the importance of IS auditing has increased. IS auditing is still frequently referred to as **EDP auditing**—a name chosen when the term electronic data processing was used to refer to computer operations. EDP auditors use a variety of methods to ensure the correct processing of data, including compliance tests, statistical sampling, and embedded auditing methods.

Compliance tests check that systems builders use high-quality systems development procedures that lead to properly functioning systems. Statistical sampling of a portion of databases can identify abnormalities that indicate systematic problems or security breaches. Embedded auditing methods include reporting triggers programmed into a system that are activated by certain processing events. The flagged records are then analyzed to determine if errors or security breaches are occurring in the system.

The most commonly used EDP auditing technique in the past has been an **audit trail**. Audit trails trace transactions from the time of input through all the processes and reports in which the transaction data are used. Audit trail records typically include program names, user name or user ID, input location and date/time stamps, as well as the transaction itself. An audit trail can help identify where errors are introduced or where security breaches might have occurred.

Managers need to participate in the identification of elements that should be captured in the audit trail to detect errors and assure compliance with all relevant laws and regulations. Furthermore, the frequency and extent of formal information system auditing is a management decision that should take into account the system's breadth and role, its relationship to other business processes, and the potential risks to the firm.

Object-Oriented Development

Just as 4GLs were a revolutionary change in the 1970s, object-oriented (OO) development was a revolutionary change in the 1980s. In fact, companies had a choice. They could choose the evolutionary approach of CASE or the revolutionary approach of OO development. OO development caught on in the early 1980s because of the PC; the graphical user interfaces were developed using objects. Developers just needed to point and click at generic items—menus, dialog boxes, radio buttons, and other graphical components—and then rearrange them to create a screen. This form of programming has come to be known as *visual programming*.

By the end of the 1980s, OO development was beginning to be noticed in IS departments for business applications. That trickle became a tidal wave when client-server systems appeared in the early 1990s, as developers attempted to simplify these extremely complex systems by reusing objects. In the early 1990s, OO system analysis and design techniques began to appear that could be used in conjunction with OO languages such as C++ and Smalltalk.

OO development is not so much a coding technique as a code-packaging technique, notes Brad Cox, an OO development pioneer. An *object* contains some private data (that other objects cannot manipulate) and a small set of operations (called *methods*) that can perform work on that data. When an object receives a request in the form of a message, it chooses the operation that will fulfill that request, it executes the operation on the data supplied by the message, and then it returns the results to the requester.

Combining data and procedures in an object, which is called *encapsulation*, is the foundation of OO development. It restricts the effects of changes by placing a wall of code around each piece of data. Data is accessed through messages that only specify *what* should be done. The object specifies *how* its operations are performed. Thus, a change in one part of a system need not affect the other parts. As you might expect, even though OO development promised significant benefits, it does have costs, especially at the outset. OO projects have gotten stuck in the mire of defining and redefining objects. Once defined, objects can be reused, another of OO's attractions. There are many other aspects of OO development, but this very brief description of objects suffices here. As will be seen later in the chapter, OO is a significant foundation for today's development efforts.

Client-Server Computing

In the 1990s, two developments became the major news: client-server systems and Web-based (or network-centric) development. Underlying these two trends, which continue today, is the increasing use of packages and system integration. As much as possible, companies prefer to buy a package rather than build an application in-house. To develop large applications, they integrate hardware and software components. For example, they buy a ready-made Web browser to become the standard access software for Web-based applications rather than write their own front-end client software. In both realms, the major construction methods are system integration and component-based development.

Client-server systems generated a lot of excitement in the early 1990s because they promised far more flexibility than mainframe-based systems. The desktop and laptop client machines could handle graphics, animation, and video, whereas the servers could handle production updating. It was a clever way to meld the pizzazz of the PC world with the necessary back-end production strengths of the mainframe world, even though mainframes were not always in the picture. The Case Example on page 356 is a typical example of the allure of client-server systems and how one company—MGM—developed its first client-server system.

Client-Server Systems

The 1990s version of distributed systems was client-server systems. This system architecture arose to take advantage of the processing capabilities of both host machines and PCs in the same system. Even though the host could handle huge databases and order processing, the PCs, laptops, and smaller devices could handle graphics, sound, and even video, which were important in some applications.

Client-server computing splits the computing workload between a *client*, which is a computer that makes a request, and a *server*, which answers the request. A request might be to print a document (handled by the print server on the LAN) or it could be a request for the gate number of one's soon-to-leave flight—a request sent by an Internet-enabled cell phone from a taxi and handled by the airline's Web site.

The most famous depiction of client-server computing comes from Gartner EXP. It shows the possibilities for splitting work between clients and servers, as illustrated in Figure 8.27.

As shown in Figure 8.27, the network presents the dividing line between what is housed on a client and what is housed on a server. The three components being split are

CASE EXAMPLE

MGM

Metro-Goldwyn-Mayer (MGM), the movie studio in Hollywood, has an extremely valuable asset: its library of TV shows and movies. The studio's first client-server application was built at the urging of end users to leverage this asset. The vice president of IS knew that the only way to meet the users' expectations for a multimedia, laptop-based system with a graphical interface was to employ client-server technology.

Previously, more than 26 disparate systems on PCs, minicomputers, and the corporate mainframe were used to maintain the rights to show MGM's films. As a result, it was not possible to get a consolidated, world-wide view of which films were being leased. The client-server system—the largest IS project in Hollywood at the time—collected and consolidated all data on the film library so that MGM would know what films it has the rights to license and to whom.

Client-server technology was chosen because it could empower MGM's 20 worldwide film-rights salespeople. They could visit the head of a cable TV network anywhere in the world with an SQL database on their laptop and built-in CD-ROM capabilities to play 20- to 30-second clips of their films. They could browse the laptop's inventory database to verify availability of films and then print the licensing deal memo on the spot. Details of the deal could then be transmitted to headquarters when convenient. Only a client-server system would provide this flexibility.

The System's Three-Level Architecture

The system's architecture had three layers. At the core was an AS/400, which acted as the central processor for the database that contains descriptions of 1,700 TV shows and movies, an index, the availability of movies in different regions, license time periods, status of bills, and so forth. MGM deliberately chose a tried-and-tested rights licensing software package to manage the database because it provided the needed processing; however, it did not support graphical interfaces, laptops, or decision support. Therefore, MGM surrounded the package with the most-tested technology possible for the client-server components. In fact, wherever possible,MGM minimized technical risk by using proven products.

The second layer was an HP 9000 server, which contained data and processing, but no presentation software. The Unix front end was built using Power-Builder. In 1 hour with Power-Builder, developers could do 8 to 10 hours of COBOL-equivalent work.

The third layer was the client machines, either desktop or laptop. They contained local processing, local databases, and presentation software. The laptops also had a database for the salespeople. They could upload and download information from their laptops via dial-up lines.

The premier skill required in this environment was systems integration. The developers needed both hardware and software expertise for Unix and NT, PowerBuilder, and SQL Windows.

The Development Environment

Even though partnering was always possible in the mainframe era, it was mandatory with client-server computing. With tools like PowerBuilder and a development life cycle that relied on prototyping, developers had to constantly interact with users. They could not seclude themselves for months. Moreover, client-server teams had no boss. The users and developers were equal; neither told the other what to do.

The role of IS at MGM changed from system development and delivery to one of cooperating and partnering. This change required a huge cultural shift in the roles and attitudes of the IS staff. Developers who formerly buried themselves in code had to conduct meetings and work side-by-side with users. In short, they had to learn people (interpersonal) skills and the business. Interestingly, the CIO felt that women had an edge because, generally speaking, they had better interpersonal skills.

With client-server systems, the hardware was cheaper than with mainframe systems, development was faster, and software support was cheaper—all by orders of magnitude. Operating costs were more expensive than MGM expected because version control of client-server software and service and systems management were more costly.

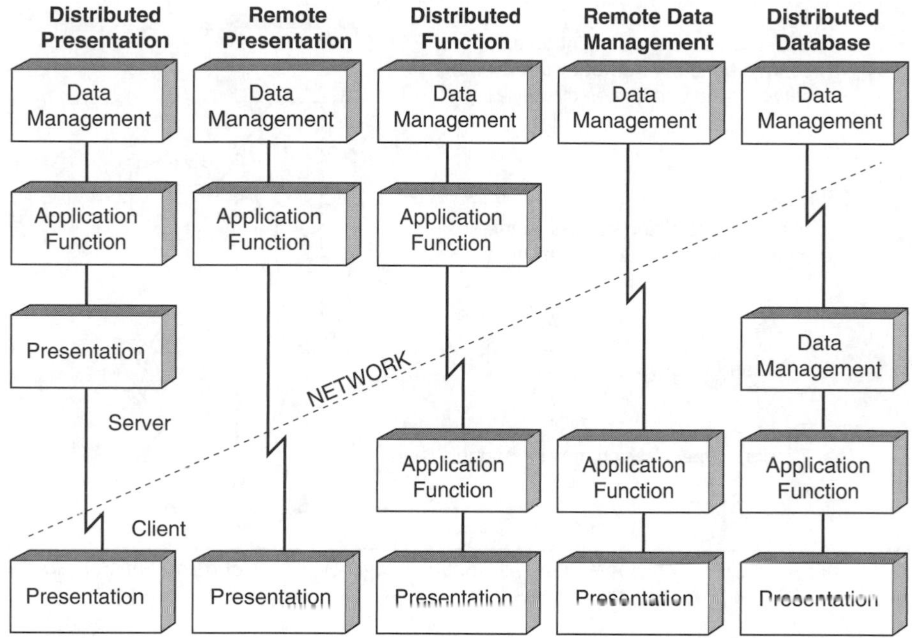

Figure 8.27 Client Server Computing. *Source:* Roger Woolfe, *Managing the Move to Client-Server,* Wentworth Research Program (now part of Gartner EXP, 56 Top Gallant, Stamford, CT 06904), January 1995.

the presentation software (what the user sees on the screen), the application itself, and the data management software. Briefly, from left to right, the spectrum is as follows:

- ***Distributed presentation*** puts all the data, all the application software, and some of the presentation software on a server. Only part of the presentation is on the client. This approach is one way to leave a mainframe-based legacy system in place while updating user screens, making them graphical rather than character based, for example. This approach is also likely for wireless Web-based computing.
- ***Remote presentation*** puts all the presentation software on the client machine but leaves the applications and data on the remote server. This approach also is a way to preserve a legacy system and simply update the face it shows users. It has been used to put transaction processing behind Web sites.
- ***Distributed function*** places all the presentation software on the client, all the data on the server, and splits the application software between the client and the server. This option is quite complex, because splitting application processing between two machines requires coordination. However, it might be the most appropriate option for applications that run packaged software, such as spreadsheets or word processing, on a client in combination with corporate applications on a mainframe. It can also be appropriate for wireless computing and for major front-end applications, such as order entry, inventory inquiry, and so on. E-mail systems use this alternative: part of the processing on the client, part on the servers.
- ***Remote data management*** places all presentation and application software on the client, leaving only data and data management software on the server. This option is popular because it keeps all application software in one place (on a *fat client*) and takes advantage of the huge processing capacity of today's PCs. Although this solution is less complex, it has the disadvantage of requiring all the machines to be updated at the same time with a new release of the software. This level of coordination can be difficult unless all the machines are under a rigorous systems management system that routinely updates them when they connect to the corporate network.
- ***Distributed database*** places all presentation and application software as well as some of the data on the client. The remaining data is on the server. It is a complex solution, especially if the numerous databases are intended to remain in sync. Even so, it is an important option used in mobile computing, where,

Tier 3
Superserver, often a mainframe, connected to the network via one or more servers, and sometimes directly as well

Tier 2
Multiple specialized servers, some possibly dedicated to middleware

LANs and WANs

Tier 1
Clients, some of which may be portable

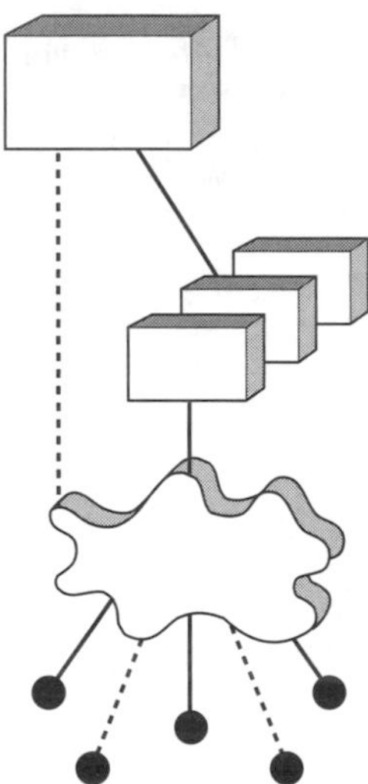

Figure 8.28 The Trend to Three-Tier Client-Server Arrangements. *Source:* Roger Woolfe, *Managing the Move to Client-Server,* Wentworth Research Program (now part of Gartner EXP, 56 Top Gallant, Stamford, CT 06904), January 1995.

for instance, each salesperson needs some data locally (probably the less dynamic data). Up-to-the-second data can be stored on the master database and accessed only when needed. This option also leads to fat client machines.

Another way to look at client-server systems is to view their architecture. The preferred architecture has been three tiered, notes Roger Woolfe. As Figure 8.28 shows, tier 3 is the superserver, perhaps a mainframe or a cluster of Web site servers. It can be connected directly to an in-house client-server network or it may be routed through tier 2 servers to the network. Companies have chosen this latter option to extend the life of their still-good-but-old legacy applications. Short-lived and fast-changing data, as well as corresponding integrity rules, are also stored at this superserver level so that the data can be shared.

Tier 2 is specialized servers. Data specific to departments or work groups is stored here, as is data that does not change often yet requires rapid retrieval. Tier 2 also houses *middleware*, or software that eases connection between clients and servers. Middleware became an important concept in client-server systems because it performs translations between disparate systems. With middleware, a major application written for UNIX can later be used to support Windows or Linux without needing to be rewritten. Without middleware, companies would be hard-pressed to serve a proliferation of new kinds of computing devices with their existing systems.

Tier 1 is the clients, either desktop or portable, connected via some sort of network.

The alternative architecture is two tier, consisting of only clients and servers or clients and a mainframe. The three-tiered architecture reduces client complexity by decreasing the number of interfaces that need to be accommodated by client machines. The drawback is that clients are more complex and access to tier 3 data is slower than to tier 2. Woolfe presents a case of a company that uses two of Gartner's client-server approaches in a three-tier architecture. That story appears on pages 360–361.

Benefits of Client-Server Computing. Client-server computing promised numerous benefits in the early 1990s. The following ones have held true. The primary benefit of client-server computing was to give people access to data or information when they needed it. This capability was especially pertinent to salespeople, who, for example, wanted to download information about customer orders from a central database using a PC while at the customer's site.

Retail chains have also used client-server systems to look into their stores to see what is selling, what is in inventory, and what is on order. Greater precision helps them keep less stock on hand and replenish inventory more on a just-in-time basis. It also lets them more closely watch the market and react to changes faster. Client-server computing has shifted the focus of computing from keeping track of the business to using information to fulfill strategic objectives.

Client-server computing also blended the autonomy of PCs with the systemwide rules and connectivity of traditional systems. This combination turned traditional computing on its head, reversing the role of the host and PCs.

Whereas the host was previously the focus of attention, in client-server computing, PCs are. This change shifted the focus of computing to end users, empowering employees, especially those who directly serve customers.

Client-server systems have also been used to streamline workflows by encouraging people to work together via networks, giving them powerful local processing power as well as access to other people and internal and external information.

Most powerfully of all, client-server computing supports new organizational structures via its connectivity. By providing a platform that supports individuals and groups who are geographically dispersed, it allows companies to experiment with dispersed work groups. In fact, experience with these technologies and their infrastructure enabled companies to more easily take advantage of the Internet. It is like a big client-server system.

However, client-server systems have not been lower in cost than mainframe systems (as first touted), because they entail so much coordination. What initially looked like simple connections between clients and servers has turned into large, often fragile, complex systems. Although client-server systems are easier for end users to use, they are far more complex for IS organizations to manage. Day-to-day management of the complex infrastructure, where servers can be in hundreds of locations, is a costly part of client-server systems.

On the human side, the systems led to organizational turmoil as people dealt with cross-boundary data flow, empowered employees, and cultural differences between people using the same data. The biggest changes were thus often organizational and cultural.

INFORMATION SECURITY

Whereas information security used to be an arcane, technical topic, even CEOs know about it today due to the importance of electronic information in running their businesses. Actually, all business executives now need to understand Internet-based threats and countermeasures and continually fund security work to protect their businesses.

As one security officer told us:

If I were an e-tailer, I might not call the Internet a bad neighborhood, but I would certainly "watch my back." My equivalent brick-and-mortar store would have automatic locks on the doors, cameras watching every aisle, and only $20 in the safe, because I would never know what kinds of thieves might show up or what kinds of attacks they might launch—from anywhere in the world. Furthermore, as an e-tailer, I would need more security than a brick-and-mortar store manager because customers can get a lot closer to the guts of my business.

The Threats

Since 1996, the Computer Security Institute and the San Francisco Federal Bureau of Investigation Computer Intrusion Squad have conducted an annual survey of U.S. security managers to uncover the types of computer crimes committed, the countermeasures being taken, and other aspects of cybercrimes. The Spring 2004 survey report (which covers 2003) contains responses from 494 computer security practitioners from a wide range of enterprises—government and private industry and from those with fewer than 99 employees to those with over 50,000 employees. Two of the report's key findings relate to threats:

- The unauthorized use of computers is declining.
- The most expensive cybercrime was denial of service.

The Unauthorized Use of Computers Is Declining. As shown in Figure 8.30, attacks on computer systems or detected misuses are declining. The largest declines from the 2003 to the 2004 report are the 18 percent drop in enterprises reporting insider abuse of Internet access, the 20 percent drop in enterprises reporting denial-of-service attacks, and the 10 percent drop in those reporting theft of proprietary information. For the first time, the survey asked about three new types of cybercrimes: abuse of wireless networks (15 percent reported experiencing this abuse), misuse of public Web applications (10 percent reported this occurring), and defacement of a Web site (7 percent reported occurrences). Every respondent reported experiencing a Web site incident, but 89 percent reported only 1 to 6 occurrences. Only 11 percent had more than 6 incidents.

The Most Expensive Cybercrime Was Denial of Service. For the 5 previous years, the security breach that caused the greatest financial losses was theft of proprietary information. But in 2003, it was denial of service, resulting in over $26 million in losses (versus $11 million from theft of proprietary information, the second-highest amount), as shown in Figure 8.31. The report authors speculate that this shift may have occurred because of the greater number of viruses in 2003 that unleashed denial-of-service attacks, such as MyDoom.

A related and important finding was that reported losses from security breaches decreased—from $201 million in the 2003 report to $141 million in the 2004 report—whereas the number of respondents reporting loss estimates

CASE EXAMPLE

AN AEROSPACE COMPANY

A corporate enterprise systems group develops systems for use across the company. The group's goal is to never again build monolithic applications. Instead, it intends to build systems—even million-dollar systems—from off-the-shelf hardware and software components.

The Software

All the client-server systems use the same structure, with application code on the clients, data on the servers, and communication middleware shared between them. The software is written using object-oriented technology, and most of it comes from an object-oriented component library.

The Data

The heart of the architecture is a repository, which allows reuse of objects. The repository holds *metadata*: information about the data being used. This repository lets developers build sets of common data under the auspices of an enterprise master database, so data elements have common definitions. When in use, data is split between operational data in production systems and data warehouses, which are updated daily via replication software.

The Network

The network is an integral part of this architecture. Each company site has three components: desktop machines, servers, and one or more site hubs. Each of these components uses standard, plug-in equipment; thus, the architecture can be used anywhere in the world. To cope with the increased networking demands of client-server systems, the company is migrating from Ethernet to the higher-speed Asynchronous Transfer Mode (ATM) network. The conversion takes place at each site hub.

The applications communicate to a site hub (a gateway), which plugs into the public telephone network, forming a ring structure of ATM switches. The speed of the ring is 600 mbps. (See Figure 8.29.)

The Architecture

The client-server architecture is *remote data management,* to use the Gartner terminology. Data resides on servers, and applications reside on clients. The company chose this approach because it discovered that only 5 to 6 percent of the average PC is utilized. The company plans to use the remaining 94 to 95 percent of spare desktop capacity for application code.

The company also uses the *distributed function* approach, but only on a few complex systems, because this approach requires more effort than remote data management.

The *distributed presentation* and *remote presentation* approaches do not take full advantage of the spare PC capacity, so they are not used. The company also does not plan to use the distributed database approach, where databases are housed on client machines, because it is just too complex. The client machines must be polled to get the data, which is impractical except for highly structured workflow applications or conversation-oriented applications, such as Lotus Notes.

In short, the company uses the distributed function and remote data management configurations because they minimize total costs. The company's migration strategy has been first to build the architecture and then to build applications using as many reusable components as possible.

actually increased from previous years. For the 2004 report, 269 of the 484 respondents provided loss estimates.

Although down, financial fraud is still a major threat. The 2002 CSI/FBI report discussed it in more detail. Credit card information is the single most commonly traded financial instrument for attackers, states the report. This can be sold, used to buy things, or traded. No data of value should be stored on Web servers, recommends the report. Data should be stored in back-end database servers, and communications with front-end Web servers should be restricted and watched very carefully. See page 364.

RSA Security Inc., a prominent, long-time network security firm, notes that it is easier to guard a bank vault than to guard every house in town. That is why many

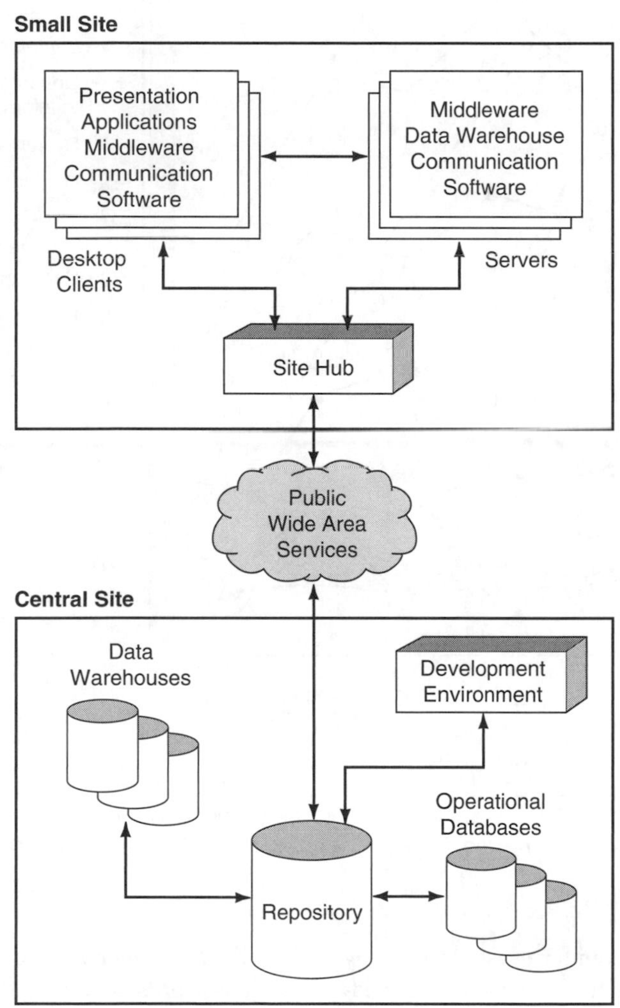

Figure 8.29 The Company's Distributed System Architecture

companies are outsourcing their data center operations to data center specialists with vault-like security.

Mobile computing and telecommuting also increase the possibility for cybercrime because the greater number of network openings provides more opportunities for illegal entry. E-commerce sites are also open to everyone, including hackers. And because the Internet does not have intrinsic security protocols, this public space is vulnerable.

In addition, the hacker community has become "a public club," says RSA, with hacker Web sites and newsgroups available to anyone who wants to learn hackers' tricks. Furthermore, hacker tools are becoming increasingly sophisticated and easier to use; and they are continually

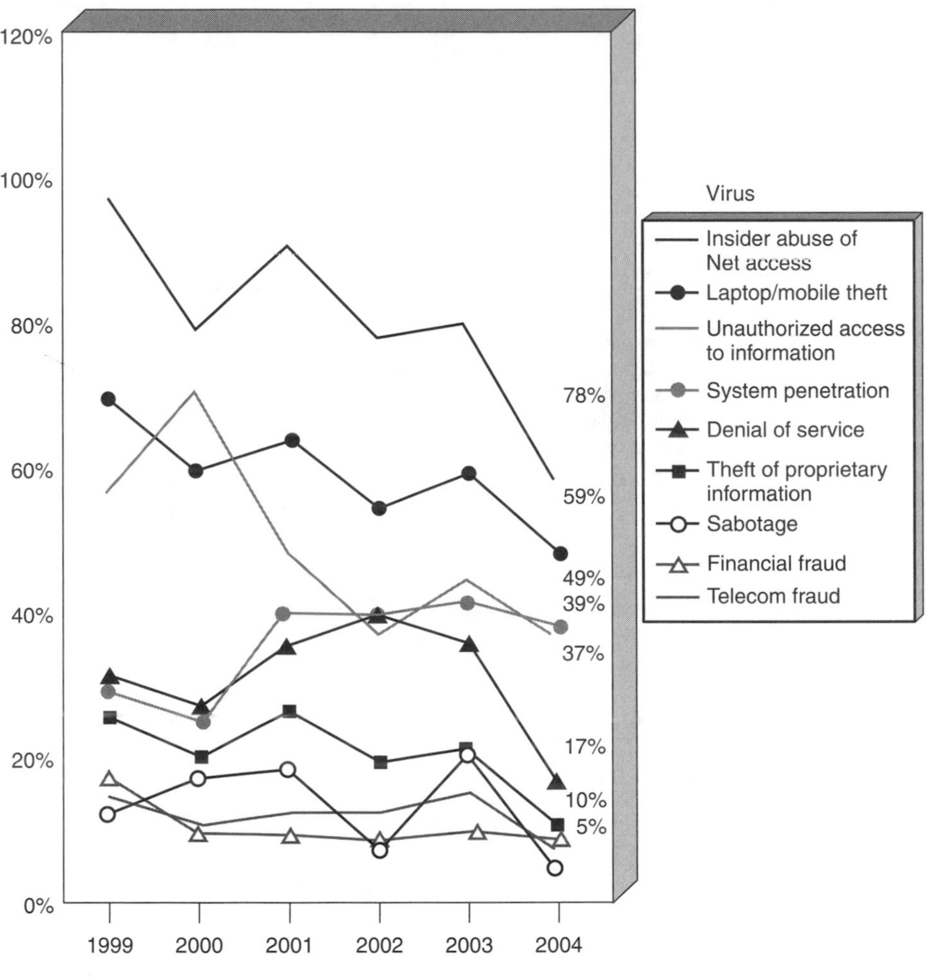

Figure 8.30 Types of Attacks or Misuse Detected in the Last 12 Months (by percent). *Source:* Reprinted with permission of Computer Security Institute, *2004 CSI/FBI Computer Crime and Security Survey,* Computer Security Institute, San Francisco, CA, www.gosci.com, Spring 2004.

being revised to outsmart the countermeasures used by companies to protect themselves. It has become a cat-and-mouse game of a continual one-upmanship. Securing an online business is not a one-shot deal; it requires constant vigilance.

RSA describes the following nine approaches hackers use:

1. *Cracking the password.* Guessing someone's password is easier than most people think, says RSA, because some people do not use passwords, others use the word "password," and still others use easy-to-remember words such as their child's name, a sports team, or a meaningful date. Hackers also use software that can test out all combinations, which is called brute force password detection.
2. *Tricking someone.* To get users to divulge their passwords, a con artist calls up an employee posing as a network administrator who needs the employee's password to solve an immediate (fictitious) network problem. It happens more than you think, says RSA.
3. *Network sniffing.* Hackers launch software that monitors all traffic looking for passwords or other valuable information. Because most network traffic is in clear text rather than encrypted (appearing as gibberish), sniffing can find information and write it to a file for later use.
4. *Misusing administrative tools.* Helpful tools can be turned against a network. For example, a well-known program written to uncover weak spots in a

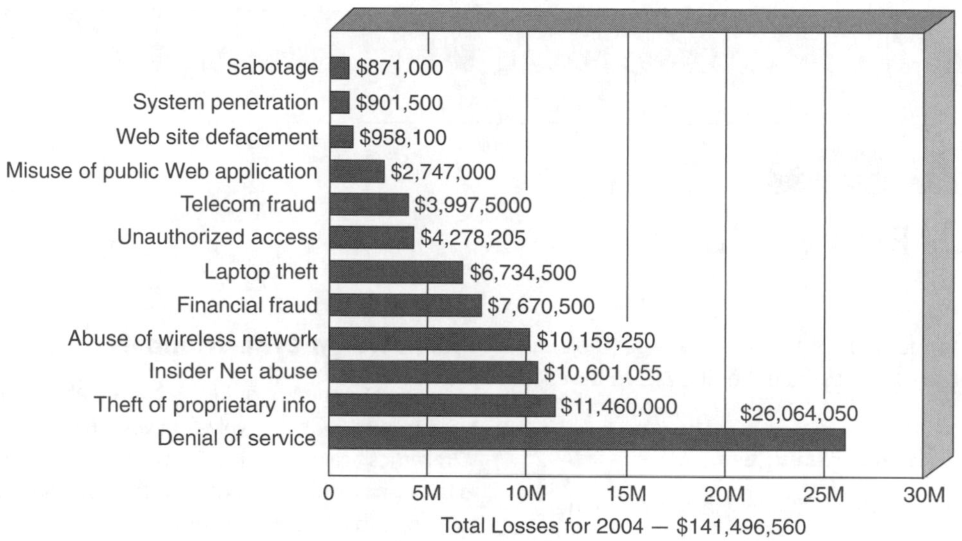

Figure 8.31 Dollar Amount of Losses by Type. *Source:* Reprinted with permission of Computer Security Institute, *2004 CSI/FBI Computer Crime and Security Survey,* Computer Security Institute, San Francisco, CA www.gosci.com, Spring 2004.

network, which is important for network administrators, has been used by hackers to find weak spots in target companies' networks. Interestingly, the program's name is Satan.

5. *Playing middleman.* Placing oneself between two communicating parties and either substituting one's own information in place of one of the parties' information or denying one party access to a session, such as denying a competitor access to an important online auction, is another common ploy.
6. *Denial of service.* This tactic floods a party, such as a Web site, with so much useless traffic that the site becomes overwhelmed and freezes. Legitimate messages are locked out, essentially shutting down the business for a period of time.
7. *Trojan horse.* A malicious program can be housed inside an innocent one or, worse yet, one that appears to be helpful.
8. *Viruses.* These pieces of software run without permission. Their most common entry point has been as e-mail attachments. Once such an attachment is opened, the program is released and performs its task, such as destroying files (a worm) or replicating itself in e-mails sent to everyone in the e-mail directory. Internet-based viruses have attracted lots of attention, not just for PCs, but for wireless devices as well.
9. *Spoofing.* By masquerading as a legitimate IP address, hackers can gain access to a site. A site can masquerade as another Web site and redirect traffic to a fraudulent look-alike site that, for example, allows credit card information to be captured for later use.

Security's Five Pillars

Five pillars make up today's security techniques, says RSA.

1. *Authentication:* Verifying the authenticity of users
2. *Identification:* Identifying users to grant them appropriate access
3. *Privacy:* Protecting information from being seen
4. *Integrity:* Keeping information in its original form
5. *Nonrepudiation:* Preventing parties from denying actions they have taken.

Authentication. *Authentication* means verifying someone's authenticity. They are who they say they are. People can authenticate themselves to a system in three basic ways, says RSA: by something they know, something they have, and something they are. "Something they know" means "something only they know," generally a password or a mother's maiden name, for example. "Something they have" means "in your possession." In computer security, one possibility is a token that generates a code a user enters into the computer to gain access to, say, an e-mail system. Users just have to remember not to lose the token. Or they may have a digital certificate, which will be discussed shortly. "Something they are" generally means a physical characteristic, such

CASE EXAMPLE

CREDIT CARD FRAUD

A major problem is the theft of large numbers of credit card records. Here are two examples from the 2002 CSI/FBI report.

One Bug in a Software Package

In one case, MSNBC reported that a bug in one shopping cart software product used by 4,000 e-commerce sites exposed customer records at those sites. The FBI issued a public warning, but one small e-commerce site did not receive this warning message because it had bought the software through a reseller.

Within days, cybercriminals charged thousands of dollars on the credit cards of users of this small site, buying phone cards, gambling at gambling sites, and buying software off the Web. Instructions on taking advantage of the flaw circulated on the Internet underground, the URLs of other companies that did not obtain the patch were posted on chat rooms, and cybercriminals could even pick up the URLs using search engines.

Two Foreign Cybercriminals

The U.S. Department of Justice has a Web site that describes past cybercrimes. One involves two Russians who committed 20 crimes against two U.S. banks that offer online banking and a U.S. online credit card company. The two stole 56,000 credit card numbers, bank account information, and other personal financial information. Then they tried to extort money from the cardholders and the banks, threatening to publicize the sensitive information they had unearthed.

They also used the stolen credit card numbers to establish fake e-mail accounts, which they used to act as fake sellers and fake winning bidders on online auctions; they paid themselves using the stolen credit card numbers.

They gained access to this information by taking unauthorized control over many computers, including one belonging to a school district. They then used these compromised computers to commit their crimes. The Moscow computer crime unit worked with the FBI to apprehend these cybercriminals. It often takes such international cooperation to fight cybercrime. Power notes that this one case is just an indication of what is happening.

as a fingerprint, retinal scan, or voice print. These characteristics fall under the area called *biometrics*. Each type of user authentication has its strengths and weaknesses. RSA recommends choosing two of the three, which is called *two-factor authentication*.

Identification. *Identification* is the process of issuing and verifying access privileges, like being issued a driver's license, RSA says. First, you must show proof of identity to get your license. Once you receive your license, it becomes your proof of identity, but it also states your driving privileges (able to drive an automobile but not a truck or a bus). Therefore, identification is like being certified to be able to do certain things.

In the Internet world, identification is moving toward application-level security, says RSA; that is, authentication for each application. It requires users to sign on for each application, which many feel is a large burden. Some companies are taking a single sign-on approach.

Data Privacy and Data Integrity. These mean keeping information from being seen (*privacy*) or changed (*integrity*). Both are especially important when information travels through the Internet because it is a public space where interception is more possible. The most common method of protecting data is encryption, to be discussed shortly.

Nonrepudiation. *Nonrepudiation* means that neither party in a sale or communication of sensitive information can later deny that the transaction or information exchange took place. Nonrepudiation services can prove that someone was the actual sender and the other the receiver; no imposter was involved on either side.

Management Countermeasures

The major problem these days, notes RSA, is that enterprises cannot have both access to information and airtight security at the same time. Due to online commerce, companies want unimpeded information flow among a complex set of alliance partners. Thus, it is no longer feasible to define *good* as "inside the network" and *bad* as "outside the network," as in the past. Today, companies must make trade offs between absolute information security and efficient flow of information. Although they might think technology can solve security loopholes, the human dimension is equally important—making employees cognizant of security threats they may encounter and teaching them how to strengthen the company's security measures. Today, due to the importance of computers in company operations, security decisions are not just technical; they are being influenced by business managers, which affects the bottom line.

The 2004 CSI/FBI Computer Crime and Security Survey had five key findings that relate to how companies are managing security and the security management policies they have put in place.

- Most organizations evaluate the return on their security expenditures.
- Over 80 percent conduct security audits.
- The percentage of organizations reporting cybercrimes to law enforcement declined.
- Most do not outsource cybersecurity.
- Most respondents view security awareness training as important.

Most Organizations Evaluate the Return on Their Security Expenditures. For the first time, the CSI/FBI survey asked how managers quantify the costs and benefits of their security expenditures, because the report's authors note that there has been considerable discussion in security circles about how to evaluate these investments. The survey found that 55 percent of the respondents measure value on return on investment, whereas 28 percent use internal rate of return and 25 percent use net present value.

On the subject of budgets, 46 percent of the respondents spend between 1 and 5 percent of their IT budget on security, 16 percent spend less than 1 percent, 12 percent spend more than 5 percent, and 14 percent did not know how much their organization spends on security. Even more interesting is security expenditures per employee. Economies of scale turn out to be significant. For example, on average, firms with less than $10 million in annual revenue spend about $500 a year per employee on security ($163 on capital investments and $334 on operating expenses), whereas firms with over $1 billion in revenue spend only $110 a year ($30 on capital investments and $82 on operating expenses), on average. The smaller firms spend over four times as much!

Over 80 Percent Conduct Security Audits. As the 2004 CSI/FBI report notes, industry literature has long recommended that firms begin a security program by conducting an audit, but until this survey, no one had surveyed the prevalence of this practice. The survey found that 82 percent of the respondents conduct security audits. However, the report authors were surprised that this figure was not higher. Because it is such a well-known practice, they wonder why the other 18 percent are not conducting audits.

The Percentage of Organizations Reporting Cybercrimes to Law Enforcement Declined. Although organizations may be willing to estimate cybercrime losses for the CSI/FBI survey and to conduct internal security audits, they apparently are not so willing to make the incidents public. Figure 8.32 shows the four ways organizations respond to a security breach: patch the hole, do not report the breach, report it to law enforcement, report it to legal counsel. As the figure shows, 91 percent patch the hole, 48 percent do not share information about the incident with others (the same percentage as in 1999), and only 20 percent report it to law enforcement—a significant downward trend.

Why not report an incident? The CSI/FBI survey found that 51 percent do not report a cybercrime to law enforcement because the negative publicity would hurt their stock price or their corporate image. Some 35 percent do not report incidents because they believe a competitor will use that information to its advantage. Only 20 percent see a civil remedy as the best course to take (hence, a reason to report a crime). And even though organizations may be aware of law enforcement's interest, they do not see that as sufficient reason to report a security breach. So there is not as much sharing of cybercrime information as some would hope.

Most Do Not Outsource Cybersecurity. A new question asked on the 2004 CSI/FBI 2004 survey was whether organizations outsource their cybersecurity function. The survey found that 63 percent do not outsource any cybersecurity function, and only 7 percent outsource more than 20 percent of their cybersecurity function. The report authors imply that they expect cybersecurity outsourcing to increase.

A related new question was whether the organizations purchase insurance to manage cybersecurity risks. Such insurance is available, and the survey found that 28 percent have taken it out. The report authors believe that more organizations will purchase such insurance in the future.

Most Respondents View Security Awareness Training as Important. Even though most organization see training as being important, a high percentage of respondents believe that their organization is not doing enough such training. They believe that employees especially need training with regards to the organization's security policy, network security, access control systems, and security management.

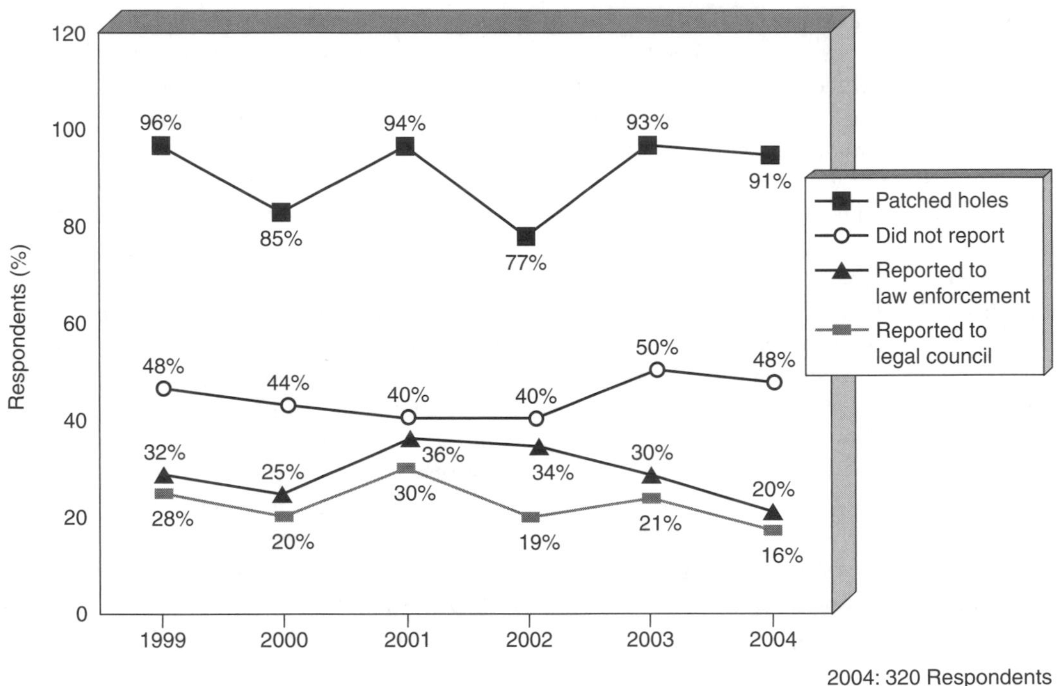

Figure 8.32 If your organization has experienced computer intrusion(s) within the last 12 months, which of the following actions did you take? *Source:* Reprinted with permission of Computer Security Institute, *2004 CSI/FBI Computer Crime and Security Survey*, Computer Security Institute, San Francisco, CA, www.gosci.com, Spring 2004.

Because airtight security is not possible, companies need to prioritize their risks and work on safeguarding against the greatest threats. To give an example of one company's approach to overall network security, consider the case from a Gartner EXP report on page 371.

Technical Countermeasures

The trend in computer security is toward policy-based management: defining security policies and then centrally managing and enforcing those policies via security management products and services. Hence, for example, a user authenticates to a network once, and then a rights-based system gives that user access only to the systems to which the user has been given the rights. A finance employee might have the rights to company finance records, but a manufacturing employee might not.

Figure 8.33 shows the types of security technologies used by the 494 security managers in the 2004 CSI/FBI survey. Some 99 percent use antivirus software, 98 percent use firewalls, and 71 percent use server-based access control lists.

To explain a bit more about countermeasures, following are three techniques used by companies to protect themselves: firewalls, encryption, and virtual private networks (VPNs).

Firewalls. To protect against hacking, companies install *firewalls*, which are hardware or software that controls access between networks. Firewalls are widely used to separate intranets and extranets from the Internet, giving only employees or authorized business partners access to the network. Typically implemented on a router, firewalls perform their job by filtering message packets to block illegal traffic, where "illegal" is defined by the security policy or by a proxy server, which acts as an intermediary server between, say, the Internet and the intranet. Proxy servers can look deeper into traffic than do packet filters, which just look at the header information on each packet. However, proxy servers are slower than packet filters. Some products perform both. Without policy management, says RSA, firewalls may not be effective because they may just be treated as stand-alone devices. The most effective security programs create layers of security.

Encryption. To protect against sniffing, messages can be encrypted before being sent over the Internet. Two classes of encryption methods are in use today: secret key encryption

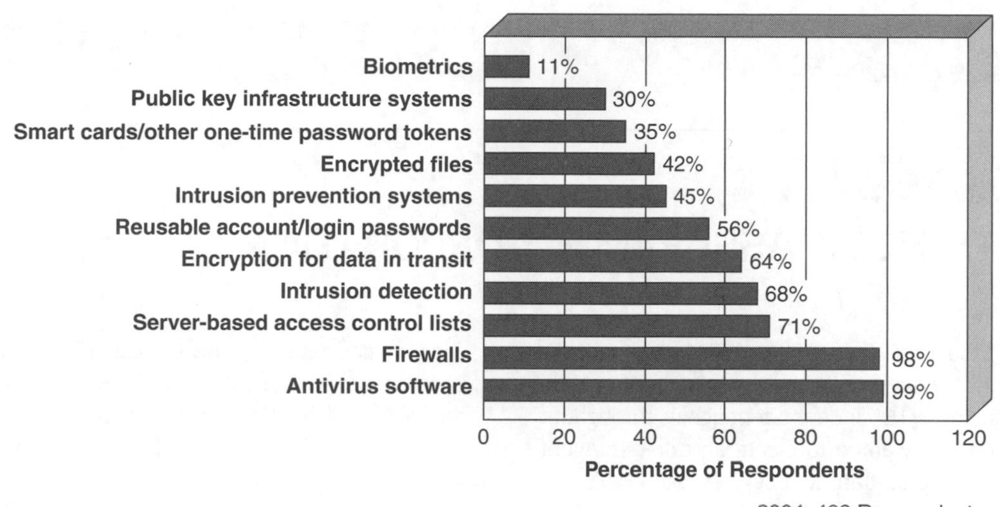

Figure 8.33 Security Technologies Used. *Source:* Reprinted with permission of Computer Security Institute, *2004 CSI/FBI Computer Crime and Security Survey*, Computer Security Institute, San Francisco, CA, www.gosci.com, Spring 2004.

and public key encryption. The most common secret key method is the Data Encryption Standard (DES) developed by IBM, the National Security Agency, and the National Bureau of Standards. Using this method, sender and receiver use the same key to code and decode a message. The level of security is a function of the size of the key. DES is widely used and available in many software applications.

The most common public key encryption method is RSA, named for the three developers: Rivest, Shamir, and Adleman. To send an encrypted message using RSA, two keys are necessary: a public key and a private key. As its name implies, the public key is known to many people and is not kept secret. However, the private key must be kept secret. The two keys are used to code and decode messages; a message coded with one can only be decoded with the other.

Figure 8.34 shows how an encrypted message is sent. First the message is encrypted using the receiver's public key. The message is now secure—it can only be decoded using the receiver's private key, which is only known to the receiver. Note that the sender uses the receiver's public key, not a key belonging to the sender. If a secure message is to be sent back to the original sender, then the public key of the original sender would be used. Thus, for two-way secure communications, both parties must have a set of keys.

The RSA method is incorporated into all major Web browsers and is the basis for the Secure Socket Layer (SSL) used in Internet communications. However, full two-way secure communication requires all parties to have a public and private key. Most individuals do not have such keys, so most B2C applications requiring encryption, such as for the transmission of credit card numbers, are only secure from the consumer to the merchant, not from the merchant to the consumer.

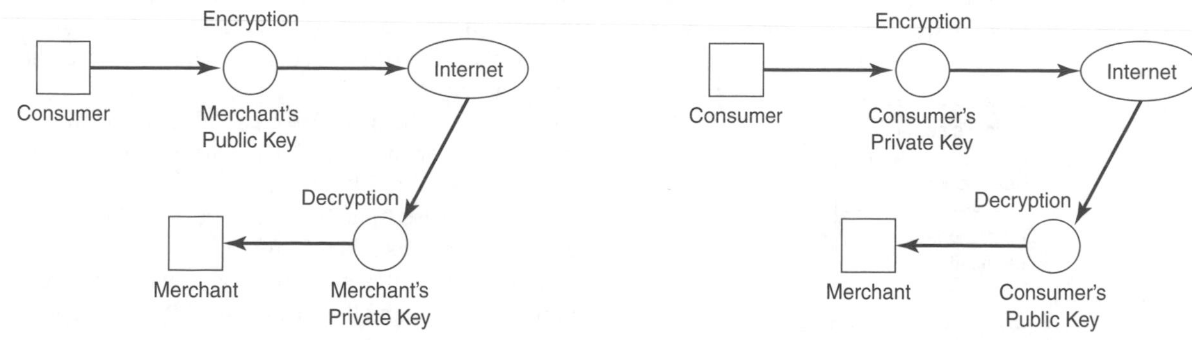

Figure 8.34 Sending an Encrypted Message

Figure 8.35 Sending a Digital Signature

CASE EXAMPLE

PLYMOUTH ROCK ASSURANCE CORPORATION

Plymouth Rock Assurance Corporation (PRAC), with headquarters in Boston, Massachusetts, sells personal automobile insurance through some 165 independent agents throughout the state. The company wanted to create an extranet, Agent Web, where an agent could transact business with PRAC.

The two main issues were ensuring that communications between the agents and the Web site were both secure and fast. Without secure links, the agents said they would not use Agent Web, and PRAC did not want agents to have to wait for page downloads.

PRAC considered using frame relay to get the speed, but that technology turned out to be more expensive than they wanted. So they looked into DSL, which would provide 20 times the speed of a regular dial-up modem. They also looked into creating a VPN from the local sites to the Agent Web site to ensure secure transmission of data back and forth.

They settled on using the services of HarvardNet, a local Massachusetts provider of Internet services, which offers a DSL-based VPN service. PRAC chose HarvardNet because its geographic footprint closely matched the geographic locations of the independent agents. Furthermore, the cost of providing these agents' offices with DSL was just one-third the cost of frame relay. HarvardNet's RemoteConnect VPN service would also allow PRAC to extend its secure corporate network to all these remote independent agent sites. Creating the DSL-based VPN provides both the sub-second response time and the secure communication links PRAC wanted to provide to the agents to streamline claims processing and reduce paper.

In addition, PRAC decided to turn over all the operations of Agent Web to HarvardNet. HarvardNet now hosts Agent Web and handles the VPN network management so that PRAC's IS department only needs to focus on the applications of Agent Web.

To protect against spoofing, firms need a way to authenticate the identity of an individual. This verification requires a form of digital ID. The most common form of digital signature uses the RSA encryption method. Because the private key is known only to one person and a message encrypted with that key can only be decoded with the matching public key, the private key provides a way of verifying that the message came from a certain individual. Figure 8.35 shows the basic process.

For digital signatures to work, though, a trusted third party must issue the keys to individuals and firms. These parties are called *certification agencies* and can be government agencies or trusted private companies. The agency issues a digital certificate containing the user's name, the user's public key, and the digital signature of the certification agency. See Figure 8.36. The digital certificate can then be attached to a message to verify the identity of the sender of the message.

User's name
User's public key
Digital signature of certificate issuer

Figure 8.36 A Digital Certificate

Virtual Private Networks (VPNs). Most offices now have a local ISP, so no matter where they are located in the world, the least costly way to create companywide networking is to utilize the Internet and its TCP/IP protocols. However, the Internet is not secure because, for one thing, none of the TCP/IP protocols authenticate the communicating parties.

One approach to security has been to obtain a VPN from a CLEC or an ISP. A VPN runs over a private IP network, so it is more affordable than leased lines, and it is secure. VPNs use tunneling technology and encryption to keep data secure as it is transmitted.

Tunneling creates a temporary connection between a remote computer and the CLEC's or ISP's local data center, which blocks access to anyone trying to intercept messages sent over that link. Encryption scrambles the message before it is sent and then decodes it at the receiving end. While in transit, the message cannot be read or changed; hence, it is protected.

VPNs can be used in three ways, according to PwC.

1. ***Remote access VPNs*** give remote employees a way to access an enterprise's intranet securely by dialing a specific ISP, generally a large one with local telephone numbers in many cities. The ISP establishes a secure tunnel through its network to the corporate network, where the user can access e-mail and the intranet. This option offloads network management to the ISP, something most IS executives want to do.
2. ***Remote office VPNs*** give enterprises a way to create a secure private network with remote offices. The ISP's VPN equipment encrypts all transmissions.
3. ***Extranet VPNs*** give enterprises a way to conduct e-business with trading partners, advisers (such as legal firms), suppliers, alliance partners, and customers. These partners dial a specific ISP, which then establishes a secure link to the extranet.

As an example of using a VPN, consider Plymouth Rock Assurance Corporation on page 368.

Information security has become an important management topic, yet it has no clear-cut answers. It is too costly to provide all the security a company wants, and performing security checks on packets takes a lot of processor power, which can slow performance. Even with world-class technical security, management needs to make sure that all employees follow security policies, because companies are only as safe as their weakest link. In fact, that weakest link could be a supplier or contractor with secure access to a company's systems, yet poor security of its own. One final thought: Security is as much a human problem as a technical problem.

SUMMARY

Systems thinking is a hallmark of good management in general. Systems thinking is also important to many basic concepts on which modern information systems are defined. Three systems characteristics especially important for IS work are: determining the system boundary, component decomposition, and designing system interfaces.

This chapter introduced a generic life cycle model for software systems, as well as some of the processes and techniques for systems analysis and design used by IS professionals for developing software. Procedurally oriented techniques for structured system development include notation systems for modeling processes and data separately. Object-oriented (O-O) techniques, including a new modeling language (UML), have become more prevalent as newer software applications have required graphical user interfaces, multimedia data, and support for "real-time" transactions. O-O approaches will also be important in the development of Web services. Common IS control mechanisms to minimize business risks due to internal and external threats are described; many of these controls need to be identified with the help of business managers and then addressed during the development and maintenance of an information system.

In the past, information security was not a hot topic among executives of corporations, but in today's world even CEOs are aware of the importance of keeping electronic information secure in running their businesses. All executives must now know and understand Internet-based threats and countermeasures in order to protect their businesses.

CHAPTER REVIEW QUESTIONS

1. Define the term *system.* Give an example of a business system and use a context diagram to show its boundary, environment, inputs, and outputs.
2. What is a subsystem? Give an example of a business subsystem and identify some subsystems with which it relates.
3. What is business processing reengineering and how is it important for IS work?
4. How will logical and physical representations of a To-Be system differ?
5. Describe the relationships between a context diagram, as in Figure 8.11, and the top-level and second-level diagrams of a data flow diagram, as in Figures 8.13 A and B.
6. What is a data dictionary and why is it important?
7. Why are software objects more reusable than other types of computer code?
8. Compare a context diagram (using DFD modeling) and a use case diagram (using UML). What is the same and what is different?
9. Briefly describe some common information system controls that need to be implemented by business managers and not IS professionals.

10. What is an audit trail and why is it a useful mechanism for controlling business risks due to an information system?
11. What are the five pillars that make up today's security techniques? Describe them.

CHAPTER DISCUSSION QUESTIONS

1. Explain and give an example that supports the following statement: Each time we change characteristics of one or more of the components of an organization (structure, people, processes, information technology), we must consider compensating changes in other components.
2. Explain the function of hierarchical decomposition in systems analysis and design. Discuss the reasons for viewing and analyzing systems in this way.
3. Why do informal systems arise? Why should systems analysts be aware of them?
4. Some observers have characterized business process reengineering (BPR) as evolutionary, others as revolutionary. Develop an argument to support one of these sides.
5. Explain why many companies were unable to implement new cross-functional processes that were identified by BPR project teams in the early 1990s, before ERP packages became widely available.
6. Describe why analysts begin with the As-Is system, rather than starting with the design of a To-Be system.
7. Develop a context diagram and a top-level DFD to model the data flows involved in registering for classes at your college or university. Then model the student registration system in a use case diagram and write a textual description for one of the use cases.
8. Web services have been called a second wave of net-centric computing that will have broad implications for software development approaches in the future. Develop an argument to support or refute this viewpoint.
9. Explain why some organizations have adopted more rigid control mechanisms in recent years and whether or not you think they are justified, given the added costs to implement them.
10. Discuss security measures that should be built into a system. How does a company balance the needs of a consumer for privacy and protection with the needs of the business for personal information?

CASE STUDY: AN INTERNET SERVICES COMPANY

This firm provides services to Internet professionals and performs security assessments.

PLANNING AND BUILDING FOR SECURITY

When establishing network connections, the firm's starting point is to deny all access to and from the Internet. From there, it opens portals only where required, and each opening has a firewall and only permits specific functions, such as FTP or e-mail.

In essence, the company has put a perimeter around itself. It determines the worth of the information inside and spends the appropriate level of money to protect those assets. It can be hard to define the perimeter, though. For example, the company does work from client sites and that work needs to be protected as well.

It recognizes that it must also stay vigilant within the perimeter to avoid having a "soft chewy center." It uses a layered approach with numerous ways to protect each layer and some redundancy. For example, it worries about telephone hackers as well as computer hackers.

The IS organization is responsible for all in-house systems and all security. A central authority oversees all servers and workstations. In addition, all machines run the latest virus-detection software. When a system reboots, it accesses the central server where its virus definitions are checked. If they are not the latest ones, the newest versions are downloaded.

Finally, the company has disaster recovery plans that include having servers geographically separated. It recommends that clients do the same so that e-business sites can remain operational, at least partially, if some of the servers are hit by an attack or become overloaded.

MONITORING

The company views security on the Internet as a war of escalation. Every few weeks someone finds a clever new way to penetrate software, and a new type of attack is launched. Once the security team has closed one hole, attackers will find and attack another. The best the security team can hope to achieve is to deter attackers by closing more and more holes.

The security team therefore believes it needs to constantly "check the locks," which it does in the following ways:

- The team keeps track of the latest bugs found in systems. The company belongs to suppliers' bug alert communities. When it receives an alert, the team looks to see whether it applies to the company's systems. If so, the team assesses the vulnerability and takes needed action.
- The team keeps up-to-date on the latest security attacks that have taken place around the world by subscribing to security organizations and constantly visiting their Web sites for the latest news.
- The team subscribes to hacker e-mail lists and bulletin boards to see what the bad guys are doing and talking about. The security team believes it must think like the enemy.
- Team members personally explore some threats by setting up a test system and trying various attacks on it—attacks they have read about on the e-mail lists and bulletin boards. It is fun for the security staff, it provides a break from the normal work, and it presents a welcome technical challenge.
- The team logs and monitors all incoming and outgoing traffic. A dedicated team manages the firewalls.
- A senior security person scans the company's Web sites monthly from a remote site, comparing the services being run on the servers with the official inventory of services that should be running on the servers. Major surprises are investigated. This person also checks to ensure that no servers are running known compromised software.

EDUCATION: THE KEY TO IMPROVING SECURITY

The greatest security challenge is employee and customer apathy; they always say, "This cannot happen to us." Hence, the greatest security need is employee and customer education. The company tries to balance education with a taste of what could happen so that its security message is taken seriously without frightening employees and clients so much that they think any countermeasure is useless. Management has learned that fear-mongering becomes counterproductive if it is too scary or used too often.

Education is a two-way street, though. Businesspeople need to determine the value of the assets, but they also need input from IS on what is technically feasible to guard specific assets. For example, the company has alerted all its high-profile clients about the possibility of denial-of-service attacks. The bigger and more well known the company and its Web site, the more it needs to be prepared for such attacks by having the technology and plans in place to identify and deal with attacks when they occur. Management warns, "If you have a determined adversary, they are going to keep trying until they get you."

The company has found that business-people do understand security when it is related to money. They understand that they, not the technicians, are the ones who need to justify security expenses because only they understand the worth of protecting different kinds of information. For example, they understand that protecting Web servers that contain public information requires keeping the servers from crashing. That type of protection costs less than safeguarding servers that house proprietary company or confidential client information, which must also protect the data from prying eyes; not everyone can access it.

Case Study Discussion Questions

Question One

Are security problems a dilemma without a solution? Discuss how this company handled its security issues. Will there ever be a site that is 100% foolproof in terms of security? What ideas do you have for making a company site secure?

Question Two

Go to the Internet and investigate the latest security measures that various companies are taking to prevent hackers from stealing information.

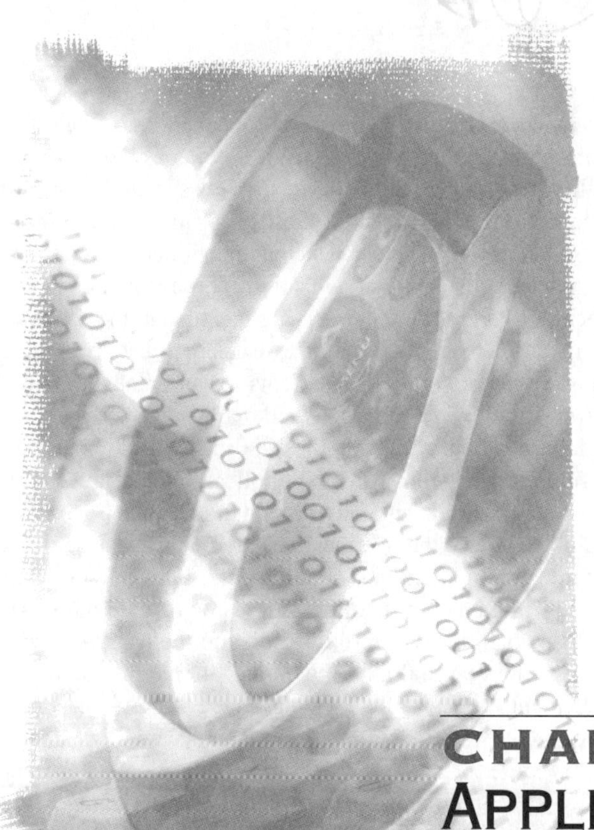

CHAPTER 9
Application Development by Information Systems

Until the late 1980s, software applications that were custom-developed systems for a specific firm were very common. If an organization had its own information systems (IS) professionals, the organization's own IS staff most likely developed these custom applications in-house. If an organization did not have the resources (or IS expertise) to develop custom applications, an outside vendor would be employed either to provide IS contract personnel on a temporary basis or to completely develop the custom software for the organization. Today's firms are likely to purchase software packages whenever they can. However, custom software development skills are still in high demand in manufacturing and service firms, as well as in software vendor and consulting firms.

This chapter describes two common approaches to developing customized applications: a traditional systems development life cycle (SDLC) approach and an evolutionary prototyping approach. Although our methodology descriptions assume that the IT project is being managed in-house, most of what we describe holds true for application development approaches used today within software houses. A key difference, of course, is that when custom applications are being built for a specific organization—rather than for many organizations—business managers and end users who will use the application on a day-to-day basis will play key roles in the development process.

This chapter also covers two newer development approaches: rapid application development (RAD) and an "agile" development approach, including some characteristics of an "extreme programming" approach.

Systems Development Life Cycle Methodology

In Chapter 8 we introduced three generic phases of a systems **life cycle process**: Definition, Construction, and Implementation. We turn now to a detailed discussion of these three phases in the development of a new software application using a highly structured approach. This traditional life cycle process for developing customized applications is referred to as the **systems development life cycle (SDLC)**.

The SDLC approach also provides a baseline for understanding what is involved in developing an application system, whether by IS professionals employed by a manufacturing or service firm, by IS professionals employed by a software development firm or consultancy, or by some combination of internal and external IS specialists. The processes for purchasing a software package or developing an application as an end user (described in Chapter 11) will also be better understood after becoming familiar with the traditional SDLC approach.

The SDLC Steps

The generic SDLC methodology includes three phases and eight steps. This template is shown in Figure 9.1. The specific steps in this figure can vary across organizations. For example, an organization could have developed its own version of an SDLC methodology that includes a total of five steps or even ten steps. Nevertheless, an organization's internally developed SDLC methodology should also essentially correspond to the steps for each of the three phases in Figure 9.1.

The overall thrusts of the three phases of the SDLC are quite straightforward. The Definition phase is critical: It defines precisely what the system must do in sufficient detail for IS specialists to build the right system. In the Construction phase, the IS specialists produce a working system according to the specifications set forth in the earlier phase. These include many of the structured techniques—data flow diagrams, E-R models, structure charts—and IS control concerns discussed in Chapter 8.

A key characteristic of the SDLC approach is extensive formal reviews by project team members and business management at the end of each major step. Without formal approvals, the project team cannot begin the next step of the methodology. The completion of each phase therefore represents a milestone in the development of the system.

In the Implementation phase, the new system is installed, becomes operational within the organization, and is maintained (modified) as needed so that it continues to reflect the changing needs of the organization. These last two steps—Operations and Maintenance—are included in the life cycle as a way to formally recognize that large custom applications are major capital investments for an organization that will have ongoing operational and maintenance costs.

In large organizations in the 1980s it was not uncommon to find many custom software applications that were more than a decade old. These systems had often been modified multiple times—the Maintenance step—in response to the organization's changing requirements. As we will learn later in this chapter, it often took a major external crisis, such as potential system failures due to the program's handling of the year 2000, for the organization to invest in a replacement system after having made significant dollar investments in these systems over many years.

In Figure 9.2 a typical breakdown of IS costs is presented for these three phases for a medium-sized project with a total development cost of $1 million. This breakdown does not include costs that a business unit might bear for training or replacing a business manager who is working on the project team. As can be seen from this hypothetical example, the Requirements Definition step is the costliest. As will be emphasized in the following sections, this is a hallmark of the SDLC approach: Extensive, upfront time is spent determining the business requirements for the new custom software application in order to avoid expensive changes

Definition Phase
- Feasibility Analysis
- Requirements Definition

Construction Phase
- System Design
- System Building
- System Testing

Implementation Phase
- Installation
- Operations
- Maintenance

Figure 9.1 The Systems Development Life Cycle

Development Activities	Percentage of Total Cost	Dollar Cost
Definition Phase		
Feasibility analysis	5	$ 50,000
Requirements definition	25	250,000
Construction Phase		
System design	15	150,000
Coding and initial testing	15	150,000
System testing	13	130,000
Documentation and procedures	12	120,000
Implementation Phase		
Installation planning, data cleanup, and conversion	15	150,000
Total	100%	$1,000,000

Figure 9.2 Cost Breakdown for $1 Million SDLC Project

later in the process due to inadequate definition of the requirements.

Most SDLC methodologies result in a lot of documentation. In the early steps, before any computer code is even written, the specific deliverables from each step are written materials. An SDLC step is not complete until a formal review of this documentation takes place.

The traditional SDLC approach has often been referred to as the "waterfall" model (Boehm, 1981): The outputs from one step are inputs to the next step. However, in practice, an organization could have to take more of a "spiral" approach, returning to earlier steps to change a requirement or a design as needed. Later in this chapter (see the section entitled "Newer Approaches") we will discuss an approach that builds on both the waterfall and spiral concepts: rapid application development (RAD).

Initiating New Systems Projects

Organizations use a number of approaches to decide which new applications to invest in. In many organizations the process begins with the submission of a formal proposal by a business department. Some large organizations require that these proposals first be reviewed and prioritized by a committee at the department or division level. When substantial investments and resources are involved, the department might be required to wait for an annual approval and prioritization process to occur. Very large, high-budget projects could also require approval by the corporation's top management executive committee and board of directors. Some organizations require that a business sponsor, rather than an IS manager, present his or her proposals to these approval bodies. Smaller, low-budget projects might be approved on a much more frequent basis with fewer hurdles.

At a minimum, a proposal that describes the need for the software application with a preliminary statement of potential benefits and scope will be prepared by business management or an IS manager assigned to a particular business unit (an account manager). The extent to which IS professionals need to be involved in this preliminary phase varies greatly across organizations.

Once the proposal has been approved and IS resources are formally assigned to the project, the formal SDLC process begins. For some projects, the initial approval might only be an endorsement to proceed with a feasibility analysis, after which additional approvals will be required. The documents for the feasibility analysis then become the basis for a decision on whether or not to invest in the custom application.

Descriptions of each of the eight steps outlined in Figure 9.1 follow.

Definition Phase

Feasibility Analysis. For this first step of the SDLC process, a project manager and one or more systems analysts are typically assigned to work with business managers to prepare a thorough analysis of the feasibility of the proposed system. Three different types of feasibility will be assessed: *economic, operational*, and *technical*.

The IS analysts work closely with the sponsoring manager who proposed the system and/or other business managers to define in some detail what the new system will do, what outputs it will produce, what inputs it will accept, how the input data might be obtained, and what databases might be required. An important activity is to define the scope or boundaries of the system—precisely who would it serve, what it would do, as well as what it would not do—and what data processing would and would not be included. The IS analyst is primarily responsible for assessing the system's technical feasibility, based on a knowledge of current and emerging technological solutions, the IT expertise of in-house personnel, and the anticipated infrastructure needed to both develop and support the proposed system. The business manager is primarily responsible for assessing the system's operational feasibility. In some organizations, business analysts who are knowledgeable about IT, but are not IT professionals, play a lead role in this process.

Both business managers and IS analysts work together to prepare a cost/benefit analysis of the proposed system to determine the economic feasibility. Typical benefits include costs to be avoided, such as cost savings from personnel, space, and inventory reductions; new revenues to be created; and other ways the system could contribute business value overall. However, for many applications today, some or all of the major benefits might be intangible benefits; they are hard to measure in dollars. Examples of intangible benefits include better customer service, more accurate or more comprehensive information for decision making, quicker processing, or better employee morale. (For a further discussion of system justification, see the section later in this chapter entitled "Managing an SDLC Project.")

The IS analyst takes primary responsibility for establishing the development costs for the project. This requires the development of a project plan that includes an estimated schedule in workweeks or months for each step in the development process and an overall budget estimate through the installation of the project. Estimating these project costs and schedules is especially difficult when new technologies and large system modules are involved. (Note that these costs usually do not include user department costs, which might be substantial during both the Definition and Implementation phases.)

The deliverable of the Feasibility Analysis step is a document of typically 10 to 20 pages that includes a short executive overview and summary of recommendations, a description of what the system would do and how it would operate, an analysis of the costs and benefits of the proposed system, and a plan for the development of the system. Sometimes referred to as a systems proposal document, this document is typically first discussed and agreed to by both the executive sponsor and the IS project manager and then reviewed by a management committee that has authority for system approvals and prioritization.

Before additional steps are undertaken, both IS and business managers need to carefully consider whether to commit the resources required to develop the proposed system. The project costs up to this point have typically been modest in relation to the total project costs, so the project can be abandoned at this stage without the organization having spent much money or expended much effort. As described earlier, the approval of a large system request might not actually occur until after the completion of a formal feasibility analysis. For large projects, the executive sponsor of the application is typically responsible for the presentation of a business case for the system before the approving body.

Requirements Definition. If the document produced from the feasibility analysis receives the necessary organizational approvals, the Requirements Definition step is begun. Both the development of the "right system" and developing the "system right" are highly dependent on how well the organization conducts this step in the SDLC process. This requires heavy participation from user management. If this step is not done well, the wrong system might be designed or even built, leading to both disruptive and costly changes later in the process.

Although in the past new systems often automated what had been done manually, most of today's systems are developed to do new things, to do old things in entirely new ways, or both. Although the executive sponsor plays a key role in envisioning how IT can be used to enable change in what the sponsor's people do and how they do it, the sponsor is often not the manager who helps to define the new system's requirements. Rather, the sponsoring manager must make sure that those who will use the system and those managers responsible for the use of the new system are involved in defining its detailed requirements.

Also referred to as systems analysis or logical design, the requirements definition focuses on processes, data flows, and data interrelationships rather than a specific physical implementation. The systems analyst(s) is responsible for making sure these requirements are elicited in sufficient detail to pass on to those who will build the system. It might appear easy to define what a system is to do at the level of detail with which system users often describe systems. However, it is quite difficult to define what the new system is to do in the detail necessary to write the computer code for it. Many business applications are incredibly complex, supporting different functions for many people or processes that cross multiple business units or geographic locations. Although each detail might be known by someone, no one person knows what a new system should do in the detail necessary to describe it. This step can therefore be very time-consuming and requires analysts who are skilled in asking the right questions of the right people and in conceptual system design techniques. In addition, there might be significant disagreements among the business managers about the nature of the application requirements. It is then the responsibility of the IS project manager and analysts to help the relevant user community reach a consensus. Sometimes outside consultants are used to facilitate this process.

Furthermore, some new applications are intended to provide decision support for tasks that are ill-structured. In these situations, managers often find it difficult to define precisely what information they need and how they will use the application to support their decision making. Information needs might also be highly variable and dynamic over time. As noted in Chapter 8, many of today's large systems development projects might also arise in conjunction with reengineering an organization's business processes. Redesign of the organization, its work processes and the development of a new computer system could go on in parallel. The ideal is to first redesign the process, but even then work processes are seldom defined at the level of detail required for a new business application.

Because defining the requirements for a system is such a difficult and a crucial task, analysts rely on a number of techniques and approaches. Examples of these were described in detail in Chapter 8. Later in this chapter we also describe an evolutionary prototyping approach that can be used to help define systems requirements—for the user interface in particular.

The deliverable for the Requirements Definition step is a comprehensive *system requirements document* that contains detailed descriptions of the system inputs and outputs and the processes used to convert the input data into these outputs. It typically includes several hundred pages with formal diagrams and output layouts, such as shown in Chapter 8. This document also includes a revised cost/benefit analysis of the defined system and a revised plan for the remainder of the development project.

The system requirements document is the major deliverable of the Definition phase of the SDLC. Although IS analysts are typically responsible for drafting and revising the requirements specifications document, business managers are responsible for making sure that the written requirements are correct and complete. Thus, all relevant participants need to carefully read and critique this document for inaccuracies and omissions. Case studies have shown that when key user representatives do not give enough attention to this step, systems deficiencies are likely to be the result.

The deliverable from this step is typically subject to approval by business managers for whom the system is being built as well as by appropriate IS managers. Once formal approvals have been received, the system requirements are considered to be fixed. Any changes typically must go through a formal approval process, requiring similar sign-offs and new systems project estimates. All key participants therefore usually spend considerable time reviewing these documents for accuracy and completeness.

Construction Phase

System Design. In this step, IS specialists design the physical system, based on the conceptual requirements document from the Definition phase. In system design, one decides what hardware and systems software to use to operate the system, designs the structure and content of the system's database(s), and defines the processing modules (programs) that will comprise the system and their interrelationships. A good design is critical because the technical quality of the system cannot be added later; it must be designed into the system from the beginning.

As shown in Figure 9.3, a quality system includes adequate controls to ensure that its data are accurate and that it provides accurate outputs. It provides an audit trail that allows one to trace transactions from their source and confirm that they were correctly handled. A quality system is highly reliable; when something goes wrong, the capability to recover and resume operation without lost data or excessive effort is planned for. It is also robust—insensitive to minor variations in its inputs and environment. It provides for interfaces with related systems so that common data can be passed back and forth. It is highly efficient, providing fast response, efficient input and output, efficient storage of data, and efficient use of computer resources. A quality system is also flexible and well documented for both users and IS specialists. It includes options for inputs and outputs compatible with its hardware and software environment and can be easily changed or maintained. Finally, it is user-friendly: It is easy to learn and easy to use, and it never makes the user feel stupid or abandoned.

To ensure that the new system design is accurate and complete, IS specialists often "walk through" the design first with their colleagues and then with knowledgeable business managers and end users, using graphical models such as those described in Chapter 8. This type of technique can help the users understand what new work procedures might need to be developed in order to implement the new system.

The major deliverable of the System Design step is a detailed design document that will be given to programmers. Models created by various development tools, such as diagrams of the system's physical structure, are also an important part of the deliverable. The documentation of the system will also include detailed descriptions of all databases and detailed specifications for each program in the system. Also included is a plan for the remaining steps in the Construction phase. Again, both users and IS managers typically approve this document before the system is actually built.

System Building. Two activities are involved in building the system—producing the computer programs and developing the databases and files to be used by the system. IS specialists perform these activities. The major involvements of users are to answer questions of omission and to help interpret requirements and design documents. The procurement of any new hardware and support software (including the database management system selection) is also part of this step, which entails consultation with IS planners and operations personnel.

System Testing. Testing is a major effort that might require as much time as writing the code for the system. This step involves testing by IS specialists, followed by user testing. First, each module of code must be tested. Then the modules are assembled into subsystems and tested. Finally, the subsystems are combined and the entire system is integration tested. Problems might be detected at any level of testing, but correction of the problems becomes more difficult as more components are integrated, so experienced

Accurate	Reliable
Auditable	Robust
Changeable	Secure
Efficient	User friendly
Flexible	Well documented

Figure 9.3 Characteristics of High Quality Systems

project managers build plenty of time into the project schedule to allow for problems during integration testing. The IS specialists are responsible for producing a high-quality system that also performs efficiently.

The system's users are also responsible for a critical type of testing—*user acceptance testing*. Its objective is to make sure that the system performs reliably and does what it is supposed to do in a user environment. This means that users must devise test data and procedures that completely test the system and that they must then carry out this extensive testing process. Plans for this part of the application testing should begin after the Definition phase. Case studies have shown that end-user participation in the testing phase can contribute to end-user commitment to the new system, as well as provide the basis for initial end-user training.

Both user and IS management must sign off on the system, accepting it for production use, before it can be installed. **Documentation** of the system is also a major mechanism of communication among the various members of the project team during the development process: Information systems are simply too complex to understand when they are described verbally.

Once the users sign off on this part of the testing, any further changes typically need to be budgeted outside of the formal development project—that is, they become maintenance requests.

Implementation Phase

The initial success of the Implementation phase is highly dependent on business manager roles. Systems projects frequently involve major changes to the jobs of the people who will use the system, and these changes must be anticipated and planned for well before the actual Implementation phase begins.

Installation. Both IS specialists and users play critical roles in the Installation step, which includes building the files and databases and converting relevant data from one or more old systems to the new system. Depending on the extent to which the data already exist within the organization, some of the data conversion burden might also fall on users. In particular, data in older systems could be inaccurate and incomplete, requiring considerable user effort to "clean it up." The clean-up process, including the entering of revised data, can be a major effort for user departments. Sometimes the clean-up effort can be accomplished in advance. In other situations, however, the data clean-up is done as part of the new system implementation. This means users that have a lot of data verifications to do and conversion edits to resolve, sometimes without the benefit of additional staff, as they also learn the new system.

Another crucial installation activity is training the system's end users, as well as training other users affected by the new system. If this involves motivating people to make major changes to their behavior patterns, planning for this motivation process needs to start well before the Implementation phase. User participation in the earlier phases can also help the users prepare for this crucial step. Similarly, user training needs to be planned and carefully scheduled so that people are prepared to use the system when it is installed but not trained so far in advance that they forget what they learned. If user resistance to proposed changes is anticipated, this potential situation needs to be addressed during training or earlier.

Installing the hardware and software is the IS organization's responsibility. This can be a challenge when the new system involves technology that is new to the IS organization, especially if the technology is on the "bleeding edge." The major problems in system installation, however, usually lie in adapting the organization to the new system—changing how people do their work.

Converting to the new system might be a difficult process for the users because the new system must be integrated into the organization's activities. The users must not only learn how to use the new system but also change the way they do their work. Even if the software is technically perfect, the system will likely be a failure if people do not want it to work or do not know how to use it. The **conversion** process therefore might require attitudinal changes. It is often a mistake to assume that people will change their behavior in the desired or expected way.

Several strategies for transitioning users from an old system to a new one are commonly used (see Figure 9.4). This is a critical choice for the effective implementation of the system, and this choice needs to be made well in advance of the Implementation phase by a decision-making process that includes both IS and business managers. Good management understanding of the options and trade-offs for the implementation strategies discussed below can reap both short-term and long-term implementation benefits.

In the *parallel* strategy, the organization continues to operate the old system in parallel with the new system until the new one is working sufficiently well to discontinue the old. This is a conservative conversion strategy because it allows the organization to continue using the old system if there are problems with the new one. However, it can also be a difficult strategy to manage because workers typically must operate both the old system and the new while also comparing the results of the two systems to make sure that the new system is working properly. When discrepancies

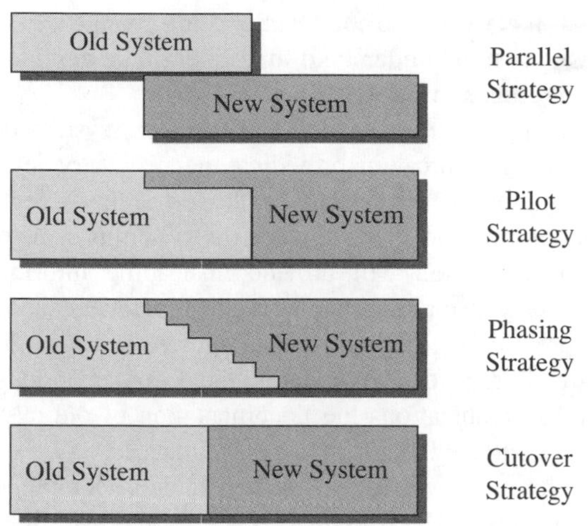

Figure 9.4 Implementation Strategies

are found, the source of the problem must be identified and corrections initiated. Parallel conversion can therefore be very stressful. A parallel strategy also might not even be feasible due to changes in hardware and software associated with the new system.

The *pilot* strategy is an attractive option when it is possible to introduce the new system in only one part of the organization. The objective is to solve as many implementation problems as possible before implementing the system in the rest of the organization. For example, in a company with many branch offices, it might be feasible to convert to the new system in only one branch office and gain experience solving data conversion and procedural problems before installing the system companywide. If major problems are encountered, companywide implementation can be delayed until they are solved. Pilot approaches are especially useful when there are potentially high technological or organizational risks associated with the systems project.

For a large, complex system, a *phased* conversion strategy might be the best approach. For example, with a large order processing and inventory control system, the firm might first convert order entry and simply enter customer orders and print them out on the company forms. Then it might convert the warehouse inventory control system to the computer. Finally, it might link the order entry system to the inventory system, produce shipping documents, and update the inventory records automatically. The downside to this approach is that it results in a lengthy implementation period. Extra development work to interface new and old system components is also typically required. On the other hand, a phasing strategy enables the firm to begin to achieve some benefits from the new system more rapidly than under other strategies.

In the *cutover* (or cold turkey) strategy, the organization totally abandons the old system when it implements the new one. In some industries this can be done over holiday weekends in order to allow for a third day for returning to the old system in the event of a major failure. The cutover strategy has greater inherent risks, but it is attractive when it is very difficult to operate both the old and new systems simultaneously. Some also argue that the total "pain is the same" for a system implementation, whether implemented as a cutover or not, and that this strategy moves the organization to the new operating environment faster.

Combinations of these four strategies are also possible. For example, when implementing system modules via a phased conversion strategy, one still has the option of a parallel or cutover approach for converting each phase of the system. Similarly, a pilot strategy could include a parallel strategy at the pilot site.

Operations. The second step of the Implementation phase is to operate the new application in "production mode." In the Operations step, the IS responsibility for the application is turned over to computer operations and technical support personnel. The project team is typically disbanded, although one or more members may be assigned to a support team.

New applications are typically not moved into production status unless adequate documentation has been provided to the computer operations staff. Implementing a large, complex system without documentation is highly risky. Documentation comes in at least two flavors: system documentation for IS specialists who operate and maintain the computer system and user documentation for those who use the system.

Successful operation of an application system requires people and computers to work together. If the hardware or software fails or people falter, system operation might be unsatisfactory. In a large, complex system, thousands of things can go wrong, and most companies operate many such systems simultaneously. It takes excellent management of computer operations to make sure that everything works well consistently and to contain and repair the damage when things do go wrong.

In Part IV we consider what it takes to successfully schedule and run large applications on a large computer system in a reliable and secure production environment.

Maintenance. The process of making changes to a system after it has been put into production mode (i.e., after the Operations stage of its life cycle) is referred to as

Maintenance. The most obvious reason for maintenance is to correct errors in the software that were not discovered and corrected prior to its initial implementation. Usually a number of bugs in a system do elude the testing process, and for a large, complex system it might take many months, or even years, to discover them.

Maintenance could also be required to adapt the system to changes in the environment—the organization, other systems, new hardware and systems software, and government regulations. Another major cause for maintenance is the desire to enhance the system. After some experience with a new system, managers typically have a number of ideas on how to improve it, ranging from minor changes to entirely new modules. The small changes are usually treated as maintenance, but large-scale additions might need approval as a new development request.

Because both business and technology environments change rapidly, periodic changes to large systems are typical. In the past the total costs over a typical system's life cycle have been estimated to be about 80 percent on maintenance and only 20 percent on the original development of the application. As a result, many IS organizations have to allocate a significant number of their IS specialists to maintaining systems, rather than developing new ones. In the early 1990s maintenance resources were consuming as much as 75 percent of the total systems development resources in many large organizations (see Figure 9.5). The IS organization is responsible for making the required changes in the system throughout its life, as well as for eliminating any bugs that are identified prior to launching the new system in a production mode.

To make a change in a system, the maintenance programmer must first determine what program(s) must be changed and then what specific parts of each program need to be changed. The programmer must also understand the logic of the part of the code that is being changed. In other words, one must understand the system in some detail in order to change it.

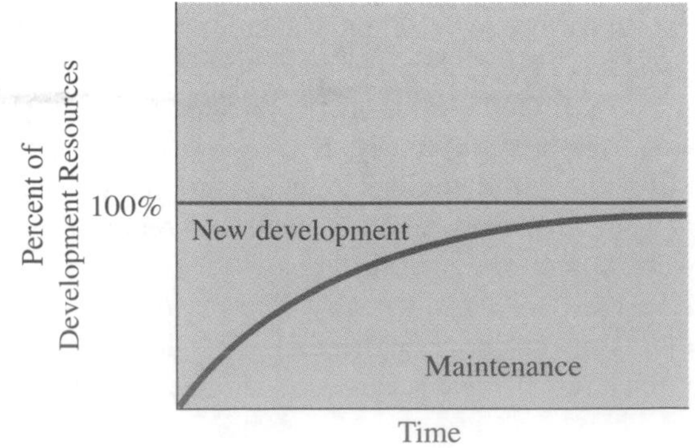

Figure 9.5 Percent of Development Resources Devoted to Maintenance

Because systems can be very complex, system documentation is critical in providing the necessary level of understanding. This brings up another difficulty—the documentation must be changed when the system is changed or the documentation will provide misleading information about the system rather than assistance in understanding it. Most programmers are primarily interested in programming and are not rewarded for updating the documentation, so in many IS organizations the documentation of old systems becomes outdated and includes inaccuracies.

Furthermore, when changes are made in complex systems, a **ripple effect** might be encountered such that the change has an unanticipated impact on some other part of the system. For example, a change in a program can affect another program that uses the output from the first program. A change to a line of code can affect the results of another line of code in an entirely different part of that program. Another change must be made to correct those problems and that change might cause unanticipated problems elsewhere.

Another major problem with maintenance is that most IS professionals prefer to work on new systems using new technologies rather than maintain old systems. Maintenance is therefore often perceived as low-status work, although it is critical to the business. Maintenance is often the first assignment of a newly hired programmer, and most organizations do not have mechanisms to ensure that really good maintenance people are rewarded well.

From the business manager's perspective, the major maintenance challenges are getting it done when it is needed and dealing with new system problems introduced as part of the maintenance process. A high proportion of operational problems are caused by errors introduced when making maintenance changes. Changes to production systems need to be carefully managed. Maintenance changes are typically made to a copy of the production system and then fully tested before they are implemented. An effective **release management** process for changing from an older to a newer version of the system is critical to avoid introducing large numbers of new problems when maintaining operational systems.

If adequate numbers of IS specialists are not available for systems maintenance projects, the manager often must suffer long delays before needed changes are made. Figure 9.6 graphically displays the widening gap that can occur between the organization's needs and the system's performance over time. Also, as a system gets older and is repeatedly patched, the probability of performance problems becomes even greater and reengineering or replacement solutions might be required.

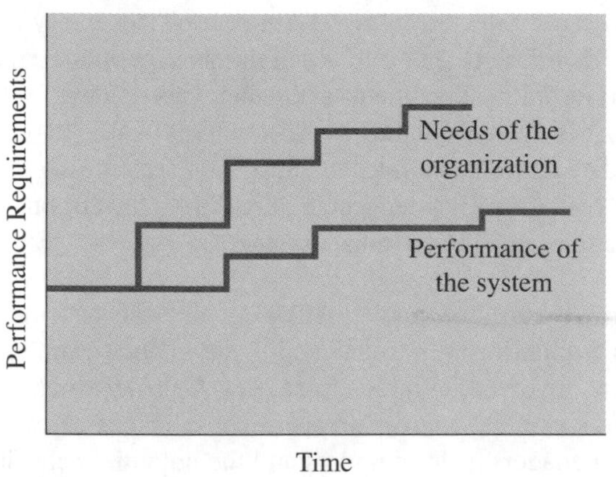

Figure 9.6 The Widening Gap Between the Organization's Needs and the System's Performance

The SDLC Project Team

Most application systems are developed by a temporary project team. When the system project is completed, the team is disbanded. Most project teams include representatives from both the IS organization and relevant business departments. If several organizational units or several levels of people within a unit will use the system, the project team might include representatives from only some of these different units, including higher-level managers and experienced end users who will work with the new application on a day-to-day basis. The selection of the project team is therefore critical to the success of a given systems project.

The project team also can vary in membership during the system's life cycle: A few members might be assigned full-time to the project for its entirety, while others might join the project team only temporarily as their specific knowledge or skills are required. In addition to an IS manager in a project leadership role, other IS personnel will be assigned as needed for the specific application, including systems analysts, application programmers, data administration specialists, telecommunications specialists, and others. It is also not unusual for IS specialists from outside the organization to also be used on systems projects. The IS specialists hired from a contract firm might bring specific IS knowledge to the project or might be needed due to the lack of internal resources available to assign to the project. These personnel could be so well integrated into the project that they are almost indistinguishable from the firm's internal IS personnel.

Historically, the **project manager** for a custom application was always an IS manager. Today, however, a business manager with information technology (IT) management knowledge might be asked to be the project manager, or a project might have two project managers: a business manager responsible for all user activities, especially for the implementation phase, and an IS manager responsible for the activities of all IS personnel. Some guidelines on whether the manager of a specific project should come from the IS organization, a business unit, or both, are provided in the sidebar "Who Should Lead the IT Project?" The practitioner press suggests that assigning both IT and business managers to lead IT projects is a way to tighten the overall alignment between the IT organization and the business. According to a recent report, Cisco Systems, Inc., is giving IT and business leaders joint responsibility for every IT project (Hoffman, 2003).

Whether or not this role is shared, the project manager(s) is held responsible for the success of the project—for delivering a quality system, on time, and within budget. Managing a systems project typically involves coordinating the efforts of many persons from different organizational units, some of whom work for the project only on a part-time or temporary basis. The project manager must plan the project, determine the SDLC tasks that must be carried out and the skills required for each task, and estimate how long each will take. The skills of the IS resources assigned to the project can be just as important as the number of resources assigned.

The system documentation produced at each step of the SDLC methodology provides a major tool for communication across team members and for assessing the quality of the development effort throughout the life of the system. Most organizations require that systems for which an SDLC process is appropriate include business management beyond those on the project team to provide formal sign-offs at each milestone of the project.

WHO SHOULD LEAD THE IT PROJECT?

If the project involves new and advanced technology,
Then it should be managed by someone from the IS department.
If the project's impact would force critical changes in the business,
Then it should be managed by someone from the business unit.
If the project is extremely large and complex,
Then it should be managed by a specialist in project management.
If a project shares all of the above characteristics,
Then senior management should consider multiple project leaders.

[Radding, 1992, based on Applegate]

The **systems analyst** role is also a critical one. These IS professionals are trained to work with business managers and end users to determine the feasibility of the new system and to develop detailed system requirements for the custom application. During the Construction phase, they work with other IS specialists in designing the system and help to monitor the adherence to the system requirements. A good systems analyst has problem-solving skills, a knowledge of IT capabilities, and a strong understanding of the business activities involved in the application. The role of the systems analyst needs to be played well in order for *multiple* user perspectives to be taken into account. Sometimes the systems analyst also provides the important function of providing checks and balances for IS specialists eager to work with new, but unproven, technologies by ensuring that the business risks associated with new technologies are accounted for in project decisions.

Other key roles, including key business roles (sponsors, champions), are discussed in the chapter on IT project management.

Managing an SDLC Project

All systems projects are typically measured by three primary success criteria: (1) on-time delivery of an IS that (2) is of high quality and meets business requirements and (3) is within project budget.

Particularly critical for the success of custom development projects using an SDLC methodology are three characteristics: manageable project size, accurate requirements definition, and executive sponsorship.

Manageable Project Size. Experience has convincingly shown that very large custom IT projects are very difficult to deliver within budget. On the other hand, projects that take fewer technical people a year or less to complete are more likely to meet the success criteria for the project. This suggests that large systems should be broken down into relatively independent modules and built as a sequence of small, manageable projects, rather than as a single monster project.

Accurate Requirements Definition. The SDLC waterfall process is based on the premise that requirements for a new system can be defined in detail at the beginning of the process. The downside is that if the requirements are not well defined, there could be large cost overruns and the system could be unsatisfactory. Early studies have shown that about half of the total number of requirements errors (or omissions) is typically detected in the Requirements Definition step. Further, as shown in Figure 9.7, an error detected in the Implementation phase costs about 130 times as much to fix as an error detected in the Definition phase. Every effort must therefore be put into obtaining as accurate a requirements definition document as possible. This requires systems analysts skilled in eliciting requirements as well as in process and data representation techniques. It also requires *access to business users* knowledgeable about both current business operations and the envisioned system.

Executive Sponsorship. Although all large systems projects require business sponsorship, the intensity and length of time involved with the typical SDLC project means that executive-level sponsorship is critical to success. Key business managers need to understand the potential benefits of the proposed system and be dedicated to contributing resources to the systems project team, as well as the sustained usage of the new custom application. Because some business managers and end users will also be assigned to the project team, business sponsors need to be willing to dedicate these resources to the project team, sometimes on a full-time basis for the life of the project.

Although not every project team has end users as formal team members, end users frequently participate by providing information about current work processes or procedures and evaluating screen designs from an end-user perspective. This, too, takes time away from normal business activities. User involvement in a systems project has in fact been associated with user acceptance and usage of the new system (Hartwick and Barki, 1994). However, business managers must be willing to dedicate these business resources throughout the project as needed, not just at the time of implementation.

Beath and Orlikowski (1994) have pointed out that systems development methodologies can differ in their assumptions about IS and user roles over the life of the project. For example, two methodologies that have been practiced more commonly outside of the United States (the ETHICS method and the Soft Systems Methodology) are specifically designed to facilitate more user involvement.

System implementation also requires managing organizational changes. Unless there is strong business sponsorship, there will not be a strong initiative to make changes to the business as part of the systems project effort.

SDLC Advantages and Disadvantages

The SDLC process is a highly structured approach to the development of large, complex applications for one or more business units. A summary of the advantages and disadvantages of the SDLC approach is provided in Figure 9.8 and is discussed in the following paragraphs.

In the hands of competent IS specialists and knowledgeable business managers, the SDLC process sets up formal

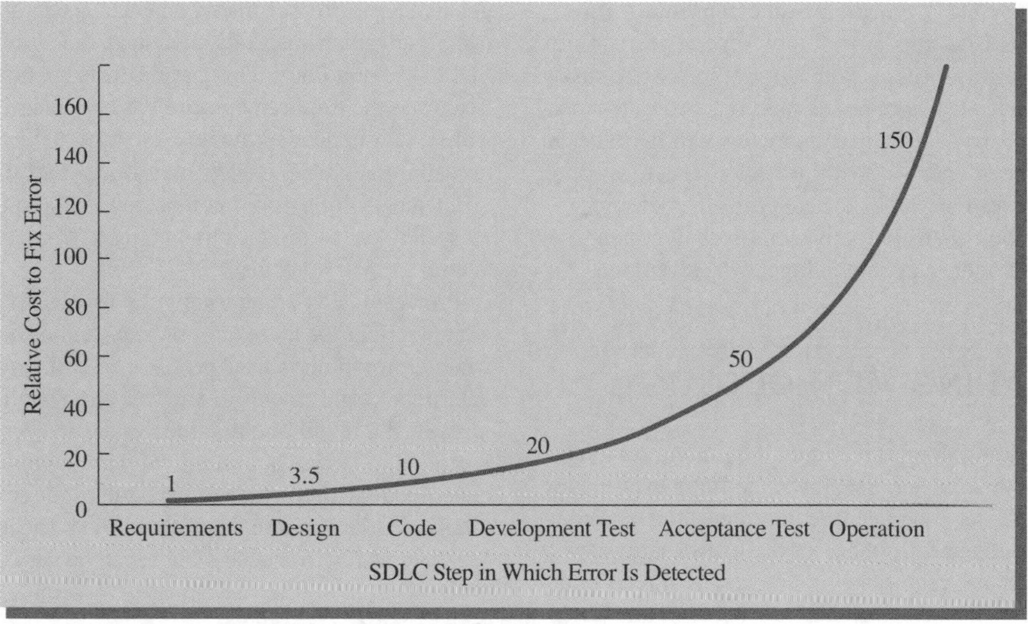

Figure 9.7 Costs of Error Correction by SDLC Step (Adapted from Boehm, 1976).

steps with clear IS and user roles, formal checkpoints, and techniques for analysis, design, testing, and implementation. These tools and the rigorous discipline associated with an SDLC methodology help the systems project manager produce a well-engineered system on time and within budget.

The major disadvantages are inherent in the methodology. First, the project's success depends on the accurate and complete specification of detailed requirements at the beginning of the development process (Definition phase). There are several serious problems with this dependency. For example, many customized applications today are unique solutions. Because the project begins with an incomplete understanding of what this unique information system will do, it might be necessary to try several approaches before discovering the optimal one. New technologies might also be involved, and until the capabilities of these technologies are better understood, it might be hard to develop a firm set of requirements. Another problem with upfront detailed requirements specification is that today's business environment is changing so rapidly that there can be significant differences in business needs between the time the requirements are specified and the time the system is installed.

Note that the SDLC process also requires a full cost/benefit analysis based on the initial Definition phase. The justification process can be difficult to accomplish using traditional approaches such as return on investment (ROI) calculations when new technologies are involved or requirements are incomplete.

Advantages

- Highly structured, systematic process
- Thorough requirements definition
- Clear milestones with business management sign-offs

Disadvantages

- Does not account well for evolving requirements during project
- Time-consuming (and costly) process
- Top-down commitment required

Figure 9.8 Advantages and Disadvantages of Traditional SDLC Approach

Second, the SDLC process is time-consuming. In the 1980s the typical systems project took several years. Third, because the SDLC process is both lengthy and costly, strong executive sponsorship is required. Without strong business sponsorship, business managers and users will be reluctant to dedicate their time to a systems project instead of working on other activities for which they are typically measured.

Below we look at an alternative approach to systems development that addresses some of these disadvantages.

PROTOTYPING METHODOLOGY

The SDLC methodology is based on the premise that business requirements for the system will be static over the life of the project. Thus, the system requirements must be completely and finally specified before the Construction phase is begun. Once the requirements have been agreed upon, changing them leads to significant project costs and potential schedule delays.

In the second half of the 1980s, the growing availability of fourth generation nonprocedural languages and relational database management systems began to offer an alternative approach. These tools make it possible to initially build a system (or part of a system) more quickly and then revise it after users have tried it out and provided their feedback to the developers. Thus, rather than first initially defining the system and then building it, the initial system can be revised based upon the user's experience and understanding gained from the earlier versions.

This approach is very powerful because, although most people find it very difficult to specify in great detail exactly what they need from a new system, it is quite easy for them to point out what they do not like about computer screens that they can try out and use.

This general approach is most commonly known as **prototyping**. It is a type of **evolutionary development** process. The prototyping concept can also be applied to a process in which a real system is developed for the user to try out as well as for situations in which only a "toy" (nonoperational) prototype is developed. For example, prototype input and output screens are often developed for users to work with as part of the requirements definition or detailed design steps. Other examples of prototyping include a "first-of-a-series" prototype in which a completely operational prototype is used as a pilot and a "selected features" prototype in which only some essential features are included in the prototype and more features are added in later modules (Kendall and Kendall, 1999).

In the next section we first discuss prototyping as a complete alternative to the traditional SDLC methodology: its steps, project management considerations, and its overall advantages and disadvantages in comparison to an SDLC methodology. This approach is particularly attractive when the requirements are hard to define, when a critical system is needed quickly, or when the system will be used infrequently (or even only once)—so that operating efficiency is not a major consideration. Note that these are all system characteristics that apply to some types of managerial support systems.

Prototyping as an alternative to an SDLC methodology is impractical for large, complex system efforts. However, when prototyping is used *within* an SDLC process to help determine requirements of a new custom application, it can increase the likelihood that the system project is a success. Prototyping provides a practical way for organizations to experiment with systems where the requirements are not totally clear and where the probability of success is unclear but the rewards for success appear to be very high.

The Prototyping Steps

Figure 9.9 presents the steps for an evolutionary methodology for developing a new, working system. The process begins with the identification of the *basic* requirements of the initial version of the system (step 1). The analyst/ builder(s) and user(s) meet and agree on the inputs, the data processing, and the system outputs. These are not complete detailed requirements; rather, this is a starting point for the system. If several builders and users are involved, a joint application design (JAD) session may be used to determine requirements (see the description of JAD in the section entitled "Newer Approaches" later in this chapter).

In step 2 the system builders produce an initial prototype system according to the basic requirements agreed on in step 1. The system builders select the software tools, locate the necessary data and make these data accessible to the system, and construct the system using higher-level languages. This step should take from a few days to a few weeks, depending on the system's size and complexity.

When the initial prototype is completed, it is given to the user with instructions similar to the following: "Here is the initial prototype. I know that it is not what you really need, but it's a beginning point. Try it and write down everything about it that you do not like or that needs to be added to the system. When you get a good list, we will make the changes you suggest."

Step 3 is the user's responsibility. He or she works with the system, notes the things that need to be improved, and then meets with the analyst/builder to discuss the changes. In step 4 the builder modifies the system to incorporate the desired changes. In order to keep everyone actively involved speed is important. Sometimes the builder can sit down with

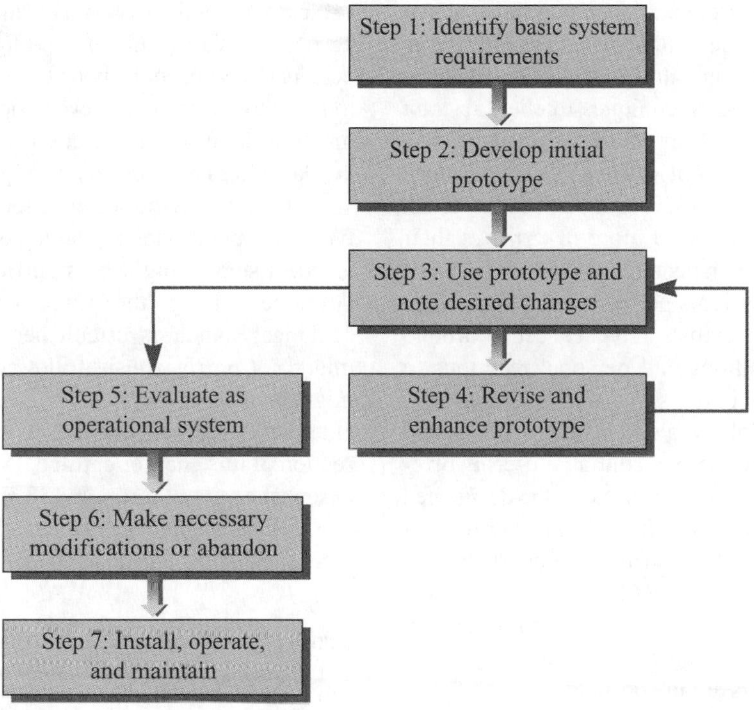

Figure 9.9 The Prototyping Life Cycle

the user and make the changes immediately; for larger systems, the changes might take several weeks. Steps 3 and 4 are repeated until the user is satisfied with the current version of the system. These are *iterative steps* within the prototyping process. When the user is satisfied that the prototype has been sufficiently developed, step 5 begins.

Step 5 involves evaluating the final prototype as an operational system. It should be noted, however, that not all prototypes become operational systems. Instead, it might be decided that the prototype system should simply be thrown away. Or, it could be decided that no additional costs should be devoted to the application because a system could not be developed that solved the original problem. That is, the prototyping process helped the organization decide that the system benefits do not outweigh the additional development or operational costs, or both, or that the expense of developing an operationally efficient system is too high. At this point it could also be decided that the system will be implemented but that the system needs to be built using different tools in order to achieve performance efficiencies.

If the prototype is to become an operational system, in step 6 the builder completes the Construction phase by making any changes necessary to improve operational efficiency and to interface the new application with the operational systems that provide it with data. This is also the step in which all necessary controls, backup and recovery procedures, and the necessary documentation need to be completed. If the prototype is only slightly modified, this step differs from the end of the Construction phase of an SDLC methodology in that most (or all) of the system has already been tested. Step 7 is similar to the Implementation phase of the SDLC: The new system is installed and moved into operational status. This is likely to be a much easier Implementation phase than under the traditional SDLC process because at least some of the intended users are already familiar with the system. Step 7 also includes maintenance. Because of the advanced tools that likely were used to build it, changes might be easier to make.

The Prototyping Project Team

Managing an evolutionary development process is clearly a joint IS and user management responsibility. Whether the project manager role is played by IS alone, business personnel alone, or both IS and business personnel, both groups need to jointly determine when to continue to request revisions to a prototype and when to end the iterative tryout-and-revise steps. The business manager needs to determine whether a satisfactory solution has been developed, and the IS manager needs to determine whether all relevant technology capabilities have been explored.

Because only basic requirements are being defined, the systems analyst and prototype builder (which might be one and the same) need to have some different skill sets than required for the SDLC process. Techniques to elicit abstract requirements and an emphasis on detailed documentation under the SDLC process are replaced by a heavy reliance on skills to build systems quickly using advanced tools. The initial prototypes are assessed more in terms of their look-and-feel from a user perspective and less in terms of technical quality from a systems performance perspective. Interactions between IS specialists and users center around creative development solutions and personal reactions to user-system interfaces and outputs.

A prototyping methodology also requires a dedicated business user role. Because there is continual user involvement with the various versions of the system, the designated business user needs to be able to be freed from other responsibilities to work with the application and to suggest changes over the life of the project. Sometimes more than one person plays this critical end-user role, which will require a structure and process for reaching agreement when suggested changes from different users are in conflict.

Managing a Prototyping Project

Managing new development projects with a methodology based on an iterative or evolutionary process requires a different mindset than managing projects using an SDLC methodology based on a highly structured development approach. IS project managers and system builders need to approach the project differently: The objective is to respond quickly to user requests with a "good enough" prototype multiple times rather than to produce a tightly engineered actual system at the outset of the project. This might require some cultural changes within the IS organization. IS professionals who have built their careers on skills and attitudes required by an SDLC approach might need to acquire new skills for prototyping approaches.

IS managers also find managing prototyping projects more problematic because it is difficult to plan how long it will take, how many iterations will be required, or exactly when the system builders will be working on the system. Project managers need to have sufficient IS resources available for system building in order to quickly respond to user requests for system changes within an agreed-upon timetable. Users who will be trying out each prototype version must be committed to the process and must be willing and able to devote the time and effort required to test each prototype version in a timely fashion. IS managers might rightfully feel that they have less control over the project's scope. One of the potential hazards of prototyping is that the iterative steps will go on and on and that the project costs will keep accumulating. Good working relationships between IS personnel and users responsible for the project are required to move to the prototype evaluation step (step 5) at the optimal time. Joint IS-user accountability would appear to be a key to success for these types of projects.

Depending on the software tools used to build the prototype, the operational efficiency of a prototype that is evaluated in step 5 might be significantly inferior to systems developed using the traditional SDLC methodology. Technical standards established by the organization also might not be rigorously followed, and the documentation might be inadequate. A substantial investment in computer-aided software engineering (CASE) tools (see the final section of this chapter entitled "Newer Approaches"), database management tools, and IS specialist training might be required before an IS organization can successfully implement the end prototype as the final system.

Prototyping Advantages and Disadvantages

The advantages of the evolutionary development methodology address the disadvantages inherent in the SDLC methodology. First, only *basic* system requirements are needed at the front end of the project. This means that systems can be built using an evolutionary approach that would be impossible to develop via an SDLC methodology. Furthermore, prototyping can be used to build systems that radically change how work is done, such as when work processes are being redesigned or a totally new type of managerial support tool has been envisioned but never seen. It is virtually impossible to define requirements for these kinds of systems at the beginning of a systems development process. Prototyping also allows firms to explore the use of newer technologies, because the expectations under an evolutionary methodology are that the builders will get it right over multiple iterations, rather than the first time.

Second, an initial working system is available for user testing much more quickly. In some cases business managers might actually use a working prototype to respond in some way to a current problem or at least to quickly learn that a given systems approach will not be the best solution. Although the complete process might take several months, users might have a working prototype in a few weeks or months that allows them to respond to a problem that exists now and is growing in importance; often a business manager cannot wait many months, let alone years, for a particular system to be built.

Third, because of the more interactive nature of the process, with hands-on use of working system models, strong top-down commitment based on a well-substantiated justification process might be less necessary at the outset of the project. Instead, the costs and benefits of the system can be derived after experience with an initial prototype.

Fourth, initial user acceptance of an application developed with an evolutionary process is likely to be higher than with an SDLC process. This is partly because the evolutionary process results in more active involvement and more joint control of the process on the part of the user.

The disadvantages of an evolutionary methodology are related to the evolutionary build process. The end prototype typically lacks some of the security and control features found in a system developed with an SDLC process. It also might not undergo the same type of rigorous testing. Documentation of the final version can be less complete because of the iterative nature of the process.

In the past the operational inefficiencies of fourth generation tools also contributed to the inadequacies of end prototypes. However, with recent advancements in hardware and software tools for developers and end users, these issues have become much less important than implementing a system that meets user needs. As described earlier, these potential deficiencies are assessed in step 5 and corrected in step 6 of the evolutionary methodology in Figure 9.9.

Another potential disadvantage is related to managing user expectations. Frequently, a prototype system appears to be so good that users are reluctant to wait for a well-functioning, well-documented operational system.

Prototyping within an SDLC Process

As fourth generation tools have become commonplace, the incorporation of a few steps of an evolutionary process into an SDLC methodology has also become common. In the following paragraphs we describe two ways that prototyping is commonly incorporated into an SDLC process.

First, prototyping is used in the Definition phase to help users define the system requirements, particularly for the user interface (computer screens and navigation). As shown in Figure 9.10, the SDLC process still begins with a feasibility analysis. However, for the requirements definition step, IS specialists use screen-painting tools to produce initial versions of screens and reports that users can experiment with. This might be an example of a nonoperational prototype, in which the screen designs are not connected to a live database. After the requirements have been determined with the help of the prototype, the remainder of the steps in the SDLC process remain the same. However, the system builders can also make use of the screens during the design and build steps, and they may actually use computer code generated by the prototyping tools in the final system.

Definition Phase
- Feasibility Analysis
- *Prototyping* to Define Requirements

Construction Phase
- System Design
- System Building
- System Testing

Implementation Phase
- Installation
- Operations
- Maintenance

Figure 9.10 SDLC with Prototyping to Define Requirements

The second way prototyping is used is more complex, and includes a pilot implementation of a working prototype. This type of prototype is typically a first-of-a-series type of pilot system. Unlike the pilot rollout strategy discussed for the Implementation stage of the SDLC process, in which a complete system is first implemented in only a portion of the organization, here the intent is to use a scaled-down prototype in only a minimal number of locations within the organization in order to assess its feasibility in an operational setting. As shown in Figure 9.11, the Definition phase of the SDLC process is replaced by three steps in a Prototyping/Piloting phase. After basic requirements are determined (step 1), a working prototype

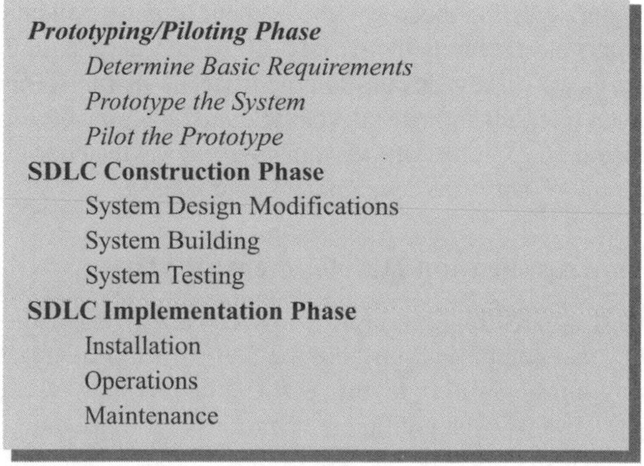

Figure 9.11 Prototyping/Piloting Phase Replaces SDLC Definition Phase

is developed (step 2). The initial prototype is sufficiently developed to demonstrate a technical solution using hardware and software components that typically had not been used before in the organization. In step 3 the prototype is extended to become a working prototype that can be piloted with a subset of the targeted users.

This prototyping/piloting approach within an SDLC is especially useful for large, risky projects that involve technological risks or organizational risks, or both. For example, one major objective might be to demonstrate the basic capabilities or provide a proof-of-concept test of a technical solution. A second major objective might be to get executive sponsors to buy in to the proposed system. By working with a prototype with live data, business managers can evaluate the potential benefits (and risks) of the new application in an operational setting. The expectation is that this is only a prototype, developed at minimal cost, which will be modified before the actual system is built.

For example, changes in functionality based on using the prototype in a pilot setting, as well as changes in the technology, are anticipated before the final system will be implemented at all locations. The prototype is used to help "sell" the system to key users as well as those who have budgeting authority. If the pilot is successful, what was learned from using the working prototype can now be incorporated into the design that will be used for the building of the actual system. The learning from the pilot step also helps users prepare for the organizational changes needed to implement the full system. The remaining steps match the typical SDLC process.

NEWER APPROACHES

The demands for speedier development of new application systems have steadily increased over the past decade. In this section we briefly discuss two approaches that have been proven to result in faster development of high-quality customized applications of a certain size: a RAD methodology and "agile" software development approaches.

Rapid Application Development (RAD)

Rapid application development (RAD) is a hybrid methodology that combines aspects of the SDLC methodology and prototyping. Similar to the SDLC methodology, several RAD variants exist within organizations and consultancies. The goal is to produce a system in less than a year. Some organizations adopting RAD approaches require that all projects fit within a short timebox—such as 6 months (Clark et al., 1997).

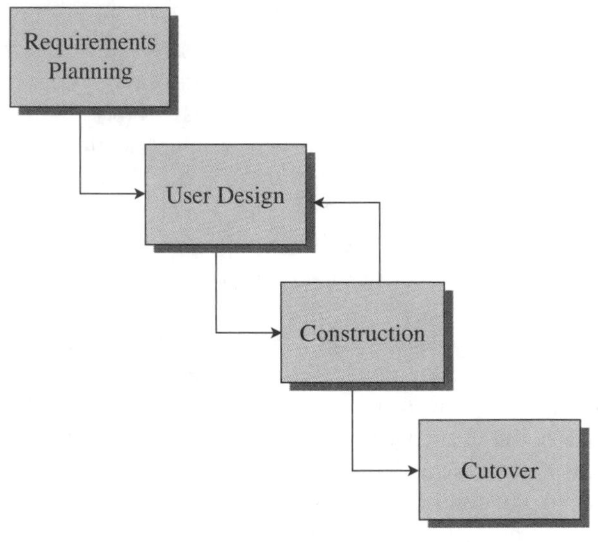

Figure 9.12 Four-Step RAD Life Cycle

The RAD life cycle developed by guru James Martin includes four steps, with iterations between steps 2 and 3, similar to a prototyping methodology (see Figure 9.12). The Requirements Planning step incorporates elements of the traditional IT project proposal initiation and steps from the SDLC Definition phases. For the User Design step, JAD sessions and software automation (CASE) tools are used to accomplish the work more quickly.

A JAD session could last several hours or could be held over several consecutive days. It is often held at a location removed from the participants' usual workplace so that the task can be concentrated on without interruption. A remote location also helps set up a forum for user representatives to work through areas of disagreement; achieving shared understanding is especially important when cross-functional systems are being developed. The JAD session is led by a facilitator who is not only skilled in systems analysis and design techniques but is also skilled in managing group interactions; a person outside the organization is sometimes used in this facilitator role in order to have a neutral third party who can help resolve conflicts and keep the group focused on the JAD session outcomes.

Joint application design (JAD) is a technique in which a team of users and IS specialists engage in an intense and structured process in order to minimize the total time required for gathering information from multiple participants.

Computer-aided software engineering (CASE) is any software tool used to automate one or more steps of a software development methodology.

EXCELERATOR: AN EARLY FRONT-END CASE TOOL

Excelerator, a software product by Intersolv, Inc., provides a set of integrated tools to support the development of system specifications, production of the system documentation, and management of the project. In addition to screen and report generators, it has an intelligent drawing tool to support the development of diagrams for process and data modeling. The CASE tool maintains a comprehensive database (repository) of all diagrams, data element specifications, processing logic, and other documentation associated with the project, and makes it electronically accessible to all members of the project team with the appropriate security levels. For example, a data dictionary entry is automatically generated for each data flow and data store in a data flow diagram (process model). It also includes its own design analyzers that checks for violations of system decomposition rules and other consistency checks.

As shown in Figure 9.13, CASE tools include *front-end* analysis tools such as diagramming tools, analysis tools, and computer display and report generator tools to support requirements definition and system designs; *back-end* tools for generating code (in one or more computer languages) from diagrams and other design documents; and *central repositories* for the processing logic, data structures, other specifications and project management documents for a software system. Full-cycle CASE systems, also called **Integrated-CASE** or **I-CASE** tools, combine front-end and back-end functions to produce a working system. A description of an early front-end CASE tool is provided in the sidebar entitled "Excelerator: An Early Front-End Case Tool."

Returning to Figure 9.12, in the Construction phase computer code is generated using the CASE tool. The business team members help validate screens and other design features, and an iterative approach is then used to make design changes and generate new code for validation. A cutover approach is used to convert the organization to the new system. By using this implementation approach, system testing must be undertaken at virtually the same time that user training and other organizational preparations are being accomplished.

The structured checkpoints and system reviews that are hallmarks of an SDLC approach are also used in a RAD approach. However, unlike the traditional SDLC approach, when users sign off on the CASE-based design document, the expectation is that they will also be involved in the Construction step, during which additional design changes can be made as necessary. Besides intensive usability testing with end-user involvement, rigorous quality assurance procedures are also built into the RAD methodology.

RAD is a methodology that works well in a business environment characterized by rapid change. The smaller design teams and shorter development times associated with RAD also can lead to considerably lower total development costs. For example, the U.S. Navy has reported system development savings of up to 50 percent and annual maintenance savings of 20 percent (Valacich et al., 2001). On the other hand, increased speed can sometimes also have its downside. For example, noncritical functionality

- *Diagramming tools:* support graphic representations for process, data, and control structure diagrams
- *Computer display and report generators:* used to prototype user interface for input (screen displays, forms) and reports as part of requirements definition
- *Analysis tools:* automatic checkers for missing, inconsistent, or incorrect specifications in diagrams, forms, and reports
- *Central repository:* integrated storage of system specs, diagrams, reports, and project management documents
- *Documentation generators:* produce technical and user documentation in vstandard formats
- *Code generators:* automatic generation of program and database definition code from diagrams, forms, reports, and other design documents

Figure 9.13 Types of CASE Tools (Adapted from Valacich, George, and Hoffer, 2001).

Advantages
- Dramatic savings in development time
- Focuses on essential system requirements
- Ability to rapidly change system design at user request

Disadvantages
- Quality may be sacrificed for speed
- Time-consuming commitments for key user personnel
- Possible shortcuts on internal standards and module reusability

Figure 9.14 RAD Advantages and Disadvantages

or quality standards might be sacrificed, such as consistent user interfaces across screens and data element naming standards.

Figure 9.14 summarizes some of the advantages and disadvantages of RAD. Like prototyping, a RAD methodology is highly dependent on involvement by key users. If these key users are not freed up to work on the RAD project, the custom application might still be produced quickly, but is less likely to be an optimal software solution for the business.

In recent years a more "agile" software development discipline has emerged as an alternative methodology for smaller projects (e.g., project teams not larger than 20). The objective is to deliver software with very low defect rates, based on a set of four key values:

- Simplicity
- Communication
- Feedback
- Courage

A "whole team" approach is taken in which business representatives (customers) and technical team members (programmers) work side-by-side in an open workspace on a daily basis.

In one agile approach, called **Extreme Programming (XP)**, the programmers write production code in pairs. By using simple designs and frequent testing, the team produces small, fully integrated releases that pass all the customers' acceptance tests in a very short time period (e.g., every 2 weeks). The programming pairs then might disband to form new pairs and thus quickly share their specialized knowledge and completed code. Another hallmark of the XP approach is the obsession with feedback and testing. As team-tested programs are released to a collective repository, any pair of programmers can improve any of the collective code at any time, following the common coding standards adopted by all teams.

MANAGING SOFTWARE PROJECTS USING OUTSOURCED STAFF

Although hiring on-site contractors to help with custom software projects has been a widespread practice for decades, today there is a renewed focus on keeping down the costs of software development by outsourcing portions of the project to off-site workers, especially offshore workers in a different labor market. Other advantages of using external resources for custom development work are to make use of technical expertise not available in-house and to be able to complete the project more quickly.

Off-site outsourcing can involve contracting with companies within the same country or region ("onshore") or not ("offshore"). According to Poria (2003), the offshore alternative is likely a very favorable option when the following conditions exist:

- The system requirements can be well-defined and will remain relatively stable over the project.
- Time is of the essence and 7x24 hour availability of resources to work on the project is advantageous.
- The cost of the project (or program) is an important consideration.

Guidelines for effectively managing the day-to-day interactions with an offsite outsourcer have also been developed. For example, some of the key guidelines published by a Sourcing Interests Group (and summarized in McNurlin and Sprague, 2003) are as follows:

Manage expectations, not staff. The outsourcer's staff is not under the direct control of the client company, so a facilitative mode of working is best in which the focus is on the outcomes.

Take explicit actions to integrate the offsite workers. Managing projects across workgroups requires more formality, such as explicit, agreed-upon outcomes and measures. In-house staff might even benefit from moving to the outsourcer's firm in order to work side-by-side with them and learn how they work together internally.

Communicate frequently. Managers responsible for the relationship with the outsourcers need to keep the lines of communication open.

Abandoning informal ways may result in increased rigor. Because of their business model, a service provider might have more disciplined processes than the client organization, which can lead to higher quality solutions.

TECHNOLOGIES FOR DEVELOPING SYSTEMS

One of the toughest jobs in IS management is developing new systems. It seems to be an area in which Murphy's Law—if anything can go wrong, it will—reigns supreme. In spite of the complexity of system development, the IT field has made significant progress in improving the process of building systems. The traditional approach, with variations, of course, appears in many textbooks and professional books. Two of the first books to describe a life cycle approach for developing systems were published in 1956 and 1957, both written by Richard Canning.

During the 1970s, a relatively well-defined process called the *system development life cycle* emerged. This life cycle improved the development process significantly. However, continued backlogs, cost overruns, and performance shortfalls underscored the difficulty and complexity of the system development process.

The 1980s saw progress in more friendly languages and automation of portions of development, such as code generation. Yet, maintenance continued to eat up 70 to 80 percent of the system development resources in most companies.

The 1990s began with the promise of significantly increasing developer productivity and reducing maintenance by relying more on packages and by building systems by linking together components. The business process reengineering movement spawned the growth of integrated enterprise systems and the widespread adoption of ERP systems. Then, all of a sudden, in the late 1990s, e-business and Internet-based systems appeared.

In the 2000s, the Internet brought the need for faster system development and integrated enterprise systems; that is, systems that pull together various aspects of the enterprise. New tools for rapid development became available; they relied on reusable components and open systems architectures. As a result, application development projects became application integration projects; systems were built by integrating prebuilt components.

These days, you could say that every application is a network application. The network is becoming the system. Web-based applications were the first generation of Internet-centric computing. The new field, Web Services, is touted as the second. In it, small modules of code perform specific functions and can be called by other modules to perform that work, all via the Internet. The Web Services world is upon us. In addition, the trend toward increasing the interconnectedness of supply chains is leading companies to build inter-organizational systems, which is a far more complex undertaking than single-company systems.

FOUNDATIONS OF SYSTEM DEVELOPMENT

In the early years, system development was considered a "craft." Since then, the goal has been to make it more scientific. In the 1970s, structured system development emerged to make the process more standard and efficient. It was characterized by the following elements:

- Hand coding in a third-generation language (such as COBOL)
- A structured-programming development methodology
- An automated project management system
- A database management system
- A mix of online and batch applications in the same system
- Development of mostly mainframe applications
- Programming by professional programmers only
- Various automated, but not well-integrated, software tools
- A well-defined sign-off process for system delivery
- User participation mainly in requirements definition and installation phases

This development approach supposedly followed the famous "waterfall" approach, shown in Figure 9.15. However, says Bob Glass, a well-known author in software development, this unidirectional waterfall was much touted but rarely used. Development did not proceed in a straight line from requirements through operation; a lot of

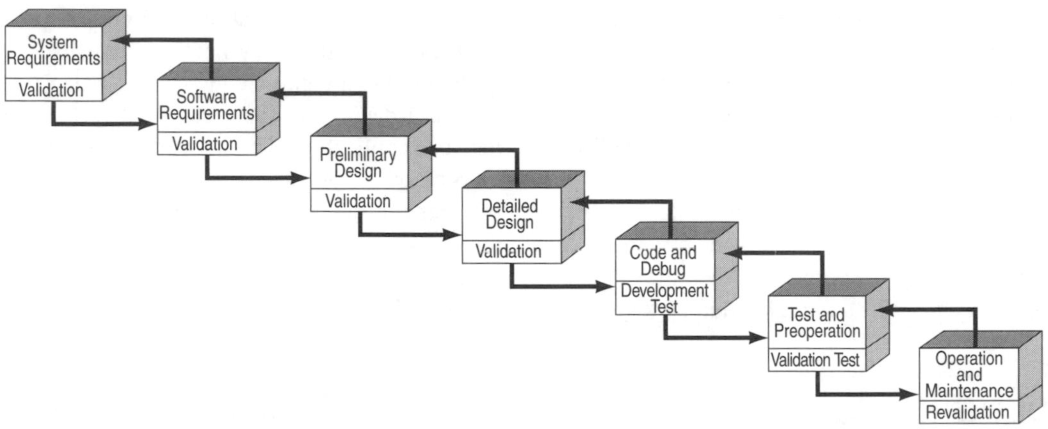

Figure 9.15 The "Waterfall" Development Life Cycle. *Source:* Barry Boehm, *Software Engineering Economics* (Upper Saddle River, NJ: Prentice Hall, 1981).

backtracking and iteration occurred. Developers really always followed the spiral approach, says Glass, which is generally attributed to Barry Boehm and shown in Figure 9.16.

Structured Development

Structured development methodologies accompanied this system development life cycle and were meant to handle the complexities of system design and development by fostering more discipline, higher reliability and fewer errors, and more efficient use of the resources.

More Discipline. By establishing standards for processes and documentation, the structured methodologies attempted to eliminate personal variations. At first they seemed to threaten programmers' creativity, but their discipline did increase productivity and permit developers to deal with greater complexity. The complexity was handled through successive decomposition of system components, coupled with preferred practices for conducting analysis, design, and construction. The result was a more disciplined system development process.

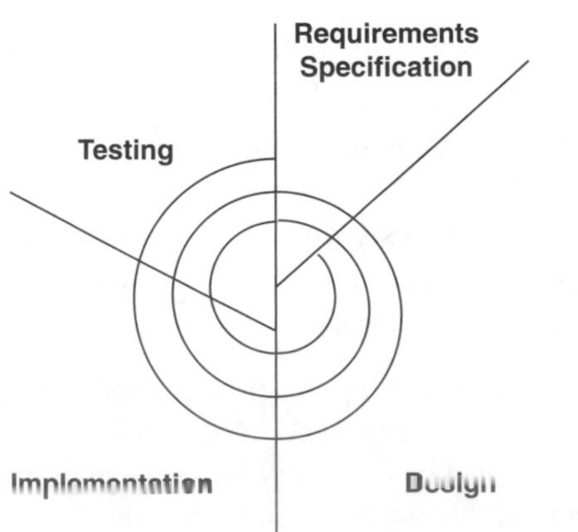

Figure 9.16 The Spiral Model of Systems Development. *Source:* Barry Boehm, "A Spiral Model of Software Development and Enhancement," *IEEE Computer*, Vol. 21, No. 5, May 1988, pp. 61–72.

Higher Reliability and Fewer Errors. The structured methodologies recognized that mistakes of both omission and commission were likely at all stages of system building. One of the main tools for coping with this tendency was (and still is) inspections, performed at every development stage and at every level of system decomposition. The goal has been to catch errors as early as possible. The methodologies also recognized that iteration would be required to redo parts of a system as mistakes were uncovered.

More Efficient Use of Resources. The project management approaches usually included in the structured methodologies contributed to cost savings, increased productivity, and better allocation of human resources. By imposing a time and cost control system, the classic approach decreased (but did not eliminate) the tendency for system development efforts to incur cost and time overruns.

Fourth-Generation Languages

In the early 1980s, two major developments occurred. One was the availability of fourth generation languages (4GLs); the second was software prototyping. Fourth-generation languages are really more than computer languages; they are programming environments. Their major components are listed in Figure 9.17.

The heart of a 4GL is its DBMS, which is used for storing formatted data records as well as unformatted text,

- Database management system (DBMS)
- Data dictionary
- Nonprocedural language
- Interactive query facilities
- Report generator
- Selection and sorting
- Screen formatter
- Word processor and text editor
- Graphics
- Data analysis and modeling tools
- Library of macros
- Programming interface
- Reusable code
- Software development library
- Backup and recovery
- Security and privacy safeguards
- Links to other DBMSs

Figure 9.17 Features and Functions of Fourth-Generation Languages

graphics, voice, and perhaps even video. Almost as important is the data dictionary, which stores the definitions of the various kinds of data. The language that programmers and users use is nonprocedural, which means that the commands can occur in any order, rather than the sequence required by the computer. The commands can be used interactively to retrieve data from files or a database in an ad hoc manner or to print a report (using a report generator). The screen formatter allows a user or programmer to design a screen by simply typing in the various data input field names and the locations where they are to appear or by choosing graphics from a menu. Some 4GLs include statistical packages for calculating time series, averages, standard deviations, correlation coefficients, and so on.

Previously, developers only had third-generation languages, such as COBOL and PL/1. The advent of 4GLs allowed end users to develop some programs and programmers to use a different development method: prototyping. Formerly, system requirements were fully defined before design and construction began. With prototyping, development could be iterative.

Computer-Aided Software Engineering

Even though the structured programming and analysis techniques of the 1970s brought more discipline to the process of developing large and complex software applications, they required tedious attention to detail and lots of paperwork. Computer-aided software engineering (CASE) appeared in the 1980s to automate structured techniques and reduce this tediousness.

Definition. CASE, as defined by Carma McClure, a CASE pioneer, is any automated tool that assists in the creation, maintenance, or management of software systems. In general, a CASE environment includes:

- An information repository
- Front-end tools for planning through design
- Back-end tools for generating code
- A development workstation

Often not included, but implied and necessary, are a software development methodology and a project management methodology.

An information repository. A repository forms the heart of a CASE system and is its most important element, says McClure. It stores and organizes all the information needed to create, modify, and develop a software system. This information includes, for example, data structures, processing logic, business rules, source code, and project management data. Ideally, this information repository should also link to the active data dictionary used during execution so that changes in one are reflected in the other.

Front-end tools. These tools are used in the phases leading up to coding. One of the key requirements for these tools is good graphics for drawing diagrams of program structures, data entities and their relationships to each other, data flows, screen layouts, and so on. Rather than store pictorial representations, front-end tools generally store the meaning of items depicted in the diagrams. This type of storage allows a change made in one diagram to be reflected automatically in related diagrams. Another important aspect of front-end design tools is automatic design analysis for checking the consistency and completeness of a design, often in accordance with a specific design technique.

Back-end tools. These tools generally mean code generators for automatically generating source code. A few CASE tools use a 4GL. Successful front-end CASE tools provide interfaces to not just one, but several, code generators.

Development workstation. The final component of a CASE system is a development workstation, and the more powerful the better, to handle all the graphical manipulations needed in CASE-developed systems.

Timeboxing. One of the most intriguing approaches to system development in the 1980s was the "timebox," a technique that uses CASE to guarantee delivery of a system within 120 days. Today, IS departments that aim for speed turn to a development technique known as rapid application development (RAD). The following case illustrates the use of timeboxing and RAD.

CASE EXAMPLE

DUPONT CABLE MANAGEMENT SERVICES

DuPont Cable Management Services was formed to manage the telephone and data wiring in DuPont's office buildings in Wilmington, Delaware. AT&T had owned and managed the wiring for DuPont's voice networks, but then responsibility passed to DuPont's corporate telecommunications group. At DuPont's Wilmington headquarters campus, cabling is complex and wiring changes are continual. The average telephone is moved one and a half times a year. Much of the telephone moving cost is labor to find the correct cables and circuit paths.

When the cable management services group was formed, the manager realized he needed a system to maintain an inventory of every wire, telephone, modem, workstation, wiring closet connection, and other pieces of telephone equipment. Technicians could then quickly locate the appropriate equipment and make the change. Although several cable management software packages were available, none could handle the scale or workload required by DuPont. The only option was to build a custom system.

The system had to be flexible, because the company's telecommunications facilities would need to handle new kinds of equipment for data and video. Furthermore, because cable management services were not unique to DuPont, the manager believed he could sell cable management services to other large companies. Therefore, the system needed to be tailorable. So that he did not have to hire programmers, the manager decided to use DuPont Information Engineering Associates (IEA), another DuPont business service unit, to build the system.

DuPont Information Engineering Associates (IEA)

IEA believed it could significantly speed up development by combining a code generator with software prototyping and project management. The resulting methodology was called rapid iterative production prototyping, or RIPP.

Using RIPP, a development project could take as few as 120 days to complete; it had four phases.

- ***Phase 1: Go-Ahead.*** Day 1 is the go-ahead day. IEA accepts a project, and the customer agrees to participate heavily in development.
- ***Phase 2: System Definition.*** Days 2 through 30 are spent defining the components of the system and its acceptance criteria. At the end of this phase, IEA presents the customer with a system definition and a fixed price for creating the application.
- ***Phase 3: The Timebox.*** The following 90 days are the "timebox," during which the IEA–customer team creates design specifications, prototypes the system, and then refines the prototype and its specifications. The final prototype becomes the production system.
- ***Phase 4: Installation.*** On Day 120, the system is installed. The customer has 3 months to verify that the system does what it is supposed to do. If it does not, IEA will refund the customer's money and remove the system.

Cable Management's Use of IEA

The cable management group contracted with IEA to develop the cable tracking system. After spending the first 30 days defining the scope of the project,IEA estimated that the system would require two timeboxes to complete, or about 210 days.

During the first timebox, IEA developed those portions that the cable management group could concisely define. During those 90 days, one cable management engineer worked full-time on the project, another worked part-time, and IEA had a project leader and two developers. The system they developed included display screens, the relational database, basic system processes, and reports.

At the end of the 90 days, IEA delivered a basic functional system, which DuPont began using. The second timebox added features uncovered during this use. Both parties agreed that this phase was ambiguous, which might affect the 90-day limitation. So they extended the project to 110 days. By that time, the development team had entered DuPont's complete wiring inventory, enhanced the basic system, and delivered a production version.

In all, the system took about 9 months to develop. The department manager realized that was fast, but he did not realize how fast until he talked to other telecommunications executives who told him their firms had spent between 2 and 3 years developing cable management systems.

The cable management group was pleased with its system. It was initially used only to manage voice wiring, but has since been extended to handle data communications wiring.

Object-Oriented Development

Just as 4GLs were a revolutionary change in the 1970s, object-oriented (OO) development was a revolutionary change in the 1980s. In fact, companies had a choice. They could choose the evolutionary approach of CASE or the revolutionary approach of OO development. OO development caught on in the early 1980s because of the PC; the graphical user interfaces were developed using objects. Developers just needed to point and click at generic items—menus, dialog boxes, radio buttons, and other graphical components—and then rearrange them to create a screen. This form of programming has come to be known as *visual programming*.

By the end of the 1980s, OO development was beginning to be noticed in IS departments for business applications. That trickle became a tidal wave when client-server systems appeared in the early 1990s, as developers attempted to simplify these extremely complex systems by reusing objects. In the early 1990s, OO system analysis and design techniques began to appear that could be used in conjunction with OO languages such as C++ and Smalltalk.

OO development is not so much a coding technique as a code-packaging technique, notes Brad Cox, an OO development pioneer. An *object* contains some private data (that other objects cannot manipulate) and a small set of operations (called *methods*) that can perform work on that data. When an object receives a request in the form of a message, it chooses the operation that will fulfill that request, it executes the operation on the data supplied by the message, and then it returns the results to the requester.

Combining data and procedures in an object, which is called *encapsulation*, is the foundation of OO development. It restricts the effects of changes by placing a wall of code around each piece of data. Data is accessed through messages that only specify what should be done. The object specifies *how* its operations are performed. Thus, a change in one part of a system need not affect the other parts. As you might expect, even though OO development promised significant benefits, it does have costs, especially at the outset. OO projects have gotten stuck in the mire of defining and redefining objects. Once defined, objects can be reused, another of OO's attractions. There are many other aspects of OO development, but this very brief description of objects suffices here. As will be seen later in the chapter, OO is a significant foundation for today's development efforts.

Client-Server Computing

In the 1990s, two developments became the major news: client-server systems and Web-based (or network-centric) development. Underlying these two trends, which continue today, is the increasing use of packages and system integration. As much as possible, companies prefer to buy a package rather than build an application in-house. To develop large applications, they integrate hardware and software components. For example, they buy a ready-made Web browser to become the standard access software for Web-based applications rather than write their own front-end client software. In both realms, the major construction methods are system integration and component-based development.

Client-server systems generated a lot of excitement in the early 1990s because they promised far more flexibility than mainframe-based systems. The desktop and laptop client machines could handle graphics, animation, and video, whereas the servers could handle production updating. It was a clever way to meld the pizzazz of the PC world with the necessary back-end production strengths of the mainframe world, even though mainframes were not always in the picture. The case example on page 390 is a typical example of the allure of client-server systems and how one company—MGM—developed its first client-server system.

INTERNET-BASED SYSTEMS

HKEx's system is actually a good introduction to Internet-based systems. AMS/3 is not Internet based, but it allows Internet access for online trading as well as other actions. The Internet has opened up the options HKEx can offer. Internet users have become so sophisticated that Internet-based systems must now be scalable, reliable, and integrated both internally and externally with the systems of customers and business partners. In developing such systems, companies have learned they must negotiate programming language differences. For example, a system may have to port old COBOL applications to Java, reconcile interface discrepancies, and interface with back-end legacy applications, often without documentation or past experience with those systems.

Internet-based systems are where the system development action is occurring. This section discusses three aspects of Internet-based systems: a framework, a language, and an environment. We examine these aspects for the following reasons:

- *Application servers* because they appear to provide the preferred framework for developing Internet-based systems
- *Java* because customers are demanding open systems; they do not want to be tied to a single vendor's proprietary technology. Java is a fairly open language

CASE EXAMPLE

MGM

Metro-Goldwyn-Mayer (MGM), the movie studio in Hollywood, has an extremely valuable asset: its library of TV shows and movies. The studio's first client-server application was built at the urging of end users to leverage this asset. The vice president of IS knew that the only way to meet the users' expectations for a multimedia, laptop-based system with a graphical interface was to employ client-server technology.

Previously, more than 26 disparate systems on PCs, minicomputers, and the corporate mainframe were used to maintain the rights to show MGM's films. As a result, it was not possible to get a consolidated, world-wide view of which films were being leased. The client-server system—the largest IS project in Hollywood at the time—collected and consolidated all data on the film library so that MGM would know what films it has the rights to license and to whom.

Client-server technology was chosen because it could empower MGM's 20 worldwide film-rights salespeople. They could visit the head of a cable TV network anywhere in the world with an SQL database on their laptop and built-in CD-ROM capabilities to play 20- to 30-second clips of their films. They could browse the laptop's inventory database to verify availability of films and then print the licensing deal memo on the spot. Details of the deal could then be transmitted to headquarters when convenient. Only a client-server system would provide this flexibility.

The System's Three-Level Architecture

The system's architecture had three layers. At the core was an AS/400, which acted as the central processor for the database that contains descriptions of 1,700 TV shows and movies, an index, the availability of movies in different regions, license time periods, status of bills, and so forth. MGM deliberately chose a tried-and-tested rights licensing software package to manage the database because it provided the needed processing; however, it did not support graphical interfaces, laptops, or decision support. Therefore MGM surrounded the package with the most-tested technology possible for the client-server components. In fact, wherever possible, MGM minimized technical risk by using proven products.

The second layer was an HP 9000 server, which contained data and processing, but no presentation software. The Unix front end was built using Power-Builder. In 1 hour with Power-Builder, developers could do 8 to 10 hours of COBOL-equivalent work.

The third layer was the client machines, either desktop or laptop. They contained local processing, local databases, and presentation software. The laptops also had a database for the salespeople. They could upload and download information from their laptops via dial-up lines.

The premier skill required in this environment was systems integration. The developers needed both hardware and software expertise for Unix and NT, PowerBuilder, and SQL Windows.

The Development Environment

Even though partnering was always possible in the mainframe era, it was mandatory with client-server computing. With tools like PowerBuilder and a development life cycle that relied on prototyping, developers had to constantly interact with users. They could not seclude themselves for months. Moreover, client-server teams had no boss. The users and developers were equal; neither told the other what to do.

The role of IS at MGM changed from system development and delivery to one of cooperating and partnering. This change required a huge cultural shift in the roles and attitudes of the IS staff. Developers who formerly buried themselves in code had to conduct meetings and work side-by-side with users. In short, they had to learn people (interpersonal) skills and the business. Interestingly, the CIO felt that women had an edge because, generally speaking, they had better interpersonal skills.

With client-server systems, the hardware was cheaper than with mainframe systems, development was faster, and software support was cheaper—all by orders of magnitude. Operating costs were more expensive than MGM expected because version control of client-server software and service and systems management were more costly.

that has evolved from client-side programming to being a server-side application development standard.

- *Web Services* because they are touted as the development environment of the future

Application Servers

Originally conceived as a piece of middleware to link a Web server to applications on other company systems, the application server has grown into a framework for developing Internet-based applications. Figure 9.18 illustrates the basic application server architecture. A set of application servers is connected to create a single virtual application server. This virtual server takes requests from clients and Web servers (on the left), runs the necessary business logic, and provides connectivity to the entire range of back-end systems (on the right).

In addition to providing middleware and integration functions, application servers have become application development platforms, with a wide range of development and automatic code generation tools. They can provide common functions, such as security and database connectivity, notes Radding, they can store business logic components (forming the building blocks for applications), and they provide development capabilities inherited from CASE [now called integrated development environments (IDEs)]. In short, they aim to increase programmer productivity by automating and managing many of the technical tasks in developing and running Internet-based applications. They also provide scalability. As demands on applications grow, a company can increase the power of its virtual application server by either installing more servers or replacing smaller servers with larger ones. The application server also provides automatic load balancing among the multiple servers.

Java

If companies are to develop Internet-based systems quickly, as the e-business environment demands, they need component-based development tools. If, in addition, the systems being developed are to be portable and scalable, then the companies need to employ an open system architecture. For both component-based tools and open systems, industry standards are necessary. Currently, some of the most widely used standards for Internet-based systems development have evolved from Java.

Java was originally developed to provide applets that run on Web clients. However, it quickly evolved into a full programming language with the goal of providing platform independence; that is, Java applications could run on any system through a *Java virtual machine*. This promised application portability was dubbed "write-once, run-anywhere." That promise has not been met, though. Java performed poorly relative to other languages, such as C++. Therefore, companies have not converted their client applications to Java. However, Java has evolved into a standard platform for developing server-side applications.

The two major components in the Java server-side platform are Enterprise JavaBeans (EJBs) and the Java 2 Enterprise Edition (J2EE) software specification. EJBs emerged on the developer scene in 1998 when Sun Microsystems unveiled a specification for creating server-based applications using software components. EJBs are

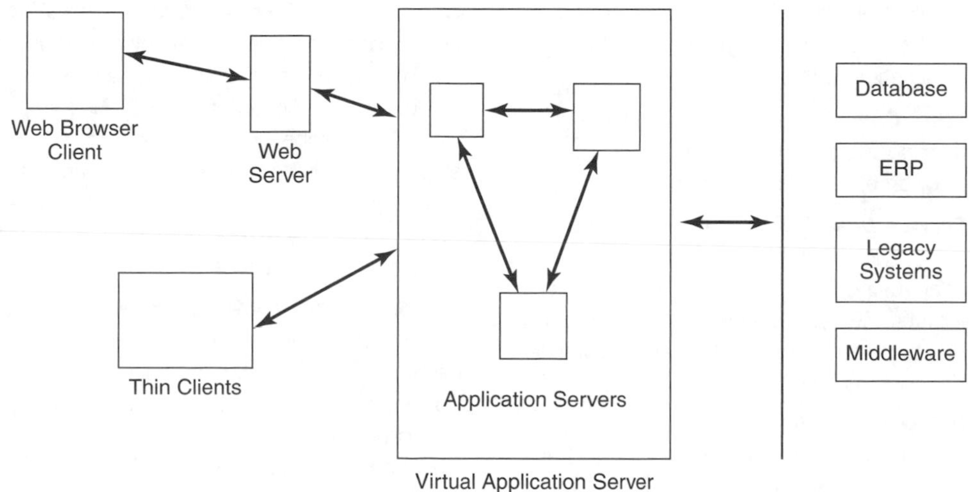

Figure 9.18 An Application Server Architecture

preconfigured pieces of code that IS staff no longer have to build from scratch. They can be as simple as an order entry form or as complicated as a virtual shopping cart that even protects shopper privacy. Use of EJBs can greatly enhance programmer productivity. Microsoft competes with its own version of components called COM (Com-ponent Object Model) components. (Note the term *object*. OO programming has become increasingly important in system development.)

J2EE defines a standard for developing Internet-based enterprise applications. It simplifies enterprise application development by basing it on a collection of standard server-side application programming interfaces (APIs), providing a set of services to modular components, and handling many of the core functions for the applications. Compo-nents include an API for database access, security modules that protect data in the Internet environment, and modules supporting interactions with existing enterprise applications. J2EE also supports XML.

Together, J2EE and EJBs provide an alternative to building online business systems from scratch or buying packaged online business systems because of their multi-vendor platform capability and pre-built, reusable components.

Web Services

The vision of Web Services is that modules of code can be assembled into services, which, in turn, can be linked to create a business process at the moment it is needed and run across enterprises, computing platforms, and data models. There are a couple of ways to build a Web Service. One is to wrap an XML wrapper around an existing piece of code that performs a specific function, thus exposing it. Then give that Web Service an Internet address and let others use it, for a fee.

John Hagel III and John Seely Brown point out that this is what Citibank has done. In the late 1990s when online exchanges were popping up like weeds, Citibank noticed that although the purchasing process was handled electronically, the actual exchange of money was generally handled manually or through special banking networks. Citibank had expertise in electronic payments, so

CASE EXAMPLE

BUILDING A WEB SERVICE

A graphical example of building a Web Service from an existing in-house application is shown in Figure 9.19. Following is a much simplified description of that process.

Step 1: Expose the Code. A currency conversion Web Service is created by exposing the currency conversion code of a credit card processor by encapsulating it in an XML wrapper.

Step 2: Write a Service Description. A description of the currency conversion service is written using WSDL (Web Services Definition Language). Housed in an XML document, this description describes the service, how to make a request to it, the data it needs to perform its work, the results it will deliver, and perhaps the cost to use it.

Step 3: Publish the Service. The currency conversion service is then published by registering it in a UDDI (Universal Discovery, Description, and Integration) registry. Publishing means that its service description, along with its URL (its address), is housed in the registry for others to find. The registry is essentially a Web Services yellow pages.

Step 4: Find a Currency Conversion Web Service. The currency conversion service can now be found by, say, a pricing Web Service. The pricing Web Service sends a request in the form of an XML document in a SOAP (Simple Object Access Protocol) envelope to one or more registries. This special envelope is also based on XML. This particular request of the UDDI registry asks for a listing of currency conversion Web Services. The reply is sent in an XML document in a SOAP envelope back to the requestor.

Step 5: Invoke a Web Service. The pricing service can now bind to and invoke the selected currency conversion service by sending it an XML message in a SOAP envelope asking it to, say, convert US $1,250.25 into Australian dollars. The currency conversion service performs the task and returns the answer in an XML document in a SOAP envelope and quite likely invokes a payment Web Service to be paid for performing that conversion service.

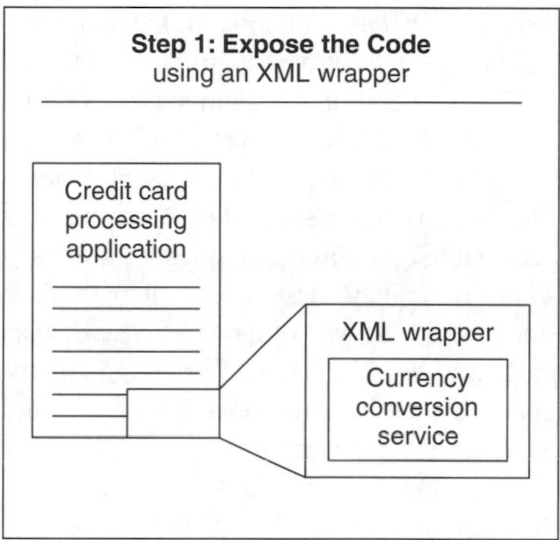

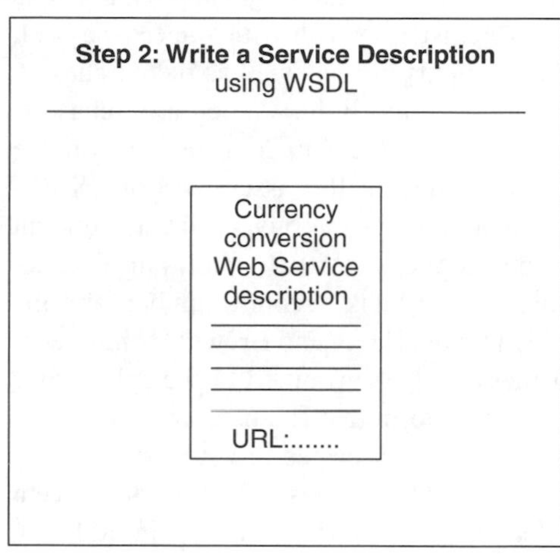

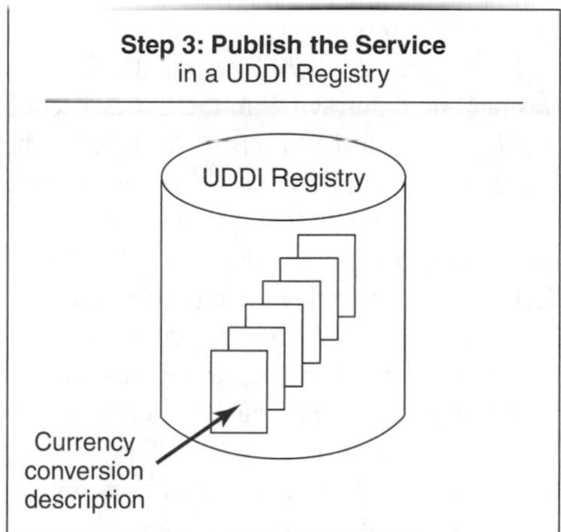

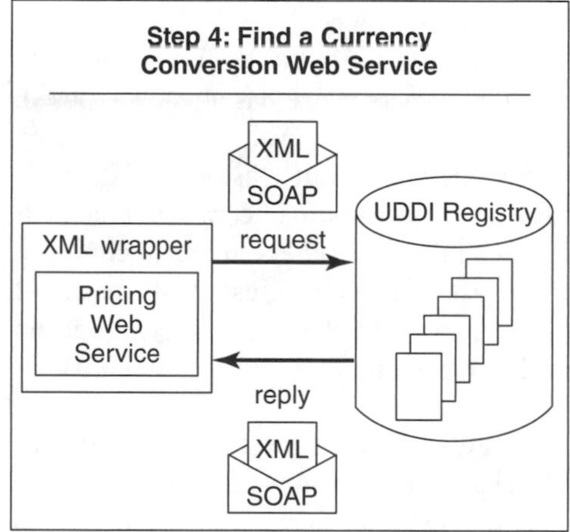

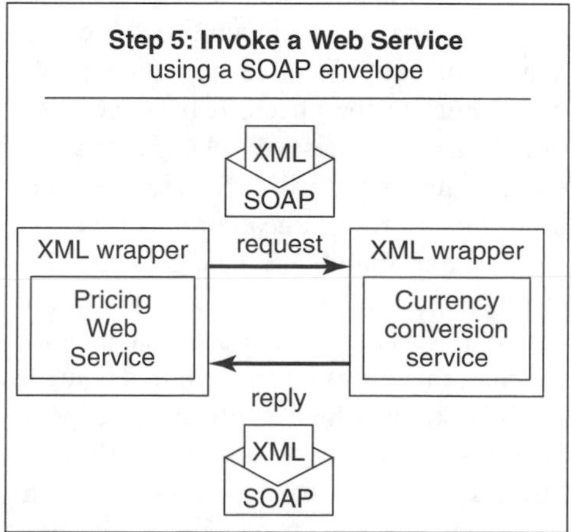

Figure 9.19 Building a Web Service

it created a payment processing Web Service called CitiConnect.

When a company plans to purchase, say, office supplies through an online exchange, the company can utilize CitiConnect by first registering with CitiConnect the bank accounts to withdraw funds from as well as the purchasing employees and their spending limits. When a purchase is made, the buyer clicks on the CitiConnect icon on the screen. That click automatically assembles an XML-wrapped message that contains the buyer's ID, the amount of the purchase, the supplier's ID, the withdrawal bank account number, the deposit bank account number, and the timing of the payment, note Hagel and Brown. Using predefined rules, that message is then routed to the appropriate settlement network to perform that financial transaction.

The benefits of this Web Service are substantial, note Hagel and Brown. Settlement times are 20 to 40 percent shorter, and settlement costs are half or less. In addition, Citibank has extended its brand into a new market, and the exchanges have happier customers.

This arrangement also illustrates the second way to build a Web Service: use one someone else has already exposed. Commerce One drew on Citibank's Web Service, allowing Commerce One to focus on the other aspects of its business. Hagel and Brown believe companies will couple their own Web Services with those of others to create complex, yet flexible, best-in-class systems. To illustrate the basics of building a Web Service, consider the simplified example on page 398, followed by a case about Bekins on page 403.

Preparing for On-the-Fly Web Services Development. Although Web Services can help enterprises develop systems faster, the technology might have other ramifications as well—ramifications that CIOs would do well to prepare for, before they actually happen. One possibility is end user development of Web Services, believes Jonathan Sapir, of InfoPower, a company that offers an SOA-based development platform. He believes that companies are experiencing a crisis in software development because their IS organizations cannot keep up with users' requests for changes to applications. Due to the increasingly volatile business environment, systems need almost continual enhancement. When they do not get it, they do not change as fast as the business environment.

This "crisis" situation has occurred before. When corporate databases first appeared, only programmers had the tools and know-how to generate reports from them. But those reports did not solve individuals' needs. When report writers and query languages appeared, end users eagerly learned them to query the databases on their own, reducing the time needed to answer their questions. Likewise, programmers wrote large financial programs to manage corporate finances, but those programs did not meet the needs of individual accountants. Thus, when spreadsheets arrived in the 1970s, accountants (and others) eagerly used them to write personal applications. In fact, the spreadsheet was the "killer app" that drove the initial growth of the PC industry.

Today, Web Services and service-oriented architectures have set the stage for yet another round of even-more-powerful, on-the-fly end user development, believes Sapir. The need is here; so is the IT savvy. Many people have been using computers for at least 20 years—some, for their whole life. They play games, manage their finances, buy stock, and perform other online tasks that are a form of programming. They would develop their own personal programs if they had the tools. End user tools based on Web Services and SOA are coming, and they will again let users write personal applications. The difference this time is that these applications will useWeb Services standards, so they will be packaged as services that others can find, use, and even build upon.

Sapir foresees people computerizing their part of the business on their own with these user-friendly tools, thereby shifting computerization from top-down to bottom-up. To do so, though, people will need to view business needs as a series of small events that are handled throughout the day as they occur, rather than consolidated and addressed after-the-fact in one large development effort by the IS organization.

This bottom-up shift has come before, as noted, with minicomputers, then PCs, as well as with spreadsheets and fourth-generation languages. Each time, most IS organizations were caught unprepared. They had not laid down an infrastructure, provided tools or training, nor established principles for end user development using the new technologies. Companies ended up with "personal silos of data and apps" that were difficult to share and were not maintained nor backed up. IS departments had to catch up to bring order to the chaos. It behooves CIOs to respond to users' current requests for changes to applications by piloting a companywide Web Services platform and tools that users can use to get ahead of the curve.

Most importantly, IS management needs to implement a management system to manage the eventual intertwining of Web Services—before it happens. Without a Web Services management system, it is going to be awfully difficult to know which applications depend on which Web Services. Corporate executives will not want their major business processes to be based on applications that are not well managed. This management aspect of Web Services is a looming issue CIOs need to address, believes Sapir, before users take development into their own hands, as they have done so eagerly in the past.

Software Prototyping

"A prototype is a software system that is created quickly–often within hours, days, or weeks–rather than months or years." Franz Edelman, a pioneer in the use of software prototyping, described the process of software prototyping as "a quick and inexpensive process of developing and testing a trial balloon." Its purpose is to test out assumptions about users' requirements, about the design of the application, or perhaps even about the logic of a program.

With only conventional programming languages, such as COBOL, it was much too expensive to create both a prototype and a production version. Therefore, only production systems were developed. With end user tools, people can get prototypes up and running quickly. The prototype is relatively inexpensive to build because the language creates much of the code.

Prototyping is an iterative process. It begins with a simple prototype that performs only a few of the basic functions. Through use of the prototype, system designers or end users discover new requirements and refinements to incorporate in each succeeding version. Each version performs more of the desired functions and in an increasingly efficient manner.

Both 4GLs and prototyping have proven to be important underpinnings for today's application development world.

SUMMARY

The choice among the traditional systems development life cycle (SDLC), prototyping, RAD, and the newer "agile" methodologies for developing a customized application is essentially an IS management decision. Within firms that have their own capable IS staffs, the methodology choice might be based on factors such as the degree to which system requirements can be easily determined, and the application's functionality, size, and complexity. Custom application development using the multistep SDLC methodology, with well-defined signoffs, is now the traditional way to develop new computer systems and to maintain them; it is still the preferred approach when the system is large, complex, and serves multiple organizational units. A prototyping methodology is a more effective approach for small, simple projects. A prototyping approach is also used within an SDLC methodology to help users and IS professionals begin with a set of basic requirements and then develop a fuller set of functional requirements. A combination prototyping/ piloting approach within an SDLC methodology is especially useful when the systems project is characterized by significant technological risks or organizational risks, or both, that can be tested out early in the project using a prototype.

Whether the traditional SDLC, prototyping, or some combination of the two is used, it is the responsibility of both business managers and IS specialists to ensure that the system that is installed meets the needs of the business at the time of installation. IS specialists typically hold primary responsibility for most system analysis and all system building steps. However, the systems project may be managed by an IS manager, a business manager, or both.

Rapid application development (RAD) methodologies have become more important as businesses seek to deliver high-quality applications within shorter time frames. A RAD methodology combines the iterative development benefits of prototyping with the quality controls of the SDLC; this approach also typically relies on JAD sessions and software automation (CASE) tools to generate code. In recent years there has also been a movement to develop more "agile" development methods based on the principles of simplicity and feedback, with relatively small project teams. One of the characteristics of an agile method called Extreme Programming is an obsession with testing code early and often, in order to have zero defects.

The traditional approach to system development from the 1960s evolved to give the process more discipline, control, and efficiency. It was valuable in moving programming and system analysis from pure free-form "art" to a better defined "craft." Problems remained, though, with long development times, little user involvement, and lack of flexibility in the resulting systems. The tools and methods of the 1970s and 1980s—4GLs, software prototyping, CASE, and OO development—permitted more rapid development and even experimental development; some were seen as revolutionary techniques to conventional developers.

The 1990s brought the need for integrated enterprise systems and Internet-based systems. Both required more flexibility and speedier development with a significant amount of integration, both internal and external to the company. With the integration efforts, companies realized the importance of focusing less on technical issues and more on the impacts of IT on business strategy, organization, and people. Widely reported failures of large ERP projects reinforced this need to concentrate on the business.

Most recently, the IT industry has responded with new tools and approaches. Application servers support integration across a wide range of new and legacy systems, Java supports Internet-based application development, and Web Services promise to make the Internet the heart of systems building. We have indeed entered a new era of application development where the focus is on the Internet, inter-organizational development, and ecosystem applications.

CHAPTER REVIEW QUESTIONS

1. Describe the three phases and eight steps in the SDLC methodology.
2. What are the key activities performed by IS professionals in each step of the SDLC?
3. Select three characteristics of a high-quality application system (as shown in Figure 9.3) and provide a rationale for why each is important.
4. How key is documentation under the SDLC methodology? What are the difficulties of keeping documentation current and how can they be overcome?
5. Describe a distinct advantage of each of the four strategies for implementing a new system, as shown in Figure 9.4.
6. Why is an accurate and complete requirements definition especially critical when using the SDLC "waterfall" approach?
7. Describe the steps of a pure prototyping methodology as an alternative to the SDLC approach.
8. Which disadvantages of an SDLC methodology are addressed by a prototyping system?
9. Describe two ways that a prototyping approach can be used within the Definition phase of a traditional SDLC methodology.
10. Why are JAD techniques a key characteristic of RAD methodologies?
11. Describe how a RAD methodology builds on the strengths of both an SDLC methodology and prototyping.
12. Why does the use of contractors increase the complexity of an IT project? What situations would be best served for using outside contractors as opposed to using in-house staff?

CHAPTER DISCUSSION QUESTIONS

1. Why was the SDLC methodology for developing application systems widely adopted in U.S.-based organizations by the early 1990s?
2. Who defines the requirements of a new system? Is it IS department managers or business managers? How can you reconcile these two points of view and effect a compromise?
3. If so much time is put into the development of new application systems using SDLC, why do so many of them fail?
4. Compare the role of the systems analyst in the development of an application system using the SDLC and using a prototyping approach.
5. Is an end prototype a poor technical solution? Why or why not?
6. Discuss why an application might be built using prototyping as part of the SDLC methodology, rather than by a pure prototyping methodology alone.
7. What is the role of a project manager in an in-house development of a customized application? When should IS and business managers serve as co-leaders of a project?
8. How critical is good documentation to a system? Can today's advanced tools alleviate some of the documentation burden?
9. How do modern tools (such as CASE), techniques (such as JAD), and new methodologies (such as extreme programming) help IS organizations overcome the disadvantages of the traditional SDLC methodology?
10. Search online for the topic of offshore outsourcing of IT project work. How prevalent is it? Could it be a problem for the U.S. now or in the future?

CASE STUDY: BEKINS

Bekins, the moving company, is using Web Services in its HomeDirectUSA business unit, which specializes in the home delivery of household appliances, large-screen televisions, and other large, expensive furniture. Bekins uses some 1,000 independent moving agents across the United States to move furniture when Bekins' own fleet cannot.

Formerly, Bekins faxed or phoned these agents to arrange deliveries, but the process was slow and not equitable to all the agents. To automate the process, Bekins used Web Services technology to create an online brokering system called Tonnage Broadcast Exchange (TBE). When Bekins receives an order to deliver, say, a refrigerator, that its centrally managed fleet cannot handle, it uses TBE to "tender" that job to its agents (and perhaps other shippers). All agents are sent the tender at the same time based on pre-established criteria; so the system is fair. Once an agent accepts a job, it becomes unavailable to the others. The results have been lower tendering costs, faster customer service, and better utilization of agents' trucks. Furthermore, because the system is so efficient, Bekins can offer lower-margin jobs to the agents, increasing its shipping volume and revenues.

BEKINS' E-COMMERCE PLATFORM

In 1999, Bekins made two key IT decisions about how it would develop future systems. One, it chose Java, rather than Microsoft's NET, as its e-commerce platform. Two, it chose IBM's WebSphere to develop and deploy future applications. TBE uses two systems that initiated Bekins' new e-commerce environment. The first system was the Shipment Tracking System, which lets Bekins' customers (such as manufacturers and retailers) and consumers track shipments via the Web. Retailers like this system because its accuracy lets them bill their customers for home delivery faster. The second Java-based system was the Customer Order Management and Inventory System, which lets customers and shipping agents enter shipping orders via the Web. This system improved order accuracy up to 40 percent and allows customers to see the inventory Bekins is holding.

The TBE system, which is also based on the Java platform and built using WebSphere, advances Bekin's e-commerce platform by adding Web Services technologies. These technologies allow Bekins to link an agent's transportation management system into TBE almost instantly once the agent has readied its system to exchange messages using the Web Services standards: XML, SOAP, WSDL, and UDDI.

TBE runs on Bekins' mainframe. Each business partner has a client-side Java application running on one of its servers. When an agent wants to accept a tender from Bekins, its client-side application accesses the private TBE UDDI registry to find out how to communicate with the SOAP servlets. The SOAP servlet transmits the acceptance message to Bekins, where an XML parser translates it. A Java interface then passes it to Bekins' customer order management system, where it is booked as an order in the DB2 database.

BUILDING TBE

The TBE development team consisted of an XML expert, two Java developers (one senior and one junior), an architect who knew IBM's WebSphere and DB2 database, and two COBOL programmers. They developed TBE in just 5 months' time, partly due to their experience and partly due to WebSphere, which provided the framework and sample code they built upon.

The team followed a formal development methodology with the developers focusing on creating TBE's components and the architect helping put the pieces together. The project was divided into five phases:

1. Code the core of TBE in Java (to be hosted on a Bekins' mainframe)
2. Convert the Java objects to Web Services
3. Deploy the Web Services
4. Code the client side of TBE (to be run on each agent's server)
5. Test the integration of the various parts of TBE

Building TBE required commitments from several moving partners because it was to be an inter-organizational system. Three partners were readying their companies to use Web Services technologies internally to integrate their own systems. Another seven acted as beta test sites for TBE using actual data. The tests gave Bekins confidence that TBE met its partners' requirements. TBE went live with 10 percent of the agents. Agents have been coming online since. Agents not ready to participate in TBE using Web Services technologies can access the system through a Web portal. Involving its partners in the development proved important, but equally important was their comfort with the new Web Services environment.

Case Study Discussion Questions

Question One

What lessons can a company learn from the way Bekins constructed its Web Services technology?

Question Two

How did Bekins maintain a fair system for its agents? Could this have derailed the whole process if the agents didn't buy into the idea?

Question Three

How can partnering with clients best be managed, so as to keep everyone happy?

Question Four

What flaws do you see in this system, if any?

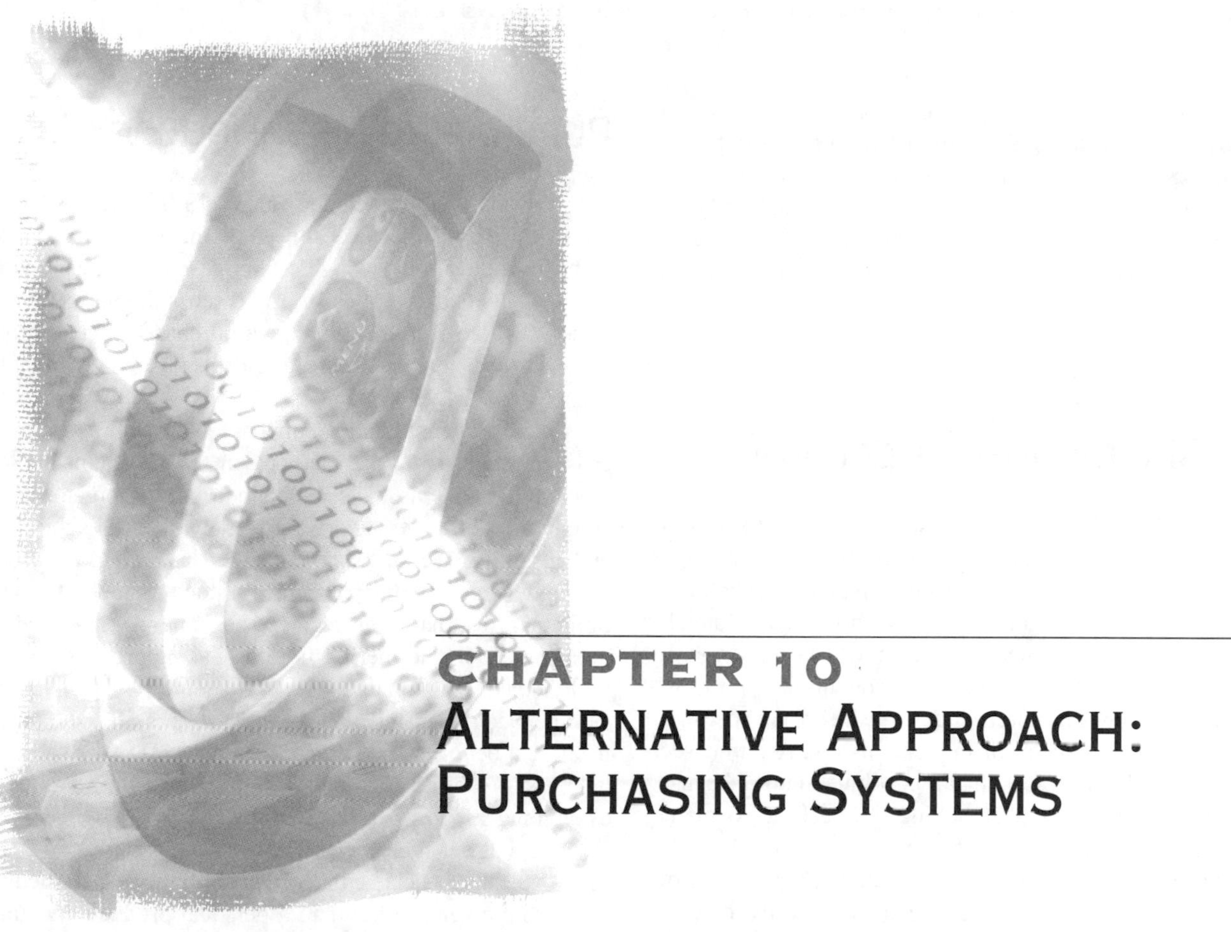

CHAPTER 10
ALTERNATIVE APPROACH: PURCHASING SYSTEMS

IN MOST LARGE COMPANIES TODAY, SOFTWARE IS BOTH CUSTOM DEVELOPED by in-house information systems (IS) staff and procured from an outside source. In fact, the trend for more than a decade has been for midsized and larger organizations to purchase application packages rather than custom develop their own solutions with in-house IS personnel, whenever it is feasible and cost-beneficial to do so. Capital expenditures for implementing purchased software packages are therefore a large part of the total IS budget. Of course, many small businesses have no, or very few, IS professionals, so they essentially procure all their software from outside sources.

Firms in the software industry have grown across the globe over the past decades, so that today companies can choose from thousands of products that can be purchased as "off-the-shelf" packaged software. The software industry firms that survive attract new and seasoned IS professionals to be their employees so that they can quickly develop information technology (IT) solutions to respond to new marketplace needs. Firms that purchase a software package also typically need to purchase services from the software vendor to help install and maintain the software for their business. Besides working with the software vendor, the purchasing firm's own system and business analysts work on project teams with business managers to purchase and install new systems. Some team members also typically are part of an ongoing support team for the business users after a new purchased system has been installed.

Packaged software applications are often built today with standard Windows or Web browser interfaces for the end user. These types of interfaces are also available for large client/server systems. Some of these enterprise-level systems have industry-specific versions of their packages to facilitate their implementation. Other software vendors develop packages for a specific industry only, such as sales and inventory management systems for retailers, commercial loan systems for banks, claim-processing systems for insurance companies or healthcare providers. Wherever there is a sizable market for a standard package, a software company is likely to be developing applications to sell to that market.

For firms that have their own IS department resources, a make-or-buy analysis is undertaken in order to decide whether to procure a product or service from an outside source or to produce the software or perform the service using internal IS resources. This chapter offers you a better understanding of the overall business and IT benefits that an organization needs to consider when it has a choice between purchasing a software application and developing a customized application. It describes in detail the process steps for selecting, preparing for, and implementing a software application package, as well as some of the project team roles and keys to success.

THE MAKE-OR-BUY DECISION

The choice between building a custom application and purchasing a software package—a **make-or-buy decision**—should be made jointly by the business managers who need the software and the IS professionals who have the knowledge to assess the technical benefits and risks. For organizations with their own skilled IS personnel, the two most obvious advantages of purchasing software are (1) cost savings and (2) faster speed of implementation. A purchased package usually costs less than a custom solution because the software vendor will be selling the package to many organizations. That is, the companies that purchase the software will be sharing the development and upgrade costs of the package. A software package also typically can be implemented sooner than a custom application because it already exists; in today's fast-changing business environments, this can be a very important advantage.

However, there also are some downsides. One major downside of buying an application solution is that a purchased package seldom exactly fits a company's needs. For the organization that is buying a package to replace an older, custom-developed system, this type of change can have several important ramifications for the business. Most commonly, it means that business users might be asked to "give up" features of the older custom software that the package does not support. This downside alone means that organizations should have a very good process in place that will help them make the best trade-off decisions for the organization. As described below, this requires a methodology that will take into account knowledge of the package's capabilities as well as informed business and technical judgments about how well the package will meet the organization's needs.

At the end of this chapter we also briefly discuss a procurement option that includes contracting with a vendor to "host" (run) one or more applications for a business firm under a leasing contract (see the section of this chapter entitled "New Purchasing Option: Application Service Providers").

PURCHASING METHODOLOGY

Let's turn now to the detailed steps of a life-cycle process for selecting, modifying, and implementing these large software application packages. After describing the individual steps in detail, we then briefly discuss the project team roles, how to effectively manage a purchased system project, and the major advantages and disadvantages of purchasing a packaged system.

Although at first glance it appears relatively easy to purchase packaged software, many instances of systems implementation problems have arisen because an organization simply did not understand what was involved in acquiring and installing the software package that was purchased. Our description of the purchasing steps assumes that an initial approval has been received for a new system that is of sufficient size to merit a full purchasing process. As we will discuss, the package selection should be a joint decision between business managers who can assess the organizational benefits and risks and IS professionals who can help assess the benefits and risks from a technical as well as ongoing support perspective.

Note that our focus here is on what has been referred to as a "dedicated" package that offers a solution to a particular business problem, rather than a personal productivity suite (such as Microsoft Office). Our discussion also assumes that an organization has its own IS specialists. Organizations that have no IS specialists will need to rely on the vendor or outside consultants, or both, to provide the necessary IS expertise.

The Purchasing Steps

The template for the purchasing process steps is shown in Figure 10.1. The steps for purchasing application packages fit into the three life-cycle phases introduced in Chapter 8: Definition, Construction, and Implementation. In the systems development life cycle (SDLC) methodology described in Chapter 9, detailed systems specifications (what the system is to do) are documented in the Definition phase; the system is built in the Construction phase; and the system is installed, operated, and maintained in the Implementation phase.

Because customized application development using an SDLC process historically came first, the process for purchasing packages is referred to here as a *modified SDLC approach*. In the Definition phase, an organization not only defines its system needs but also then uses these requirements to identify potential vendors and solutions and then collect enough information to be able to evaluate them. In comparison to the SDLC process for custom software, the

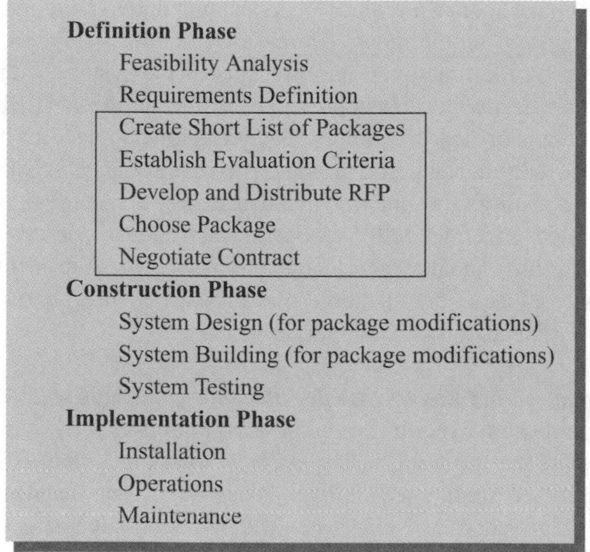

Definition Phase
Feasibility Analysis
Requirements Definition
Create Short List of Packages
Establish Evaluation Criteria
Develop and Distribute RFP
Choose Package
Negotiate Contract
Construction Phase
System Design (for package modifications)
System Building (for package modifications)
System Testing
Implementation Phase
Installation
Operations
Maintenance

Figure 10.1 The Purchasing Process

Definition phase is expanded to include five additional steps, beginning with creating a short list of potential packages.

Since an off-the-shelf packaged solution has already been designed, built, and tested by a vendor, the Construction phase is radically reduced. An exception here is when the package has not yet been fully released and the purchasing organization contracts with the vendor to serve as an **Alpha** or **Beta** site for the software vendor. Being involved as an Alpha site often means that the company can play a significant role in determining the final functionality and user interface design for the new package; in turn, this is a major commitment to providing both business and IS resources to work with the vendor. Being involved as a Beta site typically means significant involvement in a user acceptance test role for the software vendor (such as described in Chapter 10): A vendor does Beta testing with organizations that are not Alpha sites in order to closely monitor the system for potential errors in a different setting.

The Implementation phase includes the same steps as in the SDLC. For a purchased system, however, the software vendor might be highly involved in the Installation. Further, the maintenance of the package is usually a task performed by the vendor. The negotiation of this part of the purchase contract is therefore a critical step.

Initiating the Purchasing Process. Similar to the decision for customized application investments, organizations use a number of approaches to decide whether to invest in a purchased system. Some organizations do not require a detailed formal request to begin an investigation of a possible system purchase because there is an assumption that fewer IS resources are needed. At a minimum, the business manager prepares a document that briefly describes the proposed application needs and outlines the potential benefits that the application will provide to the organization.

A high-level cost estimate for a proposed purchase will need to be developed with both business manager and IS analyst input. Estimating the system costs involves much more than identifying the purchase costs of candidate packages. For example, Figure 10.2 provides a hypothetical

Stages	Cost of Building System	Cost of Buying System
Definition Phase		
Feasibility Analysis	$ 50,000	$ 50,000
Requirements Definition	250,000	200,000
Construction Phase		
System Design	150,000	—
Coding and Testing	150,000	—
System Testing	130,000	100,000
Documentation and Procedures	120,000	25,000
Implementation Phase		
Installation Planning, Data Cleanup, and Conversion	150,000	175,000
Software Purchase Price	—	100,000
Total	$1,000,000	$ 650,000

Figure 10.2 Comparison of Costs and Building versus Purchasing a System

comparison of the costs for a $1 million custom-developed system using in-house resources (a midsized system) with the costs for selecting and purchasing an off-the-shelf package with the same overall functionality. The total cost for the purchased solution ($650,000) is about two-thirds of the total cost of building the system in-house. Note, however, that the software purchase price ($100,000 for purchasing the licenses to the software package) is less than one-sixth of the total costs—a characteristic that is often not fully realized by business managers who don't have extensive experience with purchasing packaged software. Further, in the Construction phase costs for this example, there is an assumption that no major modifications to the package are required and that linkages with other systems are not a part of this project.

As when building the system using the SDLC, a systems project team should be established and given the responsibility for acquiring the software. The team should include representatives from the business units that will implement the system, IS analysts, and other IS specialists who will operate and support the packaged system and other systems that will interface with the package. Some of the specific team roles will be described later in this chapter.

Definition Phase. The Definition phase begins with the same two steps as in the SDLC process. However, five additional steps are specific to the purchasing process.

Feasibility Analysis. Similar to the SDLC, the objective of this step is to determine whether the proposed system is economically, technically, and operationally feasible. When purchasing a system, the feasibility of purchasing rather than building a system solution is also being considered. This step would therefore include a preliminary investigation of the availability of packaged systems that might be suitable candidates, including a high-level investigation of the software features and capabilities provided by the vendors. In this step a more detailed cost-benefit analysis is undertaken for project budgeting and monitoring purposes.

Requirements Definition. The requirements definition is a critical step in the SDLC approach. The SDLC deliverable is a detailed specification of what the system must do in terms of the inputs it must accept, the data it must store, the processes it must perform, the outputs it must produce, and the performance requirements that must be satisfied. It must be accurate, complete, and detailed because it is used to design and program the system and because it determines the quality of the resulting system.

When purchasing the system, this step is equally critical. In order to select the best software package, one must first have at least a high-level conceptual understanding of the system requirements. Here, however, the focus is on defining the functional requirements of the system to the degree needed for developing a request for proposal (RFP) from a short list of vendors. The requirements need to be more fully developed than the basic requirements used to build a prototype but less detailed than the requirements elicited under an SDLC process when they are used to design the actual system. Research has shown that uncertainty about an organization's needs is a significant barrier to packaged software adoption.

Create Short List of Suitable Packages. In this step the organization's requirements are used to eliminate all but a few of the most promising candidate packages that were identified in the feasibility analysis step. For example, packages should be eliminated if they do not have particular required features or will not work with existing hardware, operating system and database management software, or networks. Further research on the vendor's capabilities can be undertaken to eliminate vendors due to problems experienced with other users of the package, a vendor's inadequate track record or firm size, or other concerns about long-term viability. Independent consultants with expertise on specific types of applications or specializing in a given industry can also be key resources here and might be able to help the project team eliminate inappropriate candidates.

Establish Criteria for Selection. In this step both business and IS team members need to work together to determine relevant criteria about the candidate packages and vendors in order to choose the best one. Some criteria can be categorized as mandatory requirements, whereas others could be categorized as desirable features.

Some areas in which detailed criteria should be developed are shown in Figure 10.3. For example, the vendor's

The Package
- Functional capabilities of the packaged system
- Technical requirements the software must satisfy
- Amount and quality of documentation provided

The Vendor
- Business characteristics of the vendor firm
- Vendor support of the package—initial and ongoing

Figure 10.3 Key Criteria for Software Package Selection

business characteristics could include items such as how long the vendor has been in the software business, the number of employees, financial reports over the past 5 years, its principal products, its yearly software sales revenue, and the location of its sales and support offices. The packaged system's functional capabilities should include the degree to which the package allows for multiple options and the ease with which it can be tailored to fit company needs using parameters or other approaches that do not require system coding.

The technical requirements to be evaluated include the hardware and system software (system platform) required to run the system and the database requirements for the package. This information allows one to evaluate how well the package will conform to current organizational standards for hardware, software, and networks. The types, amount, and quality of the documentation provided should also be evaluated, as well as the quality and amount of vendor support available, including training, consulting, and system maintenance.

In addition to detailing the evaluation criteria, consideration should be given to the measures that will be used in the evaluation process. It is not uncommon to evaluate packages using a scale with numbers (such as 1 through 10) or qualitative labels (such as outstanding, good, average, fair, or poor). If a scale with numbers is used, each criterion can be assigned an importance weight, and a weighted score can be computed for each evaluation category for each package. Although quantitative scores might not be the sole means for selection, they help to quantify differences among the candidate packages.

Develop and Distribute the RFP. A **request for proposal (RFP)** is a formal document sent to potential vendors inviting them to submit a proposal describing their software package and how it would meet the company's needs. In organizations with prior experience purchasing software, a template for the RFP could already have been developed. A sample table of contents is shown in Figure 10.4. However, the specific requirements sought in Section III in this example will greatly depend on the type of package and the specific business needs.

The project team uses the criteria for selection to develop the RFP. The RFP gives the vendors information about the system's objectives and requirements, the environment in which the system will be used, the general criteria that will be used to evaluate the proposals, and the conditions for submitting proposals. Specific questions might need to be developed to capture the system's performance characteristics, whether source code is provided,

	Page
I. Introduction	
A. Structure and Scope of the RFP	3
B. Objective of RFP	3
C. Company Background and Philosophy	3
D. Hardware/Software Environment	4
E. Current Business Environment	5
II. Guidelines for Vendor Response	
A. Guidelines	6
B. Vendor Response	8
C. General Evaluation Process	10
III. Requirements	
A. Vendor Information	12
B. Vendor Support/Training	13
C. Documentation	15
D. Package Hardware and System Software Environment	17
E. Application and Database Architecture	21
F. Tuning and Measurement	26
G. Functional Requirements	28
IV. Costs	
A. Summary	33
B. Non-Recurring	35
C. Recurring	37
D. Price Guarantee	39
E. Maintenance Agreement	40
F. New Releases	41
V. Signature Page	42

Figure 10.4 Sample RFP Table of Contents

and whether the purchasing organization is allowed to modify the package without voiding the vendor warranty. In addition to pricing information for the package itself, any additional costs for training and consulting need to be ascertained. The RFP can also be used to capture historical information about the package, such as the date of the first release, the date of its last revision, and a list of companies in which the package has been implemented—including contact information to obtain references from these companies.

This step ends when the RFP is sent to the short list of qualified vendors.

Evaluate Vendor Responses to RFP and Choose Package. In this step the vendor responses to the RFP are evaluated and additional actions are taken to evaluate the candidate packages and their vendors. The overall objective of the evaluation process is to determine the extent of any discrepancies between the company's needs as specified by the requirements and the weighting system and the capabilities of the proposed application packages. Aggregate evaluations (scores) need to be calculated for each set of criteria and for the overall package. The team then uses these figures to discuss the major strengths and weaknesses of the candidate packages. This can be a large data collection and analysis task and might involve independent evaluations by all project team members. Both IS and business team members might need to confer not only with other project team members, but also with other members of their departments.

In addition to evaluating the vendors' responses from the formal RFP process, two other types of data collection are commonly pursued, at least for the leading candidate packages. First, demonstrations of the leading packages can usually be arranged. Sometimes it is feasible for the vendor to set up a demo on-site at your organization; at other times, another location is required—either at a vendor location or at another company that has installed the package. Detailed requirements for software demos should be provided to the vendors to ensure equitable conditions for demonstrating system performance, because response times and other characteristics of system performance can vary greatly depending on the hardware and system software being used to run the package. An example of demo specifications for a financial modeling package, and a form for evaluating the demo specified, are provided in Figures 10.5A and 10.5B.

Second, references from users of the software package in other companies are usually obtained. Each vendor might be asked to provide a reference list as part of the RFP. One especially effective technique is to require the vendor to provide the names of users as well as IS specialists for each customer organization on their reference list. Task force members can then divide up the names with, for example, IS specialists contacting their counterparts in companies that have already implemented the package. Site visits to one or more of these companies might also be possible. Evaluations of the vendor's consulting and training services can also be obtained from these sources.

Presentation Directions

The format must follow the outline provided.

The mainframe to which the PC is connected for this presentation must be an IBM running under MVS. If your MVS is not exactly like ours (as outlined in the RFP) you must provide a written explanation of how the differences (i.e., response time, color, etc.) affect the demonstration.

The presentation is limited to 2 hours, including 30 minutes for questions at the end. You will be given 30 minutes to set up.

With the data and formulas provided, create a relational database so that the following Profit and Loss (P&L) statements can be modeled and reported.

Fiscal 2000 Plan:

Item P&L: by month with total year at the right.
Control Unit P&L: by item with total at the right.
Business Unit P&L: by Control Unit with total at the right.

Fiscal 2001 Projection:

Business Unit P&L: by Control Unit with total at the right.

Combined Fiscal 2000 & Fiscal 2001:

Control Unit Change Analysis: by item for total Fiscal 2000 vs. proj. Fiscal 2001.
Business Unit Change Analysis: by Control Unit for total Fiscal 2000 vs. proj. Fiscal 2001.

Provide a listing of the populated database relations and/or tables.

Provide an example listing of the programs/models and report format files for each type of P&L and Change Analysis above.

Figure 10.5A Example of Requirements for Vendor Demonstration

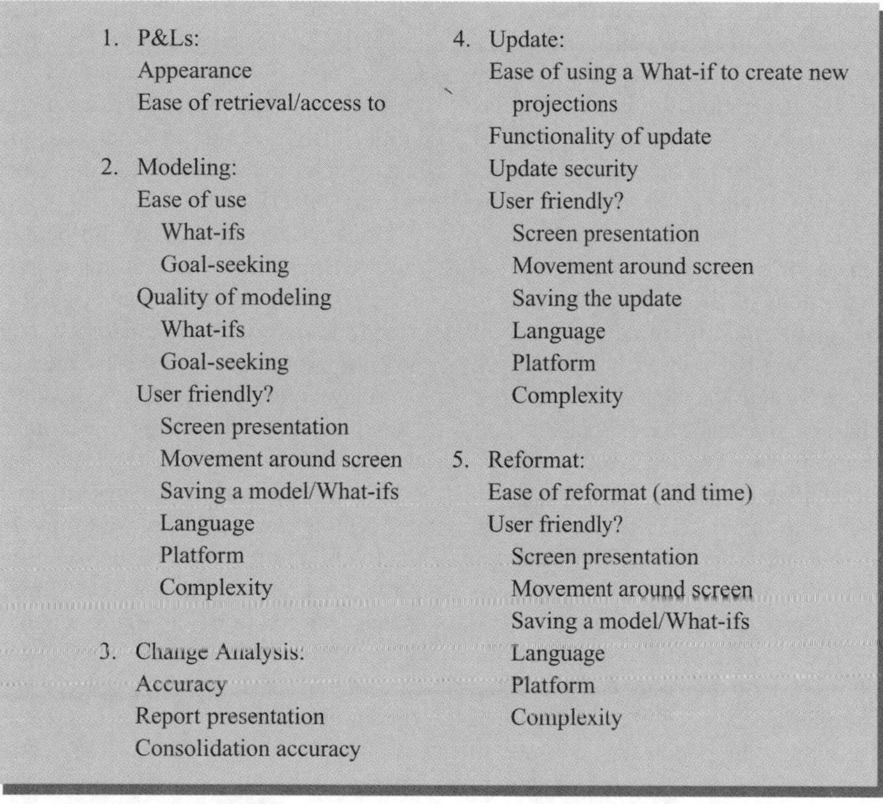

1. P&Ls:
   Appearance
   Ease of retrieval/access to

2. Modeling:
   Ease of use
     What-ifs
     Goal-seeking
   Quality of modeling
     What-ifs
     Goal-seeking
   User friendly?
     Screen presentation
     Movement around screen
     Saving a model/What-ifs
     Language
     Platform
     Complexity

3. Change Analysis:
   Accuracy
   Report presentation
   Consolidation accuracy

4. Update:
   Ease of using a What-if to create new projections
   Functionality of update
   Update security
   User friendly?
     Screen presentation
     Movement around screen
     Saving the update
     Language
     Platform
     Complexity

5. Reformat:
   Ease of reformat (and time)
   User friendly?
     Screen presentation
     Movement around screen
     Saving a model/What-ifs
     Language
     Platform
     Complexity

Figure 10.5B Example of Evaluation Worksheet for Vendor Demonstration

Based on all the above information sources, the project team needs to assess how well the company's needs match with the capabilities of the available packages (see Figure 10.6). This is a critical step that requires both business and technical expertise. The results of this process step will also have broad ramifications for the project's success.

Once the discrepancies between the package's capabilities and the company's needs are identified, the team needs to choose the best way to deal with these discrepancies for the top candidate packages. Assuming that the company decides that it still wants to invest in one of these packages, there are three major alternatives to choose from. As shown at the bottom of Figure 10.6, the company can change its own procedures to fit the package, investigate the feasibility and costs of modifying the package, or implement the package "as is" and work around the differences.

An important factor when choosing among these alternatives is fully understanding the additional development effort and costs that would be required to modify the package in order to tailor it to the company's needs and integrate it into the company's environment. These alternatives therefore need to be made in collaboration with internal IS specialists and the vendors of the top candidate packages in order to be sure that the extent of the discrepancies have been fully identified and that the feasibility and advisability of modifying a given package have been fully considered.

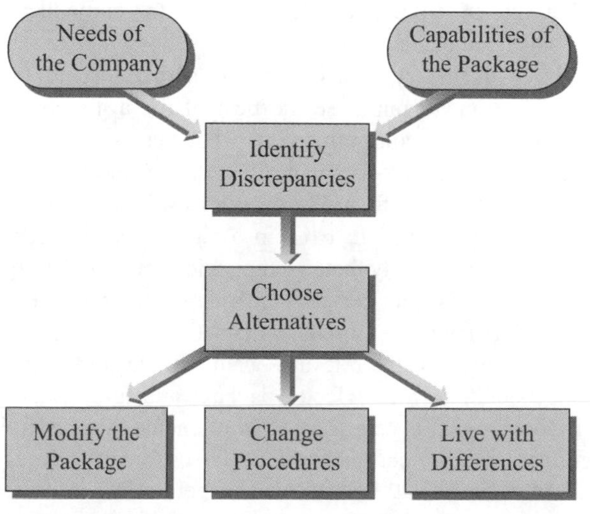

Figure 10.6 Matching Company Needs with Capabilities of the Package

If system modifications are a viable alternative, the plans for which organization will be responsible for programming the changes and the total costs of these changes will need to be taken into consideration. Further, the impacts of modifying the package need to be evaluated for not just the initial system project, but also for subsequent maintenance and package upgrade projects. For example, many companies that purchase today's large complex enterprise system packages, such as an ERP system, are advised to avoid reprogramming portions of the package in order to avoid the costs of continually modifying new releases of the package in the future (see the section below entitled "Special Case: Enterprise System Packages").

Instead, many purchasing companies have decided to take the middle alternative in Figure 10.6: Change Procedures. That is, they decide that it is better for the company to change its own procedures to match the way the software package operates than to modify the package. A company might in fact even find that the procedural assumptions incorporated into the package are better ways of doing things than those specified by the company during the Requirements Definition step of the process. This could occur if the software vendor has worked with one or more leading organizations in the same industry in order to develop the software package. For example, the vendors of today's large ERP packages might have worked with industry consortia to develop modules around industry-specific processes, and then the vendors can market their packages as having "best practices" for the industry embedded in their software package.

The decision to purchase a system is therefore not only a commitment to purchase the best of the available systems, but also a commitment to whatever organizational compromises need to be made in order to implement the system. Packaged software is a vendor's solution to a problem that is perceived to exist in a significant number of firms. Thus, it is likely that discrepancies between the organization's needs and the package's capabilities will exist. Before finalizing the purchase decision, the project team should ensure that the relevant business managers support the decision to buy the selected package and agree that they will do whatever is necessary to implement it successfully. Similarly, the project team should ensure that the IS specialists agree that the system can operate in the current environment and that they can satisfactorily support it in-house as required.

Negotiate Contract. The deliverables from this stage are a legal contract with the vendor of the selected software package and a detailed plan for the remainder of the life-cycle steps. The contract with the software vendor specifies not only the software price, number of licenses, and payment schedule, but also functional specifications, acceptance-testing procedures, a timetable of the delivery process, protection of trade secrets, repair and maintenance responsibilities, liabilities due to failures, required documentation, and options to terminate the agreement (Gurbaxani and Whang, 1991).

Contract negotiations should be an integral part of the purchase process. When working with vendors to determine how to reduce the discrepancies between the company's needs and the packages' capabilities, one is actually prenegotiating a contract with the selected vendor.

Many organizations have software purchasing specialists who work with system project managers in the contract writing and negotiation steps. Because the contract will be the only recourse if the system or the vendor does not perform as specified, the use of an attorney also reduces the likelihood of future legal wrangling or a loss of rightful claims. Once the project is underway, the project manager needs to be familiar enough with the contractual agreement in order to know whether an unanticipated need for vendor services will require a formal change to the vendor contract.

The contract type also has implications for the risk level of the purchasing company. For example, under a fixed-price contract, the buyer knows in advance the total price that will be incurred for a specified product and vendor services. Under a cost-reimbursement type of contract, in which the buyer agrees to pay the vendor's direct and indirect costs, the purchasing company assumes a much greater risk.

Construction Phase. In the SDLC process, the Construction phase includes three steps: system design, system building, and system testing. With purchasing, the extent to which the first two steps are needed depends on whether or not the purchased package is modified, as well as the complexity of the package itself.

Significant savings in time and money might be realized if no major modifications are made to the package's code. Looking back at the cost comparisons in Figure 10.2, the Construction phase costs are the major source of the total cost savings from purchasing a package vs. building a custom application: Even when adding in the software purchase price itself (shown under Implementation Phase), the costs for the Construction phase of a purchase package are less than half as great as the Construction costs for the customized solution. However, as stated earlier, the example in Figure 10.2 assumes that no major modifications to the package are required and that linkages with other systems are not a part of this project. The $350,000 difference in total costs between the cost of building and the cost of purchasing this particular system could therefore quickly vanish if the assumption of no system modifications does not hold true.

If no modifications to the system are to be made, the firm can move to the system testing step after the purchase contract is signed. Many off-the-shelf packages for single functions, such as accounting applications, are often not modified because the business practices they support are quite standardized and the vendor did not develop the package with modifications in mind (Rockart and Hofman, 1992). Packaged systems have typically been Beta-tested in companies in the targeted industry before they are sold on the open market. Despite the fact that the package might have been thoroughly tested and already used in other organizations, user acceptance testing still needs to be conducted to ensure that the system works properly with the company's data and on preexisting or newly installed hardware. This could require significant time and effort because the purchasing organization is not familiar with the system's detailed design. The vendor provides user documentation for those who will use the system and technical systems documentation for those who install the system and operate it. However, new procedures for the system's business users might need to be developed to fit the purchasing organization.

If the package is modified, there might be several options to consider for how to accomplish the changes: a contract with the vendor, a contract with a third party, or modifying the software with in-house resources. Many vendors routinely contract to make the desired modifications. If a vendor will furnish only the machine-language code for the application—not the source code in which the program was written—the only alternative might be to contract with the vendor to make the modifications.

If the vendor or another outside supplier makes the modifications, the purchaser also needs to test them. User acceptance testing is especially important and typically requires significant time and effort by the business users. Revised user and system documentation also needs to be reviewed. If the purchaser modifies the package, the system design and building activities in the SDLC methodology will likely be followed, similar to the way these steps would be for traditional custom development. Because IS staff must devote substantial effort to understanding the details of the software package's design and structure in order to modify it, it is not uncommon for the initial estimates of the time and costs for these steps to be insufficient.

The scope of the project might also include modifications to existing company systems in order to interface them with the new package. Creating these interface programs can be difficult and costly, and integration testing is typically time-consuming. According to Keen (1991), the total costs of system modifications can be hard to predict and the total life-cycle costs for a purchased system can be up to seven times greater than the original estimate.

Implementation Phase. The Implementation phase of the SDLC involves installation, operations, and maintenance. As seen in Figure 10.1, these are all major activities in the purchasing life cycle.

Installation. The installation stage in the SDLC involves installation planning, training, data cleanup, and conversion. The installation of a packaged system also includes all these activities. A key factor in a successful installation of a packaged system is the quality of vendor support during this step (Lucas et al., 1988). The package's size and complexity can also greatly affect the installation plan. For example, large ERP system packages can entail multiple years of work by in-house IS specialists as well as outside consultants to prepare for the initial installation of these integrated systems. This is because not only do these systems include many optional choices with which to configure the system to fit the organization, but also because ERP systems typically require significant changes in day-to-day business processes. As a result, the costs for installation planning, data cleanup and conversion efforts to install such packages exceed those for a custom application effort (see Figure 10.2). In large organizations, especially those with different types of business units in different geographic locations, it is also often necessary to implement the package in phases, which can also increase project costs.

Special attention also needs to be given to the training needs for a purchased system as part of the implementation activities. Depending on the extent to which the new system will require significant changes in how employees currently do their jobs, the project might require a large investment in preparing the users for the new system, including in-house or vendor-led training programs. Business managers and representative users must be actively involved in these activities and committed to devoting the time necessary to anticipate and resolve problems that arise.

To help organizations that will be making significant changes in the way people do their jobs, many consulting firms have developed an expertise in what is referred to as "change management." Some of the change management activities are specifically designed to help overcome resistance by business users to the new system being implemented. For projects implementing complex enterprise systems, for example, the systems budget for change management activities can be greater than the budgeted cost for the initial software purchase.

Operations. Ongoing operations tasks for a new application are similar whether the company purchases the system or builds it using the SDLC. However, a key to success in the initial days of operation for a new packaged system is good lines of communication with the vendor in order to quickly resolve any problems. Long-term success depends on the degree to which the organization has successfully integrated the system into the company's ongoing operations.

Maintenance. As described above, it is common for a vendor to do package maintenance, and this needs to be specified in the software purchase contract. A well-designed contract can lead to considerable cost avoidance to a firm over the life of the system. The potential downside, however, is that the purchasing company becomes totally dependent upon the vendor for future system changes. Because the vendor must balance the desires and needs of all the organizations that use the system, a purchasing company might not get all the changes it wants and it might even have to accept some changes it does not want. The worst case scenarios here are as follows: (1) the purchased system has a significantly shorter useful life than originally intended, so the system costs may exceed the expected benefits for the company that purchased the software, or (2) the vendor goes out of business before the company achieves its expected return on the packaged software investment.

If the original package was modified, the installation of a vendor's new version of the package might not be the optimal solution for the purchasing organization. With the vendor's help, the company needs to compare the functionality of the new version of the package with its current modified version and then decide on the best way to deal with these discrepancies. The choices are similar to those shown in Figure 10.6, except the "do nothing" choice means that the organization might be left operating a version of the package that the vendor might or might not continue to support. If the organization modified the original package in-house or built extensive interfaces to the package's earlier version, the implementation of a new version of the package can also result in considerable maintenance costs for the organization.

In the case of large ERP system packages, the purchasing organization needs to anticipate that new releases of the software might be relatively frequent, and the vendor might continue to support prior package releases only for a certain time period. When implementing a system upgrade that includes significant new functionality, the company will need to decide whether to first implement the new version of the system and then initiate projects to make better use of the business capabilities supported by the new release or whether to implement the new business capabilities as part of the system upgrade project.

Project Team for Purchasing Packages

Successfully implementing a packaged application typically requires a major commitment on the part of business managers and users because of the extensive changes in business processes and procedures that are needed to effectively implement the purchased software. As a result, it is not uncommon for business managers to be asked to take a **project manager** role for a packaged application system project. However, because IS expertise is still required in order to manage the technical aspects of implementing a package, IS managers also need to play project leadership roles. As mentioned previously, small organizations that have no IS specialists will need to rely on the software vendor or outside consultants, or both, to provide the necessary IS expertise.

The software vendor initially provides information on the package capabilities in response to an RFP. Vendors of leading packages might then be asked to provide a demonstration and to consult with the purchaser about potential system modifications or new interfaces to older systems. The vendor company might also be contracted to perform modifications to the package prior to implementation in order to reduce mismatches between the packaged system's capabilities and the organization's needs after a careful assessment of the benefits and risks of doing so. The vendor could also play a major role in the system installation, as well as provide ongoing maintenance support for the purchasing organization. In the case of large enterprise system packages, it is also common for companies to contract with a consulting firm (that might have been certified by the software vendor) as a **third-party implementation partner** on the project.

Because of the initial and ongoing dependence on the software vendor, purchasing specialists (contract specialists) within the purchasing company can also be critical to the success of a packaged system implementation, whether or not they are formal members of the project team. For example, if an RFP is sent to vendors, a purchasing specialist will help prepare or at least review the RFP document before it is distributed to vendors. Firms with prior software purchasing experience might have developed boilerplate sections to be adapted to the type of purchase. Purchasing specialists are also skilled in negotiating contracts that provide for contingency actions that can reduce financial and other business risks for the purchasing company. For example, many of today's contracts include specific agreements about levels of service during an installation period (see the section entitled "Service Level Agreements" in Chapter 15).

As described earlier under the negotiate-contract step, attorneys (which may also be purchasing specialists) should oversee the writing and approval of the external contract with software vendors. All associated licensing agreements should also be reviewed in order to minimize the associated costs and risks for the business.

Managing a Purchased System Project

Purchased system projects are successful when the organization has selected a product, and a vendor, that is able to satisfy the firm's current and future system needs. This requires an effective project team with members who have the business and technical skills and knowledge needed, including the skills and knowledge needed for the project team roles described above. Unlike the traditional SDLC process in which a long Construction phase buffers the Definition phase from the Implementation phase, the purchase of a software package might entail large capital expenditures by the company within just a few months. The right business managers, end users, and IS specialists need to be a part of the project team to ensure that the best package is purchased from the best vendor and that both technical and business risks have been adequately considered.

A typical problem with managing the life cycle of a purchased system project is ensuring that adequate attention is given to the steps in the initial Definition phase. A common mistake is that business managers learn about a particular packaged solution from another company or a salesperson at an industry conference and they begin negotiating with the vendor without adequate attention to the functional requirements definition step. Project teams that do not do a good job identifying their requirements will not be able to do a good job assessing the discrepancies between the company's needs and the capabilities of candidate packages. This increases the short-term and long-term investment risks, because a contract with an external vendor is not as easily changed as a project agreement between users and internal IS developers. It is therefore critical that the Definition phase be performed well.

For the project team members from the business side who also have implementation responsibilities, it is also imperative that they be *representative* business managers and users. Steps should be taken to ensure that they are committed to the project goals at the outset, including the time schedule and budget.

The success of the Implementation phase also depends on how well the Definition phase was performed, because this is where the team members assessed the organizational changes needed to successfully implement the purchased system. As discussed earlier, users of the packaged system might be asked to make significant changes in how they do their jobs in order to conform to a package's features. This requires a well-planned installation step under the leadership of committed business managers who are very knowledgeable about the needed changes.

In addition, purchased system projects introduce several new types of risks. First, the success of the project is highly dependent on the performance of a third party. The quality of the implemented system will depend not only on the vendor's software engineering capabilities, but also on how well the implementing organization understands the package's capabilities and on the vendor's training and installation capabilities. As discussed earlier, a key aspect of the vendor selection process is the accurate assessment of the vendor's capabilities, not just an evaluation of the current software package.

The project's initial success, as well as the long-term effectiveness of the system being installed, is also highly dependent on the contract negotiation process. In most situations system implementation does not simply involve "turning the key." Vendor expertise might be required to install the package, build interfaces to existing systems, and perhaps modify the package itself to better match the purchasing organization's needs. Service expectations between the purchaser and vendor need to be a part of the contract developed at the end of the Definition phase. The contract will be the only recourse for the purchaser if the system modifications, vendor training, or the implementation of the package do not go well.

Purchasing Small Systems. The discussion in this chapter has focused on the purchasing process for large, complex systems. If a smaller, simpler system is being considered, the time and effort put into the process can, of course, be scaled back. However, a small system can still be a major investment for a small business. Unfortunately, many small businesses have limited experience with and knowledge of evaluating and installing such systems. The services of a hardware vendor, a local software supplier, as well as external consultants might therefore be needed.

Purchasing Advantages and Disadvantages

Figure 10.7 summarizes the advantages and disadvantages of purchasing packaged systems, as well as some potential long-term advantages and disadvantages for buying packaged software solutions.

Advantages. The primary project advantage is that, compared to customized application development, less time is needed to implement the system. Nevertheless, for midsized systems, the entire process will still require several months, and for large-scale enterprise software implementations (with packages such as ERP systems) the process can take several years.

A second major advantage is that packaged software implementations can be very attractive from an economic standpoint. For example, a small business can obtain a complete accounting system for less than $25,000, which is very low compared to the cost of developing a comparable customized application. Assuming that the vendor has more than 10,000 installations of this small package ($250 million in revenues), the vendor will have an incentive to spend millions of dollars on improving the package in order to issue new releases. Everyone comes out a winner because each purchaser has cost avoidance from purchasing a package, and the vendor makes a large enough profit to stay in business and provide upgrades and other support services on an ongoing basis. As shown in Figure 10.2, the initial purchase price of a software package might be a relatively small fraction of the total cost of acquiring and installing a software package.

A third temporary advantage is that in-house IS resources could be freed up to develop mission-critical applications that could provide the firm a competitive advantage if software packages can be implemented for relatively common processes that provide no specific strategic advantage.

Purchasing Advantages
- Reduced time to implement
- Lower overall acquisition costs
- High application quality (debugged)
- Reduced need for internal IS resources
- Infusion of external expertise (IS, business)

Purchasing Disadvantages
- Risks due to lack of package knowledge
- Risks due to extent of organizational changes required
- Initial and ongoing dependence on vendor

Figure 10.7 Advantages and Disadvantages of Purchasing Packaged Software

Two potential long-term advantages are application quality and the infusion of external expertise. The quality of a software package might be substantially better than that of a custom system, because a vendor can afford to spend much more time and effort developing the system than an individual company. The documentation can be much better than the typical in-house documentation, and new releases of the package might incorporate improvements recommended by companies that are using the system. Furthermore, each release is usually thoroughly tested, including a Beta test in a client organization.

Finally, a packaged solution is a quick way to infuse new expertise—both IT expertise and business expertise—into the organization. Given the fast pace of technological change, most organizations today find it difficult to train and retain IS personnel with expertise in new, emerging technologies. Software vendors often have the funds and motivation to develop systems using newer technologies. Packaged solutions for a particular industry, or large ERP systems, also frequently have best-in-class processes and procedures embedded in the software. By purchasing the software, companies can also adopt better business processes.

Disadvantages. Two major project risks are also associated with implementing purchased packages. One risk is the lack of package knowledge. The package implementation can require significant training for IS as well as business personnel, which increases the implementation costs. Because of an organization's relative unfamiliarity with the software package, the organization might also not be as quick to leverage the capabilities of the package as it would be to leverage the capabilities of a system that members of the organization had designed and custom developed. Some organizations also make the mistake of initially modifying the package, or adding other functionality, only to learn later that the package could have provided the same functionality if it had been implemented differently.

Another related project risk is that since implementing a packaged system often requires significant business process changes, there are greater project risks. Knowledgeable business managers and skilled IS specialists need to be significantly involved in the Definition phase to understand what organizational changes need to be made. Furthermore, there often is more user resistance due to the extent of changes required in order to implement the packaged solution.

The long-term disadvantage is that the organization becomes dependent on an external IT provider not only for the initial installation and perhaps some package modifications, but also for the ongoing maintenance of the package. Although in many cases this can result in a strategic alliance of value to both the vendor and purchaser, the purchaser might not fully anticipate the coordination costs associated with managing the vendor relationship. In addition, of course, there is the risk that the vendor will go out of business or be unresponsive to the needs of the purchasing firm.

SPECIAL CASE: ENTERPRISE SYSTEM PACKAGES

By the end of the 1990s, the majority of U.S.-based Fortune 500 companies and more than one-fourth of European-based midsized organizations had invested in a first wave of enterprise system packages: enterprise resource planning (ERP) systems. Most companies purchased these systems in order to achieve business benefits, but ERP investments are also IT platform investments.

One of the primary business benefits associated with ERP systems is to enable access to integrated data, sometimes real-time data, for better management decision making. Since most ERP systems are built to support cross-functional business processes, interfaces across separate functional systems do not need to be maintained. Further, ERP modules that can be "configured" to be used by different types of firms in different industries enable those firms that have already conducted projects to reengineer their business processes to now implement them; building custom systems to support new cross-functional processes would require a much larger system investment over a much longer time.

For the IS departments within the large firms that were among the first to purchase an ERP package, this could also be the first time that their IS personnel would be asked to configure a package in the best way possible, rather than to custom develop an application based on the requirements of their business users. IS personnel also needed to be sent to training classes, typically conducted by the software vendor, so that they could learn the packaged software as well as learn new vendor-specific languages for writing interfaces and queries. New "business analyst" skill sets could also be required to effectively manage the process steps for a packaged software project, rather than a customized life cycle methodology.

Another key characteristic of the early ERP projects was the heavy reliance on third-party consultants who were not employees of the software vendor, such as consultants in the Big 4 or smaller consulting firms. These "implementation partners" were usually invaluable for helping an organization quickly learn how the software package operates, as well as how the complex business process options embedded in each module would work. Because of the large scope and complexity of some of these ERP package implementations, one of the key management challenges, then, could have been to what extent to rely on the external consultants to lead an ERP project and how to make sure the purchasing company captured the needed knowledge to continue to operate and "fine tune" the configurations after the consultants left. Nevertheless, even with the help of third-party consultants, many initial ERP implementation projects were not successful.

According to Brown and Vessey (2003), five factors need to be managed well for an ERP project to be successful. These factors are described in some detail below.

- *Top management is engaged in the project, not just involved.* Because enterprise systems demand fundamental changes in the way a company performs its business processes, its business executives need to be visibly active in the funding and oversight of the project. Lower-level managers will not have the clout needed to ensure that not only will the ERP modules be configured to align with the best business process solutions for the company, but also that all relevant business managers buy in to the organizational changes that will be necessary to take advantage of the software package's capabilities.
- *Project leaders are veterans, and team members are decision makers.* Because ERP system implementations are extremely complex, the leaders of the project need to be highly skilled and have a proven track record with leading a project that has had a major impact on a business. The team members who are representing different business units and different business functions (e.g., finance, marketing, manufacturing) need to also be empowered to make decisions on behalf of the unit or function they represent. If the team members do not have decision-making rights, the project leaders will likely not be able to meet the agreed-upon project deadlines.
- *Third parties fill gaps in expertise and transfer their knowledge.* As described above, ERP systems are typically implemented with the help of third-party implementation partners (consultants), as well as the software vendor. The skillsets of the consultants needed will depend on the skillsets and experiences of the purchasing company's own business and IT managers. If there are no internal project leaders

with the necessary project management skills, consultants should also be used to help manage the project. However, before the consultants leave, the internal staff needs to acquire the knowledge needed to continue to operate the new system. Many organizations develop agreements with consultants that explicitly refer to the transfer of knowledge to internal staff as a part of the consultant contract.

- *Change management goes hand-in-hand with project planning.* Many of the early adopters of ERP systems underestimated the need for project resources to help prepare the business for implementing the new system. ERP systems typically require training not only in how to use the new system, but also in how to perform business processes in new ways to take advantage of the package's capabilities. Because of the tight integration of the ERP modules, workers also typically need to learn much more about what happens before and after their own interactions with the system. Companies with the fewest problems at the time of implementation began to plan for these types of changes as part of the overall project planning activities.
- *A satisficing mindset prevails.* Because of the integrated nature of the modules of an ERP package, companies typically implement the package in as "vanilla" a form as possible. This typically means that business personnel will be asked to "give up" some functionality that they had in a system that the ERP is replacing. In other words, the company needs to be in a "satisficing" mindset, as opposed to expecting an "optimal" solution. For companies with many business units across the globe, business managers will also typically be asked to accept some less-than-optimal ways of doing things in order to have a standard configuration across the enterprise. A typical rule-of-thumb here is to try and keep a standard solution for about 80 percent of the package configuration, recognizing that some local customization will even be required due to specific country or regional regulations.

Brown and Vessey also point out that later adopters of a new kind of enterprise system always have the advantage of learning from the mistakes of early adopters. For example, companies that purchased an ERP package in the second half of the 1990s could talk with other companies in their industry who had already implemented an ERP and then they could benchmark their own implementation plans in order to avoid making costly mistakes. These authors also suggest that much of what is learned from ERP projects will help the early adopters of the next wave of enterprise systems (e.g., customer relationship management and supply chain management systems).

Other researchers (e.g., Ross, 1998) have emphasized the importance of recognizing that large, complex enterprise system initiatives really don't end with the initial "Go Live" date. Rather, managers should anticipate that there will be a period of time following the initial implementation in which the system and new processes become more stabilized (a "shakedown" period). After the new ways of doing business have become more routinized and the technical operations of the new system are running smoothly, the company can begin to make smaller changes (continuous improvement) to help it achieve the promised business benefits from implementing this new type of software package. For example, many companies report having achieved cost efficiencies in materials procurement within the first calendar year after an ERP implementation, but other value-chain improvements might not be realized for several more years.

NEW PURCHASING OPTION: APPLICATION SERVICE PROVIDERS (ASPs)

A new trend related to implementing packaged solutions began to emerge in the IT industry during the first decade of the new millennium: **application service providers** (ASPs). Under this kind of purchasing option, the purchaser elects to use a "hosted" application rather than to purchase the software application and host it on its own equipment. The ASP is therefore an ongoing service provider, and the ASP option is a different kind of "make vs. buy" decision. Instead of having a software licensing agreement with a firm that developed the software, a company pays a third party (ASP) for delivering the software functionality over the Internet to company employees and sometimes the company's business partners.

The two major *advantages* associated with purchasing a package, which were discussed at the beginning of this chapter, are also advantages for choosing an ASP: (1) cost savings and (2) faster speed of implementation. A subscription-based service with an ASP typically involves monthly fees rather than large up-front IT investments in both the software package and additional infrastructure investments to host the package. For companies with widely dispersed employees requiring remote access, an ASP solution can also reduce network access and other service delivery costs. Because the package is also typically already up and running on the ASP's host computer, the implementation project should also be less time-consuming.

However, there are also some potential downsides, including dependence on an external vendor not just for the software package, but also for ongoing operations. Good processes for making the best purchasing decision and contracting for the needed service levels are even more critical when an organization enters into an ASP agreement. A purchasing process that carefully assesses the capability of an ASP to provide reliable performance and the likelihood of the ASP surviving in the marketplace are especially important for ASP contracts, because this market is still in its infancy. Some of these risks appear to be diminished when the ASP host is also a large software vendor—such as SAP or PeopleSoft for ERP modules or Siebel Systems for CRM modules.

Metrics for vendor performance and penalties for noncompliance should be a key part of the contract. As described in the sidebar "A Dream vs. a Nightmare," if you do not do a good job with the ASP selection process up front, you risk paying the price later.

SUMMARY

Purchasing packaged software is an alternative to custom software development that has been increasingly pursued by organizations of all sizes since the early 1990s. The fact that packaged solutions can be implemented more quickly than a custom-developed solution with the same, or similar, functionality is a major advantage in today's fast-changing business environment. A major disadvantage can be increased dependence on a vendor that could go out of business.

The process for purchasing an application is based on the same life-cycle phases as a custom approach: Definition, Construction, and Implementation. Even if an application is to be purchased, an organization first must define its basic system needs before attempting to select the best off-the-shelf application solution. The Definition phase also includes the development of an RFP to be sent to software vendors and an evaluation of the vendor responses. If successful, the Definition phase ends with a vendor contract, which should be negotiated with the help of contract specialists.

The time spent on Construction phase activities varies greatly depending on whether or not the source code of the package is modified, which may be done by the vendor, another outside supplier, or the purchasing company. In the case of large packaged systems for which there are expected to be frequent future releases (such as ERP modules), modifications are typically kept to a bare minimum. In contrast, the Implementation phase for a software package can be more challenging than for a custom application because of the purchasing company's lack of familiarity with the details of how the package operates as well as the need for large-scale changes in the way the company will operate once the new package has been implemented. The software vendor might be heavily involved in the installation step and is also typically relied on for ongoing maintenance. Large enterprise system vendors (such as SAP) typically release new versions on a frequent basis and support older versions of the package only for a set period of time.

Expertise in the implementation of packaged systems has become an important IT capability. In some firms new manager positions have been created in order to manage relationships with IT vendors. A new procurement option is to pay an application service provider to host a software application for remote access by company employees via the Internet.

CHAPTER REVIEW QUESTIONS

1. What are the major trade-offs in a make-or-buy decision?
2. Summarize the five additional steps for purchasing a system that are not part of the Definition phase of a traditional SDLC process.
3. What is an RFP and what critical tasks does it facilitate in the purchasing process?
4. Why is making a lot of modifications to a packaged system sometimes a risky approach, and what are the alternatives?
5. Summarize how the phases of the traditional SDLC are similar to or different from the phases of the modified life-cycle approach in support of the cost comparisons in Figure 10.2?
6. Describe the role of the vendor for each of the three phases of the purchasing life cycle.
7. Describe why the methodology for purchasing a small system could differ from purchasing a large system.
8. Describe what a purchasing company might want to learn from a vendor demonstration of a packaged system.

9. What are the most important advantages and disadvantages of purchasing a package?
10. What are some of the major differences between a process to implement an ERP package and the process to implement a less complex package?
11. What is an ASP and why is this an attractive purchasing alternative?

CHAPTER DISCUSSION QUESTIONS

1. Critique the following statements: It would cost us $800,000 to build this system, but we can purchase an equivalent package for $125,000. Therefore, we can save the company $675,000 by purchasing the software package.
2. What are the options for a business when the best packaged-system solution is not a perfect fit with the needs of the organization?
3. If you run a small business without any attached IS specialist, what would be your three most important concerns when purchasing software?
4. If you're the in-house manager of a company that has a lot of IS expertise, how would you decide when to purchase a system from an outside vendor versus when to develop it in-house?
5. Why is an assessment of the financial stability of the vendor a critical consideration when evaluating responses to an RFP?
6. Choose one of the five factors associated with successful ERP implementation and comment on how different this really is (or isn't) from other packaged system implementations.
7. Many midsized firms are investing in ERP system packages, such as SAP and PeopleSoft. Comment on what you think might be particularly important parts of the decision-making process when the purchasing organization has only a small IS department.
8. Revise Figure 10.3 to make it a list of criteria for assessing an application service provider (ASP).

CASE STUDY: A DREAM VS. A NIGHTMARE

It was an IT manager's worst nightmare. The OshKosh B'Gosh Inc. online store was open, but the orders went nowhere: The communications link between the clothing retailer and the company that hosted its Web application had gone down. Resolving the nightmare was further complicated because the ASP with which OshKosh had contracted had subcontracted with another firm to host their application. And OshKosh's telecommunications carrier needed to get into the hosting site to repair the equipment. According to CIO Jon Dell-Antonia at OshKosh, "It was like the Three Stooges and the Keystone Cops combined. If I went through the whole litany, you'd be rolling on the floor laughing. But we were not laughing at the time."

One common mistake companies make when choosing an ASP vendor is that they involve their application specialists in the meetings with the prospective ASPs, but not their computer operations specialists. According to an analyst with the Gartner Group, customers should concentrate not just on the A in ASP—the application that will be provided—but also the S—the service. You need to carefully document your needs first, before you start talking to an ASP.

[Adapted from Anthes, 2000]

Case Study Discussion Questions

Question One

How could OshKosh B'Gosh Inc. have avoided this crisis? Would it have helped to have a trial opening date where they accepted fake orders? What would you have done in this situation?

Question Two

If you have an online store opening, what problems should you anticipate and solve for in advance?

Question Three

What backup systems would you put in place in order to avoid mishaps of communication between vendors?

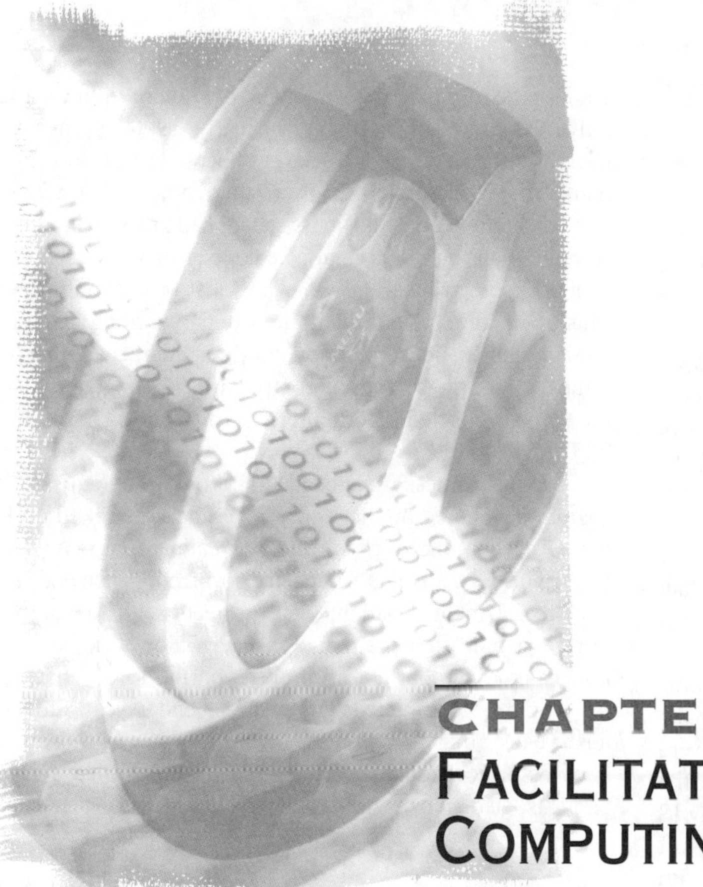

CHAPTER 11
FACILITATING USER COMPUTING

THIS CHAPTER FOCUSES ON MANAGEMENT ISSUES ASSOCIATED WITH WHAT has been referred to as end-user computing. Under the broad definition we will use here, end-user computing includes the use of all the managerial support applications discussed in Chapter 6, as well as the development of applications using personal productivity tools (such as Microsoft Office), reporting tools for enterprise systems, Web-authoring tools, and so forth.

This chapter's overall objectives are to prepare you to be an effective manager of employees who are using computer applications, as well as to be knowledgeable about the benefits and risks associated with application development by workers who are not information systems (IS) specialists. An underlying theme of our discussion is that in order for end-user computing resources to be effectively leveraged, IS and business managers must both take responsibility for their management. In other words, end-user computing policies and procedures need to become institutionalized as an enterprise-wide management concern, not just as an IT management issue. Nevertheless, IS managers need to take a leadership role in providing a secure and reliable computing and communications infrastructure.

The first part of this chapter discusses end-user computing that involves *systems development* activities by users who are not IS specialists. As early as the 1970s, workers in accounting, finance, marketing, and other business departments used mainframe tools designed for end users to analyze data and to generate reports. Today's end users typically develop applications on microcomputer platforms using spreadsheet, database management, statistical analysis, and other business intelligence tools with graphical interfaces.

The second part of this chapter talks about how to effectively leverage end-user computing resources overall. Today's business managers generally recognize the productivity gains associated with end-user computing but are concerned with managing the growing costs of supporting computer users. For example, the initial purchase of a personal computer is generally only 20 percent of the total cost of supporting an employee using a networked computer over its typical 3-year life cycle. That is, the **total cost of ownership (TCO)** for desktop and portable computers includes the costs of providing application software, network access, communications services, and ongoing training and support services. This chapter therefore provides some guidelines for supporting and controlling these information technology (IT) resources, as well as the benefits and challenges associated with supporting telecommuting environments.

THE EMERGENCE OF USER APPLICATION DEVELOPMENT

When microcomputers first became available in the late 1970s, many IS specialists viewed them as inappropriate for business application development. After all, the first microcomputers were distributed by mail order to hobbyists as electronic toys with limited processing and storage capabilities compared to the mainframe and minicomputers installed in most businesses. However, when IBM Corp. introduced its first desktop microcomputer (called the "personal computer") in late 1981, microcomputers on the desktops of users began to be accepted as useful business tools. At that time IBM was the premier source of computer systems and services for the Fortune 500, and the fact that IBM thought microcomputers could play a significant business role became a wake-up call for IS managers.

Nevertheless, the growth of end-user computing was primarily an end-user "pull" phenomenon. Well into the mid-1980s, business managers in many organizations were purchasing PCs on office equipment budgets without the knowledge or support of IS professionals. That is, many IS managers were aware of PC purchases but took a hands-off approach: They viewed IBM's early desktop PCs—with less than 640K of RAM and only floppy disk storage devices—as similar to business calculators. Yet, even without proactive IS management support of desktop PCs, there was a widespread diffusion of microcomputers into businesses during this first decade of microcomputer technology for two primary reasons (see Figure 11.1).

First, during the 1980s the price/performance ratios of microcomputers continued to decline. Other PC vendors entered the marketplace, which led to frequent releases of hardware with more functionality at lower prices. Affordable nonprocedural languages (4 GLs like FOCUS, query languages like structured query language [SQL]) were also available for developing microcomputer applications, and end users could become somewhat proficient in them after only a 2-day workshop. By the early 1990s these user-friendly tools had easy-to-use interfaces that did not even require the user to know SQL or other command structures. Further, literally every business school had invested in microcomputer labs and undergraduate courses that included education in spreadsheet and other personal productivity tools. This tremendous rise in computer literacy among U.S. college graduates, not to mention children and teenagers, continues to fuel the growth of computer usage in general (see the sidebar entitled "Computer Use by Young People Hits 90 Percent Mark").

Second, business users began to submit more requests for custom-developed applications that could be worked on by the IS staffs in their organizations, creating a large *backlog* of systems requests that had been prioritized. When and if IS resources became available, the projects with the highest priority would become active projects. However, business managers knew that not all projects on the formal backlog list would be completed within the calendar year and that next year's budgeting process would bring even more new systems project requests. This typically meant that a company also had an "invisible backlog" of systems projects that

- **Availability of low-cost microcomputers**
  - High-level languages for end users
  - Computer literacy among college graduates and professionals
- **Increased user frustrations about new systems development project backlogs**

Figure 11.1 Primary Drivers for End-User Computing

COMPUTER USE BY YOUNG PEOPLE HITS 90 PERCENT MARK

A new government-sponsored analysis of computer and Internet use found that computer usage among young people is higher than among the adult population. About 90 percent of people between the ages of 5 and 17 use computers, and more children and teens use computers at school than at home. There is no notable difference between girls and boys. About 59 percent of young computer users also use the Internet. 60 percent of 10-year-olds and 80 percent of 16-year-olds are Internet users, and 99 percent of public schools provide Internet access.

Like adults, young people go online for a variety of reasons. Three in four use the Internet for school assignments. More than half use computers for writing e-mail, sending instant messages to friends, or playing games. However, young people are more likely to access the Internet at home than at school. Since schools now have one computer with Internet access for every five students, some suggest that the heavy home usage is because many teachers aren't yet comfortable enough with the online tool to incorporate it into their classes.

[Adapted from Associated Press, 2003]

> A company's **systems backlog** includes the systems development requests by business users that members of the IS organization are not currently working on.

business management wanted but had not even formally requested due to low expectations for completion.

As business demands for more computer applications grew in the 1980s, the visible and invisible backlogs also grew, and dedicating non-IS personnel to user application development became a more attractive option (Kaiser, 1993). That is, small applications and reports could be developed quickly, as needed, without IS specialists, using tools designed for non-IS specialists.

Computer-literate business managers therefore began to invest in computing capabilities to support their own data access, reporting, and decision support needs. In many organizations the experts in the use of the new productivity tools (such as spreadsheets on a microcomputer) are in a business department, not in an IS department.

USER-DEVELOPED VERSUS IS-DEVELOPED APPLICATIONS

In Chapter 10 we described the make-or-buy decision between developing custom applications using internal IS specialists and purchasing a software package. Here we discuss the trade-offs for a different type of alternative: user-developed versus IS-developed custom applications. We begin with a discussion of the potential advantages and disadvantages of systems development by users who are not IS professionals. Then we describe three factors that need to be taken into account when making a decision about whether a specific system should be developed by end users or not: application characteristics, tool characteristics, and developer characteristics.

The overall challenge in managing user application development is to find the best combination of trade-offs that will maximize the potential benefits without creating unacceptable levels of risk.

Potential Advantages and Disadvantages

Understanding the potential advantages and disadvantages of user-developed applications is critical for making good choices about whether a new application should be user-developed or IS-developed. The lists of advantages and disadvantages in Figure 11.2 are discussed below.

Looking first at the *advantages*, **user application development** presents the opportunity for users to have total control over the initial development of the application, as well as its ongoing maintenance. Independence from IS department resources can sometimes be advantageous (Rivard and Huff, 1988). This is because users do not have to wait for IS resources to be available to work on their project; rather, the business manager can determine when the development effort is initiated. Further, users do not have to explain their information requirements to someone who might not understand the business problem; users often find it easier to communicate their computer support needs among themselves than to an IS specialist who might have only minimal knowledge about the specific area of business in which the application will be used. Also, users gain total control over the systems budget. This increased flexibility can be very attractive to the business manager: There is no cost chargeback from an internal IS organization or contractual obligations with an outside vendor if the manager's own employees develop the application. Finally, managers in organizations where an organizational committee with representatives from multiple business units determines the

POTENTIAL ADVANTAGES
Increased user control over systems development project
Increased user acceptance of systems solution
Frees up IS resources (and may reduce development backlog)
Increased IT management knowledge of users

POTENTIAL DISADVANTAGES
Loss of quality controls
Increased operational risks due to developer turnover
Potential labor/time inefficiencies
Loss of integration opportunities/capabilities

Figure 11.2 Potential Advantages and Disadvantages of User-Developed Applications

priorities for systems requests can avoid the risk of having a systems request turned down or delayed because it was not given a high enough priority. In other words, business manager control over the development of a new system can result in a timelier response to a local business unit need.

Another advantage associated with user-developed systems is the possibility of greater user acceptance of the application solution. End users tend to be more involved throughout the development process because they might be physically near the user developer. User-developed systems are also typically smaller systems that are likely to be developed using a prototyping process, which involves significant end-user involvement. Because the business unit totally "owns" the application, user application development also eliminates the possibility of "we-they" finger-pointing.

Two potential advantages for the organization as a whole are also shown in Figure 11.2. First, when IS expertise is a scarce organizational resource, it is best for the organization to use its IS resources to work on high-priority projects that require high levels of IS skills. The prolific IS guru James Martin recognized this advantage at the time of the introduction of the IBM microcomputer. In his book *Application Development Without Programmers* (1982), he shocked many IS professionals by advocating a large number of powerful software products for end users—including fourth generation languages and report writers. McLean (1979) also was an early predictor of the rise of application development by non-IS professionals. Within U.S.-based labor markets, the costs of end-user computing via a mainframe computer platform were already low enough to provide a compelling business case for user-developed applications.

> *The continuing drop in cost of computers has now passed the point at which computers have become cheaper than people.*
>
> —JAMES MARTIN, 1982

The last potential advantage of user application development listed in Figure 11.2 is also a motivator for a textbook, such as this one, that focuses on what business managers need to know about IT management. Every organization should be striving to increase the IT management knowledge of its business employees, and user application development is an experience that can contribute to this goal. As described in Chapter 1, this is an important business capability because of the role of IT as an enabler of a company's business strategy. In fact, research has shown a correlation between the IT management knowledge of key business managers and the progressive use of IT within that firm (Boynton, Zmud, and Jacobs, 1994).

However, organizations also need to manage the potential risks associated with applications that are not developed by IS specialists. These business risks are reflected in the four potential *disadvantages* shown in Figure 11.2.

First, a major concern for business as well as IS managers is the potential loss of quality controls. By virtue of their training, IS professionals are knowledgeable about how to design quality controls into a new information system: input controls, output controls, and processing controls. As in any profession, products developed by those with less training and experience will, on the average, be of lower quality. Undetected bugs in processing logic, the lack of audit trails, inadequate backup and security procedures, and undocumented systems are much more common in user-developed systems than in those developed by a trained IS professional (Schultheis and Sumner, 1991). A mid-1990s study by a leading consulting firm found that about one-third of spreadsheets contained errors (Panko, 1996). These shortcomings support the worst fears of the IS community and obviously are a major concern for all business managers (see the sidebar entitled "Errors in Spreadsheets").

In addition to quality concerns about the application design, user-developed systems also involve increased operational risks. In other words, user-developed applications that are used on an ongoing basis can pose operational risks similar to a "production system" operated by the IS department. However, the responsibilities for operations and continued maintenance of a user-developed application typically belong to the business unit that owns it and might by managed by a single employee who developed it. A common operational risk, therefore, is that the user developer could move to a different unit, or even a different organization, with little advance notice. For database applications in particular, the loss of the original user developer often results in abandoned user-developed systems due to the lack of resident operational and systems maintenance expertise within the business unit (Klepper and Sumner, 1990). The risk exposure is even greater when the application is being used as a decision support tool for decisions with high impact or as a regular transaction processing and reporting system at the workgroup or department level.

Another potential risk is the organizational inefficiencies that result when systems are being developed by persons with little or no IS training. Depending on the type and size of the application, there is an organizational cost associated with having an untrained, or partially trained, user spend considerable amounts of time on what could be much more efficiently achieved by an IS professional. There is also a learning curve associated with end-user development.

When systems are developed outside of a centralized IS organization, there is also a greater likelihood of considerable

ERRORS IN SPREADSHEETS

End users produce countless spreadsheet models each year, often to guide mission-critical decisions. In recent years several cases of spreadsheet errors have been reported. Given the reluctance of organizations to publicize embarrassments, these few cases might be only the tip of the iceberg. Some consultants have claimed that something like a third of all operational spreadsheet models contain errors. One Price Waterhouse consultant reported auditing four large spreadsheet models for a client and finding 128 errors.

Several academic researchers have done experiments to identify the different types of errors contained in spreadsheets. Even in relatively simple spreadsheets that do not require specialized business area knowledge, laboratory subjects made errors in 38 percent of their models. In a debugging phase, only 16 percent of the subjects who had made spreadsheet errors were able to identify and fix all their errors. Every research study known to us that looked for errors in user-developed systems has found them, and found them in abundance.

Spreadsheet errors can be of two types: quantitative and qualitative. Most researchers have looked at *quantitative errors*, which include the following:

- *Mechanical errors* Typing errors, pointing errors, and other simple slips. Mechanical errors can be frequent, but they have a high chance of being caught by the person making the error.
- *Logic errors* Incorrect formulas due to choosing the wrong algorithm or creating the wrong formulas to implement the algorithm. Pure logic errors result from a lapse in logic, whereas domain logic errors occur because the developer lacks the required business area knowledge. Some logic errors are also easier to identify than others: easy-to-proof errors have been called Eureka errors, and difficult-to-proof errors have been called Cassandra errors.
- *Omission errors* Things left out of the model that should be there. They often result from a misinterpretation of the situation. Human factors research has shown that omission errors have low detection rates.

Qualitative errors are flaws that do not produce immediate quantitative errors. Some qualitative errors lead to quantitative errors during later "what-if" analyses or when updates are made to a spreadsheet model. Other qualitative errors might cause users to misinterpret the model's results or make maintenance difficult, leading to increased development costs and the potential for new errors.

To err is human. We do not make mistakes all the time, but we consistently make a certain number, even when we are being careful. To reduce error rates requires aggressive techniques—similar to the discipline followed by developers of more complex applications.

[Adapted from Panko, 1996, and Panko and Halverson, 1996]

time spent "reinventing" an application with similar functionality. Duplicated efforts within the same department, let alone across business units within an organization, are common if each individual unit works independently of any IS personnel. A similar problem is faced by organizations with IS specialists decentralized to multiple business units if no mechanisms are in place to identify duplicated efforts.

Another potentially serious problem for a business unit and the organization as a whole is the possible proliferation of unit-specific customized applications that inhibit information access and sharing with others in the organization, both now and in the future. When business units throughout an organization independently develop applications using software and data definitions of their own choosing, the result is dozens, or even hundreds, of isolated islands of automation: The risks are not only unsharable data, but also conflicting information reports supposedly based on the same transaction data. (Incompatibilities across departmental systems are also a problem faced by organizations when business units have the authority to independently purchase different packaged systems for the same functions, such as payroll or the purchasing of supplies.)

The organizational risks associated with user application development therefore increase considerably when user-developed solutions are allowed to proliferate without adequate coordination. The management challenge is to find the right balance between business and IS controls without severely limiting the potential benefits.

Assessing the Application Risks

Let us turn now to the issue of whether a specific application should be developed by users or by IS professionals. As summarized in Figure 11.3, three types of factors should be considered: characteristics of the application to be developed, the tools available for user development, and the human resources needed for both a quality application and reliable operations and maintenance over the life of the completed application.

Application Characteristics. Several characteristics of the application need to be taken into account. First, the organizational risks associated with user application development differ depending on the intended scope (or organizational

Application Characteristics
Scope (personal, departmental, organizational)
Criticality/Impact (risk exposure)
Size and usage (one-time, periodic, ongoing)
Business problem complexity (commonality of task, problem structure)

Tool Characteristics
Tool sophistication/complexity
Interconnectedness

Developer Characteristics
User developer skills, experience, and availability
IS specialist skills, experience, and availability

Figure 11.3 Application, Tool, and Developer Characteristics

usage) of the completed application. Some firms make decisions based on just two categories of risk: applications developed for personal use only and those intended to be used by more than one person. Pyburn (1986-87), however, has defined three categories of application scope that typically have significantly different risk levels:

- Personal applications developed and used (operated) by the primary user for personal decision making, often replacing work formerly done manually
- Departmental applications developed by a single user but operated and used (and perhaps enhanced) by multiple users in a department; departmental applications often evolve from applications originally developed for personal use
- Organizational applications used by multiple users across a number of departments

Personal applications typically have the least risk, whereas organizational applications have the greatest risk.

In addition to scope, the potential impact of managerial decisions based on the application, as well as the actual size of the application and its intended frequency of usage, also need to be considered. Small, one-time applications are typically good candidates for user-developed applications, but the application also needs to be assessed in terms of risk exposure for the organization as a whole.

Finally, the complexity of the business problem supported by the application needs to be assessed in two different dimensions: the task's commonality and the task's problem structure. If the application is addressing an ill-structured analytical problem, a combination of business and IS specialist expertise could be required to develop the best software application to address it. Supporting business tasks that are already well understood (common), such as a system to track the status of multiple departmental projects or to track communications with various suppliers, are usually better candidates for user-developed solutions.

Tool Characteristics. Two important tool characteristics to consider are the complexity of the software tools to be used to develop the system and the degree to which the application is to be interconnected with other applications or databases. User tools vary greatly in complexity and technology sophistication. For example, spreadsheet functions are relatively simple to design and spreadsheet applications are relatively simple to implement, whereas data mining tools based on neural network technology can be much more complex.

As shown in Figure 11.4, applications also can vary greatly, depending on how much they rely on other applications for data inputs. At one extreme, "isolated" applications do not use data from any other computer-generated source and do not provide inputs to other applications. Stand-alone applications might depend on data generated by other applications, but the data is manually input. Application integration can also be accomplished in two ways: (1) manually via a specific user command (such as via file import or export commands) or (2) automatically. As organizations have implemented local area networks (LANs) and client/server computing environments, these two types of integration have become increasingly common.

Stage	Extent of Interconnectedness
Isolation	The application does not use data from another application or create data to be used for another application
Stand-alone	The application utilizes computer-generated data, which is manually entered into the application from hardcopy reports or other printouts
Manual Integration	Data is electronically transferred from another application, but this is done manually (e.g., data import command)
Automated Integration	The application is electronically connected with one or more corporate databases or applications; data is routinely transferred to this application using automated scripts designed into the applications
Distributed Integration	The application regularly utilizes data distributed via network and maintained by organizational systems under the control of IS specialists

Figure 11.4 Extent of Interconnectedness (Adapted from Huff, Munro, and Martin, 1988).

If a more integrated application is to be developed, with sophisticated tools that access data distributed via an organizational network, then an IS-developed solution could be the only suitable long-term solution. However, it is not uncommon for a stand-alone user-developed application to first be developed by users and then later to be used as a prototype for a more integrated application by IS specialists.

Developer Characteristics. The application developer characteristics to be considered include the relevant skills and experience of the potential developers, as well as their availability to work on the project. A second consideration here is the *availability* of these developer resources in relation to the time constraints faced by the users.

As discussed previously, reduced dependence on IS professionals can be a considerable advantage if user developers have, or can be trained to have, the skills required for a given application. Many non-IS professionals have considerable IT-related expertise and might also even have some training in IS development methodologies. The difficulty is that the business managers in the unit responsible for the application might not have the knowledge to adequately assess the development skills needed before the project to develop the application is underway. Consultation with IS experts inside or outside the organization is therefore required to adequately assess these characteristics.

USER DEVELOPMENT METHODOLOGY

When IS specialists develop systems, IS professionals select the methodology used to develop the application. One of the responsibilities of the IS project leader is to monitor adherence to the organizational standards for the selected methodology, as well as to monitor the project's status according to the agreed-upon process steps and user-approved milestones.

For user-developed systems, the user developer (or the accountable business manager) typically chooses the development methods to be used. Panko (1988) suggests that the most appropriate methodology for a user-developed application depends on three of the application characteristics in Figure 11.5: scope, size, and business problem complexity. Many user-developed applications do not require a strict adherence to all the steps described in earlier chapters for a systems development life cycle (SDLC). For example, small and simple applications intended to be used by the person developing the application (personal scope) could be developed with a simplified ("collapsed") life-cycle approach. However, when the application for personal use is somewhat larger and more complex, a more disciplined approach needs to be taken to ensure a quality application. The Definition phase would involve thinking through what you want the system to do (inputs, processing, outputs) and

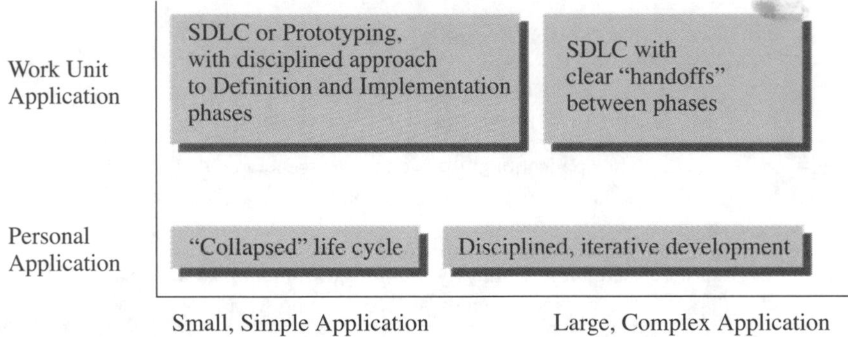

Figure 11.5 Guidelines for Choosing the Development Approach (Based on Panko, 1989).

then constructing and testing it. The developer, who is also the intended user, could try it out, modify it, and then repeat these steps as needed. However, a disciplined approach should continue to be adhered to in order to ensure that the programming logic and all modifications to the application are adequately tested.

If the application is for other users (a workgroup or department), then one or more of the intended users should be involved in the application's development, even if a formal project team is not designated for work on the application. If a large, complex application is being developed for multiple users, it should be developed using an SDLC methodology (as described in Chapter 9) with formalized user and developer roles. The Definition phase should include a reassessment of whether the project should be user-developed or IS-developed, using factors such as those summarized earlier (see Figure 11.3 in the section of this chapter entitled "Assessing the Application Risks"). This recommendation assumes, however, that the user developers are knowledgeable about the SDLC methodology and have the systems and project management skills to ensure the development of a high-quality application.

Prototyping and other iterative methods are especially well suited for user-developed applications because the end users are typically physically near the developer, the design can be tried out, and today's end-user development tools with graphical interfaces support prototyping well. As described in Chapter 9, a basic set of requirements should first be defined in order to develop the prototype; selected users then try out the prototype and suggest changes; the prototype is then modified until there is agreement that the application meets the business users' needs.

A key learning point for most first-time user developers is not to move to the Construction phase, or the building of the prototype, too soon. It is common for user developers to underestimate what it takes to define a system's requirements, especially if other users will also be using the application. In contrast, the IS professional always develops applications for other users and is typically trained in various systems analysis techniques as well as interviewing techniques to elicit requirements. The larger and more complex the system, the more critical the need for developers to devote more time to the up-front requirements analysis and Definition phase in general. In the Construction phase the design steps should take into account security features, such as input and output controls (including application backup and recovery controls).

IS professionals have also learned that a simple system that works reliably is much more useful than an elaborate failure. For user-developed applications, it is therefore often a good idea to start with a limited version of the system and then to expand it after some experience with this initial version. Indeed, user-developed systems can also become catalysts for larger systems to enable a new business strategy, which in the end will require custom development work by IS professionals.

User Development Guidelines

Figure 11.6 lists a number of important questions that can be used as a guide for user developers during the Definition and Construction phases. The first four questions need to be answered in the Definition phase when defining the system's requirements. Determining the data sources and the needed controls up front will help ensure a high-quality application. For example, can the needed data be obtained from another system, or will the data have to be collected and keyed into this system? If the data must be keyed into the system, how can the application be designed to help control for accuracy and completeness? If the data are to be extracted from other systems, separate modules might need to be constructed in order to perform this function. Today's office productivity suites, for example, allow for

DEFINITION PHASE
What outputs should the system produce?
What processes are necessary to produce the needed outputs?
What should the system be able to do?
What input data are needed?
    How can data best be obtained?
    How can data accuracy, completeness, and timeliness be assured?
CONSTRUCTION PHASE
What data must be stored in the system?
    How should data be organized?
    How can data be maintained?
How can this system be decomposed into modules?
    How do these modules relate to each other?
    In what sequence should the modules be executed?
How can the system be recovered if anything happens?
Is an audit trail necessary?
What level of documentation is necessary?
What system tests need to be run?

Figure 11.6 Questions to Guide User Developers

automatic linking of database tables (created with a database management system such as Microsoft Access) to spreadsheets that use these data for decision analysis. The data flow diagrams and other analysis tools introduced in Chapter 8 can prove helpful in these Definition tasks.

Figure 11.6 also provides questions for the Construction phase. Designing the data to be stored in the system is a critical activity. One must decide what different files or tables are required and what data elements will be stored in each record. Designing a database structure is one of the most difficult, and least understood, tasks for novice user developers. Data entry "forms" can be developed using a database package such as Access to facilitate record additions, changes, and deletions. A frequent design error is to use a spreadsheet program for an application that really needs database management functions such as those provided by a database management tool. These are all Construction issues in which access to IS consultants or a user developer highly experienced in database application design can help a user group avoid a costly reworking of a poorly designed system.

It is also important to consider data recovery needs; if the application is stored on a server and a multiuser version of the system is being used, some backup and recovery procedures should already be in place. However, the user developer needs to assess whether these are sufficient.

Designing an audit trail enables the tracing of activities through the system to validate transaction processing and adherence to organizational and accounting rules. This is closely related to the recovery process, and the provisions made for recovery can provide a basic audit trail.

The documentation that is necessary for a user-developed application depends upon the application's characteristics. Personal systems often have little or no formal documentation. However, if this is a system that a successor to the current user developer will also be expected to use, formal documentation should be provided and kept up to date; it should also include documentation that is not embedded in the application itself, in the event of a system crash. The documentation for a multiuser system, or a stand-alone application used by different people in different workgroups, typically requires detailed user documentation, such as that produced by IS specialists. If user-developed systems are regularly audited, it is obviously a good idea to consult with these auditors while defining and constructing the system to ensure that the organization's auditing concerns are adequately addressed.

Significant time and a rigorous test process are needed to ensure that an application works the way it is intended to. The lack of adequate testing for decision support applications can lead to serious consequences for a business. Errors in spreadsheet applications, for example, are known to have caused losses ranging from hundreds of thousands to millions of dollars (Galletta et al., 1996), and the user developer's postdevelopment debugging practices might be a major cause (Panko, 1996; Panko and Halverson, 1996).

USER DEVELOPER EXPERIENCES

CONTACT MANAGEMENT SYSTEM

This program was designed to better manage the contacts each member of the C workgroup has with external contacts, in order to help improve the efficiency and productivity of all members. The Contact Management System stores information about employees in the C workgroup, contacts at various sites, and the sites themselves. Contacts with other sites are captured and categorized according to their contact method. Information about a contact includes the parties involved, the time and date, the subjects discussed, and a synopsis of the communication. Reports include all contacts by individuals within a given time period, contacts on a specific topic, and contacts regarding a specific project. Visual Basic and Access were the primary tools used for this application.

The methodology used was a modified software development life-cycle approach using prototyping. I discussed the requirements of the program with several competent peers who had a desire to be a player in the development of the system. We met and discussed potential uses for the system and discussed requirements for expansion of the system to meet future goals. We utilized Visual Basic's rapid development environment to "test drive" possible screen layouts. This worked quite well, as the others were able to actually see rather than just listen to ideas and concepts for the user interface. As with most projects, this one did not progress as rapidly as predicted; the current version lacks some of the overly ambitious original goals. These will be implemented in the near future in a later release. There is a high level of anticipation for a fully functional product among the users who are currently using the program to enter the data to create the database. Their use of the product at this time is helping to finalize the interface for the final release.

Lessons Learned. During the development of this project, a number of important lessons were learned. Most important was the need to stay in touch with the end users of the product throughout the development cycle. Not only does this assure that their needs are being met and the program will be useful to their productivity, but it also entices excitement, which is vital to the acceptance of the final product. Even with rapid development tools, the several months required to develop a quality product can be enough of a lapse in the anticipation of the end users such that acceptance of the product is less than enthusiastic. Another valuable lesson learned was that when the program gets close to being completed is always when the intricate, hard-to-find bugs seem to be seen.

TRACKING DATABASE

This application is a Lotus Notes project tracking database for my workgroup. It is used to track activities between my workgroup in the parent company related to current and prospective customers. In my workgroup, projects are segmented by customer. The process starts with a customer inquiry, followed by actual work done, and concluding with problem resolution. With the current version of this application, my group can track different kinds of activities with a customer: action items, call reports, incoming correspondence, internal correspondence, outgoing correspondence, meeting reports, and miscellaneous activity. The database was tailored from a template provided with Lotus Notes to meet the needs of my workgroup.

I employed the prototyping methodology. Before beginning the project, my manager and I discussed the tracking system I envisioned; I convinced him that this application would help us manage our work more effectively. In the requirements definition phase, a colleague and I developed a list of the requirements for our tracking database. During this phase, we reviewed the Lotus Notes tracking database template to verify the compatibility of our requirements with those of the template. Many of the requirements we desired, like checkboxes for project type and technology type, and activities such as internal e-mail, were not a part of the Notes template. However, many of the structural needs of our system were included in the template.

I spent most of the first couple of days working with the Lotus Notes tool to become proficient as a user before diving into the developer world. I wanted to be sure I fully understood how Lotus Notes worked, how users interfaced with it, and what its capabilities were. The Notes tool is very intuitive and, after only a couple of days, I began work on the tailored project tracking database. My goal was to have a usable prototype as quickly as possible so I could take it to three key users: my manager and two colleagues. I chose one colleague who was very computer literate and one that seems to merely know where the "ON" switch is on his workstation. I had a usable prototype in 3 days.

As expected, the majority of my effort was after the working prototype was rolled out to key users. While using the new tracking system, the key users were able to identify several items they now wanted in the system and also found a few bugs. The bugs were corrected quickly but the changes/additions to the system required several iterations. Within a few weeks, we had a fully operational system.

As with any application where the developer resides within the department, new iterations, though minor, continue. Tweaking the tracking system in this manner has allowed us to reach a point where the application is so useful that our entire department depends heavily on it for up-to-the-minute information on projects.

Lessons Learned. One key lesson I learned in developing this system overshadows all others. I learned that managing user expectation is paramount to user satisfaction early in a project. My "key users" believed that since I had a prototype with the user screens developed very rapidly, that the workable system with "everything they wanted" would follow equally as fast. Another lesson I learned is the value of the prototyping methodology: It enabled our group to develop a powerful system with little time and little money invested.

[Evening MBA students, Indiana University]

For example, studies have found that many spreadsheet developers apparently do not attempt to reduce their spreadsheet errors systematically; it also is not a common practice to have others check their programs. Since research on the work practices of IS professionals has found that spotting errors by inspection is difficult for the original programmer, user developers should regularly involve others in debugging their applications rather than relying wholly on self-testing.

Although automatic audit features and separate audit programs (especially for spreadsheet programs) are more prevalent today than in the 1990s, research shows that organizations need to devote much more attention to spreadsheet error detection. Studies have shown that as many as one-third of spreadsheet models are likely to contain errors. The sidebar entitled "Errors in Spreadsheets" describes the types of errors that are typical in spreadsheets and some reasons why they are so common.

Complex, modular systems of course require more planning and coordination for testing and installation than simple applications for use by the person who developed the application. Even users formally educated in IS development methodologies typically face a significant learning curve as a user developer. This learning involves both tool learning and process learning. In the sidebar entitled "User Developer Experiences," knowledge workers who are not IS professionals describe the methods they used to develop their first multiuser applications and the lessons that they learned. In both instances, the user developers were also developing applications in which they were using an end-user development tool that was new to them.

User Development Roles

Depending on the development approach used, the scope of the application (personal, departmental, organizational), and its intended usage, a formal project team for the application might or might not be created. However, essentially all the roles described in Chapter 9 for custom-developed applications need to be played by the users alone or with the help of consultants. For example, consultant skills could be needed for understanding relational database and object-oriented concepts or for understanding how best to utilize a sophisticated end-user tool. IS employees within the same organization are typically the first choice for the consultant role, although sometimes the tool to be used, the skillsets needed, or the lack of availability of these IS resources results in contractual arrangements with external consultants.

For most user-developed applications, a business manager (or the business manager accountable for the application) plays the **project manager** role; for many business employees, project management is already a well-honed skill. However, developers also need to be familiar with the basic steps of a life cycle methodology, the advantages and pitfalls of alternative approaches such as an iterative or prototyping methodology, and documentation standards and best practices for auditing controls and system recovery.

Depending on the organizational context, there could also be an internal auditor or other type of oversight role to ensure that user-developed applications do not expose the organization to unacceptable levels of risk. In some organizations, the IS organization, an oversight committee of senior business managers, an internal auditing department, or all three might be formally accountable for ensuring that user-developed applications do not expose the organization to unacceptable levels of risk. Williford (2000) has identified four review methods, which range from a formal audit to a "best-guess" informal review that involves periodically questioning IS department staff about potentially problematic applications. Many organizations began taking a formal inventory of user-developed applications for the first time as part of their Year 2000 compliance initiatives and have continued this approach in lieu of a more formal (and expensive) audit.

We began this chapter by stating that in order for user computing to be effective at the individual, departmental, and organizational levels, IS and business unit managers must have a shared set of responsibilities that is appropriate for their organizational context. In the next section we present a framework to describe what types of support and control actions are commonly used, depending on the organization's overall strategy for facilitating computing by non-IS professionals.

STRATEGIES AND TACTICS FOR MANAGING USER COMPUTING

Effective management of end-user computing requires not only good procedures for making decisions about when to develop an application without the formal help of IS specialists, but also structures and personnel to support and control end-user computing activities on a ongoing basis. Figure 11.7 presents a framework that can be used to assess an organization's effectiveness in leveraging end-user computing technologies and personnel.

The box at the far left in Figure 11.7, labeled Organizational Context, explicitly acknowledges that factors such as

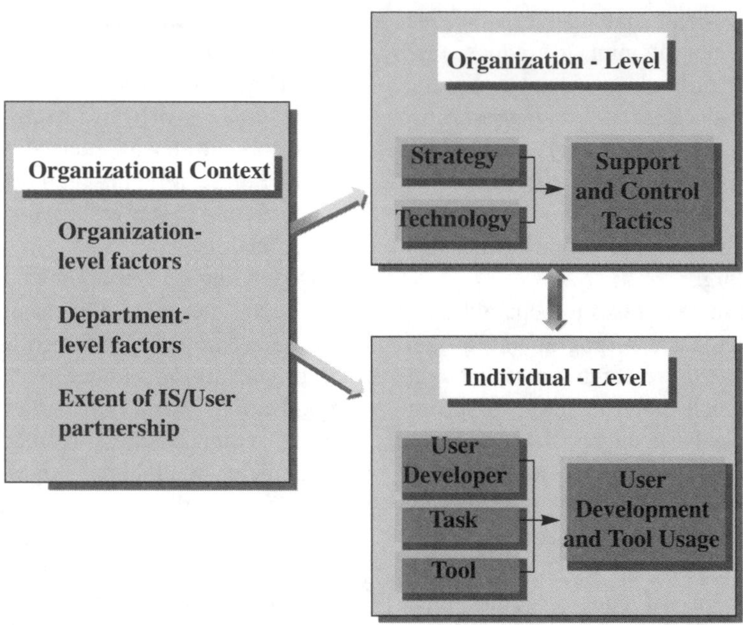

Figure 11.7 Framework for Leveraging End-User Computing (Based on Brancheau and Brown, 1993).

the organization's business strategy, the way the IS professional resources are organized, the special characteristics of a given user department, and the extent of IS/user "partnering" within the organization will influence the strategies and tactics used for end-user computing as well as factors at the individual level. For example, if systems development groups have been decentralized to business unit control, there is a greater likelihood that "local" IS professionals will have a high degree of business-specific knowledge and might be more heavily relied on for playing a *consultant* role in user application development projects. Similarly, if a highly computer-literate business manager heads a given user department, there is a greater likelihood that a large amount of user application development activity will be occurring in that department. Whether or not that user department should seek a high degree of independence from the IS organization depends on the business manager's IT management knowledge and the history (status) of the IS/business partnering on other development projects.

The two-headed arrow between the Organization-Level and Individual-Level boxes on the right in Figure 11.7 reflects the linkages between an organization's strategy and tactics for end-user computing and factors at the individual end-user level. This arrow again suggests that there is no single best way to manage end-user computing; rather, an organization's approach needs to take into account unique aspects of its own organization and its own individual users.

The Individual-Level box lists four factors that were part of our discussion on user application development approaches: characteristics of the user developer, the business problem (task) being worked on, the end-user tool, and the user development process and tool usage. As pointed out in the previous section, highly skilled user developers and highly sophisticated end-user technologies exist in organizations today, but not every user department will have the same level of skills. Therefore, a one-size-fits-all approach to the development of applications by users is likely to be ill-fated.

The Organization-Level box in Figure 11.7 has three factors that are the responsibility of an organization's management—*both* IS and business managers:

- *Strategy.* The strategic objectives and overall approach to end-user computing
- *Technology.* The range and accessibility of end-user tools
- *Tactics for Support and Control.* Support services, control policies and procedures

Strategies for End-User Computing

Some IS organizations did not have an explicit strategy for managing end-user computing when desktop PCs were first being brought into the organization in the early 1980s

At that time both mainframe and microcomputer tools were being used for user application development, but end-user training and support for the mainframe tools was much more likely to be in place than end-user training for microcomputer tools. The mainframe tools, of course, were installed by the IS department. However, many IS managers took a laissez-faire approach to end-user computing with desktop computers: IS managers might or might not have signed-off on business unit requests to purchase hardware and software, but end users were typically left on their own to install the equipment, learn the software, and manually organize and enter their own data into a stand-alone application. The early microcomputers were even viewed by some managers as inexpensive tools similar to calculators, in which business units were "free" to invest. LANs to connect microcomputers were not common until a decade later (the early 1990s), and few policies and procedures might have been put in place.

As shown in Figure 11.8, a laissez-faire approach was a common starting place for all organizations in the 1980s because microcomputer technologies were a new, emerging phenomenon. Although this approach still can be found, it much less common: Most organizations today have developed an explicit strategy and support staff for managing end-user computing.

Three other management approaches commonly used today can be identified based on the degree to which the organization has sought to *expand* (increase) end-user computing activities and the degree to which it seeks to *control* these activities. As shown in Figure 11.8, firms that invest heavily in end-user computing resources, but with minimal concerns about formal controls, can be said to have an *Acceleration* strategy. Their objective is to enable users to acquire and learn to use end-user technologies in order to develop their own computing solutions to business problems, with few constraints. In contrast, firms with a *Containment* strategy have opted to invest in end-user computing more slowly and carefully. Very specific controls are put in place and users are typically restricted to standard tool purchases and stricter guidelines for application development, backup, and security.

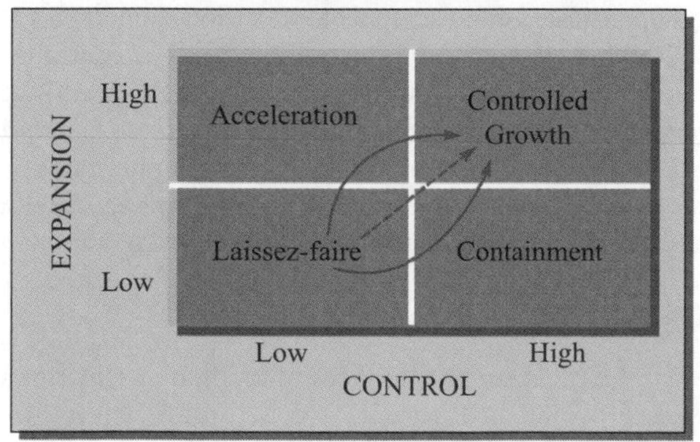

Figure 11.8 End-User Computing Strategies (Based on Munro et al., 1987–1988; Brancheau and Amoroso, 1990).

The *Controlled Growth* strategy (high expansion, but also high control) is perceived to be the most advanced or mature approach. Initially, it was expected that firms would move first to an acceleration or containment strategy and then gradually increase controls or support levels to reach a controlled growth stage. However, many organizations actually have taken a middle ground or a balanced approach, as depicted by the dotted line in Figure 11.8. This balanced strategy involves starting with small investments in end-user computing resources as well as few controls and then increasing both investments in resources and controls as the number of end users and end-user applications increases.

Finally, organizations in a mature (Controlled Growth) stage of end-user computing may still choose an Acceleration or Containment approach for introducing a new end-user technology within their organizations. For example, many organizations initially took an Acceleration approach to end-user development of Web content for organizational intranets in the late 1990s but then evolved to more restrictive approaches. Other organizations, however, chose a Containment strategy that involved committee governance and early rules for Web page content and look-and-feel (see the sidebar entitled "Different Strategies for Managing Intranets"). Today's organizations are faced with the choice among these same strategies (Laissez-Faire, Acceleration, Containment) for managing personal digital assistants (PDAs) and cellular communications devices for business computing. However, as more business employees demand linkages with personal productivity software tools and remote access to e-mail communications, organizations are likely to evolve to more "balanced" approaches.

Centralized Support (Information Center) Approaches. Some firms have established a centralized support unit for managing end-user computing activities, usually within an IS organization. The term **information center (IC)** was commonly used to describe this approach in the 1980s, because the term had previously been used to refer to supporting end-users via an separate mainframe computer on which was loaded a full copy, or extract, of one or more production databases as well as software tools for end users to develop queries, generate reports, and build decision models. By the late 1980s, the IC term was commonly used for any centralized support unit, often reporting to an IS organization, with a mandate to support end-user comput-

DIFFERENT STRATEGIES FOR MANAGING INTRANETS

As Web authoring tools designed for non-IS specialists (such as Microsoft FrontPage) became readily available in the late 1990s, managers had to develop a strategy for managing their intranets while they learned more about the best ways to do so for their organizations. (Note: intranets are internal company networks that use Internet technologies and protocols.) For example, Boeing initially took a "let-the-flowers-bloom" approach (Acceleration strategy) and deliberately sought to keep intranet restrictions to a minimum to facilitate exploration with Web tools in different units across the organization. A standard Web authoring tool was distributed without cost to user departments, and it led to a very quick growth of Web pages developed by users on the intranet. According to Graeber Jordan, who was a senior manager responsible for e-commerce at Boeing at that time, the proliferation of internal Web pages resulted in a new norm of electronic communication inside the organization, rather than communication via hard copies of newsletters, updated documents, or status reports (Jordan, 1997).

Other organizations chose a Containment strategy, in which the IS organization or a central committee first established the rules for Web page content and set specific parameters for look-and-feel formats and then continued to serve as an oversight committee. Individual employees in each department were formally designated as responsible for their department's Web pages. A separate technical committee was used to make recommendations about new technologies and to track performance for the oversight group.

Organizations like Boeing that began with an Acceleration strategy eventually implemented more rules and standards, and organizations that began with a Containment strategy also moved to a Controlled Growth strategy over time. Some of the challenges faced were how to develop a common set of terms to improve internal document searching and how to monitor and manage the deletion of outdated content.

ing. IC managers also typically were charged with implementing appropriate control policies and procedures to help manage the business risks of user-developed applications.

A critical success factor for the effectiveness of a centralized support unit is its staffing. As with other personnel responsible for customer services, effective support staff for end-user computing need to have not only product knowledge (in this case technical knowledge), but also the ability to relate well to users. The ability to provide quick turnaround time in response to user requests for help is a key performance measure for this staff. It is also common for "power users" from a business unit to be hired into a central support unit to provide consulting and troubleshooting support for other users. In the early 1990s, a typical staffing ratio was one support member for each 100 PCs, but today ratios as low as 35 staff members supporting 10,000 users have been reported (McNurlin and Sprague, 1998).

IS/Business Partnering Approaches. Other organizations have adopted a less centralized approach to supporting users. For example, an approach based on strong user/IS partnerships and joint accountability between IS and business management, originally referred to as a *managed free economy* approach, has five components:

- An explicit strategy that reflects a support and control philosophy
- A user/IS working partnership
- An end-user support unit that is well integrated with other IS units
- An emphasis on end-user education (IS development methods, quality controls)
- A targeting of critical (high-impact) end-user applications

Focusing on applications with high payoffs was also advocated more than a decade ago by end-user computing consultants (Karten, 1990). Figure 11.9 summarizes Karten's comparison of a reactive support role (that predominated at that time) versus a more proactive support role in which investments are made in end-user applications that have the potential for significantly affecting the business. In this Stage Two role, both IS and business managers work together to focus on how to better leverage technology investments, as well as the increasing numbers of users with high levels of IT literacy ("power users") who also have an interest in developing sophisticated end-user tools for decision support.

Whether or not an organization adopts a centralized or a more distributed strategy for facilitating end-user computing, all organizations need to formulate an appropriate strategy and to implement a set of support services and control policies to help realize this strategy. Below, we present some common support and control tactics.

Common Support Tactics

A list of typical support services to facilitate user computing is provided in Figure 11.10. Services such as troubleshooting (help desk), consulting, training, assistance with tool selection, maintenance, and upgrading are all services that are commonly offered today. This list also

STAGE ONE	STAGE TWO
Reactive services	Proactive services
Individual solutions, quick-and-dirty	Departmental solutions, in-depth
Product training	Business problem-solving
All needs supported	High-payoff needs supported
Computer literacy training	Information literacy education
One-way relationships	Alliance; IS/user partnerships

Figure 11.9 Reactive Stage One vs. Proactive Stage Two Support Roles

- *Troubleshooting* A hotline or help desk 24/7 or as needed
- *Consulting* One-on-one consulting on application development, query tools, and so on
- *Training* Technology (tool) training in classroom setting as well as self-paced e-learning modules
- *IS education* System development methodologies, security procedures, and so on
- *Product research and evaluation* Identifying and evaluating new end-user tools and recommending products for trial by users
- *Tool selection and purchasing* Hardware, software, network solutions
- *Tool installation, maintenance, and upgrading* Hardware, software, networks
- *Information sharing* Formalizing communications between support personnel and end users, as well as across end user groups; typical sharing mechanisms include newsletters, Web pages on an intranet, and periodical meetings for users to evaluate new tools and share development and technology "tips"

Figure 11.10 Common Support Services

distinguishes between tool training and IS education: Training refers to learning to use a specific tool. IS education is not tied to a specific tool and addresses "best practices"—such as methodologies for developing computer applications. Sharing solutions to common problems is frequently accomplished today via Web pages on an intranet and often includes postings of answers to frequently asked questions (FAQs).

Supporting end users today also involves preparing end users for new software releases. This typically involves not only retraining users, but also refitting end-user workstations with more memory or disk storage space to support the new software. During the late 1990s many organizations adopted a 3-year replacement strategy for personal computer hardware. The rationale was twofold: (1) to take advantage of new software functionality and (2) to avoid expensive maintenance and repair costs for older PCs. However, some organizations have also found that for users who need only word processing and an Internet browser, for example, 5-year-old PCs might be sufficient (Delaney, 2003).

To save costs and keep focused on core services, many organizations contract the provisioning of user support services out to IT vendors. For example, the outsourcing of user training has become more popular as firms have begun to standardize their suites of office productivity tools. However, it should be noted that by turning over classroom training to an outside firm, an end-user support organization can lose a valuable opportunity for education on company-specific IS issues as well as an opportunity to establish a support-service relationship with end users. In other words, cost efficiencies alone should not be the only criterion for choosing whether to provide a support service in-house or via a third-party supplier. Other firms have attempted to reduce classroom training costs by providing self-paced training alternatives. Progressive firms are providing e-training via a Web-based interface to a "learning portal" that is either run by the organization or hosted by an outside vendor (see the sidebar entitled "Reinventing Training at Cisco Systems").

Another frequently outsourced service is **help desk** (hotline) support. In the past, organizations used help desk positions as an initial training ground for entry-level IS positions; in a very short time, the new employee gained a first-hand appreciation of the difficulties faced by the organization's end users. However, just as many companies today are outsourcing some of their customer service support to persons in countries with different time zones or lower labor costs, or both, many IT help desks are being outsourced to gain cost efficiencies. Like other business units with help desks, IS help desk personnel frequently are guided by expert system applications to help them diagnose a problem in order to respond to telephone inquiries from end users. Today's network administrators also have an array of tools to help them troubleshoot hardware problems at remote sites.

In addition, the software industry has made great strides in improving online self-help for the end user. For example, tools have more sophisticated help functions that include searching by key words as well as context-specific help functions. The vendors of office suites have developed various types of online "assistants"—including wizards that help users create graphs in spreadsheet programs, create tables for common entities in database management programs, and format text, spreadsheets, data entry forms, and reports. In recent versions vendors have provided cartoon characters that pop up to offer help to the user. Software tips change based on recent keystrokes by the user of the particular application and animated examples help to train end users in a specific task.

However, the costliest changes in demand for facilitating end-user computing are control actions related to security issues: preventing computer abuse due to viruses, worms, and other hacker software and preventing unsolicited bulk e-mail messages (referred to as **spam**). We briefly address both of these in the next section.

REINVENTING TRAINING AT CISCO SYSTEMS

Tom Kelly, VP of worldwide training at Cisco Systems, joined the company with a clear mandate: to make Cisco a model of Web-based excellence in the one part of its business in which it was a laggard—Cisco's training division. According to Kelly: "There are very few high-tech companies that truly respect how much learning has to happen to allow them and their people to stay current." The learning model that Kelly is building at Cisco distinguishes between "structured learning" and "emergency learning," and tries to customize each form to the needs of the individual. Each person will be able to create a customized Web page, tentatively called My Future. The My Future page will serve as a learning portal where people can chart a long-term, structured learning plan; get all relevant short-term updates; and automatically receive critical information based on their job title, area of operation, field of interest, and learning preferences time critical content for emergency-learning situations. Ultimately, Kelly says, e-learning will be most effective when it no longer feels like learning—when it's simply a natural part of how people work.

[Adapted from Muoio, 2000]

Common Control Tactics

Management actions directed at controlling end-user computing typically have taken the form of policies or procedures. A list of common policies and procedures for end-user computing, which include approvals for purchasing hardware and software and keeping inventories of these tools, is provided in Figure 11.11. Many organizations place the primary responsibility for developing these policies and procedures in the hands of a centralized support unit, usually within an IS department. In some organizations an IS steering committee is responsible for establishing policies, including hardware and software standards, and the IS manager of the central support unit has the primary responsibility for monitoring compliance with these standards. The degree to which organizational policies are guidelines versus mandates, and the manner in which they are enforced, varies widely across organizations and across different departments within the same organization (Speier and Brown, 1997). However, the willingness of business unit managers and individual users to comply with computing standards has increased in recent years as the advantages for access to common computing and communications networks have increased.

Keeping users up to date on the latest policies and procedures has been a challenging management issue, organizations have typically done a better job communicating them to new workers via orientation programs

Required (or recommended) product standards (hardware and software)
Requirements (recommendations) for workstation ergonomics
Approval process for product purchases
Requirements for product inventorying
Upgrade procedures

Application quality review process
Guidelines to identify high-impact applications and sensitive data
Policies for corporate data access
Guidelines for program and data backup procedures
Requirements for audit trails
Documentation standards

Policies to control unauthorized access and file-sharing
Policies to control unauthorized software copying
Virus protection procedures
Spam filtering procedures

Figure 11.11 Common Policies and Procedures

than to older ones. Today, end-user computing policies and forms for technology and password approvals are typically accessible to all employees via the company's intranet. Changes in policies and procedural deadlines can also be broadcast to all end users via e-mail.

Organizational compliance with copyrights and licensing agreements is usually a formal responsibility of the senior IS manager. Software copyright compliance has been a weak area of end-user computing control in the past, but many organizations invested in mechanisms to monitor software licenses and to inventory software on all networked machines as part of their Year 2000 compliance initiatives, and this management area is much stronger today. Although enforcing control policies for software copyrights is easier to accomplish in networked environments in general, software vendors are reportedly still losing significant revenues due to software copyright violations. To put pressure on companies to proactively monitor for copyright and software licensing violations, the large software vendors have created alliances such as the Business Software Alliance (BSA) through which they file civil suits for copyright infringement (see the sidebar entitled "Software Companies Search for Pirates").

As mentioned above, however, the greatest control challenges today are preventing, and recovering from, external threats. Although laws against hackers have existed, and been enforced, in the United States for more than a decade, IS managers are facing increasingly frequent and more costly digital attacks from viruses and worms. Although security procedures can be implemented centrally and users can be given procedures to follow to avoid these security risks, the company's network is only as secure as its weakest link. For 2003 alone, estimates of economic damage worldwide due to viruses, worms, and other hacker attacks was estimated to be more than $120 billion, which would be more than twice as large as the estimated damage for the preceding year (Langley, 2003).

Another control issue concerns the use of peer-to-peer or **file-sharing applications,** which can slow down internal networks (due to using up bandwidth) as well as create major security problems (by giving an external computer access to an internal network, creating the potential for spreading viruses). File-sharing applications therefore intensify the problems of Internet abuse, because users expose their files for search and download by other users. Further, just as the original Napster Web site facilitated access to illegal copies of songs, most file-sharing software also is facilitating the sharing of copyrighted music and videos. Lawsuits by copyright owners against individual users are also increasing the pressure on organizations to detect or block peer-to-peer access (see sidebar "New Control Challenge: File-Sharing Applications").

The current lack of U.S. laws imposing penalties for sending commercial e-mail messages also makes it difficult for organizations, and their employees, to set up controls to block unwanted e-mail. According to recent estimates (Spam Calculator, 2003), the typical time lost by an employee for

SOFTWARE COMPANIES SEARCH FOR PIRATES

One of the most lucrative squealing operations in America is run out of the K Street lobbying district in Washington, D.C. The Business Software Alliance (BSA) does all the things that most D.C. lobby groups do, but it also has "power of attorney" to enforce the copyright claims of its members against companies using pirated software. The members of the BSA include large software companies like Microsoft. If the BSA finds out that your company is using more software than you have paid for, they can demand not only that you buy the programs, but also that you pay a penalty—a negotiated settlement fee that will serve as a reminder of the error of your ways. The alternative is to face a civil suit for copyright infringement, something few companies would want to risk.

The BSA has engaged in hundreds of enforcement actions over the years, bringing in a total of $70 million, including $12 million in 2002. The companies caught tend to be otherwise upstanding members of their local Chambers of Commerce, who for some reason or another are not paying for all the programs they are using; for some reason, they just do not view software inventories as important. For example, one Illinois engineer had a run-in with the BSA over unlicensed copies of the AutoCad engineering program: the penalty was $115,000. In addition to penalties, companies sometimes also endure the added indignity of having their managers being quoted in a BSA press release as lamenting how sorry they are and saying how much they respect intellectual property.

The BSA has a Report Piracy button on its Web site and a toll-free number. The money that is collected goes into the BSA's antipiracy program and is in fact, according to the software vendors, a "drop in the bucket" compared with the billions lost because of software piracy.

[Based on Gomes, 2003]

NEW CONTROL CHALLENGE: FILE-SHARING APPLICATIONS

File-sharing applications are challenges to corporate policies because they intensify the problems of old-fashioned Internet abuse. Although each uses a different architecture, these applications allow users to trade files with each other. (The old Napster music-sharing software, for instance, turned an individual's computer into a miniserver.) Users can search for and download files located on the hard drives of other users on the network. At the same time, users expose their files for search and download by other users. Almost all material that passes through file-sharing applications is copyrighted. Most of the applications help users search for MP3 music files, but some are sophisticated enough to handle the transfer of bigger files such as movies. The battle over copyright laws and file-sharing applications led to the shutdown of the original Napster site.

Corporations have long sought to regulate workers' Web access to avoid wasted time and controversial uses. Now they are increasingly taking aim at employees' use of peer-to-peer software such as Kazaa and Morpheus because they are under growing pressure from the copyright owners. In March 2003 music record companies sent about 300 U.S. corporations a letter warning that their networks had been used to swap songs. If a CIO or other company official knows of illegal use of file-sharing applications, he or she should take action.

[Adapted from Mathews, 2003; Pender, 2000]

each spam e-mail received is only about 3 seconds; nevertheless, if an organization has a 220-day work year and 1,000 employees using e-mail, and 40 percent of their e-mail messages are spam, the annual cost in lost productivity to the organization (as well as monthly IT maintenance costs) approaches $200,000. Filtering technologies exist for identifying and destroying viruses and for bypassing e-mail messages identified as spam, but they are deterrents against moving targets; Hackers and spammers can also buy the same software and devise ways to work around them.

Support and control tactics need to continually be modified in response to new technologies, new ways of working, and new external threats. We conclude this chapter by addressing the special case of facilitating user computing when the users are working remotely as telecommuters.

SPECIAL CASE: SUPPORTING TELECOMMUTERS

Providing support for workers outside of the physical walls of a business has become an important IT management and business management capability. Recent estimates are that about 20 million "white collar" workers in the United States, 10 million in Europe, and more than 2 million in Japan are part-time or full-time telecommuters, spending at least part of their workday or workweek at customer work sites, on the road, in home offices, or in satellite office facilities. Given the accelerated diffusion of mobile communication and computing devices and wireless networks, the number of telecommuters is likely to double before 2010.

However, not all "white collar" work (knowledge work) is suited to a telecommuting arrangement and not all telecommuters have the same needs for remote work support. One way to think about these job differences is to categorize them into three types which differ in terms of how

> **Telecommuters** spend at least a part of their regular business hours using IT to perform their jobs outside of a company's physical facilities, using a mobile office, an office in their personal home, or at a temporary office at a shared work center away from the company's main office.

"tethered" an employee's job is to the building that provides permanent office space for an organization's employees.

- *Office-bound.* Office-bound employees are "tethered" to an office in a building, where they typically use IT that might or might not be portable.
- *Travel-driven.* Travel-driven employees take their office with them to whatever location they are working in, which can change during the workday or workweek. For example, many sales force personnel have travel-driven jobs; they were likely to be among the first employees within their organizations to become telecommuters.
- *Independent.* Independent workers do not have a permanent office work space owned or leased by an employer. Instead, the worker uses IT in a home office or a mobile office, or both.

However, by the end of the 1990s many organizations in the United States were implementing telecommuting options for individual employees who weren't necessarily independent or travel-driven workers, but who required more flexibility in their work arrangements. For example, an employee might normally go to an office building to work but occasionally would work at home. Some companies' programs were designed to facilitate working at home for different types of projects that might require uninterrupted work time. Other telecommuters might simply be "day extenders"—employees working full days at a permanent office but then working at home during evenings and perhaps weekends.

For those knowledge workers in positions that are not highly office-bound, the benefits from implementing telecommuting programs can be compelling. According to self-reports by telecommuters, a very high percentage of workers say that they are more productive, due to a variety of factors (including the ability to focus better and to save in commuting time). Some companies have also realized dramatic savings from real estate costs. One of the cases in this textbook describes how a division within a large company in the IT industry (IBM) was able to avoid major real estate costs by setting up sales employees with equipment and telecommunications line access, initially for home offices and subsequently for mobile offices. Over a period of 5 years more than 12,500 employees at IBM gave up dedicated office space in company buildings and the company achieved multimillion dollar savings on an annual basis (Agpar, 1998). Lucent Technologies and AT&T have reported similar dramatic savings for enterprise-wide telecommuting programs.

Further, in some geographic regions within the United States with major environmental problems (for example, Los Angeles), companies of a certain size must comply with state or local regulations designed to improve the physical environment; for example, designated companies of a certain size might be required to have only a certain percentage of employees physically commuting to a work building within a given workweek. Governments have also set up tax incentives for companies to document how their telecommuting programs help to reduce highway congestion (and therefore air pollution).

Individual telecommuters have also reported personal benefits that they believe also contribute positively to their overall performance, such as the following.

- *Increased workday flexibility.* Remote workers gain flexibility in their work schedules that can reduce work stress and could allow them to avoid rush-hour traffic.
- *Improved work/life balance.* Employees who work at home typically are able to spend more time with family members by working very early in the morning or very late in the evening.
- *Easier accommodation of communications across time zones.* Employees who need to communicate with others in different time zones sometimes find it easier to integrate meeting times that extend their workdays if they can communicate from their homes.

Given these organizational and individual benefits, why have the number of telecommuters not increased more rapidly? One answer is that telecommuting programs typically involve an initial investment in technology, as well as ongoing IT support solutions. For example, today's telecommuters typically require portable equipment (which is still more expensive than the equivalent desktop equipment) and remote access, with sufficient bandwidth, to corporate data networks and services (see the sidebar entitled "Data Communications for Teleworkers.") Although the costs of mobile devices and networks continue to decline and not all telecommuters might need high speed connections, there are also still ongoing security and support issues that the IT organization needs to address. Telecommuters might also

Six Leadership Secrets For Managing Remote Workers

1. Aim to build trust through every interaction.
2. Create symbols and structures that unify the dispersed work group.
3. Establish ongoing opportunities for the team to learn more about each other, both professionally and personally.
4. Develop a daily alignment tool to focus the effort of the team.
5. Be scrupulously fair in treating all team members.
6. Be crystal clear about project objectives.

[Based on Kostner,1996]

Figure 11.12 Six Leadership Secrets for Managing Remote Workers

require immediate help desk support outside of normal work hours, due to more flexible work schedules and time zone differences. However, in large organizations, 24/7 user support at some level has become the norm.

Other reasons for the relatively slow diffusion of telecommuting arrangements over the past decade are not technology obstacles, but managerial and behavioral obstacles. For example, it has been learned that organizations need to redesign some of their work processes in order to effectively accommodate telecommuters. In particular, performance appraisal systems need to be revised to focus on performance outcomes so that the telecommuter is not penalized for different (and less visible) approaches to achieving work objectives. Some companies only allow "proven stars," not newcomers, to telecommute, and some managers believe that telecommuting weakens loyalty to the company (Dunham, 2000).

Another obstacle to telecommuting programs has been that many employees feel a sense of isolation. Remote workers don't have the opportunity for informal social interactions that working in an office building fosters. Some organizations have therefore instituted regular meetings that include telecommuters in order to increase social interactions with supervisors and among coworkers and make electronic communications more meaningful. Some telecommuters have also voiced concerns about not having the same opportunities for career advancement due to the belief that being "out-of-sight" would mean that they are less well known and therefore less likely to be considered for a given career opportunity. Many organizations have developed training programs for not only telecommuters, but also supervisors of telecommuters, in order to help avoid some of these nontechnical obstacles. Some guidelines for managers of remote workers, based on a very readable book by Jaclyn Kostner, are summarized in Figure 11.12.

Telecommuting programs also need to take into account security and legal issues. For example, it might be necessary to develop or modify written policies about the employee's responsibility for maintaining the confidentiality of company data accessed remotely and the use of company equipment for personal reasons. Employers of telecommuters also have the right to inspect home offices that contain company equipment, and this right should also be a part of a written agreement with the employee.

SUMMARY

The development of applications by business employees who are not IS specialists has become commonplace. The pervasiveness of user-developed applications is partly due to the clear advantages associated with these applications. However, business managers should carefully consider the potential disadvantages associated with user-developed applications when characteristics of the application to be developed, the technologies to be used, and the skills and experience of the available user developers suggest that the business risks will outweigh the benefits. User developers should also use a development methodology that is appropriate for the specific application. Consultation with IS professionals and auditing personnel should be encouraged throughout the development project, as appropriate.

Effective management of end-user computing in general requires strategies and tactics that take into account unique organizational context characteristics and the range and maturity of user development activities within the specific organization. IS and business managers need to approach end-user computing management as a user/IS working partnership and focus on supporting user applications with high payoffs. Today's network technologies make it easier to provide some support services and to enforce some control policies and procedures. In particular, the increasing use of networks has made it easier to place the tasks of hardware and software inventorying and upgrading, as well as the enforcement of some security controls and procedures, in the hands of network administrators rather than individual users. The IT industry has also become more responsive to some support needs by embedding context-specific support and control mechanisms in the end-user technologies.

In order to foster organizational learning, effective strategies for managing new and emerging end-user technologies typically differ from those used for mature end-user computing environments. Supporting telecommuters requires not only new technology solutions, but also addressing unique managerial challenges. Although new technologies help facilitate teamwork by a mobile workforce across multiple time zones, both employees and managers need special training programs to increase the likelihood of successful performance.

CHAPTER REVIEW QUESTIONS

1. What is meant by user application development? How does this differ from end-user computing in general?
2. What are some of the reasons why business users would want to develop computer applications rather than rely on IS professionals?
3. What are some of the major business risks associated with user application development?
4. Describe one characteristic each of the potential application, tool, and developer that should be assessed when evaluating whether or not a given application should be user-developed, including what you see as potential business risk.
5. Choose three Definition questions that the user developer should address. Explain why they could be important.
6. What are some of the key causes of spreadsheet errors in user-developed applications?
7. Compare the Acceleration and Containment strategies for managing end-user computing and provide a rationale for why a firm might choose one or the other.
8. Contrast the managed free economy approach with the centralized support approach for managing end-user computing.
9. What initial approach did Boeing take to managing its intranet, and what do you see as the risks associated with it?
10. What support services do you think are more important today and why?
11. Describe how a company policy could minimize some of the business risks associate with end-user computing.
12. Why are organizations concerned about spam in their employees' personal mailboxes?
13. Why are today's organizations more vigilant about enforcing copyright laws?
14. What are some of the technology challenges associated with supporting telecommuters?
15. What changes might a supervisor need to make to accommodate employees who are telecommuters?

CHAPTER DISCUSSION QUESTIONS

1. From the perspective of the organization as a whole, discuss what you see as some of the primary trade-offs between the benefits and risks of user application development.
2. Describe a situation in which one of the advantages of user-developed applications might be more important to a business manager than an IS manager. Then describe a situation in which one of the disadvantages might be more important to a business manager than an IS manager.
3. Using the factors shown in Figure 11.3, describe a scenario in which you think a business manager should and should not endorse having a new application developed by users rather than IS professionals.
4. Describe the extent to which you think each of the support services listed in Figure 11.10 is being offered in an organization familiar to you.
5. Develop a few guidelines for spreadsheet developers to help prevent spreadsheet errors.
6. Describe an organizational context in which you think a centralized support unit, such as an information center, would be an appropriate delivery mechanism for support services.
7. The number of telecommuters in the U.S. did not grow as fast over the past decade as predicted. Comment on the reasons that are suggested in the text. Then give an additional reason why these types of

arrangements have not been embraced by as many organizations as expected. Do you see this changing in the next decade?

8. Choose any three of the "secrets" for managing remote workers presented in Figure 11.12 and provide a rationale for why they might be important.

CASE STUDY: DATA COMMUNICATIONS FOR TELEWORKERS

Teleworkers need to have access to all the same data communication services that are available to employees with a permanent office, although not always at the same speeds. Virtual private networks (VPN) and other remote access technologies provide seamless, location-independent access to corporate data resources. The importance of sufficient bandwidth cannot be overemphasized: It does not make sense to lower the productivity of a highly-paid professional with low bandwidth or an unreliable connection if a faster and more reliable option is available at a marginal increase in cost. Broadband connections using xDSL, cable modems, or satellite connections are the norm if connections are regularly made from the same location. For mobile workers, wireless connections are increasingly available at airports, hotels, and restaurants/coffee shops, as is connectivity in densely populated areas. Further, e-mail, instant messaging, and access to core corporate systems are increasingly available on mobile phones and PDAs: In many cases these capabilities are all a mobile worker needs in addition to voice communication.

[Based on Topi, 2003]

Case Study Discussion Questions

Question One

It seems a given that teleworkers should have the same access to information as in-house workers. Presumably, the costs for such access aren't a barrier anymore with today's widespread access. What about security issues though? Is this an issue for companies when considering teleworkers?

Question Two

Find someone who is a teleworker and investigate the pros and cons of the position. Speculate on whether or not there will be an increase in these workers and defend your answer.

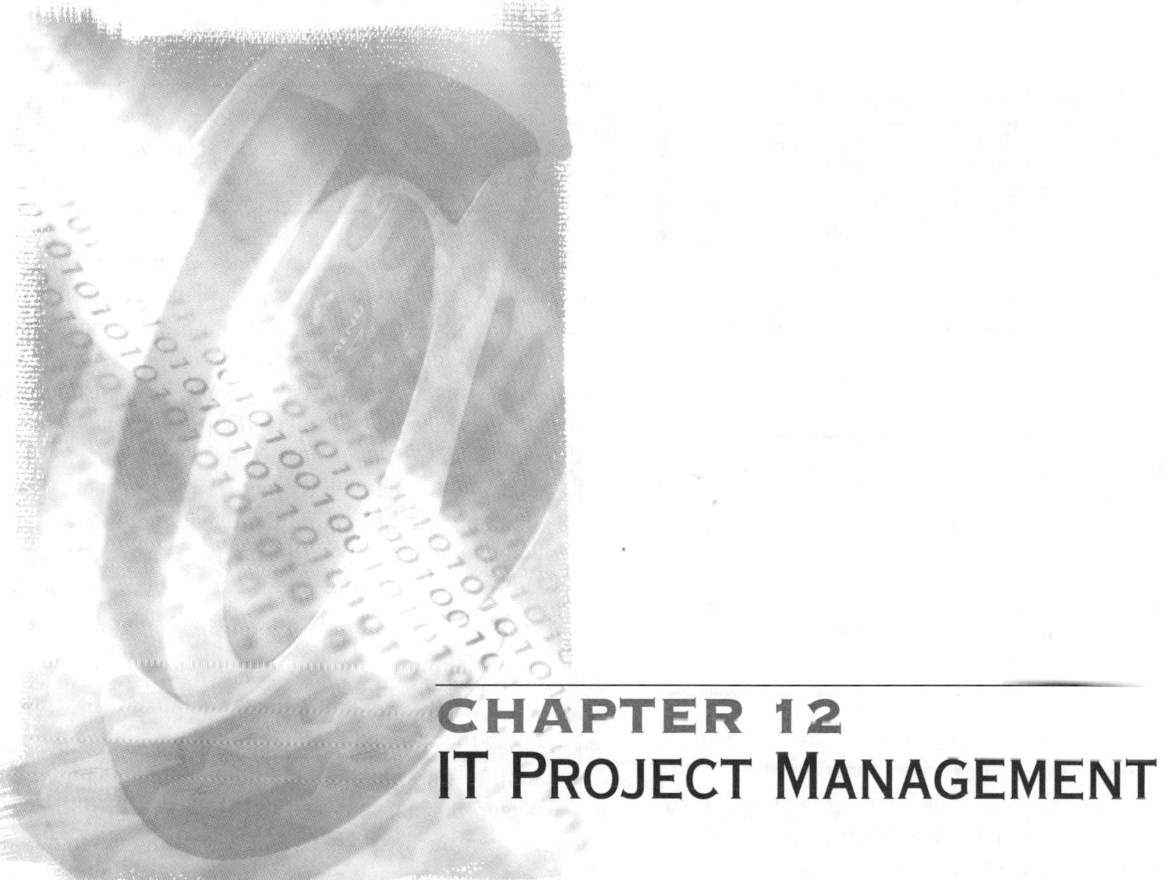

CHAPTER 12
IT PROJECT MANAGEMENT

THE OVERALL GOALS OF SYSTEMS PROJECTS ARE TO IMPLEMENT A QUALITY system that meets the needs of the targeted business and its users on schedule and within budget. Achieving these project goals requires not only a good systems methodology but also effective project management. The systems development methodologies (systems development life cycle [SDLC], prototyping, rapid application development [RAD], purchasing life cycle) discussed in the previous chapters are disciplined methods for acquiring an information technology (IT) solution. **Project management** for systems projects requires knowledge of these methodologies as well as other generally accepted practices for managing systems projects.

The project management practices described in this chapter include those applicable to managing projects in general, as well as practices that are specific to systems projects. Some of these techniques have their roots in military projects; since World War II, private sector firms have honed these techniques in industries highly dependent on project work, such as the construction, automotive, and aerospace industries.

The Project Management Institute (PMI), an international society of project workers, has certified thousands of project management professionals in generally accepted techniques since initiating its certification program in 1984 (Frame, 1994). The management competencies certified by the PMI include four areas traditionally associated with project management: (1) project scope, (2) time, (3) cost, and (4) human resources. However, to accommodate changing project demands in today's more chaotic world, four additional competencies are now certified by the PMI: (5) managing project communications, (6) contracts, (7) quality management, and (8) risk management. Managers of systems projects therefore need to be skilled in application systems methodologies and techniques, as well as skilled in the eight competencies summarized in Figure 12.1.

Although projects vary by size, scope, time duration, and uniqueness, most projects share the three following life cycle characteristics (PMI, 1996):

1. Risk and uncertainty are highest at the start of the project.
2. The ability of the project stakeholders to influence the outcome is highest at the start of the project.
3. Cost and staffing levels are lower at the start of the project and higher toward the end.

Project management experts also distinguish between project management and **program management**. Program management refers to a long-term undertaking that is typically made up of multiple projects. For example, in some organizations, a "program office" might be established to ensure that individual

Project scope	Project communications
Project time	Contracts
Project cost	Quality management
Human resources	Risk management

Figure 12.1 Eight Project Management Competencies

A **project** is a temporary endeavor undertaken to create a unique product or service. It typically is a one-time initiative that can be divided into multiple tasks, which require coordination and control, with a definite beginning and ending.

A **program** is a group of projects managed in a coordinated way to obtain benefits not available from managing them individually (PMI, 1996).

projects are coordinated with other projects currently underway in the same organization and that monetary and human resources are being leveraged for the benefit of the program as a whole. A program office headed by an information systems (IS) program manager might be a permanent unit, charged with overseeing multiple software development and maintenance projects in different stages of completion, each of which has its own objectives, schedule, and budget. In organizations with no permanent program office, one might be temporarily set up for a very large enterprisewide implementation project, such as an enterprise resource planning (ERP) project.

In the next sections we first discuss the growing issue of how to manage an organization's portfolio of IT projects. Then we describe some of the major approaches to managing the key stages of an IT project once it has been prioritized and initially funded: project initiation, project planning, project execution and control, and project closing. In the project execution and control section we focus on two IT project management capability areas that are especially important for successfully managing complex IT projects: managing risks and managing business change. The chapter ends with some guidelines for two special IT project contexts: (1) managing large, complex software implementation projects and (2) managing IT integration projects after two businesses have merged.

IT PORTFOLIO MANAGEMENT

As organizations have become highly dependent on IT and their investments in IT have become a very high percentage of their total capital investments, there has been an increasing

An organization's **IT portfolio** includes the set of IT project initiatives currently in progress, as well as requests for IT projects that have not yet been funded.

emphasis on **IT portfolio management**. Typically, a steering team of senior business leaders and the senior IT executive are held accountable for managing the organization's current portfolio of IT projects and pending requests. An organization's IT portfolio usually includes investments in both "sustaining" and "strategic" IT projects (Denis et al., 2004). For example, IT infrastructure investments are typically needed to "sustain" the organization's expected availability and reliability measures. Strategic investments typically include new application software packages for one or more business functions as well as new custom applications for a single department.

A major part of the IT portfolio management responsibilities are to continually assess whether the organization is investing in the right set of IT projects given its current competitive environment. New IT project requests are usually submitted using an agreed-upon template that includes the expected business benefits and estimates for the level of investment needed to do the project. An example of an IT project request using an organizational template is provided in Figure 12.2.

Some executive decision makers also want to be able to review an initial return on investment (ROI) analysis, or other formal financial assessment of the capital expenditure, at the time of the initial request. For large projects, however, it is more common to require instead only a rough order of magnitude (ROM) cost estimate. At a minimum, the request should include information about three types of business risks (McNurlin and Sprague, 2004):

- the risk of not doing the project
- the risks that it is the wrong project for what is trying to be achieved
- the risk that the project will fail (for technical or organizational reasons)

To help the steering team of executives prioritize a new request for an IT project against other new requests or existing IT project, an evaluative categorization scheme for all sustaining and strategic projects is typically applied. One such scheme, based on Denis et al. (2004), would be as follows:

- *Absolute Must.* A mandate due to security, legal, regulatory, or end-of-life-cycle IT issues
- *Highly Desired/Business-Critical.* Includes short-term projects with good financial returns and portions of very large projects already in progress

PROJECT DESCRIPTION	**MAJOR MILESTONES**
Implement Learning Delivery system to build and deliver virtual classes, conference calls, Web meetings, and other e-learning events. Implementation target is 18 months from project initiation.	· Project Scope and Approval · Publish RFP · Vendor Screening/Evaluation/Selection · Architecture Review · Implementation · Training · Go-Live
BUSINESS BENEFIT Creates dependable, cost-effective, scalable solutions that offer all learners rich distance learning experience to expand their knowledge in the way that works best for them. Cite savings and revenue generation expected. **DEPENDENCIES/RED FLAGS** Project budget, Resource & skill sets, Technology	**LEVEL OF EFFORT / COST** · 100 hrs ERP Interface · 300 hrs Build Learning · 100 hrs customization · Estimated Licensing, Time & Materials (500 hrs x hrly rate = $$$$) · Total Cost of Ownership (annual or per user) · FTE support required

Figure 12.2 Project Prioritization Template (Vavra and Lane, 2004).

- *Wanted.* Valuable, but with longer time periods for returns on investment (more than a 12-month period)
- *Nice to Have.* Projects with good returns, but with lower potential business value

In most organizations projects in the top two categories would most likely be funded for the budget year in which they were submitted. The "Wanted" projects would be carefully assessed and might involve the most contentious categorization decisions. The "Nice to Have" projects can be useful for helping to distinguish the projects that belong in the other categories. Many practitioners also emphasize that a team-based approach to the IT prioritization process results not only in a current prioritized list of projects but also in a better understanding among the organization's business and IT executives about the rationales for why a given IT request was funded, or not funded, and the IT budget implications for both sustaining and strategic IT investments.

Today many organizations reassess their IT project prioritization lists on a quarterly basis. Besides assessing new requests, the executive team is charged with monitoring the status of all current IT projects in order to ensure that the company's IT investments are staying aligned with the company's business goals. At AT&T, for example, a team of business and IT managers now evaluates each ongoing project on a regular basis using a Continue-Hold-Stop rating scheme (Hoffman, 2003).

PROJECT INITIATION

The first phase of a project life cycle is the project initiation phase. A key deliverable for this phase is a project charter that states in some detail the project's specific objectives, its intended scope, and any underlying assumptions and estimated results based on the feasibility analysis step of the IT project.

The scoping of a project involves setting boundaries for the project's size and the range of business functions or processes that will be involved. A high-level diagram is used to capture the major actors (entities) that provide inputs or receive outputs from the proposed system. (For examples, see the context diagram and use case diagram descriptions in Chapter 8). A statement of scope for an ERP package implementation project would include the specific ERP package modules to be purchased (e.g., finance/accounting, materials management) as well as the number of divisions and geographic locations within the enterprise to be included in the proposed project.

As described in Chapter 8, three types of feasibility analyses are typically conducted for systems projects as part of the Definition phase of a systems life cycle: economic feasibility, operational feasibility, and technical feasibility. Some of the technology feasibility questions to consider are the expected maturity level of the technologies to be used and the ease with which the needed technical expertise can be acquired (bought) or transferred to sufficient numbers of internal IS specialists. According to Applegate et al. (1996), potential "technical shortfalls" are frequently not adequately taken into account.

The economic feasibility investigation usually involves a formal cost-benefit analysis based on the overall objectives and scope of the project in order to estimate the project budget. For projects with benefits that are easily measured, an ROI will be easy to calculate. However, for projects that involve a business innovation, such as building a new organizational capability, it is much more difficult to quantify the potential benefits. For these types of strategic application projects, a technique such as rank-ordering the alternatives can be used to overcome total reliance on ROI measures that could be very difficult to calculate (see Figure 12.3).

Several other types of feasibility concerns can also be studied in order to better understand the best way to manage a systems project and its interdependencies, including schedule feasibility, legal and contractual feasibility, and political feasibility. Schedule feasibility takes into account the potential impact of externally imposed deadlines, such as the effective date of a new federal regulation or a seasonal date of importance for competing in a given industry. Legal and contractual feasibility concerns might need to be investigated to understand the issues related to partnering with one or more IT vendors for delivering the product solution. Political feasibility involves an assessment of support for the proposed system on behalf of key organizational stakeholder groups, which could or could not be captured as part of an operational feasibility study. For example, a systems innovation with major potential impacts for the way an organization conducts its business could require special capabilities that organizational members do not yet possess, or the innovation could be perceived as a major competitive threat to one organizational group but not another.

The executive team that is charged with the management of the IT portfolio of investments typically approves the project charter before additional resources are committed. If approved, the charter document also serves as a tool for the project manager, and the IS and business oversight committee, to monitor adherence to the agreed-upon project objectives and scope over the life of the project.

Project Manager Characteristics

The project initiation phase also includes the identification of a project leader responsible for managing the project. As discussed in Chapter 9, a systems project can be led by an IS manager, a business manager, or both: (1) a business manager responsible for overseeing all user activities and managing the business changes associated with the project as well as (2) an IS manager who is the project's technical director, responsible for the activities of all IS specialists and any IT vendors associated with the project. The choice of who will play this leadership role depends not only on the degree to

Rank Alternatives	Even if it is not possible to compute explicit numerical values, it may be possible to estimate with enough accuracy to rank the alternatives.
Sensitivity Analysis	Use sensitivity analysis to deal with uncertainties. If a precise value is not known for a parameter, repeat the analysis with alternative values.

Figure 12.3 Alternatives to ROI for Justifying Investments.

Leadership Skills: Sets example, energetic, vision (big picture), delegates, positive attitude

Organizational Skills: Planning, goal-setting, analyzing

Communication Skills: Listening, persuading

Team-Building Skills: Empathy, motivation, esprit de corps

Coping Skills: Flexibility, creativity, patience, persistence

Figure 12.4 Nontechnical Skills for Superior Project Management

which the application project could affect a business unit or division, but also on the degree to which the project requires technical team members, both internal and external.

Given the eight generic project management competencies summarized above in Figure 12.1, an effective manager of systems projects needs a variety of both technical and business skill sets. Figure 12.4 identifies five nontechnical skills that have been associated with superior project management.

Further, Meredith and Mantel (1989) point out that because a major characteristic of any project is "uniqueness" and therefore all projects are learning experiences for the project manager, effective project managers create ways to learn from the experiences of others and are "fire fighters" by avocation. In other words, no amount of planning can take into account the variety of unexpected changes that occur during the course of the project. Frame (1994) emphasizes that today's project managers should also be politically savvy—aware of what not to do as well as what to do—and have a high tolerance for ambiguity.

According to Highsmith (2000), systems projects for environments in which there are high levels of change and uncertainty can require a different "species" of project manager than those traditionally successful with less dynamic systems project environments. For example, the successful e-business project manager of the late 1990s was skilled in the ability to create a collaborative project environment with the right level of "creative tension" that helped move the project team toward some indefinite goal. This is a quite different skill than the one needed for creating and monitoring detailed task lists for a more clearly defined systems solution.

Project Sponsor and Champion Roles

Two key business manager roles have also been associated with successfully managed systems projects: the project sponsor and the project champion.

Many organizations require that each systems project have a designated business sponsor. The **sponsor** participates in the development of the initial project proposal and the feasibility studies and may personally argue for the approval of the systems project before an IS advisory board. The sponsor role is typically played by the business manager who financially "owns" the project.

Once the systems project has been initiated, the sponsor provides the funds for the project and plays an oversight role during the life of the project to help ensure that the projected system benefits are achieved after the system is installed. For example, the sponsor typically takes responsibility for ensuring that the most appropriate ("best") business managers or system end users are assigned to the project team and that these project team members are empowered to make decisions for the business units they represent without having to "ask for permission." The sponsor also is relied on to provide business personnel who are not formal team members as needed for certain life cycle steps of the project—such as providing information about current work processes or procedures in the Definition phase, evaluating screen designs of a prototype system from an end-user perspective early in a Construction phase, or performing system tests at the end of a Construction phase. Because the business unit often cannot easily spare the most capable business managers and users for part- or full-time project work, the business sponsor also must make the financial and human resource arrangements needed to "free up" these project team members from their normal tasks and responsibilities so that they can put forth the level of effort that is needed for the project to succeed.

For systems projects that involve multiple business functions, the sponsor is likely to be the CEO. For systems projects that are major hardware and telecommunications infrastructure investments only, the head of the IS organization might play the formal sponsor role.

The second business leadership role associated with successful IT projects is the role of **project champion**. In essentially all cases, the champion role needs to be played by a business manager who (1) has high credibility as an organizational spokesperson among the user community to be affected by the new system solution and (2) is successful at continually communicating the business vision and benefits associated with the project. In some situations the project sponsor and the champion are the same person. However, when the project sponsor's daily responsibilities are too far removed from the business activities to be affected by the new system, the champion role might not receive enough attention if left to an executive-level sponsor.

Personal traits of an effective project champion include an enthusiasm that never wanes and the capability to "rally the troops" as problems arise that require exceptional efforts.

In contrast to the sponsor role, the champion role is not always a formally designated one, although the champion's contribution to the project's success is widely recognized among both management and users.

PROJECT PLANNING

Three major project planning components are the project schedule, budget, and staff (project team). These components are obviously interrelated, and poor planning for one component can severely affect another. Good estimation techniques are especially important for systems projects that involve immature or emerging technologies. In general, conservative (rather than optimistic) estimations are recommended, as well as control mechanisms that focus on the areas of greatest project uncertainty and organizational vulnerability. Although we emphasize below some proven techniques for good project planning and control, it should also be kept in mind that experienced project managers will tailor their approaches to match the special circumstances of a given project or organizational situation (see the sidebar entitled "256 Project Characteristics to Be Managed").

Scheduling

Developing a project schedule typically involves a **work breakdown analysis**: identifying the phases and sequence of tasks that need to be accomplished to meet the project goals—as well as the goals for other organizational and external party obligations—and then estimating the time of completion for each task. For systems projects, the project phases as well as the detailed activities for each step and their sequence can typically be derived from the systems methodology being used for the project.

> **256 PROJECT CHARACTERISTICS TO BE MANAGED**
>
> Projects can have an overwhelming number of different characteristics. They can be high-risk or low-risk, long-term or short-term, state-of-the-art or routine, complex or simple, single-function or cross-functional, large or small, technology-driven or market-driven, contracted out or performed in-house, and so on. These eight characteristics alone can lead to 256 different combinations that might entail a different approach to project planning, execution, or control.
>
> [Adapted from Roman, 1986]

Time estimates are typically based on the relevant past experiences of the organization or the project manager, or both. Other sources for time estimates include benchmarking studies for similar projects in other organizations, activity estimates embedded in software estimation packages, and project databases of system consultants.

The detailed work activity list, the task interdependencies, and the time estimates for each task are then used to develop a master schedule for the project that identifies the **project milestone** dates and deliverables. The level of detail provided in a master schedule depends upon project characteristics such as size, functional complexity, and task interdependencies, as well as organizational practices.

Some project milestone dates will also be highly influenced by time demands particular to the organization. In particular, system implementation activities are frequently scheduled to coincide with calendar periods when transactions affected by the new system solution are much lower in number or can even be temporarily left unprocessed during the conversion process. For example, it is very common for major system tests and new system cutovers in U.S.-based organizations to be scheduled for 3-day holiday weekends. In other situations a project implementation date near the end of a fiscal period will be targeted in order to minimize historical data conversions.

The project scheduling process is somewhat different when an organization has adopted a timeboxing philosophy. The term **timeboxing** refers to an organizational practice in which a system module is to be delivered to the user within a set time limit, such as 6 months. This technique is a characteristic of the rapid application development (RAD) methodology (discussed in Chapter 9). Because the intent of timeboxing is to deliver new IT solutions as rapidly as possible, a work plan might be designed in which a given module is initially implemented during the timebox without full functionality, and then the functionality is increased in subsequent releases.

A common pitfall in developing a master schedule is a failure to understand the interdependencies among project tasks and subtasks. Including a customer verification step as part of the master scheduling process can help identify misunderstandings at an early stage of the project planning cycle.

Effective scheduling is critical to the project's success and is a key input to the project budgeting component. However, the master schedule is also meant to be a living

> **Work breakdown** is a basic management technique that systematically subdivides blocks of work down to the level of detail at which the project will be controlled.

document. A good planning process therefore also provides for change-control procedures to request schedule changes. Aside from a process to request the necessary management approvals, changes to the master schedule should be documented with the date of the change, the nature and reason for the change, and the estimated effects of the change on other project components (budget, resource allocations) and related project tasks.

Budgeting

The project budget documents the anticipated costs for the total project. These costs are typically aggregated into meaningful categories at the level at which the project costs will be controlled.

There are two traditional approaches to estimating project costs: bottom-up and top-down. The project work plan from the scheduling process is typically used for a bottom-up process: Cost elements are estimated for the lowest level of work plan tasks and then aggregated to provide a total cost estimate for the project. According to Frame (1994), a top-down approach "eschews" the cost details and provides instead estimates for major budget categories based on historical experience. A top-down approach (also called parametric cost estimating) could be used in the project initiation stage because not enough is known about the project to do a work breakdown analysis. However, once a master schedule has been developed, a bottom-up process is recommended, especially if the project is large and complex. These two approaches can also be used as checks for each other.

No matter which approach is used, the budgeting process needs to build in cost estimates to cover project uncertainties associated with changing human resources, immovable project deadlines (that could require overtime labor), as well as changes in technology and contract costs outside the organization's control.

Like the master schedule, the project budget is a living document of anticipated total costs. A good planning process therefore also provides change-control procedures to request approvals for deviations from an estimated budget. Changes to the budget should be documented with the date of change, the nature and amount of the requested budget deviation, the reason for the change, and the estimated effects of the change on other project components (scope, schedule, resource allocations).

According to Frame (1994), inexperienced estimators typically fall into three estimation traps: They (1) are too optimistic about what is needed to do the job, (2) tend to leave components out, and (3) do not use a consistent methodology, so they have difficulty recreating their rationales. Training in estimating processes (such as that provided by the American Association of Cost Engineers) and organizational checklists of items to include in estimates can help the amateur estimator quickly improve.

Even for the experienced project manager, cost estimations can be complicated by many types of unknowns, including the lack of precedents, unpredictable technical problems, and shifting business requirements. Projects that use standard components and an evolutionary methodology are generally the easiest to estimate. Both budget padding and lowballing are apparently widely used, but both these techniques can also cause dysfunctional consequences (see the sidebar entitled "Highballing vs. Lowballing Project Costs").

Staffing

Project staffing involves identifying the IT specialist skill mix needed for the project, selecting personnel who collectively have the skills needed and assigning them to the project, preparing them for the specific project work as team members, and providing incentives to achieve the project goals.

In project work the human resource is a critical production factor. As part of the project planning, the project manager should be able to estimate the skill type, proficiency level, quantity, and time frame for human resources to execute each project phase and critical task. Some human resources need to be dedicated to the project full-time, whereas others will be shared with other project teams. Still others might not be formal team members but will be relied on for their expertise at critical points.

HIGHBALLING VS. LOWBALLING PROJECT COSTS

Budget padding is a common approach. Often there is no useful precedent to serve as a guide for a budget projection; past authorizations can be misleading or only partially applicable. Further, sometimes project budgets receive across-the-board cuts, favoring those who have submitted a padded budget in the first place. Budget padding is therefore sometimes the best defensive measure to ensure that adequate resources will be provided to get a job done.

Lowballing project costs can be conscious or unconscious. Sometimes lower estimates are provided in order to gain initial project approval. Other times the technical glitches that can arise are underestimated. Sometimes ignorance of an environmental event invalidates what was thought to be a well-informed estimate.

[Adapted from Frame, 1994, and Roman, 1986]

Wherever possible, individual employees with the best qualifications for the project work should be selected. However, in an organizational setting this is not always possible, due to the size and talent of the specialist pool internal to the organization. Because of the diverse set of specialist skills that might be needed across projects, it is not uncommon for at least a portion of the team members to undergo specialized training in anticipation of a project. Some IS organizations use a skill set "centers" approach in which IS specialists belong to a **center of excellence** managed by a coach who is responsible for developing talent and selecting personnel for project assignments based not only on project needs but also on individual development needs (see the sidebar entitled "Centers of Excellence at Bell Atlantic").

For systems projects it is also not uncommon to hire outside contractors for project work for quality or quantity reasons. This is especially desirable if a distinct specialty is required for a single project but it does not make economic sense to develop these resources in-house. It also might be impractical to use internal resources if a project requires more resources for just a short period of time. The downside in this case is that the company can become highly dependent on a talent base that is temporary. By the late 1990s, many companies began to focus on decreasing dependence on outside contractors by developing their own IT specialist talent. One way to do this is to build in a requirement for "knowledge transfer" from consultants with special expertise to internal employees as part of the consultant contract.

Another key aspect of systems project team staffing is the selection of business personnel who are not IS specialists as formal team members or as "extended" team members who help with defining the systems requirements, testing, and training over the life of the project. Careful selection of business employees can obviously be a critical step in the staffing process. IS specialists depend on users for their functional expertise (sometimes referred to as subject matter expertise, or SME). Often, formal documented procedures are not the way that work tasks really get done, and the systems team must elicit these differences as part of the Definition phase. Further, in many systems implementations, major changes in the ways of doing business are part of the project's objectives. For example, business process changes are typical when implementing a new software package that has not been modified for the implementing organization. Business personnel with enough authority to work with both business leaders and business workers who will use the new software need to be selected with the help of the executive sponsor.

Even after a well-managed selection process, there is sometimes a need for special team-building exercises to build team spirit and to help team members who have not worked together before get to know each other quickly. However, as pointed out by Frame (1994), a sports team analogy for project teams is inappropriate (see the sidebar entitled "IT Project Teams Are Not Like Sports Teams").

The degree to which team-building is needed will depend on the characteristics of the project, the prior experiences of the team members, and the degree to which the systems methodology to be used is new to the team members. Team-building and fostering ongoing motivation are easiest when team members are in the same physical location (co-located), there is a stable roster of team members, and the project manager is able to manipulate the appropriate motivating factors.

Because project incentives can influence individual performance and productivity, projects that require especially intense efforts, personal sacrifices (such as postponed vacations), and possibly geographic relocation might also have project-based incentives to help ensure that the project goals are achieved. The dot-com IT start-up culture within the United States epitomized this highly intensive lifestyle for which stock options were the primary reward. Similar behaviors are sometimes needed for IT projects with highly aggressive schedules in order to meet a schedule deadline. Unlike a dot-com start-up, however, the duration of the project is usually known and the rewards can be more certain! When designing incentives, it should be kept in mind that an individual's response to the same incentive can vary over time due to changing personal needs. For example, key project team members on ERP package implementation projects could be asked to make multiyear commitments to the project in return for special project completion bonuses or even stock options.

CENTERS OF EXCELLENCE AT BELL ATLANTIC

Beginning in the summer of 1994, Bell Atlantic began to implement 12 skill centers, also called Centers of Excellence. Each skill center was a semipermanent team of technical specialists or people trained in a specific IT skill, such as client/server, database management, or quality assurance. Each skill center was a "virtual homeroom" managed by a coach who was responsible for assigning IT personnel to specific application projects in order to achieve the project goals as well as the employee's career goals. The objective was to build an IT talent base of skilled IT professionals. Processes were developed to anticipate the skill sets needed for new development projects and to move people from older (e.g., COBOL) skill sets to newer ones.

[Adapted from Clark et al., 1997]

IT PROJECT TEAMS ARE NOT LIKE SPORTS TEAMS

The reason that project teams do not look like sports teams is that they entail the employment of borrowed resources. . . . Imagine sports events being carried out like projects: Each week the composition of the team would change, players would get their weekly playing assignments through a lottery system, team size could fluctuate, the rules of the game would be dynamic, and coaches would have no power over their players. When applied to a sports example, the standard practices employed in project management appear laughable.

[Frame, 1994]

For systems projects not as large and intensive as a major ERP implementation, the best approach is often to simply monitor factors related to how the project is being conducted that have been found to be potential demotivators. For example, the 10 items in Figure 12.5 were among 25 factors found to be counterproductive in a project environment of skilled professionals. As will be discussed below, effective communication among those associated with a project can be key to avoiding some of these demotivators.

Planning Documents

Two documents are typically created from the project planning phase: a **statement of work (SOW)** for the customer and a project plan to be used by the project manager to guide, monitor, and control the execution of the project plan.

The SOW document is a high-level document that describes what the project will deliver and when. It is in effect a contract between the project manager and the executive sponsor. It therefore can be used as a high-level guide for business managers to plan for their own unit implementation as well as to monitor the project's progress toward the project goals of on-time completion within budget.

All program managers or committees that oversee the project typically review the project plan. For example, an IS program manager and other project managers initially review the project plan, and then a project steering committee of business managers and IS leaders might be asked to endorse it.

Two types of project management charts are also typically developed during the planning phase and used during project execution: (1) PERT (or CPM) charts and (2) Gannt charts. As will be seen below, these are two complementary techniques for project scheduling and resource planning.

A PERT chart (a Program Evaluation and Review Technique developed for a missile/submarine project in 1958) graphically models the sequence of project tasks and their interrelationships using a flowchart diagram. (Note: Some organizations use an alternative method called CPM [Critical Path Method] developed by DuPont about the same time.) As shown in Figure 12.6, each major task is represented as a symbol (such as a circle or rectangle) and lines (arrows) are used to show predecessor and successor tasks. A PERT chart depicts what is referred to as a critical path—a sequence of activities that will take the longest to complete. Any delays in completing the activities on the critical path will result in slippage on the project schedule. A PERT chart therefore helps managers estimate the effects of task slippage and shows the tasks not on the critical path for which there will be some slack resources. Researchers have found that projects in which PERT (or CPM) techniques are used are less likely to have cost and schedule overruns (Meredith and Mantel, 1989).

1. Poor planning, direction, and control
2. Improper organization
3. Excessive staffing
4. Inadequate attention of management to productivity and the elimination of counterproductive elements
5. Internal communication problems
6. Insensitivity to people
7. Improper use of employees
8. An inadequate personal performance evaluation system
9. Ineffective interface with customers
10. Too many internal political machinations

Figure 12.5 Counterproductive Characteristics of Project Team Environments (Based on productivity study by Hughes Aircraft Company in Roman, 1986).

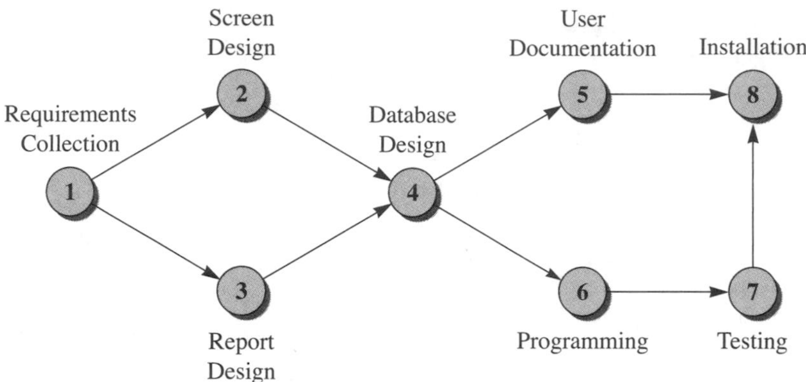

Figure 12.6 PERT Chart Example (Reprinted from Valacich, George, and Hoffer, *Essentials of Systems Analysis & Design*, Prentice Hall, 2001).

A Gannt chart graphically depicts the estimated times (and later, the actual times) for each project task against a horizontal time scale. Tasks are presented in a logical order along with a bar graph depicting the estimated time duration for each task on an appropriate linear calendar (minutes, hours, days, or weeks) for the number of months and years planned for the life cycle of the project (see Figure 12.7). The precedence relationships in the PERT/ CPM chart are reflected in the start and end dates of the activities, and overlapping tasks can be easily seen. Although time periods for tasks can also be shown on PERT or CPM charts, Gannt charts are particularly useful for displaying a project schedule and for tracking the progress of a set of tasks against the project plan (as discussed below).

An important project management skill is to determine at what level of detail to plan the project tasks. Too much detail can be stifling and result in too much time being spent on tracking rather than on more critical project tasks. Too little detail can result in inadequate project management controls and both missed deadlines and cost overruns.

PROJECT EXECUTION AND CONTROL

The *project plan* documents described in the preceding section are best recognized as living documents that need to be refined and reassessed throughout the life of the project. In large, complex projects, the planning activities still continue after a project team has been selected and some initial tasks have been undertaken, and the revised plan goes through the same endorsement procedures described above a few months into the project.

Software project management tools such as Microsoft Project are commonly used to help the project manager and other team leaders initiate and monitor the project tasks. In some cases an organization develops its own project management tools, or a consulting firm might provide such a system. Our focus here is not on the software tools used, but on three general project management practices: communication, coordination, and measuring progress.

Communication about the project to all affected stakeholders and potential users is key to successful implementation for systems projects in particular. For large projects with major business impacts, a project "kickoff" event is frequently scheduled at which the project's sponsor or champion explicitly communicates the project outcomes and perhaps also presents some general ground rules for project team members to make decisions on behalf of their constituents.

After this event, it is the project manager's responsibility to have an external communications plan appropriate for the project. This includes communicating on a regular basis (typically weekly or monthly) the project status to any oversight groups, all key stakeholders, and the user community that will be affected by the project. Using the planning charts mentioned earlier, variances from the forecasted project budget and project milestones can be reported in a way that highlights deviations from the project plan and their causes (see Figure 12.8).

Some organizations have also adopted a red yellow-green light approach to signal what is "on track," potential problem areas, and project problems (see the sidebar entitled "Red, Yellow and Green Lights"). This helps top managers focus on corrective actions for exceptional circumstances, such as changes in execution to avoid a bottleneck or major revisions to a project plan to better manage project risks. When outside

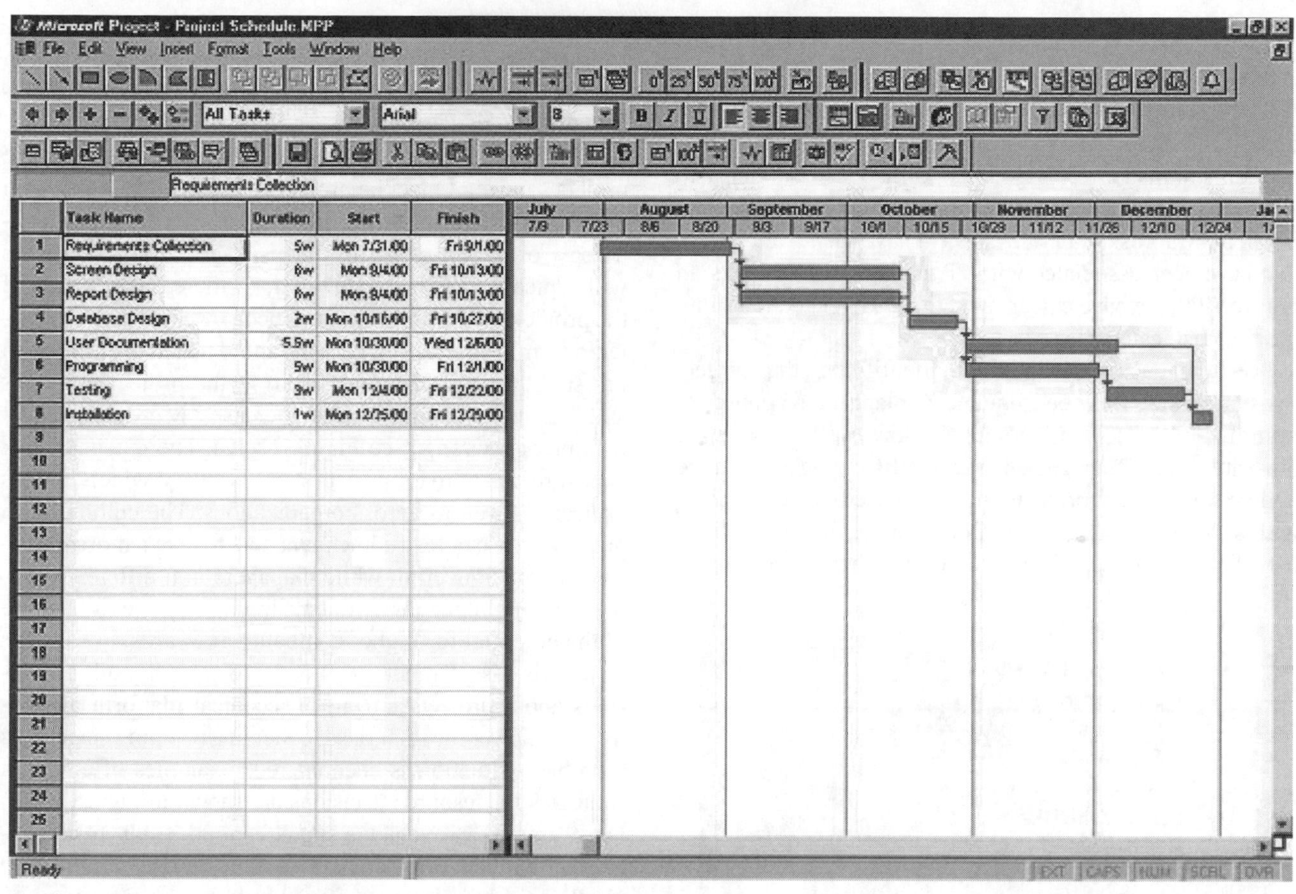

Figure 12.7 Gannt Chart Example (Reprinted from Valacich, George, and Hoffer, *Essentials of Systems Analysis & Design*, 1st Edition. Copyright © 2001. Reprinted by permission of Pearson Education, Inc., Upper Saddle River, NJ).

- **Schedule Status**
  1. Scheduled and actual or forecasted completion dates
  2. Explanations of deviation(s)

- **Budget Status**
  1. Total project funding
  2. Expenditures to date of report
  3. Current estimated cost to complete
  4. Anticipated profit or loss
  5. Explanation of deviation, if any, from planned expenditure projection

Figure 12.8 Status Reporting (Roman, 1986).

consultants are used, the tracking of consultant costs and utilization is also a key project manager responsibility.

Good communications among the project team members are also critical for task coordination and integration. The mechanisms here include both formal mechanisms (such as weekly meetings of team leaders) and informal mechanisms (such as e-mail communications and in-the-hall progress reporting).

Managing Project Risks

One of the goals of project management is to reduce the risk of failing to achieve the project objectives. All projects carry some risks. Risks can be due to a variety of causes, including human error, project scope changes, unanticipated technology changes, or internal politics. For example, Bashein, Markus, and Finley (1997) have identified 10 risk that have been associated with IT management projects. In Figure 12.9, we have categorized these IT-related risks into the four risk categories.

Risk management involves identifying the project risks, assessing their consequences, planning responses to minimize the risks, and monitoring how well the risks are mitigated and managed. Risk identification should be undertaken at the project's outset, based on experience with similar projects. A common approach is to develop a list of risk factors and then to weight them according to their potential impact, as shown in Figure 12.10. Another approach is to graph the potential impact of a given risk in relation to the extent to which it can be controlled by managers within the firm, as shown in Figure 12.11.

Organizational Risks
- Competitive risk
- Reputation risk
- Technical risk

Personnel Risks
- Personnel and expertise risk
- Nonuse and unintentional misuse risk
- Internal abuse risk

Systems Project Risks
- Control design risk
- Project delay risk

External Security Risks
- External fraud, theft, or crime risk
- Extraordinary event risk

Figure 12.9 Ten IT-Related Risks and Potential Consequences (Bashein, Markus, and Finley, 1997).

The highest level of project risk typically occurs at the project's outset. Once the project is underway and the team members learn more about a customer's needs, a new technology, or a vendor's software package, the project risks will typically decrease. However, in the earliest stages of the project fewer resources have been invested and it is easier to terminate the project. After more resources have been invested, the organization's stake in the project increases and thus its risk exposure also increases: More will be lost if things go wrong (see Figure 12.12). The extent of risk exposure for a given project can also vary widely across projects as well as across organizations. The culture of an organization can lead some managers to take a more defensive approach overall, while managers in a different organization might purposely pursue high-risk projects because of the potential for higher competitive rewards.

The risk assessment for a given project can result in decisions about project staffing or technical platform alternatives that lower the total risks, either in a planning stage or as a problem situation is encountered. Examples of common strategies for resource decisions are shown in Figure 12.13. For example, an exchange strategy could result in subcontracting with vendors, and a reduction strategy could result in allocating the "best and brightest" to a project team to minimize the potential for failure. Sometimes the project budget includes monetary resources allocated to a contingency fund that can be used at the discretion of project team members to resolve anticipated thorny problems that cannot be specifically defined at the outset of the project.

One of the major pitfalls in monitoring the risks of projects already underway is to ignore negative feedback. Keil and Robey (1999) warn that project managers need to be careful not to "turn a deaf ear" to bad news or to downplay symptoms of what could be major problems. Recognizing this type of problem was found to be an important first step in turning around a widely publicized IT project crisis faced by the city of Denver in the 1990s—the 16-month-late, \$2-billion-over-budget project to automate airport-wide baggage handling (see the sidebar entitled "Baggage Handling Problems at the Denver International Airport"). Another lesson learned from an analysis of the Denver project crisis is that an outside consultant could be needed to evaluate a troubled project and to help devise alternative courses of action.

According to Hamilton (2000), good risk management depends on accurate and timely information on project characteristics that managers view as likely indicators of risk. Deviations from expectations need to be clearly highlighted, and this information needs to reach the right

RED, YELLOW, AND GREEN LIGHTS*

Some organizations use a traffic light approach to signal the status of a project on a regular basis.

- Green indicates a project is on track.
- Yellow flags potential problems.
- Red means a project is behind; the executive sponsor and project manager need to figure out a way to get the project back on track.

* Referred to in some organizations as RAG, with Amber instead of Yellow.

Technology Risk Assessment			
Risk Factor			**Weight**
1. Which of the hardware is new to the company?[a]			5
None		0	
CPU	High	3	
Peripheral and/or additional storage	High	3	
Terminals	High	3	
Mini or micro	High	3	
2. Is the system software (nonoperating system) new to IT project team?			5
No		0	
Programming language	High	3	
Database	High	3	
Data communications	High	3	
Other (Please specify)	High	3	
3. How knowledgeable is user in area of IT?			5
First exposure	High	3	
Previous exposure but limited knowledge	Medium	2	
High degree of capability	Low	1	
4. How knowledgeable is user representative in proposed application area?			5
Limited	High	3	
Understands concept but has no experience	Medium	2	
Has been involved in prior implementation efforts	Low	1	
5. How knowledgeable is IT team in proposed application area?			5
Limited	High	3	
Understands concept but has no experience	Medium	2	
Has been involved in prior implementation efforts	Low	1	

[a]This question is scored by multiplying the sum of the numbers attached to the positive responses by the weight.

Figure 12.10 Project Implementation Risk Factors and Weights (Reprinted from Applegate et al., 4th edition, 1996).

people at the right time in order for further investigation and corrective actions to be taken.

Managing Business Change

When new systems are implemented, they typically involve major changes in business processes, which in turn require changes in the way employees do their work and information flows into and out of their work activities. **Change management**, or the ability to successfully introduce change to individuals and organizational units, is therefore key to successfully implementing a new system.

When a new information system will affect organizational power structures, strategies and tactics to deal with these political aspects of the project need to be explicitly developed. According to Markus (1983), the sources for resistance to the implementation of a new information system can often be anticipated by comparing the distribution of power implied by the new system and the distribution of power existing in the organization prior to the new system. Faced with potential shifts in organizational responsibilities, key stakeholders could consciously, or unconsciously, employ counterimplementation tactics that result in preventing or delaying the completion of a new system or in modifying its initial requirements. Examples of explicit or implicit tactics include

- withholding the people resources needed for a task (including designating a representative who is not qualified to make the decisions needed)
- raising new objections about the project requirements, resulting in schedule delays
- expanding the size and complexity of the project (rescoping)

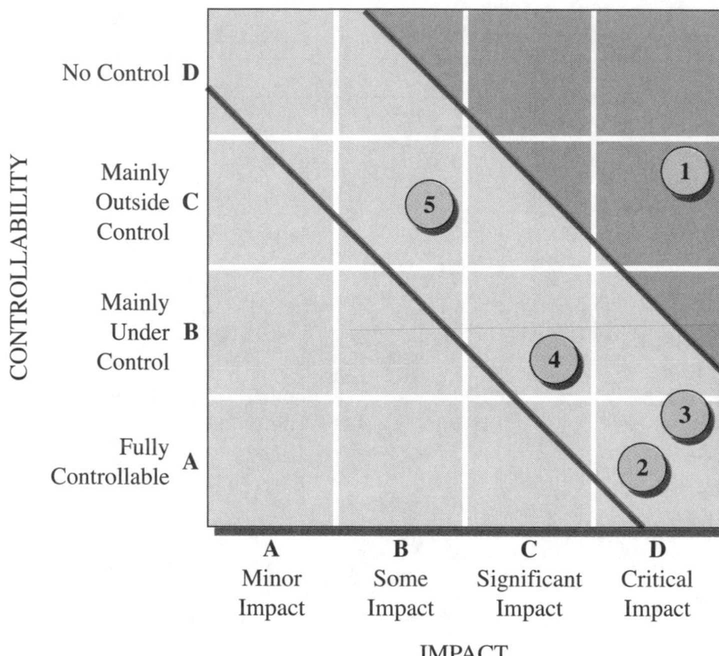

Figure 12.11 Risk Controllability and Impact Grid (Adapted from Hamilton, 2000).

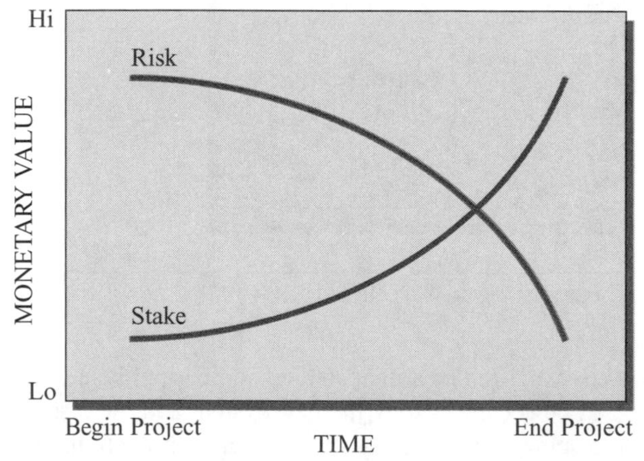

Figure 12.12 Risk Exposure: Risk Versus Stake (Adapted from Frame, 1994).

Recognizing from the beginning of a project the potential political implications and then devising solutions to avoid them is usually more effective than overtly trying to overcome resistance tactics. Devising system solutions that will be viewed as desirable by all stakeholders is of course an ideal outcome. One key way to achieve this type of win-win situation is to involve potential objectors in the implementation process so that they are involved in negotiating the requirements as well as the implementation schedule for a new system.

As business managers have come to recognize the importance of change-management practices in general, researchers have proposed multistage models for managing changes in organizations. Most of these change models have their roots in the simple three-stage **Lewin/Schein change model** shown in Figure 12.14.

In the first stage, Unfreezing, those individuals affected by the new system must realize the need for change. To help motivate change, a work environment in which it is "safe to change" needs to be created. That is, those individuals who need to change have to be convinced that giving up the old ways of doing things will not personally disadvantage them.

The Moving stage requires knowledge transfer and training. Until the knowledge and skills required for the new roles are acquired, change cannot take place. New ways to work need to be assimilated, and adequate time needs to be allocated for the people to learn these new skills and behaviors.

In the last stage, Refreezing, the new behavior becomes the accepted way of doing things. New incentive systems could be needed to reinforce the new behaviors, and the change might not be routinized until new informal norms have also been adopted within relevant workgroups across an enterprise.

Based on a study of successful and failed efforts to transform an organization, Kotter (1995) has proposed the

Exchange Strategy: An unknown risk or known critical risk is exchanged for a more acceptable level of risk. For example, the risk can be shifted to a third party by subcontracting with another organization under a fixed-cost contract for a specific project deliverable.

Reduction Strategy: By allocating to the project the best human resources available, a specific project risk can be reduced.

Avoidance Strategy: An alternative technical approach to a problem may be chosen in order to avoid risk exposure.

Figure 12.13 Common Strategies for Managing Risks (Based on Roman, 1986).

following eight-step model for leaders of major organizational change efforts.

1. Establish a Sense of Urgency
2. Form a Powerful Guiding Coalition
3. Create a Vision
4. Communicate the Vision
5. Empower Others to Act on the Vision
6. Plan for and Create Short-Term Wins
7. Consolidate Improvements and Produce Still More Change
8. Institutionalize New Approaches

The first four steps bring an organization to the Moving stage (described above) by establishing a sense of urgency for the change and both creating and communicating a vision to help direct the change effort. The eighth step is similar to the Refreezing stage. According to Kotter, for a change to be institutionalized, it must be rooted in the organization's norms and values.

Today's common wisdom is that modern organizations and their people need to be able to accept change easily. This suggests that the institutionalization step, or Refreezing stage, might be pursued somewhat differently than when it was originally conceived. That is, a more typical organizational goal today is to have a workforce that has been reskilled but is also "change-ready," rather than becoming refrozen (Clark et al., 1997). Change-ready personnel also view change as a desirable, ongoing state for competing in today's business world.

Kotter and other change-management researchers have recently emphasized that major organizational change efforts cannot be entirely planned in advance. Instead, change efforts should be expected to be somewhat "messy" and "full of surprises" (Kotter, 1995). A successful change-management effort therefore requires both planned (preplanned) activities as well as "improvisational" responses to unforeseen circumstances (Orlikowski and Hofman, 1997). Similar to risk management, then, a major systems project trap is to ignore negative feedback. Paying careful attention to those in the organization who are closest to the people who will be affected by the systems project will help avoid implementation failure.

- Unfreezing
  - Establish a felt need
  - Create a safe atmosphere
- Moving
  - Provide necessary information
  - Assimilate knowledge and develop skills
- Refreezing

Figure 12.14 Three Stages of Lewin/Schein Change Model

Three major categories of change-management activities have been associated with successful IT projects: communicating, training, and providing incentives. Communication activities are part of good project management, and communicating the need for change (the vision) is one of the first activities that needs to be addressed. The second category, training, is part of the installation step in a systems life cycle implementation phase. According to the practitioner press, however, the amount of user training required for an initial implementation success is typically underestimated. The third category, incentive system changes (such as performance rewards), helps motivate the attitudes and behaviors needed for the Lewin/Schein moving stage and helps institutionalize the behaviors for a Refreezing stage. Special project incentives may be used for high-risk projects and be under the control of the project manager(s). However, long-term incentive schemes to influence behavioral changes are clearly beyond the scope of a single project.

Finally, it should be noted that project budgets often do not include change-management activities. Moreover, the lack of recognition of the need for change-management activities has been reported to be the greatest barrier to implementation success in IT projects that involve major business processing reengineering efforts (Grover, Jeong, and Teng, 2000).

PROJECT CLOSING

A project close-out process provides a formal opportunity to codify what has been learned as part of a post-project review step. The process begins when the IT project deliverables have been completed and a formal user acceptance has been obtained or after a failed project has been terminated. According to management guru Margaret Wheatley (Wheatley and Kellner-Rogers, 1996), in today's much more complex business environments, one of the best survival strategies is to share expertise. Yet if there is no formal post-project review step, project team leaders typically do not take the time to document what actions helped the project succeed, as well as any lessons learned that could improve the likelihood of success on a future project (Russell, 2000).

Some common questions for team members to respond to are as follows (based on Schwalbe, 2004):

- What went right on this project?
- What went wrong on this project?
- What would you do differently on the next project, based on your experience with this project?

The team member responses can be aggregated and summarized in a lessons-learned section of the report.

Project managers should also be required to document whether or not the project met its budget, schedule, scope, and other project success criteria, as well as to share their own set of "lessons learned" from managing the project. Once collected, these lessons then need to be made accessible to other project team leaders, perhaps as part of a knowledge management initiative within the IT organization.

Continuous improvements in managing IT projects based on past learnings are a hallmark of a high-quality software development capability. For example, the **Capability Maturity Model (CMM)** of the Software Engineering Institute (SEI) at Carnegie Mellon University categorized a firm's software development capability on one of five levels. Organizations in the first (Initial) level of the CMM have software development processes that are primarily ad hoc. Organizations that have established project management processes to track IT projects on cost, schedule, and scope are at a second (Repeatable) level. Standard processes across all IS staff and process steps are characteristics of the third (Defined) level, and well-defined process measurements are characteristics of the fourth (Managed) level.

Organizations that reach the fifth (Optimizing) level of the CMM are still somewhat rare. Attaining this level requires continuous project management improvements based on the software development process measurements for the organization's prior IT projects.

SPECIAL ISSUE: MANAGING COMPLEX IT PROJECTS

Experienced IT project managers or IT program managers are increasingly likely to be asked to lead large, complex systems projects across an enterprise, such as ERP package implementations. Consulting firms are also frequently contracted to help with these complex projects because of their experiences in implementing the same package in other organizations.

According to Accenture consultant Hugh Ryan (2000), complexity must be accepted as a key characteristic of systems development and implementation projects in today's world. To deliver quality solutions in this type of environment, managers must realize that complexity is inescapable and that they must manage the associated risks. A multiyear field review of how large, complex projects were implemented led to the identification of three factors that are critical to success:

1. The business vision was an integral part of the project.
2. A testing approach was used at the program level (not just at the individual application level).
3. The projects used a phased-release approach (rather than a single-release rollout strategy).

Another source of project complexity comes from the use of outside contractors on a project. As shown in Figure 12.15, project complexity increases when contract workers are offsite rather than onsite during the project and when project team members are located in a different country, commonly referred to as "offshore."

The management of offsite and offshore workers and projects is becoming an important IT project management

Type of Resource	Project Characteristics
Onsite Contract Worker	Delivery team in the U.S. Hourly charges Managed by the client company
Onsite Project Teams	Delivery team in the U.S. Hourly charges; may also be milestone fees Managed by the client company
Onsite-Offshore Projects	Project management and internal customer services in the U.S. Delivery team offshore Fees normally project-based Requires client investment in development infrastructure Requires client efforts in building trust
Pure Offshore Projects	Project management by offshore vendor Fees normally project-based Requires client investment in development infrastructure Requires client and vendor efforts in building trust Requires increased efforts to transfer intellectual capital

Figure 12.15 Complexity Increases with Offsite and Offshore Resources (Adapted from Poria, 2004).

capability as more programming work in particular is being outsourced to countries with significantly lower labor costs.

SPECIAL ISSUE: POST-MERGER IT INTEGRATION PROJECTS

The past two decades have witnessed an increasing number of mergers and acquisitions in which businesses seek to achieve business growth by combining with another organization. Although senior IT leaders are not always a part of the team that selects and prices the firm to be acquired, they are depended on to quickly and effectively merge IT operations to enable the newly merged organization to meet its strategic objectives for the merger. For example, if the merging firms' call center operations for customers are to be highly integrated, then so too must the IT platforms and applications to support these operations. Well-honed IT project management skills, and a program management structure, have been associated with effective IT integration in a merger situation.

Another key to success is retaining the IT talent needed for the postmerger IT integration efforts. According to a recent study by McKinsey and Company (Kay and Shelton, 2000), 76 percent of the top executives surveyed across the globe believed that retaining key talent was a "critical" success factor for postmerger integration in general. This is because many mergers have cost-reduction goals that require personnel cuts, and key employees typically receive job inquiries from other employers within 5 days after a merger announcement.

Attractive retention contracts therefore need to be quickly offered to those personnel whose IT skills and business knowledge are critical to the postmerger success. If the intent is to keep an IT professional only until a specific IT integration project is completed, the retention package should be "generous" enough so that the employee stays loyal to the firm during the period of time needed for the integration project. To help ensure that the employee's special knowledge is transferred to IT staff who will be remaining with the company, a knowledge transfer stipulation could be made part of a project completion bonus.

Tips for Good IT Project Management

Most people would agree that a successful project has the following characteristics, notes Michael Matthew:

- It is delivered on time.
- It comes in on or under budget.
- It meets the original objectives.

However, some people do not realize that success also means that the project meets users' and the organization's needs, which may have changed since the original objectives were stated. Projects that do not give users what they want cannot be deemed a success. Following are some tips from Matthew on how to better assure IT project success.

Establish the Ground Rules. Define the technical and architectural specifications for the systems following four guidelines:

- Adhere to industry standards.
- Use an open architecture.
- Web-enable the system.
- Power with subsystems.

These principles should help ensure no nasty surprises along the way, as well as provide the ready ability to update/switchover systems in the future. The basic tenet is that the systems should be as simple as possible while fulfilling all of the (reasonable) user requirements.

Foster Discipline, Planning, Documentation, and Management. In many respects, these elements are what project management is really all about. It does not matter how well the requirements have been specified or whether the "perfect" solution has been selected, if the process is not controlled properly, anything can happen or, more realistically, potentially nothing will happen.

A firm timeline for system rollout needs to be formally established and signed off. Once this task has been done, the project team needs to work backward from the critical dates and map out the timing for the intermediate steps and include any interdependencies. Teams should take the critical date and subtract some time to factor in unforeseen contingencies. The project must progress with the target critical date in mind, which requires strong discipline.

The project also needs to follow a sound methodology and have key points planned and documented (and reported on) using a product such as Microsoft Project. All members of the team need to be aware of their responsibilities and timelines. Nothing should be left assumed. In addition, regular meetings and updates of the project plan are needed, along with proper documentation of the system development effort. Senior management needs to be able to see this documentation whenever they want. Management, key users, and even vendor personnel should be included on project steering groups, which should meet regularly to make sure the project continues on track. Such meetings also provide a venue for airing problems and raising issues that might affect others.

In addition, it is desirable to have an overall IT project steering committee. Regular project manager meetings from the various projects are key to keeping each other informed of their progress and for raising issues that might affect other projects.

Obtain and Document the "Final" User Requirements. Documenting user requirements is critical because it is the only way the team can evaluate the project outcome. Scope creep (users asking for more and more functions) causes many system failures. Documenting requirements helps lock in the scope of the work and reduce the possibility of costing problems and time overruns due to additional requests. Documenting user requirements can be done via a variety of methods, including facilitation sessions and one-on-one interviews.

A common mistake is writing user specs in technical jargon, notes Matthew. Some IT consultants make this mistake to "maintain the IT mystique." However, this approach can do harm. Similarly, IT project teams should not accept overly technical sign-off requests from software houses. These developers need to prove they can fulfill the users' requirements.

Obtain Tenders from All Appropriate Potential Vendors. Today, much software is bought rather than built in-house. This option needs to be considered when beginning a project, notes Matthew. In fact, companies that do not have expertise in the area under consideration might want to call in consultants to make a recommendation. Their extensive contacts in the IT community can significantly improve selection of the package or packages. Or consultants may simply help the IT project team create the selection criteria for evaluating bids and selecting a winner.

Include Suppliers in Decision Making. If development is to be handled by an outside firm, then create a joint project team. The supplier, or suppliers, will undoubtedly appoint their own project managers for their respective assignments. They need to be part of the governing team.

Convert Existing Data. Data conversion needs to be properly planned to make sure that the output data is complete and accurate. Although this task might appear quite simple, it is often the area that creates the biggest headaches. Here, perhaps, the oldest maxim in the IT industry applies: garbage in, garbage out.

Follow through after Implementation. After successfully implementing the systems, project managers need to cross their t's and dot their i's in terms of documentation, future maintenance processes, and so on.

The bottom line is that IT project management is no different from any other form of project management. Success requires good planning, along with good communication, and ensuring active participation of all appropriate parties, says Matthew. These elements, along with some hard work, will better ensure a successful system.

SUMMARY

IT project management requires competencies in general project management techniques, as well as systems methodologies. Today's IT projects can be led by an IS manager, a business manager, or both. The business manager roles of sponsor and champion are also critical to the project's success. The planning phase includes project scheduling, budgeting, and staffing. PERT charts, Gannt charts, and project management software are typically used to help execute and control project team activities.

Managing IT project risks involves assessing potential consequences, developing responses for risk minimization, and ongoing monitoring. Successfully managing business change as part of the IT project requires preplanned change management activities, as well as timely responses to unforeseen situations. Capturing lessons learned as part of a project closing phase has been associated with higher software quality and success with future projects.

The successful management of complex software projects often requires outside consulting help as well as exceptional skills in system testing and release management. The successful management of post-merger IT integration projects also requires paying special attention to human resource issues, including how to retain the necessary IT talent.

CHAPTER REVIEW QUESTIONS

1. Describe the difference between project management and program management.
2. What role could the Project Management Institute play in helping an organization better manage its IT projects?
3. Who is involved in managing an IT portfolio, and why is this a growing concern?
4. What information is typically included in an initial IT project request? In a project charter?
5. What skills have been identified as important for good project managers?
6. Describe the business manager roles of project sponsor and project champion.
7. What is a work breakdown analysis and why is it important?
8. Why is timeboxing a common approach for projects using new approaches such as RAD?
9. Contrast the strengths of bottom-up and top-down approaches to project budgeting.
10. What are some of the key management issues today for IT project staffing?
11. Describe the key uses of PERT, CPM, and Gannt charts.
12. Describe one technique used to manage IT project risks.
13. Describe one technique to manage business change (change management).
14. Compare and contrast the Lewin/Schein model with the Kotter framework. What is the same and what is different?
15. Describe one key to success for managing large complex system projects.
16. Why are IT project staffing issues of special importance for postmerger IT integration projects?

CHAPTER DISCUSSION QUESTIONS

1. If a person has been certified by the PMI but has never been on an IT project team, would you even consider hiring that person to manage an IT project? Justify your answer.
2. Several approaches for time and budget estimation are characterized as "dysfunctional" in this chapter. Provide an argument to support or refute one of these statements.
3. Select an IT project that you are familiar with and comment on whether there was a formal project sponsor and champion, how well these project roles were carried out, and how this positively or negatively affected the project.
4. Use the Web to identify at least two project management software products for projects in general. Briefly contrast their features and costs.
5. Select an IT project with which you are familiar and evaluate how well the budget and schedule were estimated and controlled.
6. Reread the red-yellow-green reporting mechanism (see sidebar) and comment on what you see as the pros and cons of this approach.
7. A large number of U.S.-based mergers over the past two decades have failed to achieve the forecasted business benefits of the merger. One hypothesis for this high failure rate is that the organizations did not execute well their integration of the two businesses, including their IT systems. Develop a rationale for why this hypothesis could (or could not) be true.

CASE STUDY: BAGGAGE HANDLING PROBLEMS AT THE DENVER INTERNATIONAL AIRPORT

Twice the size of Manhattan, the Denver International Airport (DIA) at 53 square miles was designed to be the USA's largest airport. By 1992, there was a growing realization that baggage handling would be critically important in an airport of this size and that this issue could not be off-loaded to the airlines that would be operating out of DIA. Consequently, commitment began to grow for the inclusion of an airport-wide, information technology (IT) based baggage handling system that could dramatically improve the efficiency of luggage delivery. BAE Automated Systems, Inc., a world leader in the design and implementation of material handling systems, was commissioned by the City of Denver to develop the system. An information system composed of 55 networked computers, 5,000 electric eyes, 400 radio frequency receivers, and 56 barcode scanners was to orchestrate the safe and timely arrival of every suitcase and ski bag at DIA. Problems with the baggage system, however, kept the new airport from opening as originally scheduled in October 1993. Soon the national and international media began to pick up the story, and the DIA came under investigation by various federal agencies. By the time the airport opened in late February 1995, it was 16 months behind schedule and close to $2 billion over budget. Additionally, DIA might never have opened at all if Mayor Webb had not found a way for the City of Denver to abandon its previous commitment to build an airport-wide automated baggage handling system. When DIA did eventually open, it did so with two concourses served by a manual baggage system and one concourse served by a scaled-down, semiautomated system.

[Montealegre and Keil, 2000]

Case Study Discussion Questions

Question One

Find out more about Denver's automatic baggage handling system and how this IT project crisis was characterized in the news.

Question Two

Why did the Denver automatic baggage system fail? Was there any way it could have succeeded?

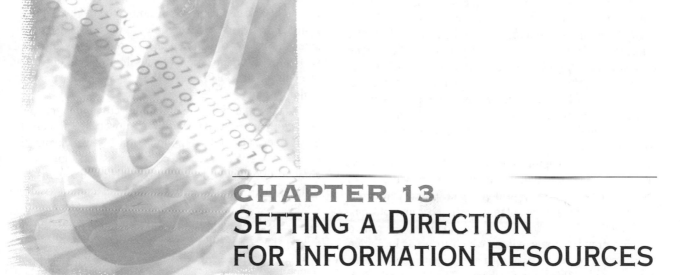

CHAPTER 13
SETTING A DIRECTION FOR INFORMATION RESOURCES

IN PREVIOUS CHAPTERS THE TECHNICAL AND OPERATIONAL GROUNDWORK crucial to an understanding of the management of the information resources in an organization was established. You should now be familiar with many of the issues of computing hardware and software, telecommunications and networking, the variety of information technology (IT) applications, and the development and maintenance of application software systems. The successful management of an organization's information resources in today's competitive business environment must combine this knowledge with a thorough understanding of business strategy to guide the development of information resources for the firm.

This chapter deals with one of the critical components for effectively managing IT in an organization—setting a direction for its information resources. The development of an overall management system for the information resources in an organization is not complete without a clear understanding by information systems (IS) professionals and business managers about how the information resources of the organization will be developed.

This chapter asserts that an information resource planning system must include: (1) an assessment of current information resources, (2) the establishment of an information vision and the IT architecture, and (3) the formulation of strategic and operational IS plans needed to move an organization's information resources from their current status toward the desired vision and architecture. It would not be appropriate here to outline detailed instructions for a specific planning system because planning needs and styles differ greatly from organization to organization and many approaches seem to work. However, the basic issues and concepts for an effective information resources planning effort are addressed in this chapter.

Likewise, the exact organization structure for IS varies widely among firms. Many large organizations have multiple IS departments, but they are treated as a single organization here. Although some parts of the detailed planning process are typically internal to the IS organization, it is helpful for the business manager to understand and to be involved in the overall process. Therefore, this chapter structures the entire IS planning process in rather broad terms. The focus is on those areas where the business manager should be involved. Examples from a variety of organizations are used to explain the concepts.

This chapter points out some of the reasons companies should set an IS direction, defines some terms, explains the planning process and each of the steps in it, and focuses on the issues that should be addressed.

WHY SET A DIRECTION FOR INFORMATION RESOURCES?

Organizations need a plan for the development of their information resources for several reasons. In some firms the management of all the diverse applications of IT is not, and never will be, organized under a single person. Yet most firms want to share information among diverse parts of the firm (and sometimes outside the firm) and use that information for strategic or operational advantage. Discussion and agreement on a common structure (or architecture, as defined later in this chapter) for the varied applications of IT in an organization can provide a shared understanding among IS professionals and business managers of how the company can best use its information resources.

Developing a plan for a company's information resources helps communicate the future to others and provides a consistent rationale for making individual decisions. Sometimes an information resources plan is created because business managers have expressed concern about whether there is some grand scheme within which to make individual decisions. The plan for information resources development provides this grand scheme. The decentralization of IS decisions and information resources makes the establishment of a well-understood overall information resources direction critical to making consistent, timely decisions by both business managers and IS professionals.

Planning discussions often help business managers and IS professionals in making basic decisions about how the "business" of IS will be conducted—defining the organization's basic style and values. Such discussions might be part of comprehensive programs that attempt to define or refine the culture of the overall company. In 2002, for example, a growing medical device manufacturing company believed it was necessary to instill a greater awareness about the concept of quality in the entire business to compete more effectively in the global marketplace. The effort led that company's IS director to consider more precisely the quality-related values to be embraced by the IS organization. For the first time, the IS organization began to consider the role of quality in the shared beliefs of people within the IS organization. Discussion focused on various IS quality issues such as excessive rework in the design of major systems.

Traumatic incidents sometimes create the need for an information resources direction-setting process. In September 2003, telecommunications network redundancy was a significant architecture discussion topic among some IS directors within the financial services industry. A tornado had destroyed much of a telecommunications company's critical switching center, and the extensive damage reduced data and voice circuit availability for several days. As a result, banks and other organizations that depended on the constant availability of the public telephone network for certain operations, such as automatic teller machines (ATMs), were forced to reexamine contingency plans associated with the unavailability of telecommunications service. Some organizations realized that IS management had not thought seriously about what to do when faced with such a loss. The result in many firms was an extended set of discussions on network architecture and network plans.

> **BUSINESS AND IT ALIGNMENT**
>
> Alignment of IT strategy with the organization's business strategy is a fundamental principle. IS managers must be knowledgeable about how new technologies can be integrated into the business (in addition to the integration among the different technologies and architectures) and must be privy to senior management's tactical and strategic plans. Both IS and business executives must be present when corporate strategies are discussed. IS executives must be able to delineate the strengths and weaknesses of the technologies in question.
>
> [Adapted from Luftman and Brier, 1996]

THE OUTPUTS OF THE DIRECTION-SETTING PROCESS

IS managers have developed project plans and budgets for many years. However, the task of formally developing and communicating an overall information resources plan, with an explicit information vision and architecture, is relatively new to many organizations. Some organizations have several years experience in developing such outputs formally. For others, building an information vision, for example, might be a very new activity. As a result, the deliverables at each step in the process take on somewhat different meanings from organization to organization. It therefore makes sense to define each output or deliverable in the planning process.

Information Resources Assessment

As outlined in earlier chapters, any organization has a set of information resources—both technological and human—through which business managers conduct the organization's business.

> An **information resources assessment** includes inventorying and critically evaluating these resources in terms of how well they are meeting the organization's business needs.

An information resources assessment includes reviewing the quality and quantity of the organization's technological resources—the hardware, software, networks, and data components of an information resources system. The human asset portion of an information resources assessment includes a review of the quantity and training/experience level of both users and IS professionals, as well as the management systems and values that drive IS decisions in the organization.

Information Vision and Architecture

At a recent meeting of IS directors, the following ideas emerged about the meaning of the information vision and architecture concept. Some executives described the term as a "shared understanding of how computing and telecommunications technology will be used and managed in the business." Others reported that they generate a "comprehensive statement about our future information resources that is part philosophy and part blueprint." The group held that a vision and architecture statement must be "specific enough to guide planning and decision making but flexible enough to avoid restatement each time a new information system is developed." Finally, several in the group asserted that a "vision and architecture statement should provide the long-term goal for the IS planning effort"—the vision and architecture statement represents the overall design target.

Several ideas common to these descriptions suggest a definition. First, the information vision and architecture statement is an ideal view of the future and not the plan on how to get there (the information resources plan is discussed later). Second, the vision and architecture statement must be flexible enough to provide policy guidelines for individual decisions but more than just fluff. Third, deliberation about both vision and architecture must focus on the long term, but exact dates are usually not specified. Finally, there is some difference between a vision and an architecture, although some firms combine the two concepts into a single statement.

With these ideas in mind, the terms can be defined as follows:

> An **information vision** is a written expression of the desired future about how information will be used and managed in the organization.
>
> The **information technology architecture** depicts the way an organization's information resources will be deployed to deliver that vision.

Much like the design of a future complex aircraft or a skyscraper, an information vision and an IT architecture together translate a mental image for the desired future state of information use and management into a comprehensive set of written guidelines, policies, pictures, or mandates within which an organization should operate and make decisions. Either the vision or the architecture might take the form of a set of doctrinal requirements (like the Ten Commandments). Other organizations create architectural diagrams or blueprints much like a building architect uses a diagram to represent a mental image of the future. As is true for a business vision, the information vision and architecture might also be a written statement. For example, one organization found it sufficient to define its information vision by stating, "We must provide quality data and computing products and services that meet our clients' needs in a timely and cost-effective manner." Regardless of the form, statements about vision and architecture should provide the business, managerial, and technical platform for planning and executing IS operations in the firm.

Information Resources Plans

The information resources planning process should generate two major plan outputs—the strategic IS plan and the operational IS plan.

> The **strategic IS plan** contains a set of longer-term objectives that represent measurable movement toward the information vision and technology architecture and a set of associated major initiatives that must be undertaken to achieve these objectives.

At the strategic level, these initiatives are not typically defined precisely enough to be IS projects. Instead, the IS strategic plan lists the major changes that must be made in the deployment of an organization's information resources over some time period, usually multiple years.

The **operational IS plan** is a precise set of shorter-term goals and associated projects that will be executed by the IS department and by business managers in support of the strategic IS plan.

The operational IS plan incorporates the precise results that will be accomplished, and often the budgets for each project are identified in the plan. In essence, the operational plan crystallizes the strategic plan into a series of defined projects that must be accomplished in the short term.

The process of generating each of these outputs and how they are linked together is discussed in more detail in the next section.

THE PROCESS OF SETTING DIRECTION

IS and Business Planning

Previous chapters have argued that IS decisions must be tightly aligned with the direction of the business. Such a maxim exists whether for the design of a particular application system or for the overall direction of the organization's information resources. Figure 13.1 depicts the relationship between setting the direction for the business as a whole and setting the overall direction for information use and management in that business. This process may be applied for the entire company, a division, or an individual business manager's department. On the left side of the chart are the general steps required to set direction for the business. On the right are the required planning steps for the organization's information resources. Note the many arrows depicting how the output of a step affects both the next step on the same side (left or right) of the figure as well as steps on the other side of the figure. This chart provides the outline for the rest of the chapter.

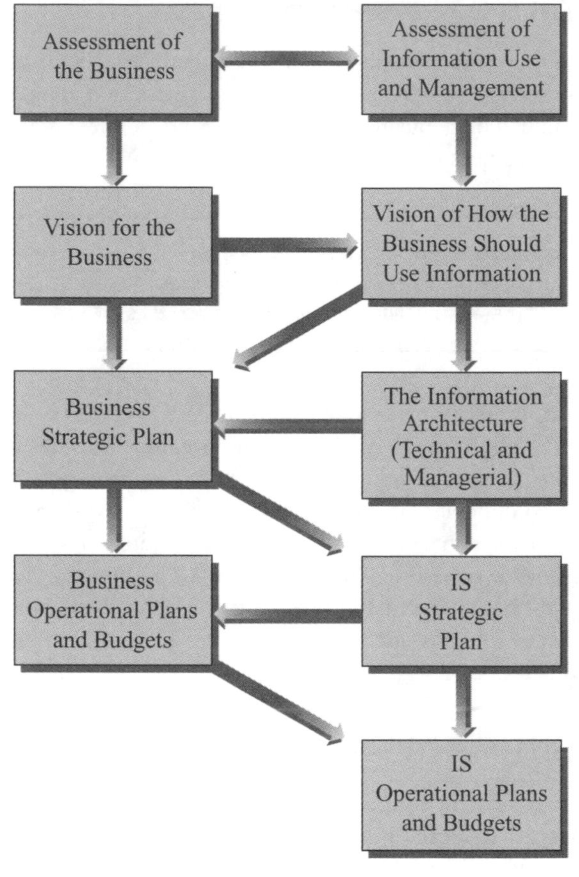

Figure 13.1 The Information Resources Planning Process

Assessment

Any organizational planning process starts with an assessment step, both for the business and for its information resources. Current performance is compared to a previous plan, to competitors, or to a set of past objectives. Operating data are collected. Surveys are often conducted to measure customer attitudes on performance. Competing organizations are benchmarked to determine both what is possible and what is being achieved at other organizations. Both a business assessment and an information resources assessment should be conducted. More on the information assessment step is presented later in this chapter.

Vision

The second basic step in any planning process should be to envision an ideal state at some distant point in the future. This step defines what the organization wants to become or to create. It does *not* define how to achieve this vision. For the information resources area, a technology architecture is added to the information vision for the organization.

Strategic Planning

Strategic planning is the third step and should be conducted for both the business and its information resources. **Strategic planning** is the process of constructing a viable fit between the organization's objectives and resources and its changing market and technological opportunities. The aim of any strategic planning effort is to shape the company's resources and products so that they combine to produce the needed results. Strategic *business* planning sets the basic course for the use of all resources, usually over an extended time period. It is designed to be general in nature and typically does not specify precise budgets, schedules, or operating details. Instead, it translates the organization's vision into a set of major initiatives that describes how to accomplish the organization's vision of its future. Review of the strategic plan is exercised by regularly examining the status of the major initiatives contained in it.

In parallel with the business plan, a strategic IS plan should be built considering the vision for the use of information and the overall management of IT in the company, as well as the role of the IS department. The strategic IS plan lays out the results desired for a specified time period and the necessary major initiatives.

Operational Planning

Operational planning lays out the major actions the organization needs to carry out in the shorter term to activate its strategic initiatives. It typically includes a portfolio of projects that will be implemented during some time frame in order of priority or urgency. Specific, measurable goals are established, and general estimates of costs and benefits are prepared. Quite often, capital expenditures are identified and justified. Responsibility for achievement of the objectives, actions, and projects is also specified in this plan. Review of the operational plan is more precise, often on a time-and-cost basis at the project level. Specific details, responsibilities, and dates of projects that move to the implementation stage are identified in the budget, including staffing requirements, facility scheduling, specific demand and usage forecasts, and detailed expense estimates. Once set in motion, the operational plan is naturally less flexible than the strategic plan. The operational plan relies heavily on the operating budget for control purposes. Quite often, companies develop both long-term (3 to 5 years) as well as short-term (1 year) operational business plans.

The operational IS plan, although usually coinciding in length with the business operational plan, is likely even more project-specific than its business plan counterpart. This difference is a natural result of the operational plan's purpose—to translate the general information resources direction, as defined in the strategic IS plan, into specific systems development projects or other efforts for the IS department (such as a capacity upgrade) that also meet specific initiatives for the business. In addition to defining methods by which the IS department plans to complete projects for other units in the organization, the operational IS plan lists internal projects designed to enable the IS department to better meet the needs of its internal customers.

The operational IS plan also identifies specific accomplishments to be achieved on multiyear application systems development projects. Suggestions are made for improvements in IS department operating procedures and for increasing infrastructure capacity. Specific goals, actions, due dates, and budgets are proposed for software purchases. The time of professional IS staff is allocated to major systems development projects.

Traditional Planning in the IS Organization

In many IS organizations the process of overall information resources planning has not been structured in the same way as the business planning process. Traditionally, the emphasis of IS planning was on major application systems internal development project planning rather than on overall organizational planning. Because of this emphasis on internal development projects, many IS organizations adopted a bottom-up, immediate needs-based approach to information resources planning, referred to as **needs-based IS planning**. When a specific, urgent business need called for a new information system, some form of formal project planning process was invoked to address the situation.

Over time, this **project-oriented IS planning** process was found to be largely reactive and often did not ensure that the proposed system meshed well with the organization's overall business plan. In some cases not enough consideration was given to the impact that one proposed system might have on another proposed or existing system. This orientation toward IS planning, although practical from the perspective of the IS department and perhaps the individual business manager, often resulted in lost strategic business opportunities, incompatible systems and databases, unacceptable implementation time frames, and a host of other problems. The needs-based IS planning approach often failed to adequately consider the organization's total information requirements across operating units, possible economies of scale, and avoidance of duplication of efforts. As demand for information to be shared across functional organizational lines increased and the distinction between classes of IT blurred, the shortcomings of the needs-based approach to IS planning led many companies to seek better ways to set a direction for their information resources. Thus, the concept of developing a strategic IS plan, driven by the business strategic plan and seeking to conform to an agreed-upon information vision and technology architecture for the organization, began to be used more extensively.

Although both the business planning and information resources planning processes are important for overall organizational effectiveness, the rest of this chapter deals in detail only with the right-hand side steps of Figure 13.1.

ASSESSING CURRENT INFORMATION RESOURCES

The information resources planning process should begin with an assessment of the use of information and IT in the entire organization and an assessment of the IS organization itself. The information resources assessment step is usually conducted by a committee of business managers and IS professionals, perhaps with the aid of outside experts. Outside facilitators can bring needed objectivity and experience to the process, but their value must be weighed against the added cost. Alternatively, the assessment might be conducted totally by an outside organization and presented to top business and IS department management or the IS oversight committee. As with all such outside studies, however, there is the distinct possibility that this approach might develop a "not invented here" response by the IS organization and some business managers. If carefully orchestrated, however, an outside information resources assessment can be very successful.

Measuring IS Use and Attitudes

The information resources assessment, however it is conducted, should measure current levels of information resources use within the organization and compare it to a set of standards. These standards can be derived from past performance in the organization, technical benchmarks, industry norms, and "best of class" estimates obtained from other companies. In addition to use measures, the attitudes of users and staff of the IS organization are important. Opinions about the performance of the IS organization in relating its activities to the needs and direction of the business must be measured. Likewise, a technical assessment of the IT infrastructure should be conducted. Figure 13.2 contains a portion of an information resources assessment conducted in late 2001 for a Michigan-based food products company. The company president initiated the assessment after the IS director was terminated, and a team of business managers and IS personnel facilitated by an outside consultant undertook it. As should be clear from the example, the assessment will likely lead to substantial changes in overall information resources direction at this organization.

Reviewing the IS Organizational Mission

Another important part of the assessment step is a review of the IS department's mission. The **IS mission** statement should set forth the fundamental rationale (or reason to exist) for the activities of the IS department. The activities of the IS department must be assessed in light of this mission.

ASSESSING THE ORGANIZATION

In conducting an information systems department assessment, ask these questions:

- Do key executives understand the impact of IT on the company's competitive position?
- Do they understand what is possible with current and forthcoming technologies?
- Do they know how the capabilities and economies of IT will change the way the business is operated and managed?
- Does the company have the right balance between innovation and managing scarce technology resources?

[Adapted from Hildebrand, 2000]

The IS organization's mission can vary substantially from one organization to another. Some IS departments are assigned the task of improving efficiency in the firm, typically by automating processes in order to reduce costs. Often, IS departments are also engaged in improving the information environment for knowledge workers in the organization, giving them the data and software tools needed to do their job better. Finally, many IS organizations have been assigned the role of helping the organization achieve strategic or competitive advantage in the marketplace, offering information-enhanced services or through some application that attracts and holds customers.

It is not uncommon in the assessment process to find an imbalance of performance in these three areas. Traditional needs-based planning approaches often do not address the requirements of all three of the above mission areas. Instead, efficiency usually receives the majority of the planners' attention. Unfortunately, satisfying immediate needs of just one of the areas might contribute little to the other elements of the IS department mission.

Involving business managers in the assessment exercise is one way to ensure that the IS mission statement defines the most appropriate role of the IS department. This involvement also allows business managers throughout the organization to understand better why the IS department needs a mission statement and a strategic plan. Figure 13.3 contains a mission statement for the IS organization of a West Coast machinery manufacturer developed by staff in the IS organization in 2003 and based on what they thought business managers wanted from the organization. The identified roles include an emphasis on secure data storage for the official records of the organization, maintaining processing capacity, managing the data network, providing access to external information resources, and offering systems development capability. Although all

- **A *single* information system does not exist in our organization.**
  A variety of disconnected information systems exists throughout our organization. Some systems are contained in isolated PCs, some on isolated mainframes/minis. Such disintegration causes needless effort on the part of staff.

- **Substantial potential exists for "cleaning up" the automation of existing work processes.**
  Significant manual processing of information currently occurs in such areas as the compilation of statistics, reporting, billing information given to finance, typing, and administrative functions. There are several work steps that our software does not treat, and there are steps where the software has a different set of requirements than is practiced at our company. Consequently, staff must override the software or supplement it manually.

  Our organization maintains several paper-based "shadow" systems created to fill in where information systems do not connect. These paper systems are costing our organization a significant loss in time.

- **Significant gaps exist in automation of the "value-added" process in our company.**
  Many of the steps involved in the value-added process are conducted either manually or, if the computer is used, operate from old data. Automating and integrating these steps will offer a significant strategic advantage for our company.

- **There is a perception that the IS organization is not a company-wide support organization.**
  The staff feels that IS seems to focus almost exclusively on the order processing function. IS has not been seen as a source of leadership for solving problems that are in other functions and PC-based. Staff associated with the distribution function seem to receive better service on their information requests and have software upgrades made more easily.

- **Except for the last year and a half, IS appears to have been a "stepchild" of senior management.**
  The staff questions whether senior management is really committed to making IS an integral part of our company. Senior management is still seen by some staff as too distant from information resource management. Active participation by senior management will be required if leadership is expected from IS.

- **There is a significant perception among the user population that IS is not particularly responsive to their needs.**
  Turnover of personnel in the PC support positions has been high, resulting in staff not understanding its role.

  There seems to be a general lack of trust between the user community and the IS organization. Requests for new software are denied with little explanation. Many people feel standards are enforced in situations that should not be subject to arbitrary standards.

- **IS personnel seem dedicated to IS and the company.**
  A strong team spirit exists in IS to operate in the current adverse situation (i.e., without a director).

- **The level of user training and support is substantially below needs and expectations.**
  Training on software is inconsistent. There is a strong feeling among staff that "tunnel training" exists (only taught enough to perform specific job). Opportunities to use software to extract data and be creative do not exist.

- **While the workload in IS is heavy at times, current staffing levels should be sufficient to meet current expectations.**
  Current IS staff are performing their regular duties consistently without a director, but nonroutine functions, many of which were previously performed by the director, are not being done. Personnel seem willing, but have not been trained in these functions, many of which require a high level of system knowledge.

  There are a number of users within our organization who would like to see IS take on a much more active role. Such a role will increase human resource requirements, both in numbers and skill levels.

- **The Internet is not used extensively.**
  Very few personnel have access from their desktops. Opportunities for use of the Internet by management seem to have been disregarded by the IS department.

Figure 13.2 Example Information Resources Assessment

Information Services is responsible for a wide variety of computing systems and services for the people of our corporation.

In this role, the department:

- Provides a secure location for housing and accessing the official electronic data records of the company.
- Maintains central/shared computer processing capacity and support for file maintenance and information reporting.
- Manages a corporate data network that delivers services to departmental servers and individual workstations linked to its data center.
- Provides integrated IS development for departments in order to advance organizational strategies (systems development services are available for corporate, local area network, workstations, and supply chain applications).

Figure 13.3 IS-Prepared Mission Statement Example

these are important technical functions, this "inside-out" view of the IS organization's mission might not match a statement developed from a user-based perspective.

Figure 13.4 provides a mission statement for the same IS organization developed by some of the business managers in the organization (in this case, the nine senior managers of the corporation). The second paragraph in particular makes it clear that these business managers see the IS organization as not being in the computing business at all, but as the provider of "management tools" to increase organizational effectiveness and the developer of the information infrastructure and services needed to improve decision making in the business. Operating an IS department with this latter mission statement would clearly require a major reconsideration of the basic activities of the IS organization compared to those represented in the first statement. Indeed, some assessments reveal that an outdated mission statement is the root cause of internal customer concern about the IS department.

Assessing Performance versus Goals

The traditional goal of many IS applications was to reduce cost by increasing the operating efficiencies of structured, repetitive tasks, such as the automation of the payroll function. The scope of IS applications has expanded dramatically in recent years to include systems to assist in the decision-making process for unstructured problem situations and in providing ways by which competitive advantage is achieved for the organization. This broader scope in the uses of IT has

In order to meet the challenges outlined within the company Vision Statement and support the strategic objectives and values of our company, the mission of Information Services is to provide reliable information, data, and computing services to all clients, both within and, where appropriate, outside of the company.

To accomplish this role, it will be necessary to exercise leadership in identifying new management tools based on evolving information technology that enables management to increase their effectiveness in operating and managing the business. The department's ultimate objective is the development of an integrated information infrastructure and associated services required to facilitate the decision-making process.

Figure 13.4 Internal Client-Prepared Mission Statement Example

Table 13.1 Objectives for the IS Department

Achievement Area	2003 Objectives	2003 Performance	2004 Objectives
Percent of internal client satisfaction with applications development services	80%	71%	85%
Percent of knowledge workers with a networked workstation	75%	78%	85%
Percent of scheduled hours data network is available to internal clients	99%	99%	99%
IS department personnel turnover	12%	14%	8%
Percent of departmental computing equipment purchases that comply with the supported equipment list	85%	88%	85%
Percent of total organization computing resource capacity connected to data network	80%	85%	85%
Cost per transaction on common systems	$0.025	$0.0285	$0.02
Percent of targeted systems converted to client/server architecture	95%	87%	99%
Percent of internal client workstations with access to the Internet	85%	92%	95%

required IS and business managers to assess the IS organization based on objectives in addition to reducing cost.

Table 13.1 shows the objectives of an IS organization at a regional bank in the Midwest. Nine objectives for 2003 were identified in an earlier planning process, and data were collected during late September 2003 to estimate actual performance for the year. The assessment report noted that on some measures, such as the number of customers and network availability, actual performance during the year exceeded expectations. On other measures, notably customer satisfaction with certain services and conversion to a client/server architecture for certain systems, actual results were far short of the goal. These conclusions and a new set of objectives for the year 2004 were used as input to later steps in the information resources planning process shown in Figure 13.1.

CREATING AN INFORMATION VISION

After assessing the current use and management of an organization's information resources, the shared business and IS leadership expectations of how information will be used in the business should be specified. Developing these expectations requires both an understanding of the future direction of the business and an understanding of the role information can play in winning the competitive race.

Vision creation starts with speculation on how the business's competitive environment will change and how the company should take advantage of it. Once this business vision is specified (and written), the implications for how information should be used in the firm in the future should be outlined. The information vision for the organization may then be written.

An example might be useful to explain the process. A $35 million printing company in Atlanta was taken over by new management in early 2003 as the result of an acquisition. During three off-site, full-day discussion sessions that were held to create a new vision and direction, the group developed the following set of basic specifications for the company:

- We will compete in five major market segments, each supplied by distinct business units.
- We will have revenues of at least $100 million by 2008 and be known for our quality and leading-edge technology.
- We will be a leading "national player" in the printing industry.
- We will exploit new business lines or market niches via acquisition or joint ventures or by spinning off existing operations.

- Our centralized administrative units (personnel, accounting, purchasing, etc.) will operate in support of all business units.
- We will achieve strategic advantage in each market via our "information-based" decisions.
- Our profit margins will exceed 10 percent of revenue.

These fundamental propositions about the company in the future led to the following basic business strategy decisions:

- We must improve gross margins and lower overhead costs while achieving moderate sales growth.
- We must increase the productivity of every person in the company.
- We must shorten the job fulfillment cycle time (from customer order to delivery).
- We must strive toward "zero defects" in all we do (quality objectives and monitoring systems will exist).
- We must be able to receive jobs electronically from all our customers.
- We must improve company-wide internal management systems (e.g., budgeting, personnel evaluation).

Senior management and senior professionals in the IS department then reviewed these business priorities along with the business vision. After several sessions, they jointly arrived at a shared vision for information use and management in the company. They chose to represent this vision via the following set of bullet points.

- Our corporate network will be able to service a large number of remote nodes at high speed.
- User demand on our information system each year will experience:
  1. Medium growth in transaction volume on existing common systems.
  2. High growth in ad hoc requests for information on all shared and personal systems.
  3. High growth in transaction volume from new applications on shared and personal systems.
- New data fields will be defined and managed each year.
- The entire job acquisition and fulfillment cycle will be supported by an integrated, comprehensive, and accurate database.
- Our corporate network will be able to send and receive large files from external customers at high speed.
- All internal customers will regularly use the Internet for research and communication.
- Business managers will know how to use information to make decisions and how to use the capabilities of our information resources effectively.
- Each business unit and functional department will manage its information resources within an overall IT architecture.
- All existing business support processes (e.g., purchase order processing) will be automated via expert systems to free up time of critical human resources.
- Internal customers will have workstation tools to make all information easily accessible.

Taken together, these statements represent a specification of how senior management wants information to be used and managed in the future. These statements are not a plan—how the IS department working with business managers will create this environment must still be determined. Instead, these statements represent a vision of what is desired. The architectural decisions on how to deploy the company's data, software, people, and other IS assets are also not all specified. That is the next step.

DESIGNING THE ARCHITECTURE

Now that a vision for future information use in the organization has been formulated, the IS organization, often in cooperation with business managers, must design an IT architecture. This architecture specifies how the technological and human assets and the IS organization should be deployed in the future to meet the information vision. The plan for migrating the organization's current information resources to the deployment specified in the architecture is developed later.

Components of Architecture

Several models have been developed that define the elements that make up an architecture for IT. Traditionally, the treatment takes on a very technical definition of an IT architecture. Later models have expanded the dimensions to include more managerial and fewer technical aspects of information resources.

In keeping with the classification of IS assets outlined in earlier chapters, it makes sense to structure an IT architecture into its technological and human components. Each component in turn contains several elements. Figure 13.5 contains a list of the elements of each component.

The **technological assets** component of the IT architecture contains desired specifications about future hardware

TECHNOLOGICAL COMPONENT
- Hardware
- Software
- Network
- Data

HUMAN COMPONENT
- Personnel
- Values/Culture
- Management System

Figure 13.5 Elements of an Information Technology Architecture

and operating systems, network, data and data management systems, and applications software. Some of the tradeoffs and issues in developing the specifications about these elements are dealt with in more detail in other chapters. Figure 13.6 contains an example of the technology elements of an IT architecture developed by the IS department of a rapidly growing, privately held personnel outsourcing company in Ohio in 2001. By carefully examining this part of an architecture, you should be able to picture the technical IT system being designed.

The **human assets** component of an IT architecture defines the **values architecture** and the **management system architecture** parts of an IT system. Together, these

- An effective IT architecture is dependent on a high-quality process by which data are collected and transformed into information.
- The company's process for information creation will apply regardless of the diverse source of data, the division, or location.
- The process of transforming our data into information will be carefully designed.
- Our core data will always be stored in a secure place.
- The entire information creation process will be supported by an excellent technical IT infrastructure.
- All company staff will be attached to a high-speed electronic network that provides easy access to a variety of data and computing resources both within and outside the company.
- Small, ad hoc reporting systems created to access existing core data are not covered by these specifications.
- All information systems that contain or use core data will be available on the electronic network.
- All information systems that contain or use core data will be of an "open" design.
- All systems development processes will follow the protocol developed by the Systems Development Policy Committee.
- All data management systems in the company will be relational and be selected from a list of supported data management software maintained by the Information Services organization and approved by the Data Committee.
- The Information Services organization will maintain a list of supported word processing, spreadsheet, statistical, and e-mail software.
- The Data Committee will regularly publish a list of data collection and data maintenance standards.
- A corporate data model for our core data will be developed and regularly maintained by the Data Committee, using outside consultants.
- Each manager in the company will be held responsible for the integrity of the core data maintained by his/her organization.
- Information Services will provide support for a set of hardware/operating system platforms that are approved by the Information Resources Management Committee.
- Data analysis methodologies will be regularly reviewed by the Data Committee.

Figure 13.6 Example Technology Component of an IT Architecture

- Trained external customers will be able to see appropriate information stored in our systems via secure access from the Internet.
- The entire information creation process will be supported by a responsive management system.
- The Data Committee will exercise overall responsibility for the quality and cost of using data and information in carrying out the mission of our company.
- The Information Resources Management Committee will be responsible for ensuring that the infrastructural components of individual systems comply with the architecture.
- The Systems Development Policy Committee will develop and maintain policies relating to information systems development.
- The Data Committee will oversee and update the company's data architecture.
- The Information Resources Management Committee will approve an information systems funding system.
- The head of the Information Services organization (i.e., the CIO) will lead and support the development and maintenance of an enterprise-wide information system for the organization.
- The Director of Network Services will be responsible for maintaining and improving the technical infrastructure, both within the organization and secure links to the Internet.
- The Director of Customer Development will provide for longer-term internal customer development and support.
- The Director of Data Quality will support the improvement of data integrity throughout the company.
- The Information Systems Director will be responsible for maintaining and improving existing information systems.
- Support for the development of new application systems and the maintenance/upgrade of existing systems will be housed in the Information Services organization.
- Each manager in our company will be responsible for budgeting and executing a data/systems training plan that meets our data training requirements.
- Each Vice President will ensure that each department within the organization has developed its own information systems plan.
- A plan for the migration of each information system in the company to be compatible with this architecture will be established by the Data Committee and approved by the Executive Staff.
- Each member of the staff will take at least 24 hours of IT training each year.

Figure 13.7 Example Human Component of an IT Architecture

elements specify the "business" parts of managing the IS department, how business managers will be involved, and how IS decisions will be made. These areas are dealt with in more detail in Chapter 15. Figure 13.7 shows the companion human assets component of the Ohio outsourcing firm's IT architecture developed in 2001. By carefully reviewing this part of the architecture, you should be able to understand the future culture, organizational structure, and management system for this organization's information resources.

THE STRATEGIC IS PLAN

According to Figure 13.1, the next two IS planning steps involve creating plans for the development of an organization's information resources. After the current information resources situation is assessed and a vision and an architecture are established, the first plan that should be developed for an organization's information resources is the strategic IS plan. The strategic IS plan is a statement of the major objectives and initiatives (not yet defined precisely enough to be projects) that the IS organization and business managers must accomplish over some time period to move the company information resources toward the information vision and to fit the business strategic plan. The plan should also contain a set of measurable results to be achieved during this time period in order to act as benchmarks for assessing progress toward the vision. The plan might also contain the results of an internal and external strategic analysis performed as part of the strategic IS planning process.

The Strategic IS Planning Process

The development of the IS strategic plan is accomplished in four basic steps: setting objectives or goals, conducting an external analysis, conducting an internal analysis, and establishing strategic initiatives. Although they are treated here in sequence, most planning processes involve iterations through these four steps.

Setting Objectives. The setting of IS objectives is done in much the same way as strategic objectives are specified for any business or functional organization. Measures are identified for each of the key result areas for the organization. IS objectives are often established in such areas as IS department service image, IS personnel productivity, and the appropriateness of technology applications. Goals relating to increased effectiveness, access to external resources, and breadth of business manager involvement in IS applications are also possible.

A sample of strategic IS objectives for a regional bank in the Midwest was shown in Table 13.1. This organization assigned the IS department goals in several areas, including internal customer satisfaction, breadth of workstation coverage, data network performance, IS department personnel turnover, supported equipment list acceptance, pervasiveness of the data network, cost per transaction on common systems, client/server conversion progress, and Internet access. Although the choice of which results to set as goals will vary with the organization's circumstances, each objective should provide some clear benchmark toward achieving the vision and architecture for IT.

Conducting Internal and External Analyses. The second step in the development of a strategic IS plan is a review of the external environment within which the organization's information resources must be developed over the planning period, say 3 to 5 years. This step should include reviews of the company's strategic business plan as well as an IT forecast. Quite often the result of this process is a series of statements called opportunities (areas in which new systems could be created or where the IS organization could take some action to the company's long-term advantage) and threats (external factors that might affect IS performance that could be corrected or for which some countermeasure could be developed).

Along with the external analysis, a review of the internal strengths and weaknesses of the IS department and how well business managers play their role in the entire IT process is also conducted. The list of strengths indicates areas where the IS department is particularly strong. Likewise, the list of weaknesses displays areas where the IS department or the role of the business manager should improve. The internal analysis parts of this step are often conducted during the assessment phase of the planning process described earlier in this chapter. These four statements together make up a **SWOT** (strengths, weaknesses, opportunities, and threats) strategic situation analysis.

A sample SWOT analysis for the Ohio outsourcing company mentioned earlier that was input into its strategic IS plan is shown in Figure 13.8. Note that the company (via a working group of business managers and IS managers) identified seven strengths related to the organization's information resources. Most relate to technical skills of IS professionals and the quality of their transaction processing systems. Six weaknesses in the use or management of information are listed, ranging from personnel issues within the IS organization to limited departmental applications beyond routine transaction processing.

These strengths and weaknesses act as either leverage points (strengths) or as limiting factors (weaknesses) for new strategic initiatives. The threats and opportunities lists contain both factual and attitudinal issues that must be dealt with in the plan. Both user and technology issues should be mentioned in the opportunities and threats sections.

Establishing Strategic Initiatives. Figure 13.9 contains a set of strategic initiatives resulting from a 2002 strategic information resources planning effort for a medium-sized energy company. Each statement represents an important initiative needed to enhance the role of IT at this corporation. Some of these initiatives will require substantial investment and create new operating costs for implementation. Yet none of the initiatives is spelled out well enough to be immediately translated into action. The operational planning step is required to translate these initiatives into actual projects.

Strengths

- Major transaction control systems are relatively new, functionally adequate, well-documented, maintainable, and operationally efficient.
- The IS department has demonstrated effectiveness in adding new technologies (e.g., its own access to the Internet).
- The IS department has demonstrated competence and effectiveness in applications development that facilitate group decision support.
- There is a stable, competent professional IS staff with expertise in designing and programming transaction processing systems.
- Our IS outsourcing partner seems to manage a reliable, cost-effective data center.
- There is a substantial use of our in-house electronic mail operation, frequented by most business managers in the company.
- There is substantial information technology expertise among business managers in both line and staff organizations.

Weaknesses

- A single point of IS contact for end-user operational problem diagnosis and resolution has not been established.
- There are limited data center performance measurement systems.
- There has been only limited transaction-based systems development productivity.
- There is a high degree of technology specialization (narrowness) among IS professional staff and a limited degree of business orientation.
- There is limited departmental use of information technology beyond simple decision support and participation in common transaction processing systems.
- Few business managers make effective use of the Internet.

Opportunities

- The IS department enjoys a high degree of credibility among the large and growing internal customer community.
- The role of the business manager in collaborating with the IS department has been institutionalized, facilitating ease of future system implementation.
- There is a growing base of internal customers who understand a wide range of information technologies and want to use IT for their business.
- The Internet provides data and interaction capabilities that would be of substantial strategic use to the firm.

Threats

- The IS department's effectiveness is threatened by pockets of internal customer negativism, especially among top management.
- Some business managers are developing a high degree of technical competence, which they employ in a nonintegrated fashion by developing separate workstation-based systems.
- The accelerating pace of technological change and proliferation of information technologies pose risks of control loss, obsolescence, and difficulty in maintaining IS professional staff competence.
- The extensive internal communication networks and internal customer accessibility to external databases pose security risks to our data.
- The IS department is still not an integral part of the company's business planning process.

Figure 13.8 Example SWOT Analysis

Management wants the Information Services and Systems department to develop its own long-range plan utilizing the vision, mission, values, and principles of operation outlined previously. The following is a listing of initiatives we feel should be undertaken in the ultimate formulation of this plan:

1. Manage development and operations of network architecture and security in accordance with business and internal customer requirements.

2. Help departments build individual information plans, utilizing Information Services and Systems departmental expertise and knowledge of overall company system requirements.

3. Create and maintain a short list of approved hardware and software that can be efficiently utilized within the designed network to meet end-user requirements.

4. Coordinate with other departments in the evaluation and design of telecommunication and data communication systems that meet the company's strategic and operational needs.

5. Provide and annually update a prioritized list of uses of external data that would strategically help the company.

6. Encourage active client participation in network utilization through training programs and help sessions that increase the efficiency and effectiveness of the overall company decision-making process.

7. Restructure the information services and systems departmental organization to better accomplish the mission of the department.

8. Develop a structured timetable and system of application backlog reductions.

9. Formulate a written standardization process for application development.

Figure 13.9 Sample Strategy Agenda

Tools for Identifying IT Strategic Opportunities

While building the strategic IS plan, organizations often seek help in identifying ways in which IT can provide strategic advantage. Several tools for finding new strategic insights have proven useful. None of the tools discussed here explicitly considers how an opportunity, once identified, can be translated into a comprehensive IS plan for the organization. The tools, however, have proven valuable in finding specific opportunities for IT applications and showing the role that IT might play in achieving certain business objectives. Because using these tools might result in IT applications during the operational planning process that help change the firm's strategic direction, their use is most important to effective strategic IS planning.

Critical Success Factors. One well-known method for identifying strategic IT opportunities is to define information needs and processes critical to the success of a business function like sales or to the entire organization, called **critical success factors (CSFs)**. Any recent text on strategic management should contain a fuller discussion of CSFs. Generally, however, CSFs define a limited number of areas (usually four to six) that, if executed satisfactorily, will contribute most to the success of the overall performance of the firm or function. Many CSFs have either short-term or long-term impact on the use of IT. Once identified, the factors can be stated as opportunities for the application of IT. An analysis might then be conducted to determine more precisely how IT can be used to accomplish the needed task.

Analysis of Competitive Forces. It is generally accepted that competitive advantage can come about by changing the balance of power between a business and the other actors in the industry. As seen from the strategic systems examples in earlier chapters, a company interested in finding a strategic initiative can

- Inhibit the entry of new competitors by raising the stakes for competing in the market or by redefining the basis for competition in at least one dimension (e.g., price, image, customer service, product features).
- Slow the application of substitute products/services by providing difficult-to-duplicate features.
- Make products/services more desirable than those of current competitors by providing unique product features or customer services or by shifting some customer product selection criterion (e.g., by being a low-cost provider).
- More strongly link with customers by making it easy for them to do business with the company and difficult to switch to a competitor.
- More strongly link with suppliers to obtain lower-cost, higher-quality materials.

An analysis of these competitive sources can identify ways in which competitive advantage can be achieved through IT. But where exactly might opportunities exist? Figure 13.10 lists various questions that IS strategic planners can ask about suppliers, customers, and competitors to identify opportunities for the strategic use of IT. An individual manager can study these questions as well and use them to stimulate discussion in a brainstorming session aimed at suggesting possible applications of IT.

Value Chain Analysis. Another technique frequently used to suggest strategic IS initiatives is the classic **value chain analysis** method described by Porter and Millar (1985). As depicted in Figure 13.11, the value chain includes five primary and four support activities within an organization that can each add value for the customer in the process of producing, delivering, and servicing a product or service.

IT can be used in each activity to capture, manipulate, and distribute the data necessary to support that activity and its linkages to other activities. To be of strategic or competitive importance, automating an activity in this chain must, for instance, make the process run more efficiently or lead to differentiation of the product or service.

For example, an organization's goal of market differentiation by a high level of on-time delivery of products requires that operations, outbound logistics, and service activities (such as installation) be highly coordinated, and the whole process might need to be reengineered to be Web-enabled. Thus, automated IS in support of such coordination could have significant strategic value. In automotive manufacturing, for example, Internet-based systems that facilitate sharing of design specifications among design, engineering, and manufacturing (which might be widely separated geographically) can greatly reduce new vehicle development time and cost. Significant advantage also can be gained at the interfaces between the activities, where incompatibility in departmental objectives and technologies can slow the transition process or provide misinformation between major activities.

From a broader perspective, an organization's value chain is actually part of a larger system of value creation, called a supply chain, that flows from suppliers, through the firm, to other firms providing distribution, and ultimately to the end customer. Opportunities for improvement in the supply chain could thus be intercompany, such as using the Internet to automate the automobile ordering process from dealers to manufacturers. As a result, exchanging information over the Internet has been of strategic importance in several industries. It is also important to remember that activities in a value chain are not necessarily sequential because many activities can occur in parallel. In fact, significant competitive advantage can occur by using IT to allow these activities to be done in parallel, thereby developing or delivering products sooner. Thus, competitive advantage can result from improvements in either the internal value chain or the interorganizational supply chain.

A series of idea-generation and action-planning sessions is often used to generate possible strategic applications of IT for the organization. The idea-generation sessions typically include example strategic applications from other organizations (to stimulate ideas by analogy). Small groups then brainstorm on possible strategic opportunities that address the competitive assessment. Questions such as those in Figure 13.10 can be used to stimulate ideas for IT applications. A critical element of this brainstorming process is that criticism and negative comments about new ideas are prohibited.

Subsequent evaluation of these ideas involves the degree of competitive advantage expected, cost to implement, technical and resource feasibility, and risk. Based upon these criteria, ideas are then grouped into ranked categories. Top priority ideas are identified and used in the strategic IS planning process.

The constructs and opportunity identification techniques discussed here are nothing more than tools for creating a strategic IS plan. Like any tools, they can be misused or misinterpreted to the detriment of the information resources planning process and ultimately the organization. Although tools and concepts help, the key to the development of a viable strategic IS plan is clearly the ability of the IS department and business managers to work together.

Suppliers

- Can we use IT to gain leverage over our suppliers?
  - — Improve our bargaining power?
  - — Reduce their bargaining power?
- Can we use IT to reduce purchasing costs?
  - — Reduce our order processing costs?
  - — Reduce supplier's billing costs?
- Can we use IT to identify alternative supply sources?
  - — Locate substitute products?
  - — Identify lower-price suppliers?
- Can we use IT to improve the quality of products and services we receive from suppliers?
  - — Reduce order lead time?
  - — Monitor quality?
  - — Leverage supplier service data for better service to our customers?
- Can we use IT to give us access to vital information about our suppliers that will help us reduce our costs?
  - — Select the most appropriate products?
  - — Negotiate price breaks?
  - — Monitor work progress and readjust our schedules?
  - — Assess quality control?
- Can we use IT to give our suppliers information important to them that will in turn yield a cost, quality, or service reliability advantage to us?
  - — Conduct electronic exchange of data to reduce their costs?
  - — Provide master production schedule changes?

Customers

- Can we use IT to reduce our customers' cost of doing business with us?
  - — Reduce paperwork for ordering or paying?
  - — Provide status information more rapidly?
  - — By reducing our costs and prices?
- Can we provide some unique information to our customers that will make them buy our products/services?
  - — Billing or account status data?
  - — Options to switch to higher-value substitutes?
  - — By being first with an easy-to-duplicate feature that will simply provide value by being first?
- Can we use IT to increase our customers' costs of switching to a new supplier?
  - — By providing proprietary hardware or software?
  - — By making them dependent upon us for their data?
  - — By making our customer service more personalized?
- Can we use external database sources to learn more about our customers and discover possible market niches?
  - — By relating buyer behavior from us to buying other products?
  - — By analyzing customer interactions and questions to us to develop customized products/services or methods of responding to customer needs?

Figure 13.10 Questions to Identify Opportunities for Strategic Information Technology Applications

- Can we use IT to help our customers increase their revenues?
  - By providing proprietary market data to them?
  - By supporting their access to their markets through our channels?

Competitors

- Can we use IT to raise the entry barriers of new competitors into our markets?
  - By redefining product features around IT components?
  - By providing customer services through IT?
- Can we use IT to differentiate our products/services?
  - By highlighting existing differentiators?
  - By creating new differentiators?
- Can we use IT to make a preemptive move over our competition?
  - By offering something new because we have proprietary data?
- Can we use IT to provide substitutes?
  - By simulating other products?
  - By enhancing our existing products?
- Can we use IT to match an existing competitor's offerings?
  - Are competitor products/services based on unique IT capabilities or technologies and capabilities generally available?

Figure 13.10 *Continued*

SUPPORT ACTIVITIES	**Firm infrastructure**	Planning models				
	Human resource management	Automated personnel scheduling				
	Technology development	Computer-aided design			Electronic market research	
	Procurement	Online procurement of parts				
PRIMARY ACTIVITIES		**Inbound logistics**	**Operations**	**Outbound logistics**	**Marketing and sales**	**Service**
	Examples of IT application	Automated warehouse	Flexible manufacturing	Automated order processing	Telemarketing Laptops for sales representatives	Remote servicing of equipment Computer scheduling and routing of repair trucks

Figure 13.11 Strategic Information Systems Opportunities in the Value Chain

THE OPERATIONAL IS PLAN

After the strategic IS plan has been developed, the initiatives identified in it must be translated into a set of defined IS projects with precise expected results, due dates, priorities, and responsibilities.

The Long-Term Operational IS Plan

Operational planning differs from strategic planning in its focus, its linkage to the business, and in the specificity with which IS projects are defined and addressed (see Figure 13.1). The long-term operational IS plan is generally developed for a 3-to-5-year time period and focuses on project definition, selection, and prioritization. Resource allocation among projects and tools for providing continuity among ongoing projects are also components of the long-term plan.

The first step in preparing the long-term operational IS plan is to define long-term IS operating objectives. Key changes in the business direction should be identified and their possible impact on IS activities should be assessed. The inventory of available information resources is then reviewed to determine which needs can be met over the planning period. Alternatives to new systems are developed in light of the constraints identified by the information resources inventory process conducted earlier.

IS development or acquisition projects must next be defined and selected. The criteria for evaluating projects include availability of resources, degree of risk, and potential of the project to contribute value to the organization's objectives. Clearly, politics often play more than a minor role in the final project selection process.

Many IS planners have taken a cue from financial analysts by adopting a portfolio view of the IS long-term operational plan. They attempt to select new systems to be developed or purchased based on their association with and impact on other projects in the current systems development portfolio. Factors to consider include, but are not limited to, the level of risk of the various projects in the portfolio, the expected time until completion, their interrelation with other projects, their nature (such as being transaction processing oriented), and the amount of resources required. IS planners then seek to balance the projects in the portfolio.

Firms that ignore portfolio balance and concentrate solely on implementing lower risk transaction processing systems, for example, might lose the opportunity to develop higher risk systems offering potential competitive advantage. Conversely, a project portfolio of nothing but risky applications with unknown chances for success and uncertain economic benefits might place the firm itself in financial jeopardy. Table 13.2 shows a portion of the systems development and enhancement project portfolio developed for the Ohio-based outsourcing company referred to earlier in the chapter.

Table 13.2 IS Long-Range Operational Plan Project Portfolio

System/Project	This Year	Next Year	In Two Years	New (N) or Replacement (R)	Make (M) or Buy (B)	Risk Assessment	Project Size	Comments
Executive and retiree personal income tax assistance		X		N	B	Low	Small	Manual assistance currently provided
Fixed assets accounting		X	X	R	B	Medium	Large	Improved asset management and ability to respond to tax law changes
Corporate competitive database	X	X		N	M	High	Medium	Improved analytical capabilities, access
Common tactical sales information system		X	X	N	M/B	High	Large	An ongoing series of installations of capabilities to enhance the effectiveness of the sales organization
Order entry by field organization	X			N	M	Medium	Small	Provide more timely processing of customer orders

Table 13.3 Sample 2004 Operational IS Plan

Title	Priority	Business Requirement
CRM/Fulfillment	High	Further develop our customer relationship management (CRM)/fulfillment application; position the company as a leading provider in this area.
Server Consolidation	High	Combine the existing two servers into one. Further improve and customize our enterprise resource planning system, focusing on supply chain management, assembly, warehouse, and corporate portal.
Field Scheduling System	High	Develop a business-focused scheduling system to work with our existing cost estimating and accounting system.
Call Center Billing System	Medium	Develop and enhance the current online help desk system. Add more functional e-mail management functions.
LAN/WAN Management	Medium	Build better monitoring tools and routing protocols.
Network Infrastructure	Low	Convert telephone system to Internet Protocol.

Each IS project in the portfolio must then be subjected to a more detailed project planning process, as described in earlier chapters. The IS and other information resources enhancement projects are portrayed in the form of a budget for review by management. Once the long-term operational IS plan has been approved, it should be publicized throughout the organization. Publication of the plan will help instill a sense of commitment on the part of the organization that will hopefully have a positive impact on users. As with all business functions, the IS plan should be reviewed and updated as necessary, at least annually.

The Short-Term Operational IS Plan

The short-term operational IS plan is usually created for a 1-year time period. Its focus is on specific tasks to be completed on projects that are currently underway or ready to be started. It is linked to the firm's business priorities by the annual budget. Immediate hardware, software, and staffing needs, scheduled maintenance, and other operational factors are highlighted in detail in the short-term plan. An example of the major projects in a short-term operational plan for 2004 is contained in Table 13.3. Sometimes the long-term and short-term operational plans are combined into a single document.

GUIDELINES FOR EFFECTIVE PLANNING

Planning for the development of an organization's information resources can be a very complex, time-consuming process. Planning efforts attempt to make provisions for the rapid rate of change in IT and capture the often hazy definition of exactly what a strategic system is supposed to do. The first step in developing an organizational planning focus, as opposed to only a project focus, is to change the way in which the IS organization's professionals view their jobs. These changes include adoption of a service orientation by the IS staff in order to view users as partners. Change must also be viewed by IS professionals as a constant process to be exploited, not just an intermittent disturbance to be controlled.

Business managers can take certain actions to increase the likelihood of adoption of the proposed mindset. By taking these actions, they also increase the likelihood of the successful creation and implementation of an IS plan.

1. Early clarification of the purpose of the planning process is essential. The IS planning group must know what they are being called upon to perform prior to their work. IS professionals and business managers will not adopt the shared vision necessary for success of the direction-setting process if they do not understand the purpose of the effort, its scope, and its relevance to their individual efforts.
2. The information resources planning effort should be developed in an iterative, not serial, process. An extended planning process that generates reams of paper that are left untouched will not be as effective as a short process that generates a plan that is reviewed and modified periodically to reflect the new realities facing the organization. Many IS plans have long implementation periods. Needs and situations might change, calling for the revision of the original plan before it is implemented.

3. The plan should reflect realistic expectations. IS application development managers have received much bad press over the years, not all of it undeserved, for "promising the sky" and delivering something far short of that. Business managers must believe that objectives are attainable or they simply will not internalize them.
4. The process of setting realistic expectations should involve business management. Input into the planning process by business managers can result in much more feasible plans, greater probability of acceptance, and systems that more closely resemble those needed by the business.
5. The resulting plans should integrate all applications of IT if possible. The boundaries between technical computing, business computing, networking, videoconferencing, the Internet, and other IT application areas are increasingly blurred. Separate plans for each of these areas will result in duplication of effort, lack of integration, lost opportunities, and lower economies of scale. IS planners should seek to integrate these various applications at every possible chance. Integration of these various activities will result in the adoption of one overall strategy that will eliminate the sending of confusing messages to users. For example, a very confusing message is sent when telecommunications is centrally planned and is a free service while scientific computing is treated as a scarce resource and charged for by the use-unit.
6. An effective IS plan will also take into consideration the barriers and constraints facing all organizations. Very important, but often overlooked, is simple human resistance to change. The best-planned, most technically well-designed systems often meet with resistance and even defeat if adequate consideration is not given to how people will react to them on both an individual and group basis.

BENEFITS OF INFORMATION RESOURCES PLANNING

The cost of developing an IS plan can be substantial, especially in terms of IS leadership's and business managers' time, but companies have found that significant benefits can come from such endeavors. Both the resulting documents and the processes used to create the assessment, the vision and architecture, and the strategic and operational plans contribute to these benefits.

Better IS Resource Allocation

A good plan forms the basis for more specific IS resource allocation. In most organizations IS management is charged with creating budgets that reflect business priorities for the IS organization over the next several years. A planning process that contains a vision and an architecture demonstrates *what* the group should be trying to create. Likewise, a good plan explains *how* the organization will get there. Budget requests then make a lot more sense to those outside the IS department.

Communicating with Top Management

Top management insists on a rationale for major capital or staffing investments in the IT arena. Many IS directors often request significant operating or capital budget increases—well above that available to other departments. A solid IS plan, clearly linked to the business's direction, can help explain the need for such expenditures by showing a nontechnical context for priorities.

Helping Vendors

Having an IT architecture and plan also helps those from whom the IS organization buys products and services. Most hardware, software, and communications vendors have a defined range of products built around their own definitions or conclusions on the future architecture their customers will want. An explicit IT architecture and plan is an effective way for the IS director to communicate with vendors on the need for certain capabilities in future products.

Creating a Context for Decisions

Another important function of an information resources plan is to create a clear context within which business managers and IS professionals can make individual decisions. In many organizations it is possible to come to work every day, move from one meeting to another and from one project to another, and not really understand the organization's overall direction. It is critical to communicate the overall direction of information use and management widely throughout the firm so everyone can understand that the organization is focused on the same defined target.

Achieving Integration and Decentralization

Most IS organizations are focused on achieving tighter integration of their common systems and networks while simultaneously decentralizing the technology and operational activities. Developing an overall information resources plan forces discussion on how exactly to go about achieving these seemingly opposite objectives. The issues can then be discussed in much more detail, often without the emotion that arguments surrounding a specific decision would provide. Such intense discussions might promote a greater understanding of the trade-off between autonomy and integration and result in a commitment to a particular course of action. In this way, later specific issue discussions are more focused and efficient.

Evaluating Options

The range of architecture options for IT applications is broad and growing. Personal workstation-based, local area network (LAN)-based, and Internet-based solutions to problems might all seem feasible and appropriate. Moreover, the number of IT vendors is growing rapidly. A clear IS plan can provide guidance in selecting one vendor over another. It allows an organization to take advantage of a range of options and see how they best fit into some overall architecture for the future. Otherwise, the organization runs the risk of being "vendor-driven," as well as responding only to current needs rather than designing long-term solutions to major future business problems.

Meeting Expectations of Management

Today, senior management in most organizations has higher expectations than ever on what IT can do strategically for the company. Company executives are looking for new sources of competitive advantage. In a global competitive arena, where many organizations have excellent scientists, design engineers, and new product development specialists, company leaders want to use IT as another source of distinction in the market. The development of an explicit vision and architecture for IT generates discussion on the role of this critical resource in meeting the firm's objectives.

ROLES IN THE INFORMATION RESOURCES PLANNING PROCESS

Both business managers and IS professionals have crucial roles to play if the IS plan is to be linked to the business direction and contain creative IS applications.

Role of the Business Manager

It should be clear that the business manager's active participation in the information resources planning process is integral to the successful development of a comprehensive, realistic IS plan that is well-linked to the organization's business plan. Because business managers typically have a better understanding of the nature of the organization's business activities, they should be given the responsibility of sharing their visions of what the need for IT will be in the organization. Architectures, strategies, and specific plans will then all evolve from a shared vision of the future.

Vision, of course, is not enough. The business manager's vision must be articulated in such a manner that it can be communicated to others. Employee understanding of a well-communicated, clear vision of the firm is a prerequisite to the planning process. Once this understanding of the vision is achieved, it becomes possible to develop an IS plan that is truly consistent with the organization's needs.

Business managers must also accept most of the responsibility for identifying specific projects that might contribute to the realization of the vision. Responsibility does not cease with the identification of an IT opportunity. Successful planning and implementation of any plan is an iterative process, containing built-in review and feedback mechanisms. As a possessor of vision and a representative of the business, the business manager must stay involved in the planning and system development activities in order to provide the feedback and input necessary to ensure that work is proceeding on course with the organization's needs. Failure to do so can be disastrous. Remember, IS professionals are not mind readers, even though they are often asked to be.

Role of the IS Professional

The changing use of IT in organizations has caused a dramatic change in the responsibilities of IS professionals. In the formative years of IT, the IS professional was typically technically oriented and rewarded for writing code that made the most effective use of the available IT resources. The user's needs sometimes had to be sacrificed in order to achieve desired hardware and software efficiencies. The data processing department had a certain mystique about it that caused most people not to question the programming wizard. Because only they knew the capabilities of the computer, the IS professionals were the ones who did most IS planning. The result was sometimes a piecemeal approach not in line with future business needs.

Times, of course, have changed. In their day-to-day activities, many IS professionals now act more in a consulting and planning role than in a programming one. They must help the business manager understand how his or her ideas for competitive advantage can get built into a new information system. They must be able to create a project plan for acquiring the new system.

The increased IT sophistication of business managers and the recognition that the firm's IS function should be afforded the same strategic status as such functions as marketing, finance, and manufacturing have also changed the role of the IS professional in the information resources planning process. IS professionals must be able to combine their technical skills with a sharp understanding of planning and how the organization works (and should work) to accomplish its goals.

SEVEN PLANNING TECHNIQUES

Due to the importance and the difficulty of systems planning, it is valuable to use a framework or methodology. Over the years, a number of techniques have been proposed to help IS executives do a better job of planning. The seven presented here take different views of IS planning, including looking at the assimilation of IT in organizations, defining information needs, understanding the competitive market, categorizing applications into a portfolio, mapping relationships, and surmising about the future. The seven planning techniques discussed are:

1. Stages of growth
2. Critical success factors
3. Competitive forces model
4. Value chain analysis
5. Internet value matrix
6. Linkage analysis planning
7. Scenario planning

Stages of Growth

Richard Nolan and Chuck Gibson published a landmark paper in 1974 entitled "Managing the Four Stages of EDP Growth." They observed that many organizations go through four stages in the introduction and assimilation of a new technology.

- *Stage 1: Early Successes.* The first stage is the beginning use of a new technology. Although stumbling occurs, early successes lead to increased interest and experimentation.
- *Stage 2: Contagion.* Based on the early successes, interest grows rapidly as new products and/or services based on the technology come to the marketplace. They are tried out in a variety of applications; growth is uncontrolled and therefore rises rapidly. This proliferation stage is the learning period for the field, both for uses and for new products and services.
- *Stage 3: Control.* Eventually it becomes apparent that the proliferation must be controlled. Management begins to believe the costs of using the new technology are too high and the variety of approaches generates waste. The integration of systems is attempted but proves difficult, and suppliers begin efforts toward standardization.
- *Stage 4: Integration.* At this stage, the use of the particular new technology might be considered mature. The dominant design of the technology has been mastered, setting the stage for newer technologies, wherein the pattern is repeated. An organization can be in several stages simultaneously for different technologies.

Nolan has since used the Stages of Growth theory to describe three eras, as shown in Figure 13.12. Underlying the three organizational learning curves pictured is the dominant design of each era. The DP (Data Processing) Era's dominant design was the mainframe, the Micro Era's design was the PC, and the Network Era's is the Internet. The eras overlap each other slightly at points of "technological discontinuity," states Nolan, which occur when proponents of the proven old dominant design struggle with the proponents of alternative new and unproven designs. Inevitably, one new dominant design wins out.

The importance of the theory to IS management is in understanding where a technology or a company currently resides on the organizational learning curve. If, for example, use of Web Services is in the trial-and-error Stage 2, where experimentation and learning take place, then exerting too much control too soon can kill off important new uses of the technology. Management needs to tolerate, even encourage, experimentation.

Because the management principles differ from one stage to another, and because different technologies are in different stages at any point in time, the Stages of Growth model continues to be an important aid to the systems planning process.

Critical Success Factors

In 1977, Jack Rockart and his colleagues at the Center for Information Systems Research (CISR), Sloan School of

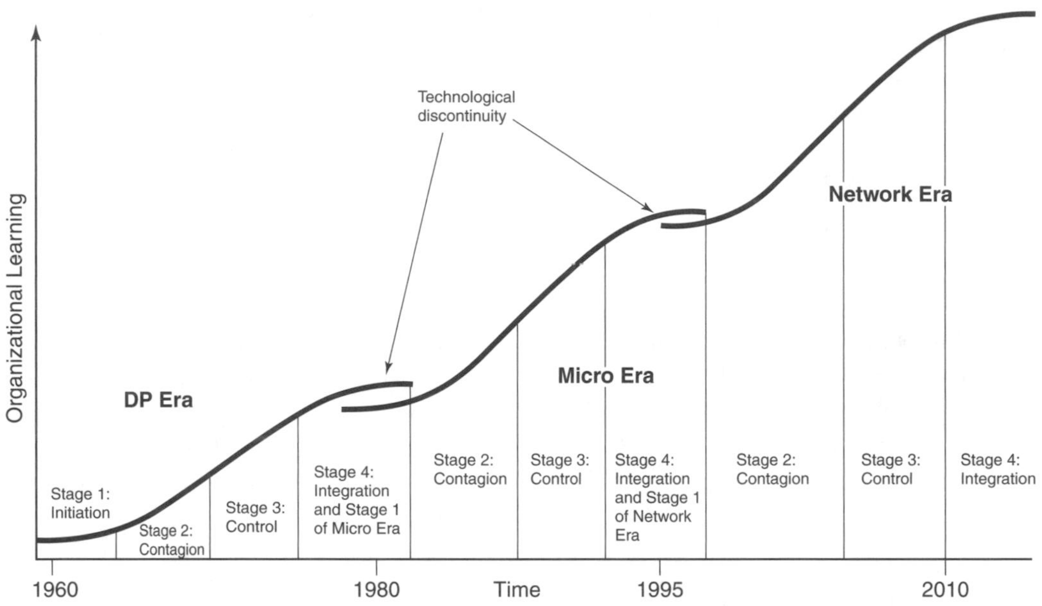

Figure 13.12 Stages of Growth. *Source:* Reprinted with permission from R. L. Nolan, "Information Technology Management from 1960–2000," in *A Nation Transformed by Information,* Alfred D. Chandler and James W. Cortad (Eds.), Oxford, 2000.

Management, at the Massachusetts Institute of Technology (MIT), began developing a method for defining executive information needs. The result of their work is the Critical Success Factors (CSF) method. It focuses on individual managers and their current information needs, whether factual or opinion information. The CSF method has become a popular planning approach and can be used to help companies identify information systems they need to develop.

For each executive, critical success factors (CSFs) are the few key areas of the job where things must go right for the organization to flourish. Executives usually have fewer than 10 of these factors that they each should monitor. Furthermore, CSFs are both time sensitive and time dependent, so they should be reexamined as often as necessary to keep abreast of the current business climate. These key areas should receive constant attention from executives, yet CISR research found that most managers had not explicitly identified these crucial factors.

Rockart finds four sources for these factors. One source is the *industry* that the business is in. Each industry has CSFs relevant to any company in it. A second source is the *company itself* and its situation within the industry. Actions by a few large, dominant companies in an industry most likely provide one or more CSFs for small companies in that industry. Furthermore, several companies may have the same CSFs but, at the same time, have different priorities for those factors.

A third source of CSFs is the *environment*, such as consumer trends, the economy, and political factors of the country (or countries) in which the company operates. A prime example is that prior to, say, 1998, few chief executives would have listed "leveraging the Internet" as a CSF. Today, most do.

The fourth source is *temporal organizational factors*, or areas of company activity that normally do not warrant concern but are currently unacceptable and need attention. A case of far too much or far too little inventory might qualify as a CSF for a short time.

In addition to these four sources, Rockart has found two types of CSFs. One he calls *monitoring*, or keeping abreast of ongoing operations. The second he calls *building*, which involves tracking the progress of "programs for change" initiated by the executive. The higher an executive is in the organization, the more *building* CSFs are usually on his or her list. Rockart sees CSFs varying from organization to organization, from time period to time period, and from executive to executive.

One way to use the CSF method is to use current corporate objectives and goals to determine which factors are critical for accomplishing the objectives, along with two or three prime measures for each factor. Discovering the measures is the most time-consuming portion, says Rockart. Some measures use hard, factual data; they are the ones most quickly identified. Others use softer measures, such as opinions, perceptions, and hunches; these measures take more analysis to uncover their appropriate sources. IS plans can then be developed based on these CSFs.

Competitive Forces Model

The most widely quoted framework for thinking about the strategic use of IT is the competitive forces model proposed by Michael Porter of the Harvard Business School in his book *Competitive Strategy*. Porter believes companies must contend with five competitive forces, as shown in Figure 13.13.

One force is the *threat of new entrants* into one's industry. For instance, the Internet has opened up a new channel of marketing and distribution, which, in turn, has allowed all kinds of unexpected new entrants into numerous markets. Travel Web sites, for example, are threats to travel agencies.

The second force is the *bargaining power of buyers*. Buyers seek lower prices and bargain for higher quality. Web-based auction sites, shopping bots, and intelligent agents are all giving buyers more shopping options and more information about potential suppliers, thus increasing their bargaining power. In fact, much of the power of the Internet has to do with this force.

A third force is the *bargaining power of suppliers*. For example, the Internet enables small companies to compete against large ones in uncovering requests for bids and bidding on them—leveling the playing field.

The fourth force is *substitute products or services*. The Internet provides a myriad of examples here. E-mail is a substitute for paper mail. Music downloads are substitutes for CDs. Book and music Web sites are substitutes for book and music stores.

The fifth force is the *intensity of rivalry among competitors*. IT-based alliances can change rivalries by, for instance, extending them into value-chain-versus-value-chain competition rather than just company-versus-company competition.

Porter presents three strategies for dealing with these competitive forces. His first is to *differentiate products and services*. By making them different—that is, better in the eyes of customers—firms may be able to charge higher prices or perhaps deter customers from moving to another product, lower the bargaining power of buyers, and so on. It is probably the most popular of his three strategies.

Porter's second strategy is to be the *lowest-cost producer*. He warns that simply being one of the low-cost

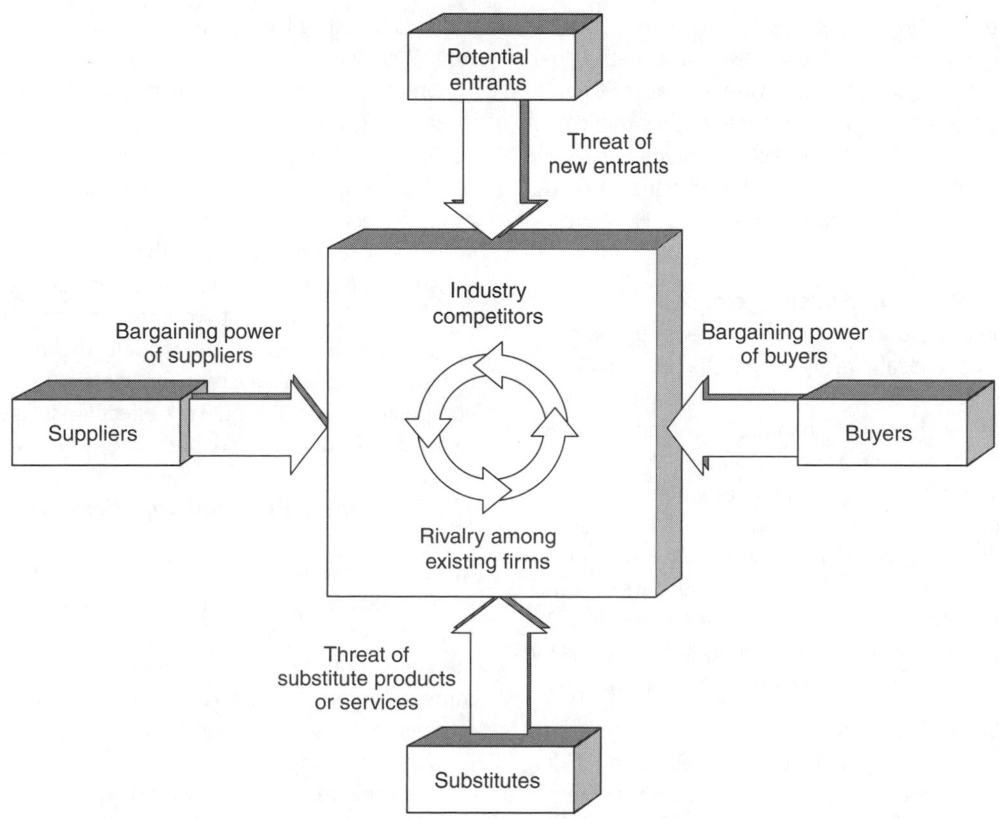

Figure 13.13 Michael Porter's Competitive Analysis Model. *Source:* Michael E. Porter, *Competitive Strategy* (New York: The Free Press, 1980).

producers is not enough. Not being the lowest causes a company to be stuck in the middle, with no real competitive advantage.

His third strategy is to find a *niche*, such as focusing on a segment of a product line or a geographical market. Companies that use this strategy can often serve their target market effectively and efficiently, at times being both the low-cost producer and having a highly differentiated product as well.

This framework guides IS planning because all five forces and all three strategies can be enabled by or implemented by technology. Once management analyzes the forces and determines company strategy, the necessary information systems can be included in the plan. In a widely referenced 2001 article in the Harvard Business Review, Porter analyzes the Internet using this framework. His main points appear below and on page 491.

Value Chain Analysis

Five years after proposing the five forces model in 1980, Porter presented the valuc chain in Competitive Advantage in 1985; it, too, became a popular strategic planning tool. As shown in Figure 13.14, a value chain for a product or service consists of major activities that add value during its creation, development, sale, and after-sale service. According to Porter, primary activities and support activities take place in every value chain.

FRAMEWORK EXAMPLE

FIVE FORCES ANALYSIS OF THE INTERNET

In the main, the Internet tends to dampen the profitability of industries and reduce firms' ability to create sustainable operational advantages, argues Michael Porter, because it has "a leveling effect on business practices." He reaches this sobering conclusion by looking at the effect the Internet can have on industry profitability using his five forces framework, described in his 1980 book *Competitive Strategy*. Here are his points.

The Bargaining Power of Buyers Increases. On the demand side of the value chain, the Internet opens up new channels for companies to deal directly with customers, rather than through intermediaries. Thus, the Internet can decrease the bargaining power of the other channels and their intermediaries, thereby potentially increasing profitability.

However, the Internet gives buyers more information, both about competitors and products, strengthening their bargaining power and lowering industry profitability. The Internet can also decrease switching costs—the cost a buyer pays to switch from buying from one firm to buying from someone else. This also increases buyer bargaining power. In total, the increase in buyer bargaining power decreases industry profitability.

Barriers to Entry Decrease. Due to the Internet's new channel to buyers, industries may not be so reliant on building up sales forces to sell their goods, making it easier for others to enter the industry because they can compete without having these high fixed costs. Furthermore, location need not be as much of a limiting factor. Small companies can sell to the world via a Web site.

On the other hand, network effects, which increase barriers to entry, are difficult to garner, argues Porter. A *network effect* occurs when the value of a product or service increases as the number of users increases. eBay illustrates this effect: the more buyers, the more eBay is a desirable marketplace for sellers. And the more sellers, the more eBay attracts buyers.

It is a virtuous circle. However, Porter argues that a self-limiting mechanism is at work. A company first attracts customers whose needs it meets well. The needs of later customers may be less well met—presenting an opening for other competitors. Thus, the network effect limits itself. Yet, where it exists, it presents a formidable barrier to entry.

The Bargaining Power of Suppliers Increases. On the supply side, the Internet can make it far easier for a company to purchase goods and services, which reduces the bargaining power of suppliers. This trend would seem to increase industry profitability. But, at the same time, suppliers can more easily expand their market, finding new customers, thereby increasing supplier bargaining power. Lower barriers to entry also erode the former advantage of a company over its suppliers.

Electronic exchanges, which expand marketplaces, can benefit both buyers and suppliers. However, they can reduce the leverage of former intermediaries between suppliers and end users. This decrease gives companies new competitors (their former suppliers), which can reduce industry profitability.

Finally, in giving equal access to all suppliers, the Internet tends to diminish differentiation among competitors—again reducing industry profitability.

The Threat of Substitute Products and Services Increases. An industry can increase its efficiency by using the Internet, thereby expanding its market and improving its position over substitutes. For example, online auctions can decrease the power of classified ads and physical marketplaces because the online auctions may be more convenient to buyers. Online exchanges, especially those with many buyers and sellers, can thus discourage substitutes.

On the other hand, the Internet has opened up entirely new ways to meet customer needs. Thus, the threat of substitutes can increase significantly, probably greater than its ability to ward them off through increased efficiencies.

Rivalry Among Competitors Intensifies. Proprietary offerings are more difficult to sustain in the Internet's open-system environment, states Porter, because products and services are easier to duplicate. Hence, there can be more intense rivalry among competitors. Furthermore, due to the Internet's global nature, companies can extend their range of competition, so there can be more competitors in a marketspace.

Also, the Internet can change the cost structure, emphasizing fixed costs (Web sites rather than call centers, for example) and reducing variable costs (serving one more customer can be much less expensive via a Web site rather than a call center). This change in cost structure can lead companies to compete on price (which hurts industry profitability) rather than on convenience, customization, specialization, quality, and service (all of which can increase industry profitability).

Even partnering with complementary products and services, while seeming to increase a market, may instead decrease profitability if it leads to standardized offerings. Microsoft's operating systems has had that effect on the PC industry. The industry now competes on price; its profitability has decreased.

Outsourcing, another form of partnering, can also depress industry profitability if the companies outsource to the same providers and their products thereby become more alike.

Overall, states Porter, the Internet tends to decrease industry profitability. But not all industries need to see this happen to them. It depends on how their companies react. They can react destructively by competing on price or compete constructively by competing on differentiating factors. However, it will be harder to distinguish themselves on operational efficiencies alone, says Porter, because the Internet can make duplication easier. Instead, firms should focus on their strategic position in an industry and how they will maintain profitability (not growth, market share, or revenue). Success depends on offering distinct value.

The five primary activities deal with creating a product or service, getting it to buyers, and servicing it afterward. These activities form the sequence of the value chain:

1. Inbound logistics: Receive and handle inputs
2. Operations: Convert inputs to the product or service
3. Outbound logistics: Collect, store, and distribute the product or service to buyers
4. Marketing and sales: Provide incentive to buyers to buy the product or service
5. Service: Enhance or maintain the value of the product or service

The four supporting activities underlie the entire value chain:

1. Organizational infrastructure
2. HR management
3. Technology development
4. Procurement

By studying how a firm performs the primary and support activities for a product or service, a firm can explore how it might add more value at every activity. Alternatively, it could determine where another company could add more value, and team up with that firm, outsourcing that activity to that partner.

Virtual Value Chains. Jeff Rayport and John Sviokla distinguish between market*places*, where physical products and physical location are important, and market*spaces*, where information substitutes for physical products and physical location. In the world of Internet commerce, they ask, "How can companies create value in marketspace?" or "How can they create value in marketspace and marketplace concurrently, leveraging off each other?" They draw on Porter's value chain in their answer.

In the traditional value chain, note Rayport and Sviokla, companies treat information as a support element, not as a source of value itself. To compete in marketspace, companies need to use information to create new value for customers (such as FedEx and UPS did in opening up their tracking systems to consumers via their Web sites). Creating value in marketspace also involves a value chain, but it is a

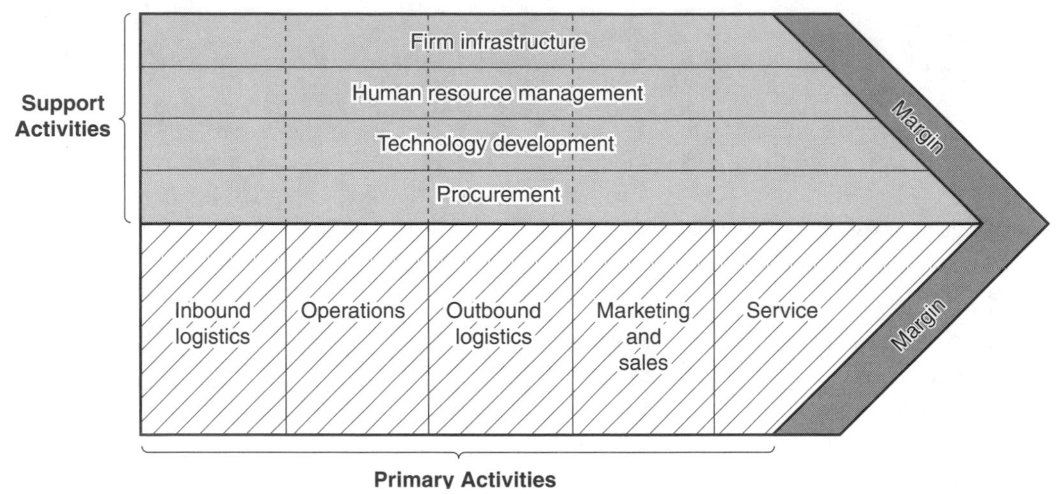

Figure 13.14 The Value Chain. *Source:* Michael E. Porter, *Competitive Advantage* (New York: The Free Press, 1985).

virtual value chain, because the steps are performed with information and through information. At every step, value via information can be added in five ways: gather it, organize it, select it, synthesize it, or distribute it. The IS organization should therefore play a major role in marketspace.

Rayport and Sviokla have observed that companies seem to follow an evolution in using information to add value: first by making operations visible, then by putting in place mirroring capabilities, and finally by creating space-based customer relationships.

Making operations visible. Companies first create ways to see their physical operations through information. That is, they foster visibility of operations, generally through their production systems, allowing employees to coordinate activities across the physical value chain, sometimes in ways that lead to competitive advantage. Frito-Lay's field employees input information on store-by-store sales as well as information about competitors' promotions and new competitive products. With all this field data, managers can better schedule production to match demand, route trucks most efficiently, and tailor promotions to suit local buying patterns. Frito-Lay can more quickly react to marketplace changes. This sort of visibility, say Rayport and Sviokla, lays the foundation for a virtual value chain.

Mirroring capabilities. Second, companies begin to substitute virtual activities for physical ones. A case in point from a report by Roger Woolfe appears on page 491.

Another example is virtual worldwide teams, such as design teams in the United States, Europe, and Asia that work on designs and prototypes in a virtual information space. Time and space are no longer limitations. The teams can be located anywhere, work can progress 24 hours a day, and many more virtual designs can be created and tested in a shorter time and for less cost than in the physical world. This mirroring of capabilities, note Rayport and Sviokla, marks the beginning of creating a parallel virtual value chain.

Space-based customer relationships. Third, companies draw on their flow of information to deliver value to customers in new ways. In essence, they create new space-based customer relationships. USAA, the insurance company for military officers, exemplifies this third step, note Rayport and Sviokla. For many years, USAA collected information about customers and made it available companywide so that employees could provide advice and answer questions anytime a customer called (visibility). The company then discovered it could create customer risk profiles and customize policies. From that point, it created new product lines, such as insurance for boat owners (mirroring capabilities). From there, USAA expanded to new areas, such as offering financing to boat purchasers. In fact, it even offers to replace stolen items in a theft claim, rather than send the insured a check, a service many seem to prefer. USAA is managing its information to create new value for customers.

When searching for strategic uses of information, Rayport and Sviokla point out that many of the rules differ from those of the physical marketplace. Digital assets are not used up in consumption; therefore, information can be reused in many forms at a low cost. New economies of scale are present, so small companies can effectively compete against large ones, due to lower overhead, while still covering large geographic areas. New economies of scope allow insurance companies to offer financing and even discount

CASE EXAMPLE

AN AUTOMOBILE MANUFACTURER

This auto manufacturer has dealerships around the United States. Many of the dealerships have a satellite dish, as does headquarters. In addition to other uses, these dishes are used by the manufacturer's rental car subsidiary to auction off good, clean used vehicles (with fewer than 10,000 miles) to dealers to sell.

For 30 minutes at a specified time, an auctioneer is able to sell 60 vehicles online. As a car comes up for bid, the dealers view it on a monitor at their premises. They can see it from several directions, read its ratings (on cleanliness and condition), and use a mouse to bid against the other dealers online. Headquarters staff monitor the progress of the auction and advise the auctioneer on, say, lowering minimum bids to ensure that every vehicle is sold. The auctions are held once or twice a month.

The dealers have been extremely satisfied with this system because it saves them from having to travel to auctions, and they can get good-quality used cars without much effort. In addition, the manufacturer guarantees satisfaction. If, after taking delivery of a vehicle, the dealer decides he does not want it, he can send it back.

buying programs to policyholders, as USAA is doing, for example. Finally, transaction costs are lower in marketspace; thus companies can capture information that they were not able to capture in the past, as Frito-Lay is doing.

To take advantage of these four changes, though, a significant mindshift is required from supply-side thinking to demand-side thinking, say Rayport and Sviokla. That is, companies need to sense and respond to needs rather than make and sell products and services. That shift appears to be a significant strategic opportunity for companies, and IS should play a role in identifying and helping the company take advantage of it.

E-Business Value Matrix

At a Networld+Interop conference, Peter Alexander of Cisco Systems described a portfolio planning technique used at Cisco to ensure it develops a well-rounded portfolio of IT projects. The approach is further described in Hartman et al.'s *Net Ready*. These days, that portfolio revolves around the Internet.

It can be difficult for executives to prioritize projects, said Alexander, because of the wealth of opportunities. A portfolio management approach is therefore of great value to senior and functional executives to ensure that they are working on a broad front that will lead to success in the Internet economy.

The portfolio management approach Cisco uses is called the e-business value matrix, and every IT project is meant to be placed in one of four categories to assess its value to the company. As shown in Figure 13.15, the value of each project is assessed as high or low in two categories: criticality to the business and newness of the idea (newness not just to the company, but to the world). The result is four categories of projects: new fundamentals, operational excellence, rational experimentation, and breakthrough strategy.

New Fundamentals. These projects provide a fundamentally new way of working in overhead areas, not business-critical areas. They are low risk and focus on increasing productivity. They can provide significant cost savings by measurably improving operations.

	Criticality to Business	*Newness of Idea*
New fundamentals	Low	Low
Operational excellence	High	Low
Rational experimentation	Low	High
Breakthrough strategy	High	High

Figure 13.15 E-Business Value Matrix. *Source:* Adapted from a speech by Peter Alexander and *Net Ready: Strategies for Success in the E-conomy* by Amir Harment, John Sifonis, and John Kador (New York: McGraw-Hill, 2000).

These projects should be managed as quick hits: Implement a project to increase productivity in finance within 3 to 6 months, said Alexander, then move on to another area. Often, such projects can be implemented by IS with little user involvement during development. However, an important point to remember is that these systems aim at the grass roots of the company. Thus, they can lead to a cultural shift, such as shifting to working via an intranet.

Operational Excellence. These projects are of medium risk because they may involve reengineering work processes. They do not aim for immediate returns, but rather intend to increase such areas as customer satisfaction and corporate agility. In essence, they revolve around providing faster access to information. These projects can be important in improving IS credibility because of their high visibility. An example is an executive dashboard for quickly viewing operational metrics. Such a system is highly visible to executives.

These projects have about a 12-month horizon. They should involve cross-functional teams (to ensure that the reengineering does indeed take place), and they should use tested technology.

Rational Experimentation. These projects test new technologies and new ideas. Hence, they are risky. However, every company needs some of these projects to hope to move ahead of competitors. When described as experiments, they set the realistic expectation that they may fail. The goal is to prove the concept in, say, several months' time or less. One example could be Web Services; another could be desktop video conferencing. When treated as experiments, these projects will not hurt the company if they fail. If they do pan out, however, they could prove a new business or IT model and thus become one of the other three types.

These incubator-type projects should be managed as experiments with short time frames and incremental funding. The team may be full-time, but it does not need to move out of IT. Participants should not be penalized if one of these projects fails.

Breakthrough Strategy. These projects potentially have a huge impact on the company, and perhaps even on the industry, if they succeed. They capture the imagination, but they are high risk. The typical response, once someone sees the potential is, "If this works, it would change . . . " An example of a breakthrough strategy is eBay. Its auction business model altered people's thinking about global buying and selling. Another example is extranets for customers. When successful, they move to the operational excellence cell.

Breakthrough strategy projects require strong functional buy-in. One way to get this commitment is to brainstorm with functional partners on the possibilities. Because they are generally bet-the-farm types of projects, they need to be managed like start-ups. They need venture-capital-like funding, not month-to-month milestones. For example, the project may request $10 million with the possibility of failure, but also offer the possibility of huge upside returns.

These IT-based projects need dedicated staff from numerous functions. To attract top talent and foster the intense communication and collaboration needed among the team members, they probably need to be housed in a "skunk works" setting by being set apart organizationally and reporting to the CEO or CFO, who protects them from corporate politics and from the "but this is the way we've always done it" mindset. Finally, the skunk works team needs to be given financial incentives if the project succeeds.

In conclusion, Alexander stated that IS departments can get functional buy-in if they create such a portfolio of IT projects and then manage that portfolio properly. A key to success is leadership. All the C-level executives need to evangelize and empower others to make these projects happen. They need to encourage risk and accept failure of the right kind. Because C-level involvement is key, executives may need to be educated on their role.

To illustrate this portfolio approach, see examples of Cisco IT projects on page 493.

Linkage Analysis Planning

Linkage analysis planning examines the links organizations have with one another with the goal of creating a strategy for utilizing electronic channels. This approach to strategic systems planning is espoused by Kenneth Primozic, Edward Primozic, and Joe Leben in their book *Strategic Choices*. The methodology includes the following three steps:

1. Define power relationships among the various players and stakeholders.
2. Map out the extended enterprise to include suppliers, buyers, and strategic partners.
3. Plan electronic channels to deliver the information component of products and services.

Define Power Relationships. To create a strategy for building electronic links among enterprises, Primozic's team believes that management must first understand the power relationships that currently exist among these various players. For this analysis, they begin with Michael Porter's classic model of competitive forces. To this model, they add technology, demographics, global competition,

CASE EXAMPLE

CISCO SYSTEMS

Cisco Systems manufactures computers that provide the infrastructure for the Internet. Cisco uses the e-business value matrix described by Alexander to manage its portfolio of IT projects, placing a value on each project based on the newness of the idea it employs and the criticality of the system to the company.

Here are examples of systems in each of the four cells in the matrix: new fundamentals, operational excellence, rational experimentation, and breakthrough strategies.

New Fundamentals

Cisco's expense reporting system, Metro, is a fundamentally new way of handling expense reporting. Its goal is to reduce costs in this overhead area.

To submit an expense report, an employee goes to a Web page to build the report online. As the report is filled in, the system checks to see whether the employee has adhered to company policy.

When submitted, the system routes the report to the employee's manager and explains the purpose of the expense report, the total expenses, and whether any policies were violated. If the manager does nothing, the employee's credit card account and personal account are credited in 2 days' time.

This system quickly delivered major cost savings, because Cisco now only needs three people to manage expense reports for all 31,000 employees. Although abuse is possible, the cost of potential losses from questionable charges is a fraction of the cost of having a larger administrative staff.

Operational Excellence

Cisco's executive dashboards for each functional area are seen as operationally differentiating the company from its competitors. In fact, Cisco executives have said, "I cannot live without this system because . . . it allows me to model sales programs, . . . it allows me to manage the supply chain, . . . it allows me to do trend analysis on component availability, and so on."

Each dashboard is a Web front end to the company's data warehouse. In essence, it is an executive information system that allows executives to drill down into the data to pull up a snapshot of, say, the company's revenues, bookings, or margins (the fundamentals of the company) at a point in time by business unit, region, entire enterprise, product line, and so on. For example, executives can see how well a division is progressing in meeting its forecasts.

Furthermore, the system allows the CFO to close the company's books within 1 day of the end of each quarter, and the company expects to reduce this lag to just 2 to 3 hours.

Such a system is not excellence in product, it is excellence in IT; and it is operational excellence, said Alexander.

Rational Experimentation

Cisco has a continual stream of such experiments going on in IT. One experiment has been multicast streaming video. Executives are watching to see the business value of this new technology to the various functional areas. For example, they have made all-company meetings available online to employees through IP TV. If this technology proves useful, it could be used for new product training.

Breakthrough Strategy

Cisco views its development of a virtual supply chain as a breakthrough strategy. Of the 26 factories that build Cisco products, only 5 are owned by Cisco. Thus, the company's ability to sense and respond is not tied to capital assets. It is a function of their building an effective supply chain. Although not easy, they believe it is critical to their business. If their gamble on virtual manufacturing goes awry, it would present an enormous problem. However, they see it as worth the effort because the returns will be extremely high if they succeed.

Cisco takes its portfolio of IT projects and Internet initiatives so seriously that CEO John Chambers holds a review of leading Internet capabilities each quarter. At these reviews, each functional area describes how it is implementing Internet capabilities that are ahead of its peers in the industry. Most company CEOs do not make this effort, said Alexander. If they did, they would see spectacular returns, he believes.

government regulations, and "whatever is important in your environment." The goals of this step are to identify who has the power and determine future threats and opportunities for the company.

The analysis begins by identifying linkages, which are relationships the organization has with other entities. The links are represented by lines between organizations (shown in boxcs). Once identified, management needs to determine who is managing each link. Oftentimes, no one is, which should be of concern. From here, the team picks the most important link and decides how the firm can control that link. The authors believe that successful organizations will be those that control the electronic channels or the electronic linkages among enterprises.

The discussion of how to gain power within one's world of linkages brings up a host of questions. Two important ones are: How might alliances with other firms across industries or even with competitors help us? How do we need to restructure ourselves to seize an opportunity or ward off a threat?

Map Out Your Extended Enterprise. These questions lead to the second step in this approach to planning—mapping the extended enterprise. An extended enterprise includes all of one's own organization plus those organizations with which one interacts, such as suppliers, buyers, government agencies, and so forth (see Figure 13.16).

The purpose of this step is to get management to recognize the existence of this extended enterprise and then begin to manage the relationships in it. Primozic and colleagues believe successful managers will focus on extended enterprises. They see two fundamental principles to managing these relationships:

1. The enterprise's success depends on the relationships among everyone involved, which includes employees, managers, suppliers, alliances, distribution channels, and so forth.
2. Managing information as a strategic tool is crucial because some 70 percent of the final cost of goods and services is in their information content.

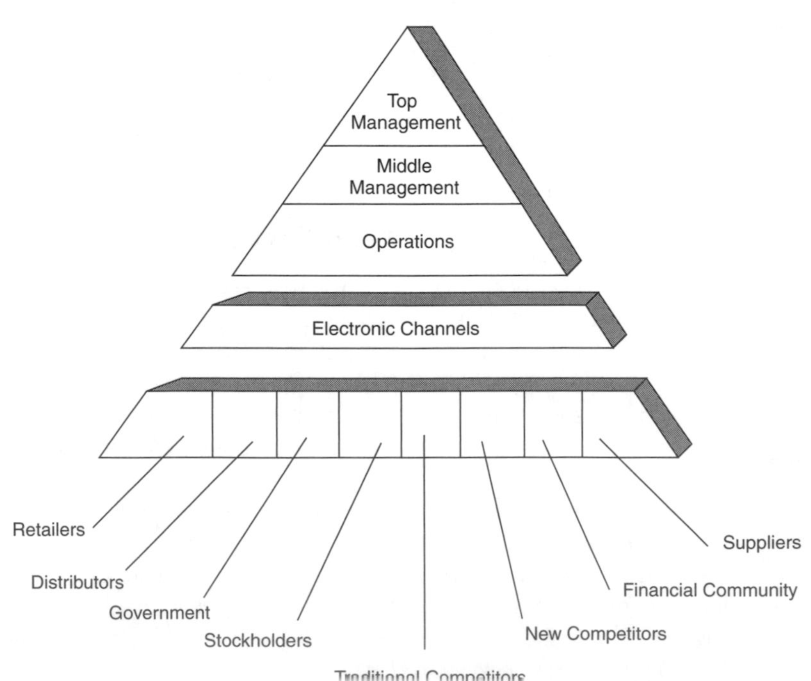

Figure 13.16 The Extended Enterprise. *Source:* K. I. Primozic, E. A. Primozic, and J. F. Leben, *Strategic Choices: Supremacy, Survival, or Sayonara* (New York: McGraw-Hill, 1991).

CASE EXAMPLE

ELECTRIC POWER RESEARCH INSTITUTE

The Electric Power Research Institute (EPRI), with headquarters in Palo Alto, California, is a large private research firm serving more than 700 electric member utilities. EPRI's 350 staff scientists and engineers manage some 1,600 R&D projects at any one time. The projects, which study such subjects as power generation, superconductivity, electronic and magnetic fields, and acid rain, are conducted by more than 400 utility, university, commercial, government, and other R&D contractors on behalf of the members.

The Challenge

EPRI's mission is to deliver the information and knowledge from its research projects to the 400,000 employees in the 768 member utilities to help them be more competitive. Management realized EPRI had to compress the "information float," the elapsed time from the availability of research findings to the use of those results in industry.

The institute was suffering from "info-sclerosis," the hardening and clogging of its information arteries. Due to the volume of research findings—gigabytes of information—moving information in and out of EPRI was extremely difficult. In addition, because of the documentation and publishing process, the results often were unavailable for up to 24 months, so the reports were not as timely as they could be. Nor were the results accessible, because they were in massive reports. Solving this information delivery challenge was critical to EPRI's survival.

The Vision

The vision was to assist members in exploiting EPRI's product—knowledge—as a strategic business resource, whenever and from wherever they choose. To accomplish this vision, EPRI built an electronic information and communication service.

As described by Marina Mann and her colleagues, their delivery vehicle is EPRINET, an online channel that includes

- A natural-language front end for accessing online information
- Expert system-based products that contain the knowledge of their energy experts
- E-mail facilities for person-to-person communications
- Video conferencing to foster small-group communications

Using Linkage Analysis Planning

To focus the EPRINET effort and to identify the services and products that would offer strategic business advantages to members, EPRI used linkage analysis in a 3-day workshop led by Kenneth Primozic. The workshop began with management stating that (1) EPRI was both an R&D organization and a knowledge provider and (2) the goal was to leverage knowledge as a strategic asset.

From this starting point, Primozic asked, "Who is linked to EPRI in creating and distributing knowledge?" The participants identified the cocreators as contractors, research firms, universities, the government, and technology firms. They identified the recipients as the utility industry, universities, research labs, government policies, and knowledge as capital—as shown in Figure 13.17. Each represented a link to EPRI; therefore, the group then studied the present and future power relationships in each buyer–seller link. During these discussions, they saw how some current customers, such as universities or research labs, could become future competitors and change the power relationship in a link.

Management's goal was to leverage knowledge, so the group listed all the ways leverage could be achieved. Then they focused on the most important way, which turned out to be treating knowledge as capital. During this analysis, management defined the following CSFs for giving EPRINET a sustainable competitive advantage:

- Establish the right mix of product offerings, a mix that allows people to pick, choose, and combine at the lowest possible cost.
- Keep all customers in mind, including utility executives, research engineers, and operations people.

(Case continued)

(*Case continued*)

- Use IT—specifically expert systems and natural language—to make the system easy to use and access.
- Create a range of "knowledge packages" targeted to specific audiences.
- Establish a timely, reliable, secure global distribution channel.

Once EPRINET was made available, a marketing campaign began. The number of users has climbed steadily since. Frequent users report that the system is indeed broadening the number of people they can stay in contact with and allowing them to uncover EPRI research findings that they would not have found otherwise.

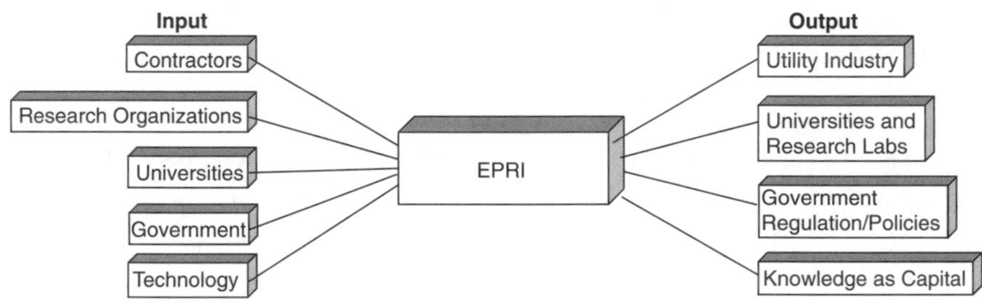

Figure 13.17 EPRI'S Linkage Analysis. *Source:* M. M. Mann et al., "EPRINET: Leveraging Knowledge in the Electric Utility Industry," *MIS Quarterly,* September 1991, pp. 403-421.

An extended enterprise diagram might deal only with external players, such as the government, stockholders, traditional competitors, the financial community, and so forth. Such a chart includes everyone whose decisions affect the organization or who are affected by its decisions. The analysis then moves to discussing how the links might change and how each link should be managed.

In the extended enterprise, each relationship will prosper only when it is win-win, say the authors. For example, in return for maintaining a buyer's parts inventory and providing just-in-time delivery, a supplier should be paid electronically upon delivery of goods. Such an arrangement profits both parties.

Competitive advantage will depend increasingly on being able to exploit the collective resources of one's extended enterprise, say Primozic and colleagues. Such enterprises often require electronic channels to execute business transactions, which leads to the third step in their planning approach—planning the electronic channels.

Plan Your Electronic Channels. An electronic channel is an electronic link used to create, distribute, and present information and knowledge as part of a product or service or as an ancillary good. These channels focus on the information component of products. The authors believe that those who control the electronic channels will be the winners because they will be able to address new niche markets as they arise. Furthermore, as use of IT leads to a faster-paced world, organizations with the longest electronic reach into their extended enterprise will have the advantage.

The authors use linkage analysis charts to help executives conceptualize the key issues they face in an extended enterprise and focus on the factors that are critical to their future success. This methodology has been used by the Electric Power Research Institute, whose story is told on pages 495–496.

Scenario Planning

The final strategic planning approach is scenario planning. Peter Schwartz, who has written the definitive book on scenario planning, *The Art of the Long View*, states that *scenarios*, which get their name from the theatrical term for a script or a play, are stories about the way the world might be in the future. Such stories can help people spot and adapt to aspects of their lives that are actually changing today. They help people find appropriate paths to each of the plausible futures described in the scenarios.

The goal of scenario planning is not to predict the future (because that is hard to do) but to explore the forces that could cause different futures to take place and then decide on actions to take if those forces begin to materialize.

M. Lynne Markus, of Bentley College, points out that long-term planning has traditionally extrapolated from the past and has not factored in low-probability events that could significantly alter trends. Thus, these straight-line projections have provided little help.

Markus identifies four steps in scenario planning:

1. *Define a decision problem and time frame to bound the analysis.* In thinking about the future of IS, for instance, IS management might ask, "How will IS be managed 10 years from now?" An individual IS employee might then ask, "What skills would I need to succeed in that organization, and what do I need to do to get those skills?"
2. *Identify the major known trends that will affect the decision problem.* Generally, scenario planners think about trends in categories: the business environment, government and regulations, societies and their concerns, technologies, financial considerations, the global environment, and such. Each trend is then judged by asking, "What impacts will this trend have on the decision problem?" "What are the directions of each impact?" Trends with unknown impacts or contradictory impacts are classified as "uncertain."
3. *Identify just a few driving uncertainties.* Driving uncertainties are those around which others tend to cluster. Often scenario analysts choose just two, with two possible states for each, leading to four scenarios. The goal is to explore quite different futures, not the most likely future, notes Markus.
4. *Construct the scenarios.* Each scenario, based on a driving uncertainty, needs to be plausible. To create this plausibility, scenario writers include a "triggering event," something that redirects the future into the desired space. For example, a triggering event could be a world event (the September 11, 2001, tragedy certainly qualifies), an action by a group (a major court decision), or a business event (the collapse of a large company). The scenarios depict the end state (at the selected point in time) and how that path got taken.

With these scenarios in hand, executives and planners then decide how well their current strategies would fare in each case. Then they ask, "Is there a better strategy, perhaps one that would cover more bases?" Also, they should determine what factors they should monitor closely to quickly spot changes in trends.

To give a brief glimpse of a scenario effort, on pages 486–487 are four scenarios Markus created around the question, "What will in-house IS management look like in 10 years?"

SUMMARY

Based on the successes and failures of past IS planning efforts, we see two necessary ingredients for good strategic planning efforts. One is that the plans must look toward the future. This point may seem obvious, but in turbulent times, the future is not likely to be an extrapolation of the past. Therefore, a successful planning effort needs to support "peering into an unknown future"—most likely in a sense-and-respond fashion.

A second necessary ingredient is that IS planning must be intrinsic to business planning. This point may also seem obvious, but, again, unless the planning process specifically requires joint development, the systems plans may not be relevant because they do not align with corporate strategy. A misalignment is not so likely with the advent of Internet commerce, but it is also not yet natural in many companies.

To ensure that IT is effectively utilized in today's competitive, rapidly changing world, the organization must engage in a proactive, future-based information resources planning process. To develop a meaningful IS plan, the firm must have a clear understanding of both the technology and the information resources planning process. The process must begin with a thorough assessment of the current situation. The IS mission, goal accomplishment, information use intensity, and business manager attitudes must all be reviewed.

The definition and development of an information vision and architecture is a difficult conceptual task. Yet the value of an explicit vision and architecture statement, over a period of time, usually exceeds the creation and maintenance costs. Organizations often create visions or architectures that explicitly deal with only some of the issues mentioned in this chapter. It is not always possible to deal with all critical issues in a short time. Therefore, it is important to revisit a vision/architecture statement regularly to resolve issues not dealt with earlier and to determine if the information vision still meets the needs of the business. In any case, attention to architecture decisions is critical for the business manager and IS organization leadership.

Planners must have an understanding of the environment in which they make their plans. Such understanding includes knowledge not only of the competitive marketplace in which the company operates but also of the strengths and weaknesses of its own IS department, its relative maturity, and the ways by which the IS plan will be linked to the business plan.

The information resources planning process should be documented and controlled. Documentation ranges from the broad objectives stated in the strategic IS plan to the detailed staffing requirements and expense forecasts made in the short-term operational IS plan. The overall IS plan should provide a well-documented road map from which the firm can navigate. The IS plan should mirror and be clearly linked to the business plan.

A number of tools exist for the development of an IS plan. The methodology most appropriate for the organization should be determined as the result of a conscious thought process. A number of tools can be used to identify strategic opportunities to be assimilated into the IS plan. As firms continue to realize the increased importance of information resources planning, greater emphasis will be placed on comprehensive planning methodologies.

CHAPTER REVIEW QUESTIONS

1. How does the information technology architecture differ from an informative vision?
2. List the critical IT issues about which Figure 13.2 makes an explicit statement. Why do you think these particular areas were specified?
3. What important issues are not addressed in Figure 13.2 that would normally be part of a complete information resources assessment? Why weren't these issues covered?
4. How would you respond to the criticism that a particular architecture is not feasible based on today's technology?
5. What are the benefits of stating an architecture by means of a picture rather than a text statement? What are the problems?
6. Consider the objectives for the IS department shown in Table 13.1. What other functions or responsibilities normally assigned to the IS organization should have objectives?
7. Describe the basic steps in the development of an IS strategic plan
8. Contrast the critical success factors (CSFs) and SWOT (strengths, weaknesses, opportunities, and threats) approaches to strategic IS planning.

CHAPTER DISCUSSION QUESTIONS

1. In addition to the reasons listed in the chapter, what other issues or events might cause an organization to recognize the need for an information resources plan?
2. What are the major implications for the business manager if a review of current practices indicates substantial inconsistency in the information vision and architecture for the company? For the IS director?
3. Compare and contrast the mission statements contained in Figures 13.3 and 13.4.
4. How might the human assets architecture described in Figure 13.7 have an impact on the company's technological assets architecture?
5. What are the user implications of the technological assets architecture shown in Figure 13.6?
6. What are some of the most important problems that would likely be encountered in working toward the architectures in Figures 13.6 and 13.7?
7. Through which media can an information vision and architecture be represented? What are the advantages of each approach?
8. Making assumptions when necessary, construct an IT architecture that is consistent with the Atlanta printing company's information vision explained in the section of this chapter entitled "Creating an Information Vision."
9. Given the rapid rate of change in IT capabilities, do you believe that strategic IS planning efforts are worthwhile, let alone realistic? Why or why not?
10. As information technologies continue to advance, is it reasonable to assert that in many instances the strategic IS plan will drive the business strategic plan instead of being driven by it? Why or why not? Can you think of an example where this might be the case?
11. Do you believe that strategic advantages obtained by the effective use of IT are sustainable? Why?
12. In what phases of the IS planning process is the business manager most likely to be involved? What are his or her responsibilities likely to be during each of the stages?
13. What role do you envision the business manager playing in plan justification as the benefits of proposed systems become increasingly difficult to quantify?

CASE STUDY: SCENARIOS ON THE FUTURE OF IS MANAGEMENT

The question M. Lynne Markus of Bentley College pondered in developing her scenarios was, "What will IS management look like in 10 years?" In studying IT and IT industry trends, business management trends, and societal trends, she noted that a straight-line extrapolation of the trends would have all organizations acquiring their IT-enabled products and services from external providers through a variety of arrangements, including partnerships, long-term contracts, and spot transactions. To explore the future of IS management, she settled on two driving uncertainties:

- How will companies coordinate IT? Will they use traditional hierarchical coordination mechanisms or pooled organizational forms?
- How will companies manage their data, or content? Will they benefit from managing their own proprietary data or will content be managed by fee-charging external service providers?

These lead to four possible scenarios, as shown in Figure 13.18.

Scenario 1: The Firewall Scenario—Locking the Barn Door after the Horse Got Loose. In this scenario, organizations maintain traditional arm's length relationships with suppliers and customers, and they believe data is proprietary. After a defining event, in which several companies go out of business from crashes in their computer systems that bring their business to a standstill, corporate managements take a concerned look at their IT operations. Many take on a bunker mentality; their main concerns are security and control. If they outsource their infrastructure to highly regarded outsourcers, they retain tight control over the vendors. All software is off-the-shelf and integrated by professional services firms. All data is housed in virtual bomb shelters. In essence, IS staff become general contractors and enforcement agencies.

Scenario 2: The Worknet Enterprise Scenario—Look Ma, No Hands. In this scenario, tough privacy legislation is enacted following highly publicized information leaks. Most companies then outsource data management to specialist service providers who comply with the new laws. However, the

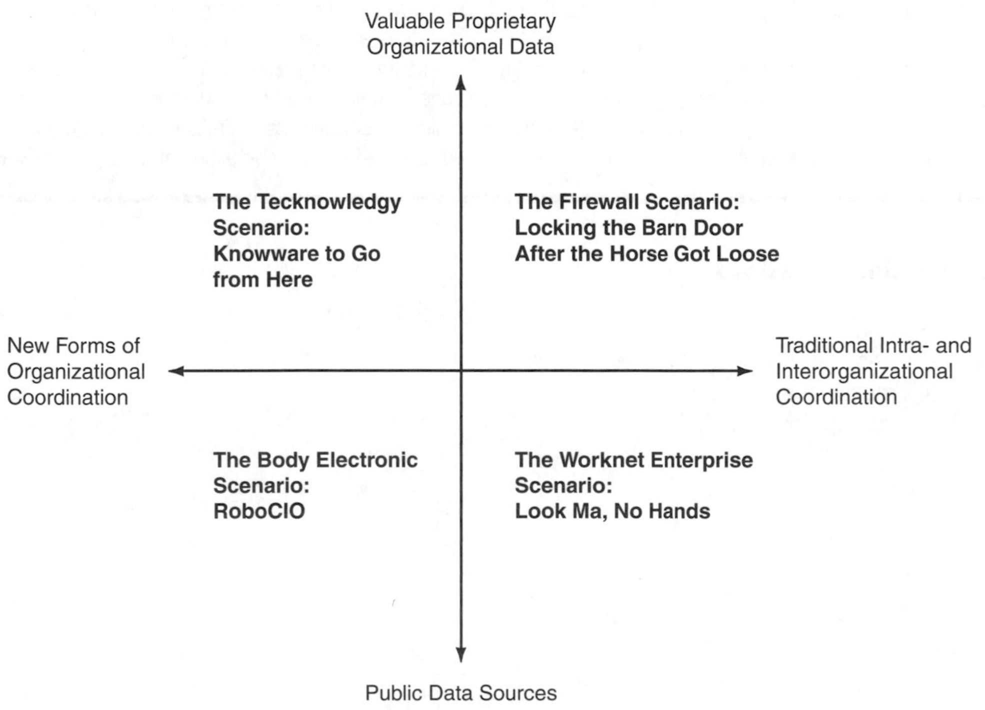

Figure 13.18 Four Scenarios on the Future of IS Management. *Source:* M. Lynnne Markus, "The Futures of IT Management," *The Data Base for Advances in Information Systems,* Vol. 27, No. 4 1996, pp. 68–84.

promised global network does not materialize, so companies cannot turn over their entire IT infrastructures to providers.

Companies continue their traditional arm's length relationships with other firms, but they use IT to mediate workflows between organizations. The result is that competition shifts to networked value chains, called worknets. Within these worknets, data is shared, generally through service providers that run interenterprise software packages for the worknet. Thus most IS organizations have handed over their IT work to their worknet's technology consortium, significantly reducing the costs of interworking with these partners. These consortia, themselves, are like self-managing virtual IS departments, so the IS staff in the contracting firms are mainly either change agents or information brokers tasked with helping the business uncover new uses of IT and implementing them.

Scenario 3: The Body Electric Scenario—RoboCIO. The triggering events in this scenario are availability of cheap, integrated networking services, plug-and-play computing devices, and portable health and pension plans (due to new legislation). As a result, new forms of organizations flower and data is more likely shared than guarded. In general, people own parts of the small, independent work units (cells) in which they work. Some work under a corporate umbrella; but many are autonomous, combining to deliver goods or services and then disbanding.

The standards for the global IT infrastructure that allow this interworking were created by a global consortium, and vendors adhere to the recommendations. The result is a highly flexible plug-and-play network of interconnected service providers and their services, called Technoos. Cells do virtually no IT work themselves, but they do need to find appropriate IT products and services. This searching is fairly automated and is called "value questing." The other piece of IT work is "IT facilitation," which involves helping cells change how they work when they either form a new alliance or adapt to a new type of software that changes their processes. Specialists can offer both services or they can be handled in-house as part of other jobs.

Scenario 4: The Tecknowledgy Scenario—Knowware to Go from Here. In this scenario, the growth of the Internet and the Web lead to an open information society. Any kind of information is available, for a price. People specialize in having (or knowing how to get) certain kinds of knowledge. Various kinds of intellectual capital have different, well-publicized value. Companies organize themselves to best develop and share knowledge. Those that learn fastest and share best are the most successful.

Knowware (advanced groupware) flourishes because it helps people and organizations share knowledge. In fact, knowware is the information technology most people use. It is part of organizational processes; it is how they work. Vendors maintain knowware, which handles administrative work as well, so few companies have IS departments. They rely fully on external providers. The downside is that changing knowware packages is unthinkable because the one a company adopts forms the foundation of its business. Many jobs even require prior knowledge of the knowware product in use in a company. Thus, the main IS job within companies is facilitation, ensuring that knowledge processes are maintained and employees understand them.

Case Study Discussion Questions

Question One

Which one of these scenarios do you think was more prevalent five years ago? Which is most common today?

Question Two

What do you think IS management will look like in the future?

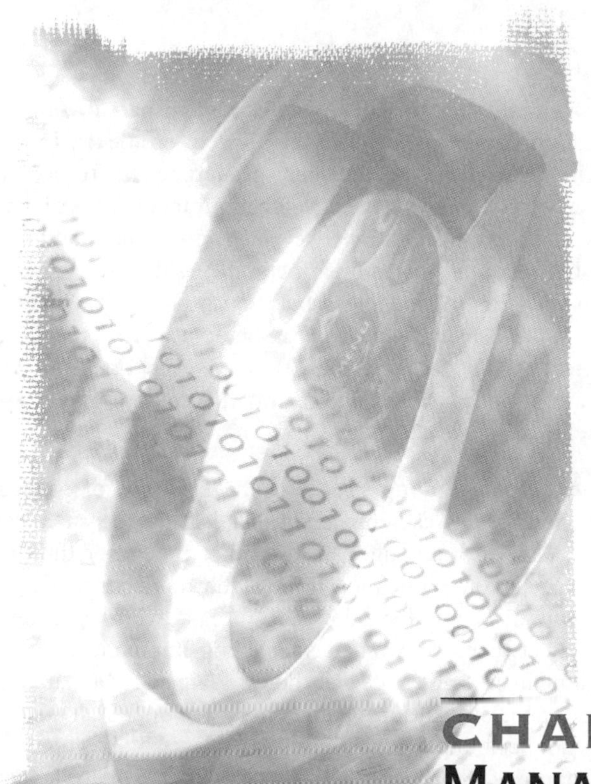

CHAPTER 14
MANAGING TECHNOLOGY RESOURCES

WAY BACK IN 1964, PAUL BARAN AT THE RAND CORPORATION WROTE a paper about distributed systems. At the time, computing meant mainframes and hardwired terminals; distributed systems were just theory. Today, distributed systems are the architecture of choice.

Definitions. To start, we need to point out that the two terms *architecture* and *infrastructure* are often used interchangeably, which can make discussions of distributed systems confusing. In this book, we make the following distinction:

> *An IT* architecture *is a blueprint. A blueprint shows how a system, house, vehicle, or product will look and how the parts interrelate. The more complex an item, the more important its architecture, so that the interrelationships among the components are well defined.*

> *An IT* infrastructure *is the implementation of an architecture. In a city, the infrastructure includes its streets and street lighting, hospitals and schools, utilities, police and fire departments, and so on. In a corporation, the IT infrastructure includes the processors, software, databases, electronic links, and data centers, as well as the standards that ensure that the components work together, the skills for managing the operation, and even some of the electronic processes themselves.*

The term *infrastructure* has become important in computing. Rather than talk about hardware, software, data, and communications as the components of computing, people now often refer to applications and infrastructure. The infrastructure provides the electronic highways, processing, and storage sites, whereas the applications use these facilities to produce value for the organization. Suffice it to say, when you hear *infrastructure*, think of city streets or electronic highways. At the end of this chapter, we delve into both architecture and infrastructure in a bit more depth after looking at the various kinds of distributed systems.

The Evolution of Distributed Systems. In the first IT architecture—mainframes doing batch processing—some input came from "dumb" terminals and some output went to "dumb" terminals. These "slave" user devices had no processing capabilities. All the processing was done by the "master" (the mainframe), and most was for corporate needs, such as payroll and billing. With the advent of minicomputers, computers moved into departments, but the master–slave model persisted. Processing was centralized; although gradually distribution or sharing of processing among mainframes and minicomputers began to occur.

With the microcomputer, though, the model changed significantly because processing power moved first onto desktops, then into briefcases, and now into handhelds, game consoles, MP3 players, and so on. In the 1990s, this distribution of processing led to processing being thought of as being split between a *client* that requests services and a *server* that provides those services. This concept of requesting services continues today and will be more important in the future as Web Services continues to develop (as discussed later in this chapter).

Throughout this evolution, stand-alone processors (or processors with dedicated terminals) appeared first and then were gradually linked to other computers. As that happened, the notion of a distributed architecture developed. Today, we have the Internet, an example of a global distributed system. Devices and computers of all sizes from any vendor that uses the appropriate standards use the Internet to send messages and files to each other, perform processing for each other, and house data for each other. The Internet has become the center of a worldwide distributed system. It is because of this global electronic infrastructure that the e-business revolution is taking place.

To get a grounding in this important notion in computing, we now delve into distributed system thinking.

Four Attributes of Distributed Systems

The degree to which a system is distributed can be determined by answering four questions:

1. Where is the processing done?
2. How are the processors and other devices interconnected?
3. Where is the information stored?
4. What rules or standards are used?

Distributed Processing. This is the ability for more than one interconnected processor to be operating at the same time, typically for processing an application on more than one computer. The goal in distributed processing is to move the appropriate processing as close to the user as possible and to let other machines handle the work they do best (such as house and manage video databases or process airline reservations).

An advanced form of distributed processing permits *interoperability*, which is the capability for different machines using different operating systems on different networks to work together on tasks. They exchange information in standard ways without requiring changes in functionality or physical intervention.

Charlie Bachman, a pioneer in the database and distributed systems fields, pointed out that only two forms of interoperability are possible. One is the transparent communication between systems using system protocols. In this form, the *systems* decide when to interoperate. To use the Internet, companies have developed protocols for standard file and job transfers to permit this form of interoperability. The second form of interoperability is the interactive or two-way flow of messages between user applications. In this form, *user applications* can be activated by receiving messages; this activity, of course, is supported on the Internet. Both kinds of interoperability are important, says Bachman.

Connectivity among Processors. This type of connectivity means that each processor in a distributed system can send data and messages to any other processor through electronic communication links. A desirable structure for reliable distributed systems has at least two independent paths between any two nodes, enabling automatic alternate routing in case one node goes down. Planned redundancy of this type is critical for reliable operation. Such redundancy has not been implemented in most LANs, which is one reason they have been so fragile. It is, however, a major feature of the Internet as well as most corporate WANs.

Distributed Databases. These are being defined in at least two ways. One divides a database and distributes its portions throughout a system without duplicating the data. Any portion is accessible from any node, subject to access authorization. Users do not need to know where a piece of data is located to access it, because the system knows where all data is stored.

The second type of distributed database stores the same data at several locations with one site containing the master file. Synchronization of data is a significant problem in this approach, which is why it has not been the preferred way to distribute data.

An interesting development in this area is edge servers on the Web. An *edge server* is defined as being on the edge of the Internet, which means it is close to a set of users (such as a city). It holds a copy of an organization's Web site. Many edge servers, located strategically around the world, hold the same information. The edge server concept arose to accelerate Web page downloads to site visitors so they would not leave the site because they had to wait too long to see a page appear on their screen. Edge servers—essentially distributed databases—have become an integral part of the Internet.

Systemwide Rules. These rules mean that an operating discipline for the distributed system has been developed and is enforced at all times. These rules govern communication between nodes, security, data accessibility, program and file transfers, and common operating procedures. Since the 1990s, these systemwide rules have been increasingly based on the *open system* concept. Products using open standards can operate together in one or more distributed systems, such as the Internet. One goal of users is to avoid being locked into the proprietary products of one vendor. Interestingly, the meaning of open systems has expanded over time as open systems have become a reality.

In the 1980s, open systems referred mainly to telecommunication and meant that a company intended to implement products that followed the OSI (Open Systems Interconnection) Reference Model whenever they became available. At that time, OSI implementation was not a reality, just a target.

About 1990, the definition of open systems expanded to include operating systems, specifically UNIX, because it runs on more platforms than any other operating system and is not owned by any one company. At that time, UNIX was tentatively seen as appropriate for mainline business computing. Today, it is an important operating system for servers on the Internet. In business computing, it has gained a foothold, but it has not displaced proprietary operating systems, such as Microsoft's Windows.

At the same time, in the data world, *open* meant structured query language (SQL), the standard intermediary language for accessing relational databases. SQL remains the standard today.

In the early 1990s, the definition shifted to the interfaces between applications. *Open* meant standardized interfaces that would allow products to interoperate across multivendor networks, operating systems, and databases. Application program interfaces (APIs) came into being. They define the way data is presented to another component of a system—a machine, a database, even an e-mail system. APIs allow individual products to be innovative, yet connectable, and they have made writing distributed systems far easier.

Today, the term *open* includes the already mentioned definitions and stresses interconnectivity. In this realm, the OSI reference model remains the definition of *open*. Most people, however, are only familiar with its widest implementation: the network protocol used in the Internet, TCP/IP. Corporate networks, both LANs and WANs, now use TCP/IP to ease interconnection to the Internet.

An interesting twist on the term *open* hit critical mass not long ago. When the Internet first arrived, it allowed programmers to offer software for free (or for a small donation), which many did. This freeware has come to be called *open source*, which means the source code can be downloaded by anyone and can be modified. (In purchased software, you only receive the compiled code, which is undecipherable.) The open source movement led to developers taking some freeware, improving it, and reposting it to the Internet. In the 1990s, Linus Torvalds offered his operating system, Linux, as open source; he has since gained a huge following. Developers around the world have contributed to it, improved it, and extended it. Because it is free, it is being used in a growing number of companies.

The term *open systems* keeps expanding because it truly is the crux of distributed systems, allowing products from multiple vendors to work together.

Although some people see the main reason for distributing systems as improving the use of computer resources, that is just a technical reason. The organizational impetus behind distributed systems is to move responsibility for computing resources to those who use them. The next section briefly addresses the business reasons for distributing applications and the responsibilities that go with them.

When to Distribute Computing Responsibilities

IS management needs a corporate policy for deciding when the development, operation, and maintenance of an application should be distributed. Individual end users and departments should not be left on their own to make these decisions, especially when enterprise connectivity and interenterprise connectivity are important. Although technical considerations are critical, they should not be the determining factors behind a system architecture. Rather, the major reason for choosing a particular distributed system architecture hinges on: *Who should make the key management operating decisions?*

Decision-making responsibilities are being pushed down and out in organizations, with local sites and teams being given more autonomy and responsibility for the resources they use. One such resource is IT. People who make the decisions about how their portion of the business operates also should be making the decisions about how they use IT. Teamwork between IS management and business management is important in designing a distributed processing architecture that supports the business's goals.

Francis Wagner, a computing pioneer, once said he believes people perform best when they are responsible for their own mistakes. If they have no one to blame but themselves, then the quality of their performance increases. The result is a more effective use of corporate resources.

Therefore, a driving force behind distributed processing is the desire to give more people more control over their work. This autonomy can happen at any of seven levels: ecosystem, company, division, site, department, team, or individual.

Professor James Wetherbe suggested asking the following three business questions before distributing IT functions and the responsibilities that go with them. Systems responsibilities can be distributed *unless* the following are true.

Are the Operations Interdependent? When it is important for one operation to know what another is doing, those operations are interdependent; thus, their planning, software development, machine resources, and operations need to be centrally coordinated to synchronize their operation. Two industries in which interdependency is important are manufacturing and airlines, which is why they have continued to have large centralized systems even in this era of distributed systems.

Are the Businesses Really Homogeneous? If the operations do not need to know what the other is doing, then many systems functions can be decentralized, unless the operations truly have a lot in common.

For example, in the fast food business, each franchise has the same information processing needs, which makes them homogeneous. But they do not need to know what the other is doing; thus, they are not interdependent. Under these circumstances, processing may be distributed, but planning, software development, and hardware selection should be centralized, to keep processing costs down and to more easily migrate to new systems.

Deciding whether the information processing in two parts of a business is truly homogeneous is not always obvious, says Wetherbe. For instance, not all retail chains are the same. One major retailer found that it needed to create two information systems for handling credit charges—one for its upscale stores and one for its discount stores. The needs of the two types of stores were so different that a single system would not suffice. However, corporate IS does control planning, which gives the retailer the ability to seize marketing opportunities quickly when it can reuse systems built by either operation. He says that centralized planning is important whether processing is distributed or not.

Does the Corporate Culture Support Decentralization? Even if the business units do quite different things and do not need to know what the other is doing, corporate culture might dictate that some functions be centralized.

Wetherbe cites the example of a large company with 60 widely diverse business units. Although it might appear logical for this company to distribute all functions, management chose to centralize finance, HR, and systems planning. They want to offer corporatewide career opportunities with as little retraining as possible. With central staff doing systems planning and coordination, the company can more easily move people and reuse systems.

If none of these three criteria—interdependency, homogeneity, or corporate culture—forces centralization, each business unit can direct its own IT activity, with the central organization coordinating the plans.

Two Guiding Frameworks

Now that we have briefly addressed why to distribute systems, we now look at how to distribute systems via two guiding frameworks: one from an organizational perspective and the other from a technical perspective.

An Organizational Framework. One possible distributed system structure looks at serving seven organizational levels. Figure 14.1 illustrates the seven levels.

1. Business ecosystem or value chain (interenterprise)
2. Enterprise
3. Country or region
4. Site (plants, warehouses, branch offices)
5. Department or process
6. Work group or team
7. Individuals

The top level deals with organizations that work closely together, such as buyers and sellers or partners in a business ecosystem. The other six exist within a single organization; they may or may not link to other organizations. The current hot levels are one (interenterprise computing) and five, where companies are changing from a functional orientation to a process orientation. In the area of SCM, for example, companies want to electronically share information about customer orders and the status of internal operations with suppliers so that those suppliers can have the specific parts on hand when needed. Interenterprise and process thinking require linking disparate systems in different organizations. This linkage can be made firm-to-firm or through intermediaries, such as electronic exchanges, which act as matchmakers over the Internet. The Internet is playing an important role in creating interenterprise electronic links for processes.

Work groups and teams have also become tremendously important as companies change how they work. We see two types of work groups at level 6. One type of work

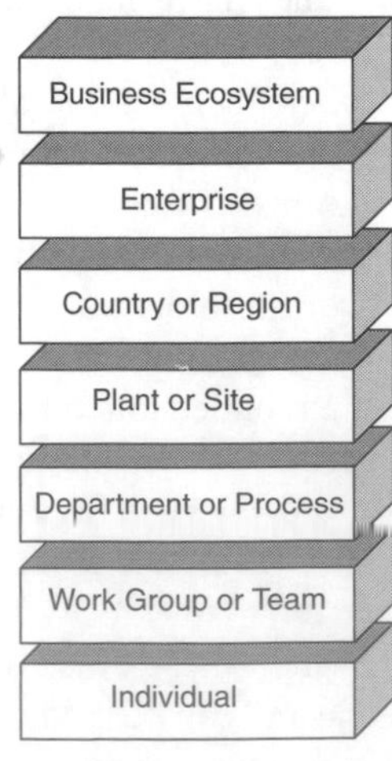

Figure 14.1 A Seven-Level Organizational Framework

group is people who do essentially the same work. Anyone in the group can substitute for any other, if necessary. Such groups are found in the customer service centers of small ISPs, where the reps need to be able to answer questions on every facet of linking to the Internet. In large ISPs, reps often specialize in answering questions on specific operating systems. Both groups need systems to support their work with customers.

The second type of group or team is self-managed work teams. They contain all the people who serve a particular set of customers or offer a particular product. These people represent all the necessary functions, such as manufacturing, marketing, customer service, and so forth. The intent is to give them more autonomy and decision-making power to serve their customers better. By allowing them to manage themselves, it is hoped they will provide more personalized and faster service. They need their own systems. However, these systems will be far different from the ones needed by the ISP reps.

In all, systems are needed for each of the seven organizational levels. Interorganizational links can occur at all six internal levels as well.

A Technical Framework. Way back in 1982, Einar Stefferud, David Farber, and Ralph Dement developed a conceptual framework for distributed systems. It uses the acronym SUMURU, meaning "single user, multiple user, remote utility." Surprisingly, SUMURU is as appropriate today as it was in 1982, perhaps even more so because distributed systems are today's architecture. Their framework includes four components: processors, networks, services, and standards. Figure 14.2 summarizes the SUMURU components, and Figure 14.3 illustrates the architecture.

Processors. The authors see three levels of processors, usually with associated information storage. The name of their architecture, SUMURU, comes from these three levels of processors. *Single-user systems* (SUs) can operate in a standalone mode but also will be connected to local networks. Today, SUs are the clients in distributed systems. *Multiple-user systems* (MUs) serve local groups of users. Today, they are work group servers in corporate LANs. These MUs also provide (1) backup facilities for other MUs, (2) heavier-duty processing for SUs, (3) program libraries for themselves and SUs, and (4) database management for central files. Ideally, say the authors, SUs are scaled-down versions of the MUs, able to run the same software (to reduce software development and maintenance) but without all the features needed for shared operation on an MU.

Remote utility systems (RUs) provide heavy-duty computing, corporate database management, remote processing, and backup for MUs. For most organizations, RUs are the corporate hosts, although they are increasingly becoming external service providers (ESPs) that run corporate data centers or corporate applications. They may house and operate a company's Web site operation, its extranet, and even its intranet. Or they may handle the HR functions for a firm. In addition, Web sites on the Internet can be considered RUs, especially if they provide subscription services to firms.

Networks. The authors see a network architecture consisting of two levels. *Local networks* (LNs) provide high-speed information transfer as well as close coupling between several SUs and a local MU. Today, these are LANs. MUs may provide personal files, shared files, and program libraries for SUs, and they can be the gateway between the LNs and remote networks.

Remote networks (RNs) provide connections among MUs and connections to both in-house and commercial RUs. RNs, which today include metropolitan area networks (MANs), WANs, cell phone and satellite networks, and the Internet, generally have lower transfer speeds than LNs, but they still should have enough bandwidth to provide downloads within reasonable time limits.

Processors	***Services***
Single-user systems (SU)	Terminal access
Multiple-user systems (MU)	File transfer
Remote utility systems (RU)	Computer mail
Networks	***Standards***
Local networks (LN)	Operating systems
Remote networks (RN)	Communications protocols
	Database systems

Figure 14.2 Components of the SUMURU Distributed System Architecture. *Source:* E. Stefferud, D. Farber, and R. Dement, "SUMURU: A Network Configuration for the Future," *Mini-Micro Systems*, May 1982, pp. 311–312.

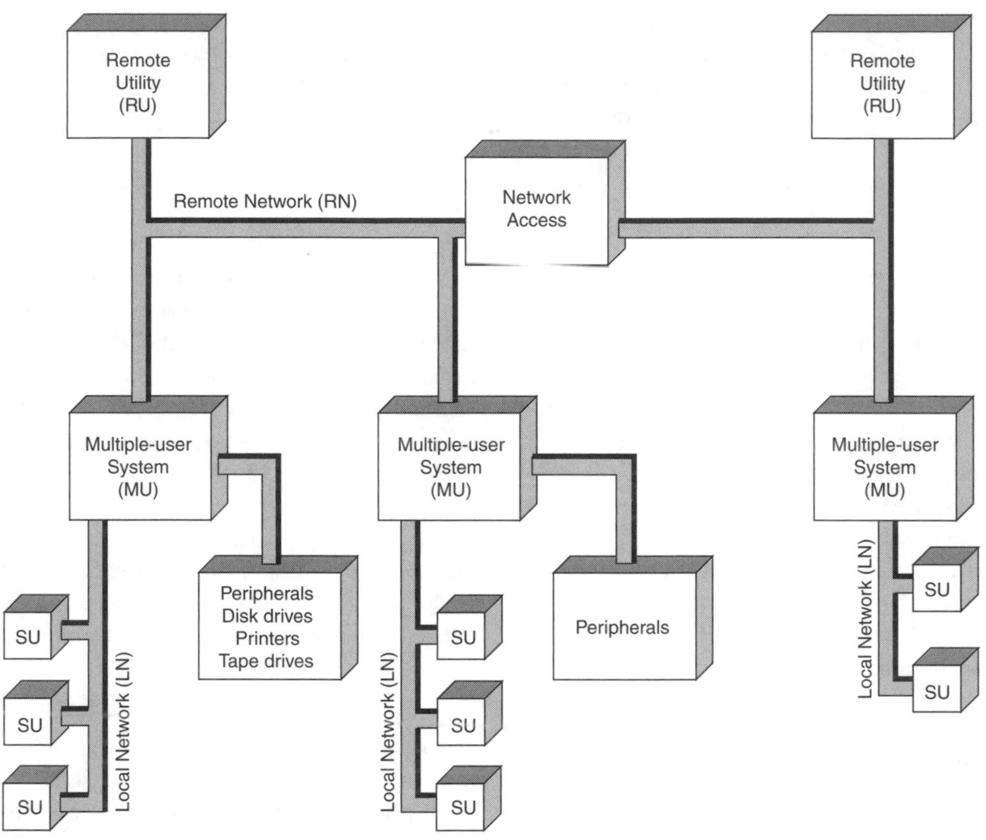

Figure 14.3 The SUMURU Architecture. *Source:* E. Stefferud, D. Farber, and R. Dement, "SUMURU: A Network Configuration for the Future," *Mini-Micro Systems*, May 1982, pp. 311–312.

Services. The authors see three main types of services in this network architecture. One service is *access* to any SU, MU, or RU, subject only to management constraints, not technical barriers. Users must also have *file transfer* capabilities to send and receive files, which means having both read and write privileges at both ends of the transfer. Finally, the system must provide an *e-mail* service. Note that all three are available to PCs via the Internet. The challenge today is providing the same capabilities to handheld devices via wireless computing.

Standards. Standards are needed in three areas: operating systems, communication protocols, and DBMSs. Operating system standards are designed to minimize barriers to transferring and using programs and data. Ideally, the selected operating systems should run on more than one vendor's equipment. Standard communication protocols are needed for access, file transfers, and e-mail. In the communication area, TCP/IP (which is used in the Internet) has become the de facto standard. In the database arena, no distributed DBMS has become a standard, although SQL has become the language of choice for accessing different databases.

We believe this distributed system framework has stood the test of time; it is still an appropriate design guide for distributed system architects. Although not often used these days, it provides a clear conceptual framework for understanding the various components of a distributed system.

Now we turn to some specifics: seven system structures that have been called distributed.

SEVEN TYPES OF DISTRIBUTED SYSTEMS

As noted earlier, the distributed systems field has been continually evolving. The seven forms of distributed systems basically developed as follows.

Host-Based Hierarchy

A hierarchy of processors was the first distributed system structure. It was favored by mainframe vendors because the large host computer at the top controlled the terminals below. It is a master–slave relationship. More than one level of processors can be part of this hierarchy, as shown in Figure 14.4, with the total workload shared among them. The important characteristic of this structure is that the host computer is the central and controlling component. The other important characteristic is that the processing is done on the computers. The terminals are simply access devices; they have no processor or hard disk.

It is not always clear just where to store the data in such a system. One view is to store all data at the top. Another is to have the master records at the top but selected subsets at intermediate levels; the master records are then updated periodically and revised records are sent to the intermediate files. Still another view is to store master records where they are most used and periodically provide updated records to the top for backup purposes. In any of these views, though, it is assumed that any processor can access any data record in the hierarchy, as long as it is authorized to do so.

Thin clients are diskless computers meant to obtain their applications from a server (perhaps on the Internet). They are an intriguing flashback to this form of distributed computing, but they have two important distinctions from the terminals of old. One, they initiate requests; terminals of old did not. Two, they can do local processing; terminals could not. It is not the same master–slave relationship as with mainframes and terminals. Thin-client thinking is being used for handhelds requesting tasks over the Internet.

Decentralized Stand-Alone Systems

Decentralized stand-alone systems do not really form a distributed system at all. They are basically a holdover from the 1960s, when departments put in their own minicomputers with no intention of connecting them to the corporate host or to other departmental systems. Hence, they are decentralized, not distributed (see Figure 14.5). Over the years, many such "islands of computing" have appeared and still exist. They have been connected to allow a little data to flow, but this flow has been mostly upward to the corporate host.

A major goal in introducing ERP systems was to replace such disparate systems—in finance, manufacturing, administration—with a single platform of interconnectable modules to serve these various functions.

Peer-to-Peer LAN-Based Systems

LANs have been the basis for distributed systems of desktop machines since the 1980s. This approach began in the office system arena with LANs providing the links between PCs, print servers, and gateways to other networks. As shown in Figure 14.6, this structure has no hierarchy. No computer is more superior than another. Communications among the components are *peer to peer* rather than through a hierarchy using a central hub. It is the key characteristic of this structure. A new development in this area is peer-to-peer wireless LANs, as discussed in the next chapter.

Hybrid Enterprisewide Systems

The typical structure of distributed systems today draws on these three forms of distributed systems linking them via three kinds of networks: MANs, WANs, and the Internet. This system is illustrated in Figure 14.7. Today's distributed systems mix and match hierarchical host-based processing favored for corporate and Web site computing with departmental processing favored by departments such as

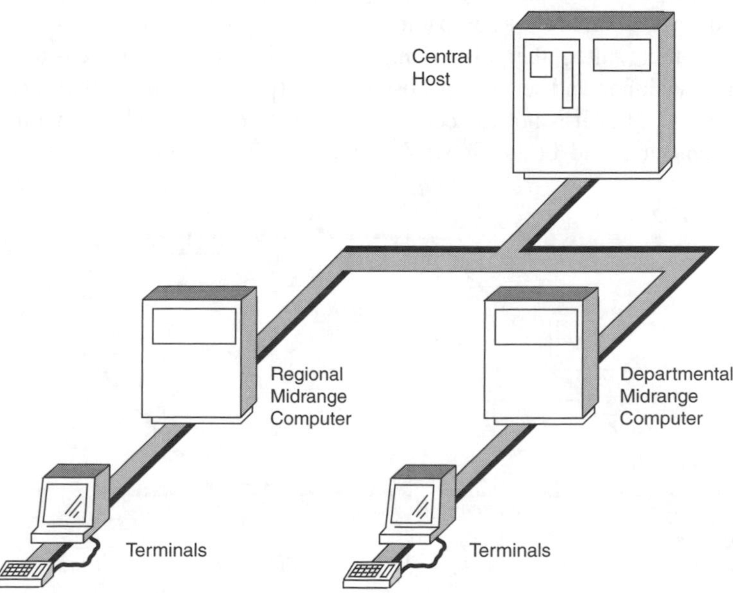

Figure 14.4 Host-Based Hierarchy

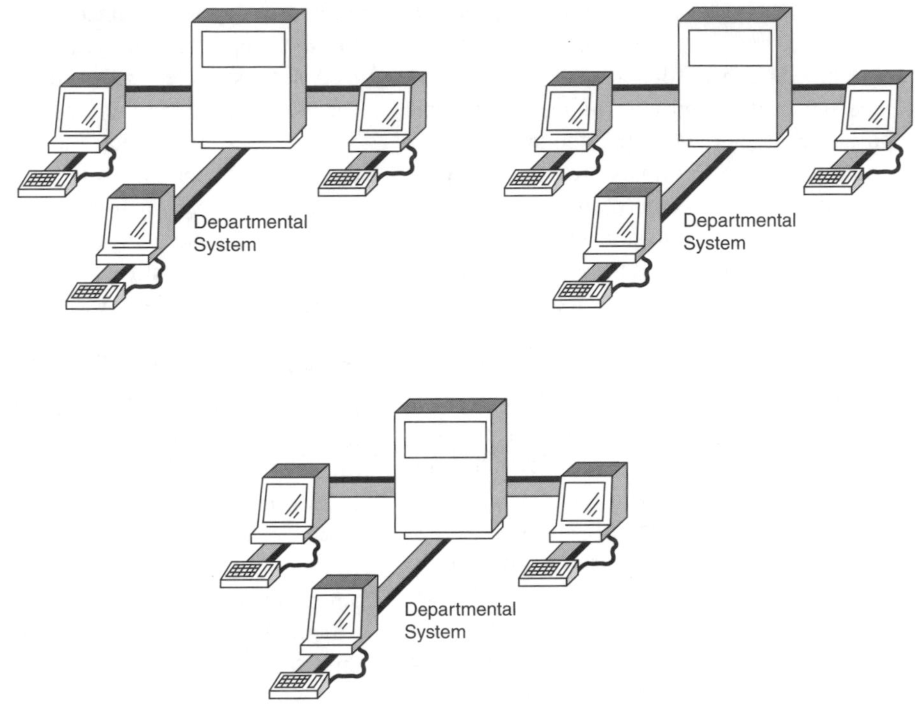

Figure 14.5 Decentralized Stand-Alone Systems

manufacturing and engineering and the LAN-based systems used in offices. This hybrid structure is likely to be the structure of choice for many years as companies link their various islands of automation and increasingly link to systems in other organizations.

One important point is that this hybrid approach does not necessarily put all the machines under the aegis of a host mainframe computer. In fact, a number of companies have gotten rid of their mainframe(s) altogether, dispersing applications to departmental machines and servers. A host computer is shown in Figure 14.7, but it is not the central control. For some applications, it could be the host; for others, it could be merely just another server, perhaps a "compute server."

A second important point is that this structure allows companies to automate business processes that span several functions within the organization or work cooperatively with systems in other enterprises. Interenterprise computing is the tenet of e-business. For example, to obtain sporting event tickets, once you enter your order on a ticketing Web site, the system needs to verify that the seats are available (probably on another system), it needs to verify that your credit is good (on another system), and if both are satisfied, it processes the order. Currently, tickets are

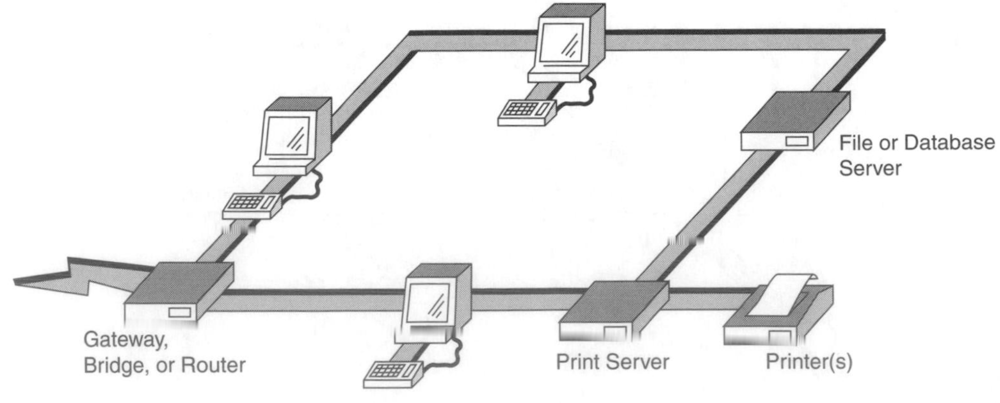

Figure 14.6 Peer-to-Peer LAN-Based System

mailed to you, but if your printer had an IP address (which is possible), your tickets could be electronically sent to a ticket broker (yet another system) who then sends them to your printer where they are printed out.

Such cooperating processes allow companies to take advantage of specialized computer programs, while at the same time extending the usefulness of some legacy systems. The process of pulling together such individual applications or components is called *system integration.* On pages 510–511 is an example of a mainstream application that uses these distributed processing principles and was built via system integration.

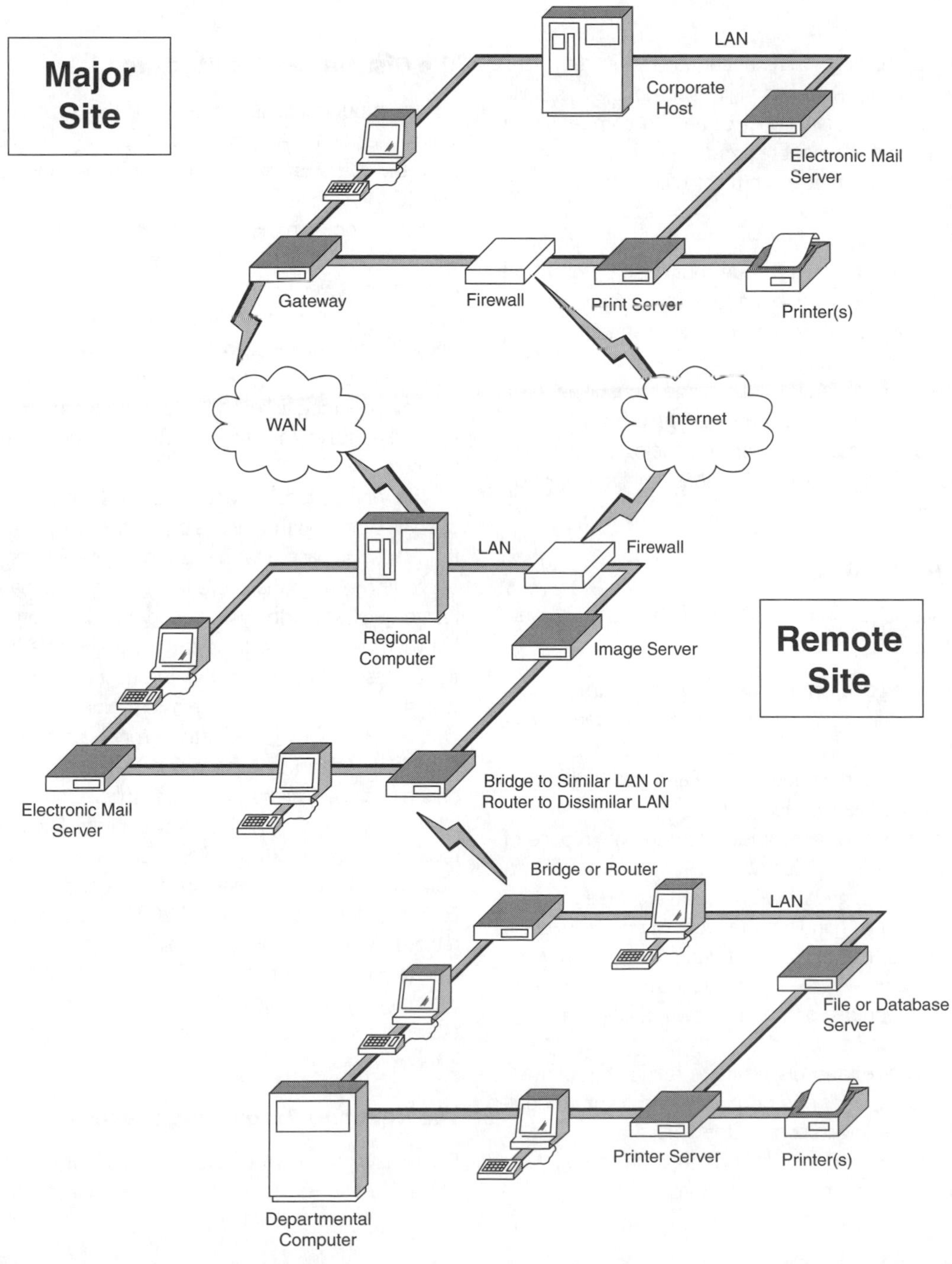

Figure 14.7 Hybrid Enterprisewide System

CASE EXAMPLE

NORTHWEST AIRLINES

When Northwest Airlines, with headquarters in St. Paul, Minnesota, merged with Republic Airlines, it doubled its business and became a major national carrier. To compete as a world-class carrier, management realized they had to revamp a number of core systems. One system calculates revenue from passengers.

At the time, Northwest sampled a small percentage of its passenger tickets to estimate revenue, but this approach did not yield accurate passenger or revenue data. To improve accuracy, it needed to audit all redeemed tickets—something few major airlines did at the time.

With the help of Accenture, the large consulting firm, Northwest built a system that integrates products from 11 vendors and just about as many different technologies, including expert systems, imaging, relational databases, high-resolution workstations, servers, and LANs.

Management's Goals

Management established six major goals for the passenger revenue accounting (PRA) system:

1. Enforce pricing and commission rules to ensure services are properly priced and travel agencies sell them at correct fares.
2. Calculate corporate earned income and track and reconcile air transport liability accounting.
3. Cope with the volume explosion and the rapid pace of change in the airline industry.
4. Unhook volume growth from staff increases so the department could handle more work without equivalent staff increases. The department had grown 700 percent to 600 people. At that projected growth rate, the department would soon need its own building unless it changed the way it worked.
5. Gather, organize, and disseminate marketing information for making decisions on pricing and flight scheduling and responding to competitors' moves.
6. Provide the flexibility to audit and report on special deals with travel agents and corporate purchasers.

The Distributed Architecture

Data communication is an integral part of this distributed system, which uses both LANs and a MAN among three buildings. The host IBM 3090 is linked to the backbone Ethernet LAN via an SNA-TCP/IP gateway.

The Ethernet backbone acts as a MAN, linking numerous Ethernet subnetworks. Ten of the subnetworks connect a Sun application server to about 40 diskless Sun workstations, which run UNIX. Northwest minimizes traffic across the backbone by designing the network to keep most client-to-server traffic on each subnet. Northwest also has an image server for storing images of redeemed ticket coupons. Several specialized servers perform the ticket auditing each night using expert system technology.

The workstations provide the PRA auditors with windows to the data stored on the various systems: the mainframe that stores the ticket database, external computer reservation systems, the application servers that store tickets with discrepancies, and the image database. The system accommodates large file transfers between these workstations and the mainframe because part of the processing is done on the IBM host and part is done on the workstations. For these file transfers, Northwest created a standard way for COBOL applications (on the mainframe) to talk to C applications (on the workstations). The workstations also draw on the host applications via 3270-terminal emulation on the Suns.

Image processing is also a key element. Each day, Northwest receives some 50,000 auditor coupons from travel agents and 100,000 lift coupons (redeemed ticket stubs) from passengers. Formerly, Northwest employed 20 to 40 people full-time just to retrieve these coupons from their huge storage basement. Now, Northwest scans both types of coupons, creating a photograph-like image and an index for each one. The images are stored on optical disks in jukeboxes, which store the platter-like disks in a jukebox fashion.

The Revenue Accounting Process

Each day, Northwest receives data from three sources: (1) magnetic tapes of ticket sales taken from computer reservation systems and consolidated by regional clearinghouses, (2) audit coupons from travel agents, and (3) lift coupons redeemed from passengers as they board a plane.

The sales data is stored in a DB2 relational database and processed on the IBM mainframe. If all the information is not provided, the sales data is queued to an auditor, who adds the missing information by viewing the appropriate auditor coupon image. Then, the sales data for performing the nighttime audits is downloaded to Sun servers, and a C program retrieves all the travel agency rules that apply to each ticket.

At night, the sales data is run through expert systems, which apply the appropriate rules to recalculate the lowest fare, commission, and taxes. If the recalculation does not match the travel agency's auditor coupon data, the recalculation and corresponding coupon image are made available to an auditor for review.

The next morning, Northwest auditors view the various pieces of data in different windows on their workstations and they decide how to handle the discrepancies. Because all the coupon images are available electronically, handling one box of coupons takes 2 to 3 hours rather than 2 to 3 days.

When passengers' redeemed flight coupons are received by the department, the verified sales data is credited as earned income. Monthly books now close on the seventh of the month, which is one-half the time previously required. Thus, earned revenue can be recognized 50 percent faster.

Lessons Learned

Northwest learned the following four major lessons about developing complex distributed systems such as PRA.

1. ***Benchmark and prototype new technologies to verify vendors' claims.*** Do not let vendors run the benchmarks by themselves. In image processing, for instance, have the vendors scan most of the kinds of documents in the application, especially if different kinds of paper and different colors of ink are common.
2. ***An open architecture works on mission-critical applications.*** PRA integrated a variety of technologies. By using an open architecture, Northwest reduced its risk in building such a system. Risk was further controlled by creating an interface to these systems that shielded the developers from the technicalities of the new technologies. Finally, integration was demonstrated early through a small test project.
3. ***Large distributed system projects need vendor coordinator.*** Due to the complexity of PRA, a clean design for creating a stable set of specifications for the vendors was unlikely; therefore, a big challenge was keeping the right people on the Northwest, Accenture, and vendor teams informed of current status. To fill this role, a full-time coordinator made sure all the various project teams stayed in close contact with each other. Otherwise, the various components would not have worked together.
4. ***Use of a computer-based development methodology was mandatory.*** Management believes that Northwest could not have done a project of this size without the tools and approaches of a computer-based methodology. For one thing, it allowed developers to work on different components in parallel. Without it, they could not have supported the team of up to 170 developers. Furthermore, it allowed users to play a larger role in development; even to the point of using the design tool to document user procedures, design reports, and supply the text in the help system. Finally, it allows them to use the data definitions from PRA in other systems, which will substantially shorten development time and improve system quality.

The huge system, which took 65,000 workdays to complete, has become a model for airline revenue accounting systems. Managers from more than a dozen airlines around the world have visited Northwest to study it.

To illustrate the versatility of Java-based computing, following are two case studies from IBM's Web site. IBM, like most vendors, has wholeheartedly embraced the integration of the Internet into business computing, using the Java language to do so.

Server-based Computing. With more and more employees carrying their offices with them on laptop computers, security and operational concerns have increased. Laptops do not have strong security features, updating them en masse is not easy, and even individual downloads can require help-desk support.

The solution companies are turning to is *server-based computing*, where applications reside on corporate servers rather than on the laptops. With server-based computing, applications can be securely accessed by any device, they can be updated directly on the server, and they do not have to be tailored to run on specific machines.

CASE EXAMPLE

CHUBB & SON INSURANCE COMPANY

Chubb is a multinational property and casualty insurance company. Management decided to take advantage of the Internet by converting legacy systems to Java-based systems. For example, they converted their cargo certificate issuance system into an extranet application. The application is used to insure ocean shipments and has proven especially important for customers outside the United States. Importers, exporters, freight forwarders, and banks can draw on this application to round out the services they offer shippers.

Likewise, Chubb has put its builder's risk application on its extranet. This application is used to provide insurance policies to builders of small inland marinas. The application is like "an underwriter in a box" so that agents can rate, quote, and book a policy immediately, making Chubb easy to do business with.

Similarly, Chubb launched a self-service accident benefit life application on the Internet so that consumers can obtain travel insurance at various travel sites at the same time they purchase tickets online.

All three applications feed into Chubb's mainframe but have a Java-based Web front end so that client machines only need access to the Web to perform the application. Users do not need special application software on their machines.

Chubb has used a number of IBM technologies to convert these applications, including VisualAge for Java and WebSphere Application Server. Chubb's goal is not only to make the applications Web-centric, but also to deliver them in record time. Chubb believes that by moving to thin-client delivery, where Java applets are delivered to client machines on demand, they can reduce their total cost of ownership by 30 to 40 percent.

Previously, Chubb developed applications in the client-server world using IBM's VisualAge Smalltalk, which is an object-oriented language. When Visual-Age for Java became available, Chubb decided to try it out to move client-server applications to the Web. Much to Chubb's pleasure, IS management discovered developers could reuse some 15 percent of their code (even some of the most difficult-to-write portions), so the migration to Web-centricity was not as difficult as they had anticipated.

CASE EXAMPLE

THE SABRE GROUP

IBM has worked with the SABRE Group (the airline reservation company) and Nokia (the cell phone manufacturer) to create a real-time, interactive service delivered via cell phone.

The service allows business travelers to not only receive updates from airlines (anytime, anyplace) but to even initiate changes. For example, if a meeting runs significantly over and the travelers realize they are going to miss their flight, they can request flight details using their Internet-enabled Nokia phone and make new travel arrangements. Travelers can also make or change hotel reservations, rental car reservations, and so forth. Likewise, if a flight is delayed or cancelled, the service notifies travelers so they can adjust their itineraries.

The service draws on SABRE's online corporate travel purchasing system and Nokia's server, which transmits the travel information to a wireless network and to its Internet-enabled phones. The service utilizes XML (eXtended Markup Language), a language that allows objects to be identified by type, which is important for constructing a user's Web site screen on-the-fly, custom-tailored to that user. It also uses Java, a language for writing small applets used to deliver applications over the Internet. In this case, SABRE is using Java to translate its travel information into XML. Finally, it is using Wireless Markup Language (WML), a language for presenting XML information to Internet-enabled devices.

Server-based computing is also replacing the need to install servers at remote offices. Small offices, with, say, 10 workstations, can be handled just as well by a remote server, which IS staff at the headquarters can maintain more easily. In some cases, all that is needed at the remote offices are thin clients.

The example below illustrates server-based computing.

Peer-to-Peer Computing. One of the most intriguing forms of Internet-based computing is peer-to-peer (P2P) computing. With P2P, tasks are distributed over a wide number of computers (peers) connected to the Internet. It is a grassroots movement, much like the open source movement, but some corporations now take it seriously.

The most infamous example of P2P was Napster, a central directory of music, and the PCs on which the music was located. Using Napster software, people could find music titles at the Napster site and then download that music from the listed PCs. Everyone swapped with everyone. Napster was infamous because the music industry contended it infringed on copyright laws by encouraging music piracy. It eventually closed down.

Author Jeremy Rifkin says that the Napster dispute goes to the heart of two economies: the old economy that is made up of buyers and sellers and the e-economy that has clients and servers. He believes the Napster model will eventually win out because it allows worldwide distribution of intangibles (even an entire music collection) faster than ringing up the sale of a single CD. Furthermore, Web distribution reduces traditional production costs—including distribution, packaging, inventory, and merchandising. At the same time that sales of hard goods aim to maximize production, distribution via Web sites aims to pool risks and share savings.

The issue has been how to make money in the P2P environment. Rifkin believes subscriptions will replace sales. People will pay for access rather than for ownership. Why buy one CD when you can have unlimited access to a continually growing gigantic music collection for a month? he asks. In physical markets, physical property is purchased. In networks, access to experiences is purchased. When hyperspeed and continuous change are the norm, it makes less sense to own and more sense to subscribe. Furthermore, continual connection provides other benefits, such as a steady stream of new music or other intangibles. Thus, says Rifkin, Napster is just the tip of the iceberg.

Web Services

The forms of Internet-based computing just described could be considered first-generation Internet-based distributed systems. Web Services are said to be the second generation. The term refers to software modules that have a URL,

CASE EXAMPLE

3i

3i, which stands for "Investors In Industry," is a U.K.-based venture capital firm. To expand beyond England to Southeast Asia and the United States, the company needed to give its investment professionals anytime-anywhere access to its systems. With this access, staff members could conduct business and complete a deal on the spot with just a laptop and a modem. To permit such location-independent remote and mobile working with up-to-date information in users' laptops, 3i turned to server-based computing.

3i called on Specialist Computer Centre in England to create new data centers in the United Kingdom and elsewhere. These centers consist of Citrix application server software installed on Hewlett-Packard servers.

Remote employees dial in to one of the centers through a secure modem service, which uses both authentication to verify their identify and encryption to jumble the messages. Using Microsoft Windows terminal server software and Citrix software, the staff create their own virtual offices. They have secure access to 120 in-house applications, all of which are housed on a variety of devices. The sessions are managed by the Citrix software.

From the IS department's point of view, the applications are much easier to manage because the software is housed in one place. Thus, updates are made once and remote employees always use the latest version. If employees had the software on their machines, all laptops would need to be updated at once, which is a difficult task.

The arrangement has allowed 3i to expand globally and let its employees work wherever they happen to be.

that is, an Internet address, so that they can be called upon to perform their function (as a service) via the Internet. Today, we use the Web for people-to-computer communication. We access a Web page by typing in its URL. Gottschalk and his colleagues call this the *eyeball Web*.

Web Services, on the other hand, is computer-to-computer use of the Internet. One computer program or Web Service makes a request of another Web Service to perform its task (or set of tasks) and pass back the answer. Gottschalk et al. call this the *transactional Web*, and they believe it will be dominated by program-to-program, business-to-business interactions. In essence, many Web Services calling upon each other form a highly distributed system.

Web Services is a very hot topic for many reasons. For one, people see it as the next generation of distributed services because it allows the building of large, complex systems by linking together any number of modules that each perform one or a few tasks. Two, it makes the Internet the hub of computing, which aims to ease interenterprise computing (something many enterprises want). Three, it permits flexible systems not possible in the past, because a Web Service can choose which other Web Service(s) to utilize at the time it needs one. Traditionally, sequences of steps have had to be hard wired (preprogrammed) ahead of time. With the dynamic binding of Web Services, this decision can be made at execution time, making systems far more flexible. Four, Web Services can possibly release companies from having to build and maintain so much software in-house. The promise is that they can rent functionality via Web Services either on a subscription basis or as needed. Five, Web Services will draw on existing systems. Web Services can be used as a *wrappering* technology, state Gottschalk et al. Companies can *wrap* (encapsulate) some functionality from an existing application in an XML envelope and *expose* it for use by others by publishing its existence in a special directory. (Two new terms used in the Web Services world are *wrapping* and *exposing*.) Thus, a bank with a credit authorization system can publish it as a Web Service that others can use, for a fee. Or a company that allows customers to configure their own product online (a computer, a bicycle, a car) may actually be using a Web Service (built in-house or obtained from a third party) to offer that functionality on their Web site to people or to the computers of, say, their largest customers.

The promises go on. Needless to say, vendors are now vying to be the providers of the platforms on which Web Services run. Companies are experimenting with Web Services, either to test out this loosely coupled, service-oriented architecture in-house or with a trusted trading partner. This architecture is different from the tightly coupled structure of most computer programs where one program calls another program. Drawing on object-oriented tenets, in Web Services, one module (a Web Service) sends a message to another Web Service, provides it some data, asks it to perform its specialized function on that data, and then expects an answer. Such message-based systems will allow systems in one company to work with systems in many other companies without first having to hard code the links between each other. The firms can use software standards and communications protocols to make the interconnections.

Web Services Standards. The world of Web Services will be possible because of three software standards (XML, WSDL, and UDDI) and three communication protocols (SOAP, HTTP, and TCP/IP), note John Hagel and John Seely Brown of 12 Entrepreneuring.

- ***XML (eXtended Markup Language).*** XML is a language for describing data in a standardized way so that different applications can use the same data. Web Services are created by wrapping XML around a piece of software that performs a function. The XML wrapper describes the services its bundle provides.
- ***WSDL (Web Services Definition Language).*** Web Services make themselves known by publishing their description in an XML document using WSDL. This service description describes the service, how to make a request to it, the data it needs to perform its work, and the results it will deliver. WSDL provides the standard language for creating these descriptions so that they can be understood by Web Services requestors.
- ***UDDI (Universal Discovery, Description, and Integration).*** The descriptions are stored in a UDDI registry, a "yellow pages" of Web Services. An application or a Web Service can find another Web Service by either knowing its URL or by searching UDDI repositories for services that meet the parameters it seeks.
- ***SOAP (Simple Object Access Protocol).*** Web Services communicate using SOAP, an XML-based communication protocol that works over any network and with any equipment. A Web Service interacts with another by sending a request for service to that other Web Service, "directly binding to it and invoking it," state Gottschalk et al. The two do not have to be preprogrammed to work together. Web Services can be combined in any pattern of use.
- ***HTTP (Hypertext Transfer Protocol).*** Web sites have addresses that use the HTTP protocol. Web Services draw on this same protocol to indicate the address where they can be located.

- ***TCP/IP (Transmission Control Protocol/Internet Protocol).*** The Internet is true to its name; it is a network of networks because it uses a protocol that permits transmitting messages across networks. This protocol is TCP/IP, and it is the protocol used by Web Services as well.

The Significance of Web Services. Hagel and Brown, two leading thinkers in the IT field, believe Web Services offers the computing architecture of the future, and thus will significantly change the job of CIOs. Rather than own and maintain their own systems, companies will buy their IT as services over the Internet, state Hagel and Brown. Thus, within the next few years, old assumptions about managing IT will be overturned.

Today, after some four decades of viewing IT as proprietary and running systems in-house, enterprises have a "mishmash of disparate systems," which they have most recently tried to replace enterprisewide via ERP systems, state Hagel and Brown. In so doing, they have created rigid business processes, making it difficult for them to respond to market changes or restructure themselves.

Web Services offers a completely new IT architecture, one based on the Web and openness. Rather than build proprietary systems, companies can obtain the functionality they need from the Internet. Some Web Services will be proprietary, some public; some will be subscription based and others on demand.

Hagel and Brown see a three-tier Web Services architecture:

1. *Application services* are the top tier. These perform specific business activities, such as credit card processing, shipment scheduling, or loan risk analysis.
2. The *service grid* is the middle tier. It provides utilities used by the application services. One type of utility is *shared utilities*, such as security utilities (to authenticate requestors and authorize access), and billing and payment utilities (to handle charges for using a Web Service). Another type of utility is *service management utilities*, which handle the management and billing of Web Services. *Resource knowledge management utilities*, a third type, provide directories and registrars for requestors and services to find one another and interact. *Transport management utilities*, a fourth type, handle messaging and transportation of files. Until this service grid is robust, though, companies will not use Web Services for their critical business activities, say Hagel and Brown, because they will not have a trusted environment for running important systems.
3. *Software standards* and *communication protocols* (the six listed earlier) reside in the bottom tier. They provide the foundation for the utilities and the application services. Without these standards and protocols, Web Services cannot speak the same language nor connect.

The difference between the past and this future is stark, the two authors note. Consider a loan application. Rather than have one large, integrated, in-house application that handles all the steps in the loan approval and funding process, each step in a Web Services environment will be performed by a different Web Service. In fact, the Web Services will be so specialized that the most appropriate one can be chosen at each processing step. Hence, the application data from a hospital will be sent to a Web Service specializing in risk analysis of hospital loans, whereas the data from a restaurant will be sent to the service that specializes in restaurant risk analysis. Each of these Web Services may draw on other specialized services to do even more specialized processing, depending on the data in the application and the amount of the desired loan.

This modularity of Web Services permits the handling of a huge variety of possibilities by mixing and matching. In addition, it will allow easier cross-company system linking. As a result, companies only pay for the functionality they use when they use it, which reduces the number of IT assets companies need to house and maintain in-house. The providers handle the maintenance of their own services and are forced to stay abreast by the competitive nature of the Web Services marketplace.

Moving to Web Services will require organizational changes in IS. It will require the outsourcing of IT activities to providers (as they emerge) and the designing of their own Web Services offerings based on their enterprise's business acumen. On page 516 is an example of what one enterprise is doing.

The seven systems discussed in this section are the different types of distributed systems that have emerged. To conclude this chapter, we come back around to the beginning of the chapter and discuss the subjects of architecture and infrastructure.

DEFINING THE OVERALL IT ARCHITECTURE

An architecture is a blueprint. It shows how the overall system, house, vehicle, or other product will look and how the parts interrelate. As Roger Woolfe and Marcus Blosch note in their Gartner EXP report *IT Architecture Matters,* the intent of an IT architecture is to bring order to the otherwise chaotic world of IS by defining a set of guidelines

CASE EXAMPLE

GENERAL MOTORS

General Motors formed eGM in 1999 to explore how it should interact with car buyers using the Internet. For 3 years, eGM was run by Mark Hogan, who gave innumerable speeches describing the progress his business unit was making. eGM was then folded into GM's IT organization and Hogan was promoted. Hagel and Brown point out that during his tenure at eGM, Hogan became a strong advocate of the Web Services architecture, going so far as to believe it could be used to move GM from its supply-driven, build-to-stock business model to a demand-driven, build-to-order business model. That change would be an enormous (some say impossible) feat.

eGM began modestly, note Hagel and Brown, building Web sites to connect GM to both consumers and dealers. Moving to a demand-driven business model (where every vehicle is built for a specific customer after the customer orders it) would require GM and its 8,000 dealers to collaborate electronically and quite differently. There would be no way to shift the business this dramatically using conventional IT architectures because that would require standardizing the systems used by the dealers, which was too costly a task for GM and its dealers to consider.

However, Web Services provides a way to create such a new business platform without replacing the disparate systems the dealers use or trying to get them all to agree to standard new systems. By exposing existing (and new) functionality in both GM and dealer systems using the Web Services standards, GM can roll out new business processes incrementally at a reasonable cost.

GM began the evolution by first enhancing its existing supply-driven model, state Hagel and Brown, offering new functions via a Web Services architecture. For example, it offers a locate-to-order Web Service to dealers, which allows them to easily find a specific car a customer might want in the inventory of other GM dealers. Another Web Service is order-to-delivery, which shortens the time to deliver a custom-ordered vehicle. Through such incremental steps, GM "paves the way," state Hagel and Brown, to eventually convert to a make-to-order business model.

By taking this incremental route on this new platform, GM can achieve payback with each new Web Service, hopefully avoiding the huge disruption that an abrupt traditional system change would cause, and evolve as the Web Services model evolves. Economically, achieving this goal brings enormous paybacks, note the two authors. GM could cut its $25-billion inventory and working capital in half and potentially shave $1,000 off the cost of each vehicle. Furthermore, by gradually evolving new processes and adopting shared terminologies and meanings, GM and its dealers can influence their parts suppliers as well, fostering industrywide change.

and standards and then adhering to them. Designing a system architecture used to be considered strictly a technical issue. More and more, though, because the architecture needs to support how the company operates, it reflects the business strategy. Furthermore, as the business changes, the architecture needs to keep pace.

The Job of Chief Technology Officer. Due to the increased importance of IT architectures, the job title of chief technology officer (CTO) or chief architect has appeared. The CTO is generally the chief architect and reports to the CIO, who is in charge of the use of IT. In a few cases, CIOs have changed their title to CTO to emphasize their role as the technical head within their firm.

In the dot-com world, the title CTO was far more prevalent than CIO because these CTOs viewed CIOs as the executives who ran traditional IT organizations, including operations and maintenance. These CTOs preferred the title CTO to reflect their more strategic role as chief architect of the company's Web presence. Furthermore, most dot-coms began life outsourcing all or most of their IT operations, so the CTO title appeared more appropriate. The dot-coms that have survived, though, now have CIOs at the helm because the job has broadened beyond the architectural aspects of IT.

An Enterprise Architecture Framework

For more than 25 years, John Zachman, an independent consultant, has been preaching the value of enterprise architecture and the modeling of data, processes, and networks. He offers the most comprehensive view of this subject we have seen, so we briefly describe it here.

The real world (an airplane, an enterprise, or a skyscraper) is so complicated that we cannot get our brain around it at one time, says Zachman, so we abstract out single variables. To completely describe an IS architecture, we need to look at the roles people play and the components they deal with. Together, these create the rows and columns of a framework.

The Rows: Planner, Owner, Designer, Builder, Subcontractor, and Consumer or User. No single architectural representation is available for an information system, says Zachman, because building complex products requires six roles: planner, owner, designer, builder, subcontractor, and consumer. Six perspectives, six models. For instance, an airframe manufacturer needs a statement of the objectives for the planner, an architect's drawings for the owner, an architect's plans for the designer, a contractor's plans for the builder, and detailed representations for the subcontractors. The completed airplane is the consumer's view. The same is true in IT. An information system needs a scope statement, a model of the enterprise, a model of the information system, a technology model, and a description of the components to produce the finished functioning system. These components make up the rows in Zachman's enterprise architecture framework, shown in Figure 14.8.

Each role has its own constraints. For instance, the owner is constrained by the use of the end product. The designer is constrained by physical laws. The builder is constrained by the state-of-the-art and the technology available. For these reasons, six models, rather than one, are needed, and they need to be kept in sync through configuration management.

The Columns: Data, Function, Network. Another significant factor is the lack of a single graphical representation for the components of a complex information system. As in engineering, systems need three components: data models (What is it made of?), functional models (How does it work?), and network models (Where are the components located?). These represent the physical manifestations of the system.

	Data (What)	**Function (How)**	**Network (Where)**
Scope Planner			
Enterprise Model Owner			
Information System Model Designer			
Technology Model Builder			
Components Subcontractor			
Functioning System Consumer or User			

Figure 14.8 An Architectural Framework. *Source:* Adapted from John Zachman, Zachman International, 2222 Foothill Blvd., Suite 337, LaCanada, CA 91011.

In addition, systems need a who (people), a when (time), and a why (motivation), says Zachman. These three elements represent the soft side of systems. Together, the six are all we need to know to build a complex system. So, the good news is that defining an enterprise architecture is not an infinite problem. The bad news is that no one has done it yet. But a few are making progress. The entire enterprise architecture framework is shown in Figure 14.9.

Using the Framework. The cells in the framework contain models that can be used to describe any complex thing—an enterprise, an airplane, even a bicycle. All of these models exist, the question is whether an enterprise spends the time to make them explicit.

For instance, your organization has a data model, whether it has been explicitly defined or whether it just grew haphazardly without an underlying design. That model is intended to work as your enterprise works. A problem occurs, though, when IT or users bring in a package that follows a different data model. If the rules in that model are inconsistent with the rules in your company, you will either spend a lot fixing the package, says Zachman, or you will require people to change how they work to be consistent with the package. Models are important because they allow people to properly evaluate packages. They also help builders align with what owners want. And they can help companies realize what changes need to be made when they move to a new business model, such as deciding to reorganize around customer groups rather than around products.

The most important reason to make a firm's enterprise system architecture explicit is to be able to make changes to the enterprise and not disintegrate as those changes are made, says Zachman.

To better understand IT architecture development, consider the case of FMC, noted in Woolfe and Blosch's Gartner EXP report on pages 520–521.

In e-commerce, IT architecture is a crucial component of business planning. To give a second example of an architecture, consider the one underlying American Airlines' Web site on page 510 and the business rationale used in creating it.

The Coming Architecture: Service-Oriented Architecture

As noted, the importance of an architecture is that it spells out the relationships among the components of an airplane, bicycle, building, system, and such. In information systems, the architecture spells out how the software components interact with each other. In the past, these interactions have been hard coded point-to-point (one to another); this is efficient, but costly to maintain. Changing one component might require changing the others that interact with it.

A relatively new system architecture has caught the attention of the field because it moves these interactions away from being hard coded and point-to-point. This new architecture is called Service Oriented Architecture (SOA). Its emergence parallels that of Web Services because it uses the same architectural concept and it can be implemented with Web Services.

Rather than think about how to get information out of one system and into another, this architecture thinks about how to expose the data and functions in a way that other systems can easily use—as a service in a wrapper with a well-defined interface that performs a business process. The wrapping hides the technical complexities developers have had to incorporate in their point-to-point interfaces. Ideally, one service would open a new account, another would update a customer account, a third would close an account, and so on. Applications that needed to provide one of these services would use the existing one, rather than their own version.

The current thinking is that an SOA provides this holy grail of how to attain reusable code, which has long eluded IS organizations. An additional benefit of this architecture is that CIOs can leverage their past systems investments, because functions in legacy systems can be exposed as services and then used in new applications. Thus, SOA supports the integration of heterogeneous systems, which has bedeviled IS organizations for years. SOAs also can help CIOs converse with their business peers because the services are essentially business processes, rather than IT services. Discussions about systems are about the business, rather than the technology.

SOA also addresses the need for IS organizations to be more agile, that is, able to more quickly build systems to address new business needs. Each service can be upgraded to use a new technology without affecting the other services. Companies can build on the systems they already have and continually upgrade either technologies or the use of SOA piecemeal, rather than in one fell swoop. In short, SOA is evolutionary, not revolutionary. That is why it is attracting so much attention.

To briefly delve into the jargon, to achieve the much-desired code reusability an SOA must support *loosely-coupled, coarse-grained, standards-based* interactions. This means, first, that a requestor of a service must simply know where to find it (loose coupling) rather than have a preprogrammed link to it (tight coupling). Second, the interactions must be at the business-service level (coarse grained), rather than at the technical-function level (fine grained). And third, the interactions must use interfaces

	Data *What*	Function *How*	Network *Where*	People *Who*	Time *When*	Motivation *Why*
Objectives/ Scope (Contextual) *Planner*	List of things important to the business Entity = Class of business thing	List of processes the business performs Function = Class of business process	List of locations in which the business operates Node = Major business location	List of Organizations/agents important to the business Agent = Class of agent	List of events significant to the business Time = Major business event	List of business goals/ strategies Ends/Means = Major bus goal/ critical success factor
Enterprise Model (Conceptual) *Owner*	e.g., Semantic model Ent = Business entity Reln = Business relationship	e.g., Business process model Proc = Business process I/O = Business resources	e.g., Logistics network Node = Business location Link = Business linkage	e.g., Organization chart Agent = Organization unit Work = Work product	e.g., Master schedule Time = Business event Cycle = Business cycle	e.g., Business plan End = Business objective Means = Business strategy
System Model (Logical) *Designer*	e.g., Data model Ent = Data entry Reln = Data relationship	e.g., "Application architecture" Proc = Application function I/O = User views	e.g., Distributed system architecture Node = I/S function (processor, storage, etc.) Link = Line characteristics	e.g., Human interface architecture Agent = Role Work = Deliverable	e.g., Processing structure Time = System event Cycle = Processing cycle	e.g., Knowledge architecture Ends = Criterion Means = Business rules
Technology Model (Physical) *Builder*	e.g., Data design Ent = Segment/Row/etc Reln = Pointer/Key/etc	e.g., System design Proc = Computer function I/O =Screen/Device formats	e.g., System architecture Node = Hardware/System software Link = Line specifications	e.g., Human/technology Interface Agent = User Work = Job	e.g., Control structure Time = Execute Cycle = Component cycle	e.g., Knowledge design Ends = Condition Means = Action
Detailed Represen-tations (out-of-context) *Sub-Contractor*	e.g., Data definition Ent = Field Reln = Address	e.g., Program Proc = Language stmt I/O = Control block	e.g., Network architecture Node = Addresses Link = Protocols	e.g., Security architecture Agent = Identity Work = "Transaction"	e.g., Timing definition Time = Interrupt Cycle = Machine cycle	e.g., Knowledge definition End = Subcondition Means = Step
Functioning System	e.g., Data	e.g., Function	e.g., Network	e.g., Organization	e.g., Schedule	e.g., Strategy

Figure 14.9 Enterprise Architecture—A Framework. *Source:* Adapted from John Zachman, Zachman International, 2222 Foothill Blvd., Suite 337, LaCanada, CA 91011.

CASE EXAMPLE

FMC CORPORATION

FMC, with headquarters in Philadelphia, Pennsylvania, is a global $2-billion chemical manufacturer with 6,000 employees focusing on three areas: agricultural, industrial, and specialty chemicals. It is first or second in the areas in which it competes, and half its sales come from outside the United States.

In 2000, FMC was a $4-billion conglomerate. In 2001, it split into two equal halves, FMC (to focus purely on chemicals) and FMC Technologies. IS spent all of 2001 pulling the IT architecture apart. The deadline for establishing separate IS operations was January 1, 2002.

Designing Two New IT Architectures

FMC outsources its telecommunications, data networking, voice mail, Web hosting, virtual private networks, remote access, and some data center operations. It worked with its outsourcers to pull the infrastructure apart and architect two new IT infrastructures. Headquarters was moved from Chicago to Philadelphia, yet no IS staff moved; FMC now has 130 IS headquarters staff.

The CIO, Ed Flynn, created a new position to report directly to him: Architecture and Technology Director. During 2001, this director had a virtual organization. He led five sub-teams—data, applications, integration, desktop, and platform—each with five to six team members from FMC and FMC Technology IS staffs. In addition, he supervised an emerging technologies subteam to look out into the future. None of the team members was full-time on a team; they also had their day-to-day jobs.

The five teams' tasks were to

- Describe the "today architecture" (inventory their area)
- Define the "tomorrow architecture" (how their area would look on January 1, 2002)
- Detail the "next-minute steps" (how to get from today to tomorrow)

They accomplished their task in 2001 with only a few transition service agreements on January 1 (where FMC and FMC Technologies would buy services from one another).

Lessons from the Work

"The split taught us we could get workable solutions by having subteams with subject matter experts define the technical architecture, and overlay them with an architecture steering team to add the enterprise and business viewpoints," says Flynn. The top team consisted of Flynn and some of his direct reports. They implemented some of the recommendations from the subteams and took those requiring corporate action to senior management.

Another lesson from the effort was that the "today architecture" can be created by IS staff. However, it then needs to be put into a framework the business folks can understand, because they need to help define the "tomorrow architecture." Then the work continues as a joint effort to define the "next-minute steps."

"Before the split, we had already standardized on SAP as our transaction backbone and on Windows for our desktops and laptops. But getting those standards was a brutal fight—probably because we were our own worst enemy. We had not defined 'tomorrow,' so everyone's 'today' answer would work," says Flynn.

"When we have a tomorrow architecture, and everyone agrees on it, we have fewer next-minute battles because the architecture limits the choices. We saw this happen in the corporate split. Once we agreed on the tomorrow architecture, we were no longer the people who said 'no.' Being a purely chemical company now also helps us with standardization," says Flynn.

Because the chemical business is so cost competitive, FMC wants low-cost IT; therefore, the operating policy is to use common tools, common processes, and replicable solutions. "You have to architect to be able to do that," says Flynn.

Designing a New "Tomorrow" IT Architecture

Flynn's organization is now using the same approach, starting with a clean slate, to architect a new tomorrow IT architecture. If they can pull the corporate architecture apart in 1 year, they believe they should be able to lay out a new tomorrow architecture in a year, even though the scope is broader. The new architecture will include applications in the operating units. "Tomorrow" means 2004–2005, which is when Flynn expects Voice-over-IP and Web Services to kick in.

The organization for the current architecture effort is the same as the one used for the split—the same subteams, the same steering committee. In fact, some of the business folks who helped support SAP after implementation in the mid-1990s stayed in IS and have been on the architecture efforts, bringing their business knowledge with them.

Once the new architecture is defined and bought off by senior management, it will be communicated and implemented via FMC's capital planning process. The expenditures must track the defined next-minute steps, some of which could have timeframes attached to them. "We may even get to the level where we talk about standards, and all purchases will have to adhere to these standards," says Flynn.

Flynn envisions this rearchitecting process as being ongoing. Each new effort will start with today as its reference point, draw on the work of the emerging technologies group to peer into the future, and create a new "tomorrow" architecture.

CASE EXAMPLE
THE SABRE SYSTEM

The architecture underlying American Airlines' Web site is modular. The existing SABRE computer reservation system serves as the reservation service module. Other modules perform the functions related to the Web. They include an input-output module for turning browser-entered data into data that can be processed by SABRE, and vice versa; an authentication module to verify users' identity; a session management module to manage each Web user's interaction with the system; and so on.

Due to this component-based architecture, it was fairly easy to add new functions, states Patricia Seybold. Electronic ticketing, for example, was housed in its own module using appropriate components.

However, as so often happens, when American looked at the underlying databases, it found customer profiles in one database, AAdvantage member profiles in another, and NetSAAver subscriber profiles in a third. In a huge redesign, American consolidated and linked these databases to have just one profile for each flyer.

Another challenge was figuring out how to present a personalized Web site to each flyer. It required creating a data architecture, which, in turn, required tagging all the content shown on the Web site so that different pieces could be presented to different groups of flyers for different purposes. The decision was made to create an object database that would contain the tagged pieces of information. Tagging took much longer than anyone projected. To use this database to present personalized Web sites, American used Broadvision's One-on-One software and worked with two system integrators and design firms, says Seybold.

Finally, to do electronic booking, which required a more flexible database than the existing fares database, American created a separate fares database that contains tags such as "skiing" and "golf" attached to appropriate destinations. This database is accessed by business rules created by the system based on the choices customers make in their profiles. With this database, the system can make appropriate recommendations of places to travel based on the preferences stored in the profiles.

American's Web site architecture has numerous pieces, including links between systems, components, modules, databases, data elements, and business rules.

based on industry standards that have been adopted by vendors so that they work across proprietary platforms (standards based).

An SOA can achieve loose coupling between services in several ways. The most recent is to create the services using Web Services protocols (discussed earlier). Although CIOs may eventually migrate to this option, Web Services is so new that the pioneers have generally not taken this route. A second alternative is to use a publish-and-subscribe approach, which is what Delta Air Lines has done. A third is to implement messaging-and-integration middleware. Credit Suisse (see pages 523–524) has used the concept of an "information bus" to build its SOA.

THE IMPORTANCE OF THE IT INFRASTRUCTURE

In the arena of IT infrastructure, the best work to date has been performed by Peter Weill, director of the Center for Information Systems Research at MIT, and Marianne Broadbent, Associate Dean, Executive MBA Program, Melbourne Business School. They describe the structure of the IT infrastructure, how local, firmwide, and public infrastructures mesh, and the different ways companies justify infrastructure investments. Such investments are a vital part of corporate IT portfolios, yet they are the most difficult to cost-justify beforehand and to measure benefits of afterwards.

The Structure of the IT Infrastructure

Weill and Broadbent define *IT infrastructure* as "the shared and reliable services that provide the foundation for the enterprise IT portfolio." The shared characteristic differentiates an IT infrastructure from IT investments used by just one function. On top of this infrastructure sit applications that perform the business's processes. Thus, infrastructure does not provide direct business performance benefits. Rather, it enables other systems that do yield business benefits, which is what makes infrastructure so difficult to cost-justify.

Weill and Broadbent divide the IT infrastructure into four layers, as shown in Figure 14.10, underlying local applications. Local applications are fast changing. They include such applications as an insurance claims system, a bank loan system, or a customer service support system. Due to their fast-changing nature, they are not part of the infrastructure, but they do draw on it.

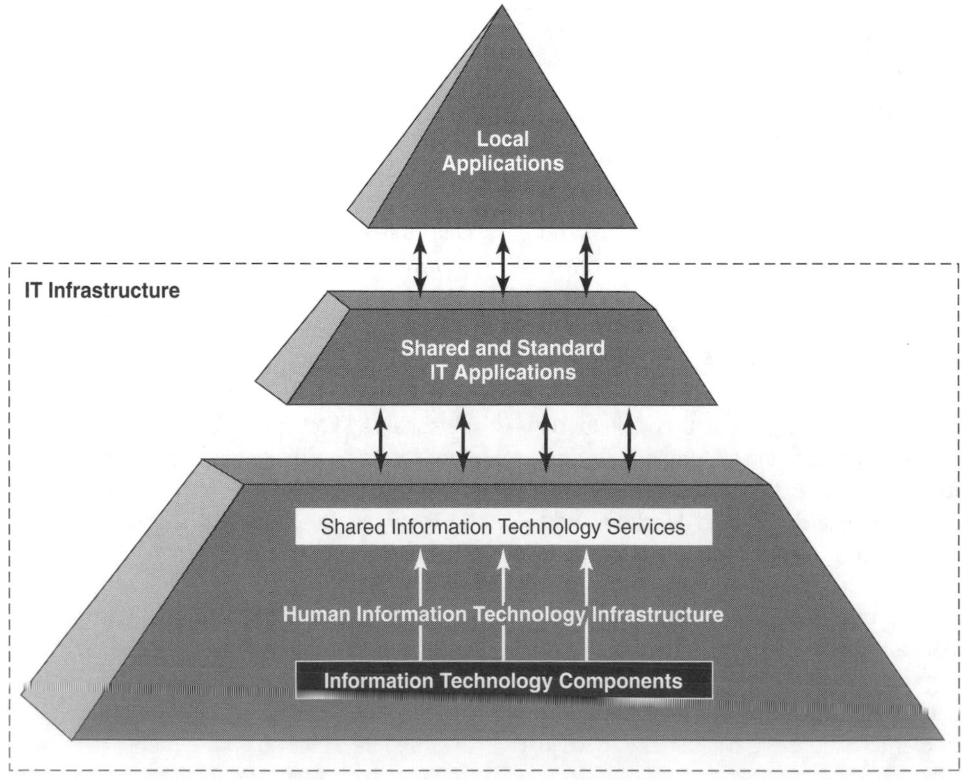

Figure 14.10 The Structure of the IT Infrastructure. *Source:* Adapted from Peter Weill and Marianne Broadbent, *Leveraging the New Infrastructure: How Market Leaders Capitalize on IT* (Boston: Harvard Business School Press, 1998).

CASE EXAMPLE

CREDIT SUISSE

Credit Suisse, with headquarters in Zurich, Switzerland, is a global financial services company with 60,000 employees operating in 50 countries. Credit Suisse is pioneering the implementation of enterprisewide SOAs. Its former architecture depended on proprietary middleware. Maintenance had become increasingly expensive, because as the number of computing platforms and technologies grew, so did the number of interfaces and the amount of time needed to change the interfaces when applications changed.

To address this maintenance problem, Credit Suisse revamped its IT infrastructure to be a service-oriented architecture by implementing two "information buses"—a service bus and an event bus.

The Service Bus

The front-end bus, that is, the bus that integrates front-end and back-end applications, is the service bus, shown in Figure 14.11. The architecture uses Orbix from Iona Technologies, which is a set of tools for integrating applications that run on mainframes, Unix, and Windows platforms. Through Orbix, Credit Suisse is reusing business procedures, business logic, and data formerly locked up in its applications.

The service bus takes a request–reply approach. Through Orbix, each business service is exposed by being stored in a central repository. When a front-end application has a request, it triggers a call to Orbix, which sends the request to the appropriate business service and waits for a reply (from a back-end application), which it then forwards to the requesting application. Thus, the bus uses a demand-pull model—the request from one application pulls the reply from another.

Credit Suisse took this approach so that it could integrate the software functions housed in the multiple generations of technology it has in-house, by presenting its core business applications as a collection of reusable business services. The SOA gives it a way to design new applications that draw on these business services using a documented interface. Because of the interface, developers do not need to worry about the software or database underlying each business service.

The Event Bus

The event bus integrates the back-end systems. It also uses a service-oriented architecture, but it uses a supply-push mode of operation, implemented using publish-and-subscribe. When an event occurs in one system, it is "published." All of the systems that need to know about that *event* are "subscribed" and are notified of the event that has taken place (the update is pushed to them). An *event* is a change in the state of an object, such as a customer. Credit Suisse has developed specific message types to run over the event bus; each is for a different type of event. The purpose of the event bus is to ensure that all systems are using the same up-to-date data. It connects all back-end systems: host applications, ERP systems, new nonhost applications, databases, data warehouses, and external data feeds.

A typical use of the event bus is to replicate the data in Credit Suisse's customer information file from its legacy application (developed in-house) and to copy it to a trading application that stores its own copy of this data. The event bus also allows Credit Suisse to transform the data between applications (that is, convert it from the format used in one system to that used in another) and to route data based on its content. The event bus was built using IBM technologies (Websphere MQ/Integration Broker).

Benefits

The SOA effort began in 1999. By December 1999, Credit Suisse had five SOA-based applications drawing on 35 business services that were being used by 800 users. The numbers have grown since then. Two years later it had 50 applications running on the information bus, drawing on 500 business services and being used by 15,000 internal users. In addition, customers using Credit Suisse's online trading and Web-based e-banking applications generated some 15 million invocations of the SOA-based business services each week.

Today, well over 100 applications use 800 services, invoking 800 million transactions per year on the service bus.

(*Case continued*)

(Case continued)

Actually, it is no longer quite clear what an application is, but these figures give a feel for the high volumes. The event bus, implemented in 2003, integrates over 32 back-end systems and handles over 1 million messages a day.

Credit Suisse was able to implement the architecture without disrupting applications. The effort was a major investment, but the company can now implement new applications much faster. In fact, it has found that some 80 percent of the business services needed in new applications are already in existing applications. Credit Suisse believes its development speed allows it to respond to customers' requests for new financial services faster than its competition.

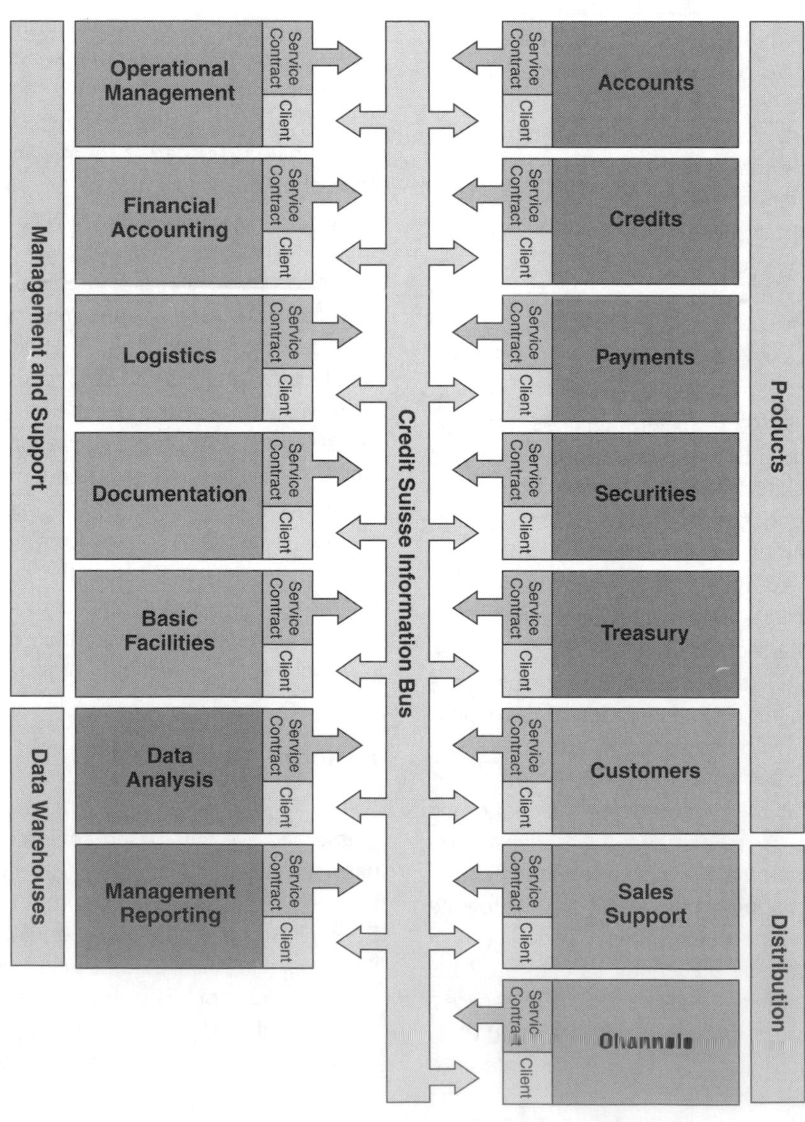

Figure 14.11 Credit Suisse's Service-Oriented Architecture. *Source:* Courtesy of Credit Suisse.

It is easiest to understand their view of infrastructure reading from bottom to top because that order describes it from the technologists' point of view to the business users' point of view. Weill and Michael Vitale, of the Australian Graduate School of Management, present the following description of the infrastructure layers, from bottom to top, in their article in the *MIS Quarterly Executive,* which discusses the infrastructure capabilities needed by e-business models:

- *IT Components.* This layer is the foundation of a firm's IT infrastructure. It consists of technology components, such as computers, printers, DBMS packages, operating systems, and such. Whereas technologists understand the capabilities of these components, business people do not. That is why IT and business people have had such a difficult time talking about infrastructure at this level. They are not speaking a common language, note Weill and Vitale.
- *Human IT Infrastructure.* The translation of the IT component layer into business terms occurs at this layer and is handled by humans. This layer consists of experts' knowledge, skills, experience, and standards to bind IT components into services that business people can understand.
- *Shared IT Services.* This layer is the business view of the IT infrastructure, and it presents the infrastructure as a set of services that users can draw upon and share to conduct business. Weill and Broadbent's recent refinement, working with Mani Subramani of the University of Minnesota, identifies 70 infrastructure services grouped into 10 clusters. Examples of services are Web sites, wireless applications, firewalls on secure gateways, and large-scale data processing facilities.
- *Shared and Standard IT Applications.* These applications, which are at the top of the IT infrastructure, change less regularly than the fast-changing local applications above the infrastructure. They include such stable applications as accounting, budgeting, and HR.

Again, the importance of this four-level description of IT infrastructure is that it gives technologists and business users a common language. Business users can discuss where they need specific services, and technologists can translate those services into the technical components that underlie them.

To take this infrastructure discussion a bit further, Weill and Broadbent note that it sits on top of the public infrastructure, as shown in Figure 14.12 that is, the Internet, industry networks, vendors, and telecommunications companies. Also note in this figure that in some cases the firmwide infrastructure provides corporatewide services. In other cases, it provide infrastructure for individual business units.

Similar to Public Infrastructure. IT infrastructure is strikingly similar to public infrastructure, such as roads, hospitals, sewers, and schools, note Weill and Broadbent.

- Both are provided by a central agency and funded by some form of taxation.
- Both are long-term and require large investments.
- A central agency provides an essential service that users are not motivated or able to provide.
- Both enable business activity by users that would otherwise not be economically feasible.
- Flexibility is valued in both because they must be in place before the precise business activity is known.
- Both are difficult to cost-justify in advance as well as to show benefits in hindsight.

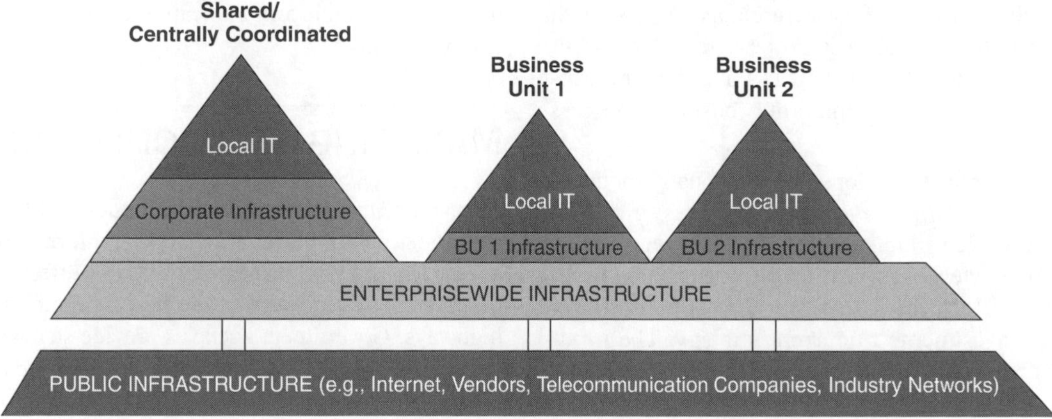

Figure 14.12 IT Infrastructure. *Source:* Adapted from Peter Weill and Marianne Broadbent, *Leveraging the New Infrastructure: How Market Leaders Capitalize on IT* (Boston: Harvard Business School Press, 1998).

- Both require a delicate investment balance: Too little investment leads to duplication, incompatibility, and suboptimal use, whereas too much discourages user investment and involvement and may result in unused capacity.

Three Views of Infrastructure

The benefits a firm actually realizes from its infrastructure investments depend on its objectives for the infrastructure. A firm might invest in infrastructure for the following three reasons, note Weill and Broadbent:

1. Economies of scale (utility)
2. Support for business programs (dependent)
3. Flexibility to meet changes in the marketplace (enabling)

Utility. Companies that view their infrastructure as a utility see it as a necessary and unavoidable service that must be provided by IS. Expected benefits are cost savings achieved through economies of scale. Normally, firms with this perspective treat infrastructure costs as an administrative expense, and they act to minimize these expenses. Therefore, they offer the fewest infrastructure services. For instance, they might promote use of networks for messaging but not as part of inter- or intraorganizational business processes. This objective requires the lowest investment, but it also only results in lowering costs (not in reengineering the business). Outsourcing may be viewed favorably because the IT infrastructure is not seen as strategic.

Dependent. A business that ties its infrastructure investments to specific, known business programs, takes the dependent view. The infrastructure is treated as a business expense because investments are tied to business plans, and its value is measured by short-term business benefits. Firms with this view include infrastructure planning in current business planning. They also see the network as critical. Furthermore, this view of infrastructure appears to smooth the way for simplifying business processes. In fact, Weill and Broadbent surmise that this view is a minimum requirement for successfully implementing business process reengineering.

Enabling. A firm that develops and continually modifies its infrastructure in *coalignment* with its business strategy—where infrastructure influences strategy and vice versa—takes the enabling view of infrastructure. The primary benefit is long-term flexibility, thus the firm does not limit infrastructure investments to current strategy. The infrastructure is intended to provide the foundation for changing direction in the future, if need be. Thus, infrastructure costs are seen as business investments. For example, the firm might use networks extensively in business processes, both within the firm and with customers and suppliers.

Needless to say, the appropriate viewpoint is not a technical decision; it is a top management decision. It is IS management's job to make this clear to senior management and show them the options. Teamwork among the various levels of management is absolutely necessary to align technical investments with business strategy.

No view is superior, though; different views are appropriate for different strategies. Moving from utility to dependent to enabling increases up-front investments and the number of IT infrastructure services provided.

To see how one organization has approached investing in infrastructure, consider the city of Sunnyvale, California in the case on page 516.

Although the concepts behind distributed systems were conceived more than 40 years ago, the use of distributed systems moved into a new era with the Internet. Before the Internet, the bulk of distributed systems were in-house, only linking systems within an enterprise. The Internet turned attention outward because it provides the infrastructure for global distributed systems. IS management can turn its attention outward toward customers, suppliers, and its business ecosystem. With IT providing the foundation for electronic collaboration within such an ecosystem, CIOs are also working closely with top management to ensure that the firm's IT infrastructure not only meshes with corporate strategy but is also flexible enough to support changes in strategy. Building a comprehensive infrastructure is the challenge facing CIOs and CTOs. Many of them got caught flat-footed with the Internet. It crept up behind them in the mid-1990s. They now realize how important infrastructure is to corporate success. Even though they might outsource the operation of their infrastructure, they and their top management peers must do the strategic thinking behind selecting infrastructure elements.

With the overall technical framework for systems provided, we now turn to the essential technologies used in distributed systems—telecommunications, information resources, and operations.

MANAGING TELECOMMUNICATIONS

Once built, the network, with its nodes and links, provides the infrastructure for the flow of data, information, and messages. This flow is managed not by IS professionals, but by users, just as users manage the flow of vehicles on physical highways. Government agencies provide standards and laws for the flow of highway traffic that are enforced by the police and highway patrol. In the same way, IS departments select and enforce telecommunications standards for information traffic while governments divvy up the spectrum for different wireless uses. This analogy could be pursued in more detail, but the point is clear: Telecommunications is the basis for the way people and companies work today. It provides the infrastructure for moving information, just as a transportation system, such as shipping lanes, railroad right of ways, and the airspace, provides the infrastructure for the movement people and goods.

This analogy presents telecommunications as a linking mechanism, which it is. However, the Internet has also

CASE EXAMPLE

CITY OF SUNNYVALE, CALIFORNIA

The city of Sunnyvale, California, in the heart of Silicon Valley, is rated as one of the best-run cities in the United States. Its performance-based budgeting system, which has been honed over the past 25 years, has fostered citywide fiscal soundness and day-to-day accountability by city administrators. This budgeting process, along with the city's 20-year planning horizon, is aiding the IS department in creating and financing the city's information infrastructure.

Sunnyvale's director of information technology was hired to move the city into the future. He thus concentrated on building the city's information infrastructure because the city sees infrastructure as its foundation for the future. Says the director,

> *If the city of Sunnyvale is to succeed in leveraging technological resources to deal with increasing customer demands, as well as improve efficiency and customer service, the IS department must first take responsibility for capturing accurate information and delivering that information in a timely manner.*

This statement is the driving force behind the city's IS department. The driver for investing in infrastructure is quality of service. To provide high-quality service to customers, the infrastructure users (city departments) must have timely and accurate information to do their jobs. For this to happen, the IS department must have the right pieces of information at the right place at the right time. The IS director believes the city needs to develop an expandable infrastructure to leverage technology and capitalize on opportunities.

The infrastructure provides connectivity between the city's traditional mainframes with attached terminals/PCs, numerous stand-alone LANs, and the outside world. It is based on a fiber-optic backbone, Internet-based computing, and relational database technology. A three-level distributed architecture is used, with enterprise servers, midtier servers, and desk-top clients. The architecture encompasses more than traditional computing equipment, though. For example, the 401 copiers throughout the city will someday be replaced by laser printers so that employees can send a request for 50 copies of a report from their desktop rather than ask a secretary or clerk to make the copies.

The information infrastructure is like the foundation for a home, says the director. It needs to withstand all the weight, all the noise, and all the things you want to plug into it. Because IT is changing so rapidly, the city must think long-term about its infrastructure to ensure that it can be easily expanded and upgraded. Unfortunately, traditional fiber-optic vendors have not been able to support upgradability. As a result, the city laid a new type of fiber-optic conduit. From the end, it looks like a honeycomb with 19 cells, only 2 of which were used initially. New fiber bundles can easily be blown through the spare cells in the future using a special gas, thus making it easy to upgrade the fiber backbone to accommodate new services such as video teleconferencing or combined voice and data transmission.

Infrastructure investments are paid through chargeback. When the IS department places equipment on someone's desk, installs a software package on a computer, or hooks up a PC to a LAN, that equipment, software, or communication link immediately begins generating its own replacement funds. Sunnyvale charges back everything on rental rates, because it knows everything will eventually need to be replaced.

"Super" rules guide technology investments. One such rule is that the city will standardize on products to make effective use of resources. Another unwritten super rule is that a person using a computer at, say, the senior center will have the same access and response time as someone working next to the mainframe. Another IT super rule is that all projects are subject to review by an executive body that represents all city departments. Thus, continuous buy-in, support, and fine-tuning of demands forms an improvement cycle. An outcome of this super rule is a more participative executive body—one that understands departmental priority and guides the city's IT goals as a high-performance team. A joint environment is established for a consistent framework from which all departments can benefit.

view of telecommunications, that of e, a place where people can "exist" ere organizations can conduct busi- in fact, a place where organizational processes exist. It is an online world, a sort of cybercity. This view, too, is providing the foundation for the online economy.

However, even more is happening. Just about everything about telecommunications is shifting, from the industry itself to the protocols (the languages networks use to communicate with each other).

MANAGING INFORMATION RESOURCES

Managing information resources initially meant managing data, first in files, then in corporate databases that were well structured, carefully defined, and generally under the jurisdiction of the IS department. Next, the term expanded to include information; that is, data that has meaning. There also has been much talk of managing knowledge. With the emergence of the Internet, talk has turned to managing content, which includes text, graphics, sound, video, and animation.

To begin, a few definitions are in order:

- *Data* consists of facts devoid of meaning or intent, where meaning and intent are supplied by a particular use.
- *Information* is data in context, which means the data has been given an explicit meaning in a specific context. In this book, we will often use the term content to refer to information. This term arose with the emergence of the World Wide Web. Content includes information presented electronically in a variety of media: charts, text, voice, sound, graphics, animation, photographs, diagrams, and video.
- *Knowledge* is information with direction or intent, where intent is derived from strategies or objectives.

As the breadth of the kinds of information resources has expanded, so has the job of managing them. Oftentimes, that job ends up in the IS organization, even though it may not have started there. For example, when PCs came on the scene, people created their own personal files to do their work. They depended on these files, but no one else did until they were shared. Then, when shared files were destroyed and had no backup, all of a sudden a department might not be able to function. Therefore, users asked IS to back up the file or house it on a computer that was regularly backed up. Thus, IS became involved. The same has occurred with Web content. When departments and field offices initially created their own Web sites, IS often was not in the picture. However, as the need for recovery, version control, corporate consistency, and such appeared, people again looked to IS to put in the necessary management procedures. Thus, IS has been continually managing new forms of information resources in addition to the ones it has already been managing.

- Corporate databases are still a major responsibility of IS organizations, and management of data has gotten increasingly complex as it has become distributed. Not only is data now global in some cases, but the data is housed in a variety of *database models*, such as hierarchical, relational, and object-oriented ones. Production databases support transaction processing of airline reservations, customer orders, and such. Data warehouses house gigantic amounts of historic data to be analyzed with data mining techniques to support decision making for such applications as CRM.
- Information, in the form of documents (electronic or paper) and Web content, has exploded the size of the databases that organizations now manage. Furthermore, with the digitization of sound files, photographs, video, and 3D models, file sizes are growing at a fast clip. Unlike structured data, these unstructured forms of information are not easy to index for retrieval purposes.
- Knowledge management is becoming a key to exploiting the intellectual assets of organizations. The types of knowledge organizations are attempting to manage include explicit knowledge (know-what), which can be housed in a file or a process, as well as tacit knowledge (know-how), which is generally in people's heads and is difficult to make explicit.

MANAGING DATA

As noted, data are facts devoid of meaning or intent. Data are primarily facts about entities, such as individual employees, customers, parts, or transactions. Well-structured data records hold a set of attributes that describe each entity. Database management systems (DBMSs) are the main tools for managing these entities in the business world. DBMSs have been around since the 1960s and are based on two major principles: a three-level conceptual model and several alternative data models for organizing the data.

The Three-Level Database Model

One of the easiest-to-understand discussions of database technology is by James Bradley in his description of the three-level database model. The concept is still an underpinning of the DBMS field. The following discussion is based on Bradley, Martin, and Atre. It begins with the level that the application developer sees.

- *Level 1* is called the external, conceptual, or local level. As Figure 14.13 illustrates, this level contains the various user views of the corporate data. Each application program has its own view. This level is not concerned with how the data is physically stored or what data is used by other applications.
- *Level 2* is called the logical or enterprise data level. It encompasses all an organization's relevant data under the control of the data administrators. Data and relationships are represented at this level by the DBMS. This level contains the same data as Level 3, but with the implementation data removed.
- *Level 3* is called the physical or storage level. It specifies the way the data is physically stored. A data record consists of its data fields plus some implementation data, generally pointers and flag fields. The end user, of course, need not be concerned with these pointers and flags; they are for use by the DBMS only.

The advantage of this three-level model is that Level 2 absorbs changes made at Level 3, such as using a new physical storage method, so that individual application programs in Level 1 do not need to be changed when the physical layer changes. Furthermore, data only needs to be stored once in Level 2, and different programs can draw on it and vary the relationships among the data.

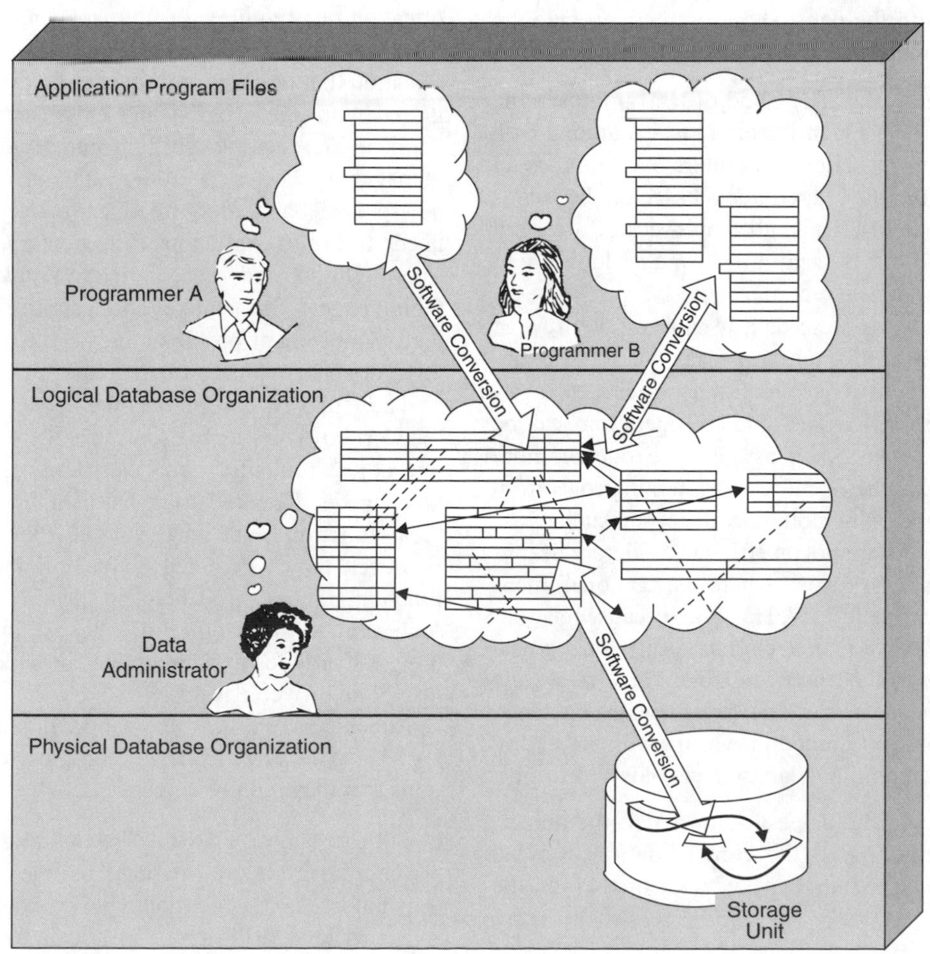

Figure 14.13 The Three-Level Database. *Source:* James Martin, *Principles of Database Management* (Upper Saddle River, NJ: Prentice Hall, 1976).

Four Data Models

The second major concept in database management is alternative ways of defining relationships among types of data. Data models are methods to structure data to represent the real world and the way data is accessed. Four main data models are in use today: hierarchical, network, relational, and object.

Hierarchical Model. In this model, each data element is subordinate to another in a strict hierarchical manner, like the boxes on an organization chart. This model uses the terminology *parent* and *child* to represent these relationships, and each data item can have only one parent.

Network Model. In this model, each data item can have more than one parent. Assembly parts lists illustrate this structure; the same part can be used in more than one assembly. In both the hierarchical and network models, the data relationships are stated explicitly, generally by pointers stored with the data. These pointers provide the means by which programs access the desired data records.

Relational Model. Edgar F. Codd of IBM proposed the relational model in 1970. In it, relationships among data items are not expressly stated by pointers. Instead, it is up to the DBMS to find the related items based on the values of specified data fields. Thus, all employees of a certain department are found by searching for the department number in each employee record.

Relational databases store data in tables. Each row of the table, called a *tuple*, represents an individual entity (person, part, account). Each column represents an attribute of the entities. Various kinds of operations can be performed on the data, such as selecting one or more columns, projecting one or more rows, joining rows from several tables by matching column values, and such.

Relational systems are not as efficient as hierarchical or networked database systems, where navigational maps through the data are predefined. However, because relational systems allow people to create relationships among data on the fly, they are much more flexible. Thus, they were first used to handle end user queries and they are now widely used in high-volume transaction systems with huge files. Relational has become the database technology of choice.

Object Model. As the newest data model, the object-oriented approach expands the view of data by storing and managing *objects*, each of which consists of the following:

- A piece of data
- Methods, or procedures that can perform work on that data
- Attributes describing the data
- Relationships between this object and others

Objects are important because they can be used with any type of data, whether a traditional name or address, an entire spreadsheet, a video clip, a voice annotation, a photograph, or a segment of music. A collection of objects is called an *object database*.

Object data management techniques draw from the past. They retain traditional DBMS features, including end user tools, high-level query languages, concurrency control, recovery, and the ability to efficiently handle huge amounts of data. They include two other important concepts as well. One is object management, which is the management of complex kinds of data, such as multimedia and procedures. The other concept is rule management, that is, managing large numbers of complex rules for reasoning and maintaining integrity constraints between data.

Stonebraker and Kemnitz provide an example of an application that requires object management as well as data management and rule management. It is a newspaper application that needs to store text and graphics and be integrated with subscription and classified ad data. In this application, customer billing requires traditional data management, whereas storage of text, pictures, and the newspaper's banner require object management. Finally, it needs the rules that control the newspaper's layout. One rule might be, "Ads for competing retailers cannot be on facing pages." Stonebraker and Kemnitz believe that most data management problems in the future will require all three dimensions: data, object, and rule management.

The tenets of objects become even more important in the world of Web Services because the XML modules utilize object principles. You can think of objects as little black boxes. They tell you what data they need to perform their function and what output they will give you. However, they will not tell you how they perform their function. If they need help performing their work, they send a request to another module. So, in addition to handling all varieties of data, objects provide a programming discipline to Web Services.

Silberschatz, Stonebraker, and Ullman give the following examples of typical, yet complex, database applications that may require objects.

- CAD data for a large office building must maintain and integrate information from the viewpoints of hundreds of subcontractors. For example, when an electrician drills a hole in a beam to run an electrical wire, the system should, ideally, recalculate the stresses on the beam to ensure that its load-bearing capabilities have not been compromised.

- Large retail chains record every product code scanned by every cashier in every store. Corporate buyers explore this data using ad hoc queries to uncover buying patterns. This procedure, called *data mining*, is growing, not only in retailing, but also in medicine, science, and many other fields.
- Databases of insurance policies now store photographs of damaged property, handwritten claim forms, audio transcripts of appraisals, images of insured objects, and even video walk-throughs of houses. These images contain so much data that these databases are enormous.

Just as there is essentially one worldwide telephone system and one worldwide computer network, some believe there will eventually be one worldwide file system. Achieving this vision requires collaboration among nations, which is actually happening in some areas. The Human Genome Project is one example. Defense contractors want a single project database that spans all subcontractors and all portions of a project. Auto companies want to give their suppliers access to new car designs. Both of these applications require inter-company databases. The challenge is making these databases behave as though they are part of a single database.

Finally, security is of major importance in today's DBMSs. Distributed, heterogeneous Internet-linked databases exacerbate the problem. Companies may want to permit access to some portions of their databases while restricting other portions. This selective accessibility requires reliably authenticating inquirers. Unless security and integrity are strictly enforced, users will not be able to trust the systems.

CASE EXAMPLE

MONSANTO

Monsanto, based in St. Louis, Missouri, is a $9-billion provider of agricultural products, pharmaceuticals, food ingredients, and chemicals. It is heavily international, with some 50 percent of revenues outside the United States. It has always had a tradition of being decentralized. The CEO's vision includes five global themes.

1. Being responsive and efficient in meeting customer needs
2. Thinking and acting from a global perspective
3. Taking some risks to enter new markets
4. Treating the earth as a closed system where consumption and contamination of finite resources cannot be sustained
5. Creating an environment of trust, honesty, openness, and initiative where people can thrive

To accomplish these (and other) goals, Monsanto established three large enterprise-wide IT projects. One is to redevelop operational and financial transaction systems using SAP. The second is to develop a knowledge-management architecture, including data warehousing. The third is to link transaction and decision support systems via common master data, known as enterprise reference data (ERD), as shown in Figure 14.14. Monsanto wants to be "small but connected" to benefit from both global integration and local flexibility. ERD is a key to achieving both simultaneously. The Center of Technical Expertise is implementing all three initiatives.

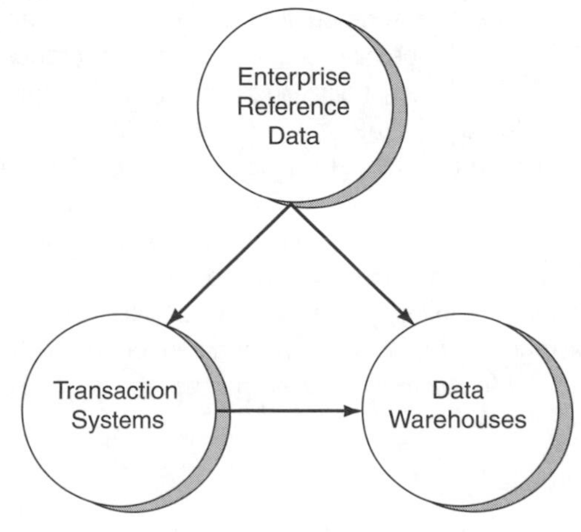

Figure 14.14 The Role of Enterprise Reference Data. *Source:* Courtesy of the Monsanto Corporation.

(*Case continued*)

(Case continued)

Transaction Systems. The worldwide operations and finance project is dominated by SAP, an ERP product that covers all core business transactions, including finance, order processing, inventory management, product planning, and manufacturing resource planning. SAP is international and handles multiple languages and multiple currencies.

Monsanto is too large and complex to operate SAP as a single installation. Hence, they have created a distributed SAP architecture with separate instances of SAP for reference data, finance, and operations in each business unit. The master reference data integrates these distributed components.

Knowledge Management. To convert SAP data to knowledge, Monsanto uses data warehouses, which are targeted at mid- to upper-level management. These warehouses focus on the big picture of the company and contain data from internal and external sources that can be sliced and diced with drill-down capability from summary data to supporting details. Again, the reference data allows the warehouses to compare and leverage information across Monsanto.

ERD. ERD, a separate use of SAP, is the repository for most master table information in the company. The information includes vendors, customers, suppliers, materials, finance, and control tables. Each table has multiple views. For instance, materials has separate views for purchasing, engineering, accounting, and safety, among others. The beauty of using a system such as SAP is that it can ensure referential integrity (adherence to complex relationship rules) of the data.

The sole source of master data is ERD, but the data can be distributed wherever it is needed in transactional SAP systems as well as in the data warehouses. However, as comprehensive as SAP is, it still does not contain all the reference data. Monsanto stores external data, such as crop statistics and economic trends, outside SAP.

The purpose of ERD is to enable integration. Vertical integration enables closer coordination with suppliers, which will reduce Monsanto's working capital and improve customer service. Horizontal integration across Monsanto's business units enables team marketing, leveraged purchasing, and interplant manufacturing. For example, common vendor and material tables enable Monsanto to leverage purchasing across the company. With total purchases of about $5.5 billion a year, even a few percentage points of leverage can yield significant savings. Without ERD, Monsanto had to rely on limited polls of many purchasing functions—a process that could not be sustained.

Getting Corporate Data into Shape

Turning data into a corporate resource is not easy for a large company with a history of decentralization. To accomplish its task, Monsanto has had to change its entire data management process. To start, it created a formal department known as ERD Stewardship. This department is independent of MIS or any other function and its job is to set data standards and enforce quality—hence its nickname, "the data police."

Another new function in ERD management is entity specialists. These key managers have the greatest stake in the quality of the data. For example, the specialist for vendor data is the vice president of purchasing. In cases of no obvious specialists, a steward has been appointed.

The third part of ERD management is the analysts who manage the data. In many cases, they are the same people who maintain systems, but they must now adhere to the new ERD rules. This requirement has led to a large cultural change because these folks formerly only maintained local data. Now they maintain a global resource that the entire company uses. The idea of tweaking a system to fix a local discrepancy, which was formerly a common occurrence, can now cause a major disruption in operations or a bad decision based on faulty data.

Getting the data right in the first place is a large undertaking, one that can easily take several work years per table to extract the data, put it in a common format, eliminate the duplicates, add missing data, and load into the ERD. Even with tools, it is labor intensive. Where possible, Monsanto is using standard external codes, such as Dun & Bradstreet numbers, universal product codes, or European article numbers, so that the company's trading partners can recognize the reference data for electronic commerce purposes. Unfortunately, none of these number schemes is truly universal, so the need to build, maintain, and cross-reference reference data appears to be unavoidable. Monsanto is working through this process and is already reaping bottom-line benefits from better integration (horizontally and vertically) and greater flexibility.

Getting Corporate Data into Shape

Attempts to get corporate data under control began in the late 1960s and early 1970s with DBMSs. Not long after that, the *database administration* function appeared to manage DBMSs and their use. Then, in the 1970s, the broader role of *data administration* was created to manage all the computerized data resources of an organization. These two functions have remained important.

The Problem: Inconsistent Data Definitions. In a nutshell, the problem has been incompatible data definitions from application to application, department to department, site to site, and division to division. How has this inconsistency happened? Blame expediency. To get application systems up and running quickly, system designers have sought the necessary data either from the cheapest source or from a politically expedient source, that is, using data from existing files and adding other new data. In effect, data has been dribbled from application to application. The result has been data showing up in different files, with different names, or the same name for different data items, or the same data in different files with different update cycles.

Use of such data may be acceptable for routine information processing, but it is far from acceptable for management uses. Management cannot get consistent views across the enterprise with such variations. Also, changes in data and programs are hard to make because a change can affect files anywhere in the organization. Furthermore, such inconsistency makes it difficult to change the tracking and reporting of the organization's products, markets, control structure, and other elements needed to meet changing business conditions.

If a major role of the IS organization had been managing data rather than getting applications running as quickly as possible, then a quite different scenario would have occurred. All the types of data of interest would first be identified. Then the single source of each data type would be identified, along with the business function that creates that data. Finally, a transaction system would be built to collect and store that data, after which all authorized users and applications would have access to it.

This data-driven approach does not result in one huge database to serve the entire enterprise, but it does require administrative control over the data as well as designing databases to support users from the outset. It starts out by describing the data the enterprise needs. Then the approach is selected that provides the data that gives a good balance between short-term, application-oriented goals and long-term, data-oriented goals.

The Role of Data Administration. The use of DBMS reduced, to some extent, the problems of inconsistent and redundant data in organizations. However, installing a DBMS is not sufficient to manage data as a corporate resource. Therefore, two additional thrusts have moved organizations in this direction: broader definition of the data administration role and effective use of data dictionaries.

Database administration concentrates on administering databases and the software that manages them. Data administration is broader. One of its main purposes is determining what data is being used outside the organizational unit that creates it. Whenever data crosses organizational boundaries, its definition and format need to be standardized under the data administration function.

The data dictionary is the main tool by which data administrators control standard data definitions. All definitions are entered into the dictionary, and data administrators monitor all new definitions and all requests for changes in definitions to make sure that corporate policy is being followed.

ERP. To bring order to the data mess, data administration has four main functions: clean up the data definitions, control shared data, manage data distribution, and maintain data quality. Interestingly, many companies did not take these four jobs seriously until the mid-1990s when they needed consistent data to either install a company-wide ERP package, such as SAP; support a data warehouse effort; or, in some instances, consolidate country-based databases on an intranet so that everyone in the company, worldwide, could draw from the same data pool.

ERP, in particular, has been the main driving force for getting some data into shape in many companies. It provided the means to consolidate data to give management a corporate-wide view of operations.

One of the benefits of ERP is that it gives companies a ready-made IT architecture. But, as John Langenbahn of Mead Corporation wondered (in Chapter 1), does it reduce flexibility because divisions of a company need to move in concert with each other? McGrane of MeadWestvaco, Langenbahn's successor, thinks not, because once a decision is made it can be implemented quickly and across the entire corporation. However, the question of flexibility of ERP still remains.

Once enterprises get their data in shape, that data can more easily be turned into information. That is the next subject in this chapter.

MANAGING INFORMATION

Information is data in context, which means the data has been given an explicit meaning in a specific context. We often hear such statements as "Information is power" or "We are in the information age." These and similar statements would lead you to believe that managing information is a key corporate activity. Indeed it is, and it is becoming increasingly so. In fact, some believe that information management, rather than technology management, is the main job of the IS department. We believe both are important. The technology can be viewed as the infrastructure and the information as the asset that runs on that infrastructure. Yet, information is just an intermediary—an intermediary for action. In this important intermediary position, the management of information is important. We begin this discussion by discerning four types of information.

Four Types of Information

One view of information resources is shown in the 2 × 2 matrix in Figure 14.15. The rows depict two *structures* of information—record based and document based—and the columns depict two *sources* of information—internal and external. Record-based data contains mainly facts about entities, such as patients, vehicles, and parts, and is housed in data records. The discussion up to this point in this chapter has dealt with record-based data. Document-based information, on the other hand, deals with concepts, such as ideas, thoughts, and opinions, and is housed in documents, messages, and video and audio clips. Figure 14.16 lists various differences between the two.

Internal record-based information was the original focus of IS organizations, because it is the type of information that computer applications generate and manage easily. External record-based information can now be accessed over the Internet or through other electronic means via public databases. End users themselves have generally handled the procurement of this kind of data by subscribing to database services.

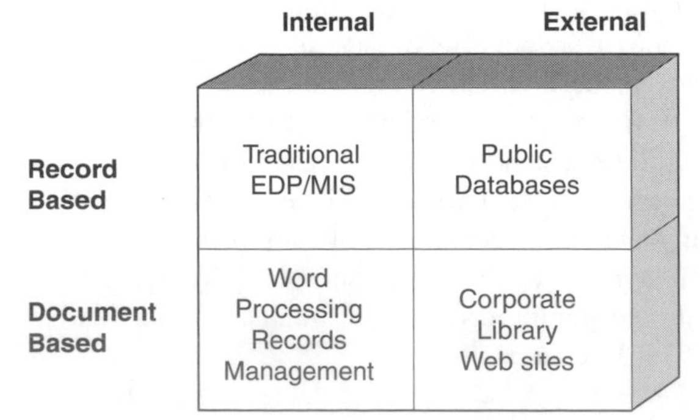

Figure 14.15 Four Types of Information

However, internal and external document-based information have received little attention from IS organizations until recently, because it has been so difficult to manipulate in computers. Intranets changed that. Documents are now an integral part of information on these sites. Even in companies where the administrative vice president or the corporate librarian believe documents are their realm, after a short time, they gladly turn over responsibility for the technical issues to IS.

In short, in the past, these four realms of information have been the responsibility of different functions, as shown in Figure 14.17. Today, the IS organization is likely to be involved in some way in each area. In fact, because the two types of information have such different characteristics, they are being managed in quite different ways. The following discussion notes that division. Managing record-based information is illustrated by the use of one technology: data warehouses. Managing document-based information is illustrated by two technologies: document management and Web content management.

Data Warehouses

Data warehouses appeared in the early 1990s, a bit before ERP systems. Like ERP systems, they, too, spurred getting record-based data into shape. Data warehouses house data used to make decisions. The data is generally obtained periodically from transaction databases—five times a day, once a week, or maybe just once a month. The warehouse thus presents a snapshot at a point in time.

Data warehouses differ from operational databases in that they do not house data used to process daily transactions. Operational databases are meant to be updated to hold the latest data on, say, a customer's flight reservation, the amount of product in inventory, or the status of a customer's order. Data warehouses are not. They are not updated as events occur, only at specific points in time. In addition, unlike transaction databases, data warehouses are used with tools for exploring the data. The simplest tools generate preformatted reports or permit ad hoc queries. Yet warehouses are reaching beyond reporting on internal data. They are being combined with purchased data, such as demographic data, late breaking news, and even weather

	Data Records	Documents
Item of interest	Entity	Concept or idea
Attribute of item	Field	Set of symbols
All attributes for item	Record	Logical paragraph
All related items	File	Document
A group of related files	Database	File cabinet
A collection of databases	Application system	Library, records center
Data models (representational approaches)	Hierarchical, relational, etc.	Keywords, hypertext

Figure 14.16 Structure of Information

reports, to uncover trends or correlations that can give a company a competitive edge. For example, a retailer might put the umbrellas and raincoats by the front door because a surprise storm is moving in.

The most common type of data in a warehouse is customer data, which is used to discover how to more effectively market to current customers as well as non-customers with the same characteristics. As a result, the marketing department has, in large part, been the driving force behind warehouses. They want to use customer data—from billing and invoicing systems, for example—to identify customer clusters and see the effect different marketing programs have on these clusters.

Data warehouses are seen as strategic assets that can yield new insights into customer behavior, internal operations, product mixes, and the like. However, to gain the benefits, companies must take the often-delayed step of reconciling data from numerous legacy systems. When the perceived benefits appear to outweigh the costs, companies tackle the tremendous task.

Due to the strategic nature of such uses of data, warehousing projects need sponsorship from top management,

	Typical Corporate Authority	Information Sources	Technologies Used
Internal record-based information	Information systems department	Transaction processing Organizational units	DBMS Data dictionaries Enterprise data analysis techniques
Internal document-based information	Administrative vice president Word processing center Records management	Corporate memos,letters, reports,forms, e-mail	Word processing Micrographics Reprographics Text-retrieval products
External record-based information	End users Corporate planning Financial analysis Marketing	Public databases	Internet-based services Public networks Analysis packages
External document-based information	Corporate library	Public literature News services Catalogs and indexes Subscriptions Purchased reports	Bibliographic services Environmental scanning Public networks

Figure 14.17 The Scope of Information Management

not only to provide funding and guide the project in truly strategic uses, but also to ensure that departments cooperate and yield up their data for cross-correlations.

Key Concepts in Data Warehousing. As with all other areas of IT, data warehousing has its own set of terms and concepts. Here are few of them.

Metadata: Defining the data. One of the most important elements in a data warehouse is its metadata; that is, the part of the warehouse that defines the data. Metadata means "data about data." Metadata explains the meaning of each data element, how each element relates to other elements, who owns each element, the source of each element, who can access each element, and so on.

Metadata sets the standard. Without it, data from different legacy systems cannot be reconciled, so the data will not be clean; that is, comparable. Without comparable data, the warehouse is not of much use. So an important aspect of data warehousing is creating and then enforcing common data definitions via metadata definitions.

Because the world continues to change, so, too, does the metadata. Thus, a metadata librarian is needed to keep it up-to-date, to enforce the standards, and even to educate users about metadata features of the warehouse. Metadata can be used not only to understand the data in the warehouse, but also to navigate through the warehouse.

Quality data: The biggest challenge. Once metadata definitions have been established, the largest job of data warehousing teams is cleaning the data to adhere to those standards. This cleaning process is onerous, lament warehousing teams, because legacy data often has definitions that have changed over time, gaps, missing fields, and so on. Sometimes, the source data was not even validated properly, for instance, to ensure that the postal code field contained the right number and type of characters.

The older the data, the more suspect its quality. However, because users want to track items over time, even with poor quality, data warehousing teams cannot discard the old, poor-quality data. They must find ways to align it with the more recent data, generally by estimating the data that should be in the missing fields, realigning figures based on the newer formulas, and so forth. This grueling manual task is one of the largest the warehousing team must perform.

Data marts: Subsets of data warehouses. When data warehousing was first espoused, the ideal was to build one huge, all-encompassing warehouse. However, that goal has not always proved feasible or practical. For one thing, search times can be excruciatingly long in huge warehouses. For another, the cost may be too high.

Thus, the concept of data marts became popular. A *data mart* is a subset of data pulled off the warehouse for a specific group of users. A data mart is less expensive to build and easier to search. For these reasons, some companies have started their data warehouse work by first building data marts. Then they populate the data warehouse by drawing from these marts. This approach is the reverse of what was espoused just a few years ago when purists believed that data should go from a data warehouse to data marts.

The main challenge in following this mart-to-warehouse approach is that the company must have unifying metadata, so that the data in all the marts uses the same definitions. Otherwise, the data cannot be meaningfully correlated in the warehouse.

Steps in a Data Warehousing Project. A typical data warehousing project has five main steps.

1. ***Define the business uses of the data.*** Warehousing projects that are run solely by IS departments without a sponsoring user department are generally unsuccessful. The data needs a business use to demonstrate payback.
2. ***Create the data model for the warehouse.*** This means defining the relationships among the data elements. This process can be quite a challenge, especially when commingling data from a number of systems.
3. ***Cleanse the data.*** This notorious step requires moving the data out of the operational systems and then transforming it into the desired standardized format. Specific tools can help cleanse standard kinds of data, such as names and addresses, but defining the transformations is often manual, as is filling in gaps.
4. ***Select the user tools.*** Consider the users' point of view and then select the tools they will use and train them to use them.
5. ***Monitor usage and system performance.*** Warehouse teams need to be particularly alert to changes in use. In many cases, usage begins slowly. But when it catches on, performance can degrade seriously as the system and the team are swamped with requests. If, however, the team monitors use and creates standard queries that serve groups of users rather than individuals, the team can reduce its workload and speed up system response time as well.

The following lengthy case example illustrates numerous ways one company is using its data for competitive advantage. The case illustrates use of ERP, data warehousing, and the Web, not only for internal use of data, but as the basis for new revenue-generating services to customers and suppliers. It shows how innovative companies can use advanced information management technologies This case is based on a paper that won one of the awards in the Society for Information Management's annual paper

CASE EXAMPLE

OWENS & MINOR

Owens & Minor (OM), headquartered in Richmond, Virginia, distributes name-brand medical and surgical supplies from 14,000 suppliers to over 4,000 hospitals, integrated health-care systems, and group purchasing organizations throughout the United States. OM employs 2,700 people and had sales of $3.8 billion in 2001.

As Don Stoller, Director of Information Management, and his co-authors point out, OM is in the middle of its value chain. The supply side begins with raw material suppliers who sell to manufacturers (such as Johnson & Johnson), who sell to OM (the distributor), who then sells to health-care providers (such as hospitals), who sell to patients. In this field, distributors compete for contracts between manufacturers and health-care providers.

In the mid-1990s, OM bought a competitor, doubling OM's size to $3 billion. However, merging the two cultures proved so difficult that OM recorded its first loss. This loss spurred management to implement a new three-part strategy:

1. Achieve operational excellence
2. Follow and support patient care
3. Turn information into knowledge and then into profit

This strategy depended on building a leading-edge IT infrastructure and an IT R&D culture, which it did. In 1999, it won an award for its industry-leading ebusiness infrastructure. Here is what OM did.

Achieving Operational Excellence

OM augmented its ERP system to automate order forecasting, which improved inventory turns, reduced ordering rates from five times a week to once a week, and improved customer service. OM also installed an activity-based costing system to separate the cost of its products from the cost of delivery. Thus, customers, such as hospitals or purchasing groups, could pay just for the delivery service they wanted. Some wanted delivery to a loading dock; others wanted delivery to an emergency room. Some customers saved large amounts of money with this new option, and OM increased its sales. A new warehouse management system that uses handheld devices also increased OM's operational efficiency.

Following and Supporting Patient Care

OM implemented an Internet-based inventory management system, called OM-Direct, so that customers could order over the Internet, even using handheld devices. For example, when a hospital signs up for this service, it can ask OM to place bar codes on the products and establish replenishment levels. Then, when a hospital employee scans the bar code with, say, a Palm device, enters the on-hand inventory of that product, and uploads the data to OM's system, the system automatically reorders the product, if needed. Some 1,100 customers signed up for OM-Direct during its first 2 years.

To serve smaller customers and suppliers, such as physicians' offices, small hospitals, and small specialist suppliers, OM teamed up with trading exchanges to provide online marketplaces for these members to buy and sell products and even use OM-Direct. The exchanges have encouraged these customers to start using the Internet for ordering, even though they only offer 1,700 of OM's 150,000 products.

Turning Information into Knowledge and Profit

Most interestingly, OM initiated a data warehousing and decision-support initiative, building one subject area at a time (sales, inventory, accounts receivable, and so on), and permitting queries across the subject areas. During the first year, much of the work was handled by a system integrator familiar with building data warehouses. After that, it became the responsibility of a 12-person OM team that included a director, a manager, three developers who add new subject areas and load data, one data administrator, and six business analysts, who work with the users.

Initially, the warehouse was for internal use only. Within the first 30 months, some 500 OM employees in sales, marketing, supply chain management, finance, and other departments had learned to use the BusinessObjects tool to make queries or create reports from the warehouse, report Stoller et al.

For several reasons, the warehouse team then investigated offering decision support over the Web. Customers were asking sales reps for more information; some requesting up to

(Case continued)

(Case continued)

30 reports a month. Why not let the customers serve themselves? Also, the Web would allow casual users, such as customers or executives who do not want to learn Business-Objects, to access the data in the data warehouse. Furthermore, OM realized that customers and suppliers were asking for information to run their own businesses because they did not have the systems or technology in-house. Delivering this information over the Web could give OM a competitive advantage by strengthening its relationships with trading partners, giving it a market-leading feature to entice new customers, and even turning the data warehouse into a new service; in fact, a new source of revenue.

To assist its trading partners, OM created an extranet and asked a pilot set of customers and suppliers to list the kinds of information they needed to, say, reduce their costs or better manage their inventories. From these lists, the OM warehousing team created queries and let these partners pilot test the system for 4 months. During that time, OM debated whether to offer this service for free or for a fee. It decided to charge money, reasoning that the information would appear more valuable if it had a price. Furthermore, the fees would be reasonable, especially compared with the up-front data warehousing costs partners would be able to avoid.

When the service, called Wisdom, was rolled out, it became the first "e-business intelligence application" in the medical and surgical supply distribution industry, state Stoller et al.

All users have a profile of the information they can access. Every access is checked by the security system. Every query contains the user's account number so that the system knows which information can be used to answer the query. The browser interface is easy to use; people point and click on over 50 predefined queries, or, more recently, make ad hoc queries.

OM has continued to improve the service. Suppliers and customers can now add external data, such as data from other manufacturers, into OM's data warehouse so they can study more relationships and perform more "what if" investigations.

For example, a typical-size hospital spends $30 million a year buying all its medical and surgical supplies. Hospital groups can have a difficult time analyzing purchases across all their hospitals, because each has a disparate system. Rather than invest in consolidating the systems themselves, hospital groups would rather purchase data about their own transactions from, say, a distributor, who is well placed in the value chain to have that information.

OM has thus become an important "infomediary," note Stoller et al., because hospital purchasing staffs may have a much easier time getting the purchasing information they need from OM than from their own hospital. They can then discover, for instance, which purchases were "on contract" with OM, and thus had the lower contract price, and which were not. Oftentimes, up to 40 percent of hospital purchases are off-contract, which costs these hospitals money they need not spend. Furthermore, purchasing managers can see how many suppliers they use for the same product and negotiate higher-volume discounts from just one or two. They can also see ordering frequency and optimize it by increasing order volumes, perhaps. In addition, they can more easily spot delivery problems.

OM's Wisdom service turns out to be equally valuable to suppliers, such as Johnson & Johnson. Wisdom has over 30 queries and 100 reports for suppliers to watch their products move out to consumers. They can analyze their marketshare in specific regions, analyze product shelf life, coordinate shipping from several locations, see on-contract purchasing (and help customers increase the levels), analyze drop shipments (which are more expensive than OM distribution), and so forth.

Wisdom has become a valuable service to both OM suppliers and customers, and it becomes more valuable the more sales or purchases go through OM rather than through other distributors. In fact, Wisdom led to over $60 million in new business in 1 year because it is providing visibility throughout OM's value chain. Because partners pay for its use, there is constant pressure to keep it market leading, note Stoller et al.

The next step is to turn the data warehouse into an industry-wide warehouse by asking suppliers and customers to place all their data there. If this occurs, conceivably, other distributors might become paying customers of Wisdom as well. Or, as OM and three competitors have agreed, they will establish an independent, neutral health care information exchange.

CASE EXAMPLE

HICSS PERSONAL PROCEEDINGS

The Hawaii International Conference on System Sciences has been held each January since 1967. It brings together academics and professionals to discuss research papers from a wide variety of computer-related subjects.

The conference proceedings have made an important contribution to the literature for many years. But with more than 450 papers averaging 10 pages each in length, the proceedings have grown to 4,500 pages in 9 volumes weighing 25 pounds. As a result, conference management decided to produce a paper book of abstracts with a CD-ROM of the full papers tucked in a sleeve inside the back cover. This publishing approach reduced the paper problem, but many participants wanted to see the full papers during the presentations and discussions. They had been using the paper versions to take notes and to understand additional details of the presentation.

Conference management then introduced personal proceedings. A month before the conference, participants can use a Web site to choose 20 papers they would like to have in their personal paper proceedings. The papers they choose are printed on a Xerox Docutech machine with their name on the cover and delivered to them at the conference. Additional papers can be printed individually at the conference using the conference print-on-demand service for a nominal fee. This new use of print-on-demand technology has helped the conference meet the participants' needs while cutting costs and reducing paper.

competition. This competition attracts some of the best in-depth descriptions of IS management in practice. The company is Owens & Minor.

Document Management

Now we turn to managing document-based information. Management of *internal* document-based information has traditionally rested with the vice president of administration, who has traditionally overseen records management (document records, not data records). Technologies used to manage documents have included micrographics (microfilm and fiche) and computer output microfilm (COM), generally in stand-alone systems. That is, until the Internet arrived. Now corporate intranets house many former paper-based internal documents.

External document-based information, on the other hand, has generally been the responsibility of corporate librarians. Yet, as the amount of such external information grows and as more of it has become computerized, it is increasingly being included in IS executives' jurisdiction. Again, it has been the Web that has brought these external documents to the attention of CIOs, yet many of them consider documents to be the least manageable form of information.

Even in today's Internet-rich world, paper still plays a major role in most enterprises. And while paper is around, there is a need to move seamlessly between digital and printed versions of documents. Hence, the importance of document management. The field of electronic document management (EDM) uses new technologies to manage information resources that do not fit easily into traditional databases. EDM addresses organizing and managing conceptual, descriptive, and ambiguous multimedia content.

Using IT to manage documents is a challenge for enterprises because most of their valuable information is in documents, such as business forms, reports, letters, memos, policy statements, contracts, agreements, and so on. Moreover, most of their important business processes are based on or driven by document flows. While computer systems have mostly handled facts organized into data records, far more valuable and important are the concepts and ideas contained in documents. Reports drawn from computerized databases fill important roles in status assessment and control. Oftentimes they must be accompanied by a memo or textual report that explains and interprets the report. Meetings, phone conversations, news items, written memos, and non-computerized reports are usually rated more important by managers. Technology applied to handling documents promises to improve these forms of communication.

A document can be described as a unit of "recorded information structured for human consumption." It is recorded

CASE EXAMPLE

TAPIOLA INSURANCE GROUP

Tapiola is a group of three insurance companies with headquarters in Espoo, Finland, a suburb of Helsinki. By Finnish law, an insurance company can sell only one type of insurance; therefore, each of Tapiola's three companies sells either life, non-life, or pension insurance. Tapiola calls itself "an insurance department store."

Some 90 percent of insurance in Finland is sold by five insurance groups; Tapiola is the fourth-largest group. It has 14 percent of the market with 1.5 million customers and 3 million policies. Each year its mailroom sends out 4 million letters, so printing is an important and expensive part of its operation.

Formerly, the Tapiola group offered 150 kinds of insurance policies and had 300 different insurance policy forms. Half of the forms were in Swedish and half were in Finnish because both are official languages in Finland. The policy forms were preprinted by an outside print shop, generally on sprocket-fed computer paper. Then the forms were filled in by printers connected to their IBM mainframes.

This mode of operation presented several problems. If a change was made to a form, the inventory of old forms had to be discarded. Reprinting new forms often took weeks. That time represented possible lost revenue. Also, the computer printers could print on only one side of each sheet of paper. Finally, for more complex policies, Tapiola had to use large-size computer paper that was often unwieldy to handle and mail.

Document-Processing Goals

The production manager and the insurance applications development manager looked around for an alternate way to print policies and statements. They had several goals. One was, of course, to reduce costs. A second goal was to stop using preprinted forms. Their third goal was to give Tapiola marketing people new ways to advertise insurance products by making computer-generated letters to customers more flexible. The fourth and most important goal was to make Tapiola "the most personal insurance company in Finland." These two systems managers wanted their computer-generated correspondence to prospective and current policyholders to appear more "human," as if a Tapiola employee had used a typewriter to write a personal reply to an inquiry or request for information.

Centralized Solution

To overcome the computer-generated appearance of their output, they switched to plain paper printers from Rank Xerox, the European subsidiary of Xerox Corporation. Xerox is best known for its photocopiers, but it is increasingly creating products for electronic document processing where a document can include text, data, images, and graphics. Conversion of the output equipment at Tapiola took 15 months, during which time it reduced its 300 preprinted forms to 4.

Four New Forms

The four new forms are actually four types of standard European A4-cut paper. (In the United States, the equivalent would be the 8-1/2 x 11 sheet of paper.) The first form is a plain white A4 sheet of paper. It is used for internal communications within Tapiola.

The second form is the same blank white paper with four holes punched along the left-hand side to fit in the standard European four-ring binder. (In the United States, the standard is a three-ring binder.) This form is also mainly for internal use.

The third form has the Tapiola logo preprinted in green in the upper left-hand corner, and both sides of the paper have the word "Tapiola" printed in tiny, faint green letters over most of the page. This form is the standard company stationery, and it has become one of Tapiola's standard computer printout forms for communicating with the outside world.

The fourth form is the same as the third except that it has a 4 x 6-inch (10 x 15-cm) perforated area in the lower right-hand corner. This form is used for all their insurance policy bills. The tear-off portion can be paid at any bank; the money and information about the payment go directly from the bank to Tapiola.

Programming and Conversion

Reprogramming the IBM applications was extremely easy, because only the output routines needed to be changed. That programming took 2 work years of application programmer time. In addition, one systems programmer spent 6 months working with Xerox on the IBM to Xerox system software interfaces. One forms designer spent 15 months redesigning all

300 preprinted forms into 240 printing formats for the application programmers. About 60 forms disappeared altogether because they were found to be unnecessary; the remaining 240 forms are not all different because one-half of them are in Swedish and the other half are in Finnish.

The conversion was done in two stages. First, customer policy statements were printed in a form-like manner on two sides of the new-size paper. These looked somewhat like the old forms so that policyholders could understand the changeover. Then, the terse, table-like data was replaced with text to make the statements look more like personal letters.

Envelope Stuffing

Interestingly, these redesigns of customer documents were the easy part of the conversion. The more difficult and sensitive part was making sure that each envelope contained the correct pieces of paper. Because Tapiola was now using smaller sheets of paper, each envelope often needed to include several sheets, and, of course, Tapiola did not want to put a cover letter for one policyholder into the same envelope as a statement for another policyholder.

To solve this problem, the company found an envelope insertion machine made by PMB Vector in Stockholm, Sweden. This machine contains a microprocessor that can read an eight-dot code printed at the top of each sheet of paper. Thus, the Xerox printer not only prints the correspondence but, at the same time, it prints a code at the top of each sheet of paper–one code for all pages to go in one envelope. The Vector insertion machine makes sure that each envelope only contains pages with the same code.

Decentralized Expansion

This document-processing conversion was just one part of the effort to improve and humanize customer correspondence. In the midst of the document redesign, Tapiola also decided to move some printing of customer correspondence to its 62 branch offices.

To illustrate how a remote printer is used, consider the case of a female policyholder who has received medical care. She can mail the medical bills to Tapiola or visit her local office in person. If she visits them and presents her bills to a Tapiola employee, that employee uses a desktop machine to access the policyholder's data from the central database. If she has brought all the proper documents needed for reimbursement, the employee can initiate a direct electronic payment from a Tapiola bank account to her personal bank account, no matter which bank they both use.

Once a day, Tapiola transmits all such electronic transactions to its bank, and those transactions are cleared that same day. (The five major Finnish banks have collaborated and created a sophisticated and fast banking system.) The employee then gives the policyholder a letter verifying the transaction. That letter is generated by the central IBM computer but is printed on the local Xerox printer. If the policyholder is missing some information, the employee can create a personalized letter explaining what is missing by assembling phrases stored in the central database and then printing the letter on-site.

The people at Tapiola Data recommend that other IS organizations become involved in electronic document management by first looking at the output their computers are generating. It was not difficult to mix traditional host computing with document processing technology.

A poll of Finnish citizens showed that Tapiola is seen as a dynamic company, and it has the best reputation among young people of all the insurance groups. The people at Tapiola Data believe their use of document-processing technology is helping to build and reinforce this image.

and stored; therefore, a speech or conversation for which no transcript is prepared is not a document. This definition accommodates "documents" dating back to cuneiform inscriptions on clay tablets. What has changed are the ways information is represented and the ways documents are processed. Information previously represented primarily by text is now also represented by graphical symbols, images, photographs, audio, video, and animation. Documents previously created and stored on paper are now digitally created, stored, transported, and displayed.

Applying technology to process traditional documents changes what documents can accomplish in organizations. A definition more oriented to technology comes from *Byte* magazine.

A document is a snapshot of some set of information that can

- *incorporate many complex information types;*
- *exist in multiple places across a network;*
- *depend on other documents for information;*
- *change on the fly (as subordinate documents are updated);*
- *have an intricate structure or complex data types such as full-motion video and voice annotations; and*

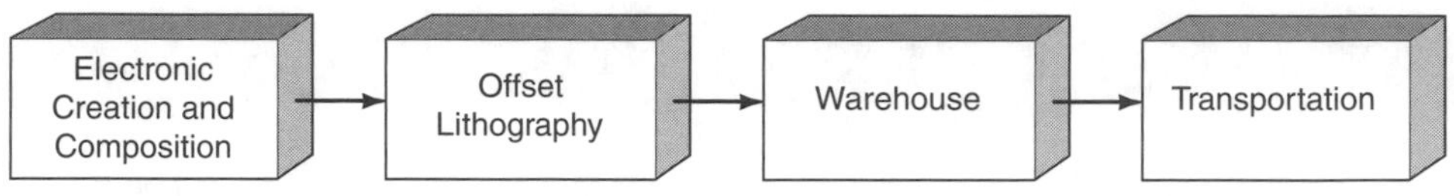

Figure 14.18 Traditional Publishing Process

- *be accessed and modified by many people simultaneously (if they have permission to do so).*

It is hard to think of anything more pervasive and fundamental to an organization than documents. The impact of applying emerging technologies to document management is potentially significant. EDM promises to advance the management of conceptual information, thereby improving the levels of support and productivity for manager and professional. With documents as the primary vehicle for business processes, EDM contributes to business process redesign and quality improvement. Numerous EDM applications generate value. In this section, we will examine three:

1. To improve the publishing process
2. To support organizational processes
3. To support communications among people and groups

The concept of just-in-time (printing, publishing, and forms processing) pervades the design philosophy in all three areas.

Improving the Publishing Process. Technology enables a major restructuring of the process of publishing and distributing paper documents. For those organizations that produce documents as a product or as support for a product, this change is reengineering their document production processes. The stages of the traditional process, designed primarily for high-volume and high-quality documents, is shown in Figure 14.18. The document is created, generally with the use of electronic tools, and a photographic plate is made for an offset printing press. The offset press requires long print runs to amortize the extensive setup costs. Thus, a large quantity of documents is produced and stored in a warehouse and then documents are shipped to their destination when they are required. R. R. Donnelley & Sons Company, the country's largest publisher, estimates that 60 percent of the total cost of delivering these documents is in storage and transportation.

Figure 14.19 shows the steps in the revised publishing/ distribution process using newer technologies. Documents are stored electronically, shipped over a network, and printed when and where they are needed. The major benefits result from reducing obsolescence (revisions are made frequently to the electronically stored version), eliminating warehouse costs, and reducing or eliminating delivery time.

Below is an example of how a traditional printing process has been changed by emerging technologies.

Supporting Communications among People and Groups. The value of documents is that they transfer information across time and space. Of course, the Internet can handle such communication, but when all members of a group do not have Internet access, or do not use it frequently, companies may need to continue to rely on paper documents. EDM can be used to facilitate such communications among people and groups. In the broadest sense, all EDM applications support this function. The case on pages 540–541 illustrates using various technologies to communicate with customers via paper and ensure that each customer gets the right pieces of paper.

Supporting Organizational Processes. Documents are still the vehicle for accomplishing many processes in organizations. Typical examples include processing a claim in an insurance company, hiring a new employee, or making a large expenditure. The documents are primarily forms that flow through the organization carrying infor-mation, accumulating input and approval from a sequence of people. Many such workflow systems still rely heavily on the physical circulation of paper forms.

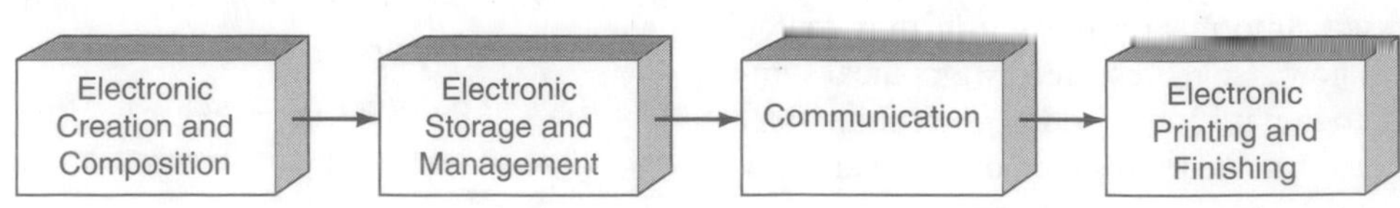

Figure 14.19 Reengineered Publishing Process

CASE EXAMPLE

TENNESSEE VALLEY AUTHORITY

The Tennessee Valley Authority (TVA) is the largest supplier of power in the United States, serving some 8 million customers in the eastern United States by generating energy using fossil, hydroelectric, and nuclear fuels. Not long ago, the nuclear division, which has three facilities, revamped its maintenance management system—a system that relies on documents, such as manuals from vendors, drawings, and work instructions, that are regulated by government.

TVA spends more than $48 million a year creating maintenance work orders and then planning and performing the work. One plant alone processes 14,000 work orders a year. Government regulations that oversee the documentation of this work contribute significantly to TVA's high maintenance costs.

The improvement project was handled by a team from various parts of the nuclear operation. They analyzed and charted the existing work processes, determined which improvements were most needed, and investigated how those improvements could be achieved. They spent 350 hours interviewing people and looked at 15 other utilities.

One thing they discovered was that the work orders were inextricably linked to document workflow and the ways procedures were managed. Previously, the three areas—work order management, document workflow, and procedure management—had been viewed as separate, and thus managed separately. Upon investigation, the team realized that every work order included accompanying diagrams, documentation, and procedure instructions. However, the three were not always in sync. For example, a work order might be planned several months in advance, but in the meantime, procedures might be changed, yet those changes were not noted when the work order was about to be performed.

The new process designed by TVA electronically combines maintenance orders in one system with procedural document management in another system and eliminates a number of existing systems that did not talk to one another. Maintenance workers can now access documentation on equipment, parts, and records as well as work instructions from desktop machines. Work orders are generated electronically and then routed for approval with the most current drawings and procedures electronically attached. In addition, the documents are indexed by, say, piece of equipment, and the three plants now use the same systems. Thus, maintenance people can review past activity and better plan for the future.

The system has been successful, but the team underestimated the change management effort needed. They did not realize they had to bring many employees up-to-speed on using computers; some had not used keyboards. In addition, the team realized they should have set expectations differently. Rather than emphasize the benefits of the new systems to each employee (because sometimes the new systems required more work of some employees), the team should have emphasized the benefits of the system to TVA, which were significant.

The average amount of human time spent processing a work order has decreased by almost half, from 39 hours to 23 hours; labor savings are large. More importantly, maintenance workers now have captured data for improving processes.

Using IT to support these processes generates significant value in reducing physical space for handling forms, faster routing of forms (especially over geographical distances), and managing and tracking forms flow and workload. Two trends in organizations have increased the importance of workflow systems: total quality management and business process reengineering.

In addition to improving transaction-oriented business processes with EDM, many organizations are improving the management processes of reporting, control, decision making, and problem solving as well. Several EISs now supply documents to supplement the more traditional data-based reports. Organizations with a custom-developed EIS also add so-called soft information in the form of documents.

To give an example of how one organization improved a work process via a new document management system, consider the Tennessee Valley Authority.

Content Management

We now turn to the other form of document-based information: Web content. Many corporate intranets now house documents that used to be paper based. In some cases, these documents appear in PDF form on the intranet, which is like taking a photograph of the pages so that the pages cannot be changed.

The question for CIOs has become: How should we manage all the internal and external content on our Web sites? The field that addresses this question is called *content management*. It deals with managing Web-based content of all types, writes Chuck Tucker in the Gartner EXP report entitled *Dealing in Web Currency*. A major reason content has become important to CIOs, he notes, is because it is a core management discipline underlying online business. Without production-level Web content management processes and technologies, large-scale online-business is not possible. The content on Web sites attracts customers, answers questions, and handles transactions. If the content is not refreshed frequently, perhaps as news occurs, or if it is full of errors, or if it cannot handle transaction volumes, a company's Web channel will stave off rather than attract customers.

Content is no longer static; it is active. It can cause actions to happen. An underlying reason is the adoption of XML. XML is used to put tags on data that give that data meaning. Computers use the meanings to manipulate the data and perform work. In essence, use of XML moves Web content from being in a human-only readable format to being in a computer-readable format. Thus, the content can be passed to back-end transaction processing systems and cause an action to take place, such as ordering a book or configuring a recently ordered computer. XML is an intrinsic part of managing Web content because it is the language for manipulating the content to work with transaction applications, which is the basis for e-commerce.

In the beginning, when Web sites were new, Web content was managed as follows: Someone in a department, usually HR or marketing, decided to use this new communication channel. They designed a format, decided on the sections on the site, and wrote the content or gathered it from written documents. The department then gave all this content to the Webmaster to publish. When new material needed to be added, they gave it to the Webmaster, who turned it into HTML and published it to the Web site. Before long, the Webmaster became the publishing bottleneck; time to publish got longer and longer. This homegrown method was not only inefficient, but it also did not present a good image to Web site visitors.

To create a content management strategy, states Tucker, companies need to understand the three phases of the content management life cycle and the goals for each one. As shown in Figure 14.20, the three phases, which can be viewed as input—process—output, are:

1. Content creation and acquisition
2. Content administration and safeguarding
3. Content deployment and presentation

Managing Content Creation and Acquisition. Each phase needs a different emphasis to be effective, notes Tucker. Content creation and acquisition, for instance, needs to focus on *creating content quality*. That is why it might be wise to buy some content from specialists, which is called syndicated content, rather than create it in-house. For example, why create a stock ticker or a weather report or a news feed? Draw on the ones that already exist.

High-quality in-house content comes from subject matter experts and local employees. Thus, the best organizational structure is to distribute content creation and maintenance to employees in HR, marketing, sales, and field offices. They should be responsible not only for creating their content, but also for keeping it updated and fresh.

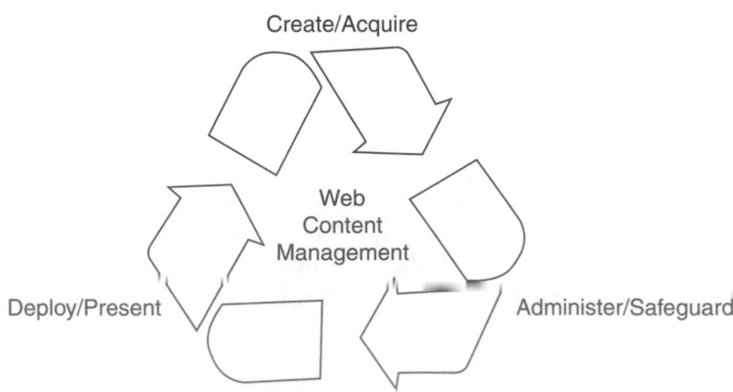

Figure 14.20 The Web Content Management Life Cycle. *Source:* Tueber, Chuck, *Dealing in Web Currency,* Gartner EXP, 56 Top Gallant, Stamford, Ct, June 2001.

To avoid anarchy, though, these dispersed experts should be directed centrally and use centrally created formats and an automated workflow system that moves their work along. The system might even send them reminder e-mails of publishing deadlines. Finally, to improve content quality, it is wise to create a feedback loop so that comments from Web site visitors reach these content creators. Then these creators know what types of content attract visitors and customers.

Content Administration and Safeguarding. The emphasis in this phase, like any operational phase, is *efficiency*, states Tucker. The goal is to achieve the most with the least effort. Content management software tools can help. These tools are used to identify types of content and the business rules that apply to each type. For example, publication of press releases on a Web site should follow business rules that state that each release will first be approved by the manager of corporate communications, each press release will use the standard press release format, and each release will move to the archive file 1 month after being published. Business rules form the heart of content administration. They present the parameters for the automated workflow for each type of content, thus relieving the Webmaster bottleneck.

So, whereas content creation should be distributed, content administration should be centralized. This struc-ture permits overall central guidance of distributed creative efforts. However, it does present some vexing challenges. One involves the approval process of foreign-language content. Companies that create an approval process believing that all content will be in, say, English, create translation bottlenecks for themselves if they expect all drafts to be translated into English for approval and then translated back into the original language once the document is approved. Companies need to consider multilanguage issues when creating their workflows, selecting their content management software, and designing their Web sites.

Content Deployment and Presentation. The third phase of the content management life cycle is the output phase, distributing content to Web site visitors. The emphasis in this phase should be on *effectiveness*, that is, presenting the content so that it attracts visitors, allows them to navigate the site easily, and leads them to the desired actions, notes Tucker.

Because this phase can determine the success of a firm's e-commerce efforts, it is best to design a Web site beginning with this phase, then move on to ensuring content quality and processing efficiency. The Eastman Chemical Company example that follows illustrates this outside-in viewpoint; most companies take an inside-out view. Eastman redesigned its site to take its customers' point of view rather than its internal organizational point of view. The change had a major positive impact.

Today, most Web sites need certain features to attract and keep visitors. Two such features are personalization and localization. Personalization means allowing Web site visitors to customize how they view the page. For instance, some visitors to consumer sites may want lots of sports news but little international news. On the other hand, business visitors to corporate sites might want the site to open to the products they buy or recent news pertinent to their industry. Web content software gives site builders the ability to offer site visitors viewing options. Once selected, the choices are stored in the users' profile and referenced every time they visit the site. Companies can also use personalization to offer complementary products, such as corkscrews to wine buyers, notes Tucker, or take into account a customer's past buying record.

Localization, on the other hand, means tailoring a site to a culture, market, or locale. For instance, a site may be designed to present its content in the language of the country or region of the visitor. Likewise, localization may mean making appropriate currency conversions automatically. Localization is crucial for companies involved in global e-commerce.

Finally, a growing issue in deployment is multichannel distribution; that is, being able to display the site in the manner appropriate to each type of device, from PC to cell phone. Ideally, the information comes from a common repository, rather than existing in several places, and is put in the appropriate form when requested, notes Tucker. Otherwise, if the same content is stored in several places, it can get out of sync. Central storage is important to maintain content quality.

In summary, the way to manage content is to understand the goal of each phase of the content life cycle—quality, efficiency, or effectiveness—and design the phase with that goal in mind. In addition, there should be a feedback loop, so that Web site visitors can tell Web site content creators which content is most useful to them. Such a loop can then drive continual improvement in the Web site.

To illustrate how one company is managing its Web content, consider Eastman Chemical on pages 535–536, whose story appeared in Tucker's report entitled *Dealing in Web Currency*.

Managing Blogs. The term *blog* is short for *"Web log"* or "weblog." A blog is a Web site where an individual makes intermittent Web postings. It is akin to a personal online journal. People write and post on blogs as a form of

CASE EXAMPLE

EASTMAN CHEMICAL COMPANY

Eastman Chemical Company, which is located in Kingsport, Tennessee, is a global manufacturer of chemicals, fibers, and plastics. Founded in 1920 to make chemicals for Eastman Kodak, it was spun off in 1994. Annual sales were $5.4 billion in 2001.

Management considers the company a leader in using IT. Eastman.com was operational in 1994, several years before most companies had Web sites. Originally the site was used for HR and recruiting. Over time, as more content was added, the site became a hodge-podge of different sections targeted at different audiences, structured like Eastman's organization chart.

Redesigning the Web Site to Take the Customer Viewpoint

In mid-1999, Eastman initiated a companywide effort to become more customer focused and launched a major e-commerce program. This was the catalyst for rethinking the Web site design. The redesign was championed by the vice presidents of e-commerce and corporate communications because their departments jointly managed content.

The e-commerce group provides the tools and processes for employees to create and update Web content. The corporate communications department enforces corporate content policy and approves all Web content for correct use of trademarks, brands, terminology, and so on.

In line with the corporate refocus, the two groups decided to change the Web site structure from presenting an inside-out view based on Eastman's corporate structure to presenting an outside-in view with sections devoted to the markets the company serves.

A packaging customer who bought plastics from two Eastman operations formerly had to search the site to find who supplied plastics. Once found, each section had a different navigational system. In the redesign, a single section on food packaging was created for all Eastman operations dealing with packaging.

Eastman worked with a Web design company on the new site architecture, site map, and layout.

Upgrading the Content Management Software

At the same time, Eastman searched for content management software to replace home-grown software in use since 1994. The flat HTML files created a maintenance bottleneck because each page had to be updated separately and required a programmer to translate the content into HTML.

Eastman selected a content management product to create pre-approved templates for employees to use, then forward the pages to corporate communications for approval. This approach eliminated the programmer bottleneck. The software manages employees' rights to update, add, and publish content. Each user ID has a security level and permissible functions associated with it.

Pulling all the business content together for the new site turned out to be a massive effort. Once the content had been compiled, cataloged, and approved, moving from the old system and server to the new system and new content proved to be a second major undertaking.

Benefits of the Site Redesign

The benefits of the redesign were far greater than expected. Within 6 months, overall traffic doubled, and hits to the new market sections, where Eastman sells its products, increased from 30 percent to 60 percent of total hits. Today, traffic has tripled, and 70 percent of the hits are in the market sectors. Adding new content significantly helped increase traffic, but so, too, did the customer focus.

Eastman underestimated the value of the technical product data sheets published on the site, especially to people outside the United States who previously were unable to get this information easily or quickly. More than 50 percent of the site traffic is from outside the United States. Customers report that the technical data has also significantly accelerated their internal decision-making processes.

To manage the technical data, Eastman uses an internally developed product catalog. Formerly, a data sheet could exist in multiple locations, which led to quality problems, because each had to be updated separately. With the product catalog, the data is stored once and is pulled into a data sheet when needed. Thus, Eastman can ensure that everyone sees the same data on a chemical, even in two different markets.

The site has a public part that anyone can access and a protected part for customers only. Once customers are registered and have a user name and password, they can place orders, look at their order history and status, and browse the product catalog in this protected part. They can also personalize their view of the site to some extent and create their own catalog of the products they normally order.

Since the redesign, Eastman has continued to expand the site. It recently improved search capabilities and added a synonym directory, which has proven important because site visitors often use different names for the same product.

Moving Forward: Globalization and Localization

Globalization and localization are major issues. Eastman has a presence in more than 30 countries and sells in all major regions of the world. A significant portion of sales comes from overseas, so the company wants to allow a site visitor to choose one of, say, eight languages and see the relevant content in that language. If it had treated English as a foreign language during the 1999 redesign, it could add other languages easily. Thinking globally in all content management decisions is a necessity.

Another major challenge is finding a workable global approval process. Checking for adherence to content policies by corporate communications is quick today because all content is in English. However, translation into multiple languages and adaptation to local cultures can significantly complicate and lengthen this approval process. Retranslation into English for corporate approval is too expensive to be feasible. The e-commerce and corporate communications departments are currently working on creating a workable translation and approval process for content originating in other languages.

Eastman has learned that it is best to push content management to the source as much as possible so as not to create bottlenecks at central control points. It also learned the value of consistent organization throughout the Web site. This helps present a cohesive image of the company to site visitors. Having the content management system pull information from the product catalog also ensures data consistency.

self-expression. What do they write about? They write about whatever comes to mind. They may write about their private life or their work life. Most blogs also invite comments from others, which appear on the blog as well. Blogs are a different form of Web content, but they still need to be managed. Enterprises need to establish guidelines for employees who choose to blog.

Blogs are powerful tools for democratizing online expression, notes Dan Farber. According to Farber, "Combine blogs with social networks and presence services (such as instant messaging and global positioning), and you have a new person-to-person, information-sharing connection fabric." In short, individuals can compete with major media via blogs, and they can have major impacts such as influencing politics or company policies. Some forward-thinking companies have recognized the power of this immediate form of publishing and communication. One corporate use of blogs is for crisis management. A blog can be more appropriate than e-mail in managing a crisis (such as a fire or a security breach). All the postings can be on one site, in journaling style, rather than passed as disconnected e-mails, notes Farber.

What readers seem to trust about blogs, that they do not trust about conventional media, is their opinionated and personal nature. These characteristics present both opportunities and challenges to organizations. For example, Farber notes that Microsoft employee Robert Scoble's popular blog about the company's forthcoming version of Windows, Longhorn, is not vetted by Microsoft. It's Scoble's opinions. But he does admit that he talks to the company's public relations department to be sure he does not divulge company-confidential information, notes Farber. Scoble's blog can be found at http://radio.weblogs.com.0001011

Employees who are not careful about the information they blog can find themselves in trouble. A hypothetical case study of a blogger who works for a disposable-glove manufacturer is presented in the September 2003 issue of the *Harvard Business Review.* Known as "Glove Girl," her highly popular blog has increased sales of a company glove, but she has also talked about competitors' products, potential deals, and industry statistics—all from her own point of view, not the company's. This case poses the question, "What should company management do about Glove Girl?" to four experts. It's a question all top management teams should be asking themselves.

One of the experts is Ray Ozzie, Chairman and CEO of Groove Networks, a company that provides software for group collaboration. He notes in his comments that he believes employee blogs are "more often than not" good for companies. But companies need policies to guide employees in expressing themselves via Weblogs or Web sites, while both protecting the company and reflecting positively on it. He notes that in 2002 his company developed such a policy, shown in the following case example, to address four concerns:

1. That readers would see blogs as official company communications rather than personal opinions
2. That confidential information would be disclosed, intentionally or not
3. That a party—the company, an employee, a customer, or other—could be disparaged on a blog
4. That a blog might violate the quiet period imposed by securities regulations, during which time a company cannot discuss an upcoming securities-related event

Ozzie's advice in the case, and to executives in general, is to create a policy for their firm and to become more familiar with blogging—even perhaps write their own blog, as he does at www.ozzie.net, to "communicate convincingly with employees, markets and shareholders.

CASE EXAMPLE

GROOVE NETWORKS

Employee Guidelines for Personal Web Site and Weblogs

In general, the company views personal Web sites and Weblogs positively, and it respects the right of employees to use them as a medium of self-expression.

If you choose to identify yourself as a company employee or to discuss matters related to the company's technology or business on your Web site or weblog, please bear in mind that, although you and we view your Web site or weblog as a personal project and a medium of personal expression, some readers may nonetheless view you as a de facto spokesperson for the company. In light of this possibility, we ask that you observe the following guidelines:

- Please make it clear to your readers that the views you express are yours alone and that they do not necessarily reflect the views of the company. To help reduce the potential for confusion, we would appreciate it if you put the following notice–or something similar–in a reasonably prominent place on your site (e.g., at the bottom of your "about me" page):

  The views expressed on this Web site/weblog are mine alone and do not necessarily reflect the views of my employer.

If you do put a notice on your site, you needn't put it on every page, but please use reasonable efforts to draw attention to it–if at all possible, from the home page of your site.

- Take care not to disclose any information that is confidential or proprietary to the company or to any third party that has disclosed information to us. Consult the company's confidentiality policy for guidance about what constitutes confidential information.
- Please remember that your employment documents give the company certain rights with respect to concepts and developments you produce that are related to the company's business. Please consult your manager if you have questions about the appropriateness of publishing such concepts or developments on your site.
- Since your site is a public space, we hope you will be as respectful to the company, our employees, our customers, our partners and affiliates, and others (including our competitors) as the company itself endeavors to be.
- You may provide a link from your site to the company's Web site, if you wish. The Web design group has created a graphic for links to the company's site, which you may use for this purpose during the term of your employment (subject to discontinuation in the company's discretion). Contact a member of the Web design group for details. Please do not use other company trademarks on your site or reproduce company material without first obtaining permission.

Finally, the company may request that you temporarily confine your Web site or Weblog commentary to topics unrelated to the company (or, in rare cases, that you temporarily suspend your Web site or weblog activity altogether) if it believes this is necessary or advisable to ensure compliance with securities regulations or other laws.

MANAGING OPERATIONS

A discussion of managing the essential information technologies is not complete without describing operational issues facing CIOs. Due to mergers, the Internet, e-commerce, increasing attacks on networks, and the September 11, 2001, terrorist attacks, the subject of computer operations has been receiving a lot of attention. Systems operations are important because if they are not professionally run (and backed up properly), a company could suffer a computer or network crash that could shut down its business for some period of time. It is not a trivial area, especially as companies become increasingly reliant on networks and computers to run their businesses. Furthermore, poorly run IS shops cause IS executives to end up fighting fires instead of setting policy. Or they may find themselves looking for a new job or their operations outsourced. Actually, this last option is often seen as a welcome relief by many IS executives.

As shown in Figure 14.21, the main change in operations is a shift in viewpoint. Traditionally, managing operations meant managing inward; that is, managing one's own operations staff, including those who work in the data center, data administration, network administration, and systems programming. Today, it is just as likely to mean managing outward; that is, managing the company's relationships with IT ESPs who have taken over the day-to-day operational work.

WHAT ARE OPERATIONS?

In a lecture at the University of California at Los Angeles (UCLA), William Congleton described the important operational issues he faced in one IS department.

Why Talk About Operations?

Keeping the shop running is getting increasingly difficult, Congleton says. The reasons become apparent at budget time. His total annual IS department budget had the following split:

- 33 percent for systems and programming, of which 70 percent was for maintenance and 30 percent was for new development
- 10 percent for department administration and training
- 57 percent for operations

Thus, one reason operations are important is because they involve more money than any other part of the IS organization.

At his company, operations included computer hardware at 64 locations, including 12 seaports, 12 parts warehouses, and 12 sales offices. Hardware included computers, disk drives, backup drives, printers, and PCs. Operations also included communication lines and equipment and software, such as operating systems, compilers, and networking

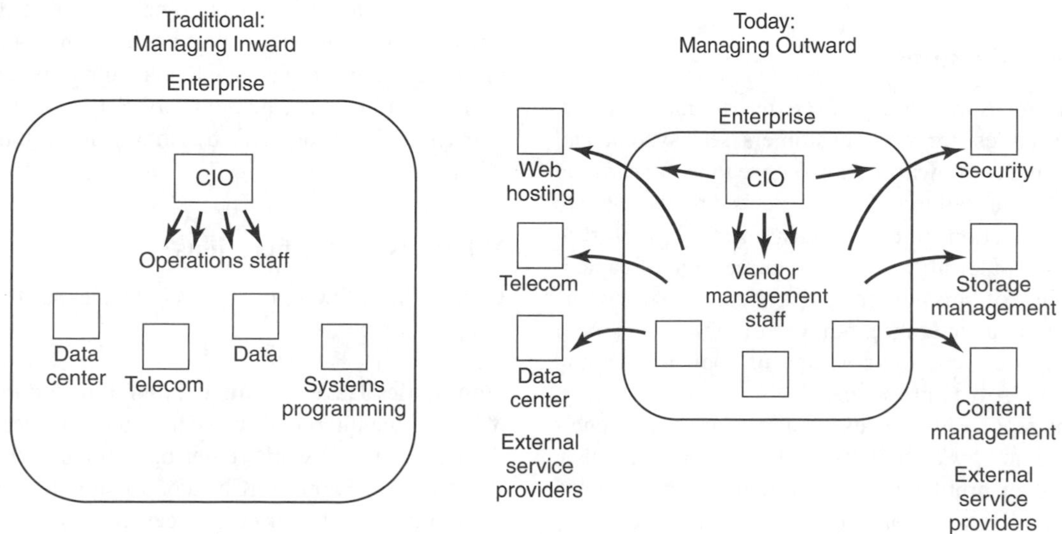

Figure 14.21 The Shifting Operations Perspective

software. In addition, the budget included data center personnel, such as systems consulting for developers and operators who scheduled and ran production jobs, performed backups, delivered reports, and monitored the machines and network. Operations also included disaster recovery planning and security.

"Putting all these things together sometimes gave me more excitement than I could stand," quips Congleton, "plus they were more expensive than I wanted. Therefore, achieving a 10 percent reduction in operations had a far greater effect than a 10 percent reduction in any other area. That is why operations are important."

Solving Operational Problems

Systems operations problems are obvious to the entire company: Response times are slow, networks are down, data is not available, or data is wrong. What can be done to improve operations? Congleton describes three strategies. One is to buy more equipment. As equipment costs drop, this solution might appear the most cost-effective, unless you run out of room for the equipment. The second approach is to continuously fight fires and rearrange priorities, getting people to solve the problem at hand. This solution really only moves the problem of poor management from one hot spot to another. The third solution is to continually document and measure what you are doing to find out the real problems, not just the apparent ones. Then set standards. This is the solution Congleton prefers. It is needed no matter who runs operations, the in-house staff or an outsourcer, and no matter whether the systems are legacy transaction systems or new Web-based front ends.

Operational Measures

Operational measures are both external and internal. External measures are what customers see: system and network uptime (or downtime), response time, turnaround time, and program failures. These aspects directly relate to customer satisfaction. Internal measures are of interest to IS people: computer utilization as a percentage of capacity, availability of mission-critical systems, disk storage utilization, job queue length, number of jobs run, number of jobs rerun due to problems, age of applications, and number of unresolved problems.

Problems reported by the external measures can generally be explained by deviations in the internal measures. To help uncover problems related to equipment capacity, quality of applications, or improper use of systems by users, numerous vendors sell monitoring software and devices. Other measurement systems log performance of computer and telecommunications equipment, says Congleton. Storage management systems manage space more efficiently. Schedulers schedule jobs. Library management systems keep track of versions and backups of files and programs. Plenty of tools are available to help IS organizations measure how efficiently their equipment is being used.

The Importance of Good Management

Tools are useless, however, unless IS management has created a culture that recognizes and values good operations, says Congleton. It is hard to find good computer operations managers because the absence of prestige (and sometimes pay) does not attract individuals with the proper combination of skills and training. This reality is unfortunate, he says, because in a good environment, an operations job can be particularly rewarding, both financially and professionally.

The skills required of an operations manager are similar to those needed in a factory or oil refinery. The factory manager must schedule work to meet promised delivery dates, monitor performance as work flows through the key pieces of equipment, and respond quickly to production breakdowns. In a well-run factory, the manager can usually recover from one or two individual problems. In a badly-run factory, a manager faces many little problems and often does not know where to start to fix the problems. The same is true in computer and telecommunications centers where the "factory equipment" is the disk drives, database machines, host computers, servers, network gateways, network routers, and the like.

In conclusion, CIOs need to be concerned about operations, says Congleton, by putting the proper operations environment in place. The key to managing operations is the same as in any management job: Set standards and then manage to those standards by finding an outstanding operations manager.

What's New in Operations?

Over the past few years, several changes have taken place in operations.

Companies Have "Cleaned Their Operational House." Y2K and the Internet forced companies to "clean house" in their data and network center operations, says Rosemary LaChance of Farber/LaChance, a company that provides consulting on automating data center operations.

In the late 1990s, companies were fearful that their old computer applications could not handle processing in the year 2000 because many of the programs left out the digits "19" in, say, "1993." Once the millennium hit, these programs would think the year 2000 was the year 1900, yielding erroneous results.

Y2K forced companies to not only look at their existing software, but also their computer operations, says LaChance; in particular, their standards and policies. Formerly, operations were managed reactively. They upgraded hardware but they rarely updated processes. Companies would not spend the money to improve procedures, thinking, "If it ain't broke, don't fix it."

Y2K, and then the Internet, required management to think about the processes that computer operations supported and ask, "How are we going to do what we say we will do? How will we be able to add services or outsource operations? Will we be able to support e-commerce?" The resulting changes have led to far better operational structures because management took the time to define the rules for operations and put better policies and procedures in place.

"Had they not gone through Y2K, most companies would not have been operationally prepared for the Internet," says LaChance. Although automation provides discipline, the rules must be in place to automate. Y2K forced companies to define such rules as how to gain access to systems. They also got rid of such outdated procedures as transferring data via tapes (moving to more efficient and less costly online data transfers), and distributing reports on paper (moving to making them available via the company intranet).

In short, Y2K gave computer operations the attention it needed but had not gotten. Companies were forced to move from a survival mode ("Let's just get this job run") to a planning mode ("What do we need to support e-enablement?"). However, challenges remain. Computer operators still cannot link identified problems with changes, so they still have integration and change management problems. That piece of the operations structure is still missing.

More Operations Managers Are Managing Outward. The picture Congleton paints is based on the traditional managing inward view where enterprises manage their own data centers. By and large, that view remains true. However, as the next section on outsourcing points out, a growing number of companies are turning to a third party to run their data centers. Even more are contracting with a network provider to manage their networks. These changes do not mean that CIOs relinquish responsibility for operations. It just means they need to ensure that their people are properly managing the service providers.

Even for companies keeping their own data centers, an increasing number are taking advantage of operational services provided by third parties, especially for Internet-based operations. For example, some host their Web site at a company that specializes in Web hosting. Offloading Web operations allows enterprises to forgo large equipment and facility investments, expensing operational costs instead. Furthermore, they offload the job of finding the needed talent to the specialist. Finding qualified employees can be an acute problem in the IT field. It is easier to attract and retain IT talent when a company's core business is IT because staff can see a career path, the company is more likely to buy the latest tools and equipment, and the culture is more likely to be IT-friendly.

Operations Are Being Simplified. Another trend is to simplify operations by centralizing applications in one place rather than distribute them on PCs. Programs are then downloaded when requested.

Certain Operations Are Being Offloaded. Yet another trend in operations is to offload certain kinds of operations or certain aspects of computer and network operations. Often, these relate to the Internet. For example, a relatively new area is Web event management, which means hosting a real-time event on the Web. When successful, such events, called Webcasts, lead to huge spikes in Web site hits. To avoid being swamped and having the Web site crash, companies offload the operational aspects of these events to third parties that specialize in hosting such activities. An example of such a Webcast is on page 552.

In conclusion, the focus of CIOs in operations is changing. Their attention used to be focused on ensuring that they had the in-house expertise to keep systems and networks up and running. Their attention now is toward determining where best to perform the various kinds of operations, in-house or with a third party, and then manage accordingly. In an increasing number of cases, the choice is to use an outside specialist; that is, outsourcing IS functions.

OUTSOURCING IS FUNCTIONS

In the IT world, *outsourcing* means turning over a firm's computer operations, network operations, or other IT function to a provider for a specified time; generally, at least a few years. In 1989, outsourcing became a legitimate management strategy by CIOs. Until that time, the only companies that outsourced their IS operations were those that were poorly run. However, in 1989, Kodak outsourced its well-run IS operations to become a more competitive company. That surprising move caused top executives around

CASE EXAMPLE

MICROSOFT

When Microsoft officially announced a new version of Windows, it did so not only at a major launch event in San Francisco, California, but also via a public Internet broadcast and a private Webcast to 6,000 original equipment manufacturer (OEM) system builders in 83 countries.

This private global Webcast to OEMs was handled by Akamai. Akamai specializes in providing e-business infrastructure through 12,000 edge servers in 66 countries. They are called *edge servers* because they are at the edge of the Internet; that is, close to end users. This approach gives users in far-flung locations fast downloads of Web content, streaming media, and applications from Web sites hosted on these servers. Like the Internet, Akamai's global distributed system has no central control; therefore, if a server, data center, or even a major network link (a backbone) fails, data can be routed around these failures. Having no single point of failure makes the network fail-safe.

Akamai has also gotten into hosting broadcasts of live events via its customers' Web sites–Webcasting–which requires high bandwidth capabilities to accommodate streaming media; that is, live audio and video. In addition, Akamai's Netpodium service allows such events to be interactive with dispersed audiences.

The Microsoft Webcast for the system builders was the largest online seminar Microsoft had held. It originated at Microsoft's headquarters in Redmond, Washington, and began with an introduction by Microsoft's OEM team. The Webcast then joined the San Francisco event with an on-site commentator and special presenters.

At their sites, the system builders could use Netpodium to send questions to the presenters. They sent some 1,800 and received real-time responses. In addition, Netpodium was used by the presenters to poll the system builders at several points during the event.

Microsoft was pleased with the private Webcast because it set a record for attendance, global reach, and audience participation.

the world to consider the use of outsourcers. Today, CIOs are expected to investigate outsourcing sufficiently to satisfy executive management that their IS operations are as efficient and effective in-house as they would be if they were outsourced; otherwise, they should outsource what they do not do well.

The Driving Forces Behind Outsourcing

At a meeting of the Chicago Chapter of the Society for Information Management, Mel Bergstein of DiamondCluster Int'l. gave an overview of outsourcing. His main message was that outsourcing is another step in the evolution of the IT field.

Outsourcing descended on IS departments as a follow-on to the merger and acquisition activities in the 1980s, says Bergstein. In the 1960s, only 10 percent of the U.S. economy had global competition. In the 1970s, that rose to 70 percent. In response, companies had to focus on core businesses in the 1980s, which led to the huge amount of merger and acquisition activity. This activity was also driven by a new market for corporate control. High-yield bonds allowed a few people to buy a company and leverage it with debt. Companies were priced based on their shareholder value; that is, their discounted cash flow.

These two drivers—focus and value—are still leading companies to restructure and focus on core businesses by asking themselves, "Where do we really add value?" As examples, some apparel companies no longer cut, sew, manufacture, or distribute goods because they see their core businesses as design and marketing. Likewise, some publishers no longer manufacture books. They manage and finance projects, and outsource everything else.

Thus, outsourcing is part of the drive for focus and value, and it is not solely an IT issue, says Bergstein; it is a business issue. Because top management must stress value, they must consider outsourcing in all their functions.

Changing Customer–Vendor Relationships

IS outsourcers perform the same activities for a company that an IS organization performs in-house. Over time, the amount of work done by outsiders has increased, says Bergstein, as the following expansion in customer–vendor relationships illustrates.

Traditionally, IS organizations bought professional services, such as planning (or consulting), building or maintaining applications, building or maintaining networks, and training. They also bought products, which may or may not have included training. They also bought transactions, such as payroll check processing from a service bureau or credit reports from a credit rating service. Purchasing transactions allows buyers to shift fixed costs to variable costs and gives sellers higher margins because they take on the risks.

With the high use of packages and the need to integrate them to create integrated systems, companies have contracted with systems integrators. They generally handle the entire life cycle—planning, development, maintenance, and training—for major systems projects. Finally, the most bundled approach to contracting for IT services is outsourcing, where the outsourcer contracts to handle all or most of certain IT activities. The main difference between the latter two options is that systems integration is project based, whereas outsourcing is time based.

This five-option continuum, shown in Figure 14.22, demonstrates how the IT field has moved, says Bergstein. As you move from the more traditional professional services category (on the left) to outsourcing (on the right), four changes occur in the vendor-customer relationship:

1. IS management loses an increasing amount of control because more of the activities are turned over to outsiders.
2. Providers take more risks as they offer options on the right.
3. Providers' margins improve as they offer services on the right.
4. The importance of choosing the right provider becomes more important to the right, because more is at risk in using an outside source.

Outsourcing's History

In 1989, essentially only one kind of outsourcing involving IT was available. Since then, the field has expanded significantly. Here is a glimpse of its history, based largely on attendance at the semiannual conferences of the Sourcing Interests Group, founded and led by Barry Wiegler since 1991.

IT Outsourcing. IT outsourcing essentially began with "big bang" deals, or megadeals, which consisted of outsourcing all of a company's data center operations for up to 10 years. These deals involved selling existing equipment to the outsourcer, transferring all software licenses, moving significant numbers of in-house IS personnel to the outsourcer's payroll, negotiating how the outsourcer would help

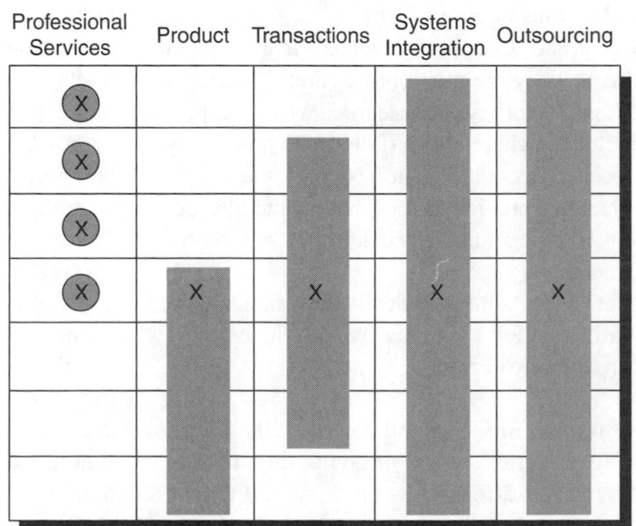

Figure 14.22 Customer-Vendor Relationships. *Source:* Mel Bergstein, DiamondCluster Int'l., Chicago, IL.

in the transition and which party would carry which costs, establishing desired service levels and ways to measure performance, and specifying every single service to be provided—because if it was not in the contract, it would be an added cost.

In those early days, the goal of these large data center contracts was purely financial. Companies wanted to remove the huge IT infrastructure investments from their books and shift those fixed costs to variable costs; and they wanted to save money, generally about 15 percent. The deals were front loaded, with the outsourcers losing money or breaking even the first year or two, but then becoming profitable after that as the costs of technology dropped, as they leveraged licenses across clients, as they shared expertise across clients, and as they invested in productivity tools that made them more efficient.

Several problems occurred, though. An "us versus them" mindset often set in because neither the clients nor the outsourcers handled the transition well. A lot of finger-pointing took place as outsourcers tried to charge for services clients thought were included in the contract. In addition, service levels did not always live up to expectations or interpretations of the contract language differed.

Furthermore, cultures clashed. Former employees might have kept their same desk, but once they became an employee of the outsourcer, they became a provider and were treated differently. Users had higher expectations of outsourcers than of their IS organizations. In short, companies learned that managing the relationship was really the tough job. Formerly, they had thought that negotiating the deal was the difficult part, so they had not carefully defined governance structures; that is, how the relationship would be managed.

Today, the IT outsourcing industry has matured. Providers have learned that heavy-handed treatment of clients can backfire. They are much more careful in transition planning. Clients' attorneys have learned what is important in a contract and where the pitfalls lie. Those early contracts have been renegotiated, and although the clients may not have changed providers, they have generally become more adept at renegotiating because they now know what they really need.

Of course, not all outsourcing deals were megadeals, but even the small deals felt like a big bang to the employees who moved to the outsourcer.

Transitional Outsourcing. In the early 1990s, a new type of computing arose: client-server computing. IT outsourcing had been around for a few years, so CIOs with their hands full supporting legacy systems looked into using outsourcing to transition to client-server computing. They chose one of two routes. Either they outsourced maintenance of their legacy systems so their staff could concentrate on building new client-server systems or they outsourced client-server development to specialists and kept maintenance in-house. In either case, once the new systems were brought in, the legacy systems they replaced were shut down.

Then, in the late 1990s, when the immense size of Y2K compliance surfaced—to retrofit old applications so they would work after the year 2000—most companies outsourced as much of their Y2K work as they could. Because of the enormous volume of work, offshore outsourcing to India, Ireland, and other countries grew significantly. Unlike traditional IT outsourcing, however, contracts were generally shorter and did not include operations. This project-based outsourcing has been called *transitional outsourcing*.

Best-of-Breed Outsourcing. All through the 1990s, IS departments outsourced different pieces of their work—mainly infrastructure support and IS Lite. However, CIOs learned that although selecting one outsourcer with broad capabilities might be easiest to manage, no single company was best in class in all areas. Thus, selective outsourcing began, where one outsourcer handled desktop operations, another data center operations, and a third network management. Even though the concept was good for getting best-of-breed providers, coordination among the multiple providers became a nightmare.

A more recent trend has been *collaborative outsourcing*, where one company becomes the prime contractor for numerous facets of IS operations but some of the work is provided by other ESPs. Often an operations partner, a development partner, and a telecommunications partner collaborate to bid on the work, but one is the prime partner. Thus, teams of large ESPs bid against other teams for contracts. In some cases, these contracts take on quite a bit more than simply operations; the work includes development of new systems as well. Best-of-breed outsourcing has perpetuated the tradition of long and complex outsourcing contracts.

Shared Services. When IT outsourcing began to gain credibility, executives wondered, "Can we get the same economies of scale by pulling disparate noncore functions together into one shared services group?" In many cases, they felt they could. So they "insourced" to themselves, creating a shared services organization to handle such functions as IT, legal, facilities management, real estate, mail room, finance, and on and on. The goal was to improve efficiencies and save money. Generally, companies created a center of expertise in each area, with all the centers reporting to one shared services vice president.

IT was not always included, but, as in the case of MeadWestvaco Corporation, it was. Some executives believe having IT in shared services gives them the ability to leverage the IT underpinnings of the other services. Shared services also centralize the management of outsourced functions because, in many cases, the functions are centralized and then outsourced. Shared services groups have become adept at negotiating and managing contracts and supplier relationships because these tasks are a main part of their job.

Business Process Outsourcing. As the IT outsourcing field matured, data center outsourcing, desktop outsourcing, and other standard IT outsourcing areas became so well understood that they became commodity services; hence, profit margins dropped as the number of competitors rose. To move into higher-margin services, ESPs began specializing in specific functional areas, offering to handle specific business processes as well as their IT underpinnings. This *business process outsourcing* (BPO) is defined as outsourcing all or most of a reengineered process that has a large IT component.

Improving a noncore process by tapping the expertise and investments of a provider that focuses solely on that process (rather than cut costs) has been the main goal in BPO. Companies are outsourcing logistics, customer service, and many other essential, yet peripheral, functions to the experts.

Balboa Travel, a travel agency in San Diego, California, handed over its ticket accounting to Unisys. Each week, travel agencies must report the tickets they have sold to the Airline Reporting Corporation. The process is important, yet burdensome, and the president of Balboa Travel did not want to hire a programmer to maintain such a reporting system, which is what he would have had to do if he had not outsourced the work. Unisys provides him a more sophisticated service than he could afford in-house. It lets him offer his clients—corporate travel departments—reports about their employees' travel habits via an extranet. Balboa is also able to do data mining on its ticket sales to uncover trends that will help it offer new and better travel services.

As is obvious, BPO moves IT-based outsourcing out beyond the IS organization; it involves business units as well. BPO outsourcing is often quite a bit more complex than IT outsourcing because it requires clients to change their business processes to fit with the processes of the service provider. Furthermore, some clients want to retain parts of a process, so complex coordination may be necessary between the two firms as well.

BPO has brought a mindset change to the field. Whereas IT outsourcing moves suppliers and customers closer to one another in terms of working together, the two parties still do not have the same goals. Clients want to save more money, whereas outsourcers want to make more money. In BPO, though, when providers take over an entire process, they can be measured and paid based on outcomes rather than transactions. Outcome-based outsourcing gives the two parties common goals. The client focuses on "what" needs to be done; the provider focuses on "how" to do it.

Rita Terdiman noted this phenomenon in a speech to the Sourcing Interests Group. As shown in Figure 14.23, BPO deals aim to be more like joint ventures and alliances, moving them to the right side of the chart. Therefore, trust, joint financial investments, and partnering are part of the deal.

As an example of BPO, consider ANZ Banking Group and its outsourcing of its procurement function, as described in a Sourcing Interests Group research report on pages 556–557.

E-Business Outsourcing. With the arrival of business use of the Internet, outsourcing enabled companies to quickly get Web sites up and handling business. In large companies, e-business outsourcing started with marketing departments outsourcing the development of their corporate Web site. Once developed, IS took over operations. However, in dot-coms and Internet-based operations, outsourcing all or most of the IS function has been the preferred mode of operation for several reasons. Even with the dot-com crash, this is still a legitimate way to mobilize for e-business.

One, outsourcing allows a company to move fast. When a firm cannot spend a year developing a system, outsourcing the e-business infrastructure can help it get a site up and running within months, perhaps weeks. Two, companies can remain flexible, which can mean staying small and focusing only on a few key functions. Generally, IT has not been seen as a core differentiating area when tailorable off-the-shelf products and services have been available. Three, outsourcing does not tie up a firm's funds in computer and networking equipment, which could become obsolete fairly soon. A company can rent rather than buy. It can draw on best-of-breed as well as change course quickly if need be, swapping out one ESP and swapping in another, to keep pace with the market.

Unlike traditional IT outsourcing, with e-business outsourcing, machines do not need to be purchased from the client, personnel do not have to be moved, and software licenses do not need to be transferred. The outsourcing starts from scratch. Some large companies have followed this route as well to get into e-business, for the same reasons.

Utility computing. E-business outsourcing and IT outsourcing are combining into a new form of managed services outsourcing that is being referred to by various names: *utility computing, on-demand computing, virtual*

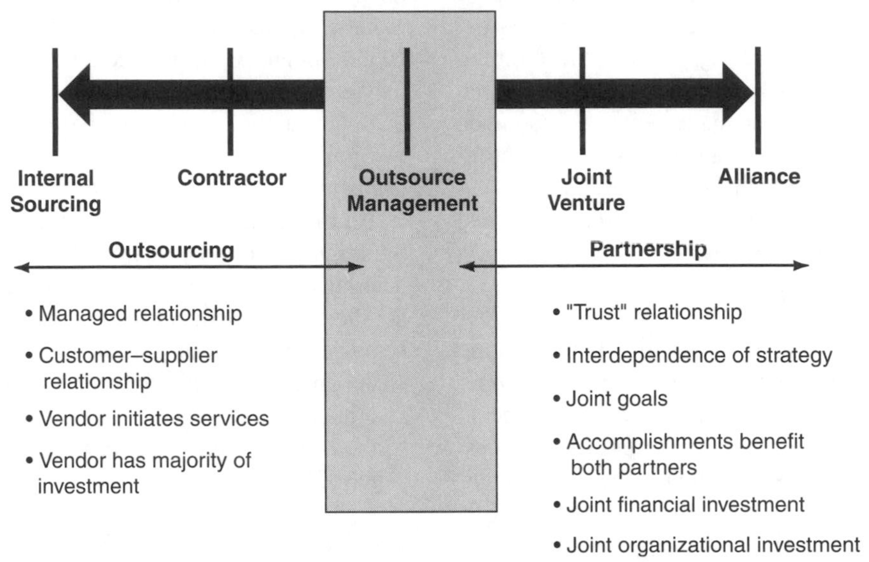

Figure 14.23 The Outsourcing Management Spectrum. *Source:* Courtesy of Gartner EXP, 56 Top Gallant, Stamford, CT.

CASE EXAMPLE

ANZ BANKING GROUP LTD.

ANZ is Australia's third-largest bank, with AU$150 billion in assets; it operates in 28 countries and has 22,000 staff. ANZ's cost-to-income ratio had been 63 percent; it is now at 47 percent, with a target of about 45 percent.

The bank's challenge in outsourcing procurement was not to reduce costs, but to gain greater quality purchases and lower ANZ's annual spend of AU$1.36 billion. ANZ outsourced its entire procurement operation, except strategy, in Australia and New Zealand to PwC, now part of IBM Global Services, in May 1999 for 5 years, with a 2-year option to continue. ANZ moved fixed asset management and accounts payable into strategic sourcing at the time; neither of them has been outsourced yet. The contract was worth AU$850 million in 1999; as of 2002 it was worth AU$950 million.

The benefit objectives of outsourcing to PwC were to leverage PwC's already global capability, reduce transaction costs (which has occurred), and better manage ANZ's spend information (which was poor at the time).

Lessons Learned

Peter Donald, General Manager of Strategic Sourcing at ANZ, recounts a number of lessons he has learned in outsourcing procurement.

Be Prepared to Change the Contract as Your Environment Changes. At ANZ, the total number of contracts managed by procurement has risen from 600 to 900, and could well rise to over 1,000. Furthermore, a new goods and services tax in 2001 has forced new issues into the relationship.

Originally, ANZ and PwC had the stretch goal of saving AU$100 million over the 5 years. That goal changed to save AU$170 million over just 2 years' time—a substantial change.

Donald thus recommends reviewing the arrangement regularly and being prepared to change it.

Make Step Changes in Technology and Processes to Save Time and Money. ANZ moved to Web-enabled PeopleSoft; 50 percent of the activity now goes through this e-procurement system. This step change was made easier because ANZ had outsourced to PwC, giving ANZ management the time to concentrate on strategic issues. Formerly, the bank had spend leakage of AU$50 million to AU$100 million a year to maverick buying and such. Over the next 12 months, due to the PeopleSoft front end and PwC's operations, ANZ stopped much of that leakage.

Focus on Having an Effective Transition. The transition should be managed so that there is little or no noise from the business units. Some people look for ways to make noise. ANZ experienced some early problems, but PwC recovered quickly, actually more quickly than Donald expected. The lesson was to understand beforehand how a provider can recover, so they can do so quickly.

Do Your Best to Make the Outsourced Group Appear Seamless to Employees. Some employees look for ways to find fault. Seamlessness can be difficult to achieve if the provider's staff advertise themselves to employees. This is not a good idea. It is always nice to get a pat on the back, like the one Donald received from a line manager who had prepared a requisition for office supplies on his desktop on Friday 4 p.m. and received the supplies Monday morning. His note to Donald: "Congratulations."

Focus Early on What You Want, and Don't Get Sidetracked. Everyday operations are going well, so Donald is pleased with the service delivery. The outsourcing gives him and his staff more time to manage strategically to capture the AU$130 million in savings. Thus, he wants more strategic input from PwC than he has been receiving. He wants PwC to push him and his staff to improve. His advice to others is to be sure global input is reaching you, if that is what you want.

Along the same strategic lines, Donald wants PwC to work closely with ANZ on large projects. Thus, PwC has moved its commodity management people closer to ANZ's business so that they better understand the procurement strategy being developed with the business units on large projects.

Keep Incentive Mechanisms Simple and Transparent. When incentive mechanisms are excessively complex, too much effort is required from both sides. Complex incentives may also promote the wrong behavior. For instance, the provider may focus on the stretch targets rather than the daily bread-and-butter issues.

PwC receives a fixed but declining management fee over the term, so there is an incentive to lower ANZ's cost base. There are other incentives as well, which are working fine, says Donald. For instance, PwC risks 50 percent of its profits when it fails to meet the stated minimum service levels. This has only happened in one quarter of the last 19.

Be Able to Benchmark Performance. Benchmark data is important in evaluating the outsourcing of procurement. Donald uses CAPS, which provides very good data. However, because he reports to the market every 6 months, he needs that data more frequently than once a year or once every 2 years.

Understand, to a Fair Degree of Detail, the Value Chain You Plan to Embrace. Little things can catch you up. For example, information security issues need to be addressed so that third parties in ANZ's supply chain have access through its firewalls.

data centers, autonomic (self-healing) systems, and *grid computing* (a take-off on the term *electricity grid*). The idea is that computing power can be treated like electricity: You plug in and only pay for what you use.

Numerous vendors, especially IBM, HP, and Sun, are promoting access rather than ownership. By supplying computer processing, network bandwidth, and applications on demand, they are selling the idea of turning clients' fixed IT costs into variable costs. Clients can then scale their IT infrastructure or handle spikes in computing demand without having to buy more IT assets.

To educate themselves and their business on the utility computing concept, CIOs can test it by using an IT outsourcer in a high-need area, such as e-mail, security, or redundancy, notes Thickins. It is important to understand the amount of consulting this form of outsourcing requires, the chargeback mechanism (for only paying for use), the contract terms, where it could provide benefits, and so on. Mobil Travel Guide, on page 558, illustrates the convergence of e-business and IT outsourcing into utility computing in one of its high-need areas: its Web site.

CASE EXAMPLE

MOBIL TRAVEL GUIDE

The Mobil Travel Guide provides travelers in the United States and Canada with information on destinations, route planning, resorts, restaurants, and other travel-related information. Its printed versions have been published for 45 years and sold in bookstores and other retail outlets.

Mobil put the guide online, but the information was static and the site could not handle the spikes in demand that took place around holidays and during the summer. Site visitors endured long response times.

Mobil wanted to upgrade its site (www.mobiltravelguide.com) to provide real-time data, such as custom travel planning, 24-hour service, and rewards at hotels and restaurants. But rather than making the large investment to upgrade its own IT resources, Mobil turned to IBM to host and manage the site, which runs on Linux-based servers. Mobil signed up for IBM's on-demand utility computing service, so that it only pays for the processing, storage, and networking capacity it uses. IBM ensures that its infrastructure can scale up to handle the demand spikes.

Mobil did not have to make the major upfront investments in IT assets and it does not need to be concerned with having enough capacity to handle peak loads. Furthermore, the Web-based portion of the system is housed on IBM's cache servers around its network, thereby providing users with faster response times and Mobil with lower per-transaction costs than if the site was housed on Mobil's servers.

Mobil believes it is saving 35 percent in maintenance and software costs by outsourcing to IBM—and it is only paying for what it uses of IBM's world-class, highly scalable e-business infrastructure.

Thus, in 15 years' time, IT outsourcing has expanded significantly, from outsourcing data center operations to outsourcing business processes and from domestic outsourcing to offshoring, which is discussed shortly.

Managing Outsourcing

Numerous aspects to managing outsourcing need to be handled well to create a successful working relationship. Here are just four—organizational structure, governance, day-to-day working, and supplier development. All are based on research reports published by the Sourcing Interests Group.

Organizational Structure. Managing outsourcing is different from managing internal staff because, for one thing, it is a joint effort between parties that may not have the same goals, as noted earlier. Therefore, during contract negotiations, the two parties need to figure out and negotiate how they are going to jointly manage the contract they sign. In fact, governance needs to be explicitly addressed in the contract.

Typically, parties establish layers of joint teams. A top-level team of a couple of executives from each firm generally has the final word on conflict resolution. An operational team with members from both companies oversees day-to-day functioning. They hold a formal meeting, say, once a week to once a month; but they are generally in daily contact. Also, some joint special-purpose teams may be created from time to time to deal with pressing issues. Some companies have ongoing standing committees, such as a pricing committee or a change management committee, to oversee the use of formal change management procedures.

Although joint committees are a common management structure, each side needs a single executive in charge of their side of the relationship. On the client side, this executive is the relationship manager. This job position has not been prevalent in IS departments, but we believe it is going to become the norm as companies move toward IS Lite. Needless to say, the skills of a relationship manager are far different from those of a data center manager. A relationship manager needs to be good at negotiating, cajoling, and being an effective liaison between end users and service providers.

To illustrate how one company has managed its outsourcing, we look at Eastman Kodak Company on pages 559–560, because it created a thoughtful and effective governance structure. The following description comes from the Sourcing Interests Group; it focuses on the outsourcing between Eastman Kodak and IBM Global Services.

CASE EXAMPLE

EASTMAN KODAK COMPANY

Eastman Kodak Company, with headquarters in Rochester, New York, is an international manufacturer of imaging and chemical products. In 1989, the company rocked the IS world by announcing strategic relationships with four suppliers to manage significant portions of its IS organization. Until that time, outsourcing had been viewed as a desperation move to improve poorly-run IS departments. Because Kodak's unit was well run, and benchmarked accordingly, its pioneering stance caused many IS executives—and a few CEOs and CFOs as well—to seriously reconsider outsourcing.

Kodak announced that one ESP would operate its data centers and networks, another would manage its telecommunications, a third would handle PC support, and a fourth would manage voice messaging. Initially the agreement with IBM to manage the data centers was U.S. based; it was later expanded to include Canadian operations, other U.S. divisions, and eventually six international sites. Kodak encourages IBM to leverage its data center for both Kodak and other companies' work for improved efficiencies. Due to efforts on both sides, the Kodak-IBM relationship has worked well. They developed trust and good processes. When issues arise, the relationship has effective processes to deal with them.

Outsourcing Management Structure

Kodak views its outsourcing management role as exercising leadership, staying in control, and managing the high value-added functions for flexibility. Kodak sets the tone for its key IT relationships. The key themes have been collaborative (not adversarial), long-term mutual benefits (not short-term), and making systemic improvements on a global basis (not local). The management structure has six elements: a management board, an advisory council, a supplier and alliance management group, a relationship manager for each relationship, ad hoc working groups, and client surveys.

Management Board. This board meets twice a year and includes senior management from both companies. It focuses on strategic issues in addition to any policies or practices on either side that are getting in the way of mutual success. It has dealt with international strategies, IT architecture, telecommunications directions, disaster recovery plans, and so forth.

Advisory Council. This council meets monthly and has 15 members. It handles technical and operational issues by focusing on what Kodak wants, not on how the services currently are delivered. Kodak's trust in IBM has grown; thus it leaves more of the "how" details up to this ESP. The advisory council reviews service levels, usage measurements and forecasts, tactical plans, migration objectives, business recovery plans, and the like.

Supplier and Alliance Management Group. This group manages the longer-term outsourcing relationships as well as other contracts with large IT suppliers. It works closely with IS management. This group of 10 people includes a manager, the relationship manager for each primary alliance, plus support staff and supplier management for other IT sourcing. Initially, this group managed only the alliances. Contracts with major vendors were handled in other groups. Eventually all these functions were brought together to increase their focus, leverage global agreements, and align the management of alliances and suppliers. About one-half of the staff have IS backgrounds; the other half come from purchasing.

Relationship Manager. This manager is key to the success of a strategic relationship, Kodak believes, because this manager is the focal point between the company and its ESP. The job of each of Kodak's four relationship managers is to ensure that Kodak receives more than just delivery on the contract. Thus, they also manage value creation. The relationship managers negotiate, coordinate, and manage agreements and ensure that service level agreements (SLAs) are established. SLAs are very precise descriptions of each service to be delivered, when, by whom, for what price, and such. Relationship managers also assist in pricing and billing strategies.

Working Groups. These groups were not part of Kodak's original outsourcing management structure; they were added to deal with specific technology areas. They are chartered by the advisory council. Their goals are to facilitate changes in processes, promulgate standards, achieve business recovery in case of disruption, and promote effective use of IS services. They have

(*Case continued*)

(Case continued)

proven to be effective vehicles for talking about important issues, such as the timing and appropriateness of upgrading to new releases of software. The groups are represented mainly by operational staff. For example, database administrators from the major sites are in one working group.

Client Surveys. These surveys are sent out twice a year to nearly 5,000 internal users of the services. Feedback on quality, cycle time, and product and service leadership are assessed and shared with the ESPs. Improvement plans are mutually developed to close perceived performance gaps.

Because Kodak's outsourcing has such a large scope, draws on four main suppliers, and covers a large geographic area, the company has discovered that it needs all of these forms of coordination for effective supplier management.

Governance. The foundations of governing an outsourcing relationship are laid out in the contract, which can be hundreds of pages long (with appendices). A major governance item in the contract is the service level agreements (SLAs) because they are used to gauge supplier performance. For every contracted service, its SLA spells out responsibilities, performance requirements, penalties, bonuses, and so on. Completeness is an important attribute of good SLAs; generally everything should be detailed, perhaps even with times of deliveries, who will deliver what to whom, and so on.

Another important component of SLAs is metrics. An SLA needs to be measurable to be of use. Establishing metrics can be tricky because, in many cases, IS departments have not kept good measures of their own performance. In BPO, the situation is even worse; companies do not know how many people are in the process, departmental costs do not reflect overhead or IT costs, and so on. Measures are needed to establish benchmarks against which vendors want to demonstrate improvements. Clients also need metrics to negotiate better deals. Clients who do not know their own performance levels negotiate from weakness; they know less than the vendor because they have not tracked details, and vendors are not apt to correct mistaken impressions. Furthermore, clients are likely to overlook important details, which will later cost them money.

In addition to SLAs, parties establish governance rules to be used when either party is making a decision so that both are "singing from the same hymnal." Most parties in strong relationships say they put the contract in the drawer after it has been signed and work from trust and agreed-upon rules. It is only when trust in one another breaks down that they turn to the contract. Figure 14.24 lists some governance rules from a number of different enterprises.

Day-to-Day Working. The Sourcing Interests Group reports provide advice from outsourcing executives on how to manage day-to-day interactions between two parties. Here are a few of those recommendations.

Manage expectations, not staff. The outsourcer's staff is no longer under the purview of the client, so command-and-control is not a wise option—it only results in an acrimonious relationship. Facilitation becomes the mode of working. Rather than say "do this," the approach becomes "how can we solve this together?" Furthermore, relationship managers have the important role of influencing users' expectations so that delivery meets business objectives.

Realize that informal ways of working may disappear. More formality is inevitable as outcomes are measured and are more tightly controlled, especially if the relationship is handled strictly by the book, which happens in some cases. This increased formality can be a shock to people who are used to, say, getting a small job done by calling their friend "Joe" in the IS department. Once Joe works for the ESP, he may no longer be able to provide that service; he must follow the work authorization process defined in the contract. This change can cause unhappiness as users see providers as "them," making them the scapegoat. The two parties need to find ways to reduce this tendency.

Loss of informal ways of working can add rigor. Rigor frequently improves work quality. Users may think twice before requesting changes and prepare better definitions of what they want. Furthermore, better processes can streamline work, improve effectiveness, and potentially reduce unnecessary work. Service providers do introduce new discipline; the client should prepare employees for this change and assist them in adapting because it is generally best to use the provider's processes. This is one reason why transition planning is so important: to help client personnel move to new procedures with the least disruption and disgruntlement.

Integration of the two staffs requires explicit actions. Integration does not happen naturally. Explicit policies are likely to be needed. Some examples are to (1) grant outsourcing staff access to appropriate work areas, not unduly restrict them; (2) hold joint celebrations and social events;

- Service levels must stay in the top 25 percent as benchmarked against the client's peers.
- Escalation of problems becomes more painful as it goes higher to encourage early resolution.
- The supplier is the grand project manager and is responsible for managing multiple vendors.
- Work style is based on respect and confidence; there should be no personalization of problems.
- Add significant value.
- Aim to operate in an "open book"manner, sharing key operating information with each other.
- New services can be put out for bid.
- No exclusive agreements.
- Meet our standards.
- Let us know about potential problems before they happen.
- Spend our money as if it were your own.

Figure 14.24 Examples of Outsourcing Governance Rules. *Source:* Reprinted with permission of Sourcing Interests Group, Bell Canyon, CA, www.sourcinginterest.org.

(3) invite each other to meetings; and (4) perhaps even have a client executive move to the provider for 2 years to learn how they work internally. However, integration generally can only go so far; the client still needs to remain in control and guide the relationship. Furthermore, the more side-by-side the parties work, the more likely they will experience scope creep in which the provider takes on more work.

The best way to manage day-to-day is to communicate frequently. One executive said he carried around a top-10 list in his shirt pocket, which he revised every week. They were the most important items he had to handle. The list kept him on focus and turned out to be his best informal management technique.

Supplier Development. A topic that is receiving increased attention in the production sourcing arena—that is, buying parts and services that go into one's own products and services—is supplier development. It means assisting one's suppliers to improve their products and services, generally by improving their processes. Although supplier development has not been prevalent in IT outsourcing, we think it will be. It will likely be prevalent in BPO.

An example of supplier development from manufacturing, not IT, from a Sourcing Interests Group research report appears on page 562.

Offshoring

To round out our discussion of outsourcing, we turn to the topic receiving much attention today: sending work offshore. In the late 1990s, when labor markets were especially tight and IS organizations needed to retrofit their systems to make them Y2K compliant, the use of offshore outsourcers to maintain IT applications grew dramatically. Offshore, of course, is relative. For U.S. companies, *near-shore* means outsourcing to Canadian and Mexican companies, whereas *offshore* means Ireland, India, the Philippines, and other countries. For European companies, near-shore is Ireland, Poland, and other Eastern European countries.

Companies turn to offshoring to tap lower labor costs and an ample supply of qualified people. During the recent economic downturn, offshoring gave companies a way to cut costs. The trickle of IT jobs in the late 1990s has turned into a steady stream of white-collar work going offshore. Application maintenance and development, call centers, customer service, back-office processing, BPO, claims processing, and other functions can all be moved offshore.

Now that the U.S. economy is improving, offshoring has become a political issue, because companies are not expanding their domestic labor force as rapidly as some had expected. There's an outcry that offshoring is taking jobs away from domestic workers. Politicians are trying, at the very least, to "shame" companies into not moving domestic work abroad. But as with manufacturing jobs in the 1980s, offshoring is unstoppable because the economics are so strong. Once one company in an industry lowers its costs by moving work to lower-wage countries, its competitors need to reduce their costs as well. That may mean that they, too, need to offshore.

For all the "this is terrible" talk, offshoring might actually be good for developed countries, because increasing the living standards in other countries increases their citizens' demands for consumer products that can, in turn, be supplied by highly efficient companies in developed countries.

Furthermore, white-collar offshoring has been inevitable, argues author Daniel Altman, because service sector productivity in the United States has not kept up with manufacturing sector productivity. In the early 1950s, each service sector employee produced about $39,000 in output (in 2000 dollars), he notes; in manufacturing, the output was $48,000. Now, 50 years later, service productivity

CASE EXAMPLE

HONDA MOTOR COMPANY

When Dave Nelson was head of purchasing for Honda Motor Company, he became widely known for his pioneering work in supplier development. To him, supplier development means being involved in improving suppliers' capabilities. The benefits include receiving higher quality goods, getting lower prices, tapping suppliers' expertise, and improving one's supply chain. In e-business, where alliances are so crucial, working together to improve processes will be of major importance.

In manufacturing, Nelson undertakes supplier development by sending two of his supply development engineers to a supplier, for free. They team up with two supplier engineers with the goal of cutting labor hours and inventory of a single part bought by Nelson by 50 percent in 13 weeks' time. The team works under two main guidelines: No supplier employees will be laid off. They will all have a job elsewhere in the company, perhaps teaching others how to improve their processes. Two, Nelson splits any savings 50/50 with the supplier.

The team of four starts by cleaning and painting the area where the part is produced. That single act gets everyone's attention. Then they ask for suggestions from the workers on how to improve the process. They map the existing process and try to implement (quickly and in any way possible) every suggestion so that the workers can test it out. Generally, once the workers see they are being heard, the suggestions pour in.

The results can be dramatic. As one small example, one assembly line of 15 women on one shift and 10 on another made 1,500 air conditioning hoses a day using 15 machines. In total, the women walked 13 miles a day and hauled 3 tons of material. After redesign, only five women were needed on one shift to make 1,550 hoses, and they only needed to walk 50 yards and haul 100 pounds.

Nelson says supplier development is like "walking around picking up money off the floor." So why isn't it more prevalent? He believes it is because manufacturing companies still maintain their internal focus. Although they now outsource most parts production—up to 70 percent at Honda—firms have not shifted their resources to managing suppliers. They still treat suppliers as outsiders rather than departments of their own company. Management has to be sold on the idea of investing in supplier management, and sold even more on supplier development. They need proof that supplier management will yield bottom-line benefits.

has increased to $54,000 (a 47 percent increase), whereas manufacturing productivity is at $207,000 (a 330 percent increase)!

Manufacturers have faced international competition, whereas service firms have not. Manufacturers have been forced to increase their productivity to stay in business—mainly by increasing the quality of their products, notes Altman. It should come as no surprise that service companies are tapping cheaper sources of labor now that they can because of globally available telecommunications technology, he notes. This global competition in services will force American companies to increase the productivity of their workforce in the same way and increase the quality of their services, Altman believes.

Offshore outsourcing differs in some unique ways from domestic outsourcing. In two reports, the Sourcing Interests Group (SIG) explores IT offshoring and the areas CIOs and their staff need to consider. Here are four points from those reports.

Offshoring Options Are Broadening. India has become the premier IT and BPO offshoring country because its huge, highly educated workforce speaks English and is hardworking. College graduates in India apply for jobs that only high school graduates will apply for in the United States, such as working in a customer service center. Hence, the quality of work is often higher, while the labor costs are lower. Furthermore, in IS, all of the major IT outsourcers in India have achieved the highest level (Level 5) in the Capability Maturity Matrix, which means their processes produce high-quality software. Most IS organizations in the United States and in other developed countries are not even up to Level 3. So the quality of software from these Indian firms is very high—as long as the specifications for the work are clear and truly what the customer wants.

After having good initial IT experiences in India, client companies are offshoring higher-value white-collar work beyond short-term software maintenance projects to ongoing software maintenance work, new development projects, and even BPO. The types of firms offering offshore options are also broadening. U.S. outsourcers are building their own offshore capabilities or acquiring existing offshore providers, often in India, sometimes in China, to lower their own costs. Client companies not wanting to deal directly with unfamiliar overseas providers can now tap offshore resources through onshore outsourcers. In fact, as noted in the SIG reports, all large IT outsourcing deals will likely have an offshore component. Global sourcing is becoming the norm.

Both Parties Need Cultural Training to Bridge Cultural Differences. Offshoring does bring cultural differences into sharp relief, which can hinder success unless properly handled. Outsourcers and offshore advisory firms (who advise clients on the offshore marketplace) now realize that both parties need cultural training to overcome management and communication gaps.

For clients, offshorers now routinely put client employees who will deal with the offshore employees through a cultural integration program. Here is a brief description of the program at Syntel, a large U.S.-based IT provider that uses an offshore (India) model, as recounted in one of the SIG reports:

> *We initially hold a 1.5-day workshop, and then a follow-up orientation a few months later. We find that clients often restructure their operations during the first few months, sometimes bringing in new people. These new people need the orientation, also, which is why we repeat the orientation.*
>
> *In the workshop we talk about how lifestyles and cultures differ between the U.S. and India. In fact, we tailor each workshop to the client's location because Midwest employees differ from New Yorkers, for example. We illustrate, for instance, how the same words have different meanings in the two countries. We point out differences in dress, foods, even eating times. We show a video of these differences, we have people wear the native dress, and we demonstrate how Indians prepare a lunch, which we then serve. We have learned that U.S. employees often have a third-world view of India that is not accurate. Our goal in the orientation is to familiarize them with today's modern India.*

On the provider side, offshorers often put their own employees through an accent neutralization program if they have an accent the client country will find difficult to understand. This practice is especially prevalent for Indian providers with American clients. Providers also teach their employees about the client's company culture (going so far as to hang the same posters on the walls as the client has on its walls) and the client country's culture (going so far as to familiarize employees with holidays and keep them up-to-date on sports teams and major sporting events).

Communication Issues Need to Be Addressed from the Outset. Different cultures have different communication norms, even when they speak the same language. These differences show up immediately when people from two cultures try to negotiate an offshore contract. The differences need to be addressed, beginning with the negotiations.

Here is just one example. The word "yes" in Asia typically means, "I hear what you are saying," whereas in the United States it means "I can do what you ask" or "I agree with you." When conversing, an Indian might nod his head "yes," which an American might misinterpret as an agreement. The American is then surprised at the next meeting when there has been no agreement after all.

There are substantially more risks in negotiating offshore than onshore contracts because of such communication misunderstandings, notes the global law firm of Mayer, Brown, Rowe & Maw LLP in a SIG report. The firm uses many mechanisms to mitigate these risks. Here are just five:

- Avoid colloquialisms, such as sports analogies ("we've got to punt on this"), because these statements do not bridge cultures.
- Simplify communications by using short, concise sentences with common words, rather than the typical legal practice of lengthy, convoluted sentences and paragraphs.
- Have the offshore provider write a "statement of work," to gauge their understanding of what they think they are being asked to do.
- Get all commitments in writing.
- Include a person on the client negotiating team who knows the offshore country culture so that he or she can explain the country's norms to the client team as issues arise and prevent the offshorer's team from holding side discussions in their own language at the bargaining table. A "country-wise" member can significantly change negotiating dynamics.

Communication issues continue throughout offshore relationships. This is why migrating the work, which is often fairly quickly defined in onshore contracts, can require lengthy discussions in offshore deals. Common understandings do not exist, so every step in moving work from one country to another, and who pays for what, must be agreed upon. Furthermore, country laws and norms must be taken into account.

Country Laws Need to Be Followed. Offshoring contracts must bridge a myriad of differences between cultures. To preclude dealing with some legal issues, offshore vendors now typically sign their contract in the client's country. For example, as noted earlier, Syntel is a U.S. company. Its contracts with U.S. clients are signed in the United States, and are governed by U.S. law.

Even so, clients need to be aware of data privacy laws, which may not allow customer data to leave its home country or enter certain other countries. The European Union (EU), for instance, does not allow personal data to be moved outside of EU countries. Likewise, clients need to understand the enforceability of intellectual property laws in the outsourced country. Lack of enforceability may preclude moving some IT work to a country, such as China, which does not have enforceable intellectual property laws. Likewise, taxation, employment, immigration, and other laws can significantly affect an offshoring arrangement. All of these must be taken into account.

CASE EXAMPLE

EXULT

Exult provides full-service human resources (HR) outsourcing to Global 500 companies. The range of administrative processes Exult provides can be grouped into four main areas. One, Exult maintains and manages employee data and HR records, thereby facilitating various HR functions for clients. Two, Exult manages clients' payroll, compensation, and benefits processes. Three, it provides recruiting and flexible staffing services. Four, Exult provides learning, global mobility, and relocation services to help clients deploy their people most effectively.

Exult is mature in outsourcing relationships because outsourcing is its primary business. Furthermore, most Exult executives were either on the buyer or seller side of outsourcing before joining the company.

In October 2001, Exult signed two contracts with two Indian companies to maintain its core HR computer systems, which include both PeopleSoft and SAP platforms as well as systems built on those two platforms. This was the first time Exult outsourced any IT services.

"We chose to outsource application maintenance to India for three reasons: to garner cost savings, to increase system quality, and to achieve scale (that is, increase our access to resources as we grow our business)," says Steve Unterberger, executive vice president of business model architecture at Exult. He is responsible for Exult's service delivery model.

Exult chose two providers rather than one to ensure that resources could be scaled up as needed. Having only one provider could constrain growth. Management also wanted a fallback position, so that one provider could back up the other if need be. Finally, having two providers would let Exult migrate work offshore faster, moving one client to one provider and another client to the other provider. There would be no single point-of-capacity limit.

Choosing the Providers

"We led the project, but we called on two advisors: neoIT to do the detailed review and content, and TPI to structure the contract," says Unterberger. He continues, "We contracted with neoIT because of their experience contracting with Indian firms. Our goal was to get the best arrangement for ourselves and our clients. To do that, we needed to understand the Indian market and its practices. NeoIT helped us achieve that."

The Exult internal outsourcing team was composed of Unterberger and Exult's top people in sourcing, IT management, application management, IT connectivity and infrastructure, and IT security and privacy.

Early in the considerations, Exult and neoIT made a 4-day trip to India and visited 9 providers. "Our goal for that first trip was to meet as many companies as we could, to see firsthand how they compared. We knew the only way we could expect to have a clear view of the Indian marketplace was to personally visit India. There are five or six main cities where the major providers are located, so it's easy to see many companies in a short time. We met management, walked around operations, and chose employees at random and talked to them. They showed us real customer service reporting, work processes, and quality measures," says Unterberger.

"We were able to accomplish a lot very quickly because we were clear about what we needed. We knew the specific skills, competencies, and commitments we needed because these are spelled out in our contracts with our clients. So we were able to quickly direct conversations to get to the points we wanted to cover. We looked for a demonstrated ability to scale, a track record for managing people, and good IT maintenance processes," says Unterberger.

"That trip taught us that India has an incredible number of people who are very disciplined and highly motivated. In the end, we came away convinced that many companies could satisfy our needs. I returned from that trip with a real zeal, believing that anyone who is not investigating Indian providers is doing their company a disservice," says Unterberger.

Following the trip, neoIT and Exult ranked the providers and selected two using neoIT's neoQA process. "NeoIT was a very good advisor during this whole process, in two ways. First, they suggested other companies for us to consider—companies not typically on the big list. That was helpful because it kept everyone on their toes. Second, they knew where to push and not push, and they were able to distinguish for us the areas specific to Indian-based firms that we might have overlooked without their guidance," says Unterberger.

Negotiating the Deals

The negotiations were straightforward, and neoIT did help Exult avoid some pitfalls in pricing, taxes, staffing commitments, and telecom. "The providers have standard things they will do, but they do not volunteer them. You have to know to ask," says Unterberger. He states, "Telecom is one of those areas because, while the people costs in India are lower than the U.S., telecommunications costs are on a par with the U.S. We had also been forewarned that interconnecting would be the pacing factor in getting up and running—and, in fact, it was."

The agreements with the two providers are expected to be for 5 years, but each statement of work aligns with an Exult client and that client's agreement with Exult. These client relationships range from 5 to 10 years in length. The contracts specify service level commitments.

"All the companies have a similar model for training and knowledge transfer, so there is a well-known discipline in migrating the work. Our transition went according to plan," says Unterberger. He states, "We transitioned client by client; some clients went to one provider, some to the other."

"Data privacy was managed through extensive planning and review. We built upon the commitments in our own client contracts. The data is only accessed remotely from India, and the development environments work only with encrypted data. Backup data is stored in the client country, as are business resumption facilities. We spent a lot of time working through these data privacy issues to ensure there were no misunderstandings," says Unterberger.

Migration and Ongoing Management

The current split of IT maintenance work is as follows:

- Seventy percent of the staff members are offshore in India; they handle most of the ongoing maintenance of the HR systems.
- Fifteen percent are provider employees and work onshore at Exult; they handle quick turnaround work and coordinate change control and testing with the offshore staff.
- Fifteen percent are Exult employees who work onshore; they handle client communications and specifying system requirements.

Exult has the ability to influence key positions, and the providers are quick to rotate people when issues arise.

"The offshore companies are very good at engineering discipline. Taking advantage of that capability, though, requires us buyers to work within those highly disciplined Indian maintenance processes rather than try to change them," says Unterberger. According to Unterberger, Exult had to transition its retained IT managers to:

1. Shift from managing people to managing outcomes
2. Take the time to learn how the Indian staff work and think
3. Be open to suggestions from the Indian staff on how to improve the quality of our HR software.

"Transitioning IT managers to manage offshore work requires new skills because they are familiar with having direct control over their people," says Unterberger. He states, "They need to become more general managers and know which levers to pull to obtain results from afar."

According to Unterberger, "Exult also draws on neoIT in managing the relationships day-to-day. NeoIT has a person who acts as our eyes and ears in India because we are not there every day," says Unterberger

Exult is very pleased with the results. From an economic standpoint, the arrangements have exceeded all the goals. From a quality standpoint, Exult has spent time getting the onshore and offshore processes to work harmoniously.

The list of issues in offshoring can be truly mind-numbing. However, as the trend continues to grow, common practices are arising that make the negotiating task less daunting and the resulting arrangement less risky and more likely to succeed. As an example from the SIG report of a company using offshoring for its IT maintenance work, consider Exult, which is itself an example of a BPO company. It manages human resources for other firms.

Use Offshoring to Advantage. A main criticism of offshoring is that it decreases the skills and know-how of the client's IS organization. This need not be so. Kate Kaiser of Marquette University and Stephen Hawk of the University of Wisconsin-Parkside describe an 8-year arrangement between an unnamed financial services firm in the United States and an unnamed IT outsourcer in India. In their recent article in *MIS Quarterly Executive*, the two authors note that the U.S. firm wanted to reduce its system development costs but also increase its in-house IS staff's knowledge—a fairly unusual dual goal. To do so, the two firms have evolved their relationship to "IT cosourcing," which Kaiser and Hawk define as "when the vendor and client collaborate so closely that the vendor can replace or augment the client's IT competencies." In essence, resources from both firms are used to meet the client's needs. Project teams are mixed, and team leadership can come from either firm—both of which require the vendor to have a large onsite presence. Two mechanisms, in particular, have ensured that the U.S. firm's IS staff gain competencies rather than lose them: formalized knowledge transfer between the two firms and a dual project-management hierarchy.

To formalize knowledge transfer from the Indian staff to the U.S. staff, U.S. staff members are sometimes *formally* assigned to projects to learn from an Indian mentor. The two firms initially made such assignments *informally*, but that approach did not improve skills. So the two firms formalized learning-oriented mechanisms, such as mentoring. At the U.S. firm, each IS employee has a development plan, which includes career goals and steps to achieve the needed skills. For the Indian firm, job assignments with the U.S. client include such tasks as mentoring a specific U.S. team member in specific areas. The cost of mentoring is included in the cost of the project.

To create the dual project management hierarchy, the hierarchies of the two firms now mirror each other to improve communication across them. Furthermore, the tiers of leadership in projects can come from either firm, depending on the circumstances. The Indian firm may lead to provide mentoring. The U.S. client may lead for business reasons. Again, the roles of each job are formally agreed upon, and mentoring or other knowledge-transfer skills are part of the cost of the project.

Both mechanisms increase the cost of outsourcing, note Kaiser and Hawk, because, for one thing, dual leadership requires more Indian staff to be located in the United States. But the additional cost improves the in-house staff's technical and application skills, which the firm believes is well worth the added expense, because they highly value their employees' career development.

Redefine Services Using Offshoring, Automation, and Self-Service. Uday Karmarkar, research director of UCLA's Center for Management in the Information Economy, like author Daniel Altman, believes that outsourcing of services is inevitable and that the real concern of service firms should be their loss of competitiveness, not the loss of jobs in their own country. He believes that the service economy is in the midst of restructuring itself, which is terribly painful when it happens in any industry. Offshoring, automation, and self-service are all combining to cause "the industrialization of services," he believes. Like manufacturing firms before them, service firms therefore need to find new ways to add value. He suggests looking in five places for determining new strategies for surviving and using offshoring, automation, and self-service to execute these strategies.

Understand customers. Companies that understand niches of customers, and serve them well, will themselves do well, believes Karmarkar, especially as they move their services to the Web. Edmunds, a company that has published books for car buyers for many years, now focuses on its car-buyer Web site. The site has been so well designed that it has won numerous awards. Edmunds understands its customers and caters to them, states Karmarkar.

Understand demographics. Look for underserved niches, like Wells Fargo Bank has done in offering specific services to the Hispanic population in the western United States. The bank now opens 22,000 Hispanic accounts a month by understanding and catering to this growing group, notes Karmarkar.

Stay in touch with customers. Do not outsource customer service, Karmarkar recommends. Many have done it and found that they lose touch with their customers. Some have realized the effect and brought the function back in-house. A far better strategy is to deliver responsive and error-free service, he believes.

Offer end-to-end service. Customers are most interested in buying services from firms that offer end-to-end services. For example, Virgin Atlantic Airways provides its business-class passengers with limousine service to the airport and drive-through check-in. People are willing to pay for such pampering to relieve themselves of hassles. This is an important strategy some service firms are delving into by using data mining to understand preferences of customer clusters and then catering to those preferences, notes Karmarkar.

Dominate the screen. As information moves online, companies are vying to control "the screen," that is, where the information ends up. Service companies have a shot at dominating the screen, because the design of the service and the interface (rather than the technology or the appliance) will determine success, states Karmarkar. For example, NTT DoCoMo, the telecommunications company in Japan, knows how to sell content on cell phones and appliances—from service providers to consumers. Due to this skill, NTT has claimed a disproportionate degree of control over the information chain, notes Karmarkar; it dominates the screen. In short, service companies need to understand what kinds of information various clusters of customer want and cater to them. For many service firms, that catering will be via the Web and mobile devices, using offshoring, self-service, and automation where each can contribute the most value.

In conclusion, outsourcing has become a strategic alternative. With the rapid pace of business change, the best hope of many enterprises is to tap the expertise of companies that are keeping pace rather than trying to do everything themselves. That is why so much inter-company collaboration is taking place. However, outsourcing does not mean relinquishing responsibility. In fact, taken to its extreme, it can mean devoting resources to assist suppliers improve their processes. We believe it is a coming focus in the world of IS Lite.

PLANNING FOR BUSINESS CONTINUITY

Sadly, the terrorist attacks on September 11, 2001, taught a lot of U.S. companies that there is a big difference between disaster recovery and business continuity. In the past, executives expected their IS organization to focus on disaster recovery; that is, getting computers and networks up-and-running after a hurricane, flood, fire, or other disaster. September 11 taught them a broader issue—business continuity—that is, getting the business back up and running. Business continuity involves far more than IT equipment, notes Chuck Tucker in the Gartner EXP report, *September 11: Business Continuity Lessons.*

Business continuity broadens the discussion to include safeguarding people during a disaster, documenting business procedures (instead of relying on certain employees who may become unavailable), and giving employees the tools and space to handle personal issues first so that they can then concentrate on work. Tucker notes that business continuity includes:

- Alternate workspaces for people with working computers and phone lines
- Backup IT sites that are not too close but not too far away (to be within driving distance but not affected by a regional telecommunication disaster)
- Up-to-date evacuation plans that everyone knows and has practiced
- Backed up laptops and departmental servers, because a lot of corporate information is housed on these machines rather than in the data center
- Helping people cope with a disaster by having easily accessible phone lists, e-mail lists, and even instant messenger lists so that people can communicate with loved ones and colleagues

In short, business continuity is a business issue. IT disaster recovery is just one component of it. Disaster recovery practitioners agree that (1) disaster contingency planning needs to be an integral part of doing business, and (2) commitment of resources to a disaster recovery process must be based on an assessment by top management of cost versus risk. Companies essentially have two options for disaster recovery: use of internal or external resources.

Using Internal Resources

Organizations that rely on internal resources for disaster recovery generally view this planning as a normal part of systems planning and development. They cost-justify backup processing and telecommunications based on company needs during foreseeable emergencies. Companies use the following approaches to backing up their computer systems, data, and communication links with company resources:

- Multiple data centers
- Distributed processing
- Backup telecommunications facilities
- LANs

Multiple Data Centers. Over the past few years, to save money organizations have consolidated their multiple computer centers or outsourced them to a provider operating mainly from one data center. September 11 caused many executives to rethink the wisdom of having all corporate computing in one location. Multiple centers can provide emergency backup for critical services.

For backing up data, companies create protected disk storage facilities, sometimes called direct access data storage, or DASD farms. These farms are regularly refreshed with current operating data to speed recovery at an alternate data center. They are normally company-owned, unattended sites and remote from the primary data center. They house disk controllers and disk drives that can be accessed either online or in batch mode.

Distributed Processing. Other organizations use distributed processing to deal with disaster recovery. They perform critical processing locally rather than at a data center so that operations can continue uninterrupted when a disaster hits a data center. Companies that use this approach standardize hardware and applications at remote locations so that each local processing site can provide backup for the others.

Distributed processing solutions to disaster recovery can be quite costly when data redundancy between central and remote sites is required. Therefore, this alternative is most commonly used for applications that must continue to operate, such as order entry and financial transaction systems.

Backup Telecommunications Facilities. Companies appear to be handling tele-communications backup in two ways: (1) by utilizing duplicate communications facilities and (2) by using alternate technologies that they redeploy in case of an emergency. However, as Tucker notes, in New York City, companies signed up with different telecommunications carriers (without checking their carriers' routing), thinking that they had alternate communication routes. Then they discovered that 30 percent of Manhattan's telecommunications traffic, from many different carriers, went through Verizon's West Street switching office, which was destroyed on September 11.

Some companies turn to alternate communication technologies when their communication links fail, such as when the infamous Hinsdale fire destroyed the Hinsdale Illinois Bell Telephone Company central office switching station. The station handled 118,000 long distance lines, 30,000 data lines, and 35,000 local voice lines, reports Jeff Bozman. It served as a hub for some 30 local exchanges in northeastern Illinois. The fire disrupted telephone service to the area for 4 weeks. Local companies used at least two alternative technologies to handle their telecommunication needs during this emergency.

MONY Financial Services in Syracuse, New York, switched a satellite link from its smaller San Juan, Puerto Rico, office to its large Hinsdale office by installing a VSAT dish on the roof, reports Crockett. It was used to communicate via satellite to a communication hub in New York City and from there via land lines to Syracuse. The San Juan office then instituted its own communication backup plan, using terrestrial lines to communicate to Syracuse.

Zurich Insurance Company, in Schaumburg, Illinois, established a line-of-site microwave link between headquarters and an AT&T switching office located about 2 miles away, reports Crockett. In fact, 38 temporary microwave links were established in the Chicago area.

September 11 taught the importance of restoring or relying on more personal forms of communication—e-mail, handhelds, instant messaging, intranets, and even paging systems. Business no longer relies just on data in data center computers; much of it is now stored in laptops, departmental servers, and e-mail. Before September 11, few IS organizations had disaster recovery plans for these computers and systems.

LANs. Servers on one LAN can be used to back up servers for other networks. As with mainframe DASD farms, data servers used for such backup need to be refreshed regularly to keep their data up-to-date. Keeping up-to-date is accomplished by linking the networks. Network master control programs permit the designating of alternate devices when primary ones fail.

Using External Resources

In many cases, a cost-versus-risk analysis may not justify committing permanent resources to contingencies; therefore, companies use the services of a disaster recovery firm. These services include:

- Integrated disaster recovery services
- Specialized disaster recovery services
- Online and off-line data storage facilities

Integrated Disaster Recovery Services. In North America, major suppliers of disaster recovery services offer multiple recovery sites interconnected by high-speed telecommunications lines. Services at these locations include fully operational processing facilities that are available on fewer-than-24-hours notice. These suppliers often have environmentally suitable storage facilities for housing special equipment for their clients.

Subscription fees for access to fully operational facilities are charged on a per-month basis. Actual use of the center is charged on a per-day basis. In addition, a fee is often charged each time a disaster is declared. Mobile facilities, with a mobile trailer containing computer equipment, can be moved to a client site and are available at costs similar to fully operational facilities. Empty warehouse space can be rented as well.

Recognizing the importance of telecommunications links, major disaster recovery suppliers have expanded their offerings to include smaller sites that contain specialized telecommunications equipment. These sites allow users to maintain telecommunications services when disaster recovery facilities are in use. They house control equipment and software needed to support communication lines connecting recovery sites with client sites.

Needless to say, companies now in the business of hosting corporate Web sites also handle disaster recovery for those sites.

September 11 pointed out a shortcoming of regional disasters: The backup sites fill up fast. In fact, one firm located in the World Trade Center declared a disaster with its provider 4 minutes after the first plane hit and was told that the closest available workspace facilities were hundreds of miles away. This company resorted to triage instead, notes Tucker, asking some employees to work from home and giving their workspaces at other locations to the displaced employees.

Specialized Disaster Recovery Services. Some suppliers of backup services can accommodate mainframe clients who also need to back up midrange machines. Others provide backup solely for midrange systems. Some will even deliver a trailer with compatible hardware and software to a client location.

Telecommunications firms also offer a type of recovery service, through network reconfiguration, where network administrators at user sites can reroute their circuits around lines with communication problems. Specialized telecommunications backup services also exist. Hughes Network Systems, in Germantown, Maryland, helped a company that had 49 of its pharmacies affected by the Hinsdale telephone switching station fire. Within 72 hours, Hughes installed a temporary network of VSATs at 12 sites. The 37 remaining sites had small satellite dishes installed within 2 weeks. Other firms offer data communications backup programs, where they will store specific telecommunications equipment for customers and deliver that equipment to the customer's recovery site when needed.

Online and Off-Line Data Storage. Alternate locations for storage of data and other records have long been a part of disaster planning. Services generally consist of fire-resistant vaults with suitable temperature and humidity controls. Several suppliers offer "electronic vaulting" for organizations that need to have current data off-site at the time a disaster occurs. These suppliers use two methods to obtain current data from their clients. One method uses computer-to-computer transmission of data on a scheduled basis. The other uses dedicated equipment to capture and store data at a remote location as it is created on the client's computer. This latter method assures uninterrupted access to data from an operationally ready disaster recovery facility selected by the client.

In summary, when disaster recovery needs do not shape the architecture of an enterprise's computer systems, the cost of reconfiguring the systems to provide the needed redundancy and backup can be prohibitive. In these cases, external backup alternatives may be a more cost-effective form of insurance. For e-business, however, mere backup capability does not suffice. Disaster recovery must be an integral part of system design, because companies need immediate roll-over to backup facilities when operations are interrupted.

To illustrate the use of disaster recovery facilities, consider the case of Household International.

SUMMARY

Distributed systems dominate the computing landscape, with the Internet now at the heart. Distributing processing, databases, and communications allow companies to move more quickly because they can more easily snap in new products and services into their existing systems. The advent of Web Services is fueling the use of the Internet to extend the tenets of distributed systems even further.

The telecommunications world is big, and getting bigger by the day. It is complex, and becoming more complex. Some see it as a global electronic highway system where the goal is to establish links and interoperability. Others see it as a cyberspace where commerce is conducted and businesses operate.

The business world of old depended on communications, of course, but not to the extent of online commerce. The Internet unleashed e-mail, then Web sites for getting noticed globally, and now it is used for transactions and business. Although worldwide communication over the Internet enables global business, it also has the opposite effect: customized personal service to individuals anywhere, anytime.

As can be seen by the wide-ranging discussion in this chapter, the job of managing information resources is widening significantly. Not only must IS departments get corporate data in shape, but they must also create and build an infrastructure for managing the full range of information types. In some ways, the Internet helps because it gives companies an easily accessible place to store information. On the other hand, the Internet contributes mightily to the information glut we all face.

The subject of managing computer operations is, perhaps surprisingly, at an all-time high because of the emergence of e-commerce, the increasing use of outsourcing, news-grabbing computer viruses, attacks on major Web sites, and terrorism. Outsourcing, security, business continuity—all are important operational issues. As enterprises increasingly rely on computing and telecommunications to work closely with others, they open themselves up to more threats by electronic means. As we noted in the security section, one security manager would not call the Internet a bad neighborhood, but he would watch his back. That attitude increasingly means being vigilant to outside threats, just as outsourcing means learning to work with outsiders. In short, the view of operations is shifting from managing inward to managing outward, on all fronts.

This chapter covered a lot of ground. You learned about distributed systems, the importance of communications, managing information, and managing operations.

CHAPTER REVIEW QUESTIONS

1. How does this chapter differentiate the two terms *architecture* and *infrastructure?*
2. What four questions should you pose to determine the degree to which a system is distributed?
3. What one factor does choosing a distributed system architecture hinge on?
4. What are the seven types of distributed systems?
5. What are the three software standards that make Web Services possible?
6. What are the three communication protocols that make Web Services feasible?
7. List some benefits that a company might realize from investing in its infrastructure.
8. Cite definitions for these terms: *data, information,* and *knowledge.*
9. What are the advantages of a three-level database model?
10. List four data models and describe each one.
11. What are some of the steps required for a data warehousing project?
12. How has the storage and transmission of documents affected technology?
13. Explain the difference between managing operations inward and outward.
14. What are some of the problems that management must address with offshoring?
15. What are the differences between disaster recovery and business continuity? What are some key ways to maintain continuity given a crisis?

CHAPTER DISCUSSION QUESTIONS

1. Discuss how the term "open" has evolved in its meaning over the history of computer technology.
2. Do you agree with the statement that Francis Wagner made when he said that people perform best when they are responsible for their own mistakes? Discuss how this philosophy works in decision-making responsibilities.
3. How is homogeneity determined in a business? Is it always obvious?
4. Discuss SUMURU and why it still works today.
5. Discuss Hagel and Brown's three-tire Web Services architecture. Do you agree with it?
6. Fill in the architectural framework model in Figure 14.8 with a fictitious company and situation that you create.
7. Discuss how outsourcing has changed over the years.
8. Discuss the pros and cons of offshoring. What do you think is the future of offshoring? How will it affect the U.S.?

CASE STUDY: HOUSEHOLD INTERNATIONAL

Household International, with headquarters in Prospect Heights, Illinois, is a major provider of consumer lending, banking, insurance, and commercial financial services in the United States. The company also provides similar services in the United Kingdom, Canada, and Australia through subsidiaries.

The core of its consumer finance business is serviced by some 700 consumer lending branches and 60 bank branches throughout the United States. Household is also a large credit card issuer in the United States and operates a major credit card service center in California. Household's major data center is in its corporate offices. The center is linked to the branch network via leased lines with regional connections to more than 10,000 remote devices and terminals.

Typical of large financial services institutions, Household justified its disaster recovery planning based on legal and regulatory requirements and the need to maintain uninterrupted customer service. The centralized design of its data network simplified recovery planning but made the headquarters data center critical to recovery.

The company established a full-time staff to prepare, maintain, and exercise (test out) disaster recovery plans. After exploring several alternatives, including adding reserve processing capacity to their network, Household decided to rely on Comdisco Disaster Recovery Services. Comdisco is a major supplier of alternate site data processing services in North America.

Services provided by Comdisco included use of facilities at one or more of its recovery centers throughout North America and hot site equipment and software to provide immediate operational support on request. In addition, Comdisco provided technical assistance in disaster planning, testing, and the use of recovery centers. Household viewed the monthly cost of these services as their most economical recovery alternative.

After 6 months, all critical banking applications had been tested at the alternate site and contingency procedures had been developed for the branch offices. Household had also begun developing contingency plans for the consumer lending operation and testing application programs at the alternate site. In addition, they had begun developing business recovery priorities and operating procedures for end users.

In the midst of this effort, nature intervened. At 9:00 a.m. on a Friday after meeting with key personnel, Household declared a disaster. More than 9 inches of rain had fallen on the Chicago area in 12 hours. Widespread flooding had closed major highways, leaving thousands of homes and businesses without power or telephone service. A retention pond at corporate headquarters had overflowed, causing an overnight runoff into the basement of the headquarters building where the data center was located. By 10:30 a.m. the water had risen to 31 inches—9 inches above the 22-inch false floor—and it rose even further before the disaster ended.

With telephone lines down and the company PBX out of service, the recovery coordinator relied on plans made early in the year. Computer operations were transferred to the Comdisco alternate site 20 miles away. Fortunately, Household made the call to Comdisco early; other clients who called later were relocated to sites as far as 800 miles (1,300 kilometers) away. Because five Chicago-area businesses declared disasters, Comdisco's hot site resources in Illinois were quickly saturated.

At the backup site, work began on restoring vital bank and check processing systems. Critical processing for most branches resumed within 24 hours. Teller systems at branches used local computers, so they operated without interruption. How-ever, online information on the current status of customer accounts was not available until the following Monday.

After pumping out the flooded data center, the data processing staff found extensive damage to disk drive motors and circuit boards below the high-water mark. However, they were able to quickly restore the communication control units. They were then able to use these units as the links for all communications between the backup site computers and the remote computers in the branches. The local telephone company used a central switch to establish a link between the disaster recovery alternate site and the Household home office.

By the third day, all the important work that had been moved to key Household locations was up and running, and communication links among these locations were working. Communica-tion links to all offices were available by the sixth day.

A few days after the disaster, more than 220 analysts and programmers were assigned to work at the alternate site on a 24-hour schedule. The disaster recovery coordinator arranged for special food service, dressing facilities, and rest areas at the alternate site. Workspaces were created using rented furniture and equipment.

Special meetings were held with senior management to establish recovery priorities for the consumer lending operation. Daily meetings, chaired by the executive vice president of IS, were attended by nearly all managers and vendors affected by the disaster—some 40 to 50 people in all. These meetings became the day-to-day means for reporting status, handling special problems, and developing recovery schedules. The meetings turned out to be the best means for communicating quickly and making decisions using the existing organization. The meetings lasted several hours each day and covered a wide range of topics. Thus, no special organizational structure was used for managing the disaster; however. the disaster recovery manager played a key role in coordinating the recovery.

The company left the backup site on the fifteenth day. Eighteen days after the disaster, normal operations had been fully restored.

LESSONS LEARNED

Household learned six lessons from this disaster, which it offers as recommendations to others.

1. Consider the risks of a natural disaster when selecting a data center location. Areas with high exposure to flooding, heavy rainfall, fire hazards, or earthquakes will be more costly to protect.
2. Create a plan to return to the primary site after the disaster. This plan is just as important as the plan to move to an alternate site.
3. Do not expect damaged equipment to always be replaced in kind or restored to original condition. Therefore, make plans for new configurations, and regularly monitor sources of equipment and supplies to assure early delivery of replacements.
4. Test hot site resources under full workload conditions to ensure that sufficient computer capacity is available to meet high-priority needs.
5. Plan for alternate telecommunications routing for multiple-site operations during a disaster. Household's original telecommunications disaster recovery plan called for key sites around the country to handle the headquarters processing load in case of a home office disaster. The quick recovery of the communication control units at headquarters allowed Household to use an alternate plan: rely mainly on processing at the nearby disaster recovery site. Thus, for 16 days they operated with both the headquarters center and the disaster recovery center. The other key Household centers handled mainly their normal work, but their computers were available if needed.
6. Maintain critical data at the alternate site or at another nearby location for fast system recovery.

Household has used its experience to refine and complete the plans started before the rainstorm. In addition, Comdisco services have been extended to other subsidiaries under a corporate-wide contract. In retrospect, key participants believe that early restoration of the headquarters computer center, the existence of computer and telecommunications backup procedures, staff familiar with the backup plans, and use of normal management channels were all important in their rapid recovery.

Case Study Discussion Questions

Question One

Do some research online to find out how various companies are handling disaster preparation and recovery operations. Is it more feasible and economical to use an outside vendor for this disaster preparation or prepare for it in-house?

Question Two

Using the lessons learned by Household International, prepare an outline/plan to implement in case your company experienced a natural disaster. Depending on the disaster, are there different levels at which the company could function? Don't forget to factor in the needs of the personnel who run the company.

Question Three

Pick one of the disasters (natural or otherwise) that has occurred in the past few years. How did people cope? What worked and what didn't for businesses to get up and running again?

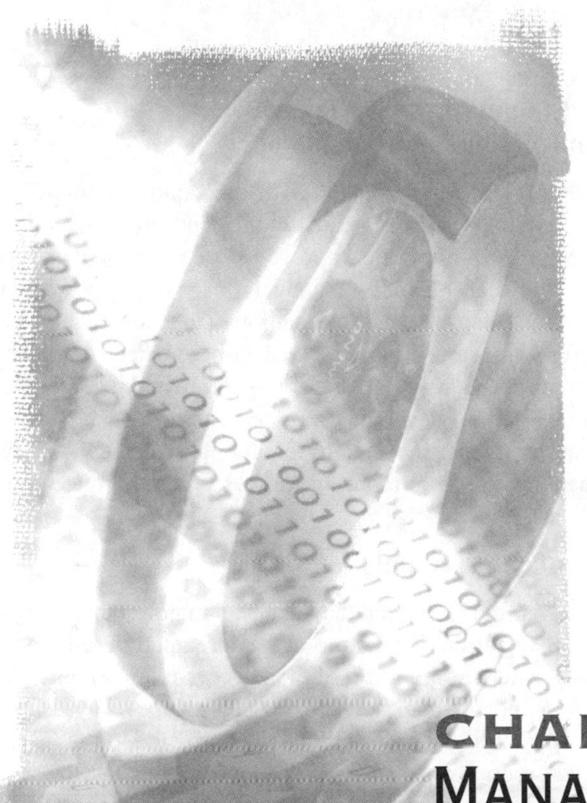

CHAPTER 15
MANAGING THE INFORMATION SYSTEMS FUNCTION

To create an effective management system for information resources, information systems (IS) leaders must create a vision, an architecture, and an overall plan for the deployment of an organization's information resources. But laying out an IS plan for reaching the information vision/architecture is only part of the task. IS leaders, with input from business managers throughout the organization, must actively manage the technology and human resources that comprise the organization's information resources. In addition, these leaders—both IS and business managers—must resolve a series of issues in order to create an effective management system for the organization's information resources. Success is attained only by actively implementing that plan via projects, policies, and an effective organization in order to build an overall management system.

Many organizations are making dramatic changes in their IS management system. Some organizations are switching from either highly centralized or highly decentralized IS organizations to a more cooperative, client/server-type structure to parallel the trend in information technology (IT) architecture. IS organizations, like other functions, suffered through the downsizing of the 1990s and early 2000s as companies worked to become more globally competitive for customers and shareholders. Also common in the early 2000s is outsourcing a portion of the IS department to an independent organization, sometimes to an offshore company. This organization may be a subsidiary of the corporation but usually is a separate service company in the business of running data centers, telecommunication networks, or systems development groups. Another major theme in IS management today is helping the organization participate in a global marketplace. As covered in this chapter, managing global systems raises unique factors and issues for an organization. Last, but certainly not least, IS organizations are responding to the fundamental influence of Internet technology as a medium for conducting business both up and down the supply and distribution channel and within the organization.

This chapter first identifies the causes of the increasing complexity in managing the IS function. Some of the issues involved in managing the human and technical resources in an IT system are then identified. Finally, the issues related to making the IS organization an effective player in the business are discussed.

THE CHALLENGES FACING IS LEADERSHIP

Almost from its inception, major external developments have required the IS function to undergo significant changes in the basic definition of its mission and the way it carries out its role. Why has the evolution of IS management—from highly centralized, low-level management units to a mixture of centralization and decentralization across all units and levels—taken place? Basically, the changes reflect trends in the technology, applications, and data; an increased understanding of IT by business managers; and changes in business environmental factors. Many of these developments have been addressed throughout this book. A few of the more critical influences are reviewed here.

These developments serve to make it difficult for IS professionals and their customers (the business managers) to determine how best to manage the IS function. Complicating this confusion is the fact that in today's (and tomorrow's) business environment, the way in which the IS function is managed and its contribution to the business are critical success factors for the entire organization. Today, IT is so pervasive that it requires the attention of every organizational unit and business manager. Ensuring payback from IT investment, being able to respond quickly to changing requirements, and leveraging technology for increased business value are now basic to conducting a successful business or other organization.

Rapid Technological Change

Small and inexpensive electronic technologies have made it possible for each knowledge worker, business manager, department, and small business to acquire sophisticated computer and communications equipment. In fact, many managers today have more data on their workstation's hard drive than in their file cabinets. With this distribution of technology comes a need for local responsibility for operations, backup and recovery, security, development, education, and planning. Even with these needs to manage the distributed technology, there is still the need to ensure that desktop and departmental systems do not become isolated.

Exploding Applications and Data

There has been very rapid growth in the number of available software systems for almost every imaginable application. Likewise, the growth of the Internet has made vast amounts of data (certainly not all of it useful) available to organizations. Gone are the days when the IS department developed the vast majority of software in-house. Also gone are the days when people could be sure that the data they are accessing have been checked for accuracy. Software development is now fragmented. Some systems are purchased; some are built in house. Database management has become a more critical part of the IS department's responsibilities and that of the business manager as well.

Growth in Business Management Understanding of Technology

There is now a greater IT skill level among non-systems professionals, which creates higher and more diverse expectations for new and improved systems and greater confidence that business managers can develop and run systems themselves. More senior management than ever before are comfortable with data-based decisions. They want to see data—and a lot of it—before making decisions. More use and development of systems by business managers stimulates the need for additional systems (a learning phenomenon—the more one knows, the more one wants).

Frequent External Shocks

External developments have caused major changes in the IS organization. For example, the deregulation (and resulting greater competition) of the telecommunications industry forced organizations to manage aspects of data and voice communications previously entrusted to the vendor. International regulations on transborder data flows and vast differences in labor rates have caused organizations to reconsider where new systems are built and operated and where data entry is most economically conducted. The terrorist threats following the events of September 11, 2001, have caused many organizations to mount a serious effort to do a better job of protecting people, facilities, and data. The shortage of highly qualified IS professionals in the late 1990s and the economic downturn in the United States in the early 2000s encouraged organizations to expect greater productivity from existing IS staff and resulted in the distribution of more systems work to non-IS professionals.

MANAGING THE ASSETS IN AN IS ORGANIZATION

In many organizations the IS function has undergone a sequence of frequent and often nonlinear changes over the last several decades in response to rapid changes in technology and business manager expectations. The job of IS leadership (for both professionals and business managers) starts with setting a vision for how the organization should use information, an architecture for the deployment of information resources to support that vision, and a plan to achieve the architecture. In addition, IS leadership must manage the organization's assets—its human resources, organizational data, the physical infrastructure, and the applications portfolio. Here the focus is on the other assets critical to an effective IS function. The business manager must be an active participant in this leadership process.

The most important asset in the IS organization is clearly its people. These individuals must be kept up-to-date in the rapidly changing world of IT if they are to be effective for the organization and themselves. How IS professionals should be treated and challenged is critical for both IS leadership and business managers to understand. It is also important for IS leadership and business managers to cooperate in making basic decisions about the other two major assets of an IT system: the physical infrastructure (hardware and networks) and the applications portfolio. In both these areas difficult technological tradeoffs must be considered and key decisions must be made. Most important, these decisions can have a major impact on the business. For example, a policy to buy rather than build applications software (popular in most organizations) usually increases the speed with which a new system can be up and running. However, using a packaged software product can severely restrict the ways in which the business can operate and perhaps even limit the ability of the business to grow. It is because of these potential types of impacts that business managers need to be involved (at least enough to understand the implication for the business) in decisions about how the organization's technological resources will be managed. The key issues and tradeoffs in determining the physical infrastructure and the applications portfolio follow the human resources discussion.

Developing Human Resources

An effective IT management system will allocate significant resources to the continuing professional development of both IS personnel and business managers. A full treatment of human resource management practices for IS personnel can be found in a number of human resources textbooks. The subject is too specialized to be treated here. However, in an environment of rapid change in technology and business demand, significant effort in technology training for both IS professionals and other employees is required. The IS field is diverse and traditionally specialized. Although senior IS executives are more and more becoming general business managers, most IS professionals, whether based in the IS organization or in business units, have specific technical duties and require specialized training. With the life cycles for software products shortening, it is not uncommon for organizations to have technology training underway all the time.

Figure 15.1 lists the generic job titles and a brief description for many possible IS management positions in a typical IS organization. Depending on the IS department structure, these positions might reside in a business unit, in a divisional group, in the corporate IS unit, or in all three. All these roles are essential for the high-quality operation of the systems in the organization. This list does not include the programmers, analysts, computer operators, trainers, and consultants. Each of these professionals has substantial training requirements as well.

The business manager community and IS leaders share in the responsibility of providing IT training for all users. Figure 15.2 shows the IT training requirements for employees in a major metropolitan healthcare organization. In 2003 senior management committed the organization to a policy that all employees should have at least 24 hours of IT training each year. The required courses had to be taken in the first year of employment.

Improving the Physical Infrastructure

In addition to developing the most valuable asset (people), business managers and IS professionals must develop policies and procedures to manage an IT system's physical assets—the computer hardware and the network—on a global basis. These assets have always represented a very large investment in IT. As hardware costs have decreased and personal workstations have proliferated, many business managers have forgotten that the aggregate monetary value of network and hardware assets is now higher than ever—even in a smaller organization.

Failure of the computer network once affected only a few administrative workers. Today, however, employees at all levels in the organization all around the world interact with the computer network for essential aspects of their work. Thus, network or computer failure now has a high degree of visibility—it might disrupt plant managers, division heads, vice presidents, and even sometimes the CEO. Computer power is like electrical power—if it goes out, everything comes to a halt until service is restored. A recent week-long outage of the corporate e-mail system at an Indianapolis outsourcing company caused the firm to lose several days of files with losses in terms of time and missed opportunities estimated at several million dollars.

Furthermore, with the advent of strategic application systems, the impact of infrastructure management is no longer restricted to company employees. Poor infrastructure management might have a direct impact on the company's customers or suppliers. For example, problems with a bank's network directly affect those customers who enter transactions into the bank's automatic teller machine (ATM)

Selected IS Management Positions

CIO
Most senior executive responsible for leading in the introduction of information technology across the whole organization

IS Director
Responsible for the day-to-day operations of all aspects of IS for the organization

Systems Development Manager
Coordinates all new systems development projects, allocates systems analysts and project managers to projects, schedules development work

Systems Maintenance Manager
Coordinates all systems maintenance projects, allocates the time of systems analysts and project managers to projects, schedules maintenance work

IS Planning Manager
Analyzes business and develops an architecture for hardware and software to support systems in the future; may also forecast technology trends

Data Center Manager
Supervises the day-to-day operations of the data center and possibly also data entry, the data network, and the computer file library; schedules computer jobs, manages downtime, and plans computer system capacity

Manager of Web-Based Technologies
Evaluates new ways to use the Internet, fosters experimental projects to test Web-based technologies in the organization, consults with users on appropriate application of new technologies, and approves new technologies for use in the organization

Telecommunications Manager
Plans, designs, and coordinates the operation of the corporate data and voice network

Systems Programming Manager
Provides support and maintenance of systems software (operating system, utilities, programming language compilers, etc.); interacts with vendors to install updates and request changes

Database Administrator
Plans databases and coordinates use of data management software

Project Manager
Supervises analysts and programmers working on the development or maintenance of an applications system and coordinates with customers of the system

Quality Assurance Manager
Coordinates activities that set standards and checks compliance with standards to improve the quality and accuracy of systems

Computer Security Manager
Develops procedures and policies and installs and monitors software to ensure the authorized use of computing resources

Figure 15.1 Selected IS Management Positions

IS Training Architecture

Required courses:

Hourly	Professional	Executive
Lotus Notes—Basics Windows—Basics Basic Network Navigation Microsoft Office MS Word—Basics MS Word—Advanced MS Excel—Basics MS Access—Basics	Lotus Notes—Basics Windows—Basics Windows—Advanced Basic Network Navigation Microsoft Office MS Word—Basics MS Word—Advanced MS Excel—Basics MS Excel—Advanced MS Access—Basics	Lotus Notes—Basics Windows—Basics Basic Network Navigation Microsoft Office MS Word—Basics MS Word—Advanced MS Excel—Basics MS Excel—Advanced MS Access—Basics Microsoft Project

Electives:

Windows		UNIX	Internet
MS Access—Basics MS Access—Intermediate MS Access—Advanced MS Excel—Basics MS Excel—Intermediate MS Excel—Advanced ArcView	Lotus Notes—Basics Lotus Notes—Advanced PC Anywhere MS PowerPoint—Basics MS PowerPoint—Advanced MS Project—Basics MS Project—Advanced MS Word—Advanced	UNIX—Basics UNIX—Advanced	HTML XML MS Front Page—Basics MS Front Page—Advanced

Figure 15.2 IS Training Architecture

system. Problems with an airline's reservations system might affect travel agents worldwide. In today's world, most people depend on the successful management of one or more IT networks every day.

The same basic functions that must be performed to manage any asset successfully should be applied to the IT global physical infrastructure. It must be planned, acquired, made available, and so on. Because of the high degree of specialized skills and training required to perform these functions, however, most business managers outsource the management of the infrastructure either to the organization's IS department or to an outside vendor. For this reason, the focus here is on infrastructure management policy issues where business managers will be most affected. More information on the elements in a physical infrastructure may be found in earlier chapters.

The following are some of the issues that must be resolved in an infrastructure management system, typically through policy statements:

1. **Location.** Clearly, most organizations today operate in a distributed computing environment. However, the physical location of the hardware on a network can be a critical issue from cost, control, and security standpoints. Physically distributing equipment, other than personal workstations, can create additional costs for managing the hardware and safeguarding data. Many computers and telecommunications switches benefit significantly from being housed in a secure, environmentally controlled location. Quite often, however, physical location connotes a sense of control to many business managers. A division general manager might be comforted by locating the division's servers in a room on divisional premises rather than in the IS data center in corporate headquarters a few blocks away. Likewise, some countries might be better hosts than others for location of complex data centers.
2. **The Workstation.** Policies on the future design and role of the IT workstation should be determined.

Which workstations should have independent intelligence and which should be a network device slaved to some central server? Should telecommunications, such as with Voice over Internet Protocol (VoIP), and computer components of the workstation be physically integrated? Should videoconferencing capability be integrated into the manager workstation? What is the most appropriate location for each type of computing work? At the workstation? At a central server? At a remote hardware resource? On a local area network (LAN)? Or at some departmental server? What level of access should the workstation have to outside resources on the Internet? In answering all these questions, cost, convenience, and security tradeoffs must be made.

3. **Supported Operating Systems.** Some vendors of technology hardware still offer a proprietary operating system, although more commonality exists now than in the past. How many and which operating systems will the organization support? Will the organization support newer operating systems such as Linux? Each different operating system creates more difficulty in sustaining a seamless network, and support costs increase rapidly as new operating systems are added. Confining the company to one operating system, however, reduces bargaining power, limits access to the best software, and makes the organization more dependent on the fortunes of a particular vendor. For example, if all workstations are required to operate only with the latest version of Microsoft Windows, the company's future in part depends on how well Microsoft sustains its leadership.
4. **Redundancy.** Because organizations are so dependent today on their networks, many business managers want full redundancy of the key nodes and paths in the IT network. Yet full redundancy can be *very* expensive. How much redundancy should there be in the design of the network? Should there be full redundancy only for major nodes and high-volume pathways? The cost for full path redundancy can be very expensive because there must be at least two different paths to every node in the network from every other node. Likewise, "hot" backup sites that allow failed critical nodes to return to operation quickly are also expensive. The lack of redundancy, however, can be very expensive in terms of lost user time if the network or a critical node is not available for some period. Business managers need to express their views on the trade-offs between the cost of downtime due to network unavailability and the cost of providing continuous access.
5. **Supported Communications Protocols.** As with operating systems, some hardware vendors support their own proprietary communications protocols as well as some mix of standard communications protocols. For example, most vendors support the American Standard Code for Information Interchange (ASCII) file transfer protocol, the Ethernet protocol for LANs, and the Transmission Control Protocol/Internet Protocol (TCP/IP) for use of the Internet. However, there are many other protocols to be considered. Although the selection process is complex, some set of communications protocols should be established as standards in the firm.
6. **Bandwidth.** What bandwidth, or transmission capacity, should be provided between hardware nodes in the network? The decision, of course, depends on the applications to be used. Image and graphical applications require much greater transmission rates for effective use than do text-only applications. Content-rich applications are growing rapidly on the Internet. Should every workstation on the network have broadband connectivity (e.g., 1.5 megabits/second)? How much bandwidth can a company afford on a global basis? Should a company provide excess capacity to allow company employees to try new applications? Or should the network be designed to meet only current needs? Specifications about the desired technical infrastructure to meet the vision for information use are critical to help drive individual decisions. Business managers should make their views known on this issue.
7. **Response Time on the Network.** In many organizations, hundreds of users are simultaneously interacting with the network, and each of them is directly affected by the system's **response time**—the delay between when the enter key is pressed and when the response from the system appears on the screen. If this delay is reasonable and consistent, the system is satisfactory. If the delay is excessively long—3 or 4 seconds when one is used to subsecond responses—it can be very frustrating and significantly hamper perceived productivity. Yet the costs needed to reduce response delays tend to increase exponentially below some level, so input from business managers is critical in making this decision.
8. **Security versus Ease of Access.** If steps are taken to make the network and its nodes more secure, quite often the result is to reduce ease of access for users of the network. In some companies, for example, company employees cannot dial in directly to the data center from home because of security concerns.

Instead, the employee calls the data center and an operator calls the user back after verification. In other organizations, systems can be much more easily accessed from the desk, from home, or from a hotel room in another part of the world. Yet horror stories about hackers breaching the security of well-known companies' Web sites make easy access a worrisome feature. Organizations should make an explicit decision to operate somewhere along the spectrum between maximum ease of access and maximum security. Business managers should provide input to the decision.

9. **Breadth of Network Access.** How ubiquitous should access to the network be? Should everyone in the organization have access to all corporate data? Or should access be restricted to only those who have a "need to know"? Some organizations have gone on record as striving for access by all personnel. As soon as such a commitment is made, however, training and other support requirements increase significantly. Business managers should provide input to this policy decision.
10. **Access to External Data Services.** What should be the range of data services that a business manager may receive via the network? Should access to customer and supplier databases be allowed? How active will the company be in electronic commerce and electronic data interchange with customers and suppliers? Should the network provide access to personal data services? At many firms viewing the results of athletic events (or even the events themselves) is permitted from the workstation at the desk. Others restrict even external e-mail. Some organizations provide broad access to a variety of commercial services. Some prohibit such access. Business managers must clearly state their need for such access.

Figure 15.3 shows a policy statement that addresses many of these issues for a multidivisional company in the medical device industry. The statement was the result of an assessment conducted by a major IS consulting firm in 2002 that criticized the organization for not having policies for the use of the IT physical infrastructure.

Managing the Applications Portfolio

The third IT asset discussed in this chapter is the applications software portfolio. Earlier chapters in this book have discussed alternative methods for the acquisition of individual applications. However, business managers and the IS department need to cooperate to manage the bundle of applications as a critical organizational asset.

In contrast to the physical infrastructure, too often the software portfolio is not managed as an asset. Frequently, the business manager's focus is on an individual application or a small number of applications. Applications development and maintenance costs are treated as a current expense. Software, and particularly software maintenance, is treated as an expense to be minimized rather than as an essential activity that preserves or enhances the value of a critical asset.

Most organizations have a substantial investment in their software portfolio. Some have thousands of programs and millions of lines of code that are the result of investing millions of dollars in thousands of staff-years of system development. These applications are critical assets without which the company could not operate, but many companies have never seriously thought about managing these programs as costly and critical assets. Some companies do not even know exactly what software resources they possess. They might not know the condition of their application systems, and some have no plan for replacement or renovation of critical obsolete systems.

Treating software as an asset changes how the portfolio is viewed and managed. A company should know what software it owns, where it is located, what it does, how effective it is, and what condition it is in. Companies should treat maintenance of software just as they treat plant maintenance—as an activity that is necessary to preserve the asset's value. Software managers are obligated to evaluate the effectiveness of the software inventory and to plan, organize, and control this inventory to maximize the return it provides to the company.

The development and maintenance of IS applications should be subject to a set of policy guidelines derived from the organization's IT architecture. Figure 15.4 contains a statement developed in early 2004 that outlines how applications should be developed in a distributed computing environment at a major personnel services company. The statement imposes a standard set of management controls on company-critical, computer-based applications being developed and supported by all company business units. These guidelines, developed by a committee representing the organization's central IS department, business unit IS groups, and users, define controls that must be applied to critical applications.

Other issues that applications portfolio policies should deal with include the following:

1. **Assumed User.** For any applications system, some assumption is made about who will use the application. Data entry operators were assumed to be the users of

The Infrastructure of the Information Technology Network

An IT infrastructure through which video, voice, data, image, and text information may be created, accessed, manipulated, and transmitted electronically will allow our company to enhance its position in the industry. The continued enhancement of such an integrated network must be a key priority and requires the establishment of policies.

The policies are as follows:

- A standard workstation shall be used uniformly in offices, laboratories, meeting rooms, and all other facilities.
- Every shareable node on the network will operate with UNIX as one of its operating systems.
- A common set of physical distribution facilities (servers and LANs) shall be used throughout the company.
- Each physical distribution subsystem shall be designed in such a way that it can be replaced or modified without affecting the performance of the other subsystems.
- Each divisional chief executive shall designate the organization responsible for the design, operation, maintenance, and allocation of the appropriate physical distribution facilities.
- Strong consideration shall be given to the installation of adequate pathways and substantial reserve transmission capacity when new physical distribution facilities are installed or existing ones enhanced.
- The public network will be used among locations for voice, data, and video and a private data network will be developed at each site.

Figure 15.3 The Infrastructure of the Information Technology Network

many transaction processing systems. As more individuals inside and outside the company become potential users and the technology skills of people grow, some clarity about likely IS users is required. What is the training level required? Should all help facilities be resident in the system? How deep into the applications system can external users get? The design requirements for the user interface and associated security are thereby likely to change and should be made explicit. Business managers must provide input to this policy issue.

2. **Application Location.** With the immense popularity of personal workstations, many applications have been developed for the workstation that would work much better on a more centralized, shareable resource. Where (at what network node) should a particular type of application be performed? For example, where in the network should word processing normally be done? For most organizations that decision seems clear. Most people find it convenient to do word processing on their personal computers. On the other hand, some organizations encourage users to save files on department servers, citing the improved ability to share and back up files. There are also many other issues about where certain applications should be performed in the network. Guidelines need to be developed with business manager input to assign applications to places in the network.
3. **Process-Driven or Data-Driven Design.** It must also be determined whether future applications development is going to be data-driven or **process-driven**. Most past systems have been designed to represent a process and to collect and manipulate only the data necessary to operate the particular process. For example, under the process approach, the job classification information system would be designed

Distributed Applications Development Policy

- Information systems development in departments is best done on distributed computers when the object of the analysis (e.g., an asset type or set of transactions): (a) is local and self-contained; (b) has sufficient commitment in the department for funding systems development and operations over the life of the system; (c) is unlikely to be needed outside the department; and (d) has total life cycle development and operational cost less than on a central resource.
- Support for the development of distributed information systems is available on a coordinated basis at each division. Support participants include the local IS organization and corporate IS personnel.
- Distributed information systems development is normally expected to have been identified as a priority in an approved departmental information resources plan.
- Support software standards for information systems should be used. The list of supported software is determined at the local site in cooperation with the corporate IS organization.
- The department should be prepared to commit approximately 25 percent of the initial hardware, software, and personnel investment associated with systems development each year for the ongoing support of the system.
- Documentation standards for all application systems are published on a regular basis by the corporate IS organization. These standards may be supplemented by standards published by the local IS organization.
- The hardware on which the system is developed should be supported by the local IS organization and/or the corporate IS organization and should be attached to either the local network or to the companywide network or both.
- Units engaging in information systems development activity should review their internal policies and procedures to bring them into compliance with these policies.

Figure 15.4 Example Distributed Applications Development Policy

to mirror the job of the personnel analyst, who must review a particular job description and make a decision on rank classification. The system would require collection of the necessary information to help make that decision. The process approach is efficient for that one particular application.

Other decisions, however, such as hiring, require much of the same data. The hiring information system would collect some of the same data, add more data, and store the data in that system. Now there are two different representations of several data fields, each collected for a particular process. The alternative **data-driven** approach is to concentrate on all the data needed in an area or department and to collect these data into a database. Each application would be designed to access this common database and extract only the needed information.

4. **Evaluation Criteria for New Applications Systems.** What should the requirements be for justifying new systems? Should a return-on-investment analysis be required? Should a risk assessment be performed on every application? Most organizations attempt to adopt some decision rules, such as expected return on investment, risk analysis, cost-benefit analysis, or expected payback period. These methods might prove to be beneficial when systems with benefits that are not easily quantifiable are considered for implementation. Business managers should actively participate in the process to determine how systems will be evaluated.

INFORMATION TECHNOLOGY MANAGEMENT SYSTEM ISSUES

Faced with the challenges mentioned above and assuming that the critical assets are being well managed, what major issues do IS leaders and their business manager partners need to deal with in designing a successful IT management system? What are the areas that most need attention? Eight areas are explained in the sections that follow.

The reader should realize that the IS organization introduces dramatic (and often traumatic) changes for its customers when it introduces new systems or technologies. The overall effectiveness of these changes is often related more to how well the change is managed than to the quality of the new system or technology. To be sure, many other issues are critical in certain organizations. For example, how to best effect the integration of systems across many organizations might well be critical for a multidivisional company.

1. Agreeing Upon the Role of the IS Organization

The IS organization's role is changing, and it will likely change even more. How IT is best managed depends on how the senior management of the organization sees information and IT as a part of the overall business vision. Therefore, the senior business management of an organization should ensure that there is a clear, shared understanding of the IS department's mission.

What mission or role the IS organization takes on, how it performs these duties, and how it organizes to get its job done will vary from organization to organization. As a general trend, senior business managers expect a future-oriented IS organization that can anticipate their information needs while simultaneously meeting today's information requirements. This challenge means that senior business leadership expects the IS unit to align its activities closely with the overall business activities and direction. IS must exercise leadership in providing IT solutions that will help the business in the future while also providing systems that solve today's problems. More specifically, these expectations mean

- demonstrating an understanding of the business through an awareness of business plans and strategies and close communication with business managers
- responding quickly with systems to meet changing business conditions (not waiting years for a strategically important system to be built)
- helping to reengineer business processes to be more responsive to customers, to bring product to market faster, or to improve business process quality
- ensuring that the business can participate, and maybe lead, in the growing development of e-commerce
- keeping the final customer, not just internal operations, in mind
- building systems that provide direct and identifiable benefits to the final customer, thus building stronger customer relationships
- helping business managers make better decisions with information
- using IT for sustainable competitive advantage and increased market share
- helping the business integrate IT into every appropriate part of the business

It is important to note that the traditional dominant expectation of the IS function—saving money through cost efficiencies (such as workforce reduction due to automation)—is not included in this set. Although such short-term tangible benefits are still important (yet often difficult to attribute solely to a new information system), expectations today are more comprehensive and complex than merely reducing cost.

Many CEOs and other senior executives were skeptical until the late 1990s and early 2000s that their businesses were getting enough value or return from the sizeable investment made in IT. However, that set of attitudes is definitely changing. It is now more common for business leaders to attribute gains in productivity and effectiveness to the integration of IT into the business. Indeed, many economics experts claim that the slowness of job growth in the economic recovery during 2002 and 2003 was due to the major progress made in improving productivity via IT. Because employees were much more productive, additional personnel did not need to be hired even though sales improved. These leaders also admit that IT applications significantly change the way their organizations operate and compete. Some even claim that good systems are critical to the organization's success. It is therefore clear that effort must be expended to develop a shared understanding of what the IS organization's role should be.

THE DIFFICULTY OF CHANGE

Let it be noted that there is no more delicate matter to take in hand, nor more dangerous to conduct, nor more doubtful in its success, than to set up as a leader in the introduction of changes. For he who innovates will have for his enemies all those who are well off under the existing order, and only lukewarm supporters in those who might be better off under the new.

[Machiavelli, 1513]

In general, the role of the IS organization (both central and distributed units) is to be the steward of the organization's information and IT resources, much as the finance organization is the steward of financial resources. More specific roles include the following:

- Deploy IT resources throughout the organization in support of the organization's effort to participate in e-commerce.
- Facilitate the productive and effective use of these resources today, not just in the future.
- Lead the development of an information vision and an architecture for IT that will support the rapid deployment of new and improved systems (through both original software development and packaged products).
- Communicate this vision and architecture to the entire organization and show the implications for the business.
- Maintain managerial control and integrity over important information resources.
- Administer corporate data and the movement of data between systems.
- Make current and new IT available at the lowest possible cost.
- Help business managers become comfortable with information technologies and knowledgeable about their effective use.
- Develop a partnership with business managers to exploit technology for business value and to influence the products and services offered by the organization.

Cooperative efforts between IS leadership and senior business leaders have often proved useful in clarifying how IT is to be exploited in the firm and what the role of the IS function should be. Figure 15.5 contains an example statement of the values and beliefs about IT that was drafted by a joint IS leadership/senior business management task force. The statement was developed at a $350 million manufacturer of industrial painting systems in late 2003.

The need for stating these shared beliefs came from an assessment of the company's IT management system. That review revealed that the expectations of senior business management and IS leadership differed widely. Indeed, the statement in Figure 15.5 took several months of discussion to develop due to these different perceptions of the participants. Item 1 was derived from business management's belief that the IS organization spent more time generating ideas on the possible use of IT than it did delivering systems that worked. Item 2 was included because IS management felt regional managers and product managers in the company were developing systems in a haphazard, uncoordinated, and undocumented way. The interaction in developing this statement served to "clear the air" on these views. An outside facilitator later used this statement to help the organization focus on the development of the company's first e-commerce strategy and to set data sharing and other policies.

2. Selecting Effective IS Leadership

The second key factor in determining the success of the IT management system and the IS function is, not unsurprisingly, the leader. The leader's level of authority in the organization, his or her business experience and skills, and his or her leadership style are all important. Most important, however, is that the leader and his or her attributes fit the mission and expectations laid out for the IS function.

In most organizations someone can be identified as the executive to whom all centralized IT management activities report. In some enterprises this person might be the IS department manager, director, or vice president; in other organizations, this person might be a finance or administrative executive. Starting in the mid-1980s, some organizations created the role of **chief information officer (CIO)** to lead IT management. More recently, some organizations (especially those involved heavily on the Internet) have established a **chief technology officer (CTO)** to focus on how IT can be used to enhance the conduct of the business.

A true CIO is part of the organization's officer team and is one of those executives responsible for making the strategic decisions for the whole organization. It is clear that some mix of business and technical skills and duties is required for IT leadership—regardless of the title. Figure 15.6 is a fictitious advertisement for a CIO. It makes clear the challenges inherent in many senior IS leadership positions. The role defined for the CIO says much about what an organization can expect from its IS organization.

Above all, the CIO is responsible for guiding and unifying the entire organization's IT resources—Internet applications, office applications, transaction processing, telecommunications, and possibly the reengineering efforts for examining business processes. Although different divisions, lines of business, or subsidiaries might have their own information executives, central IS leadership is charged with coordinating all the resources. Often, the CIO does not have responsibilities for day-to-day IS operations.

Clearly CIOs should be able to act as business executives. They are, however, expected to bridge the gulf between the more technical IS organization and general business managers. Therefore, they need to be willing to learn some aspects of IT. Traditional IS managers spent

Values Statement

1. **We stress implementation of ideas.** We have generated many new ideas and concepts that will help us develop our systems. We must refine these concepts and implement these ideas. Good ideas without implementation are insufficient.
2. **We believe in a planned, coordinated approach.** Individual decisions will be based on a well-developed and communicated information technology plan within each regional and corporate staff area. Each area will explicitly recognize information needs in the annual plan. Because many good ideas have been thought of or are being used by areas of our operations, we stress the importance of communicating these ideas to other individuals and operating units. Planning will take place at the regional level; planning and coordination will take place at the corporate staff level.
3. **Information technology will be made a valuable resource in our jobs.** We will make IT services valuable to everyone in the organization. We recognize the change that is required. We will encourage the responsible use of this important asset throughout the organization. We will help all users of information understand the effective and responsible use of the technology.
4. **We welcome the organizational impacts of information technology advances.** Improving technology will provide the potential to increase service to our clients and reduce our overall cost. These changes will create opportunities to reconsider organizational span of control, reporting lines, and communication paths. We will assess potential improvements on a regular basis and implement those changes that demonstrate enhancements to accomplish our mission.
5. **Data will be shared.** Data are not "owned" by a particular individual or department, but belong to the whole organization. Data will be made easily accessible to all authorized users. Each individual within our company should be able to access appropriate information based on her or his responsibility. Policy guidelines will be established for data to be shared.
6. **We encourage innovation in the use of information.** We are committed to the creative use of information to identify and respond to basic changes in the company's environment. We will challenge the status quo in how we use information to do our jobs. We will encourage our people to apply information technology in new ways so as to benefit our clients and owners.
7. **We expect to use information technology more frequently in our relationships with customers and suppliers.** We see the use of the Internet as an important supplement to our sales force. We hope to employ reverse auction technology to save cost on commodity purchases. We will share important data with our trading partners.

Figure 15.5 Example Values Statement

most of their time interacting with other IS professionals and users, focusing on specific user needs. In contrast, CIOs should spend the greatest percentage of time interacting with peer general managers as part of managing the business as a whole. CIOs need to be able to see the advantages of IT and where to apply it broadly in the business. This role is most suited to those persons who can explain what IT is currently accomplishing and what can be done with IT in business terms.

Although the position is now a reality in many organizations, the role of the CIO is still emerging. In some cases, therefore, the CIO might not yet have the authority needed to carry out the responsibilities of the position. Not all CIOs report directly to the company CEO or president. Few small and medium-sized companies have a CIO. However, some smaller firms have hired a senior IS consultant as a part-time CIO. Usually, it is organizations on the frontier of information management that have a true CIO—such

Wanted

Bright, versatile, industrious individual to lead the effort in determining the information vision for the company, creating partnerships with internal clients, and ensuring that IT delivers business value. Person must be able to understand how to apply information technology to corporate strategy and transform the company so that its business processes are based on information technology. Must be able to work well under pressure and have strong analytical capabilities. Outstanding interpersonal and communication skills are required because the individual will interact with all information suppliers and customers inside and outside the company. Must add value as a member of the senior management team.

Figure 15.6 Example of a CIO Job Advertisement

information-intensive enterprises as banks, insurance companies, and airlines—although more and more manufacturing and retailing firms have created the position and are effectively implementing the concept.

Senior IS Management Issues. Various studies in recent years have tracked the major concerns of senior IS executives, including the CIO. Although the exact list and ranking of issues vary from year to year, some general patterns have emerged. The following concerns summarize the kinds of expectations the business has for IS management:

- *Improving data and IT planning, especially linking IS to the business.* With rapidly changing businesses and technologies (e.g., selling products and services over the Internet), such planning is not easy, but it is essential to anticipate information needs and manage resources prudently.

WHAT MAKES A GREAT CIO?

Know the business. Learn and master every aspect of it—net income, EPS (earnings per share), EBITDA (earnings before interest, taxes, depreciation, and amortization), its management, its products, its vendors, its sales channels, its customers, its competition. Hire the best people you can and delegate. The CIO belongs in the executive room working with the chairman, the CEO, and other executives in understanding and influencing the business strategy, as well as in identifying opportunities where IT can be a competitive advantage for the enterprise.

[Adapted from Karlgaard, 2003]

- *Gaining business value through IT.* Systems that enable the organization to achieve sustained competitive advantage give the IS organization visibility and attention that can help to make many other changes in IT management possible.
- *Facilitating organizational learning about and through IT.* This issue is consistent with the evolution of the IS organization away from an exclusively "doing" role and towards an enabling one. In particular, training on how to use information to make better decisions can now be an important function of senior IS leadership.
- *Refining the IS unit's role and position.* CIOs are concerned about the IS organization's ability to be proactive and what responsibilities should be distributed to achieve the greatest payoff for the whole enterprise.
- *Guiding systems development by business managers.* The development of systems by business managers or other employees directly or by IS staff in line organizations is now a major alternative way to have systems built. Determining the proper standards for programming languages, systems justification procedures, documentation, and database management is a difficult policy challenge for the CIO.
- *Managing organizational data as an asset.* Much of Chapter 5 was devoted to this issue, which has been rising in the list of top concerns for the CIO.
- *Measuring IS effectiveness.* Frequently the strategic and decision support systems being introduced today are difficult to justify with hard benefit numbers. Further, it is difficult to show the contribution

of information and IT planning and architecture work. Thus, IT resources might be cut in hard times unless real contributions can be demonstrated.

- *Integrating information technologies.* Often, the primary role of the CIO is the unification of IS services and technologies. The history of isolated islands of automation, each with strong and protective organizational homes, usually makes integration a difficult political as well as technical problem.
- *Developing systems personnel.* Finding and retaining staff knowledgeable in such strategic technologies as enterprise resource planning (ERP) systems, Web design tools, and global telecommunications networks are of special concern. Motivating systems personnel to be productive and aware of business needs is also of high concern to the CIO and other IS managers.

3. Creating an Active Partnership with Business Managers

If the CIO is truly an officer of the business, then he or she will not be the only person at that level concerned with IT issues. In many organizations issues at the officer level are issues for all senior managers regardless of title. Cross-functional management, where problems are addressed in partnership among peers, is now the culture of most businesses. Even when there is no strong consensus or collaborative culture, senior IS leadership should not address all IT concerns alone.

It is essential for the CIO (as well as other senior IS managers) to build strong working relationships with other top managers. This result cannot be achieved unless the senior IS person is a peer in authority and responsibility, the IS department's mission and vision are clearly communicated, and other business managers view IT as an area that cannot be delegated to lower-level personnel.

What must be defined is a true business-IS partnership, a cooperative relationship. Business managers must welcome such partnerships and overtly communicate this receptivity to their peers and subordinates. The CIO and other senior IS managers must be committed to working on non-IT issues. In many organizations one senior business manager, recognizing the power of such an alliance, has championed the partnership concept.

Partnership is a critical strategy for IS management. It is based on sustaining a long-term relationship between IS and business management. Partners share key common goals. Partners seek benefits not possible to each party individually. Partnership is based on mutual trust as well as shared benefits, responsibilities, and risks. Its goal is to achieve a greater contribution for IT to the benefit of the organization. Each partner understands and appreciates the critical stakeholders and business processes that influence the organization's performance. A partner respects the distinctive resources and competencies of other partners.

Although these attributes of a true partnership are the goal, partnerships sometimes start by clearly defining the authority of the partners (as a sort of "prenuptial agreement"). Figure 15.7 contains an example of a statement developed in mid-2003 that defines the authority of both business departments and the IS department. In this mid-sized manufacturer of electric motors, relations between IS and several business departments had deteriorated to the point where such a statement was needed prior to building a better relationship.

The statement in Figure 15.7 created the IS Policy Committee that is now the focal point for the developing partnership. Although working IS/business partnerships can be implemented in several ways, by far the most frequent is the steering committee for IS management. An **IS steering committee**, issue forum, or advisory board can be used to ensure frequent interaction. Much discussion of such groups has centered on how they have been misused or abused. Inadequate authority, narrow perspectives, uninformed or inappropriate membership, and a host of other problems can hamper these committees. When properly set up, however, such groups can be used effectively to

- set priorities for systems development and IS direction
- check progress against an established direction
- allocate scarce resources (especially IS staff) to achieve business objectives
- communicate concerns, issues, and possible remedies
- provide education and the development of shared mind-sets
- develop shared responsibility and ownership of actions

Such groups are not a substitute for a good CIO and good IS management. Instead, they work best when there is proactive and responsive IS management already in place. Partnership means cooperation, dealing with problems jointly, and managing the business, not empires. A good steering committee, along with professional IS leadership, can be an effective part of the management system for IT exploitation in the business.

Expectations/Responsibilities Statement

1. All user departments will be fully accountable for their use of information resources, including the skill level of people using information technology resources.
2. User departments will pay an annual fee to the IS department for workstations to include capital, software, and maintenance costs.
3. The IS department will set and enforce standards for user workstation hardware, software, and network connections.
4. User departments will pay for use of shareable information technology resources through a fair division of overhead.
5. Senior management will be kept engaged in information technology issues via regular communications by IS staff.
6. The IS department will actively initiate communication with all user departments.
7. The IS department will build its plan and budget with full knowledge of company business plans.
8. Members of the IS department will serve as internal business process improvement consultants and consultants on the use of the Internet in making the supply chain more efficient.
9. The IS department will be represented on issue-oriented or business planning teams where information definition and/or collection is crucial.
10. Policy affecting users will be determined by the IS Policy Committee, which will be chaired by a senior business executive.

Figure 15.7 Example Expectations/Responsibilities Statement

4. Determining an Outsourcing Strategy

Many organizations have hired outside professional IS services organizations to run part of their IS operations. This approach to IT management is commonly called **outsourcing**. For many companies internal computer operations have never held a monopoly position. Public data banks, market research data processing firms, and other computing services with special software or data have been around for decades. With the cost-cutting emphasis in business since the mid-1980s, however, there has been renewed interest in outsourcing data center operations (sometimes called IS facilities management) to external service organizations. Besides the data center, an organization might outsource the management of telecommunications or traditional transaction processing systems programming. More recently, **application service providers** (**ASPs**) have developed that provide total systems to organizations ranging from single purpose applications like competitive intelligence to broad applications like ERPs.

Much of the outsourcing movement has been driven by the need to downsize and to respond to other significant organizational changes taking place (mergers, acquisitions, and divestitures). With these changes often come sudden shifts in demands for computing power. Sometimes the value of IS outsourcing to a company that is aggressively acquiring other firms is the speed and efficiency with which the outsourcing firm can integrate the systems of acquired firms into those of the acquirer. Alternatively, some companies report 10 to 20 percent cost savings from the economies of scale and competitive pricing provided by data center suppliers.

Outsourcing allows a company with greatly fluctuating computer processing demands to pay only for what it uses, rather than building a data center for peak load and letting it sit underutilized during other periods. For example, a using organization often pays an ASP on the basis of the number of "seats" (users) or on the number of transactions per month. Companies can invest the savings in fixed costs toward identifying and developing other high-impact IT applications. The trend toward outsourcing might also be related to the establishment of a CIO, who often is not tied emotionally to the existing data center and does not feel that the IS function has to manage the hardware to prove its value to the firm. A CIO might view data centers much as a manufacturing plant, which is a candidate for outsourcing when such an operation is not in the strategic core of the business.

Some firms have chosen to outsource IS operations because it is difficult to keep pace with technological change. Keeping up with the latest techniques requires hiring and retaining highly skilled IS staff, which might be difficult, especially in nonurban areas. Others believe that a large outsourcing supplier, with experience in many organizations, can reduce the cost of providing IS services and provide better customer service. Still other senior executives were not satisfied with the service being delivered by in-house staff and chose to outsource the job to a specialist. However, in late 2003 many firms reported that outsourcing, if not done properly, could in fact cost the company more in hard costs and various soft costs, such as delays, than if those functions were handled internally (see the sidebar entitled "Outsourcing: Look Who's Out of Sorts").

The decision to outsource must be viewed as both a remedy for service failures or cost issues and as a strategic choice. Likewise, outsourcing must be done selectively. In one of the early efforts at outsourcing, Eastman Kodak Company outsourced its data centers to IBM, its telecommunications to Digital Equipment Corporation, and its microcomputer systems management to Businessland, Inc. Kodak did not see these areas as core to its vision for IT or as a significant strength for competitive advantage. The savings from outsourcing were used in other parts of the business where Kodak felt a greater return on investment could be achieved. Other organizations, however, have outsourced critical strategic IS functions in response to short-term emergencies and subsequently have lost the competitive advantage its prior investment in IS staff had brought.

As discussed in earlier chapters, outsourcing systems development and integration is also possible and popular. Contracted systems development and programming, as well as purchasing of system and applications software, both common today, are forms of outsourcing. Because the bulk of IS costs are in personnel, and because many IS personnel work in systems development, major cost-reduction benefits might come from outsourcing if the outsourcing partner is able to bring improved productivity tools to the process.

When certain information systems have strategic value to the firm, healthy organizations should not see outsourcing, especially of sensitive development and planning activities, as a viable option. Security and privacy issues and the strategic value of some data might mean that certain applications should not be developed or operated outside the organization. For example, some systems development in support of research and product development might be considered too sensitive to outsource. Further, it might be quite difficult to bring systems development or operations back in-house if prices for outsourcing services increase or if there is a change in the need for strategic control of these system functions or for technical know-how. Hiring staff and familiarizing them with company operations, building data centers, and setting methods and procedures cannot be done quickly. Organizations with highly variable needs for computing power, however, are increasingly considering the outsourcing option.

The ideal outsourcing arrangement is a win-win partnership between the company and the outsourcer. The outsourcer should know and care about the business as much as client executives do. Sometimes an outsourcer will specialize in particular industries (for example, retail or health care) to gain a depth of knowledge. In such instances care should be taken to ensure that the outsourcer is not put in a situation where its personnel could leak competitive information. An outsourcer can also help the firm make sound technology decisions, not just solutions convenient for the outsourcer. The outsourcing contract should accommodate growth and expansion in the business. Finally, the firm should select an outsourcer who can operate over the full geographic area of the company's operations.

Several key factors in selecting an outsourcing vendor are

- vendor reputation, which includes understanding the business and technology standards
- quality of service, which means a clear comparative advantage over in-house services
- flexible pricing, which means cost effectiveness because, as processing volume increases or new services are added, costs can escalate

OUTSOURCING: LOOK WHO'S OUT OF SORTS

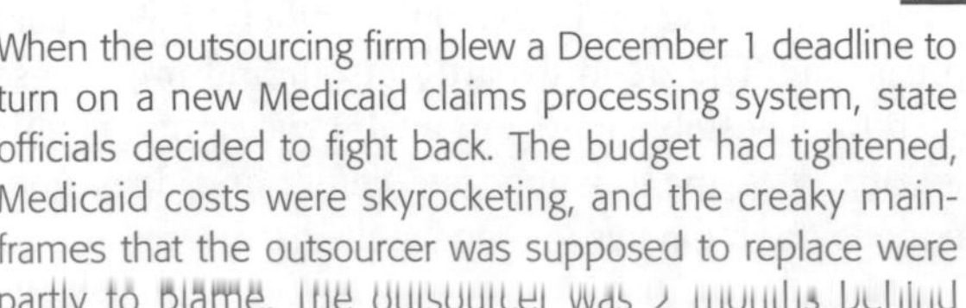
When the outsourcing firm blew a December 1 deadline to turn on a new Medicaid claims processing system, state officials decided to fight back. The budget had tightened, Medicaid costs were skyrocketing, and the creaky mainframes that the outsourcer was supposed to replace were partly to blame. The outsourcer was 2 months behind schedule. The state is levying a $32,000 fine.

[Adapted from Park, 2003]

5. Designing an Equitable Financing System

IT services are expensive, IT systems are complex, and IS personnel are among the best-paid employees in the company. At the same time, the value of IS services is not always clear. Systems often take years to build and are sometimes over budget. The direct business impacts (e.g., reduced personnel costs) of new systems might not be as evident as they were in the past. More and more systems are being built in order to compete better, and the impact on sales increases is not always easy to predict.

An effective IT management system must carefully measure IT costs, enable the understanding of the financial impacts of new and existing systems, and find a way to fund IS operations and new systems. Measuring the organization's investment in IT and calculating the impact of this investment on the organization's performance are still not well-understood activities. Most benefits are indirect or confounded by other organizational changes.

Managing IT Costs. The typical measures used for tracking IT costs include

- total IT budget as a percentage of total organization revenues, income, premiums, deposits, or other indicators of overall financial activity of the organization
- total IT budget as a percentage of total organization budget
- IS personnel costs as a percentage of total organization professional personnel salaries and wages
- the ratio of hardware and software costs to IS personnel costs
- the costs for IT hardware and software per managerial or knowledge worker

None of these measures is perfect or complete by itself, and organizations should track several of them. Sizable changes in these measures might be more significant than the absolute values. Further, high or low values are not by themselves necessarily bad or good. All these measures require interpretation to match them with IS and business directions. Organizations that try to be pioneers and leaders should expect, for example, to have higher values on many of these measures than less aggressive firms.

Even in combination, these measures must be used cautiously because of various definitional and measurement problems:

- Some IT costs are hidden because of the highly distributed nature of information processing in most organizations. Not all costs appear as IS department budget items, and certainly not all are spent in the IS organization. Personal computer hardware, software, training, and services can be purchased as general office expenses or other expense categories.
- No relationship to benefits is directly included in these measures. Costs without benefits give a very incomplete picture.
- Benefits happen after many of the development costs occur, and the lag is not considered in these measures. Direct benefits can occur quickly, but secondary benefits of technology diffusion and new ways of doing business might not emerge for years.

Measuring Benefits. There is no simple, reliable way to measure the value added benefits of IT. IT costs are easier to find; IT value is typically much more intangible (as is the value of a business education). Organizations must capture and track measures of IS performance over time to best utilize such indicators, so that values can be interpreted, changes explained, and reasonably helpful comparisons made. Some organizations now treat investment in IT like research. No matter how IT investments are valued, it is the job of the business manager, not the IS manager, to justify the investment.

Controlling IS Costs. A primary mechanism for financial control of IT is the IS organization's budget. One way to divide costs creates four primary groups—personnel, equipment and software, outside services, and overhead. But not all organizations use these areas. Furthermore, statistics from studies on IS budgets vary widely across industries. Because of these reporting and measurement issues, some individual statistics can be misleading, but some general observations appear to be valid:

- The most common measure, IT expenditures as a percent of revenue, varies widely by industry and size of firm. Information-intensive industries spend the highest percentage on IT. Smaller firms suffer from a lack of economies of scale and can spend a higher percentage (all else being equal) than larger companies.
- Personnel costs are the largest piece of the IT budget, typically more than 50 percent (depending on the industry) of the total. Although increased productivity aids have helped to keep this percentage from growing much larger, the demand for new systems makes reduction of IS development staff budgets difficult to achieve unless outsourcing is employed.

Obviously, the size of the IS budget depends on the demand for new systems. As the applications portfolio increases, greater budget pressures occur due to enhancement and maintenance requirements. Without sizable productivity gains, it is easy to incur double-digit annual IS department budget increases.

Chargeback Systems. Some senior business managers believe that the best way to hold IS and line organizations accountable for the impact of systems on the organization is to have the IS unit operate as a business within a business. In this instance the IS unit operates like a profit center, with a flexible budget and an agreed-upon transfer pricing scheme. This design places control of IS spending directly in the hands of those business managers who use the services. Instead of a vague annual negotiation process of capital expenditure approvals and cost allocations, the IS head or CIO and senior business managers must agree on prices for IT services that allow the IS department to make a profit or at least break even.

For business managers, the business unit or organization is affected directly by an IS **chargeback** process. If done well, a chargeback system can be a way to better understand true costs. Certainly there are many positive aspects to charging for IS services, but as with any profit-center and transfer-pricing scheme, short-term and long-term costs and benefits become difficult to balance. Business managers adapt behavior to take advantage of the pricing structure. For example, discounts for overnight processing might cause a business manager to rely less on online reporting. Thus, it is important for every business manager to understand why chargeback schemes are put in place and what characterizes a good process.

Organizations usually adopt a chargeback process for IS services for one or more of the following reasons:

- To assign costs clearly to those who consume and benefit from IT
- To control wasteful use of IT resources by encouraging users to compare the benefits with the costs and eliminate unprofitable use
- To overcome the belief that IT costs might be unnecessarily high
- To provide incentives by subsidizing the price of certain services or innovative uses of technologies
- To change the IS department's budgeting process to be more business driven, thus rewarding the IS organization for improved service and greater efficiency rather than technological change for its own sake
- To encourage line managers to be knowledgeable consumers of IS because they must directly pay for such support

A major problem in any chargeback system is that many IT costs are joint costs not easily attributed to one single organization, such as the cost to store and maintain a shared database or to place the order fulfillment process on the Internet. Further, some costs are essentially fixed, such as systems software and many components of a data center complex. Thus, calculating costs and reducing expenditures as demand varies might not be as easy as one would wish.

Also, in applications in which the benefits of IT might be difficult to determine, as in education, research, and customer service, chargeback can limit creative uses of technology.

Transfer prices can be developed for a broad and comprehensive range of IS activities, including charges for

- personnel time
- computer usage or wall-clock time (or computer cycles used)
- disk file space
- number of transactions processed
- amount of computer main memory used (per unit of time)
- number of screens or Web pages accessed

Charges might be cost-based (to recover all costs) or market-based (to be comparable to market alternatives). A combination of clearly identifiable direct costs plus an allocation of other overhead costs (space, administrative staff, and so on) might be used.

Chargeback systems for IT activities can be a great source of irritation between the IS organization and business managers unless a mutually agreed-upon structure for charging can be developed. A successful chargeback system should incorporate the following characteristics:

- *Understandable.* An understandable chargeback system reports use in business terms that business managers can relate to their own activities, not just to computer operations. For example, charges per customer order, invoice, or report relate more to business activity than does the number of computer input/output operations performed or machine cycles used.
- *Timely.* Charges should be reported soon after the activity to which they are related so that use and cost can be closely linked and those who can control the costs can accurately monitor the total costs.
- *Controllable.* The activity for which business managers are charged must be something they can control (e.g., charges for rerun computer jobs because of operator errors would not be controllable). Further, business managers must have a choice to use alternative services or to substitute one kind of usage with another (e.g., switching between two alternative database management systems or trading computer time for data storage).
- *Accountable.* Managers responsible for generating IS activity must be identifiable and must be held accountable for their charges. Otherwise the charges are meaningless and useless.

- *Clearly linked to benefits.* Managers must see a link between costs and benefits so they can balance the value of the IS services against what is being spent.
- *Consistent with IS and organizational goals.* Charges should be designed to achieve the goals set for the business and the goals of the IS organization. Thus, charges should encourage use of important IT services, efficient use of scarce technology and services, the desired balance of internal and external sourcing of IS services, and the development of systems that comply with accepted architectural standards.

Chargeback systems must be periodically evaluated to check that the desired results are being achieved. In any case, the chargeback or funding mechanism for the IS organization is one of the keys to having an effective IT management system.

6. Deploying Global Information Systems

In the past, managing in a global environment was the sole domain of large multinational corporations whose operations spanned the globe. Today, virtually all organizations, regardless of size, must deal with the effects of competing in a global economy. Improved telecommunications infrastructures in many countries, coupled with a steadily falling cost of technology ownership, have lowered the barriers to entry for competitors worldwide. As a result, IT managers have expanded their focus to include threats and opportunities extending well beyond their own domestic borders.

Global IT managers face a number of daunting tasks. For example, systems and standards must be coordinated across geographical, legal, and temporal borders; multinational teams have members who are dispersed across countries in multiple time zones and have radically differing languages and cultures; and potentially devastating security threats can originate from a single computer located anywhere in the world. Successful navigation of the international waters of technology management can, however, result in substantial returns for an organization.

Region and Country Issues. The heterogeneous nature of the multiple environments in which global IT managers operate makes managing such systems highly complex. Variations in language and culture affect leadership and communication styles. Time zone differences and physical distance make coordination a complex task. Among the unique factors influencing the global management of IT are the following:

1. **Country telecommunications infrastructures.** To fully realize the benefits of integrated global information systems, countries must be able to provide transnational companies with the necessary telecommunications infrastructure and its associated worldwide connectivity. Landlines in many developing countries, such as those in sub-Saharan Africa, are limited and are often supplanted by easy-to-setup wireless infrastructures. Unfortunately, cellular networks do not yet provide the bandwidth necessary for enterprise-wide applications and satellite connections are expensive.

   Many governments have become increasingly aware of the need for more state-of-the-art telecommunications capabilities to attract foreign direct investments. For example, Nigeria's improved telecommunications infrastructure has contributed to an increase in foreign investments in that country (Odo, 2003). Many global companies, including IBM, base their Asian headquarters in the tiny island nation of Singapore to take advantage of the fact it is one of the most wired countries in the world (Collett, 2003). Indeed, many emerging economies in Asia have created special zones for foreign subsidiaries where the telecommunications is world-class, even if the infrastructure in the rest of the country is limited. Malaysia, for example, has developed a 270-square-mile area designated as the Multimedia Super Corridor (MSC) to act as a global technological hub for the region. The MSC is supported by a high-capacity global telecommunications infrastructure with a 2.5 to 10 gigabit digital fiber-optic backbone that will link the region to the rest of the world through a 5-gigabit international gateway (MSC Web site, 2003). Global IT managers must be aware of what different countries will be able to provide before making decisions on global systems rollouts and multinational development efforts.
2. **Legal and security considerations.** In addition to being technically knowledgeable and culturally sensitive, the global IT manager must also keep constantly abreast of current legal and ethical issues in the countries of operation. Governmental regulations on technology transfers, intellectual property and copyrights, privacy laws, and transborder data flows are but a few of the areas that must be monitored. For example, the European Union's Data Protection Directive requires that companies exporting data about EU citizens across borders meet Europe's very stringent privacy standards. Failure to comply can lead to hefty fines imposed on the offending company. Such privacy requirements place a heavy burden on all non-EU companies to meet Europe's "no privacy, no trade" policy.

   In addition, global electronic commerce has led to considerable legal argument over issues of jurisdiction regarding intellectual property and Web content. For example, which country's laws should apply when objectionable Web content may be viewed in any country in the world? In November 2000 a French judge ruled that Yahoo! must ban the sale of Nazi memorabilia on its auction Web site as it was in violation of French law to do so (Essick, 2000). In 2002 an Australian judge ruled that a Melbourne-based businessperson had the right to sue Dow Jones, the financial publisher, for an allegedly defamatory article published on a U.S.-based Internet site (Legard, 2002).

Network security has also become a global concern for IT managers. With the promise of global connectivity comes the danger of network attacks from locations around the world. According to a 2003 survey by mi2g Ltd. (CIO.com Web site, 2003), Brazil leads the world as the originating point of hacker attacks on systems around the world (95,000 attacks). Brazil was followed by Turkey (14,795 attacks), with the United States a distant third (2,995 attacks). The attendees at the 2003 United Nations Conference on Global Information Security pointed out that it was critical to have greater information sharing on technology threats, illustrating the global nature of interconnecting systems today and the involvement of governments in determining information assurance policies.

3. **Language and culture.** Among the most common problems facing global IT managers dealing with a culturally diverse group of international workers is the issue of differences in language. Fluency in English is often mistaken for an understanding of western idioms. A baseball expression ("hit a home run") might make as little sense in a country whose national sport is cricket as would "bowling a googly" in the United States. Further, body language and gestures have different connotations in different countries.

   Cultural differences also play an important role in determining the effectiveness of global technology management. Global managers must understand the differences in the way individuals from various cultures interact with one another and their superiors. House, et al. (2002), identified nine dimensions of culture:

   - *Uncertainty avoidance.* Extent to which members of a society avoid uncertainty (through social norms or bureaucratic processes) to improve predictability of future events
   - *Power distance.* Degree to which members of a society expect and accept that power is distributed unequally within a firm
   - *Collectivism-I.* Extent to which organizations and society reward collective distribution of resources and collective action
   - *Collectivism-II.* Degree to which individuals see themselves as part of a group, whether it is an organization or family
   - *Gender egalitarianism.* Extent to which a society or organization minimizes gender role differences and gender discrimination
   - *Assertiveness.* Degree to which individuals are assertive, confrontational, and aggressive in societal relationships
   - *Future orientation.* Extent to which society engages in future-oriented activities such as planning, investing in the future, and delaying gratification
   - *Performance orientation.* Extent to which group members are encouraged and rewarded for performance improvement and excellence
   - *Humane orientation.* Extent to which a collective encourages and rewards individuals for being fair, generous, altruistic, caring and kind to others

   Global IT managers need to adapt their management style to the cultural and social context in which they are operating. For example, when dealing with individuals from a society characterized by high power distance, the manager should be aware that those employees might be less comfortable with contradicting their superiors than are their western counterparts. This might require, for example, different communication mechanisms for project team members to avoid potential problems.

4. **Time zone differences.** Managing across time zones is often frustrating. With employees around the world separated by as much as 10 to 15 hours, finding times for synchronous meetings and discussions can be very difficult. For example, setting a 10:00 A.M. meeting in a Seattle corporate headquarters translates to 10:30 P.M. in the New Delhi office and 4:00 A.M. in Sydney, Australia.To deal with the problem fairly and avoid resentment in foreign offices, meeting times are sometimes rotated through time zones, alternating between the local workday times of the foreign and domestic offices.

   It should be noted that there are also advantages to operating across multiple time zones. By handing off work from one location to another, projects can "follow the sun." For example, when an employee leaves for the day at the U.S. office, he or she can hand off the project work to an employee in the Bangalore, India, office who is just coming in for the day. Under this model, project work continues around the world, around the clock.

Global Systems Integration and Standardization. Systems integration has long been acknowledged as a critical process for most organizations. Controlling and integrating a multitude of diverse systems is exceptionally difficult in global companies. To avoid the pitfalls of nonintegration, global technology managers often rely on creating worldwide standards for systems development. For example, Unilever, the multibillion dollar consumer products company, decided to standardize its global IT servers across 80 countries to run on Linux, thus allowing the company to deploy common systems worldwide without having to worry about incompatible platforms (Weiss, 2003). In what is considered to be the company's biggest technology change ever, MasterCard International has created a globally integrated payment platform by moving its 25,000 card issuers worldwide to a standardized virtual private network (VPN)-based system (Mearian, 2002). Nestlé's commitment to an "e-revolution" has resulted in consolidation of over 140 financial systems across 70 countries to a mere handful (Wheatley, 2001).

Global Outsourcing. Since the intensive Y2K reprogramming efforts of the mid and late1990s, companies have looked increasingly beyond their own national borders for partners to help design, develop, and maintain their information systems. Although India remains the leader in offshore outsourcing, many other countries vie for a share of this market. The Philippines, Vietnam, Malaysia, Brazil, Russia, Bulgaria, and South Africa are some locations that offer highly trained IS personnel at costs that seem to be a fraction of what is required in the United States. In a 2003 survey of 252 corporate IT managers in the United States, 44 percent identified cost savings as the primary reason most global companies outsource (King, 2003a). Other drivers of offshore outsourcing include the desire to gain access to skilled personnel around the world, reduce fixed IT costs, exploit follow-the-sun development to improve time to market, and compensate for gaps in the organization's internal capabilities.

Of course, there are drawbacks to global outsourcing. For example, cost savings are often overestimated or elusive, there is a perceived loss of strategic control over IT operations, there are increased security concerns, and there is a loss of jobs in the domestic market. In late 2003 several U.S. companies were criticized in the press for moving jobs overseas at a time when many Americans were unemployed.

Nevertheless, IT managers must be aware of the emerging trends in global outsourcing. A 2003 Gartner, Inc., research report suggests that by 2004, 80 percent of all CIOs will be using offshore resources for at least part of their technology operations. Some of the key trends in global outsourcing include:

- *Offshore development centers.* With increasing commitments to offshore projects, some companies have established a permanent offshore presence. In this model of offshore insourcing, foreign technology workers are employees of U.S.-based companies and receive the same training, software tools, and development process guidelines as their domestic counterparts. The main difference between these workers is salary. Global Exchange Services, Inc., estimates that for every $100 spent on its IT workers in the United States, it spends only $30 on employees in Bangalore, India (King, 2003b). Other benefits of moving from offshore outsourcing to offshore insourcing include the ability to retain knowledge and expertise across multiple projects, greater productivity, and a sense of belonging for foreign workers who are thousands of miles away from the outsourcing company.
- *Near-shore sourcing.* For certain critical projects where the costs of failure are high, IT managers often feel more comfortable sending work to low-cost countries that are geographically closer to home and in an overlapping time zone. Further, since September 11, 2001, security risks in certain countries are forcing managers to look to locations closer to home. For the United States, Canada has emerged as a popular near-shore outsourcing destination.
- *Multisourcing.* It used to be commonplace for an outsourcing firm to establish a relationship with a single offshore provider for all its systems development and IT infrastructure needs. Now companies

NEW FRONTIERS: BUSINESS TRANSFORMATION OUTSOURCING

No longer merely a cheaper way to develop and test code, offshore outsourcing is now taking on more strategic areas. Business transformation outsourcing (BTO) looks to global outsourcing vendors to provide innovative technology solutions to existing business process problems.

In expanding the nature of outsourcing relationships, BTO attempts to integrate traditional IT outsourcing (ITO) and business process outsourcing (BPO) to provide a more robust outsourcing model. The ultimate goal is to achieve a technology-based transformation of business in which outsourcing vendors go beyond simply doing what they are told and become strategic partners in nurturing business innovation.

[Adapted from Bendor-Samuel, 2003 and Marguilius, 2003]

often rely on multiple service providers in a number of countries, based on price and the skills that are needed for the portfolio of IT projects. Electronic Data Systems Corporation (EDS), for example, has a "best-shore" policy in which it sends offshore work to the most appropriate offshore development centers for a given project.

Managing Global Virtual Teams. Traditionally, most team-based projects have involved individual team members in the same geographical location. Today, however, the focus is often on bringing together the best possible talent for a project, regardless of their location. This change has given rise to global virtual teams in which individual members who actively collaborate on a project are dispersed across thousands of miles and multiple time zones. It is very likely that the success of global systems will hinge on the effective management of such teams. Carmel (1999) identified six "centripetal" forces that, if addressed properly, can lead to more effective virtual teams. Though Carmel's research focuses on software development teams, the issues can easily be applied to the management of any globally dispersed project team. The six forces are as follows:

- *Telecommunications infrastructure.* Clearly, when team members are not co-located, reliable electronic communications are critical. Today, team members must have access to high-bandwidth network connections as well as necessary secure communication software.
- *Collaborative technology.* To get the most out of globally dispersed teams, it is often useful to have a common IT platform for collaboration that allows for easy coordination of team activities and leveraging worldwide intellectual capital. Examples of such packages include Microsoft's Sharepoint Portal and IBM's Websphere Collaboration Portal.
- *Development methodologies.* Given the differences in operating environments of team members, it is important to agree to a mutually acceptable project methodology or process that all participants will follow. The project manager must be sure that all project members are educated on the specific methodology.
- *Architecture and task allocation.* The team manager must be able to divide the project into smaller, relatively independent pieces. By reducing the coupling between these project pieces, a number of coordination overhead costs are reduced. Carmel and Agarwal (2001) argue that reducing coordination complexity is an important tactical approach to dealing with the issues of geographical distance in such teams.
- *Team building.* The need for a cohesive, focused team is important for all projects, whether co-located or dispersed. Extreme distances, both geographical and cultural, can often make the need for careful team building critical to project success. Some ways to foster such cohesion are constant communication, face-to-face milestone meetings, understanding cultural nuances and differences in communication styles, using expatriate managers (executives who leave their home country to work abroad), encouraging lateral communication between team members, and providing all team members a 360-degree view of the project via project tools.
- *Managerial techniques.* A global team manager must posses certain unique traits and abilities. Carmel refers to these as the *MERIT* qualities, that is, those of (1) a *Multiculturalist*, who is able to switch easily between cultural styles of management and communication; (2) an *E-facilitator*, who can build team loyalty and cohesiveness through e-mail and other electronic communications, even when team members cannot meet; (3) a *Recognition promoter*, who understands that virtual teams must rely on the manager to keep them in the headquarters' spotlight and tout the accomplishment of the team members; (4) an *Internationalist*, who enjoys the challenges of dealing with multiple cultures and country environments; and, finally, (5) a *Traveler,* who understands that electronic communication will never completely replace the benefits of face-to-face meetings and social contact.

In summary, the job of the global IT manager is a challenging one. It requires an in-depth knowledge not only of technological and business issues, but also of world history, culture, geography, religion, politics, and international law. With ever-improving global communication networks and connectivity, global technology management is destined to become a pervasive issue in IT governance.

7. Designing an Appropriate IS Organization and Governance System

Just as the IS leader must be selected to fulfill the expectations for IT in the total organization, the IS organization itself must be designed to fit the information needs of the business. A wide variety of IS organization structures are found in small to large organizations and in all kinds of industries, and this variety has been broadened by today's distributed technologies. Although the alternatives are numerous, this section focuses on the more common IS organizational designs as well as some alternatives that establish the IS organization as a separate business.

The Classic IS Organization. The earliest attempts to design organizations for the IS department followed a functional design. As can be seen in Figure 15.8, the classic IS organization had two primary functional areas: systems development and maintenance, and operations. Systems development activities included systems analysis and programming, as well as the installation of custom and purchased applications. Operations activities included computer processing and computer storage management (often run as part of a data center), network operations and maintenance, equipment maintenance, and systems programming.

At the outset these two primary IS activities were typically managed within the same unit. In midsized and small organizations, in particular, there was typically a single, centralized (or corporate) IS organization unit. However, in large organizations, each business division might have had its own IS organization—with separate systems development and operations staff—with little or no coordination across divisions. This design in large organizations resulted in what came to be called a decentralized IS organizational approach.

Decentralized IS designs are often found in organizations with highly autonomous business units that see no major benefits from sharing IS applications and resources with other business units. Stated differently, the business units want total control of their IS resources. In contrast, highly centralized IS designs are most often instituted in businesses that are most concerned about cost efficiencies, because all business units share the costs of purchasing and running computers, networks, and applications.

Newer Designs for the IS Organization. In all but the smallest organizations, however, two hybrid IS governance designs are often found instead. These are a federal design and a customized design (see Figure 15.9). Organizations that choose a **federal design** are attempting to achieve the benefits of *both* the centralized and decentralized designs. These companies are seeking cost efficiencies from centralizing their operations activities under a single corporate IS unit while decentralizing their applications activities to their business divisions—in order to give each business unit autonomous control over its local application needs.

A **customized design** is a mixed design found in many large enterprises. In this design some business divisions have a centralized IS unit handle all their IT needs. Other divisions within the same parent organization have a federal or decentralized design in order to locally address their own IT needs with their own local IS staff.

It is important to note that decisions on how to distribute IS decision-making authority and oversight are separate from decisions on how to distribute computer processing power, storage equipment, and network hubs. The discussion here focuses on centralized versus decentralized decision-making authority for a set of IS activities, not on the economies of locating data processing operations close to a supplier or a specific business user.

Separate IS Business. Many firms have adopted a design for the IS organization in which the IS unit is responsible for its own financial and market survival. In this approach the business units treat the IS unit much like

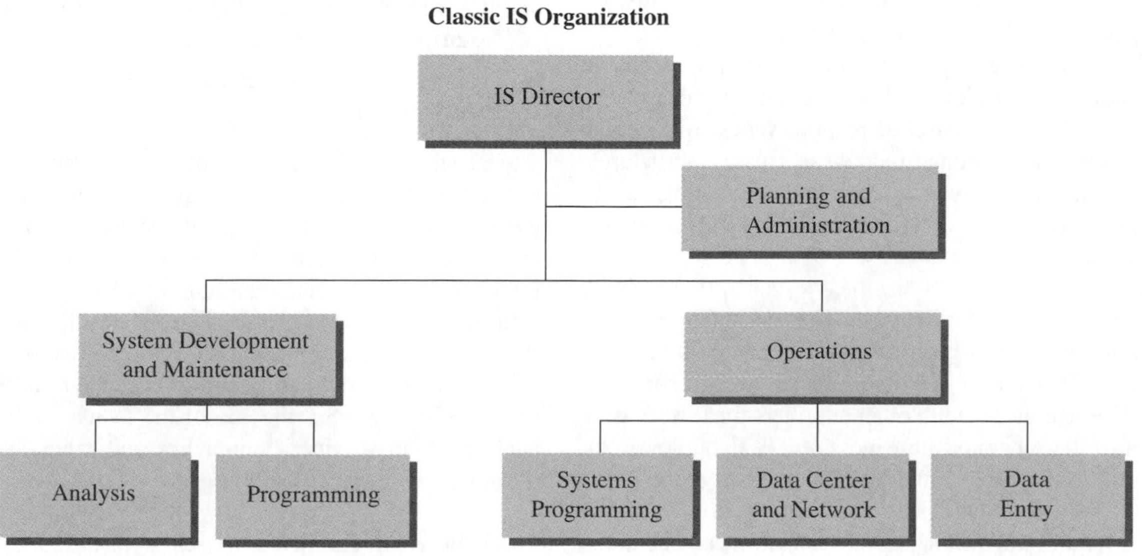

Figure 15.8 Classic IS Organization Structure

	Centralized	Decentralized	Federal	Customized
Operations				
Infrastructure Planning	C	D	C	C
Computer Operations	C	D	C	C or D
Telecom/Network Operations	C	D	C	C or D
Applications				
Application Planning	C	D	D	C or D
Systems Development & Maintenance	C	D	D	C or D
End-User Support	C	D	D	C or D

C = Centralized decision making (decision rights consolidated into a single unit)
D = Decentralized decision making (decision rights dispersed to multiple units)

Figure 15.9 Common Designs for the IS Organization (Based on Brown, 2003).

a vendor, with separate cost and revenue accounting. There are two common designs for this "business within a business" approach. First, the company might create a separate IS subsidiary company. Here the IS organization operates much like an independent business with its own board of directors and governance process. Second, many other organizations have chosen to combine the IS organization and other support organizations in a "shared services" model. These groups often include human resources, legal, physical facilities maintenance, and transportation. These organizations might or might not be created as a separate legal entity. For example, Ashland Inc. operates a shared services organization in Rotterdam, the Netherlands, to support all Ashland operations in Europe.

The primary objective for both of these approaches is to gain more cost efficiencies from the same number of resources and also to increase the responsiveness of IS units to customers' needs. Sometimes these separate structures are also created as a way to determine if contracting out IS activities is more effective than performing all IS activities with internal staff.

Creating a separate IS business organization gained popularity during the late 1990s and early 2000s because the design puts the IS organization into a competitive market position. The business units in the parent company are usually free to contract with other suppliers for IS services. Sometimes the separate IS business unit is also allowed to provide IT services to outside, noncompeting organizations. Multiple shared services organizations might also be set up in large, international firms. Sometimes these units compete for service contracts with other shared services units that primarily serve other regions.

Selecting the Best Organization Design. The IS organization structure needs to be aligned with the organization as a whole. The choice among the organization designs described above should depend on the following factors:

- How the rest of the business enterprise is organized, including global operations
- Other business characteristics, such as the type of customer markets, products, and geographical spread of the business units
- The conceptual and actual role of IT within the organization
- The reporting level of the most senior IS leader or officer within the organization
- The types of technologies managed by the IS organization

Since the late 1990s many firms have moved to more centralized IS organization designs in order to take advantage of commercial software developments. These developments include packaged enterprise systems with cross-functional modules for back-office transactions (ERP systems), front-office transactions (e.g., customer relationship management [CRM] systems), and business or competitive intelligence systems. However, the trend toward more hybrid IS organization designs seen at the end of the 1980s might emerge again as Web services approaches and other distributed technology approaches reemerge.

Governance Mechanisms. Each of the designs discussed above has its own strengths and weaknesses in terms of achieving cost efficiencies and cross-unit synergies. Thus, one approach that many businesses use to minimize the weaknesses of a given organization design is to implement additional decision mechanisms to achieve coordination across multiple IS units, multiple business units, and business and IS units. Four common types of mechanisms are shown in Figure 15.10.

The most common type of coordinating mechanism is the implementation of a formal group that brings together stakeholders from different reporting units. For example, IS steering committees (or "advisory boards") are formal group mechanisms for linking a central IS unit and multiple business units for strategic and tactical decision making. Typically, business leaders serve on a steering committee for the senior IS leader of a centralized IS unit in order to achieve consensus on which application project requests from the business units are to be worked on first and to make IT infrastructure decisions. Another type of group governance system is a center of excellence team in which individuals from multiple reporting units are virtually (if not physically) linked for tasks such as sharing best practices and researching opportunities for new technologies.

Recent research has found that some organizations also view integrator role positions as critical for achieving cross-unit coordination. For example, in firms with a centralized IS organization design, an account manager might be assigned to "manage the account" of a specific business unit. Often the person in this integrator role will have an office physically adjacent to other business managers in the company.

Two other types of mechanisms in Figure 15.10—informal networking practices and human resource practices—are used to link IS and business managers, or IS managers who report to different business units, in a less formal way. In these cases as well, the intent of these mechanisms is to help build interpersonal networks among organizational members that will promote information and knowledge sharing to help grow and sustain the business.

8. Ensuring Regular Performance Measurement

Another key element in a modern IT management system is the regular evaluation of the IS organization by its internal customers. Some business managers complain that they are not sure they are getting their money's worth from the IS function. More important, many organizations simply do not know what the impact of IT investments has been. Often, promised cost savings were never realized, project budgets were exceeded, head count was not reduced or personnel were simply moved to other jobs, and

Four Types of IS Governance Mechanisms

Mechanism	Description
Formal Groups	Formally established councils or teams with specific linking or oversight responsibilities for IT activities (such as IS steering committees)
Formal Roles	Individual positions with formal responsibility for linking activities between a central IT unit and one or more business units (such as IS managers serving as account managers for specific business units)
Informal Networking Practices	Intentional activities or practices to link managers in two or more organizational units who may engage in or impact cross-unit problem-solving (such as physical co-location)
Human Resource Practices	Human resource management initiatives to facilitate voluntary cross-unit problem-solving (such as temporary job rotations, cross-unit input to performance reviews)

Figure 15.10 Four Types of IS Governance Mechanisms (Based on Brown, 1999).

the important benefits could not be directly attributed to the use of IT. By contrast, certain general impacts are clear. Many organizations have become very dependent on IT, and IT is often being used for competitive advantage. In these instances the IS department is critical to the organization's success.

Organizations and individual managers need agreed-upon and measurable criteria by which to judge the health and contribution of the IS organization and the systems it manages. IS organizations also need metrics to judge the quality of their work. The focus of this section, however, is on the measures of most interest to the business manager.

Measures of IS Unit Success. Traditional productivity measurement approaches, such as cost-benefit analysis and return on investment, can be used to justify and evaluate individual systems. A wide variety of other criteria for evaluating the IS organization is possible, many of which are outlined in Figure 15.11. These criteria are used in

IS Evaluation Criteria

- **Meeting business objectives:** This means increasing business effectiveness and developing systems that support annual and long-term business goals and directions.
- **Responding rapidly and economically to new needs:** Reducing the length of the cycle from product idea generation to market introduction can have tremendous value in terms of cost reduction, personnel time, earlier revenue generation, and competitive advantage.
- **Expanding business or services:** Reaching new markets, adding features (often information-based) to existing products or services, or improving product service quality can be used for differentiation and revenue generation.
- **Developing an architecture and plan:** An architecture allows line managers to easily access the data now contained in data storage systems and supports the more rapid development and deployment of new systems.
- **Operating reliable and efficient technology resources:** Reliable and efficient operation of both internal systems and external services (such as order entry, reservations, and point of sale) is essential for the business to succeed.
- **Focusing on the customer:** Better customer support helps the organization to retain customers, gain new customers, and increase sales; the goal is to make it easy for the customer to do business with us and for us to know as much about the customer as he or she expects us to know.
- **Providing quality IS staff:** Indicators such as a high level of education, low turnover rate, and a large number of employees outplaced to line management jobs all suggest an IS organization of productive and useful people.
- **Reducing size of backlog:** Although a backlog of work indicates a strong demand for IS services, a large backlog can be a source of considerable frustration and unmet business opportunities; with a proper mix of end-user development, use of fourth generation languages, and purchasing package software, this backlog should be reduced to a manageable and reasonable level.
- **Satisfying users:** In the spirit of the business focusing on customer satisfaction, the IS organization can be measured by how satisfied line managers are with the technology, systems, and support services provided to them.
- **Adopting new technologies:** The IS organization can be evaluated on the basis of how soon new technologies (such as the Internet) are integrated into existing or new systems.

Figure 15.11 IS Evaluation Criteria

combination; no one or two measures adequately provide the complete picture of the IS department's contribution.

The IS evaluation criteria of Figure 15.11 require specific measures to be useful, some of which will be subjective. For example, the "meeting business objectives" criterion could be measured by an opinion survey involving such questions as:

- Does the IS plan support the corporate strategic plan?
- Would the organization be out of business without the IS unit?

Other criteria can be assessed by more quantitative and objective measures. For example, the "operating reliable and efficient technology resources" criterion could be measured by

- online response time
- network up-time as a percentage of total time during a period
- number of network crashes

As with any measurement system, an organization should measure only what is important, what needs improvement, and what is meaningful to some audience. Typically, measures of time, money, and defects are the most useful. In their classic article on the **balanced scorecard**, Kaplan and Norton (1992) called for using a set of measures that "balance" various assessment categories, including financial measures as well as the drivers of future performance:

- *Customer satisfaction.* Such measures as on-time delivery of new systems, number of defects in a system
- *Internal processes.* For IS, this could be the productivity of computer system developers, often measured by an industry standard of number of function points per month
- *Innovation and learning.* Education level of IS staff and business managers

Service Level Agreements. The IS organization can be evaluated through a **service level agreement** similar to one that would be written with an external supplier. This agreement makes expectations—from both IS and business management—explicit and defines agreed-upon criteria for a successful system and quality service.

User Satisfaction Measures. If IS is viewed as a service organization, then user satisfaction is a very important measure of IS success. Such measures are an excellent way for managers to communicate their assessment of IS to senior officers and IS executives. Although not economic in nature and not related directly to business impacts such as reduced inventory, increased customer satisfaction, or improved product quality, user satisfaction measures can easily be captured and compared over time. User attitudes about systems and the IS department affect a business manager's willingness to work with IS professionals in the kinds of partnerships discussed earlier.

Typically, an annual survey would be conducted for each major system, systems that might have problems, IS support organizations, or any area of IS that is receiving criticism; that is, a user satisfaction survey can be conducted on an application system or on an IS unit. Business managers at different levels should be surveyed separately, because their different systems perspectives and roles (for example, direct user, source of funding, supervisor) can affect their evaluation.

Figure 15.12 lists some criteria that might appear on user satisfaction surveys for a specific system and other criteria that could be customized to particular IS units, such as systems development or end-user support. The survey would ask the respondent to rate the individual system or unit on, for example, a 1-to-10 scale (low-to-high performance) or ask users to respond on a strongly-disagree-to-strongly-agree scale concerning various statements involving the criteria in Figure 15.12. The survey might ask the business manager to indicate how important each criterion is, so that a weighted assessment can be derived. The survey might also include some open-ended questions that ask for problems, complaints, praise, particular system features to add or delete, and what the customer likes best or least about the system or IS unit.

THE TOP IS JOB

The management of IT in organizations has changed drastically over the past 50 years. In the early years, the big job was to manage the technology—get it working, keep it running, and reduce the cost of doing business. Later, the main thrust was to manage the information resources of the organization, particularly to support management decision making by delivering information when and where it

Criteria for User Satisfaction Surveys

User Satisfaction Criteria for Individual Systems

- Accuracy of outputs
- Quality/readability of output format
- Completeness of outputs
- Relevance of outputs
- Completeness of or accessibility to database
- Currency of database
- Response time (or other measure of work completed)
- Availability
- Mean time between failures
- Downtime or malfunction recovery time
- Charges/costs
- Quality of system documentation
- Number and severity of security breaches
- Ease of operation
- Ease of making changes
- Increased confidence in decisions and actions based on system outputs
- Extent of achieving expected benefits

User Satisfaction Criteria for IS Units

- Quality of system specification documents
- Size of request backlog or workload
- Projects completed on time and within budget
- Speed at which requested system changes are made
- Professionalism of IS staff
- Nature of relationships with IS staff
- Business knowledge of IS staff
- Quality of user training
- User feeling of involvement in systems management

Figure 15.12 Criteria for User Satisfaction Surveys

was needed. Today, IT is pervasive in organizations and is a mandatory link between enterprises. Hence, it affects every aspect of organizational performance and is leading to the formation of "business ecosystems" in which organizations operate. Proper deployment of IT can determine an organization's growth, direction, structure, and viability.

In this book, the term *IT* is used to denote the technology, whereas *IS* is used to denote the organization that manages IT. The responsibilities of the head of IS now go far beyond operating highly efficient "production programming shops." These executives are now part of top management and help form the goals of the enterprise in partnership with the CEO, CFO, and other C-level members of top management. Yet, the CIO is the focal point for IT deployment.

WHERE IS THE ORGANIZATION HEADED?

The roles and responsibilities of the IS organization have been evolving since the first electronic data processing departments were formed in companies in the 1950s. We set the context for discussing this evolution by looking at the escalating benefits of IT, which in turn change the way executives view IS's role in the business.

The Escalating Benefits of IT

Kenneth Primozic, Edward Primozic, and Joe Leben, authors of *Strategic Choices*, present one view of the evolution of IT and the escalating benefits it provides firms. They introduce the notion of "waves of innovation," which they define as how IT is used by industries and by enterprises. They identify five waves of innovation, as shown in Figure 15.13, with *time* on the horizontal axis and *benefit* on the vertical access. The waves are

- Wave 1: Reducing costs
- Wave 2: Leveraging investments
- Wave 3: Enhancing products and services
- Wave 4: Enhancing executive decision making
- Wave 5: Reaching the consumer

Wave 1: Reducing costs. This wave began in the 1960s when use of IT focused on increasing the productivity of individuals and business areas. The goal was to achieve clerical and administrative savings by automating manual processes.

Wave 2: Leveraging investments. This wave began in the 1970s and concentrated on making more effective use of corporate assets to increase profitability. Systems were justified on return on investment and increasing cash flow.

As shown in Figure 15.13, both Wave 1 and Wave 2 are below the line, which means both focus on saving money, not making money, through better management of processing and assets. Systems are developed mainly for administration, finance, and manufacturing.

Wave 3: Enhancing products and services. This wave began in the 1980s and was the first time that attention shifted to using IT to produce revenue by gaining strategic advantage or by creating entirely new businesses. In conjunction with the new goals of using IT to grow the business or increase market share, IT was used to improve outward-looking functions, such as marketing, distribution, and customer service.

Wave 4: Enhancing executive decision making. This wave began later in the 1980s and focused on changing the fundamental structure of the organization as well as creating real-time business management systems.

The authors point out that Waves 1 and 2 can be implemented at any time, because of their internal focus, but Waves 3 and 4 can only be implemented once an industry leader has set the precedent. Companies that do not follow suit cease to be competitive.

Wave 5: Reaching the consumer. This wave began in the 1990s. IT is used to communicate directly with consumers, leading to new marketing, distribution, and service strategies. This wave changes the rules of competition, which has been precisely the focus of leading-edge firms—to restructure their industry by creating new businesses using the Internet, e-commerce, and now wireless technologies.

Waves 3, 4, and 5 are above the line because they concentrate on making money and staying in business. Due to the worldwide ubiquity of the Internet and the standard browser software for accessing the Web, most organizations have jumped to Wave 5.

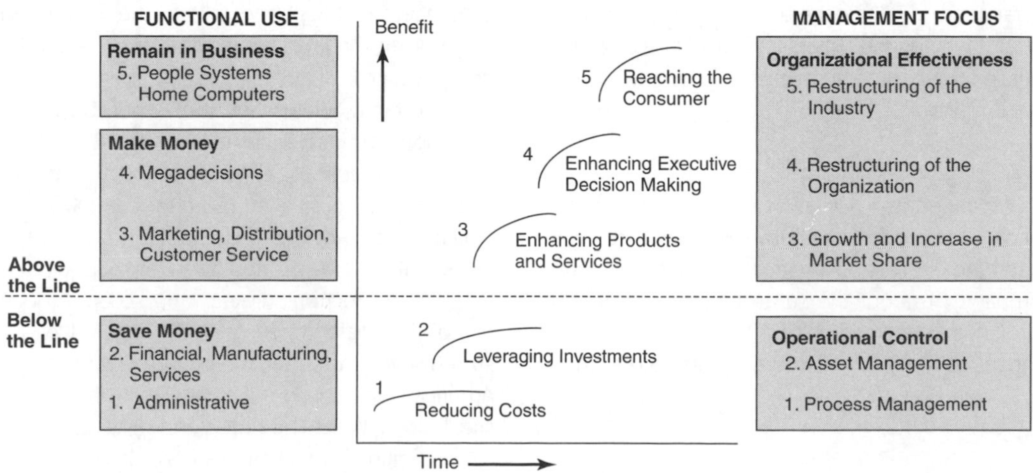

Figure 15.13 The Waves of Innovation. *Source:* Kenneth Primozic, Edward Primozic, and Joe Leben, *Strategic Choices: Supremacy, Survival, or Sayonara* (New York: McGraw-Hill, 1991).

Once companies cross "the line," top management must be involved in guiding IT use, say the authors of *Strategic Choices*, because they must steer the company in the new business environment. The risks of inappropriately using IT for competitive purposes are too great for the senior executives to abrogate leadership to technicians. Therefore, joint planning by top management and IS management must take place.

To illustrate how one company has maneuvered through these five waves, consider the example of the American Airlines SABRE system.

This SABRE example illustrates that as the benefits of IT increase, the importance of executive guidance also increases. It also raises the question, "What's the job of the IS organization?" That's the topic discussed next.

CASE EXAMPLE

THE SABRE SYSTEM

The American Airlines computer reservation system—SABRE—represents a prime example of a system that has progressed through the five waves of innovation.

Waves 1 and 2

SABRE was initially built to reduce the costs of making airline seat reservations and to leverage the reservation-making assets of the airline. The system moved American from a manual-based reservation operation to a computer-based one.

Wave 3

American then expanded the system so that it could be used by travel agents, giving them a means of making reservations directly through online terminals. American enhanced the offering by adding functions of importance to travel agents, such as tools for preparing trip itineraries. SABRE was a win-win proposition—the travel agents liked the direct access and American increased the barriers to agents switching to another carrier's reservation system.

Wave 4

American later expanded its reservation service to include hotels and rental cars. In so doing, American was transforming itself, and perhaps the entire industry, from an airline company to a travel company. At about the same time, American also added a yield-management component to SABRE, which enabled the company to reprice seats more dynamically to maximize revenue.

Wave 5

American extended its reach to the consumer in three major moves. First, it introduced EAASY SABRE, a computer reservation system that consumers can access through their PCs.

Second, American introduced its frequent flyer program, AAdvantage, thereby encouraging frequent business flyers to fly American and gain points redeemable for free trips. In addition, the airline began allying the program with credit card and long-distance telephone companies, giving AAdvantage members free airline miles when they use those credit cards and telephone companies.

Third, American enhanced its Wave 5 connections to consumers via the Web. As reported by Patricia Seybold in her book *Customers.com*, American was the first major airline to develop a Web site. This meant that passengers could not only plan their trip via the Internet, but could also buy tickets online and obtain real-time flight information, such as arrival and departure information. Even the name of the movie(s) being shown on flights could be accessed. Before the Web site, some 85 percent of telephone calls to the SABRE call center were not booking related. After the Web site, this percentage dropped significantly.

Importantly, writes Seybold, American targeted its site at the most profitable customers—its 32 million AAdvantage members—practically all of whom had access to a computer. The goal was to give them better control of their travel planning and rescheduling. Thus, on the site, AAdvantage members can see their accumulated frequent flyer points, make reservations, book electronic tickets, and so on. American promoted use of the site by offering extra frequent flyer miles; bookings spiked every time a promotion was run, notes Seybold. American has continued to enhance the functionality of the site, helping flyers find hotels and restaurants.

In addition, American has used the site to experiment with different offerings to flyers in general. One experiment proved to be a real winner. John Samuel, a marketing manager at AMR, American's parent company, asked, "How can we market to fill seats?" He and his team decided to offer to send an e-mail message every Wednesday listing "the specials of the week"—empty seats on flights the upcoming weekend—to anyone who signed up for the NetSAAver service. Not knowing what to expect, they were overwhelmed with the response—20,000 subscribers within 30 days, 100,000 in 60 days, and 775,000 in 1 year, notes Seybold.

This marketing strategy not only lets American remind subscribers of their service each week, at the subscribers' own request, but it also enables American to sell distressed inventory (the unsold seats). This additional revenue drops directly to the bottom line.

Both uses of the Internet, the AAdvantage Web site and the NetSAAver e-mail service, have required American to appropriately manage knowledge about flyers, use the Internet to interact with them, and create an e-commerce engine to support the financial interactions involved. In the knowledge management arena, for example, the airline learned that keeping Web sites pertinent requires operating like a newspaper publisher, with strict deadlines, publishing guidelines, dispersed accountability, and so forth, notes Seybold.

This example makes clear that management had to be involved as soon as SABRE moved into money-making, beginning with Wave 3, when it began offering the system to customers, the travel agents. That was a heart-of-the-business move, and it had to be led by the business executives, not the IS executives. The same has been true of its use of the Web.

Traditional Functions Are Being Nibbled Away

As SABRE demonstrates, IT has become an essential piece of business strategy; therefore, the speed of IT deployment affects when and how companies can carry out their strategy. Not keeping up in IT can even mean going out of business. The role of the IS organization is thus expanding. At the same time, management is realizing that traditional operational portions may not all need to be performed in-house. They can be performed by others. The traditional set of responsibilities for IS has included:

- Managing operations of data centers, remote systems, and networks
- Managing corporate data
- Performing system analysis and design and constructing new systems
- Planning systems
- Identifying opportunities for new systems

Although all these functions still need to be performed, the following trends are moving their performance out of IS into other parts of the organization or to other enterprises:

- *Distributed systems* have led to the migration of software applications to user areas. These applications are controlled by the users and generally purchased with their funds. Sometimes these applications are acquired following guidelines (or even standards) promulgated by the IS department; sometimes they are not.
- *Ever more knowledgeable users* have taken on increased IS responsibilities. They often identify high-leverage applications and lead multifunctional teams (which include IS staff) that acquire these systems.
- *Better application packages* have resulted in less need for armies of programmers and analysts to develop systems in-house from scratch. The job of IS has changed to *system integration*, which means integrating purchased applications so that they function together as a system. A case in point is ERP systems. Implementing these purchased systems has involved system integration rather than system development.
- *Outsourcing* has spread widely, perhaps more than most people expected, because companies see value in turning IS functions over to specialist companies. Outsourcing can be an effective strategy, based on fiscal and managerial considerations, for handling data center operations, application maintenance, network management, and PC support.

Thus, as shown in Figure 15.14, the work of the IS department is being "nibbled away." On the other hand, the IS job also is expanding.

New Roles Are Emerging

Gartner Executive Programs (EXP), part of the well-known Gartner IT analysis firm, presents analyses of the evolving IS situation and provides useful insights into the structure of IS organizations and where they are likely to

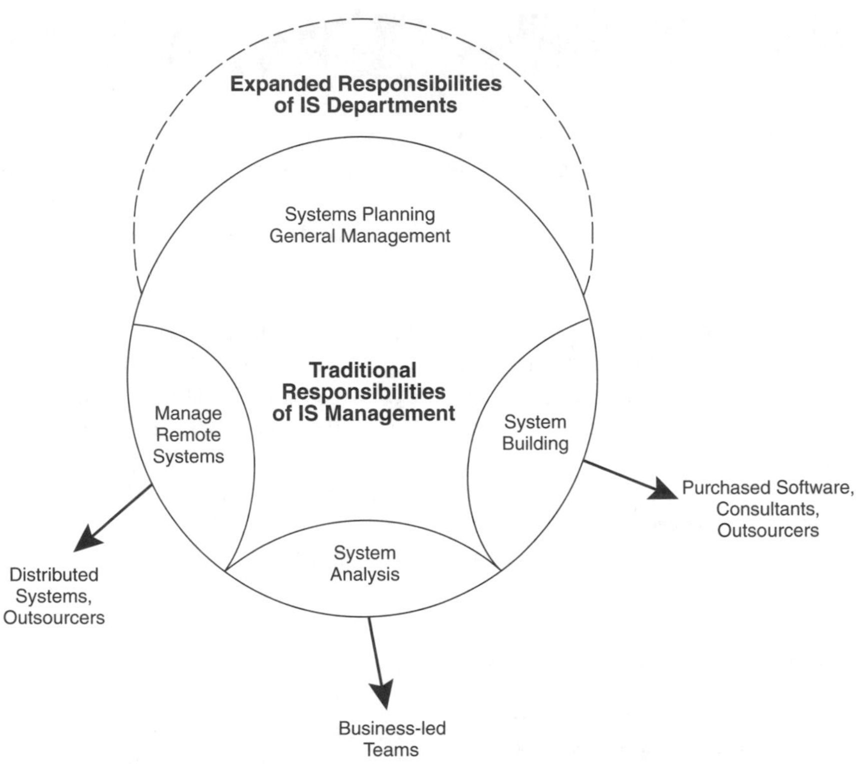

Figure 15.14 Traditional Responsibilities Being "Nibbled Away" from IS Departments

be headed. In one report, George Cox (of Wentworth Research Program, which is now part of Gartner EXP) stated that IS is not a single monolithic organization, but rather a cluster of four functions:

1. *Run operations.* Running computers and networks
2. *Develop systems.* Developing and maintaining systems, designing new systems, and updating existing ones
3. *Develop architecture.* Setting a strategy and maintaining an architecture for both IT and information, providing a framework or standard for systems operations
4. *Identify business requirements.* Helping articulate what the business needs from IT

Each of these functions requires a different set of skills and a different management strategy. A function that aims for cost efficiency and requires technical skills (such as running operations) needs to be managed differently from one that aims to add business value and requires business expertise (such as identifying business requirements).

Figure 15.15 shows the four functions on a matrix with two dimensions: the kind of impact an activity has on the organization (from cost efficiency to value added) and the type of expertise needed by the activity (from technical to business expertise).

Two technical activities that focus on cost efficiency—operations and system development and maintenance—are of less importance to the business, hence they are smaller bubbles. Meanwhile, the business-oriented activities that seek to add value to the enterprise are of far greater importance to the enterprise, hence the larger bubbles.

Companies that have failed to recognize the differences among these four areas—the relative importance of each and how to manage each properly—have, in some cases, misplaced their resources or underdeveloped their expertise. Until recently, most IS organizations invested heavily in computer operations and system development/maintenance, while neglecting the other two (developing architectures and identifying business requirements). Operations and systems development can be purchased because they are commodity-like; architecture development and business requirements identification cannot because they are unique to each organization.

Most IS organizations have had to reskill their staffs to move to these more value-added kinds of work. As shown in Figure 15.16, external services in the form of outsourcing compete well in the lower left of the matrix, the technical arena. Meanwhile, increasingly knowledgeable users assume more of the responsibility and initiative in the upper-right area of the matrix, the business-centric arena.

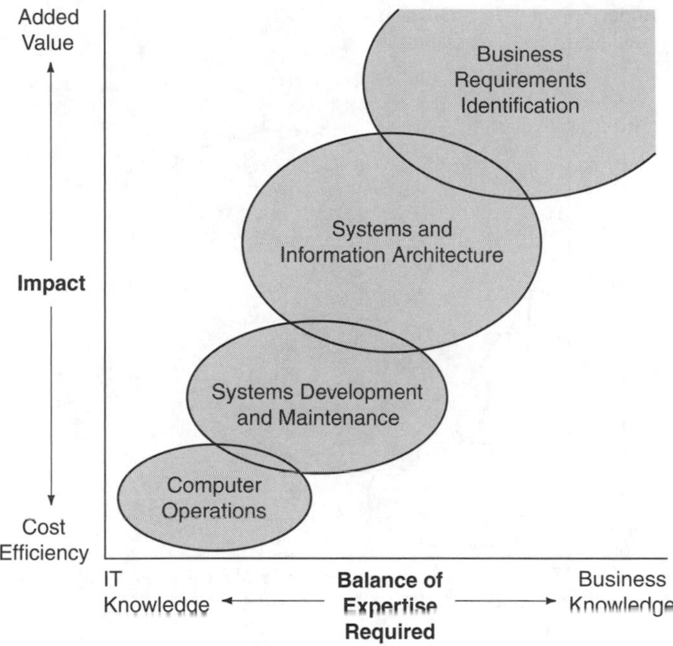

Figure 15.15 Four Major IS Activities. *Source.* George Cox, *Time to Reshape the IS Department?,* Wentworth Research Program (now part of Gartner EXP, Stamford, CT), June 1994.

Will these trends continue? Will the IS organization be squeezed into oblivion, outsourced on one end and absorbed into business units on the other? Cox thinks not! Two roles will emerge as dominant for the IS function.

First, it is not reasonable to expect an outsourcing service provider to understand and satisfy all the needs of the organization without active management and counsel. They sell commodities. Therefore, the IS organization is needed to develop and manage these contractual relationships with a variety of external suppliers. Thus, IS is becoming the broker between technical service providers and business units.

Second, a crucial role for IS organizations is development and management of the IT architecture for the enterprise, providing the framework for IT to support the business. Architecture is the biggest challenge, especially given IS organizations' systems development and operations heritage. As Cox notes, "The precious baby of a coherent framework for systems should be differentiated from the bath water of system delivery and operation." Figure 15.17 shows these two new roles and how they overlap the past roles.

In short, Cox describes the metamorphosis of IS departments as follows:

- *In computer and network operations*. IS started out being the sole provider, then moved to being the preferred provider, next was seen as a competing supplier, and finally is becoming broker and contract manager for outsourcing this work.
- *In system development and maintenance*. In-house programmers initially wrote the code, then they became software product specialists, next systems integrators, and finally brokers and contract managers for acquiring software.
- *In systems and information architecture*. IS began as technology guru and standards setter, then evolved into being custodian of technical standards, later became specialist in IT trends, and most recently morphed into IT strategist.
- *In business requirements identification*. IS initially defined the specifics of computer programs, then focused on analyzing information flows and business systems, later moved to contributing to multidisciplinary analysis teams, and finally has been partnering with the business in looking at business processes.

In short, IS organizations have moved in Figure 15.15 from lower left to upper right in their role in the business, from efficiency to value added and from technical to business expertise.

Toward IS Lite

Roger Woolfe has furthered the thinking at Gartner EXP about the role of IS departments by studying how they have responded to this evolution. He notes that whereas IS may have started as a single centralized organization, it has evolved into a federal model, where some activities (such

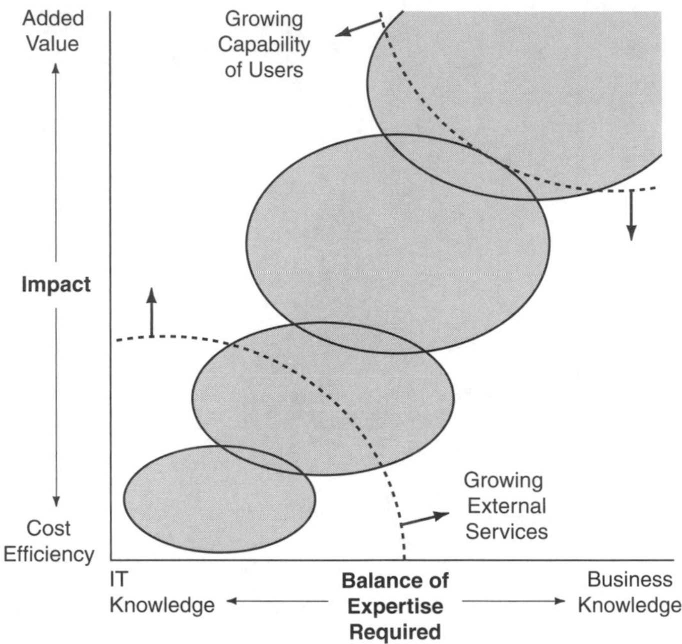

Figure 15.16 The Squeeze on Traditional IS Activities. *Source:* George Cox, *Time to Reshape the IS Department?,* Wentworth Research Program (now part of Gartner EXP, Stamford, CT), June 1994.

as standards setting and operations) are handled centrally because they can be leveraged across the enterprise, whereas other activities (such as application development) have been dispersed to business units so they can best meet local needs. Unfortunately, making this split has been far from easy and has produced continual swings between centralizing and decentralizing specific activities to try to best fit the current business environment.

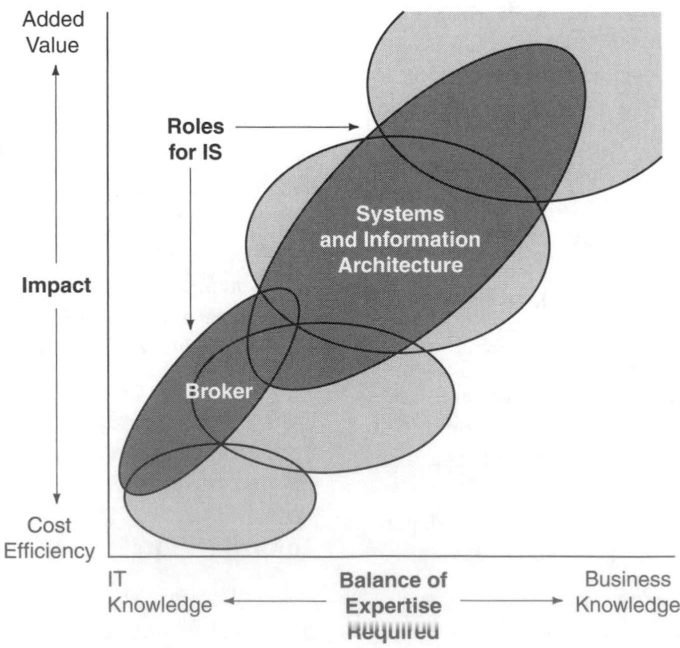

Figure 15.17 Roles for IS. *Source:* George Cox, *Time to Reshape the IS Department?,* Wentworth Research Program (now part of Gartner EXP, Stamford, CT), June 1994.

As an example, where should Web sites be developed? Initially, most were built by enterprising business people in marketing and other functions, without standards or guidance. When the importance of these sites was recognized, and the diversity began to impinge on "creating a single, powerful corporate image on the Web," Web site development was often pulled into a newly created e-commerce group. Yet the job is too large for one group, so those with responsibility for the content (in marketing, operations, and other functions) have added Web content management to their job—thus distributing that job—whereas Web site standards and operations are handled by central groups. The end result is the federal model.

However, that is not the end of the story. As Web sites take on new uses and greater importance, some companies have outsourced Web site development to specialist firms, others outsource Web operations to hosting specialists (who can provide vaultlike security and handle large spikes in demand, for instance), and they perhaps outsource hosting of Web events to still others who specialize in that activity. In short, the federal model can become quite complex with lots of players.

To make the federal model work better, companies are shifting attention from roles to processes. In this view, the IS organization can be viewed as managing three overall processes:

- Driving innovation
- Managing change
- Supporting infrastructure

Applying the federal model to these processes sharpens the distinction between IS activities performed centrally and those performed in business units. Woolfe sees the division coming from distinguishing supply-side activities from demand-side ones. *Supporting infrastructure* and aspects of *managing change* (such as delivering applications) are supply side. They involve providing networks, databases, and processing; they are best centralized because they can leverage economies of scale.

Most *managing change* and all *driving innovation*, on the other hand, are demand side. They create the demand for IT services; they are best localized in business units, which can tailor services to their needs.

To serve this split, some IS organizations have created centers of excellence to pool expertise and leverage it across the enterprise. Such centers now exist for such areas as e-commerce, supply chain management, policies and standards, help desk support, and systems integration.

The result is that much of the supply and demand sides of IS's work is being given up, as noted previously, to outsourcers and knowledgeable users. The result is that IS organizations are moving to *IS Lite*, as shown in Figure 15.18.

The remaining processes are *driving innovation*, which includes information and systems architecture, and *managing supplier and user relationships*, which includes brokering.

A company that is moving in this direction is LifeScan. Here is what its information management (IM) department is doing, as described in the paper submitted to the Society for Information Management's annual paper competition seen on pages 597–598.

Given these descriptions of how the IS department is evolving, we now look at the responsibilities of CIOs.

THE CIO'S RESPONSIBILITIES

In line with the evolution of IS departments, the emphasis of the top IS job has changed through the seven editions of this textbook as follows.

In 1986, when the first edition of this book was published, the leading IS executives were talking about their new role as architects of the enterprisewide IT infrastructure. Much of the talk centered around the strategic use of IT.

In 1989, attention shifted to helping formulate corporate policy, with an emphasis on creating a vision of the role of IT in the future. In other words, from 1986 to 1989,

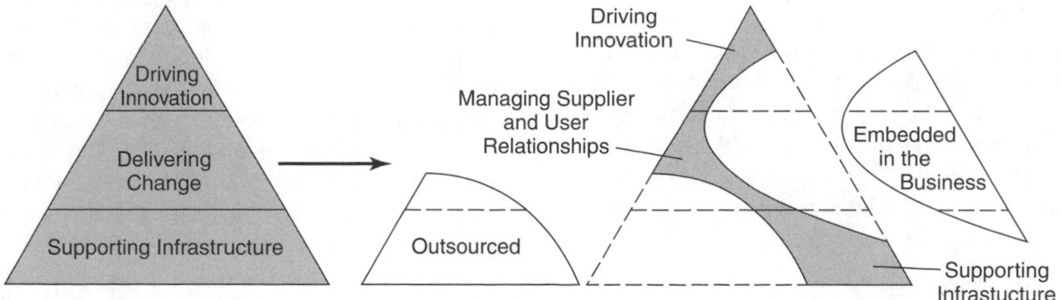

Figure 15.18 IS Lite. *Source:* Reprinted with permission from Roger Woolfe, *IS Lite*, Gartner EXP, Kuly 2000.

CASE EXAMPLE

LIFESCAN

LifeScan, a wholly owned subsidiary of Johnson & Johnson, is a world leader in blood glucose monitoring for diabetes management. Located in Silicon Valley, the company offers an array of consumer and hospital products. In 1981, LifeScan pioneered the modern era of blood glucose monitoring by eliminating wiping and timing procedures. This breakthrough took blood glucose testing out of the laboratory and into the hands of patients. LifeScan's mission is to improve the quality of life for people with diabetes.

In 1986, Johnson & Johnson acquired LifeScan, and in 1996 it began promoting greater use of IT in business strategy. The company created the board-level position of CIO and encouraged all 188 affiliates (including LifeScan) to do the same. At the time, LifeScan Information Management (IM) was led by a director—two levels below the president.

In 1998, LifeScan appointed its first CIO, Hugo Yepez, who brought with him an agenda to align the department with the business. This agenda is leading the IM department to an IS Lite type of structure.

The Alignment Road Map

Yepez has drawn on a three-stage maturation of IM departments as his road map to moving his department from supporting the business to partnering with the business. His framework defines maturity by the value the IM department delivers at each stage:

- Stage 1 IM organizations are backroom in nature. Their purpose is to keep the business running. Their value is defined through the internal IM measures of faster/better/cheaper.
- Stage 2 IM organizations work closely with business units. Hence, their value is measured from the business units' viewpoint in terms of delivery and execution. In measuring their success, some use the Balanced Scorecard because it measures performance on four dimensions—financial, internal performance, customer satisfaction, and health and growth.
- Stage 3 IM organizations partner with business units and have direct influence on business strategy. Their value is therefore gauged through the business's own performance measures. The two are integrated; there are no separate measures for IM.

Yepez believed the LifeScan IM department was at stage 1 when he arrived, but he believed it could move into stage 2 in a couple of years and into stage 3 in several more years.

To progress toward stage 2, Yepez focused on execution and measurement to gain credibility with the business units. Execution meant bringing in IM projects on time and within budget. Focusing on project execution would help move the department to a stage-2 mindset because IM staff would view their performance from the results they deliver to the business.

To deliver on their promises in implementing new systems, IM staff learned that they had to have strong project management and not allow *scope creep* (users asking for additional functions in applications as development proceeded). To deliver on promises in maintenance, IM began outsourcing work on several major systems. They use Tata Computing Systems in Calcutta, India, which has impressive software quality processes and high-quality software maintenance programmers.

LifeScan also outsourced maintenance of its desktop machines, drawing on the corporate outsourcing agreement negotiated by Johnson & Johnson's IM department. Furthermore, LifeScan has turned over computer operations to Johnson & Johnson's corporate operations department, National Computing Service. Outsourcing these supply-side IT areas has freed IM staff from *doing* the work to *overseeing* the work—performing the brokering and relationship management role in the IS Lite model.

IM also began measuring new projects, to make execution visible, by giving LifeScan employees an IM scorecard on the company intranet to show which milestones were being hit or not. The scorecard is expanded, as appropriate, to include stage 2 and stage 3 measures, such as the business impact of new systems on customer service, operations, and so on. The goal is for the board of LifeScan to be able to link IM measures to LifeScan's corporate measures to identify where IM is best supporting the business.

In the areas of driving innovation and managing change, Yepez has undertaken several initiatives to involve business units in IM work. For example, he brought in an alignment process that assists business unit executives both to determine the priority of LifeScan's business drivers and then to rank IM projects in their support of those drivers.

Being a manufacturer, LifeScan has instituted quality processes. IM is aligning itself with that quality-driven culture so that the entire company speaks the same language. In one initiative, IM is working with three other departments that develop software (for products, services, and quality assurance) to implement a companywide, quality-based software development life cycle.

In addition, all IM projects are business led, which moves ownership of systems to the business people.

Finally, IM staff members who have the skills needed in a stage 3 IM organization—those with strong project management, business process, change management, and interpersonal skills—are being promoted and given opportunities to partner with business peers. In so doing, these employees present a leadership model, one that emphasizes relationship management and brokering skills, as noted in the IS Lite model.

the focus of the top IS job had swung significantly toward addressing business issues.

In 1992, the challenge for IS executives was to use IT as a catalyst for revamping the way enterprises worked. To accomplish this task, they needed to be in a high enough position to influence the use of IT as a major underpinning of the enterprise of the future. Reflecting this higher level of responsibility, the title Vice President of MIS or Information Systems Director evolved into Chief Information Officer (CIO), a position often occupied by someone with general management expertise, rather than a traditional technology manager.

In 1998, the need to revamp business operations using IT continued with the Internet expanding the CIO's horizon beyond company boundaries out to potential customers. IT began playing a more front-office role, especially in the rapidly changing Internet marketspace.

In 2002, the CIO had become the technical member of top management. The emphasis of the job was to make sure that the electronic infrastructure for e-commerce and e-business was being put into place, to ensure that IS staff were working as partners with business units on value-adding initiatives, and to rapidly deploy new IT uses.

In 2004, IS executives had a more sobering role than the high-flying "let's get into e-commerce fast" days of the late 1990s and early 2000s. Far more emphasis was placed on justifying IT investments, building a portfolio of IT projects that balanced risk and return, ensuring that the right people were involved in making IT decisions, and working outward with customers and suppliers to build interlinking systems.

Today, the cost emphasis remains, thus the use of outsourcing continues to grow (amid controversy). However, CIOs are expected to do much more with not much more money. They are under pressure to implement protective measures to safeguard the privacy of customer data, to install increasingly sophisticated security so that viruses and other attacks do not cripple systems, and to add new financial reporting features to satisfy government regulations, such as the Sarbanes-Oxley Act in the United States. At the same time, they have to keep the IT innovations coming. It's a tall order.

CIO Roles in Three Eras

In looking at the role of CIOs, Jeanne Ross of MIT and David Feeny of Templeton College, Oxford University, divide the world of computing into three eras: mainframe, distributed, and Web based. They distinguish between the three eras because they see discontinuities between them. Each era is defined by technology innovations, resulting in new uses of IT, and consequently new roles for CIOs. Figure 15.19 shows how these eras intersect.

The Mainframe Era. This era dominated from the 1960s to the early 1980s. Ross and Feeny see the role of the data processing or information systems manager (the top IS job titles back then) as being the *operational manager* of a specialist function, IS. The focus was delivery. Deliver applications on time and within budget. Make sure operations run reliably. In short, as functional heads, they needed to deliver on promises to be credible.

The Distributed Era. This era started at the end of the 1970s and saw major changes. PCs became commonplace. LANs and WANs proliferated, linking computers of all sizes. The client-server concept arose (a client requests a service of a server). Eventually, companies recentralized IT by establishing standards for desktop machines and implementing ERP systems to coordinate companywide data. This turbulent era was very different from the stable mainframe era. Thus, the role of CIOs was very different, say Ross and Feeny. In fact, they believe CIOs took on four more roles (in addition to being the operational manager): organizational designer, technology adviser, technology architect, and informed buyer.

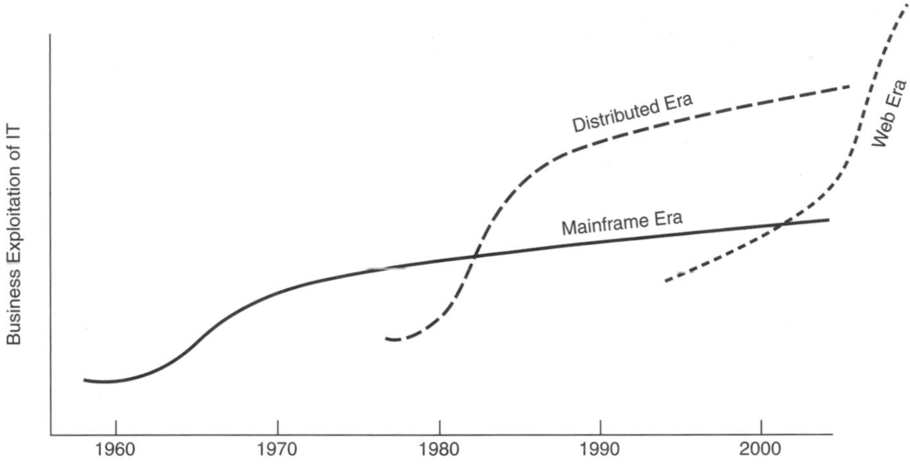

Figure 15.19 Major IT Eras. *Source:* Reprinted with permission from Pinnaflex Educational Resources, Cincinnati, Ohio 2002.

As *organizational designer*, the CIO's job was to make the IS organization responsive to the business. The result, in general, was to create a federal structure, with a central IS organization responsible for corporatewide IT and business-unit IS groups mainly developing applications for their business unit.

As *technology advisor*, the CIO's job was to align business and IS by educating business management on IT opportunities and helping the business solve their problems. In this job, CIOs spent a lot of their time outside the IS organization, working with their business peers as a technology advisor.

As *technology architect*, the CIO's role was to understand future capabilities, design the IT architecture for the entire enterprise, and then sell the business on adopting the appropriate technical standards. However, the role still had an operational aspect, ensuring that service levels remained high, no matter how many external service providers were involved.

Finally, as *informed buyer*, the CIO's role was to draw on external resources (third parties) by offloading work to them to leverage internal IS resources, such as expertise, money, space, location, and such, and thereby lower the overall cost of IS.

CIOs who mastered all four roles came to enjoy the status of being a member of the executive team, generally reporting to the CEO. Of the four roles, the most important was technology advisor, because that role provided the CEO and other top executives with an understanding of IT, its role in the enterprise, and their role in guiding its use. In short, as a strategic partner with the business, the CIO's job was to align IT with the business.

The Web Era. This era started in the mid-1990s for some. It arose, of course, from the emergence of the Internet, and especially the Web, as a business tool. With this era in its infancy, Ross and Feeny speculate that the main role of CIOs will be that of *business visionary*. By that, they mean that the CIO will need to believe and then convince others that the Internet will lead to new business models. The Internet is about fundamental business change, not technology. The challenge for enterprises is to think through possible business models; CIOs could lead this charge. Ross and Feeny even go so far as to say that CIOs who do well in this era will become leading contenders to become CEOs. Of course, CIOs still need to draw on the five former roles, but their key role will be to help the business leverage the Internet. In short, as a business visionary, their role is to be a main driver of strategy.

Obviously, this cut-and-dried pattern is an approximation of reality, note Ross and Feeney, but it demonstrates the thrust of change in the CIO's role.

Chuck Gibson, who has presented executive education seminars for years, notes that the relationship between CIOs and other senior executives, especially CEOs, has changed over time as well. In essence, it has diversified.

At one end of the relationship spectrum is the traditional relationship between CEOs and CIOs. The CIO is expected to implement technology to support business plans in a boss-subordinate, and somewhat distant, relationship Behind this relationship is the view and practice of business and IT services as separable, and IT in a support role.

The emergence of dot-coms, though, demonstrated a much closer relationship between technologists and CEOs, Gibson points out. This closeness represents the other end of the spectrum. In dot-coms, the business is inseparable from IT. Acting as a team to respond to change and build the infrastructure and applications quickly, CEOs know a lot more about IT and dot-com CIOs know a lot more about running the business because both see the two as inseparable.

One of the reasons for the breadth of this relationship spectrum is our current place in history, says Gibson. We are at the technological discontinuity on the Stages of Growth diagram where the Micro Era is ending and the Network Era is beginning. Today, both eras coexist, but the relationships, issues, and discussions of Micro Era executives are different from those of Network Era executives. Whereas Micro Era executives are talking about implementing and extending their ERP system (inside-out view), Network Era executives are talking about how to achieve customer-led product design (outside-in view).

Of course, these approaches fall along a spectrum, but the point is that not all CEO–CIO teams today talk about the same issues they did, say, 5 years ago before the dot-coms merged IS and business. Moreover, the issues, roles for IS, and relationships required between CEOs and CIOs across businesses are more diverse. As a result, it is far less appropriate to generalize about CEO–CIO discussions; the context now sets the agenda, and agendas now vary. Gibson speculates that as established companies integrate their business operations with their Internet operations, the relationship between CEO and CIO will become closer and discussion points may coalesce as the requirements of the Network Era come into clearer focus and apply more generally to all businesses.

Given these two historical overviews, we look at four aspects of the CIO role these days:

1. *Leading*: Creating a vision by understanding the business
2. *Governing*: Establishing an IS governance structure
3. *Investing*: Shaping the IT portfolio
4. *Managing*: Establishing credibility and fostering change

Leading: Creating a Vision by Understanding the Business

If CIOs are to play an important role in shaping a business's use of IT, they must understand the business. With that understanding, they can then create a vision of their firm's use of IT.

Understanding the Business. In the past, studying a business generally meant learning how it was run. However, studying internal operations is no longer enough. Today, it is important to understand the environment in which the business operates because the business's close relationships with other firms affect how the business competes. Here are seven approaches CIOs are using to understand a business and its environment.

- Encourage project teams to study the marketplace
- Concentrate on lines of business
- Sponsor weekly briefings
- Attend industry meetings with line executives
- Read industry publications
- Hold informal listening sessions
- Partner with a line executive.

Encourage project teams to study the marketplace. To learn about the business, broaden the kinds of information that project teams seek in their study of the business. Then have them describe their findings to IT management. For example, the project study might begin with a broad overview of the company, gathering the following information about the company and its industry:

- Current industry environment
- Business goals and objectives
- Major practices of competitors
- Pertinent government regulations
- The inputs, outputs, and resources of the firm.

Such an overview study can be conducted for a business unit or a product in a few weeks. The study is apt to uncover some surprises, revealing things about the industry and the company that even business unit people might not know, especially now that e-commerce initiatives are no longer being touted, but are going on nevertheless. IT management can be briefed on the findings, educating them about the markets in which their firm participates.

Concentrate on lines of business. IT researchers Robert Benson and Marilyn Parker have long studied how to manage information on an enterprisewide basis. IT needs to serve individual lines of business rather than the entire company, they found, because planning for an entire enterprise overlooks both competitive and performance matters. They believe that a line of business is where business and technology planning can be linked.

A *line of business* is an organizational unit that conducts business activities with common customers, products, and market characteristics, says Benson. For example, certain schools in a university have one line of business—undergraduate education. Others have two—undergraduate and graduate education. The customers, products, and market characteristics for the two schools are different, thus they are different lines of business.

Information technology can serve lines of business in two ways. One is by supporting current operations, which Benson and Parker call *alignment*. The second is by using systems to influence future ways of working, which they call *impact* (Figure 15.20). They recommend asking the following questions about each line of business to decide what each one needs:

1. Are we in IT organized to serve that line of business?
2. Do we have an account manager in IS who has responsibility for that line of business?
3. Do we have someone within that line of business who oversees IT activity and talks the business language?
4. Do we have a sponsor in the line of business?
5. Do we have the attention of the line's management?
6. Does the line of business offer an opportunity to use systems in new ways?

By becoming familiar with lines of business, CIOs can better help them use IT to support current operations and influence the future, say Benson and Parker.

Sponsor weekly briefings. Another way to learn about the business is to sponsor short briefings for IT management and staff that are presented by line management or staff. We have attended such meetings and have found them to be most informative. They were about one-half hour long, with one speaker describing a part of the business. Managers and staff from different departments were invited to talk to a small group of IS managers and staff about their business and its marketplace: the products and services they offered versus what the competitors offered, the strengths and weaknesses of the firm and competitors, growth projections, possible changes in the market, and so on.

For example, in the aircraft industry an engineer could give the basics of the commercial aircraft business: sizes of planes, passenger capacity, distance capability, expected competition, changes in the industry, 5-year market projections, and so on. In the financial services industry, a manager could describe various types of customers and how each is using the Internet, products now offered by the firm and competitors, the impact of globalization and the Internet on financial markets, and so on. At such briefings, it is helpful if the presenter provides a written summary of the ideas presented, so attendees can take something away with them. A brief question-and-answer period also is useful.

To understand the business, people need to understand the marketplace. Few employees are given exposure to this breadth of knowledge. By sponsoring short presentations by the people closest to a business, IS management can help fix that problem without cutting into work time too greatly.

Attend industry meetings with line executives. Another way to learn about the business is to accompany a line executive to an industry conference—not a computer conference. We have found that attending a conference is one of the quickest ways to uncover issues currently facing an industry. These conferences contain the jargon used in the industry and the approaches others have used to market products, handle regulations, respond to competition, and so on. Attending a conference with a line executive can be even more enlightening because he or she can explain what the company is or is not doing in areas discussed by the speakers. Such joint attendance also is likely to foster a new friendship.

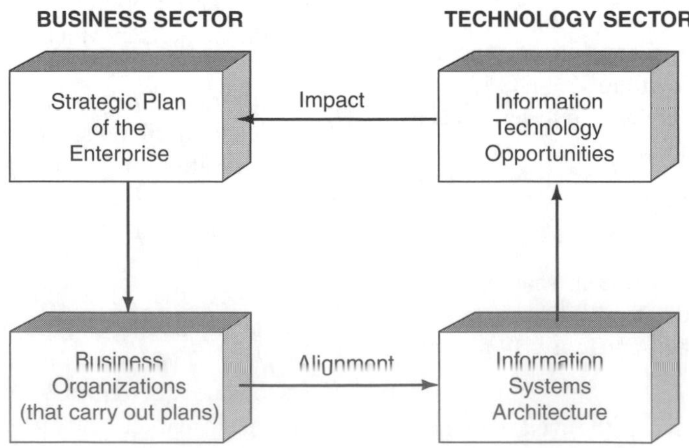

Figure 15.20 The Enterprisewide Information Management Model. *Source:* Marilyn Parker and Robert Benson with Ed Trainor, *Information Economics: Linking Information Technology and Business Perfromance* (Upper Saddle River, NJ: Prentice Hall, 1988).

Read industry publications. One of the best ways to stay abreast of an industry is to read its publications, perhaps those that are online. Getting a well-rounded view of an industry may require reading several publications a month. News publications can provide information on new products, current issues, company changes, and so on. Newsletters, reports, and research journals generally provide better analyses of industry trends, discussions of ongoing research, and projections about the future.

One CIO spreads this job around in his department. Every staff member is responsible for reading certain periodicals and routing interesting articles and URLs to others.

Hold informal listening sessions. In his book *Thriving on Chaos*, consultant Tom Peters presents hundreds of suggestions on how managers can learn to not just cope with a chaotic business environment, but to thrive on it. In numerous places in the book, Peters urges people to simply listen and learn. His ideas are appropriate for IS management in their dealings with their customers, both those internal to the firm and external to it.

Yogi Berra, the famous baseball player, once said, "You can see a lot by observing." Similarly, Peters urges employees to learn a lot by listening to others' needs. Because product life cycles are shrinking, companies need to spot new trends earlier. Becoming a listening-intensive organization can help. Peters recounts several instances where people have created informal meetings to break down barriers among people who usually do not talk with one another. These get-togethers are held in a setting that is not charged with tension; participation is voluntary. Their purpose is to offer the opportunity to just chat. For instance, one hospital administrator set aside one early morning each week to offer coffee and rolls in her office, with an open invitation for doctors and administrators to drop by and chat. She had some lonely breakfasts at first, she told Peters, but the chats eventually evolved into the "real staff meeting" of the week. Another hospital administrator held an informal staff meeting at lunchtime every 2 weeks at a local pub and invited some doctors. The doctors felt honored to be invited, and their attendance helped break down stereotypes on both sides and improve communications.

Partner with a line executive. The Society for Information Management presents a Partners in Leadership Award each year to honor an IS-business executive team who, through their alliance, have achieved significant business results. This award has been well received and is highly sought. It recognizes the partnering needed to successfully guide and deploy IT these days.

Through these approaches, CIOs and their staff can learn the businesses of the organization. Unless these or similar specific steps or mechanisms are implemented and become commonplace, the job of learning the business will be displaced by urgent, but less important, day-to-day work. With this knowledge, CIOs are in a better position to foster a vision of their firm's use of IT.

Creating a Vision of the Future and Selling It. CIOs used to be seen as followers because IT supported the business. Today, it still does, but as noted earlier, business and technology now coevolve because technology breakthroughs allow companies to operate in new ways. Thus, CIOs have become the technical leaders of their enterprises. As such, they are not only involved in defining their enterprise's IT architecture and establishing its enterprisewide technical standards, but they also must ensure that the enterprise buys into those plans. The reality in many enterprises is that top-down command only goes so far and often hits roadblocks. CIOs and their direct reports often have to sell the vision.

What is a vision? A *vision* is a statement of how someone wants the future to be or believes it will be. It is used to set the direction of an organization. Beath and Ives present several corporate visions:

- Otis Elevator: Any salesperson can order an elevator in a day.
- USAA, an insurance company for current and retired military officers: Policy holders can accomplish their objective in a single phone call or Web site visit.
- Rittenhouse Homes: Customers can get a house designed and built from a retail store.
- Fidelity Investments: Mutual funds can be repriced on an hourly, rather than daily, basis.

Once a vision is in hand, then a strategy can be formulated on how to bring the vision into being. For instance, a vision might be to become the leading manufacturer of a certain kind of pump. The strategy could be to assign salespeople to specific large customer firms rather than to a geographic area. Once the strategy is decided, planning comes into play to map out the steps for carrying out that strategy. In this case, plans are needed for when and how to make the new assignments, who will make the selections, how smaller customers will be handled, by whom, and so on.

Why develop a vision? A vision of a desirable future can provide stability when it sets direction for an organization. In the past, long-term strategies were created. They told *how* companies were going to get somewhere. Such multiyear plans are fine as long as the future is relatively predictable. However, in today's environment, people cannot

CASE EXAMPLE

BP (BRITISH PETROLEUM)

BP's main business activities are the exploration and production of crude oil and natural gas; the refining, marketing, supply, and transportation of these resources; and the manufacturing and marketing of petrochemicals. As of November 2002, BP was a $140-billion business (by market capitalization), with more than 100,000 employees serving 20 million customers daily through almost 29,000 service stations. An intense period of merger and acquisition activity has seen the absorption of Amoco, ARCO, Castrol, and Veba Aral in Germany.

The Business Is in the Business Units

BP's business units drive the business. There are 150 business units operating in over 100 countries. Ten years ago there were eight levels of organization separating executive management from business unit management. Today, this separation has been, and continues to be, radically simplified.

Business units have their own balance sheet and are held accountable via a performance contract, which is negotiated with the executive committee of their business stream. In exchange for delivering on their contracts, the business units have the freedom to operate independently.

Headquarters must convince the business units of the wisdom of BP-wide practices. Many decisions are made by peer groups—networks of business units in a business stream. They resemble federations and are a vehicle for sharing knowledge among peers. They are also where the businesses must justify the resources they seek.

Overarching this distribution of power is a set of groupwide policies based on shared core values. At the center is learning and sharing, which drive collegial behavior and enable peer-group decision making. The glues for BP's decentralized business approach are operational excellence and strong core values.

Digital Business Underpins Transformation

In 1999, John Leggate's organization issued a rare companywide mandate for a common operating environment (COE). All Amoco employees were moved to BP's operating environment. Then, in 2000, all BP desktops and laptops were moved to Windows 2000 and Office 2000. COE 3, the latest generation, bridges time and distance by providing the hardware and software needed for employees to live and work on the Web.

In early 2000, Leggate formed Digital Business (DB). This moved IT out of the beleaguered role of technology provider into a strategy-creation role. DB comprises four central groups, which deliver overarching strategy, enterprise infrastructure and projects, and policies and standards while supporting differentiated service offerings driven by the business streams:

- *DB Strategy and Chief of Staff:* Aligns DB's strategic intent with the corporation and business objectives while developing clear business plans and objectives that move the agenda forward. BP's underpinning performance-management processes are used to ensure delivery of the strategy.
- *DB Chief Technology Office (CTO):* Explores the external market to bring research and development (R&D) technology into BP to move its strategic direction forward, transforming BP into a digital corporation. The CTO group ensures that BP stays in tune with the external market through deployment of appropriate technological advancements.
- *DB Projects:* Undertakes the enterprisewide projects necessary to move its strategic infrastructure architecture forward.
- *DB Operations:* Provides overarching operational policies and standards across the globe to ensure a secure and reliable enterprise infrastructure as well as deliver some operations for the business streams. This is accomplished through an operations peer group to ensure connectivity, alignment, and compliance among the business streams.

Living on the Web

To make "living on the Web" a reality, DB is moving processes and systems to the Web and simplifying both at the same time. BP is handing processes to service providers to consolidate, simplify, and then operate. For example, BP has externalized its human resource (HR) processes through the use of an external provider, Exult. Exult, which is located in California, has integrated the numerous HR databases and is managing the processes via the Web.

The paradox of business simplification is deciding where to seek commonality and standards and where to seek flexibility and innovation.

Socializing Technical Directions

DB's visionary role is to provide thought leadership. Its implementation role is to socialize the idea of a new common good to the point where people accept it. Corporate edicts are not commonly used in BP's culture.

Socialization can take quite some time, especially when a common approach costs more than a local solution. It requires face-to-face enrollment and starts with conversations with the business leaders. From there, local governance boards decide how to implement the general principle locally.

BP's chief technology officer has established a powerful network of architects to help create consensus and drive choices that benefit BP as a whole. All of the architects on the various network teams work in the businesses. The role of each team is to create "the framework for conversation" with the business units about architecture for a specific area, such as wireless, Web Services, and so on. They use a template method to define an area of interest and drive toward consensus.

To educate communities of interest, DB reveals data, such as showing waste so a community will seek ways to reduce it. For example, BP had 36 systems reporting health and safety in 1999. Once the health and safety community knew this fact, it decided how to decrease the number. The rationalization was not centrally managed. The same is happening with the 100 maintenance management systems.

Technical choices are now made through business-based networks of experts. Similar communities handle major system upgrades. They define the global direction, evolve standards collegially, and then look to service providers to supply the components. These communities know they should not permit divergent local actions; thus, they must make difficult choices between corporate fit and local need.

Going Forward: Foster Learning and Focus on Exploitation

A major challenge is fostering learning. Today, too much prompting is needed to get BP employees to look at what others within BP are doing elsewhere in the world. Becoming a connected corporation helps, but the key is behavioral and cultural change.

Within the IT realm, the major question is, "How do we get 100,000 people to fully utilize BP's resources to change our underlying business?" The real leverage comes from the new value a new system opens up. Therefore, adoption and exploitation of the new technology and systems become a major challenge but a necessary component to realizing the value of the business transformation. This involves much effort in change management to train and influence employees to accept and use the new technology.

Bright people have been attracted to DB because it is involved in the most important conversation: where BP is going, digitally. Leggate's executive team has a broad portfolio of skills, which is critical when a leadership team is not only creating the future but is also responsible for selling it. Some have deep technical knowledge. Others are more commercially oriented people who want to use digital technology as a transformational tool. They all signed up because the agenda is vast and enthralling.

predict important future events because those events are likely to appear random, not linear or rational. In such times, direction setting and short-term explorations within that space are most appropriate. Today, most corporate visions have an IT underpinning—leveraging the Internet for business purposes. That vision sets their direction.

To illustrate how one CIO is leading his enterprise via his vision and how he has structured his organization to sell that vision to the very independent-thinking business units, consider John Leggate, Group Vice President and Chief Information Officer at BP. His approach is described in the Gartner EXP report entitled *Glocalizing Your IS* (meaning, simultaneously globalizing and localizing an IS organization) on pages 614–615.

Encouraging champions of IT projects. As the rate of change in the IT field has increased, we have heard CIOs say they need to encourage IT experimentation, especially by people in the operating units, to advance company IT experience and evolve the IT vision. Here are the ideas of two researchers and one user company on how to do that—by supporting IT champions.

A *champion* is someone with a vision who gets it implemented by obtaining the funding, pushing the project over hurdles, putting his or her reputation on the line, and taking on the risk of the project, state Professors Cynthia Beath and Blake Ives.

The first step in encouraging champions is to be able to recognize these people. They are likely to be people you

CASE EXAMPLE

AETNA LIFE AND CASUALTY

In 2000, ING acquired Aetna Life and Casualty, a financial services company with headquarters in Hartford, Connecticut. ING is headquartered in Amsterdam, The Netherlands. Aetna is now ING Life Insurance and Annuity Company.

Before being acquired by ING, much of Aetna's IT work had been decentralized; therefore, the corporate administration department focused on three functions, which they called "plan, build, and run." The operations group ran data center and telecommunication operations. The corporate technology services group assisted divisions in selecting, building, and implementing computer systems. The people and technology group also helped divisions build and implement successful systems; they emphasized the human perspective.

The planning function was the responsibility of the corporate technology planning group, which was meant to be a catalyst for introducing new technology. Its charter was to help the insurance company understand and use breakthrough technologies. By *breakthrough*, they meant technologies that would increase performance by at least 100 percent. "We constantly seek to make the future credible by encouraging innovation, experimentation, and evaluation," a member of this group told us. They saw their job as encouraging end users to talk about new technologies and test them out in real-life situations. The corporate technology planning group fostered discussions and experimentation in three ways.

They Sought Out Business Champions

The group tested technologies by cosponsoring business projects, acting as a magnet to attract people who wanted to experiment with a technology. They held workshops on specific technologies, published one-page issue papers describing certain technologies, and talked to people in a wide number of functions.

Their goal was to find business champions who thought a technology might solve their business problem. These champions also needed to be willing to share the funding and direction of a pilot project using that technology. The users agreed to let the planning group study their use and write about it. For a project to be funded, it had to have a business champion and be aimed at solving a business problem.

In several cases, the group found champions who recognized the need to test several technologies, some with expected results and others that might change future work life dramatically. These were *smart champions*, because they saw the value of investing in a portfolio of new technologies.

They Studied Pilot Projects

In one pilot project of a 500-user communication system, the planning group did systematic research during the pilot, using before-and-after questionnaires to measure how attitudes changed. They looked to see whether "telephone tag" increased or decreased. They held focus group discussions. In addition, they had some users keep daily diaries of their activities.

Based on this research, they concluded that the system would benefit a majority of employees. To then promote its use, they created a brochure and videos, which they handed off to the corporate operations group for the marketing and management of the system.

They Established Steering Committees

Steering committees can be surrogate champions to guide and build support for a new technology. When the corporate technology group saw a technology that appeared interesting, they sometimes held a one-day magnet session to find champions. Sometimes they found steering committees rather than individual champions when a topic was really hot. In one case, 200 people volunteered to do pilot projects. Because it made too large a group, a smaller steering committee was formed. It put on four seminars, got end users thinking about how they might use the technology, and oversaw some projects.

Challenges They Encountered

The technology planning group encountered three challenges.

One was simply getting people's attention. When a technology was not immediately available, people did not want to take any action. However, many technologies require a learning curve. Even when a technology is not readily available, people should be experimenting with it so that the company has in-house knowledge when products do begin to appear. Thus, making a future technology credible to people was one hurdle.

Keeping people in an experimental mode was another challenge. Once people were funded for a pilot, they wanted to do it right. They did not want to create a quick-and-dirty system; they wanted to create a production-quality system. It was hard to get people to create only quick, experimental systems.

The third challenge was making sure that the use would really pay off. The planning group did not want small productivity improvements; they wanted orders-of-magnitude improvements— at least two-to-one to three-to-one payoffs. They constantly asked users: How do you know you will get this payback?

The group's goals were education and action. They wanted end users to be comfortable using future technologies and to achieve a good payback at the same time. For more ideas on how to stimulate innovation, see *Managing Organizational Innovation.*

Such an approach puts companies in a better position to spot new opportunities, to experiment with them, and then to put them into widespread use before their competitors. In a fast-changing world, nimbleness—a sign of being open to accepting emerging technologies—is needed.

already know about, and they may be doing things that make you uncomfortable, say Beath and Ives. For instance, they are probably already circumventing established project approval processes, they are creating isolated information systems, and they may be using nonstandard equipment. They may already be pursuing a vision of how IT can help their business, whether systems people assist them or not.

These people are opinion leaders, and they have a reputation for creative ideas or being involved with innovations. They also have developed strong ties to others in their organization, and they command respect within the firm. They have the organizational power to get strategic innovations implemented.

According to the authors, IS champions need three things from IS management: information, resources, and support.

They need information. Championing an IT innovation is an information-intensive activity, note Beath and Ives. Therefore, champions need information, facts, and expertise for persuading others that the technology will work. IS staff can help champions gather and assess information about a technology's capabilities, its costs, risks of operation, and how it might be used in an experiment. IS staff also can help by sharing their expertise and by putting champions in contact with other experts, such as vendors or users of a new technology.

IS staff can assist champions in understanding current applications and data relevant to their project. Finally, they can help champions understand how the company manages change, because systems people are continually involved in implementing system changes throughout the enterprise.

They need resources. The authors cite Rosabeth Kanter, author of *Change Masters*, who says champions most need staff time. Giving champions free staff time is especially helpful during the evaluation and persuasion portions of a project. However, systems management can go even further, by assigning, say, information center consultants to help champions.

In addition to staff time, champions are likely to need material resources, such as hardware and software. These resources can be loaned to them free of charge or provided in some other way.

They need support. Finally, champions need supporters, people who approve of what they are doing and give legitimacy to their project. It is important that IS management corroborate statements made about the technology by the champion. The champion does not need to know how the technology works, only how it might be used. The IS organization should handle the technical aspects. Beath and Ives urge demonstrating the champion's claims about the technology and promoting the technology to build enthusiasm for it and to win support from others.

Finally, IS management can assist a champion win endorsement of upper management by helping to create the plans for introducing the new technology. The IS department can assist by contacting vendors and choosing an appropriate implementation approach. All of these supportive actions will improve the quality of the proposal and strengthen it in the eyes of management.

Beath and Ives encourage IS management to make it easier for IT champions to arise and succeed. One company that supported champions is Aetna Life and Casualty (see pages 616–617).

Governing: Establishing an IS Governance Structure

The term *governance* has become prominent, not only in IT circles, but in business circles as well. IT governance is *"the assignment of decision rights and the accountability framework to encourage desirable behavior in the use of IT,"* state Peter Weill and Richard Woodham of MIT's Sloan School of Management. Governance differs from management in that governance is about deciding who makes decisions, whereas management is about making decisions once decision rights have been assigned.

Governance has become important in the business world because financial scandals have shown that there was not much true governance in place in some very large enterprises. Decisions were made by a few top executives, subordinates did not question their superiors, and boards rubber-stamped decisions. There were no checks and balances.

Governance has become important in the IS world because IT expenditures have become so large and so diverse that management has had to find a way to bring order to all the decision making. However, centralizing all IT decisions is not the solution, because business units and local employees legitimately need a voice in the decisions to tailor their business to the local culture and customers. Striking a balance between global and local needs (glocalizing) is a major emphasis in IS these day. The main discussions are at the governance level, assigning decision rights. Just as the U.S. Constitution assigns rights to the states and powers to the federal government, enterprises now see the need to do the same. Finally, a third reason for the rising importance of governance is the issue of creating an IT portfolio that is in sync with business needs and stays that way.

Assigning Decision Rights. Peter Weill of MIT and Marianne Broadbent, formerly of Gartner EXP and now at Melbourne Business School, have undertaken the most comprehensive study of IT governance, surveying 256 companies in 23 countries and conducting over 20 in-depth interviews. From their research, they see IT governance as having three components, as shown in Figure 15.21: (1) six governance styles of who makes which decisions (the rows), (2) five key IT decision areas (the columns), and (3) governance mechanisms used to carry out IT governance (the cells). The IT governance arrangements matrix in Figure 15.21 illustrates "a good general-purpose IT governance design that balances decision rights for a multi-business unit enterprise," state Broadbent and Weill.

Six governance styles (the rows). A governance style defines who has a *decision right* (the right and responsibility to make a decision) and an *input right* (the right to provide input to a decision but not make the decision). The six governance styles are:

1. A *business monarchy* is where C-level executives (increasingly including the CIO) hold the right to make decisions. A mechanism used to carry out this governance style could be an executive committee or perhaps an IT council with executive committee members.
2. An *IT monarchy* is where IT executives hold the right to make decisions. A mechanism could be an IT leadership council that includes corporate and business unit CIOs.

Decision Domain / Style	IT Principles		IT Infrastructure Strategies		IT Architecture		Business Application Needs		IT Investment and Prioritization	
	Input	Decision	Input	Decision	Input	Decision	Input	Decision	Input	Decision
Business Monarchy										Cap appr comm
IT Monarchy				IT leaders		IT leaders				
Feudal										
Federal	Exec comm Biz leaders		Exec comm Biz leaders		Biz leaders Biz proc own				Exec comm Biz leaders	
Duopoly		Exec comm IT leaders					Biz leaders Biz proc own Biz/IT rel mgs	Biz leaders Biz proc own		
Anarchy										

Governance mechanisms ☐ Input rights ■ Decision rights

Exec comm	*Executive committee/C-levels*	Cap appr comm	*Exec comm subgroup includes CIO*
Biz leaders	*Business unit heads/presidents*	Biz proc own	*Business process owner*
IT leaders	*CIO, CIO offices and biz unit CIOs*	Biz IT rel mgs	*Business/IT relationship managers*

Figure 15.21 IT Governance Arrangements Matrix. *Source:* Marianne Broadbent and Peter Weill, *Taylor IT Governance to Your Enterprise,* Gartner EXP Club Report, October 2003.

3. *Feudal* is where business unit leaders (or their delegates) have decision or input rights. Feudal governance might use a business-only committee as a mechanism.
4. *Federal* means that the rights are shared by C-level executives and one other tier of the business hierarchy, such as business-unit presidents. In IT governance, an IT group might also be involved as a third participant. The federal style is akin to the U.S. government structure, with a central nationwide government and dispersed state governments. A mechanism for implementing this IT governance style is committees that draw from several organizational levels.
5. A *duopoly* is where one IT group and one business group share a right. A mechanism might be an IT–business-unit committee that draws up a service-level agreement for IT to provide services to the business unit.
6. *Anarchy* is where individual process owners or end users hold a right. The anarchy governance style is rare in the five main IT decision areas, note Weill and Broadbent, because it is not effective in guiding IT in a large enterprise.

Five decision areas (the columns). There are five key decision areas in IT.

1. *IT principles* are high-level statements about how IT will be used to create business value. Three examples of IT principles follow:
   - Corporate IT is responsible for infrastructure; business units are responsible for business-unit applications.
   - Technical reporting relationships must match corporate reporting relationships.
   - IT purchasing from major vendors must be centrally coordinated to minimize costs and ensure consistency.

As shown in Figure 15.21, Weill and Broadbent found that an IT duopoly (with business and IT executives) provides the business-IT collaboration needed to set the principles that support the business. Input often comes from other business groups (federal).

2. *IT infrastructure strategies* state the approach for building shared and standard IT services across the enterprise. This decision area is technical, so it is generally made by an IT monarchy, as shown in Figure 15.21, often with federal input.
3. *IT architecture* states the technical choices that will meet business needs. Again, this is a technical decision area, so it is generally left up to the IT monarchy, with federal input.
4. *Business application needs* is where the business defines its application needs. As shown in Figure 15.21, these decisions, and input to them, are generally federal.
5. *IT investment and prioritization* defines the process for moving IT-based investments through justification, approval, and accountability. Often, the capital appropriation committee (a business monarchy) approves IT and all other capital investments. As in other decision areas, input comes from various sources (federal style).

The arrangement matrix differs, of course, among enterprises. Those seeking synergies among their business units are more likely to enforce top-down decisions. Those with autonomous business units are likely to emphasize local decision making. Enterprises with pulls both for synergy and local autonomy may make extensive use of IT principles to guide faster decision making in their sprawling enterprise. Such is the case with Duke Energy International, as described in the October 2003 Gartner EXP report on IT governance on page 620.

Investing: Shaping the IT Portfolio

IT investments have become so large and important to company success that the subject of how to make investments properly has gained increased attention. Business executives used to blame CIOs for poor IT investments. That view is becoming less tenable because CIOs can only implement good systems. They are not responsible for changing business practices to take advantage of those systems. That's the job of line executives.

Following are two perspectives on this IT investment topic: one strategic (*what* to invest in) and one tactical (*how* to make investment decisions). Both show the importance of having business and IT thinking behind IT investing.

A Strategic View of Making IT Investments. Diana Farrell, director of the McKinsey Global Institute, conducted a fascinating study of 20 industries (8 in the U.S., 6 in Germany, and 6 in France) to discern the connections (if any) among IT, competition, innovation, and productivity from 1990 to 2000.

The bottom line of the study is that a "new" economy did indeed emerge in the 1990s, *but only in* the six industries she studied where there was intense competition that was not throttled by government regulation. These six industries were retailing, securities brokerage, wholesaling, semiconductors, computer assembly, and telecommunications.

Farrell found that intense competition forced executives in these industries to innovate—by investing in IT, by

CASE EXAMPLE

DUKE ENERGY INTERNATIONAL

Duke Energy, headquartered in Charlotte, North Carolina, manages a dynamic portfolio of natural gas and electric supply, delivery, and trading businesses. Its international division, Duke Energy International (DEI), operates regional energy businesses, primarily in Latin America; however, the company formerly had interests in the Asian Pacific and Europe as well.

DEI CIO Max Kennedy has been accountable for DEI IT performance and governance and reports to the president of DEI, Richard McGee. The regional energy businesses also have CIOs who report to their regional managing director.

DEI Differentiates Itself by Being Nimble

Product and service innovation, combined with speed and flexibility, are the key drivers in DEI's regional businesses. The company can be nimble and capture opportunities because business governance is local. Lines of communication are short, so decisions can be made quickly.

For example, when DEI still owned interests in Australia, a gas plant operated by another firm encountered a maintenance problem and had to be shut down. Within a few hours, a half-million-dollar deal had been signed with Duke Energy to supply replacement gas. Competitors could not get near Duke Energy's speed; it was the mindset under which the region operated and was one of its strengths.

IT Governance Is Based on Principles and Relationships

The regions also have pressures for synergy with Duke Energy International and among themselves. Principles play an important role in achieving synergy while maintaining agility. DEI's Information Management (IM) organization has principles for organizational and personal governance. Kennedy has espoused eight principles in managing IM:

1. Agree on the reason for being
2. Have a vision for IM
3. Put a clear organizational design in place
4. Implement successful IT governance
5. Implement demand management
6. Design useful reporting information flows
7. Manage business–IM value relationships
8. Implement global collaborative networks

As an example, part of the "Manage business–IM value relationship" principle is the guideline to establish multilevel relationships between IM and the business at different levels in the hierarchy. Such relationships are strong because more than one set of two people hold them together. This principle also is used to prepare top technical staff for their next job, which involves relationship management.

The regional CIOs follow Kennedy's three-point stewardship and escalation guidelines to help them answer the question, "When am I free to decide on my own versus when should I involve others?" The guidelines are:

- I involve others if the consequences of my actions will come to bear on those others.
- I do not involve others if the consequences of my actions will come to bear just on me.
- I inform others when the consequences of my actions will be of benefit to others.

In general, regional CIOs would prefer to use the U.S. IM solutions, which could be done about 70 percent of the time, to leverage the lower negotiated licensing prices and to tap their technical expertise. They would only differ when the cost was too high or the product did not have adequate support in the region.

In essence, DEI's IM organization aims to foster relationships with the business. Relationships increase nimbleness, help identify opportunities to save costs, and lead to innovation.

improving their business processes, and by offering new products and services. These innovations, in turn, increased productivity. Thus, notes Farrell, the "real" new economy has a virtuous circle: competition leads to innovation, which leads to productivity increases. See Figure 15.22.

As just one of many examples given by Farrell, the mobile telecommunications industry in France and Germany in the 1990s faced little government intervention, so there was intense competition among the national providers. Industry productivity increased 25 percent from 1990 to 2000. In the

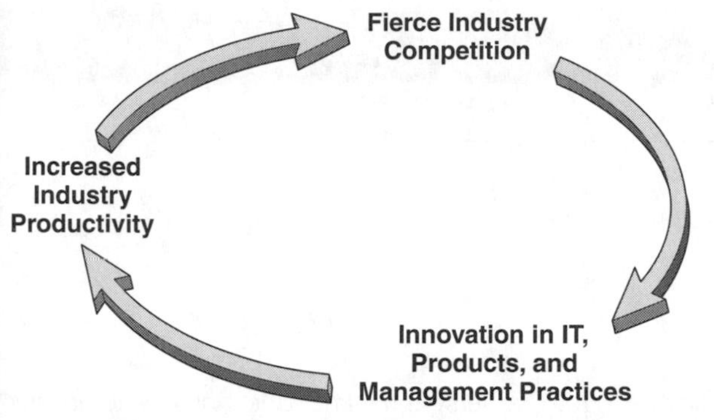

Figure 15.22 The Virtuous Circle of the "Real" News Economy. *Source:* Based on material from Diana Farrell. "The Real New Economy," *Harvard Business Review,* October 2003, pp. 105–112.

United States, on the other hand, regulation erected barriers to offering nationwide mobile telecommunications services, and productivity increased only 15 percent.

The McKinsey study also found that all IT investments were not alike. IT investments in industries that depended on information processing (such as large retailers that handled millions of transactions a day) and that faced growing competition had the greatest productivity increases—but only under three conditions:

1. The IT investments targeted the main levers of productivity,
2. The IT investments were made in the right sequence and at the right time, and
3. The IT investments were complemented with innovations in management practices.

Targeting IT investments. Firms that concentrated their IT spending on "levers that matter" gained the greatest productivity. Because productivity equals outputs divided by inputs, a lever either increases outputs (such as offering new higher-value services) or decreases inputs (such as reducing inventory or working capital). But the "levers that matter" differ among industries.

For example, the applications that mattered most for the big-box retailers, such as Wal-Mart, Kmart, and Target in the United States, that sell high volumes and have low margins were warehousing and transportation systems that more tightly linked them to their suppliers and increased the retailers' inventory turns. On the other hand, for specialty retailers whose items have short shelf lives, the applications that mattered the most dealt with assortment and allocation planning systems that reduced their inventory-holding costs and the amount of out-of-style merchandise in their stores. Concludes Farrell: Smart companies invest heavily in IT applications that increase productivity and seek the least expensive option for all their other IT systems.

Sequencing and timing IT investments. Companies that reaped the highest productivity generally sequenced their IT investments so that new ones built on existing ones. Wal-Mart and Kmart present contrasting examples, notes Farrell (see page 622).

Timing is also important, notes Farrell. The question is whether to lead or to follow IT trends. Based on her study, she recommends that companies rush into a new technology only when it advances company goals, builds on company strengths, and cannot be easily replicated by competitors. Jumping on a trend just because "everybody is doing it" signals that the new technology is not likely to provide enough differentiation to increase the company's standing against its competitors.

Complementing IT investments. IT investments do not reap anticipated results until accompanying management practices change to take advantage of potentially better ways of working. This lesson about the symbiotic relationship between IT and its use has been illustrated time and again for decades. And it's still true.

Farrell again uses Wal-Mart as an example. She notes that Wal-Mart simplified its logistics practices as it automated the flow of products to and from its distribution centers. It also redefined its relationships with suppliers when it was more tightly coordinating its information systems with theirs. The most famous shift was with Procter & Gamble and how it supplied Pampers baby diapers to Wal-Mart stores. The relationship shifted from an arms' length buyer–seller relationship to more of a trusted-partner one. The two shared confidential information, made decisions jointly, and reduced duplicate processes, thereby cutting inventory costs, improving efficiency, and better matching supply and demand.

In conclusion, Farrell believes that the reason the link between productivity and IT investments has not been easy to demonstrate is that it depends on three factors: investing in levers that matter, getting the investment sequence and timing right, and pairing new systems with new processes and work practices that take advantage of the new IT capabilities. Furthermore, IT is not the only contributor to increased productivity.

A Tactical View of Making IT Investments. In hindsight, it may be easy to see which IT investments were good and which were not so good. However, at the moment of decision, the choice may not be so clear because of the complex and volatile nature of business. The recent approach to making IT investments is to view all company

CASE EXAMPLE

WAL-MART VERSUS KMART

The sequence of IT investments at Wal-Mart and Kmart offer one example of the effect of getting the sequence right, notes Diana Farrell of McKinsey Global Institute.

In the 1990s, Wal-Mart first installed systems to automate the flow of products in its internal supply chain—from suppliers to its distribution centers and warehouses. Once this internal flow was being well-managed, Wal-Mart turned outward to its suppliers to more closely coordinate its own operations with theirs in hopes of improving effectiveness and reducing costs. With the flow along its supply chain as a base, Wal-Mart again turned to its customers, using IT to better plan its merchandising mix and replenishment. Last, it built a data warehouse, pulling data from these systems and other sources, to answer complex questions to hone operations. During the 1990s, Wal-Mart's productivity increased.

Kmart, on the other hand, did not get the sequence of IT investments right in the 1990s, says Farrell. As a result, its productivity decreased. Kmart first used IT to better target its marketing promotions rather than investing in supply chain systems to manage fluctuations in product volume. As a result, increases in customer demand from its successful promotions could not be met because Kmart could not get enough of the products into its stores. Demand was higher than supply. Kmart lost potential sales.

systems as a portfolio and to make investment decisions from that viewpoint, rather than judging each investment only on its own merits. Investment guidelines, such as those provided by Farrell, can then be used in the decision making.

There are numerous approaches for prioritizing projects. On pages 623–625 is one example, as used by AXA Financial.

Sy Aslan has helped numerous clients in strategic planning, decision making, and IT project prioritization—including clients of UMT. When people talk about prioritizing IT projects, Aslan says the process is really about team decision making; prioritization is just one aspect. He offers the following lessons he has learned over the years in this area.

Realize That the Benefits Come More from the Discussions Than the Prioritizations. A team-based approach to prioritizing projects offers numerous benefits. The foremost benefit is the business-based discussions that take place as people describe their needs and their projects, debate how projects support the business and the extent of that support, and explain the rationale behind their votes.

When the discussions are structured, focused, and well moderated, the participants better understand the business goals, better support others and other business units, and are more committed to the selected portfolio of projects, says Aslan.

Discussions during prioritization lead to healthier teamwork and better decision processes, both of which reduce political maneuvering and simplify future project reviews. The discussions also generate new ideas, surface incorrect assumptions, and create an environment for in-depth discussions of the organization's mission and goals.

Discussions also lead to better definitions of projects (and even company strategies) and to deeper understanding of the insides of projects. They bring to light what is not needed and crystallize how each project supports specific business needs, if indeed they do.

After a prioritization discussion, the participants can identify which projects can be delayed and how dependent projects are on one another. Discussion also saves time and reduces the amount of noise in prioritization. Low-value and questionable projects are no longer submitted to the group for approval because people know others will scrutinize the submissions.

Put Projects into Categories Where They Are Comparable. Once projects have been defined it becomes clear that they belong in different categories and thus require different treatment, says Aslan. One category is *R&D*. These projects cannot produce immediate tangible

CASE EXAMPLE

AXA FINANCIAL

The AXA Group is a global financial services organization with 140,000 employees and headquarters in France. Some 10,000 employees work in the United States at AXA Financial. Its retail businesses include AXA Advisors, LLC; The Equitable Life Assurance Society of the U.S.; Alliance Capital Management; and Sanford C. Bernstein & Co. Its wholesale division (AXA Distributors, LLC) works with brokerage houses, large banks, and independent financial planners that sell Equitable Life products through their own channels. As of June 30, 2002, AXA Financial had approximately $441 billion in assets under management, and its IT group employed 650 people.

Paul Bateman leads the enterprise governance process, which resides within the IT organization yet spans AXA Financial. He spends about half his time working with the business units. He was hired to manage AXA Financial's IT portfolio. Prior to his hire, senior management believed IT provided competitive differentiation and made so many significant investments in IT infrastructure and applications that the company needed to get more control of its growing portfolio. In 2000, some 200 high-priced, significant projects were in development.

Bateman introduced a governance process to instill more efficient management controls. A key principle of the process is that all projects and investments are *not* created equal. Each one's merit depends on its economics, not on an executive's emotional attachment to it or other nonfinancial factors. This new governance process has brought discipline and a way to value projects.

Introducing a New Methodology

Bateman first undid the level playing field by introducing a methodology to help AXA Financial executives define a hierarchy of importance and prioritize projects against that hierarchy. He called on the people at United Management Technologies (UMT) to demonstrate their portfolio prioritization methodology. He had been exposed to it while at Citigroup and found that UMT had since increased the methodology's functionality, making it best in class. He proposed it to senior management, and they agreed to bring the methodology into AXA Financial.

To begin acquainting the company with the new governance model, Bateman held a series of kick-off meetings with the CFO from each area, including retail and wholesale sales, marketing and product development, service delivery, and IT. Needless to say, they were pleased with the financial emphasis of the approach.

Then he introduced it to the executive vice presidents (EVPs)—the business-unit heads—explaining the need to begin managing the portfolio of major IT projects the way fund managers manage their portfolios. Once the EVPs agreed with the concept, Bateman described the UMT tools that could help.

The top-level project review committee is the governance committee, which is cochaired by the company's CEO and CIO. It also includes the CFO and the EVPs. By representing all the lines of business, the committee ensures that approved projects benefit the entire company. This committee helped develop the governance model, which initially was called *IT governance*, but has since become *enterprise governance*, because the process is now used to prioritize more than IT projects.

The Prioritization Process

The process begins each year with the EVPs turning in their wish lists of all projects they would like for the coming year, as if they had an unlimited checkbook. Last year, the lists totaled close to 300 projects.

Winnowing the Wish List. Next, the EVPs are asked to split those projects into three categories: must-have (or else AXA Financial would incur revenue or operational risks), should-have, and nice-to-have. Taking out the nice-to-haves still left over 170 projects.

Selecting Business Objectives. To reduce the 170, AXA used the UMT methodology, which begins by having the enterprise state the objectives upon which the projects will be judged. Although the CEO has set out an AXA Financial-wide vision and goals, the business units are too diverse for a single list of objectives. Therefore, each business unit developed its own objectives with the CEO's strategic goals in mind. Bateman and UMT assisted each business unit to arrive at four to six measurable objectives (such as increase customer satisfaction) that could be tracked and that aligned with the CEO's strategic direction.

Prioritizing the Objectives. Each business unit, led by the EVP and including his or her direct reports, then ranked the

(Case continued)

(Case continued)

objectives using UMT's pair-wise methodology. One at a time, the business unit decided how one objective compared with each other objective on a scale of importance. They had seven choices: extremely more important, strongly more important, moderately more important, of equal importance, moderately less important, strongly less important, or extremely less important.

As each decision was made, a color-coded choice was recorded by a facilitator on a matrix displayed on a large screen in front of the group. The side benefit of this ranking exercise was the business discussion it elicited among department members. Executives' assumptions and rationale for their decisions often surfaced when they debated how much more or less important, say, *increasing customer satisfaction* was compared with *increasing market share*. The pairwise comparison approach made it easy to debate two objectives solely on their own merit. The model took care of the final overall ranking among the objectives.

Ranking Projects Using the Objectives. Given this list of prioritized objectives, the committee moved on to ranking each project against how much that project supported each objective—extremely supports, strongly supports, moderately supports, low support, or no support.

There were several keys to performing this step confidently. One key was understanding what, say, *strongly supports* meant. Some business units quantified each level of support beforehand to vote from a level playing field.

Another key to success was each staff member's understanding of each project well enough to make these decisions, which meant having well-defined and consistently defined projects.

A third key was not having too many projects and too many objectives, or else the ranking process would take too long.

As in the objective-ranking meeting, a major benefit of this project-ranking meeting was the personal revelations that surfaced when members explained why they voted that a project *strongly supports* an objective, whereas others voted that the same project provided *low support*. When done well, these discussions yielded both insights and a group consensus. A high comfort level emerged with the results.

Following these two rankings, each EVP had a prioritized list to present to the enterprise governance committee. By this time, the total number of projects had been culled from the over 170 to approximately 70. One by one, the EVPs defended their own list, explaining why each project was included. The committee then decided which ones would advance to the funding phase.

Funding the Projects. To help the governance committee decide which projects would be funded, a business case application was then filled out for each one. The application asked for financial projections for the current year plus 5 more. Financial calculations for net present value, rate of return, cash flow, and payback period were then determined using the business case application.

Of course, not all projects are alike. For those that aim to produce income, the committee focuses on payback period. For those that will implement infrastructure improvements, the committee looks at operational efficiencies to be gained or extenuating circumstances (such as the vendor no longer supporting a system).

Thus, the process uses four filters: the EVP's wish list filter, the must-have/should-have filter, the UMT prioritization filter, and the business case filter. The result is a list of projects that *can* be funded.

Throughout the year, the governance committee meets two to three times a month for 2 hours. It reviews the launch dates for new products and works backward to determine when the support mechanisms, such as the underlying IT system, need to be in place.

Projects costing over $250,000 require the full 5-year analysis and approval of the governance committee. Projects requiring less funding need a mini-business case; these are reviewed monthly by the governance committee to ensure that they are strategically linked to company goals. The EVPs have learned to do their own filtering of projects, only taking the ones they know will pass muster at the governance committee meetings.

AXA Financial then uses ProSight portfolio management software to manage its portfolio of ongoing projects. The plan is for the governance committee to begin reviewing this data to keep tabs on the progress of projects, as well as their budgets.

Benefits of the Project Prioritization Process

The UMT-based process provides the enterprise governance committee with a panoramic view of the business, thus discussions of IT projects no long center around budgets. Rather, they center around business strategy, such as looking at the cross-functional nature of a product and how it fits on the road map laid out by the CEO. The attendees benefit from these discussions because they have both a view and a say in that future. Knowing the pending projects in the other areas has significantly increased cross-functional communications. Bateman acts as the secretary for the meeting, recording what has been approved and listing follow-up items. "It is a disciplined way of helping AXA Financial manage its future," he notes.

Another benefit is that approved projects are no longer questioned because they have the blessing of the CEO. The group discussions that precede the approvals also create a powerful group-concurrence effect.

Now that AXA Financial has been using the UMT methodology and the ProSight monitoring software for 2 years, it is turning its attention to comparing planned benefits to actual benefits because it is beginning to receive actual performance numbers. Bateman is working to refine the estimation techniques so that they are more accurate. Furthermore, once a project has been implemented, its projected savings are being taken out of the appropriate budgets by the CFOs.

This enterprise governance structure is now seen as a best practice throughout the AXA Group. It is now being introduced to and adapted by some of AXA's European and Canadian operations.

Future Plans

Due to the success of the enterprise governance process in funding and tracking new projects, Bateman is always looking at ways to expand the use of governance tools to other areas of the business. The ongoing goal is to continually search for ways to increase the value of money spent. AXA Financial has started a zero-based budgeting process (based on activity-based costing) where each business looks at the activities it performs each day and calculates the number of people and the time spent on each activity.

As an example, they could then potentially integrate the discipline of a zero-based budgeting process with the UMT prioritization tool. This approach would give the company a new way to see options to further increase the value of investments.

Another way to improve value throughout the IT organization is to ensure that project proposals list, say, two or three options. For instance, one option could be to deliver 80 percent of the functionality the first year for $1 million; the other option could be to deliver 100 percent in 1 year for $2 million. Options would yield better business cases and save the company money. In the past 2 years, the enterprise governance process has deferred approximately $20 million in expenses. The business cases showed the money would have been poorly spent. Bateman and his team are looking at ways to improve the governance process further, to help ensure that the governance committee is making informed investment decisions in support of future growth.

benefits. Furthermore, there is no certainty they will yield any value in the future. These projects should only compete with each other for some percent of the IT budget.

On the other end of the scale is the *volume* category. Volume projects are sure things. For example, when a business unit experiences increased demand, it may need to invest in more IT volume to capture the revenue from that demand. Because these projects support sure growth and have a secure return on investment (ROI), they should not compete with any other project. All that is needed is the assurance of the capacity planning people that the underlying computer system has indeed reached its capacity limit and the investment and action plan are sound.

Finally, it is also wise to have a minimum consideration level, for example, $25,000. Managers should be able to finance projects below that threshold from their discretionary budget. However, these projects should be reviewed by a higher-level sponsor and project outcomes should be part of the manager's performance evaluation.

Address Project Risks. Project managers should address three types of risk in their proposals:

- Risk that the project will fail
- Risk of not doing the project
- Risk that it is the wrong project for what is trying to be achieved

Every project carries with it a *risk of failure*. This risk can range from total failure to failure to yield some of the expected benefits. To properly prioritize projects, they all need to be at the same risk level and have the same probability of success. To evaluate risk of failure, project managers should be able to document answers to at least these four questions:

1. What is the probability the project will be completed on time?
2. Will it be completed within budget?
3. Could it be impacted by an internal issue (over which the company has control)?
4. Could it be impacted by an external issue (over which the company has little or no control)?

When a project has a higher risk than is defined as acceptable by the selection process, the project manager should identify mitigation methods, calculate the cost of the risk, and add that cost to the project, says Aslan.

The second type of risk is *not doing the project*. Here, people need to consider the reason for the project and the problems it will prevent once it is up and running, says

Aslan. For example, a project that will introduce virus protection across the network will prevent virus damage. Consider the project as insurance against this damage and use simple actuarial methods to calculate the value of such insurance (probability of the damaging event multiplied by the cost if the event does occur). The calculated insurance value should be added to the project benefits.

The third risk is *doing the wrong thing*. Three examples are introducing a technology that will be quickly replaced by a superior one, supporting a temporary market trend, and developing a system for a process that is not effective or efficient. These projects may be successful, but they will be deemed useless very quickly.

The best mitigation approach for this risk goes back to the basic tenet of project prioritization: team discussion. The team needs to surface the assumptions that support the project and then play scenario games: Create three scenarios about the business and the project's future. Make one scenario a disaster, the second rosy, and the third an extension of the team's pessimism or optimism by a few degrees. Then have the team ask itself, "What effect will this project have in each scenario?" The ensuing discussion will expose holes in thinking and offer mending approaches. The project may be cancelled, divided into phases, consolidated with another, or recreated in a different version.

The prioritization process takes into consideration costs and benefits. In essence, reviewing the risk is the response to the financial manager saying, "I need proof that this project will achieve its benefits within the stated budget."

Prioritize Quarterly and Apportion Your Budget Accordingly. In our constantly changing business world, it is not wise to close the list of approved projects for a long period of time. New project requirements arise frequently, and some of these projects may be more important than others already approved. Also, in most cases, the constraints for undertaking projects are not only budgetary, but also people resources and possibly dependencies and timing. If a prioritization team starts the year allocating its entire annual budget, it may find little leeway for change during the year. People will hold onto their budget allocation as if it were an entitlement.

A quarterly prioritization provides more agility. The first option is to allocate part of the budget as reserve to be allocated at a later time. For example, allocate two-thirds of the budget in the first quarter and save the remainder for the following quarters. Another option is to state that any project that gains approval but does not start in the quarter automatically goes into the next quarter's evaluation—and so does its allocation. People are happy with this approach, says Aslan, because they know they always have a chance to introduce a new project or reexamine a rejected one. The options are not exclusive. Any combination or variation that allows the team to be flexible in the face of change is a good process.

Once a project starts, it should be tracked by the project life cycle monitoring system. If costs change, say, more than 10 percent, that increase should trigger a reconsideration of the project's cost, risks, and benefits. In doing so, the team should only consider the benefits against what is yet to be spent, even if lots of money has already been poured into the project, because the value of the entire project rests on that unspent portion.

Be Consistent. The main hindrance to team decision making is lack of consistency. To an individual team member, a group decision-making process seems cumbersome. Individuals have a tendency to find shortcuts and change the process on the run. When a new prioritization process is introduced, people become disenchanted. They do not want to learn the new approach; they secretly revolt and revert to their own old method, which contributes to even more inconsistency.

It is important to have a consistent process and an agreed-upon method for changing the prioritization process. Surprisingly, one of the hardest things to keep consistent is the project definition, says Aslan. Without such consistency, it is difficult to compare projects. To achieve consistency, it is important to introduce principles, such as, "a project should be completed within 18 months." Such rules should not be hindrances, but breaking them should require a valid reason.

Consistency comes from understanding the team decision-making process. People need to realize that the process is a balancing act. There is no black and white. For example, they need to see they can either move quickly or scrutinize the details, but not both. If people do not understand how to balance the two, they act as a pendulum. They opt for speed, but fail, so they revert to scrutiny, even when it is not necessary. When they fail again, they go back to speed. The team needs to learn how to balance speed and scrutiny, says Aslan.

Consistency requires patience. Avoid shortcuts. Ensure that the details are well thought-out, recommends Aslan. Some team members will become impatient with the discussion of small, but important points, such as possible future resource conflicts. They need to realize that the value of prioritization comes in such discussions. A well-facilitated session will maximize the team's patience and the discussion value.

Managing: Establishing Credibility and Fostering Change

CIOs are in the change business. Information systems bring about change. But before a CIO and the IS organization will be heard as a voice for change, they must be viewed as being successful and reliable. To foster change, a CIO must establish and then maintain the credibility of the IS organization.

Establishing Credibility. Management consultant Joseph Izzo believes that IS organizations have two missions: to maintain today's systems and to work on tomorrow's systems. These two missions have distinctly different goals and therefore need to be managed separately and specifically. The "today" operation should concentrate on providing service, says Izzo, whereas the "tomorrow" operation needs to focus on helping the business operate better. The first job of IS management is to get the "today" operation in shape. Until that task is accomplished, CIOs will have little credibility with top management.

Managing the "today" organization better. The "today" organization includes computer operations, technical support (including network support), the help desk, and the maintenance and enhancement of existing applications. Because their main mission is service, the service levels of these various operations need to be measured and used to manage them.

To run the "today" operation, Izzo suggests hiring managers for each of these functions who are like supervisors—that is, they are delivery-oriented and demand a high level of service from their people.

An increasing number of companies outsource these IT support functions to companies that specialize in this work. This outsourcing releases in-house staff for higher-value work, generally reduces costs, and should result in gradually increasing levels of service. But reaping these benefits requires negotiating good contracts and managing the suppliers.

Once the "today" organization is in shape, then IS management has the credibility to be heard when talks about the need to change business practices to take advantage of a potential new system.

Fostering Change. IS staff members are often so enthralled with the technical aspects of a new system that they presume a technically elegant system is a successful system. Not so. Many technically sound systems have turned into implementation failures because the people side of the system was not handled correctly. In essence, IT is all about managing change. New systems require changing how work is done. Focusing only on the technical aspects is only half the job. The other job is change management.

Change management is the process of assisting people to make major changes in their working environment. In this case, the change is caused by the introduction of a new computer system. Management of change has not always been handled methodically; thus, choosing a change management methodology and using it is a step toward successfully introducing new computer systems.

Change disrupts peoples' frame of reference if it presents a future where past experiences do not hold true, says ODR, a change management firm in Atlanta, Georgia. People resist change, especially technological change, when they view it as a crisis. They cope by trying to maintain control. In the case of an impending new computer system, which they do not understand fully or are not prepared to handle, they may react in several ways. They may deny the change; they may distort information they hear about it; or they may try to convince themselves, and others, that the new system really will not change the status quo. These reactions are forms of resistance.

ODR offers a methodology to help companies manage technological change. They use specific terms from the field of organizational development to describe the types of people involved in a change project.

- The *sponsor* is the person or group that legitimizes the change. In most cases, this group must contain someone in top management who is highly respected by the business unit because change must be driven from the business unit.
- The *change agent* is the person or group who causes the change to happen. Change agents are often the IS staff. They can introduce the change, but they cannot enforce its use.
- The *target* is the person or group who is being expected to change and at whom the change is aimed.

Using surveys completed by a project's sponsors, change agents, and targets, ODR aims to:

- Describe the *scope* of the change
- Assess the *sponsors'* commitment to the project
- Assess the *change agents'* skills
- Evaluate the support or resistance of the *targets*

By evaluating each area, the change agents can determine (1) whether the scope of the project is doable, or whether the organization is trying to change too much at one time, (2) whether the sponsors are committed enough to push the change through, or whether they are sitting back expecting the organization to change on its own,

(3) whether the change agents have the skills to implement the change, or whether they are not adept at rallying support, and (4) which groups are receptive to the change and which are resistant. Once these assessments have been made, ODR assists IS project teams to understand the risks their projects face and identify what they can do to mitigate those risks.

Working Across Organizational Lines. CIOs now find that the systems they implement affect people outside their firm. The interconnectedness permitted by the Internet, and the desire of supply-chain members to increase their supply-chain efficiency, is pulling some CIOs to working as much with these external members of their supply chain as with their own internal people.

On the supplier side, companies and IS organizations alike are rationalizing their supplier base, depending on fewer, deeper relationships. This trend is causing CIOs to work more closely with suppliers' executives to whom they outsource their help desk, PC acquisition–maintenance–disposal, data center, network management, and other functions. The result is more disclosure of future plans, more joint planning, more joint working, and so forth. Some suppliers are treated more as partners than suppliers. This trend has opened up the need for vendor relationship management techniques.

On the customer side, CIOs are being increasingly called upon to describe the company's IT-enabled vision to customer executives to get their buy-in to building inter-business systems. When dealing with suppliers and customers, CIOs and others on the executive team all become involved in fostering change. Here is an example of a CIO who is working with his peers on his firm's executive team to manage change not only in their own company, but at customer companies as well. It is based on the Gartner EXP report, *Managing Your Stakeholders*, written by Andrew Rowsell-Jones, et al (see pages 629–630).

The Rexam case illustrates a number of points about CIOs' current role. One, CIOs are working outside as much as inside these days. Two, they are working in concert with their peers in the company in selling and implementing their visions. Three, to stay ahead, CIOs need to keep their staffs experimenting with new technologies. Four, selling the vision occurs one customer, supplier, or executive at a time. This means CIOs, and others, need to assess how IT-ready a customer, supplier, executive, department, or group is.

The Office of the CIO?

Darwin John, former CIO of the U.S. Federal Bureau of Investigation, Scott Paper, and the Mormon Church, believes that the work of CIOs has become so broad and complex that it should by handled by a team—an office of the CIO—rather than an individual.

When he was CIO, John says he divided his time into thirds: one-third managing the IS organization, one-third working with peers to manage the enterprise, and one-third networking with people outside the enterprise. Today, he says, there are just not enough thirds to go around, because every function has become dependent on IT. Furthermore, CIOs must bring in and integrate new technologies and be highly involved in business planning, because they are part of top management.

One way to divide the job, notes John, is to have an office of the CIO with four positions:

- **Chief information officer (CIO).** This executive heads IS and works with top management, customers, and suppliers.
- **Chief technology officer (CTO).** This executive heads IT planning, which involves architecture and exploration of new technologies.
- **Chief operations officer (COO).** This executive heads day-to-day IS operations.
- **Chief project officer (CPO).** This executive oversees all projects and project managers.

An alternative two-way split is to have co-CIOs, with one focusing on all things external to the IS organization (such as planning and relationships with the business, customers, and suppliers) and the other focusing on all things internal (such as operations and projects).

With IT so crucial to enterprise success, and the know-how needed to run it so deep and so wide, management needs to become a team effort. A few firms have created such an office of the CIO; others have created such a team without designating it as "the office of the CIO."

Whither CIOs?

Neil Fligstein, a sociologist at the University of California at Berkeley, makes an interesting observation about the possible future importance of CIOs by looking at history. He notes that different periods of recent history have seen executives with different backgrounds "running the show," depending on the corporate growth driver at the time:

- *Manufacturing.* In the early 1900s, manufacturing was the growth driver, thus manufacturing executives often rose to became CEO.
- *Sales and marketing.* In the 1930s through the 1950s, growth came through sales. By 1959, nearly 25 percent of the top American corporations had

CASE EXAMPLE

REXAM

Rexam PLC is one of the world's top five consumer packaging companies and the world's top beverage can maker. Rexam Beverage Can Americas, which covers all the Americas, has sales of $1.6 billion and only 2,500 employees. Globally, Rexam has sales of $4.5 billion and only 20,000 employees.

The beverage can business is over 100 years old, and the business processes in the industry have been mostly based on lowest cost. To invest in new business processes takes a strong business case. Some processes have been automated, yet many remain manual.

Rethinking Interactions with Customers

Three years ago, Paul Martin joined Rexam as CIO of Rexam Beverage Can Americas. When he visited the plants to see how the company did business, he found that most orders were received by phone or fax, keyed into spreadsheets, held for days in anticipation of changes, and then faxed to a plant near the customer, where they were rekeyed into back-office systems. The result: multiple chances for errors and shipments of the wrong products to customers.

"There's a way to leverage the Internet here," Martin told others. Their response, "Our customers will never interact with us via the Internet, or place an order online. You will hit a brick wall." Martin's reply, "If we can demonstrate the value to them, they will." He set about proving his point.

Phase 1: CRM Made Simple

"Our goal is to entangle our customers with e-technology, which means, we will deliver incredible value by creating an environment that delivers such exceptional service that our customers will think twice about leaving Rexam for a lower price," said Martin.

Rather than invest in a large customer relationship management (CRM) system, Martin's staff and some consultants built a platform and some applications based on feedback from Rexam's sales group and customers. The system includes online ordering via the Internet and captures customer feedback about quality problems. It also provides customers with a range of reports and business intelligence tools to slice and dice the data in many ways. The system also introduced invoice reporting and put accounts receivable online to reduce billing errors and to expedite payment to Rexam. Every day Rexam can reduce Days Sales Outstanding, its cash flow improves by $4 million. That is a big impact.

The system benefits customers as well. They can inquire about invoice information online—the bill of lading number, filling location, plant making the cans, and so forth. They no longer need to call Rexam's accounts receivable group for this information. Furthermore, when an online order is changed, the system automatically notifies the customer about the change, so both parties stay more in sync. The parties interact more, but the complexity of these interactions is hidden in the system, offloading it from the employees on both sides.

Testing the System with Customers

To test the value of the system to customers, Rexam approached its largest beverage can customer. The director of procurement saw the potential value, so he said, "Let's test it in one bottling location that rarely changes its orders."

After the 3-month test, the bottler's response was highly positive. The system did indeed eliminate faxes and phone calls to Rexam, which was a huge plus, and the bottler could get needed information in real time.

The customer wanted more. In an e-mail, the procurement officer wrote, "I've got some feedback for you. We see benefits, . . . and we'd like some additional features. We'd like to see shipment history for 3 months because that will help our internal forecasting."

In response, Rexam gave them 12 months of shipping history to use in reviewing orders and pull patterns. The customer rolled out the system to 27 U.S. bottling locations the first year, standardizing the ordering system. Rexam has entangled this customer with e-technology in both interactions between the two firms and in assisting the customer with its internal operations.

Phase 2: Knock Customers' Socks Off

The goal in phase 2 is: Knock their socks off, meaning, impress customers so much that they will not leave Rexam. This phase involves redefining "world-class" for the beverage can industry. In part, it involves implementing SAP, reengineering Rexam

(Case continued)

(Case continued)

processes, and using mySAP to create customer portals to leverage the ordering system and permit collaborative online forecasting. This prospect excites customers, because they have learned that Rexam knows more about some aspects of their business than they do. As a service for its customers, Rexam keeps customers' packaging inventory. Rexam's goal is to reduce these inventories through the collaborative forecasting and scheduling system.

Rexam also plans to design new can labels online so that customers can see the artwork in 3D–a significant advance from the digital pictures they now receive via e-mail.

Finally, the CRM system contains pictures and contact information of its employees. In the future, Martin's group will ask customers if they would like PC-based video conferencing. If so, it will install a small video camera on their PCS. By clicking on a Rexam employee's picture, the system dials that person to initiate video conferencing–all part of Rexam's goal to "knock their socks off."

The CIO's Role

Complexity in Martin's job now comes from Rexam's suppliers and customers more than from its employees. Martin spends as much time giving presentations to these stakeholders as he does to Rexam employees. The key to gaining their buy-in is the value Rexam brings to them. He demonstrates the value of online ordering using the Internet and interlinking systems.

He is able to spend this much time externally because his IS director has taken over management of key development efforts. "This frees me up to do what the CEO wants me to focus on: strategy and getting our external relationships under control," says Martin.

The beverage can market has flat growth, just 1 to 2 percent a year. Generally, the only way to improve margins is to cut costs. However, last year prices increased for the first time in 25 years. In renegotiating contracts this year, the vice president of sales is adding a new clause to the contracts to leverage the firm's innovative e-business and SAP work. In essence, the clause states, "if we (Rexam) deliver exceptional value in innovation, Six Sigma, and e-business, we can come back to you to collect additional fees."

Obviously, customers have been asking what this new clause means. In response, Martin visits these customers and gives them a presentation about what Rexam is doing in these areas and the potential benefits to them. "The CEO sees me as a business person. These are not IT projects; these are company projects. It's my job to translate our systems solutions to their business problems," says Martin.

The Steering Committee's Role

When Martin presented the $11-million business case for the SAP and e-business initiatives, the CEO asked, "How long will this take to deliver?" The answer: 3 years. "I need it in 18 months," replied the CEO, "It's very important to our strategy. We need this foundation in place."

To meet that aggressive schedule, the work has been guided by the executive steering committee, made up of the CEO, CFO, CIO, and heads of operations, supply chain, and sales. It meets every other week for an hour, not to prioritize projects (everyone agreed on those), but to guide implementation, resolve roadblocks, validate new business process designs, and spur progress. None of the members, including the CEO, has missed a meeting.

The committee first defined Rexam's future state so they would all be "reading from the same page." They have since focused on the vision and achieving behavioral change. "We are transforming our internal business processes and the way customers and suppliers interact with us," notes Martin. "Everyone on the executive team understands the impact of these changes on their own organization. So we divvy up the work. We have all put in the plans and procedures to be ready for the new systems." The executive committee's role has been to lay out the game plan. Phase 2 has been simplified tremendously by the committee members agreeing on the agenda.

former sales and marketing executives as CEOs, notes Fligstein.

- *Finance.* In the 1970s and 1980s, the large corporations consisted of portfolios of businesses and were best managed by executives who knew how to manage portfolios: chief financial officers (CFOs). They bought and sold businesses like you would buy and sell stock, to get the highest return.
- *Information technology.* The financial scandals in the late 1990s and early 2000s, though, have hurt CFOs' reputations. Furthermore, given the revolutionary effects IT is having on the world, perhaps CIOs now have the most appropriate background to be future CEOs, says Fligstein. It's an open question at the moment.

PROJECT MANAGEMENT

Today, much organizational work is performed via projects. In IS as well as other functions, being able to manage a project to completion, and deliver the expected outcome within the allotted time and budget, has become an increasingly valuable skill. This section explores six aspects of project management:

1. What is project management?
2. The job of a project manager
3. A day in the life of an IT project manager
4. Change management (an area IS teams have not always handled well)
5. Risk management (another area IS teams have not always handled well)
6. Some tips for good IT project management

What Is Project Management?

Project management is simply the management of a project, notes Michael Matthew of Matthew & Matthew consulting firm. This definition may sound simple and self-evident, but that does not make it easy. Many people get confused or concerned about IT project management because it involves the "T" word: *technology*. In reality, IT project management is not much different from other forms of project management, such as those used to construct an office building or a bridge.

A *project* is a collection of related tasks and activities undertaken to achieve a specific goal.Thus, all projects (IT or otherwise) should:

- Have a clearly stated goal
- Be *finite*, that is, have a clearly defined beginning and end

It has been said that IT project management is 10 percent technical and 90 percent common sense or good business practice. Indeed, many of the best IT managers do not have a background in IT at all, but they possess the important skills of communication, organization, and motivation. Perhaps the most difficult component of IT project management is keeping in mind, and under control, all the interdependencies of the numerous tasks being undertaken.

"A *project* is a temporary endeavor undertaken to achieve a particular aim and to which project management can be applied, regardless of the project's size, budget, or timeline," states the Project Management Institute (PMI). *Project management* is "the application of knowledge, skills, tools, and techniques to project activities to meet project requirements," states PMI's 2000 edition of *A Guide to the Project Management Body of Knowledge* (PMBOK, 2000 Edition).

PMI, which was founded in 1969 in Philadelphia, Pennsylvania, has established the standard for project management and is the leading association in educating project managers in all fields, including IT. It has some 125,000 members in 240 countries and over 10,000 Project Management Professionals (PMPs) who have passed its rigorous set of tests and been certified as PMPs. PMI views project management as encompassing five processes (initiating, planning, executing, controlling, and closing) and nine knowledge areas. To become a certified PMP, a person must pass tests covering all nine knowledge areas:

1. *Integration*, which involves ensuring that the various elements of a project are properly coordinated
2. *Scope*, ensuring that the project includes all the work required, and only the work required
3. *Time*, ensuring timely completion of the project
4. *Cost*, ensuring that the project is completed within the approved budget
5. *Quality*, ensuring that the project satisfies the needs for which it was undertaken
6. *Human resources*, making the most effective use of the people involved
7. *Communication*, ensuring timely and appropriate generation, collection, dissemination, storage, and disposition of project information
8. *Risk*, identifying, analyzing, and responding to project risks
9. *Procurement*, acquiring goods and services

To explore project management in a bit more detail, here is one view of the job of a project manager.

The Job of a Project Manager

Project management was once viewed as a specialty, with roots in construction, engineering, and IT, note Craig Anderson, a practice leader in KPMG's Queensland, Australia, office, and Michael Matthew, a partner in Matthew & Matthew in Sydney, Australia. But now, business managers need project management skills to implement change in a disciplined and successful manner. Business project management is evolving from IT project management. Both IT and business project managers are responsible for the following tasks:

- Setting up the project
- Managing the schedule
- Managing the finances
- Managing the benefits

- Managing the risks, opportunities, and issues
- Soliciting independent reviews

Setting Up the Project. Each project needs a project charter or document to serve as the one source of truth for the project and the first point of call when there are differences of opinion in the project, note Anderson and Matthew. It should spell out the following:

- ***Why.*** A brief background of the project (i.e., the result of a strategic review) and the business objectives to be achieved.
- ***What.*** A description of the non-financial benefits to flow from the project and a list of the key outputs to be produced.
- ***When.*** A list of the milestones and expected timing (a high-level project plan).
- ***Who.*** A definition of the project team and an analysis of the stakeholders of the project and their expectations.
- ***How.*** A definition of the work that needs to be undertaken to achieve the project, its scope, and specific exclusions.This definition also needs to address how much the project is expected to cost (a detailed financial breakdown) and expected benefit.

Risks, opportunities, prerequisites, assumptions, and the communications plan also should be included.Then this document needs to be approved.

Managing the Schedule. The schedule or project plan is the heart of a project because it communicates the activities that need to be completed to achieve the benefits, when they need to be completed, and who needs to complete them. First develop a high-level plan of the entire project. Next, break down the business objectives into deliverables and then into the pieces of work to produce these deliverables (and the time required). Do not plan the details of the entire project at the outset, recommend Anderson and Matthew, because that is too difficult and the project will change. Instead, plan the details of a stage at its outset based on the work completed and the deliverables yet to be achieved.

Then baseline the schedule, affixing a starting point so that you can gauge progress.Tracking is essential for anticipating completion and taking corrective actions when issues arise. Many automated tools are available to help project managers manage the schedule.

Anderson and Matthew make four recommendations on managing the schedule. One, focus on the date that tasks are completed rather than the percentage of the overall project that has been completed.Two, review progress at least monthly, preferably weekly or fortnightly for shorter projects.Three, focus on tasks to be completed, not those that have been finished. And four, reforecast when new evidence comes to light.

Managing the Finances. At its most basic level, the financial plan describes the project's costs, who is accountable for them, the expected financial benefits from the project, and the cash flow. These projections flow from the project plan and are determined by the resources committed to the project, when these resources are committed, and external costs, such as contractors or general expenses.

The greatest areas of contention in most projects are project costs and benefits. Whereas outsiders may focus on deliverables, insiders will focus on financials. Just as with the project plan, once authorizations have been obtained, it is a good idea to baseline the costs and track them as you do the project plan, recommend Anderson and Matthew, because the approved figures are only estimates. They will change over time. As the project manager, you will need to know how much has been spent and how much money is left.

Managing the Benefits. Four benefits can emerge from IT and business projects: profitability, cost reduction, changes to working capital, or adherence to legal or regulatory reform. Benefits are much more difficult to estimate than costs. Anderson and Matthew offer four suggestions for managing benefits. One, be realistic (most people overestimate benefits). Two, make sure the benefits are greater than the estimated costs. Three, base costs and benefits on the same assumptions. And four, forecast for various scenarios.

It also is important to forecast the timing of benefits. Discounted cash flow is one technique to compare the timing of benefits and costs. And again, a project manager should track benefits throughout the life of the project by asking, "Why are we doing this?" The answer might need to change if the business environment changes, as often happens in long-term projects.

Managing Risks, Opportunities, and Issues. Every project encounters the following:

- ***Risk.*** A potential threat that may prevent the project from achieving its business benefits
- ***Opportunity.*** A project going better than planned
- ***Issue.*** Something that threatens the success of the project

All possible risks and opportunities should be listed at the project outset and then analyzed to determine each one's likelihood and impact. Risk mitigators for high risks need to be built into the project plan. Likewise, major opportunities need to be built into the plan to maximize potential benefits. Both risks and opportunities need to be monitored.

Ongoing monitoring of risks and opportunities is one of the weakest areas of project management, note Anderson and Matthew. A good project manager continuously monitors the risks and opportunities along with the schedule, costs, and benefits. One of the most effective tools for monitoring risks and opportunities is a risk log.

Likewise, issues management is an ongoing task. Once an issue is identified by a project team member, it should follow a standard resolution process, recommend Anderson and Matthew. An issue should be brought to the project manager's attention, its impact assessed, and then it should be assigned to a team member for resolution and its resolution monitored.

Soliciting Independent Reviews. Reviews help the project manager and project sponsor assess the "health" of a project. As the project progresses, team members often focus on delivering on specific objectives. They lose sight of the overall project benefits. An independent review can identify overlooked risks and opportunities. However, this review is not the same as a progress report. It should look at whether the project is still appropriate, whether its approach is the most effective, whether the deadline will be achieved, and if the costs are as expected.

To give a flavor of what project management work actually entails, an example of a day in the life of a project manager, excerpted from a blog on ITToolbox's Web site (www.Ittoolbox.com) appears on pages 634–637.

Change Management

IS staff members are often so enthralled with the technical aspects of a new system that they presume a technically elegant system is a successful system. However, many technically sound systems have turned into implementation failures because the people side of the system was not handled correctly. IT is all about managing change. New systems require changing how work is done. Focusing only on the technical aspects is only half the job. The other job is change management.

Change management is the process of assisting people to make major changes in their working environment. In this case, the change is caused by the introduction of a new computer system. Management of change has not always been handled methodically, so choosing a change management methodology and using it is a step toward successfully introducing new computer systems.

Change disrupts people's frame of reference if it presents a future where past experiences do not hold true, says ODR, a change management firm in Atlanta, Georgia. People resist change, especially technological change, when they view it as a crisis. They cope by trying to maintain control. In the case of an impending new computer system that they do not understand fully or are not prepared to handle, they may react in several ways. They may deny the change; they may distort information they hear about it; or they may try to convince themselves, and others, that the new system really will not change the status quo. These reactions are forms of resistance.

ODR offers a methodology to help companies manage technological change. They use specific terms from the field of organizational development to describe the types of people involved in a change project.

- The *sponsor* is the person or group that legitimizes the change. In most cases, this group must contain someone in top management who is highly respected by the business unit because change must be driven from the business unit.
- The *change agent* is the person or group who causes the change to happen. Change agents are often the IS staff. They can introduce the change but they cannot enforce its use.
- The *target* is the person or group who is being expected to change and at whom the change is aimed.

Using surveys completed by a project's sponsors, change agents, and targets, ODR aims to:

- Describe the scope of the change
- Assess the sponsors' commitment to the project
- Assess the change agents' skills
- Evaluate the support or resistance of the targets

The goal of these initial evaluations is to determine whether the change can be made successfully with the current scope, sponsors, change agents, and targets. By evaluating each area, the change agents can determine (1) whether the scope of the project is doable or whether the organization is trying to change too much at one time, (2) whether the sponsors are committed enough to push the change through or whether they are sitting back expecting the organization to change on its own, (3) whether the change agents have the skills to implement the change or whether they are not adept at rallying support, and (4) which groups are receptive to the change and which are resistant. Once these assessments have been made, ODR assists IS project teams to understand the risks their project faces and what they can do to mitigate those risks.

As an example of an organization that used this approach and successfully implemented nine change management projects, consider BOC Group, as described by Neil Farmer on pages 640–641.

CASE EXAMPLE

A DAY IN THE LIFE OF AN IT PROJECT MANAGER

Larry Cone is an independent IT project management consultant in Pennsylvania. He has managed over 100 IT projects. On January 28, 2004, Cone began a highly informative and entertaining blog about his day-to-day experiences, starting with his managing a project to implement a content management system for a medical publisher.

The blog appears on ITToolbox.com, a Web site for IT professionals, that features blogs from IT professionals, providing site visitors a look at the day-to-day challenges these professionals face and how they address them. The following are brief excerpts from Cone's blog.

January 28, 2004: The Project Manager's Prayer

A few years back I got together with a group of like-minded IT project managers and did a formal review of projects we had done that had run into trouble. We tried to figure out just when the seeds of disaster were sown. In the majority of cases, a project that ran into trouble was in trouble at the beginning. Most often the project had been scoped improperly, but sometimes there were governance issues or management support issues. Another common problem was "missing" project phases, such as a needed trial or pilot phase. The pilot phase may be in the project plan, but without allowance for a substantial revision and test cycle post-pilot. All of these problems were "baked in" at the beginning.

Thus, the Project Manager's Prayer: "Bless our Beginnings". That's where we most need a blessing, and most need vigilance, because all too often the seeds of our later pain are sown well before the project kickoff meeting.

February 3, 2004: Project Benefits–Mapping the Minefield

The client has a number of different publications that have transitioned from paper to electronic over the past 5 years. It has become increasingly clear that customers want the ability to search electronically across several or all of the publications. The goal of the project is to make this not merely possible, but effective, and to turn content access into a competitive advantage.

This is a relatively small project, so I'm where I like to be—in the thick of user and customer interviews, capturing requirements. I think I have a feel for the "real" needs of a business, and I enjoy helping to capture and document those needs. I've done 15+ interviews, with an ear for three things:

- *Use cases*—I ask for details of the "typical" user, their job title, their business situation, the query they would run, and the information they would want to retrieve. I think we are all clear that successful systems start with understanding the use cases—whether it's A/R or fly-by-wire.
- *Issues*—a catch-all term for stuff—important or no. Here is where I carefully capture and document everyone's pet peeve, favorite feature, annoyance, or beef. Why? The stakeholders need to feel like they have been heard. That favorite feature may not make it into release 1 or even release 21, but if they look they see it on the Issues list. This gains me credibility and builds trust.
- *Benefits*—I listen for potential benefits at every turn, and carefully capture and collate them. I've got 18 on the list, so far. I've published the benefits list back to the users, and asked them to rank them in order of importance to them.

I use the proposed benefits list to smoke out hot issues as early as possible. Is there a creaky user registration process that frustrates everyone? A high ranking for improving the process tells me this. Who other than the VP of Sales thinks that the real point of the system is to increase cross-sells across publications? How many think that the most important outcome is to reduce training and support costs? How highly does protection of intellectual property rank?

February 7, 2004: Project Benefits—A Trail through the Swamp

I asked the management team to rank the benefits list, and got a 95 percent response rate, after some cajoling. The results held some relief, and some surprises.

A close inspection of the benefits signposts tells me a lot about what will make the project a success. I can take each of the top-rated benefits, and capture a checklist of three or four features or subsystems necessary for their delivery. Take, for example the highly ranked *cross-sell of subscriptions* benefit. To deliver increased cross-publication sales activity, I'd better make sure that the system logs every subscriber that looks at content in a different publication, and forwards that sales lead information to the sales team in the form of reporting.

February 10, 2004: It's All About the Interface

In my project, as we work through business requirements specification, I'm doing interviews with managers, customers, and users. Not surprisingly, they don't talk about business requirements—they talk about application interface details. They bring up Google, and show me how well it works. They take me to housewares shopping sites, and show me how you can cross-link from a lamp to other lamps with similar attributes. They describe features of search sites that they have used successfully, that allowed them to save their last search, or apply parentheses and Boolean logic to their current search.

Meanwhile, I'm trying to figure out how many "components" there are in the system, the nature of the interfaces between the components, and which ones we will buy, which ones we will build, and which ones we have already. I know that we are going to buy a software package as the core of the solution, and I'm trying to formulate a map of the overall solution, with my eye on the RFP to come, and how we will ask for what we need. I suspect that most of the user interface details will come with the package.

February 15, 2004: Inventories of Content—Part I

This project, like many others, will be successful when a bunch of "stuff" that is now in an old place will be accessible in a new place, and in a new way. In this case the "stuff" is medical content documents.

Thus the need for an inventory of online content. I wasn't surprised when there was no such inventory available, so I went about building one.

I started with the current print catalog, and built a spreadsheet framework containing a row for every area described in the published catalog. For the columns, I created fields for facts of interest. These included how many documents, what format they were in currently, how they were delivered to the Web where the underlying content was stored, the from and to date ranges, who was responsible, and how often the content was updated. I set up the spreadsheet, and logged onto the Web, and went looking for content.

February 20, 2004: Inventory of Content—Part II

I ended up with the first comprehensive inventory of online content—useful to the client in and of itself. For me it is a checklist of how much stuff there is, where it is, and in what format it is. This is the set of stuff that must be searchable and accessible at the end of the project. And if I can deliver that, I will be truly content.

February 24, 2004: Magic Happens

We have been interviewing customers, users and management for about 8 weeks now on the way to defining our content management system requirements. We have inventoried the content areas involved, and created use cases and benefits analyses from the interview contents. We have come to one of the most interesting parts of the project—where "Magic Happens."

I'm talking about the moment when an analyst rereads the requirements, and sits down with a pad of paper, or a white board. She reads and reviews, and starts coalescing the many individual statements like "User clicks on search result link, and if he has access rights to the document, he links through and the document appears" into solution components. There is an aha! moment where the analyst draws a circle on the white board and labels it "Document Access Control."

Then more circles appear, and lines connecting them, and a solution takes shape.

For me, that is a Magical Moment.

March 1, 2004: Structure–Function

We left the analyst in front of the white board, drawing circles and arrows. She was engaged in the primal act—creation. Out of the formless requirements void was emerging the light of a solution, an architecture. Or at least the components of a solution.

Well, we don't need to code this system; we are going to buy it (most of it, anyway). But we need more than a formless functions and features list. Why?

Well—I'm a confirmed believer in structure–function; that is, the critical relationship between a system's structure and its function. We want to buy the solution that supplies most of our needed functionality. We also want to buy the solution that makes sense architecturally—has components that perform the high level functions that map to our high-level needs.

March 4, 2004: Trade Shows, Tom Peters, and Martinis

In the Blog alternate universe, we are wrapping up a requirements/content inventory/high-level components document

(Case continued)

(Case continued)

package for this content management system package. In the real world, we are a few weeks ahead. We have convened a "blue ribbon" RFP evaluation committee, and I'm trying to develop a vendor shortlist to work from.

A great place to do that is a trade show, and I've gotten a bit of luck. The AIIM 2004 Enterprise Content and Document Management Show is in the Javits Center in NYC next week.

I'll be heading up there to see some demos, talk to some vendors, and try to get a general sense for the budget of this project. I need to do some expectation setting with my client's senior management. In an informal setting, I can ask some questions, and formulate some ideas about pricing and budget.

March 18, 2004: Project Management Tools–The Hourglass

I have been running IT projects for quite a while, and I have accumulated a set of tools that I use in my work. I thought you might be interested in a tour through my personal toolbox.

Opening my toolbox, the first tool I see is one of my oldest, the Project Manager's Hourglass.

Like most of my tools, the hourglass is a conceptual tool. Here is how I visualize it: It consists of 2 brushed aluminum plates, 6-inches square, set 12 inches apart by 4 steel rods threaded and bolted through holes in the corners. Inside the cage of the rods is a blown-glass hourglass, containing about 2 cups of black basaltic sand.

It is a precision tool for a precision job—the job of measuring the end of the analysis phase of a software project. Here is how I use it.

When the analysis phase of a project starts, I mentally turn over the hourglass. It could be a user requirements gathering phase, a data analysis phase, or a user interface design phase. As the project goes on, I keep my eye on the Hourglass. At some point, the sand runs out. When it does, I say, "Enough analysis; lets wrap up this phase."

March 23: Project Management Tools–The Scope Axe

Continuing on the theme of project management tools, we are taking a tour of my personal project management toolbox. I open the toolbox and I see one of my favorites and most used tools, the scope axe.

Most projects run into trouble at some point, and as the project continues, the options for the project manager are progressively reduced. As discussed earlier, most problems stem from unanticipated tasks or complexity. The initial reaction is to add budget and resources to handle this, but the wise project manager will get out his scope axe.

Use project creep to have the hard discussions with your users and your sponsors, and chop off some scope. You don't have to amputate it completely, just restructure the phases to push the particular scope area to a later time.

April 20, 2004: If You Measure It, They Will Come (Back)

In my Project Manager's toolbox, I always carry the indispensable measuring tape. It's like the old saw (pun intended): "if you can't measure it, you can't manage it." And, there are lots of things to measure.

Overall, there are three areas of measurement, corresponding to the golden triangle of project management: time, resources, and functionality. The triangle is used because it is a symbol of balance and stability; change any one side without adjusting the others and you get a distortion. Just so in a real project: change the timeline without adjusting the amount of resources or the functionality or both and you are either smarter now than you were before (when you built the triangle) or you are a masochist.

May 25, 2004: Project Management Tools–My Pants Are on Fire I

In a Letter to the Editor about a recent *Business 2.0* magazine article, the author used the phrase "Pants on Fire" to describe the state of an IT project manager. It was a thought-provoking phrase, and it got me thinking about how a PM's pants reach the point of ignition, and what PM tools can combat the dreaded "Pants on Fire."

In my view, "Pants on Fire," or POF, refers to the project state in which:

1. Things have gotten out of control
2. They are getting worse fast
3. The project can still be recovered, and
4. The project will fail if you don't do something quickly.

I'm unaware of a generalized project manager's pants extinguisher tool, but here are some thoughts on remedying the POF state.

In situations relating to run-away scope, I would reach for my scope axe, and hack away at the burning part, and try to remove or defer it to a later phase. Or at least reduce the size of the overall fire down to more manageable proportions.

Another POF situation is the technical fire. A recent example occurred in a project "parallel" to one of mine in a client setting.

A software product release in Beta was experiencing infrequent but catastrophic database response problems with SQL Server. I didn't get the exact details, but every few hours the Beta system database server would choke and hang with some sort of resource problem. Release schedules were slipping, the Beta client was concerned, the product management leadership team wanted hourly updates–you get the scenario.

The PM, an experienced hand, rang the fire alarm, flew in technical experts, and cashed in a pile of chits in Redmond. His actions were effective on several fronts: Management saw lots of activity and saw that the situation was being strongly addressed. The experts didn't come up with a fix but did help isolate the failure scenario. His coders were able to code around the failure scenario, and keep the Beta moving.

I'm interested in readers' comments about Pants on Fire scenarios, and tools used to combat the POF situation.

(In April, Cone's project issued a Request for Proposal to vendors of content management products. By July, the proposals had been received and the decisions on which to accept were being made.)

Risk Management

Not all IT-based projects succeed. In fact, many fail—especially the really large projects, such as those implementing ERP or CRM systems. Thirty to 70 percent of IT projects fail. Why do IT projects fail? Because they do not overcome their risks, either technical or business ones, notes Chuck Gibson, a long-time IT consultant and senior lecturer at the MIT Sloan School of Management, in an *MIS Quarterly Executive* paper on risk management.

Technical risks might be a vendor package not scaling up as expected or the project's scope creeping so much that the project becomes too complex to implement. Although technical risks cannot always be anticipated, they can be contained with the right technical corrections, notes Gibson. *Business risk*, on the other hand, is the risk that the business does not change properly to use the new system. Business change is necessary to achieve business results from IT. Lack of business change can come from the appropriate new work environment not being put in place or people's skills and attitudes not being updated to take advantage of the new environment.

Business risks are not as easily righted as technical risks, notes Gibson. Instilling the right business changes requires using the project management approach that reduces the main risks. When the risks change, the project management approach probably needs to change to keep the project on track. Gibson proposes eight project management approaches, from the *Big Bang* approach (which is appropriate when all the main business risks are low) to the *Mitigate or Kill the Project* approach (which is appropriate when all the main risks are high).

To ascertain which project management approach is most likely to yield the needed business changes, Gibson proposes using a three-step process whenever the main risks in a project change: assess the risk, mitigate the risks, and adjust the project management approach.

Step 1: Assess the Risks. The business case for an IT project should include the business risks. Based on his experience and research, Gibson believes the three predominant risk factors are *leadership* of the business change, *employees' perspective* on the change, and the *scope and urgency* of the change.

To visually see a project's overall risk from these three factors, Gibson creates a decision tree. It shows the eight possible combinations of the three factors (Figure 15.23). A plus sign (+) on a factor means "positive support for the business change"; it increases the likelihood of success by reducing the risk. A minus sign (−) on a factor means "negative support for the business change"; it decreases the likelihood of success by increasing the risk. The factor that is the greatest contributor to project success or failure should be placed on the left. In this example, it is leadership, which is often, but not always, the case. On the far right are the eight project management approaches, one for each path through the decision tree.

A project leader is the executive (or executives) responsible for the change. The project leaders should be business executives, not IT executives, notes Gibson, because the business (not IS) is being required to change. To assess whether a project's leadership contributes to success or failure (whether it is a plus or a minus on the decision tree), Gibson recommends asking six questions:

1. Are they committed to the business case?
2. Do they understand the extent of change in work behavior required for the project to succeed?

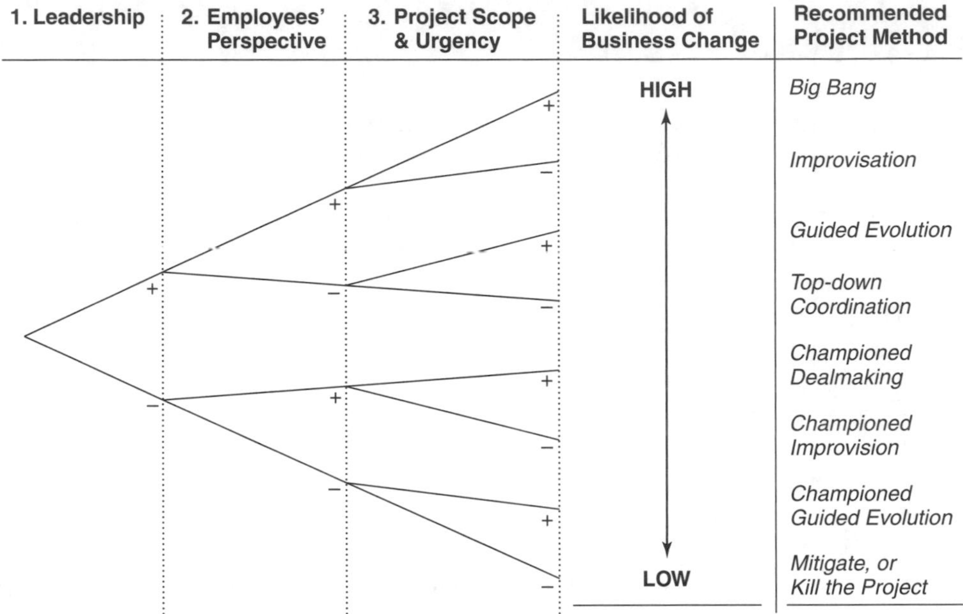

Figure 15.23 Risk Management Decision Tree. *Source:* C. Gibson, "IT-Enabled Business Change: An Approach to Understanding and Managing Risk," *MIS Quarterly Executive,* Vol. 2, No. 2, September 2003, pp. 104–115. Used with permission.

3. Are they formally motivated to pull off the change, such as built into their performance goals?
4. Are they at the appropriate organizational level and have the formal power to influence the needed changes in work behavior?
5. Do they have experience with a project of similar scope, urgency, and people impact?
6. Do they have informal power, such as respect and credibility?

The answers are likely to be mixed, notes Gibson, so give each a weight to ascertain whether the leadership factor should be a plus or minus on the decision tree.

To assess employees' perspectives, he recommends asking two questions. One, "How will the affected people react?" Will they embrace the change, follow orders, follow others, wait and see, resist, or sabotage the change? Two, "Why are they likely to react this way?" This assessment should also yield a single plus or minus on the decision tree.

To assess the project's scope and urgency, Gibson suggests asking three questions: "Is the scope wide?" (A wide scope is a minus.) "Is the change scope deep and severe?" (A major change in processes is a minus.) "Is there urgency?" (Urgency is a minus because it increases risk.) Overall, the scope and urgency factor on the decision tree gets a plus or a minus. The result of these three analyses yields a path through the decision tree that indicates both the project's level of risk and the appropriate project management approach.

Step 2: Mitigate the Risks. Mitigation means "thoughtful management action based on anticipation of high change risk," states Gibson. Some examples are provided in the Dow Corning case.

Step 3: Adjust the Project Management Approach. Gibson divides project management styles into whether they are authoritative or participative and whether the project's budget and time frame are rigid or adjustable; see Figure 15.24. The resulting four project management

	Management Style	
Project Budget and Deadlines	**Authoritative**	**Participative**
Fixed	Big Bang	Guided Evolution
Adjustable	Top-down Coordination	Improvisation

Figure 15.24 Four Approaches to Project Management. *Source:* C. Gibson, "IT-Enabled Business Change: An Approach to Understanding and Managing Risk," *MIS Quarterly Executive,* Vol. 2, No. 2, September 2003, pp. 104–115. Used with permission.

approaches are appropriate for the least risky projects, he believes, which are the four top paths in the decision tree.

The *Big Bang* approach is authoritative and has a fixed budget and deadline. This approach is only appropriate when all three factors are positive. *Improvisation* is participative and has an adjustable budget and deadline. This is the approach to use when leadership and employee perceptions are positive, but scope or urgency place the project at risk, because the committed workforce can adapt to difficult tasks, states Gibson. The *Guided Evolution* approach is participative, but it has a fixed budget and deadline. This is the project management approach to use when only the employee-perception factor is negative, because that negativity can be overcome by involving the employees through strong leadership, motivating them to accept the change. *Top-down Coordination* is an authoritative approach with an adjustable budget and deadline. This method only works when the leadership factor supports the business change and when the leadership is respected, full time, and highly experienced in leading business change, notes Gibson.

The projects on the bottom half of the decision tree, where the leadership factor is negative, are the riskiest. The only project management approaches that will lead to the success of such projects, believes Gibson, are those that have a champion in the user organization. These champions generally have to be willing to bet their job on the project's success. In actuality, these four options "are not in the realm of responsible senior management," notes Gibson, but they do happen. And champions can pull them off, generally by gaining adherents through informal channels—except when all three factors are negative. That's when *Mitigate or Kill the Project* is the only option.

To learn about outsourcing, refer back to Chapter 14. Managing operations is also covered in Chapter 14.

SUMMARY

The nature of how organizations manage information systems and technologies is changing. Increasingly, IT is managed like other business units, with expectations for contribution to the organization and with shared responsibilities for all managers.

The IS organization's major assets (its human resources, physical infrastructure, and applications portfolio) must be treated as assets whose value needs to be increased whenever possible. In order to improve the value of assets, investment, whether in training or capital expenditures, is required.

In addition, IS leaders and their business counterparts must develop strong partnerships in their organization. Steering committees and other governance mechanisms must be designed. The importance of IT is reflected in many organizations by the establishment of a chief information officer or other senior IS executive responsible for linking the IT and business plans.

Organizations have not settled on one best way to organize the IS unit. The globalization of companies makes structuring this function even more difficult. Although history suggests that the IS function has periodically shifted between centralization and decentralization, today many organizations have very distributed IS functions.

These issues and more must be dealt with in the design of an effective management system for IT. Only when combined with direction setting (setting a vision, an architecture, and an IS plan) and excellent management of its technology assets can an IS organization perform most effectively.

CHAPTER REVIEW QUESTIONS

1. Why have IT management and structure changed in the past 10 years? That is, what changes in IT or the business have caused the IS unit to be restructured or to take on a new mission?
2. How have the perspectives of IS professionals changed in the past 10 to 15 years?
3. Why are strictly financial measures like return on investment and cost-benefit analysis insufficient for evaluating information systems?
4. What are the major responsibilities of the chief information officer? How are these different from the traditional IS director?
5. Outline the essential characteristics of the classic, federal, customized, and separate unit IS organization structures discussed in this chapter.
6. What is IT outsourcing? Is it good or bad?
7. What is the largest cost in the IS budget today?
8. What are the characteristics of a good IS chargeback system?
9. What are some unique issues concerning IT management that arise in multinational firms or firms doing business in many countries?
10. What should be the nature of the partnership between IT and business managers?

CHAPTER DISCUSSION QUESTIONS

1. If you were to write an IS department mission statement, what key words would you have used 10 years ago compared to the words you would use today?
2. Consider an organization with which you are familiar. Develop a policy for managing the applications portfolio.
3. As the manager of a major business unit (division), what would you do to implement a corporate infrastructure policy, such as the one in Figure 15.3?
4. What financial measures can be used to assess the contribution the IS organization makes to the business? What are the caveats involved with these measures?
5. What type of person in an organization should be considered for a chief information officer position? That is, what type of individual would be a prime candidate for such a job?
6. This chapter emphasizes the need for a partnership between IS and business managers for managing IT. Define your concept of a management partnership and relate this to making people accountable for business operations and functions.
7. Review the various pros and cons of distributing the systems development organization between central IS and line management organizations.
8. What type of organization would benefit most from creating an IS subsidiary? What type of organization would benefit most from outsourcing IS operations?
9. Under what circumstances would you recommend that an organization adopt a direct chargeback scheme for IS services?
10. As the manager of a statewide ATM network, how would you evaluate the quality of the IS organization serving you? If you were director of consumer marketing for a major appliance manufacturer, how would you evaluate the quality of the IS services you receive?
11. What arguments would you use to justify a career in IS management as a way to senior management in an organization?
12. How should the role of the IS department change as more of the business transactions with other firms (B2B commerce) are conducted over the Internet? How should the role of the business manager change?

CASE STUDY: THE BOC GROUP

The BOC Group is an industrial gas manufacturer with global headquarters in Windlesham, England, and U.S. headquarters in Murray Hill, New Jersey. The company operates in 60 countries and sells industrial gases such as oxygen for steel making, carbon dioxide for food freezing, and so on.

The industry is mature and highly competitive, so companies compete on price and service. To improve the company's competitive position, management committed $35 million to reengineer BOC's core processes. In all, nine reengineering projects were initiated. All succeeded over a 30-month time frame—a significant achievement.

The company established nine full-time teams, each to improve a selected process. Following completion, all team members were guaranteed a return to their former (or equivalent) job. Each team was co-led by a business and information management (IM) process leader because IT was a major component of most of the projects. Each team also sat together in a bullpen setting.

For the first 6 months, each team studied its chosen business process. The research was not parceled out among team members: every team member studied everything. Thus, IM team members were like all the other members. They studied the existing processes and then had a say in how implementation should be handled; they supplied input into the training plan; and they helped devise the customer communication plan. They were often significant influencers because the other team members respected their opinions and their technical knowledge.

GARNERING TRUE EXECUTIVE SPONSORSHIP

Although the president was the executive sponsor for all the teams, he was not intimately involved in each project. Thus, the real executive sponsors were vice presidents and directors. Although they understood the need for the changes and were committed to the concepts behind them, day-to-day operational pressures put a strain on true sponsorship. To address this problem, BOC called on ODR to teach sponsorship to the nine sponsors in a 2-day event.

The sponsors were reticent to go off-site for 2 days to talk about managing change. They believed employees did what they were asked to do. The sponsors did not understand the full impact of the changes on employees nor how employees would be assimilating the changes. They also did not realize their sponsorship job included building sponsorship down through company levels.

During the 2-day event, the ODR facilitator described the sponsorship job in basic here's-what-is-needed terms, and he challenged the nine sponsors to ask the important questions, such as: "What in our culture might make our project not work? What has failed in the past at BOC? Are we asking too much? Is this realistic?" The facilitator pressed the sponsors to question the company's capacity to assimilate change. He got them to be honest and identify obstacles. They were, indeed, challenged. Up to that point, they had not addressed these questions.

The workshop did the job. It opened their eyes to their sponsorship role, which turned out to be crucial to the success of all the projects. They had underestimated the involvement required from the total organization. They had been sitting back expecting their teams to make change happen. But the teams could only put the tools in place; the organization had to make change happen. The workshop taught the sponsors the difference. They left understanding how they needed to drive change through the organization. The facilitator led them into planning their own strategies and examining possible consequences.

ONE CHANGE PROJECT

One of the reengineering projects changed the way BOC processed the paperwork for delivering gas products and invoicing customers. Previously, drivers received a batch of shipping tickets each morning from a clerk. These tickets described their route for the day. When they dropped off a cylinder of gas or picked up an empty one, they marked it on a full-size sheet of paper and handed it to the customer. They also returned handwritten notes to the clerk for entry into the system.

The solution was to replace the paper with a point-of-delivery handheld device (PODD). Schedules would be made at night and downloaded electronically to the PODDs. Loaders would use this information to load the trucks during the night. In the morning, the drivers would pick up their PODD, which contained their route for the day. When they delivered a cylinder, the PODD would accept the customer's signature and then print out a delivery document the size of a grocery store receipt. At the end of the day, the driver hung the PODD back on the rack and the billing data was automatically transmitted to headquarters.

To arrive at this solution, the team, as a whole, studied the process from order to delivery to billing. In working as a unified team, the IM folks began to act as business folks, and vice versa. At the end, the two were indistinguishable because they had absorbed each other's knowledge.

This interaction was a much-appreciated by-product of the process. Once the entire team devised the solution, the IM staff built the technical infrastructure.

Involving Middle Management. To engage middle managers in the nine reengineering projects, BOC established an advisory council for each one. Each advisory council's job was twofold, upward and downward. The upward job was to give feedback on recommended changes, pointing out implementation issues. The downward job was to describe the recommendations to employees and get their buy-in.

The PODD advisory council had 11 members, which included drivers, logistics, IM, field people, and managers. They met several times, and they had more influence than they realized. Their upward feedback significantly affected the PODD team's decisions and their downward communication gave the field people a way to be heard. Through all the advisory councils, BOC created a cascade of influencers, which was a key contributor to their success.

Training the Drivers. The PODD team developed a handheld device that was so logical and intuitive that little training was needed. However, to make the drivers comfortable and ensure success of the project, the team created a 6-hour training program.

The training theme was "A day in a driver's life," and the purpose was to show the truck drivers how to use the PODD to do their job. The lead trainer (a former truck driver) first led the drivers through "A perfect day" scenario where nothing went wrong. With PODD in hand, each driver followed the lead trainer in going through an entire day's use of the PODD, from loading cylinders into the truck to dropping off the PODD at night. This rapid scenario gave them the overall feel of its use. The drivers made mistakes, but as they corrected their own mistakes, they became more and more comfortable with the PODD.

The drivers then worked at their own pace through three successively harder scenarios following a laminated sheet of instructions that included cylinder bar codes and other pertinent information. The drivers who got through all three had no problem with the PODD. Those who got through two might need a little support. Those who struggled would need a trainer to ride with them for a day or two.

To ensure that the drivers were fully comfortable with the PODD, the PODD team offered to ride with any driver for a day. Many accepted, not just to build their confidence, but because they enjoyed the company of another person. Whenever the driver raised a question during that day, the team member usually responded, "What do you think you should do?" Generally the driver's answer was right, which built self-confidence.

Due to all the training, the PODD team encountered little resistance from the drivers. In fact, the drivers were so pleased the company was investing in them that they proudly showed their PODD to their customers; they were the only drivers in the industry to have them.

The project was successful because the PODD team had assessed its people aspects at the outset and mitigated the identified risks by holding the sponsorship event, involving middle management via the advisory council, and thoroughly training the truck drivers.

Case Study Discussion Questions

Question One

What made the BOC's approach to reengineering their core processes successful?

Question Two

Would this approach work in every company, given the buy-in of all employees or are there some types of companies where it wouldn't work?

GLOSSARY

3G Teams Teams of three generations (25+, 35+, 45+) that work together.

Action Labs An approach to planning where frontline employees identify and interactively refine local-level strategies by having to get them funded at action lab meetings with top management.

Active Desktop A feature of newer versions of Microsoft Windows, which Microsoft describes as a customizable "dashboard" for the PC. With Active Desktop, the user may place both Windows icons (shortcuts to programs) and HTML elements (links to frequently visited Web sites) on the Windows home screen.

Advanced Technology Group A group within the IS department that is responsible for spotting and evaluating new technologies, often by conducting a pilot project.

Agent An electronic entity that performs tasks, either on its own or at the request of a person or a computer.

Aggregation Combining formerly separate pieces of infrastructure, providing companies with an e-business infrastructure on very short notice.

AI *See* Artificial intelligence.

Alpha testing The testing of a commercial software package inside a customer organization, similar to a user acceptance test in an SDLC approach, during which changes to the package are typically made. *See also* Beta testing.

American National Standards Institute (ANSI) The United States standard-setting body for many IT standards.

Analog network The electronic linking of devices, where messages are sent over the links by having some analogous physical quantity (e.g., voltage) continuously vary as a function of time. Historically, the telephone network has been an analog network.

Analog technology Signals sent as sine waves rather than ones and zeros (as in digital technology).

ANSI *See* American National Standards Institute.

Applet An application program written in the Java object-oriented programming language; usually stored on a Web server and downloaded to a microcomputer with a mouse click and executed by a Java-compatible Web browser. A major advantage of a Java applet is that it can be run on virtually any IT platform. *See also* Web browser, IT platform.

Application independence The separation, or decoupling, of data from application systems. Application independence means that applications are built separately from the databases from which applications draw their data; application independence results in lower long-term costs for systems development.

Application Program Interface (API) An interface created for a software product that, like a standard, allows programmers to write to, link to, and utilize that software's interface in their applications.

Application Service Provider (ASP) An information technology vendor that hosts applications for which it holds the licenses, typically using Web-based front ends and Internet access. The vendor provides one or more complete applications to client organizations on a pay-per-use or flat-fee basis. The vendor may be the vendor of the software (e.g., SAP or PeopleSoft) or a third-party service provider. ASP aggregators host multiple applications with a common interface. *See also* Outsourcing.

Application suite *See* Office suite.

Applications software All programs written to accomplish particular tasks for computer users. Examples include programs for payroll computation, inventory record keeping, word processing, and producing a summarized report for top management.

Archie An Internet application, or tool, that allows the user to search the publicly available anonymous File Transfer Protocol (FTP) sites to find the desired computer files. *See also* File Transfer Protocol.

Architecture A blueprint that shows how a system, house, vehicle, or product will look and how the parts interrelate.

Arithmetic/logical unit The portion of a computer system in which arithmetic operations (such as addition and multiplication) and logical operations (such as comparing two numbers for equality) are carried out.

ARPANET The forerunner of the Internet; a network created by the U.S. Department of Defense to link leading U.S. research universities and research centers.

Artificial intelligence (AI) The study of how to make computers do things that are currently done better by people. AI research includes six separate but related areas: natural languages, robotics, perceptive systems (vision and hearing), genetic programming (also called evolutionary design), expert systems, and neural networks.

Artificial intelligence (AI) shell *See* Expert system shell.

Assembler A program (software) that translates an assembly language program—a program containing mnemonic operation codes and symbolic addresses—into an equivalent machine language program.

Assembly language Second generation computer language in which the programmer uses easily remembered mnemonic operation codes instead of machine language operation codes and symbolic addresses instead of memory cell addresses. Such a language is considerably easier to use than machine language, but it still requires the programmer to employ the same small steps that the computer has been built to understand.

Asynchronous Transfer Mode (ATM) An approach to implementing a network, especially a WAN or a backbone network, based on high-speed switching technology to accomplish fast packet switching with short, fixed-length packets. With ATM, connectivity between devices is provided through a switch rather than through a shared bus or ring, with line speeds up to 1.24 billion bits per second possible. *See also* Packet switching.

ATM *See* Asynchronous Transfer Mode.

Attribute In data modeling, the actual elements of data that are to be collected, for example, customer last name, customer first name, customer street, and customer city.

Audit trail An EDP auditing technique that allows a business transaction to be traced from the time of input through all the processes and reports in which the transaction data are used. An audit trail is used to identify where errors are introduced or security breaches may have occurred.

Authentication Assuring that the digital signature of the user is valid.

Authorization Assuring that the correct user is accessing a network, application, or stored files or documents.

B2B Business-to-business e-commerce utilizing electronic applications for transactions and communications between two or more businesses. B2B e-commerce includes direct-to-customer sales with business customers.

B2C Business-to-consumer e-commerce utilizing electronic applications for transactions and communications between a business seller (or a business intermediary or distributor) and individual end-consumers.

Backbone In a telecommunications network, the underlying foundation to which the other elements attach. For example, NSFNET served as the backbone for the Internet until 1995 by providing the underlying high-volume links of the Internet to which other elements attached. *See also* Backbone network.

Backbone network A middle-distance network that interconnects local area networks in a single organization with each other and with the organization's wide area network and the Internet. The technology employed is at the high end of that used for local area networks, such as FDDI, Fast Ethernet, or ATM running over fiber-optic cabling or shielded twisted pair. *See also* Asynchronous Transfer Mode, Fast Ethernet, Fiber Distributed Data Interface.

Backbone systems Mainline corporate transaction processing systems.

Back-end systems Computer systems that handle an enterprise's operational processing, as opposed to front-end systems that interact with users.

Back-end tools Tools, such as code generators, in computer-aided software engineering suites that automatically generate source code.

Balanced scorecard A management technique that translates an organization's goals and strategy into a "scorecard" of measures in order to predict financial performance.

Bandwidth The difference between the highest and the lowest frequencies (cycles per second) that can be transmitted on a single medium. Bandwidth is important because it is a measure of the capacity of the transmission medium.

Bar code label A label consisting of a series of bars used to identify an item; when the bar code is scanned, the data are entered into a computer. There are a variety of bar code languages, the most widely known of which is the Universal Product Code, or UPC, used by the grocery industry. The use of bar codes is very popular for high-volume supermarket checkout, department store sales, inventory tracking, time and attendance records, and health care records.

Baseband coax A simple-to-use and inexpensive-to-install type of coaxial cable that offers a single digital transmission channel with maximum transmission speeds ranging from 10 million bits per second (bps) up to 1 billion bps. Baseband coax was widely used for LANs and for long-distance transmission within the telephone network, although much of this coax has now been replaced by fiber-optic cabling.

Batch processing A mode of transaction processing in which a group or "batch" of transactions of a particular type is accumulated and then processed as a single batch at one time. For example, all sales for a firm would be accumulated during the day and then processed as a single batch at night.

Baud Number of signals sent per second; one measure of data transmission speed. Baud is often equivalent to Hertz (another measure of transmission speed) and to bits per second.

Benchmarking A procedure used to compare the capabilities of various computers in a particular organizational setting by running a representative set of real jobs (jobs regularly run on the organization's existing computer) on each of the machines and comparing the resulting elapsed times.

Best-of-breed outsourcing Outsourcing specific functions, each to the most appropriate provider, rather than outsourcing all functions to one provider who may not be the best for all the functions.

Beta testing The testing of a commercial software package at one or more organizations after the package has been modified based on Alpha testing at one or more customer sites. *See also* Alpha testing.

Bit Widely used abbreviation for a *bi*nary digi*t,* i.e., a 0 or a 1. Coding schemes used in computer systems employ particular sequences of bits to represent the decimal numbers, alphabetic characters, and special characters.

Blogs Self-published journals posted electronically on the Web.

Bluetooth Short-range radio technology that has been built into a microchip, enabling data to be transmitted wirelessly at a speed of 1 million bits per second. The use of Bluetooth technology eliminates the need for many cables and permits the control of Bluetooth-equipped appliances from a cellular phone—all from a remote location, if desired.

Boundary Identifies the scope of a system. A boundary segregates the system from its environment.

Bricks-and-clicks Companies with a dual physical and Internet presence, becoming a hybrid of *Brick-and-Mortar* firms and *dot-coms.*

Bridge A hardware device employed in a telecommunications network to connect two local area networks (LANs) or LAN segments when the LANs use the same protocols, or set of rules. A bridge is smart enough to forward only messages that need to go to the other LAN.

Broadband A general designation applied to the higher-speed alternatives for accessing the Internet from a home or small office, namely digital subscriber line (DSL), cable modem, and satellite connections.

Broadband coax A type of coaxial cable—more expensive and harder to use than baseband coax—that originally used analog transmission, but increasingly employs digital transmission. A single broadband coax can be divided into multiple channels so that a single cable can support simultaneous transmission of data, voice, and television. Broadband data transmission rates are similar to those for baseband coax, and high transmission speeds are possible over much longer distances than are feasible for baseband coax. Broadband coax is still widely used for cable television and LANs that span a significant area, often called metropolitan area networks.

Browser *See* Web browser.

Bull-whip effect Where a small change by a customer results in a huge change upstream. For instance, a customer order triggers a company to generate an order to its supplier, who, in turn, generates its own larger order to its suppliers, and so on; moving upstream through the supply chain increases greater variance from the original order. If the customer then cancels the order, that cancellation ripples through the supply chain.

Business continuity Involves not only disaster recovery (recovering data and programs from back-up and instituting communication links, for example) but also having back-up work procedures and office space for displaced employees to work with telephone lines and computers so that the business can continue operating.

Bus topology A network topology in which a single length of cable (coax, fiber-optic, or twisted pair)—not connected at the ends—is shared by all network devices; also called a linear topology.

Business intelligence The focus of newer fourth generation languages; these software tools are designed to answer queries relating to the business by analyzing data (often massive quantities of data), thereby providing "intelligence" to the business that will help it become more competitive.

Business intelligence system *See* Competitive intelligence system.

Business process The chain of activities required to achieve an outcome such as order fulfillment or materials acquisition.

Business Process Outsourcing (BPO) Outsourcing all or most of a reengineered process that has a large IT component.

Business process reengineering (BPR) The redesign of business processes to achieve dramatic improvements in efficiency and responsiveness by taking advantage of information technology. Also referred to as business process redesign.

Business Visionary One of the CIO's roles where the CIO will need to believe, and then convince others, that the Internet will lead to new business models. This makes the CIO's role a main driver of strategy.

Byte A memory cell that can store only one character of data. *See also* Memory.

Cable modem A high-speed, or broadband, connection to the Internet using the coaxial cables already used by television. Cable television companies had to reengineer the cable television system to permit the two-way data flow required for Internet connections. Cable modem speeds may be degraded as the number of users goes up because users are sharing the bandwidth of the coaxial cable.

Cache memory A very high-speed storage unit used as an intermediary between elements of a computer system that have a significant mismatch in speeds (e.g., the very fast data channel and relatively slow direct access storage device). An entire block of data is moved from the slower element to cache memory, so that most requests for data from the faster element can be satisfied directly from the very high-speed cache memory.

CAD *See* Computer-aided design.

CAE *See* Computer-aided engineering.

CAM *See* Computer-aided manufacturing.

Capability Maturity Model (CMM) A five stage model of software development and IT project management processes that are designed to increase software quality and decrease development costs due to standard, repeatable approaches across multiple projects within the same organization. The model was developed by the Software Engineering Institute at Carnegie Mellon University. A level-5 CMM certification is required for some contractors to bid on software development projects for high-risk, government-sponsored projects today, such as for custom development projects for the U.S. Department of Defense.

CAPP *See* Computer-aided process planning.

CASE *See* Computer-aided software engineering.

Case-Based Reasoning (CBR) Expert systems that draw inferences by comparing a current problem (or case) to hundreds or thousands of similar past cases. CBR is best used when the situation involves too many nuances and variations to be generalized into rules.

CD An abbreviation for compact disk, a commonly used optical storage device with a standard capacity of 700 megabytes of data or 80 minutes of audio recording. *See also* CD-ROM, CD-R, CD-RW, DVD, DVD-ROM, DVR-R, DVD-RW, Optical disk.

CD-R An abbreviation for compact disk-recordable, formerly called a WORM (write once-read many) disk, a type of optical disk that can be written on by the user once and can then be read many times. CD-R technology is appropriate for archiving documents, engineering drawings, and records of all types.

CD-ROM An abbreviation for compact disk-read only memory; the first common type of optical disk storage for personal computers. CD-ROM can only be read and cannot be erased and is particularly useful for distributing large amounts of relatively stable data to many locations.

CD-RW An abbreviation for compact disk-rewritable, a type of optical disk that can be written on and read many times, then rewritten and read many times, and so on. Rewritable optical disks are the most versatile form of optical storage, and falling prices make them an attractive alternative to the standard floppy disk.

Cellular telephone A telephone instrument that can be installed in a car or carried in a pocket or briefcase; this instrument can be used anywhere as long as it is within the 8 to 10 mile range of a cellular switching station.

Center of excellence An organizational structure in which internal experts in a technology, IT process, or both, are brought together in order to provide internal consulting and transfer their knowledge to others in the organization. For example, a multinational firm may establish an SAP center of excellence in order to more effectively leverage what personnel throughout the company have learned about how best to design and implement SAP software modules for the company's business processes.

Central processing unit (CPU) The name given to the combination of the control unit, which controls all other components of a computer, and the arithmetic/logical unit, in which computations and logical comparisons are carried out; also referred to as the processor.

Champion A person inside or outside IS who has a vision and gets it implemented by obtaining the funding, pushing the project over hurdles, putting his or her reputation on the line, and taking on the risk of the project.

Change management The process of assisting people to make major changes in their work and working environment.

Chaos theory As applied to business, a theory that states that "order is free" when groups and organizations are allowed to be self-organizing because, as in scientific chaos theory, randomness (chaos) works within boundaries, which are called strange attractors. As a result, there is order in chaos.

Chargeback The process that is used to internally charge client units for IS services provided. These internal charges may be established to recover costs or may represent market prices.

Check digit One or more digits appended to a critical value for validation purposes; the check digit has some mathematical relationship to the other digits in the number.

Chief information officer (CIO) The executive responsible for information technology strategy, policy, and service delivery at the corporate level; a general manager responsible for IS leadership, similar to a chief financial officer who is responsible for the finance function. Sometimes CIOs have no direct operating responsibilities because the organization has decentralized these responsibilities to IT leaders reporting to division heads. In dot-com businesses, the CTO may also play a CIO role. *See also* Chief technology officer.

Chief technology officer (CTO) Senior manager responsible for identifying and recommending ways in which information technology (IT) can be applied in an organization. The title is most often used in dot-com businesses or companies with a substantial presence on the Internet. *See also* Chief information officer.

CIM *See* Computer-integrated manufacturing.

CIO *See* Chief information officer.

Circuit switching When a virtual (temporary) circuit is created between caller and receiver and that circuit is theirs alone to use; no other parties can share it during the duration of their telephone call. Most appropriate for voice calls.

Cleansed data Data processed to make it usable for decision support; referred to in conjunction with data warehouses. Opposite is *dirty data* (data from different databases that does not match, has different names, uses different time frames, etc.).

Cleartext Nonencrypted versions of passwords and messages.

Clicks-and-mortar A term that emerged in the late 1990s to refer to traditional companies (bricks-and-mortar, including catalog retailers) that had implemented new business strategies based on e-commerce opportunities. Used synonymously with the term "clicks-and-bricks."

Clickwrap contract A contract not really bargained over in any way, but presented as a take-it-or-leave-it offer. Generally speaking, these contracts are legally enforceable. The use of the term *clickwrap contract* is an extension to the "shrinkwrap licenses" used in purchased software.

Client-server Splitting the computing workload between the "client," which is a computer used by the user and can sit on the desktop or be carried around, and the "server," which houses the sharable resources.

Client/server system A particular type of distributed system in which the processing power is distributed between a central server computer, such as a midrange system or a powerful workstation, and a number of client computers, usually desktop microcomputers. The split in responsibilities between the server and the client varies considerably between applications, but the client often handles data entry and the immediate output, while the server maintains the larger database against which the new data are processed. *See also* Distributed systems.

Closed network A network that is offered by one supplier and to which only the products of that supplier can be attached.

Coax *See* Coaxial cable.

Coaxial cable (coax) A common transmission medium that consists of a heavy copper wire at the center, surrounded by insulating material, then a cylindrical conductor such as a woven braided mesh, and finally an outer protective plastic covering. The two kinds of coaxial cable in widespread use are baseband coax for digital transmission and broadband coax for both analog and digital transmission.

Collaboration A term used as a synonym for groupware. *See also* groupware.

Collaborative environment *See* Collaboration.

Collaborative outsourcing Where one service provider becomes the prime contractor for numerous facets of an operation, but some of the work is provided by other external service providers (ESPs).

COM *See* Computer output microfilm.

Commercial software package *See* Software package.

Communities of Practice (CoPs) Networks of people who work together in an unofficial way to get work accomplished using unofficial procedures that may be outside the company's formal corporate culture.

Compact disk *See* CD.

Competitive forces model A model of five competitive forces faced by companies within the same industry, developed by Michael E. Porter for strategic assessment and planning.

Competitive intelligence system An executive information system (EIS) that emphasizes competitive information. *See also* Executive information system.

Competitive Local Exchange Carriers (CLECs) Telecom carriers that compete with incumbent local exchange carriers (ILECS) and provide new kinds of connection options to businesses and homes, such as cable modems, optical fiber, wireless, and satellite.

Compiler A program (software) that translates a third generation or fourth generation language program into an equivalent machine language program, translating the entire program into machine language before any of the program is executed.

Computer-aided design (CAD) The use of computer graphics (both two-dimensional and three-dimensional) and a database to create and modify engineering designs.

Computer-aided engineering (CAE) The analysis of the functional characteristics of an engineering design by simulating the product performance under various conditions.

Computer-aided manufacturing (CAM) The use of computers to plan and control manufacturing processes. CAM incorporates computer programs to control automated equipment on the shop floor, automated guided vehicles to move material, and a communications network to link all the pieces.

Computer-aided process planning (CAPP) A computer-based system that plans the sequence of processes that produce or assemble a part. During the design process, the engineer retrieves the closest standard plan from a database and modifies that plan rather than starting from scratch.

Computer-aided software engineering (CASE) A set of integrated software tools used by IS specialists to automate some or all phases of an SDLC process. Upper-CASE tools support project management, the Definition phase, and the initial steps of the Construction phase, including the creation of a DD/D. Lower-CASE tools are back-end code generators and maintenance support tools. *See also* Integrated-CASE.

Computer-integrated manufacturing (CIM) A broad term that encompasses many uses of the computer to help manufacturers operate more effectively and efficiently. CIM systems fall into three major categories: engineering systems, which are aimed at increasing the productivity of engineers; manufacturing administration, which includes systems that develop production schedules and monitor production; and factory operations, which include those systems that actually control the operation of machines on the factory floor.

Computer output microfilm (COM) A computer output method using microfilm or microfiche (a sheet of film) as the output medium. A computer output device called a COM recorder accepts the data from memory and prepares the microfilm output at very high speeds.

Computer telecommunications network The type of network emanating from a single medium-sized, large, or very large computer or a group of closely linked computers; usually arranged in a tree topology.

Computer virus A small unit of code that invades a computer program or file. When the invaded program is executed or the file is opened, the virus makes copies of itself that invade other programs or files in that computer. It may also erase files or corrupt programs. Viruses are transmitted from one computer to another when an invaded computer program or file is transmitted to another computer.

Computer worm A computer virus that has the ability to copy itself from machine to machine over a network.

Connectivity Allowing users to communicate up, down, across, and out of an organization via a network.

Consequentialism An ethical theory that judges an action by evaluating all of its consequences; if the consequences are predominantly good, the action is ethical, but if the consequences are predominantly bad, the action is unethical.

Content Refers to information presented electronically in a variety of media: charts, text, voice, sound, graphics, animation, photographs, diagrams, and video.

Contention bus A design standard for a local area network based on a bus topology and contention for the use of the bus by all devices on the network. Any device may transmit a message if the bus is idle, but if two devices start to transmit at the same time, a collision will occur and both messages will be lost. *See also* CSMA/CD protocol.

Context diagram A logical model that identifies the entities outside the boundaries of a system with which the system must interface. *See also* Data flow diagram.

Control unit The component of a computer system that controls all the remaining components. The control unit brings instructions (operations to be performed) from memory one at a time, interprets each instruction, and carries it out—all at electronic speed. *See also* Central processing unit, Stored-program concept.

Controller A hardware unit used to link input/output or file devices to the CPU and memory of large computer systems (through the data channel). The controller is a highly specialized microprocessor that manages the operation of its attached devices to free the CPU from these tasks (e.g., a DASD controller handles direct access storage devices, and a communications controller handles multiple terminals or PCs acting as terminals).

Conversion The process of changing to a new system, such as with a pilot or cutover (cold turkey) conversion strategy.

Cookie As used with the Web, a message given to a Web browser by a Web server. The browser stores the message on the user's hard drive, and then sends it back to the server each time the browser requests a page from the server. The main purpose of cookies is to identify users and possibly prepare customized Web pages for them.

Cooperative processing Computer systems that cooperate with each other to perform a task. The systems may span internal business functions or even span enterprises.

Copyright A law that aims to protect an expression in a tangible form; a copyright protects the expression, not the idea.

Cordless telephone A portable telephone instrument that can be used up to about 1,000 feet from its wired telephone base unit; this permits the user to carry the instrument to various rooms in a house or take it outdoors.

Corporate data model A chart that describes all the data requirements of a given organization. This chart shows what data entities and relationships between the entities are important for the organization.

Corporate information policy The foundation for managing the ownership of data; a policy describing the use and handling of data and information within the corporation.

Corporate memory The knowledge or information accumulated by a business, which is often stored in its software, databases, patents, and business processes.

Corporate portal An intranet where employees, customers, and suppliers gain access to a company's information, applications, and processes. This approach moves the software from being decentralized (on PCs) to being centralized (on a server).

Countermeasures Mechanisms used by people and enterprises to protect themselves from security breaches, such as stealing data or machines, destroying files, redirecting traffic, shutting down Web sites, and unleashing computer viruses.

Coverage model A common data model used in geographic information systems in which different layers or themes represent similar types of geographic features in the same area (e.g., counties, highways, customers) and are stacked on top of one another.

CPU *See* Central processing unit.

Cracker A person who breaks into a computer system to steal information, wipe out hard drives, or do other harm.

Credit bureau An organization that acquires computer records from banks and other creditors and from public records of such things as lawsuits, tax liens, and legal judgments. These records are compiled and then sold to credit grantors, rental property owners, employers, insurance companies, and many others interested in a consumer's credit record.

Critical success factor (CSF) One of a limited number of organizational activities that, if done well, will contribute most to the success of the overall performance of the firm or function.

CRM *See* Customer relationship management system.

CSF *See* Critical success factor.

CSMA/CA Protocol An abbreviation for Carrier Sense Multiple Access with Collision Avoidance, the protocol used in a wireless design for a local area network. CSMA/CA is quite similar to CSMA/CD used in traditional Ethernet, but it makes greater efforts to avoid collisions. *See also* CSMA/CD Protocol.

CSMA/CD Protocol An abbreviation for Carrier Sense Multiple Access with Collision Detection, the protocol used in the contention bus design for a local area network. With this protocol, any device may transmit a message if the bus is idle. However, if two devices start to transmit at the same time, a collision will occur and the messages will become garbled. Both devices must recognize that this collision has occurred, stop transmitting, wait some random period of time, and then try again.

CTO *See* Chief technology officer.

Customer capital The strength of a company's franchise with its customers and its relationships and networks of associates. This form of capital may be either human (relationships with the company) or structural (products used from the company).

Customer relationship management (CRM) system A computer application that attempts to provide an integrated approach to all aspects of interaction a company has with its customers, including marketing, sales, and support. A CRM system often pulls much of its data from the organization's data warehouse; most CRM packages depend upon capturing, updating, and utilizing extensive profiles of individual customers.

Customized design A mixed type of IS organization design, found in many large enterprises, where some business units have a centralized IS unit handle all their IT needs, while other divisions within the same parent organization have a federal or decentralized design in order to locally address their own IT needs with their own local IS staff.

Cyberspace A "space" on the Internet where people "exist" in a virtual world.

Cybersquatting The act of registering domain names that clearly referred to known companies, anticipating that those companies would eventually want the domain name and would be willing to pay for it.

Cycle time The amount of time it takes to accomplish a complete cycle, such as the time from getting an idea to turning it into a product or service.

DASD *See* Direct access storage device.

Data Electronic information that is comprised of facts (devoid of meaning or context).

Data administration The name typically given to an organizational unit created to lead the efforts in data management; the group often reports as a staff unit to the IS director, although other structures are possible.

Data analysis and presentation application An application that manipulates data and then distributes information to authorized users. These applications concentrate on creating useful information from established data sources and, because they are separate from data capture and transfer systems, can be individually changed without the expense of changing the data capture and transfer systems.

Data architecture *See* Data model.

Data capture application An application that gathers data and populates databases. These applications allow the simplification of all other applications that then transfer or report data and information.

Data center A computer installation that stores, maintains, and provides access to vast quantities of data; includes computer hardware (servers, workstations/midrange systems, mainframes, and/or supercomputers), communications facilities, system software, and technical support and operations staff.

Data channel A specialized input/output processor (hardware) that takes over the function of device communication from the CPU. The data channel corrects for the significant speed mismatch between the slow input/output and file devices and the fast and critical CPU.

Data dictionary The main tool by which data administrators control a company's standard data definitions, to make sure that corporate policy is being followed.

Data dictionary/directory (DD/D) Support software that provides a repository of metadata for each data element in a system—including the meaning, alternative names, storage format, integrity rules, security clearances, and physical location of data—that is used by the DBMS and system users.

Data-driven design An approach to systems development that concentrates on the ideal and natural organization of data, independent of how or where data are used. *See also* Process-driven design.

Data flow diagram (DFD) A common diagrammatic technique for logical As-Is and To-Be models. Symbols are used to represent the movement, processing, and storage of data in a system and both inputs from and outputs to the environment. Each process in a top-level DFD is decomposed to a lower level, and so on.

Data independence A highly desirable characteristic of data stored in a database in which the data are independent of the database structure or the physical organization of the data. Thus data can be selected from a disk file by referring to the content of records, and systems professionals responsible for database design can reorganize the physical organization of data without affecting the logic of programs.

Data integrity Data that maintains its integrity because it cannot be modified in transit or in storage.

Data mart A smaller, more focused version of a data warehouse created for "drop-in shopping," much like a neighborhood convenience mart. *See also* Data warehousing.

Data mining Searching or "mining" for "nuggets" of information from the vast quantities of data stored in an organization's data warehouse, employing a variety of technologies such as decision trees and neural networks. *See also* Data warehousing.

Data model A map or blueprint for organizational data. A data model shows the data entities and relationships that are important to an organization. *See also* Entity-relationship diagram.

Data standards A clear and useful way to uniquely identify every instance of data and to give unambiguous business meaning to all data. Types of standards include identifiers, naming, definition, integrity rules, and usage rights.

Data transfer application An application that moves data from one database to another. These applications permit one source of data to serve many localized systems within an organization.

Data warehouse A very large database or collection of databases, created to make data accessible to many people in an organization. *See also* Data warehousing.

Data warehousing The establishment and maintenance of a large data storage facility containing data on all or at least many aspects of the enterprise; less formally, a popular method for making data accessible to many people in an organization. To create a data warehouse, a firm pulls data from its operational transaction processing systems and puts the data in a separate "data warehouse" so that users may access and analyze the data without endangering the operational systems. *See also* Data mining.

Database A shared collection of files and associations between these files. A database reduces redundancy and inconsistency compared to file processing, but this lack of natural redundancy can cause risks from loss of data or breaches of authorized data access or manipulation.

Database administrator (DBA) The person in the data administration unit who is responsible for computerized databases. A DBA is concerned with efficiency, integrity, and security of database processing.

Database architecture A description of the way in which the data are structured and stored in a database.

Database machine *See* Database server.

Database management system (DBMS) Support software that is used to create, manage, and protect organizational data. A DBMS is the software that manages a database; it works with the operating system to store and modify data and to make data accessible in a variety of meaningful and authorized ways.

Database server A separate computer, attached to another computer, that is responsible for only processing database queries and updates. A database server is usually part of a local area network and serves the database needs of all the personal and larger computers on this network.

DBA *See* Database administrator.

DBMS *See* Database management system.

DBMS engine A computer program that handles the detailed retrieving and updating of data for a wide variety of other DBMSs, electronic spreadsheets, and other software. Use of a DBMS engine allows the other software to concentrate on providing a convenient user interface while the DBMS engine handles the common database access functions.

DDD *See* Direct Distance Dialing.

DD/D *See* Data dictionary/directory.

DDM paradigm A part of the architecture of a DSS: the dialog (D) between the user and the system, the data (D) that supports the system, and the models (M) that provide the analysis capabilities.

Decision support system (DSS) A computer-based system, almost always interactive, designed to assist managers in making decisions. A DSS incorporates both data and models and is usually intended to assist in the solution of semistructured or unstructured problems. An actual application that assists in the decision-making process is properly called a specific DSS; examples of specific DSSs include a police-beat allocation system, a capacity planning and production scheduling system, and a capital investment decision system.

Decision support system (DSS) generator Computer software that provides a set of capabilities to build a specific DSS quickly and easily. For example, Microsoft Excel, a spreadsheet package, can be used as a DSS generator to construct specific financial models that can be used in decision making.

Demand-pull In this business model, companies offer customers the components of a service or product, and the customers create their own personalized versions, creating the demand that pulls the specific product or service they want through the supply chain; opposite is supply-push.

Denial of service attack A method of crippling a computer by invading a large number of computers on the Internet and instructing them to simultaneously send repeated messages to a target computer, thus either overloading that computer's input buffer or jamming the communications lines into the computer so badly that legitimate users cannot obtain access.

Deontologism An ethical theory that holds that an action is either ethical or unethical based only upon whether the action conforms to certain ethical precepts without regard to its consequences in the particular case.

Desktop computer The most common type of personal computer, which is large enough that it cannot be moved around easily. The monitor and the keyboard, and sometimes the computer case itself, sit on a table or "desktop." If the computer case sits on the floor under the table or desk, it is called a "tower" unit.

DFD *See* data flow diagram.

Digital divide A term that emerged in the late 1990s to refer to societal inequities due to the lack of computer skills and access to the Internet by portions of the population. Also used to refer to a global digital divide.

Digital network The electronic linking of devices, where messages are sent over the links by directly transmitting the zeros and ones used by computers and other digital devices. Computer telecommunications networks and LANs are digital networks, and the telephone network is gradually being shifted from an analog to a digital network.

Digital signal processor (DSP) A type of semiconductor chip that converts analog images or sounds in real time (i.e., with essentially no delay) to a stream of digital signals. DSP chips are used at the heart of digital cellular telephones and in traditional products such as kitchen appliances and electric motors.

Digital subscriber line A high-speed, or broadband, connection to the Internet using already installed telephone lines. DSL service, which is available from telephone companies in many parts of the United States, uses a sophisticated modulation scheme to move data over the wires without interfering with voice traffic.

Digital video disk *See* DVD.

Direct access file A basic type of computer file from which it is possible for the computer to obtain a record immediately, without regard to where the record is located on the file; usually stored on magnetic disk. Computer files, also called secondary memory or secondary storage, are added to a computer system to keep vast quantities of data accessible within the computer system at more reasonable costs than main memory.

Direct access storage device (DASD) The device on which direct access files are stored. *See also* Direct access file.

Direct Distance Dialing (DDD) The normal way of using the long-distance telephone network in the United States in which the user directly dials the number with which he or she wishes to communicate and pays for the service based on the duration of the call and the geographical distance; may be used for voice and data communications between any two spots served by the telephone network.

Direct file organization *See* Direct access file.

Disposable application An application that can be discarded when it becomes obsolete without affecting the operation of any other application; this is made possible by application independence. Also referred to as a disposable system. *See also* Application independence.

Distributed data processing *See* Distributed systems.

Distributed systems Application systems in which the processing power is distributed to multiple sites, which are then tied together via telecommunications lines. Distributed systems have computers of possibly varying sizes located at various physical sites at which the organization does business, and these computers are linked by telecommunications lines in order to support some business process.

Document A unit of recorded information structured for human consumption. This definition accommodates "documents" dating back to cuneiform inscriptions on clay tablets—what has changed are the ways information is represented and the ways documents are processed.

Documentation Written descriptions produced during the systems development process for those who use the system (user documentation) and for IS specialists who operate and maintain the system (system documentation).

Dot-com A term used to describe a cyber business that receives revenues entirely based on customer transactions or other usage of its Web site. Also referred to as "pure-play" dot-com businesses, as distinguished from clicks-and-mortar businesses.

Dribbling Data Obtaining data for a new application from data in an existing application.

DSL *See* Digital subscriber line.

DSP *See* Digital signal processor.

DSS *See* Decision support system.

Dumb Terminals Desktop machines without processing or storage capabilities.

DVD An abbreviation for digital video disk, an optical storage device that holds much more data than a conventional CD and therefore can be used for very large files such as video; standard capacity for a two-sided DVD is 4.7 gigabytes. Also called a digital versatile disk. *See also* CD, CD-ROM, CD-R, CD-RW, DVD-ROM, DVR-R, DVD-RW, Optical disk.

DVD-R An abbreviation for digital video disk-recordable, a type of optical disk that can be written on by the user once and can then be read many times. DVD-R technology is appropriate for archiving documents, engineering drawings, and records of all types.

DVD-ROM An abbreviation for digital video disk-read only memory, a type of optical disk that can only be read and cannot be erased. DVD-ROM is particularly useful for distributing large amounts of relatively stable data to many locations.

DVD-RW An abbreviation for digital video disk-rewritable, a type of optical disk that can be written on and read many times, then rewritten and read many times, and so on. Rewritable optical disks are the most versatile form of optical storage, and falling prices make them an attractive alternative to the standard floppy disk.

Eavesdropping Intercepting messages on a computer network.

E-business Outsourcing Outsourcing e-commerce and e-business aspects of one's company, such as Web-site hosting, application hosting, telecom management, and so forth.

E-commerce Buying and selling electronically, as in handling commerce transactions.

Ecosystem A web of relationships surrounding one or a few companies.

E-mail *See* Electronic mail.

Edge Server Distributed databases on the edge of the Internet (close to a set of users), holding a copy of an organization's Web site.

EDI *See* Electronic data interchange.

EDP auditing A variety of methods used by trained auditors to ensure the correct processing of data. EDP auditing combines data processing controls with classical accounting auditing methods.

E-enablement Integrating use of the Internet into how companies work; building e-enabled relationships with consumers and other enterprises, not simply performing transactions electronically.

EIS *See* Executive information system.

Electronic channel An electronic link used to create, distribute, and present information and knowledge as part of a product or service or as an ancillary good.

Electronic commerce The electronic transmission of buyer/seller transactions and other related communications between individuals and businesses or between two or more businesses that are trading partners. By the late 1990s the Internet became the major platform for conducting electronic commerce or e-commerce. *See also* B2B, B2C, Dot-com.

Electronic data interchange (EDI) A set of standards and hardware and software technology that enables computers in independent organizations to exchange business documents electronically. Although typical transactions include purchase orders, order acknowledgments, invoices, price quotes, shipping notices, and insurance claims, any document can potentially be exchanged using EDI. The transaction standards are typically established by an industry consortium or a national or international standards body (such as ANSI).

Electronic mail A system whereby users send and receive messages electronically at their workstations. Electronic mail, or e-mail, can help eliminate telephone tag and usually incorporates such features as sending a message to a distribution list, resending a message to someone else with an appended note, and filing messages in electronic file folders for later recall.

Electronic tender An electronic communication capability in a product or service that allows that product or service to be tended; that is, cared for, attended to, or kept track of by a remote computer.

Electronic vaulting An off-site data storage facility used by organizations for backing up data against loss in case of a disaster.

Encapsulation A principle of object-oriented programming in which both data and operations (methods) to be performed using the data are stored together as an object.

Encryption An encoding system used for transmission of computer data to ensure confidentiality and security of the data.

End-user computing Hands-on use of computer resources by non-IS specialists to enter data, make inquiries, prepare reports, communicate, perform statistical analyses, analyze problems, develop Web pages, and so forth.

Enterprise modeling A top-down approach to detailing the data requirements of an organization. Enterprise modeling employs a high-level, three-tier approach, first dividing the work of the organization into its major functions (such as selling and manufacturing), and then dividing each of these functions into processes and each process into activities.

Enterprise nervous system The technical means to a real-time enterprise; a network that connects people, applications, and devices.

Enterprise resource planning (ERP) system A set of integrated business applications, or modules, to carry out the most common business functions, including inventory control, general ledger accounting, accounts payable, accounts receivable, material requirements planning, order management, and human resources. ERP modules are integrated, primarily through a common set of definitions and a common database, and the modules have been designed to reflect a particular way of doing business, i.e., a particular set of business processes. The leading ERP vendors are Oracle, PeopleSoft, and SAP.

Enterprise system Large applications designed to integrate a set of business functions or processes. Enterprise resource planning (ERP) system packages were the first wave of such systems, which today also include customer relationship management (CRM) systems and supply chain management (SCM) systems.

Entity In data modeling, the things about which data are collected, for example, a customer or a product.

Entity-relationship diagram (ERD) A common notation for modeling organizational data requirements. ER diagramming uses specific symbols to represent data entities, relationships, and elements.

E-procurement Buying items via the Web using company-tailored electronic catalogs of items for which the company has negotiated prices with the seller; e-procurement generally uses a third-party marketplace to handle the coordination between buyer and seller.

ERD *See* Entity-relationship diagram.

ERP *See* Enterprise resource planning system.

E-tailing Retailing over the Web.

Ethernet The name of the original Xerox version of a contention bus local area network design, which has come to be used as a synonym for a contention bus design. *See also* Local area network, Contention bus.

Evolutionary design *See* Genetic programming.

Evolutionary development Any development approach that does not depend upon defining complete requirements early in the development process, but, like prototyping, evolves the system by building successive versions until the system is acceptable. *See also* Prototyping, Rapid application development.

Exchanges Business-to-business electronic marketplaces where many buyers purchase goods from many sellers. These are generally organized by industry or by specialties within an industry.

Executive dashboard A type of executive information system that allows executives access to a company's data warehouse (via a display screen that resembles a car dashboard), allowing real-time analysis of how well a division, region, or other part of the business is progressing on meeting its forecasts.

Executive information system (EIS) A computer application designed to be used directly by managers, without the assistance of intermediaries, to provide the executive easy online access to current information about the status of the organization and its environment. Such information includes filtered and summarized internal transactions data, as well as "soft" data, such as assessments, rumors, opinions, and ideas.

Expert systems The branch of artificial intelligence concerned with building systems that incorporate the decision-making logic of a human expert. Expert systems can diagnose and prescribe treatment for diseases, analyze proposed bank loans, and determine the optimal sequence of stops on a truck route.

Expert systems shell Computer software that provides the basic framework of an expert system and a limited but user-friendly special language to develop the expert system. With the purchase of such a shell, the organization's system builder can concentrate on the details of the business decision being modeled and the development of the knowledge base.

Explicit knowledge Knowledge that has been articulated, codified, and made public.

Extended enterprise All of one's own organization plus those organizations with which one interacts, such as suppliers, buyers, and government agencies; interconnected single-organization networks that are not limited by industry and provide a type of electronic information consortium.

eXtensible Markup Language (XML) An emerging standard in markup languages that is used to facilitate data interchange among applications on the Web. An XML specification consists of tags that are intended to convey the meaning of data, not the presentation format.

External document-based information Electronic information that is available outside an organization and is text based, rather than numeric.

External operational measures Measures of computer operational performance that users can see, such as system and network uptime (or downtime), response time, turnaround time, and program failures. These directly relate to customer satisfaction.

External record-based information Electronic information that is available outside an organization and is numeric, rather than text based.

External Service Provider (ESP) A company that provides services to a firm, often acting as an outsourcer. There are numerous types of ESPs, such as those that provide Web-site hosting, back-up and recovery, and application hosting.

Extract file A file extracted from a company's transaction database and placed in a decision support database or a data warehouse where it can be queried by end users.

Extranet An e-commerce application in which a business has electronic access to a trading partner's intranet using a Web browser. *See also* Intranet.

Extreme Programming (XP) A so-called "agile" software development approach in which programmers develop computer code in a very short time period using programming pairs, common coding approaches, and frequent testing of each other's work.

E-zines Web pages owned by frustrated writers who publish their own electronic magazines.

Factory automation The use of information technology to automate various aspects of factory operations. Factory automation includes numerically controlled machines, material requirements planning (MRP) systems, computer-integrated manufacturing (CIM), and computer-controlled robots.

Fast Ethernet An approach to implementing a high-speed local area network, operating at 100 million bits per second (mbps). Fast Ethernet uses the same CSMA/CD architecture as traditional Ethernet and is usually implemented using either a cable of four twisted pairs (this is called 100 Base-T) or a multi-mode fiber-optic cable (this is 100 Base-F). *See also* Contention bus, CSMA/CD protocol, Ethernet.

FDDI *See* Fiber Distributed Data Interface.

Feasibility analysis An analysis step in the systems development life cycle in which the economic, operational, and technical feasibility of a proposed system is assessed.

Federal design A type of IS organization design that centralizes certain functions where economies can be substantial and decentralizes other functions to be closer to the IS customer. Often operations activities are centralized under a single corporate IS unit to achieve cost efficiencies, while systems development activities are decentralized to business units to give these units autonomous control over local application needs.

Federated databases A way of organizing databases where each retains its autonomy, where its data is defined independently of the other databases, and where its database management system takes care of itself while retaining rules for others to access its data.

Feeding the Web Promoting the platform on which a firm bases its offerings because the firm's prosperity is linked to the platform's prosperity.

Fiber Distributed Data Interface (FDDI) An American National Standards Institute (ANSI) standard for building a local area network that offers a transmission speed of 100 million bits per second and fault tolerance because of its double-ring architecture; FDDI utilizes either fiber-optic cabling or a cable containing four twisted pairs.

Fiber optics A transmission medium in which data are transmitted by sending pulses of light through a thin fiber of glass or fused silica. Although expensive to install and difficult to work with, the high transmission speeds possible with fiber-optic cabling—100 million bits per second (bps) to 100 billion bps—are leading to its use in most new long-distance telephone lines, in backbone networks to connect multiple LANs, and in LANs where very high speeds or high security needs exist.

File-sharing application A computer program that facilitates the sharing of files across computers, client-to-client, using peer-to-peer networking rather than a traditional server. See also P2P.

File Transfer Protocol (FTP) An Internet application, or tool, that allows users to send and receive files, including programs, from one computer system to another over the Internet. The user logs onto the two computer systems at the same time and then copies files from one system to the other.

Filtering Using a software program (a filter) to automatically route messages or documents according to their content.

Firewall An electronic device, such as a router, personal computer, or workstation, that inhibits access to an organization's internal network (intranet) from the Internet.

Flash memory A type of memory used in digital cameras and music players, as well as in keychain drives for PCs. *See also* Keychain drive.

Formal system The way an organization or business process was designed to work. *See also* Informal system.

Foundry As used in the semiconductor industry, a foundry operation involves the production of chips for other companies that have been designed by those companies.

Fourth generation language A computer language in which the user gives a precise statement of what is to be accomplished, not how to do it. No procedure is necessary; the order of statements is usually inconsequential. Examples include IFPS, SAS, FOCUS, and CA-Ramis.

Free agent A type of telecommuter who works as an independent contractor.

Freeware Software given away for free, generally via the Internet but also on CD-ROMs.

Front-end intelligence An interface for interacting with the user, most useful when it is decentralized, flexible, personalized, and sensitive to context.

Front-end tools Tools in a computer-aided software engineering suite that are used by analysts and designers to create the design of a computer system.

FTP *See* File Transfer Protocol.

Full-duplex transmission A type of data transmission in which data can travel in both directions at once over the communication line.

Functional information system An information system, usually composed of multiple interrelated subsystems, that provides the information necessary to accomplish various tasks within a specific functional area of the business, such as production, marketing, accounting, personnel, or engineering.

Gateway A hardware device employed in a telecommunications network to connect two or more local area networks (LANs) or to connect two different types of networks, such as a backbone network and the Internet, where the networks may use different protocols. The gateway, which is really a sophisticated router, forwards only those messages that need to be forwarded from one network to another. *See also* Router.

Genetic programming The branch of artificial intelligence that divides a problem into multiple segments, and then links solutions to these segments together in different ways to breed new "child" solutions; after many generations of breeding, genetic programming might produce results superior to anything devised by a human. Genetic programming has been most useful in the design of innovative products, such as a satellite support arm and an energy-efficient light bulb.

Geodatabase model A relatively new approach for representation and analysis of spatial data that draws on object-oriented database concepts; this approach results in fewer problems with data accuracy while accommodating raster, vector, address, coordinate, and other spatial data in one database.

Geographic information system (GIS) A computer-based system designed to capture, store, manipulate, display, and analyze data spatially referenced to the Earth; a GIS links data to maps so that the data's spatial characteristics can be easily understood.

Gigabit Ethernet An approach to implementing a high-speed local area network, operating at 1 billion bits per second (gbps) and higher. One-gigabit

Ethernet (1 GbE) comes in several versions, including 1000 Base-T running over a cable of four twisted pairs, 1000 Base-SX running over multimode fiber-optic cabling, and 1000 Base-LX running over either multimode fiber or single-mode fiber depending on the distances involved (much longer distances are possible with single-mode fiber). 1 GbE is often used in backbone networks. *See also* Backbone network, Fast Ethernet.

GIS *See* Geographic information system.

Glocalizing Striking a balance between global and local needs.

Gopher A menu-driven Internet application, or tool, that allows the user to search for publicly available data posted on the Internet by digging (like a gopher) through a series of menus until the sought-after data are located. Gopher has largely disappeared, subsumed by the greater capabilities of the World Wide Web.

Graphical user interface (GUI) An interface between a computer and a human user based on graphical screen images such as icons. With a GUI (pronounced gooey), the user selects an application or makes other choices by using a mouse to click on an appropriate icon or label appearing on the screen. Windows 2000, Windows XP, and the OS/2 operating system employ a GUI.

Grid computing The cooperative utilization of many (even several thousand) computers in a network to solve a problem that requires a lot of parallel computer processing power.

Group support system (GSS) A variant of a decision support system (DSS) in which the system is designed to support a group rather than an individual. The purpose of a GSS is to make group sessions more productive by supporting such group activities as brainstorming, issue structuring, voting, and conflict resolution.

Group technology (GT) A computer-based system that logically groups parts according to physical characteristics, machine routings through the factory, and similar machine operations. Based on these logical groupings, GT is able to identify existing parts that engineers can use or modify rather than design new parts.

Groupware Application software designed to support groups; the functionality varies but may include electronic mail, electronic bulletin boards, computer conferencing, electronic calendaring, group scheduling, sharing documents, meeting support systems, electronic forms, and desktop videoconferencing.

GSS *See* Group support system.

GT *See* Group technology.

GUI *See* Graphical user interface.

Hacker A person who breaks into a computer for the challenge of it without intending to do any harm.

Hacking/cracking The unauthorized access to a host computer. This access may be a direct intrusion or via a computer virus or Trojan horse.

Half-duplex transmission A type of data transmission in which data can travel in both directions over the communication line, but not simultaneously.

Handheld computers The smallest type of computing device, which can easily be held in one hand while using the other hand to enter instructions or data via a keyboard or stylus; also called palmtop computer or personal digital assistant.

Hardware The physical pieces of a computer or telecommunications system, such as a central processing unit, a printer, and a terminal.

Help desk A support service for the users of IT that can be accessed via phone or e-mail. The service is either provided by IS specialists within the organization that owns, operates, or develops the resource, or is provided by IS specialists external to the organization that have been contracted to provide this service (i.e., an outsourcing vendor).

Hertz Cycles per second; one measure of data transmission speed. Hertz is usually equivalent to baud (another measure of transmission speed) and to bits per second.

Heuristics Rules that draw upon experience, common sense, ways of doing business, and even rules and regulations.

Hierarchical decomposition The process of breaking down a system into successive levels of subsystems. This recursive decomposition allows a system to be described at various levels of detail, each appropriate for a different kind of analysis or for a different audience.

Homepage A person's or organization's base page on the World Wide Web.

HTML *See* Hypertext Markup Language.

HTTP *See* Hypertext Transfer Protocol.

Hub A simple network device employed in a telecommunications network to connect one section of a local area network (LAN) to another. A hub forwards every message it receives to the other section of the LAN, whether or not the messages need to go there. Another use of a hub is to create a shared Ethernet LAN; in this case, the hub is a junction box containing up to 24 ports into which cables can be plugged. Embedded inside the hub is a linear bus connecting all the ports.

Human assets A component of the IT architecture outlining the ideal state of the personnel, values, and management systems aspects of an IT system.

Human capital Knowledge, skills, and innovativeness of employees as well as company values, culture, and philosophy.

Hypertext As used on the World Wide Web, the linking of objects, such as text, pictures, sound clips, and video clips, to each other so that by clicking on highlighted text or a small icon, the user is taken to the related object.

Hypertext Markup Language (HTML) A specialized language to "mark up" pages to be viewed on the World Wide Web. The "markups" consist of special codes inserted in the text to indicate headings, boldfaced text, italics, where images or photographs are to be placed, and links to other Web pages, among other things.

Hypertext Transfer Protocol (HTTP) The underlying protocol used by the World Wide Web. HTTP defines how messages are formatted and transmitted and what actions Web browsers and Web servers should take in response to various commands.

I-CASE *See* Integrated-CASE.

IC *See* Information center.

Identity theft The act of appropriating an individual's personal information without that person's knowledge to commit fraud or theft. An identity thief uses information such as name, address, social security number, credit card number, and/or other identifying information to impersonate someone else and obtain loans or purchase items using his or her credit.

IM *See* Instant messaging.

Imaging A computer input/output method by which any type of paper document—including business forms, reports, charts, graphs, and photographs—can be read by a scanner and translated into digital form so that it can be stored in the computer system; this process can also be reversed so that the digitized image stored in the computer system can be displayed on a video display unit, printed on paper, or transmitted to another computer or workstation.

In-line system A computer system in which data entry is accomplished online (i.e., a transaction is entered directly into the computer via some input device) but the processing is deferred until a suitable batch of transactions has been accumulated.

Incumbent Local Exchange Carriers (ILECs) Formerly called Regional Bell Operating Companies (RBOCs), telecom companies spun off from AT&T in 1984.

Indexed file organization A method of organizing a computer file or database in which the control keys only are arranged in sequence in a separate table, along with a pointer to the complete records associated with each key. The records themselves can then be arranged in any order.

Inference engine A portion of an expert system's software that contains the reasoning methods used to search the knowledge base and solve the problem.

Informal system The way the organization or business process actually works. *See also* Formal system.

Information Data (usually processed data) that are useful to a decision maker.

Information age Though defined a multitude of ways, this book refers to the information age as when the number of U.S. information workers surpassed the number of U.S. workers in all other sectors combined (information workers exceeded 50 percent of the U.S. workforce).

Information architecture A blueprint or definitions of corporate data—such as customers, products, and business transactions—that is used consistently across the firm's applications.

Information center (IC) An organizational unit whose mission is to support end-user computing by providing services such as education and training, application consulting, assistance in selecting hardware and software, facilitating access to computerized data, and so forth. An IC may also be responsible for policy setting for end-user computing, including the selection of standards for PC tools.

Information repository The heart of a computer-aided software engineering (CASE) system that stores and organizes all information needed to create, modify, and develop a software system.

Information resources The intangible information assets of a firm, including data, information, knowledge, processes, patents, and so on.

Information resources assessment The act of taking inventory and critically evaluating technological and human resources in terms of how well they meet the organization's business needs.

Information system (IS) A computer-based system that uses information technology, procedures (processes), and people to capture, move, store, and distribute data and information.

Information systems (IS) organization The organizational department or unit that has the primary responsibility for managing information technology (IT).

Information technology (IT) Computer hardware and software for processing and storing data, as well as communications technology for transmitting data.

Information technology architecture A written set of guidelines for a company's desired future for information technology (IT) within which people can make individual decisions that will be compatible with that desired future; should include components relating to beliefs or values, data, the technology infrastructure, applications, and the management system for IT.

Information vision A written expression of the desired future for information use and management in an organization.

Infrastructure The implementation of an architecture, including in IT the processors, software, databases, electronic links, and data centers as well as the standards that ensure the components work together, the skills for managing the operation, and even some of the electronic processes themselves.

Inheritance A principle of object-oriented approaches in which subclasses inherit all of the properties and methods of the class to which they belong.

Insourcing Moving responsibility for specific services to a group within the company rather than to an external service provider. Commonly the insourcer is the shared services group.

Instant messaging (IM) A synchronous communication system (a variant of electronic mail) that enables the user to establish a private "chat room" with another individual to carry out text-based communication in real time over the Internet. Typically, the IM system signals the user when someone on his or her private list is online, and then the user can initiate a chat session with that individual.

Institutional DSS A decision support system built by DSS professionals using a DSS language that is intended to be used for the long term to support the organization's operations rather than to support an individual or small group for a short time.

Instruction An individual step or operation in a program, particularly in a machine language program. *See also* Machine language, Program.

Integrated-CASE (I-CASE) A set of full-cycle, integrated CASE tools, in which system specifications supported by the front-end tools can be converted into computer code by the back-end tools included in the system. *See also* Computer-aided software engineering.

Integrated Services Digital Network (ISDN) A set of international standards by which the public telephone network offers extensive new telecommunications capabilities—including simultaneous transmission of both voice and data over the same line—to telephone users worldwide.

Intellectual capital A preferred term for knowledge, to distinguish it from the other kinds of capital that firms possess.

Intellectual property Any product of the human mind, such as an idea, an invention, a literary creation, a work of art, a business method, an industrial process, a chemical formula, a computer program, or a presentation.

Interactive system A computer system in which the user directly interacts with the computer. In such a system, the user would enter data into the computer via some type of input device and the computer would provide a response almost immediately, as in an airline reservation system. An interactive system is an online system in which the computer provides an immediate response to the user.

Inter-Exchange Carriers (IXCs) Long-distance telecom carriers.

Internal document-based information Information that is available in-house and is text based, such as internal reports, memos, and so forth.

Internal operational measures Metrics of the performance of a firm's IT operations that are of interest to its computer operations staff, such as computer usage as a percentage of capacity, availability of mainline systems, disk storage utilized, job queue length, number of jobs run, number of jobs rerun due to problems, age of applications, and number of unresolved problems.

Internal record-based information Information that is available in-house and is alphanumeric rather than textual.

Interface The point of contact where the environment meets a system or where two subsystems meet. Special functions such as filtering, coding/decoding, error detection and correction, buffering, security, and summarizing occur at an interface, which allows compatibility between the environment and system or two subsystems. *See also* Graphical user interface.

Internet A network of networks that use the TCP/IP protocol, with gateways (connections) to even more networks that do not use the TCP/IP protocol. The two primary applications on the Internet are electronic mail and the World Wide Web. *See also* B2B, B2C, Electronic commerce, Electronic mail, Transmission Control Protocol/Internet Protocol, World Wide Web.

Internet2 A not-for-profit consortium of more than 200 universities, working in partnership with more than 60 leading technology companies and the U.S. government, to develop and deploy advanced network applications and technologies. Internet2 operates the Abilene very high-performance network as the backbone network for the Internet2 universities.

Internet era A computing era usually considered to have begun with the widespread dissemination of Web browsers in the mid-1990s.

Interoperate Different products working together, driven by the open systems movement.

Interorganizational Systems (IOS) Systems that require at least two parties with different objectives to collaborate on the development and operation of a joint computer-based system.

Interpreter A software program that translates a third generation or fourth generation language program into an equivalent machine language program, executing each source program statement as soon as that single statement is translated.

Intranet A network operating within an organization that employs the TCP/IP protocol. Because the protocol is the same, the organization may use the same Web browser, Web crawler, and Web server software as it would use on the Internet. A firewall typically is used to separate the intranet from the public Internet.

IS *See* Information system.

IS mission The reason(s) for the existence of the IS organization. Typical reasons include reducing the organization's costs, creating an effective information technology system, and exercising leadership in creating competitive advantage for the organization.

IS steering committee A committee of business managers whose function is to advise the head of IS on policy matters and often to decide which proposed systems will be developed by IS.

ISDN *See* Integrated Services Digital Network.

IT *See* Information technology.

IT Governance The assignment of decision rights and the accountability framework to encourage desirable behavior in the use of IT. Governance differs from management in that governance is about deciding who makes decisions, while management is about making decisions once decision rights have been assigned.

IT platform The set of hardware, software, communications, and standards an organization uses to build and operate its information systems.

IT portfolio management A disciplined approach to managing IT investments to best align with the current and anticipated needs of a business for not only the short term, but also the long term. The typical IT investment portfolio includes investments in hardware, custom software, packaged software, and communications networks.

J2EE *See* Java 2 Enterprise Edition.

JAD *See* Joint application design.

Java 2 Enterprise Edition (J2EE) A platform for application development on the Web, using the OOP paradigm, created by an alliance of companies led by Sun Microsystems. J2EE programming is done in Java, and the programs will run on any platform. J2EE is a collection of Java-based technologies for Web application development; popular J2EE products are Websphere from IBM, Weblogic from BEA, and SunOne from Sun.

Java virtual machine A self-contained operating environment, existing for all major operating systems, in which Java programs are run. The Java virtual machine behaves as if it is a separate computer and thus implements the "write once, run anywhere" portability that is Java's goal.

JCL *See* Job control language.

Job control language (JCL) The specialized computer language by which computer users communicate with the operating system. The term JCL is used primarily in the context of IBM mainframe computers.

Joint application design (JAD) A technique in which system requirements are defined by a team of users and IS specialists during an intensive effort led by a trained facilitator. JAD sessions are often held at special facilities with CASE tool support.

Keiretsu Japanese term referring to the associations of independent and interdependent businesses working in concert.

Keychain drive The newest and smallest portable direct access storage device for PCs, making use of flash memory rather than a magnetizable disk. This device, which plugs into the USB port of a PC, goes by various names, of which keychain drive is perhaps the most descriptive, because the device is not much larger than the average car key.

KM *See* Knowledge management.

KMS *See* Knowledge management system.

Knowledge Information with direction or intent derived from strategies or objectives.

Knowledge brokers A way to promote knowledge sharing by giving titles to employees who excel at knowledge sharing.

Knowledge infrastructure A support system that manages information, enables understanding, and supports learning.

Knowledge management (KM) The sharing and transferring of knowledge for the purpose of disseminating and reusing valuable knowledge that, once applied, enhances learning and improves performance; in other words, the strategies and processes of identifying, creating, capturing, organizing, transferring, and leveraging knowledge to help individuals and firms compete.

Knowledge management system (KMS) A system for managing organizational knowledge that enables individuals and organizations to enhance learning, improve performance, and, hopefully, produce long-term sustainable competitive advantage.

Knowledge worker A typical employee in the Information Age for whom information and knowledge are both inputs and outputs of his or her work activities.

Knowware Advanced groupware information technology that helps people and organizations share knowledge.

LAN *See* Local area network.

Laptop computers The type of personal computer that can easily be carried by a user and used on the user's "lap." A laptop PC is the size of a small briefcase and weighs less than 10 pounds. The terms "laptop" and "notebook" PC are now used almost interchangeably, although the notebook PC originally was a smaller machine than a laptop.

Legacy systems Mainframe computer applications that handle the day-to-day transactions of the company in a centralized, rather than distributed, manner. Alternatively, any system that does not use current technology.

Lewin/Schein change model A model for managing changes that describes planned change in an organization as consisting of three stages—unfreezing, moving, and refreezing.

Life-cycle process *See* Systems development life cycle.

Line executive A business executive who manages a profit-oriented business unit, such as manufacturing, rather than a supporting staff unit, such as finance.

Linkage analysis planning A planning approach that studies the links between an organization and its suppliers and customers.

Listserv An Internet application, or tool, that is essentially a mailing list such that members of a group can send a single electronic mail message and have it delivered to everyone in the group.

Local area network (LAN) A local data-only network, usually within a single organization and generally operating within an area no more than 2 or 3 miles in diameter, that contains a number of intelligent devices (usually microcomputers) capable of data processing. LANs are usually arranged in one of four topologies: contention bus, token bus, token ring, and wireless. *See also* Contention bus, Token bus, Token ring, Wireless LAN.

Local Exchange Carrier (LEC) Telecom companies that only handle local, not long distance, telephone calls.

Logic bomb A program that is introduced into a computer and set to take action at a certain time or when a specified event occurs.

Logical system or model A depiction of the function and purpose (the what) of a system without reference to, or implications for, how the system is implemented; includes both As-Is and To-Be models. *See also* Physical system or model.

Loosely/tightly coupled groups Loosely coupled groups are where the activity of each member is relatively independent of the other members (such as salespeople who have their own sales territories). Tightly coupled groups are where the work of each member is tied closely to the work of the other members.

Lower-CASE *See* Computer-aided software engineering.

M-commerce Shorthand for mobile commerce; the utilization of electronic applications and communications via handheld devices and wireless technologies.

Machine language The form of a computer program that the control unit of the computer has been built to understand. In general, each machine language instruction consists of an operation code that tells the control unit what basic machine function is to be performed and one or more addresses that identify the specific memory cells whose contents will be involved in the operation.

Magnetic ink character recognition (MICR) A computer input method used for check processing in the United States. Identifying information and the amount are recorded in magnetizable ink at the bottom of the check; a computer input device called a magnetic ink character reader magnetizes the ink, recognizes the numbers, and transmits the data to the memory of the bank's computer to permit the check to be processed.

Magnetic tape unit A computer file device that stores (writes) data on magnetic tape and retrieves (reads) data from tape back into memory; the usual device on which sequential access files are stored. *See also* Sequential access file.

Mainframes The type of computer system that is used as the main, central computing system of most major corporations and government agencies, ranging in cost from $1,000,000 to $20,000,000 or more and in power from 200 to 8,000 MFLOPS; used for large business general processing, as the server in client/server applications, as a large Web server, and for a wide range of other applications.

Maintenance The process of making changes to a system after it has been placed in operation, including changes required to correct errors, to adapt the system to changes in the environment, and to enhance the system's functionality. Vendors of a purchased system may be contracted to carry out maintenance as part of the purchase contract.

Make-or-buy decision Within the context of systems development, the choice between customized application development and purchasing a software package.

Management systems architecture The portion of an information technology architecture that specifies the management process for IS in an organization.

Manufacturing Automation Protocol (MAP) A communications protocol (a set of rules) for communicating between automated equipment on a factory floor. MAP, which was pioneered by General Motors and has now been accepted by most major manufacturers and IT vendors, ensures an open manufacturing system in which communication between equipment from various vendors is possible.

Manufacturing resources planning (MRP II) A computer-based manufacturing administration system that usually incorporates three major components—the master production schedule, which sets the overall production goals; material requirements planning, which develops the detailed production schedule; and shop floor control, which releases orders to the shop floor based on the detailed schedule and actual production to date.

MAP *See* Manufacturing Automation Protocol.

Marketspace A nonphysical marketplace where information substitutes for physical products and physical location.

Massively parallel processor (MPP) A parallel processor computer with some large number of parallel CPUs; in general, 32 or more parallel CPUs is considered an MPP if the different CPUs are capable of performing different instructions at the same time, or 1,000 or more parallel CPUs is considered an MPP if the different CPUs must all carry out the same instruction at the same time. *See also* Parallel processor.

Material requirements planning (MRP) A computer-based system that accepts the master production schedule for a factory as input and then develops a detailed production schedule, using parts explosion, production capacity, inventory, and lead time data; usually a component of a manufacturing resources planning (MRP II) system.

M-commerce Conducting commerce via small wireless devices, such as buying an item from a vending machine using a cell phone or personal digital assistant (PDA).

Mead's Law Says that *N* transistors on a sliver of silicon yield N^2 performance and value.

MegaFLOPS (MFLOPS) Shorthand for millions of floating point operations per second, a commonly used speed rating for computers. MegaFLOPS ratings are derived by running a particular set of programs in a particular language on the machines being investigated.

Memory The primary area for storage of data in a computer system; also referred to as main memory or primary memory. In a computer system all data flows to and from memory. Memory is divided into cells, and a fixed amount of data can be stored in each cell.

Mesh topology A network topology in which most devices are connected to two, three, or more other devices in a seemingly irregular pattern that resembles a woven net, or a mesh. Examples of a mesh topology include the public telephone network and the network of networks that makes up the Internet.

Metadata Information about a data entity, such as its definition, how it was calculated, its source, when it is updated, who is responsible for it, and so forth.

Metcalfe's Law A theory in which the value of a network to each of its members is related to the square of the number of users; more formally, the value is proportional to $(n^2 - n)/2$, where "n" is the number of nodes on the network.

MFLOPS *See* MegaFLOPS.

MICR *See* Magnetic ink character recognition.

Microcomputers The category of computers with the least cost ($200 to $3,000) and the least power (20 to 400 MFLOPS), generally used for personal computing and small business processing and as a Web client and a client in client/server applications; also called micros or personal computers (PCs).

Microwave Considered a transmission medium, although strictly speaking it is line-of-sight broadcast technology in which radio signals are sent out into the air. With transmission speeds of 50 thousand bits per second (bps) to 100 million bps, microwave transmission is widely used for long-distance telephone communication and for corporate voice and data networks.

Middleware A term that covers all of the software needed to support interactions between clients and servers in client/server systems. Middleware usually includes three categories of software: server operating systems to create a "single-system image" for all services on the network; transport stack software to allow communications employing a standard protocol to be sent across the network; and service-specific software to carry out specific services such as electronic mail.

Midrange systems The subcategory of computers that can be viewed as "small mainframes" in that their technical architecture is derived from mainframe architecture; formerly called minicomputers or superminicomputers. It is now difficult to distinguish midrange systems from workstations because of significant overlaps, resulting in the creation of the workstations/midrange systems category. *See also* Workstations/midrange systems, Workstations.

Mid-tier servers A network topology that has several tiers of servers, such as local work group servers, departmental servers, and an enterprise server (the corporate mainframe).

Minicomputers *See* Midrange systems.

MIPS An acronym for millions of instructions per second executed by the control unit of a computer; a commonly used maximum speed rating for computers.

Modem An abbreviation for modulator/demodulator, a device that converts data from digital form to analog form so that it can be sent over the analog telephone network and reconverts data from analog to digital form after it has been transmitted.

Module A self-contained unit of software that performs one or more functions. Ideally it has well-defined interfaces with the other modules in the program so that changes in a module affect the rest of the program only through the outputs from that module. *See also* Subsystem.

Moore's Law Computer processing power will double every 18 months. This law, stated by Gordon Moore, a founder of Intel, has proven true since 1959.

MP3 A standard coding scheme for compressing audio signals into a very small file (about one-twelfth the size of the original file) while preserving the original level of sound quality when it is played. MP3 is the most popular Internet-audio format that allows users to download music from the Internet.

MPP *See* Massively parallel processor.

MRP *See* Material requirements planning.

MRP II *See* Manufacturing resources planning.

Multimedia The use of a microcomputer system to coordinate many types of communication media—text, graphics, sound, still images, animations, and video. The purpose of a multimedia system is to enhance the quality of and interest in a presentation, whether it is a corporate briefing or a school lesson.

Multiprocessing The method of processing when two or more CPUs are installed as part of the same computer system. Each CPU works on its own job or set of jobs (often using multiprogramming), with all the CPUs under control of a single operating system.

Multiprocessor A computer configuration in which multiple processors (CPUs) are installed as part of the same computer system, with each processor or CPU operating independently of the others. *See* Multiprocessing, Parallel processor, Symmetric multiprocessor.

Multiprogramming A procedure by which the operating system switches back and forth among a number of programs, all located in memory at the same time, to keep the CPU busy while input/output operations are taking place; more specifically, this is called event-driven multiprogramming.

Multitasking The terminology used for microcomputers to describe essentially the same function as multiprogramming on larger machines. In preemptive multitasking, the operating system allocates slices of CPU time to each program (the same as time-driven multiprogramming); in cooperative multitasking, each program can control the CPU for as long as it needs it (the same as event-driven multiprogramming). *See also* Multiprogramming, Time-sharing.

Natural language A computer language (often termed a fifth generation language) in which the user writes a program in ordinary English (or something very close to it). Little or no training is required to use a natural language.

Needs-based IS planning The process of assembling the IS plan by addressing only the stated needs of users.

Negotiation support system (NSS) A special type of group support system designed to support the activities of two or more parties in a negotiation. The core components of an NSS are an individual decision support system for each party in the negotiation and an electronic communication channel between the parties.

.NET A platform for application development on the Web, using the OOP paradigm, created by Microsoft. .NET programming can be done in variety of languages, including VB.NET, C#, and J#, but can only be run on a Windows platform.

Network army A set of individuals and communities aligned by a cause. They have moral and intellectual influencers as opposed to formal leadership, and are only as permanent as their common agenda. Their communications are open, in forums that anyone can join.

Network effect When the value of a product or service offered on a platform (such as a gaming platform or an operating system) increases as the number of users increases, thereby creating a "virtuous" circle of upward spiraling product value and customers. The opposite is a downward spiraling "vicious" circle where a product continually loses its value and its customers.

Network interface card (NIC) In general, a specialized card that must be installed in a computer to permit it to access a particular type of network, usually a local area network. For wireless LANs, the NIC is a short-range radio transceiver that can send and receive radio signals.

Network operating system (NOS) *See* Server operating system.

Network protocol An agreed-upon set of rules or conventions governing communication among elements of a network, or, more specifically, among layers or levels of a network.

Networking The electronic linking of geographically dispersed devices.

Neural networks The branch of artificial intelligence concerned with recognizing patterns from vast amounts of data by a process of adaptive learning; named after the study of how the human nervous system works, but in fact uses extensive statistical analysis to identify meaningful patterns from the data.

NIC *See* Network interface card.

Nonprocedural language *See* Fourth generation language.

Nonrepudiation Not allowing a party in an electronic transaction to repudiate, which means claiming that the transaction never took place; nonrepudiation is an important cornerstone of electronic security.

Normalization The process of creating simple data structures from more complex ones; this process consists of a set of rules that yields a data structure that is very stable and useful across many different requirements.

NOS *See* Network operating system.

Notebook computers The type of personal computer that can easily be carried by the user; this type of PC is similar in size to a student's notebook and it typically weighs no more than 5 or 6 pounds. The terms "laptop" and "notebook" PC are now used almost interchangeably, although the notebook PC originally was a smaller machine than a laptop.

NSS *See* Negotiation support system.

Object A chunk of program code encompassing both data and methods. *See also* Object-oriented programming.

Object-oriented programming (OOP) A type of computer programming based on the creation and use of a set of objects and the development of relationships among the objects. The most popular OOP languages are C++ and Java. *See also* Object, Object-oriented techniques.

Object-oriented techniques A broad term that includes object-oriented analysis and design techniques as well as object-oriented programming.

Object program The machine language program that is the result of translating a second, third, or fourth generation source program.

Object-to-Object Communication The potential for objects such as smart tags to talk to one another.

OCR *See* Optical character recognition.

Office automation The use of information technology to automate various aspects of office operations. Office automation involves a set of office related functions that might or might not be integrated in a single system, including electronic mail, word processing, photocopying, document preparation, voice mail, desktop publishing, personal databases, and electronic calendaring.

Office suite A collection of personal productivity software packages for use in the office (e.g., word processing, spreadsheet, presentation graphics, database management system) that are integrated to some extent and marketed as a set. Microsoft Office is the leading office suite; other suites include Corel WordPerfect Office, Lotus SmartSuite, and Sun StarOffice.

OLAP *See* Online analytical processing.

Online analytical processing (OLAP) Querying against a database, employing OLAP software that makes it easy to pose complex queries along multiple dimensions, such as time, organizational unit, and geography. The chief component of OLAP is the OLAP server, which sits between a client machine and a database server; the OLAP server understands how data are organized in the database and has special functions for analyzing the data. *See also* Data mining.

Online processing A mode of transaction processing in which each transaction is entered directly into the computer when it occurs and the associated processing is carried out immediately. For example, sales would be entered into the computer (probably via a microcomputer) as soon as they occurred, and sales records would be updated immediately.

Online system *See* Online processing.

OOP *See* Object-oriented programming.

Open/closed groups Open groups are where almost anyone can join. Closed groups are where membership is restricted. A "gray scale" between open and closed indicates the degree of difficulty to gain membership.

Open network or open system Though the term "open" keeps expanding, this book refers to open networks/systems as those based on national or international standards so that the products of many manufacturers work with each other.

Open source Software where the complete source code is distributed with any and all distributions, and where anyone can modify and redistribute the code.

Open systems Systems (usually operating systems) that are not tied to a particular computer system or hardware manufacturer. An example is the UNIX operating system, with versions available for a wide variety of hardware platforms.

Open Systems Interconnection (OSI) Reference Model An evolving set of network protocols developed by the International Standards Organization (ISO), which deals with connecting all systems that are open for communication with other systems (i.e., systems that conform to certain minimal standards) by defining seven layers, each of which will have one or more protocols.

Operating system Very complex software that controls the operation of the computer hardware and coordinates all the other software. The purposes of an operating system are to get as much work done as possible with the available resources and to be convenient to use.

Operational IS plan A precise set of shorter-term goals and associated projects that will be executed by the IS department and by business managers in support of the strategic IS plan.

Operational planning The process of outlining the shorter-term goals and tactics that detail how the IS organization and other organizations are implementing the strategic IS initiatives.

Optical character recognition (OCR) A computer input method that directly scans typed, printed, or hand-printed material. A computer input device called an optical character reader scans and recognizes the characters and then transmits the data to the memory or records them on magnetic tape.

Optical disk A medium upon which computer files can be stored. Data are recorded on an optical disk by using a laser to burn microscopic pits on its surface. Optical disks have a much greater capacity than magnetic disks.

OSI *See* Open Systems Interconnection Reference Model.

Outsourcing Contracting with an outside organization to perform one or more functions. IT outsourcing most often involves the operation of computers and networks.

P2P Peer-to-peer networking, in which client computers also act as servers. For example, computers running the same P2P application can gain access to files stored on other computers running the application at that time.

Packet assembly/disassembly device (PAD) A telecommunications device used to connect an organization's internal networks (at each of its locations) to the common carrier network in order to set up a packet-switched network.

Packet-switched network A network employing packet switching; examples include vBNS+, the Internet, and many WANs. *See also* Packet switching.

Packet switching A method of operating a digital telecommunications network (especially a WAN) in which information is divided into packets of some fixed length that are then sent over the network separately.

Rather than tying up an entire end-to-end circuit for the duration of the session, the packets from various users can be interspersed with one another to permit more efficient use of the network.

PAD *See* Packet assembly/disassembly device.

Palmtop computers *See* Handheld computers.

Parallel processor (PP) A multiprocessor configuration (multiple CPUs installed as part of the same computer system) designed to give a separate piece of the same program to each of the processors so that work on the program can proceed in parallel on the separate pieces.

Partnering Allying with another organization that has different core competencies, often on a strategic alliance basis, for mutual benefit.

Partnership A coordinating strategy for IS management. Partnership creates strong working relationships between IS personnel and peer managers in business functions and often results in more effective information systems and IS management.

Patent A law that aims to protect inventions (things or processes for producing things) but not abstract ideas or natural laws.

PBX network The type of network emanating from a *p*rivate *b*ranch e*x*change, or PBX, which is a digital switch operated by a built-in computer with the capability of simultaneously handling communications with internal analog telephones, digital microcomputers and terminals, mainframe computers, and the external telephone network; usually arranged in a star or a tree topology.

PC *See* Microcomputers, Laptop computers, Notebook computers.

PDA *See* Personal digital assistant.

Perceptive systems The branch of artificial intelligence that involves creating machines possessing a visual or aural perceptual ability, or both, that affects their physical behavior; in other words, creating robots that can "see" or "hear" and react to what they see or hear.

Personal Area Network (PAN) A network that allows computers in a "personal area" to communicate wirelessly, much like Wi-Fi.

Personal computers *See* Microcomputers.

Personal digital assistant The smallest microcomputers, also called palmtop or handheld computers, which weigh under a pound and cost from $200 to $800.

Personalization Coordinating disparate pieces of intelligence to form personalized offerings.

Personal productivity software Software packages, usually microcomputer-based, designed to increase the productivity of a manager or other knowledge worker; examples are word processing, spreadsheets, database management systems, presentation graphics, and Web browsers.

Physical system or model A depiction of the physical form (the how) of an information system. *See also* Logical system or model.

Planning Developing a view of the future that guides decision making today.

Platform A major trend in interorganizational systems that provides the infrastructure for the operation of a business ecosystem, a region, or an industry. Examples are American Airlines' SABRE computer reservation system, or the video game industry's PlayStation, Nintendo, and Xbox platforms.

Pocket PC The name given to handheld or palmtop PCs running Microsoft's Windows Mobile for Pocket PC operating system (formerly known as Windows CE). Pocket PCs on the market include the Hewlett-Packard iPaq line, the Dell Axim, and products from Toshiba, Audiovox, and ViewSonic.

Portal A standardized entry point to key information on the corporate network. Many organizations have created carefully designed portals to enable employees (and perhaps customers and suppliers) to gain easy access to information they need. *See also* Intranet.

PP *See* Parallel processor.

Privacy Includes the freedom from intrusion, the right to be left alone, the right to control information about oneself, and freedom from surveillance.

Private branch exchange (PBX) network *See* PBX network.

Private programs Computer programs created and used by only one person.

Procedural language *See* Third generation language.

Procedural-oriented techniques *See* Structured techniques.

Process-centered organization A company whose perspective has shifted from tasks to processes; an approach to designing an organization where the business processes are the driving structures

Process-driven design An approach to systems development that designs systems based on the process they are intended to support. With such an approach, only the data necessary to operate the particular process are collected and manipulated.

Processor *See* Central processing unit.

Process owner A person in an organization responsible for an end-to-end process such as the ordering process or a research and development process.

Productivity language Another name for a fourth generation language. This type of language tends to make the programmer or user more productive, which explains the name.

Program A complete listing of what the computer is to do for a particular application, expressed in a form that the control unit of the computer has been built to understand or that can be translated into such a form. A program is made up of a sequence of individual steps or operations called instructions. *See also* Control unit, Instruction.

Program management Techniques for coordinating multiple projects in order to obtain benefits not achievable from managing each project individually.

Program structure chart A common diagrammatic technique for showing the flow of control for a computer program.

Project champion A business manager who has the motivation or influence, or both, to drive a systems project through to successful implementation; helps to remove obstacles and motivate users to accept changes associated with the system. *See also* Sponsor.

Project management Techniques for managing a one-time endeavor (project) that includes multiple tasks, including the management of project scope, time, cost, and human resources.

Project manager The manager accountable for delivering a project of high quality, on time and within budget; may be an IS manager, a business manager, or both.

Project milestone A significant deliverable for a project and its assigned deadline date for completion.

Project-oriented IS planning An approach to building the IS plan that assembles the IS plan from individual projects.

Proprietary software Software sold only in its compiled state, undecipherable by humans, and whose code is not allowed to be changed except by the developer.

Proprietary systems Systems (usually operating systems) that are written expressly for a particular computer system. Examples are Windows 2000 and Windows XP, which are Microsoft's current operating systems for personal computers, and MVS and VM, which are the two alternative large machine operating systems offered by IBM.

Prototyping A systems methodology in which an initial version of a system is built very quickly using fourth generation tools and then is tried out by users, who recommend changes that are the basis for building an improved version. This iterative process is continued until the result is accepted. *See also* Rapid application development.

Public key encryption A methodology for encrypting and decrypting text to ensure identity of the parties. A message sender uses the assigned private key to encrypt the message and the recipient uses the sender's public key (known to anyone) to decrypt it, thus validating the sender's identity. The process also works in reverse; sending a message encrypted using a person's public key that can only be decrypted and read by that person using their private key.

Pull technology Refers to the mode of operation on the Internet where the client must request data before the data are sent to the client. For example, a Web browser represents pull technology in that the browser must request a Web page before it is sent to the user's screen. *See also* Push technology.

Push technology Refers to the mode of operation on the Internet where data are sent to the client without the client requesting the data. Examples of push technology include electronic mail and the delivery of news or stock quotations to the user's screen. *See also* Pull technology.

Quality of service Refers to the ability of a network to provide a range of assured levels of performance.

Query language A 4 GL, nonprocedural special-purpose language for posing queries to the database, often built into the DBMS, that allows users to produce reports without writing procedural programs by specifying their content and format.

Quick hit DSS A system that is quite limited in scope, is developed and put into use quickly, and helps a manager come to a decision. The term "ad hoc" has also been used to distinguish from institutional DSS, although some quick hit systems become regularly used.

RAD *See* Rapid application development.

Radio frequency identification (RFID) An approach to item identification being considered as a possible successor to bar codes. RFID tags, which are about the size of a postage stamp, combine tiny chips with an antenna. When a tag is placed on an item, it automatically radios its location to RFID readers on store shelves, checkout counters, loading bay doors, and possibly shopping carts. With RFID tags, inventory is taken automatically and continuously. RFID tags can cut costs by requiring fewer workers for scanning items; they can also provide more current and more accurate information to the entire supply chain.

RAID *See* Redundant array of independent disks.

Rapid application development (RAD) A hybrid systems development methodology based upon a combination of SDLC, prototyping, JAD techniques, and CASE tools, in which the end-prototype becomes the actual system. *See also* Prototyping, Joint application design, CASE.

Raster-based GIS One of two basic approaches for representation and analysis of spatial data in which space is divided into small, equal-sized cells arranged in a grid; these cells (or rasters) can take on a range of values and are "aware" of their location relative to other cells. Weather forecasting employs a raster-based approach.

Rationalized data Using the same data name for all uses of the same data.

Real-time enterprise Where organizations can know how they are doing at the moment, rather than have to wait days, weeks, or months for analyzable data.

Reduced instruction set computing chip *See* RISC chip.

Redundant array of independent disks (RAID) A type of storage system for large computers in which a large number of inexpensive, small disk drives (such as those used in microcomputers) are linked together to substitute for the giant disk drives that were previously used.

Reengineering Not to be confused with the term "business process reengineering," this term, "system or application reengineering," is much narrower and refers to rebuilding software for a new platform or new programming language.

Regional Bell Operating Company A regional telephone company formed by the 1984 deregulation of AT&T. Formerly, these companies were part of AT&T.

Relational databases Databases that store data in tables.

Relational DBMS A particular type of database management system (DBMS) that views each data entity as a simple table, with the columns as data elements and the rows as different instances of the entity. The records are then related by storing common data, e.g., customer number, in each of the associated tables. Relational DBMSs are the most popular type of DBMS today.

Relationship tech New peer-to-peer relationships that are forming—between customer and firm, between customer and customer—which question past ways of working (such as recommender systems).

Release management A documented process for migrating a new system, or a new version of an older system, from a development environment to a production (operations) environment within a given organization.

Repetitive stress injury (RSI) Injury occurring from repetitive motions, such as frequent mouse clicking.

Repudiation Refusing a computer-based transaction, such as when one party reneges on an agreement after the fact, the other party may be left paying for the transaction processing unless it is repudiated.

Request for proposal (RFP) A document that is sent to potential vendors inviting them to submit a proposal for a system purchase. It provides the objectives and requirements of the desired system, including the technical environment in which it must operate; specifies what the vendor must provide as input to the selection process; and explains the conditions for submitting proposals and the general criteria that will be used to evaluate them.

Response time The elapsed time between when a user presses the enter key to send data over the network and when the response from the system appears on the screen.

RFID *See* Radio frequency identification.

RFP *See* Request for proposal.

Ring topology A network topology in which all network devices share a single length of cable—with the ends of the cable connected to form a ring.

Ripple effect The result that occurs when a change in one part of a program or system causes unanticipated problems in a different part of the program or system. Then changes necessary to correct that problem may cause problems somewhere else, and so on.

RISC chip Very fast processor chip based on the idea of reduced instruction set computing, or RISC; originally developed for use in high-powered workstations, but now used in other machines, especially midrange systems.

Router A hardware device employed in a telecommunications network to connect two or more local area networks (LANs), where the networks may use different protocols. The router forwards only those messages that need to be forwarded from one network to another. *See also* Gateway.

RSI *See* Repetitive stress injury.

Rules-Based Systems A common way to store knowledge in an expert system knowledge base, where rules are obtained from experts drawing on their own expertise. Rules generally present this knowledge in the form of if-then statements, and are appropriate when knowledge can be generalized into such specific statements.

Rummler-Brache approach An approach for deciding how to reengineer an organization.

SA&D *See* Systems analysis and design.

SAA *See* Systems Application Architecture.

Satellite communication A variation of microwave transmission in which a communications satellite is used to relay microwave signals over long distances.

Satellite connection A high-speed, or broadband, connection to the Internet using a satellite dish at the home or office to communicate with a satellite.

Scan-Based Trading (SBT) An arrangement between a retail store and product supplier whereby the scan data from point-of-sale checkout systems for products sold determines the amount the retailer pays the supplier.

Scenario A way to manage planning assumptions by creating a speculation of what the future might be like by drawing on trends, events, environmental factors, and the relationships among them.

SCM *See* Supply chain management system.

Scope creep Users asking for additional functions in applications as development proceeded.

SDLC *See* Systems development life cycle.

Secure Sockets Layer (SSL) A protocol for providing security over the Internet.

Self-Managed Work Groups Groups or teams that handle most supervisory tasks on their own, without a supervisor.

Self-Organizing Systems Entities, such as ecosystems, organisms, or organizations, that deal with their environment by responding to each stimulus in an appropriate manner, rather than in a predetermined manner, so they self-organize when needed.

Sense-and-Respond Strategy Making An approach to strategy making that endorses keeping in close contact with the business world, continually sensing for important changes, and then responding quickly to changes by conducting experiments that test different possible futures—as opposed to betting on one strategy for the future.

Sequential access file A basic type of computer file in which all of the records that make up the file are stored in sequence according to the file's control key (e.g., a payroll file will contain individual employee records stored in sequence according to the employee identification number); usually stored on magnetic tape. Computer files, also called secondary memory or secondary storage, are added to a computer system to keep vast quantities of data accessible within the computer system at more reasonable costs than main memory.

Sequential file organization *See* Sequential access file.

Server operating system Support software installed on the network server that manages network resources and controls the network's operation. The primary server operating systems are Microsoft's Windows NT, Windows 2000, and Windows 2003, Novell's NetWare, several variations of UNIX, and Linux.

Service level agreement An agreement between IS and a client that specifies a set of services to be provided, the amount of those services to be provided, the quality of these services and how it is to be measured, and the price to be charged for these services.

SFC *See* Shop floor control system.

Shared Ethernet The original Ethernet design, which employs a contention bus as its logical topology but is usually implemented as a physical star arrangement. The usual way of creating a shared Ethernet LAN is to plug the cables from all the devices on the LAN into a hub, which is a junction box containing up to 24 ports into which cables can be plugged. Embedded inside the hub is a linear bus connecting all the ports. *See also* Ethernet, Switched Ethernet.

Shared services A department or division formed by consolidating and centralizing services formerly operated by business units. These services can include legal, travel, finance, IT, food service, fleet management, accounting, telecom, and others. It is a form of insourcing; business units draw on the expertise in shared services when needed.

Shop floor control (SFC) system A computer-based system that provides online, real-time control and monitoring of machines on the shop floor; for example, the SFC system might recognize that a tool on a particular milling machine is getting dull (by measuring the metal that the machine is cutting per second) and signal this fact to the human operator on duty.

Short message service An "always on" telecom service for communicating quickly and wirelessly using a small handheld device; the messages are typed using a shorthand, code words, abbreviations, or short phrases.

Simplex transmission A type of data transmission in which data can travel only in one direction over the communication line. Simplex transmission might be used from a monitoring device at a remote site back to a central computer.

Smart tags Communicating objects with a small chip that contains information and a radio frequency identification device (RFID). They can carry far more information than bar codes because they carry the history of an item.

SMP *See* Symmetric multiprocessor.

SNA *See* Systems Network Architecture.

Sniffing The interception and reading of electronic messages as they travel over the communication networks. Usually for attempting to unveil passwords to gain access to a system.

Software The set of programs (made up of instructions) that control the operations of the computer system.

Software package Computer software that is sold as a self-contained "package" so that it may be distributed widely. In addition to the computer programs, a package may include comprehensive documentation of the system, assistance in installing the system, training, a hot-line consulting service for dealing with problems, and even maintenance of the system.

SONET *See* Synchronous Optical Network.

Source program A program written in a second, third, or fourth generation language.

SOW *See* Statement of work.

Spaghetti code The way code in many legacy systems appears to a programmer because it has been patched so many times that the logic of the application weaves in and out like a plate of spaghetti.

Spam Unsolicited electronic mail that is broadcast to a large list of e-mail users in an attempt to reach potential customers. Spam is the Internet equivalent to the "junk mail" that is physically sent as bulk mail and delivered by a postal service to recipients who often discard it without even opening it.

Specific DSS *See* Decision support system.

Speech recognition software Software package used to convert the human voice into digitized computer input so that users can "dictate" a document or message to the computer and, eventually, control the computer by oral commands.

Spiral diagram A way of viewing the application development process as a spiral, as opposed to a waterfall.

Sponsor The business executive who is responsible for funding a new system and ensuring that the necessary resources are available to a systems project team. Also may be called business owner. *See also* Project champion.

Spoofing A way of misleading or defrauding a Web surfer by setting up a Web site that mimics a legitimate site. The spoofer may use some means, such as a message board, to direct the victim to the spurious site, or he or she may simply use a close variant of the site's Uniform Resource Locator (URL) to con people who make a typing mistake.

SQL A standard query and data definition language for relational DBMSs. This standard, endorsed by the American National Standards Institute (ANSI), is used in many personal computer, midrange system, and mainframe computer DBMSs.

Stages of growth The four stages that many organizations go through in the introduction and assimilation of new technologies. These are *early successes* (leading to increased interest and experimentation), *contagion* (the learning period for the field), *control* (integration of systems is attempted but proves difficult), and *integration* (use of the particular new technology is mature). An organization can be in several stages simultaneously for different technologies.

Star topology A network topology that has some primary device at its center with cables radiating from the primary device to all the other network devices.

Statement of work A high-level document that describes the deliverables of the project and the key project milestones, which can be used as a contract between the project manager and the executive sponsor of a systems project. *See* Project milestone.

Status access system A system for monitoring what is going on in the company and in the outside world.

Stored-program concept The concept of preparing a precise list of exactly what the computer is to do (this list is called a program), loading or storing this program in the computer's memory, and then letting the control unit carry out the program at electronic speed. The listing or program must be in a form that the control unit of the computer has been built to understand.

Straight-through processing A system where transaction data is entered just once in a process or a supply chain.

Strategic Having a significant, long-term impact on the growth rate, industry, and revenue of an organization.

Strategic IS plan A set of longer-term objectives that represent measurable movement toward the information vision and technology architecture and a set of associated major initiatives that must be undertaken to achieve these objectives.

Strategic planning The process of constructing a viable fit between the organization's objectives and resources and its changing market and technological opportunities.

Strategy Stating the direction you want to go and how you intend to get there.

Structural capital The capabilities embedded in hardware, software, databases, organizational structure, patents, and trademarks that support employees as well as relationships with customers.

Structural dependence A characteristic of a database in which, if the structure of the database changes, all programs accessing the data must be changed as well; hierarchical and network databases both have this undesirable characteristic.

Structural independence A characteristic of a database in which programs that access the data do not need to know the database's structure; in other words, if the structure of the database changes, programs accessing the data do not have to be changed; relational databases have this desirable characteristic.

Structure chart *See* Program structure chart.

Structured programming A technique of writing programs so that each program is divided into modules or blocks, where each block has only one entry point and only one exit point. In this form, the program logic is easy to follow and understand, and thus the maintenance and correction of such a program should be easier than for a nonstructured program.

Structured Query Language (SQL) A database language for making queries of a database that has become the standard.

Structured techniques A body of structured approaches and tools to document system needs and requirements, functional features and dependencies, and design decisions. Also referred to as procedurally oriented techniques. *See also* Structured programming.

Subsystem A component of a system that is itself viewed as a set of interrelated components. A subsystem has a well-defined purpose that must contribute to the purpose of the system as a whole. *See also* Module, Hierarchical decomposition.

Supercomputers The most expensive and most powerful category of computers, ranging in cost from $1,000,000 to $100,000,000 and power from 4,000 to 100,000,000 MFLOPS; used for numerically-intensive computing and as a very large Web server.

Superminicomputers Large minicomputers; the upper end of the minicomputer or midrange systems category. *See also* Midrange systems, Workstations/midrange systems.

Supply chain management (SCM) system A computer-based system for the distribution and transportation of raw materials and finished products throughout the supply chain and for incorporating constraints caused by the supply chain into the production scheduling process.

Supply-push In this business model, companies are organized to build a supply of products or services and then "push" them out to end customers, on store shelves, in catalogs, and such; the opposite is demand-pull.

Support software Programs that do not directly produce output needed by users, but instead support other applications software in producing the needed output. Support software provides a computing environment in which it is relatively easy and efficient for humans to work, enables applications programs written in a variety of languages to be carried out, and ensures that computer hardware and software resources are used efficiently. Support software includes operating systems, language compilers, and sort utilities.

Support systems Systems that can help knowledge workers perform knowledge-based work.

Switch A hardware device employed in a telecommunications network to connect more than two local area networks (LANs) or LAN segments that use the same protocols. For example, a switch might connect several low speed LANs (16 Ethernet LANs running at 10 mbps) into a single 100 mbps backbone network running Fast Ethernet.

Switched Ethernet A newer variation of Ethernet that provides better performance than shared Ethernet at a higher price. A switch is substituted for the shared Ethernet's hub, and the LAN operates as a logical star as well as a physical star. The switch is smarter than a hub—rather than passing all communications through to all devices on the LAN, which is what a hub does, the switch establishes separate point-to-point circuits to each device and then forwards communications only to the appropriate device. *See also* Ethernet, Shared Ethernet.

SWOT analysis A situation analysis conducted as part of strategic IS planning; SWOT refers to strengths, weaknesses, opportunities, and threats.

Symmetric multiprocessor (SMP) A multiprocessor computer configuration in which all the processors (CPUs) are identical, with each processor acting independently of the others. The multiple CPUs equally share functional and timing access to and control over all other system components, including memory and the various peripheral devices, with each CPU working in its own allotted portion of memory.

Synchronous Optical Network (SONET) American National Standards Institute (ANSI) approved standard for connecting fiber-optic transmission systems; this standard is employed in a range of high-capacity leased lines varying from the OC-1 level of 52 mbps to the OC-768 level of 39.812 gbps.

System A set of interrelated components that must work together to achieve some common purpose.

System decoupling Reducing the need to coordinate two system components. Decoupling is accomplished by creating slack and flexible resources, buffers, sharing resources, and standards.

System development The process of building a system, originally by writing code to create an application and then linking together applications to form a system; a newer process is system integration.

System development methodology A framework of guidelines, tools, and techniques for developing computer systems. *See also* Systems development life cycle, Prototyping.

System integration The current process of building systems by piecing together hardware components, software packages, database engines, and network products from numerous vendors into a single, cohesive system.

System requirements A set of logical and physical capabilities and characteristics that a new (or modified) system is required to have upon its implementation (or installation).

System-wide rules An operating discipline for distributed systems that is enforced at all times and governs security, communication between nodes, data accessibility, program and file transfers, and common operating procedures.

Systems analysis and design (SA&D) Major activities performed by IS specialists that are part of systems development and implementation methodologies. *See also* Systems development life cycle, Prototyping, Rapid application development.

Systems analyst IS specialist who works with users to develop systems requirements and help plan implementations and who works with systems designers, programmers, and other information technology (IT) specialists to construct systems based on the user requirements.

Systems Application Architecture (SAA) An evolving set of specifications, under development by IBM, defining programming, communications, and a common end-user interface that will allow applications to be created and moved among the full range of IBM computers. IBM has stated its intention of supporting both SNA and OSI protocols in its future efforts under the SAA umbrella.

Systems backlog The number of new systems development requests or maintenance requests, or both, that have not yet been assigned IS resources to work on them. An "invisible backlog" refers to systems requests not even formally submitted by business managers due to the size of the existing "visible" backlog.

Systems development life cycle (SDLC) The traditional methodology used by IS professionals to develop a new computer application that includes three general phases: Definition, Construction, and Implementation. Also referred to as a "waterfall" process because of its sequential steps. The SDLC methodology defines the activities necessary for these three phases, as well as a framework for planning and managing a development project. Operations and maintenance are included in the Implementation phase. A modified SDLC approach is used to purchase packaged systems.

Systems integrator A firm that will take overall responsibility for managing the development or integration of large, complex systems involving the use of components from a number of different vendors.

Systems Network Architecture (SNA) A set of network protocols created by IBM to allow its customers to construct their own private networks using the wide variety of IBM communication products, teleprocessing access methods, and data link protocols. SNA was first created in 1974 and is still widely used.

Systems software *See* Support software.

T-1 lines The most common leased communication lines, operating at a data transmission rate of 1.544 million bits per second. These lines, which may be leased from AT&T or another long-distance carrier, often provide the basis for a wide area network (WAN).

Tablet computer A variation of a personal computer where the user writes on an electronic tablet (usually the video screen folded flat on top of the PC) with a digital pen. Please note that a tablet PC can also be used as a standard notebook computer.

Tacit knowledge Knowledge "known" but not easily explained to others.

TCO *See* Total cost of ownership.

TCP/IP *See* Transmission Control Protocol/Internet Protocol.

Tech clubs Cross-organizational groups that meet informally, but are supported and sanctioned by top management.

Technological assets A component of the IT architecture that contains desired specifications about future hardware and operating systems, network, data and data management systems, and applications software.

Technology camel A way to distinguish levels of comfort with any technology using five clusters, which, when graphed on a chart, look a lot like a two-humped camel.

Telecommunications Communications at a distance, including voice (telephone) and data (text/image) communications. Other similar terms used almost interchangeably with telecommunications include data communications, datacom, teleprocessing, telecom, and networking.

Telecommuter A person who works at home or at another location that is not part of a regular office environment and who uses computers and communications to connect to organizational resources to accomplish his or her work; includes mobile workers, other "road warriors," and free agents. *See also* Free agent.

Telnet An Internet application, or tool, that allows users to log onto a remote computer from whatever computer they are using at the time, as long as both computers are attached to the Internet.

Terminal A computer-related device that has input (keyboard, mouse) and output (video display) capabilities, but does essentially no processing, and thus operates as a "slave" to a "master" computer, usually a midrange system or a mainframe. For some applications, a microcomputer may emulate a terminal so that it can operate with a large computer system.

Thin clients Network computers that are used much like telephones; they have no hard disk or house applications, but rather just a browser, memory, keyboard, and a modem.

Third generation language A programming language in which the programmer expresses a step-by-step procedure devised to accomplish the desired task. Examples include FORTRAN, COBOL, BASIC, PASCAL, and C.

Third-party implementation partner Outside consultants who are contracted to manage a packaged software implementation project at a client's site as employees of an independent consulting firm, not employees of the vendor of the software package. For example, the large enterprise system vendors typically certify large consulting firms (such as the "Big 4"), IT industry consultants (such as IBM), and smaller consulting firms on different versions of their software packages, and these third-party businesses provide employees who work on project teams at the client site, while the vendors' employees only provide on-site technical support as needed.

Three-tier client/server system A variation of a client/server system in which the processing is split across three tiers, the client and two servers. In the most popular three-tier system, the user interface is housed on the client, usually a PC (tier 1), the processing is performed on a midrange system or workstation operating as the applications server (tier 2), and the data are stored on a large machine (often a mainframe or midrange system) that operates as the database server (tier 3).

Timebox A methodology for building a system in which the developers promise to deliver specific portions of the system within a specific timeframe (a timebox); the intent is to better control project delivery schedules.

Timeboxing Establishing a maximum time limit for the delivery of a project or project module; typically 6 months or less.

Time-sharing A procedure by which the operating system switches among a number of programs, all stored in memory at the same time, giving each program a small slice of CPU time before moving on to the next program; also called time-driven multiprogramming.

Token bus A design standard for a local area network based on a bus topology and the passing of a token around the bus to all devices in a specified order. In this design, a given device can transmit only when it has the token and thus collisions can never occur. The token bus design is central to the Manufacturing Automation Protocol (MAP).

Token ring A design standard for a local area network based on a ring topology and the passing of a token around the ring to all devices in a specified order. In this design, a given device can transmit only when it has the token and thus collisions can never occur.

Total cost of ownership (TCO) Total cost of ownership for a computer system or device, including initial investment and implementation as well as ongoing support costs. For example, the TCO for a desktop PC includes not only the purchase and installation of the PC hardware, but also the software and network installation costs, as well as the cost of supporting the use of the PC (user training, help desk, software upgrades, backups, etc.)

Total Quality Management (TQM) A management technique that focuses on managing the quality of a service or product, often through statistical quality control techniques, in order to achieve higher customer satisfaction and reduce costs as well.

Trademarks A law to protect names, symbols, and other icons used to identify a company or product.

Transaction processing system A very common type of computer application in which transactions of a particular type are processed in order to provide desired output. Examples include the processing of employee work records (transactions) to produce payroll checks and accompanying reports and the processing of orders (transactions) to produce invoices and associated reports. Transaction processing systems might be batch, online, or in-line.

Transborder data flow Electronic movement of data across a country's national boundary. Such data flows may be restricted by laws that protect a country's economic, political, or personal privacy interests.

Transitional outsourcing The outsourcing of legacy systems for maintenance so that the in-house staff can focus on developing replacement client/server systems.

Transmission Control Protocol/Internet Protocol (TCP/IP) A popular network protocol used in many versions of the UNIX operating system, many packet-switched networks, the Internet, and intranets operating within organizations. Although not part of the OSI model, TCP/IP corresponds roughly to the network and transport layers of the seven-layer model.

Tree topology A network topology that has some primary device at the top of the tree, with cables radiating from this primary device to devices further down the tree that, in turn, may have cables radiating from them to other devices still further down the tree, and so on; also called hierarchical topology.

Trojan horse A security-breaking program that is introduced into a computer and serves as a way for an intruder to re-enter the computer in the future. It may be disguised as something innocent such as a screen saver or a game.

T-shaped managers Executives who have both a vertical role (such as running a business unit) and a horizontal role (such as sharing knowledge with their peers in other business units).

Twisted pair The most common transmission medium, with two insulated copper wires (about 1 millimeter thick) twisted together in a long helix. Data transmission speeds of 14,400 to 56,000 bits per second (bps) are possible with twisted pairs on the analog telephone network, with higher speeds of 128,000 bps up to 1.544 million bps attainable over the digital telephone network or up to 100 million bps on local area networks (LANs).

Two-tier client/server system The original implementation of a client/server system in which the processing is split between the client (usually a PC) and the server (workstation, midrange system, or mainframe). If most of the processing is done on the client, this is called a fat client or thin server model; if most of the processing is done on the server, this is called a thin client or fat server model.

Ubiquitous IT An environment in which computer and communications devices are almost everywhere and become an unremarkable part of almost all aspects of people's lives.

UML *See* Unified Modeling Language.

Unified Modeling Language (UML) A general-purpose notational language for specifying and visualizing complex software, especially large, object-oriented projects. Examples of such UML-based CASE tools are IBM's Rational Rose and Borland's Together.

Uniform Resource Locator (URL) An address for an Internet file; the address includes the name of the protocol to access the resource (usually http), a domain name for the computer on which the file is located, and perhaps specific locator information. For example, the Web URL for the publisher of this textbook is *http://www.prenhall.com.* Also known as Universal Resource Locator.

Upper-CASE *See* Computer-aided software engineering.

URL *See* Uniform Resource Locator.

Usenet newsgroups An Internet application, or tool, setting up discussion groups, which are essentially huge electronic bulletin boards on which group members can read and post messages.

User application development Development of business applications by employees who are not IS professionals, but rather are primarily in traditional business roles such as accountants, financial analysts, production schedulers, engineers, and brand managers. In most but not all instances, the people who develop the applications also directly use them in their work.

User-friendly A perceptual measure of how easy it is to navigate and use particular hardware or software from the perspective of a person who is not an IS specialist.

User interface That part of a system through which the user interacts with the system. As examples, it might use a mouse, a touch-screen, menus, commands, voice recognition, a telephone keypad, output screens, voice response, and printed reports. *See also* Graphical user interface.

Utilitarianism An ethical theory, a variation of consequentialism, in which *all* the parties that will be affected by an action must be identified and the consequences for each party delineated and quantified, with beneficial results measured on the positive scale and the harmful results measured on the negative scale. If the outcomes are not certain, then probabilities must be assigned to each outcome for each of the affected parties so that the expected return can be calculated. The action is ethically justified if the expected value of the positives and negatives is positive, that is, if the good outweighs the bad.

Value added network (VAN) Formerly, the name given to the practice of contracting with an outside vendor to operate a packet-switched wide area network (WAN) for an organization. Today such a packet-switched WAN is usually called a managed network.

Value assessment framework A systematic way to separate potential benefits of IT investments by organizational levels.

Value chain A technique for describing a chain of business processes from product/service conception through cessation of the product/ service, where each of the processes adds some kind of value.

Value chain analysis A method developed by Michael E. Porter to identify possible strategic uses of information technology. A firm's value chain contains the activities in the business that add value to a firm's products or services.

Values architecture That part of an IT architecture that specifies the basic beliefs of the managers and employees about IT in the organization.

VAN *See* Value added network.

vBNS+ A very high-speed network, operated by MCI and developed through a cooperative agreement between MCI and the National Science Foundation (NSF), that links NSF-supported supercomputer centers across the United States and provides points-of-presence (POPs) where other users may link to vBNS+ from the Internet.

Vector-based GIS One of two basic approaches for representation and analysis of spatial data in which features in the landscape are associated with either a point (e.g., customer address, power pole), a line (road, river), or a polygon (lake, county, zip code area). The vector-based approach is in widespread use in public administration, public utilities, and business.

Vector facility A specialized multiprocessor configuration (multiple CPUs installed as part of the same computer system) used to handle calculations involving vectors. Parallel microprocessors perform the same operation simultaneously on each element of the vector. A vector facility can be attached to a mainframe or other large computer to handle numeric- or compute-intensive portions of programs.

Veronica An Internet application, or tool, that allows the user to search publicly available Gopher sites using key words until the sought-after data are located. Veronica, like Gopher, has largely disappeared, with both subsumed by the greater capabilities of the World Wide Web.

Vertically integrated information system An information system that serves more than one vertical level in an organization or an industry, such as a system designed to be used by an automobile manufacturer and the associated independent dealers.

View integration A bottom-up approach to detailing an organization's data requirements. View integration analyzes each report, screen, form, and document in the organization and combines each of these views into one consolidated and consistent picture of all organizational data.

Virtual circuit A temporary circuit created between caller and receiver where that circuit is theirs alone to use; no other parties can share it during the duration of their telephone call.

Virtual memory A procedure by which the operating system switches portions of programs (called pages) between main memory and DASD so that portions of enough programs are stored in main memory to enable efficient multiprogramming. To the user it appears as though an unlimited amount of main memory is available, whereas in fact most of each program is stored in DASD.

Virtual organization An organization that regularly uses the services of workers who are not regular (long-term) employees or have no real office or headquarters, or both. *See also* Free agent.

Virtual private network (VPN) The equivalent of a private packet-switched network that has been created using public telecommunications lines. A VPN provides a moderate data rate (up to 2 mbps) at a very reasonable cost, but the network's reliability is low. Most commonly, a VPN is created using the Internet as the medium for transporting data, employing encryption and other security mechanisms to ensure that only authorized users can access the network and that the data cannot be intercepted. *See also* Packet-switched network, Packet switching.

Virtual reality (VR) The use of computer-based systems to create an environment that seems real to one or more senses (usually including sight) of the human user or users. Examples of practical uses of VR include tank crew training for the U.S. Army, the design of an automobile dashboard and controls, and retail store layout.

Virtual team A work team where members of the team are not co-located, and where they are not necessarily even in the same time zone. A virtual team is often supported by groupware or a group support system that facilitates a "different time, different place" meeting format.

Virus *See* Computer virus.

Vision A statement of how someone wants the future to be or believes it will be; it is used to set direction for an organization.

Visual programming A type of computer programming built around a graphical programming environment and a paint metaphor for developing user interfaces. The most popular visual programming languages are Visual Basic and Java.

Voice response unit A computer output method using the spoken voice to provide a response to the user. This output method is gaining increasing acceptance as a provider of limited, tightly programmed computer output, often in conjunction with touch-tone telephone input.

VPN *See* Virtual private network.

VR *See* Virtual reality.

W3C World Wide Web Consortium, an international consortium of companies involved with the Internet and the World Wide Web. W3C is the chief standards body for the Web with the purpose of developing open standards; among W3C's standards are Hypertext Transfer Protocol (HTTP) and Hypertext Markup Language (HTML).

WAN *See* Wide area network.

WAP *See* Wireless access point.

Waterfall approach A way to view the system development process as a series of steps that, when diagrammed, appear as a waterfall.

WATS *See* Wide Area Telephone Service.

Waves of innovation Primozic, Primozic, and Leben's presentation on how IT is used by industries and by enterprises, one view of the evolution of IT, and the escalating benefits it provides firms. They identify five waves of innovation, with *time* on the horizontal axis and *benefit* on the vertical access.

Web Shorthand for World Wide Web. *See* World Wide Web.

Web browser Software application that runs on a microcomputer, enabling the user to access Web sites and Web pages; the most common Web browsers are Microsoft Internet Explorer and Netscape Navigator.

Web cast Broadcast of a live event over the World Wide Web.

Web services This second-generation Internet-based system environment gives software modules URLs (Internet addresses) so they can be called upon to perform their function as a service via the Internet.

Web site A personal or organizational site on the World Wide Web. In just a few years, company Web sites have become standard business practice in most companies, large and small.

Web surfing (surfing the Web) Slang term for continuously following hyperlinks hidden behind highlighted words on Web pages that, when clicked, jump to another Web page.

Wi-Fi An abbreviation for wireless fidelity, this name is commonly used to refer to a wireless LAN.

Wide area network (WAN) A type of network over which both voice and data for a single organization are communicated among the multiple locations (often far apart) where the organization operates, usually employing point-to-point transmission over facilities owned by several organizations, including the public telephone network; also called a long-haul network.

Wide Area Telephone Service (WATS) A service available from the telephone company in which an organization pays a monthly fee for unlimited long-distance telephone service using ordinary voice circuits. WATS is an easy way to set up a wide area network (WAN) and costs less per hour than standard Direct Distance Dialing (DDD).

Wireless Considered a transmission medium, although strictly speaking it is broadcast technology in which radio signals are sent out into the air. Examples are cordless telephone, cellular telephone, wireless LAN, and microwave.

Wireless access point (WAP) A radio transceiver that serves as the central device in a wireless LAN and that connects the LAN to other networks. The WAP receives the signals of all computers within its range and repeats them to ensure that all other computers within the range can hear them; it also forwards all messages for recipients not on this wireless LAN via the wired network.

Wireless LAN A local area network employing wireless communication between the various devices in the network. Compared to a wired LAN, a wireless LAN is easier to plan and install, less secure, and more susceptible to interference. Most wireless LANs operate in the range of 6 to 11 million bps, with a few newer wireless LANs operating at speeds up to 54 mbps.

Word A memory cell that can store two or more characters of data; alternatively, the amount of data handled by the CPU as a single unit. *See also* Memory.

Work breakdown analysis Identification of the project phases and detailed activities for each phase, including the task sequencing and time estimates, usually based on a particular systems methodology.

Worknets Informal groups of people whose collective knowledge is used to accomplish a specific task.

Workscape The virtual workplace, which includes the Internet.

Workstations Generally, any computer-related device at which an individual may work, such as a personal computer or a terminal. Specifically, the subcategory of computers based on powerful microprocessor chips and RISC chips—really grown-up, more powerful microcomputers. Because of strong price-performance characteristics, workstations have made inroads into the domain of traditional midrange systems so that it is almost impossible to decide which machines should be considered "workstations" and which should be considered "midrange systems," resulting in the creation of the workstations/midrange systems category. *See also* Workstations/midrange systems, Midrange systems, RISC chip.

Workstations/midrange systems A broad middle-of-the-road category of computers stretching all the way from microcomputers to the much larger mainframes and supercomputers, with costs ranging from $3,000 to $1,000,000 and power ranging from 40 to 4,000 MFLOPS; used for departmental computing, specific applications such as computer-aided design and graphics, midsized business general processing, and as a Web server, file server, local area network server, and a server in client/server applications. Historically, workstations and midrange computers were considered as distinct categories of computers, but they now overlap so much in cost, power, and applications that they have been combined in a single category. *See also* Workstations, Midrange systems.

World Wide Web An Internet application, or tool, that uses a hypertext-based approach to traverse, or "surf," the Internet by clicking on a link contained in one document to move to another document, and so on; these links may also connect to video clips, recordings, photographs, and images.

Worm *See* Computer worm.

WORM disk *See* CD-R.

WWW *See* World Wide Web.

XML *See* eXtensible Markup Language.

XP *See* Extreme programming.

Year 2000 (Y2K) problem Computer calculation errors that would have occurred (without programming changes) beginning with the year 2000 due to the earlier coding of a four-digit year as a two-digit data element; sometimes called the "millennium bug." Billions of dollars were spent worldwide to achieve Y2K compliance for computer software and hardware.

Zero latency Reacting quickly to new information (with no wait time).

ACRONYMS AND ABBREVIATIONS

1G/2G/3G/4G First, Second, Third, and Fourth Generation (of wireless systems)

3i Investors in Industry

4GLs Fourth Generation Languages

ACM Association for Computing Machinery

AI Artificial Intelligence

AIS Association for Information Systems

AM Amplitude Modulation

AmEx American Express

AMS/3 Third-Generation Automatic Order Matching and Execution System

ANSI American National Standards Institute

AOL America Online

AOP Advanced Optimization Planning

API Application Program Interface

ARPANET Advanced Research Projects Agency Network

ASP Application Service Provider or Active Server Page

AT&T American Telephone and Telegraph

ATM Asynchronous Transfer Mode or Automated Teller Machine

B2B Business to Business

B2C Business to Consumer

BCG Boston Consulting Group

BLISS Banking and Loan Insurance Software System

BMW Bavarian Motor Works

BPO Business Process Outsourcing

BPR Business Process Redesign/Reengineering

C/C++ Programming Languages Used with UNIX

CAD/CAM Computer-Aided Design/Computer-Aided Manufacturing

CAPS Center for Advanced Purchasing Studies

CAS Credit Authorization System

CASE Computer Aided Software Engineering

CBR Case-Based Reasoning

CC Computer Center

CCITT Consultive Committee for International Telegraphy and Telephony

CDMA Code Division Multiple Access

CDPD Cellular Digital Packet Data

CD-ROM Compact Disc—Read Only Memory

CEMEX Cementos Mexicanos (a cement company)

CEO Chief Executive Officer

CFO Chief Financial Officer

CIO Chief Information Officer

CIR Corporate Information Resources

CIRANO Center for Interuniversity Research and Analysis on Organizations

CIS Corporate Information Services

CISR Center for Information Systems Research

CLEC Competitive Local Exchange Carrier

CMA Cash Management Account

COBOL Common Business Oriented Language

COE Common Operating Environment

COM Computer Output Microfilm or Component Object Model

COO Chief Operations Officer

CRAMM United Kingdom Central Computer and Telecommunication Agency Risk Analysis and Management Method

CRM Customer Relationship Management

CSC Computer Sciences Corporation

CSF Critical Success Factor

CTO Chief Technology Officer

CU Credit Unions

CXO A Group of "Chiefs" (CEO, CFO, CIO, COO, etc.)

DARPA Defense Advanced Research Projects Agency

DASD Direct Access Data Storage

DB Digital Business

DB2 Database 2 (an IBM product)

DBMS Database Management System

DDM Dialog, Data, and Modeling

DES Data Encryption Standard

DGMS Dialog Generation and Management System

DNS Distributed Name Service

DOS Disk Operating System

DP Data Processing

DPI Dots Per Inch

DSA Decision Support Application

DSL Digital Subscriber Line

DSS Decision Support System

DVD Digital Video Disc

EAI Enterprise Application Integration

EDI Electronic Data Interchange

EDM Electronic Document Management

EDP Electronic Data Processing

EDS Electronic Data System

EIS Executive Information System *or* Enterprise Information Solutions

EJB Enterprise Java Bean

E-mail Electronic Mail

EMR Electro Magnetic Radiation

EPRI Electric Power Research Institute

ERD Enterprise Reference Data

ERP Enterprise Resource Planning

ES Enterprise System

ESOP Employee Stock Ownership Plan

ESP External Service Provider

ESS Executive Support System

EUC End User Computing

EVP Executive Vice President

E-zines Electronic magazines

FAQ Frequently Asked Questions

Fax Facsimile

FBI Federal Bureau of Investigations

FDA U.S. Food and Drug Administration

FDDI Fiber Distributed Data Interface

FT *Financial Times*

FTC Federal Trade Commission

FTP File Transfer Protocol

GDSS Group Decision Support System

GOTOs Go-to's, in computer programming code

GPRS General Packed Radio System

GPS Global Positioning Satellite

GSM Global System for Mobile Communication

GSS Group Support System

GTE General Telephone Company

HEC Hautes Etudes Commerciales

HICSS Hawaii International Conference on System Sciences

HKEx Hong Kong Exchanges and Clearing

HP Hewlett-Packard

HR Human Resources

HTML HyperText Markup Language

HTTP HyperText Transfer Protocol

IBM International Business Machines Corporation

IC Intellectual Capital

ID Identification

IDE Integrated Development Environment

IDS Integrated Data Store or Intrusion Detection System

IEA Information Engineering Associates

IFTF Institute for the Future

IIML Indian Institute of Management, Lucknow

ILEC Incumbent Local Exchange Carrier

IM Information Management or Instant Messaging

INR Indian Rupes

IOS Inter-Organizational System

IP Internet Protocol

IPng Internet Protocol Next Generation

IR Information Resources

IS Information Systems

ISDN Integrated Services Digital Network

ISM Information Security Management

ISO International Standards Organization

ISP Internet Service Provider

ISS Internet Security System

IT Information Technology

IXC Inter-exchange Carrier

J2EE Java 2 Enterprise Edition

JAD Joint Application Design

JDS Job Diagnostic Survey

JIT Just-In-Time

Kbps Kilobytes Per Second

LAN Local Area Network

LEC Local Exchange Carrier

LLC Limited Liability Company

LN Local Network

LTL Less-Than-Truckload

Mac Apple's Macintosh Computer

MAN Metropolitan Area Network

MBMS Model Base Management System

Mbps Megabytes Per Second

MGM Metro-Goldwyn-Mayer

MIPS Millions of Instructions Per Second

MIS Management Information Systems

MIT Massachusetts Institute of Technology

MOM Message-Oriented Middleware

MU Multiple-User system

MVS Multiple Virtual System

NASA National Aeronautics and Space Administration

NBC National Broadcasting Corporation

NC Network Computer

Net, The The Internet

NetBIOS Network BIOS, a proprietary network transfer protocol

NFL National Football League

NIC Network Interface Card

NOC Network Operations Centers

NT Network Technology

NTT Nippon Telephone and Telegraph

NYNEX A New York-Based Telecom Company

OEM Original Equipment Manufacturer

OLAP Online Analytical Processing

OLTP Online Transaction Processing

OM Owens & Minor

OO Object-Oriented

OPEC Organization of Petroleum Exporting Countries

OR/MS Operations Research/Management Science

ORB Object Request Broker

OSI Open System Interconnection

OSS Open Source Software

OX Operations Expediter System

PAN Personal Area Network

PARC Xerox's Palo Alto Research Center

PBX Private Branch Exchange

PC Personal Computer

PCS Personal Communication Service

PDA Personal Digital Assistant

PDF Portable Document Format (proprietary file format in Adobe)

PIN Personal Identification Number

PL/1 Programming Language/1

PLL Phase Lock Loops

PODD Point of Delivery Device

POTS Plain Old Telephone Service

PPSR Personal Property Securities Register Service

PRA Passenger Revenue Accounting

PRAC Plymouth Rock Assurance Corporation

PROFS Professional Office System

PSTN Public Switched Telephone Network

PTT Postal, Telephone, and Telegraph Authority

PwC Pricewaterhouse Coopers

QoS Quality of Service

R&D Research and Development

RAD Rapid Application Development

RBOC Regional Bell Operating Company

RCA Radio Corporation of America

RF Radio Frequency

RFID Radio Frequency Identification

RIPP Rapid Iterative Production Prototyping

RN Remote Network

ROI Return On Investment

RPC Remote Procedure Call

RSA Encryption method named for developers Rivest, Shamir, & Adleman

RU Remote Utility

SAP Systeme Anwendung Produkte (System Application Product)

SAP R/3 SAP Release 3; the client-server version

SBT Scan-Based Trading

SCM Supply Chain Management

SEC U.S. Securities and Exchange Commission

SEI Software Engineering Institute at Carnegie Mellon University

SET Secure Electronic Transactions

SLBG Sara Lee Bakery Group

SLICE Simple Low Cost Innovative Engine

SMS Short Message Service

SNA System Network Architecture

SOAP Simple Object Access Protocol

SOHO Small Office/Home Office

SQL Structured Query Language

SSL Secure Sockets Layer

SSP Security Service Providers

STS Sociotechnical System

SU Single-User systems

SUMURU Single User, Multiple User, Remote Utility

TCO Total Cost of Ownership

TCP/IP Transmission Control Protocol/Internet Protocol

TDL Teleport Denver, Ltd.

TDMA Time Division Multiple Access

TQM Total Quality Management

TV Television

TVA Tennessee Valley Authority

UCC Uniform Commercial Code

UCLA University of California at Los Angeles

UDDI Universal Discovery, Description, and Integration

UHF Ultra High Fidelity

UMT United Management Technologies

UNIX "Unics" Operating System; an attempt at a pun

UPS United Parcel Service

URL Uniform Resource Locator

VAN Value Added Network

VoIP Voice-Over Internet Protocol

VPN Virtual Private Network

VSAT Very Small Aperture Terminal

WAN Wide Area Network

WAP Wireless Application Protocol

Web World Wide Web

Wi-Fi Wireless Fidelity

WiNS Wire Nova Scotia

WISP Wireless Internet Service Providers

WSDL Web Services Definition Language

XML Extensible Markup Language

Y2K Year 2000

INDEX

FIGURE INDEX